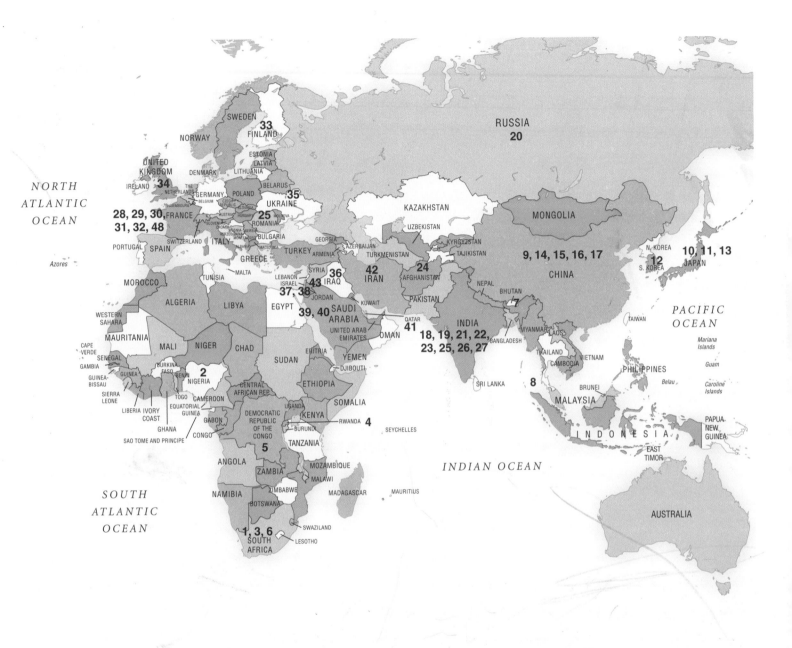

11th edition

sociology

Richard T. Schaefer
DePaul University

Boston   Burr Ridge, IL   Dubuque, IA   New York   San Francisco   St. Louis
Bangkok   Bogotá   Caracas   Kuala Lumpur   Lisbon   London   Madrid   Mexico City
Milan   Montreal   New Delhi   Santiago   Seoul   Singapore   Sydney   Taipei   Toronto

Published by McGraw-Hill, an imprint of The McGraw-Hill Companies, Inc., 1221 Avenue of the Americas, New York, NY 10020.

This book is printed on recycled, acid-free paper containing a minimum of 50% total recycled fiber with 10% postconsumer de-inked fiber.

1 2 3 4 5 6 7 8 9 0 QPD/QPD 0 9 8 7

ISBN: 978-0-07-340414-1
MHID: 0-07-340414-4

Editor in Chief: *Michael Ryan*
Publisher: *Frank Mortimer*
Sponsoring Editor: *Gina Boedeker*
Director of Development: *Rhona Robbin*
Marketing Manager: *Leslie Oberhuber*
Senior Developmental Editor: *Thom Holmes*
Editorial Coordinator: *Evan Bock*
Editorial Assistant: *Rachel Bara*
Editorial Supplement Coordinator: *Jessica Bodie Richards*
Production Editor: *Carey Eisner*
Manuscript Editor: *Sheryl Rose*
Design Manager: *Cassandra Chu*
Text Designer: *Maureen McCutcheon*
Cover Designer: *Cassandra Chu*
Art Editor: *Emma Ghiselli*
Photo Research: *Editorial Image, LLC*
Senior Photo Research Coordinator: *Nora Agbayani*
Production Supervisor: *Richard DeVitto*
Composition: *10/12 Minion by Professional Graphics Inc.*
Printing: *45# Publishers Matte Plus, Quebecor World*

Cover: Frank Wing

Credits: The acknowledgments/credits for this book begin on page 597 and are considered an extension of the copyright page.

Library of Congress Cataloging-in-Publication Data

Schaefer, Richard T.
    Sociology / Richard T. Schaefer. -- 11th ed.
       p. cm.
    ISBN-13: 978-0-07-340414-1 (alk. paper)
    ISBN-10: 0-07-340414-4 (alk. paper)
  1.   Sociology. 2.   Social problems. 3.   United States--Social policy. I.   Title.
    HM586.S33 2008
    301—dc22

                                         2007032038

The Internet addresses listed in the text were accurate at the time of publication. The inclusion of a Web site does not indicate an endorsement by the authors or McGraw-Hill, and McGraw-Hill does not guarantee the accuracy of the information presented at these sites.

www.mhhe.com

dedication

To my brother, Douglas, a teacher of college students for over 40 years

ABOUT the author

Richard T. Schaefer
Professor, DePaul University
B.A. Northwestern University
M.A., Ph.D. University of Chicago

Growing up in Chicago at a time when neighborhoods were going through transitions in ethnic and racial composition, Richard T. Schaefer found himself increasingly intrigued by what was happening, how people were reacting, and how these changes were affecting neighborhoods and people's jobs. His interest in social issues caused him to gravitate to sociology courses at Northwestern University, where he eventually received a B.A. in sociology.

"Originally as an undergraduate I thought I would go on to law school and become a lawyer. But after taking a few sociology courses, I found myself wanting to learn more about what sociologists studied, and fascinated by the kinds of questions they raised." This fascination led him to obtain his M.A. and Ph.D. in sociology from the University of Chicago. Dr. Schaefer's continuing interest in race relations led him to write his master's thesis on the membership of the Ku Klux Klan and his doctoral thesis on racial prejudice and race relations in Great Britain.

Dr. Schaefer went on to become a professor of sociology, and now teaches at DePaul University in Chicago. In 2004 he was named to the Vincent DePaul professorship in recognition of his undergraduate teaching and scholarship. He has taught introductory sociology for over 35 years to students in colleges, adult education programs, nursing programs, and even a maximum-security prison. Dr. Schaefer's love of teaching is apparent in his interaction with his students. "I find myself constantly learning from the students who are in my classes and from reading what they write. Their insights into the material we read or current events that we discuss often become part of future course material and sometimes even find their way into my writing."

Dr. Schaefer is author of the seventh edition of *Sociology: A Brief Introduction* (McGraw-Hill, 2008) and of the third edition of *Sociology Matters* (McGraw-Hill, 2008). He is also the author of *Racial and Ethnic Groups,* now in its eleventh edition, and *Race and Ethnicity in the United States,* fourth edition. Together with William Zellner, he coauthored the eighth edition of *Extraordinary Groups,* published by Worth in 2007. Dr. Schaefer serves as the general editor of the three-volume *Encyclopedia of Race, Ethnicity, and Society,* forthcoming from Sage in 2008. His articles and book reviews have appeared in many journals, including *American Journal of Sociology; Phylon: A Review of Race and Culture; Contemporary Sociology; Sociology and Social Research; Sociological Quarterly;* and *Teaching Sociology.* He served as president of the Midwest Sociological Society in 1994–1995.

Dr. Schaefer's advice to students is to "look at the material and make connections to your own life and experiences. Sociology will make you a more attentive observer of how people in groups interact and function. It will also make you more aware of people's different needs and interests—and perhaps more ready to work for the common good, while still recognizing the individuality of each person."

brief contents

contents

PART 1 *The Sociological Perspective*

PART 2 *Organizing Social Life*

PART 3 *Social Inequality*

PART 4 *Social Institutions*

Photo Essay: What Is a Family? 342

Sociology in the Global Community: One Wife, Many Husbands: The Nyinba 344

Research in Action: Arranged Marriage, American-Style 350

Research in Action: The Lingering Impact of Divorce 356

Photo Essay: Why Do Sociologists Study Religion? 368

Research in Action: Income and Education, Religiously Speaking 372

Research in Action: Islam in the United States 378

Research in Action: The Church of Scientology: Religion or Quasi-Religion? 381

Taking Sociology to Work: Ray Zapata, Business Owner and Former Regent, Texas State University 395

Sociology on Campus: The Debate over Title IX 398

Research in Action: Violence in the Schools 401

PART 5 *Changing Society*

chapter-opening EXCERPTS

Every chapter in this textbook begins with an excerpt from one of the works listed here. These excerpts convey the excitement and relevance of sociological inquiry and draw readers into the subject matter from each chapter.

boxed features

social policy SECTIONS

MAPS summingUPtables photo essays

preface

Without a doubt, you have thought about sociological issues before opening this book. Have you or a childhood friend ever spent time in day care? Are your parents or a friend's parents divorced? Are you concerned about plagiarism or binge drinking on your campus? Did you need a student loan to attend college? Chances are you have been touched by most or all of these issues. If you are like most students, you've also spent a great deal of time thinking about your future career. If you major in sociology, what occupations can you choose from?

These are just some of the topics of immediate personal interest that are dealt with in this book. Sociologists also address broader issues, from bilingual education to the existence of slavery in the 21st century. Sociology includes the study of immigration, poverty, overpopulation, and the process and problems of growing old in different cultures. In the aftermath of disasters such as Hurricane Katrina and the terrorist attacks of September 11, 2001, sociologists have been called on to explain their social consequences—how they affected people of different ages, social classes, and racial and ethnic groups, and how our government responded. These topics, along with many others, are of great interest to me, but it is the sociological explanations for them that I find especially compelling. The introductory sociology class provides the ideal laboratory in which to study our own society and those of our global neighbors.

Making Sociology Relevant

Sociology examines and questions even the most familiar patterns of social behavior. It can help students to better understand their own lives and those of people from other cultures.

After more than 30 years of teaching sociology to students in colleges, adult education programs, nursing programs, an overseas program based in London, and even a maximum-security prison, I am firmly convinced that the discipline can play a valuable role in teaching critical thinking skills. The distinctive emphasis on social policy found in this text shows students how to use the sociological imagination in examining such public policy issues as welfare reform, global immigration, gay marriage, and the AIDS crisis.

My hope is that through their reading of this book, students will begin to think like sociologists and will be able to use sociological theories and concepts in evaluating human interactions and institutions. From the introduction of the concept of sociological imagination in Chapter 1, this text stresses the distinctive way in which sociologists examine human social behavior, and how their research can be used to understand the broader principles that guide our lives.

The first ten editions of *Sociology* have been used in more than 500 colleges and universities. This book is often part of a student's first encounter with the engaging ideas of sociology. Many who have read it have gone on to make sociology their life's work. Equally gratifying for me is hearing that *Sociology* has made a difference in the lives of other students, who have applied the knowledge they gained in the course to guide their life choices.

The 11th edition of *Sociology* builds on the success of earlier editions by continuing to emphasize three important goals:

- **Comprehensive and balanced coverage of theoretical perspectives throughout the text.** Chapter 1 introduces, defines, and contrasts the functionalist, conflict, and interactionist perspectives. We explore their distinctive views of such topics as social institutions (Chapter 5), deviance (Chapter 8), the family (Chapter 14), education (Chapter 16), and health and medicine (Chapter 19). In addition, the feminist perspective is introduced in Chapter 1. Other theoretical approaches particular to certain topics are presented in later chapters.

- **Strong coverage of issues pertaining to gender, age, race, ethnicity, and class in all chapters.** Examples of such coverage include social policy sections on bilingualism (Chapter 3), welfare (Chapter 9), global immigration (Chapter 11), and gay marriage (Chapter 14); chapter-opening excerpts on globalization in India (Chapter 10), the so-called Lipstick Jihad in Iran (Chapter 12), and the unequal childhoods of young people in the United States (Chapter 14); boxes on interracial and interethnic friendships (Chapter 11), naturally occurring retirement communities, or NORCs (Chapter 13), and squatter settlements (Chapter 20); and sections on the social construction of race (Chapter 11), gender equity in education (Chapter 16), and the informal economy (Chapter 18).

- **Emphasis on cross-cultural and global content throughout the book.** The 11th edition greatly extends coverage of globalization. Chapters 1, 10, and 23 provide expanded coverage of global terms and concepts, as well as of social, economic, and technological issues that increasingly influence cultural encounters around the world. A world map, found on the inside front cover of the book, provides a quick guide to passages that consider sociological issues as they are manifested in other countries. Among the topics examined are:

Neglect of children in Eastern European orphanages (Chapter 4)
The global "McDonaldization of society" (Chapter 6)
The status of women around the world (Chapter 12)

Issues of aging around the world (Chapter 13)
Transmission of cultural values through education
(Chapter 16)
Homelessness worldwide (Chapter 20)
Population policy in China (Chapter 21)
Transnationals (Chapter 23)

I take great care to introduce the basic concepts and research methods of sociology and to reinforce this material in all chapters. The most recent data are included, making this book more current than all previous editions.

Special Features

Integrated Learning System

The text, its accompanying *Reel Society* Interactive Movie CD-ROM, and the Online Learning Center Web site work together as an integrated learning system to bring the theories, research findings, and basic concepts of sociology to life for students. Offering a combination of print, multimedia, and Web-based materials, this comprehensive system meets the needs of instructors and students with a variety of teaching and learning styles. The material that follows describes the many features of the text, CD-ROM, and Online Learning Center, as well as the supplementary materials that support those resources.

Poster Art

Each chapter opens with a reproduction of a poster or piece of graphic art that illustrates a key theme or concept of the chapter. Accompanying captions help readers to grasp the relevance of the artwork to the chapter.

Chapter-Opening Excerpts

The chapter-opening excerpts convey the excitement and relevance of sociological inquiry by means of lively passages from writings of sociologists and others who explore sociological topics. These excerpts are designed to expose students to vivid writing on a broad range of topics and to stimulate their sociological imaginations. For example, Chapter 1 opens with Barbara Ehrenreich's account of her experiment in survival as a low-wage worker, drawn from her best-selling book *Nickel and Dimed.* Chapter 5 opens with a description of Philip Zimbardo's now-classic mock prison study. And in the opening to Chapter 21, Kai Erikson reflects on the connection between population, the economy, and environmental disasters.

Chapter Overview

The opening excerpt is followed by a chapter overview that provides a bridge between the opening excerpt and the content of the chapter. In addition, the overview poses questions and describes the content of the chapter in narrative form.

Key Terms

I have given careful attention to presenting understandable and accurate definitions of each key term. These terms are highlighted in bold italics when they are introduced. A list of key terms and definitions in each chapter—with page references—follows the end of the chapter. In addition, the glossary at the end of the book includes the definitions of the textbook's key terms and the page references for each term.

Sociology in the Global Community

These sections provide a global perspective on topics such as aging, Al Jazeera, and the 2004 tsunami.

Research in Action

These sections present sociological findings on topics such as divorce, school violence, political apathy among young people, and naturally occurring retirement communities (NORCs).

Social Inequality

These sections illustrate various types of social stratification. Featured topics include privilege and discrimination in employment, disability as a master status, and affirmative action.

Taking Sociology to Work

These sections profile individuals who majored in sociology and use its principles in their work. While these people are employed in a variety of occupations and professions, they share a conviction that their background in sociology has been valuable in their careers.

Sociology on Campus

These sections apply the sociological perspective to issues of immediate interest to today's students. Title IX, plagiarism, and financial aid are among the featured topics.

Use Your Sociological Imagination

In the spirit of C. Wright Mills, these short, thought-provoking sections encourage students to apply the sociological concepts they have learned to the world around them. Through open-ended "what-if" questions, students step into the shoes of researchers, famous sociologists, and people of other cultures and generations.

Illustrations

The photographs, cartoons, figures, and tables are closely linked to the themes of the chapters. The maps, titled Mapping Life Nationwide and Mapping Life Worldwide, show the prevalence of social trends. A world map highlighting those countries used as examples in the text appears on the inside front cover.

Think About It

Selected tables and figures include stimulating questions that prompt students to interpret the data and think about their deeper meaning. Students search for trends in the data, wonder about the underlying reasons for the trends, and apply the implications to their own lives.

Photo Essays

Nine photo essays enliven the text. Each begins with a question that is intended to prompt students to see some part of everyday life with new eyes—those of a sociologist. For instance, the essay in Chapter 1 asks "Are You What You Own?" and the essay in Chapter 8 asks "Who Is Deviant?" The photos and captions that follow suggest the answer to the question.

Social Policy Sections

The Social Policy sections that close all but one of the chapters play a critical role in helping students to think like sociologists. They apply sociological principles and theories to important social and political issues being debated by policymakers and the general public. Four sections are new to this edition. All the Social Policy sections now present a global perspective.

Cross-Reference Icons

When the text discussion refers to a concept introduced earlier in the book, an icon in the margin points the reader to the exact page.

Summing Up Tables

Twenty-eight Summing Up tables help to pull together coverage of the major theoretical perspectives, providing helpful study aids for students as they review the chapters.

Chapter Summaries

Each chapter includes a brief numbered summary to aid students in reviewing the important themes.

Critical Thinking Questions

After the summary, each chapter includes critical thinking questions that will help students analyze the social world in which they participate. Critical thinking is an essential element in the sociological imagination.

Self-Quizzes

Each chapter includes a 20-item quiz that allows students to test their comprehension and retention of core information presented in the chapter. Answers to the questions are presented at the end of the quiz.

Technology Resources

Suggested activities at the end of each chapter take students online to analyze pertinent social issues. Updates, exercises, and hyperlinks related to these Web-based activities are displayed on the book's Web site (**www.mhhe.com/schaefer11**).

Endpapers

The inside front cover features a world map highlighting selected countries mentioned in the book. Page numbers indicate the relevant passages, many of which stress the effects of globalization in the United States and other countries. The inside back cover features two summary tables: one that highlights the book's coverage of race, class, and gender and another that summarizes its applications of sociology's major theoretical approaches.

What's New in the 11th Edition?

The most important changes in this edition include the following (refer as well to the chapter-by-chapter list of changes on pages xxiii–xxvii and to the *Visual Preview* on pages xxxi–xxxvi).

Content

- Five new chapter-opening excerpts, drawn from sociological writings, convey the excitement and relevance of sociological inquiry: "Body Ritual among the Nacirema" by Horace Miner (Chapter 3); *Growing Up Digital: The Rise of the Net Generation* by Don Tapscott (Chapter 7); *Stripped: Inside the Lives of Exotic Dancers* by Bernadette Barton (Chapter 8); *The Shame of the Nation* by Jonathan Kozol (Chapter 16); and *Is Voting for Young People?* by Martin P. Wattenberg (Chapter 17).

- Five new Social Policy sections help students to apply sociological principles and theories to important social and political issues currently under debate by policymakers and the general public: Regulating the Net (Chapter 5); Media Concentration (Chapter 7); The Death Penalty in the United States and Worldwide (Chapter 8); and Global Immigration (Chapter 11).

- Seven new Sociology in the Global Community boxes provide a global perspective on current social and cultural issues: Cultural Survival in Brazil (Chapter 3); McDonald's and the Worldwide Bureaucratization of Society (Chapter 6); It's All Relative: Appalachian Poverty and Congolese Affluence (Chapter 9); Cutting Poverty Worldwide (Chapter 10); One Wife, Many Husbands: The Nyinba (Chapter 14); The Mysterious Fall of the Nacirema (Chapter 21); and One Laptop per Child (Chapter 23).

- Eleven new Research in Action boxes highlight sociological research on a wide variety of topics: What's in a Name? (Chapter 2); Decision Making in the Jury Room (Chapter 6); Hired Guns (Chapter 6); Labeling a Behavior as a Crime: Road Rage (Chapter 8); The Shrinking Middle Class (Chapter 9); Growing Up Latina (Chapter 11); Arranged Marriage, American-Style (Chapter 14); Income and Education, Religiously Speaking (Chapter 15); The Church of Scientology: Religion or Quasi-Religion? (Chapter 15); Organizing for Controversy on the Web (Chapter 22); and The Internet's Global Profile (Chapter 23).

- Two new Social Inequality boxes, American Indians: First Here, Among the Last to Vote (Chapter 17) and Medical Apartheid (Chapter 19), help students to see the far-reaching consequences of social stratification.

- Eight new Taking Sociology to Work boxes describe the varied careers of some real people who majored in sociology: a brand planner for an advertising agency (Chapter 7); a research assistant in an urban poverty program (Chapter 9); a human rights advocate (Chapter 10); a program coordinator for a women's health organization (Chapter 12); a congressional aide (Chapter 17); a product manager (Chapter 18); an independent consultant in health care research (Chapter 19); and a community organizer (Chapter 20).
- Three new photo essays, How Does Television Portray the Family? (Chapter 7), What Is Our Work? (Chapter 18), and What Is Medical Care? (Chapter 19), help to spark students' interest in sociology.

Pedagogy

- A new Summing Up table, "Sociological Perspectives on Social Change," summarizes theoretical coverage in Chapter 23.
- Eight new U.S. and world maps illustrate important sociological trends and developments.

Supplements

- *Reel Society:* Interactive Movie CD-ROMs, version 2.0. This two-disk set features an interactive movie that demonstrates the sociological imagination through the use of actors and scenarios involving campus life. See page xxviii for a complete description of *Reel Society* 2.0.
- Updated Online Learning Center Web site features include interactive quizzes, diagnostic midterm and final exams, links to additional information about the chapter-opening excerpts and their authors, and SurveyMaker, software that allows students to construct and electronically disseminate their own polls for class research projects.
- Four 60-minute VHS videotapes feature brief clips (5–10 minutes each) from *NBC News* and the *Today Show* that dramatize sociological concepts, serve as lecture launchers, and generate class discussion. These videotapes are accompanied by a guide that is available on the Online Learning Center Web site (**www.mhhe.com/schaefer11**).

This edition has been thoroughly updated. It includes the most recent data and research findings, many of which were published in the last three years. Recent data from the Census Bureau, Bureau of Labor Statistics, *Current Population Reports,* the Population Reference Bureau, the World Bank, the United Nations Development Programme, and the Centers for Disease Control have been incorporated.

A more complete, chapter-by-chapter listing of the most significant new material in this edition follows.

What's New in Each Chapter?
Chapter 1: Understanding Sociology

- Revised photo essay, "Are You What You Own?" featuring new photos of families in Japan, Mexico, and South Africa

- Table: "Sections of the American Sociological Association"
- Discussion of how sociologists and other social scientists study the impact of events such as Hurricane Katrina and the 2007 shootings at Virginia Tech, with map, "Poverty Rates in Hurricane Katrina Disaster Area," and photos
- Updated discussion of sociology and common sense, with new examples
- Discussion of the functionalist perspective on cow worship in Indian society, with photo
- Improved definition of the conflict perspective
- Updated discussion of the feminist perspective
- Discussion of the interactionist perspective on the new NBA dress code, with figure: "Enforcing Symbols: The NBA Dress Code"
- Updated and expanded Research in Action box, "Looking at Sports from Four Theoretical Perspectives," including (a) coverage of the feminist perspective and (b) new example of women in sports, professional race car drivers, with photo
- Discussion of new research on illegal drug use and the spread of HIV/AIDS
- Figure: "Sociology Degrees Conferred in the United States by Gender"

Chapter 2: Sociological Research

- Updated Mapping Life Nationwide map: "Educational Level and Household Income in the United States"
- Expanded discussion of independent versus dependent variables, with new example
- Updated discussion of correlation, with new example
- Updated figure: "Impact of a College Education on Income"
- Updated Research in Action box, "Polling in Baghdad," including results of recent poll on U.S. intentions in declaring war on Iraq
- Research in Action box: "What's in a Name?" with figure
- Three "Use Your Sociological Imagination" exercises
- Updated discussion of the Exxon Corporation's attempt to reduce the multibillion-dollar penalty for negligence in the *Exxon Valdez* disaster through funding of research on jury verdicts
- Updated figure: "Percent of Television Shows That Contain Sexual Content"
- Revision of Appendix I to concentrate on figures rather than tables, including two new figures, "Changing Attitudes toward the Legalization of Marijuana" and "Legalization of Marijuana by Gender and Age"

Chapter 3: Culture

- Chapter-opening poster: Nike billboard in Hong Kong
- Chapter-opening excerpt from "Body Ritual among the Nacirema" by Horace Miner

- Use Your Sociological Imagination feature on cultural differences
- Sociology in the Global Community box: "Cultural Survival in Brazil"
- Mapping Life Worldwide map: "Languages of the World: How Many Do You Speak?"
- Discussion of the creation of new symbols to warn future societies of the existence of a hazardous waste dump, with figure, "A Timeless Alert"
- Discussion of the "clash of civilizations" thesis (cultural and religious identities have become more important sources of conflict than national or political loyalties)
- Discussion of Indian movie superhero Krrish as an example of the insight media provide into society's values, with photo
- Case study: "Culture at Wal-Mart"
- Discussion of the argot spoken by those who engage in the extreme sport of *parkour*
- Discussion of the new subculture that has developed in India among employees at international call centers, with photo
- Figure, "A Palestinian World View," showing a map of the world drawn by a high school student in Gaza
- Updated Social Policy section on bilingualism, with discussion of legislative proposals regarding treatment of illegal immigrants

Chapter 4: Socialization

- Discussion of Genie, a neglected 13-year-old discovered in 1970, with sketch she did at age 18
- Discussion of the prolonged transition from adolescence to adulthood in the United States
- "Use Your Sociological Imagination" feature on the transition from adolescence to adulthood
- Figure: "How Young People Use the Media"
- Discussion of socialization to the use of a new telecommunications technology (cell phones) in developing countries
- Revised Social Policy section featuring (a) updated discussion of the percentage of preschoolers in day care, with figure, "Child Care Arrangements for Preschoolers," and (b) figure, "Child Care Costs in Industrial Nations"

Chapter 5: Social Interaction and Social Structure

- Use Your Sociological Imagination feature
- Redefinition of the key term *sociocultural evolution*
- Social Policy section, "Regulating the Net," with key term treatment of *net neutrality* and figure, "Identity Information Revealed Online by College Students"

Chapter 6: Groups and Organizations

- Chapter-opening poster: "The In Crowd"
- Research in Action box: "Decision Making in the Jury Room"
- Sociology in the Global Community box: "McDonald's and the Worldwide Bureaucratization of Society"
- Discussion of voluntary associations for youths as training grounds for civic engagement
- Research in Action box: "Hired Guns"
- Three Use Your Sociological Imagination exercises
- Discussion of how electronic communication is contributing to the fragmentation of work
- Revised Social Policy section, "The State of the Unions," with new graph, "Union Membership in the United States," and discussion of government-controlled unions in China

Chapter 7: The Mass Media

- Chapter-opening excerpt from *Growing Up Digital: The Rise of the Net Generation* by Don Tapscott
- Discussion of new children's television program in Gaza, sponsored by Hamas, with photo
- Photo essay: "How Does Television Portray the Family?"
- Taking Sociology to Work box, "Nicole Martorano Van Cleve, Former Brand Planner, Leo Burnett USA"
- Mapping Life Worldwide map: "Branding the Globe"
- Section on media monitoring
- Updated discussion of the overseas market for U.S. films, with photo
- Two Use Your Sociological Imagination exercises
- Discussion of the unequal network TV coverage devoted to women's sports, with figure, "Network Sports Coverage"
- Updated discussion of gender differences in use of the Internet
- Discussion of audience networks, with figure: "Two Audience Networks"
- Figure illustrating the demographics of Internet usage: "Who's on the Internet?"
- Social Policy section, "Media Concentration"

Chapter 8: Deviance and Social Control

- Chapter-opening poster: "Body Art Goes Postal"
- Chapter-opening excerpt from *Stripped: Inside the Lives of Exotic Dancers* by Bernadette Barton
- Discussion of differential treatment of "learners" of different races in Milgram's obedience experiment
- Discussion of changes in campus security measures following the Virginia Tech shootings as a form of social control
- Updated Mapping Life Nationwide map: "The Status of Medical Marijuana"

- Use Your Sociological Imagination feature
- Updated Sociology on Campus box: "Binge Drinking"
- Updated photo essay, "Who Is Deviant?" featuring a beach in a Middle Eastern country
- Research in Action box: "Labeling a Behavior as a Crime: Road Rage"
- Key term treatment of *differential justice*
- Updated coverage of marital rape laws
- Key term treatment of *index crimes*
- Expanded discussion of computer crime, including identity theft
- Table: "National Crime Rates and Percentage Change"
- Social Policy section on the death penalty, with figure, "Executions by State"

Chapter 9: Stratification and Social Mobility in the United States

- Mapping Life Nationwide double map: "The 50 States: Haves and Have-Nots," showing median household income and people below the poverty line by state
- Use Your Sociological Imagination exercise
- Research in Action box: "The Shrinking Middle Class"
- Updated table: "Prestige Rankings of Occupations," with new Think About It feature
- Expanded discussion of U.S. income distribution, illustrated by pyramid graph with inset emphasizing the steep height of the top 0.5 percent of the distribution
- Discussion of U.S. public opinion regarding income inequality, compared to opinion in other countries
- Updated figure, "Poverty in Selected Countries"
- Sociology in the Global Community box: "It's All Relative: Appalachian Poverty and Congolese Affluence"
- Updated discussion of the accuracy of the federal government's definition of poverty
- Taking Sociology to Work Box, "Jessica Houston Su, Research Assistant, Joblessness and Urban Poverty Research Program"

Chapter 10: Global Inequality

- Chapter-opening poster: "Hungry? 38 Million Empty Plates Every Day"
- Subsection, "Worldwide Poverty," with Mapping Life Worldwide map, "Poverty Worldwide," and key term treatment of *gross national product*
- Discussion of the relative value of government aid, charitable aid, and remittances sent from the United States to foreign countries, with figure, "Foreign Aid Donated by Eight Countries"
- Sociology in the Global Community box: "Cutting Poverty Worldwide"

- Use Your Sociological Imagination exercise
- Updated case study: "Stratification in Mexico," with Mapping Life Nationwide map, "The Borderlands," expanded to include remittances and Border Patrol apprehensions
- Updated Social Policy section on universal human rights, including discussion of transnational trafficking in human beings, with table, "Human Trafficking Report"
- Taking Sociology to Work box, "Bari Katz, Program Director, National Conference for Community and Justice"

Chapter 11: Racial and Ethnic Inequality

- Discussion of discriminatory classified ads posted on Craigslist.org and Roommate.com
- Use Your Sociological Imagination exercise
- Updated coverage of racial profiling
- Expansion of Summing Up table, "Sociological Perspectives on Race and Ethnicity," to include labeling theory
- Research in Action box: "Growing Up Latina," with photo of Latina sorority
- Social Policy section on global immigration, with Mapping Life Worldwide map, "World Immigration since 1500," and figure, "Legal Migration in the United States, 1820–2010"

Chapter 12: Stratification by Gender

- Comparative data on the sharing of housework in several nations
- Two Use Your Sociological Imagination exercises
- Expansion of the section on the emergence of a collective consciousness, including key term treatment of *feminism*
- Section on the intersection of social inequality, including key term treatment of *matrix of domination,* with figure, "Matrix of Domination"
- Taking Sociology to Work box, "Abigail E. Drevs, Former Program and Volunteer Coordinator, Y-ME Illinois"

Chapter 13: Stratification by Age

- Two Use Your Sociological Imagination exercises
- Sociology in the Global Community box: "Aging, Japanese Style"
- Figure: "Expected Retirement Age"

Chapter 14: The Family and Intimate Relationships

- Chapter-opening double poster: "Fine, turn the page; Matt's used to being ignored" and "Sure, toss the paper; Kelly's always been treated like trash"
- Sociology in the Global Community box: "One Wife, Many Husbands: The Nyinba," with photo
- Use Your Sociological Imagination exercise

- Research in Action box: "Arranged Marriage, American-Style," with photo
- Expanded coverage of international adoption
- Updated treatment of single-parent families

Chapter 15: Religion

- Updated photo essay: "Why Do Sociologists Study Religion?"
- Use Your Sociological Imagination exercise
- Research in Action box: "Income and Education, Religiously Speaking," with two-part figure
- Coverage of the feminist perspective on religion and social control, with photo of Mary Baker Eddy
- Inclusion of the feminist perspective in Summing Up table, "Sociological Perspectives on Religion"
- Discussion of fundamentalism as a form of religious belief, with key term treatment of *fundamentalism*
- Research in Action box: "The Church of Scientology: Religion or Quasi-Religion?" with key term treatment of *quasi-religion*
- Updated case study, "Religion in India," including discussion of Hindu tolerance of cloning and stem cell research as a factor in India's leadership in biotechnology
- Updated Social Policy section on religion in the schools, including key term treatment of *intelligent design* and new cartoon

Chapter 16: Education

- Chapter-opening excerpt from *The Shame of the Nation* by Jonathan Kozol
- Discussion of recent changes in China's history curriculum
- Three Use Your Sociological Imagination exercises
- Subsection on the feminist view, including discussion of the gender gap in education and the "absence of men" on some college campuses
- Expansion of Summing Up table, "Sociological Perspectives on Education," to include the feminist view
- Mapping Life Nationwide map, "Average Salary for Teachers"
- Figure: "Public High School Graduates by Race and Ethnicity, 2014 (projected)"
- Updated Social Policy section on the No Child Left Behind Act

Chapter 17: Government and Politics

- Chapter-opening poster from Saudi Arabia, "We All Say No to Terrorism"
- Chapter-opening excerpt from *Is Voting for Young People?* by Martin P. Wattenberg
- Taking Sociology to Work box, "Joshua Johnston, Congressional Aide, Office of Congressman Norm Dicks"
- Figure: "Voter Turnout Worldwide"

- Two Use Your Sociological Imagination exercises
- Subsection, "Race and Gender in Politics"
- Social Inequality box, "American Indians: First Here, Among the Last to Vote"
- Updated section, "Political Activism on the Internet"

Chapter 18: The Economy and Work

- Chapter-opening poster from *Time* magazine, "India Inc."
- Taking Sociology to Work box, "Amy Wang, Product Manager, Norman International Company"
- Updated case study of capitalism in China, with (a) discussion of the social problems connected to China's rapid economic growth, (b) discussion of government censorship of the Internet, (c) figure, "World's Largest Economies, 2020 (Forecast)," and (d) cartoon
- Photo essay: "What Is Our Work?"
- Three Use Your Sociological Imagination exercises
- Subsection on microfinancing
- Updated Social Policy section on global offshoring, with discussion of offshoring as "the third Industrial Revolution"

Chapter 19: Health and Medicine

- Chapter-opening poster: "This Chicken Received More Medication in Its Lifetime than a Child from East Timor"
- Discussion of the cultural beliefs many immigrants hold and the challenges they pose to the practice of medicine, with table
- Photo essay: "What Is Medical Care?"
- Three Use Your Sociological Imagination exercises
- Discussion of the effects of poor medical care early in life on one's health later in life
- Social Inequality box: "Medical Apartheid"
- Taking Sociology to Work box: "Lola Adedokun, Independent Consultant, Health Care Research"
- Discussion of concerns about the U.S. mental health system raised by the shootings at Virginia Tech
- Updated Social Policy section on the AIDS crisis (moved from Chapter 5), with (a) updated Mapping Life Worldwide map, "Adults and Children Living with HIV/AIDS," and discussion of (b) the increasing accessibility of HIV treatment in developing countries and (c) controversy over the production of generic drugs in developing countries

Chapter 20: Communities and Urbanization

- Two Use Your Sociological Imagination exercises
- Taking Sociology to Work box, "Christie Taylor, Program Coordinator, African American Health Coalition"
- Expanded section on rural areas, including discussions of (a) their racial and ethnic diversity, (b) their place in the

global economy, (c) the migration of Gulf Coast residents to rural areas following Hurricane Katrina, (d) constraints on higher education, and (e) depopulation and economic stagnation in the northern Rockies and western Great Plains

- Revised Social Policy section, "Seeking Shelter Worldwide," with (a) Mapping Life Nationwide map, "Homeless Estimates by State," and discussions of (b) public opinion on the issue of homelessness and (c) innovative new programs to address the problem

Chapter 21: Population and the Environment

- Chapter-opening poster: Hudson Valley Development Commission, "Stop the Plant"
- Discussion of the Sierra Club's debate over restricting immigration
- Updated Mapping Life Nationwide map, "Where Americans Moved after 2000"
- Section on the environment expanded into two major sections, "Sociological Perspectives on the Environment" and "Environmental Problems"
- New subsection on global warming, with cartoon
- Discussion of the impact of the environment on health
- Use Your Sociological Imagination exercise
- Sociology in the Global Community box, "The Mysterious Fall of the Nacirema"

Chapter 22: Collective Behavior and Social Movements

- Chapter-opening poster from the Hurricane Poster Project, "Help: Need Food, Water, Electricity"
- Three Use Your Sociological Imagination exercises
- Completely revised and retitled Sociology in the Global Community box, "Women and New Social Movements in India," including (a) a historical overview of social movements in India and women's involvement in them and (b) discussion of Indian women's resource mobilization through microfinancing and lobbying for increased representation in Parliament
- Research in Action box, "Organizing for Controversy on the Web"
- Table, "Can You Match the Person with the Disability?" in Social Policy section on disability rights

Chapter 23: Globalization, Technology, and Social Change

- Table: "The United States: A Changing Nation"
- Summing Up table: "Sociological Perspectives on Social Change"

- Four Use Your Sociological Imagination exercises
- Research in Action box, "The Internet's Global Profile," with three bar graphs
- Sociology in the Global Community box, "One Laptop per Child"
- Updated and expanded Research in Action box, "The Human Genome Project"

Support for Instructors and Students

Print Resources

Study Guide The study guide, prepared by Rebecca Matthews, Ph.D. Sociology, Cornell University, includes standard features such as detailed key points, definitions of key terms, multiple-choice questions, fill-in questions, and true–false questions. All study guide questions are keyed to specific pages in the textbook, and page references are provided for key points and definitions of key terms.

In addition to the questions in the study guide, students can test their mastery of the subject matter by taking the quizzes on the *Reel Society* CD-ROM and on the Online Learning Center Web site. Students therefore have three different sets of questions to draw on for review.

Primis Customized Readers An array of first-rate readings are available to adopters in a customized electronic database. Some are classic articles from the sociological literature; others are provocative pieces written especially for McGraw-Hill by leading sociologists.

McGraw-Hill Dushkin Any of the Dushkin publications can be packaged with this text at a discount: Annual Editions, Taking Sides, Sources, Global Studies. For more information, please visit the Web site at **www.dushkin.com.**

Digital and Video Resources

VHS Videotapes Four 60-minute VHS videotapes feature brief clips (5–10 minutes each) from *NBC News* and the *Today Show* that dramatize sociological concepts, serve as lecture launchers, and generate class discussion. Each is accompanied by a guide that is available on the Online Learning Center Web site (**www.mhhe.com/schaefer11**).

PageOut: The Course Web Site Development Center All online content for *Sociology*, 11th edition, is supported by WebCT, eCollege.com, BlackBoard, and other course management systems. Additionally, McGraw-Hill's PageOut service is available to get you and your course up and running online in a matter of hours, at no cost. PageOut was designed for instructors just beginning to explore Web options. Even the novice computer user can create a course Web site with a template provided by McGraw-Hill (no programming knowledge is necessary). To learn more about PageOut, ask your McGraw-Hill representative for details, or visit **www.mhhe.com/pageout.**

Reel Society: *Interactive Movie CD-ROMs, Version*

2.0 This two-disk set features an interactive movie that demonstrates the sociological imagination through the use of actors and scenarios involving campus life. The program allows students to interact with the concepts described in the textbook in a relevant and meaningful context. Students are asked to take on the role of one of the characters and influence key plot turns by making choices for the character. A wide variety of issues and perspectives (such as culture, socialization, deviance, inequality, race and ethnicity, social institutions, and social change) are addressed in order to relate major sociological concepts and theories to the students' lives. There are also interactive quiz questions on the CDs. These CD-ROMs, a breakthrough in the use of media to teach introductory sociology students, can serve as an integral companion to the book. An instructor's guide to using the CD-ROMs, written by Rebecca Matthews, Ph.D. Sociology, Cornell University, is available on the Instructor's Edition Online Learning Center (see below).

John Tenuto of College of Lake County (in Illinois) served as the academic consultant throughout the development of this program. The script for *Reel Society* was reviewed by the following instructors: Jan Abu Shakrah, Portland Community College; Grant Farr, Portland State University; Rebecca Matthews, Ph.D. Sociology, Cornell University; Kenneth L. Stewart, Angelo State University (in Texas); and Cheryl Tieman, Radford University (in Virginia). In addition, students from George Mason University in Virginia offered their reactions to the script during a focus group.

There are several ways for instructors and students to use *Reel Society.* Students can follow the storyline from start to finish or choose only those scenes for a given chapter or topic. In either case, the movie segments are augmented by a robust array of review and assessment features, including self-quizzes. Instructors are provided with their own version of *Reel Society,* which allows them to choose which of the program's review features to show in class, if any.

Online Learning Center Web Site

The Online Learning Center Web site that accompanies this text (**www.mhhe.com/schaefer11**) offers a rich array of resources for instructors and students, which were developed by Lynn Newhart of Rockford College in Illinois and Rebecca Matthews, Ph.D. Sociology, Cornell University. Here you will find the author's audio introductions to each chapter, as well as interactive quizzes and maps, social policy exercises, PowerPoint slides, census updates, chapter glossaries, vocabulary flash cards, video clips, additional information about the chapter-opening excerpts and their authors, diagnostic midterm and final exams, links to the book's Internet exercises, and other resources. You can use any of the material from the Online Learning Center in a course Web site that you create using PageOut.

eInstruction: *The Classroom Performance System*

The Classroom Performance System (CPS) is a wireless response system that allows instructors to receive immediate feedback from students. CPS units include easy-to-use software for instructors' use in creating questions and assessments and delivering them to students. The units also include individual wireless response pads for students' use in responding. Suggested questions, prepared by Rebecca Matthews, Ph.D. Sociology, Cornell University, appear on the Instructor's Edition of the Schaefer Web site, **www.mhhe.com/schaefer11,** and on the Instructor's Resource DVD-ROM. CPS also runs alongside the PowerPoint slides that supplement Schaefer's *Sociology: A Brief Edition.* For further details, go to **www.mhhe.com/einstruction.**

PowerPoint Slides

Adopters of *Sociology* can also receive a set of more than 600 PowerPoint slides developed especially for this edition by Richard T. Schaefer and Gerry Williams. The slides are included on the Instructor's Edition Online Learning Center (described below). The set includes bulleted lecture points, figures, and maps. Instructors are welcome to create overhead transparencies from the slides if they wish to do so.

Instructor's Edition Online Learning Center with Computerized Test Bank

Schaefer's highly valued instructor resources are all available for download from the Instructor's portion of the Online Learning Center located at **www.mhhe.com/schaefer11.** Teaching aids available include the Instructor's Resource Manual, Test Banks I and II in computerized and Word formats, the instructor's guide to the *Reel Society* CD, and PowerPoint slides for the convenience of instructors who choose to give multimedia lectures. The Instructor's Resource Manual, prepared by Richard T. Schaefer, Clayton Steenberg of Arkansas State University, and Rebecca Matthews, Ph.D. Sociology, Cornell University, provides sociology instructors with detailed chapter outlines, learning objectives, additional lecture ideas (among them, alternative social policy issues), class discussion topics, essay questions, topics for student research (along with suggested research materials for each topic), and suggested additional readings. Media materials are suggested for each chapter, including videotapes and films. The test banks were written by Clayton Steenberg of Arkansas State University and Rebecca Matthews, Ph.D. Sociology, Cornell University. Multiple-choice and true–false questions are included for each chapter; they will be useful in testing students on basic sociological concepts, application of theoretical perspectives, and recall of important factual information. Correct answers and page references are provided for all questions.

McGraw-Hill's EZ Test is a flexible and easy-to-use electronic testing program. The program allows instructors to create tests from book-specific items. It accommodates a wide range of question types and instructors may add their own questions. Multiple versions of the test can be created and any test can be exported for use with course management systems such as WebCT, BlackBoard, or PageOut. EZ Test Online is a new service that gives you a place to easily administer your EZ Test–created exams and quizzes online. The program is available for Windows and Macintosh environments.

Primis Online   Professors can customize this book by selecting from it only those chapters they want to use in their courses. Primis Online allows users to choose and change the order of chapters, as well as to add readings from McGraw-Hill's vast database of content. Both custom-printed textbooks and electronic eBooks are available. To learn more, contact your McGraw-Hill sales representative, or visit our Web site at **www.primisonline.com**

Acknowledgments

Since 1999, Elizabeth Morgan has played a most significant role in the development of my introductory sociology books. Once again, in the Eleventh Edition, Betty has been involved from the preliminary plans for the vast array of changes right through checking the page proofs with me. Her impact is found on literally every page of this book.

I deeply appreciate the contributions to this book made by my editors. Thom Holmes, a senior developmental editor at McGraw-Hill, challenged me to make this edition better than its predecessor. Rhona Robbin, director of development and media technology, oversaw the project.

I have received strong support and encouragement from Frank Mortimer, publisher; Gina Boedeker, sponsoring editor; and Leslie Oberhuber, senior marketing manager. Additional guidance and support were provided by Evan Bock, editorial coordinator; Rachel Bara, editorial assistant; Carey Eisner, production editor; Cassandra Chu, design manager; Nora Agbayani, senior photo research coordinator; David Tietz, photo researcher; Emma Ghiselli, art editor; Richard DeVitto, production supervisor; and Judy Brody, permissions editor.

Academic Reviewers

This edition continues to reflect many insightful suggestions made by reviewers of the first ten hardcover editions and the seven paperback brief editions. The tenth and eleventh editions have benefited from constructive and thorough evaluations provided by sociologists from both two-year and four-year institutions.

I would also like to acknowledge the contributions of the following individuals: Lynn Newhart of Rockford College in Illinois for her work on the Online Learning Center; Clayton Steenberg of Arkansas State University and Rebecca Matthews, Ph.D. Sociology, Cornell University, for their work on the Instructor's Resource Manual and the test banks; Rebecca Matthews for her work on the study guide; Thom Holmes of McGraw-Hill and John Tenuto of Lake County College in Illinois for their work on the *Reel Society* CD-ROM; and Rebecca Matthews for her work on the instructor's guide to accompany the *Reel Society* CD-ROM, and on a series of exam questions based on *Reel Society* scenarios.

As is evident from these acknowledgments, the preparation of a textbook is truly a team effort. The most valuable member of this effort continues to be my wife, Sandy. She provides the support so necessary in my creative and scholarly activities.

I have had the good fortune to be able to introduce students to sociology for many years. These students have been enormously helpful in spurring on my own sociological imagination. In ways I can fully appreciate but cannot fully acknowledge, their questions in class and queries in the hallway have found their way into this textbook.

Richard T. Schaefer
www.schaefersociology.net
schaeferrt@aol.com

*As a full-service publisher of quality educational products, McGraw-Hill does much more than just sell textbooks to your students. We create and publish an extensive array of print, video, and digital supplements to support instruction on your campus. Orders of new (versus used) textbooks help us to defray the cost of developing such supplements, which is substantial. Please consult your local McGraw-Hill representative to learn about the availability of the supplements that accompany Sociology. If you are not sure who your representative is, you can find him or her by using the Rep Locator at **www.mhhe.com**.*

Jan Abu Shakrah, *Portland Community College*

Anora Ackerson, *Kalamazoo Valley Community College*

Randall Adams, *Tennessee Tech University*

Grace Auyang, *University of Cincinnati*

Therese Baker-Degler, *California State University–San Marcos*

Stanley Baran, *Bryant University*

Jeffrey Basham, *Ohlone College*

Johnnie Bell, *Northeast Alabama Community College*

Gregg Busch, *West Virginia University at Parkersburg*

Stella Capek, *Hendrix College*

Michael S. Carolan, *Colorado State University*

Judy Carr, *Southwest Missouri State University*

Denise Cobb, *University of Arkansas–Little Rock*

Kelly Dagan, *Illinois College*

Estelle Disch, *University of Massachusetts–Boston*

Kevin D. Dougherty, *Calvin College*

Robyn Driskell, *Baylor University*

Susan Dumais, *Louisiana State University*

Kevin Everett, *Radford University*

Catherine Felton, *Central Piedmont Community College*

Jan Fiola, *Minnesota State University*

Jeremy Freese, *University of Wisconsin–Madison*

Kathleen French, *Kapiolani Community College*

Tom Gerschick, *Illinois State University*

Naomi Gerstel, *University of Massachusetts*

Michael D. Grimes, *Louisiana State University*

William Gronfein, *IUPUI*

Jennifer F. Hamer, *Wayne State University*

Chad M. Hanson, *Casper College*

Brooke Harrington, *Brown University*

Doug Hartmann, *University of Minnesota*

Jeremy Hein, *University of Wisconsin–Eau Claire*

William Hoynes, *Vassar College*

Scott Kauzlarich, *Ellsworth Community College*

Kevin Keating, *Broward Community College*

Robert O. Keel, *University of Missouri–St. Louis*

Harold Kerbo, *California Polytechnic State University*

Keith Kerr, *Texas A&M*

Dustin Kidd, *Temple University*

Ramsey Kleff, *Virginia Union University*

Jerome Koch, *Texas Tech University*

Nelson F. Kofie, *Prince George's Community College*

Kevin T. Leicht, *University of Iowa*

Robert J. Mahoney, *Rockhurst College*

Martin Marger, *Michigan State University*

Matthew Oware, *DePauw University*

Ralph Pyle, *Michigan State University*

Charles Quiste-Adade, *Central Michigan University*

Paul D. Roof, *College of Charleston*

William G. Roy, *UCLA*

Carol Schmid, *Guilford Technical Community College*

J. William Spencer, *Purdue University*

Jim Thomas, *Northern Illinois University*

Leona Tompkin, *University of Toledo*

Lisa Troyer, *University of Iowa*

Debra Van Ausdale, *Syracuse University*

Candace Warner, *Columbia State Community College*

Rollin J. Watson, *Somerset Community College*

Keith Whitworth, *TCU*

Melissa J. Wilde, *Indiana University*

Stephani Williams, *Arizona State University*

J. Russell Willis, *Grambling State University*

visual preview

Teaching Students to Think Sociologically

The eleventh edition of *Sociology* continues its tradition of teaching students how to think critically about society and their own lives from a wide range of classical and contemporary sociological perspectives.

"Use Your Sociological Imagination" Sections

Within each chapter are challenging questions designed to stimulate a student's sociological imagination. Students can respond to these questions using the associated Online Learning Center for the book and e-mail their answers to their instructors.

Provocative Book Excerpts

Each chapter opens with a lively excerpt from the writings of sociologists and others, clearly conveying the excitement and relevance of sociological inquiry. These excerpts are effectively linked by the author to the content of the chapter.

Sociology's Global View Map

Sociology explores key sociological issues from the viewpoints of many global cultures. This map serves as a quick guide to selected passages focusing on global issues and topics.

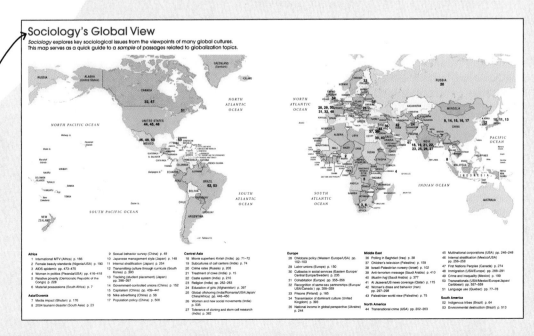

Analyzing a Broad Range of Contemporary Issues

Page thumbnail (150)

150

Chapter 6

(social Policy) and Organizations

The State of the Unions

The Issue

How many people do you know who belong to a labor union? Chances are you can name a lot fewer people than someone could 50 years ago. In 1954, unions represented 39 percent of workers in the private sector of the U.S. economy; in 2005 they represented only 12.5 percent (see Figure 6-2). What has happened to diminish the importance of organized labor? Have unions outlived their usefulness in a rapidly changing global economy that is dominated by the service sector (AFL-CIO 2001; Bureau of Labor Statistics 2005)?

The Setting

Labor unions consist of organized workers who share either the same skill (as in electronics) or the same employer (as in the case of postal employees). Unions began to emerge during the Industrial Revolution in England, in the 1700s. Groups of workers banded together to extract concessions from employers (e.g., safer working conditions, a shorter workweek), as well as to protect their positions. They frequently tried to protect their jobs by limiting entry to their occupation based on gender, race, ethnicity, citizenship, age, and sometimes rather arbitrary measures of skill levels. Today we see less of this protection of special interests, but individual labor unions are still the target of charges of discrimination, as are employers.

The power of labor unions varies widely from country to country. In some countries, such as Britain and Mexico, unions play a key role in the foundation of governments. In others, such as Japan and Korea, their role in politics is very limited, and even their ability to influence the private sector is relatively weak. In the United States, unions can sometimes have a significant influence on employers and elected officials, but their effect varies dramatically by type of industry and even region of the country: see Figure 6-3 (M. Wallerstein and Western 2000).

Few people today would dispute the fact that union membership is declining. Among the reasons for the decline are the following:

1. **Changes in the type of industry.** Manufacturing j... traditional heart of the labor union, have declined, giv... to postindustrial service jobs.
2. **Growth in part-time jobs.** Between 1982 and 1998 t... ber of temporary jobs in the United States rose 577... while total employment increased only 41 percent. ... 2000 did laws governing collective bargaining allow... rary workers to join a union.
3. **The legal system.** The United States has not made i... ularly easy for unions to organize and bargain, and so... ernment measures have made it more difficult. A d...

FIGURE 6-2

Union Membership in the United States

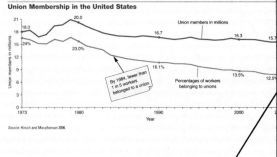

Union members in millions

By 1984, fewer than 1 in 5 workers belonged to a union.

Percentages of workers belonging to unions

Source: Hirsch and Macpherson 2006.

Hallmark Social Policy Sections

These discussions provide a sociological perspective on contemporary social issues such as the death penalty, global immigration, gay marriage, and offshore service jobs. Providing a global view of the issues, each section includes an overview of the subject plus questions to stimulate critical thinking and discussion.

Page thumbnail (168)

social INEQUALITY ●●●

7-1 The Color of Network TV

Today, 40 percent of all youths in the United States are children of color, yet few of the faces they see on television reflect their race or cultural heritage. As of spring 2007, only 5 of the nearly 60 primetime series carried on the four major networks featured performers of color in leading roles, and only 2—*Ugly Betty* and *George Lopez*—centered on minority performers. What is more, the programs were debuted earlier in the evening, when young people are most likely to watch television, are the *least* diverse of all.

When minority groups do appear on television and in other forms of media, their roles tend to reinforce the stereotypes associated with their ethnic or racial groups. In 2004, nearly half of all Middle Eastern characters shown on television were criminals, compared to only 5 percent of White characters. Latino roles were just as stereotyped. Recently, Latinas have been featured as maids on *Will and Grace* (Rosario), *Dharma and Greg* (Celia), and even the animated *King of the Hill* (Lupino), to name just three shows.

In a rare exception to this pattern, in 2006 *The West Wing* featured the election of a Latino president, played by Puerto Rican American Jimmy Smits. Ironically, the character of Jed Bartlett, who was president through most of the long-running series, is played by Martin Sheen. Sheen, born Ramon Estevez, rarely mentions his Hispanic roots.

Producers, writers, executives, and advertisers blame one another for the rampant underrepresentation of racial and ethnic minorities. Television programming is dictated by advertisers, a former executive claims; if advertisers said they wanted blatantly biased programming, the networks would provide it. Jery Isenberg, chairman of the Caucus for Producers, Writers & Directors, blames the networks, saying that writers would produce a series about three-headed Martians if the networks told them to.

Beyond these excuses, real reasons can be found for the departure from the diversity exhibited in past shows and seasons. In recent years, the rise of more networks, cable TV, and the Internet has fragmented the broadcast entertainment market, siphoning viewers away from the general-audience sitcoms and dramas of the past. Both the UPN and WB networks produce situation comedies and even full evenings geared toward African American audiences. With the proliferation of cable channels such as Black Entertainment Television (BET) and the Spanish-language Telemundo and Univision, as well as Web sites that cater to every imaginable taste, there no longer seems to be a need for broadly popular

A rare sight on prime-time television: In CW's *Girlfriends*, which debuted in 2000, all the leading roles are played by African Americans.

series such as *The Cosby Show*, the tone and content of which appealed to Whites as well as Blacks in a way the newer series do not. The result of these sweeping technological changes has been a sharp divergence in viewer preferences.

Meanwhile, mainstream network executives, producers, and writers remain overwhelmingly White. Most of them live far from ethnically and racially diverse inner-city neighborhoods and tend to write and produce stories about people like themselves. Marc Hirshfeld, an NBC executive, claims some

> *Marc Hirshfeld, an NBC executive, claims some White producers have told him they don't know how to write for Black characters.*

White producers have told him they don't know how to write for Black characters. Stephen Bochco, producer of *NYPD Blue*, is a rare exception. His series *City of Angels* featured a mostly non-White cast, like the people Bochco grew up with in an inner-city neighborhood. The series ran for 23 episodes before being canceled in 2000.

In the long run, media observers believe, the major networks will need to integrate the ranks of gatekeepers before they achieve true diversity in programming. Adonis Hoffman, director of the Corporate Policy Institute, has

urged network executives to throw open their studios and boardrooms to minorities. Hoffman thinks such a move would empower Black writers and producers to present a true-to-life portrait of African Americans. There are some signs of agreement from the networks. According to Doug Herzog, president of Fox Entertainment, real progress means incorporating diversity from within.

Why should it matter that minority groups aren't visible on major network television, if they are well represented on other channels such as UPN, WB, BET, and Univision? The problem is that Whites as well as minorities see a distorted picture of their society every time they turn on network TV. In Hoffman's words, "African Americans, Latinos and Asians, while portrayed as such, are not merely walk-ons in our society—they are woven into the fabric of what has made this country great" (A. Hoffman 1997:M6).

Let's Discuss

1. Do you watch network TV? If so, how well do you think it represents the diversity of U.S. society?
2. Have you seen a movie or TV show recently that portrayed members of a minority group in a sensitive and realistic way—as real people rather than as stereotypes or token walk-ons? If so, describe the show.

Sources: Bielby and Bielby 2002; Braxton 2007; Children Now 2004; Directors Guild of America 2002; Gamson and Latteier 2004; A. Hoffman 1997; M. Navarro 2002; Poniewozik 2001.

168

Social Inequality Boxes

These boxes on social issues such as affirmative action, disability as a master status, and privilege and discrimination in employment highlight an important area of analysis for sociologists today.

New section thumbnails

Sociological Perspectives on the Environment

Sociologists and others may debate the potential impact ulation...

Race and Gender in Politics

Because politics is synonymous with power and autho... should not be surprised that political strength is lacking... ginaliz...

Worldwide Poverty

In developing countries, any deterioration of the econo... being of those who are least well off threatens their ver... As we saw in Chapter 9 (see Box 9-2, page 000), even t... in the developing world are poor by U.S. standards. T... are poor in developing countries are truly destitute. What would a map of the world look like if we d...

New Sections: Environmental Issues, Race and Gender in Politics, Global Poverty

Among the many new chapter sections are discussions of global warming and the environment with views representing three sociological perspectives (Chapter 21), race and gender in politics, key points regarding use of the Internet for political activism (Chapter 17), and worldwide poverty, with a Mapping Life Worldwide feature (Chapter 10).

Providing Expanded Coverage of Globalization and World Cultures

Sections on Global Issues

Every chapter has been revised with the aim of embracing examples and sociological issues affecting world cultures. Especially important are sections providing contemporary terms and definitions for thinking globally (Chapter 1); understanding fundamental global inequality (Chapter 10); the impact of global immigration (Chapter 11); global population and environmental issues (Chapter 21); and privacy and censorship in a global village (Chapter 23).

FIGURE 10–1

Fundamental Global Inequality

Deaths of children
Rural population
Total births
The burden of disease
Total population
Cultivated land
Urban population
Income
CO_2 emissions
Health spending
Exports
Military spending

0   20   40   60   80   100
Percent of total

■ Developing nations   ■ Industrial nations

Note: In this comparison, industrial nations include the United States and Canada, Japan, Western Europe, and Australasia. Developing nations include Africa, Asia (except for Japan), Latin America, Eastern Europe, the Caribbean, and the Pacific.
Source: Adapted from Sutcliffe 2002:18.

Think About It

Languages of the World: How

MAPPING LIFE WORLD

Stratification in the World System

The divide between industrial and developing nations is sharp.

Number of languages spoken as a first language in each country

Each square represents one language

Country Rankings
● Highest number of spoken languages
● Lowest number of spoken languages

---

ungry children that supper is almost ready. As they hover over ne pot, these women hope that their malnourished children will ll asleep (McNeil 2004).

Around the world, inequality is a significant determinant of uman behavior, opening doors of opportunity to some and osing them to others. Indeed, disparities in life chances are so xtreme that in some places, the poorest of the poor may not be ware of them. Western media images may have circled the lobe, but in extremely depressed rural areas, those at the bot- om of society are not likely to see them.

A few centuries ago, such vast divides in global wealth did not xist. Except for a very few rulers and landowners, everyone in he world was poor. In much of Europe, life was as difficult as it as in Asia or South America. This was true until the Industrial evolution and rising agricultural productivity produced explo- ve economic growth. The resulting rise in living standards was ot evenly distributed across the world.

Figure 10-1 compares the industrial nations of the world to he developing nations. Using total population as a yardstick, we e that the developing countries have more than their fair share f rural population, as well as of total births, disease, and child- ood deaths. At the same time, the industrial nations of the orld, with a much smaller share of total population, have much ore income and exports than the developing nations. Indus- ial nations also spend more on health and the military than her nations, and they emit more carbon dioxide (CO_2) (Sachs 005a; Sutcliffe 2002).

Revealing Photo Essays

Nine photo essays (three new to this edition) provide glimpses of ways of life in different countries. Each begins with a question intended to prompt students to see some part of everyday life with new eyes—those of a sociologist. The accompanying photos and captions suggest the answer to the question.

Are You What You Eat?

The foods people eat, along with the customs they observe in preparing and consuming their meals, say a great deal about their cultures. In some cultures, such as that of Papua New Guinea, most pork is a delicacy reserved for feasts; in others it is forbidden food. In U.S. culture, genetically modified food is accepted without much question, but in Europe it is banned. Because Swedish people put great value on natural, organic foods, 99 percent of mothers in Sweden breast-feed their in- fants—a rate much higher than that in the United States.

In India, people generally dine while sitting on the floor, as shown here, or on very low stools. Instead of utensils such as forks or chopsticks, they eat with the fingers of the right hand. While Indians have accepted some aspects of U.S.-style fast- food culture, they go to McDonald's for McCurry and McVeggie sandwiches—not for hamburgers, a food that is prohibited by the Hindu religion.

In some cultures, such as France, fine cuisine is a cultural in- stitution. The French prefer fresh local produce lovingly pre- pared, consumed slowly along with good conversation and a bottle of wine. To the French and to gourmets around the world, great chefs are celebrities.

Given their reverence for food, the French would be most un- likely to participate in a contest designed to see who can gob- ble down the most hot dogs. In the United States and Japan, these public events are quite popular. But though the Japanese admire American culture, they stop short at copying the Ameri- can habit of eating fast food on the street while rushing from one place to another. The Japanese will purchase food from a street vendor, but they will not walk around while eating it, because doing so would show disrespect for the preparer.

Coney Island, New York

(India)

60

Sociology in the Global Community Boxes

These boxes, found in most chapters, provide a global perspective on topics such as the worldwide response to the 2004 tsunami disaster, working women in Nepal, global poverty, and the impact of global media such as the Al Jazeera network.

---

sociology IN *the Global Community*

10-1 Cutting Poverty Worldwide

The goal of the United Nations' Millennium Project is to cut the world's poverty level in half by 2015. The project has eight objectives:

1. *Eradicate extreme poverty and hunger.* Poverty rates are falling in many parts of the globe, particularly in Asia. But in sub-Saharan Africa, where the poor are hard pressed, millions more have sunk deeper into poverty. As of 2001, more than 1 bil- lion people worldwide were living on less than $1 a day. These people suffer from chronic hunger. As of 2006, an estimated 100 million of the world's children were malnourished—a statistic that has nega- tive implications for their countries' eco- nomic progress.
2. *Achieve universal primary education.* While many parts of the developing world are approaching universal school enroll- ment, in sub-Saharan Africa, less than two-thirds of all children are enrolled in primary school.
3. *Promote gender equality and empower women.* The gender gap in primary school enrollment that has characterized the de- veloping world for so long is slowly clos- ing. However, women still lack equal representation at the highest levels of gov- ernment. Worldwide, they hold only about

toward reducing child mortality has slowed in recent decades.
5. *Improve maternal health.* Each year more than half a million women die during preg- nancy or childbirth. Progress has been made in reducing maternal death rates in some developing regions, but not in countries where the risk of giving birth is highest.
6. *Combat HIV/AIDS, malaria, and other dis- eases.* AIDS has become the leading cause of premature death in sub-Saharan Africa, where two-thirds of the world's AIDS patients reside. Worldwide, the dis- ease is the fourth most frequent killer. Though new drug treatments can prolong life, there is still no cure for this scourge.

> *As of 2001, more than 1 billion people worldwide were living on less than $1 a day.*

Moreover, each year malaria and tuber- culosis kill almost as many people as AIDS, severely draining the labor pool in many countries.
7. *Ensure environmental sustainability.*

water has increased, half the developing world lacks toilets and other forms of ba- sic sanitation.
8. *Develop a global partnership for develop- ment.* The United Nations Millennium Declaration seeks a global social com- pact in which developing countries pledge to do more to ensure their own de- velopment, while developed countries support them through aid, debt relief, and improved trade opportunities. However, despite the much publicized G8 summit (a meeting of the heads of state of the 8 ma- jor economies) in Gleneagles, Scotland, in 2005 and the accompanying LIVE 8 global concerts, the developed nations have fallen far short of the targets they set themselves.

Let's Discuss

1. Do you think the Millenium Project's ob- jectives are realistic, given the enormity of the obstacles that must be overcome? Why do you think the project's founders gave themselves only 15 years to accom- plish their goal?
2. How are the project's eight objectives re- lated to one another? Could some of the objectives be reached successfully with-

Relating Sociology to Students' Lives

Sociology on Campus Boxes

These boxes on topics such as cheating, social class and financial aid, and binge drinking apply a sociological perspective to several issues of immediate interest to students.

sociologyON*campus*

8-1 Binge Drinking

Wesley Allan Croley, a 20-year-old community college student, was standing around a bonfire with some friends the night of December 9, 2006. Most of the young people gathered in the field in Monroe County, Alabama, that night were drinking beer. But witnesses told investigators that Croley took a bottle of vodka from his truck, passed it around, and then finished it himself.

About 11 p.m. police responded to a 911 call from the field. Shortly after, Croley was pronounced dead at a local hospital. Forensic tests showed his blood-alcohol content was .414—more than five times the legal level for motorists in Alabama. The cause of death: acute alcohol intoxication.

Croley was not unusual in his behavior. According to a study published by the Harvard School of Public Health in 2002, 44 percent of college students indulge in binge drinking (defined as at least five drinks in a row for men and four in a row for women). For those who live in a Greek fraternity or sorority, the rates are even higher—four out of five are binge drinkers (see the figure). These numbers represent an increase from 1990s data, despite efforts on many campuses across the nation to educate students about the risks of binge drinking. The problem is not confined to the United States—Britain, Russia, and South Africa all report regular "drink till you drop" alcoholic consumption among young people. Nor does binge drinking begin in college. A national study published in 2007 by the American Academy of Pediatrics found that over a 30-day pe-

The other side of this potentially self-destructive behavior is that binge drinking represents *conformity* to the peer culture, especially in fraternities and sororities, which serve as social centers on many campuses. Most students seem to take an "everybody does it—no big deal" attitude toward the behavior. Many find that taking five drinks in a row is fairly typical. As one student at Boston University noted, "Anyone that goes to a party does that or worse. If you talk to anyone college age, it's normal."

44 percent of college students indulge in binge drinking.

Some colleges and universities are taking steps to make binge drinking a bit less "normal" by means of *social control*—banning kegs, closing fraternities and sororities, encouraging liquor retailers not to sell in high volume to students, and expelling students after three alcohol-related infractions. Yet many colleges still tolerate spring break organizers who promote "All you can drink" parties as part of a tour package.

Let's Discuss

1. Why do you think most college students regard binge drinking as a normal rather than a deviant behavior?
2. Which do you think would be more effective in stopping binge drinking on your campus, informal or formal social control?

Sources: Baggett 2007; J. Miller et al. 2007; Wechsler et al. 2002, 2004.

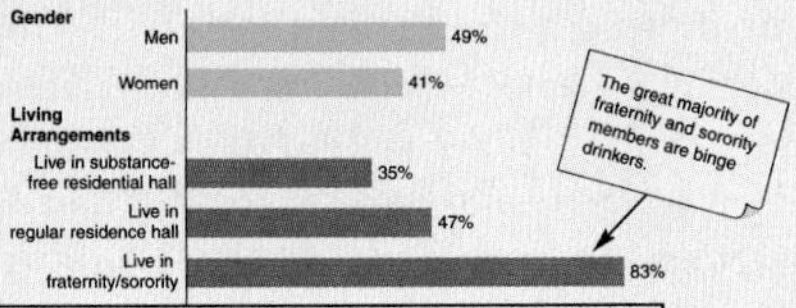
Gender
Men
49%
Women
41%
Living Arrangements
Live in substance-free residential hall
35%
Live in regular residence hall
47%
Live in fraternity/sorority
83%
The great majority of fraternity and sorority members are binge drinkers.

Research in Action Boxes

These boxes present sociological findings on relevant topics such as adolescent sexual networks, the challenge of doing research polling in Baghdad, and communication differences between male and female physicians.

researchIN*action*

11-1 Interracial and Interethnic Friendships

Do people really have close friends of different racial and ethnic backgrounds? Some sociologists have attempted to gauge the degree of White–Black interaction in the United States. But if these studies are not done carefully, they may overestimate the degree of "racial togetherness" in our society.

Sociologist Tom Smith, who directs the respected General Social Survey, has noticed that a high proportion of both White and African American respondents claim to have close friends of another race. But is that really true? When Smith and fellow researchers analyzed the survey data, they found that response rates varied with the way the question was phrased. When asked whether any of the friends they felt close to was Black, 42.1 percent of Whites said yes. Yet when asked to give the names of friends they felt close to, only 6 percent of Whites listed a close friend of a different race or ethnicity.

When asked the race of their best same-sex friend, most Americans choose someone of the same race as themselves. In a national study of adolescents, over 91 percent of non-Hispanic Whites claimed a non-Hispanic White as their best same-sex friend. (The General Social Survey yielded almost the same result for all adults.) Given the fact that over a third of the teens in the United States are either non-White or Hispanic, we might have expected to find more cross-race friendships. Members of minority groups seem more willing than Whites to cross racial and ethnic boundaries, however. A slightly lower 85 percent of Black adolescents selected a Black for a best friend, and a markedly lower 62 percent of Mexican Americans named another Mexican American.

A high proportion of both White and African American respondents claim to have close friends of another race.

Interactionists have noted significant differences in interracial and interethnic friendships. Regardless of one's racial or ethnic group, friendships that cross racial and ethnic boundaries are less likely than others to involve visits to each other's homes. They are also less likely than others to feature a sharing of personal problems.

In sum, careful research shows that to a great degree, our society's growing diversity is not reflected in our choice of friends.

Let's Discuss

1. How common are interracial and interethnic friendships where you live or go to school? Do the results of the two surveys described here strike you as familiar?
2. What might explain the gap between the percentage of Whites claiming to have a close friend who was Black and the percentage of Whites who listed a close friend of another race or ethnicity?

Sources: Hamm et al. 2005; Kao and Joyner 2004; T. Smith 1999.

are treated as second-class citizens—a charge that provoked ri- in 2005. In Australia, Aborigines who have become part of dominant society refuse to acknowledge their darker- ned grandparents on the street. And in the United States, e Italian Americans, Polish Americans, Hispanics, and Jews changed their ethnic-sounding family names to names that ypically found among White Protestant families.

Assimilation is the process through which a person forsakes his or her own cultural tradition to become part of a different culture. Generally, it is practiced by a minority group member who wants to conform to the standards of the dominant group. Assimilation can be described as a pattern in which A + B + C → A. The majority, A, dominates in such a way that members of minorities B and C imitate it and attempt to become indistinguishable from it (Newman 1973).

Assimilation can strike at the very roots of a person's identity. Alphonso D'Abruzzo, for example, changed his name to Alan Alda. The British actress Joyce Frankenberg changed her name to Jane

le 11-2

ciological Perspectives on Race and Ethnicity

{takingSOCIOLOGY TO WORK}

Bari Katz
Program Director, National Conference for Community and Justice

"Though it may sound like a cliché, I have always known that my goal in life is to change the world," says Bari Katz. Since ninth grade this sociology major has known that her mission is to end injustice and cycles of oppression, both at home and abroad.

Katz began working for human rights while studying for her B.A. and M.A. at New York University. While there she joined with the Human Rights Initiative at New York's Urban Justice Center to tackle issues such as immigration, hate crimes, and housing for the homeless. In her final year at NYU, eager to involve other students in the hands-on advocacy work she had been doing, she founded an internship program in human rights. Today, thanks to Katz's efforts, NYU students can work for human rights in New York City and South Africa.

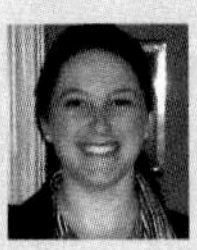

Katz is currently program director at the National Conference for Community and Justice, where she develops, implements, and evaluates programs to promote respect and understanding among all races, religions, and cultures. Her long-range goal is to educate people about social justice issues, teach them to manage conflict, and inspire them to become advocates for positive social change. For Katz, every week brings new challenges and opportunities. She trains personnel at other organizations, develops youth programs, and researches and writes on issues that affect her community. "I have the amazing opportunity to be creative, independent, and influential in affecting real change," she says.

As a student, Katz found sociology to be extremely relevant to her interest in human rights. In her sophomore year she took a class on social movements, which climaxed with class attendance at an antiwar protest. "This was the first time I realized that sociology wasn't just about theories and research—it is a discipline that applies this knowledge to social problems and real-world events," she says. Katz also took a class called Public Sociology, which emphasized the importance of connecting sociology to the larger world. As part of the course, she joined the editorial board of *Contexts*, a sociological journal aimed at bridging the gap between the academic and practical sides of the discipline.

Looking back on her education, Katz says it has been invaluable to her. Sociology gave her both analytical skills and a broad understanding of systems and societies. "My training has taught me to look at the root causes of a problem, which is a principle I use every day in designing curriculum and programs," she says.

Let's Discuss

1. Katz found that sociology supported her interest in human rights, allowing her to make it her life's work. How can sociology help you to develop your interests?
2. What human rights issues are you aware of in your own community? What could you do to support human rights?

2006, the average value of goods and services produced per citizen (or per capita gross national income) in the industrialized countries of the United States, Japan, Switzerland, Belgium, and Norway was more than $31,000. In at least 10 poorer countries, the value was just $900 or less. But most countries fell somewhere between those extremes, as Figure 10-2 shows.

Still, the contrasts are stark. Three forces discussed here are particularly responsible for the domination of the world marketplace by a few nations: the legacy of colonialism, the advent of multinational corporations, and modernization.

The Legacy of Colonialism

Colonialism occurs when a foreign power maintains political, social, economic, and cultural domination over a people for an ex-

By the 1980s, colonialism had largely disappeared. Most of the nations that were colonies before World War I had achieved political independence and established their own governments. However, for many of these countries, the transition to genuine self-rule was not yet complete. Colonial domination had established patterns of economic exploitation that continued even after nationhood was achieved—in part because former colonies were unable to develop their own industry and technology. Their dependence on more industrialized nations, including their former colonial masters, for managerial and technical expertise, investment capital, and manufactured goods kept former colonies in a subservient position. Such continuing dependence and foreign domination are referred to as ***neocolonialism***.

Taking Sociology to Work Boxes

These boxes—including eight new entries with this edition—underscore the value of an undergraduate degree in sociology by profiling individuals who majored in sociology and use its principles in their work.

Offering Distinctive Pedagogy, Illustrations, and Resources That Reinforce Content

Summing Up Tables

Twenty-eight Summing Up tables recap coverage of the major theoretical perspectives on all major topics.

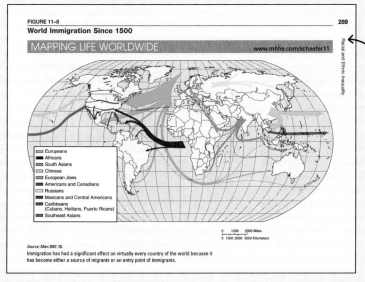

information. In addition, research proposals that involve human subjects must now be overseen by a review board, whose members seek to ensure that subjects are not placed at an unreasonable level of risk. If necessary, the board may ask researchers to revise their research designs to conform to the code of ethics.

Sometimes disclosing all the sources of funding for a study, as required in principle 7 of the ASA's *Code of Ethics*, is not a sufficient guarantee of ethical conduct. Especially in the case of both corporate and government funding, money given ostensibly for the support of basic research may come with strings attached. Ac-

summingUP

Table 2-2
Major Research Designs

Method	Examples	Advantages	Limitations
Survey	Questionnaires Interviews	Yields information about specific issues	Can be expensive and time-consuming
Observation	Ethnography	Yields detailed information about specific groups or organizations	Involves months if not years of labor-intensive data
Experiment	Deliberate manipulation of people's social behavior	Yields direct measures of people's behavior	Ethical limitations on the degree to which subjects' behavior can be manipulated
Existing sources/ Secondary analysis	Analysis of census or health data Analysis of films or TV commercials	Cost-efficiency	Limited to data collected for some other purpose

---

FIGURE 11–8   **289**
World Immigration Since 1500

MAPPING LIFE WORLDWIDE   www.mhhe.com/schaefer11

Racial and Ethnic Inequality

Legend:
- Europeans
- Africans
- South Asians
- Chinese
- European Jews
- Americans and Canadians
- Russians
- Mexicans and Central Americans
- Caribbeans (Cubans, Haitians, Puerto Ricans)
- Southeast Asians

0   1000   2000 Miles
0 1000 2000 3000 Kilometers

Source: Allen 2007: 20.
Immigration has had a significant effect on virtually every country of the world becuase it has become either a source of migrants or an entry point of immigrants.

Demographic Map Program

Two kinds of maps—Mapping Life Nationwide and Mapping Life Worldwide—are featured throughout the text. Interactive versions of many of these maps, along with accompanying questions, appear on the book's Online Learning Center Web site.

"Think About It" Figure Captions

These captions, which accompany many of the book's maps, graphs, and tables, encourage students to think critically about information presented in figures.

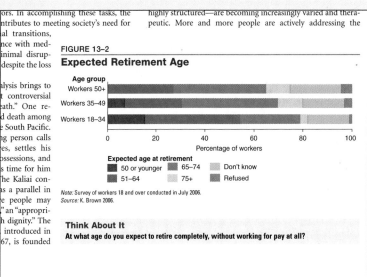

ors. In accomplishing these tasks, the ntributes to meeting society's need for al transitions, nce with med- inimal disrup- despite the loss

alysis brings to t controversial eath." One re- d death among e South Pacific. ng person calls es, settles his ossessions, and s time for him The Kaliai con- as a parallel in e people may " an "appropri- h dignity." The introduced in 67, is founded

highly structured—are becoming increasingly varied and therapeutic. More and more people are actively addressing the

FIGURE 13–2
Expected Retirement Age

Age group
- Workers 50+
- Workers 35–49
- Workers 18–34

Percentage of workers: 0, 20, 40, 60, 80, 100

Expected age at retirement
- 50 or younger
- 51–64
- 65–74
- 75+
- Don't know
- Refused

Note: Survey of workers 18 and over conducted in July 2006.
Source: K. Brown 2006.

Think About It
At what age do you expect to retire completely, without working for pay at all?

Featuring Meaningful Resources That Promote Active Learning and Review

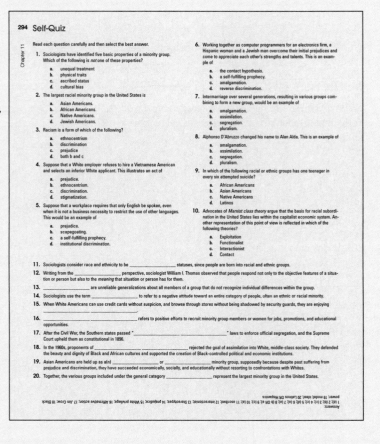

New Self-Quizzes

At the end of every chapter, a twenty-question self-quiz allows students to test their comprehension and retention of core information presented in the chapter.

Integrated Technology Resources

These resources include Internet exercises and brief descriptions of specific content on the Online Learning Center Web site for the book, including a listing of relevant topics that are explored in *Reel Society* video clips.

sociology

LA AND THE SOUTH PACIFIC // UNITED

THREE DAILY NONSTOPS TO THE SOUTH PACIFIC.

Social behavior varies, both around the world and within societies. Sociologists are interested in both the similarities and the differences in human behavior among different societies. In this billboard for an international airline, a young woman from Los Angeles shows off her tongue stud and a South Pacific islander displays a ceremonial tattooed face.

2

1

Understanding Sociology

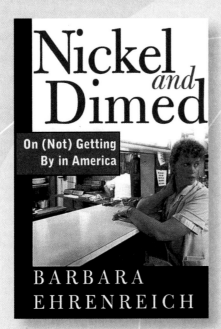

Nickel and Dimed
On (Not) Getting By in America
BARBARA EHRENREICH

> I am, of course, very different from the people who normally fill America's least attractive jobs, and in ways that both helped and limited me. Most obviously, I was only visiting a world that others inhabit full-time, often for most of their lives. With all the real-life assets I've built up in middle age—bank account, IRA, health insurance, multiroom home—waiting indulgently in the background, there was no way I was going to "experience poverty" or find out how it "really feels" to be a long-term low-wage worker. My aim here was much more straightforward and objective—just to see whether I could match income to expenses, as the truly poor attempt to do every day. . . .

In Portland, Maine, I came closest to achieving a decent fit between income and expenses, but only because I worked seven days a week. Between my two jobs, I was earning approximately $300 a week after taxes and paying $480 a month in rent, or a manageable 40 percent of my earnings. It helped, too, that gas and electricity were included in my rent and that I got two or three free meals each weekend at the nursing home. But I was there at the beginning of the off-season. If I had stayed until June 2000 I would have faced the Blue Haven's summer rent of $390 a week, which would of course have been out of the question. So to survive year-round, I would have had to save enough, in the months between August 1999 and May 2000, to accumulate the first month's rent and deposit on an actual apartment. I think I could have done this—saved $800 to $1,000—at least if no car trouble or illness interfered with my budget. I am not sure, however, that I could have maintained

> *With all the real-life assets I've built up in middle age—bank account, IRA, health insurance, multiroom home—waiting indulgently in the background, there was no way I was going to "experience poverty" or find out how it "really feels" to be a long-term low-wage worker.*

the seven-day-a-week regimen month after month or eluded the kinds of injuries that afflicted my fellow workers in the housecleaning business.

In Minneapolis—well, here we are left with a lot of speculation. If I had been able to find an apartment for $400 a month or less, my pay at Wal-Mart—$1,120 a month before taxes—might have been sufficient, although the cost of living in a motel while I searched for such an apartment might have made it impossible for me to save enough for the first month's rent and deposit. A weekend job, such as the one I almost landed at a supermarket for about $7.75 an hour, would have helped, but I had no guarantee that I could arrange my schedule at Wal-Mart to reliably exclude weekends. If I had taken the job at Menards and the pay was in fact $10 an hour for eleven hours a day, I would have made about $440 a week after taxes—enough to pay for a motel room and still have something left over to save up for the initial costs of an apartment. But were they really offering $10 an hour? And could I have stayed on my feet eleven hours a day, five days a week? So yes, with some different choices, I probably could have survived in Minneapolis. But I'm not going back for a rematch.

(Ehrenreich 2001:6, 197–198) Additional information about this excerpt can be found on the Online Learning Center at www.mhhe.com/schaefer11.

In her undercover attempts to survive as a low-wage worker in different cities in the United States, journalist Barbara Ehrenreich revealed patterns of human interaction and used methods of study that foster sociological investigation. This excerpt from her book *Nickel and Dimed: On (Not) Getting By in America* describes how she left a comfortable home and assumed the identity of a divorced, middle-aged housewife with no college degree and little working experience. She set out to get the best-paying job and the cheapest living quarters she could find, to see whether she could make ends meet. Months later, physically exhausted and demoralized by demeaning work rules, Ehrenreich confirmed what she had suspected before she began: getting by in this country as a low-wage worker is a losing proposition.

Ehrenreich's study focused on an unequal society, which is a central topic in sociology. Her investigative work, like the work of many other journalists, is informed by sociological research that documents the existence and extent of inequality in our society. Social inequality has a pervasive influence on human interactions and institutions. Certain groups of people control scarce resources, wield power, and receive special treatment. The poster that opens this chapter illustrates another common focus of sociologists, the variations in social behavior from one part of the world to another.

While it might be interesting to know how one individual is affected by the need to make ends meet, or even by the choice to wear a tongue stud or tattoo, sociologists consider how en-tire groups of people are affected by these kinds of factors, and how society itself might be altered by them. Sociologists, then, are not concerned with what one individual does or does not do, but with what people do as members of a group or in interaction with one another, and what that means for individuals and for society as a whole.

As a field of study, sociology is extremely broad in scope. You will see throughout this book the range of topics sociologists investigate—from suicide to TV viewing habits, from Amish society to global economic patterns, from peer pressure to genetic engineering. Sociology looks at how others influence our behavior; how major social institutions like the government, religion, and the economy affect us; and how we ourselves affect other individuals, groups, and even organizations.

How did sociology develop? In what ways does it differ from other social sciences? This chapter will explore the nature of sociology as both a field of inquiry and an exercise of the "sociological imagination." We'll look at the discipline as a science and consider its relationship to other social sciences. We'll meet three pioneering thinkers—Émile Durkheim, Max Weber, and Karl Marx—and examine the theoretical perspectives that grew out of their work. We'll note some of the practical applications for sociological theory and research. Finally, we'll see how sociology helps us to develop a sociological imagination. For those students interested in exploring career opportunities in sociology, the chapter closes with a special appendix.

What Is Sociology?

"What has sociology got to do with me or with my life?" As a student, you might well have asked this question when you signed up for your introductory sociology course. To answer it, consider these points: Are you influenced by what you see on television? Do you use the Internet? Did you vote in the last election? Are you familiar with binge drinking on campus? Do you use alternative medicine? These are just a few of the everyday life situations described in this book that sociology can shed light on. But as the opening excerpt indicates, sociology also looks at large social issues. We use sociology to investigate why thousands of jobs have moved from the United States to developing nations, what social forces promote prejudice, what leads someone to join a social movement and work for social change, how access to computer technology can reduce social inequality, and why relationships between men and women in Seattle differ from those in Singapore.

Sociology is, very simply, the scientific study of social behavior and human groups. It focuses on social relationships; how those relationships influence people's behavior; and how societies, the sum total of those relationships, develop and change.

The Sociological Imagination

In attempting to understand social behavior, sociologists rely on an unusual type of creative thinking. A leading sociologist, C. Wright Mills, described such thinking as the *sociological imagination*—an awareness of the relationship between an individual and the wider society, both today and in the past. This awareness allows all of us (not just sociologists) to comprehend the links between our immediate, personal social settings and the remote, impersonal social world that surrounds and helps to shape us. Barbara Ehrenreich certainly used a sociological imagination when she studied low-wage workers (Mills [1959] 2000a).

A key element in the sociological imagination is the ability to view one's own society as an outsider would, rather than only from the perspective of personal experiences and cultural biases. Consider something as simple as sporting events. On college campuses in the United States, thousands of students cheer well-trained football players. In Bali, Indonesia, dozens of spectators gather around a ring to cheer on well-trained roosters engaged in cockfights. In both instances, the spectators debate the merits of their favorites and bet on the outcome of the events. Yet what is considered a normal sporting event in one part of the world is considered unusual in another part.

The sociological imagination allows us to go beyond personal experiences and observations to understand broader public issues. Divorce, for example, is unquestionably a personal hardship for a husband and wife who split apart. However, C. Wright Mills advocated using the sociological imagination to view divorce not simply as an individual's personal problem but rather as a societal concern. Using this perspective, we can see that an increase in the divorce rate actually redefines a major social institution—the family. Today's households frequently include stepparents and half-siblings whose parents have divorced and remarried. Through the complexities of the blended family, this private concern becomes a public issue that affects schools, government agencies, businesses, and religious institutions.

The sociological imagination is an empowering tool. It allows us to look beyond a limited understanding of human behavior to see the world and its people in a new way and through a broader lens than we might otherwise use. It may be as simple as understanding why a roommate prefers country music to hip-hop, or it may open up a whole different way of understanding other populations in the world. For example, in the aftermath of the terrorist attacks on the United States on September 11, 2001, many citizens wanted to understand how Muslims throughout the world perceived their country, and why. From time to time this textbook will offer you the chance to exercise your own sociological imagination in a variety of situations. We'll begin with one that may be close to home for you.

Use Your Sociological Imagination

You are walking down the street in your city or hometown. In looking around you, you can't help noticing that half or more of the people you see are overweight. How do you explain your observation? If you were C. Wright Mills, how do you think you would explain it?

Sociology and the Social Sciences

Is sociology a science? The term *science* refers to the body of knowledge obtained by methods based on systematic observation. Just like other scientific disciplines, sociology involves the organized, systematic study of phenomena (in this case, human behavior) in order to enhance understanding. All scientists, whether studying mushrooms or murderers, attempt to collect precise information through methods of study that are as objective as possible. They rely on careful recording of observations and accumulation of data.

Of course, there is a great difference between sociology and physics, between psychology and astronomy. For this reason, the sciences are commonly divided into natural and social sciences. *Natural science* is the study of the physical features of nature and the ways in which they interact and change. Astronomy, biology, chemistry, geology, and physics are all natural sciences. *Social science* is the study of the social features of humans and the ways in which they interact and change. The social sciences include sociology, anthropology, economics, history, psychology, and political science.

These social science disciplines have a common focus on the social behavior of people, yet each has a particular orientation. Anthropologists usually study past cultures and preindustrial societies that continue today, as well as the origins of humans. Economists explore the ways in which people produce and exchange goods and services, along with money and other resources. Historians are concerned with the peoples and events of the past and their significance for us today. Political scientists study international relations, the workings of government, and the exercise of power and authority. Psychologists investigate personality and individual behavior. So what do *sociologists* focus on? They study the influence that society has on people's attitudes and behavior and the ways in which people interact and shape society. Because humans are social animals, sociologists examine our social relationships with others scientifically. The range of the relationships they investigate is vast, as the current list of sections in the American Sociological Association suggests (see Table 1-1 on page 8).

Let's consider how different social sciences would study the impact of Hurricane Katrina, which ravaged the Gulf Coast of the United States in 2005. Historians would compare the damage done by natural disasters in the 20th century to that caused by Katrina. Economists would conduct research on the economic impact of the damage, not just in the Southeast but throughout the nation and the world. Psychologists would study individual cases to assess the emotional stress of the traumatic event. And political scientists would study the stances taken by different elected officials, along with their implications for the government's response to the disaster.

What approach would sociologists take? They might look at Katrina's impact on different communities, as well as on different social classes. Some sociologists have undertaken neighborhood and community studies, to determine how to maintain the integrity of storm-struck neighborhoods during the rebuilding phase. Researchers have focused in particular on Katrina's impact on marginalized groups, from the inner-city poor in New Orleans to residents of rural American Indian reservations (Laska 2005). The devastating social impact of the storm did not surprise sociologists; as Figure 1-1 on page 9 shows, the disaster area was among the poorest in the United States. In terms of family income, for example, New Orleans ranked 63rd (7th lowest) among the nation's 70 largest cities. When the storm left tens of thousands of Gulf Coast families homeless and unemployed, most had no savings to fall back on—no way to pay for a hotel room or tide themselves over until the next paycheck.

Are You What You Own?

Use your sociological imagination to analyze the "material world" of three different societies. These photos come from the book *Material World: A Global Family Portrait*. The photographers selected a "statistically average" family in each country they visited and took pictures of that family with all the possessions in the household. Shown here are families in Japan, Mexico, and South Africa.

What do the material goods in these photographs tell you about the food, shelter, and lifestyle in each culture? Which possessions are geared toward recreation and which toward subsistence? What means of transport and communication are available to each family? What items do all three families own,

and how are those items similar? What does the clothing family members are wearing tell you about their social class? What effect might each family's size have on its economic position? Do all three families have enough material goods to meet all their members' needs? How do you think each family would react if they lived with the belongings of the other two households?

These photos make us aware that when we look at people's material possessions, we learn something about the social, economic, and geographic factors that influence their way of life. The photos may also prompt us to think sociologically about our own material possessions, and what they say about us and about our society (Menzel 1994).

{The Ukita family, Tokyo, Japan}

{The Qampie family, Soweto, South Africa}

{The Castillo Balderas family, Guadalajara, Mexico}

7

Sections of the American Sociological Association

Aging and the Life Course	Marxist Sociology
Alcohol, Drugs, and Tobacco	Mathematical Sociology
Animals and Society	Medical Sociology
Asia and Asian America	Mental Health
Children and Youth	Methodology
Collective Behavior and Social Movements	Organizations, Occupations, and Work
Communication and Information Technologies	Peace, War, and Social Conflict
Community and Urban Sociology	Political Economy of the World-System
Comparative and Historical Sociology	Political Sociology
Crime, Law, and Deviance	Population
Culture	Race, Gender, and Class
Economic Sociology	Racial and Ethnic Minorities
Education	Rationality and Society
Emotions	Religion
Environment and Technology	Science, Knowledge, and Technology
Ethnomethodology and Conversation Analysis	Sex and Gender
Family	Sexualities
History of Sociology	Social Psychology
International Migration	Sociological Practice
Labor and Labor Movements	Teaching and Learning
Latino/a Sociology	Theory
Law	

The range of sociological issues is very broad. For example, sociologists who belong to the Animals and Society section of the ASA may study the animal rights movement; those who belong to the Sexualities section may study global sex workers or the gay, bisexual, and transgendered movements. Economic sociologists may investigate globalization or consumerism, among many other topics.
Source: American Sociological Association 2008.

Sociologists would take a similar approach to studying episodes of extreme violence. In March 2007, just as college students were beginning to focus on the impending end of the semester, tragedy struck on the campus of Virginia Tech. In a two-hour shooting spree, a mentally disturbed senior armed with automatic weapons killed a total of 32 students and faculty at Virginia's largest university. Observers struggled to describe the events and place them in some social context. For sociologists in particular, the event raised numerous issues and topics for study, including the media's role in describing the attacks, the presence of violence in our educational institutions, the gun control debate, the inadequacy of the nation's mental health care system, and the stereotyping and stigmatization of people who suffer from mental illness. For more on how sociologists research unanticipated tragic events, see Box 1-2 (page 23) on the 2004 tsunami that ravaged South Asia.

Sociologists have a long history of advising government agencies on how to respond to disasters. Certainly the poverty of the Gulf Coast region complicated the huge challenge of evacuation. With Katrina bearing down on the Gulf Coast, thousands of poor inner-city residents had no automobiles or other available means of escaping the storm. Added to that difficulty was the high incidence of disability in the area. New Orleans ranked 2nd among the nation's 70 largest cities in the proportion of people over age 65 who are disabled—56 percent. Moving wheelchair-bound residents to safety requires specially equipped vehicles, to say nothing of handicap-accessible accommodations in public shelters. Clearly, officials must consider these factors in developing evacuation plans (Bureau of the Census 2005f).

Sociological analysis of the disaster did not end when the floodwaters receded. Long before residents of New Orleans staged a massive anticrime rally at City Hall in 2007, researchers were analyzing resettlement patterns in the city. They noted that returning residents often faced bleak job prospects. Yet families who had stayed away for that reason often had trouble enrolling their children in schools unprepared for an influx of evacuees. Faced with a choice between the need to work and the need to return their children to school, some displaced families risked sending their older children home alone. Meanwhile, opportunists had arrived to victimize unsuspecting homeowners. And the city's overtaxed judicial and criminal justice systems, which had been understaffed before Katrina struck, had been only partially restored. All these social factors led sociologists and others to anticipate the unparalleled rise in reported crime the city experienced in 2006 and 2007 (Kaufman 2006; Maggi 2007; Nossiter 2007).

Sociologists put their sociological imaginations to work in a variety of areas—including aging, the family, human ecology, and religion. Throughout this textbook, you will see how sociologists develop theories and conduct research to study and better understand societies. And you will be encouraged to use your own sociological imagination to examine the United States (and other societies) from the viewpoint of a respectful but questioning outsider.

Sociology and Common Sense

Sociology focuses on the study of human behavior. Yet we all have experience with human behavior and at least some knowledge of it. All of us might well have theories about why people become homeless, for example. Our theories and opinions typically come from "common sense"—that is, from our experiences and conversations, from what we read, from what we see on television, and so forth.

In our daily lives, we rely on common sense to get us through many unfamiliar situations. However, this commonsense knowledge, while sometimes accurate, is not always reliable, because it rests on commonly held beliefs rather than on systematic analysis of facts. It was once considered common sense to accept that the earth was flat—a view rightly questioned by Pythagoras and Aristotle. Incorrect commonsense notions are not just a part of the distant past; they remain with us today.

Contrary to the saying "The love of money is the root of all evil," for example, sociologists have found that in reality, affluence brings not only nicer cars and longer vacations but also better health and a significantly reduced exposure to pollution of all types. Another commonsense belief, "Love knows no reason," does not stand up to sociological research on courtship and marriage. The choice of a lifetime partner is generally limited by societal expectations and confined within boundaries defined by age, money, education, ethnicity, religion, and even height. Cupid's arrow flies only in certain directions (Ruane and Cerulo 2004).

In the United States today, "common sense" tells us that young people flock to concerts featuring Christian rock because religion is becoming more important to them. However, this particular "commonsense" notion—like the notion that the earth is flat—is untrue and is not supported by sociological research. Through 2006, annual surveys of first-year college students show a decline in the percentage who attend religious services even occasionally. Increasing numbers of college students claim to have no religious preference. The trend encompasses not just organized religion but other forms of spirituality as well. Fewer students pray or meditate today than in the past, and fewer consider their level of spirituality to be very high (Pryor et al. 2006).

FIGURE 1–1

9

Understanding Sociology

Poverty Rates in Hurricane Katrina Disaster Area

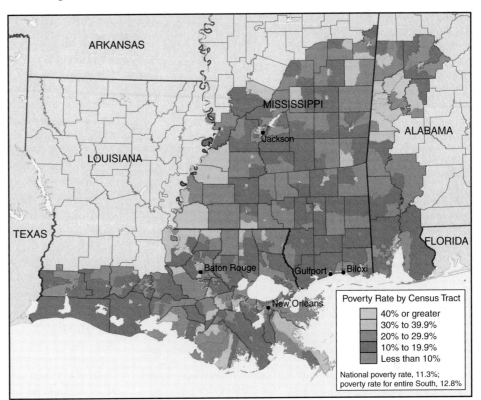

Poverty Rate by Census Tract
- 40% or greater
- 30% to 39.9%
- 20% to 29.9%
- 10% to 19.9%
- Less than 10%

National poverty rate, 11.3%; poverty rate for entire South, 12.8%

Note: Poverty data for 2000, reported in 2001. Disaster area defined by the Federal Emergency Management Agency as of September 14, 2005.
Source: Bureau of the Census 2005g.

Students at Virginia Tech mourn the loss of their classmates and professors following the deadly shooting spree in April 2007. Sociological study provides insight to assess and understand such tragic events. This specific incident immediately raised concerns about gun control, a form of social control (see Chapter 8); the role of the institution of mass media in reporting and influencing such events (see Chapter 7); violence in schools (see Chapter 16); and the role of mental health treatment in the United States today (see Chapter 19).

On August 29, 2005, shortly after Hurricane Katrina swept through the Gulf of Mexico, the U.S. Coast Guard took this aerial photograph of New Orleans. The widespread flooding shown in the photo grew worse as the week wore on, hampering the efforts of rescue teams. Sociologists want to know how the storm affected people from different communities and social classes, as well as how its impact varied with residents' income, race, and gender.

Similarly, disasters do not generally produce panic. In the aftermath of disasters such as 9/11 and Hurricane Katrina, most people respond responsibly, even heroically, by following the authorities' directions and reaching out to those in need. Some emergency responses go more smoothly than others. On September 11, 2001, New York City's command and control structures were re-created quickly, but in 2005, amid Katrina's much vaster destruction, social organizations from the local to the federal level struggled to communicate and coordinate. Regardless of the type of catastrophe or its location, however, decision making becomes more centralized in times of disaster.

Like other social scientists, sociologists do not accept something as a fact because "everyone knows it." Instead, each piece of information must be tested and recorded, then analyzed in relationship to other data. Sociologists rely on scientific studies in order to describe and understand a social environment. At times, the findings of sociologists may seem like common sense, because they deal with familiar facets of everyday life. The difference is that such findings have been *tested* by researchers.

Common sense now tells us that the earth is round. But this particular commonsense notion is based on centuries of scientific work that began with the breakthroughs made by Pythagoras and Aristotle.

What Is Sociological Theory?

Why do people commit suicide? One traditional commonsense answer is that people inherit the desire to kill themselves. Another view is that sunspots drive people to take their own lives. These explanations may not seem especially convincing to contemporary researchers, but they represent beliefs widely held as recently as 1900.

Sociologists are not particularly interested in why any one individual commits suicide; they are more concerned with identifying the social forces that systematically cause some people to take their own lives. In order to undertake this research, sociologists develop a *theory* that offers a general explanation of suicidal behavior.

We can think of theories as attempts to explain events, forces, materials, ideas, or behavior in a comprehensive manner. In sociology, a **theory** is a set of statements that seeks to explain problems, actions, or behavior. An effective theory may have both explanatory and predictive power. That is, it can help us to see the relationships among seemingly isolated phenomena, as well as to understand how one type of change in an environment leads to other changes.

The World Health Organization (2006) estimates that 900,000 people commit suicide every year. More than a hundred years ago, a sociologist tried to look at suicide data scientifically. Émile Durkheim ([1897] 1951) developed a highly original theory about the relationship between suicide and social factors. Durkheim was primarily concerned not with the personalities of individual suicide victims, but rather with suicide rates and how they varied from country to country. As a result, when he looked at the number of reported suicides in France, England, and Denmark in 1869, he also noted the total population of each country in order to determine the rate of suicide in each nation. He found that whereas England had only 67 reported suicides per million inhabitants, France had 135 per million and Denmark had 277 per million. The question then became "Why did Denmark have a comparatively high rate of reported suicide?"

Durkheim went much deeper into his investigation of suicide rates. The result was his landmark work *Suicide,* published in 1897. Durkheim refused to accept unproved explanations regarding suicide, including the beliefs that cosmic forces or inherited tendencies caused such deaths. Instead, he focused on social factors, such as the cohesiveness or lack of cohesiveness of religious, social, and occupational groups.

Durkheim's research suggested that suicide, while a solitary act, is related to group life. Protestants had much higher suicide rates than Catholics; the unmarried had much higher rates than married people; and soldiers were more likely to take their lives than civilians. In addition, there seemed to be higher rates of suicide in times of peace than in times of war and revolution, and in times of economic instability and recession rather than in times of prosperity. Durkheim concluded that the suicide rates of a society reflected the extent to which people were or were not integrated into the group life of the society.

Émile Durkheim, like many other social scientists, developed a *theory* to explain how individual behavior can be understood within a social context. He pointed out the influence of groups and societal forces on what had always been viewed as a highly personal act. Clearly, Durkheim offered a more *scientific* explanation for the causes of suicide than that of sunspots or inherited tendencies. His theory has predictive power, since it suggests that suicide rates will rise or fall in conjunction with certain social and economic changes.

Of course, a theory—even the best of theories—is not a final statement about human behavior. Durkheim's theory of suicide is no exception. Sociologists continue to examine factors that contribute to differences in suicide rates around the world and to a particular society's rate of suicide. For example, although the overall rate of suicide in New Zealand is only marginally higher than the rate in the United States, the suicide rate among young people is 41 percent higher in New Zealand. Sociologists and psychiatrists from that country suggest that their remote, sparsely populated society maintains exaggerated standards of masculinity that are especially difficult for young males. Gay adolescents who fail to conform to their peers' preference for sports are particularly vulnerable to suicide (Shenon 1995).

Use Your Sociological Imagination

If you were Durkheim's successor in his research on suicide, how would you investigate the factors that may explain the increase in suicide rates among young people in the United States today?

The Development of Sociology

People have always been curious about sociological matters—how we get along with others, what we do for a living, whom we select as our leaders. Philosophers and religious authorities of ancient and medieval societies made countless observations about human behavior. They did not test or verify those observations scientifically; nevertheless, their observations often became the foundation for moral codes. Several of the early social philosophers predicted that a systematic study of human behavior would emerge one day. Beginning in the 19th century, European theorists made pioneering contributions to the development of a science of human behavior.

Early Thinkers

Auguste Comte The 19th century was an unsettling time in France. The French monarchy had been deposed in the revolu-

Young people of marriageable age mingle at a social get-together. Though it is common wisdom that "love knows no reason," sociological research shows that the choice of a marriage partner is heavily influenced by societal expectations.

tion of 1789, and Napoleon had suffered defeat in his effort to conquer Europe. Amid this chaos, philosophers considered how society might be improved. Auguste Comte (1798–1857), credited with being the most influential of the philosophers of the early 1800s, believed that a theoretical science of society and a systematic investigation of behavior were needed to improve society. He coined the term *sociology* to apply to the science of human behavior.

Writing in the 1800s, Comte feared that the excesses of the French Revolution had permanently impaired France's stability. Yet he hoped that the systematic study of social behavior would eventually lead to more rational human interactions. In Comte's hierarchy of the sciences, sociology was at the top. He called it the "queen," and its practitioners "scientist-priests." This French theorist did not simply give sociology its name; he presented a rather ambitious challenge to the fledgling discipline.

Harriet Martineau Scholars learned of Comte's works largely through translations by the English sociologist Harriet Martineau (1802–1876). But Martineau was a pathbreaker in her own right. She offered insightful observations of the customs and social practices of both her native Britain and the United States. Martineau's book *Society in America* ([1837] 1962) examined religion, politics, child rearing, and immigration in the young nation. It gave special attention to social class distinctions and to such factors as gender and race. Martineau ([1838] 1989) also wrote the first book on sociological methods.

Martineau's writings emphasized the impact that the economy, law, trade, health, and population could have on social problems. She spoke out in favor of the rights of women, the emancipation of slaves, and religious tolerance. Later in life, deafness did not keep her from being an activist. In Martineau's

{ Harriet Martineau, an early pioneer of sociology, studied social behavior both in her native England and in the United States. }

([1837] 1962) view, intellectuals and scholars should not simply offer observations of social conditions; they should *act* on their convictions in a manner that will benefit society. That is why Martineau conducted research on the nature of female employment and pointed to the need for further investigation of the issue (Deegan 2003; Hill and Hoecker-Drysdale 2001).

Herbert Spencer

Herbert Spencer Another important early contributor to the discipline of sociology was Herbert Spencer (1820–1903). A relatively prosperous Victorian Englishman, Spencer (unlike Martineau) did not feel compelled to correct or improve society; instead, he merely hoped to understand it better. Drawing on Charles Darwin's study *On the Origin of Species,* Spencer applied the concept of evolution of the species to societies in order to explain how they change, or evolve, over time. Similarly, he adapted Darwin's evolutionary view of the "survival of the fittest" by arguing that it is "natural" that some people are rich while others are poor.

Spencer's approach to societal change was extremely popular in his own lifetime. Unlike Comte, Spencer suggested that since societies are bound to change eventually, one need not be highly critical of present social arrangements or work actively for social change. This viewpoint appealed to many influential people in England and the United States who had a vested interest in the status quo and were suspicious of social thinkers who endorsed change.

Émile Durkheim

Émile Durkheim made many pioneering contributions to sociology, including his important theoretical work on suicide. The son of a rabbi, Durkheim (1858–1917) was educated in both France and Germany. He established an impressive academic reputation and was appointed one of the first professors of sociology in France. Above all, Durkheim will be remembered for his insistence that behavior must be understood within a larger social context, not just in individualistic terms.

As one example of this emphasis, Durkheim ([1912] 2001) developed a fundamental thesis to help explain all forms of society. Through intensive study of the Arunta, an Australian tribe, he focused on the functions that religion performed and underscored the role of group life in defining what we consider to be religious. Durkheim concluded that like other forms of group behavior, religion reinforces a group's solidarity.

Another of Durkheim's main interests was the consequences of work in modern societies. In his view, the growing division of labor in industrial societies, as workers became much more specialized in their tasks, led to what he called anomie. *Anomie* refers to the loss of direction felt in a society when social control of individual behavior has become ineffective. The state of anomie occurs when people have lost their sense of purpose or direction, often during a time of profound social change. In a period of anomie, people are so confused and unable to cope with the new social environment that they may resort to taking their own lives.

Durkheim was concerned about the dangers that alienation, loneliness, and isolation might pose for modern industrial societies. He shared Comte's belief that sociology should provide direction for social change. As a result, he advocated the creation of new social groups—mediators between the individual's family and the state—which would provide a sense of belonging for members of huge, impersonal societies. Unions would be an example of such groups.

Like many other sociologists, Durkheim did not limit his interests to one aspect of social behavior. Later in this book we will consider his thinking on crime and punishment, religion, and the workplace. Few sociologists have had such a dramatic impact on so many different areas within the discipline.

Max Weber

Another important early theorist was Max Weber (pronounced "VAY-ber"). Born in Germany, Weber (1864–1920) studied legal and economic history, but gradually developed an interest in sociology. Eventually, he became a professor at various German universities. Weber taught his students that they should employ *verstehen* (pronounced "fair-SHTAY-en"), the German word for "understanding" or "insight," in their intellectual work. He pointed out that we cannot analyze our social behavior by the same type of objective criteria we use to measure weight or temperature. To fully comprehend behavior, we must learn the subjective meanings people attach to their actions—how they themselves view and explain their behavior.

For example, suppose that a sociologist was studying the social ranking of individuals in a fraternity. Weber would expect the researcher to employ *verstehen* to determine the significance

FIGURE 1-2   **13**

Early Social Thinkers

	Émile Durkheim 1858–1917	**Max Weber 1864–1920**	**Karl Marx 1818–1883**
Academic training	Philosophy	Law, economics, history, philosophy	Philosophy, law
Key works	1893—*The Division of Labor in Society*	1904–1905—*The Protestant Ethic and the Spirit of Capitalism*	1848—*The Communist Manifesto*
	1897—*Suicide: A Study in Sociology*	1921—*Economy and Society*	1867—*Das Kapital*
	1912—*Elementary Forms of Religious Life*		

of the fraternity's social hierarchy for its members. The researcher might examine the effects of athleticism or grades or social skills or seniority on standing within the fraternity. He or she would seek to learn how the fraternity members relate to other members of higher or lower status. While investigating these questions, the researcher would take into account people's emotions, thoughts, beliefs, and attitudes (Coser 1977).

We also owe credit to Weber for a key conceptual tool: the ideal type. An ***ideal type*** is a construct or model for evaluating specific cases. In his own works, Weber identified various characteristics of bureaucracy as an ideal type (discussed in detail in Chapter 6). In presenting this model of bureaucracy, Weber was not describing any particular business, nor was he using the term *ideal* in a way that suggested a positive evaluation. Instead, his purpose was to provide a useful standard for measuring how bureaucratic an actual organization is (Gerth and Mills 1958). Later in this textbook, we will use the concept of *ideal type* to study the family, religion, authority, and economic systems, as well as to analyze bureaucracy.

Although their professional careers coincided, Émile Durkheim and Max Weber never met and probably were unaware of each other's existence, let alone ideas. Such was not true of the work of Karl Marx. Durkheim's thinking about the impact of the division of labor in industrial societies was related to Marx's writings, while Weber's concern for a value-free, objective sociology was a direct response to Marx's deeply held convictions. Thus, it is not surprising that Karl Marx is viewed as a major figure in the development of sociology, as well as several other social sciences (see Figure 1-2).

Karl Marx

Karl Marx (1818–1883) shared with Durkheim and Weber a dual interest in abstract philosophical issues and the concrete reality of everyday life. Unlike the others, Marx was so critical of existing institutions that a conventional academic career was impossible. He spent most of his life in exile from his native Germany.

Marx's personal life was a difficult struggle. When a paper he had written was suppressed, he fled to France. In Paris, he met Friedrich Engels (1820–1895), with whom he formed a lifelong friendship. They lived at a time when European and North American economic life was increasingly dominated by the factory rather than the farm.

While in London in 1847, Marx and Engels attended secret meetings of an illegal coalition of labor unions known as the Communist League. The following year they prepared a platform called *The Communist Manifesto*, in which they argued that the masses of people with no resources other than their labor (whom they referred to as the *proletariat*) should unite to fight for the overthrow of capitalist societies. In the words of Marx and Engels:

> The history of all hitherto existing society is the history of class struggles. . . . The proletarians have nothing to lose but their chains. They have a world to win. WORKING MEN OF ALL COUNTRIES UNITE! (L. Feuer 1989:7, 41)

After completing *The Communist Manifesto*, Marx returned to Germany, only to be expelled. He then moved to England, where he continued to write books and essays. Marx lived there in extreme poverty. He pawned most of his possessions, and several of his children died of malnutrition and disease. Marx clearly was an outsider in British society, a fact that may well have colored his view of Western cultures.

In Marx's analysis, society was fundamentally divided between two classes that clashed in pursuit of their own interests. When he examined the industrial societies of his time, such as Germany, England, and the United States, he saw the factory as the center of conflict between the exploiters (the owners of the means of production) and the exploited (the workers). Marx viewed these relationships in systematic terms; that is, he believed that a system of economic, social, and political relationships maintained the power and dominance of the owners over the workers. Consequently, Marx and Engels argued that the working class should *overthrow* the existing class system. Marx's influence on contemporary thinking has been dramatic. His writings inspired those who would later lead communist revolutions in Russia, China, Cuba, Vietnam, and elsewhere.

Even apart from the political revolutions that his work fostered, Marx's significance is profound. Marx emphasized the *group* identifications and associations that influence an individual's place in society. This area of study is the major focus of contemporary sociology. Throughout this textbook, we will consider how membership in a particular gender classification, age group, racial group, or economic class affects a person's attitudes and behavior. In an important sense, we can trace this way of understanding society back to the pioneering work of Karl Marx.

Modern Developments

Sociology today builds on the firm foundation developed by Émile Durkheim, Max Weber, and Karl Marx. However, the field certainly has not remained stagnant over the last hundred years. While Europeans have continued to make contributions to the discipline, sociologists from throughout the world and especially the United States have advanced sociological theory and research. Their new insights have helped us to better understand the workings of society.

Charles Horton Cooley Charles Horton Cooley (1864–1929) was typical of the sociologists who came to prominence in the early 1900s. Born in Ann Arbor, Michigan, Cooley received his graduate training in economics but later became a sociology professor at the University of Michigan. Like other early sociologists, he had become interested in this "new" discipline while pursuing a related area of study.

Cooley shared the desire of Durkheim, Weber, and Marx to learn more about society. But to do so effectively, he preferred to use the sociological perspective to look first at smaller units—intimate, face-to-face groups such as families, gangs, and friendship networks. He saw these groups as the seedbeds of society, in the sense that they shape people's ideals, beliefs, values, and social nature. Cooley's work increased our understanding of groups of relatively small size.

Jane Addams In the early 1900s, many leading sociologists in the United States saw themselves as social reformers dedicated to systematically studying and then improving a corrupt society. They were genuinely concerned about the lives of immigrants in the nation's growing cities, whether those immigrants came from Europe or from the rural American South. Early female sociologists, in particular, often took active roles in poor urban areas as leaders of community centers known as *settlement houses.* For example, Jane Addams (1860–1935), a member of the American Sociological Society, cofounded the famous Chicago settlement, Hull House.

Addams and other pioneering female sociologists commonly combined intellectual inquiry, social service work, and political activism—all with the goal of assisting the underprivileged and creating a more egalitarian society. For example, working with the Black journalist and educator Ida Wells-Barnett, Addams successfully prevented racial segregation in the Chicago public schools. Addams's efforts to establish a juvenile court system and a women's trade union reveal the practical focus of her work (Addams 1910, 1930; Deegan 1991; Lengermann and Niebrugge-Brantley 1998).

By the middle of the 20th century, however, the focus of the discipline had shifted. Sociologists for the most part restricted themselves to theorizing and gathering information; the aim of transforming society was left to social workers and activists. This shift away from social reform was accompanied by a growing commitment to scientific methods of research and to value-free interpretation of data. Not all sociologists were happy with this

In a photograph taken around 1930, social reformer Jane Addams reads to children at the Mary Crane Nursery. Addams was an early pioneer both in sociology and in the settlement house movement.

emphasis. A new organization, the Society for the Study of Social Problems, was created in 1950 to deal more directly with social inequality and other social problems.

Robert Merton Sociologist Robert Merton (1910–2003) made an important contribution to the discipline by successfully combining theory and research. Born to Slavic immigrant parents in Philadelphia, Merton won a scholarship to Temple University. He continued his studies at Harvard, where he acquired his lifelong interest in sociology. Merton's teaching career was based at Columbia University.

Merton (1968) produced a theory that is one of the most frequently cited explanations of deviant behavior. He noted different ways in which people attempt to achieve success in life. In his view, some may deviate from the socially approved goal of accumulating material goods or the socially accepted means of achieving that goal. For example, in Merton's classification scheme, "innovators" are people who accept the goal of pursuing material wealth but use illegal means to do so, including robbery, burglary, and extortion. Merton based his explanation of crime on individual behavior that has been influenced by society's approved goals and means, yet it has wider applications. It helps to account for the high crime rates among the nation's poor, who may see no hope of advancing themselves through traditional roads to success. Chapter 8 discusses Merton's theory in greater detail.

Merton also emphasized that sociology should strive to bring together the "macro-level" and "micro-level" approaches to the study of society. **Macrosociology** concentrates on large-scale phenomena or entire civilizations. Émile Durkheim's cross-cultural study of suicide is an example of macro-level research. More recently, macrosociologists have examined international crime rates (see Chapter 8), the stereotype of Asian Americans as a "model minority" (see Chapter 11), and the population patterns of developing countries (see Chapter 21). In contrast, **microsociology** stresses the study of small groups, often through experimental means. Sociological research on the micro level has included studies of how divorced men and women disengage from significant social roles (see Chapter 5); of how conformity can influence the expression of prejudiced attitudes (see Chapter 8); and of how a teacher's expectations can affect a student's academic performance (see Chapter 16).

Today sociology reflects the diverse contributions of earlier theorists. As sociologists approach such topics as divorce, drug addiction, and religious cults, they can draw on the theoretical insights of the discipline's pioneers. A careful reader can hear Comte, Durkheim, Weber, Marx, Cooley, Addams, and many others speaking through the pages of current research. Sociology has also broadened beyond the intellectual confines of North America and Europe. Contributions to the discipline now come from sociologists studying and researching human behavior in other parts of the world. In describing the work of these sociologists, it is helpful to examine a number of influential theoretical approaches (also known as *perspectives*).

Major Theoretical Perspectives

Sociologists view society in different ways. Some see the world basically as a stable and ongoing entity. They are impressed with the endurance of the family, organized religion, and other social institutions. Other sociologists see society as composed of many groups in conflict, competing for scarce resources. To still other sociologists, the most fascinating aspects of the social world are the everyday, routine interactions among individuals that we sometimes take for granted. These three views, the ones most widely used by sociologists, are the functionalist, conflict, and interactionist perspectives. Together, these approaches will provide an introductory look at the discipline.

Functionalist Perspective

Think of society as a living organism in which each part of the organism contributes to its survival. This view is the **functionalist perspective,** which emphasizes the way in which the parts of a society are structured to maintain its stability.

Talcott Parsons (1902–1979), a Harvard University sociologist, was a key figure in the development of functionalist theory. Parsons was greatly influenced by the work of Émile Durkheim, Max Weber, and other European sociologists. For over four decades, he dominated sociology in the United States with his advocacy of functionalism. Parsons saw any society as a vast network of connected parts, each of which helps to maintain the system as a whole. His functionalist approach holds that if an aspect of social life does not contribute to a society's stability or survival—if it does not serve some identifiably useful function or promote value consensus among members of a society—it will not be passed on from one generation to the next.

Let's examine an example of the functionalist perspective. Many Americans have difficulty understanding the Hindu prohibition against slaughtering cows (specifically, zebu). Cattle browse unhindered through Indian street markets, helping themselves to oranges and mangoes while people bargain for the little food they can afford. What explains this devotion to the cow in the face of human deprivation—a devotion that appears to be dysfunctional?

The simple explanation is that cow worship is highly functional in Indian society, according to economists, agronomists, and social scientists who have studied the matter. Cows perform two essential tasks: plowing the fields and producing milk. If eating their meat were permitted, hungry families might be tempted to slaughter their cows for immediate consumption, leaving themselves without a means of cultivation. Cows also produce dung, which doubles as a fertilizer and a fuel for cooking. Finally, cow meat sustains the neediest group in society, the untouchables, or *dalit,* who sometimes resort to eating beef in secrecy. If eating beef were socially acceptable, higher-status Indians would no doubt bid up its price, placing it beyond the reach of the hungriest.

Manifest and Latent Functions A college catalog typically states various functions of the institution. It may inform you,

Cows (zebu), considered sacred in India, wander freely through this village, respected by all who encounter them. The sanctity of the cow is functional in India, where plowing, milking, and fertilizing are far more important to subsistence farmers than a diet that includes beef.

for example, that the university intends to "offer each student a broad education in classical and contemporary thought, in the humanities, in the sciences, and in the arts." However, it would be quite a surprise to find a catalog that declared, "This university was founded in 1895 to assist people in finding a marriage partner." No college catalog will declare this as the purpose of the university. Yet societal institutions serve many functions, some of them quite subtle. The university, in fact, *does* facilitate mate selection.

Robert Merton (1968) made an important distinction between manifest and latent functions. *Manifest functions* of institutions are open, stated, conscious functions. They involve the intended, recognized consequences of an aspect of society, such as the university's role in certifying academic competence and excellence. In contrast, *latent functions* are unconscious or unintended functions that may reflect hidden purposes of an institution. One latent function of universities is to hold down unemployment. Another is to serve as a meeting ground for people seeking marital partners.

Dysfunctions Functionalists acknowledge that not all parts of a society contribute to its stability all the time. A *dysfunction* refers to an element or process of a society that may actually disrupt the social system or reduce its stability.

We view many dysfunctional behavior patterns, such as homicide, as undesirable. Yet we should not automatically interpret them in this way. The evaluation of a dysfunction depends on one's own values, or as the saying goes, on "where you sit." For example, the official view in prisons in the United States is that inmate gangs should be eradicated because they are dysfunctional to smooth operations. Yet some guards have actually come to view prison gangs as a functional part of their jobs. The danger posed by gangs creates a "threat to security," requiring in-

creased surveillance and more overtime work for guards, as well as requests for special staffing to address gang problems (G. Scott 2001).

Conflict Perspective

Where functionalists see stability and consensus, conflict sociologists see a social world in continual struggle. The *conflict perspective* assumes that social behavior is best understood in terms of tension between groups over power or the allocation of resources, including housing, money, access to services, and political representation. The tension between competing groups need not be violent; it can take the form of labor negotiations, party politics, competition between religious groups for new members, or disputes over the federal budget.

Throughout most of the 1900s, the functionalist perspective had the upper hand in sociology in the United States. However, the conflict approach has become increasingly persuasive since the late 1960s. The widespread social unrest resulting from battles over civil rights, bitter divisions over the war in Vietnam, the rise of the feminist and gay liberation movements, the Watergate political scandal, urban riots, and confrontations at abortion clinics have offered support for the conflict approach—the view that our social world is characterized by continual struggle between competing groups. Currently, the discipline of sociology accepts conflict theory as one valid way to gain insight into a society.

The Marxist View As we saw earlier, Karl Marx viewed struggle between social classes as inevitable, given the exploitation of workers that he perceived under capitalism. Expanding on Marx's work, sociologists and other social scientists have come to see conflict not merely as a class phenomenon but as a part of everyday life in all societies. In studying any culture, organization, or social group, sociologists want to know who benefits, who suffers, and who dominates at the expense of others. They are concerned with the conflicts between women and men, parents and children, cities and suburbs, Whites and Blacks, to name only a few. Conflict theorists are interested in how society's institutions—including the family, government, religion, education, and the media—may help to maintain the privileges of some groups and keep others in a subservient position. Their emphasis on social change and the redistribution of resources makes conflict theorists more "radical" and "activist" than functionalists (Dahrendorf 1959).

An African American View: W. E. B. Du Bois One important contribution of conflict theory is that it has encouraged sociologists to view society through the eyes of those segments of the population that rarely influence decision making. Some early Black sociologists, including W. E. B. Du Bois (1868–1963), conducted research that they hoped would assist the struggle for a racially egalitarian society. Du Bois believed that knowledge was essential in combating prejudice and achieving tolerance and justice. Sociology, he contended, had to draw on scientific principles to study social problems such as those experienced by Blacks in the United States. Du Bois made a major contribution to sociology through his in-depth studies of urban life, both White and Black.

Du Bois had little patience with theorists such as Herbert Spencer, who seemed content with the status quo. He advocated basic research on the lives of Blacks, to separate opinion from fact. In this way he documented their relatively low status in Philadelphia and Atlanta. Du Bois believed that the granting of full political rights to Blacks was essential to their social and economic progress in the United States. Because many of his ideas challenged the status quo, he did not find a receptive audience within either the government or the academic world. As a result, Du Bois became increasingly involved with organizations whose members questioned the established social order. He helped to found the National Association for the Advancement of Colored People, better known as the NAACP (Wortham 2005).

The addition of diverse views within sociology in recent years has led to some valuable research, especially on African Americans. For many years, African Americans were understandably wary of participating in medical research studies, because those studies had been used for such purposes as justifying slavery or determining the impact of untreated syphilis. Now, however, African American sociologists and other social scientists are working to involve Blacks in useful ethnic medical research on diabetes and sickle cell anemia, two disorders that strike Black populations especially hard (A. Young and Deskins 2001).

The Feminist View   Sociologists began embracing the feminist perspective only in the 1970s, although it has a long tradition in many other disciplines. The *feminist view* sees inequity in gender as central to all behavior and organization. Because it clearly focuses on one aspect of inequality, it is often allied with the conflict perspective. Proponents of the feminist perspective tend to focus on the macro level, just as conflict theorists do. Drawing on the work of Marx and Engels, contemporary feminist theorists often view women's subordination as inherent to capitalist societies. Some radical feminist theorists, however, view the oppression of women as inevitable in *all* male-dominated societies, whether capitalist, socialist, or communist.

An early example of this perspective (long before the label came into use by sociologists) can be seen in the life and writings of Ida Wells-Barnett (1862–1931). Following her groundbreaking publications in the 1890s on the practice of lynching Black Americans, she became an advocate in the women's rights campaign, especially the struggle to win the vote for women. Like feminist theorists who succeeded her, Wells-Barnett used her analysis of society as a means of resisting oppression. In her case, she researched what it meant to be African American, a woman in the United States, and a Black woman in the United States (Wells-Barnett 1970).

Feminist scholarship has broadened our understanding of social behavior by extending the analysis beyond the male point of view. In the past, studies of physical violence typically failed

This postage stamp honors W. E. B. Du Bois, who challenged the status quo in both academic and political circles. The first Black person to receive a doctorate from Harvard University, Du Bois later helped organize the National Association for the Advancement of Colored People (NAACP).

Ida Wells-Barnett explored what it meant to be female and Black in the United States. Her work established her as one of the earliest feminist theorists.

to include domestic violence, in which women are the chief victims. Not only was there a void in the research; in the field, law enforcement agencies were ill-prepared to deal with such violence. Similarly, feminists have complained that studies of "children having children" focus almost entirely on the characteristics and behavior of unwed teenage mothers, ignoring the unwed father's role. They have called for more scrutiny of boys and their behavior, as well as their parents and their role models (Ferree 2005; Fields 2005).

Use Your Sociological Imagination

You are a sociologist who uses the conflict perspective to study various aspects of our society. How do you think you would interpret the practice of prostitution? Contrast this view with the functionalist perspective. Do you think your comments would differ if you took the feminist view, and if so, how?

Interactionist Perspective

Workers interacting on the job, encounters in public places like bus stops and parks, behavior in small groups—all these aspects of microsociology catch the attention of interactionists. Whereas functionalist and conflict theorists both analyze large-scale, societywide patterns of behavior, theorists who take the **interactionist perspective** generalize about everyday forms of social interaction in order to explain society as a whole. In the 1990s, for example, the workings of juries became a subject of public scrutiny. High-profile trials ended in verdicts that left some people shaking their heads. Long before jury members were being interviewed on their front lawns following a trial, interactionists tried to better understand behavior in the small-group setting of a jury deliberation room.

Interactionism (also referred to as *symbolic interactionism*) is a sociological framework in which human beings are viewed as living in a world of meaningful objects. Those "objects" may include material things, actions, other people, relationships, and even symbols. Interactionists see symbols as an especially important part of human communication (thus the term *symbolic* interactionism). Symbols have a shared social meaning that is understood by all members of a society. In the United States, for example, a salute symbolizes respect, while a clenched fist signifies defiance. Another culture might use different gestures to convey a feeling of respect or defiance. These types of symbolic interaction are classified as forms of **nonverbal communication,** which can include many other gestures, facial expressions, and postures.

Symbols in the form of tattoos took on special importance in the aftermath of September 11, 2001. Tattoo parlors in lower Manhattan were overwhelmed with requests from various groups for designs that carried symbolic significance for them. New York City firefighters asked for tattoos with the names of their fallen colleagues; police officers requested designs

incorporating their distinctive NYPD shield; recovery workers at Ground Zero sought tattoos that incorporated the image of the giant steel cross, the remnant of a massive cross-beam in a World Trade Center building. Through symbols such as these tattoos, people communicate their values and beliefs to those around them (Scharnberg 2002).

Another manipulation of symbols can be seen in dress codes. Schools frown on students who wear clothes displaying messages that appear to endorse violence or drug and alcohol consumption. Businesses stipulate the attire employees are allowed to wear on the job in order to impress their customers or clients. In 2005, the National Basketball Association (NBA) adopted a new dress code for the athletes who play professional basketball—one that involved not the uniforms they wear on court, but the clothes they wear off court on league business. The code requires "business casual attire" when players are representing the league. Indoor sunglasses, chains, and sleeveless shirts are specifically banned. Figure 1-3 illustrates the new dress code for

FIGURE 1-3

Enforcing Symbols: The NBA Dress Code

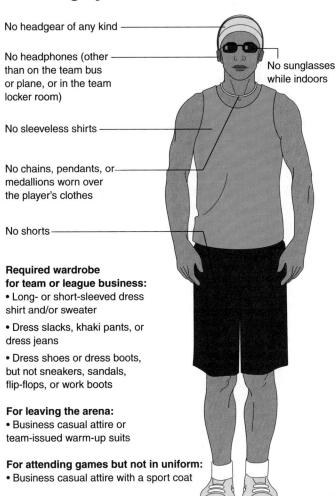

No headgear of any kind

No headphones (other than on the team bus or plane, or in the team locker room)

No sunglasses while indoors

No sleeveless shirts

No chains, pendants, or medallions worn over the player's clothes

No shorts

Required wardrobe for team or league business:
• Long- or short-sleeved dress shirt and/or sweater
• Dress slacks, khaki pants, or dress jeans
• Dress shoes or dress boots, but not sneakers, sandals, flip-flops, or work boots

For leaving the arena:
• Business casual attire or team-issued warm-up suits

For attending games but not in uniform:
• Business casual attire with a sport coat

Source: Crowe and Herman 2005:A23.

the millionaire athletes, which the NBA hopes will improve the image of its players, presenting them as responsible, serious-minded adults rather than as overgrown teens one step removed from the neighborhood court.

While the functionalist and conflict approaches were initiated in Europe, interactionism developed first in the United States. George Herbert Mead (1863–1931) is widely regarded as the founder of the interactionist perspective. Mead taught at the University of Chicago from 1893 until his death. As his teachings have become better known, sociologists have expressed greater interest in the interactionist perspective. Many have moved away from what may have been an excessive preoccupation with the large-scale (macro) level of social behavior and have redirected their attention toward behavior that occurs in small groups (micro level).

Erving Goffman (1922–1982) popularized a particular type of interactionist method known as the ***dramaturgical approach,*** in which people are seen as theatrical performers. The dramaturgist compares everyday life to the setting of the theater and stage. Just as actors project certain images, all of us seek to present particular features of our personalities while we hide other qualities. Thus, in a class, we may feel the need to project a serious image; at a party, we want to look relaxed and friendly.

The Sociological Approach

Which perspective should a sociologist use in studying human behavior? Functionalist? Conflict? Interactionist? Feminist? In fact, sociologists make use of all the perspectives summarized in Table 1-2, since each offers unique insights into the same issue. We gain the broadest understanding of our society, then, by drawing on all the major perspectives, noting where they overlap and where they diverge.

Although no one approach is correct by itself, and sociologists draw on all of them for various purposes, many sociologists tend to favor one particular perspective over others. A sociologist's theoretical orientation influences his or her approach to a research problem in important ways—including the choice of what to study, how to study it, and what questions to pose (or not to pose). (See Box 1-1 on page 20 for an example of how a researcher would study sports from different perspectives.) Whatever the purpose of sociologists' work, their research will always be guided by their theoretical viewpoints. For example, sociologist Elijah Anderson (1990) embraces both the interactionist perspective and the groundbreaking work of W. E. B. Du Bois. For 14 years Anderson conducted fieldwork in Philadelphia, where he studied the interactions of Black and White residents who

Table 1-2

Major Sociological Perspectives

summingUP

	Functionalist	Conflict	Interactionist
View of Society	Stable, well integrated	Characterized by tension and struggle between groups	Active in influencing and affecting everyday social interaction
Level of Analysis Emphasized	Macro	Macro	Micro, as a way of understanding the larger macro phenomena
Key Concepts	Manifest functions Latent functions Dysfunctions	Inequality Capitalism Stratification	Symbols Nonverbal communication Face-to-face interaction
View of the Individual	People are socialized to perform societal functions	People are shaped by power, coercion, and authority	People manipulate symbols and create their social worlds through interaction
View of the Social Order	Maintained through cooperation and consensus	Maintained through force and coercion	Maintained by shared understanding of everyday behavior
View of Social Change	Predictable, reinforcing	Change takes place all the time and may have positive consequences	Reflected in people's social positions and their communications with others
Example	Public punishments reinforce the social order	Laws reinforce the positions of those in power	People respect laws or disobey them based on their own past experience
Proponents	Émile Durkheim Talcott Parsons Robert Merton	Karl Marx W. E. B. Du Bois Ida Wells-Barnett	George Herbert Mead Charles Horton Cooley Erving Goffman

1-1 Looking at Sports from Four Theoretical Perspectives

We watch sports. Talk sports. Spend money on sports. Some of us live and breathe sports. Because sports occupy much of our time and directly or indirectly consume and generate a great deal of money, it should not be surprising that sports have sociological components that can be analyzed from the various theoretical perspectives.

Functionalist View

In examining any aspect of society, functionalists emphasize the contribution it makes to overall social stability. Functionalists regard sports as an almost religious institution that uses ritual and ceremony to reinforce the common values of a society:

- Sports socialize young people into such values as competition and patriotism.

- Sports help to maintain people's physical well-being.

- Sports serve as a safety valve for both participants and spectators, who are allowed to shed tension and aggressive energy in a socially acceptable way.

- Sports bring together members of a community (supporting local athletes and teams) or even a nation (as seen during World Cup matches and the Olympics) and promote an overall feeling of unity and social solidarity.

Conflict View

Conflict theorists argue that the social order is based on coercion and exploitation. They emphasize that sports reflect and even exacerbate many of the divisions of society:

- Sports are a form of big business in which profits are more important than the health and safety of the workers (athletes).

- Sports perpetuate the false idea that success can be achieved simply through hard work, while failure should be blamed on the individual alone (rather than on injustices in the larger social system). Sports also serve as an "opiate" that encourages people to seek a "fix" or temporary "high" rather than focus on personal problems and social issues.

- Sports maintain the subordinate role of Blacks and Latinos, who toil as athletes but are less visible in supervisory positions as coaches, managers, and owners.

Professional racer Danica Patrick. Women often have difficulty entering what are considered men's sports.

Feminist View

Feminist theorists consider how watching or participating in sports reinforces the roles that men and women play in the larger society:

- Although sports generally promote fitness and health, they may also adversely affect the health of participants, both men (through steroid use by bodybuilders and baseball players) and women (through excessive dieting by gymnasts and figure skaters).

> *Despite their differences, functionalists, conflict theorists, feminists, and interactionists would all agree that there is much more to sports than exercise or recreation.*

- Gender expectations encourage female athletes to be passive and gentle, qualities that do not support the emphasis on competitiveness in sports. As a result, women find it difficult to enter sports traditionally dominated by men, such as Indy or NASCAR.

Interactionist View

In studying the social order, interactionists are especially interested in shared understandings of everyday behavior. Interactionists examine sports on the micro level by focusing on how day-to-day social behavior is shaped by the distinctive norms, values, and demands of the world of sports:

- Sports often heighten parent–child involvement; they may lead to parental expectations for participation and (sometimes unrealistically) for success.

- Participation in sports provides friendship networks that can permeate everyday life.

- Despite class, racial, and religious differences, teammates may work together harmoniously and may even abandon previous stereotypes and prejudices.

- Relationships in the sports world are defined by people's social positions as players, coaches, and referees—as well as by the high or low status that individuals hold as a result of their performances and reputations.

Despite their differences, functionalists, conflict theorists, feminists, and interactionists would all agree that there is much more to sports than exercise or recreation. They would also agree that sports and other popular forms of culture are worthy subjects of serious study by sociologists.

Let's Discuss

1. Have you experienced or witnessed discrimination in sports based on gender or race? If so, how did you react? Has the representation of Blacks or women on teams been controversial on your campus? In what ways?

2. Which perspective do you think is most useful in looking at the sociology of sports? Why?

Sources: Acosta and Carpenter 2001; H. Edwards 1973; Eitzen 2006; Fine 1987; K. Young 2004.

lived in adjoining neighborhoods. In particular, he was interested in their "public behavior," including their eye contact—or lack of it—as they passed one another on the street. Anderson's research tells us much about the everyday social interactions of Blacks and Whites in the United States, but it does not explain the larger issues behind those interactions. Like theories, research results illuminate one part of the stage, leaving other parts in relative darkness.

Applied and Clinical Sociology

Many early sociologists—notably, Jane Addams, W. E. B. Du Bois, and George Herbert Mead—were strong advocates for social reform. They wanted their theories and findings to be relevant to policymakers and to people's lives in general. For instance, Mead was the treasurer of Hull House for many years, where he applied his theory to improving the lives of those who were powerless (especially immigrants). He also served on committees dealing with Chicago's labor problems and public education. Today, *applied sociology* is the use of the discipline of sociology with the specific intent of yielding practical applications for human behavior and organizations.

Often, the goal of such work is to assist in resolving a social problem. For example, in the last 40 years, eight presidents of the United States have established commissions to delve into major societal concerns facing our nation. Sociologists are often asked to apply their expertise to studying such issues as violence, pornography, crime, immigration, and population. In Europe, both academic and governmental research departments are offering increasing financial support for applied studies.

One example of applied sociology is the growing interest in the ways in which nationally recognized social problems manifest themselves locally. Since 2003, sociologist Greg Scott and his colleagues have been seeking to better understand the connection between illegal drug use and the spread of HIV/AIDS. The study, which will run through 2009, has so far employed 14 researchers from colleges and public health agencies, assisted by an additional 15 graduate and 16 undergraduate students. By combining a variety of methods, including interviews and observation, with photo and video documentation, these researchers have found that across all drug users, HIV/AIDS transmission is highest among users of crystal methamphetamine. Meth users are also most likely to engage in risky sexual behavior, and to have partners who do so. Fortunately, of all drug users, meth users are the ones most closely connected to health care treatment programs, which allows them to receive substance abuse education and treatment from their regular health care providers. However, their cases, brought to the forefront by Scott and his team, highlight the need for public health officials to identify other individuals who engage in high-risk sexual behavior and get them into appropriate treatment programs (G. Scott 2005).

Growing interest in applied sociology has led to such specializations as medical sociology and environmental sociology. The former includes research on how health care professionals and patients deal with disease. As one example, medical sociologists

have studied the social impact of the AIDS crisis on families, friends, and communities (see Chapter 19). Environmental sociologists examine the relationship between human societies and the physical environment. One focus of their work is the issue of "environmental justice" (see Chapter 21), raised when researchers and community activists found that hazardous waste dumps are especially likely to be situated in poor and minority neighborhoods (M. Martin 1996).

The growing popularity of applied sociology has led to the rise of the specialty of clinical sociology. Louis Wirth (1931) wrote about clinical sociology more than 75 years ago, but the term itself has become popular only in recent years. While applied sociology may simply evaluate social issues, *clinical sociology* is dedicated to facilitating change by altering social relationships (as in family therapy) or restructuring social institutions (as in the reorganization of a medical center).

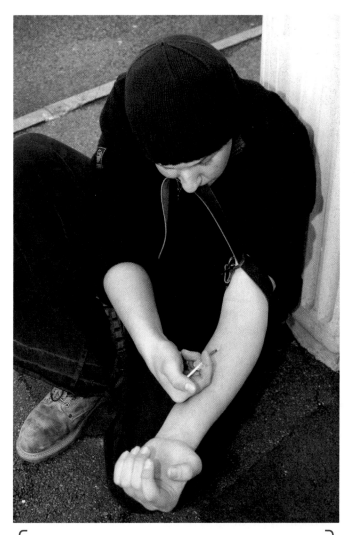

An intravenous (IV) drug user shoots up. Sociologists have studied the link between IV drug use and infection with HIV/AIDS in an attempt to develop guidelines for treatment and prevention.

The Association for Applied Clinical Sociology was founded in 1978 to promote the application of sociological knowledge to intervention for individual and social change. This professional group has developed a procedure for certifying clinical sociologists—much as physical therapists or psychologists are certified.

Applied sociologists generally leave it to others to act on their evaluations. By contrast, clinical sociologists take direct responsibility for implementation and view those with whom they work as their clients. This specialty has become increasingly attractive to graduate students in sociology because it offers an opportunity to apply intellectual learning in a practical way. A shrinking job market in the academic world has made such alternative career routes appealing.

Applied and clinical sociology can be contrasted with *basic* (or *pure*) *sociology,* which seeks a more profound knowledge of the fundamental aspects of social phenomena. This type of research is not necessarily meant to generate specific applications, although such ideas may result once findings are analyzed. When Durkheim studied suicide rates, he was not primarily interested in discovering a way to eliminate suicide. In this sense, his research was an example of basic rather than applied sociology.

www.mhhe.com/schaefer11

Use Your Sociological Imagination

What issues facing your local community would you like to address with applied sociological research? Do you see any global connections to these local issues?

Developing a Sociological Imagination

In this book, we will be illustrating the sociological imagination in several different ways—by showing theory in practice and research in action; by thinking globally; by exploring the significance of social inequality; by speaking across race, gender, and religious boundaries; and by highlighting social policy throughout the world.

Theory in Practice

We will illustrate how the major sociological perspectives can be helpful in understanding today's issues, from capital punishment to the AIDS crisis. Sociologists do not necessarily declare "Here I am using functionalism," but their research and approaches do tend to draw on one or more theoretical frameworks, as will become clear in the pages to follow.

Research in Action

Sociologists actively investigate a variety of issues and social behavior. We have already seen that research can shed light on the social factors that affect suicide rates and decision making in the jury box. Sociological research often plays a direct role in im-

proving people's lives, as in the case of increasing the participation of African Americans in diabetes testing. Throughout the rest of the book, the research performed by sociologists and other social scientists will shed light on group behavior of all types.

Thinking Globally

Whatever their theoretical perspective or research techniques, sociologists recognize that social behavior must be viewed in a global context. *Globalization* is the worldwide integration of government policies, cultures, social movements, and financial markets through trade and the exchange of ideas. While public discussion of globalization is relatively recent, intellectuals have been pondering its social consequences for a long time. Karl Marx and Friedrich Engels warned in *The Communist Manifesto* (written in 1848) of a world market that would lead to production in distant lands, sweeping away existing working relationships.

Today, developments outside a country are as likely to influence people's lives as changes at home. For example, though much of the world was already in recession by September 2001, the terrorist attacks on New York and Washington, D.C., caused an immediate economic decline not just in the United States, but throughout the world. One example of the massive global impact was the downturn in international tourism, which lasted for at least two years. The effects have been felt by people far removed from the United States, including African game wardens and Asian taxi drivers. Some observers see globalization and its effects as the natural result of advances in communications technology, particularly the Internet and satellite transmission of the mass media. Others view it more critically, as a process that allows multinational corporations to expand unchecked. We examine the impact of globalization on societies throughout the world, including our own, in Box 1-2 (on the tsunami disaster of December 2004) and throughout this text (Fiss and Hirsch 2005).

The Significance of Social Inequality

Who holds power? Who doesn't? Who has prestige? Who lacks it? Perhaps the major theme of analysis in sociology today is *social inequality,* a condition in which members of society have differing amounts of wealth, prestige, or power. The tsunami that hit countries on the Indian Ocean in 2004 highlighted the huge social gap between the impoverished people who live there and the wealthy Westerners who visit the area's luxury resorts (see Box 1-2, opposite). Likewise, in 2005 Hurricane Katrina drew attention to the social inequality among U.S. residents of the Gulf Coast. Predictably, the people who were hit the hardest by the massive storm were the poor, who had the greatest difficulty evacuating before the storm and have had the most difficulty recovering from it. Barbara Ehrenreich's research among low-wage workers uncovered some other aspects of social inequality in the United States.

Some sociologists, in seeking to understand the effects of inequality, have made the case for social justice. W. E. B. Du Bois ([1940] 1968:418) noted that the greatest power in the land is not "thought or ethics, but wealth." As we have seen,

1-2 The Global Response to the 2004 Tsunami

On December 26, 2004, an earthquake beneath the Indian Ocean set in motion a series of events that affected hundreds of millions of people around the world. The shifting ocean floor sent a series of gigantic tsunami waves toward the coasts of South Asia and Africa, completely engulfing many populated islands along the way. As the weeks passed, the outside world looked on in horror as the death toll climbed to more than 225,000.

The international relief effort that mobilized to rescue the injured, provide shelter to the homeless, and address long-term economic needs was one obvious sign of globalization. Through volunteer labor and donated money, sympathetic people and governments around the world could gain some sense of control in the face of the massive natural disaster. Beyond the humanitarian effort, however, lay more complicated aspects of globalization, including social interrelationships that span the globe and vast economic disparities between one part of the world and another.

Most of the devastation caused by the tsunami hit relatively poor areas of the world. As a result, the global economy barely flickered, and the insurance and financial markets escaped virtually unscathed. Had the tsunami hit the coast of North America or Europe, the results would have been far different. In fact, to guard against such catastrophe, a sophisticated tsunami detection and warning system had been in place in the Pacific Ocean for about 40 years, to offer some measure of protection to industrial giants Japan and the United States. No such network existed in the Indian Ocean, where neighboring countries lacked the resources to create one. Expensive warning systems and risk management plans, also common in affluent countries, were nonexistent in the area hit by the 2004 tsunami.

Though the areas affected by the tsunami were populated by some of the poorest, most vulnerable people in the world, pockets of incredible affluence could be found there as well. From the vantage point of the region's expensive resorts, vacationing Westerners used their camcorders to videotape the 30-foot waves as they pounded the coast and swept

> *The same borders that tourists cross so effortlessly confine those left homeless by the disaster to their impoverished, flood-ravaged nations.*

through the streets. Because such resorts offer almost the only form of economic development in the coastal areas, within weeks of the calamity, nations like Indonesia, Thailand, and Sri Lanka were urging tourists to return to the stricken zone. Their desperate attempt to restart the shattered tourism industry underscored the privileges that citizens of wealthy nations enjoy. Globalization permits them to pass effortlessly across national borders to visit such luxury resorts, where they pay for a single night's lodging with a sum the local people must work a year to earn. The same borders that tourists cross so effortlessly confine those left homeless by the disaster to their impoverished, flood-ravaged nations.

Another aspect of globalization was the political reaction to the disaster. Within days of the arrival of the first foreign assistance, the government of Indonesia, a predominantly Muslim country, announced that U.S. soldiers would be permitted in the disaster area only without their sidearms. All Western relief organizations were to be out of the country by March 30, whatever the needs in the stricken areas. This unusual step of turning away assistance must be viewed in a global context. At that time, the United States occupied two Muslim countries, Afghanistan and Iraq. Indonesian officials wanted to make clear that their country would not be subject to a similar occupation, however unlikely that scenario. Today, events in one part of the world impact people everywhere, in ways that cannot always be predicted.

Let's Discuss

1. Have you ever lived in or traveled to a place where the very wealthy lived side by side with the desperately poor? If so, where was it—in a foreign country or the United States? Explain the economic relationship between the two groups.
2. Which of the three major theoretical perspectives would be most useful in analyzing the social effects of the 2004 tsunami? Explain your answer.

Sources: Geist et al. 2006; Seabrook 2005; Swiss Re 2005; *The Economist* 2005a.

---

the contributions of Karl Marx, Jane Addams, and Ida Wells-Barnett also stressed this sentiment for the overarching importance of social inequality and social justice. Joe Feagin (2001) echoed it in a presidential address to the American Sociological Association.

Throughout, this book will highlight the work of sociologists on social inequality. Many chapters also feature a box on this theme.

Speaking across Race, Gender, and Religious Boundaries

Sociologists include both men and women, as well as people from a variety of ethnic, national, and religious origins. In their work, sociologists seek to draw conclusions that speak to all people—not just the affluent or powerful. Doing so is not always easy. Insights into how a corporation can increase its profits tend to attract more attention and financial support than do, say, the merits of a needle exchange program for low-income inner-city residents. Yet today more than ever, sociology seeks to better understand the experiences of all people.

Sociologists have noted, for example, that the 2004 tsunami affected men and women differently. When the waves hit, mothers and grandmothers were at home with the children; men were outside working, where they were more likely to become aware of the impending disaster. Moreover, most of the men knew how to swim, a survival skill that women in these traditional societies usually do not learn. As a result, many more men than women survived the catastrophe—about 10 men for every 1 woman. In one Indonesian village typical of the disaster area, 97 of 1,300 people survived; only 4 were women. The impact of this gender imbalance will be felt for some time, given women's primary role as caregivers for children and the elderly (BBC News 2005a).

Social Policy throughout the World

One important way we can use a sociological imagination is to enhance our understanding of current social issues throughout the world. Beginning with Chapter 2, each chapter will conclude with a discussion of a contemporary social policy issue. In some cases, we will examine a specific issue facing national governments. For example, government funding of child care centers will be discussed in Chapter 4, Socialization; global immigration in Chapter 11, Racial and Ethnic Inequality; and religion in the schools in Chapter 15, Religion. These Social Policy sections will demonstrate how fundamental sociological concepts can enhance our

critical thinking skills and help us to better understand current public policy debates taking place around the world.

In addition, sociology has been used to evaluate the success of programs or the impact of changes brought about by policymakers and political activists. For example, Chapter 9, Stratification and Social Mobility in the United States, includes a discussion of research on the effectiveness of welfare reform experiments. Such discussions underscore the many practical applications of sociological theory and research.

Sociologists expect the next quarter of a century to be perhaps the most exciting and critical period in the history of the discipline. That is because of a growing recognition—both in the United States and around the world—that current social problems *must* be addressed before their magnitude overwhelms human societies. We can expect sociologists to play an increasing role in government by researching and developing public policy alternatives. It seems only natural for this textbook to focus on the connection between the work of sociologists and the difficult questions confronting policymakers and people in the United States and around the world.

APPENDIX   Careers in Sociology

For the last two decades the number of U.S. college students who have graduated with a degree in sociology has risen steadily (see Figure 1-4). In this appendix we'll consider some of the options these students have after completing their undergraduate education.

An undergraduate degree in sociology doesn't just serve as excellent preparation for future graduate work in sociology. It also provides a strong liberal arts background for entry-level positions in business, social services, foundations, community organizations, not-for-profit groups, law enforcement, and many government jobs. A number of fields—among them marketing, public relations, and broadcasting—now require investigative skills and an understanding of the diverse groups found in today's multiethnic and multinational environment. Moreover, a sociology degree requires accomplishment in oral and written communication, interpersonal skills, problem solving, and critical thinking—all job-related skills that may give sociology graduates an advantage over those who pursue more technical degrees.

Consequently, while few occupations specifically require an undergraduate degree in sociology, such academic training can be an important asset in entering a wide range of occupations (American Sociological Association 2006a). To emphasize this point, a number of chapters in this book highlight a real-life professional who describes how the study of sociology has helped in his or her career. Look for the "Taking Sociology to Work" boxes.

Figure 1-5 summarizes the sources of employment for those with BA or BS degrees in sociology. It shows that the areas of social services, education, business, and government offer major career

opportunities for sociology graduates. Undergraduates who know where their career interests lie are well advised to enroll in sociology courses and specialties best suited to those interests. For example, students hoping to become health planners would take a class in medical sociology; students seeking employment as social science research assistants would focus on courses in statistics and methods. Internships, such as placements at city planning agencies and survey research organizations, afford another way for sociology students to prepare for careers. Studies show that students who choose an internship placement have less trouble finding jobs, obtain better jobs, and enjoy greater job satisfaction than students without internship placements (American Sociological Association 2006a; Salem and Grabarek 1986).

Many college students view social work as the field most closely associated with sociology. Traditionally, social workers received their undergraduate training in sociology and allied fields such as psychology and counseling. After some practical experience, social workers would generally seek a master's degree in social work (MSW) to be considered for supervisory or administrative positions. Today, however, some students choose (where it is available) to pursue a bachelor's degree in social work (BSW). This degree prepares graduates for direct service positions, such as caseworker or group worker.

Many students continue their sociological training beyond the bachelor's degree. More than 250 universities in the United States have graduate programs in sociology that offer PhD and/or master's degrees. These programs differ greatly in their areas of specializa-

FIGURE 1-4

Sociology Degrees Conferred in the United States by Gender

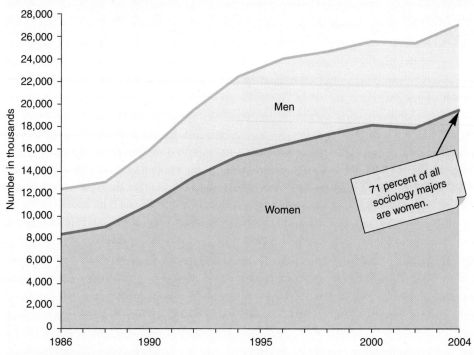

Source: Department of Education 2006.

a doctoral student in sociology will engage in four to seven years of intensive work, including the time required to complete the dissertation. Yet even this effort is no guarantee of a job as a sociology professor.

The good news is that over the next 10 years, the demand for instructors is expected to increase because of high rates of retirement among faculty from the baby-boom generation, as well as the anticipated slow but steady growth in the college student population in the United States. Nonetheless, anyone who launches an academic career must be prepared for considerable uncertainty and competition in the college job market (American Sociological Association 2006a; Huber 1985).

Of course, not all people working as sociologists teach or hold doctoral degrees. Take government, for example. The Census Bureau relies on people with sociological training to interpret data for other government agencies and the general public. Virtually every agency depends on survey research—a field in which sociology students can specialize—in order to assess everything from community needs to the morale of the agency's own workers. In addition, people with sociological training can put their academic knowledge to effective use in probation and parole, health sciences, community development, and recreational services. Some people working in government or private industry have a master's degree (MA or MS) in sociology; others have a bachelor's degree (BA or BS).

Currently, about 22 percent of the members of the American Sociological Association use their sociological skills outside the academic world, whether in social service agencies or in marketing positions for business firms. Increasing numbers of sociologists

tion, course requirements, costs, and the research and teaching opportunities available to graduate students. About 61 percent of the graduates are women (American Sociological Association 2005, 2008).

Higher education is an important source of employment for sociologists with graduate degrees. About 83 percent of recent PhD recipients in sociology seek employment in colleges and universities. These sociologists teach not only majors committed to the discipline but also students hoping to become doctors, nurses, lawyers, police officers, and so forth (American Sociological Association 2005).

Sociologists who teach in colleges and universities may use their knowledge and training to influence public policy. For example, sociologist Andrew Cherlin (2003) recently commented on the debate over proposed federal funding to promote marriage among welfare recipients. Citing the results of two of his studies, Cherlin questioned the potential effectiveness of such a policy in strengthening low-income families. Because many single mothers choose to marry someone other than the father of their children—sometimes for good reason—their children often grow up in stepfamilies. Cherlin's research shows that children who are raised in stepfamilies are no better off than those in single-parent families. He sees government efforts to promote marriage as a politically motivated attempt to foster traditional social values in a society that has become increasingly diverse.

For sociology graduates interested in academic careers, the road to a PhD (or doctorate) can be long and difficult. This degree symbolizes competence in original research; each candidate must prepare a book-length study known as a dissertation. Typically,

FIGURE 1-5

Occupational Fields of Sociology BA/MA Graduates

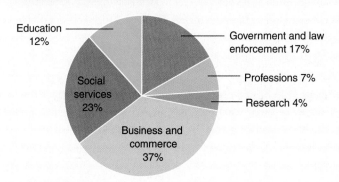

Source: Schaefer 1998b.

with graduate degrees are employed by businesses, industry, hospitals, and nonprofit organizations. Studies show that many sociology graduates are making career changes from social service areas to business and commerce. For an undergraduate major, sociology is excellent preparation for employment in many parts of the business world (American Sociological Association 2001).

Whether you take a few courses in sociology or actually complete a degree, you will benefit from the critical thinking skills developed in this discipline. Sociologists emphasize the value of being able to analyze, interpret, and function within a variety of working situations—an asset in virtually any career. Moreover, given rapid technological change and the expanding global economy, all of us will need to adapt to substantial social change, even in our own careers. Sociology provides a rich conceptual framework that can serve as a foundation for flexible career development and assist you in taking advantage of new employment opportunities (American Sociological Association 2006a).

 For more information on career opportunities for individuals with a background in sociology, visit the Online Learning Center at **www.mhhe.com/schaefer11.** Go to "Student Edition," and in the section titled "Course-wide Content," click on "Web Resources." Then click on "Career Opportunities," which will provide you with numerous links to sites offering career advice and information.

{ MASTERING THIS CHAPTER }

Summary

Sociology is the scientific study of social behavior and human groups. In this chapter, we examine the nature of sociological theory, the founders of the discipline, theoretical perspectives in contemporary sociology, practical applications for sociological theory and research, and ways to exercise the "sociological imagination."

1. The *sociological imagination* is an awareness of the relationship between an individual and the wider society. It is based on the ability to view our own society as an outsider might, rather than from the perspective of our limited experiences and cultural biases.

2. In contrast to other *social sciences,* sociology emphasizes the influence that groups can have on people's behavior and attitudes and the ways in which people shape society.

3. Knowledge that relies on "common sense" is not always reliable. Sociologists must test and analyze each piece of information they use.

4. Sociologists employ *theories* to examine relationships between observations or data that may seem completely unrelated.

5. Nineteenth-century thinkers who contributed sociological insights included Auguste Comte, a French philosopher; Harriet Martineau, an English sociologist; and Herbert Spencer, an English scholar.

6. Other important figures in the development of sociology were Émile Durkheim, who pioneered work on suicide; Max Weber, who taught the need for "insight" in intellectual work; and Karl Marx, who emphasized the importance of the economy and social conflict.

7. In the 20th century, the discipline of sociology was indebted to the U.S. sociologists Charles Horton Cooley and Robert Merton.

8. *Macrosociology* concentrates on large-scale phenomena or entire civilizations, whereas *microsociology* stresses the study of small groups.

9. The *functionalist perspective* emphasizes the way in which the parts of a society are structured to maintain its stability.

10. The *conflict perspective* assumes that social behavior is best understood in terms of conflict or tension between competing groups.

11. The *interactionist perspective* is concerned primarily with fundamental or everyday forms of interaction, including symbols and other types of nonverbal communication.

12. The *feminist view,* which is often allied with the conflict perspective, sees inequity in gender as central to all behavior and organization.

13. Sociologists make use of all four perspectives, since each offers unique insights into the same issue.

14. *Applied* and *clinical sociology* apply the discipline of sociology to the solution of practical problems in human behavior and organizations. In contrast, *basic sociology* is sociological inquiry that seeks only a deeper knowledge of the fundamental aspects of social phenomena.

15. This textbook makes use of the sociological imagination by showing theory in practice and research in action; by thinking globally; by focusing on the significance of social inequality; by speaking across race, gender, and religious boundaries; and by highlighting social policy around the world.

1. What aspects of the social and work environment in a fast-food restaurant would be of particular interest to a sociologist because of his or her sociological imagination?

2. What are the manifest and latent functions of a health club?

3. How does the merchandise that is displayed in a toy store relate to issues of race, class, and gender?

Key Terms

Anomie The loss of direction felt in a society when social control of individual behavior has become ineffective. (page 12)

Applied sociology The use of the discipline of sociology with the specific intent of yielding practical applications for human behavior and organizations. (21)

Basic sociology Sociological inquiry conducted with the objective of gaining a more profound knowledge of the fundamental aspects of social phenomena. Also known as *pure sociology*. (22)

Clinical sociology The use of the discipline of sociology with the specific intent of altering social relationships or restructuring social institutions. (21)

Conflict perspective A sociological approach that assumes that social behavior is best understood in terms of tension between groups over power or the allocation of resources, including housing, money, access to services, and political representation. (16)

Dramaturgical approach A view of social interaction in which people are seen as theatrical performers. (19)

Dysfunction An element or process of a society that may disrupt the social system or reduce its stability. (16)

Feminist view A sociological approach that views inequity in gender as central to all behavior and organization. (17)

Functionalist perspective A sociological approach that emphasizes the way in which the parts of a society are structured to maintain its stability. (15)

Globalization The worldwide integration of government policies, cultures, social movements, and financial markets through trade and the exchange of ideas. (22)

Ideal type A construct or model for evaluating specific cases. (13)

Interactionist perspective A sociological approach that generalizes about everyday forms of social interaction in order to explain society as a whole. (18)

Latent function An unconscious or unintended function that may reflect hidden purposes. (16)

Macrosociology Sociological investigation that concentrates on large-scale phenomena or entire civilizations. (15)

Manifest function An open, stated, and conscious function. (16)

Microsociology Sociological investigation that stresses the study of small groups, often through experimental means. (15)

Natural science The study of the physical features of nature and the ways in which they interact and change. (5)

Nonverbal communication The sending of messages through the use of gestures, facial expressions, and postures. (18)

Science The body of knowledge obtained by methods based on systematic observation. (5)

Social inequality A condition in which members of society have differing amounts of wealth, prestige, or power. (22)

Social science The study of the social features of humans and the ways in which they interact and change. (5)

Sociological imagination An awareness of the relationship between an individual and the wider society, both today and in the past. (4)

Sociology The scientific study of social behavior and human groups. (4)

Theory In sociology, a set of statements that seeks to explain problems, actions, or behavior. (10)

Verstehen The German word for "understanding" or "insight"; used to stress the need for sociologists to take into account the subjective meanings people attach to their actions. (12)

Self-Quiz

Read each question carefully and then select the best answer.

1. Sociology is
   a. very narrow in scope.
   b. concerned with what one individual does or does not do.
   c. the systematic study of social behavior and human groups.
   d. an awareness of the relationship between an individual and the wider society.

2. Which of the following thinkers introduced the concept of the sociological imagination?
   a. Émile Durkheim
   b. Max Weber
   c. Karl Marx
   d. C. Wright Mills

3. Émile Durkheim's research on suicide suggested that
   a. Catholics had much higher suicide rates than Protestants.
   b. there seemed to be higher rates of suicide in times of peace than in times of war and revolution.
   c. civilians were more likely to take their lives than soldiers.
   d. suicide is a solitary act, unrelated to group life.

4. Max Weber taught his students that they should employ which of the following in their intellectual work?
   a. anomie
   b. *verstehen*
   c. the sociological imagination
   d. microsociology

5. Robert Merton's contributions to sociology include

    a. successfully combining theory and research.

    b. producing a theory that is one of the most frequently cited explanations of deviant behavior.

    c. an attempt to bring macro-level and micro-level analyses together.

    d. all of the above

6. Which sociologist made a major contribution to society through his in-depth studies of urban life, including both Blacks and Whites?

    a. W. E. B. Du Bois

    b. Robert Merton

    c. Auguste Comte

    d. Charles Horton Cooley

7. In the late 19th century, before the term *feminist perspective* could even be coined, the ideas behind this major theoretical approach appeared in the writings of

    a. Karl Marx.

    b. Ida Wells-Barnett.

    c. Charles Horton Cooley.

    d. Carol Brooks Gardner.

8. Thinking of society as a living organism in which each part of the organism contributes to its survival is a reflection of which theoretical perspective?

    a. the functionalist perspective

    b. the conflict perspective

    c. the feminist perspective

    d. the interactionist perspective

9. Karl Marx's view of the struggle between social classes inspired the contemporary

    a. functionalist perspective.

    b. conflict perspective.

    c. interactionist perspective.

    d. dramaturgical approach.

10. Erving Goffman's dramaturgical approach, which postulates that people present certain aspects of their personalities while obscuring other qualities, is derivative of what major theoretical perspective?

    a. the functionalist perspective

    b. the conflict perspective

    c. the feminist perspective

    d. the interactionist perspective

11. While the findings of sociologists may at times seem like common sense, they differ because they rest on _____ analysis of facts.

12. Within sociology, a(n) _____ is a set of statements that seeks to explain problems, actions, or behavior.

13. In _____ _____'s hierarchy of the sciences, sociology was the "queen," and its practitioners were "scientist-priests."

14. In *Society in America,* originally published in 1837, English scholar _____ _____ examined religion, politics, child rearing, and immigration in the young nation.

15. _____ _____ adapted Charles Darwin's evolutionary view of the "survival of the fittest" by arguing that it is "natural" that some people are rich while others are poor.

16. Sociologist Max Weber coined the term _____ _____ in referring to a construct or model that serves as a measuring rod against which actual cases can be evaluated.

17. In *The Communist Manifesto,* _____ _____ and _____ _____ argued that the masses of people who have no resources other than their labor (the proletariat) should unite to fight for the overthrow of capitalist societies.

18. _____ _____, an early female sociologist, cofounded the famous Chicago settlement house called Hull House and also tried to establish a juvenile court system.

19. The university's role in certifying academic competence and excellence is an example of a(n) _____ function.

20. The _____ _____ draws on the work of Karl Marx and Friedrich Engels in that it often views women's subordination as inherent in capitalist societies.

TECHNOLOGY RESOURCES

Online Learning Center

1. Visit the Online Learning Center, this textbook's specific Web site, at **www.mhhe.com/schaefer11.** The student center in the Online Learning Center offers a variety of helpful and interesting resources and activities for each chapter. The resources include chapter outlines and summaries, quizzes with feedback, direct links to Internet sites, including those found in the Technology Resources sections at the end of each chapter in your text, relevant news updates, and audio clips by the author. The activities include flashcards, crossword

puzzles, interactive maps, and interactive exercises. Don't pass up this opportunity to learn more about sociology and to take advantage of resources that will help you master the material in your text and get a better grade in the course!

2. The Web site of the Hull House Museum (**www.uic.edu/jaddams/hull/hull_house.html**) provides a wealth of information about Jane Addams and her life work. To view historical photo-graphs of Hull House and the people Addams served, click on "Urban Experience."

3. Descriptions of the major sociological theorists in this chapter only begin to scratch the surface of these fascinating and creative people. Learn more at Sociology Professor (**www.sociologyprofessor.com**), a Web site where you can find biographical information on a variety of historical figures in the discipline.

*Note: Although all the URLs listed were current as of the printing of this book, these sites often change. Please check our Web site (**www.mhhe.com/schaefer11**) for updates, hyperlinks, and exercises related to these sites.*

Reel Society Video Clips

Exercise your imagination and step into the world of *Reel Society*, a professionally produced movie that demonstrates the sociological imagination through typical scenarios drawn from campus life. In this movie you will become part of the exploits of several college students, and will influence the plot by making key choices for them. You'll learn to relate sociological thought to real life through a variety of issues and perspectives. In addition to the interactive movie, *Reel Society* includes explanatory text screens and a glossary, as well as quizzes and discussion questions to test your knowledge of sociology.

Reel Society video clips, which appear on this book's Web site, can be used to spark discussion about the following topics from this chapter:

• The Sociological Imagination
• Major Theoretical Perspectives
• Speaking across Race, Gender, and Religious Boundaries

The data social scientists collect often confirm what people think, but sometimes they surprise us. In the United States today, the percentage of homes with two children, a working father, and a homemaker mother remains relatively the same at 2 percent as when this billboard was photographed in 1992.

2 Sociological Research

PARADISE LABORERS
HOTEL WORK IN THE GLOBAL ECONOMY

Patricia A. Adler and Peter Adler

"You land in paradise. Departing the airport in your canary-yellow rented convertible, you . . . head toward your vacation destination: an exclusive Hawaiian hotel. . . . Turning off the main road onto the winding driveway, you see the rich, vibrant colors of the beautiful trees and flowers lining the peaceful path. As you drive up to the lobby, a potpourri of pleasurable sensations assaults you. You smell the fragrant plumeria and gardenia blossoms, indications that you are in a tropical Eden. You hear the rumble of the waterfall and then behold its magnificence, a torrent of rushing streams tumbling over rocks and crashing into a pool below. The cascading water and its splash fill the air with moisture and your nostrils with the hydrated aroma. You have entered paradise.

As you pull up, . . . a smartly dressed bell captain approaches and opens your door, welcoming you with a resounding "aloha." A bellman wheels up his cart and unloads your bags. You give your name and hand your keys to the valet and wander toward the lobby. . . . Immediately, a beautiful Polynesian woman appears and, in soft tones, welcomes you, slipping a colorful and sweet-smelling lei over your head. . . .

You are steered toward the front desk where another Polynesian employee greets you and begins your check-in process. Discreetly, your lei greeter returns, carrying a silver tray from which she offers you glasses filled with tropical fruit punch and a sugarcane swizzle stick to chew on. . . . You gaze around at the impressive space, the many workers bustling around in diverse uniforms. They range among the different Hawaiian hotels from the flowing raiment of traditional Polynesian garb to the starched, dignified British uniforms summoning images of old-world butlers and high service.

> *Immediately, a beautiful Polynesian woman appears and, in soft tones, welcomes you, slipping a colorful and sweet-smelling lei over your head.*

After you complete your transaction, the front desk clerk summons a bellman who appears with your luggage. . . . Your bellman takes you to your room, . . . brings in your bags, lays them atop the unfolded luggage holders, and fills your ice bucket. You have arrived in the lap of luxury.

This surreal guest experience is made possible by a set of carefully planned structures surrounding and underlying what customers see. Most guests do not notice the precise ethnic and racial stratification of those attending them. They do not recognize that the lei greeters and front desk clerks are locals, selected for their Polynesian appearance; that many valets and the bell captain are "haoles" (Caucasians), selected to give an atmosphere of continental service; and that the bellmen are a combination of these two groups. At the same time guests may completely overlook the new immigrants: outdoor housekeepers sweeping the lobby or gardeners raking the leaves. . . .

Guests are also usually unaware of the complex systems that organize and track the services they receive. Valets and bellmen work on a rotation that calls them forth to fetch luggage or cars in a careful order. . . . Unbeknownst to guests, the passage of every bag through the hotel is meticulously charted. . . . All this constitutes the complex underground functioning of a large resort that makes the guest experience invisibly smooth."

(P. Adler and Adler 2004:1–2, 4) Additional information about this excerpt can be found on the Online Learning Center at www.mhhe.com/schaefer11.

This description of a tourist's arrival at a Hawaiian resort, taken from Patricia A. Adler and Peter Adler's (2004) *Paradise Laborers: Hotel Work in the Global Economy,* is based on extensive research into the global tourism industry. Over an eight-year period, the two sociologists conducted extensive fieldwork at five Hawaiian hotels, studying the staff and operations in minute detail. They interviewed employees and members of the corporate management team, took extensive notes, and spent considerable time observing the social organization of the resort business. Their research allowed them to go well beyond the postcard observations that a typical tourist might send home from vacation.

The Adlers' work in Hawaii reflects all three major sociological approaches. In noting the resorts' relatively smooth operation, despite continual employee turnover even at the highest levels, the Adlers adopt a functionalist perspective. When they focus on how members of the hotel workforce relate to one another on the job, they are employing the interactionist perspective. And when they note that those employees are divided by social class, gender, ethnicity, and immigration status, they are relying on the conflict and feminist approaches.

The Adlers' work also illustrates the enormous breadth of the field of sociology. Over the course of their careers, Patricia A. Adler and Peter Adler (1991, 1993, 1998, 2005) have published studies of college athletes, illicit drug traffickers, preadolescent peer groups, and people who engage in self-mutilation (self-described cutters, burners, and so on). Their choice of the global tourism industry as their latest subject indicates the tremendous freedom sociologists have to explore and open up new topics of inquiry.

Effective sociological research can be quite thought-provoking. It may suggest many new questions that require further study, such as why we make assumptions about people's suitability for certain jobs based merely on their gender or race. In some cases, rather than raising additional questions, a study will simply confirm previous beliefs and findings. Sociological research can also have practical applications. For instance, research results that disconfirm accepted beliefs about marriage and the family may lead to changes in public policy.

This chapter will examine the research process used in conducting sociological studies. How do sociologists go about setting up a research project? And how do they ensure that the results of the research are reliable and accurate? Can they carry out their research without violating the rights of those they study?

We will first look at the steps that make up the scientific method used in research. Then we will take a look at various techniques commonly used in sociological research, such as experiments, observations, and surveys. We will pay particular attention to the ethical challenges sociologists face in studying human behavior, and to the debate raised by Max Weber's call for "value neutrality" in social science research. We will also examine the role technology plays in research today. The Social Policy section considers the difficulties in researching the controversial subject of human sexuality.

Whatever the area of sociological inquiry and whatever the perspective of the sociologist—whether functionalist, conflict, interactionist, or any other—there is one crucial requirement: imaginative, responsible research that meets the highest scientific and ethical standards.

What Is the Scientific Method?

Like all of us, sociologists are interested in the central questions of our time. Is the family falling apart? Why is there so much crime in the United States? Is the world falling behind in its ability to feed a growing population? Such issues concern most people, whether or not they have academic training. However, unlike the typical citizen, the sociologist has a commitment to use the *scientific method* in studying society. The scientific method is a systematic, organized series of steps that ensures maximum objectivity and consistency in researching a problem.

Many of us will never actually conduct scientific research. Why, then, is it important that we understand the scientific method? The answer is that it plays a major role in the workings of our society. Residents of the United States are constantly bombarded with "facts" or "data." A television news report informs us that "one in every two marriages in this country now ends in divorce," yet Chapter 14 will show that this assertion is based on misleading statistics. Almost daily, advertisers cite supposedly scientific studies to prove that their products are superior. Such claims may be accurate or exaggerated. We can better evaluate such information—and will not be fooled so easily—if we are familiar with the standards of scientific research. These standards are quite stringent, and they demand as strict adherence as possible.

The scientific method requires precise preparation in developing useful research. Otherwise, the research data collected may not prove accurate. Sociologists and other researchers follow five basic steps in the scientific method: (1) defining the problem, (2) reviewing the literature, (3) formulating the hypothesis, (4) selecting the research design and then collecting and analyzing data, and (5) developing the conclusion (see Figure 2-1). We'll use an actual example to illustrate the workings of the scientific method.

Defining the Problem

Does it "pay" to go to college? Some people make great sacrifices and work hard to get a college education. Parents borrow money for their children's tuition. Students work part-time jobs or even take full-time positions while attending evening or weekend classes. Does it pay off? Are there monetary returns for getting that degree?

The first step in any research project is to state as clearly as possible what you hope to investigate—that is, *define the problem.* In this instance, we are interested in knowing how schooling relates to income. We want to find out the earnings of people with different levels of formal schooling.

Early on, any social science researcher must develop an operational definition of each concept being studied. An **operational definition** is an explanation of an abstract concept that is specific enough to allow a researcher to assess the concept. For example, a sociologist interested in status might use membership in exclusive social clubs as an operational definition of status. Someone studying prejudice might consider a person's unwillingness to hire or work with members of minority groups as an operational definition of prejudice. In our example, we need to develop two operational definitions—education and earnings—in order to study whether it pays to get an advanced educational degree. We'll define *education* as the number of years of schooling a person has achieved, and *earnings* as the income a person reports having received in the last year.

Initially, we will take a functionalist perspective (although we may end up incorporating other approaches). We will argue that opportunities for more earning power are related to level of schooling and that schools prepare students for employment.

Reviewing the Literature

By conducting a *review of the literature*—relevant scholarly studies and information—researchers refine the problem under study, clarify possible techniques to be used in collecting data, and eliminate or reduce avoidable mistakes. In our example, we would examine information about the salaries for different occupations. We would see if jobs that require more academic training are better rewarded. It would also be appropriate to review other studies on the relationship between education and income.

The review of the literature would soon tell us that many other factors besides years of schooling influence earning potential. For example, we would learn that the children of rich parents are more likely to go to college than those from modest backgrounds, so we might consider the possibility that the same parents may later help their children secure better-paying jobs.

We might also look at macro-level data, such as state-by-state comparisons of income and educational levels. In one macro-level study based on census data, researchers found that in states

FIGURE 2–1   **33**

Sociological Research

The Scientific Method

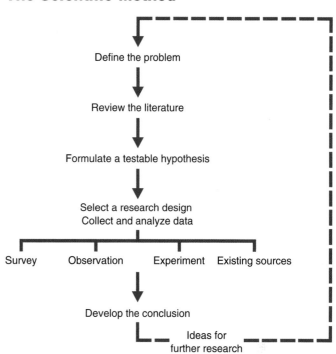

The scientific method allows sociologists to objectively and logically evaluate the data they collect. Their findings can suggest ideas for further sociological research.

whose residents have a relatively high level of education, household income levels are high as well (see Figure 2-2, page 34). This finding suggests that schooling may well be related to income, though it does not speak to the micro-level relationship we are interested in. That is, we want to know whether *individuals* who are well educated are also well paid.

Formulating the Hypothesis

After reviewing earlier research and drawing on the contributions of sociological theorists, the researchers may then *formulate the hypothesis.* A **hypothesis** is a speculative statement about the relationship between two or more factors known as variables. Income, religion, occupation, and gender can all serve as variables in a study. We can define a **variable** as a measurable trait or characteristic that is subject to change under different conditions.

Researchers who formulate a hypothesis generally must suggest how one aspect of human behavior influences or affects another. The variable hypothesized to cause or influence another is called the **independent variable.** The second variable is termed the **dependent variable** because its action *depends* on the influence of the independent variable. In other words, the researcher believes that the independent variable predicts or causes change in the dependent variable. For example, a researcher in sociology might anticipate that the availability of affordable housing

Educational Level and Household Income in the United States

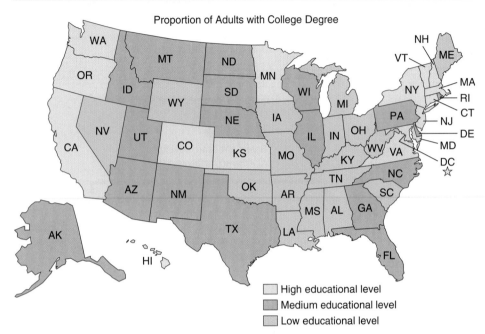

MAPPING LIFE
NATIONWIDE
www.mhhe.com/schaefer11

Proportion of Adults with College Degree

☐ High educational level
☐ Medium educational level
☐ Low educational level

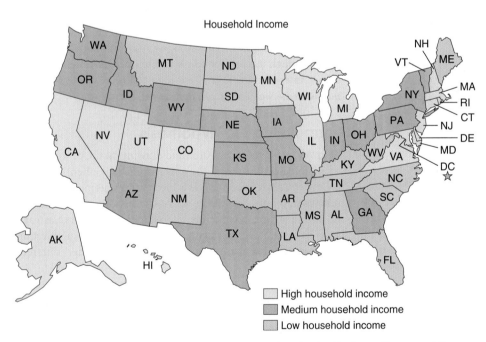

Household Income

☐ High household income
☐ Medium household income
☐ Low household income

Notes: Education data are for 2005. Cutoffs for high/medium and medium/low educational levels were 30 percent and 25 percent of the population with a college degree, respectively; median for the entire nation was 27.6 percent. Income data are 2002–2004 three-year average medians. Cutoffs for high/medium and medium/low household income levels were $45,700 and $41,000, respectively; national median household income was $44,473.

Sources: Bureau of the Census 2006a:145; DeNavas-Walt et al. 2005:23, 76.

In general, states with high educational levels (top) also have high household incomes (bottom).

(the independent variable, x) affects the level of homelessness in a community (the dependent variable, y).

Our hypothesis is that the higher one's educational degree, the more money one will earn. The independent variable that is to be measured is the level of education. The variable that is thought to depend on it—income—must also be measured.

Identifying independent and dependent variables is a critical step in clarifying cause-and-effect relationships. As shown in Figure 2-3, *causal logic* involves the relationship between a condition or variable and a particular consequence, with one event leading to the other. For instance, being less integrated into society may be directly related to, or produce a greater likelihood of, suicide. Similarly, the time students spend reviewing material for a quiz may be directly related to, or produce a greater likelihood of, getting a high score on the quiz.

A *correlation* exists when a change in one variable coincides with a change in the other. Correlations are an indication that causality *may* be present; they do not necessarily indicate causation. For example, data indicate that people who prefer to watch televised news programs are less knowledgeable than those who read newspapers and newsmagazines. This correlation between people's relative knowledge and their choice of news media seems to make sense, because it agrees with the common belief that television "dumbs down" information. But the correlation between the two variables is actually caused by a third variable, people's relative ability to comprehend large amounts of information. People with poor reading skills are much more likely than others to get their news from television, while those who are more educated or skilled turn more often to the print media. Though television viewing is correlated with lower news comprehension, then, it does not *cause* it. Sociologists seek to identify the *causal* link between variables; the suspected causal link is generally described in the hypothesis (Neuman 2000:139).

Collecting and Analyzing Data

How do you test a hypothesis to determine if it is supported or refuted? You need to collect information, using one of the research designs described later in the chapter. The research design guides the researcher in collecting and analyzing data.

Selecting the Sample In most studies, social scientists must carefully select what is known as a sample. A *sample* is a selection from a larger population that is statistically representative of that population. There are many kinds of samples, but the one social scientists use most frequently is the random sample. In a *random sample,* every member of an entire population being studied has the same chance of being selected. Thus, if researchers want to examine the opinions of people listed in a city directory (a book that, unlike the telephone directory, lists all households), they might use a computer to randomly select names from the directory. The results would constitute a random sample. The advantage of using specialized sampling techniques is that sociologists do not need to question everyone in a population (Igo 2007).

It is all too easy to confuse the careful scientific techniques used in representative sampling with the many *nonscientific* polls that receive much more media attention. For example, television viewers and radio listeners are often encouraged to e-mail their views on headline news or political contests. Such polls reflect nothing more than the views of those who happened to see the television program (or hear the radio broadcast) and took the time, perhaps at some cost, to register their opinions. These data do not necessarily reflect (and indeed may distort) the views of the broader population. Not everyone has access to a television or radio, time to watch or listen to a program, or the means and/or inclination to send e-mail. Similar problems are raised by the "mail-back" questionnaires found in many magazines and by "mall intercepts," in which shoppers are asked about some issue. Even when these techniques include answers from tens of thousands of people, they will be far less accurate than a carefully selected representative sample of 1,500 respondents.

For the purposes of our research example, we will use information collected in the General Social Survey (GSS). Since 1972, the National Opinion Research Center (NORC) has conducted this national survey 24 times, most recently in 2004. In this survey, a representative sample of the adult population is interviewed on a variety of topics for about one and a half hours. The author of this book examined the responses of the 1,875 people interviewed in 2002 concerning their level of education and income.

Ensuring Validity and Reliability The scientific method requires that research results be both valid and reliable. *Validity* refers to the degree to which a measure or scale truly reflects the phenomenon under study. A valid measure of income depends on the gathering of accurate data. Various studies show that people are reasonably accurate in reporting how much money they earned in the most recent year. *Reliability* refers to the

It seems reasonable to assume that these Columbia University graduates will earn more income than high school graduates. But how would you go about testing that hypothesis?

FIGURE 2–3

Causal Logic

Independent variable	Dependent variable
x →	y
Level of educational degree →	Level of income
Degree of lack of integration into society →	Likelihood of suicide
Availability of affordable housing →	Level of homelessness
Parents' church attendance →	Children's church attendance
Time spent preparing for quiz →	Performance on quiz
Parents' income →	Likelihood of children's enrolling in college

In *causal logic* an independent variable (often designated by the symbol *x*) influences a dependent variable (generally designated as *y*); thus, *x* leads to *y*. For example, parents who attend church regularly (*x*) are more likely to have children who are churchgoers (*y*). Notice that the first two pairs of variables are taken from studies already described in this textbook.

Think About It
Identify two or three dependent variables that might be influenced by this independent variable: number of alcoholic drinks ingested.

extent to which a measure produces consistent results. Some people may not disclose accurate information, but most do. In the General Social Survey, only 5 percent of the respondents refused to give their income or indicated they did not know what their income was. That means 95 percent of the respondents gave their income, which we can assume is reasonably accurate (given their other responses about occupation and years in the labor force).

Developing the Conclusion

Scientific studies, including those conducted by sociologists, do not aim to answer all the questions that can be raised about a particular subject. Therefore, the conclusion of a research study represents both an end and a beginning. It terminates a specific phase of the investigation but should also generate ideas for future study.

Supporting Hypotheses In our example, we find that the data support our hypothesis: People with more formal schooling *do* earn more money than others. Those with a high school diploma earn more than those who failed to complete high school, but those with an associate's degree earn more than high school graduates. The relationship continues through more advanced levels of schooling, so that those with graduate degrees earn the most.

The relationship is not perfect, however. Some people who drop out of high school end up with high incomes, whereas some with advanced degrees earn modest incomes, as shown in Figure 2-4. A successful entrepreneur, for example, might not have much formal schooling, while a holder of a doctorate may choose to work for a low-paying nonprofit institution. Sociologists are interested in both the general pattern that emerges from their data and exceptions to the pattern.

Sociological studies do not always generate data that support the original hypothesis. In many instances, a hypothesis is refuted, and researchers must reformulate their conclusions. Unexpected results may also lead sociologists to reexamine their methodology and make changes in the research design.

Controlling for Other Factors A *control variable* is a factor that is held constant to test the relative impact of an independent variable. For example, if researchers wanted to know how adults in the United States feel about restrictions on smoking in public places, they would probably attempt to use a respondent's smoking behavior as a control variable. That is, how do smokers versus nonsmokers feel about smoking in public places? The researchers would compile separate statistics on how smokers and nonsmokers feel about antismoking regulations.

Our study of the influence of education on income suggests that not everyone enjoys equal educational opportunities, a

FIGURE 2–4

Impact of a College Education on Income

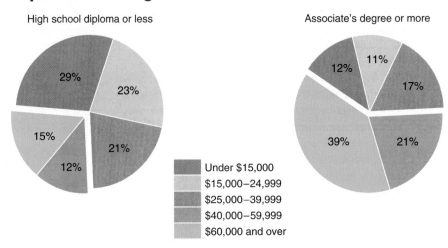

Source: Author's analysis of General Social Survey 2004 in J. A. Davis et al. 2005.

Fifty-two percent of people with a high school diploma or less (left) earn under $25,000 a year, while only 27 percent earn $40,000 or more. In contrast, 60 percent of those with an associate's degree or higher (right) earn $40,000 or more, while only 23 percent earn less than $25,000.

{ p.22 } disparity that is one of the causes of social inequality. Since education affects a person's income, we may wish to call on the conflict perspective to explore this topic further. What impact does a person's race or gender have? Is a woman with a college degree likely to earn as much as a man with similar schooling? Later in this textbook we will consider these other factors and variables. That is, we will examine the impact that education has on income while controlling for variables such as gender and race.

In Summary: The Scientific Method

Let us briefly summarize the process of the scientific method through a review of the example. We *defined a problem* (the question of whether it pays to get a higher educational degree). We *reviewed the literature* (other studies of the relationship between education and income) and *formulated a hypothesis* (the higher one's educational degree, the more money one will earn). We *collected and analyzed the data,* making sure the sample was representative and the data were valid and reliable. Finally, we *developed the conclusion:* The data do support our hypothesis about the influence of education on income.

Use Your Sociological Imagination

What might be the effects of a college education on society as a whole? Think of some potential effects on the family, government, and the economy.

Major Research Designs

An important aspect of sociological research is deciding *how* to collect the data. A ***research design*** is a detailed plan or method for obtaining data scientifically. Selection of a research design is often based on the theories and hypotheses the researcher starts with (Merton 1948). The choice requires creativity and ingenuity, because it directly influences both the cost of the project and the amount of time needed to collect the data. Research designs that sociologists regularly use to generate data include surveys, observation, experiments, and existing sources.

Surveys

Almost all of us have responded to surveys of one kind or another. We may have been asked what kind of detergent we use, which presidential candidate we intend to vote for, or what our favorite television program is. A ***survey*** is a study, generally in the form of an interview or questionnaire, that provides researchers with information about how people think and act. Among the United States' best-known surveys of opinion are the Gallup poll and the Harris poll. As anyone who watches the news during presidential campaigns knows, these polls have become a staple of political life.

When you think of surveys, you may recall seeing many person-on-the-street interviews on local television news shows. Although such interviews can be highly entertaining, they are not necessarily an accurate indication of public opinion. First, they reflect the opinions of only those people who happen to be at a certain location. Such a sample can be biased in favor of commuters, middle-class shoppers, or factory workers, depending on which street or area the newspeople select. Second, television interviews tend to attract outgoing people who are willing to appear on the air, while they frighten away others who may feel intimidated by a camera. As we've seen, a survey must be based on precise, representative sampling if it is to genuinely reflect a broad range of the population.

In preparing to conduct a survey, sociologists must not only develop representative samples; they must exercise great care in the wording of questions. An effective survey question must be simple and clear enough for people to understand. It must also be specific enough so that there are no problems in interpreting the results. Open-ended questions ("What do you think of the programming on educational television?") must be carefully phrased to solicit the type of information desired. Surveys can be indispensable sources of information, but only if the sampling is done properly and the questions are worded accurately and without bias. Box 2-1 on page 38 describes the special challenges of conducting a public opinion poll in Iraq after the defeat of Saddam Hussein's regime in 2003.

There are two main forms of the survey: the ***interview,*** in which a researcher obtains information through face-to-face or telephone questioning, and the ***questionnaire,*** in which the researcher uses a printed or written form to obtain information from a respondent. Each of these has its own advantages. An interviewer can obtain a higher response rate because people find it more difficult to turn down a personal request for an interview than to throw away a written questionnaire. In addition, a skillful interviewer can go beyond written questions and probe for a subject's underlying feelings and reasons. On the other hand, questionnaires have the advantage of being cheaper, especially in large samples.

Studies have shown that the characteristics of the interviewer have an impact on survey data. For example, women interviewers tend to receive more feminist responses from female subjects than do male researchers, and African American interviewers tend to receive more detailed responses about race-related issues

Doonesbury

BY GARRY TRUDEAU

Think About It

What would constitute a less biased question for a survey on smoking?

2-1 Polling in Baghdad

In 2003, as the U.S. Army launched the war in Iraq, pollsters watched President George W. Bush's approval rating carefully. Such periodic measures of the public pulse have become routine in the United States—an accepted part of presidential politics. But in Iraq, a totalitarian state ruled for 24 years by dictator Saddam Hussein, polling of public opinion on political and social issues was unknown until August 2003, when representatives of the Gallup Organization began regular surveys of the residents of Baghdad. Later in the occupation, Gallup extended its survey to other areas in Iraq.

Needless to say, conducting a scientific survey in the war-torn city presented unusual challenges. Planners began by assuming that no census statistics would be available, so they used satellite imagery to estimate the population in each of Baghdad's neighborhoods. They later located detailed statistics for much of Baghdad, which they updated for use in their sampling procedure. Gallup's planners also expected that they would need to hire trained interviewers from outside Iraq, but were fortunate to find some government employees who had become familiar with Baghdad's neighborhoods while conducting consumer surveys. To train and supervise these interviewers, Gallup hired two seasoned executives from the Pan Arab Research Center in Dubai.

To administer the survey, Gallup chose the time-tested method of private, face-to-face interviews in people's homes. This method not only put respondents at ease; it allowed women to participate in the survey at a time when venturing out in public may have been dangerous for them. In all, Gallup employees conducted over 3,400 person-to-person interviews in the privacy of Iraqis' homes. Respondents, they found, were eager to offer opinions and would talk with them at length. Only 3 percent of those who were sampled declined to be interviewed.

The survey's results are significant, since the more than 6 million people who live in Baghdad constitute a quarter of Iraq's population. Asked which of several forms of government would be acceptable to them, equal numbers of respondents chose (1) a multiparty parliamen-

tary democracy and (2) a system of governance that includes consultations with Islamic leaders. Fewer respondents endorsed a constitutional democracy or an Islamic kingdom. At a time when representatives of the Iraqi people had convened to establish a new form of government for the nation, this kind of information would prove invaluable.

> _Needless to say, conducting a scientific survey in the war-torn city presented unusual challenges._

In a more recent nationwide survey, conducted in October 2006, Gallup asked Iraqis about "the three main reasons for the U.S. invasion of Iraq." Their responses showed a disconnect with official U.S. policy. A large majority—76 percent—said the United States wanted "to control Iraqi oil." A sizable 41 percent thought the United States' intention was

"to build military bases," and almost a third, 32 percent, thought it was "to help Israel." Less than 2 percent of respondents thought the United States went to war "to bring democracy to Iraq."

Building on its experience in Iraq, Gallup has begun to expand its overseas polling operations. Gallup employees conduct public opinion surveys in China, a Muslim world survey, and many broad-based international polls.

Let's Discuss

1. The 97 percent response rate interviewers obtained in the 2003 survey was extremely high. Why do you think the response rate was so high, and what do you think it tells political analysts about the residents of Baghdad?

2. What might be some limitations of this survey?

Sources: ABC News 2007; Gallup 2004, 2006a; Iraq Analysis Group 2007; Moaddel 2007.

A Gallup employee interviews an Iraqi army veteran at his home in Baghdad. Pollsters had to carefully estimate the population of Baghdad's many districts, subdistricts, and neighborhoods to obtain a statistically representative sample of respondents.

from Black subjects than do White interviewers. The possible impact of gender and race indicates again how much care social research requires (D. W. Davis and Silver 2003).

The survey is an example of **quantitative research,** which collects and reports data primarily in numerical form. Most of the survey research discussed so far in this book has been quantitative. While this type of research can make use of large samples, it can't offer great depth and detail on a topic. That is why researchers also make use of **qualitative research,** which relies on what is seen in field and naturalistic settings, and often focuses on small groups and communities rather than on large groups or whole nations. The most common form of qualitative research is observation, which we consider next. Throughout this book you will find examples of both quantitative and qualitative research, since both are used widely. Some sociologists prefer one type of research to the other, but we learn most when we draw on many different research designs and do not limit ourselves to a particular type of research.

Observation

As we saw in the introduction to this chapter, Patricia A. Adler and Peter Adler gathered their information on the Hawaiian resort industry by *observing* the everyday interactions among employees. Investigators who collect information through direct participation and/or by closely watching a group or community are engaged in **observation.** This method allows sociologists to examine certain behaviors and communities that could not be investigated through other research techniques. Though observation may seem a relatively informal method compared to surveys or experiments, researchers are careful to take detailed notes while observing their subjects.

An increasingly popular form of qualitative research in sociology today is ethnography. **Ethnography** refers to the study of an entire social setting through extended systematic observation. Typically, the emphasis is on how the subjects themselves view their social life in some setting. The Adlers' study of the Hawaiian resort industry, described in the opening to this chapter, was an ethnographic study that covered hotel workers' leisure time and family lives as well as their on-the-job behavior (P. Adler and Adler 2003, 2004, 2008).

In some cases, the sociologist actually joins a group for a period to get an accurate sense of how it operates. This approach is called *participant observation.* In Barbara Ehrenreich's study of {pp.3–4 low-wage workers, described in Chapter 1, as well as in the Adlers' study of the Hawaiian resort industry, the researchers were participant observers.

During the late 1930s, in a classic example of participant-observation research, William F. Whyte moved into a low-income Italian neighborhood in Boston. For nearly four years he was a member of the social circle of "corner boys" that he describes in *Street Corner Society.* Whyte revealed his identity to these men and joined in their conversations, bowling, and other leisure-time activities. His goal was to gain greater insight into the community that these men had established. As Whyte (1981:303) listened to Doc, the leader of the group, he "learned

Peter and Patricia Adler's book *Paradise Laborers,* featured in the opening excerpt for this chapter, was based on careful, detailed observation of Hawaiian resort workers. The Adlers spent eight years studying receptionists, housekeepers, and other resort employees as they went about their daily work.

the answers to questions I would not even have had the sense to ask if I had been getting my information solely on an interviewing basis." Whyte's work was especially valuable, since at the time the academic world had little direct knowledge of the poor, and tended to rely for information on the records of social service agencies, hospitals, and courts (P. Adler et al. 1992).

The initial challenge that Whyte faced—and that every participant observer encounters—was to gain acceptance into an unfamiliar group. It is no simple matter for a college-trained sociologist to win the trust of a religious cult, a youth gang, a poor Appalachian community, or a circle of skid row residents. It requires a great deal of patience and an accepting, nonthreatening type of personality on the part of the observer.

Observation research poses other complex challenges for the investigator. Sociologists must be able to fully understand what they are observing. In a sense, then, researchers must learn to see the world as the group sees it in order to fully comprehend the events taking place around them.

This raises a delicate issue. If the research is to be successful, the observer cannot allow the close associations or even friendships that inevitably develop to influence the subjects' behavior or the conclusions of the study. Anson Shupe and David Bromley (1980), two sociologists who have used participant observation, have likened this challenge to that of walking a tightrope. Even while working hard to gain acceptance from the group being studied, the participant observer *must* maintain some degree of detachment.

The feminist perspective in sociology has drawn attention to a shortcoming in ethnographic research. For most of the history of sociology, studies were conducted on male subjects or about male-led groups and organizations, and the findings were generalized to all people. For example, for many decades studies of urban life focused on street corners, neighborhood taverns, and bowling alleys—places where men typically congregated. Although the insights gained were valuable, they did not give a true impression of city life because they overlooked the areas where women were likely to gather, such as playgrounds, grocery stores, and front stoops. The feminist perspective focuses on these arenas. Feminist researchers also tend to involve and consult their subjects more than other researchers, and they are more oriented to seeking change, raising consciousness, and trying to affect policy. In addition, feminist researchers are particularly open to a multidisciplinary approach, such as making use of historical evidence or legal studies as well as feminist theory (Baker 1999; Lofland 1975; Reinharz 1992).

How do people respond to being observed? Evidently these employees at the Hawthorne plant enjoyed the attention paid them when researchers observed them at work. No matter what variables were changed, the workers increased their productivity—even when the level of lighting was *reduced*.

Experiments

When sociologists want to study a possible cause-and-effect relationship, they may conduct experiments. An ***experiment*** is an artificially created situation that allows a researcher to manipulate variables.

In the classic method of conducting an experiment, two groups of people are selected and matched for similar characteristics, such as age or education. The researchers then assign the subjects to one of two groups: the experimental or the control group. The ***experimental group*** is exposed to an independent variable; the ***control group*** is not. Thus, if scientists were testing a new type of antibiotic, they would administer the drug to an experimental group but not to a control group.

Sociologists don't often rely on this classic form of experiment, because it generally involves manipulating human behavior in an inappropriate manner, especially in a laboratory setting. However, they do try to re-create experimental conditions in the field. For example, to see the effect of a criminal background on a person's employment opportunities, sociologist Devah Pager (2003) devised an experiment in which she sent four young men out to look for jobs, each with a carefully crafted background story (see Box 2-2).

In some experiments, just as in observation research, the presence of a social scientist or other observer may affect the be-

havior of the people being studied. The recognition of this phenomenon grew out of an experiment conducted during the 1920s and 1930s at the Hawthorne plant of the Western Electric Company. A group of researchers set out to determine how to improve the productivity of workers at the plant. The investigators manipulated such variables as the lighting and working hours to see what impact the changes would have on productivity. To their surprise, they found that *every* step they took seemed to increase productivity. Even measures that seemed likely to have the opposite effect, such as reducing the amount of lighting in the plant, led to higher productivity.

Why did the plant's employees work harder even under less favorable conditions? Their behavior apparently was influenced by the greater attention being paid to them in the course of the research, and by the novelty of being subjects in an experiment. Since that time, sociologists have used the term ***Hawthorne effect*** in referring to the unintended influence that observers of experiments can have on their subjects (S. Jones 1992; Lang 1992; Pelton 1994).

Use Your Sociological Imagination

You are a researcher interested in the effect of TV watching on schoolchildren's grades. How would you go about setting up an experiment to measure this effect?

2-2 Researching Privilege and Discrimination in Employment

At the University of Wisconsin, Devah Pager, a doctoral candidate in sociology, was looking for a topic for her dissertation. Pager was a volunteer at a homeless shelter, where she distributed mail and listened to residents' hard-luck stories. Frequently, she heard men who had prison records talk about their difficulty finding work. Moved by their stories, she wondered if there was something she could do. What if she could demonstrate a clear link between a criminal background and reduced employment prospects?

Pager set out to devise a field experiment to do just that—an experiment that would become the basis for her dissertation. She sent four polite, well-dressed young men out to look for an entry-level job in Milwaukee, Wisconsin. All four were 23-year-old college students, but they presented themselves as high school graduates with similar job histories. Two of the men were Black and two were White. One Black applicant and one White applicant claimed to have served 18 months in jail for a felony conviction—possession of cocaine with intent to distribute.

As one might expect, the four men's experiences with 350 potential employers were vastly different. Predictably, the White applicant with a purported prison record received only half as many callbacks as the other White applicant—17 percent compared to 34 percent (see the accompanying figure). But as dramatic as the effect of his criminal record was, the effect of his race was more significant. Despite his

prison record, he received slightly more callbacks than the Black applicant *with no criminal record* (17 percent compared to 14 percent). Race, it seems, was more of a concern to potential employers than a criminal background.

These results stunned Pager, along with other academicians and public policy experts. (Indeed, a parallel study, in which researchers merely asked employers their hiring intentions, showed no racial difference.) "I expected there to be an effect of race, but I did not expect it to swamp the results as it did," Pager told an interviewer. Her finding was especially

> *Race, it seems, was more of a concern to potential employers than a criminal background.*

significant because the majority of convicts who are released from prison each year (52 percent) are, in fact, Black men. Pager's research, which was widely publicized, eventually contributed to a change in public policy. In his 2004 State of the Union address, President George W. Bush announced a $300 million mentoring program for offenders who are attempting to reintegrate into society.

In August 2004, Pager received the American Sociological Association's award for best dissertation of the year. She is currently teaching at Princeton University, where she plans to replicate her groundbreaking study.

Let's Discuss

1. Do you see any weaknesses in Pager's research method? Does her study prove conclusively that prison time reduces a man's employment prospects?
2. Can you think of another method for investigating the link between a prison record and difficulty finding work? If so, explain how you would do it.

Sources: Bordt 2005; Bureau of Justice Statistics 2004; Kroeger 2004; Pager 2003; Pager and Quillian 2005.

White Privilege in Job Seeking

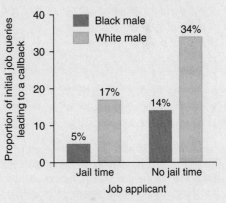

Source: Pager 2003:958.

Use of Existing Sources

Sociologists do not necessarily need to collect new data in order to conduct research and test hypotheses. The term **secondary analysis** refers to a variety of research techniques that make use of previously collected and publicly accessible information and data. Generally, in conducting secondary analysis, researchers use data in ways that were unintended by the initial collectors of information. For example, census data are compiled for specific uses by the federal government but are also valuable to marketing specialists in locating everything from bicycle stores to nursing homes. And Social Security registrations, originally meant for

government use in administering the nation's retirement system, have been used to track cultural trends in the naming of newborn children (see Box 2-3, page 42).

Sociologists consider secondary analysis to be *nonreactive*— that is, it does not influence people's behavior. For example, Émile Durkheim's statistical analysis of suicide neither increased nor decreased human self-destruction. Researchers, then, can avoid the Hawthorne effect by using secondary analysis.

There is one inherent problem, however: the researcher who relies on data collected by someone else may not find exactly what is needed. Social scientists who are studying family violence can

researchINaction

2-3 What's in a Name?

Sociologists can learn a great deal using available information. For example, every year the Social Security Administration receives thousands of registrations for newborn babies. Using these data, we can identify some cultural trends in the popularity of children's names.

As the accompanying figure shows, for example, John has been an extremely popular boy's name for over a century. In 2005, over 5,000 babies were named John, making the moniker the 18th most popular name that year. Though only about half as many babies were named Juan in 2005, that name has been gaining in popularity in recent generations, reflecting the growing impact of the Latino population in the United States.

We can see some other patterns in the annual data on name giving. In many ethnic and

> *In 2005, over 5,000 babies were named John, making the moniker the 18th most popular name that year.*

racial groups, parents choose names that display pride in their identity or the uniqueness they see in their children. Among African Americans, for example, names such as Ebony and Imani are the most popular ones for girls.

The public data contained in name registries also reveal a trend toward "American-sounding" names among immigrants to the United States. In Italy, for example, Giuseppe is a very popular boy's name. Among Italian immigrants to the United states, the English form of Giuseppe, Joseph, is the third most popular boy's name, though it ranks only 10th among other Americans. The pattern of selecting names that will allow children to "fit in" is not uniform, however. In some immigrant groups, parents tend to favor names that symbolize

Popularity of John versus Juan

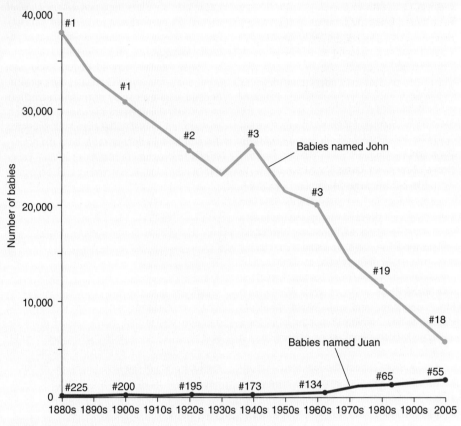

Note: Numbers indicate rank in popularity among all boys' names in that year.
Source: Baby Name Wizard 2007.

their ethnicity. For example, Kelly is popular among Irish Americans, even though it isn't a traditional girl's name in the home country. Thus, the available data on newborns' names allows sociologists to detect cultural trends that reflect changing group identities.

Let's Discuss

1. Visit www.babynamewizard.com on the Internet, and click on "NameVoyager." According to this Web site, how popular is your first name? Is it becoming more or less fashionable over time?

2. What might be the pros and cons of choosing a first name that is associated with a particular ethnic or racial group? Would your answer differ depending on whether the chosen name was Sean or Juan?

Sources: Baby Name Wizard 2007; Levitt and Dubner 2005; Lieberson 2000.

use statistics from police and social service agencies on *reported* cases of spouse abuse and child abuse. But how many cases are not reported? Government bodies have no precise data on *all* cases of abuse.

Many social scientists find it useful to study cultural, economic, and political documents, including newspapers, periodicals, radio and television tapes, the Internet, scripts, diaries, songs, folklore, and legal papers (see Table 2-1). In examining these sources, researchers employ a technique known as **content analysis,** which is the systematic coding and objective recording of data, guided by some rationale.

Using content analysis, Erving Goffman (1979) conducted a pioneering exploration of how advertisements portray women. The ads he studied typically showed women as subordinate to or dependent on others, or as taking instruction from men. They engaged in caressing and touching gestures more than men. Even when presented in leadership roles, women were likely to be shown striking seductive poses or gazing out into space.

Today, researchers who analyze film content are finding an increase in smoking in motion pictures, despite heightened public health concerns. Other researchers have found a growing difference in the way men and women use sexually explicit language. For example, an analysis of the lyrics of *Billboard* magazine's top 100 hits indicates that since 1958, male artists have increased their use of such language, while female artists have decreased theirs (American Lung Association 2003; Dukes et al. 2003).

Table 2-2 on page 44 summarizes the major research designs.

Table 2-2 on page 44 summarizes the major research designs.

Use Your Sociological Imagination

Imagine you are a legislator or government policymaker working on a complex social problem. What might happen if you were to base your decision on faulty research?

Ethics of Research

A biochemist cannot inject a drug into a human being unless it has been thoroughly tested and the subject agrees to the shot. To do otherwise would be both unethical and illegal. Sociologists, too, must abide by certain specific standards in conducting research, called a **code of ethics.** The professional society of the discipline, the American Sociological Association (ASA), first published the society's *Code of Ethics* in 1971 and revised it most recently in 1997. It puts forth the following basic principles:

1. Maintain objectivity and integrity in research.
2. Respect the subject's right to privacy and dignity.
3. Protect subjects from personal harm.
4. Preserve confidentiality.
5. Seek informed consent when data are collected from research participants or when behavior occurs in a private context.
6. Acknowledge research collaboration and assistance.
7. Disclose all sources of financial support (American Sociological Association 1997).

These basic principles probably seem clear-cut. How could they lead to any disagreement or controversy? Yet many delicate ethical questions cannot be resolved simply by reading these seven principles. For example, should a sociologist who is engaged in participant-observation research always protect the confidentiality of subjects? What if the subjects are members of a religious cult allegedly involved in unethical and possibly illegal activities? What if the sociologist is interviewing political activists and is questioned by government authorities about the research?

Because most sociological research uses *people* as sources of information— as respondents to survey questions, subjects of observation, or participants

summingUP

Table 2-1

Existing Sources Used in Sociological Research

Most Frequently Used Sources

Census data

Crime statistics

Birth, death, marriage, divorce, and health statistics

Other Sources

Newspapers and periodicals

Personal journals, diaries, e-mail, and letters

Records and archival material of religious organizations, corporations, and other organizations

Transcripts of radio programs

Videotapes of motion pictures and television programs

Web pages, Weblogs, and chatrooms

Song lyrics

Scientific records (such as patent applications)

Speeches of public figures (such as politicians)

Votes cast in elections or by elected officials on specific legislative proposals

Attendance records for public events

Videotapes of social protests and rallies

Literature, including folklore

Content analysis of popular song lyrics shows that over the last 50 years, top female artists such as Beyoncé Knowles have used fewer sexually explicit words, while male artists have used more.

in experiments—these sorts of questions are important. In all cases, sociologists need to be certain they are not invading their subjects' privacy. Generally, they do so by assuring subjects of anonymity and by guaranteeing the confidentiality of personal information. In addition, research proposals that involve human subjects must now be overseen by a review board, whose members seek to ensure that subjects are not placed at an unreasonable level of risk. If necessary, the board may ask researchers to revise their research designs to conform to the code of ethics.

We can appreciate the seriousness of the ethical problems researchers confront by considering the experience of sociologist Rik Scarce, described in the next section. Scarce's vow to protect his subjects' confidentiality got him into considerable trouble with the law.

Confidentiality

Like journalists, sociologists occasionally find themselves subject to questions from law enforcement authorities because of knowledge they have gained in the course of their work. This uncomfortable situation raises profound ethical questions.

In May 1993, Rik Scarce, a doctoral candidate in sociology at Washington State University, was jailed for contempt of court. Scarce had declined to tell a federal grand jury what he knew—or even whether he knew anything—about a 1991 raid on a university research laboratory by animal rights activists. At the time, Scarce was conducting research for a book about environmental protestors and knew at least one suspect in the break-in. Curiously, although he was chastised by a federal judge, Scarce won respect from fellow prison inmates, who regarded him as a man who "wouldn't snitch" (Monaghan 1993:A8).

The American Sociological Association supported Scarce's position when he appealed his sentence. Scarce maintained his silence. Ultimately the judge ruled that nothing would be gained by further incarceration, and Scarce was released after serving 159 days in jail. In January 1994, the U.S. Supreme Court declined to hear Scarce's case on appeal. The Court's failure to consider his case led Scarce (1994, 1995, 2005) to argue that federal legislation is needed to clarify the right of scholars and members of the press to preserve the confidentiality of those they interview.

Research Funding

Sometimes disclosing all the sources of funding for a study, as required in principle 7 of the ASA's *Code of Ethics,* is not a sufficient guarantee of ethical conduct. Especially in the case of both corporate and government funding, money given ostensibly for the support of basic research may come with strings attached. Ac-

Table 2-2

Major Research Designs

summingUP

Method	Examples	Advantages	Limitations
Survey	Questionnaires Interviews	Yields information about specific issues	Can be expensive and time-consuming
Observation	Ethnography	Yields detailed information about specific groups or organizations	Involves months if not years of labor-intensive data
Experiment	Deliberate manipulation of people's social behavior	Yields direct measures of people's behavior	Ethical limitations on the degree to which subjects' behavior can be manipulated
Existing sources/ Secondary analysis	Analysis of census or health data Analysis of films or TV commercials	Cost-efficiency	Limited to data collected for some other purpose

cepting funds from a private organization or even a government agency that stands to benefit from a study's results can call into question a researcher's objectivity and integrity (principle 1).

The Exxon Corporation's support for research on jury verdicts is a good example of this kind of conflict of interest. On March 24, 1989, the Exxon oil tanker *Valdez* hit a reef off the coast of Alaska, spilling over 11 million gallons of oil into Prince William Sound. Almost two decades later, the *Valdez* disaster is still regarded as the world's worst oil spill in terms of its environmental impact. In 1994 a federal court ordered Exxon to pay $5.3 billion in damages for the accident. Exxon appealed the verdict and began approaching legal scholars, sociologists, and psychologists who might be willing to study jury deliberations. The corporation's objective was to develop academic support for its lawyers' contention that the punitive judgments in such cases result from faulty deliberations and do not have a deterrent effect.

Some scholars have questioned the propriety of accepting funds under these circumstances, even if the source is disclosed. In at least one case, an Exxon employee explicitly told a sociologist that the corporation offers financial support to scholars who have shown the tendency to express views similar to its own. An argument can also be made that Exxon was attempting to set scholars' research agendas with its huge war chest. Rather than funding studies on the improvement of cleanup technologies or the assignment of long-term environmental costs, Exxon chose to shift scientists' attention to the validity of the legal awards in environmental cases.

The scholars who accepted Exxon's support deny that it influenced their work or changed their conclusions. Some received support from other sources as well, such as the National Science Foundation and Harvard University's Olin Center for Law, Economics, and Business. Many of their findings were published in respected academic journals after review by a jury of peers. Still, at least one researcher who participated in the studies refused monetary support from Exxon to avoid even the suggestion of a conflict of interest.

To date, Exxon has spent roughly $1 million on the research, and at least one compilation of studies congenial to the corporation's point of view has been published. As ethical considerations require, the academics who conducted the studies disclosed Exxon's role in funding them. Nevertheless, the investment appears to have paid off. In 2006, drawing on these studies, Exxon's lawyers succeeded in persuading an appeals court to reduce the corporation's legal damages from $5.3 to $2.5 billion. The case is still under appeal as Exxon attempts to further reduce the damages (Associated Press 2007; Freudenburg 2005).

Value Neutrality

The ethical considerations of sociologists lie not only in the methods they use and the funding they accept, but in the way they interpret their results. Max Weber ([1904] 1949) recognized that personal values would influence the questions that sociologists select for research. In his view, that was perfectly acceptable, but under no conditions could a researcher allow his or her personal

A floating containment barrier encircles the Exxon oil tanker *Valdez* after its grounding on a reef off the coast of Alaska. Exxon executives spent a million dollars to fund academic research that they hoped would support lawyers' efforts to reduce the $5.3 billion judgment against the corporation for negligence in the environmental disaster.

feelings to influence the *interpretation* of data. In Weber's phrase, sociologists must practice *value neutrality* in their research.

As part of this neutrality, investigators have an ethical obligation to accept research findings even when the data run counter to their own personal views, to theoretically based explanations, { pp.10–11 or to widely accepted beliefs. For example, Émile Durkheim challenged popular conceptions when he reported that social (rather than supernatural) forces were an important factor in suicide.

Some sociologists believe that neutrality is impossible. They worry that Weber's insistence on value-free sociology may lead the public to accept sociological conclusions without exploring researchers' biases. Others, drawing on the conflict perspective, as Alvin Gouldner (1970) does, have suggested that sociologists may use objectivity as a justification for remaining uncritical of existing institutions and centers of power. These arguments are attacks not so much on Weber himself as on the way his goals have been misinterpreted. As we have seen, Weber was quite clear that sociologists may bring values to their subject matter. In his view, however, they must not confuse their own values with the social reality under study (Bendix 1968).

Let's consider what might happen when researchers bring their own biases to the investigation. A person investigating the impact of intercollegiate sports on alumni contributions, for example,

Dave Eberbach
**Research Coordinator,
United Way of Central Iowa**

As a research specialist, Dave Eberbach uses his training in sociology to work for social change. Eberbach looks for small pockets of poverty that are generally hidden in state and county statistics. By zeroing in on conditions in specific neighborhoods, he empowers state and local agencies that work on behalf of the disadvantaged.

Eberbach, who is based in Des Moines, Iowa, was hired to establish a "data warehouse" of social statistics for the local United Way. Part of his job has been to demonstrate to agencies how the information in the database can be of use to them. "We have moved most of our data presentations away from charts and graphs, and on to maps of the county, the city, and the neighborhood," he explains. "This allows people to truly 'see' the big picture."

When Eberbach entered Grinnell College in 1985, he had already taken a sociology course and knew that the subject interested him. Still, he could not have foreseen all the practical uses he might have had for what he learned. "Never assume that you'll never need to know something (including statistics)," he advises. "Life has a funny way of bringing things around again."

At Grinnell, Eberbach benefited from the presence of several visiting professors who exposed him to a variety of cultural and racial perspectives. His personal acquaintance with them complemented the concepts he was learning in his sociology classes. Today, Eberbach draws on his college experiences at the United Way, where his work brings him into contact with a diverse group of people.

Sociology has also helped Eberbach in his chosen specialty, research. "I believe that I am a better 'data person' because of my sociology background," he claims. "The human context for data is as important and can get lost or misdirected by pure statistics," he explains. "My sociology background has helped me ask the appropriate questions to make effective change in our community."

Let's Discuss

1. Do you know what you want to be doing 10 years from now? If so, how might a knowledge of statistics help you in your future occupation?
2. What kinds of statistics, specifically, might you find in the United Way's data warehouse? Where would they come from?

---

may focus only on the highly visible revenue-generating sports of football and basketball and neglect the so-called minor sports, such as tennis or soccer, which are more likely to involve women athletes. Despite the early work of W. E. B. Du Bois and Jane Addams, sociologists still need to be reminded that the discipline often fails to adequately consider all people's social behavior.

In her book *The Death of White Sociology* (1973), Joyce Ladner called attention to the tendency of mainstream sociology to treat the lives of African Americans as a social problem. More recently, feminist sociologist Shulamit Reinharz (1992) has argued that sociological research should be not only inclusive but open to bringing about social change and to drawing on relevant research by nonsociologists. Both Reinharz and Ladner maintain that researchers should always analyze whether women's unequal social status has affected their studies in any way. For example, one might broaden the study of the impact of education on income to consider the implications of the unequal pay status of men and women. The issue of value neutrality does not mean that sociologists can't have opinions, but it does mean that they must work to overcome any biases, however unintentional, that they may bring to their analysis of research.

Peter Rossi (1987) admits to having liberal inclinations that direct him to certain fields of study. Yet in line with Weber's view of value neutrality, Rossi's commitment to rigorous research methods and objective interpretation of data has sometimes led him to controversial findings that are not necessarily supportive of his own liberal values. For example, his measure of the extent of homelessness in Chicago in the mid-1980s fell far below the estimates of the Chicago Coalition for the Homeless. Coalition members bitterly attacked Rossi for hampering their social reform efforts by minimizing the extent of homelessness. Rossi (1987:79) concluded that "in the short term, good social research will often be greeted as a betrayal of one or another side to a particular controversy."

Use Your Sociological Imagination

You are a sociological researcher who is having difficulty maintaining a neutral attitude toward your research topic. Your topic isn't pollution, racism, or homelessness. What is it?

www.mhhe.com/schaefer11

Technology and Sociological Research

Advances in technology have affected all aspects of our lives, and sociological research is no exception. The increased speed and capacity of computers are enabling sociologists to handle larger and larger sets of data. In the recent past, only people with grants or major institutional support could easily work with census data. Now anyone with a desktop computer and modem can access census information and learn more about social behavior. Moreover, data from foreign countries concerning crime statistics and health care are sometimes as available as information from the United States.

Researchers usually rely on computers to deal with quantitative data—that is, numerical measures—but electronic technology is also assisting them with qualitative data, such as information obtained in observational research. Numerous software programs, such as Ethnograph and NVivo 7, allow the researcher not only to record observations but to identify common behavioral patterns or concerns expressed in interviews. For example, after observing students in a college cafeteria over several weeks and putting her observations into the computer, a researcher could group all the observations according to certain variables, such as "sorority" or "study group."

The Internet affords an excellent opportunity to communicate with fellow researchers, as well as to locate useful information on social issues that has been posted on Web sites. It would be impossible to calculate all the sociological postings on Web sites or Internet mailing lists. Of course, researchers need to apply the same critical scrutiny to Internet material that they would to any printed resource.

How useful is the Internet for conducting survey research? That is still unclear. It is relatively easy to send out a questionnaire or post one on an electronic bulletin board. This technique is an inexpensive way to reach large numbers of potential respondents and get a quick response. However, there are some obvious dilemmas. How do you protect a respondent's anonymity? How do you define the potential audience? Even if you know to whom you sent the questionnaire, the respondents may forward it to others.

Web-based surveys are still in their early stages. Even so, the initial results are promising. For example, InterSurvey has created a pool of Internet respondents, initially selected by telephone, to serve as a diverse and representative sample. Using similar methods to locate 50,000 adult respondents in 33 nations, the National Geographic Society conducted an online survey that focused on migration and regional culture. Social scientists are closely monitoring these new approaches to gauge how they might revolutionize one type of research design (Bainbridge 1999; Morin 2000).

This new technology is exciting, but there is one basic limitation to the methodology: Internet surveying works only with those who have access to the Internet and are online. For some market researchers, such a limitation is acceptable. For example,

Computers have vastly extended the range and capability of sociological research, both by allowing large amounts of data to be stored and analyzed and by facilitating communication with other researchers via Web sites, newsgroups, and e-mail.

if you were interested in the willingness of Internet users to order books or make travel reservations online, limiting the sample population to those who are already online makes sense. However, if you were surveying the general public about their plans to buy a computer in the coming year or their views on a particular candidate, your online research would need to be supplemented by more traditional sampling procedures, such as mailed questionnaires.

We have seen that researchers rely on a number of tools, from time-tested observational research and use of existing sources to the latest in computer technologies. The Social Policy section that follows will describe researchers' efforts to survey the general population about a controversial aspect of social behavior: human sexuality. This investigation was complicated by its potential social policy implications. Because, in the real world, sociological research can have far-reaching consequences for public policy and public welfare, each of the following chapters in this book will close with a Social Policy section.

and Sociological Research

Studying Human Sexuality

The Issue

Reality TV shows often feature an attempt to create a relationship or even a marriage between two strangers. In a picturesque setting, an eligible bachelor or bachelorette interviews potential partners—all of them good-looking—and gradually eliminates those who seem less promising. The questions that are posed on camera can be explicit. "How many sexual partners have you had?" "How often would you be willing to have sex?"

The Kaiser Family Foundation conducts a study of sexual content on television every two years. The latest report, released in 2005, shows that more than two-thirds of all shows on TV include some sexual content, up from about half of all shows seven years earlier (see Figure 2-5, below). Media representations of sexual behavior are important because surveys of teens and young adults tell us that television is a top source of information and ideas about sex for them; it has more influence than schools, parents, or peers.

In this age of devastating sexually transmitted diseases, there is no time more important to increase our scientific understanding of human sexuality. As we will see, however, this is a difficult topic to research because of all the preconceptions, myths, and beliefs people bring to the subject of sexuality. How does one carry out scientific research on such a controversial and personal topic?

FIGURE 2–5

Percent of Television Shows That Contain Sexual Content

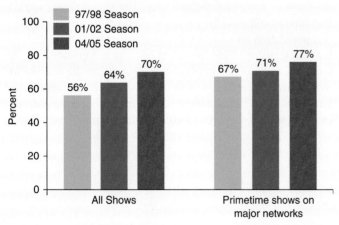

Source: Kaiser Family Foundation 2005:4.

The Setting

Sociologists have little reliable national data on patterns of sexual behavior in the United States. Until recently, the only comprehensive study of sexual behavior was the famous two-volume Kinsey Report prepared in the 1940s (Kinsey et al. 1948, 1953; see also Igo 2007). Although the Kinsey Report is still widely quoted, the volunteers interviewed for the report were not representative of the nation's adult population.

In part, we lack reliable data on patterns of sexual behavior because it is difficult for researchers to obtain accurate information about this sensitive subject. Moreover, until AIDS emerged in the 1980s, there was little scientific demand for data on sexual behavior, except for specific concerns such as contraception. Finally, even though the AIDS crisis has reached dramatic proportions (as will be discussed in the Social Policy section of Chapter 19), government funding for studies of sexual behavior is controversial. Because the General Social Survey concerns sexual attitudes rather than behavior, its funding has not been jeopardized.

Sociological Insights

The controversy surrounding research on human sexual behavior raises the issue of value neutrality (see page 45), which becomes especially delicate when one considers the relationship of sociology to the government. The federal government has become the major source of funding for sociological research. Yet Max Weber urged that sociology remain an autonomous discipline and not become unduly influenced by any one segment of society. According to Weber's ideal of value neutrality, sociologists must remain free to reveal information that is embarrassing to the government, or for that matter, supportive of government institutions.

Although the American Sociological Association's *Code of Ethics* requires sociologists to disclose all funding sources, it does not address the issue of whether sociologists who accept funding from a particular agency or corporation may also accept the agency's perspective on what needs to be studied. As we saw in our discussion of research funded by the Exxon Corporation (page 45), this question is a knotty one. As the next section will show, applied sociological research on human sexuality has run into political barriers.

Policy Initiatives

In 1987 the National Institute of Child Health and Human Development sought proposals for a national survey of sexual behavior. Sociologists responded with various plans that a review panel of scientists approved for funding. However, in 1991, the

U.S. Senate voted to forbid funding any survey on adult sexual practices. Two years earlier, a similar debate in Great Britain had led to the denial of government funding for a national sex survey (A. Johnson et al. 1994; Laumann et al. 1994a:36).

Despite the vote by the U.S. Senate, sociologists Edward Laumann, John Gagnon, Stuart Michaels, and Robert Michael developed the National Health and Social Life Survey (NHSLS) to better understand the sexual practices of adults in the United States. The researchers raised $1.6 million of *private* funding to make their study possible (Laumann et al. 1994a, 1994b).

The NHSLS researchers made great efforts to ensure privacy during the interviews, as well as confidentiality and security in maintaining data files. Perhaps because of this careful effort, the interviewers did not typically experience problems getting responses, even though they were asking people about their sexual behavior. All interviews were conducted in person, although a confidential form included questions about sensitive subjects such as family income and masturbation. The researchers used several techniques to test the accuracy of subjects' responses, such as asking redundant questions at different times and in different ways during the 90-minute interview. These careful procedures helped to establish the validity of the NHSLS findings.

The authors of the NHSLS believe that their research is important. They argue that using data from their survey allows us to more easily address public policy issues such as AIDS, sexual harassment, welfare reform, sex discrimination, abortion, teenage pregnancy, and family planning. Moreover, the research findings help to counter some "commonsense" notions. For instance, contrary to the popular beliefs that women regularly use abortion for birth control, and that poor teens are the most likely socioeconomic group to have abortions, researchers found that three-fourths of all abortions are the first for the woman, and that well-educated and affluent women are more likely to have abortions than poor teens (Sweet 2001).

Scholars in China, aware of the NHSLS, have begun to collaborate with sociologists in the United States on a similar study in China. The data are just now being analyzed, but responses thus far indicate dramatic differences in the sexual behavior of people in their 20s, compared to behavior at the same age by people who are now in their 50s. Younger-generation Chinese are more active sexually and have more partners than their parents did. Partly in response to these preliminary results, the Chinese Ministry of Health has sought U.S. assistance on HIV/AIDS prevention and research (Beech 2005; Braverman 2002).

Increasingly, researchers who study human sexual behavior are exploring sexual patterns among the Chinese.

Let's Discuss

1. Do you see any merit in the position of those who oppose government funding for research on sexual behavior? Explain your reasoning.

2. Exactly how could the results of research on human sexual behavior be used to control sexually transmitted diseases?

3. Compare the issue of value neutrality in government-funded research to the same issue in corporate-funded research. Are concerns about conflict of interest more or less serious in regard to government funding?

GettingINVOLVED

To get involved in the debate over research on human sexuality, visit this text's Online Learning Center, which offers links to relevant Web sites. Check out the Social Policy section in the OLC as well; it provides survey data on U.S. public opinion regarding this issue.

www.mhhe.com/schaefer11

APPENDIX I Using Statistics and Graphs

In their effort to better understand social behavior, sociologists rely heavily on numbers and statistics. How have attitudes toward the legalization of marijuana changed over the last 40 years? A quick look at the results of 12 national surveys shows that while support for legalization of the drug has increased, it remains relatively weak (see Figure 2-6).

Using Statistics

The most common summary measures used by sociologists are percentages, means, modes, and medians. A *percentage* shows a portion of 100. Use of percentages allows us to compare groups of different sizes. For example, if we were comparing financial contributors to a town's Baptist and Roman Catholic churches, the absolute numbers of contributors in each group could be misleading if there were many more Baptists than Catholics in the town. By using percentages, we could obtain a more meaningful comparison, showing the proportion of persons in each group who contribute to churches.

The *mean,* or *average,* is a number calculated by adding a series of values and then dividing by the number of values. For example, to find the mean of the numbers 5, 19, and 27, we add them to-

gether (for a total of 51), divide by the number of values (3), and discover that the mean is 17.

The *mode* is the single most common value in a series of scores. Suppose we were looking at the following scores on a 10-point quiz:

10	7
10	7
9	7
9	6
8	5
8	

The mode—the most frequent score on the quiz—is 7. While the mode is easier to identify than other summary measures, it tells sociologists little about all the other values. Hence, you will find much less use of the mode in this book than of the mean and the median.

The *median* is the midpoint or number that divides a series of values into two groups of equal numbers of values. For the quiz just discussed, the median, or central value, is 8. The mean, or average, would be 86 (the sum of all scores) divided by 11 (the total number of scores), or 7.8.

In the United States, the median household income for the year 2004 was $43,389; it indicates that half of all households had incomes above $43,389, while half had lower incomes (DeNavas-Walt et al. 2005:31). In many respects, the median is the most characteristic value. Although it may not reflect the full range of scores, it does approximate the typical value in a set of scores, and it is not affected by extreme scores.

Some of these statistics may seem confusing at first. But think how difficult it is to comb an endless list of numbers to identify a pattern or central tendency. Percentages, means, modes, and medians are essential time-savers in sociological research and analysis.

Reading Graphs

Tables and figures (that is, graphs) allow social scientists to display data and develop their conclusions more easily. During 2001–2005, the Gallup Poll interviewed 2,034 people in the United States, ages 18 and over. Each respondent was asked: "Do you think the use of marijuana should be

FIGURE 2–6

Changing Attitudes toward the Legalization of Marijuana

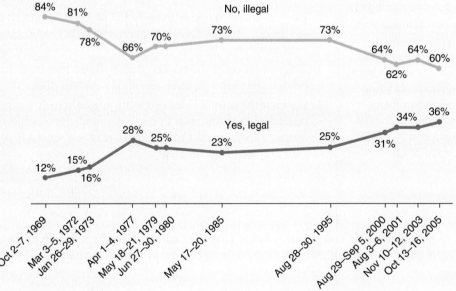

Do you think the use of marijuana should be made legal, or not?

Source: Joseph Carroll 2005.

FIGURE 2-7

Attitudes toward the Legalization of Marijuana by Gender and Age

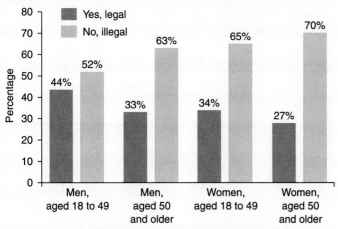

Legalization of Marijuana by Gender and Age
2001–2005 aggregate

Source: Joseph Carroll 2005.

made legal, or not?" Without some type of summary, there is no way that analysts could examine the hundreds of individual responses to this question and reach firm conclusions. One type of summary sociologists use, a ***cross-tabulation,*** shows the relationship between two or more variables. Through the cross-tabulations presented in Figure 2-7, we can quickly see that older people are less likely to favor the legalization of marijuana than younger people, and that women are less supportive of legalization than men.

Graphs, like tables, can be quite useful to sociologists. And illustrations are often easier for the general public to understand, whether they are in newspapers or in PowerPoint presentations. Still, as with all data, we need to be careful how they are presented.

APPENDIX II   Writing a Research Report

Let's say you have decided to write a report on cohabitation (unmarried couples living together). How do you go about doing the necessary library research? Students must follow procedures similar to those used by sociologists in conducting original research. First, you must define the problem that you wish to study—perhaps in this case, how much cohabitation occurs and what its impact is on later marital happiness. The next step is to review the literature, which generally requires library research.

Finding Information

The following steps will be helpful in finding information:

1. Check this textbook and other textbooks that you own. Don't forget to begin with the materials closest at hand, including the Web site associated with this textbook, **www.mhhe.com/schaefer11.**

2. Use the library catalog. Computerized library systems now access not only the college library's collection but also books and magazines from other libraries, available through interlibrary loans. These systems allow you to search for books by author or title. You can use title searches to locate books by subject as well. For example, if you search the title base for the keyword *cohabitation*, you will learn where books with that word somewhere in the title are located in the library's book stacks. Near these books will be other works on cohabitation that may not happen to have that word in

the title. You may also want to search other related keywords, such as *unmarried couples.*

3. Investigate using computerized periodical indexes if they are available in your library. *Sociological Abstracts* online covers most sociological writing since 1963. In 2007, a search of just this one database found more than 1,271 documents having either *unmarried couples* or *cohabitation* as keywords. Some dealt with laws about cohabitation, while others focused on trends in other countries. If you limited your topic to same-sex couples, you would find 133 citations. Other electronic databases cover general-interest periodicals (*Time, Ms., National Review, Atlantic Monthly,* and so forth), reference materials, or newspapers. These electronic systems may be connected to a printer, allowing you to produce your own printout complete with bibliographic information and sometimes even complete copies of articles.

4. Examine government documents. The United States government, states and cities, and the United Nations publish information on virtually every subject of interest to social science researchers. Publications of the Census Bureau, for example, include tables showing the number of unmarried couples living together and some social characteristics of those households. Many university libraries have access to a wide range of government reports. Consult the librarian for assistance in locating such materials.

5. Use newspapers. Major newspapers publish indexes annually or even weekly that are useful in locating information about specific events or issues. Academic Universe News is an electronic index to U.S. and international newspapers.

6. Ask people, organizations, and agencies concerned with the topic for information and assistance. Be as specific as possible in making requests. You might receive very different information on the issue of cohabitation from talking with marriage counselors and with clergy from different religions.

7. If you run into difficulties, consult the instructor, teaching assistant, or reference librarian at your college library.

A word of caution: Be extremely careful in using the Internet to do research. Much of the information on the Internet is simply incorrect—even if it looks authoritative, is accompanied by impressive graphics, or has been widely circulated. Unlike the information in a library, which must be screened by a highly qualified librarian, "information" on the Internet can be created and posted by anyone with a computer. Check the sources for the information and note the Web page sponsor. Is the author qualified to write on the subject? Is the author even identified? Is the Web page sponsor likely to be biased? Whenever possible, try to confirm what you have read on the Internet through a well-known, reputable source or organization. If the accuracy of the information could be affected by how old it is, check the date on which the page or article was created or updated. Used intelligently, the Internet is a wonderful tool that offers students access to many of the reliable print sources noted earlier, including government documents and newspaper archives extending back over a century.

Writing the Report

Once you have completed all your research, you can begin writing the report. Here are a few tips:

- Be sure the topic you have chosen is not too broad. You must be able to cover it adequately in a reasonable amount of time and a reasonable number of pages.

- Develop an outline for your report. You should have an introduction and a conclusion that relate to each other—and the discussion should proceed logically throughout the paper. Use headings within the paper if they will improve clarity and organization.

- Do not leave all the writing until the last minute. It is best to write a rough draft, let it sit for a few days, and then take a fresh look before beginning revisions.

- If possible, read your paper aloud. Doing so may be helpful in locating sections or phrases that don't make sense.

Remember that you *must* cite all information you have obtained from other sources, including the Internet. Plagiarism is a serious academic offense for which the penalties are severe. If you use an author's exact words, it is essential that you place them in quotation marks. Even if you reworked someone else's ideas, you must indicate the source of those ideas.

Including Citations and References

Some professors may require that students use footnotes in research reports. Others will allow students to employ the form of referencing used in this textbook, which follows the format of the American Sociological Association (ASA). If you see "(Merton 1968:27)" listed after a statement or paragraph, it means that the material has been quoted from page 27 of a work published by Merton in 1968 and listed in the reference section at the back of this textbook. (For further guidance, visit the ASA Web site, www.asanet.org, and in the sidebar on the left-hand side of the home page, click on "Publications," then "Journals," and then "ASA Journals Home." You will be connected to the ASA Journals home page. In the sidebar on the right-hand side of the page, under "Author's Corner," click on "Instructions to Authors" to view the Preparation Checklist for ASA Manuscripts.)

{ **MASTERING THIS CHAPTER** }

Summary

Sociologists are committed to the use of the *scientific method* in their research efforts. In this chapter we examined the basic principles of the scientific method and studied various techniques used by sociologists in conducting research.

1. There are five basic steps in the *scientific method:* defining the problem, reviewing the literature, formulating the hypothesis, collecting and analyzing the data, and developing the conclusion.

2. Whenever researchers wish to study abstract concepts, such as intelligence or prejudice, they must develop workable *operational definitions.*

3. A *hypothesis* states a possible relationship between two or more variables.

4. By using a *sample,* sociologists avoid having to test everyone in a population.

5. According to the scientific method, research results must possess both *validity* and *reliability.*

6. An important part of scientific research is devising a plan for collecting data, called a *research design.* Sociologists use four major research designs: surveys, observation, experiments, and existing sources.

7. The two principal forms of *survey* research are the *interview* and the *questionnaire.*

8. *Observation* allows sociologists to study certain behaviors and communities that cannot be investigated through other research methods.

9. When sociologists wish to study a cause-and-effect relationship, they may conduct an *experiment.*

10. Sociologists also make use of existing sources in *secondary analysis* and *content analysis.*

11. The *Code of Ethics* of the American Sociological Association calls for objectivity and integrity in research, confidentiality, and disclosure of all sources of financial support.

12. Max Weber urged sociologists to practice *value neutrality* in their research by ensuring that their personal feelings do not influence their interpretation of data.

13. Technology plays an important role in sociological research, whether it be a computer database or information from the Internet.

14. Despite failure to obtain government funding, researchers developed the National Health and Social Life Survey (NHSLS) to better understand the sexual practices of adults in the United States.

Critical Thinking Questions

1. Suppose your sociology instructor has asked you to do a study of homelessness. Which research technique (survey, observation, experiment, or existing sources) would you find most useful? How would you use that technique to complete your assignment?

2. How can a sociologist genuinely maintain value neutrality while studying a group that he or she finds repugnant (for example, a White supremacist organization, a satanic cult, or a group of convicted rapists)?

3. New technologies have benefited sociological research by facilitating statistical analysis and encouraging communication among scholars. Can you think of any potential drawbacks these new technologies might have for sociological investigation?

Key Terms

Causal logic The relationship between a condition or variable and a particular consequence, with one event leading to the other. (page 34)

Code of ethics The standards of acceptable behavior developed by and for members of a profession. (43)

Content analysis The systematic coding and objective recording of data, guided by some rationale. (43)

Control group The subjects in an experiment who are not introduced to the independent variable by the researcher. (40)

Control variable A factor that is held constant to test the relative impact of an independent variable. (36)

Correlation A relationship between two variables in which a change in one coincides with a change in the other. (34)

Cross-tabulation A table or matrix that shows the relationship between two or more variables. (51)

Dependent variable The variable in a causal relationship that is subject to the influence of another variable. (33)

Ethnography The study of an entire social setting through extended systematic observation. (39)

Experiment An artificially created situation that allows a researcher to manipulate variables. (40)

Experimental group The subjects in an experiment who are exposed to an independent variable introduced by a researcher. (40)

Hawthorne effect The unintended influence that observers of experiments can have on their subjects. (40)

Hypothesis A speculative statement about the relationship between two or more variables. (33)

Independent variable The variable in a causal relationship that causes or influences a change in a second variable. (33)

Interview A face-to-face or telephone questioning of a respondent to obtain desired information. (37)

Mean A number calculated by adding a series of values and then dividing by the number of values. (50)

Median The midpoint or number that divides a series of values into two groups of equal numbers of values. (50)

Mode The single most common value in a series of scores. (50)

Observation A research technique in which an investigator collects information through direct participation and/or by closely watching a group or community. (39)

Operational definition An explanation of an abstract concept that is specific enough to allow a researcher to assess the concept. (33)

Percentage A portion of 100. (50)

Qualitative research Research that relies on what is seen in field or naturalistic settings more than on statistical data. (39)

Quantitative research Research that collects and reports data primarily in numerical form. (39)

Questionnaire A printed or written form used to obtain information from a respondent. (37)

Random sample A sample for which every member of an entire population has the same chance of being selected. (35)

Reliability The extent to which a measure produces consistent results. (35)

Research design A detailed plan or method for obtaining data scientifically. (37)

Sample A selection from a larger population that is statistically representative of that population. (35)

Scientific method A systematic, organized series of steps that ensures maximum objectivity and consistency in researching a problem. (32)

Secondary analysis A variety of research techniques that make use of previously collected and publicly accessible information and data. (41)

Survey A study, generally in the form of an interview or questionnaire, that provides researchers with information about how people think and act. (37)

Validity The degree to which a measure or scale truly reflects the phenomenon under study. (35)

Value neutrality Max Weber's term for objectivity of sociologists in the interpretation of data. (45)

Variable A measurable trait or characteristic that is subject to change under different conditions. (33)

Self-Quiz

Read each question carefully and then select the best answer.

1. The first step in any sociological research project is to
   a. collect data.
   b. define the problem.
   c. review previous research.
   d. formulate a hypothesis.

2. An explanation of an abstract concept that is specific enough to allow a researcher to measure the concept is a(n)
   a. hypothesis.
   b. correlation.
   c. operational definition.
   d. variable.

3. The variable hypothesized to cause or influence another is called
   a. the dependent variable.
   b. the hypothetical variable.
   c. the correlation variable.
   d. the independent variable.

4. A correlation exists when
   a. one variable causes something to occur in another variable.
   b. two or more variables are causally related.
   c. a change in one variable coincides with a change in another variable.
   d. a negative relationship exists between two variables.

5. Through which type of research technique does a sociologist ensure that data are statistically representative of the population being studied?
   a. sampling
   b. experiments
   c. validity
   d. control variables

6. In order to obtain a random sample, a researcher might
   a. administer a questionnaire to every fifth woman who enters a business office.
   b. examine the attitudes of residents of a city by interviewing every 20th name in the city's telephone book.
   c. study the attitudes of registered Democratic voters by choosing every 10th name found on a city's list of registered Democrats.
   d. do all of the above.

7. A researcher can obtain a higher response rate by using which type of survey?
   a. an interview
   b. a questionnaire
   c. representative samples
   d. observation techniques

8. In the 1930s, William F. Whyte moved into a low-income Italian neighborhood in Boston. For nearly four years, he was a member of the social circle of "corner boys" that he describes in *Street Corner Society*. His goal was to gain greater insight into the community established by these men. What type of research technique did Whyte use?
   a. experiment
   b. survey
   c. secondary analysis
   d. participant observation

9. When sociologists want to study a possible cause-and-effect relationship, they may engage in what kind of research technique?
   a. ethnography
   b. survey research
   c. secondary analysis
   d. experiment

10. Émile Durkheim's statistical analysis of suicide was an example of what kind of research technique?
    a. ethnography
    b. observation research
    c. secondary analysis
    d. experimental research

11. Unlike the typical citizen, the sociologist has a commitment to the use of the _____ method in studying society.

12. A(n) _____ is a speculative statement about the relationship between two or more factors known as variables.

13. _____ refers to the degree to which a measure or scale truly reflects the phenomenon under study.

14. In order to obtain data scientifically, researchers need to select a research _____.

15. If scientists were testing a new type of toothpaste in an experimental setting, they would administer the toothpaste to a(n) _____ group, but not to a(n) _____ group.

16. The term _____ _____ refers to the unintended influence that observers of experiments can have on their subjects.

17. Using census data in a way unintended by its initial collectors would be an example of _____ _____.

18. Using content analysis, _____ _____ conducted a pioneering exploration of how advertisements in 1979 portrayed women as being inferior to men.

19. The American Sociological Association's *Code of* _____ requires sociologists to maintain objectivity and integrity and to preserve the confidentiality of their subjects.

20. As part of their commitment to _____ neutrality, investigators have an ethical obligation to accept research findings even when the data run counter to their own personal views or widely accepted beliefs.

{ TECHNOLOGY RESOURCES }

Online Learning Center

1. When you visit the student center of the Online Learning Center (**www.mhhe.com/schaefer11**), one of the Interactive Activities for this chapter gives you an opportunity to participate in a brief survey. After you submit your responses, you'll be able to see how other students using this book and participating in the survey answered the same questions.

2. Oral history is a type of qualitative research that is often used in ethnographic studies. Go to the Web site of the Oral History Society (**www.oralhistory.org.uk**) and read the section that guides you through the process of recording an oral history.

3. The U.S. government makes use of surveys frequently, to track trends in the American population. Some of the data they collect is accessible to you on the American FactFinder Web site (**factfinder.census.gov**). Go there to learn more about the information these surveys collect.

*Note: Although all the URLs listed were current as of the printing of this book, these sites often change. Please check our Web site (**www.mhhe.com/schaefer11**) for updates, hyperlinks, and exercises related to these sites.*

Reel Society Video Clips

Reel Society video clips, which appear on this book's Web site, can be used to spark discussion about the following topics from this chapter:

- What Is the Scientific Method?
- Ethics of Research

While this Hong Kong pedestrian appears not to notice the Nike billboard behind him, featuring NBA star LeBron James wearing the Air Zoom sneaker, the Chinese people certainly did notice. The Oregon-based Nike corporation was forced to pull its "Chamber of Fear" promotion, based on a Bruce Lee movie, after an outraged public objected to the image of a U.S. athlete defeating a kung fu master. In the global marketplace, cultural differences can undermine even the most elaborate promotional campaign.

3 Culture

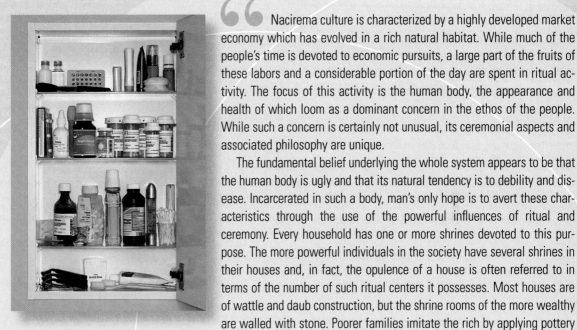

" Nacirema culture is characterized by a highly developed market economy which has evolved in a rich natural habitat. While much of the people's time is devoted to economic pursuits, a large part of the fruits of these labors and a considerable portion of the day are spent in ritual activity. The focus of this activity is the human body, the appearance and health of which loom as a dominant concern in the ethos of the people. While such a concern is certainly not unusual, its ceremonial aspects and associated philosophy are unique.

The fundamental belief underlying the whole system appears to be that the human body is ugly and that its natural tendency is to debility and disease. Incarcerated in such a body, man's only hope is to avert these characteristics through the use of the powerful influences of ritual and ceremony. Every household has one or more shrines devoted to this purpose. The more powerful individuals in the society have several shrines in their houses and, in fact, the opulence of a house is often referred to in terms of the number of such ritual centers it possesses. Most houses are of wattle and daub construction, but the shrine rooms of the more wealthy are walled with stone. Poorer families imitate the rich by applying pottery plaques to their shrine walls.

While each family has at least one such shrine, the rituals associated with it are not family ceremonies but are private and secret. The rites are normally only discussed with children, and then only during the period

> *The focal point of the shrine is a box or chest which is built into the wall. In this chest are kept the many charms and magical potions without which no native believes he could live.*

when they are being initiated into these mysteries. I was able, however, to establish sufficient rapport with the natives to examine these shrines and to have the rituals described to me.

The focal point of the shrine is a box or chest which is built into the wall. In this chest are kept the many charms and magical potions without which no native believes he could live. These preparations are secured from a variety of specialized practitioners. The most powerful of these are the medicine men, whose assistance must be rewarded with substantial gifts. However, the medicine men do not provide the curative potions for their clients, but decide what the ingredients should be and then write them down in an ancient and secret language. This writing is understood only by the medicine men and by the herbalists who, for another gift, provide the required charm.

The charm is not disposed of after it has served its purpose, but is placed in the charm-box of the household shrine. As these magical materials are specific for certain ills, and the real or imagined maladies of the people are many, the charm-box is usually full to overflowing. The magical packets are so numerous that people forget what their purposes were and fear to use them again. While the natives are very vague on this point, we can only assume that the idea in retaining all the old magical materials is that their presence in the charm-box, before which the body rituals are conducted, will in some way protect the worshipper. "

(Miner 1956:503–504) Additional information about this excerpt can be found on the Online Learning Center at www.mhhe.com/schaefer11.

In this excerpt from his journal article "Body Ritual among the Nacirema," anthropologist Horace Miner casts his observant eye on the intriguing rituals of an exotic culture. If some aspects of this culture seem familiar to you, however, you are right, for what Miner is describing is actually the culture of the United States ("Nacirema" is "American" spelled backward). The "shrine" Miner writes of is the bathroom; he correctly informs us that in this culture, one measure of wealth is how many bathrooms one's home has. In their bathroom rituals, he goes on, the Nacirema use charms and magical potions (beauty products and prescription drugs) obtained from specialized practitioners (such as hair stylists), herbalists (pharmacists), and medicine men (physicians). Using our sociological imaginations, we could update Miner's description of the Nacirema's charms, written in 1956, by adding tooth whiteners, anti-aging creams, Waterpiks, and hair gel.

When we step back and examine a culture thoughtfully and objectively, whether it is our own culture in disguise or another less familiar to us, we learn something new about society. Take Fiji, an island in the Pacific where a robust, nicely rounded body has always been the ideal for both men and women. This is a society in which traditionally, "You've gained weight" has been considered a compliment, and "Your legs are skinny," an insult. Yet a recent study shows that for the first time, eating disorders have been showing up among the young people in Fiji. What has happened to change their body image? Since the introduction of cable television in 1995, many Fiji islanders, especially girls, have begun to emulate not their mothers and aunts, but the thin-waisted stars of television programs such as *ER*. Studying culture in places like Fiji, then, sheds light on our own society (A. Becker 2007).

In this chapter we will study the development of culture around the world, including the cultural effects of the worldwide trend toward globalization. We will see just how basic the study of culture is to sociology. We will examine the meaning of culture and society, as well as the development of culture from its roots in the prehistoric human experience to the technological advances of today. We will define and explore the major aspects of culture, including language, norms, sanctions, and values. We will see how cultures develop a dominant ideology, and how functionalist and conflict theorists view culture. Our discussion will focus both on general cultural practices found in all societies and on the wide variations that can distinguish one society from another. We'll see what can happen when a major corporation ignores those variations. Finally, in the Social Policy section we will look at the conflicts in cultural values that underlie current debates over bilingualism.

Culture and Society

Culture is the totality of learned, socially transmitted customs, knowledge, material objects, and behavior. It includes the ideas, values, and artifacts (for example, DVDs, comic books, and birth control devices) of groups of people. Patriotic attachment to the flag of the United States is an aspect of culture, as is a national passion for the tango in Argentina.

Sometimes people refer to a particular person as "very cultured" or to a city as having "lots of culture." That use of the term *culture* is different from our use in this textbook. In sociological terms, *culture* does not refer solely to the fine arts and refined intellectual taste. It consists of *all* objects and ideas within a society, including slang words, ice cream cones, and rock music. Sociologists consider both a portrait by Rembrandt and the work of graffiti spray painters to be aspects of culture. A tribe that cultivates soil by hand has just as much culture as a people that relies on computer-operated machinery. Each people has a distinctive culture with its own characteristic ways of gathering and preparing food, constructing homes, structuring the family, and promoting standards of right and wrong.

The fact that you share a similar culture with others helps to define the group or society to which you belong. A fairly large number of people are said to constitute a *society* when they live in the same territory, are relatively independent of people outside their area, and participate in a common culture. Metropolitan Los Angeles is more populous than at least 150 nations, yet sociologists do not consider it a society in its own right. Rather, they see it as part of—and dependent on—the larger society of the United States.

A society is the largest form of human group. It consists of people who share a common heritage and culture. Members of the society learn this culture and transmit it from one generation to the next. They even preserve their distinctive culture through literature, art, video recordings, and other means of expression. If it were not for the social transmission of culture, each generation would have to reinvent television, not to mention the wheel.

Having a common culture also simplifies many day-to-day interactions. For example, when you buy an airline ticket, you know you don't have to bring along hundreds of dollars in cash. You can pay with a credit card. When you are part of a society, you take for granted many small (as well as more important) cultural patterns. You assume that theaters will provide seats for the audience, that physicians will not disclose confidential information, and that parents will be careful when crossing the street with young children. All these assumptions reflect basic values, beliefs, and customs of the culture of the United States.

Language is a critical element of culture that sets humans apart from other species. Members of a society generally share a common language, which facilitates day-to-day exchanges with others. When you ask a hardware store clerk for a flashlight, you don't need to draw a picture of the instrument. You share the same cultural term for a small, portable battery-operated light. However, if you were in England and needed this item, you would have to ask for an "electric torch." Of course, even within the same society, a term can have a number of different meanings. In the United States, *pot* signifies both a container that is used for cooking and an intoxicating drug.

Use Your Sociological Imagination

Besides your language, what other aspects of your culture might seem unusual to people in India, Japan, or France?

Development of Culture around the World

We've come a long way from our prehistoric heritage. The human species has produced such achievements as the ragtime compositions of Scott Joplin, the novels of V. S. Naipaul, the paintings of Jan Vermeer, and the films of Akira Kurosawa. As we begin a new millennium, we can transmit an entire book around the world via the Internet, clone cells, and prolong lives through organ transplants. We can peer into the outermost reaches of the universe or analyze our innermost feelings. In all these ways, we are remarkably different from other species of the animal kingdom.

Cultural Universals

All societies have developed certain common practices and beliefs, known as *cultural universals.* Many cultural universals are, in fact, adaptations to meet essential human needs, such as the need for food, shelter, and clothing. Anthropologist George Murdock (1945:124) compiled a list of cultural universals, including athletic sports, cooking, funeral ceremonies, medicine, marriage, and sexual restrictions.

The cultural practices Murdock listed may be universal, but the manner in which they are expressed varies from culture to culture. For example, one society may let its members choose their own marriage partners; another may encourage marriages arranged by the parents.

Not only does the expression of cultural universals vary from one society to another; within a society, it may also change dramatically over time. Each generation, and each year for that matter, most human cultures change and expand through the processes of innovation and diffusion.

Customers enjoy a cup of premium coffee at a Starbucks franchise in China. Through the process of diffusion, the Chinese, traditionally tea drinkers, have begun to appreciate a beverage associated with Western cultures.

Innovation

The process of introducing a new idea or object to a culture is known as *innovation.* Innovation interests sociologists because of the social consequences of introducing something new. There are two forms of innovation: discovery and invention. *Discovery* involves making known or sharing the existence of an aspect of reality. The finding of the DNA molecule and the identification of a new moon of Saturn are both acts of discovery. A significant factor in the process of discovery is the sharing of newfound knowledge with others. By contrast, an *invention* results when existing cultural items are combined into a form that did not exist before. The bow and arrow, the automobile, and the television are all examples of inventions, as are Protestantism and democracy.

Globalization, Diffusion, and Technology

The familiar green Starbucks logo beckons you into a comfortable coffee shop, where you can order decaf latte and a cinnamon ring. What's unusual about that? This Starbucks happens to be located in the heart of Beijing's Forbidden City, just outside the Palace of Heavenly Purity, former residence of Chinese emperors. In 2000 it was one of 25 Starbucks stores in China; seven

Are You What You Eat?

The foods people eat, along with the customs they observe in preparing and consuming their meals, say a great deal about their culture. In some cultures, such as that of Papua New Guinea, roast pork is a delicacy reserved for feasts; in others it is forbidden food. In U.S. culture, genetically modified food is accepted without much question, but in Europe it is banned. Because Swedish people put great value on natural, organic foods, 99 percent of mothers in Sweden breast-feed their infants—a rate much higher than that in the United States.

In India, people generally dine while sitting on the floor, as shown here, or on very low stools. Instead of utensils such as forks or chopsticks, they eat with the fingers of the right hand. While Indians have accepted some aspects of U.S.-style fast-food culture, they go to McDonald's for McCurry and McVeggie sandwiches—not for hamburgers, a food that is prohibited by the Hindu religion.

In some cultures, such as France, fine cuisine is a cultural institution. The French prefer fresh local produce lovingly prepared, consumed slowly along with good conversation and a bottle of wine. To the French and to gourmets around the world, great chefs are celebrities.

Given their reverence for food, the French would be most unlikely to participate in a contest designed to see who can gobble down the most hot dogs. In the United States and Japan, these public events are quite popular. But though the Japanese admire American culture, they stop short at copying the American habit of eating fast food on the street while rushing from one place to another. The Japanese will purchase food from a street vendor, but they will not walk around while eating it, because doing so would show disrespect for the preparer.

{Coney Island, New York}

{Paris}

61

3-1 Life in the Global Village

Imagine a "borderless world" in which culture, trade, commerce, money, and even people move freely from one place to another. Popular culture is widely shared, whether it be Japanese sushi or U.S. running shoes, and the English speaker who answers questions over the telephone about your credit card account is as likely to be in India or Ireland as in the United States. In this world, even the sovereignty of nations is at risk, challenged by political movements and ideologies that span nations.

There is no need to imagine this world, for we are already living in the age of globalization. African tribal youngsters wear Simpsons T-shirts; Thai teens dance to techno music; American children collect Hello Kitty items. Ethnic accessories have become a fashion statement in the United States, and Asian martial arts have swept the world.

What caused this great wave of cultural diffusion? First, sociologists take note of advances in communications technology. Satellite TV, cell phones, the Internet, and the like allow information to flow freely across the world, linking global markets. In 2008, this process reached the point where consumers could view videos on hand-held devices and surf the Internet on their wireless cell phones, shopping online at Amazon.com, eBay, and other commercial Web sites from cars, airports, and cafeterias. Second, corporations in the industrial nations have become multinational, with both factories and markets in developing countries. Business leaders welcome the opportunity to sell consumer goods in populous countries such as China. Third, these multinational firms have cooperated with global financial institutions, organizations, and governments to promote free trade—unrestricted or lightly restricted commerce across national borders.

Globalization is not universally welcomed. Many critics see the dominance of "businesses without borders" as benefiting the rich, particularly the very wealthy in industrial countries, at the expense of the poor in less developed nations. They consider globalization to be a successor to the imperialism and colonialism that oppressed Third World nations for centuries.

> *Even James Bond movies and Britney Spears may be seen as threats to native cultures.*

Another criticism of globalization comes from people who feel overwhelmed by global culture. Embedded in the concept of globalization is the notion of the cultural domination of developing nations by more affluent nations. Simply put, people lose their traditional values and begin to identify with the culture of dominant nations. They may discard or neglect their native language and dress as they attempt to copy the icons of mass-market entertainment and fashion. Even James Bond movies and Britney Spears may be seen as threats to native cultures, if they dominate the media at the expense of local art forms. As Sembene Ousmane, one of Africa's most prominent writers and filmmakers, noted, "[Today] we are more familiar with European fairy tales than with our own traditional stories" (World Development Forum 1990:4).

Globalization has its positive side, too. Many developing nations are taking their place in the world of commerce and bringing in much needed income. The communications revolution helps people to stay connected and gives them access to knowledge that can improve living standards and even save lives. For example, people suffering from illnesses are now accessing treatment programs that were developed outside their own nation's medical establishment. The key seems to be finding a balance between the old ways and the new—becoming modernized without leaving meaningful cultural traditions behind.

Let's Discuss

1. How are you affected by globalization? Which aspects of globalization do you find advantageous and which objectionable?
2. How would you feel if the customs and traditions you grew up with were replaced by the culture or values of another country? How might you try to protect your culture?

Sources: Dodds 2000; Giddens 1991; Hirst and Thompson 1996; D. Martin et al. 2006; Ritzer 2004b; Sernau 2001; Tedeschi 2006.

---

years later there were more than 190. The success of Starbucks in a country in which coffee drinking is still a novelty (most Chinese are tea drinkers) has been striking (*China Daily* 2004; Osnos 2007).

The emergence of Starbucks in China illustrates the rapidly escalating trend of globalization, introduced in Chapter 1. It affects not only coffee consumption patterns but the international trade in coffee beans, which are harvested mainly in developing countries. Our consumption-oriented culture, described in the opening to this chapter, supports a retail price of two to three dollars for a single cup of premium coffee. At the same time, the price of coffee beans on the world market has fallen so low that millions of Third World farmers can barely eke out a living. Worldwide, the growing demand for coffee, tea, chocolate, fruit, and natural resources is straining the environment, as poor farmers in developing countries clear more and more forestland to enlarge their fields.

While people in Asia are beginning to drink coffee, people in North America are discovering sushi. Some have become familiar with the *bento box,* a small lunchbox that is often used to serve sushi. More and more cultural expressions and practices are crossing national borders and having an effect on the traditions and customs of the societies exposed to them. Sociologists use the term *diffusion* to refer to the process by which a cultural item spreads from group to group or society to society. Diffusion can occur through a variety of means, among them exploration, military conquest, missionary work, and the influence of the mass media, tourism, and the Internet (see Box 3-1).

Sociologist George Ritzer coined the term *McDonaldization of society* to describe how the principles of fast-food restaurants developed in the United States have come to dominate more and more sectors of societies throughout the world (see Chapter 6). For example, hair salons and medical clinics now take walk-in appointments. In Hong Kong, sex selection clinics offer a menu of items, from fertility enhancement to methods of increasing the likelihood of having a child of the desired sex. Religious groups—from evangelical preachers on local stations or Web sites to priests at the Vatican Television Center—use marketing techniques similar to those that are used to sell Happy Meals.

McDonaldization is associated with the melding of cultures, through which we see more and more similarities in cultural expression. In Japan, for example, African entrepreneurs have found a thriving market for hip-hop fashions popularized by teens in the United States. In Austria, the McDonald's organization itself has drawn on the Austrians' love of coffee, cake, and conversation to create the McCafe, a new part of its fast-food chain. Many critical observers believe that McDonaldization and globalization serve to dilute the distinctive aspects of a society's culture (Alfino et al. 1998; Ritzer 2002, 2004a).

Technology in its many forms has increased the speed of cultural diffusion and broadened the distribution of cultural elements. Sociologist Gerhard Lenski has defined **technology** as "cultural information about how to use the material resources of the environment to satisfy human needs and desires" (Nolan and Lenski 2006:37). Today's technological developments no longer await publication in journals with limited circulation. Press conferences, often carried simultaneously on the Internet, trumpet the new developments.

Technology not only accelerates the diffusion of scientific innovations but also transmits culture. The English language and North American culture dominate the Internet and World Wide Web. Such control, or at least dominance, of technology influences the direction of diffusion of culture. Web sites cover even the most superficial aspects of U.S. culture but offer little information about the pressing issues faced by citizens of other nations. People all over the world find it easier to visit electronic chat rooms about the latest reality TV shows than to learn about their own governments' policies on day care or infant nutrition.

Sociologist William F. Ogburn (1922) made a useful distinction between the elements of material and nonmaterial culture. **Material culture** refers to the physical or technological aspects { pp.6–7 } of our daily lives, including food, houses, factories, and raw materials. **Nonmaterial culture** refers to ways of using material objects and to customs, beliefs, philosophies, governments, and patterns of communication. Generally, the nonmaterial culture is more resistant to change than the material culture. Consequently, Ogburn introduced the term **culture lag** to refer to

the period of maladjustment when the nonmaterial culture is still struggling to adapt to new material conditions. For example, the ethics of using the Internet, particularly issues concerning privacy and censorship, have not yet caught up with the explosion in Internet use and technology (Griswold 2004).

Resistance to technological change can lead not only to culture lag, but to some very real questions of cultural survival (see Box 3-2, page 64).

Use Your Sociological Imagination

If you grew up in your parents' generation—without computers, e-mail, MP3 players, and cell phones—how would your daily life differ from the one you lead today?

Biological Bases of Culture

While sociology emphasizes diversity and change in the expression of culture, another school of thought, sociobiology, stresses the universal aspects of culture. *Sociobiology* is the systematic

When a society's nonmaterial culture (its values and laws) does not keep pace with rapid changes in its material culture, people experience an awkward period of maladjustment called *culture lag*. The transition to nuclear power generation that began in the second half of the 20th century brought widespread protests against the new technology, as well as serious accidents that government officials were poorly prepared to deal with.

3-2 Cultural Survival in Brazil

When the first Portuguese ships landed on the coast of what we now know as Brazil, more than 2 million people inhabited the vast, mineral-rich land. They lived in small, isolated settlements, spoke a variety of languages, and embraced many different cultural traditions.

Today, over five centuries later, Brazil's population has grown to more than 180 million, only about 500,000 of whom are indigenous peoples descended from the original inhabitants. Over 200 different indigenous groups have survived, living a life closely tied to the land and the rivers, just as their ancestors did. But over the last two generations, their numbers have dwindled as booms in mining, logging, oil drilling, and agriculture have encroached on their land and their settlements.

Many indigenous groups were once nomads, moving around from one hunting or fishing ground to another. Now they are hemmed in on the reservations the government confined them to, surrounded by huge farms or ranches whose owners deny their right to live off the land. State officials may insist that laws restrict the development of indigenous lands, but indigenous peoples tell a different story. In Mato Grosso, a heavily forested state near the Amazon River, loggers have been clear-cutting the land at a rate that alarms the Bororo, an indigenous group that has lived in the area for centuries. According to one elder, the Bororo are now confined to six small reservations of about 500 square miles—much less than the area officially granted them in the 19th century.

> In Mato Grosso, a heavily forested state near the Amazon River, loggers have been clear-cutting the land at a rate that alarms the Bororo.

Indigenous tribes are no match for powerful agribusiness interests, one of whose leaders is also governor of Mato Grosso. Blairo Maggi, head of the largest soybean producer in the world, has publicly trivialized the consequences of the massive deforestation occurring in Mato Grosso. Though Maggi recently said he would propose a three-year moratorium on development, opponents are skeptical that he will follow through on the promise.

Meanwhile, indigenous groups like the Bororo struggle to maintain their culture in the face of dwindling resources. Though the tribe still observes the traditional initiation rites for adolescent boys, members are finding it difficult to continue their hunting and fishing rituals, given the scarcity of fish and game in the area. Pesticides in the runoff from nearby farms have poisoned the water they fish and bathe in, threatening both their health and their culture's survival.

Let's Discuss

1. Compare what is happening in Brazil today to the development of the North American West in the 19th century. What similarities do you see?
2. What does society lose when indigenous cultures die?

Sources: Chu 2005; Instituto del Tercer Mundo 2005.

---

study of how biology affects human social behavior. Sociobiologists assert that many of the cultural traits humans display, such as the almost universal expectation that women will be nurturers and men will be providers, are not learned but are rooted in our genetic makeup.

Sociobiology is founded on the naturalist Charles Darwin's (1859) theory of evolution. In traveling the world, Darwin had noted small variations in species—in the shape of a bird's beak, for example—from one location to another. He theorized that over hundreds of generations, random variations in genetic makeup had helped certain members of a species to survive in a particular environment. A bird with a differently shaped beak might have been better at gathering seeds than other birds, for instance. In reproducing, these lucky individuals had passed on their advantageous genes to succeeding generations. Eventually, given their advantage in survival, individuals with the variation began to outnumber other members of the species. The species was slowly adapting to its environment. Darwin called this process of adaptation to the environment through random genetic variation *natural selection*.

Sociobiologists apply Darwin's principle of natural selection to the study of social behavior. They assume that particular forms of behavior become genetically linked to a species if they contribute to its fitness to survive (van den Berghe 1978). In its extreme form, sociobiology suggests that *all* behavior is the result of genetic or biological factors and that social interactions play no role in shaping people's conduct.

Sociobiologists do not seek to describe individual behavior on the level of "Why is Fred more aggressive than Jim?" Rather, they focus on how human nature is affected by the genetic composition of a *group* of people who share certain characteristics (such as men or women, or members of isolated tribal bands). In general, sociobiologists have stressed the basic genetic heritage that *all* humans share, and have shown little interest in speculating about alleged differences between racial groups or nationalities (E. Wilson 1975, 1978).

Some researchers insist that intellectual interest in sociobiology will only deflect serious study of the more significant influence on human behavior, the social environment. Yet Lois Wladis Hoffman (1985), in her presidential address to the Society for the Psychological Study of Social Issues, argued that sociobiology poses a valuable challenge to social scientists to better document their own research. Interactionists, for example, could show how social behavior is not programmed by human biology, but instead adjusts continually to the attitudes and responses of others.

Certainly most social scientists would agree that there is a biological basis for social behavior. But there is less support for the extreme positions taken by certain advocates of sociobiology. Like interactionists, conflict theorists and functionalists believe that people's behavior rather than their genetic structure defines social reality. Conflict theorists fear that the sociobiological approach could be used as an argument against efforts to assist disadvantaged people, such as schoolchildren who are not competing successfully (Guterman 2000; Segerstråle 2000; E. Wilson 2000).

Elements of Culture

Each culture considers its own ways of handling basic societal tasks to be "natural." But in fact, methods of education, marital ceremonies, religious doctrines, and other aspects of culture are learned and transmitted through human interaction within specific societies. Parents in India are accustomed to arranging marriages for their children; parents in the United States leave marital decisions up to their offspring. Lifelong residents of Naples consider it natural to speak Italian; lifelong residents of Buenos Aires feel the same way about Spanish. Let's take a look at the major aspects of culture that shape the way the members of a society live: language, norms, sanctions, and values.

Language

Seven thousand languages are spoken in the world today—many more than the number of countries. Within a nation's political boundaries, the number of languages spoken may range from only one (as in North Korea) to several hundred (as in Papua New Guinea, with 820—see Figure 3-1 on page 66). For the speakers of each one, whether they number 2,000 or 200 million, language is critical to their shared culture (R. Gordon 2005).

The English language, for example, makes extensive use of words dealing with war. We speak of "conquering" space, "fighting" the "battle" of the budget, "waging war" on drugs, making a "killing" on the stock market, and "bombing" an examination; something monumental or great is "the bomb." An observer from an entirely different and warless culture could gauge the importance that war and the military have had in our lives simply by recognizing the prominence that militaristic terms have in our language. On the other hand, in the Old West, words such as *gelding, stallion, mare, piebald,* and *sorrel* were all used to describe one animal—the horse. Even if we knew little of that period in history, we could conclude from the list of terms that horses were important to the culture. Similarly, the Slave Indians of northern Canada, who live in a frigid climate, have 14 terms to describe ice, including 8 for different kinds of "solid ice" and others for "seamed ice," "cracked ice," and "floating ice." Clearly, language reflects the priorities of a culture (Basso 1972; Haviland 2002).

Language is, in fact, the foundation of every culture. *Language* is an abstract system of word meanings and symbols for all aspects of culture. It includes speech, written characters, numerals, symbols, and nonverbal gestures and expressions. Because language is the foundation of every culture, the ability to speak other languages is crucial to intercultural relations. Throughout the Cold War era, beginning in the 1950s and continuing well into the 1970s, the U.S. government encouraged the study of Russian by developing special language schools for diplomats and military advisers who dealt with the Soviet Union. And following September 11, 2001, the nation recognized how few skilled translators it had for Arabic and other languages spoken in Muslim countries. Language quickly became a key not only to tracking potential terrorists, but to building diplomatic bridges with Muslim countries willing to help in the war against terrorism.

While language is a cultural universal, striking differences may be found in the way different cultures use language. To lend authenticity to his 1990 film *Dances with Wolves,* actor-director Kevin Costner hired a Lakota woman to teach the Lakota language to the cast. Lakota is a gendered language in which women and men speak slightly different dialects. The cast members found the language so difficult to learn that the teacher decided to dispense with the complexities of gendered speech. When members of the Lakota Sioux tribe saw the film, they could not help laughing at the resulting gender confusion (Haviland et al. 2005:109).

Sapir-Whorf Hypothesis Language does more than simply describe reality; it also serves to *shape* the reality of a culture. For example, most people in the United States cannot easily make the verbal distinctions concerning ice that are possible in the Slave Indian culture. As a result, they are less likely to notice such differences.

The *Sapir-Whorf hypothesis,* named for two linguists, describes the role of language in shaping our interpretation of reality. According to Sapir and Whorf, since people can conceptualize the world only through language, language *precedes* thought. Thus, the word symbols and grammar of a language organize the world for us. The Sapir-Whorf hypothesis also holds that language is not a given. Rather, it is culturally determined and encourages a distinctive interpretation of reality by focusing our attention on certain phenomena.

In a literal sense, language may color how we see the world. Berlin and Kay (1991) have noted that humans possess the physical ability to make millions of color distinctions, yet languages differ in the number of colors they recognize. The English language distinguishes between yellow and orange, but some other languages do not. In the Dugum Dani language of New Guinea's West Highlands, there are only two basic color terms—*modla* for "white" and *mili* for "black." By contrast, there are 11 basic terms in English. Russian and Hungarian, though, have 12 color terms. Russians have terms for light blue and dark blue, while Hungarians have terms for two different shades of red (Roberson et al. 2000).

Feminists have noted that gender-related language can reflect—although in itself it does not determine—the traditional

FIGURE 3–1

Languages of the World: How Many Do You Speak?

MAPPING LIFE WORLDWIDE

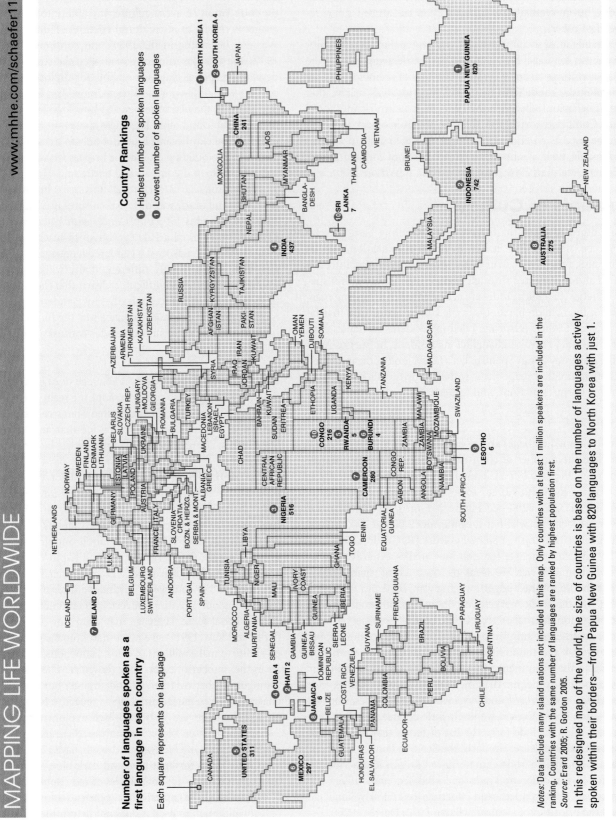

Country Rankings

❶ Highest number of spoken languages

❶ Lowest number of spoken languages

Number of languages spoken as a first language in each country

Each square represents one language

Notes: Data include many island nations not included in this map. Only countries with at least 1 million speakers are included in the ranking. Countries with the same number of languages are ranked by highest population first.

Source: Erard 2005; R. Gordon 2005.

In this redesigned map of the world, the size of countries is based on the number of languages actively spoken within their borders—from Papua New Guinea with 820 languages to North Korea with just 1.

Think About It

Considering how many languages are spoken in the United States, why do you think people in the United States are much less likely to master more than one language than people in other parts of the world?

acceptance of men and women in certain occupations. Each time we use a term such as *mailman, policeman,* or *fireman,* we are implying (especially to young children) that these occupations can be filled only by males. Yet many women work as *letter carriers, police officers,* and *firefighters*—a fact that is being increasingly recognized and legitimized through the use of such nonsexist language.

Language can also transmit stereotypes related to race. Look up the meanings of the adjective *black* in dictionaries published in the United States. You will find *dismal, gloomy or forbidding, destitute of moral light or goodness, atrocious, evil, threatening, clouded with anger.* By contrast, dictionaries list *pure* and *innocent* among the meanings of the adjective *white.* Through such patterns of language, our culture reinforces positive associations with the term (and skin color) *white* and negative associations with *black.* Is it surprising, then, that a list meant to prevent people from working in a profession is called a *blacklist,* while a lie that we think of as somewhat acceptable is called a *white lie?*

Language can shape how we see, taste, smell, feel, and hear. It also influences the way we think about the people, ideas, and objects around us. Language communicates a culture's most important norms, values, and sanctions to people. That's why the death of an old language or the introduction of a new one is such a sensitive issue in many parts of the world (see the Social Policy section at the end of this chapter).

Nonverbal Communication If you don't like the way a meeting is going, you might suddenly sit back, fold your arms, and turn down the corners of your mouth. When you see a friend in tears, you may give a quick hug. After winning a big game you probably high-five your teammates. These are all examples of *nonverbal communication,* the use of gestures, facial expressions, and other visual images to communicate.

We are not born with these expressions. We learn them, just as we learn other forms of language, from people who share our same culture. This statement is as true for the basic expressions of happiness and sadness as it is for more complex emotions, such as shame or distress (Fridlund et al. 1987).

Like other forms of language, nonverbal communication is not the same in all cultures. For example, sociological research done at the micro level documents that people from various cultures differ in the degree to which they touch others during the course of normal social interactions. Even experienced travelers are sometimes caught off guard by these differences. In Saudi Arabia, a middle-aged man may want to hold hands with a partner after closing a business deal. The gesture, which would shock an American businessman, is considered a compliment in that culture. The meaning of hand signals is another form of nonverbal communication that can differ from one culture to the next. In Australia, the thumbs-up sign is considered rude (Passero 2002).

Still, some gestures, such as the basic emotional expressions—a smile, a look of horror—may be close to universal. Not long ago, a team of linguists, social scientists, and physical scientists collaborated on a system for communicating with those

A native speaker trains instructors from the Oneida Nation of New York in the Berlitz method of language teaching. Many Native American tribes are taking steps to recover their seldom-used languages, realizing that language is the essential foundation of any culture.

who live thousands of years from now, long after people have ceased to speak our languages. The challenge was to create a series of signs and explanations that would warn future generations of the dangers posed by the Waste Isolation Pilot Plant (WIPP), a nuclear waste repository in New Mexico. For the next few centuries, warning signs engraved in English, Spanish, Russian, French, Chinese, Arabic, and Navajo will alert those in the area to the presence of the underground dump, which will remain highly radioactive for at least 10,000 years. But the signs also include pictographs that researchers hope will be understandable to people who live millennia from now, no matter what their language: see Figure 3-2 on page 68 (Department of Energy 2004; Piller 2006).

Norms

"Wash your hands before dinner." "Thou shalt not kill." "Respect your elders." All societies have ways of encouraging and enforcing what they view as appropriate behavior while discouraging and punishing what they consider to be improper behavior. ***Norms*** are the established standards of behavior maintained by a society.

For a norm to become significant, it must be widely shared and understood. For example, in movie theaters in the United States, we typically expect that people will be quiet while the film is shown. Of course, the application of this norm can vary,

A Timeless Alert

The symbols on this subsurface marker at the Waste Isolation Pilot Plant in New Mexico are an attempt to communicate the presence of hazardous waste to people who may live 10,000 years from now. Would these symbols convince you not to dig? Might future generations misinterpret them?

Cockfighting, anyone? In the United States, it's legal only in the states of New Mexico and Louisiana. However, in Puerto Rico and many other places around the world, the sport is not only legal but highly popular, and the subject of frenzied betting. What does this cultural difference tell us about social norms?

depending on the particular film and type of audience. People who are viewing a serious artistic film will be more likely to insist on the norm of silence than those who are watching a slapstick comedy or horror movie.

Types of Norms   Sociologists distinguish between norms in two ways. First, norms are classified as either formal or informal. *Formal norms* generally have been written down and specify strict punishments for violators. In the United States, we often formalize norms into laws, which are very precise in defining proper and improper behavior. Sociologist Donald Black (1995) has termed *law* "governmental social control," meaning that laws are formal norms enforced by the state. Laws are just one example of formal norms. The requirements for a college major and the rules of a card game are also considered formal norms.

By contrast, *informal norms* are generally understood but not precisely recorded. Standards of proper dress are a common example of informal norms. Our society has no specific punishment or sanction for a person who comes to school, say, wearing a monkey suit. Making fun of the nonconforming student is usually the most likely response.

Norms are also classified by their relative importance to society. When classified in this way, they are known as *mores* and *folkways*. *Mores* (pronounced "MOR-ays") are norms deemed highly necessary to the welfare of a society, often because they embody the most cherished principles of a people. Each society demands obedience to its mores; violation can lead to severe penalties. Thus, the

United States has strong mores against murder, treason, and child abuse, which have been institutionalized into formal norms.

Folkways are norms governing everyday behavior. Folkways play an important role in shaping the daily behavior of members of a culture. Society is less likely to formalize folkways than mores, and their violation raises comparatively little concern. For example, walking up a "down" escalator in a department store challenges our standards of appropriate behavior, but it will not result in a fine or a jail sentence.

In many societies around the world, folkways exist to reinforce patterns of male dominance. Various folkways reveal men's hierarchical position above women within the traditional Buddhist areas of Southeast Asia. In the sleeping cars of trains, women do not sleep in upper berths above men. Hospitals that house men on the first floor do not place women patients on the second floor. Even on clotheslines, folkways dictate male dominance: women's attire is hung lower than that of men (Bulle 1987).

Use Your Sociological Imagination

You are a high school principal. What norms would you want to govern the students' behavior? How might these norms differ from those appropriate for college students?

www.mhhe.com/schaefer11

Acceptance of Norms People do not follow norms, whether mores or folkways, in all situations. In some cases, they can evade a norm because they know it is weakly enforced. It is illegal for U.S. teenagers to drink alcoholic beverages, yet drinking by minors is common throughout the nation. (In fact, teenage alcoholism is a serious social problem.)

In some instances, behavior that appears to violate society's norms may actually represent adherence to the norms of a particular group. Teenage drinkers are conforming to the standards of their peer group when they violate norms that condemn underage drinking. Similarly, business executives who use shady accounting techniques may be responding to a corporate culture that demands the maximization of profits at any cost, including the deception of investors and government regulatory agencies.

Norms are violated in some instances because one norm conflicts with another. For example, suppose that you live in an apartment building and one night hear the screams of the woman next door, who is being beaten by her husband. If you decide to intervene by ringing their doorbell or calling the police, you are violating the norm of minding your own business, while at the same time following the norm of assisting a victim of violence.

Even if norms do not conflict, there are always exceptions to any norm. The same action, under different circumstances, can cause one to be viewed as either a hero or a villain. Secretly taping telephone conversations is normally considered illegal and abhorrent. However, it can be done with a court order to obtain valid evidence for a criminal trial. We would heap praise on a government agent who used such methods to convict an organized crime figure. In our culture, we tolerate killing another human being in self-defense, and we actually reward killing in warfare.

Acceptance of norms is subject to change as the political, economic, and social conditions of a culture are transformed. Until the 1960s, for example, formal norms throughout much of the United States prohibited the marriage of people from different racial groups. Over the last half century, however, such legal prohibitions were cast aside. The process of change can be seen today in the increasing acceptance of single parents and growing support for the legalization of marriage between same-sex couples (see Chapter 14).

When circumstances require the sudden violation of long-standing cultural norms, the change can upset an entire population. In Iraq, where Muslim custom strictly forbids touching by strangers for men and especially for women, the war that began in 2003 has brought numerous daily violations of the norm. Outside important mosques, government offices, and other facilities likely to be targeted by terrorists, visitors must now be patted down and have their bags searched by Iraqi security guards. To reduce the discomfort caused by the procedure, women are searched by female guards and men by male guards. Despite that concession, and the fact that many Iraqis admit or even insist on the need for such measures, people still wince at the invasion of their personal privacy. In reaction to the searches, Iraqi women have begun to limit the contents of the bags they carry or simply to leave them at home (Rubin 2003).

Sanctions

Suppose a football coach sends a 12th player onto the field. Imagine a college graduate showing up in shorts for a job interview at a large bank. Or consider a driver who neglects to put any money into a parking meter. These people have violated widely shared and understood norms. So what happens? In each of these situations, the person will receive sanctions if his or her behavior is detected.

Sanctions are penalties and rewards for conduct concerning a social norm. Note that the concept of *reward* is included in this definition. Conformity to a norm can lead to positive sanctions such as a pay raise, a medal, a word of gratitude, or a pat on the back. Negative sanctions include fines, threats, imprisonment, and stares of contempt.

Table 3-1 on page 70 summarizes the relationship between norms and sanctions. As you can see, the sanctions that are associated with formal norms (which are written down and codified) tend to be formal as well. If a coach sends too many players onto the field, the team will be penalized 15 yards. The driver who fails to put money in the parking meter will receive a ticket

Sanctions can be positive as well as negative. In 2000, the British actor Sean Connery was knighted by Queen Elizabeth II in recognition of his work in motion pictures.

Norms and Sanctions

Norms	Sanctions	
	Positive	Negative
Formal	Salary bonus	Demotion
	Testimonial dinner	Firing from a job
	Medal	Jail sentence
	Diploma	Expulsion
Informal	Smile	Frown
	Compliment	Humiliation
	Cheers	Belittling

and have to pay a fine. But sanctions for violations of informal norms can vary. The college graduate who goes to the bank interview in shorts will probably lose any chance of getting the job; on the other hand, he or she might be so brilliant that bank officials will overlook the unconventional attire.

The entire fabric of norms and sanctions in a culture reflects that culture's values and priorities. The most cherished values will be most heavily sanctioned; matters regarded as less critical will carry light and informal sanctions.

Values

Though we each have our own personal set of standards—which may include caring or fitness or success in business—we also share a general set of objectives as members of a society. Cultural *values* are these collective conceptions of what is considered good, desirable, and proper—or bad, undesirable, and improper—in a culture. They indicate what people in a given culture prefer as well as what they find important and morally right (or wrong). Values may be specific, such as honoring one's parents and owning a home, or they may be more general, such as health, love, and democracy. Of course, the members of a society do not uniformly share its values. Angry political debates and billboards promoting conflicting causes tell us that much.

Values influence people's behavior and serve as criteria for evaluating the actions of others. The values, norms, and sanctions of a culture are often directly related. For example, if a culture places a high value on the institution of marriage, it may have norms (and strict sanctions) that prohibit the act of adultery or make divorce difficult. If a culture views private property as a basic value, it will probably have stiff laws against theft and vandalism.

The values of a culture may change, but most remain relatively stable during any one person's lifetime. Socially shared, intensely felt values are a fundamental part of our lives in the United States. Sociologist Robin Williams (1970) has offered a list of basic values. It includes achievement, efficiency, material

comfort, nationalism, equality, and the supremacy of science and reason over faith. Obviously, not all 290 million people in this country agree on all these values, but such a list serves as a starting point in defining the national character.

In the last 20 years, extensive efforts have been made to compare values in different nations, recognizing the challenges in interpreting value concepts in a similar manner across cultures. Psychologist Shalom Schwartz has measured values in more than 60 countries. Around the world, certain values are widely shared, including benevolence, which is defined as "forgiveness and loyalty." In contrast, power, defined as "control or dominance over people and resources," is a value that is endorsed much less often (Hitlin and Piliavin 2004; S. Schwartz and Bardi 2001).

Despite this evidence of shared values, some scholars have interpreted the terrorism, genocide, wars, and military occupations of the early 21st century as a "clash of civilizations." According to this thesis, cultural and religious identities, rather than national or political loyalties, are becoming the prime source of international conflict. Critics of this thesis point out that conflict over values is nothing new; only our ability to create havoc and violence has grown. Furthermore, speaking of a clash of "civilizations" disguises the sharp divisions that exist within large groups. Christianity, for example, runs the gamut from Quaker-style pacifism to certain elements of the Ku Klux Klan's ideology (Berman 2003; Huntington 1993; Said 2001).

Each year more than 271,441 entering college students at 393 of the nation's four-year colleges fill out a questionnaire about their attitudes. Because this survey focuses on an array of issues, beliefs, and life goals, it is commonly cited as a barometer of the nation's values. The respondents are asked what values are personally important to them. Over the last 39 years, the value of "being very well-off financially" has shown the strongest gain in popularity; the proportion of first-year college students who endorse this value as "essential" or "very important" rose from 44 percent in 1967 to 73.4 percent in 2006 (see Figure 3-3). In contrast, the value that has shown the most striking decline in endorsement by students is "developing a meaningful philosophy of life." While this value was the most popular in the 1967 survey, endorsed by more than 80 percent of the respondents, it had fallen to seventh place on the list by 2006, when it was endorsed by 46.3 percent of students entering college.

During the 1980s and 1990s, support for values having to do with money, power, and status grew. At the same time, support for certain values having to do with social awareness and altruism, such as "helping others," declined. According to the 2006 nationwide survey, only 42.5 percent of first-year college students stated that "influencing social values" was an "essential" or "very important" goal. The proportion of students for whom "helping to promote racial understanding" was an essential or very important goal reached a record high of 42 percent in 1992, then fell to 34.0 percent in 2006. Like other aspects of culture, such as language and norms, a nation's values are not necessarily fixed.

Recently, cheating has become a hot issue on college campuses. Professors who take advantage of computerized services that can identify plagiarism, such as the search engine Google,

FIGURE 3–3

Life Goals of First-Year College Students in the United States, 1966–2006

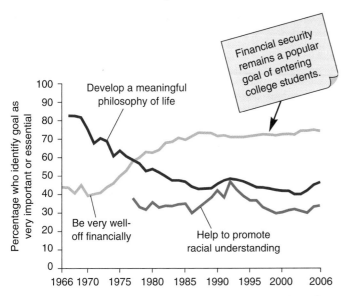

Financial security remains a popular goal of entering college students.

Develop a meaningful philosophy of life

Be very well-off financially

Help to promote racial understanding

Percentage who identify goal as very important or essential

100 90 80 70 60 50 40 30 20 10 0

1966 1970 1975 1980 1985 1990 1995 2000 2006

Sources: UCLA Higher Education Research Institute, as reported in Astin et al. 1994; Pryor et al. 2006.

Think About It

Why do you think values have shifted among college students in the last few decades? Which of these values is important to you?

have been shocked to learn that many of the papers their students hand in are plagiarized in whole or in part. Box 3-3 (page 72) examines the shift in values that underlies this decline in academic integrity.

Another value that has begun to change recently, not just among students but among the public in general, is the right to privacy. Americans have always valued their privacy and resented government intrusions into their personal lives. In the aftermath of the terrorist attacks of September 11, 2001, however, many citizens called for greater protection against the threat of terrorism. In response, the U.S. government broadened its surveillance powers and increased its ability to monitor people's behavior without court approval. In 2001, shortly after the attacks, Congress passed the Patriot Act, which empowers the FBI to access individuals' medical, library, student, and phone records without informing them or obtaining a search warrant.

Culture and the Dominant Ideology

Functionalist and conflict theorists agree that culture and society are mutually supportive, but for different reasons. Functionalists maintain that social stability requires a consensus and the support of society's members; strong central values and common norms provide that support. This view of culture became popular in sociology beginning in the 1950s. It was bor-

rowed from British anthropologists who saw cultural traits as a stabilizing element in a culture. From a functionalist perspective, a cultural trait or practice will persist if it performs functions that society seems to need or contributes to overall social stability and consensus.

Conflict theorists agree that a common culture may exist, but they argue that it serves to maintain the privileges of certain groups. Moreover, while protecting their own self-interest, powerful groups may keep others in a subservient position. The term *dominant ideology* describes the set of cultural beliefs and practices that helps to maintain powerful social, economic, and political interests. This concept was first used by Hungarian Marxist Georg Lukacs (1923) and Italian Marxist Antonio Gramsci (1929), but it did not gain an audience in the United States until the early 1970s. In Karl Marx's view, a capitalist society has a dominant ideology that serves the interests of the ruling class.

From a conflict perspective, the dominant ideology has major social significance. Not only do a society's most powerful groups and institutions control wealth and property; even more important, they control the means of producing beliefs about reality through religion, education, and the media. Feminists would also argue that if all of a society's most important institutions tell women that they should be subservient to men, this dominant ideology will help to control women and keep them in a subordinate position.

Because those with power control the media, we can gain insight into their values by studying media content. Consider Krrish, the Indian answer to Superman. Members of India's growing urban middle class, along with affluent migrants worldwide, see education

This movie poster from India shows the popular superhero Krrish. In addition to being extremely fast and strong, Krrish is supersmart—a trait that is valued highly by middle-class Indians who hope to compete in the global marketplace. When this movie character is not in rescue mode, he works as a computer specialist for a company in Singapore.

3-3 A Culture of Cheating?

On November 21, 2002, after issuing several warnings, officials at the U.S. Naval Academy seized the computers of almost 100 midshipmen suspected of downloading movies and music illegally from the Internet. Officers at the school may have taken the unusually strong action to avoid liability on the part of the U.S. government, which owns the computers students were using. But across the nation, college administrators have been trying to restrain students from downloading pirated entertainment for free. The practice is so widespread, it has been slowing down the high-powered computer networks colleges and universities depend on for research and admissions.

Illegal downloading is just one aspect of the growing problem of copyright violation, both on campus and off. Now that college students can use personal computers to surf the Internet, most do their research online. Apparently, the temptation to cut and paste passages from Web site postings and pass them off as one's own is irresistible to many. Surveys done by the Center for Academic Integrity show that from 1999 to 2005, the percentage of students who approved of this type of plagiarism rose from 10 percent to 41 percent. At the same time, the percentage who considered cutting and pasting from the Internet to be a serious form of cheating fell from 68 percent to 23 percent.

Other forms of cheating are becoming rampant, as well. The Center for Academic Integrity estimates that at most schools, more than three-quarters of the students engage in some form of cheating. Students not only cut passages from the Internet and paste them into their papers without citing the source; they share questions and answers on exams, collaborate on assignments they are supposed to do independently, and even falsify the results of their laboratory experiments. Worse, many professors have become inured to the problem and have ceased to report it.

To address what they consider an alarming trend, many schools are rewriting or adopting new academic honor codes. According to the Center for Academic Integrity, cheating on tests and papers is considerably less common

> *Cheating is considerably less common at schools with honor codes than at schools without honor codes.*

at schools with honor codes than at schools without honor codes. Cornell, Duke, and Kansas State University are just three of a growing number of schools that are instituting or strengthening their honor codes in an attempt to curb student cheating.

This renewed emphasis on honor and integrity underscores the influence of cultural values on social behavior. Observers contend that the increase in student cheating reflects widely publicized instances of cheating in public life, which have served to create an alternative set of values in which the end justifies the means. When young people see sports heroes, authors, entertainers, and corporate executives exposed for cheating in one form or another, the message seems to be "Cheating is OK, as long as you don't get caught." More than proctoring of exams or reliance on search engines to identify plagiarism, then, educating students about the need for academic honesty seems to reduce the incidence of cheating. "The feeling of being treated as an adult and responding in kind," says Professor Donald McCabe of Rutgers University, "it's clearly there for many students. They don't want to violate that trust."

Let's Discuss

1. Do you know anyone who has engaged in Internet plagiarism? What about cheating on tests or falsifying laboratory results? If so, how did the person justify these forms of dishonesty?

2. Even if cheaters aren't caught, what negative effects does their academic dishonesty have on them? What effects does it have on students who are honest? Could an entire college or university suffer from students' dishonesty?

Sources: Argetsinger and Krim 2002; Center for Academic Integrity 2006; R. Thomas 2003; Zernike 2002.

---

as the key to success in the global marketplace. Little wonder, then, that the first of Krrish's superpowers to be discovered was his intelligence. This superhero has extraordinary strength and speed, but his ability to explain the principles of accounting at age 6 was what first endeared him to his audience (Baldauf 2006).

A growing number of social scientists believe it is not easy to identify a "core culture" in the United States. For support, they point to the lack of consensus on national values, the diffusion of cultural traits, the diversity within our culture, and the changing views of young people (look again at Figure 3-3). Yet there is no way of denying that certain expressions of values have greater influence than others, even in so complex a society as the United States.

If cultural values vary within the United States, they vary even more significantly from one country to the next. The following case study illustrates what can happen when a corporation attempts to export U.S. cultural values to another country. We'll discuss the topic of cultural variation in depth in the section that follows.

CASE *study* (CULTURE AT WAL-MART)

By some measures, Wal-Mart is the largest corporation in the world. By other measures, it is the world's 14th largest economy. Indeed, the Arkansas-based retailer's annual revenue—nearly one-third of a trillion dollars—surpasses the total value of goods and services produced in many countries, such as Austria and Turkey.

Wal-Mart's rise to the status of an economic superpower has not been without criticism. Opponents have criticized its policy of shutting out labor unions, its lack of commitment to elevating women to managerial positions, the insufficiency of its health care benefits, and its negative impact on smaller retailers in the areas where its stores are located. Nonetheless, U.S. consumers have embraced Wal-Mart's "everyday low prices." The reaction has not been as positive when the discount giant has tried to enter countries where consumers hold different cultural values.

The company, now located in 15 countries, has not been an unqualified success abroad. In 2006 Wal-Mart pulled out of Germany, due in part to its failure to adjust to the national culture. German shoppers, accustomed to no-nonsense, impersonal service, found Wal-Mart employees' smiling, outgoing style off-putting. The company's "ten-foot attitude"—a salesperson who comes within 10 feet of a customer must look the person in the eye, greet the person, and ask if he or she needs help—simply did not play well there. Food shoppers, used to bagging their own groceries, were turned off by Wal-Mart's practice of allowing clerks to handle their purchases. Furthermore, German employees, who had grown up in a culture that accepts workplace romances, found the company's prohibition against on-the-job relationships bizarre.

Unfortunately, executives did not react quickly enough to the cultural clash. Despite their need for cultural know-how, they passed up the opportunity to install German-speaking managers in key positions. While the company struggled to adjust to unfamiliar cultural standards, fierce competition from German retailers cut into its profits. After an eight-year effort that cost the company one billion dollars, Wal-Mart's executives conceded defeat.

Wal-Mart's withdrawal from Germany was its second exit of the year. Earlier in 2006, the company sold all its facilities in South Korea, where its warehouse-style stores were not appreciated by shoppers accustomed to more elegant surroundings. Today, the successful U.S. retailer is learning not to impose its corporate culture on foreign customers and employees. No longer does the company plan to sell golf clubs in Brazil, where the game is rarely played, or ice skates in Mexico, where skating rinks are hard to find. More important, the corporate giant has begun to study the culture and social patterns of potential customers (Landler and Barbaro 2006; Wal-Mart 2007a; Zimmerman and Nelson 2006).

Wal-Mart's mistakes in Germany and South Korea are instructive. Even without a background in sociology, most businesspeople know that culture is fundamental to society. Yet they often fail to adjust to new cultures when they enter foreign markets. Today, as Wal-Mart prepares to enter China and India, two massive consumer markets, executives are determined to repeat the company's success in Latin America, rather than its failure in Germany and South Korea (B. Nussbaum 2006). ●

Cultural Variation

Each culture has a unique character. Inuit tribes in northern Canada, wrapped in furs and dieting on whale blubber, have little in common with farmers in Southeast Asia, who dress for the heat and subsist mainly on the rice they grow in their paddies. Cultures adapt to meet specific sets of circumstances, such as climate, level of technology, population, and geography. This adaptation to different conditions shows up in differences in all elements of culture, including norms, sanctions, values, and language. Thus, despite the presence of cultural universals such as courtship and religion, great diversity exists among the world's many cultures. Moreover, even *within* a single nation, certain segments of the populace develop cultural patterns that differ from the patterns of the dominant society.

Aspects of Cultural Variation

Subcultures   Rodeo riders, residents of a retirement community, workers on an offshore oil rig—all are examples of what sociologists refer to as *subcultures*. A **subculture** is a segment of society that shares a distinctive pattern of mores, folkways, and values that differs from the pattern of the larger society. In a sense, a subculture can be thought of as a culture existing within a larger, dominant culture. The existence of many subcultures is characteristic of complex societies such as the United States.

Members of a subculture participate in the dominant culture while at the same time engaging in unique and distinctive forms of behavior. Frequently, a subculture will develop an ***argot***, or specialized language, that distinguishes it from the wider society. Athletes who play *parkour*, an extreme sport that combines forward running with fence leaping and the vaulting of walls, water barriers, and even moving cars, speak an argot they devised especially to describe their feats. Parkour runners talk about doing *King Kong vaults*—diving arms first over a wall or grocery cart and landing in a standing position. They may follow this maneuver with a *tic tac*—kicking off a wall to overcome some kind of obstacle (Wilkinson 2007).

Such argot allows insiders—the members of the subculture—to understand words with special meanings. It also establishes patterns of communication that outsiders can't understand. Sociologists associated with the interactionist perspective emphasize that language and symbols offer a powerful way for a subculture to feel cohesive and maintain its identity.

In India, a new subculture has developed among employees at the international call centers established by multinational corporations. To serve customers in the United States and Europe, the young men and women who work there must be fluent speakers of English. But the corporations that employ them demand more than proficiency in a foreign language; they expect their Indian employees to adopt Western values and work habits, including the grueling pace U.S. workers take for granted. In return they offer perks such as Western-style dinners, dances, and coveted consumer goods. Significantly, they allow employees to take the day off only on U.S. holidays, like Labor Day and Thanksgiving—not on Indian holidays like Diwali, the Hindu festival of lights. While most Indian families are home celebrating, call center employees see only each other; when they have the day off, no one else is free to socialize with them. As a result, these employees have formed a tight-knit subculture based on hard work and a taste for Western luxury goods and leisure-time pursuits. Increasingly, they are the object of criticism from Indians who live a more conventional lifestyle centered on family and holiday traditions (Kalita 2006).

Employees of an international call center in Simla, India, socialize after finishing a seven-hour shift on the telephone. Call center employees, who are isolated from other Indians by their unusual holidays and working hours, have formed a tight-knit subculture based partly on their appreciation for Western-style consumer goods.

Another shared characteristic among some employees at Indian call centers is their contempt for the callers they serve. In performing their monotonous, repetitive job day after day, hundreds of thousands of these workers have come to see the faceless Americans they deal with as slow, often rude customers. As described in the recent Indian bestseller *One Night @ the Call Centre,* new trainees quickly learn the "35 = 10 rule," meaning that a 35-year-old American's IQ is the same as a 10-year-old Indian's. Such shared understandings underpin this emerging subculture (Bhagat 2007; Gentlemen 2006).

Functionalist and conflict theorists agree that variation exists within a culture. Functionalists view subcultures as variations of particular social environments and as evidence that differences can exist within a common culture. However, conflict theorists suggest that variations often reflect the inequality of social arrangements within a society. A conflict perspective would view the challenge to dominant social norms by African American activists, the feminist movement, and the disability rights movement as a reflection of inequity based on race, gender, and disability status. Conflict theorists also argue that subcultures sometimes emerge when the dominant society unsuccessfully tries to suppress a practice, such as the use of illegal drugs.

Countercultures By the end of the 1960s, an extensive subculture had emerged in the United States, composed of young people turned off by a society they believed was too materialistic and technological. This group included primarily political radicals and "hippies" who had "dropped out" of mainstream social institutions. These young men and women rejected the pressure to accumulate more and more cars, larger and larger homes, and an endless array of material goods. Instead, they expressed a desire to live in a culture based on more humanistic values, such as sharing, love, and coexistence with the environment. As a political force, this subculture opposed the United States' involvement in the war in Vietnam and encouraged draft resistance (Flacks 1971; Roszak 1969).

When a subculture conspicuously and deliberately opposes certain aspects of the larger culture, it is known as a ***counterculture.*** Countercultures typically thrive among the young, who have the least investment in the existing culture. In most cases, a 20-year-old can adjust to new cultural standards more easily than someone who has spent 60 years following the patterns of the dominant culture (Zellner 1995).

In the wake of the terrorist attacks of September 11, 2001, people around the United States learned of the existence of terrorist groups operating as a counterculture within their country. This was a situation that generations have lived with in Northern Ireland, Israel and the Palestinian territory, and many other parts of the world. But terrorist cells are not necessarily fueled only by outsiders. Frequently people become disenchanted with the policies of their own country, and a few take very violent steps.

Culture Shock Anyone who feels disoriented, uncertain, out of place, or even fearful when immersed in an unfamiliar culture may be experiencing ***culture shock.*** For example, a resident of the United States who visits certain areas in China and wants local meat for dinner may be stunned to learn that the specialty is dog meat. Similarly, someone from a strict Islamic culture may be shocked upon first seeing the comparatively provocative dress styles and open displays of affection that are common in the United States and various European cultures.

All of us, to some extent, take for granted the cultural practices of our society. As a result, it can be surprising and even disturbing to realize that other cultures do not follow our way of life. The fact is that customs that seem strange to us are considered normal and proper in other cultures, which may see our own mores and folkways as odd.

Use Your Sociological Imagination

You arrive in a developing African country as a Peace Corps volunteer. What aspects of a very different culture do you think would be the hardest to adjust to? What might the citizens of that country find shocking about your culture?

"IT'S ENDLESS. WE JOIN A COUNTER-CULTURE; IT BECOMES THE CULTURE. WE JOIN ANOTHER COUNTER-CULTURE; IT BECOMES THE CULTURE..."

Cultures change. Fashions we once regarded as unacceptable—such as men wearing earrings and people wearing jeans in the workplace—or associated with fringe groups (such as men and women with tattoos) are now widely accepted. These countercultural practices have been absorbed by mainstream culture.

FIGURE 3–4
A Palestinian World View

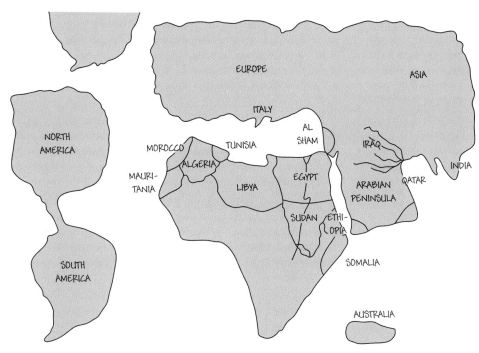

Source: Fellmann et al. 2007:76.

This map, drawn by a high school student in Gaza, reflects the emphasis on pan-Arabism in the Palestinian educational curriculum.

Think About It
What would be the major differences between this map and a map based on your own world view? What would account for those differences?

Attitudes toward Cultural Variation

Ethnocentrism Many everyday statements reflect our attitude that our own culture is best. We use terms such as *underdeveloped, backward,* and *primitive* to refer to other societies. What "we" believe is a religion; what "they" believe is superstition and mythology.

It is tempting to evaluate the practices of other cultures on the basis of our own perspectives. Sociologist William Graham Sumner (1906) coined the term **ethnocentrism** to refer to the tendency to assume that one's own culture and way of life represent the norm or are superior to all others. The ethnocentric person sees his or her own group as the center or defining point of culture and views all other cultures as deviations from what is "normal." Westerners who think cattle are to be used for food might look down on India's Hindu religion and culture, which views the cow as sacred. Or people in one culture may dismiss as unthinkable the mate selection or child-rearing practices of another culture. As Figure 3-4 shows, our view of the world is dramatically influenced by the society in which we were raised.

Table 3-2

Sociological Perspectives on Culture

	Functionalist Perspective	Conflict Perspective	Feminist Perspective	Interactionist Perspective
Norms	Reinforce societal standards	Reinforce patterns of dominance	Reinforce roles of men and women	Are maintained through face-to-face interaction
Values	Are collective conceptions of what is good	May perpetuate social inequality	May perpetuate men's dominance	Are defined and redefined through social interaction
Culture and Society	Culture reflects a society's strong central values	Culture reflects a society's dominant ideology	Culture reflects society's view of men and women	A society's core culture is perpetuated through daily social interactions
Cultural Variation	Subcultures serve the interests of subgroups; ethnocentrism reinforces group solidarity	Countercultures question the dominant social order; ethnocentrism devalues groups	Cultural relativism respects variations in the way men and women are viewed in different societies	Customs and traditions are transmitted through intergroup contact and through the media

Ethnocentric value judgments have complicated U.S. efforts at democratic reform of the Iraqi government. Before the 2003 war in Iraq, U.S. planners had assumed that Iraqis would adapt to a new form of government in the same way the Germans and Japanese did following World War II. But in the Iraqi culture, unlike the German and Japanese cultures, loyalty to the family and the extended clan comes before patriotism and the common good. In a country in which almost half of all people, even those in the cities, marry a first or second cousin, citizens are predisposed to favor their own kin in government and business dealings. Why trust a stranger from outside the family? What Westerners would criticize as nepotism, then, is actually an acceptable, even admirable, practice to Iraqis (Tierney 2003).

Conflict theorists point out that ethnocentric value judgments serve to devalue groups and to deny equal opportunities. Functionalists, on the other hand, point out that ethnocentrism serves to maintain a sense of solidarity by promoting group pride. Denigrating other nations and cultures can enhance our own patriotic feelings and belief that our way of life is superior. Yet this type of social stability is established at the expense of other peoples. Of course, ethnocentrism is hardly limited to citizens of the United States. Visitors from many African cultures are surprised at the disrespect that children in the United States show their parents. People from India may be repelled by our practice of living in the same household with dogs and cats. Many Islamic fundamentalists in the Arab world and Asia view the United States as corrupt, decadent, and doomed to destruc-

tion. All these people may feel comforted by membership in cultures that in their view are superior to ours.

Cultural Relativism While ethnocentrism means evaluating foreign cultures using the familiar culture of the observer as a standard of correct behavior, ***cultural relativism*** means viewing people's behavior from the perspective of their own culture. It places a priority on understanding other cultures, rather than dismissing them as "strange" or "exotic." Unlike ethnocentrists, cultural relativists employ the kind of value neutrality in scien-{p.45} tific study that Max Weber saw as so important.

Cultural relativism stresses that different social contexts give rise to different norms and values. Thus, we must examine practices such as polygamy, bullfighting, and monarchy within the particular contexts of the cultures in which they are found. Although cultural relativism does not suggest that we must unquestionably *accept* every cultural variation, it does require a serious and unbiased effort to evaluate norms, values, and customs in light of their distinctive culture.

Table 3-2 summarizes the major sociological perspectives on culture. How one views a culture—whether from an ethnocentric point of view or through the lens of cultural relativism—has important consequences in the area of social policy. A hot issue today is the extent to which a nation should accommodate nonnative language speakers by sponsoring bilingual programs. We'll take a close look at this issue in the Social Policy section, next.

(social Policy)
and Culture

Bilingualism

The Issue

All over the world, nations face the challenge of how to deal with residential minorities who speak a language different from that of the mainstream culture. **Bilingualism** refers to the use of two or more languages in a particular setting, such as the workplace or schoolroom, treating each language as equally legitimate. Thus, a teacher of bilingual education may instruct children in their native language while gradually introducing them to the language of the host society. If the curriculum is also bicultural, it will teach children about the mores and folkways of both the dominant culture and the subculture. To what degree should schools in the United States present the curriculum in a language other than English? This issue has prompted a great deal of debate among educators and policymakers.

The Setting

Because languages know no political boundaries, minority languages are common in most nations. For example, Hindi is the most widely spoken language in India, and English is used widely for official purposes, but 18 other languages are officially recognized in the nation of about 1 billion people. According to the 2000 Census, 47 million residents of the United States over the age of five—that's about 18 percent of the population—speak a language other than English as their primary language. Indeed, 32 different languages are each spoken by at least 200,000 residents of this country (Bureau of the Census 2003d; Shin and Bruno 2003).

Schools throughout the world must deal with incoming students who speak many different languages. Do bilingual programs in the United States help these children to learn English? It is difficult to reach firm conclusions because bilingual programs in general vary so widely in their quality and approach. They differ in the length of the transition to English and in how long they allow students to remain in bilingual classrooms. Moreover, results have been mixed. In the years since California effectively dismantled its bilingual education program, reading and math scores of students with limited English proficiency rose dramatically, especially in the lower grades. Yet a major overview of 17 different studies, done at Johns Hopkins University, found that students who are offered lessons in both English and their home languages make better progress than similar children who are taught only in English (Slavin and Cheung 2003).

Sociological Insights

For a long time, people in the United States demanded conformity to a single language. This demand coincided with the functionalist view that language serves to unify members of a society.

Immigrant children from Europe and Asia—including young Italians, Jews, Poles, Chinese, and Japanese—were expected to learn English once they entered school. In some cases, immigrant children were actually forbidden to speak their native languages on school grounds. Little respect was granted to immigrants' cultural traditions; a young person would often be teased about his or her "funny" name, accent, or style of dress.

Recent decades have seen challenges to this pattern of forced obedience to the dominant ideology. Beginning in the 1960s, active movements for Black pride and ethnic pride insisted that people regard the traditions of all racial and ethnic subcultures as legitimate and important. Conflict theorists explain this development as a case of subordinated language minorities seeking opportunities for self-expression. Partly as a result of these challenges, people began to view bilingualism as an asset. It seemed to provide a sensitive way of assisting millions of non-English-speaking people in the United States to *learn* English in order to function more effectively within the society.

The perspective of conflict theory also helps us to understand some of the attacks on bilingual programs. Many of them stem from an ethnocentric point of view, which holds that any deviation from the majority is bad. This attitude tends to be expressed by those who wish to stamp out foreign influence wherever it occurs, especially in our schools. It does not take into account that success in bilingual education may actually have beneficial results, such as decreasing the number of high school dropouts and increasing the number of Hispanics in colleges and universities.

Policy Initiatives

Bilingualism has policy implications largely in two areas: efforts to maintain language purity and programs to enhance bilingual education. Nations vary dramatically in their tolerance for a variety of languages. China continues to tighten its cultural control over Tibet by extending instruction of Mandarin, a Chinese dialect, from high school into the elementary schools, which will now be bilingual along with Tibetan. By contrast, nearby Singapore establishes English as the medium of instruction but allows students to take their mother tongue as a second language, be it Chinese, Malay, or Tamil.

In many nations, language dominance is a regional issue—for example, in Miami or along the Tex-Mex border, where Spanish speaking is prevalent. A particularly virulent bilingual hot spot is Quebec, the French-speaking province of Canada. The Québécois, as they are known, represent 83 percent of the province's population, but only 25 percent of Canada's total population. A law implemented in 1978 mandated education in French for all Quebec's children except those whose parents or siblings had

Throughout Canada, official signs are bilingual, even in regions where almost everyone speaks only English or French.

learned English elsewhere in Canada. While special laws like this one have advanced French in the province, dissatisfied Québécois have tried to form their own separate country. In 1995, the people of Quebec indicated their preference of remaining united with Canada by only the narrowest of margins (50.5 percent). Language and language-related cultural areas both unify and divide this nation of 32 million people (*The Economist* 2005b; Schaefer 2006).

Policymakers in the United States have been somewhat ambivalent in dealing with the issue of bilingualism. In 1965, the Elementary and Secondary Education Act (ESEA) provided for bilingual, bicultural education. In the 1970s, the federal government took an active role in establishing the proper form for bilingual programs. However, more recently, federal policy has been less supportive of bilingualism, and local school districts have been forced to provide an increased share of funding for their bilingual programs. Yet bilingual programs are an expense that many communities and states are unwilling to pay for and are quick to cut back. In 1998, voters in California approved a proposition that all but eliminated bilingual education: it requires instruction in English for 1.4 million children who are not fluent in the language.

In the United States, repeated efforts have been made to introduce a constitutional amendment declaring English as the nation's official language. In 2006, the issue arose once again during debates over two extremely controversial congressional proposals—a House bill that would have criminalized the presence of illegal immigrants in the United States and expanded the penalties for aiding them, and a Senate bill that offered some illegal immigrants a path to citizenship. In an attempt to reach a compromise between the two sides, legislative leaders introduced a proposal to make English the national language. As they described it, the legislation would not completely outlaw bilingual or multilingual government services. As of 2007, 28 states had declared English their official language—an action that is now more symbolic than legislative in its significance.

As Figure 3-5 shows, non-English speakers tend to be clustered along the U.S.-Mexican border, in urban areas, and in rural areas populated by Native American tribal groups. Yet bilingualism stirs passions nationwide. The release in 2006 of *"Nuestro Himno,"* the Spanish-language version of the "Star-Spangled Banner," produced a strong public reaction: 69 percent of those who were surveyed on the topic said the anthem should be sung only in English. In reaction against the Spanish version, at least one congressman defiantly sang the national anthem in English—with incorrect lyrics. And the proprietor of a restaurant in Philadelphia posted signs advising patrons that he would accept orders for his famous steak sandwiches only in English. Throughout the year, passions ran high as policymakers debated how much support to afford people who speak other languages (Joseph Carroll 2006; U.S. English 2007).

Let's Discuss

1. Have you attended a school with a number of students for whom English is a second language? If so, did the school set up a special bilingual program? Was it effective? What is your opinion of such programs?

2. The ultimate goal of both English-only and bilingual programs is for foreign-born students to become proficient in English. Why should the type of program students attend matter so much to so many people? List all the reasons you can think of for supporting or opposing such programs. What do you see as the primary reason?

3. Besides bilingualism, can you think of another issue that has become controversial recently because of a clash of cultures? If so, analyze the issue from a sociological point of view.

GettingINVOLVED

To get involved in the debate over bilingualism, visit this text's Online Learning Center, which offers links to relevant Web sites. Check out the Social Policy section in the OLC as well; it provides survey data on U.S. public opinion regarding this issue.

FIGURE 3–5

79

Culture

Non-English Speakers at Home

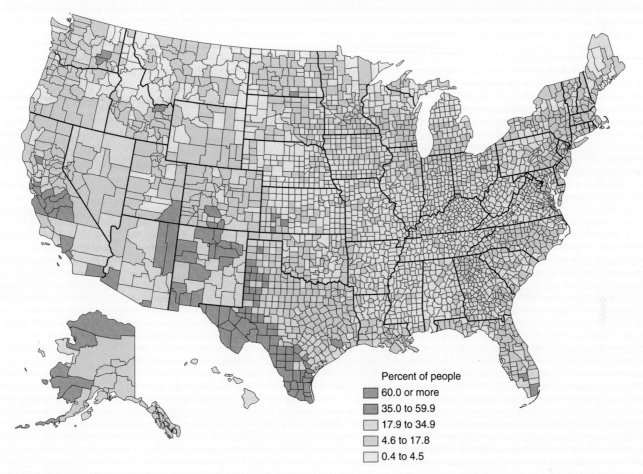

Percent of people

	60.0 or more
	35.0 to 59.9
	17.9 to 34.9
	4.6 to 17.8
	0.4 to 4.5

Note: Data are from 2000 Census for people 5 years and over. National average was 17.9 percent.
Source: Shin and Bruno 2003:8.

Summary

Culture is the totality of learned, socially transmitted customs, knowledge, material objects, and behavior. This chapter examines the basic elements that make up a culture, social practices common to all cultures, and variations that distinguish one culture from another.

1. A shared *culture* helps to define the group or *society* to which we belong.

2. Anthropologist George Murdock compiled a list of *cultural universals,* or common practices found in every culture, including marriage, sports, cooking, medicine, and sexual restrictions.

3. Human culture is constantly expanding through the process of *innovation,* which includes both *discovery* and *invention.*

4. *Diffusion*—the spread of cultural items from one place to another—has fostered globalization. But people resist ideas that seem too foreign, as well as those they perceive as threatening to their own values and beliefs.

5. *Language,* an important element of culture, includes speech, written characters, numerals, and symbols, as well as gestures and other forms of nonverbal communication. Language both describes culture and shapes it.

6. Sociologists distinguish between *norms* in two ways, classifying them either as *formal* or *informal* or as *mores* or *folkways.*

7. The formal norms of a culture will receive the heaviest *sanctions;* informal norms will carry light sanctions.

8. The *dominant ideology* of a culture is the set of cultural beliefs and practices that help to maintain powerful social, economic, and political interests.

9. In a sense, a *subculture* can be thought of as a small culture that exists within a larger, dominant culture. *Countercultures* are subcultures that deliberately oppose aspects of the larger culture.

10. People who assume that their own culture is superior to others engage in *ethnocentrism.* By contrast, *cultural relativism* is the practice of viewing other people's behavior from the perspective of their own culture.

11. The social policy of *bilingualism* calls for the use of two or more languages, treating each as equally legitimate. It is supported by those who want to ease the transition of non-native-language speakers into a host society, but opposed by those who adhere to a single cultural tradition and language.

Critical Thinking Questions

1. Select three cultural universals from George Murdock's list (see page 59) and analyze them from a functionalist perspective. Why are these practices found in every culture? What functions do they serve?

2. Drawing on the theories and concepts presented in this chapter, apply sociological analysis to one subculture with which you are familiar. Describe the norms, values, argot, and sanctions evident in that subculture.

3. In what ways is the dominant ideology of the United States evident in the nation's literature, music, movies, theater, television programs, and sporting events?

Key Terms

Argot Specialized language used by members of a group or subculture. (page 73)

Bilingualism The use of two or more languages in a particular setting, such as the workplace or schoolroom, treating each language as equally legitimate. (77)

Counterculture A subculture that deliberately opposes certain aspects of the larger culture. (74)

Cultural relativism The viewing of people's behavior from the perspective of their own culture. (76)

Cultural universal A common practice or belief found in every culture. (59)

Culture The totality of learned, socially transmitted customs, knowledge, material objects, and behavior. (58)

Culture lag A period of maladjustment when the nonmaterial culture is still struggling to adapt to new material conditions. (63)

Culture shock The feeling of surprise and disorientation that people experience when they encounter cultural practices that are different from their own. (74)

Diffusion The process by which a cultural item spreads from group to group or society to society. (63)

Discovery The process of making known or sharing the existence of an aspect of reality. (59)

Dominant ideology A set of cultural beliefs and practices that helps to maintain powerful social, economic, and political interests. (71)

Ethnocentrism The tendency to assume that one's own culture and way of life represent the norm or are superior to all others. (75)

Folkway A norm governing everyday behavior whose violation raises comparatively little concern. (68)

Formal norm A norm that has been written down and that specifies strict punishments for violators. (68)

Informal norm A norm that is generally understood but not precisely recorded. (68)

Innovation The process of introducing a new idea or object to a culture through discovery or invention. (59)

Invention The combination of existing cultural items into a form that did not exist before. (59)

Language An abstract system of word meanings and symbols for all aspects of culture; includes gestures and other nonverbal communication. (65)

Law Governmental social control. (68)

Material culture The physical or technological aspects of our daily lives. (63)

Mores Norms deemed highly necessary to the welfare of a society. (68)

Nonmaterial culture Ways of using material objects, as well as customs, beliefs, philosophies, governments, and patterns of communication. (63)

Norm An established standard of behavior maintained by a society. (67)

Sanction A penalty or reward for conduct concerning a social norm. (69)

Sapir-Whorf hypothesis A hypothesis concerning the role of language in shaping our interpretation of reality. It holds that language is culturally determined. (65)

Society A fairly large number of people who live in the same territory, are relatively independent of people outside it, and participate in a common culture. (58)

Sociobiology The systematic study of how biology affects human social behavior. (63)

Subculture A segment of society that shares a distinctive pattern of mores, folkways, and values that differs from the pattern of the larger society. (73)

Technology Cultural information about how to use the material resources of the environment to satisfy human needs and desires. (63)

Value A collective conception of what is considered good, desirable, and proper—or bad, undesirable, and improper—in a culture. (70)

Read each question carefully and then select the best answer.

1. Which of the following is an aspect of culture?

   a. a comic book
   b. the patriotic attachment to the flag of the United States
   c. slang words
   d. all of the above

2. People's needs for food, shelter, and clothing are examples of what George Murdock referred to as

   a. norms.
   b. folkways.
   c. cultural universals.
   d. cultural practices.

3. What term do sociologists use to refer to the process by which a cultural item spreads from group to group or society to society?

   a. diffusion
   b. globalization
   c. innovation
   d. cultural relativism

4. The appearance of Starbucks coffee houses in China is a sign of what aspect of culture?

   a. innovation
   b. globalization
   c. diffusion
   d. cultural relativism

5. Which of the following statements is true according to the Sapir-Whorf hypothesis?

   a. Language simply describes reality.
   b. Language does not transmit stereotypes related to race.
   c. Language precedes thought.
   d. Language is not an example of a cultural universal.

6. Which of the following statements about norms is correct?

   a. People do not follow norms in all situations. In some cases, they evade a norm because they know it is weakly enforced.
   b. In some instances, behavior that appears to violate society's norms may actually represent adherence to the norms of a particular group.
   c. Norms are violated in some instances because one norm conflicts with another.
   d. all of the above

7. Which of the following statements about values is correct?

   a. Values never change.
   b. The values of a culture may change, but most remain relatively stable during any one person's lifetime.
   c. Values are constantly changing; sociologists view them as being very unstable.
   d. all of the above

8. Which of the following terms describes the set of cultural beliefs and practices that help to maintain powerful social, economic, and political interests?

   a. mores
   b. dominant ideology
   c. consensus
   d. values

9. Terrorist groups are examples of

   a. cultural universals.
   b. subcultures.
   c. countercultures.
   d. dominant ideologies.

10. What is the term used when one places a priority on understanding other cultures, rather than dismissing them as "strange" or "exotic"?

    a. ethnocentrism
    b. culture shock
    c. cultural relativism
    d. cultural value

11. A(n) _____ is the largest form of human group.

12. _____ is the process of introducing a new idea or object to a culture.

13. The bow and arrow, the automobile, and the television are all examples of _____.

14. Sociologists associated with the _____ perspective emphasize that language and symbols offer a powerful way for a subculture to maintain its identity.

15. "Put on some clean clothes for dinner" and "Thou shalt not kill" are both examples of _____ found in U.S. culture.

16. The United States has strong _____ against murder, treason, and other forms of abuse that have been institutionalized into formal norms.

17. From a(n) _____ perspective, the dominant ideology has major social significance. Not only do a society's most powerful groups and institutions control wealth and property; more important, they control the means of production.

18. Countercultures (e.g., hippies) are typically popular among the _____, who have the least investment in the existing culture.

19. A person experiences _____ _____ when he or she feels disoriented, uncertain, out of place, even fearful, when immersed in an unfamiliar culture.

20. From the _____ perspective, enthocentrism serves to maintain a sense of solidarity by promoting group pride.

Online Learning Center

1. In this chapter you have learned that language is the foundation of every culture. For a long time, people in the United States demanded conformity to a single language. One of the interactive exercises in the student center of the Online Learning Center (**www.mhhe.com/ schaefer11**) asks you to assess how well you would adjust as an immigrant to a non-English-speaking country. Try the assessment and see whether it changes your ideas about the need for bilingual education in the United States.

2. You learned in this chapter both that nonverbal communication is an important element of culture and that there are differences in nonverbal communication around the world. Get an introduction to some common gestures used by the French at **french.about.com/ od/vocabulary/a/topgestures.htm.**

3. One of the more interesting examples of a subculture in the United States is the Gullah culture of South Carolina. Read about Gullah history, culture, and language at the Web site of the Beaufort County (South Carolina) Public Library (**www.co.beaufort.sc.us/bftlib/ gullah.htm**).

*Note: Although all the URLs listed were current as of the printing of this book, these sites often change. Please check our Web site (**www.mhhe.com/schaefer11**) for updates, hyperlinks, and exercises related to these sites.*

Reel Society Video Clips

Reel Society video clips, which appear on this book's Web site, can be used to spark discussion about the following topics from this chapter:

- Cultural Universals
- Norms

On a busy commercial street in Bangalore, India, pedestrians dressed in traditional garb stroll past a shop and billboard advertising Western fashions. Socialization comes from corporate influences as well as from those who are closest to us, such as family and friends. In today's globalized world, Western media expose children to cultural values that their parents and other authorities may not embrace.

4

Socialization

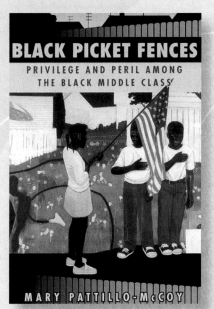

" Charisse . . . is sixteen and lives with her mother and younger sister, Deanne, across the street from St. Mary's Catholic Church and School. Charisse's mother is a personnel assistant at a Chicago university, and is taking classes there to get her bachelor's degree. Mr. Baker is a Chicago firefighter. While her father and mother are separated, Charisse sees her father many times a week at the afterschool basketball hour that he supervises at St. Mary's gym. He and Charisse's mother are on very good terms, and Charisse has a loving relationship with both parents. Mr. Baker is as active as any parent could be, attending the father/daughter dances at Charisse's high school, never missing a big performance, and visiting his daughters often.

Charisse and her sister are being raised by the neighborhood family in addition to their biological parents. "We [are] real close. Like all our neighbors know us because my dad grew up over here. Since the '60s." Charisse is a third-generation Grovelandite just like Neisha Morris. Her grandparents moved into Groveland with Charisse's then-teenage father when the neighborhood first opened to African Americans. . . . Now Charisse is benefiting from the friends her family has made over their years of residence in Groveland, especially the members of St. Mary's church, who play the role of surrogate parents. When Charisse was in elementary school at St. Mary's, her late paternal grandmother was the school secretary, and so the Baker girls were always under the watchful eye of their grandmother as well as the staff, who were their grandmother's friends. And in the evenings Charisse's mother would bring her and her sister to choir practice, where they accumulated an ensemble of mothers and fathers.

> *Charisse is a third-generation Grovelandite just like Neisha Morris. Her grandparents moved into Groveland with Charisse's then-teenage father when the neighborhood first opened to African Americans.*

After St. Mary's elementary school, Charisse went on to St. Agnes Catholic High School for girls, her father's choice. St. Agnes is located in a suburb of Chicago and is a solid, integrated Catholic school where 100 percent of the girls graduate and over 95 percent go on to college. . . .

Most of Charisse's close friends went to St. Mary's and now go to St. Agnes with her, but her choice of boyfriends shows modest signs of rebellion. . . . Many of Charisse's male interests are older than she, and irregularly employed—although some are in and out of school. She meets many of them hanging out at the mall. One evening, members of the church's youth choir sat around talking about their relationships. Charisse cooed while talking about her present boyfriend, who had just graduated from high school but did not have a job and was uncertain about his future. But in the middle of that thought, Charisse spontaneously changed her attentions to a new young man that she had just met. "Charisse changes boyfriends like she changes her clothes," her sister joked, indicating the impetuous nature of adolescent relationships.

While these young men are not in gangs or selling drugs, many of them do not seem to share Charisse's strong career goals and diligence in attaining them. Some of them would not gain the approval of her parents. However, this full list of boyfriends has not clouded Charisse's focus. "

(Pattillo-McCoy 1999:100–102) Additional information about this excerpt can be found on the Online Learning Center at www.mhhe.com/schaefer11.

This excerpt from *Black Picket Fences: Privilege and Peril among the Black Middle Class* describes the upbringing of a young resident of Groveland, a close-knit African American community in Chicago. The author, sociologist Mary Pattillo-McCoy, became acquainted with Charisse while living in the Groveland neighborhood, where she was doing ethnographic research. Charisse's childhood is similar to that of other youths in many respects. Regardless of race or social class, a young person's development involves a host of influences, from parents, grandparents, and siblings to friends and classmates, teachers and school administrators, neighbors and churchgoers—even youths who frequent the local mall. Yet in some ways, Charisse's development is specifically influenced by her race and social class. Contact with family and community members, for instance, has undoubtedly prepared her to deal with prejudice and the scarcity of positive images of African Americans in the media (W. Wilson et al. 2006).

Sociologists, in general, are interested in the patterns of behavior and attitudes that emerge *throughout* the life course, from infancy to old age. These patterns are part of the lifelong process of *socialization,* in which people learn the attitudes, values, and behaviors appropriate for members of a particular culture. Socialization occurs through human interactions. We learn a great deal from those people most important in our lives—immediate family members, best friends, and teachers. But we also learn from people we see on the street, on television, on the Internet, and in films and magazines. From a microsociological perspective, socialization helps us to discover how to behave "properly" and what to expect from others if we follow (or challenge) society's norms and values. From a macrosociological perspective, socialization provides for the transmission of a culture from one generation to the next, and thereby for the long-term continuance of a society.

Socialization also shapes our self-images. For example, in the United States, a person who is viewed as "too heavy" or "too short" does not conform to the ideal cultural standard of physical attractiveness. This kind of unfavorable evaluation can significantly influence the person's self-esteem. In this sense, socialization experiences can help to shape our personalities. In everyday speech, the term ***personality*** is used to refer to a person's typical patterns of attitudes, needs, characteristics, and behavior.

How much of a person's personality is shaped by culture, as opposed to inborn traits? In what ways does socialization continue into adulthood? Who are the most powerful agents of socialization? In this chapter we will examine the role of socialization in human development. We will begin by analyzing the interaction of heredity with environmental factors. We will pay particular attention to how people develop perceptions, feelings, and beliefs about themselves. The chapter will also explore the lifelong nature of the socialization process, as well as important agents of socialization, among them the family, schools, peers, and the media. Finally, the Social Policy section will focus on the socialization experience of group child care for young children.

The Role of Socialization

What makes us who we are? Is it the genes we are born with, or the environment in which we grow up? Researchers have traditionally clashed over the relative importance of biological inheritance and environmental factors in human development—a conflict called the *nature versus nurture* (or *heredity versus environment*) debate. Today, most social scientists have moved beyond this debate, acknowledging instead the *interaction* of these variables in shaping human development. However, we can better appreciate how heredity and environmental factors interact and influence the socialization process if we first examine situations in which one factor operates almost entirely without the other (Homans 1979).

Social Environment: The Impact of Isolation

In the 1994 movie *Nell,* Jodie Foster played a young woman hidden from birth by her mother in a backwoods cabin. Raised without normal human contact, Nell crouches like an animal, screams wildly, and speaks or sings in a language all her own. This movie was drawn from the actual account of an emaciated 16-year-old boy who appeared mysteriously in 1828 in the town square of Nuremberg, Germany (Lipson 1994).

Isabelle and Genie: Two Cases Some viewers may have found the story of Nell difficult to believe, but the painful childhood of Isabelle was all too real. For the first six years of her life, Isabelle lived in almost total seclusion in a darkened room. She had little contact with other people, with the exception of her mother, who could neither speak nor hear. Isabelle's mother's parents had been so deeply ashamed of Isabelle's illegitimate birth that they kept her hidden away from the world. Ohio authorities finally discovered the child in 1938, when Isabelle's mother escaped from her parents' home, taking her daughter with her.

When she was discovered at age six, Isabelle could not speak; she could merely make various croaking sounds. Her only communications with her mother were simple gestures. Isabelle had been largely deprived of the typical interactions and socialization experiences of childhood. Since she had seen few people, she showed a strong fear of strangers and reacted almost like a wild animal when confronted with an unfamiliar person. As she became accustomed to seeing certain individuals, her reaction changed to one of extreme apathy. At first, observers believed that Isabelle was deaf, but she soon began to react to nearby sounds. On tests of maturity, she scored at the level of an infant rather than a six-year-old.

Specialists developed a systematic training program to help Isabelle adapt to human relationships and socialization. After a few days of training, she made her first attempt to verbalize. Although she started slowly, Isabelle quickly passed through six years of development. In a little over two months she was speaking in complete sentences. Nine months later she could identify both words and sentences. Before Isabelle reached the age of nine, she was ready to attend school with other children. By her 14th year she was in sixth grade, doing well in school, and emotionally well adjusted.

Yet without an opportunity to experience socialization in her first six years, Isabelle had been hardly human in the social sense when she was first discovered. Her inability to communicate at the time of her discovery—despite her physical and cognitive potential to learn—and her remarkable progress over the next few years underscore the impact of socialization on human development (K. Davis 1940, 1947).

Unfortunately, other children who have been locked away or severely neglected have not fared so well as Isabelle. In many instances, the consequences of social isolation have proved much more damaging. For example, in 1970 a 14-year-old Californian named Genie was discovered in a room where she had been confined since the age of 20 months. During her years of isolation, no family member had spoken to her, nor could she hear anything other than swearing. Since there was no television or radio in her home, she had never heard the sounds of normal human speech. One year after beginning extensive therapy, Genie's grammar resembled that of a typical 18-month-old. Though she made further advances with continued therapy, she never achieved full language ability. Today Genie, now in her early fifties, lives in a home for developmentally disabled adults. Figure 4-1 shows a sketch Genie made of her teacher five years after she was discovered (Curtiss 1977, 1985; Rymer 1993).

Isabelle's and Genie's experiences are important to researchers because there are only a few cases of children reared in total isolation. Unfortunately, however, there are many cases of children raised in extremely neglectful social circumstances. Recently, attention has focused on infants and young children from orphanages in the formerly communist countries of Eastern Europe. In Romanian orphanages, babies once lay in their cribs for 18 to 20 hours a day, curled against their feeding bottles and receiving little adult care. Such minimal attention continued for the first five years of their lives. Many of them were fearful of human contact and prone to unpredictable antisocial behavior.

This situation came to light as families in North America and Europe began adopting thousands of the children. The adjustment problems for about 20 percent of them were often so dra-

FIGURE 4-1 **87**

Genie's Sketch

Source: Curtiss 1977:274.

This sketch was made in 1975 by Genie—a girl who had been isolated for most of her 14 years, until she was discovered by authorities in 1970. In her drawing, her linguist friend (on the left) plays the piano while Genie listens. Genie was 18 when she drew this picture.

matic that the adopting families suffered guilty fears of being ill-fit adoptive parents. Many of them have asked for assistance in dealing with the children. Slowly, efforts are being made to introduce the deprived youngsters to feelings of attachment that they have never experienced before (Groza et al. 1999; Craig Smith 2006a).

Increasingly, researchers are emphasizing the importance of the earliest socialization experiences for children who grow up in more normal environments. We now know that it is not enough to care for an infant's physical needs; parents must also concern themselves with children's social development. If, for example, children are discouraged from having friends even as toddlers, they will miss out on social interactions with peers that are critical for emotional growth.

Primate Studies Studies of animals raised in isolation also support the importance of socialization in development. Harry Harlow (1971), a researcher at the primate laboratory of the University of Wisconsin, conducted tests with rhesus monkeys that had been raised away from their mothers and away from contact with other monkeys. As was the case with Isabelle, the rhesus monkeys raised in isolation were fearful and easily frightened. They did not mate, and the females who were artificially inseminated became abusive mothers. Apparently, isolation had had a damaging effect on the monkeys.

A creative aspect of Harlow's experimentation was his use of "artificial mothers." In one such experiment, Harlow presented monkeys raised in isolation with two substitute mothers—one cloth-covered replica and one covered with wire that had the ability to offer milk. Monkey after monkey went to the wire mother for the life-giving milk, yet spent much more time clinging to the more motherlike cloth model. It appears that the infant monkeys developed greater social attachments from their need for warmth, comfort, and intimacy than from their need for milk.

While the isolation studies just discussed may seem to suggest that heredity can be dismissed as a factor in the social development of humans and animals, studies of twins provide insight into a fascinating interplay between hereditary and environmental factors.

www.mhhe.com/schaefer11

Use Your Sociological Imagination

What events in your life have had a strong influence on who you are?

The Influence of Heredity

Identical twins Oskar Stohr and Jack Yufe were separated soon after their birth and raised on different continents, in very different cultural settings. Oskar was reared as a strict Catholic by his maternal grandmother in the Sudetenland of Czechoslovakia. As a member of the Hitler Youth movement in Nazi Germany, he learned to hate Jews. By contrast, his brother Jack was reared in Trinidad by the twins' Jewish father. Jack joined an Israeli kibbutz (a collective settlement) at age 17 and later served in the Israeli army. But when the twins were reunited in middle age, some startling similarities emerged: They both wore wire-rimmed glasses and mustaches. They both liked spicy foods and sweet liqueurs, were absent-minded, flushed the toilet before using it, stored rubber bands on their wrists, and dipped buttered toast in their coffee (Holden 1980).

The twins also differed in many important respects: Jack was a workaholic; Oskar enjoyed leisure-time activities. Whereas Oskar was a traditionalist who was domineering toward women, Jack was a political liberal much more accepting of feminism. Finally, Jack was extremely proud of being Jewish, while Oskar never mentioned his Jewish heritage (Holden 1987).

Oskar and Jack are prime examples of the interplay of heredity and environment. For a number of years, the Minnesota Twin Family Study has been following pairs of identical twins reared apart to determine what similarities, if any, they show in personality traits, behavior, and intelligence. Preliminary results from the available twin studies indicate that *both* genetic factors

and socialization experiences are influential in human development. Certain characteristics, such as temperaments, voice patterns, and nervous habits, appear to be strikingly similar even in twins reared apart, suggesting that these qualities may be linked to hereditary causes. However, identical twins reared apart differ far more in their attitudes, values, chosen mates, and even drinking habits; these qualities, it would seem, are influenced by environmental factors. In examining clusters of personality traits among such twins, researchers have found marked similarities in their tendency toward leadership or dominance, but significant differences in their need for intimacy, comfort, and assistance.

Researchers have also been impressed with the similar scores on intelligence tests of twins reared apart in *roughly similar* social settings. Most of the identical twins register scores even closer than those that would be expected if the same person took a test twice. At the same time, however, identical twins brought up in *dramatically different* social environments score quite differently on intelligence tests—a finding that supports the impact of socialization on human development (Joseph 2004; McGue and Bouchard 1998; Minnesota Center for Twin and Family Research 2007).

We need to be cautious in reviewing studies of twin pairs and other relevant research. Widely broadcast findings have often been based on extremely small samples and preliminary analysis. For example, one study (not involving twin pairs) was fre-

Two twins celebrate their special identity at the annual Twins Day Festival in Twinsburg, Ohio. Every year, social scientists descend on Twinsburg to study the 3,000 pairs of twins who gather at the festival. Research points to some behavioral similarities between twins, but little beyond the likenesses found among nontwin siblings.

quently cited as confirming genetic links with behavior. Yet the researchers had to retract their conclusions after they increased the sample and reclassified two of the original cases. After those changes, the initial findings were no longer valid.

Critics add that studies of twin pairs have not provided satisfactory information concerning the extent to which separated identical twins may have had contact with each other, even though they were raised apart. Such interactions—especially if they were extensive—could call into question the validity of the twin studies. As this debate continues, we can certainly anticipate numerous efforts to replicate the research and clarify the interplay between heredity and environmental factors in human development (Horgan 1993; Plomin 1989).

The Self and Socialization

We all have various perceptions, feelings, and beliefs about who we are and what we are like. How do we come to develop them? Do they change as we age?

We were not born with these understandings. Building on the work of George Herbert Mead (1964b), sociologists recognize that our concept of who we are, the *self,* emerges as we interact with others. The *self* is a distinct identity that sets us apart from others. It is not a static phenomenon, but continues to develop and change throughout our lives.

Sociologists and psychologists alike have expressed interest in how the individual develops and modifies the sense of self as a result of social interaction. The work of sociologists Charles {pp.14, 19 Horton Cooley and George Herbert Mead, pioneers of the interactionist approach, has been especially useful in furthering our understanding of these important issues.

Sociological Approaches to the Self

Cooley: Looking-Glass Self In the early 1900s, Charles Horton Cooley advanced the belief that we learn who we are by interacting with others. Our view of ourselves, then, comes not only from direct contemplation of our personal qualities but also from our impressions of how others perceive us. Cooley used the phrase **looking-glass self** to emphasize that the self is the product of our social interactions.

The process of developing a self-identity or self-concept has three phases. First, we imagine how we present ourselves to others—to relatives, friends, even strangers on the street. Then we imagine how others evaluate us (attractive, intelligent, shy, or strange). Finally, we develop some sort of feeling about ourselves, such as respect or shame, as a result of these impressions (Cooley 1902; M. Howard 1989).

A subtle but critical aspect of Cooley's looking-glass self is that the self results from an individual's "imagination" of how others view him or her. As a result, we can develop self-identities based on *incorrect* perceptions of how others see us. A student may react strongly to a teacher's criticism and decide (wrongly) that the instructor views the student as stupid. This misperception may be converted into a negative self-identity through the following process: (1) the teacher criticized me, (2) the teacher must think that I'm stupid, (3) I *am* stupid. Yet self-identities are also subject to change. If the student receives an A at the end of the course, he or she will probably no longer feel stupid.

Mead: Stages of the Self George Herbert Mead continued Cooley's exploration of interactionist theory. Mead (1934, 1964a) developed a useful model of the process by which the self emerges, defined by three distinct stages: the preparatory stage, the play stage, and the game stage.

The Preparatory Stage During the *preparatory stage,* children merely imitate the people around them, especially family members with whom they continually interact. Thus, a small child will bang on a piece of wood while a parent is engaged in carpentry work, or will try to throw a ball if an older sibling is doing so nearby.

As they grow older, children become more adept at using symbols to communicate with others. *Symbols* are the gestures, objects, and words that form the basis of human communication. By interacting with relatives and friends, as well as by watching cartoons on television and looking at picture books, children in the preparatory stage begin to understand symbols. They will continue to use this form of communication throughout their lives.

Like spoken languages, symbols vary from culture to culture, and even from one subculture to another. In North America, raising one's eyebrows may communicate astonishment or doubt. In Peru, the same gesture means "money" or "pay me," and may constitute an unspoken request for a bribe. In the Pacific island nation of Tonga, raised eyebrows mean "yes" or "I agree" (Axtell 1990).

Children imitate the people around them, especially family members they continually interact with, during the *preparatory stage* described by George Herbert Mead.

In multicultural societies, such differences in the meaning of symbols create the potential for conflict. For example, the symbolic headscarf that is worn by Muslim women recently became a major social issue in France. For years French public schools have banned overt signs of religion, such as large crosses, skullcaps, and headscarves. Muslim students who violated the informal dress code were expelled. In 2003, amid growing controversy, a government advisory panel recommended that the French Parliament strengthen the ban by writing it into law. The issue is a particularly thorny one because of the conflicting cultural meanings these symbols carry. To many of the French, the headscarf symbolizes the submission of women—an unwelcome connotation in a society that places a high value on egalitarianism. To others it represents a challenge to the French way of life. Thus, 78 percent of the French surveyed on the issue supported the ban. But to Muslims, the headscarf symbolizes modesty and respectability. Muslim schoolchildren take this symbol very seriously (Vaïsse 2004).

According to George Herbert Mead, children begin to communicate through symbols at an early age, and continue to use them throughout their lives. This French girl is protesting a law that forbids public school students to wear Islamic headscarves and other religious insignia. The ban against the deeply symbolic head covering has sparked considerable controversy in France.

The Play Stage   Mead was among the first to analyze the relationship of symbols to socialization. As children develop skill in communicating through symbols, they gradually become more aware of social relationships. As a result, during the *play stage,* they begin to pretend to be other people. Just as an actor "becomes" a character, a child becomes a doctor, parent, superhero, or ship captain.

Mead, in fact, noted that an important aspect of the play stage is role playing. **Role taking** is the process of mentally assuming the perspective of another and responding from that imagined viewpoint. For example, through this process, a young child will gradually learn when it is best to ask a parent for favors. If the parent usually comes home from work in a bad mood, the child will wait until after dinner, when the parent is more relaxed and approachable.

The Game Stage   In Mead's third stage, the *game stage,* the child of about eight or nine years old no longer just plays roles but begins to consider several tasks and relationships simultaneously. At this point in development, children grasp not only their own social positions but also those of others around them—just as in a football game the players must understand their own and everyone else's positions. Consider a girl or boy who is part of a scout troop out on a weekend hike in the mountains. The child must understand what he or she is expected to do but must also recognize the responsibilities of other scouts as well as the leaders. This is the final stage of development under Mead's model; the child can now respond to numerous members of the social environment.

Mead uses the term **generalized other** to refer to the attitudes, viewpoints, and expectations of society as a whole that a child takes into account in his or her behavior. Simply put, this concept suggests that when an individual acts, he or she takes into account an entire group of people. For example, a child will not act courteously merely to please a particular parent. Rather, the child comes to understand that courtesy is a widespread social value endorsed by parents, teachers, and religious leaders.

At the game stage, children can take a more sophisticated view of people and the social environment. They now understand what specific occupations and social positions are and no longer equate Mr. Williams only with the role of "librarian" or Ms. Sanchez only with "principal." It has become clear to the child that Mr. Williams can be a librarian, a parent, and a marathon runner at the same time and that Ms. Sanchez is one of many principals in our society. Thus, the child has reached a new level of sophistication in observations of individuals and institutions.

Mead: Theory of the Self   Mead is best known for his theory of the self. According to Mead (1964b), the self begins at a privileged, central position in a person's world. Young children picture themselves as the focus of everything around them and find it difficult to consider the perspectives of others. For example, when shown a mountain scene and asked to describe what an observer on the opposite side of the mountain might see (such as a lake or hikers), young children describe only objects visible from their own vantage point. This childhood tendency to place ourselves at the center of events never entirely disappears. Many people with a fear of flying automatically assume that if any plane goes down, it will be the one they are on. And who reads the horoscope section in the paper without looking at their own horoscope first? Why else do we buy lottery tickets, if we do not imagine ourselves winning?

Nonetheless, as people mature, the self changes and begins to reflect greater concern about the reactions of others. Parents, friends, co-workers, coaches, and teachers are often among those who play a major role in shaping a person's self. The term *significant others* is used to refer to those individuals who are most important in the development of the self. Many young people, for example, find themselves drawn to the same kind of work their parents engage in (Sullivan [1953] 1968).

In some instances, studies of significant others have generated controversy among researchers. For example, some researchers have contended that African American adolescents are more "peer-oriented" than their White counterparts because of presumed weaknesses in Black families. However, investigations indicate that these hasty conclusions were based on limited studies focusing on less affluent Blacks. In fact, there appears to be little difference in who African Americans and Whites from similar economic backgrounds regard as their significant others (Giordano et al. 1993; Juhasz 1989).

Use Your Sociological Imagination

How do you view yourself as you interact with others around you? How do you think you formed this view of yourself?

Goffman: Presentation of the Self How do we manage our "self"? How do we display to others who we are? Erving Goffman, a sociologist associated with the interactionist perspective, suggested that many of our daily activities involve attempts to convey impressions of who we are. His observations help us to understand the sometimes subtle yet critical ways in which we learn to present ourselves socially. They also offer concrete examples of this aspect of socialization.

Early in life, the individual learns to slant his or her presentation of the self in order to create distinctive appearances and satisfy particular audiences. Goffman (1959) referred to this altering of the presentation of the self as ***impression management.*** Box 4-1 (page 92) describes an everyday example of this concept—the way students behave after receiving their exam grades.

In analyzing such everyday social interactions, Goffman makes so many explicit parallels to the theater that his view has been termed the ***dramaturgical approach.*** According to this perspective, people resemble performers in action. For example, a clerk may try to appear busier than he or she actually is if a supervisor happens to be watching. A customer in a singles' bar may try to look as if he or she is waiting for a particular person to arrive.

Goffman (1959) also drew attention to another aspect of the self—*face-work.* How often do you initiate some kind of face-saving behavior when you feel embarrassed or rejected? In response to a rejection at the singles' bar, a person may engage in face-work by saying, "There really isn't an interesting person in this entire crowd." We feel the need to maintain a proper image of the self if we are to continue social interaction.

In some cultures, people engage in elaborate deceptions to avoid losing face. In Japan, for example, where lifetime

A prospective employer reviews an applicant's qualifications for the job. To present themselves in a positive manner, both interviewer and applicant may resort to *impression management* and *face-work,* two tactics described by the interactionist Erving Goffman.

sociology ON campus

4-1 Impression Management by Students

When you and fellow classmates get an exam back, you probably react differently depending on the grades that you and they earned. This distinction is part of *impression management,* as sociologists Daniel Albas and Cheryl Albas have demonstrated. The two explored the strategies college students use to create desired appearances after receiving their grades on exams. Albas and Albas divided these encounters into three categories: those between students who have all received high grades (Ace–Ace encounters); those between students who have received high grades and those who have received low or even failing grades (Ace–Bomber encounters); and those between students who have all received low grades (Bomber–Bomber encounters).

Ace–Ace encounters occur in a rather open atmosphere, because there is comfort in sharing a high mark with another high achiever. It is even acceptable to violate the norm of modesty and brag when among other Aces, since as one student admitted, "It's much easier to admit a high mark to someone who has done better than you, or at least as well."

Ace–Bomber encounters are often sensitive. Bombers generally attempt to avoid such exchanges, because "you . . . emerge looking like the dumb one" or "feel like you are lazy or unreliable." When forced into interactions with Aces, Bombers work to appear gracious and congratulatory. For their part, Aces offer sympathy and support to the dissatisfied Bombers and even rationalize their own "lucky" high scores. To help Bombers save face, Aces may emphasize the difficulty and unfairness of the examination.

> When forced into interactions with Aces, Bombers work to appear gracious and congratulatory.

Bomber–Bomber encounters tend to be closed, reflecting the group effort to wall off the feared disdain of others. Yet, within the safety of these encounters, Bombers openly share their disappointment and engage in expressions of mutual self-pity that they themselves call "pity parties." They devise face-saving excuses for their poor performance, such as "I wasn't feeling well all week" or "I had four exams and two papers due that week." If the grade distribution in a class includes particularly low scores, Bombers may blame the professor, attacking him or her as a sadist, a slave driver, or simply an incompetent.

As is evident from these descriptions, students' impression management strategies conform to society's informal norms regarding modesty and consideration for less successful peers. In classroom settings, as in the workplace and in other types of human interaction, efforts at impression management are most intense when status differentials are pronounced, as in encounters between the high-scoring Aces and the low-scoring Bombers.

Let's Discuss

1. How do you react to those who have received higher or lower grades than you? Do you engage in impression management? How would you like others to react to your grade?
2. What social norms govern students' impression management strategies?

Source: Albas and Albas 1988.

---

employment has until recently been the norm, "company men" thrown out of work by a deep economic recession may feign employment, rising as usual in the morning, donning suit and tie, and heading for the business district. But instead of going to the office, they congregate at places such as Tokyo's Hibiya Library, where they pass the time by reading before returning home at the usual hour. Many of these men are trying to protect family members, who would be shamed if neighbors discovered the family breadwinner was unemployed. Others are deceiving their wives and families as well (French 2000).

Goffman's work on the self represents a logical progression of sociological studies begun by Cooley and Mead on how personality is acquired through socialization and how we manage the presentation of the self to others. Cooley stressed the process by which we create a self; Mead focused on how the self develops as we learn to interact with others; Goffman emphasized the ways in which we consciously create images of ourselves for others.

Psychological Approaches to the Self

Psychologists have shared the interest of Cooley, Mead, and other sociologists in the development of the self. Early work in psychology, such as that of Sigmund Freud (1856–1939), stressed the role of inborn drives—among them the drive for sexual gratification—in channeling human behavior. More recently, psychologists such as Jean Piaget have emphasized the stages through which human beings progress as the self develops.

Like Charles Horton Cooley and George Herbert Mead, Freud believed that the self is a social product, and that aspects of one's personality are influenced by other people (especially one's parents). However, unlike Cooley and Mead, he suggested that the self has components that work in opposition to each other. According to Freud, our natural impulsive instincts are in constant conflict with societal constraints. Part of us seeks limitless pleasure, while another part favors rational behavior. By interacting with others, we learn the expectations of society and then select behavior most appropriate to our own culture. (Of course, as Freud was well aware, we sometimes distort reality and behave irrationally.)

Research on newborn babies by the Swiss child psychologist Jean Piaget (1896–1980) has underscored the importance of social interactions in developing a sense of self. Piaget found that newborns have no self in the sense of a looking-glass image. Ironically, though, they are quite self-centered; they demand that all attention be directed toward them. Newborns have not yet separated themselves from the universe of which they are a part. For these babies, the phrase "you and me" has no meaning; they understand only "me." However, as they mature, children are gradually socialized into social relationships, even within their rather self-centered world.

In his well-known *cognitive theory of development,* Piaget (1954) identified four stages in the development of children's thought processes. In the first, or *sensorimotor,* stage, young children use their senses to make discoveries. For example, through touching they discover that their hands are actually a part of themselves. During the second, or *preoperational,* stage, children begin to use words and symbols to distinguish objects and ideas. The milestone in the third, or *concrete operational,* stage is that children engage in more logical thinking. They learn that even when a formless lump of clay is shaped into a snake, it is still the same clay. Finally, in the fourth, or *formal operational,* stage, adolescents become capable of sophisticated abstract thought and can deal with ideas and values in a logical manner.

Piaget suggested that moral development becomes an important part of socialization as children develop the ability to think more abstractly. When children learn the rules of a game such as checkers or jacks, they are learning to obey societal norms. Those under eight years old display a rather basic level of morality: rules are rules, and there is no concept of "extenuating circumstances." As they mature, children become capable of greater autonomy and begin to experience moral dilemmas and doubts as to what constitutes proper behavior.

According to Jean Piaget, social interaction is the key to development. As children grow older, they pay increasing attention to how other people think and why they act in particular ways. In order to develop a distinct personality, each of us needs opportunities to interact with others. As we saw earlier, Isabelle was deprived of the chance for normal social interactions, and the consequences were severe (Kitchener 1991).

We have seen that a number of thinkers considered social interaction the key to the development of an individual's sense of self. As is generally true, we can best understand this topic by drawing on a variety of theory and research. Table 4-1 summarizes the rich literature, both sociological and psychological, on the development of the self.

Socialization and the Life Course
The Life Course

Among the Kota people of the Congo in Africa, adolescents paint themselves blue. Mexican American girls go on a daylong religious retreat before dancing the night away. Egyptian mothers step over their newborn infants seven times, and students at the Naval Academy throw their hats in the air. These are all ways of celebrating *rites of passage,* a means of dramatizing and validating changes in a person's status. The Kota rite marks the

Table 4-1

Theoretical Approaches to Development of the Self

summingUP

Scholar	Key Concepts and Contributions	Major Points of Theory
Charles Horton Cooley 1864–1929 sociologist (USA)	Looking-glass self	Stages of development not distinct; feelings toward ourselves developed through interaction with others
George Herbert Mead 1863–1931 sociologist (USA)	The self Generalized other	Three distinct stages of development; self develops as children grasp the roles of others in their lives
Erving Goffman 1922–1982 sociologist (USA)	Impression management Dramaturgical approach Face-work	Self developed through the impressions we convey to others and to groups
Sigmund Freud 1856–1939 psychotherapist (Austria)	Psychoanalysis	Self influenced by parents and by inborn drives, such as the drive for sexual gratification
Jean Piaget 1896–1980 child psychologist (Switzerland)	Cognitive theory of development	Four stages of cognitive development; moral development linked to socialization

Body painting is a ritual marking the passage to puberty among young people in Liberia, in western Africa.

passage to adulthood. The color blue, viewed as the color of death, symbolizes the death of childhood. Hispanic girls celebrate reaching womanhood with a *quinceañera* ceremony at age 15. In the Cuban American community of Miami, the popularity of the *quinceañera* supports a network of party planners, caterers, dress designers, and the Miss Quinceañera Latina pageant. For thousands of years, Egyptian mothers have welcomed their newborns to the world in the Soboa ceremony by stepping over the seven-day-old infant seven times. And Naval Academy seniors celebrate their graduation from college by hurling their hats skyward.

These specific ceremonies mark stages of development in the life course. They indicate that the process of socialization continues through all stages of the life cycle. In fact, some researchers have chosen to concentrate on socialization as a lifelong process. Sociologists and other social scientists who take such a **life course approach** look closely at the social factors that influence people throughout their lives, from birth to death, including gender and income. They recognize that biological changes mold but do not dictate human behavior.

Several life events mark the passage to adulthood. Of course, these turning points vary from one society and even one generation to the next. According to a national survey done in 2002, in the United States the key event seems to be the completion of formal schooling (see Table 4-2). On average, Americans expect this milestone to occur by a person's 23rd birthday. Other major events in the life course, such as getting married or becoming a parent, are expected to follow three or four years later. Interestingly, comparatively few survey respondents identified marriage and parenthood as important milestones (S. Furstenberg et al. 2004).

One result of these staggered steps to independence is that in the United States, unlike some other societies, there is no clear dividing line between adolescence and adulthood. Nowadays, few young people finish school, get married, and leave home at about the same age, clearly establishing their transition to adulthood. The term *youthhood* has been coined to describe the prolonged ambiguous status that young people in their twenties experience (Côté 2000).

We encounter some of the most difficult socialization challenges (and rites of passage) in the later years of life. Assessing one's accomplishments, coping with declining physical abilities, experiencing retirement, and facing the inevitability of death may lead to painful adjustments. Old age is further complicated by the negative way that many societies, including the United States, view and treat the elderly. The common stereotypes of the elderly as helpless and dependent may well weaken an older person's self-image. However, as we will explore more fully in Chapter 13, many older people continue to lead active, productive, fulfilled lives, whether in the paid labor force or as retirees.

Freshman cadets at the Virginia Military Institute crawl up a muddy hill in the school's gritty indoctrination into strict military discipline, a rite of passage at the school.

Use Your Sociological Imagination

You are a religious leader who is trying to retain young adults as they grow up and separate from their families. You recognize that marriage and parenthood are no longer considered as important in the transition to adulthood as they were in the past. What rite of passage could you develop to appeal to today's young adults?

Anticipatory Socialization and Resocialization

The development of a social self is literally a lifelong transformation that begins in the crib and continues as one prepares for death. Two types of socialization occur at many points throughout the life course: anticipatory socialization and resocialization.

Anticipatory socialization refers to processes of socialization in which a person "rehearses" for future positions, occupations, and social relationships. A culture can function more efficiently and smoothly if members become acquainted with the norms, values, and behavior associated with a social position before actually assuming that status. Preparation for many aspects of adult life begins with anticipatory socialization during childhood and adolescence, and continues throughout our lives as we prepare for new responsibilities.

You can see the process of anticipatory socialization take place when high school students start to consider what colleges they may attend. Traditionally, this task meant looking at publications received in the mail or making campus visits. However, with new technology, more and more students are using the Web to begin their college experience. Colleges are investing more time and money in developing attractive Web sites through which students can take "virtual" campus tours and hear audio clips of everything from the college anthem to a sample zoology lecture.

Occasionally, assuming a new social or occupational position requires us to *unlearn* an established orientation. *Resocialization* refers to the process of discarding former behavior patterns and accepting new ones as part of a transition in one's life. Often resocialization occurs during an explicit effort to transform an individual, as happens in reform schools, therapy groups, prisons, religious conversion settings, and political indoctrination camps. The process of resocialization typically involves considerable stress for the individual—much more so than socialization in general, or even anticipatory socialization (Gecas 2004).

Resocialization is particularly effective when it occurs within a total institution. Erving Goffman (1961) coined the term *total institution* to refer to an institution that regulates all aspects of a person's life under a single authority, such as a prison, the military, a mental hospital, or a convent. Because the total institution is generally cut off from the rest of society, it provides for all the needs of its members. Quite literally, the crew of a merchant vessel at sea becomes part of a total institution. So elaborate are its requirements, so all-encompassing its activities, a total institution often represents a miniature society.

Goffman (1961) identified four common traits of total institutions:

- All aspects of life are conducted in the same place under the control of a single authority.

Table 4-2

Milestones in the Transition to Adulthood

Life Event	Expected Age	Percentage of People Who View Event as Extremely/Quite Important
Financial independence from parents/guardians	20.9 years	80.9%
Separate residence from parents	21.1	57.2
Full-time employment	21.2	83.8
Completion of formal schooling	22.3	90.2
Capability of supporting a family	24.5	82.3
Marriage	25.7	33.2
Parenthood	26.2	29.0

Note: Based on the 2002 General Social Survey of 1,398 people.
Source: T. W. Smith 2003.

Think About It
Why did so few respondents consider marriage and parenthood to be important milestones? Which milestones do you think are most important?

Prisons are centers of resocialization, where people are placed under pressure to discard old behavior patterns and accept new ones. These prisoners are learning to use weights to release tension and exert their strength—a socially acceptable method of handling antisocial impulses.

- Any activities within the institution are conducted in the company of others in the same circumstances—for example, army recruits or novices in a convent.

- The authorities devise rules and schedule activities without consulting the participants.

- All aspects of life within a total institution are designed to fulfill the purpose of the organization. Thus, all activities in a monastery might be centered on prayer and communion with God. (Davies 1989; P. Rose et al. 1979)

People often lose their individuality within total institutions. For example, a person entering prison may experience the humiliation of a *degradation ceremony* as he or she is stripped of clothing, jewelry, and other personal possessions. From this point on, scheduled daily routines allow for little or no personal initiative. The individual becomes secondary and rather invisible in the overbearing social environment (Garfinkel 1956).

Agents of Socialization

As we have seen, the culture of the United States is defined by rather gradual movements from one stage of socialization to the next. The continuing and lifelong socialization process involves many different social forces that influence our lives and alter our self-images.

The family is the most important agent of socialization in the United States, especially for children. In this chapter, we'll also discuss six other agents of socialization: the school, the peer group, the mass media, the workplace, religion, and the state. We'll explore the role of religion in socializing young people into society's norms and values more fully in Chapter 15.

Family

Children in Amish communities are raised in a highly structured and disciplined manner. But they are not immune to the temptations posed by their peers in the non-Amish world—"rebellious" acts such as dancing, drinking, and riding in cars. Still, Amish families don't become too concerned; they know the strong influence they ultimately exert over their offspring (see Box 4-2, opposite). The same is true for the family. It is tempting to say that the "peer group" or even the "media" really raise children these days, especially when the spotlight falls on young people involved in shooting sprees and hate crimes. Almost all available research, however, shows that the role of the family in socializing a child cannot be overestimated (W. Williams 1998; for a different view see J. Harris 1998).

The lifelong process of learning begins shortly after birth. Since newborns can hear, see, smell, taste, and feel heat, cold, and pain, they are constantly orienting themselves to the surrounding world. Human beings, especially family members, constitute an important part of their social environment. People minister to the baby's needs by feeding, cleansing, carrying, and comforting the baby.

Cultural Influences As both Charles Horton Cooley and George Herbert Mead noted, the development of the self is a critical aspect of the early years of one's life. But how children develop this sense of self can vary from one society to another. For example, most parents in the United States do not send six-year-olds to school unsupervised. But that is the norm in Japan, where parents push their children to commute to school on their own from an early age. In cities like Tokyo, first-graders must learn to negotiate buses, subways, and long walks. To ensure their safety, parents carefully lay out rules: never talk to strangers; check with a station attendant if you get off at the wrong stop; if you miss your stop stay on to the end of the line, then call; take stairs, not escalators; don't fall asleep. Some parents equip the children with cell phones or pagers. One parent acknowledges that she worries, "but after they are 6, children are supposed to start being independent from the mother. If you're still taking your child to school after the first month, everyone looks at you funny" (Tolbert 2000:17).

While we consider the family's role in socialization, we need to remember that children do not play a passive role. They are active agents, influencing and altering the families, schools, and communities of which they are a part.

The Impact of Race and Gender In the United States, social development includes exposure to cultural assumptions

sociologyIN *the Global Community*

4-2 Raising Amish Children

Jacob is a typical teenager in his Amish community in Lancaster County, Pennsylvania. At 14 he is in his final year of schooling. Over the next few years he will become a full-time worker on the family farm, taking breaks only for three-hour religious services each morning. When he is a bit older, Jacob may bring a date to a community "singing" in his family's horse-drawn buggy. But he will be forbidden to date outside his own community and can marry only with the deacon's consent.

Jacob is well aware of the rather different way of life of the "English" (the Amish term for non-Amish people). One summer, late at night, he and his friends hitchhiked to a nearby town to see a movie, breaking several Amish taboos. His parents learned of his adventure, but like most Amish they are confident that their son will choose the Amish way of life. What is this way of life, and how can his parents be so sure of its appeal?

Jacob and his family live in a manner very similar to their ancestors, members of the conservative Mennonite church who migrated to North America from Europe in the 18th and 19th centuries. Schisms in the church after 1850 led to a division between those who wanted to preserve the "old order" and those who favored a "new order" with more progressive methods and organization. Today the old order Amish live in about 50 communities in the United States and Canada. Estimates put their number at about 80,000, with approximately 75 percent living in three states—Ohio, Pennsylvania, and Indiana.

The old order Amish live a simple life and reject most aspects of modernization and contemporary technology. That's why they spurn conveniences such as electricity, automobiles, radio, and television. The Amish maintain their own schools and traditions and do not want

their children socialized into many norms and values of the dominant culture of the United States. Those who stray too far from Amish mores may be excommunicated and shunned by all other members of the community—a practice of social control called *Meiding*. Sociologists sometimes use the term *secessionist minorities* to refer to groups like the Amish, who reject assimilation and coexist with the rest of society primarily on their own terms.

The socialization of Amish youths pushes them to forgo movies, radio, television, cosmetics, jewelry, musical instruments of any kind, and motorized vehicles. Yet, like Jacob did, Amish youths often test their subculture's boundaries during a period of discovery called

> The old order Amish live a simple life and reject most aspects of modernization and contemporary technology.

rumspringe, a term that means "running around." Amish young people attend barn dances where taboos like drinking, smoking, and driving cars are commonly broken. Parents often react by looking the other way, sometimes literally. For example, when they hear radio sounds from a barn or a motorcycle entering their property in the middle of the night, they don't immediately investigate and punish their offspring. Instead, they pretend not to notice, secure in the comfort that their children almost always return to the traditions of the Amish lifestyle. Research shows that only about 20 percent of Amish youths leave the fold, generally to join a more liberal Mennonite

group. Rarely does a baptized adult ever leave. The socialization of Amish youths moves them gently but firmly into becoming Amish adults.

Let's Discuss

1. What makes Amish parents so sure that their children will choose to remain in the Amish community?
2. If you lived in an Amish community, how would your life differ from the way it is now? In your opinion, what advantages and disadvantages would that lifestyle have?

Sources: Kraybill 2008; Meyers 1992; Remnick 1998; Schaefer and Zellner 2007.

---

regarding gender and race. African American parents, for example, have learned that children as young as two years old can absorb negative messages about Blacks in children's books, toys, and television shows—all of which are designed primarily for White consumers. At the same time, African American children are exposed more often than others to the inner-city youth gang culture. Because most Blacks, even those who are middle class, live near very poor neighborhoods, children such as Charisse (see the chapter-opening excerpt) are susceptible to these influ-

ences, despite their parents' strong family values (Linn and Poussaint 1999; Pattillo-McCoy 1999).

The term **gender roles** refers to expectations regarding the proper behavior, attitudes, and activities of males and females. For example, we traditionally think of "toughness" as masculine—and desirable only in men—while we view "tenderness" as feminine. As we will see in Chapter 12, other cultures do not necessarily assign these qualities to each gender in the way that our culture does.

In her Michigan home, a young girl displays Razanne, a modestly dressed doll made especially for Muslim children. Because girls learn about themselves and their social roles by playing with dolls, having a doll that represents their own heritage is important to them.

As the primary agents of childhood socialization, parents play a critical role in guiding children into those gender roles deemed appropriate in a society. Other adults, older siblings, the mass media, and religious and educational institutions also have a noticeable impact on a child's socialization into feminine and masculine norms. A culture or subculture may require that one sex or the other take primary responsibility for the socialization of children, economic support of the family, or religious or intellectual leadership. In some societies, girls are socialized mainly by their mothers and boys by their fathers—an arrangement that may prevent girls from learning critical survival skills. In South Asia, fathers teach their sons to swim to prepare them for a life as fishermen; girls typically do not learn to swim. When a deadly tsunami hit the coast of South Asia in 2004, many more men survived than women.

Interactionists remind us that socialization concerning not only masculinity and femininity but also marriage and parenthood begins in childhood as a part of family life. Children ob-

serve their parents as they express affection, deal with finances, quarrel, complain about in-laws, and so forth. Their learning represents an informal process of anticipatory socialization in which they develop a tentative model of what being married and being a parent are like. (We will explore socialization for marriage and parenthood more fully in Chapter 14.)

School

Where did you learn the national anthem? Who taught you about the heroes of the American Revolution? Where were you first tested on your knowledge of your culture? Like the family, schools have an explicit mandate to socialize people in the United States—and especially children—into the norms and values of our culture.

As conflict theorists Samuel Bowles and Herbert Gintis (1976) have observed, schools in this country foster competition through built-in systems of reward and punishment, such as grades and evaluations by teachers. Consequently, a child who is experiencing difficulty trying to learn a new skill can sometimes come to feel stupid and unsuccessful. However, as the self matures, children become capable of increasingly realistic assessments of their intellectual, physical, and social abilities.

Functionalists point out that schools, as agents of socialization, fulfill the function of teaching children the values and customs of the larger society. Conflict theorists agree, but add that schools can reinforce the divisive aspects of society, especially those of social class. For example, higher education in the United States is costly despite the existence of financial aid programs. Students from affluent backgrounds therefore have an advantage in gaining access to universities and professional training. At the same time, less affluent young people may never receive the preparation that would qualify them for the best-paying and most prestigious jobs. The contrast between the functionalist and conflict views of education will be discussed in more detail in Chapter 16.

In other cultures as well, schools serve socialization functions. Until the overthrow of Saddam Hussein in 2003, the sixth-grade textbooks used in Iraqi schools concentrated almost entirely on the military and its values of loyalty, honor, and sacrifice. Children were taught that their enemies were Iran, the United States, Israel and its supporters, and NATO, the European military alliance. Within months of the regime's fall, the curriculum had been rewritten to remove indoctrination on behalf of Hussein, his army, and his Baath Socialist Party (Marr 2003).

Peer Group

Ask 13-year-olds who matters most in their lives and they are likely to answer "friends." As a child grows older, the family becomes somewhat less important in social development. Instead, peer groups increasingly assume the role of Mead's significant others. Within the peer group, young people associate with others who are approximately their own age, and who often enjoy a similar social status (Giordano 2003).

We can see how important peer groups are to young people when their social lives are strained by war or disaster. In Bagh-

Rakefet Avramovitz
**Program Administrator,
Child Care Law Center**

Rakefet Avramovitz has been working at the Child Care Law Center in San Francisco since 2003. The center uses legal tools to foster the development of quality, affordable child care, with the goal of expanding child care options, particularly for low-income families. As a support person for the center's attorneys, Avramovitz manages grants, oversees the center's publications, and sets up conferences and training sessions. One of her most important tasks has been to organize a working group that brings together people from all parts of the child care community. "The documents that come out of this forum inform the organization's work for the year," she explains.

Avramovitz graduated from Dickinson College in 2000. She first became interested in sociology when she took a social analysis course. Though she enjoyed her qualitative courses most, she found her quantitative courses fun, "in that we got to do surveys of people on campus. I've always enjoyed fieldwork," she notes. Avramovitz's most memorable course was one that gave her the opportunity to interact with migrant farm workers for an entire semester. "I learned ethnography and how to work with people of different cultures. It changed my life," she says.

Avramovitz finds that the skills she learned in her sociology courses are a great help to her on the job. "Sociology taught me how to work with people . . . and how to think critically. It taught me how to listen and find the stories that people are telling," she explains. Before joining the Child Care Law Center, Avramovitz worked as a counselor for women who were facing difficult issues. "My background in ethnography helped me to talk to these women and listen effectively," she notes. "I was able to help many women by understanding and being able to express their needs to the attorneys we worked with."

Avramovitz is enthusiastic about her work and her ability to make a difference in other people's lives. Maybe that is why she looks forward to summer at the center, when the staff welcomes several law students as interns. "It is really neat to see people learn and get jazzed about child care issues," she says.

Let's Discuss

1. What might be some of the broad, long-term effects of the center's work to expand child care options? Explain.
2. Besides the law, what other professions might benefit from the skills a sociology major has to offer?

dad, the overthrow of Saddam Hussein has profoundly changed teenagers' world, casting doubt on their future. Some young people have lost relatives or friends; others have become involved with fundamentalist groups or fled with their families to safer countries. Those youths who are left behind can suffer intense loneliness and boredom. Confined to their homes by crime and terrorism, those fortunate enough to have computers turn to Internet chat rooms or immerse themselves in their studies. Through e-mail, they struggle to maintain old friendships interrupted by wartime dislocation (Sanders 2004).

Gender differences are noteworthy among adolescents. Boys and girls are socialized by their parents, peers, and the media to identify many of the same paths to popularity, but to different degrees. Table 4-3 on page 100 compares male and female college students' reports of how girls and boys they knew became popular in high school. The two groups named many of the same paths to popularity but gave them a different order of importance. While neither men nor women named sexual activity, drug use, or alcohol use as one of the top five paths, college men were much more likely than women to mention those behaviors as a means to becoming popular, for both boys and girls.

Mass Media and Technology

In the last 80 years, media innovations—radio, motion pictures, recorded music, television, and the Internet—have become important agents of socialization. Television, and increasingly the Internet, are critical forces in the socialization of children in the United States. One national survey indicates that 68 percent of U.S. children have a television in their bedroom, and nearly half of all youths ages 8 to 18 use the Internet every day (see Figure 4-2, page 100).

These media, however, are not always a negative socializing influence. Television programs and even commercials can introduce young people to unfamiliar lifestyles and cultures. Not only do children in the United States learn about life in "faraway lands," but inner-city children learn about the lives of farm children, and vice versa. The same thing happens in other countries.

Sociologists and other social scientists have also begun to consider the impact of technology on socialization, especially as it applies to family life. The Silicon Valley Cultures Project studied families in California's Silicon Valley (a technological corridor) for 10 years, beginning in 1991. Although these families may not be typical, they represent a lifestyle that more

High School Popularity

What makes high school girls popular?		What makes high school boys popular?	
According to college men:	According to college women:	According to college men:	According to college women:
1. Physical attractiveness	1. Grades/intelligence	1. Participation in sports	1. Participation in sports
2. Grades/intelligence	2. Participation in sports	2. Grades/intelligence	2. Grades/intelligence
3. Participation in sports	3. General sociability	3. Popularity with girls	3. General sociability
4. General sociability	4. Physical attractiveness	4. General sociability	4. Physical attractiveness
5. Popularity with boys	5. Clothes	5. Car	5. School clubs/government

Note: Students at the following universities were asked in which ways adolescents in their high schools had gained prestige with their peers: Cornell University, Louisiana State University, Southeastern Louisiana University, State University of New York at Albany, State University of New York at Stony Brook, University of Georgia, and the University of New Hampshire.
Source: Suitor et al. 2001:445.

and more households probably will approximate as time goes by. This study has found that technology in the form of e-mail, Web pages, cellular phones, voice mail, digital organizers, and pagers is allowing householders to let outsiders do everything from grocery shopping to carpooling. The researchers are also finding that families are socialized into multitasking (doing more than one task at a time) as the social norm; devoting one's full attention to one task—even eating or driving—is less and less common on a typical day (Silicon Valley Cultures Project 2004).

Not just in Silicon Valley, but in Africa and other developing areas, people have been socialized into relying on new commu-

nications technologies. Not long ago, if Zadhe Iyombe wanted to talk to his mother, he had to make an eight-day trip from the capital city of Kinshasa up the Congo River by boat to the rural town where he was born. Now both he and his mother have access to a cell phone, and they send text messages to each other daily. Iyombe and his mother are not atypical. Although cell phones aren't cheap, 1.4 billion owners in developing countries have come to consider them a necessity. Today, there are more cell phones in developing countries than in industrial nations— the first time in history that developing countries have outpaced the developed world in the adoption of a telecommunications technology (K. Sullivan 2006).

FIGURE 4-2

How Young People Use the Media on a Typical Day

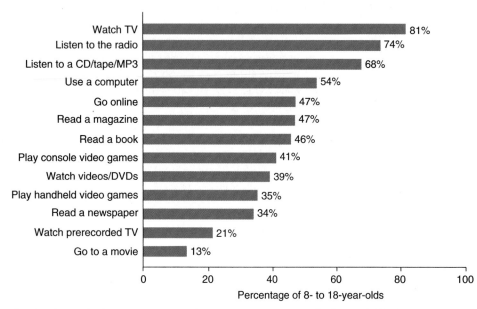

Watch TV	81%
Listen to the radio	74%
Listen to a CD/tape/MP3	68%
Use a computer	54%
Go online	47%
Read a magazine	47%
Read a book	46%
Play console video games	41%
Watch videos/DVDs	39%
Play handheld video games	35%
Read a newspaper	34%
Watch prerecorded TV	21%
Go to a movie	13%

Percentage of 8- to 18-year-olds

Note: Based on a national representative sample of 2,032 people surveyed between October 2003 and March 2004.
Source: Rideout et al. 2005:7.

Workplace

Learning to behave appropriately in an occupation is a fundamental aspect of human socialization. In the United States, working full-time confirms adult status; it indicates that one has passed out of adolescence. In a sense, socialization into an occupation can represent both a harsh reality ("I have to work in order to buy food and pay the rent") and the realization of an ambition ("I've always wanted to be an airline pilot") (W. Moore 1968:862).

It used to be that going to work began with the end of our formal schooling, but that is no longer the case, at least not in the United States. More and more young people work today, and not just for a parent or relative. Adolescents generally seek jobs in order to make spending money; 80 percent of high school seniors say that little or none of what they earn goes to family expenses. These teens rarely look on their employment as a means of exploring vocational interests or getting on-the-job training.

Some observers feel that the increasing number of teenagers who are working earlier in life and for longer hours are finding the workplace almost as important an agent of socialization as school. In fact, a number of educators complain that student time at work is adversely affecting schoolwork. The level of teenage employment in the United States is the highest among industrial countries, which may provide one explanation for why U.S. high school students lag behind those in other countries on international achievement tests.

Socialization in the workplace changes when it involves a more permanent shift from an after-school job to full-time employment. Occupational socialization can be most intense during the transition from school to job, but it continues throughout one's work history. Technological advances may alter the requirements of the position and necessitate some degree of resocialization. Today, men and women change occupations, employers, or places of work many times during their adult years. Occupational socialization continues, then, throughout a person's years in the labor market.

College students today recognize that occupational socialization is not socialization into one lifetime occupation. They anticipate going through a number of jobs. The Bureau of Labor Statistics (2006b) has found that from ages 18 to 40, the typical person holds 11 different jobs. This high rate of turnover in employment applies to both men and women, and to those with a college degree as well as those with a high school diploma.

Religion and the State

Increasingly, social scientists are recognizing the importance of both government ("the state") and religion as agents of socialization, because of their impact on the life course. Traditionally, family members have served as the primary caregivers in our culture, but in the 20th century, the family's protective function was steadily transferred to outside agencies such as hospitals, mental health clinics, and child care centers. Many of these agencies are run by the state or by groups affiliated with certain religions.

Both government and organized religion have impacted the life course by reinstituting some of the rites of passage once observed in agricultural communities and early industrial societies. For example, religious organizations stipulate certain traditional rites that may bring together all the members of

This girl's day doesn't end when school lets out. So many teenagers now work after school, the workplace has become another important agent of socialization for adolescents.

an extended family, even if they never meet for any other reason. And government regulations stipulate the ages at which a person may drive a car, drink alcohol, vote in elections, marry without parental permission, work overtime, and retire. These regulations do not constitute strict rites of passage: most 18-year-olds choose not to vote, and most people choose their age of retirement without reference to government dictates.

In the Social Policy section that follows, we will see that government is under pressure to become a provider of child care, which would give it a new and direct role in the socialization of infants and young children.

Use Your Sociological Imagination

You are Muslim (or another religion that is different from your own). How does your self-concept differ from the one you developed as a child?

socialPolicy
and Socialization

Child Care around the World

In Israel, Aisheh and Eliza run a nursery for 29 Israeli and Palestinian children, ages 4 to 6. Aisheh, who is Palestinian, speaks to the children in Arabic. Eliza, who is Jewish, speaks to them in Hebrew. The result: a bilingual, binational classroom that supports both Arab and Jewish culture—a first for Israel.

This unusual educational setting underscores the importance of early childhood socialization outside the home. Child care programs are not just babysitting services; they have an enormous influence on the development of young children—an influence that has been growing with the movement of more and more women into the paid labor force.

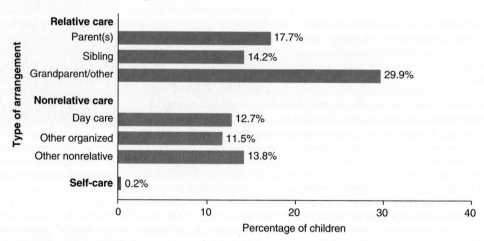

FIGURE 4–3

Child Care Arrangements for Preschoolers

Note: Data for 2002, reported in 2005.
Source: Julia Johnson 2005:2.

The Issue

The rise in single-parent families, increased job opportunities for women, and the need for additional family income have all propelled an increasing number of mothers of young children into the paid labor force of the United States. Who takes care of the children of these women during work hours?

Preschoolers typically are not cared for by their parents. Seventy-three percent of employed mothers depend on others to care for their children, and 30 percent of mothers who aren't employed have regular care arrangements. As Figure 4-3 shows, children under age 5 are more likely to be cared for on a daily basis by their grandparents than by their parents. Over a third of these children are cared for by nonrelatives in nursery schools, Head Start programs, day care centers, family day care, and other arrangements.

The Setting

Few people in the United States or elsewhere can afford the luxury of having a parent stay at home, or of paying for high-quality live-in child care. For millions of mothers and fathers, finding the right kind of child care is a challenge both to parenting and to the pocketbook.

Researchers have found that high-quality child care centers do not adversely affect the socialization of children; in fact, good day care benefits children. The value of preschool programs was documented in a series of studies conducted in the United States. Researchers found no significant differences in infants

who had received extensive nonmaternal care compared with those who had been cared for solely by their mothers. They also reported that more and more infants in the United States are being placed in child care outside the home, and that overall, the quality of those arrangements is better than has been found in previous studies. It is difficult, however, to generalize about child care, since there is so much variability among day care providers, and even among policies from one state to another (Kirp 2004; Loeb et al. 2004; NICHD 1998).

Sociological Insights

Studies that assess the quality of child care outside the home reflect the micro level of analysis and the interest of interactionists in the impact of face-to-face interaction. These studies also explore macro-level implications for the functioning of social institutions like the family. But some of the issues surrounding day care have also been of interest to those who take the conflict perspective.

In the United States, high-quality day care is not equally available to all families. Parents in wealthy neighborhoods have an easier time finding day care than those in poor or working-class communities. Finding *affordable* child care is also a problem. Viewed from a conflict perspective, child care costs are an especially serious burden for lower-class families. The poorest families spend 25 percent of their income for preschool child care, while families who are *not* poor pay only 6 percent or less of their income.

Feminist theorists echo the concern of conflict theorists that high-quality child care receives little government support because it is regarded as "merely a way to let women work." Nearly all child care workers (95 percent) are women; many find themselves in low-status, minimum-wage jobs. Typically, food servers, messengers, and gas station attendants make more money than the 1.2 million child care workers in the United States, half of whom earn less than $8.70 per hour. Not surprisingly, turnover among employees in child care centers runs at about 30 percent per year (Bureau of the Census 2006a:390; NACCRRA 2007; Clawson and Gerstel 2002).

Policy Initiatives

Policies regarding child care outside the home vary throughout the world. As Figure 4-4 shows, the cost of child care as a proportion of one's income can vary dramatically, but at least it is available in industrial nations. Most developing nations do not have the economic base to provide subsidized child care. Thus, working mothers rely largely on relatives or take their children to work. In the comparatively wealthy industrialized countries of Western Europe, government provides child care as a basic service, at little or no expense to parents. But even those countries with tax-subsidized programs occasionally fall short of the need for high-quality child care.

When policymakers decide that child care is desirable, they must determine the degree to which taxpayers should subsidize it. In Sweden and Denmark, one-third to one-half of children under age three were in government-subsidized child care full-time in 2001. In the United States, where government subsidies are very limited, the total cost of child care can easily run between $9,100 and $13,200 per family per year (NACCRRA 2007:2).

Children play at the Communicare day care center in Perth, Australia. The Australian government subsidizes children's attendance at day care and after-school programs from birth to age 12.

FIGURE 4–4

Child Care Costs in Industrial Nations

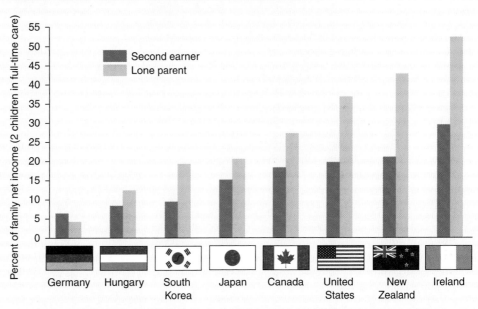

Source: Data collected by the Organisation for Economic Co-operation and Development (OECD) in 2002 and reported in Immervoll 2006.

We have a long way to go in making high-quality child care more affordable and accessible, not just in the United States but throughout the world. In an attempt to reduce government spending, France is considering cutting back the budgets of sub-sidized nurseries, even though waiting lists exist and the French public heartily disapproves of cutbacks. In Germany, reunification has reduced the options previously open to East German mothers, who had become accustomed to government-supported child care. Experts in child development view such reports as a vivid reminder of the need for greater government and private-sector support for child care (Hank 2001; L. King 1998).

Let's Discuss

1. Were you ever in a day care program? Do you recall the experience as good or bad? In general, do you think it is desirable to expose young children to the socializing influence of day care?

2. In the view of conflict theorists, child care receives little government support because it is "merely a way to let women work." Can you think of other explanations?

3. Should the costs of day care programs be paid by government, by the private sector, or entirely by parents?

GettingINVOLVED

To get involved in the debate over day care, visit this text's Online Learning Center, which offers links to relevant Web sites. Check out the Social Policy section on the Online Learning Center as well; it provides survey data on U.S. public opinion regarding this issue.

www.mhhe.com/schaefer11

{ **MASTERING THIS CHAPTER** }

Summary

Socialization is the process through which people learn the attitudes, values, and actions appropriate for members of a particular culture. This chapter examined the role of socialization in human development; the way in which people develop perceptions, feelings, and beliefs about themselves; the lifelong nature of the socialization process; and the important agents of socialization.

1. **Socialization** affects the overall cultural practices of a society; it also shapes the images that we hold of ourselves.

2. Heredity and environmental factors interact in influencing the socialization process.

3. In the early 1900s, Charles Horton Cooley advanced the belief that we learn who we are by interacting with others, a phenomenon he called the **looking-glass self.**

4. George Herbert Mead, best known for his theory of the **self,** proposed that as people mature, their selves begin to reflect their concern about reactions from others—both **generalized others** and **significant others.**

5. Erving Goffman has shown that in many of our daily activities, we try to convey distinct impressions of who we are, a process called **impression management.**

6. Socialization proceeds throughout the life course. Some societies mark stages of development with formal **rites of passage.** In the cul-

ture of the United States, significant events such as marriage and parenthood serve to change a person's status.

7. As the primary agents of socialization, parents play a critical role in guiding children into those **gender roles** deemed appropriate in a society.

8. Like the family, schools in the United States have an explicit mandate to socialize people—especially children—into the norms and values of our culture.

9. Peer groups and the mass media, especially television, are important agents of socialization for adolescents.

10. Socialization in the workplace begins with part-time employment while we are in school and continues as we work full-time and change jobs throughout our lives.

11. Religion and the state shape the socialization process by regulating the life course and influencing our views of appropriate behavior at particular ages.

12. As more and more mothers of young children have entered the labor market, the demand for child care has increased dramatically, posing policy questions for many nations around the world.

Critical Thinking Questions

1. Should social research be conducted on issues such as the influence of heredity and environment, even though many investigators believe that this type of analysis is potentially detrimental to large numbers of people?

2. Drawing on Erving Goffman's dramaturgical approach, discuss how the following groups engage in impression management: athletes, college instructors, parents, physicians, and politicians.

3. How would functionalists and conflict theorists differ in their analysis of socialization by the mass media?

Key Terms

Anticipatory socialization Processes of socialization in which a person "rehearses" for future positions, occupations, and social relationships. (page 95)

Cognitive theory of development The theory that children's thought progresses through four stages of development. (93)

Degradation ceremony An aspect of the socialization process within some total institutions, in which people are subjected to humiliating rituals. (96)

Dramaturgical approach A view of social interaction in which people are seen as theatrical performers. (91)

Face-work The efforts people make to maintain the proper image and avoid public embarrassment. (91)

Gender role Expectations regarding the proper behavior, attitudes, and activities of males and females. (97)

Generalized other The attitudes, viewpoints, and expectations of society as a whole that a child takes into account in his or her behavior. (90)

Impression management The altering of the presentation of the self in order to create distinctive appearances and satisfy particular audiences. (91)

Life course approach A research orientation in which sociologists and other social scientists look closely at the social factors that influence people throughout their lives, from birth to death. (94)

Looking-glass self A concept that emphasizes the self as the product of our social interactions. (89)

Personality A person's typical patterns of attitudes, needs, characteristics, and behavior. (86)

Resocialization The process of discarding former behavior patterns and accepting new ones as part of a transition in one's life. (95)

Rite of passage A ritual marking the symbolic transition from one social position to another. (93)

Role taking The process of mentally assuming the perspective of another and responding from that imagined viewpoint. (90)

Self A distinct identity that sets us apart from others. (89)

Significant other An individual who is most important in the development of the self, such as a parent, friend, or teacher. (91)

Socialization The lifelong process in which people learn the attitudes, values, and behaviors appropriate for members of a particular culture. (86)

Symbol A gesture, object, or word that forms the basis of human communication. (89)

Total institution An institution that regulates all aspects of a person's life under a single authority, such as a prison, the military, a mental hospital, or a convent. (95)

Self-Quiz

Read each question carefully and then select the best answer.

1. Which of the following social scientists used the phrase *looking-glass self* to emphasize that the self is the product of our social interactions with other people?
   a. George Herbert Mead
   b. Charles Horton Cooley
   c. Erving Goffman
   d. Jean Piaget

2. In what he called the *play stage* of socialization, George Herbert Mead asserted that people mentally assume the perspectives of others, thereby enabling them to respond from that imagined viewpoint. This process is referred to as
   a. role taking.
   b. the generalized other.
   c. the significant other.
   d. impression management.

3. George Herbert Mead is best known for his theory of what?
   a. presentation of the self
   b. cognitive development
   c. the self
   d. impression management

4. Suppose a clerk tries to appear busier than he or she actually is when a supervisor happens to be watching. Erving Goffman would study this behavior from what approach?
   a. functionalist
   b. conflict
   c. psychological
   d. interactionist

5. According to child psychologist Jean Piaget's cognitive theory of development, children begin to use words and symbols to distinguish objects and ideas during which stage in the development of the thought process?

   a. the sensorimotor stage
   b. the preoperational stage
   c. the concrete operational stage
   d. the formal operational stage

6. On the first day of basic training in the army, a recruit has his civilian clothes replaced with army "greens," has his hair shaved off, loses his privacy, and finds that he must use a communal bathroom. All these humiliating activities are part of

   a. becoming a significant other.
   b. impression management.
   c. a degradation ceremony.
   d. face-work.

7. Which social institution is considered to be the most important agent of socialization in the United States, especially for children?

   a. the family
   b. the school
   c. the peer group
   d. the mass media

8. The term *gender role* refers to

   a. the biological fact that we are male or female.
   b. a role that is given to us by a teacher.
   c. a role that is given to us in a play.
   d. expectations regarding the proper behavior, attitudes, and activities of males and females.

9. Which sociological perspective emphasizes that schools in the United States foster competition through built-in systems of reward and punishment?

   a. the functionalist perspective
   b. the conflict perspective
   c. the interactionist perspective
   d. the psychological perspective

10. Which of the following statements about teenagers in Baghdad is true?

   a. They have lost much of their peer group due to death and relocation.
   b. They have lost peers who have joined fundamentalist groups.
   c. If they own a computer, they use it in an attempt to stay in contact with their pre-war peer group.
   d. all of the above

11. _____ is the term used by sociologists in referring to the lifelong process whereby people learn the attitudes, values, and behaviors appropriate for members of a particular culture.

12. In everyday speech, the term _____ is used to refer to a person's typical patterns of attitudes, needs, characteristics, and behavior.

13. Studies of twins raised apart suggest that both _____ and _____ influence human development.

14. _____ are gestures, objects, and/or words that form the basis of human communication.

15. Those individuals who are most important in shaping a person's identity (e.g., parents, friends, co-workers, coaches, and teachers) are referred to as _____ _____.

16. Early work in _____, such as that by Sigmund Freud, stressed the role of inborn drives—among them the drive for sexual gratification—in channeling human behavior.

17. Preparation for many aspects of adult life begins with _____ socialization during childhood and adolescence and continues throughout our lives as we prepare for new responsibilities.

18. Resocialization is particularly effective when it occurs within a(n) _____ institution.

19. The _____ perspective emphasizes the role of schools in teaching the values and customs of the larger society.

20. As children grow older, the family becomes less important in social development, while _____ groups become more important.

Answers:
1 (b); 2 (a); 3 (c); 4 (d); 5 (b); 6 (c); 7 (a); 8 (d); 9 (b); 10 (d); 11 Socialization; 12 personality; 13 heredity, environment; 14 Symbols; 15 significant others; 16 psychology; 17 anticipatory; 18 total; 19 functionalist; 20 peer

Online Learning Center

1. The rise in single-parent families, increased job opportunities for women, and the need for additional family income have combined to propel more and more mothers of young children into the paid labor force. In the Social Policy exercise for this chapter in the Online Learning Center (**www.mhhe.com/schaefer11**) you can read about the controversies surrounding child care and working mothers.

2. Though cases in which children grow up with limited human contact are tragic, they provide valuable and fascinating information about the importance of childhood socialization. FeralChildren.com (**www.feralchildren.com/en/index.php**) provides extensive information on a number of such children.

3. Parents are a key agent of socialization. The National Fatherhood Initiative (**www.fatherhood.org**) is an organization whose purpose is to educate fathers about their crucial role in socializing their children. Explore this site to learn more about the organization's efforts.

*Note: Although all the URLs listed were current as of the printing of this book, these sites often change. Please check our Web site (**www.mhhe.com/schaefer11**) for updates, hyperlinks, and exercises related to these sites.*

Reel Society Video Clips

Reel Society video clips, which appear on this book's Web site, can be used to spark discussion about the following topic from this chapter:

- Agents of Socialization

"THE BEST PLACE TO FIND A HELPING HAND IS AT THE END OF YOUR OWN ARM."

the power of **FIVE**

Lend your helping hand to kids in your community

Fulfill the 5 Promises

1. Be somebody's buddy
2. Where to be after 3
3. Be health smart
4. Use what you know
5. Make a move

YOU HAVE THE POWER TO MAKE A DIFFERENCE!

Please visit www.americaspromise.org for more information.

WEEKLY READER.

AMERICA'S PROMISE
THE ALLIANCE FOR YOUTH®

© 2002 America's Promise – The Alliance for Youth®. Created by Weekly Reader.

Social interaction is critical to society; without it, there is no shared sense of meaning or purpose. This poster, sponsored by the nonprofit group America's Promise, encourages people to reach out to the youths in their community.

5

Social Interaction and Social Structure

"The quiet of a summer Sunday morning in Palo Alto, California, was shattered by a screeching squad car siren as police swept through the city picking up college students in a surprise mass arrest. Each suspect was charged with a felony, warned of his constitutional rights, spread-eagled against the car, searched, handcuffed and carted off in the back seat of the squad car to the police station for booking.

After being fingerprinted and having identification forms prepared for his "jacket" (central information file), each prisoner was left isolated in a detention cell to wonder what he had done to get himself into this mess. After a while, he was blindfolded and transported to the "Stanford County Prison." Here he began the induction process of becoming a prisoner—stripped naked, skin searched, deloused, and issued a uniform, bedding, soap and towel. By late afternoon when nine such arrests had been completed, these youthful "first offenders" sat in dazed silence on the cots in their barren cells. These men were part of a very unusual kind of prison, an experimental or mock prison, created by social psychologists for the purpose of intensively studying the effects of imprisonment upon volunteer research subjects. When we planned our two-week-long simulation of prison life, we were primarily concerned about understanding the process by which people adapt to the novel and alien environment in which those called "prisoners" lose their liberty, civil rights, independence and privacy, while those called "guards" gain social power by accepting the responsibility for controlling and managing the lives of their dependent charges. . . .

Our final sample of participants (10 prisoners and 11 guards) were selected from over 75 volunteers recruited through ads in the city and campus newspapers. . . . Half were randomly assigned to role-play being guards, the others to be prisoners. Thus, there were no measurable differences between the guards and the prisoners at the start of this experiment. . . .

At the end of only six days we had to close down our mock prison because what we saw was frightening. It was no longer apparent to most of the subjects (or to us) where reality ended and their roles began. The majority had indeed become prisoners or guards, no longer able to clearly differentiate between role playing and self. There were dramatic changes in virtually every aspect of their behavior, thinking and feeling. In less than a week the experience of imprisonment undid (temporarily) a lifetime of learning; human values were suspended, self-concepts were challenged and the ugliest, most base, pathological side of human nature surfaced. We were horrified because we saw some boys (guards) treat others as if they were despicable animals, taking pleasure in cruelty, while other boys (prisoners) became servile, dehumanized robots who thought only of escape, of their own individual survival, and of their mounting hatred for the guards."

> *The quiet of a summer Sunday morning in Palo Alto, California, was shattered by a screeching squad car siren as police swept through the city picking up college students in a surprise mass arrest.*

(Zimbardo 1972:4; Zimbardo et al. 1974:61, 62, 63) Additional information about this excerpt can be found on the Online Learning Center at www.mhhe.com/schaefer11.

In this study directed and described by social psychologist Philip Zimbardo, college students adopted the patterns of social interaction expected of guards and prisoners when they were placed in a mock prison. Sociologists use the term *social interaction* to refer to the ways in which people respond to one another, whether face to face or over the telephone or on the computer. In the mock prison, social interactions between guards and prisoners were highly impersonal. The guards addressed the prisoners by number rather than name, and they wore reflective sunglasses that made eye contact impossible.

As in many real-life prisons, the simulated prison at Stanford University had a social structure in which guards held virtually total control over prisoners. The term *social structure* refers to the way in which a society is organized into predictable relationships. The social structure of Zimbardo's mock prison influenced how the guards and prisoners interacted. Zimbardo and his colleagues (2003:546) note that it was a real prison "in the minds of the jailers and their captives." His simulated prison experiment, first conducted more than 30 years ago, has subsequently been repeated (with similar findings) both in the United States and in other countries.

Zimbardo's experiment took on new relevance in 2004, in the wake of shocking revelations of prisoner abuse at the U.S.-run Abu Ghraib military facility in Iraq. Graphic photos showed U.S. soldiers humiliating naked Iraqi prisoners and threatening to attack them with police dogs. The structure of the wartime prison, coupled with intense pressure on military intelligence officers to secure information regarding terrorist plots, contributed to the breakdown in the guards' behavior.

But Zimbardo himself noted that the guards' depraved conduct could have been predicted simply on the basis of his research (Zarembo 2004; Zimbardo 2004, 2005, 2007).

The two concepts of social interaction and social structure are central to sociological study. They are closely related to socialization (see Chapter 4), the process through which people learn the attitudes, values, and behaviors appropriate to their culture. When the students in Zimbardo's experiment entered the mock prison, they began a process of resocialization. In that process, they adjusted to a new social structure and learned new rules for social interaction.

In this chapter we will study social structure and its effect on our social interactions. What determines a person's status in society? How do our social roles affect our social interactions? What is the place of social institutions such as the family, religion, and government in our social structure? We'll begin by considering how social interactions shape the way we view the world around us. Next, we'll focus on the five basic elements of social structure: statuses, social roles, groups, social networks, and social institutions such as the family, religion, and government. We'll see that functionalists, conflict theorists, and interactionists approach these institutions quite differently. Finally, we'll compare our modern social structure with simpler forms, using typologies developed by Émile Durkheim, Ferdinand Tönnies, and Gerhard Lenski. The Social Policy section at the end of the chapter focuses on how the Internet has changed our social interactions.

Social Interaction and Reality

When someone in a crowd shoves you, do you automatically push back? Or do you consider the circumstances of the incident and the attitude of the instigator before you react? Chances are you do the latter. According to sociologist Herbert Blumer (1969:79), the distinctive characteristic of social interaction among people is that "human beings interpret or 'define' each other's actions instead of merely reacting to each other's actions." In other words, our response to someone's behavior is based on the *meaning* we attach to his or her actions. Reality is shaped by our perceptions, evaluations, and definitions.

These meanings typically reflect the norms and values of the dominant culture and our socialization experiences within that culture. As interactionists emphasize, the meanings that we attach to people's behavior are shaped by our interactions with them and with the larger society. Social reality is literally constructed from our social interactions (Berger and Luckmann 1966).

How do we define our social reality? Consider something as simple as how we regard tattoos. At one time, most of us in the United States considered tattoos weird or kooky. We associated them with fringe countercultural groups, such as punk rockers, biker gangs, and skinheads. Among many people, a tattoo elicited an automatic negative response. Now, however, so many people have tattoos—including society's trendsetters and major sports figures—and the ritual of getting a tattoo has become so legitimized, that mainstream culture regards tattoos differently. At this point, as a result of increased social interaction with tattooed people, tattoos look perfectly at home to us in a number of settings.

The ability to define social reality reflects a group's power within a society. In fact, one of the most crucial aspects of the relationship between dominant and subordinate groups is the ability of the dominant or majority group to define a society's values. Sociologist William I. Thomas (1923), an early critic of theories of racial and gender differences, recognized that the "definition of the situation" could mold the thinking and personality of the individual. Writing from an interactionist perspective, Thomas observed that people respond not only to the objective features of a person or situation but also to the *meaning* that person or situation has for them. For example, in Philip Zimbardo's mock prison experiment, student "guards" and "prisoners" accepted the definition of the situation (including the traditional roles and behavior associated with being a guard or prisoner) and acted accordingly.

As we have seen throughout the last 50 years—first in the civil rights movement of the 1960s and since then among such groups as women, the elderly, gays and lesbians, and people with disabilities—an important aspect of the process of social change involves redefining or reconstructing social reality. Members of subordinate groups challenge traditional definitions and begin to perceive and experience reality in a new way. For example, the world champion boxer Muhammad Ali began his career as the creation of a White male syndicate, which sponsored his early matches when he was known as Cassius Clay. Soon, however, the young boxer rebelled against those who would keep him or his race down. He broke the old stereotypes of the self-effacing

Symbols of status and power, such as this judge's robes, tend to reinforce the position of the dominant groups in society. When such symbols are associated with a member of a racial minority, they challenge prevailing racial stereotypes, changing what the interactionist William I. Thomas called "the definition of the situation."

Black athlete, insisting on his own political views (including refusing to serve in the Vietnam War), his own religion (Black Muslim), and his own name (Muhammad Ali). Not only did Ali change the world of sports; he also helped to alter the world of race relations. Viewed from a sociological perspective, then, Ali was redefining social reality by rebelling against the racist thinking and terminology that restricted him and other African Americans.

Elements of Social Structure

All social interaction takes place within a social structure, including those interactions that redefine social reality. For purposes of study, we can break down any social structure into five elements: statuses, social roles, groups, social networks, and social institutions. These elements make up social structure just as a foundation, walls, and ceilings make up a building's structure. The elements of social structure are developed through the lifelong process of socialization described in Chapter 4.

Statuses

We normally think of a person's "status" as having to do with influence, wealth, and fame. However, sociologists use the term *status* to refer to any of the full range of socially defined positions within a large group or society, from the lowest to the highest. Within our society, a person can occupy the status of president of the United States, fruit picker, son or daughter, violinist, teenager, resident of Minneapolis, dental technician, or neighbor. A person can hold a number of statuses at the same time.

Ascribed and Achieved Status Sociologists view some statuses as *ascribed* and others as *achieved* (see Figure 5-1, page 112). An ***ascribed status*** is assigned to a person by society without regard for the person's unique talents or characteristics. Generally, the assignment takes place at birth; thus, a person's racial background, gender, and age are all considered ascribed statuses. Though these characteristics are biological in origin, they are significant mainly because of the *social* meanings they have in our culture. Conflict theorists are especially interested in ascribed statuses, since they often confer privileges or reflect a person's membership in a subordinate group. The social meanings of race and ethnicity, gender, and age will be analyzed more fully in Chapters 11–13.

In most cases, we can do little to change an ascribed status. But we can attempt to change the traditional constraints associated with such statuses. For example, the Gray Panthers—an activist political group founded in 1971 to work for the rights of older people—have tried to modify society's negative and confining stereotypes of the elderly (see Chapter 13). As a result of their work and that of other groups supporting older citizens, the ascribed status of "senior citizen" is no longer as difficult for millions of older people.

An ascribed status does not necessarily have the same social meaning in every society. In a cross-cultural study, sociologist

Social Statuses

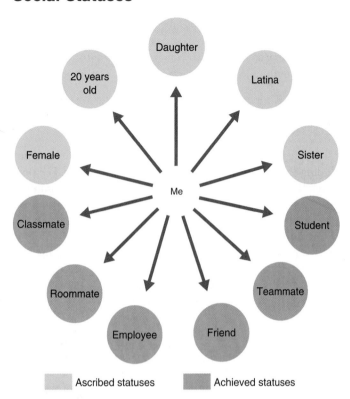

Daughter

Latina

20 years old

Sister

Female

Me

Student

Classmate

Teammate

Roommate

Friend

Employee

Ascribed statuses   Achieved statuses

Think About It

The young woman in this figure—"me"—occupies many positions in society, each of which involves distinct statuses. How would you define your statuses? Which have the most influence in your life?

Gary Huang (1988) confirmed the long-held view that respect for the elderly is an important cultural norm in China. In many cases, the prefix "old" is used respectfully: calling someone "old teacher" or "old person" is like calling a judge in the United States "your honor." Huang points out that positive age-seniority language distinctions are uncommon in the United States; consequently, we view the term *old man* as more of an insult than a celebration of seniority and wisdom.

Unlike ascribed statuses, an ***achieved status*** comes to us largely through our own efforts. Both "bank president" and "prison guard" are achieved statuses, as are "lawyer," "pianist," "sorority member," "convict," and "social worker." We must do something to acquire an achieved status—go to school, learn a skill, establish a friendship, invent a new product. But as we will see in the next section, our ascribed status heavily influences our achieved status. Being male, for example, would decrease the likelihood that we would consider child care as a career.

Master Status   Each person holds many different and sometimes conflicting statuses; some may connote higher social posi-

tion and some, lower position. How, then, do others view one's overall social position? According to sociologist Everett Hughes (1945), societies deal with inconsistencies by agreeing that certain statuses are more important than others. A ***master status*** is a status that dominates others and thereby determines a person's general position in society. For example, Arthur Ashe, who died of AIDS in 1993, had a remarkable career as a tennis star, but at the end of his life, his status as a well-known personality with AIDS may have outweighed his statuses as a retired athlete, author, and political activist. Throughout the world, many people with disabilities find that their status as "disabled" receives undue weight, overshadowing their actual ability to perform successfully in meaningful employment (see Box 5-1, opposite).

Our society gives such importance to race and gender that they often dominate our lives. These ascribed statuses frequently influence our achieved status. The African American activist Malcolm X (1925–1965), an eloquent and controversial advocate of Black power and Black pride during the early 1960s, recalled that his feelings and perspectives changed dramatically while in eighth grade. When his English teacher, a White man, advised him that his goal of becoming a lawyer was "no realistic goal for a nigger" and encouraged him instead to become a carpenter, Malcolm X (1964:37) found that his position as a Black man (ascribed status) was an obstacle to his dream of becoming

Whom do you see in this photo: a food service worker, an elderly food service worker, or an elderly woman? Our achieved and ascribed statuses determine how others see us.

social**INEQUALITY**

5-1 Disability as a Master Status

When officials in New Hampshire required a handicap access ramp for a mountain shelter, they were ridiculed. Who could climb a mountain in a wheelchair? critics asked. In the summer of 2000 that challenge impelled several intrepid climbers, some in wheelchairs, to make a 12-hour trek over rocks and rough trail so that they could enter the shelter in triumph. As a result of such feats, stereotypes of the disabled are gradually falling away. But the status of "disabled" still carries a stigma.

Throughout history and around the world, people with disabilities have been subjected to cruel and inhuman treatment. For example, in the 20th century, the disabled were frequently viewed as subhuman creatures who were a menace to society. In Japan more than 16,000 women with disabilities were involuntarily sterilized with government approval from 1945 to 1995. Sweden apologized for the same action taken against 62,000 of its citizens in the 1970s.

Such blatantly hostile treatment of people with disabilities has given way to a *medical model,* in which the disabled are viewed as chronic patients. Increasingly, however, people concerned with the rights of the disabled have criticized this model as well. In their view, it is the unnecessary and discriminatory barriers present in the environment—both physical

and attitudinal—that stand in the way of people with disabilities, more than any biological limitations. Applying a *civil rights model,* activists emphasize that those with disabilities face widespread prejudice, discrimination, and segregation. For example, most voting places are inaccessible to wheelchair users and fail to provide ballots that can be used by those unable to read print.

> *In Japan more than 16,000 women with disabilities were involuntarily sterilized with government approval from 1945 to 1995.*

Drawing on the earlier work of Erving Goffman, contemporary sociologists have suggested that society attaches a stigma to many forms of disability, a stigma that leads to prejudicial treatment. People with disabilities frequently observe that the nondisabled see them only as blind, wheelchair users, and so forth, rather than as complex human beings with individual strengths and weaknesses, whose blindness or use of a wheelchair is merely one aspect of their lives.

Though discrimination against the disabled occurs around the world, attitudes are changing. The African nation of Botswana has plans to assist its disabled, most of whom live in rural areas and need special services for mobility and economic development. In many countries, disability rights activists are targeting issues essential to overcoming this master status and becoming a full citizen, including employment, housing, education, and access to public buildings.

Let's Discuss

1. Does your campus present barriers to disabled students? If so, what kind of barriers—physical, attitudinal, or both? Describe some of them.
2. Why do you think nondisabled people see disability as the most important characteristic of a disabled person? What can be done to help people see beyond the wheelchair and the seeing-eye dog?

Sources: Albrecht 2004; Goffman 1963a; D. Murphy 1997; *Newsday* 1997; E. Rosenthal 2001; Shapiro 1993; Waldrop and Stern 2003.

a lawyer (achieved status). In the United States, the ascribed statuses of race and gender can function as master statuses that have an important impact on one's potential to achieve a desired professional and social status.

Social Roles

What Are Social Roles? Throughout our lives, we acquire what sociologists call social roles. A ***social role*** is a set of expectations for people who occupy a given social position or status. Thus, in the United States, we expect that cab drivers will know how to get around a city, that receptionists will be reliable in handling phone messages, and that police officers will take action if they see a citizen being threatened. With each distinctive social status—whether ascribed or achieved—come particular role expectations. However, actual performance varies from individual to individual. One secretary may assume extensive ad-

ministrative responsibilities, while another may focus on clerical duties. Similarly, in Philip Zimbardo's mock prison experiment, some students were brutal and sadistic guards; others were not.

Roles are a significant component of social structure. Viewed from a functionalist perspective, roles contribute to a society's stability by enabling members to anticipate the behavior of others and to pattern their own actions accordingly. Yet social roles can also be dysfunctional if they restrict people's interactions and relationships. If we view a person *only* as a "police officer" or "supervisor," it will be difficult to relate to him or her as a friend or neighbor.

Role Conflict Imagine the delicate situation of a woman who has worked for a decade on an assembly line in an electrical plant, and has recently been named supervisor of her unit. How is this woman expected to relate to her longtime friends and co-workers? Should she still go out to lunch with them,

Why Do We Gather Together?

Around the world, people cluster at bus stops, in schools, and at houses of worship. Others gather at malls, movie theaters, and government offices. They do so for many reasons—to earn a living, get an education, or just to have fun. But there is a larger purpose to these gatherings. Humans are social creatures, with a social fabric that is knit together by the give-and-take of even the most common encounters. The people we meet with, the places where we gather, our purposes in seeking others' company—these are fundamental building blocks of our society.

Our social interactions are also defined by the social structures in which they take place. Social interactions may be relatively casual and unstructured, as they are when friends spend time hanging out together at the park. Or they may be carefully organized, as they are when tribal musicians compete for the title of best drum circle at the powwow, or when mountain climbers attempt to reach the summit of the world's highest peak. In each case, the social interaction is defined by the larger social structure, whether it be the neighbors who live around the park, the organizers of the intertribal competition, or the government officials who grant climbers permission to ascend a peak.

{Base camp for a Mt. Everest expedition}

{Teen gathering in South Korea}

{Upper Mattaponi tribal powwow, Virginia}

as she has done almost daily for years? Is it her responsibility to recommend the firing of an old friend who cannot keep up with the demands of the assembly line?

Role conflict occurs when incompatible expectations arise from two or more social positions held by the same person. Fulfillment of the roles associated with one status may directly violate the roles linked to a second status. In the example just given, the newly promoted supervisor will most likely experience a sharp conflict between her social and occupational roles.

Such role conflicts call for important ethical choices. The new supervisor will have to make a difficult decision about how much allegiance she owes her friend and how much she owes her employers, who have given her supervisory responsibilities.

Another type of role conflict occurs when individuals move into occupations that are not common among people with their ascribed status. Male preschool teachers and female police officers experience this type of role conflict. In the latter case, female officers must strive to reconcile their workplace role in law enforcement with the societal view of a woman's role, which does not embrace many skills needed in police work. And while female police officers encounter sexual harassment, as women do throughout the labor force, they must also deal with the "code of silence," an informal norm that precludes their implicating fellow officers in wrongdoing (Fletcher 1995; S. Martin 1994).

Use Your Sociological Imagination

If you were a male nurse, what aspects of role conflict might you experience? Now imagine you are a professional boxer and a woman. What conflicting role expectations might that involve? In both cases, how well do you think you would handle role conflict?

This college student in India has decorated his dorm room with photos of beautiful women and fast cars. They may signify his attempt to create a new identity, the final stage in his exit from the role of high school student living at home.

Role Strain   Role conflict describes the situation of a person dealing with the challenge of occupying two social positions simultaneously. However, even a single position can cause problems. Sociologists use the term *role strain* to describe the difficulty that arises when the same social position imposes conflicting demands and expectations.

People who belong to minority cultures may experience role strain while working in the mainstream culture. Criminologist Larry Gould (2002) interviewed officers of the Navajo Nation Police Department about their relations with conventional law enforcement officials, such as sheriffs and FBI agents. Besides enforcing the law, Navajo Nation officers practice an alternative form of justice known as Peacemaking, in which they seek reconciliation between the parties to a crime. The officers expressed great confidence in Peacemaking, but worried that if they did not make arrests, other law enforcement officials would think they were too soft, or "just taking care of their own." Regardless of the strength of their ties to traditional Navajo ways, all felt the strain of being considered "too Navajo" or "not Navajo enough."

Role Exit   Often, when we think of assuming a social role, we focus on the preparation and anticipatory socialization a person undergoes for that role. Such is true if a person is about to become an attorney, a chef, a spouse, or a parent. Yet until recently, social scientists have given little attention to the adjustments involved in *leaving* social roles.

Sociologist Helen Rose Fuchs Ebaugh (1988) developed the term *role exit* to describe the process of disengagement from a role that is central to one's self-identity in order to establish a new role and identity. Drawing on interviews with 185 people—among them ex-convicts, divorced men and women, recovering alcoholics, ex-nuns, former doctors, retirees, and transsexuals—Ebaugh (herself a former nun) studied the process of voluntarily exiting from significant social roles.

Ebaugh has offered a four-stage model of role exit. The first stage begins with *doubt.* The person experiences frustration, burnout, or simply unhappiness with an accustomed status and the roles associated with the social position. The second stage involves a *search for alternatives.* A person who is unhappy with his or her career may take a leave of absence; an unhappily married couple may begin what they see as a temporary separation.

The third stage of role exit is the *action stage* or *departure.* Ebaugh found that the vast majority of her respondents could identify a clear turning point that made them feel it was essential to take final action and leave their jobs, end their marriages, or engage in another type of role exit. Twenty percent of respondents saw their role exit as a gradual, evolutionary process that had no single turning point.

The last stage of role exit involves the *creation of a new identity.* Many of you participated in a role exit when you made the transition from high school to college. You left behind the role of off-spring living at home and took on the role of a somewhat independent college student living with peers in a dorm. Sociologist Ira Silver (1996) has studied the central role that material objects play in this transition. The objects students choose to leave at home (like stuffed animals and dolls) are associated with their prior identities. They may remain deeply attached to those objects, but do not want them to be seen as part of their new identities at college. The objects they bring with them symbolize how they now see themselves and how they wish to be perceived. IPods and wall posters, for example, are calculated to say, "This is me."

Groups

In sociological terms, a ***group*** is any number of people with similar norms, values, and expectations who interact with one another on a regular basis. The members of a women's basketball team, a hospital's business office, a synagogue, or a symphony orchestra constitute a group. However, the residents of a suburb would not be considered a group, since they rarely interact with one another at one time.

Every society is composed of many groups in which daily social interaction takes place. We seek out groups to establish friendships, to accomplish certain goals, and to fulfill the social roles we have acquired. In Kuwait, men gather in groups called *diwaniyas,* which means "little guest house" in Arabic. Hundreds of these gatherings take place every night. *Diwaniyas* may be centered around a family, but are just as likely to be organized around a business, specific occupation, or politics. Men gather to exchange gossip or ideas in these groups, which range in size from 5 or 6 members to well over 100. Meetings can last an hour in the early evening or stretch well into the night. *Diwaniyas* have a rich history in Kuwait, going back over 200 years. Recently a handful of *diwaniyas* has begun to allow women to attend—a major departure from custom for this type of social group. We'll explore the various types of groups in which people interact in detail in Chapter 6, where we will also examine sociological investigations of group behavior (Marshall 2003).

Groups play a vital part in a society's social structure. Much of our social interaction takes place within groups and is influenced by their norms and sanctions. Being a teenager or a retired person takes on special meanings when we interact within groups designed for people with that particular status. The expectations associated with many social roles, including those accompanying the statuses of brother, sister, and student, become more clearly defined in the context of a group.

Social Networks

Groups do not merely serve to define other elements of the social structure, such as roles and statuses; they also link the individual with the larger society. We all belong to a number of different groups, and through our acquaintances make connections with people in different social circles. These connections are known as a ***social network***—a series of social relationships that links a person directly to others, and through them indirectly to still more people. Social networks can center on virtually any activity, from sharing job information to exchanging news and gossip or sharing sex (see Box 5-2, page 118). Some networks may constrain people by limiting the range of their interactions, yet networks can also empower people by making vast resources available to them (M. Jackson and Rogers 2007).

Involvement in social networks—commonly known as *networking*—is especially valuable in finding employment. Albert Einstein was successful in finding a job only when a classmate's father put him in touch with his future employer. These kinds of contacts—even those that are weak and distant—can be crucial in establishing social networks and facilitating the transmission of information.

In the workplace, networking pays off more for men than for women because of the traditional presence of men in leadership positions. One survey of executives found that 63 percent of the men used networking to find new jobs, compared to 41 percent of the women. Thirty-one percent of the women used classified advertisements to find jobs, compared to only 13 percent of the men. Still, women at all levels of the paid labor force are beginning to make effective use of social networks. A study of women who were leaving the welfare rolls to enter the paid workforce found that networking was an effective tool in their search for employment. Informal networking also helped them to locate child care and better housing—keys to successful employment (Carey and McLean 1997; Henly 1999).

With advances in technology, we can now maintain social networks electronically; we don't need face-to-face contacts. Online network-building companies emerged in 2004, offering their services free of charge at first. People log in to these sites and create a profile. Rather than remaining anonymous, as they would with an online dating service, users are identified by name and encouraged to list friends—even trusted friends of friends—who can serve as job contacts, offer advice, or simply share interests. One site creates "tribes" of people who share the same characteristic—a religion, hobby, music preference, or college affiliation (Tedeschi 2004).

Sociologist Manuel Castells (1997, 1998, 2000) views these emerging electronic social networks as fundamental to new organizations and the growth of existing businesses and associations. One such network, in particular, is changing the way people interact. *Texting* refers to the exchange of wireless e-mails over cell phones. It began first in Asia in 2000 and has now taken off in North America and Europe. Initially, texting was popular among young users, who sent shorthand messages such as "WRU" ("Where are you?") and "CU2NYT" ("See you tonight"). Now the business world has seen the advantages of transmitting e-mails via cell phones or PalmPilots. However, sociologists caution that such devices create a workday that never ends, and that increasingly people are busy checking their digital devices rather than actually conversing with those around them.

research**IN**action

5-2 Adolescent Sexual Networks

If you drew a chart of the sexual network at a typical American high school, what would it look like? In the mid-1990s, sociologists Peter Bearman, James Moody, and Katherine Stovel asked themselves that question. While studying romantic relationships at a high school with about 1,000 students, they had found that about 61 percent of the boys and 55 percent of the girls had been sexually active over the past 18 months. Those percentages did not differ much from the results of similar studies done during the period. What surprised the research team was what they saw when they began to chart the students' relationships.

To obtain their data, Bearman and his colleagues conducted in-home interviews with the respondents. Instead of asking students for a face-to-face interview—a technique that might have embarrassed them or distorted their answers—the researchers gave them an

> *A particularly significant implication of this study is the risk of sexually transmitted diseases (STDs) to those who participate in such a network.*

audio recording of the questions, a pair of earphones, and a laptop computer on which to record their answers. The research team also asked respondents to look at a list of all the students at the high school and identify those with whom they had had romantic or sexual relationships.

The results showed that 573 of the 832 students surveyed had had at least one sexual relationship over the past 18 months. Among those respondents, the sociologists found only 63 steady couples, or pairs with no other partners. A much larger group of 288 students—almost a third of the sample—was involved in the free-flowing network of relationships shown on the accompanying chart. (Note the comparative absence of tightly closed loops of 3 to 5 individuals.) Not shown on the chart were another 90 students who were involved in relationships outside the school.

A particularly significant implication of this study is the risk of sexually transmitted diseases (STDs) to those who participate in such a network. Through the complicated chain of relationships, even students who have only one or two sexual partners are exposing themselves to a relatively high degree of risk. But while parents and even students may be alarmed by the data, public health officials are encouraged. Experts at the Centers for Disease Control who have reviewed the network charts from this and other studies see them as blueprints for change. If experts can alter participants' behavior anywhere along these chains—by counseling abstinence, condom use, or treatment of STDs—they can significantly reduce transmission of the diseases.

Let's Discuss

1. Do the results of the study surprise you? How does the sexual network described in this study compare to the network where you went to high school?
2. Do you see any problems with the research method used in this study? Can you think of anything that might have compromised the validity of the data?

Sources: Bearman, Moody, and Stovel 2004; C. F. Turner et al. 1998; Wallis 2005.

Each dot represents a boy or girl at "Jefferson High." The lines that link them represent romantic and sexual relationships that occurred over an 18-month period. While most of the teens had just one or two partners, 288 of the 832 students interviewed were linked in a giant sexual network.

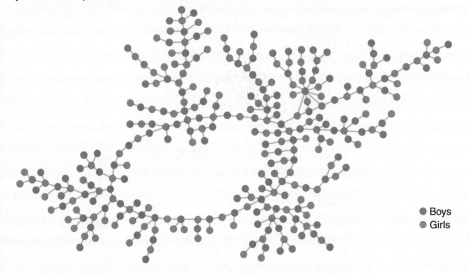

● Boys
● Girls

Other relationships (If a pattern was observed more than once, numeral indicates frequency)

Source: Bearman, Moody, and Stovel 2004:58.

In 2003, the deployment of U.S. troops in the Middle East increased many people's reliance on e-mail. Today, digital photos and sound files accompany e-mail messages between soldiers and their families and friends. Well-established networks have developed to help those who are novices at electronic communication to connect to the Internet. Meanwhile, more seasoned users, including U.S. soldiers and Iraqi citizens, have begun to post their opinions of the war in Iraq in online journals called Web logs, or blogs. Though critics are skeptical of the identity of some of the authors, these postings have become yet another source of news about the war (Faith 2005; O'Connor 2004).

www.mhhe.com/schaefer11

Use Your Sociological Imagination

If you were deaf, what impact might instant messaging, or texting, have on you?

Social Institutions

The mass media, the government, the economy, the family, and the health care system are all examples of social institutions found in our society. *Social institutions* are organized patterns of beliefs and behavior centered on basic social needs, such as replacing personnel (the family) and preserving order (the government).

A close look at social institutions gives sociologists insight into the structure of a society. Consider religion, for example. The institution of religion adapts to the segment of society that it serves. Church work has very different meanings for ministers who serve a skid row area and those who serve a suburban middle-class community. Religious leaders assigned to a skid row mission will focus on tending to the ill and providing food and shelter. In contrast, clergy in affluent suburbs will be occupied with counseling those considering marriage and divorce, arranging youth activities, and overseeing cultural events.

Functionalist View   One way to understand social institutions is to see how they fulfill essential functions. Anthropologist David F. Aberle and his colleagues (1950) and sociologists Raymond Mack and Calvin Bradford (1979) have identified five major tasks, or functional prerequisites, that a society or relatively permanent group must accomplish if it is to survive:

1. *Replacing personnel.* Any group or society must replace personnel when they die, leave, or become incapacitated. This task is accomplished through such means as immigration, annexation of neighboring groups, acquisition of slaves, or sexual reproduction. The Shakers, a religious sect that came to the United States in 1774, are a conspicuous example of a group that has *failed* to replace personnel. Their religious beliefs commit the Shakers to celibacy; to survive, the group must recruit new members. At first, the Shakers proved quite

successful in attracting members, reaching a peak of about 6,000 members in the United States during the 1840s. As of 2004, however, the only Shaker community left in this country was a farm in Maine with five members—three men and two women (Sabbathday Lake 2004).

2. *Teaching new recruits.* No group or society can survive if many of its members reject the group's established behavior and responsibilities. Thus, finding or producing new members is not sufficient; the group or society must also encourage recruits to learn and accept its values and customs. Such learning can take place formally, within schools (where learning is a manifest function), or informally, through interaction in peer groups (where instruction is a latent function).

3. *Producing and distributing goods and services.* Any relatively permanent group or society must provide and distribute desired goods and services to its members. Each society establishes a set of rules for the allocation of financial and other resources. The group must satisfy the needs of most members to some extent, or it will risk the possibility of discontent and ultimately disorder.

4. *Preserving order.* Throughout the world, indigenous and aboriginal peoples have struggled to protect themselves from outside invaders, with varying degrees of success. Failure to preserve order and defend against conquest leads to the death not only of a people, but of a culture.

5. *Providing and maintaining a sense of purpose.* People must feel motivated to continue as members of a group or society in order to fulfill the first four requirements. After the September 11, 2001, attacks on New York City and Washington, D.C.,

This memorial service for the victims of the September 11, 2001, terrorist attacks incorporated many patriotic elements, all of which helped New Yorkers to maintain a sense of purpose in extremely difficult times.

memorial services and community gatherings across the nation allowed people to affirm their allegiance to their country and bind up the psychic wounds inflicted by the terrorists. Patriotism, then, assists some people in developing and maintaining a sense of purpose. For others, tribal identities, religious values, or personal moral codes are especially meaningful. Whatever the motivator, in any society there remains one common and critical reality: if an individual does not have a sense of purpose, he or she has little reason to contribute to a society's survival.

This list of functional prerequisites does not specify *how* a society and its corresponding social institutions will perform each task. For example, one society may protect itself from external attack by amassing a frightening arsenal of weaponry, while another may make determined efforts to remain neutral in world politics and to promote cooperative relationships with its neighbors. No matter what its particular strategy, any society or relatively permanent group must attempt to satisfy all these functional prerequisites for survival. If it fails on even one condition, the society runs the risk of extinction.

Conflict View Conflict theorists do not agree with the functionalist approach to social institutions. Although proponents of both perspectives agree that social institutions are organized to meet basic social needs, conflict theorists object to the idea that the outcome is necessarily efficient and desirable.

From a conflict perspective, the present organization of social institutions is no accident. Major institutions, such as education, help to maintain the privileges of the most powerful individuals and groups within a society, while contributing to the powerlessness of others. To give one example, public schools in the United States are financed largely through property taxes. This arrangement allows more affluent areas to provide their children with better-equipped schools and better-paid teachers than low-income areas can afford. As a result, children from prosperous communities are better prepared to compete academically than children from impoverished communities. The structure of the nation's educational system permits and even promotes such unequal treatment of schoolchildren.

Conflict theorists argue that social institutions such as education have an inherently conservative nature. Without question, it has been difficult to implement educational reforms that promote equal opportunity—whether bilingual education, school desegregation, or mainstreaming of students with disabilities. From a functionalist perspective, social change can be dysfunctional, since it often leads to instability. However, from a conflict view, why should we preserve the existing social structure if it is unfair and discriminatory?

Social institutions also operate in gendered and racist environments, as conflict theorists, as well as feminists and interactionists, have pointed out. In schools, offices, and government institutions, assumptions about what people can do reflect the sexism and racism of the larger society. For instance, many people assume that women cannot make tough decisions—even

those in the top echelons of corporate management. Others assume that all Black students at elite colleges represent affirmative action admissions. Inequality based on gender, economic status, race, and ethnicity thrives in such an environment—to which we might add discrimination based on age, physical disability, and sexual orientation. The truth of this assertion can be seen in routine decisions by employers on how to advertise jobs, as well as whether to provide fringe benefits such as child care and parental leave.

www.mhhe.com/schaefer11

Use Your Sociological Imagination

Would social networks be more important to a migrant farm worker in California than to someone with political and social clout? Why or why not?

Interactionist View Social institutions affect our everyday behavior, whether we are driving down the street or waiting in a long shopping line. Sociologist Mitchell Duneier (1994a, 1994b) studied the social behavior of the word processors, all women, who work in the service center of a large Chicago law firm. Duneier was interested in the informal social norms that emerged in this work environment and the rich social network these female employees created.

The Network Center, as it is called, is a single, windowless room in a large office building where the law firm occupies seven floors. The center is staffed by two shifts of word processors, who work either from 4:00 p.m. to midnight or from midnight to 8:00 a.m. Each word processor works in a cubicle with just enough room for her keyboard, terminal, printer, and telephone. Work assignments for the word processors are placed in a central basket and then completed according to precise procedures.

At first glance, we might think that these women labor with little social contact, apart from limited breaks and occasional conversations with their supervisor. However, drawing on the interactionist perspective, Duneier learned that despite working in a large office, these women find private moments to talk (often in the halls or outside the washroom) and share a critical view of the law firm's attorneys and day-shift secretaries. Indeed, the word processors routinely suggest that their assignments represent work that the "lazy" secretaries should have completed during the normal workday. Duneier (1994b) tells of one word processor who resented the lawyers' superior attitude and pointedly refused to recognize or speak with any attorney who would not address her by name.

Interactionist theorists emphasize that our social behavior is conditioned by the roles and statuses we accept, the groups to which we belong, and the institutions within which we function. For example, the social roles associated with being a judge occur within the larger context of the criminal justice system. The status of "judge" stands in relation to other statuses, such as attor-

in other words, on the manner in which tasks are performed. Thus, a task such as providing food can be carried out almost totally by one individual, or it can be divided among many people. The latter pattern is typical of modern societies, in which the cultivation, processing, distribution, and retailing of a single food item are performed by literally hundreds of people.

In societies in which there is minimal division of labor, a collective consciousness develops that emphasizes group solidarity. Durkheim termed this collective frame of mind *mechanical solidarity,* implying that all individuals perform the same tasks. In this type of society, no one needs to ask, "What do your parents do?" since all are engaged in similar work. Each person prepares food, hunts, makes clothing, builds homes, and so forth. Because people have few options regarding what to do with their lives, there is little concern for individual needs. Instead, the group is the dominating force in society. Both social interaction and negotiation are based on close, intimate, face-to-face social contacts. Since there is little specialization, there are few social roles.

As societies become more advanced technologically, they rely on greater division of labor. The person who cuts down timber is not the same person who puts up your roof. With increasing specialization, many different tasks must be performed by many different individuals—even in manufacturing a single item, such as a radio or stove. In general, social interactions become less personal than in societies characterized by mechanical solidarity. People begin relating to others on the basis of their social positions ("butcher," "nurse") rather than their distinctive human qualities. Because the overall social structure of the society continues to change, statuses and social roles are in perpetual flux.

Once society has become more complex and division of labor is greater, no individual can go it alone. Dependence on others becomes essential for group survival. In Durkheim's terms, mechanical solidarity is replaced by *organic solidarity,* a collective consciousness resting on the need a society's members have for one another. Durkheim chose the term *organic solidarity* because in his view, individuals become interdependent in much the same way as organs of the human body.

Tönnies's *Gemeinschaft* and *Gesellschaft*

Ferdinand Tönnies (1855–1936) was appalled by the rise of an industrial city in his native Germany during the late 1800s. In his view, the city marked a dramatic change from the ideal of a close-knit community, which Tönnies termed a *Gemeinschaft,* to that of an impersonal mass society, known as a *Gesellschaft* (Tönnies [1887] 1988).

The *Gemeinschaft* (pronounced guh-MINE-shoft) is typical of rural life. It is a small community in which people have similar backgrounds and life experiences. Virtually everyone knows one another, and social interactions are intimate and familiar, almost as among kinfolk. In this community there is a commitment to the larger social group and a sense of togetherness among members. People relate to others in a personal way, not just as "clerk" or "manager." With this personal interaction comes little privacy, however: we know too much about everyone.

Social institutions affect the way we behave. How might the worshippers at this mosque in Egypt interact differently in school or at work?

ney, plaintiff, defendant, and witness, as well as to the social institution of government. Although courts and jails have great symbolic importance, the judicial system derives its continued significance from the roles people carry out in social interactions (Berger and Luckmann 1966).

Social Structure in Global Perspective

Modern societies are complex, especially compared to earlier social arrangements. Sociologists Émile Durkheim, Ferdinand Tönnies, and Gerhard Lenski developed ways to contrast modern societies with simpler forms of social structure.

Durkheim's Mechanical and Organic Solidarity

In his *Division of Labor* ([1893] 1933), Durkheim argued that social structure depends on the division of labor in a society—

In small communities like this one in Merida, Venezuela, people maintain social control through informal means such as gossip. Tönnies referred to this type of community as a *Gemeinschaft.*

"I'd like to think of you as a person, David, but it's my job to think of you as personnel."

In a *Gesellschaft,* people are likely to relate to one another in terms of their roles rather than their relationships.

Social control in the *Gemeinschaft* is maintained through informal means such as moral persuasion, gossip, and even gestures. These techniques work effectively because people genuinely care how others feel about them. Social change is relatively limited in the *Gemeinschaft;* the lives of members of one generation may be quite similar to those of their grandparents.

In contrast, the **Gesellschaft** (pronounced guh-ZELL-shoft) is an ideal community that is characteristic of modern urban life. In this community most people are strangers who feel little in common with other residents. Relationships are governed by social roles that grow out of immediate tasks, such as purchasing a product or arranging a business meeting. Self-interest dominates, and there is little consensus concerning values or commitment to the group. As a result, social control must rest on more formal techniques, such as laws and legally defined punishments. Social change is an important aspect of life in the *Gesellschaft;* it can be strikingly evident even within a single generation.

Table 5-1 (opposite) summarizes the differences between the *Gemeinschaft* and the *Gesellschaft.* Sociologists have used these terms to compare social structures that stress close relationships with those that emphasize less personal ties. It is easy to view the *Gemeinschaft* with nostalgia, as a far better way of life than the rat race of contemporary existence. However, the more intimate relationships of the *Gemeinschaft* come at a price. The prejudice and discrimination found there can be quite confining; ascribed statuses such as family background often outweigh a person's unique talents and achievements. In addition, the *Gemeinschaft* tends to distrust individuals who seek to be creative or just to be different.

Lenski's Sociocultural Evolution Approach

Sociologist Gerhard Lenski takes a very different view of society and social structure. Rather than distinguishing between two opposite types of society,

Table 5-1

123

Social Interaction and Social Structure

Comparison of the *Gemeinschaft* and *Gesellschaft*

summingUP

Gemeinschaft	Gesellschaft
Rural life typifies this form.	Urban life typifies this form.
People share a feeling of community that results from their similar backgrounds and life experiences.	People have little sense of commonality. Their differences appear more striking than their similarities.
Social interactions are intimate and familiar.	Social interactions are likely to be impersonal and task-specific.
People maintain a spirit of cooperation and unity of will.	Self-interest dominates.
Tasks and personal relationships cannot be separated.	The task being performed is paramount; relationships are subordinate.
People place little emphasis on individual privacy.	Privacy is valued.
Informal social control predominates.	Formal social control is evident.
People are not very tolerant of deviance.	People are more tolerant of deviance.
Emphasis is on ascribed statuses.	Emphasis is on achieved statuses.
Social change is relatively limited.	Social change is very evident, even within a generation.

Think About It

How would you classify the communities with which you are familiar? Are they more *Gemeinschaft* or *Gesellschaft*?

as Tönnies did, Lenski sees human societies as undergoing a process of change characterized by a dominant pattern known as **sociocultural evolution.** This term refers to long-term trends in societies resulting from the interplay of continuity, innovation, and selection (Nolan and Lenski 2006:361).

In Lenski's view, a society's level of technology is critical to the way it is organized. Lenski defines **technology** as "cultural information about the ways in which the material resources of the environment may be used to satisfy human needs and desires" (Nolan and Lenski 2006:361). The available technology does not completely define the form that a particular society and its social structure take. Nevertheless, a low level of technology may limit the degree to which a society can depend on such things as irrigation or complex machinery. As technology advances, Lenski writes, a community evolves from a preindustrial to an industrial and finally a postindustrial society.

Preindustrial Societies How does a preindustrial society organize its economy? If we know that, we can categorize the society. The first type of preindustrial society to emerge in human history was the **hunting-and-gathering society,** in which people simply rely on whatever foods and fibers are readily available. Technology in such societies is minimal. Organized into groups, people move constantly in search of food. There is little division of labor into specialized tasks.

Hunting-and-gathering societies are composed of small, widely dispersed groups. Each group consists almost entirely of people who are related to one another. As a result, kinship ties are the source of authority and influence, and the social institu-

tion of the family takes on a particularly important role. Tönnies would certainly view such societies as examples of the *Gemeinschaft.*

Social differentiation within the hunting-and-gathering society is based on ascribed statuses such as gender, age, and family background. Since resources are scarce, there is relatively little inequality in terms of material goods. By the close of the 20th century, hunting-and-gathering societies had virtually disappeared (Nolan and Lenski 2006).

Horticultural societies, in which people plant seeds and crops rather than merely subsist on available foods, emerged about 10,000 to 12,000 years ago. Members of horticultural societies are much less nomadic than hunters and gatherers. They place greater emphasis on the production of tools and household objects. Yet technology remains rather limited in these societies, whose members cultivate crops with the aid of digging sticks or hoes (Wilford 1997).

The last stage of preindustrial development is the **agrarian society,** which emerged about 5,000 years ago. As in horticultural societies, members of agrarian societies are engaged primarily in the production of food. However, new technological innovations such as the plow allow farmers to dramatically increase their crop yields. They can cultivate the same fields over generations, allowing the emergence of larger settlements.

The agrarian society continues to rely on the physical power of humans and animals (as opposed to mechanical power). Nevertheless, its social structure has more carefully defined roles than that of horticultural societies. Individuals focus on specialized tasks, such as the repair of fishing nets or blacksmithing. As human settlements become more established and stable, social institutions become more elaborate and property rights more important. The comparative permanence and greater surpluses of an agrarian society allow members to create artifacts such as statues, public monuments, and art objects and to pass them on from one generation to the next.

Table 5-2 summarizes Lenski's three stages of sociocultural evolution, as well as the stages that follow, which are described next.

Industrial Societies Although the industrial revolution did not topple monarchs, it produced changes every bit as significant as those resulting from political revolutions. The industrial revolution, which took place largely in England during the period 1760 to 1830, was a scientific revolution focused on the application of nonanimal (mechanical) sources of power to labor tasks. An *industrial society* is a society that depends on mechanization to produce its goods and services. Industrial societies rely on new inventions that facilitate agricultural and industrial production, and on new sources of energy, such as steam.

As the industrial revolution proceeded, a new form of social structure emerged. Many societies underwent an irrevocable shift from an agrarian-oriented economy to an industrial base. No longer did an individual or a family typically make an entire product. Instead, specialization of tasks and manufacturing of goods became increasingly common. Workers, generally men but also women and even children, left their family homesteads to work in central locations such as factories.

The process of industrialization had distinctive social consequences. Families and communities could not continue to function as self-sufficient units. Individuals, villages, and regions began to exchange goods and services and to become interdependent. As people came to rely on the labor of members of other communities, the family lost its unique position as the source of power and authority. The need for specialized knowledge led to more formalized schooling, and education emerged as a social institution distinct from the family.

Postindustrial and Postmodern Societies When Lenski first proposed the sociocultural evolutionary approach in the 1960s, he paid relatively little attention to how maturing industrialized societies may change with the emergence of even more advanced forms of technology. More recently, he and other sociologists have studied the significant changes in the occupational structure of industrial societies as they shift from manufacturing to service economies. In the 1970s sociologist Daniel Bell wrote about the technologically advanced *postindustrial society,* whose economic system is engaged primarily in the processing and control of information. The main output of a postindustrial society is services rather than manufactured goods. Large numbers of people become involved in occupations devoted to the teaching, generation, or dissemination of ideas. Jobs in fields such as advertising, public relations, human resources, and computer information systems would be typical of a postindustrial society (D. Bell 1999).

Bell views the transition from industrial to postindustrial society as a positive development. He sees a general decline in organized working-class groups and a rise in interest groups concerned with national issues such as health, education, and the environment. Bell's outlook is functionalist, because he portrays the postindustrial society as basically consensual. As organizations and interest groups engage in an open and competitive process of decision making, Bell believes, the level of conflict between diverse groups will diminish, strengthening social stability.

Conflict theorists take issue with Bell's functionalist analysis of the postindustrial society. For example, Michael Harrington (1980), who alerted the nation to the problems of the poor in his

Table 5-2

Stages of Sociocultural Evolution

Societal Type	First Appearance	Characteristics
Hunting-and-gathering	Beginning of human life	Nomadic; reliance on readily available food and fibers
Horticultural	About 10,000 to 12,000 years ago	More settled; development of agriculture and limited technology
Agrarian	About 5,000 years ago	Larger, more stable settlements; improved technology and increased crop yields
Industrial	1760–1850	Reliance on mechanical power and new sources of energy; centralized workplaces; economic interdependence; formal education
Postindustrial	1960s	Reliance on services, especially the processing and control of information; expanded middle class
Postmodern	Latter 1970s	High technology; mass consumption of consumer goods and media images; cross-cultural integration

The emphasis of postmodern theorists is on observing and describing newly emerging cultural forms and patterns of social interaction. Within sociology, the postmodern view offers support for integrating the insights of various theoretical perspectives—functionalism, conflict theory, feminist theory, and interactionism—while incorporating other contemporary approaches. Feminist sociologists argue optimistically that with its indifference to hierarchies and distinctions, the postmodern society will discard traditional values of male dominance in favor of gender equality. Yet others contend that despite new technologies, postindustrial and postmodern societies can be expected to display the same problems of inequality that plague industrial societies (Denzin 2004; Smart 1990; B. Turner 1990; van Vucht Tijssen 1990).

Durkheim, Tönnies, and Lenski present three visions of society's social structure. While they differ, each is useful, and this textbook will draw on all three. The sociocultural evolutionary approach emphasizes a historical perspective. It does not picture

At first glance, this scene may seem a throwback to agrarian society, but look more closely. Today's farm is actually a highly mechanized, computer-dependent operation that is networked into the global economy.

book *The Other America,* questioned the significance that Bell attached to the growing class of white-collar workers. Harrington conceded that scientists, engineers, and economists are involved in important political and economic decisions, but he disagreed with Bell's claim that they have a free hand in decision making, independent of the interests of the rich. Harrington followed in the tradition of Marx by arguing that conflict between social classes will continue in the postindustrial society.

Sociologists have recently gone beyond discussion of the postindustrial society to the ideal of the postmodern society. A ***postmodern society*** is a technologically sophisticated society that is preoccupied with consumer goods and media images (Brannigan 1992). Such societies consume goods and information on a mass scale. Postmodern theorists take a global perspective, noting the ways that culture crosses national boundaries. For example, residents of the United States may listen to reggae music from Jamaica, eat sushi and other Japanese foods, and wear clogs from Sweden. And the online social net-

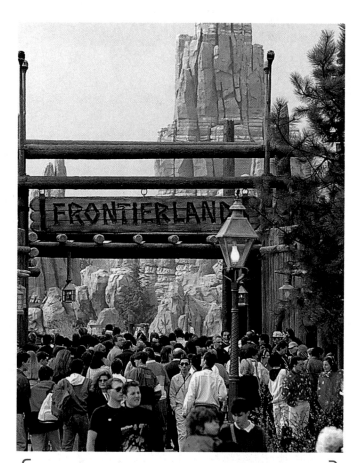

In a postmodern society, people consume goods, information, and media images en masse. In Paris, Disneyworld is popularizing U.S. media images abroad, illustrating another characteristic of postmodern societies—globalization.

different types of social structure coexisting within the same society. Consequently, one would not expect a single society to include hunters and gatherers along with a postmodern culture. In contrast, Durkheim's and Tönnies's theories allow for the existence of different types of community—such as a *Gemeinschaft* and a *Gesellschaft*—in the same society. Thus, a rural New Hampshire community located 100 miles from Boston can be linked to the city by modern information technology. The main difference between these two theories is a matter of emphasis. While Tönnies emphasized the overriding concern in each type of community—one's own self-interest or the well-being of the larger society—Durkheim emphasized the division (or lack of division) of labor.

The work of these three thinkers reminds us that a major focus of sociology has been to identify changes in social structure and the consequences for human behavior. At the macro level, we see society shifting to more advanced forms of technology.

The social structure becomes increasingly complex, and new social institutions emerge to assume some functions that once were performed by the family. On the micro level, these changes affect the nature of social interactions. Each individual takes on multiple social roles, and people come to rely more on social networks and less on kinship ties. As the social structure becomes more complex, people's relationships become more impersonal, transient, and fragmented.

Use Your Sociological Imagination

Of all the different forms of social structure described by Durkheim, Tönnies, and Lenski, which comes closest to matching your social setting?

social**Policy**
and Social Interaction

Regulating the Net

The Issue

In 1991 the first Webcam went online. The years that followed saw the widespread adoption of the cell phone and the digital camera, not to mention the Internet. By 1998, eHarmony.com, the first online dating service, had been founded. MySpace followed in 2003, and YouTube in 2005.

All these technological innovations have affected the way we shop and share information. But just as important is their impact on our social interactions. No longer are we limited to face-to-face encounters, letters and greeting cards, and long-distance telephone calls. Not only can we communicate with others instantaneously online; we can find and scan the profiles of perfect strangers. Unfortunately, people are using these complex communication systems without any real understanding of the technology underlying them, and thus of their potential for misuse (Shortliffe and Patel 2004).

The Setting

Though people of all ages use the Internet, it has become especially important to young people's social interactions. By 2005, 87 percent of those aged 12 to 17 used the Internet; every day, 11 million teens went online. Today young people supplement conventional e-mail with texting, instant messages, and shared images and video files. Increasingly, however, they regard e-mail—in widespread use for just fifteen years—as a way of

communicating with "old people" or businesses. Instead, the majority of teens make daily visits to online social networking sites, such as Facebook and MySpace—a part of the social scene that is alien to older adults (Lenhart et al. 2005, 2007).

Sociological Insights

The ease of communication that the Internet offers would seem the epitome of functionality, allowing people to access new technologies in order to conduct meetings, select colleges, find jobs, monitor their health, and even expand their religious or spiritual horizons. But through misuse or abuse, the Internet can easily become dysfunctional. About one in five (21 percent) of young people who go online report having sent an e-mail, instant message, or text message that was meant to be private but was forwarded to others by the recipient. Another dysfunction (discussed later) is the victimization of young people by online predators.

The Internet is not a level playing field. While the digital divide that separates Internet use by race and social class is narrowing, it has not disappeared. Conflict theorists have documented the gap between White and Black or Hispanic youths in the use of electronic communication. Still, the greatest divide is not that of race, ethnicity, or even social class, but of age. Low-income African Americans are more likely to send instant messages than older White adults, even those who are affluent.

Interactionists have investigated the implications of online communication for everyday social interaction. Their research shows that young people have a fairly significant network of regular online communicators, which gives them daily contact with about 20 friends. Maintaining face-to-face or even telephone contact with that many people would be difficult on a daily basis. But that is not all the Internet offers. Instant messaging has led to buddy lists (begun by AOL in 1996), which allow users to monitor which friends are online at any given moment. Most teens who go online have a buddy list of more than 25 names; about a quarter of them have over 100 buddies that they monitor 24/7. Just as they can access friends more easily online, they can also block them much more easily online than they can in person, in the workplace, or in the school cafeteria (Lenhart et al. 2005, 2007).

In any social interaction, knowing your partner is critical. Obviously, anonymity is not an issue in face-to-face conversation or even in the typical phone call. Online messages are a different matter, however, since people can easily disguise their gender, age, and other characteristics. Most online users have more than one screen name, some of them because they lost or forgot a password. But others use multiple screen names to present one image to one group of intimates and another image to others. They often use icons, or *avatars,* which have a human (or sometimes creature-like) appearance, to flesh out these images. This manipulative use of screen names allows people to engage in online impression management. Some of the profiles people create at MySpace, Facebook, Xanga, Friendster, Yahoo, Piczo, Gaianonline, and Tagged show enormous creativity and depth of detail.

This common disclosure of personal characteristics online contrasts sharply with the policies that govern disclosure of information by social institutions. The Family Educational Rights and Privacy Act (FERPA), passed in 1974, allows academic institutions to disclose only the barest of details about students. Yet millions of high school and college students have disclosed personal details about themselves not just to their friends, but to the public. As Figure 5-2 (page 128) shows, many if not most students reveal their birth date, gender, relationship status, occupation, interests (often termed "passions"), and sexual orientation in their online profiles—all of which cannot be shared under FERPA. Students may also admit to drinking, drug use, sexual promiscuity, eating disorders, and other socially disapproved behaviors.

Feminist researchers have noted that women and girls have embraced the Internet even more than men. While male dominance is well established in online game playing, women are more likely than men to engage in online chats or to access online social networks, and to do so for longer periods than men.

Policy Initiatives

Although the U.S. Constitution does not explicitly extend the right of privacy to citizens, the Fourth Amendment's protection against unreasonable searches has often been interpreted as offering that right. As a general principle, then, our social interactions should not be monitored by outsiders, including government officials.

Most parents use filtering and monitoring to oversee their children's online communications. Indeed, it is much easier for parents to monitor their children's electronic communications than their face-to-face encounters. Every time a new operating system, such as Windows Vista or Mac Leopard, is unveiled, the originator markets "parental controls" as a compelling feature.

In private companies as well, self-regulation is outstripping government regulation. For example, Google's YouTube bans nudity and takes down copyrighted material that is used without permission, but only when the rights holder files a specific complaint. One challenge to any effort to monitor such

The Internet has added a massive new dimension to social interaction—even though you may not be totally sure whom you are "talking to."

Chapter 5

Identity Information Revealed Online by College Students

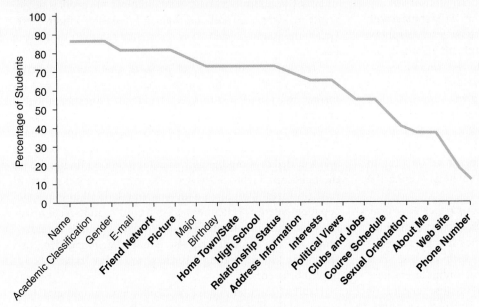

Boldface type indicates information not typically disclosed by colleges.

Note: Based on a review of 200 online profiles posted by college students in Facebook. Information on friend networks, majors, home towns/states, and clubs and jobs was drawn from more than one possible field.
Source: Adapted from Stutzman 2007:Figure 1.

sites more closely is that thousands of videos are posted daily, and millions of people may access the sites every hour (Stone 2007).

Policy issues that have led to significant legislation include the harassment or stalking of young users and the file sharing of pornographic images. Needless to say, government administrators are also concerned about the sharing of unflattering communications that seem to show officials, police, or the military behaving unprofessionally. Despite outcries by policymakers and the general public about online abuses, however, regulation has been very limited. Except for obscenity, pornography, and government-classified information, the online social world is less regulated than everyday social life (Clemmitt 2006).

Instead of regulation, policymakers have embraced the concept of **net neutrality** (short for *Internet neutrality*), or the principle that the government should remain nonselective or neutral toward online content. The driving force behind net neutrality is not Facebook profilers, but big business. Corporate supporters of net neutrality speak of their "freedoms" and condemn any effort to limit online communication as "discrimination." Google, in fact, has an executive whose title is "Vice President and Chief Internet Evangelist," whose job is to lobby Congress to block almost all regulation of online activities.

The net neutrality campaign arose around 2003, when large telephone conglomerates, seeing a future in the transmission of telephone calls over the Internet, began to monitor pending legislation to ensure the deregulation of online content. Several years earlier, in the Internet Tax Freedom Act (1998), Congress had declared a moratorium on the taxation of online commercial transactions. In 2006, continuing its hands-off policy, the Federal Election Commission declared that campaign finance laws would not apply to most online political activity (Pace 2006; *Wall Street Journal* 2006; Weil 1998).

Despite corporate pleas for net neutrality, concern has arisen that information gathered over the Internet is being shared in ways unknown to online users. Beginning in 2006, critics charged that computer applications had been developed which would allow Internet service providers to monitor and redirect online communications for commercial or government use. Citing the Fourth Amendment, they warned against "e-mail warehouses" where data is stored with little thought to who may later access it. While online communications may be less subject to regulation than everyday interactions, they are definitely less private. We will consider the implications of monitoring these communications in Chapter 7 (Tessler 2006).

The impact of new technologies over the last decade has been amazing, but research indicates that even savvy surfers still socialize in person rather than solely online. The more serious the event, the more likely it is to occur offline (Lenhart et al. 2005, 2007). Will that change someday, so that everything from Super Bowl parties to dating and fighting will occur online? What would be the social policy implications of such a shift in social interactions?

Let's Discuss

1. Do you know people whose online profiles are more revealing than their everyday interactions? If so, why do you think people are more open about themselves online?

2. Have your face-to-face social interactions ever been affected by something you learned in an online social network, such as MySpace or Friendster? If so, in what ways?

3. What role should the government take in regulating the information people post about themselves online? Would your answer differ depending on a person's age—say, under 21? Under 18?

GettingINVOLVED

To get involved in the debate over regulation of the Internet and other new forms of communication, visit this text's Online Learning Center, which offers links to relevant Web sites. Check out the Social Policy section in the Online Learning center as well; it provides survey data on U.S. public opinion regarding this issue.

www.mhhe.com/schaefer11

{ MASTERING THIS CHAPTER }

Summary

Social interaction refers to the ways in which people respond to one another. *Social structure* refers to the way in which a society is organized into predictable relationships. This chapter examines the five basic elements of social structure: *statuses, social roles, groups, social networks,* and *social institutions.*

1. People shape their social reality based on what they learn through their *social interactions.* Social change comes from redefining or reconstructing social reality.

2. An *ascribed status* is generally assigned to a person at birth, whereas an *achieved status* is attained largely through one's own effort. Some ascribed statuses, such as race and gender, can function as *master statuses* that affect one's potential to achieve a certain professional or social status.

3. With each distinctive status—whether ascribed or achieved—come particular *social roles,* the set of expectations for people who occupy that status.

4. Much of our social behavior takes place in *groups,* which are often linked to *social networks* and their vast resources.

5. *Social institutions* fulfill essential functions, such as replacing personnel, training new recruits, and preserving order. The mass media, the government, the economy, the family, and the health care system are all examples of social institutions.

6. Conflict theorists charge that social institutions help to maintain the privileges of the powerful while contributing to the powerlessness of others.

7. Interactionist theorists stress that our social behavior is conditioned by the roles and statuses we accept, the groups to which we belong, and the institutions within which we function.

8. Émile Durkheim thought that social structure depends on the division of labor in a society. According to Durkheim, societies with minimal division of labor have a collective consciousness called *mechanical solidarity;* those with greater division of labor show an interdependence called *organic solidarity.*

9. Ferdinand Tönnies distinguished the close-knit community of *Gemeinschaft* from the impersonal mass society known as *Gesellschaft.*

10. Gerhard Lenski thinks that a society's social structure changes as its culture and technology become more sophisticated, a process he calls *sociocultural evolution.*

11. The rise of the Internet has changed the nature of our social interactions, greatly expanding our social networks but raising concerns about privacy, unequal access, and the protection of young people from sexual predators.

Critical Thinking Questions

1. People in certain professions seem particularly susceptible to role conflict. For example, journalists commonly experience role conflict during disasters, crimes, and other distressing situations. Should they offer assistance to the needy or cover breaking news? Select two other professions and discuss the role conflicts people in them might experience.

2. The functionalist, conflict, and interactionist perspectives can all be used in analyzing social institutions. What are the strengths and weaknesses in each perspective's analysis of those institutions?

3. What are the pros and cons of net neutrality? Which approach do you favor, government regulation of online content or government neutrality toward that content? Explain your position.

Achieved status A social position that a person attains largely through his or her own efforts. (page 112)

Agrarian society The most technologically advanced form of preindustrial society. Members are engaged primarily in the production of food, but increase their crop yields through technological innovations such as the plow. (123)

Ascribed status A social position assigned to a person by society without regard for the person's unique talents or characteristics. (111)

Gemeinschaft A close-knit community, often found in rural areas, in which strong personal bonds unite members. (121)

Gesellschaft A community, often urban, that is large and impersonal, with little commitment to the group or consensus on values. (122)

Group Any number of people with similar norms, values, and expectations who interact with one another on a regular basis. (117)

Horticultural society A preindustrial society in which people plant seeds and crops rather than merely subsist on available foods. (123)

Hunting-and-gathering society A preindustrial society in which people rely on whatever foods and fibers are readily available in order to survive. (123)

Industrial society A society that depends on mechanization to produce its goods and services. (124)

Master status A status that dominates others and thereby determines a person's general position in society. (112)

Mechanical solidarity A collective consciousness that emphasizes group solidarity, characteristic of societies with minimal division of labor. (121)

Net neutrality The principle that the government should remain nonselective or neutral toward online content. (128)

Organic solidarity A collective consciousness that rests on mutual interdependence, characteristic of societies with a complex division of labor. (121)

Postindustrial society A society whose economic system is engaged primarily in the processing and control of information. (124)

Postmodern society A technologically sophisticated society that is preoccupied with consumer goods and media images. (125)

Role conflict The situation that occurs when incompatible expectations arise from two or more social positions held by the same person. (116)

Role exit The process of disengagement from a role that is central to one's self-identity in order to establish a new role and identity. (116)

Role strain The difficulty that arises when the same social position imposes conflicting demands and expectations. (116)

Social institution An organized pattern of beliefs and behavior centered on basic social needs. (119)

Social interaction The ways in which people respond to one another. (110)

Social network A series of social relationships that links a person directly to others, and through them indirectly to still more people. (117)

Social role A set of expectations for people who occupy a given social position or status. (113)

Social structure The way in which a society is organized into predictable relationships. (110)

Sociocultural evolution Long-term trends in societies resulting from the interplay of continuity, innovation, and selection. (123)

Status A term used by sociologists to refer to any of the full range of socially defined positions within a large group or society. (111)

Technology Cultural information about the ways in which the material resources of the environment may be used to satisfy human needs and desires. (123)

Read each question carefully and then select the best answer.

1. In the United States, we expect that cab drivers will know how to get around a city. This expectation is an example of which of the following?

   a. role conflict
   b. role strain
   c. social role
   d. master status

2. What occurs when incompatible expectations arise from two or more social positions held by the same person?

   a. role conflict
   b. role strain
   c. role exit
   d. both a and b

3. In sociological terms, what do we call any number of people with similar norms, values, and expectations who interact with one another on a regular basis?

   a. a category
   b. a group
   c. an aggregate
   d. a society

4. Which sociological perspective argues that the present organization of social institutions is no accident?

   a. the functionalist perspective
   b. the conflict perspective
   c. the interactionist perspective
   d. the global perspective

5. Social control in what Ferdinand Tönnies termed a *Gemeinschaft* community is maintained through all but which of the following means?

   a. moral persuasion
   b. gossip
   c. legally defined punishment
   d. gestures

6. Sociologist Daniel Bell uses which of the following terms to refer to a society whose economic system is engaged primarily in the processing and control of information?

   a. postmodern
   b. horticultural
   c. industrial
   d. postindustrial

7. The Shakers, a religious sect that came to the United States in 1774 has seen its group membership diminish significantly due to its inability to

   a. teach new recruits.
   b. preserve order.
   c. replace personnel.
   d. provide and maintain a sense of purpose.

8. Which sociologist saw that the "definition of the situation" could mold the thinking and personality of the individual?

   a. Philip Zimbardo
   b. Herbert Blumer
   c. William I. Thomas
   d. Erving Goffman

9. Which sociological perspective has identified five major tasks that a society must accomplish if it is to survive?

   a. the functionalist perspective
   b. the conflict perspective
   c. the interactionist perspective
   d. the clinical perspective

10. In Zimbardo's mock prison experiment at Stanford University,

   a. the social interactions between the prisoners and the guards influenced the social structure of the prison.
   b. the social structure of the prison influenced the social interactions between the prisoners and the guards.
   c. there was no relationship between social interaction and social structure.
   d. Zimbardo believed that social structure and social interaction influence each other.

11. The term _____ _____ refers to the way in which a society is organized into predictable relationships.

12. The African American activist Malcolm X wrote in his autobiography that his position as a Black man, an _____ status, was an obstacle to his dream of becoming a lawyer, an _____ status.

13. Sociologist Helen Rose Fuchs Ebaugh developed the term _____ _____ to describe the process of disengagement from a role that is central to one's self-identity in order to establish a new role and identity.

14. The mass media, the government, the economy, the family, and the health care system are all examples of _____ _____ found in the United States.

15. According to Herbert Blumer, our response to someone's behavior is based on the _____ we attach to his or her actions.

16. In studying the social behavior of word processors in a Chicago law firm, sociologist Mitchell Duneier drew on the _____ perspective.

17. According to Émile Durkheim, societies with a minimal division of labor are characterized by _____ solidarity, while societies with a complex division of labor are characterized by _____ solidarity.

18. In Gerhard Lenski's theory of sociocultural evolution, a society's level of _____ is critical to the way it is organized.

19. A(n) _____ society is a technologically sophisticated society that is preoccupied with consumer goods and media images.

20. Policymakers have embraced the concept of _____ _____, or the principle that the government should remain nonselective toward online content.

Answers:
1 (c); 2 (a); 3 (b); 4 (b); 5 (c); 6 (d); 7 (b); 8 (c); 9 (a); 10 (b); 11 social structure; 12 ascribed, achieved; 13 role exit; 14 social institutions; 15 meaning; 16 interactionist; 17 mechanical, organic; 18 technology; 19 postmodern; 20 net neutrality

TECHNOLOGY RESOURCES

Online Learning Center

1. You can assess your knowledge of the material in this chapter at any point by completing the true–false quiz at the student center in the Online Learning Center (**www.mhhe.com/schaefer11**). It will give you immediate feedback on incorrect answers. You can even take the quiz before reading the chapter as a way of familiarizing yourself with some of the key topics.

2. Proponents of educational programs in prisons argue that the social structure of a classroom environment can be used to rehabilitate people who have been incarcerated. Visit the Web site of the Center for the Study of Correctional Education (**www.csusb.edu/coe/cg/csce/index.html**)—especially the link to Research. Contrast these programs with the social environment of Zimbardo's prison experiment.

3. In this chapter you learned that social networks can be a very empowering component of social structure. The Step Up Women's Network (**www.stepupwomensnetwork.org**) is one example of a network designed to benefit women and girls, in part by providing specific opportunities for them to enhance their social networks.

Note: Although all the URLs listed were current as of the printing of this book, these sites often change. Please check our Web site **(www.mhhe.com/schaefer11)** *for updates, hyperlinks, and exercises related to these sites.*

Reel Society Video Clips

Reel Society video clips, which appear on this book's Web site, can be used to spark discussion about the following topic from this chapter:

• Social Roles

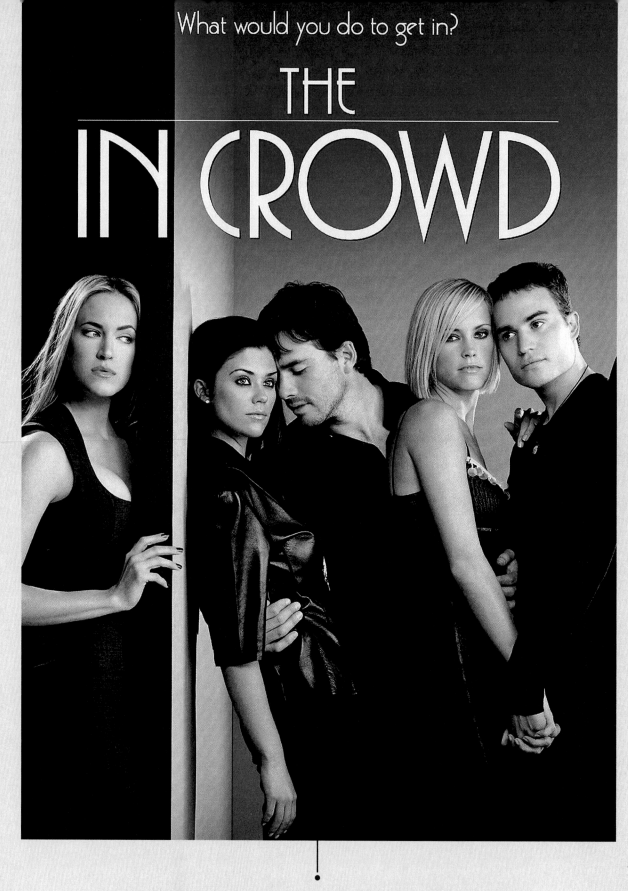

What would you do to get in?

THE IN CROWD

Groups help individuals to navigate through the larger social world, including complex organizations like educational institutions. The motion picture *The In Crowd* (2000) dramatized the group dynamics of an affluent but twisted clique of college students. Despite media concentration on such youthful in-groups, however, people of all ages value the groups they belong to.

6

Groups and Organizations

GEORGE RITZER

The McDonaldization
of Society

Revised New Century Edition

66 Ray Kroc (1902–1984), the genius behind the franchising of McDonald's restaurants, was a man with big ideas and grand ambitions. But even Kroc could not have anticipated the astounding impact of his creation. McDonald's is the basis of one of the most influential developments in contemporary society. Its reverberations extend far beyond its point of origin in the United States and in the fast-food business. It has influenced a wide range of undertakings, indeed the way of life, of a significant portion of the world. And in spite of McDonald's recent and well-publicized economic difficulties, that impact is likely to expand at an accelerating rate.

However, this is *not* a book about McDonald's, or even about the fast-food business. . . . I devote all this attention to McDonald's . . . because it serves here as the major example of, and the paradigm for, a wide-ranging process I call *McDonaldization*. . . . As you will see, McDonaldization affects not only the restaurant business but also education, work, the criminal justice system, health care, travel, leisure, dieting, politics, the family, religion, and virtually every other aspect of society. McDonaldization has shown every sign of being an inexorable process, sweeping through seemingly impervious institutions and regions of the world.

Other types of business are increasingly adapting the principles of the fast-food industry to their needs. Said the vice chairman of Toys "R" Us, "We want to be thought of as a sort of McDonald's of toys." . . . Other chains with similar ambitions include Gap, Jiffy Lube, AAMCO Transmissions, Midas Muffler & Brake Shops, Great Clips, H&R Block, Pearle Vision, Bally's. . . .

> *Ray Kroc (1902–1984), the genius behind the franchising of McDonald's restaurants, was a man with big ideas and grand ambitions.*

Other nations have developed their own variants of this American institution. . . . Paris, a city whose love for fine cuisine might lead you to think it would prove immune to fast food, has a large number of fast-food croissanteries; the revered French bread has also been McDonaldized. India has a chain of fast-food restaurants, Nirula's, that sells mutton burgers (about 80% of Indians are Hindus, who eat no beef) as well as local Indian cuisine. Mos Burger is a Japanese chain with over fifteen hundred restaurants that in addition to the usual fare, sells Teriyaki chicken burgers, rice burgers, and "Oshiruko with brown rice cake." . . .

McDonald's is such a powerful model that many businesses have acquired nicknames beginning with Mc. Examples include "McDentists" and "McDoctors," meaning drive-in clinics designed to deal quickly and efficiently with minor dental and medical problems; "McChild" care centers, meaning child care centers such as KinderCare; "McStables," designating the nationwide race horse–training operation of Wayne Lucas; and "McPaper," describing the newspaper *USA TODAY.* 99

(Ritzer 2004a:1–4, 10–11) Additional information about this excerpt can be found on the Online Learning Center at www.mhhe.com/schaefer11.

In this excerpt from *The McDonaldization of Society*, sociologist George Ritzer contemplates the enormous influence of a well-known fast-food organization on modern-day culture and social life. Ritzer defines **McDonaldization** as "the process by which the principles of the fast-food restaurant are coming to dominate more and more sectors of American society as well as of the rest of the world" (Ritzer 2004a:1). In his book, he shows how the business principles on which the fast-food industry is founded—efficiency, calculability, predictability, and control—have changed not only the way Americans do business and run their organizations, but the way they live their lives. Today, busy families rely on the takeout meals served up by fast-food establishments, and McDonald's has become a regular meeting place for social groups from adolescents to senior citizens.

Despite the runaway success of McDonald's and its imitators, and the advantages these enterprises bring to millions of people around the world (see Box 6-2, page 144), Ritzer is critical of their effect on society. The waste and environmental degradation created by billions of disposable containers and the dehumanized work routines of fast-food crews are two of the disadvantages he cites in his critique. Would the modern world be a better one, Ritzer asks, if it were less McDonaldized?

This chapter considers the impact of groups and organizations on social interaction. Do we behave differently in large groups than in small ones? How do we make large organizations manageable? What effect are current social changes having on the structure of groups? We'll begin by noting the distinctions between various types of groups, with particular attention to the dynamics of small groups. We'll examine how and why formal organizations came into existence and describe Max Weber's model of the modern bureaucracy. In a case study of the loss of the space shuttle *Columbia,* we'll see how NASA's bureaucratic culture contributed to the ship's disastrous accident. And we'll examine a special kind of organization, the voluntary association. Finally, we'll look at recent changes in the workplace, some of which are designed to counteract the failures of bureaucracies. The social policy section at the end of the chapter focuses on the status of organized labor today.

Understanding Groups

Most of us use the term *group* loosely to describe any collection of individuals, whether three strangers sharing an elevator or hundreds attending a rock concert. However, in sociological terms a **group** is any number of people with similar norms, values, and expectations who interact with one another on a regular basis. College sororities and fraternities, dance companies, tenants' associations, and chess clubs are all considered groups. The important point is that members of a group share some sense of belonging. This characteristic distinguishes groups from mere *aggregates* of people, such as passengers who happen to be together on an airplane flight, or from *categories* of people—those who share a common feature (such as being retired) but otherwise do not act together.

Consider the case of a college singing group. It has agreed-on values and social norms. All members want to improve their singing skills and schedule lots of performances. In addition, like many groups, the singing ensemble has both a formal and an informal structure. The members meet regularly to rehearse; they choose leaders to run the rehearsals and manage their affairs. At the same time, some group members may take on unofficial leadership roles by coaching new members in singing techniques and performing skills.

The study of groups has become an important part of sociological investigation because they play such a key role in the transmission of culture. As we interact with others, we pass on our ways of thinking and acting—from language and values to ways of dressing and leisure activities.

Types of Groups

Sociologists have made a number of useful distinctions between types of groups—primary and secondary groups, in-groups and out-groups, and reference groups.

Primary and Secondary Groups Charles Horton Cooley (1902) coined the term ***primary group*** to refer to a small group characterized by intimate, face-to-face association and cooperation. The members of a street gang constitute a primary group; so do members of a family living in the same household, as do a group of "sisters" in a college sorority.

Primary groups play a pivotal role both in the socialization process (see Chapter 4) and in the development of roles and statuses (see Chapter 5). Indeed, primary groups can be instrumental in a person's day-to-day existence. When we find ourselves identifying closely with a group, it is probably a primary group.

We also participate in many groups that are not characterized by close bonds of friendship, such as large college classes and business associations. The term ***secondary group*** refers to a formal, impersonal group in which there is little social intimacy or mutual understanding (see Table 6-1). Secondary groups often emerge in the workplace among those who share special understandings about their occupation. The distinction between primary and secondary groups is not always clear-cut, however. Some social clubs may become so large and impersonal that they no longer function as primary groups.

In-Groups and Out-Groups A group can hold special meaning for members because of its relationship to other groups. For example, people in one group sometimes feel antagonistic toward or threatened by another group, especially if that group is perceived as being different either culturally or racially. To identify these "we" and "they" feelings, sociologists use two terms first employed by William Graham Sumner (1906): *in-group* and *out-group*.

An **in-group** can be defined as any group or category to which people feel they belong. Simply put, it comprises everyone who is regarded as "we" or "us." The in-group may be as narrow as a teenage clique or as broad as an entire society. The very existence of an in-group implies that there is an *out-group* that is viewed as "they" or "them." An **out-group** is a group or category to which people feel they do *not* belong.

In-group members typically feel distinct and superior, seeing themselves as better than people in the out-group. Proper behavior for the in-group is simultaneously viewed as unacceptable behavior for the out-group. This double standard enhances the sense of superiority. Sociologist Robert Merton (1968) described this process as the conversion of "in-group virtues" into "out-group vices." We can see this differential standard operating in worldwide discussions of terrorism. When a group or a nation takes aggressive actions, it usually justifies them as necessary, even if civilians are hurt or killed. Opponents are quick to label such actions with the emotion-laden term of *terrorist* and appeal to the world community for condemnation. Yet these same people may themselves retaliate with actions that hurt civilians, which the first group will then condemn.

Conflict between in-groups and out-groups can turn violent on a personal as well as a political level. In 1999 two disaffected students at Columbine High School in Littleton, Colorado, launched an attack on the school that left 15 students and teachers dead, including themselves. The gunmen, members of an out-group that other students referred to as the Trenchcoat Mafia, apparently resented taunting by an in-group referred to as the Jocks. Similar episodes have occurred in schools across the nation, where rejected adolescents, overwhelmed by personal

A pizza delivery crew is an example of a *secondary group*—a formal, impersonal group in which there is little social intimacy or mutual understanding. While waiting for the next delivery, members of this crew will become well enough acquainted to distinguish those who see the job as temporary from those who view it as permanent. They will learn who looks forward to deliveries in perceived high-risk areas and who does not. They may even spend time together after work, joking or boasting about their exploits on the job, but their friendship typically will not develop beyond that point.

Table 6-1

Comparison of Primary and Secondary Groups

summingUP

Primary Group	Secondary Group
Generally small	Usually large
Relatively long period of interaction	Relatively short duration, often temporary
Intimate, face-to-face association	Little social intimacy or mutual understanding
Some emotional depth to relationships	Relationships generally superficial
Cooperative, friendly	More formal and impersonal

and family problems, peer group pressure, academic responsibilities, or media images of violence, have struck out against more popular classmates.

In-group members who actively provoke out-group members may have their own problems, including limited time and attention from working parents. Sociologists David Stevenson and Barbara Schneider (1999), who studied 7,000 teenagers, found that despite many opportunities for group membership, young people spend an average of three and a half hours alone every day. While youths may claim they want privacy, they also crave attention, and striking out at members of an in-group or out-group, be they the wrong gender, race, or friendship group, seems to be one way to get it.

"So long, Bill. This is my club. You can't come in."

An exclusive social club is an in-group whose members consider themselves superior to others.

Use Your Sociological Imagination

Try putting yourself in the shoes of an out-group member. What does your in-group look like from that perspective?

Reference Groups Both in-groups and primary groups can dramatically influence the way an individual thinks and behaves. Sociologists call any group that individuals use as a standard for evaluating themselves and their own behavior a *reference group.* For example, a high school student who aspires to join a social circle of hip-hop music devotees will pattern his or her behavior after that of the group. The student will begin dressing like these peers, listening to the same tapes and CDs, and hanging out at the same stores and clubs.

Reference groups have two basic purposes. They serve a normative function by setting and enforcing standards of conduct and belief. The high school student who wants the approval of the hip-hop crowd will have to follow the group's dictates, at least to some extent. Reference groups also perform a compari-

son function by serving as a standard against which people can measure themselves and others. An actor will evaluate himself or herself against a reference group composed of others in the acting profession (Merton and Kitt 1950).

Reference groups may help the process of anticipatory socialization. For example, a college student majoring in finance may read *The Wall Street Journal,* study the annual reports of corporations, and listen to midday stock market news on the radio. Such a student is using financial experts as a reference group to which he or she aspires.

Often, two or more reference groups influence us at the same time. Our family members, neighbors, and co-workers all shape different aspects of our self-evaluation. In addition, reference group attachments change during the life cycle. A corporate executive who quits the rat race at age 45 to become a social worker will find new reference groups to use as standards for evaluation. We shift reference groups as we take on different statuses during our lives.

Coalitions As groups grow larger, coalitions begin to develop. A *coalition* is a temporary or permanent alliance geared toward a common goal. Coalitions can be broad-based or narrow and can take on many different objectives. Sociologist William Julius Wilson (1999b) has described community-based organizations in Texas that include Whites and Latinos, working class and affluent, who have banded together to work for improved sidewalks, better drainage systems, and comprehensive street paving. Out of this type of coalition building, Wilson hopes, will emerge better interracial understanding.

Some coalitions are intentionally short lived. Short-term coalition building is a key to success in popular TV programs like *Survivor.* In *Survivor I,* broadcast in 2000, the four members of the "Tagi alliance" banded together to vote fellow castaways off the island. The political world is also the scene of many temporary coalitions. For example, in 1997 big tobacco companies joined with antismoking groups to draw up a settlement for reimbursing states for tobacco-related medical costs. Soon after the settlement was announced the coalition members returned to their decades-long fight against each other (Pear 1997).

Use Your Sociological Imagination

Do coalitions always work toward positive goals? Imagine a coalition that was formed to achieve a socially undesirable goal. Who are the members, and why did they band together?

Studying Small Groups

Sociological research done on the micro level and research done from the interactionist perspective usually focus on the study of small groups. Box 6-1 (page 140), for example, describes microsociological research on juries. The term *small group* refers

their authority in the neighborhood (Venkatesh 2000).

Size of a Group At what point does a collection of people become too large to be called a small group? That is not clear. In a group with more than 20 members, it is difficult for individuals to interact regularly in a direct and intimate manner. But even within a range of 2 to 20 people, group size can substantially alter the quality of social relationships. For example, as the number of group participants increases, the most active communicators become even more active relative to others. Therefore, a person who dominates a group of 3 or 4 members will be relatively more dominant in a 15-person group.

Group size also has noticeable social implications for members who do not assume leadership roles. In a larger group, each member has less time to speak, more points of view to absorb, and a more elaborate structure to function in. At the same time, an individual has greater freedom to ignore certain members or viewpoints than he or she would in a smaller group. It is harder to disregard someone in a 4-person workforce than someone in an office with 30 employees, harder to disregard

Members of New York City's Unatics, a unicycle club, often gather in Central Park to ride their cycles. These accomplished riders may serve as a reference group for onlookers who become interested in the sport.

to a group small enough for all members to interact simultaneously—that is, to talk with one another or at least be well acquainted. Certain primary groups, such as families, may also be classified as small groups. However, many small groups differ from primary groups in that they do not necessarily offer the intimate personal relationships characteristic of primary groups. For example, a manufacturer may bring together its seven-member regional sales staff twice a year for an intensive sales conference. The salespeople, who live in different cities and rarely see one another, constitute a small secondary group, not a primary group.

We may think of small groups as being informal and unpatterned; yet, as interactionist researchers have revealed, distinct and predictable processes are at work in the functioning of small groups. A long-term ethnographic study of street gangs in Chicago revealed an elaborate structure resembling that of a family business. A street gang there is composed of several geographically based units called sets, each of which possesses a leader, lower-ranking officers, and a rank-and-file membership. Besides staffing the economic network of the drug trade, gang members develop relationships with tenant leaders in public housing projects and participate in nondelinquent social activities important to the maintenance of

Can you outwit, outplay, outlast your competition? Maybe a coalition can help. In *Survivor: Fiji*, coalition building continued to be one of the keys to success in the long-running television series.

research IN action

6-1 Decision Making in the Jury Room

In the motion picture *Twelve Angry Men* (1957), actor Henry Ford played a juror who began as the lone voice for acquittal but in the end convinced the entire jury of the defendant's innocence. Although *Twelve Angry Men* made for great drama, recent research suggests that jurors generally do not change their minds after the first ballot. A study of 225 cases indicates that if a majority of jurors vote to convict a defendant on the first ballot, there is only a 5 percent chance that they will later acquit the defendant.

Few small groups have received as much attention from sociologists over the past decade and a half as U.S. juries. Scholars have used several research methods to investigate juries' decision making: interviews with jury members after they have reached a verdict; observation of jurors as they sit through and react to courtroom events; observation of actual jury deliberations, which presiding judges have permitted in a few instances; and experiments involving mock juries. The findings indicate that jurors do not always make decisions the way they are supposed to.

For example, a jury's decision making may occur even before the first ballot is taken. Despite judges' instructions to the contrary, many jurors form tentative verdicts early in the trial. Studies suggest that jurors who have reached an initial judgment of "guilty" or "not guilty" give disproportionate weight to testimony that reinforces their impressions, while they tend to discount testimony that undermines them.

Most research on jurors' decision making in criminal trials has focused on how jurors decide whether or not a defendant is guilty. In a significant number of criminal cases, however, a defendant is tried not on one but on several counts, and might also be found not guilty by reason of insanity. Several studies have shown that jurors are more likely to convict a defendant on at least one charge if they are given alternatives to an absolute "guilty" or "not guilty" verdict.

Researchers have paid special attention to comparisons of 6-person versus 12-person juries, because state legislatures have shown an interest in reducing jury size to save money

> *Several studies have shown that jurors are more likely to convict a defendant on at least one charge if they are given alternatives to an absolute "guilty" or "not guilty" verdict.*

and expedite judicial proceedings. In one study of criminal cases, social scientists found that when the defendant appeared to be not guilty, the size of the jury had no impact on the likelihood of conviction. However, when the defendant's guilt seemed more obvious, 12-person juries were more reluctant to convict than 6-person juries.

Today, research on juries is expanding to deal with changes in the experience of being a juror. Some jurors arrive at court expecting to see the kind of sophisticated DNA analysis or investigative methods featured on televised crime shows, such as *CSI*. Improved methods of documenting crime scenes, including the use of computer-generated re-creations, mean that today's jurors are more likely than past jurors to be exposed to images of graphic violence and gore. Mental health professionals and social scientists have documented that the trauma jurors sometimes suffer from such exposure can trigger classic symptoms of stress, including depression, anxiety, weight loss, sleep loss, and disruptions in close social relationships. As with membership in other small groups, serving on a jury can be an intense experience—especially during a long, combative criminal trial with a focus on violence and bloodshed.

Let's Discuss

1. Have you ever served on a jury? If so, were you aware of jurors who made up their minds early in the trial, despite the judge's instructions? Did you experience stress from being exposed to graphic images of violence and bloodshed?

2. Relate what you have learned about small groups to juries. Is a jury a typical small group? Why or why not? Would a large group be more effective than a small group in determining a defendant's guilt or innocence?

Sources: Abramson 1994; S. Diamond and Rose 2005; Hare 1992; MacCoun 1989; Rakowitz and Sabini 1995; Roan 1995; Sunwolf and Seibold 1998.

---

someone in a string quartet than someone in a college band with 50 members.

The German sociologist Georg Simmel (1858–1918) is credited as the first sociologist to emphasize the importance of interactive processes within groups and to note how they change as the group's size changes. The simplest of all social groups or relationships is the **dyad,** or two-member group. A wife and a husband constitute a dyad, as does a business partnership or a singing duo. The dyad offers a special level of intimacy that cannot be duplicated in larger groups. However, as Simmel ([1917] 1950) noted, a dyad, unlike any other group, can be destroyed by the loss of a single member. Therefore, the threat of termination hangs over a dyadic relationship perhaps more than over any other.

Obviously, the introduction of one additional person to a dyad dramatically transforms the character of the small group. The dyad becomes a three-member group, or **triad.** The third member has many ways of interacting with and influencing the dynamics of the group. The new person may play a *unifying* role in the triad. When a married couple has their first child, the baby may serve to bind the group closer together. A newcomer also may play a *mediating* role in a three-person group. If two roommates are perpetually sniping at each other, the third roommate may attempt to remain on good terms with both and to arrange compromise solutions to problems. Finally, a member of a triad can choose to employ a *divide-and-rule* strategy. Such is the case, for example, with a coach who tries to gain greater control over two assistants by making them rivals (Nixon 1979).

Groupthink Can mere membership in a group cause those who belong to reach faulty decisions? William H. Whyte, Jr. (1952) thought so. To describe the uncritical acceptance of or conformity to the prevailing viewpoint—a phenomenon that too often characterizes group decision making—Whyte coined the term ***groupthink.*** Simply put, group members experience a collective pressure to conform to the predominant line of thought. This social pressure effectively discourages the open expression of dissent.

In Whyte's opinion, high-level government leaders and their advisers are particularly prone to groupthink. These people confer regularly with one another, often in closed meetings in which they hear no one else's viewpoint. When decision makers are isolated from others in this way, they are liable to adopt unpopular or even disastrous policies. Of course, groupthink is not limited to the upper echelons of government. It occurs in jury rooms, corporate board rooms, and even among high school students selecting a theme for their senior prom.

There are ways to avoid the illusion of unanimity created by groupthink. Small-group studies have shown the value of having outside facilitators lead groups. Dividing an established group into smaller units also encourages the expression of new perspectives (Janis 1967; Street 1997).

The effects of group size, coalition building, and groupthink on group dynamics are but two of the many aspects of the small group that sociologists have studied. Another aspect, conformity and deviance, is examined in Chapter 8. Although it is clear that small-group encounters have a considerable influence on our lives, we are also deeply affected by much larger groups of people, as we'll see in the next section.

Understanding Organizations
Formal Organizations and Bureaucracies

As contemporary societies have shifted to more advanced forms of technology and their social structures have become more complex, our lives have become increasingly dominated by large secondary groups referred to as *formal organizations*. A ***formal organization*** is a group designed for a special purpose and structured for maximum efficiency. The U.S. Postal Service, McDonald's, and the Boston Pops orchestra are examples of formal organizations. Though organizations vary in their size, specificity of goals, and degree of efficiency, they are all structured to facilitate the management of large-scale operations. They also have a bureaucratic form of organization, described in the next section.

In our society, formal organizations fulfill an enormous variety of personal and societal needs, shaping the lives of every one of us. In fact, formal organizations have become such a dominant force that we must create organizations to supervise other organizations, such as the Securities and Exchange Commission (SEC) to regulate brokerage companies. While it sounds much more exciting to say that we live in the "computer age" than to say that ours is the "age of formal organization," the latter is probably a more accurate description of our times (Azumi and Hage 1972; Etzioni 1964).

Ascribed statuses such as gender, race, and ethnicity can influence how we see ourselves within formal organizations. For example, a study of women lawyers in the nation's largest law firms found significant differences in the women's self-images, depending on the relative presence or absence of women in positions of power. In firms in which less than 15 percent of partners were women, the female lawyers were likely to believe that "feminine" traits were strongly devalued and that masculinity was equated with success. As one female attorney put it, "Let's face it: this is a man's environment, and it's sort of Jock City, especially at my firm." Women in firms where female lawyers were better represented in positions of power had a stronger desire for and higher expectations of promotion (Ely 1995:619).

Characteristics of a Bureaucracy

A ***bureaucracy*** is a component of formal organization that uses rules and hierarchical ranking to achieve efficiency. Rows of desks staffed by seemingly faceless people, endless lines and forms, impossibly complex language, and frustrating encounters with red tape—all these unpleasant images have combined to make *bureaucracy* a dirty word and an easy target in political campaigns. As a result, few people want to identify their occupation as "bureaucrat," despite the fact that all of us perform various bureaucratic tasks. In an industrial society, elements of bureaucracy enter into almost every occupation.

Max Weber ([1913–1922] 1947) first directed researchers to the significance of bureaucratic structure. In an important sociological advance, Weber emphasized the basic similarity of structure and process found in the otherwise dissimilar enterprises of religion, government, education, and business. Weber saw bureaucracy as a form of organization quite different from {p.13} the family-run business. For analytical purposes, he developed an *ideal type* of bureaucracy that would reflect the most characteristic aspects of all human organizations. By ***ideal type*** Weber meant a construct or model for evaluating specific cases. In actuality, perfect bureaucracies do not exist; no real-world organization corresponds exactly to Weber's ideal type.

Weber proposed that whether the purpose is to run a church, a corporation, or an army, the ideal bureaucracy displays five basic characteristics. A discussion of those characteristics, as well {p.16} as the dysfunctions of a bureaucracy, follows.

1. **Division of labor.** Specialized experts perform specific tasks. In your college bureaucracy, the admissions officer does not do the job of registrar; the guidance counselor doesn't see to the maintenance of buildings. By working at a specific task, people are more likely to become highly skilled and carry out a job with maximum efficiency. This emphasis on specialization is so basic a part of our lives that we may not realize it is a fairly recent development in Western culture.

The downside of division of labor is that the fragmentation of work into smaller and smaller tasks can divide workers and remove any connection they might feel to the overall objective of the bureaucracy. In *The Communist Manifesto* (written in 1848), Karl Marx and Friedrich Engels charged that the capitalist system reduces workers to a mere "appendage of the machine" (L. Feuer 1989). Such a work arrangement, they wrote, produces extreme **alienation**—a condition of estrangement or dissociation from the surrounding society. According to both Marx and conflict theorists, restricting workers to very small tasks also weakens their job security, since new employees can be easily trained to replace them.

Although division of labor has certainly enhanced the performance of many complex bureaucracies, in some cases it can lead to **trained incapacity;** that is, workers become so specialized that they develop blind spots and fail to notice obvious problems. Even worse, they may not care about what is happening in the next department. Some observers believe that such developments have caused workers in the United States to become less productive on the job.

In some cases, the bureaucratic division of labor can have tragic results. In the wake of the coordinated attacks on the World Trade Center and the Pentagon on September 11, 2001, Americans wondered aloud how the FBI and CIA could have failed to detect the terrorists' elaborately planned operation. The problem, in part, turned out to be the division of labor between

Whistle-blower Colleen Rowley, an FBI agent, tried unsuccessfully to bring her superiors' attention to a French Moroccan who had signed up for pilot training at a local flight school, keen to operate a 747. The man later used his training to crash a hijacked jet into the World Trade Center. Rowley was photographed as she testified before the Senate Judiciary Committee in June 2002.

the FBI, which focuses on domestic matters, and the CIA, which operates overseas. Officials at these intelligence-gathering organizations, both of which are huge bureaucracies, are well known for jealously guarding information from one another. Subsequent investigations revealed that they knew about Osama bin Laden and his al-Qaeda terrorist network in the early 1990s. Unfortunately, five federal agencies—the CIA, FBI, National Security Agency, Defense Intelligence Agency, and National Reconnaissance Office—failed to share their leads on the network. Although the hijacking of the four commercial airliners used in the massive attacks may not have been preventable, the bureaucratic division of labor definitely hindered efforts to defend against terrorism, undermining U.S. national security.

2. Hierarchy of authority. Bureaucracies follow the principle of hierarchy; that is, each position is under the supervision of a higher authority. A president heads a college bureaucracy; he or she selects members of the administration, who in turn hire their own staff. In the Roman Catholic Church, the pope is the supreme authority; under him are cardinals, bishops, and so forth.

3. Written rules and regulations. What if your sociology professor gave your classmate an A for having such a friendly smile? You might think that wasn't fair, that it was against the rules.

Rules and regulations, as we all know, are an important characteristic of bureaucracies. Ideally, through such procedures, a bureaucracy ensures uniform performance of every task. Thus your classmate cannot receive an A for a nice smile, because the rules guarantee that all students will receive essentially the same treatment.

Through written rules and regulations, bureaucracies generally offer employees clear standards for an adequate (or exceptional) performance. In addition, procedures provide a valuable sense of continuity in a bureaucracy. Individual workers will come and go, but the structure and past records of the organization give it a life of its own that outlives the services of any one bureaucrat.

Of course, rules and regulations can overshadow the larger goals of an organization to the point that they become dysfunctional. What if a hospital emergency room physician failed to treat a seriously injured person because he or she had no valid proof of U.S. citizenship? If blindly applied, rules no longer serve as a means to achieving an objective, but instead become important (and perhaps too important) in their own right. Robert Merton (1968) used the term **goal displacement** to refer to overzealous conformity to official regulations.

4. Impersonality. Max Weber wrote that in a bureaucracy, work is carried out *sine ira et studio,* "without hatred or passion." Bureaucratic norms dictate that officials perform their duties without giving personal consideration to people as individuals. Although this norm is intended to guarantee equal treatment for each person, it also contributes to the often cold and uncaring feeling associated with modern organizations. We typically think of big government and big business when we think of impersonal bureaucracies. In some cases, the impersonality that is associated

"Frankly, at this point in the flow chart, we don't know what happens to these people..."

A hierarchy of authority may deprive individuals of a voice in decision making, but it does clarify who supervises whom.

promoted, and people often have a right to appeal if they believe that particular rules have been violated. Such procedures protect bureaucrats against arbitrary dismissal, provide a measure of security, and encourage loyalty to the organization.

In this sense, the "impersonal" bureaucracy can be considered an improvement over nonbureaucratic organizations. College faculty members, for example, are ideally hired and promoted according to their professional qualifications, including degrees earned and research published, rather than because of whom they know. Once they are granted tenure, their jobs are protected against the whims of a president or dean.

Although any bureaucracy ideally will value technical and professional competence, personnel decisions do not always follow that ideal pattern. Dysfunctions within bureaucracy have become well publicized, particularly because of the work of Laurence J. Peter. According to the **Peter principle,** every employee within a hierarchy tends to rise to his or her level of incompetence (Peter and Hull 1969). This hypothesis, which has not been directly or systematically tested, reflects a possible dysfunctional outcome of advancement on the basis of merit. Talented people receive promotion after promotion, until sadly, some of them finally achieve positions that they cannot handle with their usual competence (Blau and Meyer 1987).

Table 6-2 summarizes the five characteristics of bureaucracy. These characteristics, developed by Max Weber more than 80 years ago, describe an ideal type rather than an actual bureaucracy. Not every formal organization will possess all five of Weber's characteristics. In fact, wide variation exists among actual bureaucratic organizations.

Bureaucracy pervades modern life. Through McDonaldization —the worldwide diffusion not only of the fast-food restaurant, but of the principles of operating such an establishment— bureaucratization has reached new heights (see Chapter 3). As Box 6-2 (page 144) shows, the McDonald's organization provides an excellent illustration of Weber's concept of bureaucracy.

with a bureaucracy can have tragic results. More frequently, bureaucratic impersonality produces frustration and disaffection. Today, even small firms screen callers with electronic menus.

5. Employment based on technical qualifications. Within the ideal bureaucracy, hiring is based on technical qualifications rather than on favoritism, and performance is measured against specific standards. Written personnel policies dictate who gets

Table 6-2

Characteristics of a Bureaucracy

Characteristic	Positive Consequence	Negative Consequence For the Individual	Negative Consequence For the Organization
Division of labor	Produces efficiency in a large-scale corporation	Produces trained incapacity	Produces a narrow perspective
Hierarchy of authority	Clarifies who is in command	Deprives employees of a voice in decision making	Permits concealment of mistakes
Written rules and regulations	Let workers know what is expected of them	Stifle initiative and imagination	Lead to goal displacement
Impersonality	Reduces bias	Contributes to feelings of alienation	Discourages loyalty to company
Employment based on technical qualifications	Discourages favoritism and reduces petty rivalries	Discourages ambition to improve oneself elsewhere	Fosters Peter principle

summingUP

6-2 McDonald's and the Worldwide Bureaucratization of Society

In his book *The McDonaldization of Society*, sociologist George Ritzer notes the enormous influence of a well-known fast-food organization on modern-day culture and social life.

Not surprisingly, Max Weber's five characteristics of bureaucracy are apparent in McDonald's restaurants, as well as in the global corporation behind them. Food preparation and order-taking reflect a painstaking *division of labor*, implemented by a *hierarchy of authority* that stretches from the food workers up to the shift manager and store operator, and ultimately to the corporate board of directors. Store operators learn McDonald's *written rules and regulations*, which govern even the amount of ketchup or mustard placed on a hamburger, at McDonald's Hamburger University. Little bonding occurs between servers and customers, creating a pervasive sense of *impersonality*. Together with McDonald's cookie-cutter architectural designs, this lack of personal character tends to disguise a restaurant's locale—not just the town or city it serves, but often the country or continent as well. Finally, employees are expected to have specific *technical qualifications*, although most of the skills they need to perform routine tasks can be learned in a brief training period.

The real significance of McDonaldization is that it is not confined to the food-service industry. Worldwide, McDonald's brand of predictability, efficiency, and dependence on nonhuman technology have become customary in a number of services, ranging from medical care to wedding planning to education. Even sporting events reflect the influence of bureaucratization. Around the world, stadiums are becoming increasingly similar, both physically and in the way they present the sport to spectators. Swipe cards, "sports city" garages and parking lots, and automated ticket sales maximize efficiency. All seats offer spectators an unrestricted view, and a big screen guarantees them access to instant replays. Scores, player statistics, and attendance figures are updated automatically by computer and displayed on an automated scoreboard. Spectator enthusiasm is manufactured through digital displays urging applause or rhythmic chanting. At food counters, refreshments include well-known brands whose customer loyalty has

> *Worldwide, McDonald's brand of predictability, efficiency, and dependence on nonhuman technology have become customary in a number of services, ranging from medical care to wedding planning to education.*

been nourished by advertisers for decades. And of course, the merchandising of teams' and even players' names and images is highly controlled.

McDonald's reliance on the five characteristics of bureaucracy is not revolutionary. What is new is the bureaucratization of services and life events that once were highly individualized, at times even spontaneous. More and more, society itself is becoming McDonaldized.

Let's Discuss

1. Do you patronize McDonald's and other fast-food establishments? If so, what features of these restaurants do you appreciate? Do you have any complaints about them?
2. Analyze life at your college using Weber's model of bureaucracy. What elements of McDonaldization do you see? Do you wish life were less McDonaldized?

Sources: Ormond 2005; Ritzer 2004a.

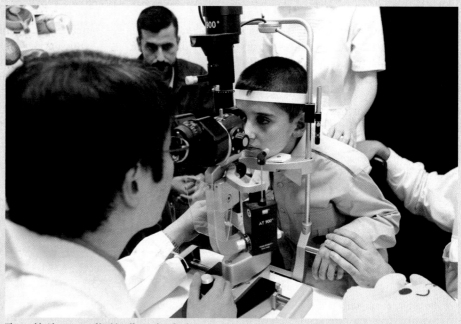

The worldwide success of highly efficient fast-food operations has led to the bureaucratization of many other services, including eye care and other forms of medical treatment.

Use Your Sociological Imagination

Your school or workplace suddenly ceases to exhibit one of the five characteristics of bureaucracy. Which characteristic is it, and what are the consequences?

Bureaucratization as a Process Have you ever had to speak to 10 or 12 individuals in a corporation or government agency just to find out which official has jurisdiction over a particular problem? Ever been transferred from one department to another until you finally hung up in disgust? Sociologists have used the term **bureaucratization** to refer to the process by which a group, organization, or social movement becomes increasingly bureaucratic.

Normally, we think of bureaucratization in terms of large organizations. But bureaucratization also takes place within small-group settings. Sociologist Jennifer Bickman Mendez (1998) studied domestic houseworkers employed in central California by a nationwide franchise. She found that housekeeping tasks were minutely defined, to the point that employees had to follow 22 written steps for cleaning a bathroom. Complaints and special requests went not to the workers, but to an office-based manager.

Oligarchy: Rule by a Few Conflict theorists have examined the bureaucratization of social movements. The German sociologist Robert Michels (1915) studied socialist parties and labor unions in Europe before World War I and found that such organizations were becoming increasingly bureaucratic. The emerging leaders of the organizations—even some of the most radical—had a vested interest in clinging to power. If they lost their leadership posts, they would have to return to full-time work as manual laborers.

Through his research, Michels originated the idea of the **iron law of oligarchy,** which describes how even a democratic organization will eventually develop into a bureaucracy ruled by a few (called an oligarchy). Why do oligarchies emerge? People who achieve leadership roles usually have the skills, knowledge, or charismatic appeal (as Weber noted) to direct, if not control, others. Michels argued that the rank and file of a movement or organization look to leaders for direction and thereby reinforce the process of rule by a few. In addition, members of an oligarchy are strongly motivated to maintain their leadership roles, privileges, and power.

Michels's insights continue to be relevant today. Contemporary labor unions in the United States and Western Europe bear little resemblance to those organized spontaneously by exploited workers. Conflict theorists have pointed to the longevity of union leaders, who are not always responsive to the needs and demands of the membership and seem more concerned with maintaining their own positions and power. (The Social Policy section at the end of this chapter focuses on the status of labor unions today.)

Bureaucracy and Organizational Culture

How does bureaucratization affect the average individual who works in an organization? The early theorists of formal organizations tended to neglect this question. Max Weber, for example, focused on the management personnel in bureaucracies, but had little to say about workers in industry or clerks in government agencies.

According to the **classical theory** of formal organizations, also known as the **scientific management approach,** workers are motivated almost entirely by economic rewards. This theory stresses that only the physical constraints on workers limit their productivity. Therefore, workers may be treated as a resource, much like the machines that began to replace them in the 20th century. Under the scientific management approach, management attempts to achieve maximum work efficiency through scientific planning, established performance standards, and careful supervision of workers and production. Planning involves efficiency studies but not studies of workers' attitudes or job satisfaction.

Not until workers organized unions—and forced management to recognize that they were not objects—did theorists of formal organizations begin to revise the classical approach. Along with management and administrators, social scientists became aware that informal groups of workers have an important impact on organizations (Perrow 1986). An alternative way of considering bureaucratic dynamics, the **human relations approach,** emphasizes the role of people, communication, and participation in a bureaucracy. This type of analysis reflects the interest of interactionist theorists in small-group behavior. Unlike planning under the scientific management approach, planning based on the human relations perspective focuses on workers' feelings, frustrations, and emotional need for job satisfaction.

The gradual move away from a sole focus on the physical aspects of getting the job done—and toward the concerns and needs of workers—led advocates of the human relations approach to stress the less formal aspects of bureaucratic structure. Informal groups and social networks within organizations develop partly as a result of people's ability to create more direct forms of communication than under the formal structure. Charles Page (1946) used the term *bureaucracy's other face* to refer to the unofficial activities and interactions that are such a basic part of daily organizational life.

A series of classic studies illustrates the value of the human {p.40 relations approach. The Hawthorne studies alerted sociologists to the fact that research subjects may alter their behavior to match the experimenter's expectations. The major focus of the Hawthorne studies, however, was the role of social factors in workers' productivity. One aspect of the research concerned the switchboard-bank wiring room, where 14 men were making parts of switches for telephone equipment. The researchers discovered that these men were producing far below their physical capabilities. The discovery was especially surprising because the men would have earned more money if they had produced more parts.

What accounted for such an unexpected restriction of output? The men feared that if they produced switch parts at a faster rate, their pay rate might be reduced, or some of them might lose their jobs. As a result, this group of workers had established their own (unofficial) norm for a proper day's work and created informal rules and sanctions to enforce it. Yet management was unaware of these practices and believed that the men were working as hard as they could (Roethlisberger and Dickson 1939).

Today, research on formal organizations is following new avenues. First, the proportion of women and minority group members in high-level management positions is still much lower than might be expected, given their numbers in the labor force. Researchers are now beginning to look at the impact this gender and racial/ethnic imbalance may have on managerial judgment, both formal and informal. Second, a company's power structure is only partly reflected in its formal organizational charts. In practice, core groups tend to emerge to dominate the decision-making process. Very large corporations—say, a General Electric or a Procter & Gamble—may have hundreds of interlocking core groups, each of which plays a key role in its division or region. Third, these organizations have traditionally been viewed as having fairly fixed boundaries. But today's production and service systems stretch across networks of independent or semi-independent companies—a fact that must be considered in studying corporate culture (Kleiner 2003; W. Scott 2004).

CASE *study* (BUREAUCRACY AND THE SPACE SHUTTLE *COLUMBIA*)

In February 2003, the space shuttle *Columbia* disintegrated as it reentered the earth's atmosphere. Seven astronauts died in the accident, which was blamed at first on a piece of foam weighing less than two pounds that had struck the spacecraft's wing during liftoff. But by August, the *Columbia* Accident Investigation Board (2003) had identified a second cause: NASA's bureaucratic organizational culture.

The board's blistering report cited NASA's emphasis on bureaucratic rules and regulations at the expense of astronauts' safety. Though engineers had voiced safety concerns over the years, especially after the shuttle *Challenger*'s explosion in 1986, their memos rarely reached the top of NASA's hierarchy, where costs and scheduling were considered paramount. In fact, the organization's culture discouraged the expression of safety concerns. When engineers tried to obtain special images of the *Columbia*'s wing during its last flight so that they could check for damage, managers denied their request. Aside from cost concerns, officials may have been unwilling to admit that something had gone wrong. In general, hierarchical organizations tend to encourage the concealment of mistakes (Vaughan 1996, 1999).

Another part of the problem was that over the years, foam debris had fallen during liftoff in about 10 percent of NASA's launches, without disastrous results. Officials had come to expect that a shower of debris might occur, and to speak of it as an "acceptable risk." Rather than treating it as a safety issue, they labeled it a maintenance problem. When the program resumed with *Discovery* in 2005, more foam debris broke off at launch, causing NASA to suspend further flights (J. Schwartz 2005).

Investigators had condemned the "acceptable risk" attitude following the *Challenger* explosion in 1986, but NASA's organizational culture had not changed. In a bureaucratic organization, bringing about real change can be extremely difficult. Those intrepid individuals who attempt to consider new alternatives often run into groupthink. Thus, in the wake of the second disaster, members of the *Columbia* Accident Investigation Board (2003:13) predicted, "The changes we recommend will be difficult to accomplish—and will be internally resisted." ●

Voluntary Associations

In the mid-19th century, the French writer Alexis de Tocqueville noted that people in the United States are "forever forming associations." By 2007, there were more than 456,000 voluntary associations in a U.S. national database. ***Voluntary associations*** are organizations established on the basis of common interest, whose members volunteer or even pay to participate. The Girl Scouts of America, the American Jewish Congress, the Kiwanis Club, and the League of Women Voters are all considered voluntary associations; so, too, are the American Association of Aardvark Aficionados, the Cats on Stamps Study Group, the Mikes of America, the New York Corset Club, and the William Shatner Fellowship (Thomson Gale 2007).

The categories of "formal organization" and "voluntary association" are not mutually exclusive. Large voluntary associations such as the Lions Club and the Masons have structures similar to those of profit-making corporations. At the same time, certain formal organizations, such as the Young Men's Christian Association (YMCA) and the Peace Corps, have philanthropic and educational goals usually found in voluntary associations. The Democratic Party and the United Farm Workers union are considered examples of voluntary associations. Even though membership in a political party or union can be a condition of employment and therefore not genuinely voluntary, political parties and labor unions are usually included in discussions of voluntary associations.

Participation in voluntary associations is not unique to the United States. This textbook's author attended a carnival in London featuring bungee-jumping, at which participants were expected to jump from a height of 180 feet. Skeptics were given assurances of the attraction's safety by being told that the proprietor belonged to a voluntary association: the British Elastic Rope Sports Association. An analysis of 15 industrial nations, including the United States, shows that active memberships in voluntary associations typically increased during the 1980s and 1990s. Only relatively inactive memberships in religious organizations and labor unions have showed a decline. On the whole, then, voluntary associations are fairly healthy (Baer et al. 2000).

Voluntary associations can provide support to people in preindustrial societies. During the post–World War II period, migration from rural areas of Africa to the cities was accompanied by a growth in voluntary associations, including trade unions, occupational societies, and mutual aid organizations developed along old tribal lines. As people moved from the {pp.121–122 *Gemeinschaft* of the countryside to the *Gesellschaft* of the city, these voluntary associations provided immigrants with substitutes for the extended groups of kinfolk in their villages (Little 1988).

Voluntary associations in the United States are largely segregated by gender. Half of them are exclusively female, and one-fifth are all-male. Because the exclusively male associations tend to be larger and more heterogeneous, in terms of the background of members, all-male associations hold more promise for networking than all-female groups. Although participation varies across the population of the United States, most people belong to at least one voluntary association (see Figure 6-1), while more than one-fourth maintain three or more memberships.

The importance of voluntary associations—and especially of their unpaid workers (or volunteers)—is increasingly being recognized. Traditionally, society has devalued unpaid work, even though the skill levels, experience, and training demands are often comparable with those of wage labor. Viewed from a conflict perspective, the critical difference has been that women perform a substantial amount of volunteer work. Feminists and conflict

AARP volunteers staff a phone bank in an effort to get out the vote in Des Moines, Iowa. The AARP is a voluntary association of people age 50 and older, both retired and working, that advocates for the needs of older Americans. A huge organization, it has been instrumental in maintaining Social Security benefits to retirees.

theorists agree that like the unpaid child care and household labor of homemakers, the effort of volunteers has too often been ignored by scholars—and awarded too little respect by the larger society—because it is viewed as "women's work." Failure to recognize women's volunteerism obscures a critical contribution women make to a society's social structure (Daniels 1987, 1988).

Besides contributing to the well-being of society, voluntary associations also serve as training grounds for civic engagement. Research shows that youthful involvement in a variety of organizations, from sports teams to debating societies and musical groups, influences a person's adult behavior. Specifically, adults who were active in voluntary associations as youths are more likely than others to participate in political activity, from voting to campaign work (McFarland and Thomas 2006).

FIGURE 6–1

Membership in Voluntary Associations in the United States

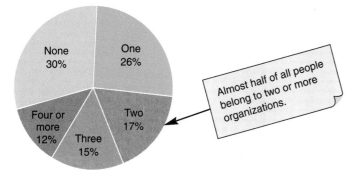

None 30%
One 26%
Two 17%
Three 15%
Four or more 12%

Almost half of all people belong to two or more organizations.

Source: J. Davis and Smith 2001:347.

Use Your Sociological Imagination

How many voluntary associations do you belong to? How do you benefit from your membership in them? How might your membership benefit others?

www.mhhe.com/schaefer11

The Changing Workplace

Weber's work on bureaucracy and Michels's thinking on oligarchy are still applicable to the organizational structure and culture of the workplace. But today's factories and offices are undergoing rapid, profound changes unanticipated a century or more ago. Besides the far-reaching impact of technological advances such as computerization, workers must cope with organizational restructuring. This section will detail the dramatic changes evident in today's workplace.

Organizational Restructuring

To some extent, individual businesses, community organizations, and government agencies are always changing, if only because of personnel turnover. But since the late 20th century, formal organizations have been experimenting with new ways of getting the job done, some of which have significantly altered the workplace.

Collective decision making, or the active involvement of employee problem-solving groups in corporate management, first became popular in the United States in the 1980s. Management gurus had noted the dazzling success of Japanese automobile and consumer products manufacturers. In studying these companies, they found that problem-solving groups were one key to success. At first, such groups concentrated on small problems at specific points in the production line. But today, these groups often cross departmental and divisional boundaries to attack problems rooted in the bureaucratic division of labor. Thus, they require significant adjustment by employees long used to working in a bureaucracy (P. Hirsch and De Soucey 2006; Ouchi 1981).

Another innovation in the workplace, called *minimal hierarchy,* replaces the traditional bureaucratic hierarchy of authority with a flatter organizational structure. Minimal hierarchy offers workers greater access to those in authority, giving them an opportunity to voice concerns that might not be heard in a traditional bureaucracy. This new organizational structure is thought to minimize the potential for costly and dangerous bureaucratic oversights.

Finally, organizational *work teams* have become increasingly common, even in smaller organizations. There are two types of

work team. *Project teams* address ongoing issues, such as safety or compliance with the Americans with Disabilities Act. *Task forces* pursue nonrecurring issues, such as a major building renovation. In both cases, team members are released to some degree from their regular duties in order to contribute to the organizationwide effort (W. Scott 2003; Huff 2007).

The common purpose of work teams, minimal hierarchy, and collective decision making is to empower workers. For that reason, these new organizational structures can be exciting for the employees who participate in them. But these innovations rarely touch the vast numbers of workers who perform routine jobs in factories and office buildings. The 40 percent of all full-time workers and 60 percent of all part-time workers who are paid hourly and who earn the minimum wage or lower know little about organizational restructuring (Bureau of Labor Statistics 2006a).

Finally, organizational restructuring has fostered growing numbers of independent consultants and outside contractors who labor off-site, with no guarantee of steady employment. Box 6-3 looks at the situation of these "hired guns."

Telecommuting

Increasingly, in many industrial countries, workers are turning into telecommuters. **Telecommuters** are employees who work full-time or part-time at home rather than in an outside office, and who are linked to their supervisors and colleagues through computer terminals, phone lines, and fax machines. One national survey showed that next to on-site day care, most office workers want virtual offices that allow them to work off-site. Not surprisingly, the number of telecommuters increased from 8.5 million in 1995 to 50 million in 2005 (Donald B. Davis and Polonko 2001; Mokhtarian et al. 2005; Turek 2006).

What are the social implications of this shift toward the virtual office? From an interactionist perspective, the workplace is a major source of friendships; restricting face-to-face social opportunities could destroy the trust that is created by "handshake agreements." Thus, telecommuting may move society further along the continuum from *Gemeinschaft* to *Gesellschaft.* And like it or not, when employees work at home, they tend to become available 24/7. On a more positive note, telecommuting may be the first social change that pulls fathers and mothers back into the home rather than pushing them out. The trend, if it continues, should also increase autonomy and job satisfaction for many employees (Castells 2001; DiMaggio et al. 2001; P. Hirsch and De Soucey 2006).

Work teams are becoming an increasingly common form of organizational restructuring. Members of this team are brainstorming ways to address the needs of the disabled.

research IN *action*

6-3 Hired Guns

Interim talent, itinerant experts, gurus for hire, hired guns—whatever you call them, they are fixtures in today's economy: the temporary workers and independent contractors who do more and more of our nation's work.

Temporary workers are not new; day laborers and temporary clerical workers have been part of the labor force for generations. But researchers have begun to focus on a more recent trend: greater organizational dependence on professionals who do contract work on a temporary basis, even contributing to an organization's decision making. The growing dominance of service industries and information systems has facilitated this increasing reliance on temporary professionals, whose skills include marketing, public relations, design, computer technology, and project management, to name just a few.

The issue of high-tech workers for hire emerged during the debates over the war in Iraq. More and more, the military is relying on outside contractors not only for everyday support services, but for security in war zones. As criticism of the war has escalated, some people have complained that military contractors

seem less accountable to civilian leaders than the military itself.

To investigate the trend toward a skilled temporary workforce, management specialists Stephen Barley and Gideon Kunda carried out two years of intensive field work in the Silicon Valley area. They found that because of corporate efforts to limit the number of permanent employees (called the "politics of headcount"), external staffing agencies were taking over

> *More and more, the military is relying on outside contractors not only for everyday support services, but for security in war zones.*

companies' human resource functions, including applicant screenings and wage negotiations.

For their part, the workers in this new high-level contingent workforce like the tremendous flexibility that temporary work gives them, as well as the relative freedom they enjoy from bureaucratic hierarchies and regulations. But they also work more than full-time employees,

and they rarely report taking downtime, much less a vacation. Though these workers have traditionally been ignored by unions, efforts are now under way to organize them (see the Social Policy section). For the last few years, organizers have been trying to address what they see as the biggest problem for contract workers, their lack of health insurance. Other challenges, such as the exclusion of contract workers from important meetings where knowledge is shared and the stigma of being a "temp," have yet to be addressed.

Let's Discuss

1. What do you think of the trend toward the temporary employment of skilled workers? How might it affect the value that you place on a college education?

2. Besides the growing dominance of service industries and information systems, what other factors might be contributing to the trend toward temporary employment of skilled workers?

Sources: Barley and Kunda 2004; *The Economist* 2006b; Free Lancers Union 2007; Price 2006; V. Smith 2004.

Use Your Sociological Imagination

If your first full-time job after college involved telecommuting, what do you think would be the advantages and disadvantages of working out of a home office? Do you think you would be satisfied as a telecommuter? Why or why not?

Electronic Communication

Electronic communication in the workplace has generated some heat lately. On the one hand, e-mailing is a convenient way to push messages around, especially with the copy button. It's democratic, too: lower-status employees are more likely to participate in e-mail discussions than in face-to-face communications, giving organizations the benefit of their experience and views.

But e-mail doesn't convey body language, which in face-to-face communication can soften insensitive phrasing and make unpleasant messages (such as a reprimand) easier to take. It also leaves a permanent record, which can be a problem if messages are written thoughtlessly (DiMaggio et al. 2001).

Electronic communication has contributed significantly to the fragmentation of work. Today, work is frequently interrupted by e-mail, pagers, and pop-up windows, as well as face-to-face interruptions. In one observation study of office workers, researchers found that employees spent an average of only 11 minutes on any given project before being interrupted. Typically, 25 minutes passed before they returned to their original tasks. While multitasking may increase a person's efficiency in some situations, it has become an integral and not necessarily helpful feature of work for many employees (Mark et al. 2005; C. Thompson 2005).

socialPolicy
and Organizations

The State of the Unions

The Issue

How many people do you know who belong to a labor union? Chances are you can name a lot fewer people than someone could 50 years ago. In 1954, unions represented 39 percent of workers in the private sector of the U.S. economy; in 2005 they represented only 12.5 percent (see Figure 6-2). What has happened to diminish the importance of organized labor? Have unions outlived their usefulness in a rapidly changing global economy that is dominated by the service sector (AFL-CIO 2001; Bureau of Labor Statistics 2005)?

The Setting

Labor unions consist of organized workers who share either the same skill (as in electronics) or the same employer (as in the case of postal employees). Unions began to emerge during the Industrial Revolution in England, in the 1700s. Groups of workers banded together to extract concessions from employers (e.g., safer working conditions, a shorter workweek), as well as to protect their positions. They frequently tried to protect their jobs by limiting entry to their occupation based on gender, race, ethnicity, citizenship, age, and sometimes rather arbitrary measures of skill levels. Today we see less of this protection of special interests, but individual labor unions are still the target of charges of discrimination, as are employers.

The power of labor unions varies widely from country to country. In some countries, such as Britain and Mexico, unions play a key role in the foundation of governments. In others, such as Japan and Korea, their role in politics is very limited, and even their ability to influence the private sector is relatively weak. In the United States, unions can sometimes have a significant influence on employers and elected officials, but their effect varies dramatically by type of industry and even region of the country: see Figure 6-3 (M. Wallerstein and Western 2000).

Few people today would dispute the fact that union membership is declining. Among the reasons for the decline are the following:

1. **Changes in the type of industry.** Manufacturing jobs, the traditional heart of the labor union, have declined, giving way to postindustrial service jobs.

2. **Growth in part-time jobs.** Between 1982 and 1998 the number of temporary jobs in the United States rose 577 percent, while total employment increased only 41 percent. Only in 2000 did laws governing collective bargaining allow temporary workers to join a union.

3. **The legal system.** The United States has not made it particularly easy for unions to organize and bargain, and some government measures have made it more difficult. A dramatic

FIGURE 6–2

Union Membership in the United States

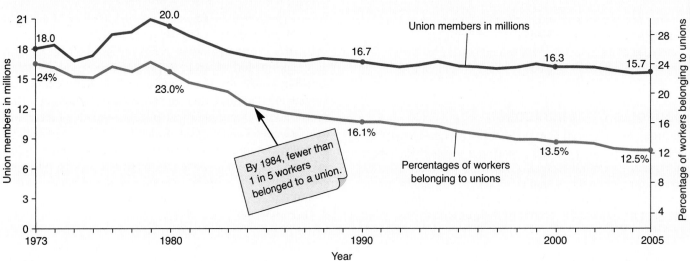

Source: Hirsch and Macpherson 2006.

FIGURE 6–3

Union Membership in the United States

MAPPING LIFE
NATIONWIDE

www.mhhe.com/schaefer11

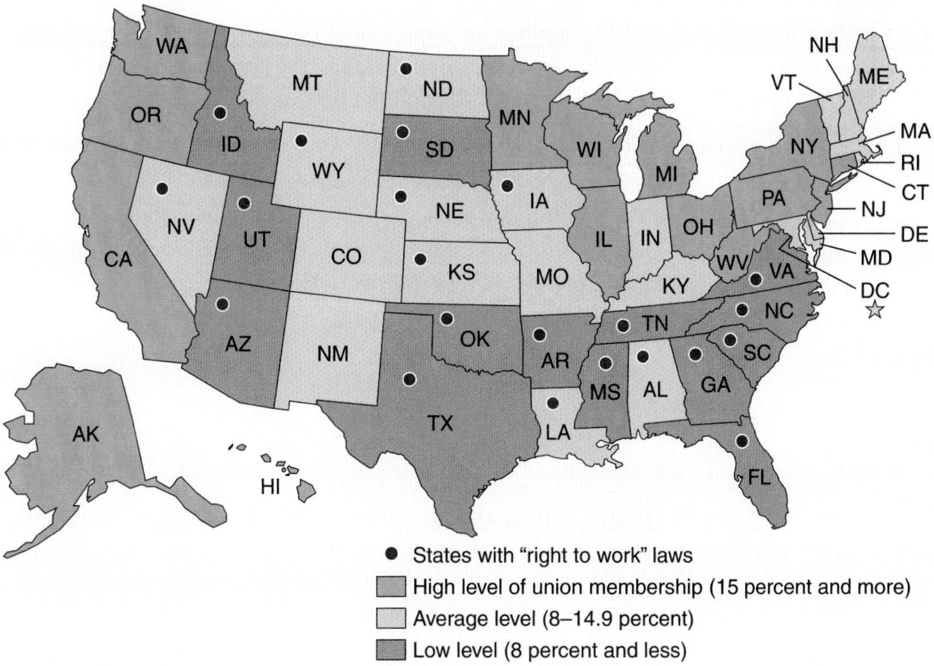

- ● States with "right to work" laws
- ▨ High level of union membership (15 percent and more)
- ▨ Average level (8–14.9 percent)
- ▨ Low level (8 percent and less)

Note: "Right to work" means that, legally, workers cannot be required to join a union or pay union dues.
Source: Developed by the author based on data from Bureau of Labor Statistics 2005; National Right to Work Legal Defense Foundation 2007.

with a sharp division of labor. However, as manufacturing has declined, unions have had to look elsewhere for growth.

Worldwide, today's labor unions bear little resemblance to those early unions organized spontaneously by exploited workers. In line with Robert Michels's iron law of oligarchy (see page 145), unions have become increasingly bureaucratized under a self-serving leadership. Conflict theorists would point out that the longer union leaders are in office, the less responsive they are to the needs and demands of the rank and file, and the more concerned with maintaining their own positions and power. Yet research shows that under certain circumstances, union leadership can change significantly. Smaller unions are vulnerable to changes in leadership, as are unions whose membership shifts in composition from predominantly White to African American or Latino.

Many union employees encounter role conflict (see page 116). For example, they may agree to provide a needed service and then organize a strike to withhold it. Role conflict is especially apparent in the so-called helping occupations: teaching, social work, nursing, law enforcement, and firefighting. These workers may feel torn between carrying out their professional responsibilities and enduring working conditions they find unacceptable.

example was President Ronald Reagan's firing of 11,000 air traffic controllers in 1981, when their union threatened they would walk off the job while seeking a new contract.

4. **Globalization.** The threat of jobs leaving the country has undercut the ability of union leaders to organize workers at home. Some say that labor union demands for wage increases and additional benefits have themselves spurred the exodus of jobs to developing nations, where wages are significantly lower and unions are virtually nonexistent.

5. **Employer offensives.** Increasingly hostile employers have taken court action to block unions' efforts to represent their members.

6. **Union rigidity and bureaucratization.** In the past, labor has been slow to embrace women, minorities, and immigrants. Furthermore, in some unions the election of leaders seems to dominate the organization's activity (Prah 2005).

Sociological Insights

Both Marxists and functionalists would view unions as a logical response to the emergence of impersonal, large-scale, formal, and often alienating organizations. This view certainly characterized the growth of unions in major manufacturing industries

Policy Initiatives

U.S. law grants workers the right to self-organize via unions. But the United States is unique among industrial democracies in allowing employers to actively oppose their employees' decision to organize (Comstock and Fox 1994).

A major barrier to union growth exists in the 22 states that have so-called right-to-work laws (see Figure 6-3). In these states, workers cannot be *required* to join or pay dues or fees to a union. The very term *right to work* reflects the anti-union view that a worker should not be forced to join a union, even if the union may negotiate on his or her behalf and achieve results that benefit the worker. This situation is unlikely to change. That is, right-to-work states will remain so; those without such laws typically have a strong union tradition or restrict union activities in other ways.

On the national level, union power is waning. In the security buildup that followed the terrorist attacks of September 11, 2001, federal officials created many new jobs and reorganized existing agencies into the Department of Homeland Security. In doing so, they specified that some 170,000 workers would not have collective bargaining rights, and that 43,000 newly federalized airport security screeners could not be unionized. These stipulations barring unions have been maintained and represent another sign of growing anti-union sentiment (Frank 2007).

In Europe, labor unions tend to play a major role in political elections. (The ruling party in Great Britain, in fact, is called the Labour Party.) Although unions play a lesser political role in the United States, they have recently faced attacks for their large financial contributions to political campaigns. Debate over campaign finance reform in Congress in 2001 raised the question of whether labor unions should be able to use dues to support a particular candidate or promote a position via "issue ads" that favor one party, usually the Democrats.

Though unions are a global force, their form and substance varies from country to country. In China, where there is only one political party, the government ordered Wal-Mart's 31,000 workers to unionize, over the corporation's objections. Chinese unions are controlled by the Communist Party, whose member-

ship has declined as the party's pervasive control has weakened. Nevertheless, these unions are more likely to listen to the government than independent unions, which respond to the workers who are their members (Lague 2006).

Let's Discuss

1. What unions are represented on your college campus? Have you been aware of union activity? Has there been any opposition to the unions on the part of the administration?

2. Do you think nurses should be allowed to strike? Why or why not? What about teachers or police officers?

3. If a union is working on behalf of all the workers of a company, should all the employees be required to join the union and pay dues? Why or why not?

GettingINVOLVED

To get involved in the debate over the labor movement, visit this text's Online Learning Center, which offers links to relevant Web sites. Check out the Social Policy section in the Online Learning Center as well; it provides survey data on U.S. public opinion regarding this issue.

www.mhhe.com/schaefer11

{ **MASTERING THIS CHAPTER** }

Summary

Social interaction among human beings is necessary to the transmission of culture and the survival of every society. This chapter examines the social behavior of *groups, formal organizations,* and *voluntary associations.*

1. When we find ourselves identifying closely with a group, it is probably a *primary group.* A *secondary group* is more formal and impersonal.

2. People tend to see the world in terms of *in-groups* and *out-groups,* a perception often fostered by the very groups to which they belong.

3. *Reference groups* set and enforce standards of conduct and serve as a source of comparison for people's evaluations of themselves and others.

4. Interactionist researchers have noted distinct and predictable processes in the functioning of *small groups.* The simplest group is a *dyad,* composed of two members. *Triads* and larger groups increase the ways of interacting and allow for *coalitions* to form.

5. As societies have become more complex, large *formal organizations* have become more powerful and pervasive.

6. Max Weber argued that in its ideal form, every *bureaucracy* has five basic characteristics: division of labor, hierarchical authority, written rules and regulations, impersonality, and employment based on technical qualifications.

7. Bureaucracy can be understood both as a process and as a matter of degree. Thus, an organization may be more or less bureaucratic than other organizations.

8. When leaders of an organization build up their power, the result can be *oligarchy* (rule by a few).

9. The informal structure of an organization can undermine and redefine official bureaucratic policies.

10. People join *voluntary associations* for a variety of purposes—for example, to share in joint activities or to get help with personal problems.

11. Organizational restructuring and new technologies have transformed the workplace through innovations such as *collective decision making* and *telecommuting.*

12. *Labor unions* are on the decline because of major shifts in the economy.

Critical Thinking Questions

1. Think about how behavior is shaped by reference groups. What different reference groups have shaped your outlook and your goals at different periods in your life? How have they done so?

2. Are primary groups, secondary groups, in-groups, out-groups, and reference groups likely to be found within a formal organization? What functions do these groups serve for a formal organization? What dysfunctions might occur as a result of their presence?

3. Max Weber identified five basic characteristics of bureaucracy. Select an actual organization familiar to you (for example, your college, a workplace, or a religious institution or civic association you belong to) and apply Weber's five characteristics to that organization. To what degree does it correspond to Weber's ideal type of bureaucracy?

Key Terms

Alienation A condition of estrangement or dissociation from the surrounding society. (page 142)

Bureaucracy A component of formal organization that uses rules and hierarchical ranking to achieve efficiency. (141)

Bureaucratization The process by which a group, organization, or social movement becomes increasingly bureaucratic. (145)

Classical theory An approach to the study of formal organizations that views workers as being motivated almost entirely by economic rewards. (145)

Coalition A temporary or permanent alliance geared toward a common goal. (138)

Dyad A two-member group. (140)

Formal organization A group designed for a special purpose and structured for maximum efficiency. (141)

Goal displacement Overzealous conformity to official regulations of a bureaucracy. (142)

Group Any number of people with similar norms, values, and expectations who interact with one another on a regular basis. (136)

Groupthink Uncritical acceptance of or conformity to the prevailing viewpoint. (141)

Human relations approach An approach to the study of formal organizations that emphasizes the role of people, communication, and participation in a bureaucracy and tends to focus on the informal structure of the organization. (145)

Ideal type A construct or model for evaluating specific cases. (141)

In-group Any group or category to which people feel they belong. (137)

Iron law of oligarchy A principle of organizational life under which even a democratic organization will eventually develop into a bureaucracy ruled by a few individuals. (145)

Labor union Organized workers who share either the same skill or the same employer. (150)

McDonaldization The process by which the principles of the fast-food restaurant are coming to dominate more and more sectors of American society as well as of the rest of the world. (136)

Out-group A group or category to which people feel they do not belong. (137)

Peter principle A principle of organizational life according to which every employee within a hierarchy tends to rise to his or her level of incompetence. (143)

Primary group A small group characterized by intimate, face-to-face association and cooperation. (136)

Reference group Any group that individuals use as a standard for evaluating themselves and their own behavior. (138)

Scientific management approach Another name for the classical theory of formal organizations. (145)

Secondary group A formal, impersonal group in which there is little social intimacy or mutual understanding. (136)

Small group A group small enough for all members to interact simultaneously—that is, to talk with one another or at least be well acquainted. (138)

Telecommuter An employee who works full-time or part-time at home rather than in an outside office, and who is linked to supervisor and colleagues through computer terminals, phone lines, and fax machines. (148)

Trained incapacity The tendency of workers in a bureaucracy to become so specialized that they develop blind spots and fail to notice obvious problems. (142)

Triad A three-member group. (140)

Voluntary association An organization established on the basis of common interest, whose members volunteer or even pay to participate. (146)

Read each question carefully and then select the best answer.

1. George Ritzer's belief that business principles of the fast-food industry have greatly influenced how we live and do business has been coined
   a. Fast Food Nation
   b. Drive-Through Life
   c. McDonaldization
   d. Burger USA

2. _____ groups often emerge in the workplace among those who share special understandings about their occupation.
   a. Primary
   b. Secondary
   c. Out-
   d. Formal

3. The purpose of a reference group is to serve a(n)
   a. normative function by enforcing standards of conduct and belief.
   b. comparison function by serving as a standard against which people can measure themselves and others.
   c. elimination function by dissolving groups that no longer have a social purpose.
   d. both a and b

4. The president of the United States need not be a good typist, and a surgeon need not be able to fill a cavity, because of the bureaucratic characteristic of
   a. division of labor.
   b. impersonality.
   c. employment based on technical qualifications.
   d. written rules and regulations.

5. Which pioneer of sociology first directed researchers to the significance of bureaucratic structure?
   a. Émile Durkheim
   b. Max Weber
   c. Karl Marx
   d. Ferdinand Tönnies

6. Minimal hierarchy involves
   a. a traditional bureaucracy.
   b. a lack of rules in the workplace.
   c. a flatter organizational structure.
   d. an absence of traditional job titles.

7. The U.S. Postal Service, the Boston Pops orchestra, and the college or university in which you are currently enrolled as a student are all examples of
   a. primary groups.
   b. reference groups.
   c. formal organizations.
   d. triads.

8. One positive consequence of bureaucracy is that it reduces bias. Reduction of bias results from which characteristic of a bureaucracy?
   a. impersonality
   b. hierarchy of authority
   c. written rules and regulations
   d. employment based on technical qualifications

9. According to the Peter principle,
   a. all bureaucracies are notoriously inefficient.
   b. if something *can* go wrong, it *will*.
   c. every employee within a hierarchy tends to rise to his or her level of incompetence.
   d. all line workers get burned in the end.

10. What are the social implications of a shift toward the virtual office as a result of the increasing number of telecommuters?
    a. Supervisors will find that performance goals must be defined more clearly, which may lead to further bureaucratization.
    b. It should increase autonomy and job satisfaction for many employees.
    c. It will lead to greater worker privacy and job security.
    d. both a and b

11. William Graham Sumner distinguished between _____ and _____.

12. Formal organizations have a(n) _____ form of organization.

13. A third member of a group may try to gain control by having the other two members become rivals. This is known as the _____-_____-_____ strategy.

14. _____ groups often emerge in the workplace among those who share special understandings about their occupation.

15. In many cases, people model their behavior after groups to which they may not belong. These groups are called _____ groups.

16. Trained incapacity, goal displacement, and the Peter principle are all examples of bureaucratic _____.

17. The iron law of oligarchy was developed by German sociologist _____ _____.

18. People who happen to be in the same place at the same time, such as members of a Broadway theatre audience, are a(n) _____.

19. When we find ourselves identifying closely with a group, it is probably a(n) _____ group.

20. Max Weber developed a(n) _____ _____ of bureaucracy, which reflects the most characteristic aspects of all human organizations.

{ TECHNOLOGY RESOURCES }

Online Learning Center

1. Everyone has been a member of in-groups and out-groups. Visit the student center in the Online Learning Center (**www.mhhe.com/ schaefer11**) and link to the Interactive Activity entitled "In-Groups, Out-Groups, and Un-words!" In this activity, you will be asked to discuss your experiences as a member of an in-group and an out-group. You can also do the word scramble, which contains key words and phrases from this chapter.

2. The Web site of the Illinois Labor History Society (**www.kentlaw. edu/ilhs/**) contains extensive information on labor unions, strikes,

and disasters in that state, past and present. Visit the site for an overview of labor history in Illinois.

3. As this chapter notes, telecommuting has important implications for social relationships. The Telework Coalition (**www.telcoa.org**) is a non-profit organization formed to educate the public about the benefits of offsite work. Explore this site for more information and resources on this growing trend.

*Note: Although all the URLs listed were current as of the printing of this book, these sites often change. Please check our Web site (**www.mhhe.com/schaefer11**) for updates, hyperlinks, and exercises related to these sites.*

Reel Society Video Clips

Reel Society video clips, which appear on this book's Web site, can be used to spark discussion about the following topic from this chapter:

- Understanding Groups

Though the mass media reflect society, they do not necessarily represent all of society. To highlight films by the native peoples of the United States, the American Indian Film Institute, founded in 1979, holds an annual motion picture festival. This poster, created by Michael Horse of the Yaqui, Zuni, and Mescalero Apache tribes, promotes the AIFI's 2003 Festival.

7

The Mass Media

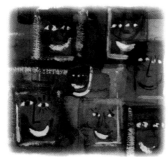

"A fascinating technological profile of a generation that will change the world." —*USA Today*

growing up digital

The Rise of the Net Generation

DON TAPSCOTT

Author of the International Bestseller
The Digital Economy

" The Net Generation has arrived! The baby boom has an echo and it's even louder than the original.

What makes this generation different from all others before it? It is the first to grow up surrounded by digital media. Computers can be found in the home, school, factory, and office and digital technologies such as cameras, video games, and CD-ROMs are commonplace. Increasingly, these new media are connected by the Internet, an expanding web of networks which is attracting a million new users monthly. Today's kids are so bathed in bits that they think it's all part of the natural landscape. To them, the digital technology is no more intimidating than a VCR or toaster.

For the first time in history, children are more comfortable, knowledgeable, and literate than their parents about an innovation central to society. And it is through the use of the digital media that the N-Generation will develop and superimpose its culture on the rest of society. Boomers stand back. Already these kids are learning, playing, communicating, working, and creating communities very differently than their parents. They are a force for social transformation.

. . . If left purely to market forces, the digital economy could foster a two-tiered society, creating a major gulf between information haves and have-nots—those who can communicate with the world and those who can't. As information technology becomes more important for economic success and societal well-being, the possibility of "information apartheid" becomes increasingly real. Such a "digital divide" may mean that for many children *N-Gen* means *Not-Generation*.

For example, in the United States there is a direct relationship between family income and access to computers and the Net. This correlation also exists between the higher- and lower-income schools. Some observers argue that this is just a temporary problem, but our research shows that the digital divide is actually widening, not disappearing. As the new technology trickles into poorer neighborhoods and schools, the better-off children are leapfrogging others—getting not only better access, but a wider range of services, faster access, the best technology, and, most importantly, increasing motivation, skills, and knowledge. This not only exacerbates the fluency gap but also the gap in different economic classes' capacity to learn and to have successful lives. Have-nots become know-nots and do-nots. . . .

Globally, most children of the new generation are not growing up digital. In fact many of them will not grow up at all. One billion people were born over the last decade—the biggest increase in human history. However, 97 percent of them were born in developing countries that often lack the ability to feed, house, and educate them. More than half of the 1.2 billion children in the world aged six to eleven have never placed a phone call. "

> *For the first time in history, children are more comfortable, knowledgeable, and literate than their parents about an innovation central to society.*

(Tapscott 1998:1–2, 11, 12) Additional information about this excerpt can be found on the Online Learning Center at
www.mhhe.com/schaefer11.

In his book *Growing Up Digital: The Rise of the Net Generation,* Don Tapscott confronts the sweeping social change caused by the introduction of new means of communication. The head of New Paradigm, a Canadian think tank devoted to information technology, Tapscott sees a huge generational divide between Baby Boomers and "N-Gen"—those who were children, adolescents, or young adults at the turn of the 21st century. Like their parents the boomers, who grew up with a new means of communication called television, the young people of N-Gen are defined by the Internet. These "children of a digital age," he writes, will change the way we live and work in ways that marketers, employers, and government planners have not even begun to imagine.

Both TV and the Net are **mass media,** a term that refers to the print and electronic means of communication that carry messages to widespread audiences. Print media include newspapers, magazines, and books; electronic media include radio, satellite radio, television, motion pictures, and the Internet. Advertising, which falls into both categories, is also a form of mass media.

The social impact of the mass media is obvious. Consider a few examples. TV dinners were invented to accommodate the millions of "couch potatoes" who can't bear to miss their favorite television programs. Today *screen time* encompasses not just television viewing but playing video games and surfing the Internet. Candidates for political office rely on their media consultants to project a winning image both in print and in the electronic media. World leaders use all forms of media for political advantage, whether to gain territory or to bid on hosting the Olympics. In parts of Africa and Asia, AIDS education projects owe much of their success to media campaigns. And during the 2003 war in Iraq, both the British and U.S. governments allowed journalists to be embedded with frontline troops as a means of "telling their story."

Few aspects of society are as central as the mass media. Through the media we expand our understanding of people and events beyond what we experience in person. The media inform us about different cultures and lifestyles and about the latest forms of technology. For sociologists, the key questions are how the mass media affect our social institutions and how they influence our social behavior.

Why are the media so influential? Who benefits from media influence and why? How do we maintain cultural and ethical standards in the face of negative media images? In this chapter we will consider the ways sociology helps us to answer these questions. First we will look at how proponents of the various sociological perspectives view the media. Then we will examine just who makes up the media's audience, not just at home but around the world. The chapter closes with a Social Policy section on the concentration of the media in the hands of a few powerful corporations.

Sociological Perspectives on the Media

Over the past decade, new technologies have made new forms of mass media available to U.S. households. These new technologies have changed people's viewing and listening habits. People spend a lot of time with the media, more and more of it on the Internet. Consumers have moved away from television and toward digital images downloaded to their computers and portable devices. Increasingly, they learn not just about the famous but about ordinary people by viewing their personal Web sites or their pages in FaceBook or MySpace. People now spend less time listening to recorded music than they did just a few years ago; they spend more time surfing the Internet. These patterns tend to vary by age group, however. Among 18- to 34-year-olds, for example, time spent watching prime-time TV—both broadcast and cable—declined by 19 percent between 1991 and 2003, as video games and the Internet took up more of their media time. What do these changes in people's viewing and listening habits signify? In the following sections we'll examine the impact of the mass media and changes in their usage patterns from the three major sociological perspectives (E. Nelson 2004).

Functionalist View

One obvious function of the mass media is to entertain. Except for clearly identified news or educational programming, we often think the explicit purpose of the mass media is to occupy our leisure time—from newspaper comics and crossword puzzles to the latest music releases on the Internet. While that is true, the media have other important functions. They also socialize us, enforce social norms, confer status, and promote consumption. An important dysfunction of the mass media is that they may act as a narcotic, desensitizing us to distressing events (Lazarsfeld and Merton 1948; C. Wright 1986).

Agent of Socialization The media increase social cohesion by presenting a common, more or less standardized view of culture through mass communication. Sociologist Robert Park (1922) studied how newspapers helped immigrants to the United States adjust to their environment by changing their customary habits and teaching them the opinions of people in their new home country. Unquestionably, the mass media play a significant role in providing a collective experience for members of society. Think {p.99–100} about how the mass media bring together members of a community or even a nation by broadcasting important events and ceremonies (such as inaugurations, press conferences, parades, state funerals, and the Olympics) and by covering disasters.

Which media outlets did people turn to in the aftermath of the September 11, 2001, tragedy? Television and the telephone were the primary means by which people in the United States bonded. But the Internet also played a prominent role. About half of all Internet users—more than 53 million people—received some kind of news about the attacks online. Nearly three-fourths of Internet users communicated via e-mail to show their patriotism, discuss events with their families, or re-connect with old friends. More than a third of Internet users read or posted material in online forums. In the first 30 days alone, the Library of Congress collected from one Internet site more than half a million pages having to do with the terrorist attacks. As a Library director noted, "The Internet has become for many the public commons, a place where they can come together and talk" (D. Miller and Darlington 2002; Mirapaul 2001:E2; Rainie 2001).

Of course, the socializing effects of the media can be used to promote the goals of dissident, even militant minorities. In the Palestinian-held Gaza Strip, Hamas—a group better known for its suicide bombing campaigns—has launched a television program meant to familiarize children with the Palestinian position on the disputed territories. In between lectures on revered sites such as Nablus and Al Aksa Mosque, the show's host, known as Uncle Hazim, takes on-air phone calls from viewers and talks with animal characters reminiscent of those on *Sesame Street*. However, not all the video content is so mild. In 2007 Al-Aqsa (Hamas) Television received an avalanche of criticism after the show introduced a costumed character resembling Mickey Mouse, called Farfur. When chastised for cheating by copying another student's work, Farfur blamed "the Jews" for destroying his home, and hence his homework. The media can have a powerful influence, especially on young children (Marcus and Crook 2007; Craig Smith 2006b).

Other problems are inherent in the socialization function of the mass media. For instance, many people worry about the effect of using television as a babysitter and the impact of violent programming on viewer behavior. Some people adopt a blame-the-media mentality, holding the media accountable for anything that goes wrong, especially with young people.

Enforcer of Social Norms   The media often reaffirm proper behavior by showing what happens to people who act in a way that violates societal expectations. These messages are conveyed when the bad guy gets clobbered in cartoons or is thrown in jail on *Law and Order*. Yet the media also sometimes glorify disap-

On Al Aksa TV in Gaza, two animal characters interact with Uncle Hazim, the popular host of a local children's show. Sponsored by the militant group Hamas, the show is meant to inculcate in the young the Palestinian people's claim to disputed territories in the Mideast.

proved behavior, whether it is physical violence, disrespect to a teacher, or drug use.

The media play a critical role in shaping people's perceptions about the risks of substance use. Increases in substance use among youths during the 1990s were linked to a decline in warnings and antidrug messages from the media; the proliferation of pro-use messages from the entertainment industry; and high levels of tobacco and alcohol product advertising and promotion. Media content analysis shows that in the 200 most popular movie rentals of 1996 and 1997, alcohol use appeared in 93 percent, tobacco use in 89 percent, and illicit drug use in 22 percent, with marijuana and cocaine use shown most often. An analysis of the 1,000 most popular songs during the same period showed that 27 percent referred to either alcohol or illicit drugs. In 1999, 44 percent of entertainment programs aired by the four major television networks portrayed tobacco use in at least one episode (Ericson 2001; Roberts et al. 1999).

In 1997, a federal law required television networks to provide one free minute for every minute the government bought for a public service announcement with an antidrug message. The networks subsequently persuaded the government to drop the free minutes in exchange for aggressive antidrug messages embedded in their programs, such as *ER* and *The Practice*. Some people objected, saying that the networks were evading their legal responsibility in using the public airwaves, but criticism really mounted when word got out that a government agency was

How Does Television Portray the Family?

The media don't just present reality; they filter and interpret it. A good example of the media's interpretive portrayal of content is the way the family has been presented on television, from the 1950s to the present.

One of the earliest and biggest hit shows on TV, *I Love Lucy* (1951–1957), starred a real-life married couple, Lucille Ball and Desi Arnaz. In a nod to audience sensibilities in the prim and proper 1950s, the two characters slept in separate beds and avoided the word *pregnant,* even when in real life Lucille was carrying the couple's first child. Viewers did glimpse signs of the cultural tension inherent in an Anglo-Latino relationship.

As the decades passed and Americans' concept of family life changed, television families changed with it. While the emphasis was on humor in *The Brady Bunch* (1969–1974), the show did foreshadow what would become a common phenomenon by the century's end—the blended family—as character Michael Paul Brady merged his family of three sons with Carol Ann Tyler Martin's family of three daughters. And though *The Cosby Show* (1984–1992) did not always embrace social commentary, it did present a realistic picture of a dual-career couple (physician and attorney) whose family was firmly rooted in the Black upper middle class.

More recent shows have continued to expand the boundaries of the televised portrayal of family life. *Family Guy* (1999–2002, 2005–present), an animated series about a dysfunctional Rhode Island family with a clueless dad, a talking dog, and a frighteningly precocious infant, offers an irreverent and relatively rare look at a working-class family. And through the story of a family that belongs to a crime syndicate, *The Sopranos* (2003–2007) provided a dramatic illustration of the impact of work on the home. Finally, in *Two and a Half Men* (2003–present), two brothers, one of whom retains custody of his son after a divorce, show that today's household comes in all varieties.

Television has also shown Latino, Korean American, childless, extended, single-father, single-mother, public-housing-project, and gay households. What TV family looks most like yours? What kinds of family are rarely, if ever, shown on television?

{I Love Lucy}

{The Brady Bunch}

{The Cosby Show}

{Family Guy}

{The Sopranos}

{Two and a Half Men}

Status Conferred by Magazines

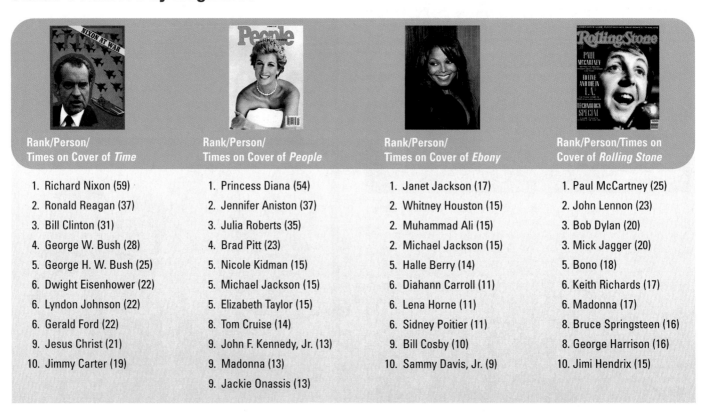

Rank/Person/ Times on Cover of *Time*	Rank/Person/ Times on Cover of *People*	Rank/Person/ Times on Cover of *Ebony*	Rank/Person/Times on Cover of *Rolling Stone*
1. Richard Nixon (59)	1. Princess Diana (54)	1. Janet Jackson (17)	1. Paul McCartney (25)
2. Ronald Reagan (37)	2. Jennifer Aniston (37)	2. Whitney Houston (15)	2. John Lennon (23)
3. Bill Clinton (31)	3. Julia Roberts (35)	2. Muhammad Ali (15)	3. Bob Dylan (20)
4. George W. Bush (28)	4. Brad Pitt (23)	2. Michael Jackson (15)	3. Mick Jagger (20)
5. George H. W. Bush (25)	5. Nicole Kidman (15)	5. Halle Berry (14)	5. Bono (18)
6. Dwight Eisenhower (22)	5. Michael Jackson (15)	6. Diahann Carroll (11)	6. Keith Richards (17)
6. Lyndon Johnson (22)	5. Elizabeth Taylor (15)	6. Lena Horne (11)	6. Madonna (17)
6. Gerald Ford (22)	8. Tom Cruise (14)	6. Sidney Poitier (11)	8. Bruce Springsteen (16)
9. Jesus Christ (21)	9. John F. Kennedy, Jr. (13)	9. Bill Cosby (10)	8. George Harrison (16)
10. Jimmy Carter (19)	9. Madonna (13)	10. Sammy Davis, Jr. (9)	10. Jimi Hendrix (15)
	9. Jackie Onassis (13)		

Source: Author's content analysis of primary cover subject for full run of the periodicals beginning with *Time,* March 3, 1923; *People,* March 4, 1974; *Ebony,* November 1945; and *Rolling Stone,* September 1967 through June 15, 2007. In case of ties, the more recent cover person is listed first.

Think About It
How do these magazines differ in the types of people they feature on their covers? Which type do you think enjoys the most status? Why?

screening scripts in advance and even working on the story lines. Many critics felt the practice could open the way for the government to plant messages in the media on other topics as well, such as abortion or gun control (Albiniak 2000).

Conferral of Status The mass media confer status on people, organizations, and public issues. Whether it is an issue such as the homeless or a celebrity such as Cameron Diaz, they single out one from thousands of other similarly placed issues or people to become significant. Table 7-1 (above) shows how often certain public figures are prominently featured on weekly magazine covers. Obviously, *People* magazine alone was not responsible for making Princess Diana into a worldwide figure, but collectively, all the media outlets created a notoriety that Princess Victoria of Sweden, for one, did not enjoy.

Another way the media confer celebrity status on individuals is by publishing information about the frequency of Internet searches. Some newspapers and Web sites carry regularly up-dated lists of the most heavily researched individuals and topics of the week. The means may have changed since the first issue of *Time* magazine hit the stands in 1923, but the media still confer status—often electronically.

Promotion of Consumption Twenty thousand commercials a year—that is the number the average child in the United States watches on television, according to the American Academy of Pediatrics. Young people cannot escape commercial messages. They show up on high school scoreboards, at rock concerts, and as banners on Web pages. They are even embedded in motion pictures (remember Reese's Pieces in 1982's *E.T.: The Extra-Terrestrial?*). Such *product placement* is nothing new. In 1951 *The African Queen* prominently displayed Gordon's Gin aboard the boat carrying Katharine Hepburn and Humphrey Bogart. But commercial promotion has become far more common today. Moreover, advertisers are attempting to develop brand or logo loyalty at younger and younger ages (Lasn 2003; Quart 2003).

{taking SOCIOLOGY TO WORK}

Nicole Martorano Van Cleve
**Former Brand Planner,
Leo Burnett USA**

When Nicole Van Cleve graduated from Northwestern University in 1999 with a degree in sociology, she had no idea how useful it would be in her business career. But she soon found that her training in observing and analyzing social phenomena was in demand, especially in consumer research. "While my friends were trying to land a job in advertising using their 'business' know-how, I leveraged what I knew best—the sociological perspective," she says.

Van Cleve was hired by Leo Burnett, Chicago's largest advertising agency, to work on the campaigns for internationally known brands. "Big brands like Hallmark, Polaroid, and Disney are socially constructed entities," she explains. "The sociological imagination is an essential tool in 'seeing' the cultural phenomenon that others might miss."

In 2003 Van Cleve became a specialist in strategic brand planning, or the development of brand images to appeal to the passions and cultural truths that drive consumer purchases. As a brand planner, she conducted and analyzed interviews, surveys, focus groups, and ethnographic studies. Once, for example, she studied families on vacation in Disneyland, which involved everything from videotaping them to conducting focus groups and reading through the diaries they kept. In the results to these studies, Van Cleve found clues to the human motivations that underlie consumers' purchasing habits and brand preferences.

Van Cleve loved the variety inherent in her work at Burnett. "In advertising, no week is ever the same," she enthuses. When she wasn't working in the field with consumers or analyzing the results of her studies, she wrote the creative briefs that inspire the agency's copy writers and art directors. Van Cleve knew that if she did her job well, the insights she developed through her consumer research would infuse the commercials and print advertisements that support her clients' brands.

Today, Van Cleve has taken her passion for sociological observation and research one step further: She is now a Ph.D. candidate in sociology at Northwestern University. "As a student, sociology gave me an intellectual passion that I never knew I had," she muses. "As a profession, sociology gave me a job that I love."

Let's Discuss

1. Can you think of some other careers in the mass media in which the sociological imagination might prove useful? If so, how?
2. What might be some ethical considerations in consumer research?

{ Product placement ("brand casting") is an increasingly important source of revenue for motion picture studios. This scene from *Talladega Nights: The Ballad of Ricky Bobby* (2006) doubles as a commercial for Wonder Bread. }

Using advertising to develop a brand name with global appeal is an especially powerful way to encourage consumption. U.S. corporations have been particularly successful in creating global brands. An analysis of the hundred most successful brands worldwide, each of which derives at least a third of its earnings outside the home country, shows that 53 of them originated in the United States; 47 others come from 11 different countries (see Figure 7-1, page 164).

Media advertising has several clear functions: it supports the economy, provides information about products, and underwrites the cost of media. In some cases, advertising becomes part of the entertainment industry. A national survey showed that 14 percent of those who viewed the 2003 Super Bowl did so *only* for the commercials. Yet related to these functions are dysfunctions. Media advertising contributes to a consumer

Branding the Globe

MAPPING LIFE WORLDWIDE

www.mhhe.com/schaefer11

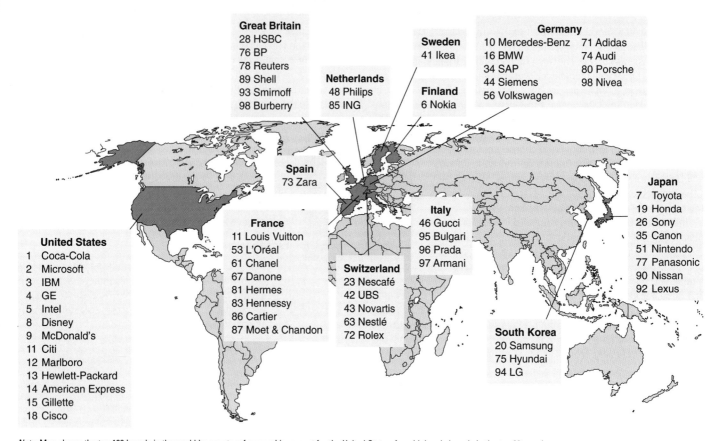

Great Britain
28 HSBC
76 BP
78 Reuters
89 Shell
93 Smirnoff
98 Burberry

Sweden
41 Ikea

Germany
10 Mercedes-Benz   71 Adidas
16 BMW   74 Audi
34 SAP   80 Porsche
44 Siemens   98 Nivea
56 Volkswagen

Netherlands
48 Philips
85 ING

Finland
6 Nokia

Spain
73 Zara

Japan
7   Toyota
19 Honda
26 Sony
35 Canon
51 Nintendo
77 Panasonic
90 Nissan
92 Lexus

Italy
46 Gucci
95 Bulgari
96 Prada
97 Armani

France
11 Louis Vuitton
53 L'Oréal
61 Chanel
67 Danone
81 Hermes
83 Hennessy
86 Cartier
87 Moet & Chandon

Switzerland
23 Nescafé
42 UBS
43 Novartis
63 Nestlé
72 Rolex

United States
1   Coca-Cola
2   Microsoft
3   IBM
4   GE
5   Intel
8   Disney
9   McDonald's
11 Citi
12 Marlboro
13 Hewlett-Packard
14 American Express
15 Gillette
18 Cisco

South Korea
20 Samsung
75 Hyundai
94 LG

Note: Map shows the top 100 brands in the world by country of ownership, except for the United States, for which only brands in the top 20 are shown.
Source: Adapted from Kiley 2006.

Based on revenue and name recognition, these are the brands that dominate the global marketplace.

Think About It
How many of these brands do you recognize?

culture that creates "needs" and raises unrealistic expectations of what is required to be happy or satisfied. Moreover, because the media depend heavily on advertising revenue, advertisers can influence media content (FAIR 2001; Horovitz 2003).

Use Your Sociological Imagination

You are a news junkie. Where do you gather your facts or information—from newspapers, tabloids, magazines, TV newscasts, or the Internet? Why did you choose that medium?

Dysfunction: The Narcotizing Effect In addition to the {p.16} functions just noted, the media perform a *dysfunction*. Sociologists Paul Lazarsfeld and Robert Merton (1948) created the term **narcotizing dysfunction** to refer to the phenomenon in which the media provide such massive amounts of coverage that the audience becomes numb and fails to act on the information, regardless of how compelling the issue. Interested citizens may take in the information but make no decision or take no action.

Consider how often the media initiate a great outpouring of philanthropic support in response to natural disasters or family crises. But then what happens? Research shows that as time passes, viewer fatigue sets in. The mass media audience becomes numb, desensitized to the suffering, and may even conclude that a solution to the crisis has been found (Moeller 1999).

The media's narcotizing dysfunction was identified over 50 years ago, when just a few homes had television—well before the advent of electronic media. At that time, the dysfunction went largely unnoticed, but today commentators often point out the ill effects of addiction to television or the Internet, especially among young people. Street crime, explicit sex, war, and HIV/AIDS apparently are such overwhelming topics that some in the audience may feel they have acted—or at the very least learned all they need to know—simply by watching the news.

Conflict View

Conflict theorists emphasize that the media reflect and even exacerbate many of the divisions in our society and world, including those based on gender, race, ethnicity, and social class. They point in particular to the media's ability to decide what is transmitted through a process called gatekeeping.

Gatekeeping   What story appears on page 1 of the morning newspaper? Which motion picture plays on three screens rather than one at the local cineplex? What picture isn't released at all? Behind these decisions are powerful figures—publishers, editors, and other media moguls.

The mass media constitute a form of big business in which profits are generally more important than the quality of the programming. Within the mass media, a relatively small number of people control what eventually reaches the audience through a process known as *gatekeeping.* This term describes how material must travel through a series of checkpoints (or gates) before reaching the public. Thus, a select few decide what images to bring to a broad audience. In many countries the government plays a gatekeeping role. A study done for the World Bank found that in 97 countries, 60 percent of the top five TV stations and 72 percent of the largest radio stations are government-owned (World Bank 2001:183).

Gatekeeping prevails in all kinds of media. As sociologist C. Wright Mills ([1956] 2000b) observed, the real power of the media is that they can control what is being presented. In the recording industry, gatekeepers may reject a popular local band because it competes with a group already on their label. Even if the band is recorded, radio programmers may reject the music because it does not fit the station's "sound." Television programmers may keep a pilot for a new TV series off the air because they believe it does not appeal to the target audience (which is sometimes determined by advertising sponsors). Similar decisions are made by gatekeepers in the publishing industry (Hanson 2005).

Gatekeeping is not as dominant in at least one form of mass media, the Internet. You can send virtually any message to an electronic bulletin board, and create a Web page or Web log (blog) to advance any argument, including one that insists the earth is flat. The Internet is a means of quickly disseminating information (or misinformation) without going through any significant gatekeeping process.

Nevertheless, the Internet is not totally without restrictions. In many nations laws regulate content on issues such as gambling, pornography, and even politics. Popular Internet service providers will terminate accounts for offensive behavior. After the terrorist attacks in 2001, eBay did not allow people to sell parts of the World Trade Center via its online auction. A World Bank study found that 17 countries place significant controls on Internet content. For example, China routinely blocks search engines like Google and AltaVista from accessing the names of groups or individuals critical of the government (French 2004a; World Bank 2001:187).

Critics of the content of mass media argue that the gatekeeping process reflects a desire to maximize profits. Why else, they argue, would movie star Julia Roberts, rather than Afghanistan's leader Hamid Karzai, make the cover of *Time* magazine? Later in this chapter we will consider the role that corporate structure plays in the content and delivery of mass media. Another criticism of the gatekeeping process is that the content that makes it through the gates does not reflect the diversity of the audience.

Media Monitoring   The term *media monitoring* is used most often to refer to interest groups' monitoring of media content. The public reaction to the shootings at Virginia Tech in April 2007 provides one example. People did not need to be constant news monitors to learn of the rampage. Ever since the mass shootings at Columbine High School near Littleton, Colorado, in 1999, news outlets of every type have descended on the sites of such school shootings, offering insight into the perpetrators and their families, covering the mass expressions of grief, and following the communities' efforts to recover. Once again, though media outlets provided valuable information and quickly reassured viewers, listeners, and readers that the shooter posed no further danger, many people criticized the reality that they constructed in their coverage.

Reactions ran the gamut. Some observers, including groups representing Asian Americans, questioned the recurring racial identifier used to describe the shooter. Indeed, when the news began to leak out that the shooter was "foreign" or "Asian," many people of color commented that they hoped he would not turn out to be one of their own, since people of color appear so rarely, if at all, in news coverage. Other observers objected to another form of stigmatization, the detailed disclosure of the shooter's history of mental illness, which seemed to some to vilify anyone who has ever suffered from a mental health problem (see Chapter 19). Still others felt that any presentation of the shooter's thinking, including the controversial release of the package of documents and videos he sent to NBC news, only served to glorify those who commit such wanton violence. Others objected to what they saw as the media's heavily anti-gun posture, which damned those who work to preserve the right to own firearms. In such emotional circumstances, the media's construction of reality certainly is not to everyone's liking, and rarely satisfies anyone completely (Asian American Journalists Association 2007; Groening 2007; Stanley 2007).

From television and newspapers to bloggers, media outlets were both applauded and harshly criticized for their coverage of the shootings at Virginia Tech in 2007.

tivities and scan the blogs they read—which are, of course, available for anyone to see. Most parents see such monitoring of children's media use and communications as an appropriate part of adult supervision. Yet their snooping sets an example for their children, who may use the technique for their own ends. Some media analysts have noted a growing trend among adolescents: the use of new media to learn not-so-public information about their parents (Delaney 2005).

Dominant Ideology: Constructing Reality Conflict theorists argue that the mass media maintain the privileges of certain groups. Moreover, powerful groups may limit the media's representation of others to protect their own interests. The term ***dominant ideology*** { **pp.71–72** describes a set of cultural beliefs and practices that helps to maintain powerful social, economic, and

Recently, use of the term *media monitoring* has expanded to include monitoring of individuals' media usage and choices without their knowledge. New technologies related to video on demand, downloading of audio/video clips, and satellite programming have created records of individual viewing and listening preferences. In 2006, Google opposed U.S. government efforts to obtain company records of users' Web-browsing activities. At the same time, members of the general public expressed concern both that companies such as Google were maintaining such records and that government agencies were interested in them. In Chapter 10 we will see that media and computer giants don't always oppose government efforts to monitor media usage. For example, Yahoo, Google, Microsoft, and Dell have cooperated with the Chinese government's efforts to restrict and monitor Internet use, raising human rights concerns in the process.

The federal government has also come under criticism recently for authorizing wiretaps of U.S. citizens' telephone conversations without judicial approval. Government officials argue that the wiretaps were undertaken in the interest of national security, to monitor contacts between U.S. citizens and known terrorist groups following the terrorist attacks of September 11, 2001. But critics who take the conflict perspective, among others, are concerned by the apparent invasion of people's privacy (Gertner 2005).

What are the practical and ethical limits of media monitoring? In daily life, parents often oversee their children's online ac-

In Johannesburg, South Africa, musical artist Lebo Mathosa celebrates MTV's launch of the first local music channel on the African continent. African artists hope the channel will offer greater exposure to indigenous musicians. Like the mass media in most parts of the world, African television is dominated by Western constructions of reality, including Western musical styles.

political interests. The media transmit messages that virtually define what we regard as the real world, even though those images frequently vary from the ones that the larger society experiences.

Mass media decision makers are overwhelmingly White, male, and wealthy. It may come as no surprise, then, that the media tend to ignore the lives and ambitions of subordinate groups, among them working-class people, African Americans, Hispanics, gays and lesbians, people with disabilities, overweight people, and older people. Worse, media content may create false images or stereotypes of these groups that then become accepted as accurate portrayals of reality. *Stereotypes* are unreliable generalizations about all members of a group that do not recognize individual differences within the group.

Television content is a prime example of this tendency to ignore reality. How many overweight TV characters can you name? Even though in real life one out of every four women is obese (30 or more pounds over a healthy body weight), only 3 out of 100 TV characters are portrayed as obese. Heavyset television characters have fewer romances, talk less about sex, eat more often, and are more often the object of ridicule than their thin counterparts (Hellmich 2001).

Minority groups are often stereotyped in TV shows. Almost all the leading roles are cast as White, even in urban-based programs such as *Friends,* which is situated in ethnically diverse New York City. Asian Americans and Native Americans rarely appear in general roles; Blacks tend to be featured mainly in crime-based dramas; Latinos are virtually ignored. Box 7-1 (page 168) discusses the distorted picture of society presented on prime-time television programs.

Another concern about the media, from the conflict perspective, is that television distorts the political process. Until the U.S. campaign finance system is truly reformed and the law enforced, the candidates with the most money (often backed by powerful lobbying groups) will be able to buy exposure to voters and saturate the air with commercials attacking their opponents.

Dominant Ideology: Whose Culture? In the United States, on the popular television contest *The Apprentice,* the dreaded dismissal line is "You're fired." In Finland, on *Dilli (The Deal),* it's "*Olet vapautettu*" ("You're free to leave"); in Germany, on *Big Boss,* it's "*Sie haben frei*" ("You're off"). Although people { pp.59, 62–63 throughout the world decry U.S. exports, from films to language to Bart Simpson, the U.S. media are still widely imitated. Sociologist Todd Gitlin describes American popular culture as something that "people love, and love to hate" (2002:177; Wentz and Atkinson 2005).

This love-hate relationship is so enduring that the U.S. media have come to rely on the overseas market. In fact, many motion pictures have brought in more revenue abroad than at home. Through early 2007, for example, *Titanic* had earned a record-breaking $600 million in the United States and another $1.4 billion at overseas box offices. Of the top 250 top-grossing movies in 2006, in fact, 246 were U.S.-made. Some Hollywood movies,

however, are so insensitive to the global audience that they fail miserably overseas. The 2005 film *Memoirs of a Geisha,* set in 20th-century Japan, greatly offended Japanese moviegoers because the title role went to the Chinese actress Ziyi Zhang. Ironically, her casting also upset the Chinese, who were outraged to see a leading Chinese actress portray a Japanese geisha. In 2006 Chinese government officials banned the film's release (Barboza 2006; Joffe 2006).

We risk being ethnocentric if we overstress U.S. dominance. For example, *Survivor, Who Wants to Be a Millionaire,* and *Iron Chef*—immensely popular TV programs in the United States—came from Sweden, Britain, and Japan, respectively. Even *American Idol* originated in Britain as *Pop Idol,* featuring

Famed Chinese actress Ziyi Zhang played a Japanese geisha in the U.S.-made film *Memoirs of a Geisha* (2005). The decision to cast her in a Japanese role backfired in both Japan and China. Though U.S. films are usually well received abroad, cultural insensitivity can damage their box-office receipts.

social**INEQUALITY** •••

7-1 The Color of Network TV

Today, 40 percent of all youths in the United States are children of color, yet few of the faces they see on television reflect their race or cultural heritage. As of spring 2007, only 5 of the nearly 60 primetime series carried on the four major networks featured performers of color in leading roles, and only 2—*Ugly Betty* and *George Lopez*—centered on minority performers. What is more, the programs shown earlier in the evening, when young people are most likely to watch television, are the *least* diverse of all.

When minority groups do appear on television and in other forms of media, their roles tend to reinforce the stereotypes associated with their ethnic or racial groups. In 2004, nearly half of all Middle Eastern characters shown on television were criminals, compared to only 5 percent of White characters. Latino roles were just as stereotyped. Recently, Latinas have been featured as maids on *Will and Grace* (Rosario), *Dharma and Greg* (Celia), and even the animated *King of the Hill* (Lupino), to name just three shows.

In a rare exception to this pattern, in 2006 *The West Wing* featured the election of a Latino president, played by Puerto Rican American Jimmy Smits. Ironically, the character of Jed Bartlett, who was president through most of the long-running series, is played by Martin Sheen. Sheen, born Ramon Estevez, rarely mentions his Hispanic roots.

Producers, writers, executives, and advertisers blame one another for the rampant underrepresentation of racial and ethnic minorities. Television programming is dictated by advertisers, a former executive claims; if advertisers said they wanted blatantly biased programming, the networks would provide it. Jery Isenberg, chairman of the Caucus for Producers, Writers & Directors, blames the networks, saying that writers would produce a series about three-headed Martians if the networks told them to.

Beyond these excuses, real reasons can be found for the departure from the diversity exhibited in past shows and seasons. In recent years, the rise of more networks, cable TV, and the Internet has fragmented the broadcast entertainment market, siphoning viewers away from the general-audience sitcoms and dramas of the past. Both the UPN and WB networks produce situation comedies and even full evenings geared toward African American audiences. With the proliferation of cable channels such as Black Entertainment Television (BET) and the Spanish-language Telemundo and Univision, as well as Web sites that cater to every imaginable taste, there no longer seems to be a need for broadly popular

A rare sight on prime-time television: In CW's *Girlfriends*, which debuted in 2000, all the leading roles are played by African Americans.

series such as *The Cosby Show,* the tone and content of which appealed to Whites as well as Blacks in a way the newer series do not. The result of these sweeping technological changes has been a sharp divergence in viewer preferences.

Meanwhile, mainstream network executives, producers, and writers remain overwhelmingly White. Most of them live far from ethnically and racially diverse inner-city neighborhoods and tend to write and produce stories about people like themselves. Marc Hirshfeld, an NBC executive, claims some

> *Marc Hirshfeld, an NBC executive, claims some White producers have told him they don't know how to write for Black characters.*

White producers have told him they don't know how to write for Black characters. Stephen Bochco, producer of *NYPD Blue,* is a rare exception. His series *City of Angels* featured a mostly non-White cast, like the people Bochco grew up with in an inner-city neighborhood. The series ran for 23 episodes before being canceled in 2000.

In the long run, media observers believe, the major networks will need to integrate the ranks of gatekeepers before they achieve true diversity in programming. Adonis Hoffman, director of the Corporate Policy Institute, has

urged network executives to throw open their studios and boardrooms to minorities. Hoffman thinks such a move would empower Black writers and producers to present a true-to-life portrait of African Americans. There are some signs of agreement from the networks. According to Doug Herzog, president of Fox Entertainment, real progress means incorporating diversity from within.

Why should it matter that minority groups aren't visible on major network television, if they are well represented on other channels such as UPN, WB, BET, and Univision? The problem is that Whites as well as minorities see a distorted picture of their society every time they turn on network TV. In Hoffman's words, "African Americans, Latinos and Asians, while portrayed as such, are not merely walk-ons in our society—they are woven into the fabric of what has made this country great" (A. Hoffman 1997:M6).

Let's Discuss

1. Do you watch network TV? If so, how well do you think it represents the diversity of U.S. society?
2. Have you seen a movie or TV show recently that portrayed members of a minority group in a sensitive and realistic way—as real people rather than as stereotypes or token walk-ons? If so, describe the show.

Sources: Bielby and Bielby 2002; Braxton 2007; Children Now 2004; Directors Guild of America 2002; Gamson and Latteier 2004; A. Hoffman 1997; M. Navarro 2002; Poniewozik 2001.

Simon Cowell. And the steamy telenovelas of Mexico and other Spanish-speaking countries owe very little of their origin to the soap operas on U.S. television. Unlike motion pictures, television is gradually moving away from U.S. domination and is more likely to be locally produced. By 2003, all the top 50 British TV shows were locally produced. *The West Wing* may appear on television in London, but it is shown late at night. Even U.S.-owned TV ventures such as Disney, MTV, and CNN have dramatically increased their locally produced programming overseas. The introduction of MTV Romania and MTV Indonesia in 2003 brought the number of local versions of the popular music channel to 38 (*The Economist* 2003b).

Nations that feel a loss of identity may try to defend against the cultural invasion from foreign countries, especially the economically dominant United States. Many developing nations have long argued for a greatly improved two-way flow of news and information between industrialized nations and developing nations. They complain that news from the Third World is scant, and what news there is reflects unfavorably on the developing nations. For example, what do you know about South America? Most people in the United States will mention the two topics that dominate the news from countries south of the border: revolution and drugs. Most know little else about the continent.

To remedy this imbalance, a resolution to monitor the news and content that cross the borders of developing nations was passed by the United Nations Educational, Scientific, and Cultural Organization (UNESCO) in the 1980s. The United States disagreed with the proposal, which became one factor in the U.S. decision to withdraw from UNESCO in the mid-1980s. In 2005, the United States opposed another UNESCO plan, meant to reduce the diminishment of cultural differences. Hailed as an important step toward protecting threatened cultures, particularly the media markets in developing nations, the measure passed the UN's General Assembly by a vote of 148–2. The United States, one of the two dissenters, objected that the measure's wording was vague (Dominick 2005:455; Riding 2005).

Use Your Sociological Imagination

How much of the media you watch or listen to reflects U.S. culture? How much reflects the cultures of the rest of the world?

www.mhhe.com/schaefer11

Feminist View

Feminists share the view of conflict theorists that the mass media stereotype and misrepresent social reality. According to this view, the media powerfully influence how we look at men and women, communicating unrealistic, stereotypical, and limiting images of the sexes. Here are three problems feminists believe arise from media coverage (Wood 1994):

1. Women are underrepresented, which suggests that men are the cultural standard and women are insignificant.

2. Men and women are portrayed in ways that reflect and perpetuate stereotypical views of gender. Women, for example, are often shown in peril, needing to be rescued by a male—rarely the reverse.

3. Depictions of male–female relationships emphasize traditional sex roles and normalize violence against women.

Educators and social scientists have long noted the stereotypical portrayal of women and men in the mass media. Women are often shown as being shallow and obsessed with beauty. They are more likely than men to be presented unclothed, in danger, or even physically victimized. When women achieve newsworthy feats in fields traditionally dominated by men, such as professional sports, the media are often slow to recognize their accomplishments. As Figure 7-2 shows, only about 6 percent of network sports coverage is devoted to women. The situation is even worse on ESPN Sports Center, where content analysis shows that only 2 percent of air time is devoted to women's sports.

A continuing, troubling issue for feminists and society as a whole is pornography. Feminists tend to be very supportive of freedom of expression and self-determination, rights that are denied to women more often than to men. Yet pornography presents women as sex objects and seems to make viewing women that way acceptable. Nor are concerns about pornography limited to this type of objectification and imagery, as well as their implicit endorsement of violence against women. The industry that creates risqué adult images for videos, DVDs, and the Internet is largely unregulated, putting its own performers at risk. A 2002 health survey of triple-X, as the porn industry refers to itself, found that 40 percent of actors and actresses had at least one sexually transmitted disease, compared to 0.1 percent of the general population. The career span of

FIGURE 7–2

Network Coverage of Women's versus Men's Sports

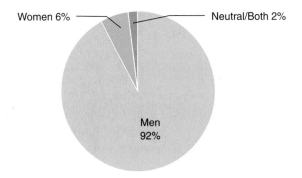

Women 6% — Neutral/Both 2%

Men 92%

Note: Based on a content analysis of 2004 televised sports news and highlights shows.
Source: Messner et al. 2006:35.

these women and men is short, usually about 18 months, but the profits for the industry are continuous and enormous (Huffstutter 2003).

As in other areas of sociology, feminist researchers caution against assuming that what holds true for men's media use is true for everyone. Researchers, for example, have studied the different ways that women and men approach the Internet. Though men are only slightly more likely than women ever to have used the Internet, they are much more likely to use it daily. According to a 2005 study, about a third of men use the Internet every day, compared to a quarter of women. Not surprisingly, men account

for 91 percent of the players in online sports fantasy leagues. But perhaps more socially significant, women are more likely than men to maintain friendship networks through e-mail (Boase et al. 2006; Fallows 2006; Rainie 2005).

Interactionist View

Interactionists are especially interested in shared understandings of everyday behavior. These scholars examine the media on the micro level to see how they shape day-to-day social behavior. Increasingly, researchers point to the mass media as the source of major daily activity; some argue that television serves virtually

FIGURE 7–3

The Internet Explosion

MAPPING LIFE WORLDWIDE www.mhhe.com/schaefer11

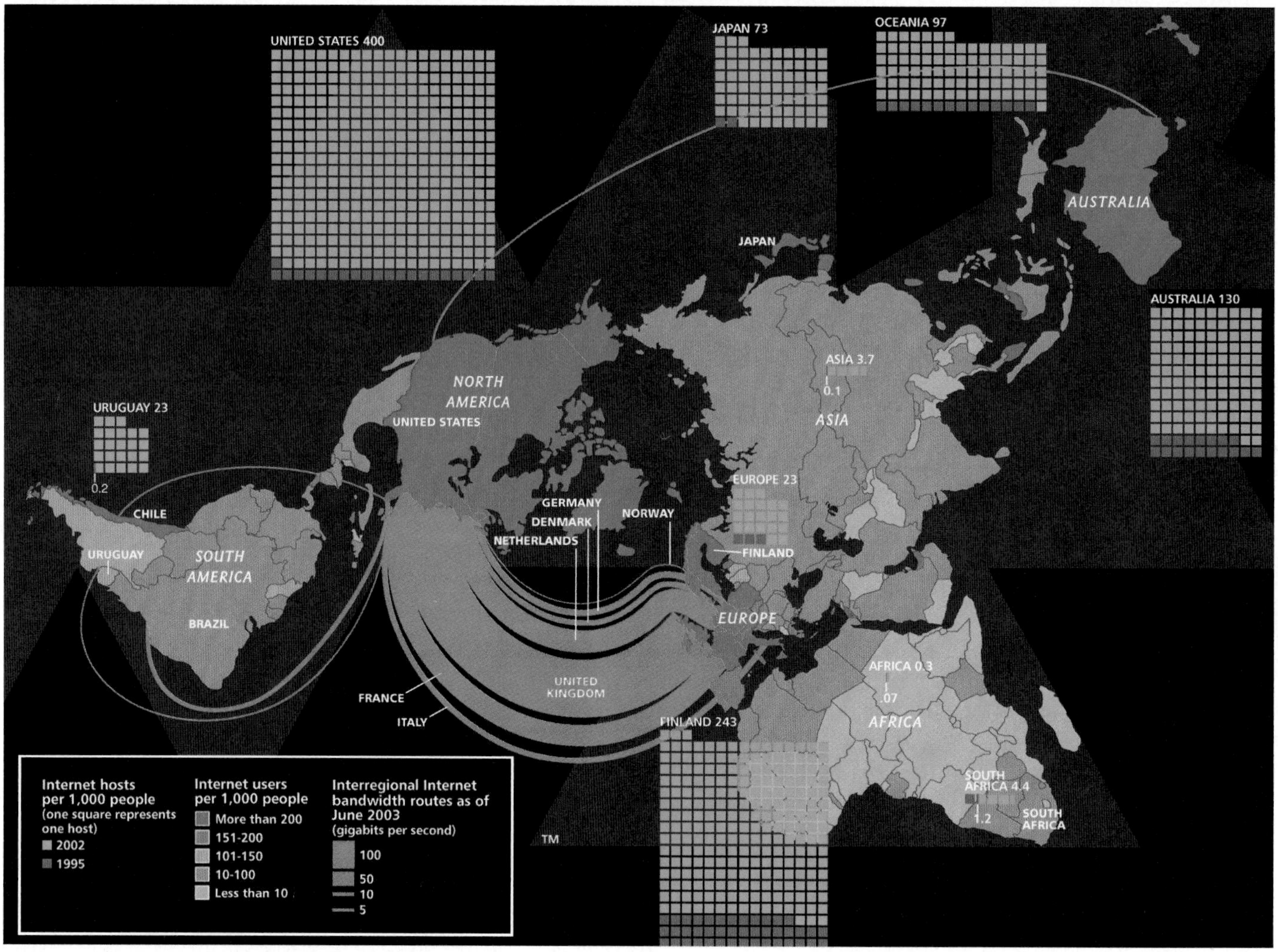

Source: National Geographic 2005:21 and the Buckminster Fuller Institute™.

In little more than a decade, the World Wide Web has exploded, touching 600 million users in every single country on earth. Still, a digital divide, measured in the form of relative bandwidth, separates rich countries from poor ones.

FIGURE 7–4

Who's on the Internet

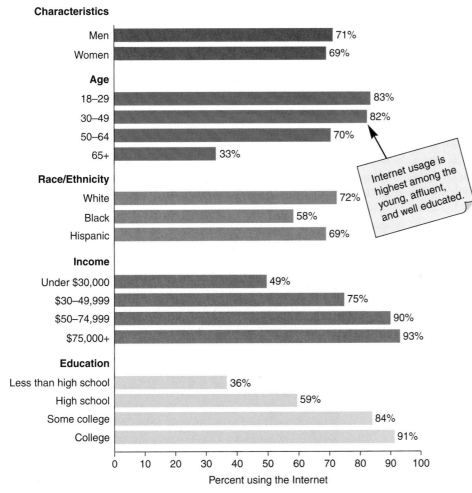

Internet usage is highest among the young, affluent, and well educated.

Note: Based on a December 2006 national survey released on January 11, 2007. Data for Blacks and Whites are for non-Hispanics. Hispanic data are for English-speaking Hispanics.
Source: Pew Internet Project 2007.

events attempt to convey self-serving definitions of social reality (M. Weinstein and Weinstein 2002).

The rise of the Internet has facilitated new forms of communication and social interaction. Grandparents can now keep up with their grandchildren via e-mail. Gay and lesbian teens have online resources for support and information. People can even find their lifetime partners through computer dating services. As Figure 7-3 shows, throughout the world, the Internet is casting an increasingly wider net over social interactions.

Some troubling issues have been raised about day-to-day life on the Internet. What, if anything, should be done about terrorists and other extremist groups who use the Internet to exchange messages of hatred and even bomb-making recipes? What, if anything, should be done about the issue of sexual expression on the Internet? How can children be protected from it? Should "hot chat" and X-rated film clips be censored? Or should expression be completely free?

Though the Internet has created a new platform for extremists and pornographers, it has also given people greater control over what they see and hear. That is, the Internet allows people to manage their media exposure so as to avoid sounds, images, and ideas they do not enjoy or approve of. The legal scholar Cass Sunstein (2002) has referred to this personalized approach to news information gathering as *egocasting*. One social consequence of this trend may be a less tolerant society. If we read, see, and hear only what we know and agree with, we may be much less prepared to meet people from different backgrounds or converse with those who express new viewpoints.

Finally, while many people in the United States embrace the Internet, we should note that information is not evenly distributed throughout the population. The same people, by and large, who experience poor health and have few job opportunities have been left off the information highway. Figure 7-4 breaks down Internet usage by gender, age, race, income, and education. Note the large disparities in usage between those with high and low incomes, and between those with more and less education. The data also show a significant racial disparity. Though educators and politicians have touted the potential benefits to the disadvantaged, Internet usage may be reinforcing existing social-class barriers.

as a primary group for many individuals who share TV viewing. Other mass-media participation is not necessarily face to face. For example, we usually listen to the radio or read the newspaper as a solitary activity, although it is possible to share it with others (Cerulo et al. 1992; Waite 2000).

Interactionists note, too, that friendship networks can emerge from shared viewing habits or from recollection of a cherished television series from the past. Family members and friends often gather for parties centered on the broadcasting of popular events such as the Super Bowl or the Academy Awards. And as we've seen, television often serves as a babysitter or playmate for children and even infants.

The power of the mass media encourages political leaders and entertainment figures to carefully manipulate their images through public appearances called photo opportunities, or photo ops. By embracing symbols (posing with celebrities or in front of prestigious landmarks), participants in these staged

The interactionist perspective helps us to understand one important aspect of the entire mass media system—the audience. How do we actively participate in media events? How do we construct with others the meaning of media messages? We will explore these questions in the section that follows. (Table 7-2, below, summarizes the various sociological perspectives on the media.)

The Audience

Ever feel like text messaging everyone you know, to encourage them to vote for your favorite performer on a certain reality program? Ever looked over someone's shoulder as he watched last week's episode of *Grey's Anatomy* on his handheld video player—and been tempted to reveal the ending to him? Ever come across an old CD and tried to remember the last time you or a friend listened to one, or heard the songs in the order in which they were recorded? In this and many other ways, we are reminded that we are all part of a larger audience.

Who Is in the Audience?

The mass media are distinguished from other social institutions by the necessary presence of an audience. It can be an identifiable, finite group, such as an audience at a jazz club or a Broadway musical, or a much larger and undefined group, such as VH-1 viewers or readers of the same issue of *USA Today*. The audience may be a secondary group gathered in a large auditorium or a primary group, such as a family watching the latest Disney video at home.

We can look at the audience from the level of both *microsociology* and *macrosociology*. At the micro level, we might consider how audience members, interacting among themselves, respond to the media, or in the case of live performances, actually influence the performers. At the macro level, we might examine broader societal consequences of the media, such as the early childhood education delivered through programming like *Sesame Street*.

Even if an audience is spread out over a wide geographic area and members don't know one another, it is still distinctive in terms of age, gender, income, political party, formal schooling, race, and ethnicity. The audience for a ballet, for example, would differ substantially from the audience for alternative music.

Use Your Sociological Imagination

Think about the last time you were part of an audience. How similar to or different from yourself were the other audience members? What might account for whatever similarities or differences you noticed?

www.mhhe.com/schaefer11

The Segmented Audience

Increasingly, the media are marketing themselves to a *particular* audience. Once a media outlet, such as a radio station or a magazine, has identified its audience, it targets that group. To some degree, this specialization is driven by advertising. Media specialists have sharpened their ability, through survey research, to identify particular target audiences. As a result, Nike would be much more likely to promote a new line of golf clubs on the Golf Channel, for example, than on an episode of *SpongeBob*. The many more choices that the growing Internet and satellite broadcast channels offer audiences also foster specialization. Members of these audiences are more likely to *expect* content geared to their own interests.

Marketing research has developed to the point that those who are interested can estimate the size of the audience for a particular performer. In fact, computer programs have been written to simulate not just specific audiences, but the connections among them. Figure 7-5 (opposite) shows the computer-drawn audience networks for two well-known performing artists, Usher and Shania Twain.

The specialized targeting of audiences has led some scholars to question the "mass" in mass media. For example, the British social psychologist Sonia Livingstone (2004) has written that the media have become so segmented, they have taken on the appearance almost of individualization. Are viewing audiences so segmented that large collective audiences are a thing of the past? That is not yet clear. Even though we seem to be living in an age of *personal* computers and *personal* digital assistants (PDAs),

Table 7-2

Sociological Perspectives on the Mass Media

summingUP

Theoretical Perspective	Emphasis
Functionalist	Socialization
	Enforcement of social norms
	Conferral of status
	Promotion of consumption
	Narcotizing effect (dysfunction)
Conflict	Gatekeeping
	Media monitoring
	Construction of reality
Feminist	Underrepresentation of women
	Misrepresentation of women
Interactionist	Impact on social behavior
	Source of friendship networks

FIGURE 7–5

173

The Mass Media

Two Audience Networks

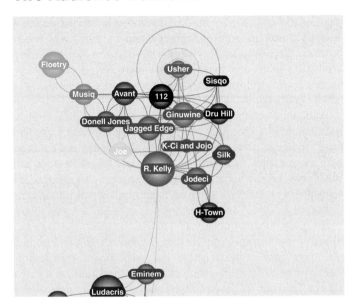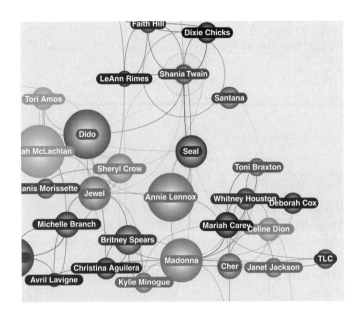

Source: Liveplasma.com 2006.

These maps, which were generated by analysis of purchasing patterns, show the audience networks for two very different performing artists, Usher and Shania Twain. Each circle represents the audience for a particular artist; the larger the circle, the more popular the artist. Usher fans are connected to Shania Twain fans by a series of links, from R. Kelly fans to Eminem fans to Nelly, Justin Timberlake, Madonna, and finally Jewel fans.

large formal organizations still do transmit public messages that reach a sizable, heterogeneous, and scattered audience.

Audience Behavior

Sociologists have long researched how audiences interact with one another and how they share information after a media event. The role of audience members as opinion leaders particularly intrigues social researchers. An ***opinion leader*** is someone who influences the opinions and decisions of others through day-to-day personal contact and communication. For example, a movie or theater critic functions as an opinion leader. Sociologist Paul Lazarsfeld and his colleagues (1948) pioneered the study of opinion leaders in their research on voting behavior in the 1940s. They found that opinion leaders encourage their relatives, friends, and co-workers to think positively about a particular candidate, perhaps pushing them to listen to the politician's speeches or read the campaign literature.

Today, film critics often attribute the success of low-budget independent films to word of mouth. This is another way of saying that the mass media influence opinion leaders, who in turn influence others. The audience, then, is not a group of passive people but of active consumers who are often impelled to interact with others after a media event (Croteau and Hoynes 2003; C. Wright 1986).

Despite the role of opinion leaders, members of an audience do not all interpret media in the same way. Often their response is influenced by their social characteristics, such as occupation, race, education, and income. Take the example of the televised news coverage of the riots in Los Angeles in 1992. The riots were an angry response to the acquittal of two White police officers accused of severely beating a Black motorist. Sociologist Darnell Hunt (1997) wondered how the social composition of audience members would affect the way they interpreted the news coverage. Hunt gathered 15 groups from the Los Angeles area, whose members were equally divided among Whites, African Americans, and Latinos. He showed each group a 17-minute clip from the televised coverage of the riots and asked members to discuss how they would describe what they had just seen to a 12-year-old. In analyzing the discussions, Hunt found that although gender and class did not cause respondents to vary their answers much, race did.

Hunt went beyond noting simple racial differences in perceptions; he analyzed how the differences were manifested. For example, Black viewers were much more likely than Latinos or Whites to refer to the events in terms of "us" versus "them." Another difference was that Black and Latino viewers were more animated and critical than White viewers as they watched the film clip. White viewers tended to sit quietly, still and unquestioning, suggesting that they were more comfortable with the news coverage than the Blacks or Hispanics.

www.mhhe.com/schaefer11

Use Your Sociological Imagination

On what occasions might you be part of an audience in which you feel you are in the minority?

The Media's Global Reach

Has the rise of the electronic media created a "global village"? Canadian linguist Marshall McLuhan predicted it would some 40 years ago. Today, physical distance is no longer a barrier, and instant messaging is possible across the world. The mass media have indeed created a global village. Not all countries are equally connected, as Figure 7-6 shows, but the progress has been staggering, considering that voice transmission was just beginning 100 years ago (McLuhan 1964; McLuhan and Fiore 1967).

Sociologist Todd Gitlin considers "global torrent" a more apt metaphor for the media's reach than "global village." The media permeate all aspects of everyday life. Take advertising, for example. Consumer goods are marketed vigorously worldwide, from advertisements on airport baggage carriers to imprints on sandy beaches. Little wonder that people around the world develop loyalty to a brand and are as likely to sport a Nike, Coca-Cola, or Harley-Davidson logo as they are their favorite soccer or baseball insignia (Gitlin 2002; N. Klein 1999).

A highly visible part of the media, whether it be print or electronic, is news. In the past, most people in the United States had little familiarity with news outlets outside their own country, with the possible exception of the British-based Reuters and BBC News. Like so many other things, however, that changed after September 11, 2001, when an Arab news network took center stage (see Box 7-2).

The key to creating a truly global network that reaches directly into workplaces, schools, and homes is the Internet. Although much of the online global transmission today is limited to print and pictures, the potential to send audio and video via the Internet will increasingly reach into every part of the world. Social interaction will then truly take place on a global scale.

FIGURE 7–6

Media Penetration in Selected Countries

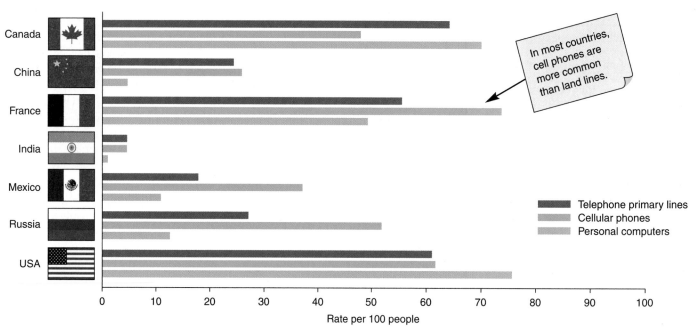

Note: Data for 2004 released in 2006.
Source: Bureau of the Census 2006a:864.

Think About It
What is the economic and political significance of media penetration?

7-2 Al Jazeera Is on the Air

A 24-hour-a-day televised news network with short bulletins every hour, followed by a fast-paced montage of news clips—all broadcast globally by satellite-linked cable stations. This could be CNN, but it's Al Jazeera, the Arabic-language television news network based in the small Persian Gulf state of Qatar. The name Al Jazeera means "island" or "peninsula," in reference to the network's home country. Founded in 1996, the channel now has 230 correspondents based at 30 foreign bureaus and an audience of about 40 million Arabs worldwide, including 150,000 Arab Americans.

Most people in the United States had never heard of Al Jazeera until October 7, 2001. That was when the channel aired the first of several videotaped messages from Osama bin Laden, the mastermind of the Al Qaeda terrorist network. U.S. news outlets also televised the messages, but stopped after the government objected to the airing of bin Laden's calls for violence against U.S. citizens.

Al Jazeera refused to acquiesce to the government request, invoking its motto, "The Opinion, and the Other Opinion Too." Al Jazeera officials insist that they promote a forum for independent dialogue and debate, an unusual practice in the Arab world, where most media outlets are state controlled. In fact, several Arab states, including Saudi Arabia, Jordan, and Bahrain, have banned or restricted Al Jazeera because of the network's critical coverage of affairs in their countries. Other Arab nations criticize Al Jazeera for giving too much airplay to U.S. news.

Though many media observers see Al Jazeera as biased, many viewers around the world might see CNN, ABC, and Fox News as biased. For example, in virtually all media outlets in the United States, the immorality of Palestinian suicide bombings is an unstated assumption. However, many people in the Arab world would regard that assumption as fundamentally wrong. Similarly, most Muslims worldwide would question why CBS's respected news show *60 Minutes* would give exposure to preacher Jerry Falwell, who called the Prophet Muhammad a terrorist. According to Kenton Keith, a former U.S. ambassador to Qatar, Al Jazeera has a slant, but no more than other news organizations. It just happens to be a slant that most Americans aren't comfortable with.

Al Jazeera does offer diverse views. On its popular talk show *The Opposing View,* two women hotly debated polygamy among Muslim men. On another popular program, *Sharia [Islamic Law] and Life,* the speaker dared to reassure Muslim women that the Koran does not force them to marry suitors designated by their parents. Ambassador Keith believes that "for the long-range importance of press freedom in the Middle East and the advantages that will

> *"You have to be a supporter of Al Jazeera, even if you have to hold your nose sometimes."*

ultimately have for the West, you have to be a supporter of Al Jazeera, even if you have to hold your nose sometimes" (Barr 2002:7).

To counter Al Jazeera's influence, in 2004 the U.S. State Department established its own satellite network, Al Hurra, in the Middle East. Based in Springfield, Virginia, and staffed by veteran Arab journalists, the new network promises balanced and objective reporting on regional issues and events. Its ultimate purpose, however, is to win over the hearts and minds of a population that is deeply suspicious of U.S. motives. Al Hurra, whose name means "The Free One," is the latest in a series of U.S. attempts at improving public relations with the Islamic world. Knowledgeable observers view the effort with some skepticism, however. Al Hurra now ranks seventh out of seven among international news channels in the Middle East, with an audience less than 4 percent the size of Al Jazeera's.

Let's Discuss

1. Do you find news outlets in the United States biased? How would you judge?
2. What do you think of the new Al Hurra network in the Middle East? Can it win over the hearts and minds of viewers there? Should the U.S. government be using taxpayers' dollars to fund the effort?

Sources: Al Jazeera 2006; Barr 2002; Daniszewski 2003; MacLeod and Walt 2005; McCarthy 2004; MediaGuardian 2001; H. Rosenberg 2003; Urbina 2002.

An Al Jazeera staff member monitors the news at the network's headquarters in Qatar. The Al Jazeera network was featured in the 2004 documentary film *Control Room.*

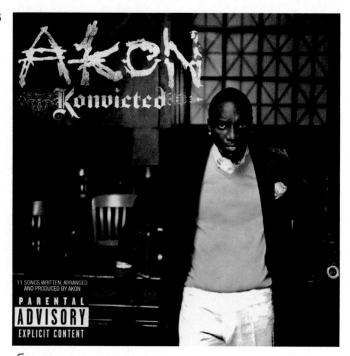

In 2006, Akon's "Smack That" became the number-one cell phone ring tone, with 1.57 million downloads. Because today's media provide multiple sevices, music fans can use the Internet to access recorded music and listen to it on their cell phones (Barnes 2007).

The Internet has also facilitated other forms of communication. Reference materials and data banks can now be made accessible across national boundaries. Information related to international finance, marketing, trade, and manufacturing is literally just a keystroke away. We have seen the emergence of truly world news outlets and the promotion of a world music that is not clearly identifiable with any single culture. Even the most future-oriented thinker would find the growth in the reach of the mass media in postindustrial and postmodern societies remarkable (Castells 2000, 2001; Croteau and Hoynes 2003, 2006).

The lack of one national home for the various forms of mass media raises a potential dilemma for users. People worry that unhealthy influences and even crime pervade today's electronic global village, and that few if any controls prevent them. For example, the leaders of Bhutan worry about the impact of newly introduced television programming on their culture and their people. Similarly, in industrial countries, including the United States, officials are concerned about everything from video poker to online pornography and the menace posed by hackers. And in the Social Policy section that follows, we'll see that just a few powerful corporations dominate the mass media, controlling the content that is presented to billions of people.

These Bhutanese householders are watching the *Oprah Winfrey Show* on their brand-new television set. The Bhutanese were introduced to television in 1999. Since then, Marshall McLuhan's global village has become a reality in their remote Asian kingdom, where rulers have become concerned about the cultural impact of Western media.

[social**Policy**]
and the Mass Media

Media Concentration

The Issue

Who owns the media production and distribution process? Increasingly, the answer is a small number of very large corporations. The social consequences of this trend toward the concentration of media ownership are a reduction in the number of information outlets and an increase in the cross-promotion of films and television shows through multiple media channels.

The Setting

The United States still has thousands of independent media outlets—small-town newspapers, radio stations, and television broadcasters—but the clear trend in the media industry is toward the consolidation of ownership. The fact is, a few multinational corporations dominate the publishing, broadcasting, and film industries, though their influence may be hard to identify, since global conglomerates manage many different product names. Walt Disney alone owns 16 television channels that reach 140 countries. But Disney is only one of several media giants. Add to the list Time Warner (HBO, CNN, AOL, *Time* and *People* magazines); Rupert Murdoch's News Corporation, founded in Australia (Fox Network Television, several book publishers, numerous newspapers and magazines, and 20th Century Fox); Sony of Japan (Columbia Pictures, IMAX, CBS Records, and Columbia Records); Clear Channel Communications (over 1,100 radio and 30 television stations); and Viacom (Paramount, DreamWorks SKG, MTV, and Black Entertainment Television), and the extent of their power becomes clear. This concentration of media giants fosters considerable cross-promotion. For example, the release of Warner Brothers' film *The Matrix Reloaded* in 2003 was heavily promoted by both CNN and *Time* magazine. In fact, *Time* somehow managed to devote its cover to the film's release in the midst of the war in Iraq.

Similar concerns have been raised about the situation in countries such as China, Cuba, Iraq, and North Korea, where the ruling party owns and controls the media. The difference, which is considerable, is that in the United States the gatekeeping process lies in the hands of private individuals, who desire only to maximize profits. In totalitarian countries, the gatekeeping process belongs to political leaders, whose desire is to maintain control of the government (P. Thomas and Nain 2004).

We should note one significant exception to the centralization and concentration of the media: the Internet. Research shows that more and more people, especially those under age 35, are receiving their media content through the Internet. Currently, the World Wide Web is accessible through independent outlets to millions of producers of media content. Obviously, the producer must be technologically proficient and must have access to a computer, but compared to other media outlets, the Internet is much more readily available. Media conglomerates, well aware of the Internet's potential, are already delivering their material via the Web. But for now, the Internet is the only medium that allows the average individual to become a media entrepreneur with a potential audience of millions (Gamson and Latteier 2004; J. Schwartz 2004).

Though concentration of ownership is not unique to the media (consider aircraft and automobile manufacturers), the media

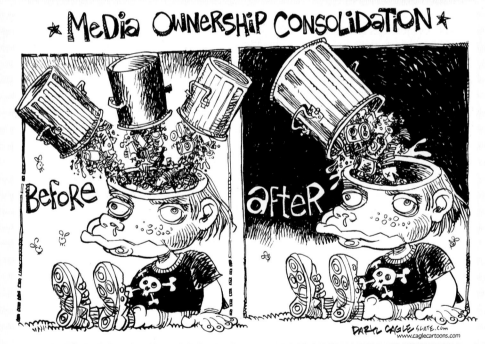

The 2003 FCC ruling that allowed further consolidation of media outlets by already huge conglomerates may have increased the companies' profitability, but it has had little positive impact on media content.

deserve special attention given the way they filter how we view reality.

Sociological Insights

Functionalists see media concentration—or the consolidation of any business—as a step toward greater economic efficiency. In their view, consolidation reduces the cost of operations, freeing capital for the development of new creative outlets. Furthermore, they believe that global trade in the media facilitates the free exchange of intellectual property, which is often hampered by arbitrary local restrictions (Croteau and Hoynes 2006).

Conflict theorists believe that media concentration stifles opportunities for minority ownership. According to the most recent FCC data, fewer than 4 percent of television stations in the United States are owned by racial and ethnic minorities; fewer than 5 percent are owned by women. Minority owners are underrepresented even in markets where minorities make up the majority of the audience. Nor is the Internet a level playing field for minorities. For example, with 10 percent of the world's population, the whole of Africa provides less than 1 percent of the Internet's online content (P. Thomas and Nain 2004; S. Turner and Cooper 2006).

Interactionists see a change in the way people get their news, though not in their interest in it. In the past people may have met or called one another to discuss the latest episode of *Survivor;* now they share the latest Internet news via e-mail or buddy list. Why wait for the evening news, or even for breaking news on CNN, when Yahoo and Google are at your fingertips?

Policy Initiatives

Any discussion of media regulation must begin with the Telecommunications Act of 1996, which marked the first overhaul of media policy since the early 1930s. The act, which covers everything from cable service to social issues such as obscenity and violence, made a significant distinction between information services, such as the Internet, and promoters of telecommunications service—that is, traditional telephone and wireless phone companies, as well as cable companies that offer phone service. Nevertheless, rapid technological development has rendered the act obsolete in many people's minds. With the convergence of telephone service, videocasting, and the Internet, not to mention the delivery of motion pictures online, such distinctions have become archaic only a decade after the act was passed.

Significantly, the act eliminated most restrictions on media ownership; those that remain appear to be on their way out, as well. In 2003 the Federal Communications Commission began considering the consolidation of newspaper and television ownership in cities with only one local newspaper and one local television station. Critics worry that once the transition to digital television is complete (perhaps by 2009), a single local media outlet could transmit a dozen signals *and* deliver the daily newspaper (Lear and McChesney 2006).

For generations, media conglomerates have battled efforts to regulate their industry, but in 2007 they began to pull back from their lobbying efforts. More and more, they are looking to new media like the Internet as their future source of profits. By 2010, if not sooner, Internet advertising revenue is projected to surpass total television ad revenues. People are now more likely to discuss the videos available on YouTube than the new season's lineup on prime-time television (Lieberman 2007).

Let's Discuss

1. Are you aware of who owns or manages the media you watch or listen to?

2. Do concerns about media concentration differ from concerns over the monopoly of certain products or services?

3. Are traditional media outlets (print, radio, and broadcast television) affected differently than the Internet by the trend toward media concentration?

GettingINVOLVED

To get involved in the debate over media concentration, visit this text's Online Learning Center, which offers links to relevant Web sites. Check out the Social Policy section in the Online Learning Center as well; it provides survey data on U.S. public opinion regarding this issue.

{ MASTERING THIS CHAPTER }

Summary

The **mass media** are print and electronic instruments of communication that carry messages to often widespread audiences. They pervade all social institutions, from entertainment to education to politics. This chapter examines how the mass media affect those institutions and influence our social behavior.

1. From the functionalist perspective, the media entertain, socialize, enforce social norms, confer status, and promote consumption. They can be dysfunctional to the extent that they desensitize us to serious events and issues (the **narcotizing dysfunction**).

2. Conflict theorists think the media reflect and even deepen the divisions in society through **gatekeeping,** or control over which material reaches the public; *media monitoring,* the covert observation of people's media usage and choices; and support of the **dominant ideology,** which defines reality, overwhelming local cultures.

3. Feminist theorists point out that media images of the sexes communicate unrealistic, stereotypical, limiting, and sometimes violent perceptions of women.

4. Interactionists examine the media on the micro level to see how they shape day-to-day social behavior. Interactionists have studied shared TV viewing and staged public appearances intended to convey self-serving definitions of reality.

5. The mass media require the presence of an audience—whether it is small and well defined or large and amorphous. With increasing numbers of media outlets has come more and more targeting of segmented (or specialized) audiences.

6. Social researchers have studied the role of **opinion leaders** in influencing audiences.

7. The media have a global reach thanks to new communications technologies, especially the Internet. Some people are concerned that the media's global reach will spread unhealthy influences to other cultures.

8. The media industry is becoming more and more concentrated, creating media conglomerates. This concentration raises concerns about how innovative and independent the media can be. In some countries, governments own and control the media.

9. The Internet is the one significant exception to the trend toward centralization, allowing millions of people to produce their own media content.

Critical Thinking Questions

1. What kind of audience is targeted by the producers of televised professional wrestling? By the creators of an animated film? By a rap group? What factors determine who makes up a particular audience?

2. Trace the production process for a new televised situation comedy (sitcom). Who do you imagine are the gatekeepers in the process?

3. Use the functionalist, conflict, and interactionist perspectives to assess the effects of global TV programming on developing countries.

Key Terms

Dominant ideology A set of cultural beliefs and practices that helps to maintain powerful social, economic, and political interests. (page 166)

Gatekeeping The process by which a relatively small number of people in the media industry control what material eventually reaches the audience. (165)

Mass media Print and electronic means of communication that carry messages to widespread audiences. (158)

Narcotizing dysfunction The phenomenon in which the media provide such massive amounts of coverage that the audience becomes numb and fails to act on the information, regardless of how compelling the issue. (164)

Opinion leader Someone who influences the opinions and decisions of others through day-to-day personal contact and communication. (173)

Stereotype An unreliable generalization about all members of a group that does not recognize individual differences within the group. (167)

Read each question carefully and then select the best answer.

1. From the functionalist perspective, the media can be dysfunctional in what way?

    a. They enforce social norms.
    b. They confer status.
    c. They desensitize us to events.
    d. They are agents of socialization.

2. Sociologist Robert Park studied how newspapers helped immigrants to the United States adjust to their environment by changing their customary habits and by teaching them the opinions held by people in their new home country. His study was conducted from which sociological perspective?

    a. the functionalist perspective
    b. the conflict perspective
    c. the interactionist perspective
    d. the dramaturgical perspective

3. There are problems inherent in the socialization function of the mass media. For example, many people worry about

    a. the effect of using the television as a babysitter.
    b. the impact of violent programming on viewer behavior.
    c. the unequal ability of all individuals to purchase televisions.
    d. both a and b

4. Media advertising has several clear functions, but it also has dysfunctions. Sociologists are concerned that

    a. it creates unrealistic expectations of what is required to be happy.
    b. it creates new consumer needs.
    c. advertisers are able to influence media content.
    d. all of the above

5. Gatekeeping, the process by which a relatively small number of people control what material reaches an audience, is largely dominant in all but which of the following media?

    a. television
    b. the Internet
    c. publishing
    d. music

6. Which sociological perspective is especially concerned with the media's ability to decide what gets transmitted through gatekeeping?

    a. the functionalist perspective
    b. the conflict perspective
    c. the interactionist perspective
    d. the dramaturgical perspective

7. Which of the following is *not* a problem feminist theorists see with media coverage?

    a. Women are underrepresented, suggesting that men are the cultural standard and that women are insignificant.
    b. Men and women are portrayed in ways that reflect and perpetuate stereotypical views of gender.
    c. Depictions of male–female relationships emphasize traditional sex roles and normalize violence against women.
    d. The increasing frequency of single moms in the media is providing a negative role model for women.

8. Which of the following is *not* true concerning how men and women use the Internet?

    a. Men are more likely to use the Internet daily.
    b. Women are more likely to use email to maintain friendships.
    c. Men account for 100 percent of players in online sports fantasy leagues.
    d. Men are slightly more likely to have ever used the Internet than women.

9. Sociologist Paul Lazarsfeld and his colleagues pioneered the study of

    a. the audience.
    b. opinion leaders.
    c. the media's global reach.
    d. media violence.

10. In his study of how the social composition of audience members affected how they interpreted the news coverage of riots in Los Angeles in 1992, sociologist Darnell Hunt found what kind of differences in perception?

    a. racial
    b. gender
    c. class
    d. religious

11. The mass media increase social cohesion by presenting a more or less standardized, common view of culture through mass communication. This statement reflects the _____ perspective.

12. Paul Lazarsfeld and Robert Merton created the term _____ _____ to refer to the phenomenon whereby the media provide such massive amounts of information that the audience becomes numb and generally fails to act on the information, regardless of how compelling the issue.

13. _____ _____ is the term used to describe the set of cultural beliefs and practices that helps to maintain powerful social, economic, and political interests.

14. Sociologists blame the mass media for the creation and perpetuation of _____, or generalizations about all members of a group that do not recognize individual differences within the group.

15. The _____ perspective contends that television distorts the political process.

16. We risk being _____ if we overstress U.S. dominance and assume other nations do not play a role in media cultural exports.

17. Both _____ and _____ theorists are troubled that the victims depicted in violent imagery are often those who are given less respect in real life: women, children, the poor, racial minorities, citizens of foreign countries, and even the physically disabled.

18. The _____ perspective examines the media on the micro level to see how they shape day-to-day social behavior.

19. We can point to a handful of _____ _____ that now dominate the publishing, broadcasting, and film industries, although they may be hard to identify, since global conglomerates manage many different product names.

20. Some 40 years ago, Canadian linguist _____ _____ predicted that the rise of the electronic media would create a "global village."

{ TECHNOLOGY RESOURCES }

Online Learning Center

1. Visit the student center in the Online Learning Center at **www.mhhe.com/schaefer11** and link to Use Your Sociological Imagination. You will be asked to become a news junkie, and to think about where you will gather your "facts" or information. Next, you will be asked to imagine yourself as part of an audience, and to think about the similarities you might share with other audience members. Use your sociological imagination to answer the questions.

2. Numerous organizations have been formed for the purpose of providing alternatives to mainstream mass media. One of them is Paper

Tiger Television (**www.papertiger.org**). Explore this site and become more aware of ways in which media gatekeeping may be challenged.

3. In China, the mass media are largely government-controlled. Browse through the English version of China's leading national newspaper, the *People's Daily* (**english.people.com.cn/**), to see how government control affects the paper's news coverage.

Note: Although all the URLs listed were current as of the printing of this book, these sites often change. Please check our Web site (**www.mhhe.com/schaefer11**) for updates, hyperlinks, and exercises related to these sites.

Reel Society Video Clips

Reel Society video clips, which appear on this book's Web site, can be used to spark discussion about the following topic from this chapter:

- Sociological Perspectives on the Media

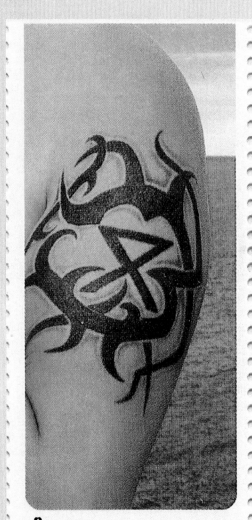

Åland 0,65 €
LASSE KÄRKKÄINEN / C.M.   2006

Åland 0,65 €
LASSE KÄRKKÄINEN / C.M.   2006

Åland 0,65 €
LASSE KÄRKKÄINEN / C.M.   2006

These three postage stamps, issued by the Åland, a small nation associated with Finland, show
the gradual evolution of tattoos from deviant to mainstream insignia. The stamp on the left
shows a hostile-looking tribal tattoo dating back to Viking times. The one in the middle features
some of the tattoos seamen favored in the 1800s. The more feminine tattoos on the right belong
to an Åland woman who survived the 2004 tsunami catastrophe in Thailand. Written in Thai,
the inscription translates "Forever in my memory."

8

Deviance and Social Control

Social Control

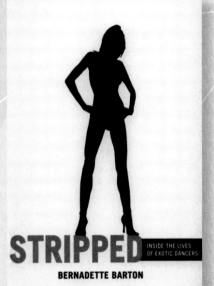

66 Brandy is considering becoming a dancer. Before she musters the courage to audition, she wants to see what the dancers actually do. Bringing a male friend to an upscale club near her home, Brandy enters the lobby of the Velvet Lounge. Mötley Crüe's classic rock song "Girls, Girls, Girls!" is playing while an attractive, elaborately made-up woman flanked by a burly bouncer takes their money at the door. Brandy gets in free because she's a woman. The lobby has a comfortable couch, some tasteful, artistic photographs of nude women, and an ever-present pot of coffee.

Brandy walks down a hallway to a hazy room lit by black lights. There is a huge-screen TV playing the sport of the season. The club is two-tiered. The first floor includes a main stage and side stages for the dancers on which at least two women perform, one clothed in an evening gown, the other topless or nude. Dancers, waitresses, bouncers, and customers maneuver through a maze of tables and comfortable, padded chairs. While Brandy is grateful that they obtained seats in a relatively inconspicuous area of the club, she is, nonetheless, acutely conscious of being a clothed woman among so many near-naked ones.

She listens to the DJ's banter encouraging the men to applaud and tip the dancers, "Hey guys, give it up for Selena!" and "Who's drunk enough out there to give me a 'Hell, yeah!'" This DJ commentary is also spiced with raunchy remarks about the performers, "Shit fellas, somebody take over the booth, I got to get me some of that," and homophobic quips like "Clap if you're not a fag!" . . .

When she glances up, Brandy spots couches ringing the entire space on the second floor; on each couch is a patron with a dancer undulating over him. From the customer's vantage point, it is a voyeur's dream. People downstairs can see the backs of the dancers performing while the clients purchasing the dances are shadowed and anonymous. Brandy buys an overpriced beer and watches the dancers circling the room soliciting table dances as well as the women performing onstage. One dancer walks to the center of the stage, removes her evening gown, displays her breasts, pivots slowly, and thrusts out her buttocks. Brandy has the opportunity to peruse the dancer's body from every angle while the performer struts and sways, eyes glassy or shut. There is a pole in the center of the stage running from the base of the floor to the ceiling. After a period of languorous posing, the dancer twirls on the pole, twisting into a back flip and hanging upside down by her ankles. Brandy is intimidated and impressed by the acrobatics. Later, she learns that most dancers balance themselves with the pole. As the dancer is virtually naked on a raised stage in front of any number of fully clothed men, the pole provides both a psychological and physical balance. When she feels vulnerable, when the stage is wet, when she's dizzy or intoxicated, the pole is something the dancer can literally hang onto. 99

From the customer's vantage point, it is a voyeur's dream. People downstairs can see the backs of the dancers performing while the clients purchasing the dances are shadowed and anonymous.

(Barton 2006:1, 2) Additional information about this excerpt can be found on the Online Learning Center at www.mhhe.com/schaefer11.

Stripped: Inside the Lives of Exotic Dancers describes sociologist Bernadette Barton's five-year ethnographic study of the women who work at strip clubs in California, Hawaii, and Kentucky. The book offers insight into how dancers like Brandy get into the business and eventually choose to become strippers. Barton reports that often, the initial excitement and financial rewards of the occupation give way to the dangers, such as drug use and prostitution.

Most people would consider dancing naked for money to be deviant. Though Barton strove to keep an open mind in conducting her fieldwork, she found herself reacting on the basis of conventional expectations. Having been a student of ballet and modern dance most of her life, she found she was distracted by the strippers' lack of rhythm and grace. But of course, it wasn't bad dancing that made the women deviant, but their lack of clothing and their overtly sexual behavior toward the club's patrons.

Is stripping truly a deviant activity, though? In today's society, women are constantly receiving the message that they are supposed to be sexy—but not too sexy. Movies, magazines, and YouTube are filled with images of naked or near-naked women, many of them in sexually provocative poses. And what about the men who patronize the clubs? They too are subject to the media's unrealistic stereotypes, but their sexual harassment of the dancers—which the clubs condone and even encourage—is behavior that most people would disapprove. Are the men who visit strip clubs deviant?

Another example of the difficulty of determining what is and is not deviant is binge drinking on campus. On the one hand, we can view binge drinking as *deviant,* as violating a school's standards of conduct and endangering one's health. On the other hand, we can see it as *conforming,* or complying with peer culture. In the United States, people are socialized to have mixed feelings about both conforming and nonconform-

ing behavior. The term *conformity* can conjure up images of mindless imitation of one's peer group—whether a circle of teenagers wearing "phat pants" or a group of business executives all dressed in gray suits. Yet the same term can also suggest that an individual is cooperative, or a "team player." What about those who do not conform? They may be respected as individualists, leaders, or creative thinkers who break new ground. Or they may be labeled as "troublemakers" and "weirdos."

This chapter examines the relationship between conformity, deviance, and social control. When does conformity verge on deviance? How does a society manage to control its members and convince them to conform to its rules and laws? What are the consequences of deviance? We will begin by distinguishing between conformity and obedience and then look at an experiment on obedience to authority. Next, we will analyze the informal and formal mechanisms societies use to encourage conformity and discourage deviance. We will pay particular attention to the legal order and how it reflects underlying social values.

The second part of the chapter focuses on theoretical explanations for deviance, including the functionalist approach employed by Émile Durkheim and Robert Merton; interactionist-based theories; labeling theory, which draws on both the interactionist and the conflict perspectives; and conflict theory.

The third part of the chapter focuses on crime, a specific type of deviant behavior. As a form of deviance that is subject to official, written norms, crime has been a special concern of policymakers and the public in general. We will look at various types of crime found in the United States, the ways crime is measured, and international crime rates. Finally, the Social Policy section considers the controversial topic of the death penalty.

Social Control

As we saw in Chapter 3, each culture, subculture, and group has distinctive norms governing appropriate behavior. Laws, dress codes, organizational bylaws, course requirements, and the rules of sports and games all express social norms.

How does a society bring about acceptance of basic norms? The term **social control** refers to the techniques and strategies for preventing deviant human behavior in any society. Social control occurs on all levels of society. In the family, we are socialized to obey our parents simply because they are our parents. Peer groups introduce us to informal norms, such as

dress codes, that govern the behavior of their members. Colleges establish standards they expect of students. In bureaucratic organizations, workers encounter a formal system of rules and regulations. Finally, the government of every society legislates and enforces social norms.

Most of us respect and accept basic social norms and assume that others will do the same. Even without thinking, we obey the instructions of police officers, follow the day-to-day rules at our jobs, and move to the rear of elevators when people enter. Such behavior reflects an effective process of socialization to the dominant standards of a culture. At the same time, we are well aware that individuals, groups, and institutions *expect* us to act "prop-

{ p.69–70 } erly." This expectation carries with it *sanctions,* penalties and rewards for conduct concerning a social norm. If we fail to live up to the norm, we may face punishment through informal sanctions such as fear and ridicule, or formal sanctions such as jail sentences or fines.

The challenge to effective social control is that people often receive competing messages about how to behave. While the state or government may clearly define acceptable behavior, friends or fellow employees may encourage quite different behavior patterns. Historically, legal measures aimed at blocking discrimination based on race, religion, gender, age, and sexual orientation have been difficult to implement, because many people tacitly encourage the violation of such measures.

Functionalists maintain that people must respect social norms if any group or society is to survive. In their view, societies literally could not function if massive numbers of people defied standards of appropriate conduct. In contrast, conflict theorists contend that the "successful functioning" of a society will consistently benefit the powerful and work to the disadvantage of other groups. They point out that in the United States, widespread resistance to social norms was necessary to win our independence from England, to overturn the institution of slavery, to allow women to vote, to secure civil rights, and to force an end to the war in Vietnam.

Conformity and Obedience

Techniques for social control operate on both the group level and the societal level. People we think of as peers or equals influence us to act in particular ways; the same is true of people who hold authority over us or occupy awe-inspiring positions. Social psychologist Stanley Milgram (1975) made a useful distinction between these two levels of social control.

Milgram used the term *conformity* to mean going along with peers—individuals of our own status who have no special right to direct our behavior. In contrast, *obedience* is compliance with higher authorities in a hierarchical structure. Thus, a recruit entering military service will typically *conform* to the habits and language of other recruits and *obey* the orders of superior officers. Students will *conform* to the drinking behavior of their peers and *obey* the requests of campus security officers.

We often think of conformity and obedience as rather harmless behaviors. When members of an expensive health club all don the same costly sportswear, we may see their conformity as unimaginative, but we do not think of it as harmful. Nevertheless, reseachers have found that under certain circumstances, both conformity and obedience can have negative consequences. Obedience, in particular, can cause immense damage—a potential that Milgram demonstrated in the laboratory.

If ordered to do so, would you comply with an experimenter's instruction to administer increasingly painful electric shocks to a subject? Most people would say no; yet Milgram's research (1963, 1975) suggests that most of us *would* obey such orders. In his words (1975:xi), "Behavior that is unthinkable in an individual . . . acting on his own may be executed without hesitation when carried out under orders."

Milgram placed advertisements in New Haven, Connecticut, newspapers to recruit subjects for a learning experiment at Yale University. Participants included postal clerks, engineers, high school teachers, and laborers. They were told that the purpose of the research was to investigate the effects of punishment on learning. The experimenter, dressed in a gray technician's coat, explained that in each test, one subject would be randomly selected as the "learner," while another would function as the "teacher." However, the experiment was rigged so that the "real" subject would always be the teacher, while an associate of Milgram's served as the learner.

At this point, the learner's hand was strapped to an electric apparatus. The teacher was taken to an electronic "shock generator" with 30 levered switches labeled from 15 to 450 volts. Before beginning the experiment, all subjects received sample shocks of 45 volts, to convince them of the authenticity of the experiment. The experimenter then instructed the teacher to apply shocks of increasing voltage each time the learner gave an incorrect answer on a memory test. Teachers were told that "although the shocks can be extremely painful, they cause no permanent tissue damage." In reality, the learner did not receive any shocks.

Social control, Finnish style. This young man is relaxing in his prison cell, not in his college dorm room. Thirty years ago Finland rejected the rigid Soviet model of imprisonment and adopted a gentler correctional system meant to shape prisoners' values and encourage moral behavior. Today, Finland's rate of imprisonment is less than half that of England and one-fourth that of the United States.

In a prearranged script, the learner deliberately gave incorrect answers and expressed pain when "shocked." For example, at 150 volts, the learner would cry out, "Get me out of here!" At 270 volts, the learner would scream in agony. When the shock reached 350 volts, the learner would fall silent. If the teacher wanted to stop the experiment, the experimenter would insist that the teacher continue, using such statements as "The experiment requires that you continue" and "You have no other choice; you *must* go on" (Milgram 1975:19–23).

The results of this unusual experiment stunned and dismayed Milgram and other social scientists. A sample of psychiatrists had predicted that virtually all subjects would refuse to shock innocent victims. In their view, only a "pathological fringe" of less than 2 percent would continue administering shocks up to the maximum level. Yet almost *two-thirds* of participants fell into the category of "obedient subjects."

Why did these subjects obey? Why were they willing to inflict seemingly painful shocks on innocent victims who had never done them any harm? There is no evidence that these subjects were unusually sadistic; few seemed to enjoy administering the shocks. Instead, in Milgram's view, the key to obedience was the experimenter's social role as a "scientist" and "seeker of knowledge."

Milgram pointed out that in the modern industrial world, we are accustomed to submitting to impersonal authority figures whose status is indicated by a title (professor, lieutenant, doctor) or by a uniform (the technician's coat). Because we view the authority as larger and more important than the individual, we shift responsibility for our behavior to the authority figure. Milgram's subjects frequently stated, "If it were up to me, I would not have administered shocks." They saw themselves as merely doing their duty (Milgram 1975).

From a conflict perspective, our obedience may be affected by the value we place on those whom our behavior affects. While Milgram's experiment shows that in general, people are willing to obey authority figures, other studies show that they are even more willing to obey if they feel the "victim" is deserving of punishment. Sociologist Gary Schulman (1974) recreated Milgram's experiment and found that White students were significantly more likely to shock Black "learners" than White "learners." By a margin of 70 percent to 48 percent, they imposed more shocks on the Black learners than on the White learners.

From an interactionist perspective, one important aspect of Milgram's findings is the fact that subjects in follow-up studies were less likely to inflict the supposed shocks as they were moved physically closer to their victims. Moreover, interactionists emphasize the effect of *incrementally* administering additional dosages of 15 volts. In effect, the experimenter negotiated with the teacher and convinced the teacher to continue inflicting higher levels of punishment. It is doubtful that anywhere near the two-thirds rate of obedience would have been reached had the experimenter told the teachers to administer 450 volts immediately (B. Allen 1978; Katovich 1987).

Milgram launched his experimental study of obedience to better understand the involvement of Germans in the annihila-

In one of Stanley Milgram's experiments, the "learner" supposedly received an electric shock from a shock plate when he answered a question incorrectly. At the 150-volt level, the "learner" would demand to be released and would refuse to place his hand on the shock plate. The experimenter would then order the actual subject (the "teacher") to force the hand onto the plate, as shown in the photo. Though 40 percent of the true subjects stopped complying with Milgram at this point, 30 percent did force the "learner's" hand onto the shock plate, despite his pretended agony.

tion of 6 million Jews and millions of other people during World War II. In an interview conducted long after the publication of his study, he suggested that "if a system of death camps were set up in the United States of the sort we had seen in Nazi Germany, one would be able to find sufficient personnel for those camps in any medium-sized American town." Though many people questioned his remark, the revealing photos taken at Iraq's Abu Ghraib prison in 2004, showing U.S. military guards humiliating if not torturing Iraqi prisoners, recalled the experiment Milgram had done two generations earlier. Under conducive circumstances, otherwise normal people can and often do treat one another inhumanely (CBS News 1979:7–8; Hayden 2004).

Use Your Sociological Imagination

If you were a participant in Milgram's research on conformity, how far do you think you would go in carrying out orders? Do you see any ethical problem with the experimenter's manipulation of the control subjects?

Informal and Formal Social Control

The sanctions that are used to encourage conformity and obedience—and to discourage violation of social norms—are carried out through both informal and formal social control. As the term implies, people use *informal social control* casually to enforce norms. Examples include smiles, laughter, a raised eyebrow, and ridicule.

In the United States and many other cultures, adults often view spanking, slapping, or kicking children as a proper and necessary means of informal social control. Child development specialists counter that such corporal punishment is inappropriate because it teaches children to solve problems through violence. They warn that slapping and spanking can escalate into more serious forms of abuse. Yet, despite a 1998 policy statement by the American Academy of Pediatrics that corporal punishment is not effective and can indeed be harmful, 59 percent of pediatricians support the use of corporal punishment, at least in certain situations. Our culture widely accepts this form of informal social control (Wolraich et al. 1998).

Formal social control is carried out by authorized agents, such as police officers, judges, school administrators, employers, military officers, and managers of movie theaters. It can serve as a last resort when socialization and informal sanctions do not bring about desired behavior. An increasingly significant means of formal social control in the United States is to imprison people. During the course of a year, 7 million adults undergo some form of correctional supervision—jail, prison, probation, or parole. Put another way, almost 1 out of every 30 adult Americans is subject to this very formal type of social control every year (Glaze and Palla 2005).

In 2007, in the wake of the mass shootings at Virginia Tech, many college officials reviewed security measures on their campuses. Administrators were reluctant to end or even limit the relative freedom of movement students on their campuses enjoyed. Instead, they concentrated on improving emergency communications between campus police and students, faculty, and staff. Reflecting a reliance on technology to maintain social control, college leaders called for replacement of the "old" technology of e-mail with instant alerts that could be sent to people's cell phones via instant messaging.

Six years earlier, in the aftermath of September 11, 2001, new measures of social control became the norm in the United States. Some of them, such as stepped-up security at airports and high-rise buildings, were highly visible to the public. The federal government has also publicly urged citizens to engage in informal social control by watching for and reporting people whose actions seem suspicious. But many other measures taken by the government have increased the covert surveillance of private records and communications.

Just 45 days after September 11, with virtually no debate, Congress passed the Patriot Act of 2001. Sections of this sweeping legislation revoked legal checks on the power of law enforcement agencies. Without a warrant or probable cause, the Federal Bureau of Investigation (FBI) can now secretly access most private records, including medical histories, library accounts, and student registrations. In 2002, for example, the FBI searched the records of hundreds of dive shops and scuba organizations. Agents had been directed to identify every person who had taken diving lessons in the past three years because of speculation that terrorists might try to approach their targets underwater (Moss and Fessenden 2002).

Many people think this kind of social control goes too far. Civil rights advocates also worry that the government's request for information on suspicious activities may encourage negative stereotyping of Muslims and Arab Americans. Clearly, there is a trade-off between the benefits of surveillance and the right to privacy.

The interplay between formal and informal social control can be complicated, especially if people are encouraged to violate social norms. Box 8-1 (page 188) considers binge drinking among

What's next in formal social control—iris checks? At Amsterdam's Schiphol airport, a security official scans a passenger's irises. Like fingerprints, iris patterns are unique, but their greater complexity makes them a more accurate form of identification. This passenger may choose to store her iris patterns on an identification card to expedite her boarding process.

sociologyONcampus

8-1 Binge Drinking

Wesley Allan Croley, a 20-year-old community college student, was standing around a bonfire with some friends the night of December 9, 2006. Most of the young people gathered in the field in Monroe County, Alabama, that night were drinking beer. But witnesses told investigators that Croley took a bottle of vodka from his truck, passed it around, and then finished it himself.

About 11 p.m. police responded to a 911 call from the field. Shortly after, Croley was pronounced dead at a local hospital. Forensic tests showed his blood-alcohol content was .414—more than five times the legal level for motorists in Alabama. The cause of death: acute alcohol intoxication.

Croley was not unusual in his behavior. According to a study published by the Harvard School of Public Health in 2002, 44 percent of college students indulge in binge drinking (defined as at least five drinks in a row for men and four in a row for women). For those who live in a Greek fraternity or sorority, the rates are even higher—four out of five are binge drinkers (see the figure). These numbers represent an increase from 1990s data, despite efforts on many campuses across the nation to educate students about the risks of binge drinking. The problem is not confined to the United States—Britain, Russia, and South Africa all report regular "drink till you drop" alcoholic consumption among young people. Nor does binge drinking begin in college. A national study published in 2007 by the American Academy of Pediatrics found that over a 30-day period, 29 percent of high school students engaged in binge drinking.

Binge drinking on campus presents a difficult social problem. On the one hand, it can be regarded as *deviant,* violating the standards of conduct expected of those in an academic setting. In fact, Harvard researchers consider binge drinking the most serious public health hazard facing colleges. Not only does it cause about 50 fatalities a year and hundreds of cases of alcohol poisoning; it increases the likelihood of falling behind in schoolwork, getting injured, and damaging property.

The other side of this potentially self-destructive behavior is that binge drinking represents *conformity* to the peer culture, especially in fraternities and sororities, which serve as social centers on many campuses. Most students seem to take an "everybody does it—no big deal" attitude toward the

> *44 percent of college students indulge in binge drinking.*

behavior. Many find that taking five drinks in a row is fairly typical. As one student at Boston University noted, "Anyone that goes to a party does that or worse. If you talk to anyone college age, it's normal."

Some colleges and universities are taking steps to make binge drinking a bit less "nor-mal" by means of *social control*—banning kegs, closing fraternities and sororities, encouraging liquor retailers not to sell in high volume to students, and expelling students after three alcohol-related infractions. Yet many colleges still tolerate spring break organizers who promote "All you can drink" parties as part of a tour package.

Let's Discuss

1. Why do you think most college students regard binge drinking as a normal rather than a deviant behavior?
2. Which do you think would be more effective in stopping binge drinking on your campus, informal or formal social control?

Sources: Baggett 2007; J. Miller et al. 2007; Wechsler et al. 2002, 2004.

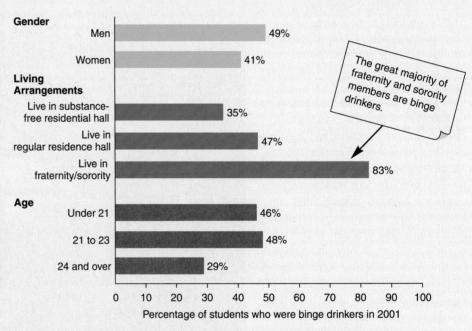

The great majority of fraternity and sorority members are binge drinkers.

Note: Based on a 2001 national survey of more than 10,000 college students. Binge drinking was defined as one drinking session of at least five drinks for men or four drinks for women during the two weeks prior to the self-administered questionnaire.
Source: Wechsler et al. 2002:208.

college students, who receive conflicting messages about the acceptability of the behavior from sources of social control.

Law and Society

Some norms are so important to a society that they are formalized into laws regarding people's behavior. *Law* may be defined as governmental social control (Black 1995). Some laws, such as the prohibition against murder, are directed at all members of society. Others, such as fishing and hunting regulations, primarily affect particular categories of people. Still others govern the behavior of social institutions (for instance, corporate law and laws regarding the taxing of nonprofit enterprises).

Sociologists see the creation of laws as a social process. Because laws are passed in response to a perceived need for formal social control, sociologists have sought to explain how and why such a perception arises. In their view, law is not merely a static body of rules handed down from generation to generation. Rather, it reflects continually changing standards of what is right and wrong, of how violations are to be determined, and of what sanctions are to be applied (Schur 1968).

Sociologists representing varying theoretical perspectives agree that the legal order reflects the values of those in a position to exercise authority. Therefore, the creation of civil and criminal law can be a most controversial matter. Should it be against the law to employ illegal immigrants, to have an abortion (see Chapter 12), to allow prayer in public schools (see Chapter 15), or to smoke on an airplane? Such issues have been bitterly debated, because they require a choice among competing values. Not surprisingly, laws that are unpopular—such as the onetime prohibition of alcohol under the Eighteenth Amendment and the widespread establishment of a 55-mile-per-hour speed limit on highways—become difficult to enforce when there is no consensus supporting the norms.

One current and controversial debate over laws governing behavior is whether people should be allowed to use marijuana legally, for medical purposes. Although the majority of adults polled in national surveys support such a use, the federal government continues to regard all uses of marijuana as illegal. In 2005 the Supreme Court upheld the federal government's position. Nevertheless, 11 states have granted citizens the right to use marijuana for medical purposes—even if that privilege rests on dubious legal grounds (see Figure 8-1).

Socialization is the primary source of conforming and obedient behavior, including obedience to law. Generally, it is { p.86 } not external pressure from a peer group or authority figure that makes us go along with social norms. Rather, we have internalized such norms as valid and desirable and are committed to observing them. In a profound sense, we want to see ourselves (and to be seen) as loyal, cooperative, responsible, and respectful of others. In the United States and other societies around the world, people are socialized both to want to belong and to fear being viewed as different or deviant.

Control theory suggests that our connection to members of society leads us to systematically conform to society's norms. According to sociologist Travis Hirschi and other control theorists, our bonds to family members, friends, and peers induce us to follow the mores and folkways of our society. We give little conscious thought to whether we will be sanctioned if we fail to conform. Socialization develops our self-control so well that we don't need further pressure to obey social norms. While control theory does not effectively explain the rationale for every conforming act, it nevertheless reminds us that while the media may focus on crime and disorder, most members of most societies conform to and obey basic norms (Gottfredson and Hirschi 1990; Hirschi 1969).

FIGURE 8–1
The Status of Medical Marijuana

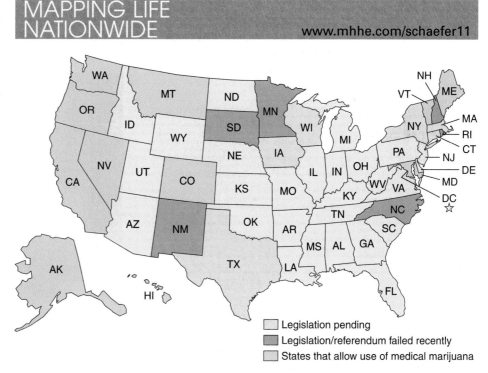

Note: Federal law confers a one-year prison sentence on those convicted of possessing a small amount of marijuana. No exception is made for medical use, even if state law allows it, as it does in California. Maryland has not legalized medical use, but has greatly reduced the penalties.

Source: Developed by author based on data from L. Greenhouse 2005 and Marijuana Policy Project 2004, 2007.

Enraged Indiana Pacers basketball player Ron Artest lunges into the stands during the final minute of a 2004 game against the Detroit Pistons. The brawl, which began after a fan hurled a full beverage cup at Artest, raised the questions of how to define improper conduct by fans and what right professional athletes have to defend themselves. Even in highly competitive sports, the amount of violence society will tolerate has limits; social control must be maintained.

What Is Deviance?

For sociologists, the term *deviance* does not mean perversion or depravity. **Deviance** is behavior that violates the standards of conduct or expectations of a group or society (Wickman 1991:85). In the United States, alcoholics, compulsive gamblers, and the mentally ill would all be classified as deviants. Being late for class is categorized as a deviant act; the same is true of wearing jeans to a formal wedding. On the basis of the sociological definition, we are all deviant from time to time. Each of us violates common social norms in certain situations.

Is being overweight an example of deviance? In the United States and many other cultures, unrealistic standards of appearance and body image place a huge strain on people—especially adult women and girls—based on how they look. Journalist Naomi Wolf (1992) has used the term *beauty myth* to refer to an exaggerated ideal of beauty, beyond the reach of all but a few females, which has unfortunate consequences. In order to shed their "deviant" image and conform to unrealistic societal norms, many women and girls become consumed with adjusting their appearances. Yet what is deviant in one culture may be celebrated in another. In Nigeria, for example, being fat is considered a mark of beauty. Part of the coming-of-age ritual calls for

young girls to spend a month in a "fattening room." Among Nigerians, being thin at this point in the life course is deviant (A. Simmons 1998).

Deviance involves the violation of group norms, which may or may not be formalized into law. It is a comprehensive concept that includes not only criminal behavior but also many actions that are not subject to prosecution. The public official who takes a bribe has defied social norms, but so has the high school student who refuses to sit in an assigned seat or cuts class. Of course, deviation from norms is not always negative, let alone criminal. A member of an exclusive social club who speaks out against a traditional policy of excluding women, Blacks, and Jews from admittance is deviating from the club's norms. So is a police officer who blows the whistle on corruption or brutality within the department.

From a sociological perspective, deviance is hardly objective or set in stone. Rather, it is subject to social definition within a particular society and at a particular time. For that reason, what is considered deviant can shift from one social era to another. In most instances, those individuals and groups with the greatest status and power define what is acceptable and what is deviant. For example, despite serious medical warnings against the dangers of tobacco, made since 1964, cigarette smoking continued to be accepted for decades—in good part because of the power of tobacco farmers and cigarette manufacturers. Only after a long campaign led by public health and anticancer activists did cigarette smoking become more of a deviant activity. Today, many state and local laws limit where people can smoke.

While deviance can include relatively minor day-to-day decisions about our personal behavior, in some cases it can become part of a person's identity. This process is called *stigmatization.*

Are tattoos a fashion statement, a personal statement, or a barrier to employment? While tattoos may not seem deviant or even unusual to many of us, in some circles they may create quite the opposite impression. Until recently, the U.S. military refused to accept applicants with tattoos, like this young man.

Deviance and Social Stigma

A person can acquire a deviant identity in many ways. Because of physical or behavioral characteristics, some people are unwillingly cast in negative social roles. Once they have been assigned a deviant role, they have trouble presenting a positive image to others and may even experience lowered self-esteem. {p.91} Whole groups of people—for instance, "short people" or "redheads"—may be labeled in this way. The interactionist Erving Goffman coined the term *stigma* to describe the labels society uses to devalue members of certain social groups (Goffman 1963; Heckert and Best 1997).

Prevailing expectations about beauty and body shape may prevent people who are regarded as ugly or obese from advancing as rapidly as their abilities permit. Both overweight and anorexic people are assumed to be weak in character, slaves to their appetites or to media images. Because they do not conform to the beauty myth, they may be viewed as "disfigured" or "strange" in appearance, bearers of what Goffman calls a "spoiled identity." However, what constitutes disfigurement is a matter of interpretation. Of the 1 million cosmetic procedures done every year in the United States alone, many are performed on women who would be defined objectively as having a normal appearance. And while feminist sociologists have accurately noted that the beauty myth makes many women feel uncomfortable with themselves, men too lack confidence in their appearance. The number of males who choose to undergo cosmetic procedures has risen sharply in recent years; men now account for 21 percent of such surgeries (American Academy of Cosmetic Surgery 2007).

Often people are stigmatized for deviant behaviors they may no longer engage in. The labels "compulsive gambler," "ex-convict," "recovering alcoholic," and "ex–mental patient" can stick to a person for life. Goffman draws a useful distinction between a prestige symbol that draws attention to a positive aspect of one's identity, such as a wedding band or a badge, and a stigma symbol that discredits or debases one's identity, such as a conviction for child molestation. While stigma symbols may not always be obvious, they can become a matter of public knowledge. Starting in 1994, many states required convicted sex offenders to register with local police departments. Some communities publish the names and addresses, and in some instances even the pictures, of convicted sex offenders on the Web.

A person need not be guilty of a crime to be stigmatized. Homeless people often have trouble getting a job, because employers are wary of applicants who cannot give a home address. Moreover, hiding one's homelessness is difficult, since agencies generally use the telephone to contact applicants about job openings. If a homeless person has access to a telephone at a shelter, the staff generally answers the phone by announcing the name of the institution—a sure way to discourage prospective employers. Even if a homeless person surmounts these obstacles and manages to get a job, she or he is often fired when the employer learns of the situation. Regardless of a person's positive attributes, employers regard the spoiled identity of homelessness as sufficient reason to dismiss an employee. (For more infor-

mation on homelessness, see the Social Policy section in Chapter 20.)

While some types of deviance will stigmatize a person, other types do not carry a significant penalty. Some good examples of socially tolerated forms of deviance can be found in the world of high technology.

Deviance and Technology

Technological innovations such as pagers and voice mail can redefine social interactions and the standards of behavior related to them. When the Internet was first made available to the general public, no norms or regulations governed its use. Because online communication offers a high degree of anonymity, uncivil behavior—speaking harshly of others or monopolizing chat room "space"—quickly became common. Online bulletin boards designed to carry items of community interest became littered with commercial advertisements. Such deviant acts are beginning to provoke calls for the establishment of formal rules for online behavior. For example, policymakers have debated whether to regulate the content of Web sites featuring hate speech and pornography.

Some deviant uses of technology are criminal, though not all participants see it that way. The pirating of software, motion pictures, and music has become a big business. At conventions and swap meets, pirated copies of movies, CDs, and DVDs are sold openly. Some of the products are obviously counterfeit, but many come in sophisticated packaging, complete with warranty cards. The vendors say they merely want to be compensated for their time and the cost of materials, or that the software they have copied is in the public domain.

Similarly, the downloading of music from the Internet, which is typically protected by copyright, is widely accepted. But file sharing, like the pirating of CDs and DVDs, has grown to the point that it is threatening the profits of copyright owners. Napster, the renegade Web site that allowed thousands of people to download from a wide selection of music files for free, has been shut down, the victim of a court challenge by the music industry. Nevertheless, its fleeting success has encouraged imitators, many of them college students who run file-sharing programs

"I swear I wasn't looking at smut—I was just stealing music."

Who Is Deviant?

What if your girlfriend started to elongate her neck by layering it with heavy brass coils? Wouldn't you think she was behaving in a bizarre way? Certainly by the standards of U.S. society, she would be. But not if you were living among the Kayan tribe in northern Thailand, where females traditionally wear up to 12 pounds of coils around the neck as a mark of beauty and tribal identity. Because deviance is socially constructed, it is subject to different social interpretations over time and across cultures.

Even within the same culture, not everyone may share the same idea of what constitutes proper or deviant behavior. For example, in the Middle East, some women feel they must cover themselves, even at the beach. And in the United States, cage fighting—a fight staged in a chain-link cage—is banned in some places but permitted in others. These highly popular events can be seen not only in person but on pay-per-view and commercially produced DVDs. Looking at ourselves and other peoples from their point of view as well as from our own helps us to understand deviance as a social construction.

{"Long-necked" girls of the Kayan tribe in Thailand}

{Muslim women at the beach, Middle East}

{Cage fight, Sioux Falls, South Dakota}

from their dorm rooms. The music industry is fighting back by urging law enforcement agents to track the pirates down and prosecute them.

Though most of these black market activities are clearly illegal, many consumers and small-time pirates are proud of their behavior. They may even think themselves smart for figuring out a way to avoid the "unfair" prices charged by "big corporations." Few people see the pirating of a new software program or a first-run movie as a threat to the public good, as they would embezzling from a bank. Similarly, most businesspeople who "borrow" software from another department, even though they lack a site license, do not think they are doing anything wrong. No social stigma attaches to their illegal behavior.

Deviance, then, is a complex concept. Sometimes it is trivial, sometimes profoundly harmful. Sometimes it is accepted by society and sometimes soundly rejected. What accounts for deviant behavior and people's reaction to it? In the next section we will examine five theoretical explanations for deviance.

Use Your Sociological Imagination

What kinds of file sharing do you and your friends regard as acceptable? What do you regard as illegal?

Sociological Perspectives on Deviance

Why do people violate social norms? We have seen that deviant acts are subject to both informal and formal social control. The nonconforming or disobedient person may face disapproval, loss of friends, fines, or even imprisonment. Why, then, does deviance occur?

Early explanations for behavior that deviated from societal expectations blamed supernatural causes or genetic factors (such as "bad blood" or evolutionary throwbacks to primitive ancestors). By the 1800s, substantial research efforts were being made to identify biological factors that lead to deviance, and especially to criminal activity. Though such research was discredited in the 20th century, contemporary studies, primarily by biochemists, have sought to isolate genetic factors that suggest a likelihood of certain personality traits. Although criminality (much less deviance) is hardly a personality characteristic, researchers have focused on traits that might lead to crime, such as aggression. Of course, aggression can also lead to success in the corporate world, in professional sports, or in other walks of life.

The contemporary study of the possible biological roots of {p.63 criminality is but one aspect of the larger debate over sociobiology. In general, sociologists reject any emphasis on the genetic roots of crime and deviance. The limitations of current knowledge, the possibility of reinforcing racist and sexist as-

sumptions, and the disturbing implications for the rehabilitation of criminals have led sociologists to draw largely on other approaches to explain deviance (Sagarin and Sanchez 1988).

Functionalist Perspective

According to functionalists, deviance is a common part of human existence, with positive as well as negative consequences for social stability. Deviance helps to define the limits of proper behavior. Children who see one parent scold the other for belching at the dinner table learn about approved conduct. The same is true of the driver who receives a speeding ticket, the department store cashier who is fired for yelling at a customer, and the college student who is penalized for handing in papers weeks overdue.

Durkheim's Legacy Émile Durkheim ([1895] 1964) focused his sociological investigations mainly on criminal acts, yet his conclusions have implications for all types of deviant behavior. In Durkheim's view, the punishments established within a culture (including both formal and informal mechanisms of social control) help to define acceptable behavior and thus contribute to stability. If improper acts were not sanctioned, people might stretch their standards of what constitutes appropriate conduct.

Kai Erikson (1966) illustrated the boundary-maintenance function of deviance in his study of the Puritans of 17th-century New England. By today's standards, the Puritans placed tremendous emphasis on conventional morals. Their persecution and execution of women as witches represented a continuing attempt to define and redefine the boundaries of their community. In effect, their changing social norms created "crime waves," as people whose behavior was previously acceptable suddenly faced punishment for being deviant (Abrahamson 1978; N. Davis 1975).

Durkheim ([1897] 1951) introduced the term ***anomie*** into sociological literature to describe the loss of direction felt in a society when social control of individual behavior has become ineffective. Anomie is a state of normlessness that typically occurs during a period of profound social change and disorder, such as a time of economic collapse. People become more aggressive or depressed, which results in higher rates of violent crime and suicide. Since there is much less agreement on what constitutes proper behavior during times of revolution, sudden prosperity, or economic depression, conformity and obedience become less significant as social forces. It also becomes much more difficult to state exactly what constitutes deviance.

Merton's Theory of Deviance What do a mugger and a teacher have in common? Each is "working" to obtain money that can then be exchanged for desired goods. As this example illustrates, behavior that violates accepted norms (such as mugging) may be performed with the same basic objectives in mind as those of people who pursue more conventional lifestyles.

On the basis of this kind of analysis, sociologist Robert Merton (1968) adapted Durkheim's notion of anomie to explain why people accept or reject the goals of a society, the socially approved means of fulfilling their aspirations, or both. Merton maintained that one important cultural goal in the United States is success, measured largely in terms of money. In addition to providing this goal for people, our society offers specific instructions on how to pursue success—go to school, work hard, do not quit, take advantage of opportunities, and so forth.

What happens to individuals in a society with a heavy emphasis on wealth as a basic symbol of success? Merton reasoned that people adapt in certain ways, either by conforming to or by deviating from such cultural expectations. His *anomie theory of deviance* posits five basic forms of adaptation (see Table 8-1).

Conformity to social norms, the most common adaptation in Merton's typology, is the opposite of deviance. It involves acceptance of both the overall societal goal ("become affluent") and the approved means ("work hard"). In Merton's view, there must be some consensus regarding accepted cultural goals and the legitimate means for attaining them. Without such a consensus, societies could exist only as collectives of people rather than as unified cultures, and might experience continual chaos.

The other four types of behavior represented in Table 8-1 all involve some departure from conformity. The "innovator" accepts the goals of society but pursues them with means that are regarded as improper. For instance, a safecracker may steal money to buy consumer goods and expensive vacations.

In Merton's typology, the "ritualist" has abandoned the goal of material success and become compulsively committed to the institutional means. Work becomes simply a way of life rather than a means to the goal of success. An example would be the bureaucratic official who blindly applies rules and regulations without remembering the larger goals of the organization. Certainly that would be true of a welfare caseworker who refuses to assist a homeless family because their last apartment was in another district.

The "retreatist," as described by Merton, has basically withdrawn (or retreated) from both the goals and the means of society. In the United States, drug addicts and vagrants are typically portrayed as retreatists. Concern has been growing that adolescents who are addicted to alcohol will become retreatists at an early age.

The final adaptation identified by Merton reflects people's attempts to create a *new* social structure. The "rebel" feels alienated from the dominant means and goals, and may seek a dramatically different social order. Members of a revolutionary political organization, such as a militia group, can be categorized as rebels according to Merton's model.

Merton's theory, though popular, has had relatively few applications. Little effort has been made to determine to what extent all acts of deviance can be accounted for by his five modes. Moreover, while Merton's theory is useful in examining certain types of behavior, such as illegal gambling by disadvantaged "innovators," his formulation fails to explain key differences in crime rates. Why, for example, do some disadvantaged groups have lower rates of reported crime than others? Why do many people in adverse circumstances reject criminal activity as a viable alternative? Merton's theory of deviance does not easily answer such questions (Clinard and Miller 1998).

Still, Merton has made a key contribution to the sociological understanding of deviance by pointing out that deviants such as innovators and ritualists share a great deal with conforming people. The convicted felon may hold many of the same aspirations as people with no criminal background. The theory helps us to understand deviance as a socially created behavior rather than as the result of momentary pathological impulses.

Interactionist Perspective

The functionalist approach to deviance explains why rule violations continue to happen despite pressure to conform and obey. However, functionalists do not indicate how a given person comes to commit a deviant act, or why on some occasions crimes do or do not occur. The emphasis on everyday behavior that is the focus of the interactionist perspective offers two explanations of crime—cultural transmission and routine activities theory.

Cultural Transmission In the course of studying graffiti writing by gangs in Los Angeles, sociologist Susan A. Phillips (1999) discovered that the writers learned from one another. In fact, Phillips was surprised by how stable their focus was over time. She also noted how other ethnic groups built on the models of the African American and Chicano gangs, superimposing Cambodian, Chinese, or Vietnamese symbols.

Humans *learn* how to behave in social situations, whether properly or improperly. There is no natural, innate manner in which people interact with one another. These simple ideas are not disputed today, but such was not the case when sociologist Edwin Sutherland (1883–1950) first advanced the idea that an individual undergoes

Table 8-1

Modes of Individual Adaptation

summingUP

Mode	Institutionalized Means (Hard Work)	Societal Goal (Acquisition of Wealth)
Nondeviant		
Conformity	Accept	Accept
Deviant		
Innovation	Reject	Accept
Ritualism	Accept	Reject
Retreatism	Reject	Reject
Rebellion	Replace with new means	Replace with new goals

Source: Adapted from Merton 1968:194.

Under cover of darkness, drag racers await the start signal on a deserted Los Angeles street. Sutherland's concepts of differential association and cultural transmission would both apply to the practice of drag racing on city streets.

the same basic socialization process in learning conforming and deviant acts.

Sutherland's ideas have been the dominating force in criminology. He drew on the **cultural transmission** school, which emphasizes that one learns criminal behavior by interacting with others. Such learning includes not only the techniques of lawbreaking (for example, how to break into a car quickly and quietly) but also the motives, drives, and rationalizations of the criminal. The cultural transmission approach can also be used to explain the behavior of those who habitually abuse alcohol or drugs.

Sutherland maintained that through interactions with a primary group and significant others, people acquire definitions of proper and improper behavior. He used the term **differential association** to describe the process through which exposure to attitudes *favorable* to criminal acts leads to the violation of rules. Research suggests that this view of differential association also applies to noncriminal deviant acts, such as smoking, truancy, and early sexual behavior (E. Jackson et al. 1986).

To what extent will a given person engage in activity that is regarded as proper or improper? For each individual, it will depend on the frequency, duration, and importance of two types of social interaction—those experiences that endorse deviant behavior and those that promote acceptance of social norms. People are more likely to engage in norm-defying behavior if they are part of a group or subculture that stresses deviant values, such as a street gang.

Sutherland offers the example of a boy who is sociable, outgoing, and athletic and who lives in an area with a high rate of delinquency. The youth is very likely to come into contact with peers who commit acts of vandalism, fail to attend school, and so forth, and may come to adopt such behavior. However, an introverted boy who lives in the same neighborhood may stay away from his peers and avoid delinquency. In another community, an outgoing and athletic boy may join a Little League baseball team or a scout troop because of his interactions with peers. Thus, Sutherland views improper behavior as the result of the types of groups to which one belongs and the kinds of friendships one has (Sutherland et al. 1992).

According to critics, however, the cultural transmission approach may explain the deviant behavior of juvenile delinquents or graffiti artists, but it fails to explain the conduct of the first-time impulsive shoplifter or the impoverished person who steals out of necessity. While it is not a precise statement of the process through which one becomes a criminal, differential association theory does direct our attention to the paramount role of social interaction in increasing a person's motivation to engage in deviant behavior (Morselli et al. 2006; Sutherland et al. 1992).

Routine Activities Theory Another, more recent interactionist explanation considers the requisite conditions for a crime or deviant act to occur: there must be, at the same time and in the same place, a perpetrator, a victim, and/or an object of property. **Routine activities theory** contends that criminal victimization increases when motivated offenders and suitable targets converge. It goes without saying that you cannot have car theft without automobiles, but the greater availability of more valuable automobiles to potential thieves *heightens* the likelihood that such a crime will occur. Campus and airport parking lots, where vehicles may be left in isolated locations for long periods, represent a new target for crime that was unknown just a generation ago. Routine activity of this nature can occur even in the home. If a parent keeps a number of liquor bottles in an easily accessible place, juveniles can siphon off the contents without attracting attention to their "crime." This theory derives its name from the fact that the elements of a criminal or deviant act come together in normal, legal, and routine activities. It is considered interactionist because of its emphasis on everyday behavior and micro-level social interactions.

Advocates of this theory see it as a powerful explanation for the rise in crime over the last 50 years. That is, routine activities have changed, making crime more likely. Homes left vacant during the day or during long vacations are more accessible as targets of crime. The greater presence of highly portable consumer goods, such as video equipment and computers, is another change that makes crime more likely (L. Cohen and Felson 1979; M. Felson 2002).

Some significant research supports routine activities theory. For example, studies of urban crime have documented the existence of "hot spots" such as tourist destinations and automated teller machines (ATMs), where people are more likely to be victimized because of their routine comings and goings. Furthermore, evidence shows that in cold climates, warmer temperatures are associated with a rise in property crimes and probably violent crimes as well—regardless of a community's population density. In good weather, people are out and about, rendering both themselves and their vacated homes more vulnerable (Cromwell et al. 1995; Hipp et al. 2004).

Labeling Theory

The Saints and Roughnecks were two groups of high school males who were continually engaged in excessive drinking, reckless driving, truancy, petty theft, and vandalism. There the similarity ended. None of the Saints was ever arrested, but every Roughneck was frequently in trouble with police and townspeople. Why the disparity in their treatment? On the basis of observation research in their high school, sociologist William Chambliss (1973) concluded that social class played an important role in the varying fortunes of the two groups.

The Saints hid behind a facade of respectability. They came from "good families," were active in school organizations, planned on attending college, and received good grades. People generally viewed their delinquent acts as a few isolated cases of sowing wild oats. The Roughnecks had no such aura of respectability. They drove around town in beat-up cars, were generally unsuccessful in school, and aroused suspicion no matter what they did.

We can understand such discrepancies by using an approach to deviance known as *labeling theory.* Unlike Sutherland's work, labeling theory does not focus on why some individuals come to commit deviant acts. Instead, it attempts to explain why certain people (such as the Roughnecks) are *viewed* as deviants, delinquents, bad kids, losers, and criminals, while others whose behavior is similar (such as the Saints) are not seen in such harsh terms. Reflecting the contribution of interactionist theorists, labeling theory emphasizes how a person comes to be labeled as deviant, or to accept that label. Sociologist Howard Becker (1963:9; 1964), who popularized this approach, summed it up with this statement: "Deviant behavior is behavior that people so label."

How do certain behaviors come to be viewed as a problem? Cigarette smoking, which was once regarded as a polite, gentlemanly activity, is now considered a serious health hazard, not only to the smoker but to others who don't smoke. Box 8-2 (page 198) considers a behavior that has only recently been identified and labeled a crime: road rage.

Labeling theory is also called the *societal-reaction approach,* reminding us that it is the *response* to an act, not the behavior itself, that determines deviance. For example, studies have shown that some school personnel and therapists expand educational programs designed for learning-disabled students to include those with behavioral problems. Consequently, a "troublemaker" can be improperly labeled as learning-disabled, and vice versa.

Traditionally, research on deviance has focused on people who violate social norms. In contrast, labeling theory focuses on police, probation officers, psychiatrists, judges, teachers, employers, school officials, and other regulators of social control. These agents, it is argued, play a significant role in creating the deviant identity by designating certain people (and not others) as deviant. An important aspect of labeling theory is the recognition that some individuals or groups have the power to *define* labels and apply them to others. This view ties into the conflict perspective's emphasis on the social significance of power.

In recent years the practice of *racial profiling*, in which people are identified as criminal suspects purely on the basis of their

Parking lots invite trouble. On college campuses, they provide an ideal setting for the convergence of a perpetrator, a victim, and an article of property (the automobile or its contents). According to routine activities theory, crimes are more likely to occur wherever motivated offenders meet vulnerable targets.

race, has come under public scrutiny. Studies confirm the public's suspicions that in some jurisdictions, police officers are much more likely to stop African American males than White males for routine traffic violations, in the expectation of finding drugs or guns in their cars. Civil rights activists refer to these cases sarcastically as DWB (Driving While Black) violations. Beginning in 2001, profiling took a new turn as people who appeared to be Arab or Muslim came under special scrutiny. (Racial profiling will be examined in more detail in Chapter 11.)

The labeling approach does not fully explain why certain people accept a label and others manage to reject it. In fact, this perspective may exaggerate the ease with which societal judgments can alter our self-images. Labeling theorists do suggest, however, that the power one has relative to others is important in determining a person's ability to resist an undesirable label. Competing approaches (including that of Sutherland) fail to explain why some deviants continue to be viewed as conformists rather than as violators of rules. According to Howard Becker (1973), labeling theory was not conceived as the *sole* explanation for deviance; its proponents merely hoped to focus more attention on the undeniably important actions of those people who are officially in charge of defining deviance (N. Davis 1975; compare with Cullen and Cullen 1978).

The popularity of labeling theory is reflected in the emergence of a related perspective, called social constructionism. According to the *social constructionist perspective,* deviance is the product of the culture we live in. Social constructionists focus specifically on the decision-making process that creates the deviant identity. They point out that "child abductors," "deadbeat dads," "spree killers," and "date rapists" have always been with us, but at times have become *the* major social concern of

8-2 Labeling a Behavior as a Crime: Road Rage

You're cut off by a honking, cursing driver as you try to merge with traffic—road rage in action! Though this kind of antisocial behavior isn't new, the concept of road rage is. Sociologists who have tried to trace its emergence want to know why it became socially significant only recently, even though bad driving dates back to the dawn of the automotive age.

It has been well documented that media portrayals of crime can influence the way we understand crime, even if the social reality is quite different. Serial killers are extremely rare, but you wouldn't know it from watching television or the movies. And though news coverage of civil disorders emphasizes the lawlessness of the crowd, most people in the immediate vicinity of such disturbances behave in a law-abiding fashion, even during the largest riots.

Thus we should not be surprised to learn that the provocative term *road rage* emerged in the media, in response to an extreme event: a series of deadly shootings committed by a driver on a Los Angeles freeway more than 20 years ago. Once the term had become established in everyday usage, the idea that aggressive behavior behind the wheel was on the increase became an accepted truism. In response to this perception, government officials launched campaigns to control aggressive driving, and legislators passed laws to distinguish road rage from other motor vehicle violations, such as tailgating or forcing another car off the road.

Like the attention the media give to serial killers, the attention given to road rage may be overdone. One research study estimates that the odds of dying because of road rage are only 1 in 9.5 million, compared to the much more significant risk of being killed in an auto accident—a chance of about 1 in 16,000. Yet the concept of road rage resonates with our notion of cars as superpowerful machines. As in Stephen King's novel *Christine* (in which an "evil" car comes to "possess" its owner), cars have acquired almost a personality of their own in the popular imagination.

> *The concept of road rage resonates with our notion of cars as superpowerful machines.*

Once a form of deviance has been designated as unique, it may draw attention away from more pressing concerns. Significantly, more common forms of aggression than road rage—such as "bar rage" or "party rage"—have not been singled out by special expressions. While road rage is far from a trivial or harmless behavior, research suggests that its importance has been exaggerated by the power of labeling.

Let's Discuss

1. What is the role of the audience in the creation of a new label such as *road rage*?

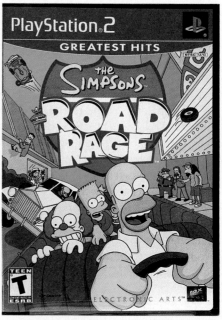

PlayStation2's interactive game Road Rage illustrates the wide usage of a label invented by the media just two decades ago.

2. Can you think of another label for deviant behavior that has come into currency only recently? If so, do you know how it originated?

Sources: Elliott 1999; Farrar 2005; Lupton 1999, 2001.

---

policymakers because of intensive media coverage (Liska and Messner 1999; E. R. Wright et al. 2000).

www.mhhe.com/schaefer11

Use Your Sociological Imagination

You are a teacher. What labels, freely used in educational circles, might you attach to your students?

Conflict Theory

Conflict theorists point out that people with power protect their own interests and define deviance to suit their own needs. Sociologist Richard Quinney (1974, 1979, 1980) is a leading exponent of the view that the criminal justice system serves the interests of the powerful. Crime, according to Quinney (1970), is a definition of conduct created by authorized agents of social control—such as legislators and law enforcement officers—in a politically organized society. He and other conflict theorists argue that lawmaking is often an attempt by the powerful to coerce others into their own morality (see also Spitzer 1975).

In the 1930s, the Federal Bureau of Narcotics launched a campaign to portray marijuana as a dangerous drug rather than a pleasure-inducing substance. From a conflict perspective, those in power often use such tactics to coerce others into adopting a different point of view.

This theory helps to explain why our society has laws against gambling, drug usage, and prostitution, many of which are violated on a massive scale. (We will examine these "victimless crimes" later in the chapter.) According to conflict theorists, criminal law does not represent a consistent application of societal values, but instead reflects competing values and interests. Thus, the U.S. criminal code outlaws marijuana because of its alleged harm to users, yet cigarettes and alcohol—both of which can be harmful to users—are sold legally almost everywhere.

In fact, conflict theorists contend that the entire criminal justice system in the United States treats suspects differently based on their racial, ethnic, or social-class background. In many cases, officials in the system use their own discretion to make biased decisions about whether to press charges or drop them, whether to set bail and how much, whether to offer parole or deny it. Researchers have found that this kind of *differential justice*— differences in the way social control is exercised over different groups—puts African Americans and Latinos at a disadvantage in the justice system, both as juveniles and as adults. On average, White offenders receive shorter sentences than comparable Latino and African American offenders, even when prior arrest records and the relative severity of the crime are taken into consideration. The Social Policy section at the end of this chapter notes marked racial disparities in the application of the death penalty (Quinney 1974).

Differential justice is not limited to the United States. In 2007, the people of India were alarmed to learn that a series of killings in the slums of New Delhi had never been investigated by police. Only after 17 bodies of recently murdered children were found in a sewer drain on the edge of a slum were police moved to act. For many onlookers, it was just the latest example of the two-tier justice system found in India and many other countries throughout the world (Gentleman 2007).

Such dramatic differences in social treatment may lead to heightened violence and crime. People who view themselves as the victims of unfair treatment may strike out, not against the powerful so much as against fellow victims. In studying crime in rural Mexico, Andrés Villarreal (2004) found that crime rates were high in the areas where land distribution was most inequitable. In areas where land was distributed more equally, communities appeared to suffer less violence and to enjoy greater social cohesion.

The perspective advanced by conflict and labeling theorists forms quite a contrast to the functionalist approach to deviance. Functionalists see standards of deviant behavior as merely reflecting cultural norms; conflict and labeling theorists point out that the most powerful groups in a society can shape laws and standards and determine who is (or is not) prosecuted as a criminal. These groups would be unlikely to apply the label "deviant" to the corporate executive whose decisions lead to large-scale environmental pollution. In the opinion of conflict theorists, agents of social control and other powerful groups can impose their own self-serving definitions of deviance on the general public.

Feminist Perspective

Feminist criminologists such as Freda Adler and Meda Chesney-Lind have suggested that many of the existing approaches to deviance and crime were developed with only men in mind. For example, in the United States, for many years any husband who forced his wife to have sexual intercourse—without her consent and against her will—was not legally considered to have committed rape. The law defined rape as pertaining only to sexual relations between people who were not married to each other, reflecting the overwhelmingly male composition of state legislatures at the time.

It took repeated protests by feminist organizations to get changes in the criminal law defining rape. Beginning in 1993, husbands in all 50 states could be prosecuted under most circumstances for the rape of their wives. There remain alarming exceptions in no fewer than 30 states, however. For example, the husband is exempt when he does not need to use force because his wife is asleep, unconscious, or mentally or physically impaired. These interpretations rest on the notion that the marriage contract entitles a husband to sex (Bergen 2006).

When it comes to crime and to deviance in general, society tends to treat women in a stereotypical fashion. For example, consider how women who have many and frequent sexual partners are more likely to be viewed with scorn than men who are promiscuous. Cultural views and attitudes toward women influence how they are perceived and labeled. The feminist perspective also emphasizes that deviance, including crime, tends to flow from economic relationships. Traditionally, men have had greater earning power than their wives. As a result, wives may be reluctant to report acts of abuse to the authorities, and lose what may be their primary or even sole source of income. In the workplace, men have exercised greater power than women in pricing, accounting, and product control, giving them greater opportunity to engage in such crimes as embezzlement and fraud. But as women have taken more active and powerful roles both in the household and in business, these gender differences in deviance and crime have narrowed (F. Adler 1975; F. Adler et al. 2004; Chesney-Lind 1989).

In the future, feminist scholarship can be expected to grow dramatically. Particularly on topics such as white-collar crime, drinking behavior, drug abuse, and differential sentencing rates between the genders, as well as on the fundamental question of how to define deviance, feminist scholars will have much to say.

We have seen that over the past century, sociologists have taken many different approaches in studying deviance, arousing some controversy in the process. Table 8-2 summarizes the various theoretical approaches to this topic.

Crime

Crime is a violation of criminal law for which some governmental authority applies formal penalties. It represents a deviation from formal social norms administered by the state. Laws divide crimes into various categories, depending on the severity of the offense, the age of the offender, the potential punishment, and the court that holds jurisdiction over the case.

The term *index crimes* refers to the eight types of crime that are tabulated each year by the Federal Bureau of Investigation (FBI). This category of criminal behavior generally consists of those serious offenses that people think of when they express concern about the nation's crime problem. Index crimes include murder, rape, robbery, and assault—all of which are violent crimes committed against people—as well as the property crimes of burglary, theft, motor vehicle theft, and arson.

Types of Crime

Rather than relying solely on legal categories, sociologists classify crimes in terms of how they are committed and how society views the offenses. In this section, we will examine five types of crime differentiated by sociologists: victimless crimes, professional crime, organized crime, white-collar and technology-based crime, and transnational crime.

Victimless Crimes When we think of crime, we tend to think of acts that endanger people's economic or personal well-being against their will (or without their direct knowledge). By contrast, sociologists use the term *victimless crime* to describe the willing exchange among adults of widely desired, but illegal, goods and services, such as prostitution (Schur 1965, 1985).

Some activists are working to decriminalize many of these illegal practices. Supporters of decriminalization are troubled by the attempt to legislate a moral code for adults. In their view, prostitution, drug abuse, gambling, and other victimless crimes are impossible to prevent. The already overburdened criminal justice system should instead devote its resources to "street crimes" and other offenses with obvious victims.

Table 8-2

Sociological Perspectives on Deviance

summing UP

Approach	Theoretical Perspective	Proponents	Emphasis
Anomie	Functionalist	Émile Durkheim Robert Merton	Adaptation to societal norms
Cultural transmission/ Differential association	Interactionist	Edwin Sutherland	Patterns learned through others
Routine activities	Interactionist	Marcus Felson	Impact of the social environment
Labeling/Social constructionist	Interactionist	Howard Becker	Societal response to acts
Conflict	Conflict	Richard Quinney	Dominance by authorized agents Discretionary justice
Feminist	Conflict/Feminist	Freda Adler Meda Chesney-Lind	Role of gender Women as victims and perpetrators

Despite widespread use of the term *victimless crime,* however, many people object to the notion that there is no victim other than the offender in such crimes. Excessive drinking, compulsive gambling, and illegal drug use contribute to an enormous amount of personal and property damage. A person with a drinking problem can become abusive to a spouse or children; a compulsive gambler or drug user may steal to pursue his or her obsession. And feminist sociologists contend that prostitution, as well as the more disturbing aspects of pornography, reinforce the misconception that women are "toys" who can be treated as objects rather than people. According to critics of decriminalization, society must not give tacit approval to conduct that has such harmful consequences (Meier and Geis 1997).

The controversy over decriminalization reminds us of the important insights of labeling and conflict theorists presented earlier. Underlying this debate are two questions: Who has the power to define gambling, prostitution, and public drunkenness as "crimes"? and, Who has the power to label such behaviors as "victimless"? The answer is generally the state legislatures, and in some cases, the police and the courts.

Again, we can see that criminal law is not simply a universal standard of behavior agreed on by all members of society. Rather, it reflects a struggle among competing individuals and groups to gain government support for their moral and social values. For example, organizations such as Mothers Against Drunk Driving (MADD) and Students Against Drunk Driving (SADD) have been successful in recent years in modifying public attitudes toward drunkenness. Rather than being viewed as a victimless crime, drunkenness is increasingly associated with the potential dangers of driving while under the influence of alcohol. As a result, the mass media are giving greater (and more critical) attention to people who are found guilty of drunk driving, and many states have instituted severe fines and jail terms for a wide variety of alcohol-related offenses.

Professional Crime Although the adage "Crime doesn't pay" is familiar, many people do make a career of illegal activities. A ***professional criminal*** (or career criminal) is a person who pursues crime as a day-to-day occupation, developing skilled techniques and enjoying a certain degree of status among other criminals. Some professional criminals specialize in burglary, safecracking, hijacking of cargo, pickpocketing, and shoplifting. Such people have acquired skills that reduce the likelihood of arrest, conviction, and imprisonment. As a result, they may have long careers in their chosen "professions."

Edwin Sutherland (1937) offered pioneering insights into the behavior of professional criminals by publishing an annotated account written by a professional thief. Unlike the person who engages in crime only once or twice, professional thieves make a business of stealing. They devote their entire working time to planning and executing crimes, and sometimes travel across the nation to pursue their "professional duties." Like people in regular occupations, professional thieves consult with their colleagues concerning the demands of work, becoming part of a subculture of similarly occupied individuals. They exchange information on places to burglarize, on outlets for unloading stolen goods, and on ways of securing bail bonds if arrested.

Organized Crime A 1978 government report devotes three pages to defining the term *organized crime.* For our purposes, we will consider **organized crime** to be the work of a group that regulates relations among criminal enterprises involved in illegal activities, including prostitution, gambling, and the smuggling and sale of illegal drugs. Organized crime dominates the world of illegal business just as large corporations dominate the conventional business world. It allocates territory, sets prices for goods and services, and acts as an arbitrator in internal disputes. A secret, conspiratorial activity, it generally evades law enforcement. It takes over legitimate businesses, gains influence over labor unions, corrupts public officials, intimidates witnesses in criminal trials, and even "taxes" merchants in exchange for "protection" (National Advisory Commission on Criminal Justice 1976).

Organized crime serves as a means of upward mobility for groups of people struggling to escape poverty. Sociologist Daniel Bell (1953) used the term *ethnic succession* to describe the sequential passage of leadership from Irish Americans in the early part of the 20th century to Jewish Americans in the 1920s and then to Italian Americans in the early 1930s. Recently, ethnic succession has become more complex, reflecting the diversity of the nation's latest immigrants. Colombian, Mexican, Russian, Chinese, Pakistani, and Nigerian immigrants are among those who have begun to play a significant role in organized crime activities (Chin 1996; Kleinknecht 1996).

There has always been a global element in organized crime. But law enforcement officials and policymakers now acknowledge the emergence of a new form of organized crime that takes advantage of advances in electronic communications. *Transnational* organized crime includes drug and arms smuggling, money laundering, and trafficking in illegal immigrants and stolen goods; see the discussion on pages 202–203 (Lumpe 2003; Office of Justice Programs 1999).

White-Collar and Technology-Based Crime Income tax evasion, stock manipulation, consumer fraud, bribery and extraction of kickbacks, embezzlement, and misrepresentation in advertising—these are all examples of **white-collar crime,** illegal acts committed in the course of business activities, often by affluent, "respectable" people. Edwin Sutherland (1949, 1983) likened these crimes to organized crime because they are often perpetrated through occupational roles.

A new type of white-collar crime has emerged in recent decades: computer crime. The use of high technology allows criminals to carry out embezzlement or electronic fraud, often leaving few traces, or to gain access to a company's inventory without leaving home. According to a study by the FBI and the National White Collar Crime Center, over 231,000 Internet crimes were reported in 2005, ranging from scams to identity theft (Internet Crime Complaint Center 2006).

When Charles Horton Cooley spoke of the self and Erving Goffman of impression management, surely neither scholar could have envisioned the insidious crime of identity theft. According to a 2007 report, each year 3.7 percent of all adults find that their personal information has been misused for criminal purposes. Unfortunately, with our society's growing reliance on electronic financial transactions, assuming someone else's identity has become increasingly easy (Baum 2006; Monahan 2007).

Sutherland (1940) coined the term *white-collar crime* in 1939 to refer to acts by individuals, but the term has been broadened more recently to include offenses by businesses and corporations as well. *Corporate crime,* or any act by a corporation that is punishable by the government, takes many forms and includes individuals, organizations, and institutions among its victims. Corporations may engage in anticompetitive behavior, environmental pollution, medical fraud, tax fraud, stock fraud and manipulation, accounting fraud, the production of unsafe goods, bribery and corruption, and health and safety violations (J. Coleman 2006).

For many years, corporate wrongdoers got off lightly in court by documenting their long history of charitable contributions and agreeing to help law enforcement officials find other white-collar criminals. In 2003, ten investment firms and two stock analysts collectively paid a $1.4 billion settlement for issuing fraudulent information to investors. While the magnitude of the fine grabbed headlines nationwide, it must be balanced against the millions of investors who were lured into buying billions of dollars' worth of shares in companies that the accused knew were either troubled or on the verge of collapse. The bottom line is that no individual served a jail sentence as part of the settlement, and no firm lost its license to do business. Prosecutors in other investigations into corporate scandals have pledged to pursue jail sentences for white-collar criminals, but to date most defendants have only been fined (Labaton 2003; J. O'Donnell and Willing 2003).

Conviction for corporate crime does not generally harm a person's reputation and career aspirations nearly so much as conviction for street crime would. Apparently, the label "white-collar criminal" does not carry the stigma of the label "felon convicted of a violent crime." Conflict theorists don't find such differential treatment surprising. They argue that the criminal justice system largely disregards the crimes of the affluent, focusing on crimes committed by the poor. Generally, if an offender holds a position of status and influence, his or her crime is treated as less serious than others' crimes, and the sanction is much more lenient.

Transnational Crime More and more, scholars and police officials are turning their attention to *transnational crime,* or crime that occurs across multiple national borders. In the past, international crime was often limited to the clandestine shipment of goods across the border between two countries. But increasingly, crime is no more restricted by such borders than is legal commerce. Rather than concentrating on specific countries, international crime now spans the globe.

Historically, probably the most dreaded example of transnational crime has been slavery. At first, governments did not regard slavery as a crime, but merely regulated it as they would the trade in goods. In the 20th century, transnational crime grew to embrace trafficking in endangered species, drugs, and stolen art and antiquities.

"BUT IF WE GO BACK TO SCHOOL AND GET A GOOD EDUCATION, THINK OF ALL THE DOORS IT'LL OPEN TO WHITE-COLLAR CRIME."

Table 8-3

Types of Transnational Crime

Bankruptcy and insurance fraud

Computer crime (treating computers as both a tool and a target of crime)

Corruption and bribery of public officials

Environmental crime

Hijacking of airplanes ("skyjacking")

Illegal drug trade

Illegal money transfers ("money laundering")

Illegal sales of firearms and ammunition

Infiltration of legal businesses

Intellectual property crime

Networking of criminal organizations

Sea piracy

Terrorism

Theft of art and cultural objects

Trafficking in body parts (includes illegal organ transplants)

Trafficking in human beings (includes sex trade)

Source: Compiled by the author based on Mueller 2001 and United Nations Office on Drugs and Crime 2005.

Tiffany Zapata-Mancilla
**Victim Witness Specialist,
Cook County State's Attorney's Office**

Tiffany Zapata-Mancilla's typical day brings her into contact with all manner of crime victims—those who have survived murder attempts, domestic assault, child abuse, robbery, and other violent crimes—as well as family members who testify on behalf of victims. She works closely with victims who have witnessed a crime, since they are invariably called to testify in a trial. "My job is to make the courtroom experience for them as comfortable as possible," she says. That may mean offering them referral for crisis counseling, a court escort, court orientation, help with impact statements, assistance with restitution, protection services, transportation, child care, emergency financial assistance, or just a hot lunch. Her caseload of 500 cases comes from the four to eight courtrooms to which she is assigned in Chicago's Cook County.

"My sociological background helps me in all situations on a daily basis," Zapata-Mancilla says. In particular, it helps her to recognize the underlying societal issues, even in what seem to be horrendous individual acts, and to help victims to recognize those issues as well. "I do not judge those who come into the courtroom; I can only judge society," she says. According to Zapata-Mancilla, that doesn't mean that individuals have no personal responsibility for their life choices. But it helps to understand that people are conditioned by the environment and society they live in. One of her cases involved a young man who was called to testify to who killed his younger brother in a gang shootout. At the time of the trial, two years later, he denied knowing

anything about the killing, and afterward went out to eat with the defendant. It appears he might have been offered a drug job in return for not testifying. Instead of taking a judgmental attitude, Zapata-Mancilla recognized the young man's need to survive. Social problems such as poverty dictate to some degree the choices people believe they need to make.

Zapata-Mancilla majored in sociology at DePaul University after becoming hooked by her introductory course. She went on to earn her master's degree in sociology there in 2001. "I was very interested in societal issues such as poverty, crime, organized crime, and gang involvement, and how they influenced the lifestyles and psychology of individuals. Sociology, for me, offers reasons, not excuses, for why individuals act and react in certain ways," she says. She also thinks she has gained a greater understanding of herself as a Latina through her studies.

Her advice for students: "Keep an open mind and don't be judgmental of others."

Let's Discuss

1. Why do you think victim witnesses need special attention?
2. What aspect of sociological study do you think best prepared Zapata-Mancilla for her job?

Transnational crime is not exclusive of some of the other types of crime we have discussed. For example, organized criminal networks are increasingly global. Technology definitely facilitates their illegal activities, such as trafficking in child pornography. Beginning in the 1990s, the United Nations began to categorize transnational crimes; Table 8-3 lists some of the more common types. In the Social Policy section of Chapter 10 we will consider the crime of trafficking in human beings in the context of universal human rights.

Bilateral cooperation in the pursuit of border criminals such as smugglers has been common for many years. The first global effort to control international crime was the International Criminal Police Organization (Interpol), a cooperative network of European police forces founded to stem the movement of political revolutionaries across borders. While such efforts to fight transnational crime may seem lofty—an activity with which any government should cooperate—they are complicated by sensitive legal and security issues. Most nations that have signed protocols issued by the United Nations, including the United States, have expressed concern over potential encroachments on their national judicial systems, as well as concern over their national security. Thus, they have been reluctant to share certain types of intelligence data. The terrorist attacks of September 11, 2001, in-

creased both the interest in combating transnational crime and sensitivity to the risks of sharing intelligence data (Deflem 2005; D. Felson and Kalaitzidis 2005).

Use Your Sociological Imagination

As a newspaper editor, how might you treat stories on corporate or white-collar crime differently from those on violent crime?

www.mhhe.com/schaefer11

Crime Statistics

Crime statistics are not as accurate as social scientists would like, especially since they deal with an issue of grave concern to the people of the United States. Unfortunately, they are frequently cited as if they were completely reliable. Such data do serve as an indicator of police activity, as well as an approximate indication of the level of certain crimes. Yet it would be a mistake to interpret these data as an exact representation of the incidence of crime.

National Crime Rates and Percentage Change

Crime Index Offenses in 2005	Number Reported	Rate per 100,000 Inhabitants	Percentage Change in Rate	
			Since 2001	Since 1996
Violent crime				
Murder	16,692	6	0.2	−24
Forcible rape	93,934	32	−.5	−13
Robbery	417,122	141	−2	−30
Aggravated assault	862,947	291	−9	−26
Total	1,390,695	469	−7	−26
Property crime				
Burglary	2,460,526	919	−2	−23
Larceny-theft	7,743,760	2,286	−8	−14
Motor vehicle theft	1,235,226	417	−3	−21
Total	10,166,159	3,744	−6	−14

Notes: Arson was designated an index offense beginning in 1979; data on arson were still incomplete as of 2006. Because of rounding, the offenses may not add to totals.
Source: Department of Justice 2006a:Tables 1, 1a.

Understanding Crime Statistics Because reported crime is very high in the United States, the public regards crime as a major social problem. However, there has been a significant decline in violent crime nationwide following many years of increases. A number of explanations have been offered, including:

- A booming economy and falling unemployment rates through most of the 1990s.
- Community-oriented policing and crime prevention programs.
- New gun control laws.
- A massive increase in the prison population, which at least prevents inmates from committing crimes outside prison.

It remains to be seen whether this pattern will continue, but even with current declines, reported crimes remain well above those of other nations, and exceed the reported rates in the United States of just 20 years earlier. Feminist scholars draw our attention to one significant variation: the proportion of major crimes committed by women has increased. In a recent 10-year period (1996–2005), female arrests for major reported crimes increased 7 percent, while comparable male arrests declined 8 percent (Department of Justice 2006a:Table 33).

Typically, the crime data used in the United States are based on the index crimes described earlier. The crime index, published annually by the FBI as part of the *Uniform Crime Reports*, includes statistics on murder, rape, robbery, assault, burglary, larceny-theft, motor vehicle theft, and arson (see Table 8-4, above). Obviously,

many serious offenses, such as white-collar crimes, are not included in this index (although they are recorded elsewhere). In addition, the crime index is disproportionately devoted to property crimes, whereas most citizens are more worried about violent crimes. Thus, a significant decrease in the number of rapes and robberies could be overshadowed by a slightly larger increase in the number of automobiles stolen, leading to the mistaken impression that *personal* safety is more at risk than before.

The most serious limitation of official crime statistics is that they include only those crimes actually *reported* to law enforcement agencies. Because members of racial and ethnic minority groups often distrust law enforcement agencies, they may not contact the police. Feminist sociologists and others have noted that many women do not report rape or spousal abuse out of fear they will be blamed for the crime.

Partly because of these deficiencies in official statistics, the National Crime Victimization Survey was initiated in 1972. The Bureau of Justice Statistics, in compiling this annual report, seeks information from law enforcement agencies, but also interviews members of over 77,200 households and asks if they were victims of a specific set of crimes during the preceding year. In general, those who administer **victimization surveys** question ordinary people, not police officers, to determine whether they have been victims of crime.

Unfortunately, like other crime data, victimization surveys have particular limitations. They require that victims understand what has happened to them and are willing to disclose such information to interviewers. Fraud, income tax evasion, and blackmail are examples of crimes that are unlikely to be reported in victimization studies. Nevertheless, 91 percent of all households have been willing to cooperate with investigators for the National Crime Victimization Survey. As shown in Figure 8-2, data from these surveys reveal a fluctuating crime rate with significant declines in both the 1980s and 1990s (Catalano 2006).

International Crime Rates If developing reliable crime data is difficult in the United States, making useful cross-national comparisons is even more difficult. Nevertheless, with some care, we can offer preliminary conclusions about how crime rates differ around the world.

During the 1980s and 1990s, violent crimes were much more common in the United States than in Western Europe. Murders, rapes, and robberies were reported to the police at much higher rates in the United States. Yet the incidence of certain other types of crime appears to be higher elsewhere. For example, England, Italy, Australia, and New Zealand all have higher rates of car theft than the United States. Developing nations have significant rates of reported homicide due to civil unrest and political conflict among civilians (International Crime Victim Survey 2004; World Bank 2003a).

Why are rates of violent crime so much higher in the United States than in Western Europe? Sociologist Elliot Currie (1985, 1998) has suggested that our society places greater emphasis on individual economic achievement than other societies. At the same time, many observers have noted that the culture of the United States has long tolerated, if not condoned, many forms of violence. Coupled with sharp disparities between poor and affluent citizens, significant unemployment, and substantial alcohol and drug abuse, these factors combine to produce a climate conducive to crime.

However, disturbing increases in violent crime are evident in other Western societies. For example, crime has skyrocketed in

FIGURE 8–2 **205**

Deviance and Social Control

Victimization Rates, 1973–2005

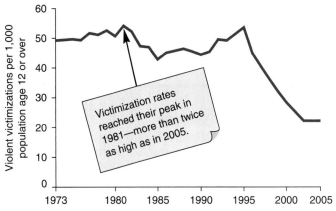

Victimization rates reached their peak in 1981—more than twice as high as in 2005.

Source: Catalano 2006:5.

Russia since the overthrow of Communist Party rule (with its strict controls on guns and criminals) in 1991. In 1998 there were fewer than 260 homicides in Moscow; now there are more than 1,000 homicides a year. Organized crime has filled the power vacuum in Moscow: one result is that gangland shootouts and premeditated "contract hits" have become more common. Some prominent reformist politicians have been targeted as well. Russia is the only nation in the world that incarcerates a higher proportion of its citizens than the United States. The country imprisons 580 per 100,000 of its adults on a typical day, compared to 550 in the United States, fewer than 100 in Mexico or Britain, and only 16 in Greece (Currie 1998; Shinkai and Zvekic 1999).

The Death Penalty in the United States and Worldwide

The Issue

On June 11, 2001, Timothy McVeigh—the man who took the lives of hundreds of innocent people by bombing the federal building in Oklahoma City—was executed by the federal government. McVeigh was the first federal death row prisoner to be put to death in nearly four decades. His execution and that of others who received the death penalty for their crimes raise many questions, both from supporters and from critics of capital punishment. How can the government prevent the execution of innocent men and women? Is it right to resort to a punishment that imitates the crime it seeks to condemn? Is life in prison enough of a punishment for truly heinous crimes?

Historically, execution has been a significant form of punishment for deviance from social norms and for criminal behavior. The death penalty has been used for centuries in North America to punish murder, alleged witchcraft, and a few other crimes. Yet for most of that time, little thought was given to its justification; capital punishment was simply assumed to be morally and religiously right.

The Setting

Worldwide, fewer than half of all nations allow the death penalty. Yet at least 2,148 prisoners in 22 countries are known to have been executed in 2005 alone, and another 5,186 defendants in 53 nations were sentenced to death that year. Ninety-four percent of all known executions in 2005 took place in China, Iran, Saudi Arabia, and the United States. Within the United States, 38 states, the military, and the federal government continue to sentence convicted felons to death for selected crimes. On the state level, more than 1,062 prisoners have been executed since 1977.

For many years, the U.S. Supreme Court waffled on the issue of capital punishment. But in 1972, in a landmark 5–4 decision in *Furman v. Georgia,* the Court held that state death penalty laws as they were administered at the time were unconstitutional, because the states allowed judges and juries too much discretion in choosing the death sentence. Before imposing the death penalty, the Justices ruled, lower courts must consider the circumstances of the crime and the character and previous record of the defendant. Four years later, in *Gregg v. Georgia,* the Court ruled specifically that capital punishment is constitutional if administered under these guidelines. According to this ruling, execution can be an ap-

propriate sentence so long as it does not involve needless pain or suffering and is not grossly out of proportion to the severity of the crime. As a result of this ruling, all states that allowed the death penalty changed their statutes to meet the Court's standards. Yet today, state laws regarding the death penalty still vary widely, as Figure 8-3 shows (Amnesty International 2007; Death Penalty Information Center 2007a).

Sociological Insights

The debate over the death penalty has traditionally focused on its appropriateness as a form of punishment and its value in deterring crime. Viewed from the functionalist perspective of Émile Durkheim, sanctions against deviant acts help to reinforce society's standards of proper behavior. In this light, supporters of capital punishment insist that fear of execution will prevent at least some criminals from committing serious offenses. Moreover, supporters see the death penalty as justified even if it does

FIGURE 8–3

Executions by State since 1976

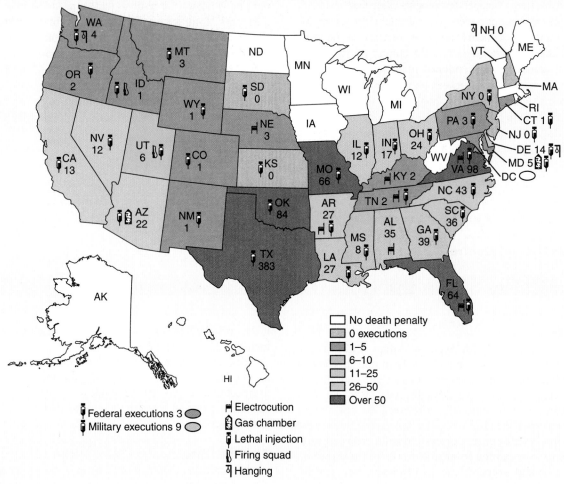

MAPPING LIFE NATIONWIDE www.mhhe.com/schaefer11

Legend:
- No death penalty
- 0 executions
- 1–5
- 6–10
- 11–25
- 26–50
- Over 50

Federal executions 3
Military executions 9

- Electrocution
- Gas chamber
- Lethal injection
- Firing squad
- Hanging

Note: As of February 16, 2007.

Source: Based on Death Penalty Information Center 2007a and NAACP Legal Defense and Educational Fund 2006.

not serve as a deterrent, because they believe that the worst criminals deserve to die for their crimes.

While proponents note the functions of the death penalty, there are some dysfunctions. Though many citizens are concerned that the alternative to execution, life in prison, is unnecessarily expensive, sentencing a person to death is not cheap. With hundreds of people housed on death row, the state of Texas spends an estimated $2.3 million *per case*—about three times the cost of imprisoning someone in a single cell at the highest level of security for a period of 40 years (Death Penalty Information Center 2007a).

The conflict perspective emphasizes the persistence of social inequality in today's society. Simply put, poor people cannot afford to hire the best lawyers, but must rely on court-appointed attorneys, who typically are overworked and underpaid. With capital punishment in place, these unequal resources may mean the difference between life and death for poor defendants. Indeed, the American Bar Association (1997) has repeatedly expressed concern about the limited defense most defendants facing the death penalty receive. Through 2007, DNA analysis and other new technologies had exonerated 14 death row inmates (Innocence Project 2007).

Another issue of critical concern to conflict theorists and researchers is the possibility of racial discrimination. Numerous studies show that defendants are more likely to be sentenced to death if their victims were White rather than Black. About 79 percent of the victims in death penalty cases are White, even though only 50 percent of *all* murder victims are White. There is some evidence that Black defendants, who constituted 42 percent of all death row inmates in 2007, are more likely to face execution than Whites in the same legal circumstances. Evidence exists, too, that capital defendants receive poor legal services because of the racist attitudes of their own defense counsel. While racism is never acceptable in the criminal justice system, it is particularly devastating when the legal process results in an execution (Death Penalty Information Center 2007a).

Policy Initiatives

Many people hesitate to endorse the death penalty, yet when confronted with a horrendous crime, they feel the death penalty should be available, at least in some cases. In most people's minds, for example, Timothy McVeigh's sentence would be an appropriate use of the death penalty. Surveys conducted in the United States since 1936 have found that the majority of people tend to favor the death penalty for a person convicted of murder, though approval has fluctuated. In 2006 support for the death penalty was at 67 percent—about the same level as has prevailed over the last 25 years (Gallup 2006b).

Recently, policy initiatives have moved in two different directions. In several death penalty states, legislators are considering broadening the range of offenses for which convicted criminals may be sentenced to execution. Child molesters who did not murder their victims would become eligible for the death penalty, along with certain repeat offenders. The countertrend, a movement away from the death penalty, is based on doubts as to whether executions can be carried out humanely. Legal actions have been taken on behalf of those convicted to die, especially by lethal injection, which is used in virtually all death penalty jurisdictions. Concerns about lethal injection range from medical ethics (the injection must be administered by a medical technician) to the effectiveness of the technique, which sometimes takes a long time to cause death (Bazar 2007; Death Penalty Information Center 2007b).

Surprisingly, only about 125 death sentences are handed out for the more than 20,000 murders that occur every year. Courts continue to face the question of how this ultimate penalty can be administered in a judicially fair manner. Policymakers, however, do not seem concerned with such questions. In recent years, federal and state legislatures have declared additional crimes to be punishable by death, curtailed appeals by death row inmates, and reimbursed far fewer lawyers for their defense of condemned criminals (Snell 2006).

Internationally, attention has focused on those nations where executions are relatively common, such as China and Iran. Foes of the death penalty see these nations as violators of human rights. In the United States, which usually regards itself as a champion of human rights, pressure to abolish capital punishment has grown, both at home and abroad.

Let's Discuss

1. Does the death penalty serve as a deterrent to crime? If so, why are crime rates in the United States comparatively high?

2. What is your position on the death penalty—should it be legal, or should it be abolished? Why?

3. Should youths who have been convicted of violent crimes be subject to the death penalty? Why or why not?

GettingINVOLVED

To get involved in the debate over the death penalty, visit this text's Online Learning Center, which offers links to relevant Web sites. Check out the Social Policy section on the Online Learning Center as well; it provides survey data on U.S. public opinion regarding this issue.

www.mhhe.com/schaefer11

Summary

Conformity and *deviance* are two ways in which people respond to real or imagined pressure from others. In this chapter, we examined the relationship between conformity, deviance, and mechanisms of *social control.*

1. A society uses *social control* to encourage the acceptance of basic norms.

2. Stanley Milgram defined *conformity* as going along with one's peers; *obedience* is defined as compliance with higher authorities in a hierarchical structure.

3. Some norms are so important to a society, they are formalized into *laws.* Socialization is a primary source of conforming and obedient behavior, including obedience to law.

4. Deviant behavior violates social norms. Some forms of *deviance* carry a negative social *stigma,* while other forms are more or less accepted.

5. From a functionalist point of view, deviance and its consequences help to define the limits of proper behavior.

6. Some interactionists maintain that people learn criminal behavior by interacting with others *(cultural transmission).* To them, deviance results from exposure to attitudes that are favorable to criminal acts *(differential association).*

7. Other interactionists stress that for a crime to occur, there must be a convergence of motivated offenders and suitable targets of crime *(routine activities theory).*

8. An important aspect of *labeling theory* is the recognition that some people are viewed as deviant, while others who engage in the same behavior are not.

9. From the conflict perspective, laws and punishments are a reflection of the interests of the powerful.

10. The feminist perspective emphasizes that cultural attitudes and differential economic relationships help to explain gender differences in deviance and crime.

11. *Crime* represents a deviation from formal social norms administered by the state.

12. Sociologists differentiate among *victimless crimes* (such as drug use and prostitution), *professional crime,* *organized crime, white-collar crime,* and *transnational crime.*

13. Crime statistics are among the least reliable social data, partly because so many crimes are not reported to law enforcement agencies. Rates of violent crime are higher in the United States than in other Western societies, although they have been dropping.

14. The majority of people in the United States approve of the death penalty for particularly horrible crimes. However, sociologists have questioned the effectiveness of capital punishment as a deterrent to crime, and have pointed out that it falls disproportionately on those who are poor and non-White.

Critical Thinking Questions

1. What mechanisms of formal and informal social control are evident in your college classes and in day-to-day life and social interactions at your school?

2. What approach to deviance do you find most persuasive: that of functionalists, conflict theorists, interactionists, or labeling theorists? Why do you consider that approach more convincing than the other three? What are the main weaknesses of each approach?

3. Rates of violent crime are higher in the United States than they are in Western Europe, Canada, Australia, or New Zealand. Draw on as many of the theories discussed in this chapter as possible to explain why the United States is such a comparatively violent society.

Anomie Durkheim's term for the loss of direction felt in a society when social control of individual behavior has become ineffective. (page 194)

Anomie theory of deviance Robert Merton's theory of deviance as an adaptation of socially prescribed goals or of the means governing their attainment, or both. (195)

Conformity Going along with peers—individuals of our own status who have no special right to direct our behavior. (185)

Control theory A view of conformity and deviance that suggests that our connection to members of society leads us to systematically conform to society's norms. (189)

Crime A violation of criminal law for which some governmental authority applies formal penalties. (200)

Cultural transmission A school of criminology that argues that criminal behavior is learned through social interactions. (196)

Deviance Behavior that violates the standards of conduct or expectations of a group or society. (190)

Differential association A theory of deviance that holds that violation of rules results from exposure to attitudes favorable to criminal acts. (196)

Differential justice Differences in the way social control is exercised over different groups. (199)

Formal social control Social control that is carried out by authorized agents, such as police officers, judges, school administrators, and employers. (187)

Index crimes The eight types of crime reported annually by the FBI in the *Uniform Crime Reports:* murder, rape, robbery, assault, burglary, theft, motor vehicle theft, and arson. (200)

Informal social control Social control that is carried out casually by ordinary people through such means as laughter, smiles, and ridicule. (187)

Labeling theory An approach to deviance that attempts to explain why certain people are viewed as deviants while others engaged in the same behavior are not. (197)

Law Governmental social control. (189)

Obedience Compliance with higher authorities in a hierarchical structure. (185)

Organized crime The work of a group that regulates relations among criminal enterprises involved in illegal activities, including prostitution, gambling, and the smuggling and sale of illegal drugs. (201)

Professional criminal A person who pursues crime as a day-to-day occupation, developing skilled techniques and enjoying a certain degree of status among other criminals. (201)

Routine activities theory The notion that criminal victimization increases when motivated offenders and suitable targets converge. (196)

Sanction A penalty or reward for conduct concerning a social norm. (185)

Social constructionist perspective An approach to deviance that emphasizes the role of culture in the creation of the deviant identity. (197)

Social control The techniques and strategies for preventing deviant human behavior in any society. (184)

Societal-reaction approach Another name for *labeling theory.* (197)

Stigma A label used to devalue members of certain social groups. (191)

Transnational crime Crime that occurs across multiple national borders. (202)

Victimization survey A questionnaire or interview given to a sample of the population to determine whether people have been victims of crime. (204)

Victimless crime A term used by sociologists to describe the willing exchange among adults of widely desired, but illegal, goods and services. (200)

White-collar crime Illegal acts committed by affluent, "respectable" individuals in the course of business activities. (201)

Read each question carefully and then select the best answer.

1. Society brings about acceptance of basic norms through techniques and strategies for preventing deviant human behavior. This process is termed
   a. stigmatization.
   b. labeling.
   c. law.
   d. social control.

2. Which sociological perspective argues that people must respect social norms if any group or society is to survive?
   a. the conflict perspective
   b. the interactionist perspective
   c. the functionalist perspective
   d. the feminist perspective

3. Stanley Milgram used the word *conformity* to mean
   a. going along with peers.
   b. compliance with higher authorities in a hierarchical structure.
   c. techniques and strategies for preventing deviant human behavior in any society.
   d. penalties and rewards for conduct concerning a social norm.

4. Which sociological theory suggests that our connection to members of society leads us to conform systematically to society's norms?
   a. feminist theory
   b. control theory
   c. interactionist theory
   d. functionalist theory

5. Which of the following statements is true of deviance?
   a. Deviance is always criminal behavior.
   b. Deviance is behavior that violates the standards of conduct or expectations of a group or society.
   c. Deviance is perverse behavior.
   d. Deviance is inappropriate behavior that cuts across all cultures and social orders.

6. Which sociologist illustrated the boundary-maintenance function of deviance in his study of Puritans in 17th-century New England?
   a. Kai Erikson
   b. Émile Durkheim
   c. Robert Merton
   d. Edwin Sutherland

7. Which of the following is *not* one of the basic forms of adaptation specified in Robert Merton's anomie theory of deviance?
   a. conformity
   b. innovation
   c. ritualism
   d. hostility

8. Which sociologist first advanced the idea that an individual undergoes the same basic socialization process whether learning conforming or deviant acts?
   a. Robert Merton
   b. Edwin Sutherland
   c. Travis Hirschi
   d. William Chambliss

9. Which of the following theories contends that criminal victimization increases when motivated offenders and suitable targets converge?
   a. labeling theory
   b. conflict theory
   c. routine activities theory
   d. differential association theory

10. Which of the following conducted observation research on two groups of high school males (the Saints and the Roughnecks) and concluded that social class played an important role in the varying fortunes of the two groups?
    a. Richard Quinney
    b. Edwin Sutherland
    c. Émile Durkheim
    d. William Chambliss

11. If we fail to respect and obey social norms, we may face punishment through informal or formal _____.

12. Police officers, judges, administrators, employers, military officers, and managers of movie theaters are all instruments of _____ social control.

13. Some norms are considered so important by a society that they are formalized into _____ controlling people's behavior.

14. It is important to underscore the fact that _____ is the primary source of conformity and obedience, including obedience to law.

15. _____ is a state of normlessness that typically occurs during a period of profound social change and disorder, such as a time of economic collapse.

16. Labeling theory is also called the _____-_____ approach.

17. _____ theorists view standards of deviant behavior as merely reflecting cultural norms, whereas _____ and _____ theorists point out that the most powerful groups in a society can shape laws and standards and determine who is (or is not) prosecuted as a criminal.

18. Organizations such as Mothers Against Drunk Driving (MADD) and Students Against Drunk Driving (SADD) have had success in recent years in shifting public attitudes toward drunkenness, so that it is no longer viewed as a _____ crime.

19. Daniel Bell used the term _____ _____ to describe the process during which leadership of organized crime was transferred from Irish Americans to Jewish Americans and later to Italian Americans and others.

20. Consumer fraud, bribery, and income tax evasion are considered _____-_____ crimes.

{ TECHNOLOGY RESOURCES }

Online Learning Center

1. If you are interested in what people in the United States think about the death penalty, visit the student center of the Online Learning Center at **www.mhhe.com/schaefer11** and link to the Social Policy exercise for this chapter. You'll see survey results showing the divided opinions Americans have on this issue.

2. Whether or not marijuana should be legal for medicinal purposes is currently a controversial question in the United States. Explore the Web site of a group that advocates legalizing marijuana for such purposes, Americans for Safe Access (**www.safeaccessnow.org**). Do you agree with their views?

3. Can ordinary Americans take action to prevent crime? The Neighborhood Watch Program of the National Sheriff's Association believes that they can. Find out how by visiting their Web site at **www.usaonwatch.org.**

Note: Although all the URLs listed were current as of the printing of this book, these sites often change. Please check our Web site **(www.mhhe.com/schaefer11)** for updates, hyperlinks, and exercises related to these sites.

Reel Society Video Clips

Reel Society video clips, which appear on this book's Web site, can be used to spark discussion about the following topics from this chapter:

• Conformity and Obedience
• Informal and Formal Social Control
• What Is Deviance?

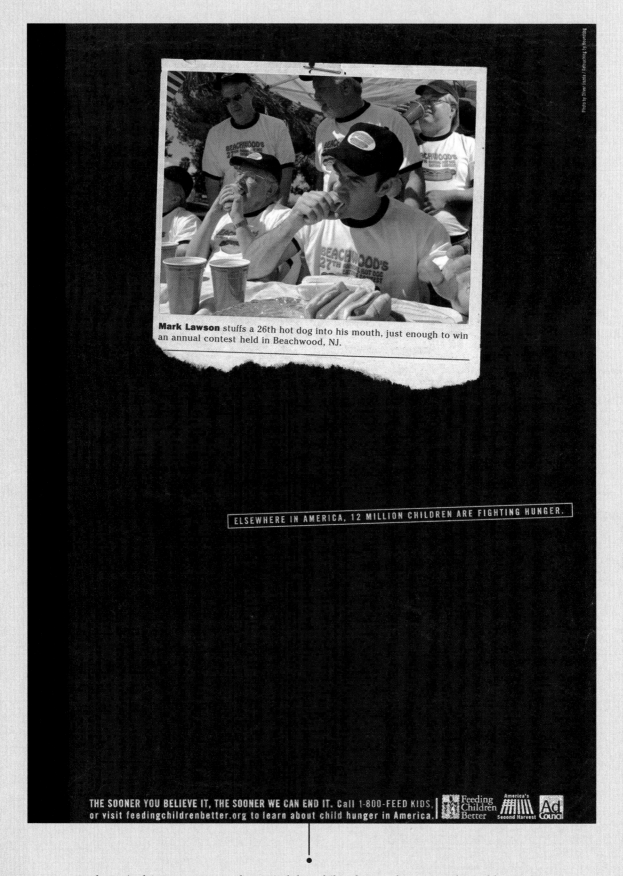

Mark Lawson stuffs a 26th hot dog into his mouth, just enough to win an annual contest held in Beachwood, NJ.

ELSEWHERE IN AMERICA, 12 MILLION CHILDREN ARE FIGHTING HUNGER.

THE SOONER YOU BELIEVE IT, THE SOONER WE CAN END IT. Call 1-800-FEED KIDS, or visit feedingchildrenbetter.org to learn about child hunger in America.

Feeding Children Better · America's Second Harvest · Ad Council

In the United States, some people overindulge while others go hungry, as this public service advertisement reminds us. Social class stratification determines the distribution of resources in our society, from necessities such as food and shelter to relative luxuries such as higher education.

Stratification and Social Mobility in the United States

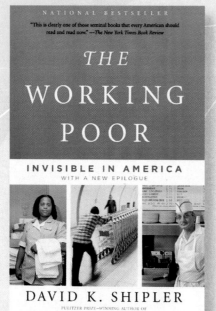

> " The man who washes cars does not own one. The clerk who files cancelled checks at the bank has $2.02 in her own account. The woman who copyedits medical textbooks has not been to a dentist in a decade.
>
> This is the forgotten America. At the bottom of its working world, millions live in the shadow of prosperity, in the twilight between poverty and well-being. Whether you're rich, poor, or middle-class, you encounter them every day. They serve you Big Macs and help you find merchandise at Wal-Mart. They harvest your food, clean your offices, and sew your clothes. In a California factory, they package lights for your kids' bikes. In a New Hampshire plant, they assemble books of wallpaper samples to help you redecorate.
>
> They are shaped by their invisible hardships. Some are climbing out of welfare, drug addiction, or homelessness. Others have been trapped for life in a perilous zone of low-wage work. Some of their children are malnourished. Some have been sexually abused. Some live in crumbling housing that contributes to their children's asthma, which means days absent from school. Some of their youngsters do not even have the eyeglasses they need to see the chalkboard clearly.
>
> . . . While the United States has enjoyed unprecedented affluence, low-wage employees have been testing the American doctrine that hard work cures poverty. . . . Moving in and out of jobs that demand much and pay little, many people tread just above the official poverty line, dangerously close to the edge of destitution. An inconvenience to an affluent family— minor car trouble, a brief illness, disrupted child care—is a crisis to them, for it can threaten their ability to stay employed. They

> *The man who washes cars does not own one. The clerk who files cancelled checks at the bank has $2.02 in her own account. The woman who copyedits medical textbooks has not been to a dentist in a decade.*

> spend everything and save nothing. They are always behind on their bills. They have minuscule bank accounts or none at all, and so pay more fees and higher interest rates than more secure Americans. . . .
>
> Breaking away and moving a comfortable distance from poverty seems to require a perfect lineup of favorable conditions. A set of skills, a good starting wage, and a job with the likelihood of promotion are prerequisites. But so are clarity of purpose, courageous self-esteem, a lack of substantial debt, the freedom from illness or addiction, a functional family, a network of upstanding friends, and the right help from private or governmental agencies. Any gap in that array is an entry point for trouble. . . . The American Myth still supposes that any individual from the humblest origins can climb to well-being. . . .
>
> But the American Myth also provides a means of laying blame. . . . A harsh logic dictates a hard judgment: If a person's diligent work leads to prosperity, if work is a moral virtue, and if anyone in the society can attain prosperity through work, then the failure to do so is a fall from righteousness. . . .
>
> There is an opposite extreme, the American Anti-Myth, which holds the society largely responsible for the individual's poverty. The hierarchy of racial discrimination and economic power creates a syndrome of impoverished communities with bad schools and closed options. The children of the poor are funneled into delinquency, drugs, or jobs with meager pay and little future. The individual is a victim of great forces beyond his control, including profit-hungry corporations that exploit his labor. "

(Shipler 2005:3–6) Additional information about this excerpt can be found on the Online Learning Center at www.mhhe.com/schaefer11.

In this excerpt from his book *The Working Poor: Invisible in America*, Pulitzer Prize–winning journalist David K. Shipler highlights a segment of the population often overlooked by social scientists and policymakers. The working poor—Black, White, Asian American, Latino—are in fact a significant segment of the U.S. labor force. Yet as the book's title suggests, they are largely invisible to the better-off people who eat at the restaurants and visit the hotels where they work. Their very presence in an otherwise prosperous economy contradicts the long-held popular belief that in the United States, anyone who works hard can get ahead. Shipler, who clearly wishes this myth were a reality, claims the term *working poor* "should be an oxymoron. Nobody who works hard should be poor in America" (Shipler 2005:ix).

The Working Poor is based on Shipler's interviews with low-income farm, factory, and service workers throughout the United States, from New Hampshire to Chicago and Los Angeles. Shipler began meeting with them in 1997 in the housing projects, sweatshops, and clinics where they lived, worked, and sought medical care. Some of them he spoke with only once or twice; others he interviewed 15 to 20 times over the course of five or six years. Though Shipler's sample population was not necessarily representative, he did study people of all races and ethnic groups. The majority of his subjects were women, as are the majority of the United States' working poor.

Ever since people first began to speculate about the nature of human society, their attention has been drawn to the differences between individuals and groups within society. The term *social inequality* describes a condition in which members of society have different amounts of wealth, prestige, or power. Some degree of social inequality characterizes every society.

When a system of social inequality is based on a hierarchy of groups, sociologists refer to it as *stratification:* a structured ranking of entire groups of people that perpetuates unequal economic rewards and power in a society. These unequal rewards are evident not only in the distribution of wealth and income, but even in the distressing mortality rates of impoverished communities. Stratification involves the ways in which one generation passes on social inequalities to the next, producing groups of people arranged in rank order, from low to high.

Stratification is a crucial subject of sociological investigation because of its pervasive influence on human interactions and institutions. It results inevitably in social inequality, because certain groups of people stand higher in social rankings, control scarce resources, wield power, and receive special treatment. As we will see in this chapter, the consequences of stratification are evident in the unequal distribution of both wealth and income in industrial societies. The term *income* refers to salaries and wages. In contrast, *wealth* is an inclusive term encompassing all a person's material assets, including land, stocks, and other types of property.

Is social inequality an inescapable part of society? How does government policy affect the life chances of the working poor? Is this country still a place where a hardworking person can move up the social ladder? This chapter focuses on the unequal distribution of socially valued rewards and its consequences. We will begin by examining four general systems of stratification, including the one most familiar to us, the social class system. We will examine three sociological perspectives on stratification, paying particular attention to the theories of Karl Marx and Max Weber. We'll also ask whether stratification is universal, and see what sociologists, including functionalist and conflict theorists, have to say about that question. We will see how sociologists define social class and examine the consequences of stratification for people's wealth and income, safety, and educational opportunities. And we will confront the question of social mobility, both upward and downward. Finally, in the Social Policy section, we will address welfare reform, an issue that is complicated by the attitudes that people, particularly those in the United States, hold toward those who do not work.

Systems of Stratification

Sociologists consider stratification on many levels, ranging from its impact on the individual to worldwide patterns of inequality. No matter where we look, however, disparities in wealth and income are substantial. Take income and poverty patterns in the United States, for example. As the top part of Figure 9-1 shows, in many states the median household income is 25 percent higher than that in other states. And as the bottom part of the figure shows, the poverty rate in many states is double that of other states. Later in this chapter we will address the meaning of such statistics. We'll begin our discussion here with an overview of the four basic systems of stratification. Then we'll see what sociologists have had to say on the subject of social inequality.

Look at the four general systems of stratification examined here—slavery, castes, estates, and social classes—as ideal types useful for purposes of analysis. Any stratification system may include elements of more than one type. For example, prior to the Civil War, you could find in the southern states of the United States both social classes dividing Whites from Whites and the institutionalized enslavement of Blacks.

FIGURE 9–1

The 50 States: Haves and Have-Nots

MAPPING LIFE NATIONWIDE

www.mhhe.com/schaefer11

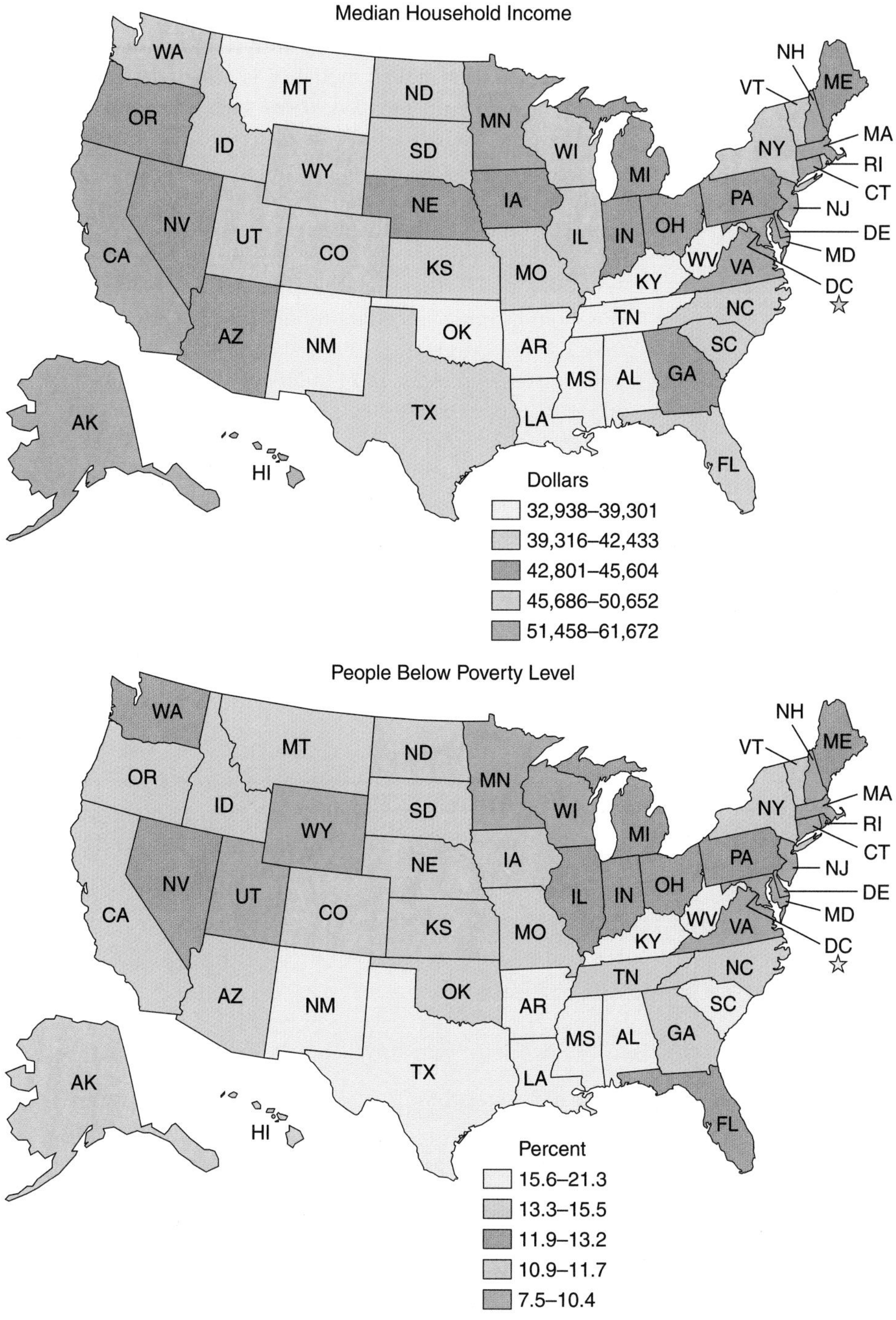

Median Household Income

Dollars
- 32,938–39,301
- 39,316–42,433
- 42,801–45,604
- 45,686–50,652
- 51,458–61,672

People Below Poverty Level

Percent
- 15.6–21.3
- 13.3–15.5
- 11.9–13.2
- 10.9–11.7
- 7.5–10.4

Source: 2005 census data presented in American Community Survey 2006: Tables R1701, R2001.

to a person by society without regard for the person's unique talents or characteristics. In contrast, **achieved status** is a {pp.111–112} social position that a person attains largely through his or her own efforts. The two are closely linked. The nation's most affluent families generally inherit wealth and status, while many members of racial and ethnic minorities inherit disadvantaged status. Age and gender, as well, are ascribed statuses that influence a person's wealth and social position.

Slavery

The most extreme form of legalized social inequality for individuals and groups is **slavery.** What distinguishes this oppressive system of stratification is that enslaved individuals are *owned* by other people, who treat these human beings as property, just as if they were household pets or appliances.

Slavery has varied in the way it has been practiced. In ancient Greece, the main source of slaves was piracy and captives of war. Although succeeding generations could inherit slave status, it was not necessarily permanent. A person's status might change, depending on which city-state happened to triumph in a military conflict. In effect, all citizens had the potential of becoming slaves or of receiving freedom, depending on the circumstances of history. In contrast, in the United States and Latin America, where slavery was an ascribed status, racial and legal barriers prevented the freeing of slaves.

Today, the Universal Declaration of Human Rights, which is binding on all members of the United Nations, prohibits slavery in all its forms. Yet around the world, millions of people still live as slaves. In many developing countries, bonded laborers are imprisoned in virtual lifetime employment; in some countries, human beings are owned outright. But a form of slavery also exists in Europe and the United States, where guest workers and illegal immigrants have been forced to labor for years under terrible conditions, either to pay off debts or to avoid being turned over to immigration authorities (Kapstein 2006).

To understand these systems better, it may be helpful to review the distinction between *achieved status* and *ascribed status,* explained in Chapter 5. **Ascribed status** is a social position assigned

Castes

Castes are hereditary ranks that are usually religiously dictated, and that tend to be fixed and immobile. The caste system is generally associated with Hinduism in India and other countries. In India there are four major castes, called *varnas*. A fifth category of outcastes, referred to as the *dalit,* or *untouchables,* is considered to be so lowly and unclean as to have no place within this system of stratification. There are also many minor castes. Caste membership is an ascribed status (at birth, children automatically assume the same position as their parents). Each caste is quite sharply defined, and members are expected to marry within that caste.

In 1950, after gaining independence from Great Britain, India adopted a new constitution that formally outlawed the caste system. Over the last decade or two, however, urbanization and technological advances have brought more change to India's caste system than the government or politics has in more than half a century. The anonymity of city life tends to blur caste boundaries, allowing the *dalit* to pass unrecognized in temples, schools, and places of employment. And the globalization of high technology has opened up India's social order, bringing new opportunities to those who possess the skills and ability to capitalize on them.

Estates

A third type of stratification system, called *estates,* was associated with feudal societies during the Middle Ages. The **estate system,** or *feudalism,* required peasants to work land leased to them by nobles in exchange for military protection and other services. The basis for the system was the nobles' ownership of land, which was critical to their superior and privileged status. As in systems based on slavery and caste, inheritance of one's position largely defined the estate system. The nobles inherited their titles and property; the peasants were born into a subservient position within an agrarian society.

As the estate system developed, it became more differentiated. Nobles began to achieve varying degrees of authority. By the 12th century, a priesthood had emerged in most of Europe, along with classes of merchants and artisans. For the first time there were groups of people whose wealth did not depend on land ownership or agriculture. This economic change had profound social consequences as the estate system ended and a class system of stratification came into existence.

Social Classes

A *class system* is a social ranking based primarily on economic position in which achieved characteristics can influence social mobility. In contrast to slavery and caste systems, the boundaries between classes are imprecisely defined, and one can move from one stratum, or level, of society to another. Even so, class systems maintain stable stratification hierarchies and patterns of class divisions, and they, too, are marked by unequal distribution of wealth and power. Class standing, though it is achieved, is heavily dependent on family and ascribed factors, such as race and ethnicity.

Income inequality is a basic characteristic of a class system. In 2005, the median household income in the United States was $46,326. In other words, half of all households had higher incomes in that year and half had lower incomes. But this fact does not fully convey the income disparities in our society. As Figure 9-2 shows, there is a broad range around the median household income. Furthermore, considerable numbers of people fall at the extremes. In 2003, about 181,000 tax returns reported incomes in excess of $1 million. At the same time, over 23 million households reported incomes under $9,000 (Bureau of the Census 2006a:317; DeNavas-Walt et al. 2006).

Sociologist Daniel Rossides (1997) uses a five-class model to describe the class system of the United States: the upper class, the upper-middle class, the lower-middle class, the working class, and the lower class. Although the lines separating social classes in his model are not so sharp as the divisions between castes, members of the five classes differ significantly in ways other than just income level.

FIGURE 9–2

Household Income in the United States, 2005

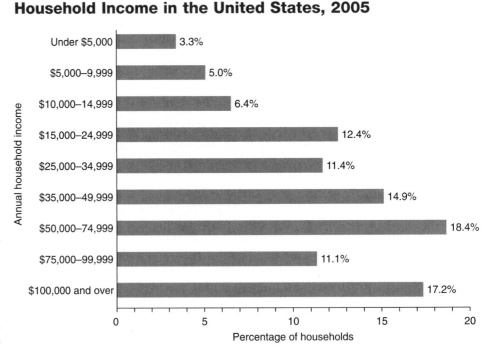

Source: DeNavas-Walt et al. 2006:31.

taking SOCIOLOGY TO WORK

Jessica Houston Su
Research Assistant, Joblessness and Urban Poverty Research Program

Jessica Houston Su chose sociology as her major "because it was the first class that appealed to my desire to understand the roots of inequality." It also helped her to make sense of what was going on around her at Dartmouth College. "I grew up in a rural, working-class community," she explains; "it was quite a culture shock to attend an affluent, Ivy League college." Learning about social structures and institutions helped Su to navigate through a new environment filled with people from many different backgrounds.

Su went through several potential majors before taking a sociology course and realizing that she was interested in almost every course the department offered. When she was hired for a work-study job in the department, she "soon realized that I was spending a lot of time reading all of the articles I was supposed to be photocopying," she jokes. "It became very obvious to me that I had found my major."

Su works at Harvard University's John F. Kennedy School of Government on a research program directed by the well-known sociologist William Julius Wilson. She is currently assigned to a large-scale longitudinal study of welfare reform in Boston, Chicago, and San Antonio. Her primary responsibility is to analyze the qualitative data from the study, gathered through ethnographic interviews with families who are affected by welfare reform, by searching for themes that might help to explain the study's quantitative data. She finds it exciting to be able to follow the same families over a long period. "I feel like I almost know some of the people," she explains.

Of all the things she learned as a sociology major, Su thinks one of the most important was the concept of social construction. "We consider many things to simply be facts of life," she explains, "but upon further investigation it is clear that most things have been socially constructed in some way." The concept of social construction has helped her to look more carefully at the world around her: "My worldview is much more nuanced and I've gained a much better understanding of how society works, both the good and the bad."

Su uses the research methods she learned in her sociology courses all the time. "I love going to work each day," she says. "I am challenged academically and I feel fulfilled knowing that I am working on something that will benefit society and perhaps influence future policy."

Let's Discuss

1. Did you experience a sense of culture shock when you entered college and were exposed to students from different social classes? If so, has studying sociology helped you to adjust to the diversity in students' backgrounds?
2. Have you begun to see the world differently since you learned about the social construction of reality? If so, what in particular do you see in a different light?

Rossides categorizes about 1 to 2 percent of the people of the United States as *upper class,* a group limited to the very wealthy. These people associate in exclusive clubs and social circles. In contrast, the *lower class,* consisting of approximately 20 to 25 percent of the population, disproportionately consists of Blacks, Hispanics, single mothers with dependent children, and people who cannot find regular work or must make do with low-paying work. This class lacks both wealth and income and is too weak politically to exercise significant power.

Both these classes, at opposite ends of the nation's social hierarchy, reflect the importance of ascribed status and achieved status. Ascribed statuses such as race clearly influence a person's wealth and social position. Sociologist Richard Jenkins (1991) has shown how the ascribed status of being disabled marginalizes a person in the U.S. labor market. People with disabilities are particularly vulnerable to unemployment, are often poorly paid, and tend to occupy the lower rung of the occupational ladder. Regardless of their actual performance on the job, the disabled are stigmatized as not earning their keep. Such are the effects of ascribed status.

Sandwiched between the upper and lower classes in this model are the upper-middle class, the lower-middle class, and the working class. The *upper-middle class,* numbering about 10 to 15 percent of the population, is composed of professionals such as doctors, lawyers, and architects. They participate extensively in politics and take leadership roles in voluntary associations. The *lower-middle class,* which accounts for approximately 30 to 35 percent of the population, includes less affluent professionals (such as elementary school teachers and nurses), owners of small businesses, and a sizable number of clerical workers. While not all members of this varied class hold degrees from a college, they share the goal of sending their children there. This class is currently under a great deal of economic pressure: Box 9-1 (page 218) discusses the shrinking size of the middle class.

Rossides describes the *working class*—about 40 to 45 percent of the population—as people who hold regular manual or blue-collar jobs. Certain members of this class, such as electricians, may have higher incomes than people in the lower-middle class. Yet even if they have achieved some degree of economic security,

217

research**IN**action

9-1 The Shrinking Middle Class

The cherished belief that the poor can rise to middle-class status has long been central to the United States' reputation as a land of opportunity. However, according to Lester C. Thurow, noted professor of economics and management at the Massachusetts Institute of Technology, the American middle class is disappearing. Using a widely accepted definition of a middle-class household as one whose income falls between 75 and 125 percent of the nation's median household income (that is, between $34,700 and $57,900), only about 22 percent of American households would have been classified as middle class in 2004, compared to 28 percent in 1967.

Closer analysis by Thurow indicates that of those who relinquished their middle-class standing during this period, about half rose to a higher ranking in the social class system, while half dropped to a lower position. In Thurow's view, these data mean that the United States is moving toward a "bipolar income distribution." That is, a broadly based middle class is slowly being replaced by two growing groups of rich and poor.

Sociologists and other scholars have identified several factors that have contributed to the shrinking size of the middle class:

- *Disappearing opportunities for those with little education.* In *The Working Poor,* highlighted at the beginning of this chapter, David Shipler tells how his grandfather rose from an eight-cent-an-hour job on the Jersey City docks to the presidency of Bethlehem Steel's steamship lines. Such opportunities are disappearing fast, yet to-

day, less than a third of adults between ages 35 and 44 have prepared themselves with a college degree.

- *Global competition and rapid advances in technology.* These two trends, which began several decades ago, have rendered workers more replaceable than they once were. Increasingly, they are affecting the more complex jobs that were once the bread and butter of middle-class workers. Experts disagree on whether they represent a permanent setback to the workforce or the

> *According to Lester C. Thurow, noted professor of economics and management at the Massachusetts Institute of Technology, the American middle class is disappearing.*

foundation for new industries that will someday generate millions of new jobs. In the meantime, however, U.S. households are struggling.

- *Growing dependence on the temporary workforce.* Some workers depend on temporary jobs for a second income, in order to maintain their middle-class lifestyle. For those workers who have no other job, these positions are tenuous at best, because they rarely offer health care coverage or retirement benefits.

- *The rise of new growth industries and nonunion workplaces.* In the past, workers in heavy industry were able to achieve middle-class incomes through the efforts of strong labor unions. But today, the growth areas in the economy are fast-food restaurants and large retail outlets. Though these industries have added employment opportunities, they are at the lower end of the wage scale.

In response to these concerns, observers note that living standards in the United States are improving. Middle-class families want large homes, college degrees for their children, and high-quality health care—the cost of which has been growing faster than inflation. The answer, for many people, is either to go without or to work longer hours at multiple jobs.

Let's Discuss

1. Does your family belong to the middle class? If so, in what generation did your family achieve that status, and how? Are your parents struggling to maintain a middle-class lifestyle?
2. For the nation as a whole, what are the dangers of a shrinking middle class?

Sources: DeNavas-Walt et al. 2006:HINC-01; Greenblatt 2005; Leonhardt 2007; Shipler 2005; Witte 2005.

---

they tend to identify with manual workers and their long history of involvement in the labor movement of the United States. Of the five classes, the working class is declining noticeably in size. In the economy of the United States, service and technical jobs are replacing those involved in the actual manufacturing or transportation of goods.

Social class is one of the independent or explanatory variables most frequently used by social scientists to shed light on social issues. In later chapters, we will analyze the relationships between social class and child rearing (Chapter 14), religious affiliation (Chapter 15), and formal schooling (Chap-

ter 16), as well as other relationships in which social class is a variable.

Use Your Sociological Imagination

How can you tell someone's social class? What indicators can be misleading?

Supersized homes like this one typically belong to upper-middle-class families, who may also enjoy vacation retreats and luxury condos in the city. These conspicuous homes mark their owners as members of a privileged 10 to 15 percent of the population—just shy of the truly wealthy 1 or 2 percent who constitute the upper class.

In Marx's view, social relations during any period of history depend on who controls the primary mode of economic production, such as land or factories. Differential access to scarce resources shapes the relationship between groups. Thus, under the feudal estate system, most production was agricultural, and the land was owned by the nobility. Peasants had little choice but to work according to terms dictated by those who owned the land.

Using this type of analysis, Marx examined social relations within *capitalism*—an economic system in which the means of production are held largely in private hands and the main incentive for economic activity is the accumulation of profits (D. Rosenberg 1991). Marx focused on the two classes that began to emerge as the feudal estate system declined, the bourgeoisie and the proletariat. The *bourgeoisie,* or capitalist class, owns the means of production, such as factories and machinery; the *proletariat* is the working class. In capitalist societies, the members of the bourgeoisie maximize profit in competition with other firms. In the process, they exploit workers, who must exchange their labor for subsistence wages. In Marx's view, members of each class share a distinctive culture. Marx was most interested in the culture of the proletariat, but he also examined the ideology of the bourgeoisie, through which that class justifies its dominance over workers.

Sociological Perspectives on Stratification

Sociologists have hotly debated stratification and social inequality and have reached varying conclusions. No theorist stressed the significance of class for society—and for social change—more strongly than Karl Marx. Marx viewed class differentiation as the crucial determinant of social, economic, and political inequality. In contrast, Max Weber questioned Marx's emphasis on the overriding importance of the economic sector, and argued that stratification should be viewed as having many dimensions.

Karl Marx's View of Class Differentiation

Karl Marx has been aptly described as both a revolutionary and a social scientist. Marx was concerned with stratification in all types of human society, beginning with primitive agricultural tribes and continuing into feudalism. But his main focus was on the effects of economic inequality on all aspects of 19th-century Europe. The plight of the working class made him feel that it was imperative to strive for changes in the class structure of society (Beeghley 1978:1).

Karl Marx would identify these coal miners as members of the *proletariat,* or working class. For generations, miners were forced to spend their meager wages at "company stores," whose high prices kept them perpetually in debt. The exploitation of the working class is a core principle of Marxist theory.

According to Marx, exploitation of the proletariat will inevitably lead to the destruction of the capitalist system, because the workers will revolt. But first, the working class must develop *class consciousness*—a subjective awareness of common vested interests and the need for collective political action to bring about social change. Often, workers must overcome what Marx termed *false consciousness,* or an attitude held by members of a class that does not accurately reflect their objective position. A worker with false consciousness may adopt an individualistic viewpoint toward capitalist exploitation ("*I* am being exploited by *my* boss"). In contrast, the class-conscious worker realizes that all workers are being exploited by the bourgeoisie, and have a common stake in revolution.

For Marx, class consciousness was part of a collective process in which the proletariat comes to identify the bourgeoisie as the source of its oppression. Revolutionary leaders will guide the working class in its struggle. Ultimately, the proletariat will overthrow the rule of both the bourgeoisie and the government (which Marx saw as representing the interests of capitalists) and will eliminate private ownership of the means of production. In Marx's rather utopian view, classes and oppression will cease to exist in the postrevolutionary workers' state.

How accurate were Marx's predictions? He failed to anticipate the emergence of labor unions, whose power in collective bargaining weakens the stranglehold that capitalists maintain over workers. Moreover, as contemporary conflict theorists note, he did not foresee the extent to which political liberties and relative prosperity could contribute to false consciousness. Many workers have come to view themselves as individuals striving for improvement within free societies that offer substantial mobility, rather than as downtrodden members of a social class who face a collective fate. Finally, Marx did not predict that Communist Party rule would be established and later overthrown in the former Soviet Union and throughout Eastern Europe. Still, the Marxist approach to the study of class is useful in stressing the importance of stratification as a determinant of social behavior and the fundamental separation in many societies between two distinct groups, the rich and the poor.

Max Weber's View of Stratification

Unlike Karl Marx, Max Weber insisted that no single characteristic (such as class) totally defines a person's position within the stratification system. Instead, writing in 1916, he identified three distinct components of stratification: class, status, and power (Gerth and Mills 1958).

Weber used the term *class* to refer to a group of people who have a similar level of wealth and income. For example, certain workers in the United States try to support their families through minimum-wage jobs. According to Weber's definition, these wage earners constitute a class because they share the same economic position and fate. Although Weber agreed with Marx on the importance of this economic dimension of stratification, he argued that the actions of individuals and groups cannot be understood *solely* in economic terms.

Weber used the term *status group* to refer to people who have the same prestige or lifestyle. An individual gains status through membership in a desirable group, such as the medical profession. But status is not the same as economic class standing. In our culture, a successful pickpocket may belong to the same income class as a college professor. Yet the thief is widely regarded as a member of a low-status group, whereas the professor holds high status.

For Weber, the third major component of stratification has a political dimension. *Power* is the ability to exercise one's will over others. In the United States, power stems from membership in particularly influential groups, such as corporate boards of directors, government bodies, and interest groups. Conflict theorists generally agree that two major sources of power—big business and government—are closely interrelated (see Chapter 17). For instance, many of the heads of major corporations also hold powerful positions in the government or military.

The corporate executives who head private companies in the United States earn the highest incomes in the nation. In fact, the gap between their salaries and those of the average worker has widened significantly over time. In 1940, half of all U.S. executives earned more than 58 times the average worker's pay; by 2006, the multiple was 104. These highly compensated individuals represent the pinnacle not just of U.S. society, but of corporate executives around the world. Heads of U.S. corporations are paid significantly better than chief executive officers (CEOs) in other industrial countries. Even when their performance is less than stellar, many of them receive handsome raises. Data reported in 2006 show that of the 49 largest U.S. corporations performing *at a loss* recently, 29 actually increased their CEOs' salaries (Dash 2006; McCall 2006).

To summarize, in Weber's view, each of us has not one rank in society but three. Our position in a stratification system reflects some combination of class, status, and power. Each factor influences the other two, and in fact the rankings on these three dimensions often tend to coincide. John F. Kennedy came from an extremely wealthy family, attended exclusive preparatory schools, graduated from Harvard University, and went on to become president of the United States. Like Kennedy, many people from affluent backgrounds achieve impressive status and power.

Interactionist View

Both Karl Marx and Max Weber looked at inequality primarily from a macrosociological perspective, considering the entire society or even the global economy. Marx did suggest the importance of a more microsociological analysis, however, when he stressed the ways in which individuals develop a true class consciousness.

Interactionists, as well as economists, have long been interested in the importance of social class in shaping a person's lifestyle. The theorist Thorstein Veblen (1857–1929) noted that those at the top of the social hierarchy typically convert part of their wealth into *conspicuous consumption,* purchasing more automobiles than they can reasonably use and building houses with more rooms than they can possibly occupy. Or they may engage in *conspicuous leisure,* jetting to a remote destination and staying just long enough to have dinner or view a sunset over some historic locale (Veblen [1899] 1964).

At the other end of the spectrum, behavior that is judged to be typical of the lower class is subject not only to ridicule but even to legal action. Communities have, from time to time, banned trailers from people's front yards and sofas from their front porches. In some communities, it is illegal to leave a pickup truck in front of the house overnight.

Use Your Sociological Imagination

www.mhhe.com/schaefer11

Refer to the photo essay on pages 6–7. How do you think Thorstein Veblen would answer the question posed in the title? What do you think he would say about the three families pictured in the essay?

Is Stratification Universal?

Must some members of society receive greater rewards than others? Do people need to feel socially and economically superior to others? Can social life be organized without structured inequality? These questions have been debated for centuries, especially among political activists. Utopian socialists, religious minorities, and members of recent countercultures have all attempted to establish communities that to some extent or other would abolish inequality in social relationships.

This family's expensive lifestyle illustrates Thorstein Veblen's concept of conspicuous consumption, a spending pattern common to those at the very top of the social ladder.

Social scientists have found that inequality exists in all societies —even the simplest. For example, when anthropologist Gunnar Landtman ([1938] 1968) studied the Kiwai Papuans of New Guinea, at first he noticed little differentiation among them. Every man in the village did the same work and lived in similar housing. However, on closer inspection, Landtman observed that certain Papuans—men who were warriors, harpooners, and sorcerers—were described as "a little more high" than others. In contrast, villagers who were female, unemployed, or unmarried were considered "down a little bit" and were barred from owning land.

Stratification is universal in that all societies maintain some form of social inequality among members. Depending on its values, a society may assign people to distinctive ranks based on their religious knowledge, skill in hunting, beauty, trading expertise, or ability to provide health care. But why has such inequality developed in human societies? And how much differentiation among people, if any, is actually essential?

Functionalist and conflict sociologists offer contrasting explanations for the existence and necessity of social stratification. Functionalists maintain that a differential system of rewards and punishments is necessary for the efficient operation of society. Conflict theorists argue that competition for scarce resources results in significant political, economic, and social inequality.

Functionalist View

Would people go to school for many years to become physicians if they could make as much money and gain as much respect working as street cleaners? Functionalists say no, which is partly why they believe that a stratified society is universal.

In the view of Kingsley Davis and Wilbert Moore (1945), society must distribute its members among a variety of social positions. It must not only make sure that these positions are filled but also see that they are staffed by people with the appropriate talents and abilities. Rewards, including money and prestige, are based on the importance of a position and the relative scarcity of qualified personnel. Yet this assessment often devalues work performed by certain segments of society, such as women's work in the home or in occupations traditionally filled by women, or low-status work in fast-food outlets.

Davis and Moore argue that stratification is universal and that social inequality is necessary so that people will be motivated to fill functionally important positions. But critics say that unequal rewards are not the only means of encouraging people to fill critical positions and occupations. Personal pleasure, intrinsic satisfaction, and value orientations also motivate people to enter particular careers. Functionalists agree, but they note that society must use some type of reward to motivate people to enter unpleasant or dangerous jobs and professions that require a long training period. This response does not address stratification systems in which status is largely inherited, such as slave or caste societies. Moreover, even if stratification is inevitable, the functionalist explanation for differential rewards does not explain the wide disparity between the rich and the poor (Collins 1975; Kerbo 2003; Tumin 1953, 1985).

222 Conflict View

The writings of Karl Marx lie at the heart of conflict theory. {p.13 Marx viewed history as a continuous struggle between the oppressors and the oppressed, which ultimately would culminate in an egalitarian, classless society. In terms of stratification, he argued that under capitalism, the dominant class—the bourgeoisie—manipulates the economic and political systems in order to maintain control over the exploited proletariat. Marx did not believe that stratification was inevitable, but he did see inequality and oppression as inherent in capitalism (E. O. Wright et al. 1982).

Like Marx, contemporary conflict theorists believe that human beings are prone to conflict over scarce resources such as wealth, status, and power. However, Marx focused primarily on class conflict; more recent theorists have extended the analysis to include conflicts based on gender, race, age, and other dimensions. British sociologist Ralf Dahrendorf is one of the most influential contributors to the conflict approach.

Dahrendorf (1959) has modified Marx's analysis of capitalist society to apply to *modern* capitalist societies. For Dahrendorf, social classes are groups of people who share common interests resulting from their authority relationships. In identifying the most powerful groups in society, he includes not only the bourgeoisie—the owners of the means of production—but also the managers of industry, legislators, the judiciary, heads of the government bureaucracy, and others. In that respect, Dahrendorf has merged Marx's emphasis on class conflict with Weber's recognition that power is an important element of stratification (Cuff et al. 1990).

Conflict theorists, including Dahrendorf, contend that the powerful of today, like the bourgeoisie of Marx's time, want society to run smoothly so that they can enjoy their privileged positions. Because the status quo suits those with wealth, status, and power, they have a clear interest in preventing, minimizing, or controlling societal conflict.

One way for the powerful to maintain the status quo is to define and disseminate the society's dominant ideology. The term {p.71 *dominant ideology* describes a set of cultural beliefs and practices that helps to maintain powerful social, economic, and political interests. For Marx, the dominant ideology in a capitalist society served the interests of the ruling class. From a conflict perspective, the social significance of the dominant ideology is that not only do a society's most powerful groups and institutions control wealth and property; even more important, they control the means of producing beliefs about reality through religion, education, and the media (Abercrombie et al. 1980, 1990; Robertson 1988).

The powerful, such as leaders of government, also use limited social reforms to buy off the oppressed and reduce the danger of challenges to their dominance. For example, minimum-wage laws and unemployment compensation unquestionably give some valuable assistance to needy men and women. Yet these reforms also serve to pacify those who might otherwise rebel. Of course, in the view of conflict theorists, such maneuvers can never entirely eliminate conflict, since workers will continue to

As popular songs and movies suggest, long-haul truck drivers take pride in their low-prestige job. According to the conflict perspective, the cultural beliefs that form a society's dominant ideology, such as the popular image of the truck driver as hero, help the wealthy to maintain their power and control at the expense of the lower classes.

demand equality, and the powerful will not give up their control of society.

Conflict theorists see stratification as a major source of societal tension and conflict. They do not agree with Davis and Moore that stratification is functional for a society or that it serves as a source of stability. Rather, conflict sociologists argue that stratification will inevitably lead to instability and social change (Collins 1975; Coser 1977).

Table 9-1 (opposite) summarizes and compares the three major perspectives on social stratification.

Lenski's Viewpoint

Let's return to the question posed earlier—Is stratification universal?—and consider the sociological response. Some form of differentiation is found in every culture, from the most primitive to the most advanced industrial societies of our time. Sociologist Gerhard Lenski, in his sociocultural evolution approach, described how economic systems change as their level of technology becomes more complex, beginning with hunting and gathering and culminating eventually with industrial society.

In subsistence-based hunting-and-gathering societies, people focus on survival. While some inequality and differentiation are {pp.122–124 evident, a stratification system based on social class does not emerge because there is no real wealth to be claimed. As a society advances technologically, it becomes capable of producing a considerable surplus of goods. The emergence of surplus resources greatly expands the possibilities for inequality in status, influence, and power, allowing a well-defined, rigid social

summingUP

Sociological Perspectives on Social Stratification

	Functionalist	Conflict	Interactionist
Purpose of social stratification	Facilitates filling of social positions	Facilitates exploitation	Influences people's lifestyles
Attitude toward social inequality	Necessary to some extent	Excessive and growing	—
Analysis of the wealthy	Talented and skilled, creating opportunities for others	Use the dominant ideology to further their own interests	Exhibit conspicuous consumption and conspicuous leisure

class system to develop. To minimize strikes, slowdowns, and industrial sabotage, the elites may share a portion of the economic surplus with the lower classes, but not enough to reduce their own power and privilege.

As Lenski argued, the allocation of surplus goods and services controlled by those with wealth, status, and power reinforces the social inequality that accompanies stratification systems. While this reward system may once have served the overall purposes of society, as functionalists contend, the same cannot be said for the large disparities separating the haves from the have-nots in current societies. In contemporary industrial society, the degree of social and economic inequality far exceeds what is needed to provide for goods and services (Lenski 1966; Nolan and Lenski 2006).

Stratification by Social Class

Measuring Social Class

We continually assess how wealthy people are by looking at the cars they drive, the houses they live in, the clothes they wear, and so on. Yet it is not so easy to locate an individual within our social hierarchies as it would be in slavery or caste systems of stratification. To determine someone's class position, sociologists generally rely on the objective method.

Objective Method In the *objective method* of measuring social class, class is viewed largely as a statistical category. Researchers assign individuals to social classes on the basis of criteria such as occupation, education, income, and place of residence. The key to the objective method is that the *researcher*, rather than the person being classified, identifies an individual's class position.

The first step in using this method is to decide what indicators or causal factors will be measured objectively, whether wealth, income, education, or occupation. The prestige ranking of occupations has proved to be a useful indicator of a person's class position. For one thing, it is much easier to determine accurately than income or wealth. The term *prestige* refers to the respect and admiration that an occupation holds in a society. "My daughter, the physicist" connotes something very different from

"my daughter, the waitress." Prestige is independent of the particular individual who occupies a job, a characteristic that distinguishes it from esteem. *Esteem* refers to the reputation that a specific person has earned within an occupation. Therefore, one can say that the position of president of the United States has high prestige, even though it has been occupied by people with varying degrees of esteem. A hairdresser may have the esteem of his clients, but he lacks the prestige of a corporate executive.

Table 9-2 (page 224) ranks the prestige of a number of well-known occupations. In a series of national surveys, sociologists assigned prestige rankings to about 500 occupations, ranging from physician to newspaper vendor. The highest possible prestige score was 100; the lowest was 0. Physician, lawyer, dentist, and college professor were the most highly regarded occupations. Sociologists have used such data to assign prestige rankings to virtually all jobs and have found a stability in rankings from 1925 to the present. Similar studies in other countries have also developed useful prestige rankings of occupations (Hodge and Rossi 1964; Lin and Xie 1988; Treiman 1977).

Gender and Occupational Prestige For many years, studies of social class tended to neglect the occupations and incomes of *women* as determinants of social rank. With more than half of all married women now working outside the home (see Chapter 12), this approach seems outmoded. How should we judge class or status in dual-career families—by the occupation regarded as having greater prestige, the average, or some other combination of the two? Sociologists—in particular, feminist sociologists in Great Britain—are drawing on new approaches to assess women's social class standing. One approach is to focus on the individual (rather than the family or household) as the basis for categorizing a woman's class position. Thus, a woman would be classified according to her own occupational status rather than that of her spouse (M. O'Donnell 1992).

Another feminist effort to measure the contribution of women to the economy reflects a more clearly political agenda. International Women Count Network, a global grassroots feminist organization, has sought to give a monetary value to women's unpaid work. Besides providing symbolic recognition

Chapter 9

Prestige Rankings of Occupations

Occupation	Score	Occupation	Score
Physician	86	Secretary	46
Lawyer	75	Insurance agent	45
Dentist	74	Bank teller	43
College professor	74	Nurse's aide	42
Architect	73	Farmer	40
Clergy	69	Correctional officer	40
Pharmacist	68	Receptionist	39
Registered nurse	66	Carpenter	39
High school teacher	66	Barber	36
Accountant	65	Child care worker	35
Elementary school teacher	64	Hotel clerk	32
Airline pilot	60	Bus driver	32
Police officer or detective	60	Auto body repairer	31
Prekindergarten teacher	55	Truck driver	30
Librarian	54	Salesworker (shoes)	28
Firefighter	53	Garbage collector	28
Social worker	52	Waiter and waitress	28
Dental hygienist	52	Bartender	25
Electrician	51	Farm worker	23
Funeral director	49	Janitor	22
Mail carrier	47	Newspaper vendor	19

Note: 100 is the highest and 0 the lowest possible prestige score.
Source: J. Davis et al. 2005:2050–2051.

Think About It
Can you name what you think are two more high-prestige occupations? Two more low-prestige occupations?

of women's role in labor, this value would also be used to calculate pension and other benefits that are based on wages received. The United Nations has placed an $11 trillion price tag on unpaid labor by women, largely in child care, housework, and agriculture. Whatever the figure, the continued undercounting of many workers' contributions to a family and to an entire economy means that virtually all measures of stratification are in need of reform (United Nations Development Programme 1995; Wages for Housework Campaign 1999).

Multiple Measures Another complication in measuring social class is that advances in statistical methods and computer technology have multiplied the factors used to define class under the objective method. No longer are sociologists limited to annual income and education in evaluating a person's class position. Today, studies use as criteria the value of homes, sources of income, assets, years in present occupations, neighborhoods, and considerations regarding dual careers. Adding these variables will not necessarily paint a different picture of class differentiation in the United States, but it does allow sociologists to measure class in a more complex and multidimensional way.

Whatever the technique used to measure class, the sociologist is interested in real and often dramatic differences in power, privilege, and opportunity in a society. The study of stratification is a study of inequality. Nowhere is the truth of that statement more evident than in the distribution of wealth and income.

Wealth and Income

By all measures, income in the United States is distributed unevenly. Nobel Prize–winning economist Paul Samuelson has described the situation in the following words: "If we made an income pyramid out of building blocks, with each layer portraying $500 of income, the peak would be far higher than Mount Everest, but most people would be within a few feet of the ground" (P. Samuelson and Nordhaus 2005:383).

Recent data support Samuelson's analogy. Figure 9-3 (opposite) shows the distribution of U.S. income in the form of a section sliced from a three-dimensional pyramid—one whose needle nose is so tall that it won't fit onto the page. The box to the right of the pyramid represents the very top of the graph, collapsed to a much smaller scale. This box includes those fortunate Americans who received an income of $500,000 or more in 2005, a very select group representing only 0.5 percent of the population. At the top of the box are the more than 9,600 taxpayers who reported an income exceeding $10 million.

As the pyramid to the left of the box in Figure 9-3 shows, 90 percent of the nation's population received an income of less than $100,000 in 2005. According to the Bureau of the Census, only the top 20 percent of Americans received an income of $91,705 or more. In contrast, members of the bottom fifth of the nation's population received just $19,178 or less. Note the bottom-heavy nature of the income distribution shown in Figure 9-3: the lower the income level, the greater the percentage of the population receiving that income (DeNavas-Walt et al. 2006:10; Dykman 2006).

There has been a modest redistribution of income in the United States over the past 75 years. From 1929 through 1970,

U.S. Income Distribution, 2005

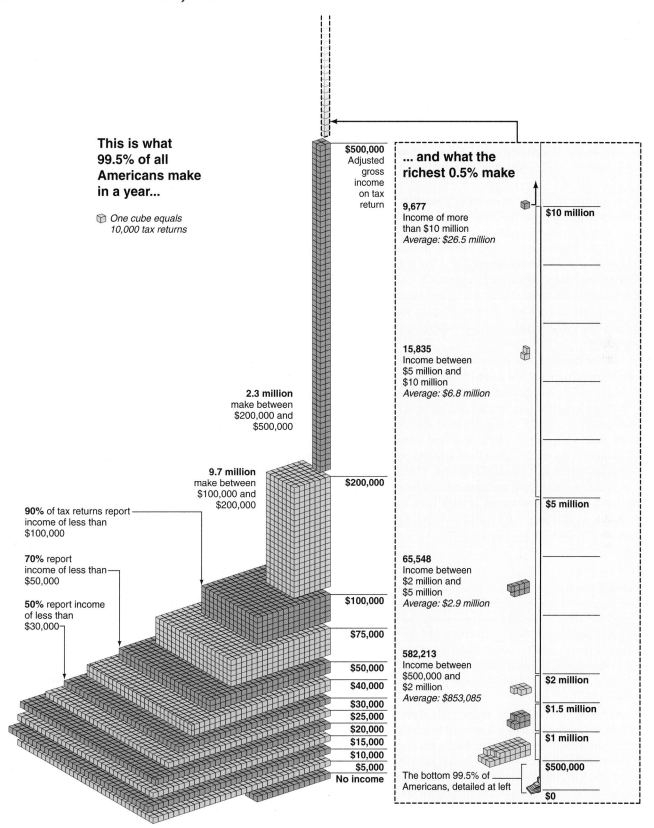

This is what 99.5% of all Americans make in a year...

One cube equals 10,000 tax returns

$500,000
Adjusted gross income on tax return

2.3 million make between $200,000 and $500,000

9.7 million make between $100,000 and $200,000

$200,000

90% of tax returns report income of less than $100,000

70% report income of less than $50,000

50% report income of less than $30,000

$100,000

$75,000

$50,000

$40,000

$30,000

$25,000

$20,000

$15,000

$10,000

$5,000

No income

... and what the richest 0.5% make

9,677 Income of more than $10 million *Average: $26.5 million*

15,835 Income between $5 million and $10 million *Average: $6.8 million*

65,548 Income between $2 million and $5 million *Average: $2.9 million*

582,213 Income between $500,000 and $2 million *Average: $853,085*

The bottom 99.5% of Americans, detailed at left

$10 million

$5 million

$2 million

$1.5 million

$1 million

$500,000

$0

Source: Dykman 2006:48–49, based on data from Bureau of Labor Statistics, Internal Revenue Service, *The State of Working America 2006/2007,* Salary.com, and Forbes.com.

the government's economic and tax policies shifted some income to the poor. However, in the last three decades—especially the 1980s—federal tax policies have favored the affluent. Moreover, while the salaries of highly skilled workers and professionals have continued to rise, the wages of less skilled workers have *decreased* when controlled for inflation. As a result, the Census Bureau reports that regardless of the measure that is used, income inequality rose substantially from 1967 through the end of the century. Former Federal Reserve Board Chairman Alan Greenspan was referring to this significant increase in income inequality when he told Congress that the gap between the rich and the poor in the United States has become so wide that a democratic society must address it (Greenblatt 2005; Grier 2005).

Americans do not appear to be seriously concerned about income and wealth inquality in the United States. In a comparison of opinions about social inequality in 27 different countries, respondents in the United States were less aware than those in other countries of the extent of inequality at the top of the income distribution. Americans would prefer to "level down" the top of the nation's earning distribution, but compared to people in other countries, they are less concerned about reducing income differentials at the bottom of the distribution (Osberg and Smeeding 2006).

Wealth in the United States is much more unevenly distributed than income. As Figure 9-4 shows, in 2001, the richest fifth of the population held 84.5 percent of the nation's wealth. Government data indicate that more than 1 out of every 100 households had assets over $2.4 million, while one-fifth of all households were so heavily in debt they had a negative net worth. Researchers have also found a dramatic disparity in wealth between African Americans and Whites. This disparity is evident even when educational backgrounds are held constant: the households of college-educated Whites have about three times as much wealth as the households of college-educated Blacks (Oliver and Shapiro 1995; Wolff 2002).

Poverty

Approximately one out of every nine people in the United States lives below the poverty line established by the federal government. In 2005, no fewer than 36.6 million people were living in poverty. The economic boom of the 1990s passed these people by. A recent Bureau of the Census report showed that one in five households has trouble meeting basic needs—with everything from paying the utility bills to buying dinner (Bauman 1999; DeNavas-Walt et al. 2006).

One contributor to the United States' high poverty rate has been the large number of workers employed at minimum wage. The federal government has raised the minimum wage over the last half century (see Figure 9-5) from 75 cents in 1950 to $6.55 in 2008 and $7.25 in 2009. But in terms of its real value adjusted for inflation, the minimum wage has frequently failed to keep pace with the cost of living. Little wonder, then, that the low-income workers David Shipler interviewed could barely scrape by (see the chapter-opening excerpt), or that Barbara Ehrenreich

FIGURE 9–4

Distribution of Wealth in the United States, 2001

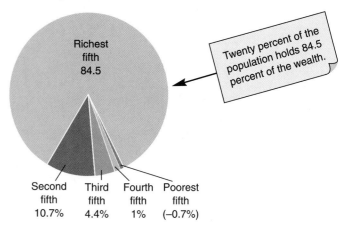

Richest fifth 84.5

Twenty percent of the population holds 84.5 percent of the wealth.

Second fifth 10.7%   Third fifth 4.4%   Fourth fifth 1%   Poorest fifth (–0.7%)

Note: Data do not add to 100 percent due to rounding.
Source: Wolff 2002.

could do no better when she experimented with life as a low-wage worker (see the excerpt that opened Chapter 1). In this section, we'll consider just how social scientists define *poverty*. We'll also take a closer look at the people who fall into that category—including the working poor.

Studying Poverty   The efforts of sociologists and other social scientists to better understand poverty are complicated by the difficulty of defining it. This problem is evident even in government programs that conceive of poverty in either absolute or relative terms. ***Absolute poverty*** refers to a minimum level of subsistence that no family should be expected to live below.

One commonly used measure of absolute poverty is the federal government's *poverty line,* a money income figure that is adjusted annually to reflect the consumption requirements of families based on their size and composition. The poverty line serves as an official definition of which people are poor. In 2005, for example, any family of four (two adults and two children) with a combined income of $19,806 or less fell below the poverty line. This definition determines which individuals and families will be eligible for certain government benefits (DeNavas-Walt et al. 2006:45).

Although by absolute standards, poverty has declined in the United States, it remains higher than in many other industrial nations. As Figure 9-6 shows, a comparatively high proportion of U.S. households are poor, meaning that they are unable to purchase basic consumer goods. If anything, this cross-national comparison understates the extent of poverty in the United States, since U.S. residents are likely to pay more for housing, health care, child care, and education than residents of other countries, where such expenses are often subsidized.

In contrast, ***relative poverty*** is a floating standard of deprivation by which people at the bottom of a society, whatever their lifestyles, are judged to be disadvantaged *in comparison with the*

FIGURE 9–5

U.S. Minimum Wage Adjusted for Inflation, 1950–2006

Note: In 2007 the federal minimum wage was raised to $5.85, with provisions for $6.55 in 2008 and $7.25 in 2009. Some states legislate different standards. Minima as of 2005 were actually lower in two states (KS and OH) and higher in 16 states (AK, CA, CT, DE, FL, HI, IL, MA, ME, MN, NJ, NY, OR, RI, VT, WA) and the District of Columbia.
Source: Author's estimate and Bureau of the Census 2006a.

nation as a whole. Therefore, even if the poor of 2005 are better off in absolute terms than the poor of the 1930s or 1960s, they are still seen as deserving of special assistance. Box 9-2 (page 228) explores the difference between relative poverty in Appalachia and relative affluence in the Congo.

Since the 1990s, debate has grown over the accuracy of the federal government's measure of poverty. If noncash benefits such as Medicare, Medicaid, food stamps, public housing, and health care and other employer-provided fringe benefits were included, the reported poverty rate would be lower. On the other hand, if out-of-pocket medical expenses and mandatory work expenses for transportation and child care were included, the poverty rate would be higher. The Census Bureau estimates that on balance, if both these recommendations were followed the official poverty rate would be 2 percent higher, and 5 million more people would fall below the poverty line (Bernasek 2006).

FIGURE 9–6

Poverty in Selected Countries

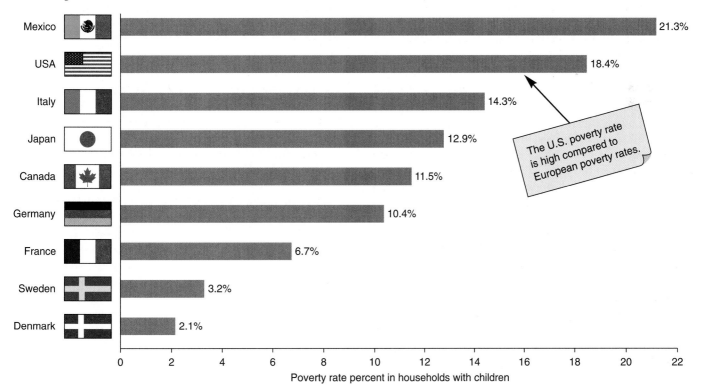

Note: Data are for 2000 except for Germany (2001) and Mexico (2002). Poverty threshold is 50 percent of nation's median income.
Source: Förster and d'Ercole 2005:36.

9-2 It's All Relative: Appalachian Poverty and Congolese Affluence

What does it mean to be well off? To be poor? To explore this question, the editors of the London-based publication *The Economist* compared the situations of two men living very different lives: an unemployed truck driver in the Appalachian Mountains and a physician in Congo.

Enos Banks makes his home in a forgotten pocket of rural poverty, described over 40 years ago in Michael Harrington's *The Other America*. Banks once worked for a coal-mining company, but a heart attack forced him to quit his job. In his 60s, he lives in a trailer and gets by on a little more than $500 a month in supplemental security income (SSI). Because he owns a truck, he is not eligible for food stamps.

On the other side of the world, in the Democratic Republic of Congo, Mbwebwe Kabamba earns about $100 or $200 more per month than Enos Banks. Kabamba is a surgeon and head of the emergency room at a hospital in Kinshasa, the country's capital. His hospital salary is only $250 a month, but he supplements it by performing surgery on the side. In Congo, the same income that impoverishes Enos Banks

places Kabamba near the middle of his society's income distribution.

Though Kabamba may seem better off than Banks, especially given the Congo's lower cost of living, such is not the case. Kabamba supports a family of 12, while Banks supports only himself. By U.S. standards, Kabamba's four-bedroom home, spacious compared to Banks's

> *By U.S. standards, Kabamba's four-bedroom home, spacious compared to Banks's trailer, is overcrowded with 12 inhabitants.*

trailer, is overcrowded with 12 inhabitants. And though Kabamba's home has a kitchen, it lacks running water, dependable electric service, and air-conditioning—services most Americans take for granted. Considered wealthy in his own country, Kabamba is worse off than a poor person in the United States.

Nevertheless, Banks's poverty is real; he occupies a position close to the bottom of the

pyramid in Figure 9-3. In absolute terms defined by his own society, Kabamba is not poor, even though he is less well off than Enos Banks. Relative to most of the world's population, however, both men are doing well.

Let's Discuss

1. Have you ever lived in or traveled to a foreign country where income and living standards were very different from those in the United States? If so, did the contrast give you a new perspective on poverty? What differences between the living standards in the two societies stand out in your mind?

2. If absolute measures of poverty, such as household income, are inconsistent from one country to the next, what other measures might give a clearer picture of people's relative well-being? Should the poverty level be the same everywhere in the world? Why or why not?

Sources: The Economist 2005f; Harrington 1962; Haub 2006

Who Are the Poor? Not only does the category of the poor defy any simple definition; it counters the common stereotypes {p.3 about "poor people" that Barbara Ehrenreich addressed in her book *Nickel and Dimed* (see the opening excerpt in Chapter 1). For example, many people in the United States believe that the vast majority of the poor are able to work but will not. Yet many poor adults do work outside the home, although only a small portion of them work full-time throughout the year. In 2005, about 31 percent of all poor adults worked full-time, compared to 66 percent of all adults. Of those poor adults who do not work, most are ill or disabled, or are occupied in maintaining a home (DeNavas-Walt et al. 2006:14).

Though many of the poor live in urban slums, a majority live outside those poverty-stricken areas. Poverty is no stranger in rural areas, from Appalachia to hard-hit farming regions to Native American reservations. Table 9-3 provides additional statistical information regarding low-income people in the United States.

Since World War II, an increasing proportion of the poor people of the United States have been women, many of whom are divorced or never-married mothers. In 1959, female house-

holders accounted for 26 percent of the nation's poor; by 2005, that figure had risen to 58 percent (see Table 9-3). This alarming trend, known as the *feminization of poverty*, is evident not just in the United States but around the world.

About half of all women living in poverty in the United States are in transition, coping with an economic crisis caused by the departure, disability, or death of a husband. The other half tend to be economically dependent either on the welfare system or on friends and relatives living nearby. A major factor in the feminization of poverty has been the increase in families with women as single heads of the household (see Chapter 14). In 2005, 28.7 percent of households headed by single mothers lived in poverty, compared to 12.6 percent of married couples in the United States. Conflict theorists and other observers trace the higher {pp.102–104 rates of poverty among women to three distinct factors: the difficulty in finding affordable child care, sexual harassment, and sex discrimination in the labor market.

In 2005, 43 percent of poor people in the United States were living in central cities. These highly visible urban residents are the focus of most government efforts to alleviate poverty. Yet according to many observers, the plight of the urban poor is grow-

Table 9-3

Who Are the Poor in the United States?

Group	Percentage of the Population of the United States	Percentage of the Poor of the United States
Under 18 years old	26%	35%
18 to 64 years old	61	55
65 years and older	13	10
Whites (non-Hispanic)	83	44
Blacks	12	25
Hispanics	11	25
Asians and Pacific Islanders	4	4
Married couples and families with male householders	82	47
Families with female householders	18	53

Note: Data are for 2005, as reported by the Bureau of the Census in 2006.
Source: DeNavas-Walt et al. 2006.

ing worse, owing to the devastating interplay of inadequate education and limited employment prospects. Traditional employment opportunities in the industrial sector are largely closed to the unskilled poor. Past and present discrimination heightens these problems for those low-income urban residents who are Black and Hispanic (DeNavas-Walt et al. 2006:14).

Along with other social scientists, sociologist William Julius Wilson (1980, 1987, 1996) and his colleagues (2004) have used the term *underclass* to describe the long-term poor who lack

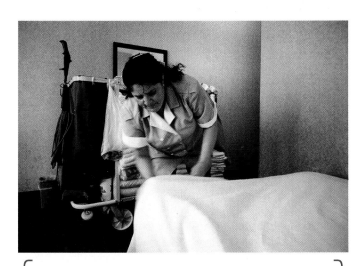

A hotel housekeeper hurries to make the bed and move on to the next room to be cleaned. At low wage rates, even full-time workers have difficulty staying out of poverty, especially if they have families.

training and skills. According to an analysis of Census 2000 data, 7.9 million people live in high-poverty neighborhoods. About 30 percent of the population in these neighborhoods is Black, 29 percent Hispanic, and 24 percent White. In central cities, about 49 percent of the underclass is African American, 29 percent Hispanic, 17 percent White, and 5 percent "other" (Jargowsky and Yang 2006; O'Hare and Curry-White 1992; Young Jr. 2007).

Conflict theorists, among others, have expressed alarm at the portion of the nation's population living on this lower rung of the stratification ladder, and at society's reluctance to address the lack of economic opportunities for these people. Often, portraits of the underclass seem to blame the victims for their own plight, while ignoring other factors that push people into poverty.

Analyses of the poor in general reveal that they are not a static social class. The overall composition of the poor changes continually, because some individuals and families near the top edge of poverty move above the poverty level after a year or two, while others slip below it. Still, hundreds of thousands of people remain in poverty for many years at a time. African Americans and Latinos are more likely than Whites to be persistently poor. Over a 21-year period, 15 percent of African Americans and 10 percent of Latinos were persistently poor, compared to only 3 percent of Whites. Both Latinos and Blacks are less likely than Whites to leave the welfare rolls as a result of welfare reform, discussed in the Social Policy section of this chapter (Mangum et al. 2003).

Explaining Poverty Why is it that poverty pervades a nation of such vast wealth? Sociologist Herbert Gans (1995), who has applied functionalist analysis to the existence of poverty, argues that various segments of society actually *benefit* from the existence of the poor. Gans has identified a number of social, economic, and political functions that the poor perform for society:

- The presence of poor people means that society's dirty work—physically dirty or dangerous, dead-end and underpaid, undignified and menial jobs—will be performed at low cost.

- Poverty creates jobs for occupations and professions that serve the poor. It creates both legal employment (public health experts, welfare caseworkers) and illegal jobs (drug dealers, numbers runners).

- The identification and punishment of the poor as deviants {p.191 upholds the legitimacy of conventional social norms and mainstream values regarding hard work, thrift, and honesty.

- Within a relatively hierarchical society, the existence of poor people guarantees the higher status of the more affluent. As psychologist William Ryan (1976) has noted, affluent people may justify inequality (and gain a measure of satisfaction) by blaming the victims of poverty for their disadvantaged condition.

- Because of their lack of political power, the poor often absorb the costs of social change. Under the policy of deinstitutionalization, mental patients released from long-term hospitals have been transferred primarily to low-income communities and neighborhoods. Similarly, halfway houses for rehabilitated drug abusers, rejected by more affluent communities, often end up in poorer neighborhoods.

In Gans's view, then, poverty and the poor actually satisfy positive functions for many nonpoor groups in the United States.

Life Chances

Max Weber saw class as being closely related to people's **life chances**—that is, their opportunities to provide themselves with material goods, positive living conditions, and favorable life experiences (Gerth and Mills 1958). Life chances are reflected in measures such as housing, education, and health. Occupying a higher position in a society improves your life chances and brings greater access to social rewards. In contrast, people in the lower social classes are forced to devote a larger proportion of their limited resources to the necessities of life.

In times of danger, the affluent and powerful have a better chance of surviving than people of ordinary means. When the supposedly unsinkable British oceanliner *Titanic* hit an iceberg in 1912, it was not carrying enough lifeboats to accommodate all passengers. Plans had been made to evacuate only first- and second-class passengers. About 62 percent of the first-class passengers survived the disaster. Despite a rule that women and children would go first, about a third of those passengers were male. In contrast, only 25 percent of the passengers in third class survived. The first attempt to alert them to the need to abandon ship came well after other passengers had been notified (D. Butler 1998; Crouse 1999; Riding 1998).

Class position also affects people's vulnerability to natural disasters. When Hurricane Katrina hit the Gulf Coast of the United States in 2005, affluent and poor people alike became its victims. However, poor people who did not own automobiles (100,000 of them in New Orleans alone) were less able than others to evacuate in advance of the storm. Those who survived its fury had no nest egg to draw on, and thus were more likely than others to accept relocation wherever social service agencies could place them—sometimes hundreds or thousands of miles from home (Department of Homeland Security 2006).

Some people have hoped that the Internet revolution would help to level the playing field by making information and markets uniformly available. Unfortunately, however, not everyone can get onto the information superhighway, so yet another aspect of social inequality has emerged—the *digital divide*. The poor, minorities, and those who live in rural communities and inner cities are not getting connected at home or at work. A recent government study found that despite falling computer prices, the Internet gap between the haves and have-nots has not narrowed. For

レオナルド・ディカプリオ　　ケイト・ウィンスレット

運命の恋。
誰もそれを裂くことはできない。

タイタニック

「T2」「エイリアン2」のジェームズ・キャメロン監督作品

TITANIC

In the movie *Titanic,* the romantic fantasy of a love affair that crossed class lines obscured the real and deadly effects of the social class divide. This poster appeared in Japan.

example, while 70 percent of all people in the United States used the Internet in 2006, that group included 93 percent of people with incomes over $75,000 but fewer than 49 percent of people with incomes less than $30,000. As wealthier people switch to high-speed Internet connections, they will be able to take advantage of even more sophisticated interactive services, and the digital divide will grow even wider (Pew Internet Project 2007).

Wealth, status, and power may not ensure happiness, but they certainly provide additional ways of coping with problems and disappointments. For this reason, the opportunity for advancement—for social mobility—is of special significance to those on the bottom of society. These people want the rewards and privileges that are granted to high-ranking members of a culture. What can society do to increase their social mobility? One strategy is to offer financial aid to college students from low-income families, on the theory that education lifts people out of poverty. Yet such programs are not having as great an effect as their authors once hoped (see Box 9-3).

9-3 Social Class and Financial Aid

Today's young people have been dubbed Generation Y, but a more appropriate name for them could be Generation Debt. Every year, millions of prospective college students and their parents struggle through the intricate and time-consuming process of applying for financial aid. Originally, financial aid programs were intended to level the playing field—to allow qualified students from all walks of life to attend college, regardless of the cost. But have these programs fulfilled their promise?

In 2004, 40 percent of first-year students at major state universities came from families with incomes of more than $100,000 a year. In other words, close to half of all students came from high-income families. This statistic should not be surprising, given the high cost of tuition, room, and board at state universities. For students from families with the lowest incomes,

> *Statistics that show the educational level in the United States rising overall obscure the widening gap between the advantaged and the less advantaged.*

the cost can be prohibitive. At any school, students from households with incomes of $75,000 and over are three times as likely to graduate as students from households with incomes under $25,000. Those moderate-income students who do graduate, and even those who fail to complete their degrees, are often saddled with heavy postgraduate debt. As of 2006, the average college graduate owed a total of $19,000 in student financial aid.

Besides the spiraling cost of an education, the widespread difficulty in paying for college stems from three trends. First, over the past few decades, colleges and universities have been moving away from making outright grants, such as scholarships, to deserving students, and toward low-interest student loans. Second, much of the assistance schools offer in the form of loans is not based strictly on

need. Since 1982, non-need-based state aid has grown by 336 percent, while need-based assistance has grown by only 88 percent. Third, interest rates on federally guaranteed loans have risen steadily, increasing the burden of repayment.

These trends in financial aid for higher education are closely tied to trends in social inequality. As noted earlier in this chapter, over the past half century, rather than declining, inequality in income and wealth has actually increased. According to one analysis of U.S. economic trends over the last 30 years, this increase in wealth and income inequality has contributed to a modest increase in educational inequality, as measured by the number of years of formal schooling students achieve. In a variation on the truism that the rich tend to get richer while the poor get poorer, the rich are getting better educations and the poor are getting poorer educations. Statistics that show

the educational level in the United States rising overall obscure the widening gap between the advantaged and the less advantaged.

Let's Discuss

1. Take a poll in your class: How many students are receiving some form of financial aid? How many have a scholarship and how many have a loan?
2. Aside from a reduction in individual social mobility, what might be the long-term effects of the shortage of need-based financial aid? Relate your answer to the trend toward globalization.

Sources: Boushey 2005; Campbell et al. 2005; Kamenetz 2006; Leonhardt 2004; Michals 2003; Trumbull 2006.

Use Your Sociological Imagination

Imagine a society in which there are no social classes—no differences in people's wealth, income, and life chances. What would such a society be like? Would it be stable, or would its social structure change over time?

Social Mobility

In the movie *Maid in Manhattan,* Jennifer Lopez plays the lead in a modern-day Cinderella story, rising from the lowly status of chambermaid in a big-city hotel to become a company supervisor and the girlfriend of a well-to-do politician. The ascent of a person from a poor background to a position of prestige, power, or financial reward is an example of social mobility. Formally defined, the term *social mobility* refers to the movement of individuals or groups from one position in a society's stratification system to another. But how significant—how frequent, how dramatic—is mobility in a class society such as the United States?

Open versus Closed Stratification Systems

Sociologists use the terms *open stratification system* and *closed stratification system* to indicate the degree of social mobility in a society. An **open system** implies that the position of each individual is influenced by his or her *achieved* status. Such a system encourages competition among members of society. The United States is moving toward this ideal type as the government attempts to reduce the barriers faced by women, racial and ethnic minorities, and people born in lower social classes.

At the other extreme of social mobility is the **closed system,** which allows little or no possibility of individual social mobility. The slavery and caste systems of stratification are examples of closed systems. In such societies, social placement is based on *ascribed* statuses, such as race or family background, which cannot be changed.

Types of Social Mobility

An airline pilot who becomes a police officer moves from one social position to another of the same rank. Each occupation has the same prestige ranking: 60 on a scale ranging from a low of 0 to a high of 100 (see Table 9-2 on page 224). Sociologists call this kind of movement **horizontal mobility.** However, if the pilot were to become a lawyer (prestige ranking of 75), he or she would experience **vertical mobility,** the movement of an individual from one social position to another of a different rank. Vertical mobility can also involve moving *downward* in a society's stratification system, as would be the case if the airline pilot became a bank teller (ranking of 43). Pitirim Sorokin ([1927] 1959) was the first sociologist to distinguish between horizontal and vertical mobility. Most sociological analysis, however, focuses on vertical rather than horizontal mobility.

One way of examining vertical social mobility is to contrast its two types, intergenerational and intragenerational mobility. *Intergenerational mobility* involves changes in the social position of children relative to their parents. Thus, a plumber whose father was a physician provides an example of downward intergenerational mobility. A film star whose parents were both factory workers illustrates upward intergenerational mobility.

Intragenerational mobility involves changes in social position within a person's adult life. A woman who enters the paid labor force as a teacher's aide and eventually becomes superintendent of the school district experiences upward intragenerational mobility. A man who becomes a taxicab driver after his accounting firm goes bankrupt undergoes downward intragenerational mobility.

Social Mobility in the United States

The belief in upward mobility is an important value in our society. Does that mean that the United States is indeed the land of opportunity? Not unless such ascriptive characteristics as race, gender, and family background have ceased to be significant in determining one's future prospects. We can see the impact of these factors in the occupational structure.

Occupational Mobility Two sociological studies conducted a decade apart offer insight into the degree of mobility in the nation's occupational structure (Blau and Duncan 1967; Featherman and Hauser 1978). Taken together, these investigations lead to several noteworthy conclusions. First, occupational mobility (both intergenerational and intragenerational) has been common among males. Approximately 60 to 70 percent of sons are employed in higher-ranked occupations than their fathers.

Second, although there is a great deal of mobility in the United States, much of it is minor. That is, people who reach an occupational level above or below that of their parents usually advance or fall back only one or two out of a possible eight occupational levels. Thus, the child of a laborer may become an artisan or a technician, but he or she is less likely to become a manager or professional. The odds against reaching the top are extremely high unless one begins from a relatively privileged position.

The Impact of Education Another conclusion of both studies is that education plays a critical role in social mobility. The impact of formal schooling on adult status is even greater than that of family background (although as we have seen, family background influences the likelihood that one will receive higher education). Furthermore, education represents an important means of intergenerational mobility. Three-fourths of college-educated men in these studies achieved some upward mobility, while only 12 percent of those who received no schooling did (see also J. Davis 1982).

The impact of education on mobility has diminished somewhat in the last decade, however. An undergraduate degree—a B.A. or a B.S.—serves less as a guarantee of upward mobility

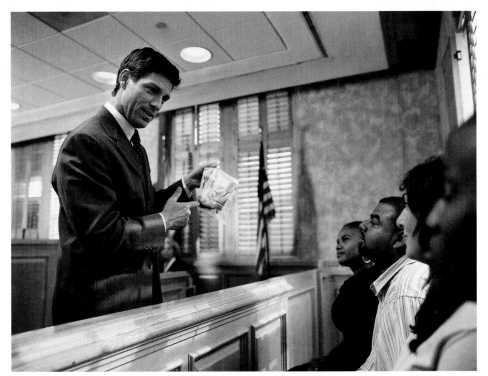

If this lawyer were the son of a car mechanic, his rise to the upper middle class would illustrate intergenerational mobility. If he had begun as a paralegal and worked his way up the occupational ladder, his career would illustrate intragenerational mobility.

(Oliver and Shapiro 1995; Sernau 2001; W. J. Wilson 1996).

The Latino population is not doing much better. The typical Hispanic has less than 10 percent of the wealth that a White person enjoys. A 2004 study suggests that in recent years, Latinos have even lost ground. Their continuing immigration accounts for part of the disparity: most of the new arrivals are destitute. But even the wealthiest 5 percent of Latino households have only a third as much net worth as the top 5 percent of White households (Kochhar 2004).

The Impact of Gender Studies of mobility, even more than those of class, have traditionally ignored the significance of gender, but some research findings are now available that explore the relationship between gender and mobility.

Women's employment opportunities are much more limited than men's (as Chapter 12 will show). Moreover, according to recent research, women whose skills far exceed the jobs offered

now than it did in the past, simply because more and more entrants into the job market hold such a degree. Moreover, intergenerational mobility is declining, since there is no longer such a stark difference between generations. In earlier decades, many high school–educated parents successfully sent their children to college, but today's college students are increasingly likely to have college-educated parents (Hout 1988).

The Impact of Race and Ethnicity Sociologists have long documented the fact that the class system is more rigid for African Americans than it is for members of other racial groups. Black men who have good jobs, for example, are less likely than White men to see their adult children attain the same status. The cumulative disadvantage of discrimination plays a significant role in the disparity between the two groups' experiences. Compared to White households, the relatively modest wealth of African American households means that adult Black children are less likely than adult White children to receive financial support from their parents. Indeed, young Black couples are much more likely than young White couples to be assisting their parents—a sacrifice that hampers their social mobility.

The African American middle class has grown over the last few decades, due to economic expansion and the benefits of the civil rights movement of the 1960s. Yet many of these middle-class households have little savings, a fact that puts them in danger during times of crisis. Studies have consistently shown that downward mobility is significantly higher for Blacks than it is for Whites

them are more likely than men to withdraw entirely from the paid labor force. Their withdrawal violates an assumption common to traditional mobility studies: that most people will aspire to upward mobility and seek to make the most of their opportunities.

In contrast to men, women have a rather large range of clerical occupations open to them. But the modest salary ranges and few

Andrea Jung, chairman and chief executive officer of Avon Corporation since 1999, is one of the few women in the United States who have risen to the top of the corporate hierarchy. Despite the passage of equal opportunity laws, occupational barriers still limit women's social mobility.

prospects for advancement in many of these positions limit the possibility of upward mobility. Self-employment as shopkeepers, entrepreneurs, independent professionals, and the like—an important road to upward mobility for men—is more difficult for women, who find it harder to secure the necessary financing. Although sons commonly follow in the footsteps of their fathers, women are unlikely to move into their fathers' positions. Consequently, gender remains an important factor in shaping social mobility. Women in the United States (and in other parts of the world) are especially likely to be trapped in poverty, unable to rise out of their low-income status (Heilman 2001).

Rethinking Welfare in North America and Europe

The Issue

- In Milwaukee, a single mother of six has just lost her job as a security guard. Once considered a success story of the welfare reform program, she has fallen victim to the economic recession that followed the boom years of the 1990s. Because she has been on welfare before, she is ineligible to receive additional assistance from the state of Wisconsin. Yet like many other workers who made the transition from welfare to work in the late 1990s, she does not qualify for unemployment benefits; food stamps are all she can count on (Pierre 2002).

- In Paris, France, Hélène Desegrais, another single mother, waited four months to place her daughter in government-subsidized day care. Now she can seek a full-time job, but she is concerned about government threats to curtail such services in order to keep taxes down (Simons 1997).

These are the faces of people living on the edge—often women with children seeking to make a go of it amid changing social policies. Governments in all parts of the world are searching for the right solution to welfare: How much subsidy should they provide? How much responsibility should fall on the shoulders of the poor?

The Setting

In the 1990s, an intense debate took place in the United States over the issue of welfare. Welfare programs were costly, and concern was widespread (however unfounded) that welfare payments discouraged recipients from seeking jobs. Both Democrats and Republicans vowed to "end welfare as we know it."

In late 1996, in a historic shift in federal policy, Congress passed the Personal Responsibility and Work Opportunity Reconciliation Act, ending the long-standing federal guarantee of assistance to every poor family that meets eligibility requirements. The law set a lifetime limit of five years of welfare benefits, and required all able-bodied adults to work after receiving two years of benefits (although hardship exceptions were allowed). The federal government would give block grants to the states to use as they wished in assisting poor and needy resi-

dents, and it would permit states to experiment with ways to move people off welfare.

Other countries vary widely in their commitment to social service programs. But most industrialized nations devote higher proportions of their expenditures to housing, social security, welfare, health care, and unemployment compensation than the United States does. Available data indicate that in Great Britain, 82 percent of health expenditures are paid for by the government; in Portugal and Canada, 70 percent; but in the United States, only 45 percent (World Bank 2006a:101–102).

Sociological Insights

Many sociologists tend to view the debate over welfare reform in industrialized nations from a conflict perspective: the "haves" in positions of policymaking listen to the interests of other "haves," while the cries of the "have-nots" are drowned out. Critics of welfare reform believe that the nation's economic problems are unfairly blamed on welfare spending and the poor. From a conflict perspective, this backlash against welfare recipients reflects deep fears and hostility toward the nation's urban, predominantly African American and Hispanic underclass.

Those who are critical of the backlash note that "welfare scapegoating" conveniently ignores the lucrative federal handouts that go to *affluent* individuals and families. For example, while federal housing aid to the poor was cut drastically in the 1980s, tax deductions for mortgage interest and property taxes more than doubled.

Those who take a conflict perspective also urge policymakers and the general public to look closely at **corporate welfare**—the tax breaks, direct payments, and grants that the government makes to corporations—rather than to focus on the comparatively small allowances being given to welfare mothers and their children. Yet any suggestion to curtail such corporate welfare brings a strong response from special-interest groups that are much more powerful than any coalition on behalf of the poor. One example of corporate welfare is the airline bailout bill that was passed in the wake of terrorist attacks on the United States in September 2001. Within 11 days the federal government had approved the bailout, whose pos-

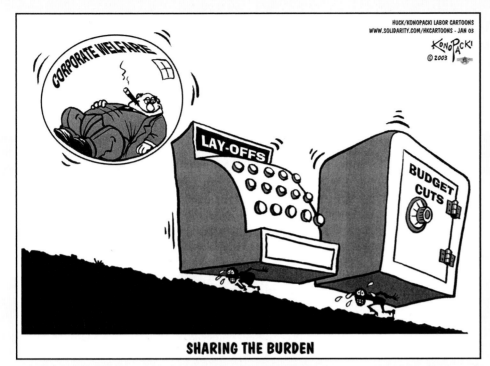

SHARING THE BURDEN

and food stamps has increased by 50 percent since 2000 (Haskins 2006; R. Wolf 2006).

European governments have encountered many of the same citizen demands as in North America: Keep our taxes low, even if it means reducing services to the poor. However, nations in eastern and central Europe have faced a special challenge since the end of communism. Though governments in those nations had traditionally provided an impressive array of social services, they differed from capitalist systems in several important respects. First, the communist system was premised on full employment, so there was no need to provide unemployment insurance; social services focused on the old and the disabled. Second, subsidies for housing and even utilities played an important role. With new competition from the West and tight budgets, some of these countries are beginning to realize that universal coverage is no longer affordable and must be replaced with targeted programs. Even Sweden, despite its long history of social welfare programs, is feeling the pinch. Still, only modest cutbacks have been made in European social service programs, leaving them much more generous than those in the United States (Petrášová 2006).

Both in North America and in Europe, people are beginning to turn to private means to support themselves. For instance, they are investing money for their later years rather than depending on government social security programs. But that solution works only if you have a job and can save money. Increasingly, people are seeing the gap between themselves and the affluent grow, with fewer government programs available to assist them. Solutions are frequently left to the private sector, while government policy initiatives at the national level all but disappear.

itive impact was felt largely by airline executives and shareholders. Relatively low-paid airline employees were still laid off, and hundreds of thousands of low-wage workers in airports, hotels, and related industries received little or no assistance. Efforts to broaden unemployment assistance to help these marginally employed workers failed (Hartman and Miller 2001).

Policy Initiatives

The government likes to highlight welfare reform success stories. Though many people who once depended on tax dollars are now working and paying taxes themselves, it is much too soon to see if "workfare" will be successful. The new jobs that were generated by the booming economy of the late 1990s were an unrealistic test of the system. Prospects for the hard-core jobless—those people who are difficult to train or are encumbered by drug or alcohol abuse, physical disabilities, or child care needs—have faded as the boom passed and the economy moved into recession (Jencks et al. 2006).

True, fewer people remained on the rolls since welfare reform was enacted in August 1996. By June 2006, only 1.8 million families were still on the rolls, down 65 percent from a high of 5.1 million in 1994. But while those families that have left the rolls are modestly better off now, most of their breadwinners continue to hold low-paying, unskilled jobs. Of those adults who remain on welfare, nearly 60 percent are not in school or in welfare-to-work programs, as the law requires them to be. This group tends to face the greatest challenges—substance abuse, mental illness, or a criminal record. Finally, while the welfare rolls have declined, the number of people who receive Medicaid

Let's Discuss

1. Do you personally know anyone who has had to depend on public assistance, such as food stamps, now or in the past? If so, what were the circumstances? Would you yourself need government assistance under such circumstances?

2. Do you think welfare recipients should be required to work? If so, what kind of support should they receive? Should any exceptions be granted to the work requirement?

3. Why do you think western and northern European countries have more generous welfare programs than the United States?

To get involved in the debate over welfare reform, visit this text's Online Learning Center, which offers links to relevant Web sites. Check out the Social Policy section on the Online Learning Center as well; it provides survey data on U.S. public opinion regarding this issue.

www.mhhe.com/schaefer11

{ MASTERING THIS CHAPTER }

Summary

Stratification is the structured ranking of entire groups of people that perpetuates unequal economic rewards and *power* in a society. In this chapter we examined four general systems of stratification, the explanations offered by functionalist and conflict theorists for the existence of *social inequality,* and the relationship between stratification and *social mobility.*

1. Some degree of *social inequality* characterizes all cultures.

2. Systems of social *stratification* include *slavery, castes,* the *estate system,* and social classes.

3. Karl Marx saw that differences in access to the means of production created social, economic, and political inequality, as well as two distinct classes, owners and laborers.

4. Max Weber identified three analytically distinct components of stratification: *class, status group,* and *power.*

5. Functionalists argue that stratification is necessary to motivate people to fill society's important positions. Conflict theorists see stratification as a major source of societal tension and conflict. Interactionists stress the importance of social class in determining a person's lifestyle.

6. One consequence of social class in the United States is that both *wealth* and *income* are distributed unevenly.

7. Many of those who live in poverty are full-time workers who struggle to support their families at minimum-wage jobs. The long-term poor—those who lack the training and skills to lift themselves out of poverty—form an *underclass.*

8. Functionalists find that the poor satisfy positive functions for many of the nonpoor in the United States.

9. One's *life chances*—opportunities for obtaining material goods, positive living conditions, and favorable life experiences—are related to one's social class. Occupying a high social position improves a person's life chances.

10. *Social mobility* is more likely to be found in an *open system* that emphasizes *achieved status* than in a *closed system* that focuses on *ascribed status.* Race, gender, and family background are important factors in social mobility.

11. Today, many governments are struggling with the question of how much tax revenue to spend on welfare programs. The trend in the United States is to put welfare recipients to work.

Critical Thinking Questions

1. Sociologist Daniel Rossides has conceptualized the class system of the United States using a five-class model. According to Rossides, the upper-middle class and the lower-middle class together account for about 40 percent of the nation's population. Yet studies suggest that a higher proportion of respondents identify themselves as middle class. Drawing on the model presented by Rossides, suggest why members of both the upper class and the working class might prefer to identify themselves as middle class.

2. Sociological study of stratification is generally conducted at the macro level and draws most heavily on the functionalist and conflict perspectives. How might sociologists use the *interactionist* perspective to examine social class inequalities in a college community?

3. Imagine you have the opportunity to do research on changing patterns of social mobility in the United States. What specific question would you want to investigate, and how would you go about it?

Key Terms

Absolute poverty A minimum level of subsistence that no family should be expected to live below. (page 226)

Achieved status A social position that a person attains largely through his or her own efforts. (215)

Ascribed status A social position assigned to a person by society without regard for the person's unique talents or characteristics. (215)

Bourgeoisie Karl Marx's term for the capitalist class, comprising the owners of the means of production. (219)

Capitalism An economic system in which the means of production are held largely in private hands and the main incentive for economic activity is the accumulation of profits. (219)

Caste A hereditary rank, usually religiously dictated, that tends to be fixed and immobile. (216)

Class A group of people who have a similar level of wealth and income. (220)

Class consciousness In Karl Marx's view, a subjective awareness held by members of a class regarding their common vested interests and need for collective political action to bring about social change. (220)

Class system A social ranking based primarily on economic position in which achieved characteristics can influence social mobility. (216)

Closed system A social system in which there is little or no possibility of individual social mobility. (232)

Corporate welfare Tax breaks, direct payments, and grants that the government makes to corporations. (234)

Dominant ideology A set of cultural beliefs and practices that helps to maintain powerful social, economic, and political interests. (222)

Estate system A system of stratification under which peasants were required to work land leased to them by nobles in exchange for military protection and other services. Also known as *feudalism*. (216)

Esteem The reputation that a specific person has earned within an occupation. (223)

False consciousness A term used by Karl Marx to describe an attitude held by members of a class that does not accurately reflect their objective position. (220)

Horizontal mobility The movement of an individual from one social position to another of the same rank. (232)

Income Salaries and wages. (214)

Intergenerational mobility Changes in the social position of children relative to their parents. (232)

Intragenerational mobility Changes in social position within a person's adult life. (232)

Life chances The opportunities people have to provide themselves with material goods, positive living conditions, and favorable life experiences. (230)

Objective method A technique for measuring social class that assigns individuals to classes on the basis of criteria such as occupation, education, income, and place of residence. (223)

Open system A social system in which the position of each individual is influenced by his or her achieved status. (232)

Power The ability to exercise one's will over others. (220)

Prestige The respect and admiration that an occupation holds in a society. (223)

Proletariat Karl Marx's term for the working class in a capitalist society. (219)

Relative poverty A floating standard of deprivation by which people at the bottom of a society, whatever their lifestyles, are judged to be disadvantaged *in comparison with the nation as a whole.* (226)

Slavery A system of enforced servitude in which some people are owned by other people. (215)

Social inequality A condition in which members of society have different amounts of wealth, prestige, or power. (214)

Social mobility Movement of individuals or groups from one position in a society's stratification system to another. (232)

Status group People who have the same prestige or lifestyle, independent of their class positions. (220)

Stratification A structured ranking of entire groups of people that perpetuates unequal economic rewards and power in a society. (214)

Underclass The long-term poor who lack training and skills. (229)

Vertical mobility The movement of an individual from one social position to another of a different rank. (232)

Wealth An inclusive term encompassing all a person's material assets, including land, stocks, and other types of property. (214)

Self-Quiz

Read each question carefully and then select the best answer.

1. Which of the following is the term used to describe a condition in which members of a society have different amounts of wealth, prestige, or power?

   a. stratification
   b. status inconsistency
   c. slavery
   d. social inequality

2. In Karl Marx's view, the destruction of the capitalist system will occur only if the working class first develops

   a. bourgeois consciousness.
   b. false consciousness.
   c. class consciousness.
   d. caste consciousness.

3. Which of the following were viewed by Max Weber as analytically distinct components of stratification?

   a. conformity, deviance, and social control
   b. class, status, and power
   c. class, caste, and age
   d. class, prestige, and esteem

4. Which sociological perspective argues that stratification is universal and that social inequality is necessary so that people will be motivated to fill socially important positions?

   a. the functionalist perspective
   b. the conflict perspective
   c. the interactionist perspective
   d. the labeling perspective

238

5. British sociologist Ralf Dahrendorf views social classes as groups of people who share common interests resulting from their authority relationships. Dahrendorf's ideology aligns best with which theoretical perspective?

   a. the functionalist perspective
   b. the conflict perspective
   c. the interactionist perspective
   d. sociocultural evolution

6. The respect or admiration that an occupation holds in a society is referred to as

   a. status.
   b. esteem.
   c. prestige.
   d. ranking.

7. Approximately how many out of every nine people in the United States live(s) below the poverty line established by the federal government?

   a. one
   b. two
   c. three
   d. four

8. Which sociologist has applied functionalist analysis to the existence of poverty and argues that various segments of society actually benefit from the existence of the poor?

   a. Émile Durkheim
   b. Max Weber
   c. Karl Marx
   d. Herbert Gans

9. The poor, minorities, and those who live in rural communities and inner cities are not as likely to have access to the Internet as other members of the United States. This situation is called

   a. the cybervoid.
   b. electronic redlining.
   c. the digital divide.
   d. none of the above

10. A plumber whose father was a physician is an example of

    a. downward intergenerational mobility.
    b. upward intergenerational mobility.
    c. downward intragenerational mobility.
    d. upward intragenerational mobility.

11. _____ is the most extreme form of legalized social inequality for individuals or groups.

12. In the _____ system of stratification, or feudalism, peasants were required to work land leased to them by nobles in exchange for military protection and other services.

13. Karl Marx viewed _____ differentiation as the crucial determinant of social, economic, and political inequality.

14. _____ _____ is the term Thorstein Veblen used to describe the extravagant spending patterns of those at the top of the class hierarchy.

15. _____ poverty is the minimum level of subsistence that no family should be expected to live below.

16. _____ poverty is a floating standard of deprivation by which people at the bottom of a society, whatever their lifestyles, are judged to be disadvantaged in comparison with the nation as a whole.

17. Sociologist William Julius Wilson and other social scientists have used the term _____ to describe the long-term poor who lack training and skills.

18. Max Weber used the term _____ _____ to refer to people's opportunities to provide themselves with material goods, positive living conditions, and favorable life experiences.

19. An open class system implies that the position of each individual is influenced by the person's _____ status.

20. _____ mobility involves changes in social position within a person's adult life.

Online Learning Center

1. When you visit the student center in the Online Learning Center at **www.mhhe.com/schaefer11,** link to Author's Audio Overview. Listen to Richard Schaefer, the author of your textbook, talk about some sociology students he taught and their prestige rankings of various occupations. These sociology students were all "lifers" in a maximum-security prison.

2. The question of where to draw the poverty line is a controversial one in the United States. The Economic Policy Institute's Web site (**www.epinet.org**) offers some tools that you can use to explore the issue. Using the online calculators, find out what a budget-conscious family in your community needs to get by. Then read more about the poverty line in the issue guides.

3. This chapter describes the digital divide among various groups in American society. The Digital Divide Network (**www.digitaldividenetwork.org**) is an organization that seeks to minimize this emerging dimension of inequality. Explore this Web site to learn more about its efforts.

*Note: Although all the URLs listed were current as of the printing of this book, these sites often change. Please check our Web site (**www.mhhe.com/schaefer11**) for updates, hyperlinks, and exercises related to these sites.*

Reel Society Video Clips

Reel Society video clips, which appear on this book's Web site, can be used to spark discussion about the following topics from this chapter:

- Systems of Stratification
- Stratification by Social Class
- Social Mobility

Hungry?

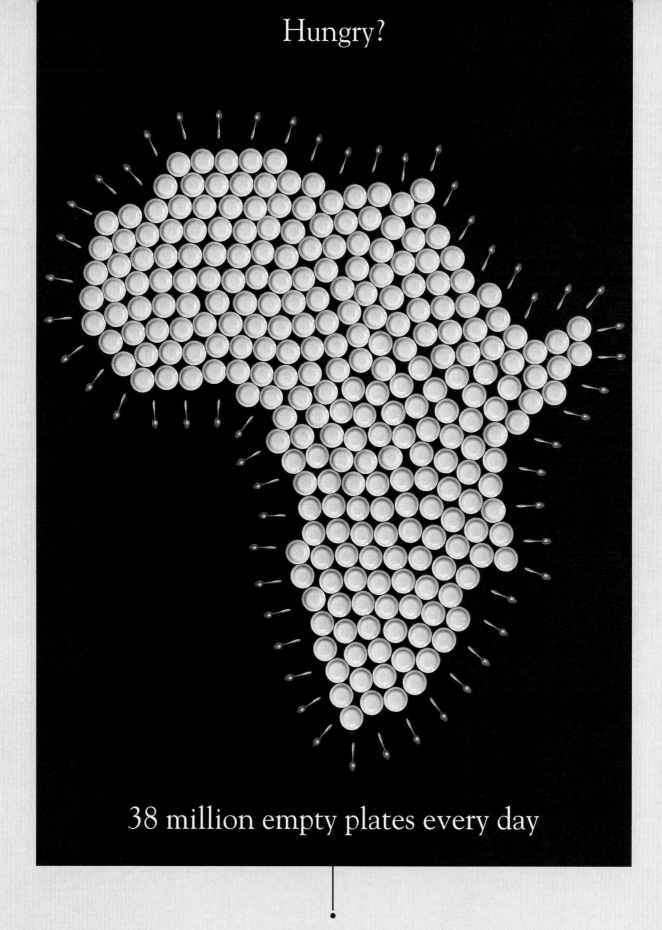

38 million empty plates every day

Though social inequality can be found everywhere in the world, dire poverty is especially
common on the continent of Africa. Twenty-six of the 27 poorest countries in the world are
located in Africa, where the quest for food, as this poster suggests, is a constant one.

10 Global Inequality

" Amit is a member of India's rising middle class. The 22-year-old left his village to study at an urban university and considers himself a connoisseur of Western fashions. He enjoys watching Arnold Schwarzenegger films and National Basketball Association games beamed to India from the United States. The foreign media reaffirm his self-image as a citizen of the world. Yet at the same time Amit complains that the media threaten Indian family arrangements. "I want an arranged marriage," Amit says, "but I fear that Fashion Television, MTV, and [music] channel V are distorting the desires of the younger generation."

India, with a population now in excess of 1 billion, is a massive experiment in "globalization"—the emergence of worldwide markets and communications that increasingly ignore national boundaries. People, jobs, goods, and media move to and from India at unprecedented speed and volume. Global consumer products entice Indians. And Indians, in turn, produce for the global market. Cable and satellite television broadcasts from around the world reach Indian homes and Hollywood has grabbed a significant share of the movie audience (India's huge "Bollywood" film industry notwithstanding). There is a fear that Western images and ideas will undermine traditional Indian culture. . . .

Over the last two decades, more of what people around the world buy and watch is produced elsewhere; more of what they produce is made for a global market; and more local policies are shaped by outside decision makers. In India, a foreign-exchange crisis in 1991 gave the International Monetary Fund leverage to demand the removal of restrictions on foreign investment and trade. With that economic liberalization, once scarce goods rapidly flowed into the Indian market. Taking advantage of cheap, well-trained labor, computer programming jobs appeared. International financiers arrived. Within five years, imports more than doubled, exports more than tripled and foreign capital investment more than quintupled.

> *Amit is a member of India's rising middle class. The 22-year-old left his village to study at an urban university and considers himself a connoisseur of Western fashions.*

Cultural globalization—international media—quickly followed as global advertisers tried to reach the new Indian market and government restrictions eased. In 1991, cable television in India reached 300,000 homes; in 1999, it reached 24 million. In 1991, only a few foreign films showed in the biggest cities, but by 2001 foreign films were dubbed into Hindi and screened throughout the country.

Given new opportunities for employment, consumption, and entertainment, affluent urban Indian men aspired to new goods and experimented with changes in family life. In contrast, studies show that the lives of middle-class Indian men have not been significantly transformed and while the research is less conclusive, the contrast seems to apply to women as well. (Unfortunately, the effects of globalization on poor urban and rural Indians have not been sufficiently studied—although we do know that rural and urban poverty have increased slightly since 1991.) "

(Derné 2003:12–13) Additional information about this excerpt can be found on the Online Learning Center at www.mhhe.com/schaefer11.

In this excerpt from the journal *Contexts,* sociologist Steve Derné describes the effects of globalization on Indian society. Derné conducted observation research in India in 1991 and again in 2001. He found that through Western media, Indians like Amit were being exposed to more and more consumer products, most of which they could not afford to purchase. Indians are considered affluent if their incomes top $2,150 a year; only about 3 percent of the population fits that description. These high-income consumers can afford some foreign goods, as well as an occasional visit to Pizza Hut, where they spend about $6 per person. (In comparison, a full dinner at an Indian restaurant costs about $1.) Even in the United States, most people cannot afford the lifestyle portrayed in movies and on television. But the disconnect between desire and reality is much greater in India and most other countries around the globe (Derné 2003).

At the same time that Western media have been flooding India with images of material wealth, U.S. college students have been questioning the labor conditions in the foreign factories that produce their college-logo-embroidered sweatshirts. Their concerns have given rise to a nationwide coalition called United Students Against Sweatshops, based on college campuses across the country. Because this issue combines women's rights, immigrant rights, environmental concerns, and human rights, it has linked diverse groups on campus. The student movement—ranging from sit-ins and "knit-ins" to demonstrations and building occupation—has been aimed at ridding campus stores of all products made in sweatshops, both at home and abroad. Pressed by their students, many colleges and universities have agreed to adopt antisweatshop codes governing the products they stock on campus. Nike and Reebok, partly in response to student protests, have raised the wages of some 100,000 workers in their Indonesian factories to about 20 cents an hour—still far below what is needed to raise a family (Appelbaum and Dreier 1999; Rivoli 2005).

Together, the apparel industry and the global consumer goods culture focus our attention on worldwide social stratification—on the enormous gap between wealthy nations and poorer nations. In many respects, the wealth of rich nations de-

Students protesting sweatshop labor in developing countries mock Nike with its own slogan: "Just do it."

pends on the poverty of poor nations. People in industrialized societies benefit when they buy consumer goods made by low-wage workers in developing countries. Yet the low wages workers earn in multinational factories are comparatively high for those countries.

What economic and political conditions explain the divide between rich nations and poor? Within developing nations, how are wealth and income distributed, and how much opportunity does the average worker have to move up the social ladder? How do race and gender affect social mobility in these countries? In this chapter we will focus on global inequality, beginning with the global divide. We will consider the impact of colonialism and neocolonialism, of globalization, of the rise of multinational corporations, of grinding poverty, and of the trend toward modernization. Then we will focus on stratification *within* nations, in terms of the distribution of wealth and income as well as social mobility. In a special case study, we will look closely at social stratification in Mexico, including the social impact of race and gender and the economic effects of industrialization. The chapter closes with a Social Policy section on universal human rights.

The Global Divide

In some parts of the world, the people who have dedicated their lives to fighting starvation refer to what they call "coping mechanisms"—ways in which the desperately poor attempt to control their hunger. Eritrean women will strap flat stones to their stomachs to lessen their hunger pangs. In Mozambique, people eat the grasshoppers that have destroyed their crops, calling them "flying shrimp." Though dirt eating is considered a pathological condition (called *pica*) among the well-fed, the world's poor eat dirt to add minerals to their diet. And in many countries, mothers have been known to boil stones in water, to convince their

People's needs and desires differ dramatically depending on where they live. On the left, eager customers line up outside a store in New York City to purchase the newly released version of X-Box 360. On the right, residents of Ethiopia line up to receive water.

hungry children that supper is almost ready. As they hover over the pot, these women hope that their malnourished children will fall asleep (McNeil 2004).

Around the world, inequality is a significant determinant of human behavior, opening doors of opportunity to some and closing them to others. Indeed, disparities in life chances are so extreme that in some places, the poorest of the poor may not be aware of them. Western media images may have circled the globe, but in extremely depressed rural areas, those at the bottom of society are not likely to see them.

A few centuries ago, such vast divides in global wealth did not exist. Except for a very few rulers and landowners, everyone in the world was poor. In much of Europe, life was as difficult as it was in Asia or South America. This was true until the Industrial Revolution and rising agricultural productivity produced explosive economic growth. The resulting rise in living standards was not evenly distributed across the world.

Figure 10-1 compares the industrial nations of the world to the developing nations. Using total population as a yardstick, we see that the developing countries have more than their fair share of rural population, as well as of total births, disease, and childhood deaths. At the same time, the industrial nations of the world, with a much smaller share of total population, have much more income and exports than the developing nations. Industrial nations also spend more on health and the military than other nations, and they emit more carbon dioxide (CO_2) (Sachs 2005a; Sutcliffe 2002).

Stratification in the World System

The divide between industrial and developing nations is sharp, but sociologists recognize a continuum of nations, from the richest of the rich to the poorest of the poor. For example, in

FIGURE 10–1

Fundamental Global Inequality

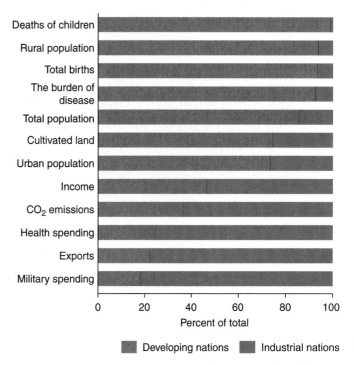

Percent of total

■ Developing nations   ■ Industrial nations

Note: In this comparison, industrial nations include the United States and Canada, Japan, Western Europe, and Australasia. Developing nations include Africa, Asia (except for Japan), Latin America, Eastern Europe, the Caribbean, and the Pacific.
Source: Adapted from Sutcliffe 2002:18.

Think About It
What is the relationship between health spending, disease, and deaths of children? Between CO_2 emissions, income, and exports?

FIGURE 10-2

Gross National Income per Capita

MAPPING LIFE WORLDWIDE

www.mhhe.com/schaefer11

Key:
GNI per capita in 2005

- $3,000 and below
- $8,000–$19,100
- $3,100–$7,995
- Over $19,200
- No available data

Note: Size based on 2000 population estimates.
Sources: Haub 2006; Weeks 2002:22–23, 2005:32–33.

This stylized map reflects the relative population sizes of the world's nations. The color for each country shows the 2005 estimated gross national income (the total value of goods and services produced by the nation in a given year) per capita. As the map shows, some of the world's most populous countries—such as Nigeria, Bangladesh, and Pakistan—are among the nations with the lowest standard of living, as measured by per capita gross national income.

"Though it may sound like a cliché, I have always known that my goal in life is to change the world," says Bari Katz. Since ninth grade this sociology major has known that her mission is to end injustice and cycles of oppression, both at home and abroad.

Katz began working for human rights while studying for her B.A. and M.A. at New York University. While there she joined with the Human Rights Initiative at New York's Urban Justice Center to tackle issues such as immigration, hate crimes, and housing for the homeless. In her final year at NYU, eager to involve other students in the hands-on advocacy work she had been doing, she founded an internship program in human rights. Today, thanks to Katz's efforts, NYU students can work for human rights in New York City and South Africa.

Katz is currently program director at the National Conference for Community and Justice, where she develops, implements, and evaluates programs to promote respect and understanding among all races, religions, and cultures. Her long-range goal is to educate people about social justice issues, teach them to manage conflict, and inspire them to become advocates for positive social change. For Katz, every week brings new challenges and opportunities. She trains personnel at other organizations, develops youth programs, and researches and writes on issues that affect her community. "I have the amazing opportunity to be creative, independent, and influential in affecting real change," she says.

As a student, Katz found sociology to be extremely relevant to her interest in human rights. In her sophomore year she took a class on social movements, which climaxed with class attendance at an antiwar protest. "This was the first time I realized that sociology wasn't just about theories and research—it is a discipline that applies this knowledge to social problems and real-world events," she says. Katz also took a class called Public Sociology, which emphasized the importance of connecting sociology to the larger world. As part of the course, she joined the editorial board of *Contexts*, a sociological journal aimed at bridging the gap between the academic and practical sides of the discipline.

Looking back on her education, Katz says it has been invaluable to her. Sociology gave her both analytical skills and a broad understanding of systems and societies. "My training has taught me to look at the root causes of a problem, which is a principle I use every day in designing curriculum and programs," she says.

Let's Discuss

1. Katz found that sociology supported her interest in human rights, allowing her to make it her life's work. How can sociology help you to develop your interests?
2. What human rights issues are you aware of in your own community? What could you do to support human rights?

2006, the average value of goods and services produced per citizen (or per capita gross national income) in the industrialized countries of the United States, Japan, Switzerland, Belgium, and Norway was more than $31,000. In at least 10 poorer countries, the value was just $900 or less. But most countries fell somewhere between those extremes, as Figure 10-2 shows.

Still, the contrasts are stark. Three forces discussed here are particularly responsible for the domination of the world marketplace by a few nations: the legacy of colonialism, the advent of multinational corporations, and modernization.

The Legacy of Colonialism

Colonialism occurs when a foreign power maintains political, social, economic, and cultural domination over a people for an extended period. In simple terms, it is rule by outsiders. The long reign of the British Empire over much of North America, parts of Africa, and India is an example of colonial domination. The same can be said of French rule over Algeria, Tunisia, and other parts of North Africa. Relations between the colonial nation and colonized people are similar to those between the dominant capitalist class and the proletariat, as described by Karl Marx.

By the 1980s, colonialism had largely disappeared. Most of the nations that were colonies before World War I had achieved political independence and established their own governments. However, for many of these countries, the transition to genuine self-rule was not yet complete. Colonial domination had established patterns of economic exploitation that continued even after nationhood was achieved—in part because former colonies were unable to develop their own industry and technology. Their dependence on more industrialized nations, including their former colonial masters, for managerial and technical expertise, investment capital, and manufactured goods kept former colonies in a subservient position. Such continuing dependence and foreign domination are referred to as *neocolonialism.*

The economic and political consequences of colonialism and neocolonialism are readily apparent. Drawing on the conflict perspective, sociologist Immanuel Wallerstein (1974, 1979a, 2000) views the global economic system as being divided between nations that control wealth and nations from which resources are taken. Through his *world systems analysis,* Wallerstein has described the unequal economic and political relationships in which certain industrialized nations (among them the United States, Japan, and Germany) and their global corporations dominate the *core* of this system (see Figure 10-3). At the *semiperiphery* of the system are countries with marginal economic status, such as Israel, Ireland, and South Korea. Wallerstein suggests that the poor developing countries of Asia, Africa, and Latin America are on the *periphery* of the world economic system. The key to Wallerstein's analysis is the exploitative relationship of *core* nations toward noncore nations. Core nations and their corporations control and exploit noncore nations' economies. Unlike other nations, they are relatively independent of outside control (Chase-Dunn and Grimes 1995).

The division between core and periphery nations is significant and remarkably stable. A study by the International Monetary Fund (2000) found little change over the course of the *last 100 years* for the 42 economies that were studied. The only changes were Japan's movement up into the group of core nations and China's movement down toward the margins of the semiperiphery nations. Yet Immanuel Wallerstein (2000) speculates that the world system as we currently understand it may soon undergo unpredictable changes. The world is becoming increasingly urbanized, a trend that is gradually eliminating the large pools of low-cost workers in rural areas. In the future, core nations will have to find other ways to reduce their labor costs. The exhaustion of land and water resources through clearcutting and pollution is also driving up the costs of production.

Wallerstein's world systems analysis is the most widely used version of **dependency theory.** According to this theory, even as developing countries make economic advances, they remain

weak and subservient to core nations and corporations in an increasingly intertwined global economy. This interdependency allows industrialized nations to continue to exploit developing countries for their own gain. In a sense, dependency theory applies the conflict perspective on a global scale.

In the view of world systems analysis and dependency theory, a growing share of the human and natural resources of developing countries is being redistributed to the core industrialized nations. This redistribution happens in part because developing countries owe huge sums of money to industrialized nations as a result of foreign aid, loans, and trade deficits. The global debt crisis has intensified the Third World dependency begun under colonialism, neocolonialism, and multinational investment. International financial institutions are pressuring indebted countries to take severe measures to meet their interest payments. The result is that developing nations may be forced to devalue their currencies, freeze workers' wages, increase privatization of industry, and reduce government services and employment.

Closely related to these problems is **globalization,** the worldwide integration of government policies, cultures, social movements, and financial markets through trade and the exchange of ideas. Because world financial markets transcend governance by conventional nation-states, international organizations such as the World Bank and the International Monetary Fund have emerged as major players in the global economy. The function of these institutions, which are heavily funded and influenced by core nations, is to encourage economic trade and development and to ensure the smooth operation of international financial markets. As such, they are seen as promoters of globalization and defenders primarily of the interests of core nations. Critics call attention to a variety of issues, including violations of workers' rights, the destruction of the environment, the loss of cultural identity, and discrimination against minority groups in periphery nations.

Some observers see globalization and its effects as the natural result of advances in communications technology, particularly the Internet and satellite transmission of the mass media. Others view it more critically, as a process that allows multinational corporations to expand unchecked, as we will see in the next section (Chase-Dunn et al. 2000; Feketekuty 2001; L. Feuer 1989; Pearlstein 2001).

{p.22}

FIGURE 10–3

World Systems Analysis at the Beginning of the 21st Century

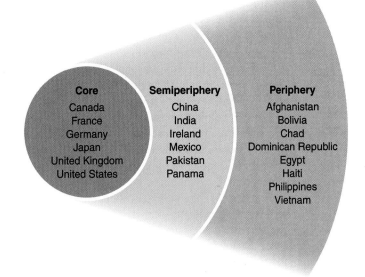

Core	Semiperiphery	Periphery
Canada	China	Afghanistan
France	India	Bolivia
Germany	Ireland	Chad
Japan	Mexico	Dominican Republic
United Kingdom	Pakistan	Egypt
United States	Panama	Haiti
		Philippines
		Vietnam

Note: Figure shows only a partial listing of countries.

Use Your Sociological Imagination

You are traveling through a developing country. What evidence do you see of neocolonialism and globalization?

Multinational Corporations

Worldwide, corporate giants play a key role in neocolonialism. The term **multinational corporations** refers to commercial or-

cent of the nation's annual growth (U.S. **247**
Trade Representative 2007).

Global Inequality

Ever since violent street demonstrations rocked Seattle in 1999, the annual meetings of the World Trade Organization (WTO) have been accompanied by protests. Dissenters charge that multinational corporations dominate world trade policy at the expense of developing nations, and that industrial nations should be held accountable for the economic and financial problems they create.

ganizations that are headquartered in one country but do business throughout the world. Such private trade and lending relationships are not new; merchants have conducted business abroad for hundreds of years, trading gems, spices, garments, and other goods. However, today's multinational giants are not merely buying and selling overseas; they are also *producing* goods all over the world (I. Wallerstein 1974).

Moreover, today's "global factories" (factories throughout the developing world that are run by multinational corporations) may now have the "global office" alongside them. Multinationals based in core countries are beginning to establish reservation services and centers for processing data and insurance claims in the periphery nations. As service industries become a more important part of the international marketplace, many companies are concluding that the low costs of overseas operations more than offset the expense of transmitting information around the world.

Do not underestimate the size of these global corporations. As Table 10-1 (page 248) shows, the total revenues of multinational businesses are on a par with the total value of goods and services exchanged in *entire nations*. Foreign sales represent an important source of profit for multinational corporations, which are constantly seeking to expand into other countries (in many cases, developing nations). The economy of the United States is heavily dependent on foreign commerce, much of which is conducted by multinationals. Over 10 percent of all goods and services produced in the United States relates to the export of goods to foreign countries, and accounts for 20 per-

Functionalist View Functionalists believe that multinational corporations can actually help the developing nations of the world. They bring jobs and industry to areas where subsistence agriculture once served as the only means of survival. Multinationals also promote rapid development through the diffusion of inventions and innovations from industrial nations. Viewed from a functionalist perspective, the combination of skilled technology and management provided by multinationals and the relatively cheap labor available in developing nations is ideal for a global enterprise. Multinationals can take maximum advantage of technology while reducing costs and boosting profits.

Through their international ties, multinational corporations also make the nations of the world more interdependent. These ties may prevent certain disputes from reaching the point of serious conflict. A country cannot afford to sever diplomatic relations or engage in warfare with a nation that is the headquarters for its main business suppliers or a key outlet for its exports.

Conflict View Conflict theorists challenge this favorable evaluation of the impact of multinational corporations. They emphasize that multinationals exploit local workers to maximize profits. Starbucks—the international coffee retailer based in Seattle—gets some of its coffee from farms in Guatemala. But to earn enough money to buy a pound of Starbucks coffee, a Guatemalan farmworker would have to pick 500 pounds of beans, representing five days of work (Entine and Nichols 1996).

The pool of cheap labor in the developing world prompts multinationals to move factories out of core countries. An added bonus for the multinationals is that the developing world discourages strong trade unions. In industrialized countries, organized labor insists on decent wages and humane working conditions, but governments seeking to attract or keep multinationals may develop a "climate for investment" that includes repressive antilabor laws that restrict union activity and collective bargaining. If labor's demands become too threatening, the multinational firm will simply move its plant elsewhere, leaving a trail of unemployment behind. Nike, for example, moved its factories from the United States to Korea to Indonesia to Vietnam in search of the lowest labor costs. Conflict theorists conclude that on the whole, multinational corporations have a negative social impact on workers in *both* industrialized and developing nations.

Chapter 10

Multinational Corporations Compared to Nations

Rank	Corporation	Revenues ($ millions)	Comparison Nation(s)	Gross Domestic Product ($ millions)
1.	Wal-Mart (USA)	$351,139	Sweden	$369,100
2.	Exxon Mobil (USA)	347,254	Turkey	342,000
3.	Royal Dutch/Shell (Britain/Netherlands)	318,845	Austria	306,200
4.	BP British Petroleum (Britain)	274,316	Poland	273,100
5.	General Motors (USA)	207,349	Columbia and Hungary	206,100
6.	Toyota Motor (Japan)	204,746	Pakistan and Chile	203,000
7.	Chevron (USA)	200,567	Finland	196,900
8.	DaimlerChrysler (Germany)	190,191	Portugal	181,300
9.	ConocoPhillips (USA)	172,451	Argentina	173,100
10.	Total (France)	168,357	Ireland	171,100

Notes: Total is an oil, petroleum, and chemical company. Where two nations are listed, the country with the larger GNI is listed first. Revenues are tabulated by *Fortune* for 2006. GNI as collected by the World Bank are for 2005.
Sources: For corporate data, *Fortune* 2007; for GNI data, World Bank 2007a:14–16.

Think About It
What happens to society when corporations grow richer than countries and spill across international borders?

Workers in the United States and other core countries are beginning to recognize that their own interests are served by helping to organize workers in developing nations. As long as multinationals can exploit cheap labor abroad, they will be in a strong position to reduce wages and benefits in industrialized countries. With this in mind, in the 1990s, labor unions, religious organizations, campus groups, and other activists mounted public campaigns to pressure companies such as Nike, Starbucks, Reebok, Gap, and Wal-Mart to improve wages and working conditions in their overseas operations (Global Alliance for Workers and Communities 2003; Gonzalez 2003).

Several sociologists who have surveyed the effects of foreign investment by multinationals conclude that although it may initially contribute to a host nation's wealth, it eventually increases economic inequality within developing nations. This conclusion holds true for both income and ownership of land. The upper and middle classes benefit most from economic expansion, whereas the lower classes are less likely to benefit. As conflict theorists point out, multinationals invest in limited economic sectors and restricted regions of a nation. Although certain sectors of the host nation's economy expand, such as hotels and expensive restaurants, their very expansion appears to retard growth in agriculture and other economic sectors. Moreover, multinational corporations often buy out or force out local entrepreneurs and companies, thereby increasing economic and cultural dependence (Chase-Dunn and Grimes 1995; Kerbo 2003; I. Wallerstein 1979b).

Worldwide Poverty

In developing countries, any deterioration of the economic well-being of those who are least well off threatens their very survival. As we saw in Chapter 9 (see Box 9-2, page 228), even the wealthy in the developing world are poor by U.S. standards. Those who are poor in developing countries are truly destitute.

What would a map of the world look like if we drew it to a scale that reflects the number of *poor* people in each country instead of the number of people, as in Figure 10-2 (page 244)? As Figure 10-4 (page 250) shows, when we focus on the poverty level rather than the population, the world looks quite different. Note the huge areas of poverty in Africa and Asia, and the comparatively small areas of affluence in industrialized North America and Europe. Poverty is a worldwide problem that blights the lives of billions of people.

In 2000 the United Nations launched the Millennium Project, whose objective is to eliminate extreme poverty worldwide by the year 2015 (see Box 10-1, page 251). While 15 years may seem a long time, the challenge is great. Today, almost 3 billion people subsist on $2 a day or less. To accomplish the project's goal, planners estimate that industrial nations must set aside 0.7 percent of their ***gross national product***—the value of a nation's goods and services—for aid to developing nations.

At the time the Millennium Project was launched, only five countries were giving at that target rate: Denmark, Luxembourg,

The influence of multinational corporations abroad can be seen in this street scene from Manila, capital of the Philippines.

States send home to relatives. In 2006, remittances from the United States to developing countries were estimated at $199 billion—twice the total of foreign aid from all countries (*The Economist* 2007a; World Bank 2006b).

Privileged people in industrialized nations tend to assume that the world's poor lack significant assets. Yet again and again, observers from these countries have been startled to discover how far even a small amount of capital can go. Numerous microfinance programs, which involve relatively small grants or loans, have encouraged marginalized people to invest not in livestock, which may die, or jewelry, which may be stolen, but in technological improvements such as small cooking stoves. In Indonesia, for example, some 60,000 microloans have enabled families who once cooked their food in a pit to purchase stoves. Improvements such as this not only enable people to cook more food at a more consistent temperature; they can become the basis of small-scale home businesses (*The Economist* 2005g).

Modernization

Around the world, millions of people are witnessing a revolutionary transformation of their day-to-day life. Contemporary social scientists use the term ***modernization*** to describe the far-reaching process by which periphery nations move from traditional or less developed institutions to those characteristic of more developed societies.

Wendell Bell (1981), whose definition of modernization we are using, notes that modern societies tend to be urban, literate, and industrial. These societies have sophisticated transportation and media systems. Their families tend to be organized within the nuclear family unit rather than the extended-family model (see Chapter 14). Thus, members of societies that undergo modernization must shift their allegiance from traditional sources of authority, such as parents and priests, to newer authorities, such as government officials.

Many sociologists are quick to note that terms such as *modernization* and even *development* contain an ethnocentric bias. The unstated assumption behind these terms is that "they" (people living in developing countries) are struggling to become more like "us" (in the core industrialized nations). Viewed from a conflict perspective, these terms perpetuate the dominant ideology of capitalist societies.

The term *modernization* also suggests positive change. Yet change, if it comes, often comes slowly, and when it does it tends to serve the affluent segments of industrial nations. This truism seems to apply to the spread of the latest electronic technologies to the developing world (see Box 10-2, page 253).

A similar criticism has been made of ***modernization theory,*** a functionalist approach that proposes that modernization and development will gradually improve the lives of people in developing nations. According to this theory, even though countries develop at uneven rates, the development of peripheral countries will be assisted by innovations transferred from the industrialized world. Critics of modernization theory, including dependency theorists, counter that any such technology transfer

the Netherlands, Norway, and Sweden. To match their contribution proportionally, the United States would need to multiply its present aid level by 45. Though in dollar terms the U.S. government delivers far more aid to foreign countries and multinational organizations than any other nation, the amount is not impressive considering the nation's tremendous wealth relative to other countries. In terms of per capita giving, the United States ranks only sixteenth highest of the 22 most advanced industrial countries—far below countries such as Great Britain, France, and Norway, as Figure 10-5 (page 252) shows (Bureau of the Census 2006a:830; Haub 2006; Kerbo 2006; Sachs 2005a; World Bank 2007).

Direct government-to-government foreign aid is only one way of alleviating poverty, however. While per capita aid from the U.S. government may not be strong, private spending by U.S. residents is. Individual charitable giving is much higher in the United States than in other industrial nations. Even more significant are remittances, the money that immigrants to the United

Poverty Worldwide

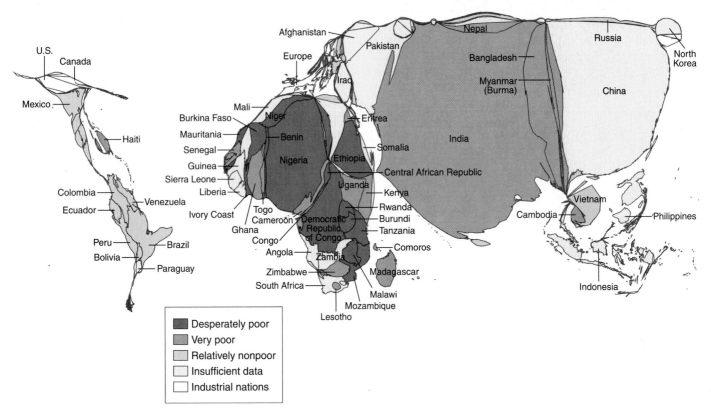

Legend:
- ■ Desperately poor
- ■ Very poor
- ■ Relatively nonpoor
- □ Insufficient data
- □ Industrial nations

Sources: Chronic Poverty Research Center 2005 in Sachs 2005b.

The scale of this map is based on the number of people in each region who are chronically poor. The colors represent the income levels of those who are poorest.

Think About It

To what degree does this map minimize those countries you have studied or might want to visit? To what degree does it emphasize parts of the world about which you know very little?

only increases the dominance of core nations over developing countries and facilitates further exploitation. (Table 10-2, on page 254, summarizes the three major approaches to global inequality.)

When we see all the Coca-Cola and IBM signs going up in developing countries, it is easy to assume that globalization and economic change are effecting cultural change. But that is not always the case, researchers note. Distinctive cultural traditions, such as a particular religious orientation or a nationalistic identity, often persist, and can soften the impact of modernization on a developing nation. Some contemporary sociologists emphasize that both industrialized and developing countries are "modern." Researchers increasingly view modernization as movement along a series of social indicators—among them de-

gree of urbanization, energy use, literacy, political democracy, and use of birth control. Clearly, some of these are subjective indicators; even in industrialized nations, not everyone would agree that wider use of birth control represents an example of progress (Armer and Katsillis 1992; Hedley 1992; Inglehart and Baker 2000).

Current modernization studies generally take a convergence perspective. Using the indicators just noted, researchers focus on how societies are moving closer together, despite traditional differences. From a conflict perspective, the modernization of developing countries often perpetuates their dependence on and continued exploitation by more industrialized nations. Conflict theorists view such continuing dependence on foreign powers as an example of contemporary neocolonialism.

10-1 Cutting Poverty Worldwide

The goal of the United Nations' Millennium Project is to cut the world's poverty level in half by 2015. The project has eight objectives:

1. *Eradicate extreme poverty and hunger.* Poverty rates are falling in many parts of the globe, particularly in Asia. But in sub-Saharan Africa, where the poor are hard pressed, millions more have sunk deeper into poverty. In 2001, more than 1 billion people worldwide were living on less than $1 a day. These people suffer from chronic hunger. As of 2006, an estimated 100 million of the world's children were malnourished—a statistic that has negative implications for their countries' economic progress.
2. *Achieve universal primary education.* While many parts of the developing world are approaching universal school enrollment, in sub-Saharan Africa, less than two-thirds of all children are enrolled in primary school.
3. *Promote gender equality and empower women.* The gender gap in primary school enrollment that has characterized the developing world for so long is slowly closing. However, women still lack equal representation at the highest levels of government. Worldwide, they hold only about 16 percent of all parliamentary seats. Numerous research studies have shown that advances in women's education and governance are critical to improved health and economic development.
4. *Reduce child mortality.* Death rates among children under age five are dropping, but not nearly fast enough. About 59 of every 1,000 children die in the first year of life in developing nations, compared to just 3 of every 1,000 in developed nations. Sadly, evidence indicates that progress toward reducing child mortality has slowed in recent decades.
5. *Improve maternal health.* Each year more than half a million women die during pregnancy or childbirth. Progress has been made in reducing maternal death rates in some developing regions, but not in countries where the risk of giving birth is highest.
6. *Combat HIV/AIDS, malaria, and other diseases.* AIDS has become the leading cause of premature death in sub-Saharan Africa, where two-thirds of the world's AIDS patients reside. Worldwide, the disease is the fourth most frequent killer. Though new drug treatments can prolong life, there is still no cure for this scourge.

> *In 2001, more than 1 billion people worldwide were living on less than $1 a day.*

Moreover, each year malaria and tuberculosis kill almost as many people as AIDS, severely draining the labor pool in many countries.

7. *Ensure environmental sustainability.* While most countries have publicly committed themselves to the principles of sustainable development (development that can be maintained across generations), sufficient progress has not been made toward reversing the loss of the world's environmental resources through rampant clear-cutting of forests and other forms of environmental destruction. Even so, many developing countries lack the infrastructure needed to support public health. Though access to safe drinking water has increased, half the developing world lacks toilets and other forms of basic sanitation.
8. *Develop a global partnership for development.* The United Nations Millennium Declaration seeks a global social compact in which developing countries pledge to do more to ensure their own development, while developed countries support them through aid, debt relief, and improved trade opportunities. However, despite the much publicized G8 summit (a meeting of the heads of state of the 8 major economies) in Gleneagles, Scotland, in 2005 and the accompanying LIVE 8 global concerts, the developed nations have fallen far short of the targets they set themselves.

Let's Discuss

1. Do you think the Millennium Project's objectives are realistic, given the enormity of the obstacles that must be overcome? Why do you think the project's founders gave themselves only 15 years to accomplish their goal?
2. How are the project's eight objectives related to one another? Could some of the objectives be reached successfully without addressing the others? If you were a government planner with the resources to address just one objective, which would you pick, and why?

Sources: Haub 2006; Katel 2005; Sachs 2005a; United Nations 2005a; Weisbrot et al. 2005; World Bank 2006a.

Foreign Aid per Capita in Eight Countries

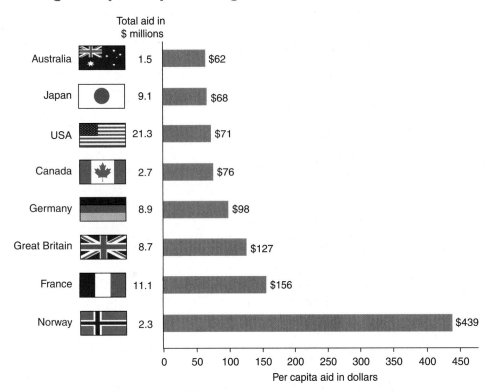

Total aid in
$ millions

Country		Total aid in $ millions	Per capita aid in dollars
Australia		1.5	$62
Japan		9.1	$68
USA		21.3	$71
Canada		2.7	$76
Germany		8.9	$98
Great Britain		8.7	$127
France		11.1	$156
Norway		2.3	$439

0   50   100   150   200   250   300   350   400   450
Per capita aid in dollars

Note: Data for 2004 released by World Bank in 2006.
Source: World Bank 2006a.

Distribution of Wealth and Income

Global inequality is staggering. World-wide, the richest 2 percent of adults own more than half the world's household wealth. In at least 22 nations around the world, the most affluent 10 percent of the population receives at least 40 percent of all income. The list includes the African nation of Namibia (the leader, at 65 percent of all income), as well as Colombia, Mexico, Nigeria, and South Africa. Figure 10-6 (page 255) compares the distribution of income in selected industrialized and developing nations (Shorrocks et al. 2006).

Women in developing countries find life especially difficult. Karuna Chanana Ahmed, an anthropologist from India who has studied women in developing nations, calls women the most exploited of oppressed people. Beginning at birth women face sex discrimination. They are commonly fed less than male children, are denied educational opportunities, and are often hospitalized only when they are critically ill. Inside or outside the home, women's work is devalued. When economies fail, as they did in Asian countries in the late 1990s, women

Use Your Sociological Imagination

When you see a developing country on television or in the movies, does the film or program emphasize the country's progress or its problems?

Stratification within Nations: A Comparative Perspective

At the same time that the gap between rich and poor nations is widening, so too is the gap between rich and poor citizens *within* nations. As discussed earlier, stratification in developing nations is closely related to their relatively weak and dependent position in the global economy. Local elites work hand in hand with multinational corporations and prosper from such alliances. At the same time, the economic system creates and perpetuates the exploitation of industrial and agricultural workers. That's why foreign investment in developing countries tends to increase economic inequality. As Box 10-3 (page 254) makes clear, inequality within a society is also evident in industrialized nations such as Japan (Bornschier et al. 1978; Kerbo 2003).

This UNICEF poster reminds affluent Western consumers that the brand-name jeans they wear may be produced by exploited workers in developing countries. In sweatshops throughout the developing world, nonunion garment workers—some of them still children—labor long hours for what we would consider extremely low wages—even if for the workers in those semiperiphery countries, those wages are relatively high.

sociologyIN *the Global Community*

10-2 The Global Disconnect

Bogdan Ghirda, a Romanian, is paid 50 cents an hour to participate in multiplayer Internet games like City of Heroes and Star Wars. He is sitting in for someone in an industrialized country who does not want to spend days ascending to the highest levels of competition in order to compete with players who are already "well armed." This arrangement is not unusual. U.S.-based services can earn hundreds of dollars for recruiting someone in a less developed country, like Ghirda, to represent a single player in an affluent industrial country.

Meanwhile, villagers in Arumugam, India, are beginning to benefit from their new Knowledge Centre. The facility, funded by a nonprofit organization, contains five computers that offer Internet access—an amenity unknown until now to thousands of villagers.

Networked Readiness Index

Top 10 Countries	Bottom 10 Countries
1. Denmark	113. Cameroon
2. Sweden	114. Paraguay
3. Singapore	115. Mozambique
4. Finland	116. Lesotho
5. Switzerland	117. Zimbabwe
6. Netherlands	118. Bangladesh
7. United States	119. Ethiopia
8. Iceland	120. Angola
9. United Kingdom	121. Burundi
10. Norway	122. Chad

These two situations illustrate the technological disconnect between the developing and industrial nations. Around the world, developing nations lag far behind industrial nations in their use of and access to new technologies. The World Economic Forum's Networked Readiness Index (NRI), a ranking of 122 nations, shows the relative preparedness of individuals, businesses, and governments to benefit from information technologies. As the accompanying table shows, the haves of the world—countries like Singapore, the United

> *For developing nations, the consequences of the global disconnect are far more serious than an inability to surf the Net.*

States, and Denmark—are network ready; the have-nots—countries like Ethiopia, Chad, and Paraguay—are not.

For developing nations, the consequences of the global disconnect are far more serious than an inability to surf the Net. Thanks to the Internet, multinational organizations can now function as a single global unit, responding instantly in real time, 24 hours a day. This new capability has fostered the emergence of what sociologist Manuel Castells calls a "global economy." But if large numbers of people—indeed, entire nations—are disconnected from the new global economy, their economic growth will remain slow and the well-being of their people will remain retarded. Those citizens who are educated and skilled will immigrate to other labor markets, deepening the impoverishment of these nations on the periphery.

Remedying the global disconnect is not a simple matter. To gain access to new technologies, people in developing nations typically must serve the world's industrial giants, as Bogdan Ghirda does. Some may benefit from investment by nongovernmental organizations, as the villagers in India have. But progress to date has been slow. In 2005, in an effort to accelerate the diffusion of new technologies, the United Nations launched the Digital Solidarity Fund. The hope is that global information technology companies can be persuaded to set aside some of their profits to help developing nations connect to the Internet.

Let's Discuss

1. For nations on the periphery, what are some of the social and economic consequences of the global disconnect?
2. What factors might complicate efforts to remedy the global disconnect in developing nations?

Sources: Castells 2000; *The Economist* 2005c; Lim 2007; T. Thompson 2005; United Nations 2005b; World Economic Forum 2007.

---

are the first to be laid off from work (J. Anderson and Moore 1993; Kristof 1998).

Surveys show a significant degree of *female infanticide* (the killing of baby girls) in China and rural areas of India. Only one-third of Pakistan's sexually segregated schools are for women, and one-third of those schools have no buildings. In Kenya and Tanzania, it is illegal for a woman to own a house. In Saudi Arabia, women are prohibited from driving, walking alone in public, and socializing with men outside their families (C. Murphy 1993). We will explore women's second-class status throughout the world more fully in Chapter 12.

Social Mobility

Mobility in Industrial Nations
Studies of intergenerational mobility in industrialized nations have found the following patterns:

1. Substantial similarities exist in the ways that parents' positions in stratification systems are transmitted to their children.

2. As in the United States, mobility opportunities in other nations have been influenced by structural factors, such as labor market changes that lead to the rise or decline of an occupational group within the social hierarchy.

10-3 Stratification in Japan

A tourist visiting Japan may at first experience a bit of culture shock after noticing the degree to which everything in Japanese life is ranked: corporations, universities, even educational programs. These rankings are widely reported and accepted. Moreover, the ratings shape day-to-day social interactions: Japanese find it difficult to sit, talk, or eat together unless the relative rankings of those present have been established, often through the practice of *meishi* (the exchange of business cards).

The apparent preoccupation with ranking and formality suggests an exceptional degree of stratification. Yet researchers have determined that Japan's level of income inequality is among the lowest of major industrial societies (see Figure 10-6). The pay gap between Japan's top corporate executives and the nation's lowest-paid workers is about 8 to 1; the comparable figure for the United States would be 37 to 1.

One factor that works against inequality is that Japan is rather homogeneous—certainly when compared with the United States—in terms of race, ethnicity, nationality, and language. Japan's population is 98 percent Japanese. Still, there is discrimination against the nation's Chinese and Korean minorities, and the *Burakumin,* a low-status subculture, encounter extensive prejudice.

Perhaps the most pervasive form of inequality in Japan today is gender discrimination. Overall, women earn only about 65 percent of men's wages. Only about 9 percent of Japanese managers are female—a ratio that is one of the lowest in the world. Even in

> *Even in developing countries, women are twice as likely to be managers as women in Japan.*

developing countries, women are twice as likely to be managers as women in Japan.

In 1985, Japan's parliament—at the time, 97 percent male—passed an Equal Employment bill that encourages employers to end sex discrimination in hiring, assignment, and promotion policies. However, feminist organizations were dissatisfied because the law lacked strong sanctions. In a landmark ruling issued in late 1996, a Japanese court for the first time held an employer liable for denying promotions due to sex discrimination.

Progress has also been made in terms of public opinion. In 1987, 43 percent of Japanese adults agreed that married women should stay home, but by 2000 the proportion had dropped to 25 percent. On the political front, Japanese women have made progress but remain underrepresented. In a study of women in government around the world, Japan ranked near the bottom of the countries studied, with only 9.4 percent of its national legislators female.

Let's Discuss

1. What factors might contribute to the relatively low level of income inequality in Japan?

2. Describe the types of gender discrimination found in Japan. Why do you think Japanese women occupy such a subordinate social position?

Sources: French 2003a, 2003b; Fujimoto 2004; Goodman and Kashiwagi 2002; Inter-Parliamentary Union 2007; Neary 2003.

summingUP

Table 10-2

Sociological Perspectives on Global Inequality

Approach	Sociological Perspective	Explanation
World systems analysis	Functionalist and conflict	Unequal economic and political relationships maintain sharp divisions between nations.
Dependency theory	Conflict	Industrial nations exploit developing countries through colonialism and multinational corporations.
Modernization theory	Functionalist	Developing countries are moving away from traditional cultures and toward the cultures of industrialized nations.

3. Immigration continues to be a significant factor in shaping a society's level of intergenerational mobility (Ganzeboom et al. 1991; Haller et al. 1990; Hauser and Grusky 1988).

Cross-cultural studies suggest that intergenerational mobility has been increasing in recent decades, at least among men. Dutch sociologists Harry Ganzeboom and Ruud Luijkx, joined by sociologist Donald Treiman of the United States (1989), examined surveys of mobility in 35 industrial and developing nations. They found that almost all the countries studied had witnessed increased intergenerational mobility between the 1950s and 1980s. In particular, they noted a common pattern of movement away from agriculture-based occupations.

Mobility in Developing Nations Mobility patterns in industrialized countries are usually associated with intergenerational and intragenerational mobility. However, in developing nations, macro-level social and economic changes often overshadow micro-level movement from one occupation to another. For example, there is typically a substantial wage differen-

FIGURE 10–6

Gender Differences and Mobility **255**

Global Inequality

Distribution of Income in Nine Nations

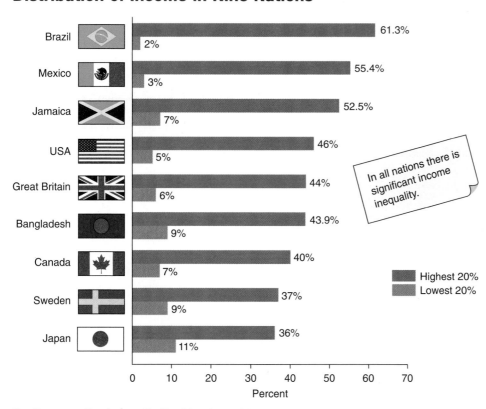

Brazil — 61.3% / 2%
Mexico — 55.4% / 3%
Jamaica — 52.5% / 7%
USA — 46% / 5%
Great Britain — 44% / 6%
Bangladesh — 43.9% / 9%
Canada — 40% / 7%
Sweden — 37% / 9%
Japan — 36% / 11%

In all nations there is significant income inequality.

Highest 20%
Lowest 20%

Percent

Note: Data are considered comparable although based on statistics covering 1993 to 2001.
Source: World Bank 2007:66–68.

tial between rural and urban areas, which leads to high levels of migration to the cities. Yet the urban industrial sectors of developing countries generally cannot provide sufficient employment for all those seeking work.

In large developing nations, the most socially significant mobility is the movement out of poverty. This type of mobility is difficult to measure and confirm, however, because economic trends can differ from one area of a country to another. For instance, China's rapid income growth has been accompanied by a growing disparity in income between urban and rural areas, and among different regions. Similarly, in India during the 1990s, poverty declined in urban areas but may have remained static at best in rural areas. Around the world, social mobility is also dramatically influenced by catastrophes such as crop failure and warfare (World Bank 2000).

Only recently have researchers begun to investigate the impact of gender on the mobility patterns of developing nations. Many aspects of the development process—especially modernization in rural areas and the rural-to-urban migration just described—may result in the modification or abandonment of traditional cultural practices and even marital systems. The effects on women's social standing and mobility are not necessarily positive. As a country develops and modernizes, women's vital role in food production deteriorates, jeopardizing both their autonomy and their material well-being. Moreover, the movement of families to the cities weakens women's ties to relatives who can provide food, financial assistance, and social support.

In the Philippines, however, women have moved to the forefront of the indigenous peoples' struggle to protect their ancestral land from exploitation by outsiders. Having established their right to its rich minerals and forests, members of indigenous groups had begun to feud among themselves over the way in which the land's resources should be developed. Aided by the United Nations Partners in Development Programme, women volunteers established the

In developing countries, people who hope to rise out of poverty often move from the country to the city, where employment prospects are better. The jobs available in industrialized urban areas offer perhaps the best means of upward mobility. This woman works in an electronics factory in Kuala Lumpur, Malaysia.

Pan-Cordillera Women's Network for Peace and Development, a coalition of women's groups dedicated to resolving local disputes. The women mapped boundaries, prepared development plans, and negotiated more than 2,000 peace pacts among community members. They have also run in elections, campaigned against social problems, and organized residents to work together for the common good (United Nations Development Programme 2000:87).

Studies of the distribution of wealth and income within various countries, together with cross-cultural research on mobility, consistently reveal stratification based on class, gender, and other factors within a wide range of societies. Clearly, a worldwide view of stratification must include not only the sharp contrast between wealthy and impoverished nations but also the layers of hierarchy *within* industrialized societies and developing countries.

Use Your Sociological Imagination

Imagine that the United States borders a country with a much higher standard of living. In this neighboring country, the salaries of workers with a college degree start at $120,000 a year. What is life in the United States like?

www.mhhe.com/schaefer11

CASE*study* (STRATIFICATION IN MEXICO)

In May 2003, on a stretch of highway in southern Arizona, the open doors of an abandoned tractor trailer revealed the dead bodies of 19 Mexicans. The truck had been carrying a group of illegal immigrants across the Sonoran Desert when the people hidden inside began to suffer from the intense desert heat. Their story was not unusual. Each year several hundred illegal immigrants die attempting to traverse the U.S.–Mexican border in the hot, arid corridor that connects the state of Sonora in Mexico to the state of Arizona in the United States.

Why do Mexicans risk their lives crossing the dangerous desert that lies between the two countries? The answer to this question can be found in the income disparity between the two nations—one an industrial giant and the other a partially developed country still recovering from a history of colonialism and neocolonialism. In this section we will look in some detail at the dynamics of stratification in Mexico, a country of 102 million people. Since the early 20th century there has been a close cultural, economic, and political relationship between Mexico and the United States, one in which the United States is the dominant party. According to Immanuel Wallerstein's analysis, the United States is at the core while neighboring Mexico is still on the semiperiphery of the world economic system.

Mexico's Economy

If we compare Mexico's economy to that of the United States, differences in the standard of living and in life chances are quite dramatic, even though Mexico is considered a semiperiphery nation. Gross national income is a commonly used measure of an average resident's well-being. In 2005 the gross national income per person in the United States came to $41,950; in Mexico, it was a mere $10,030. About 87 percent of adults in the United States have a high school education, compared to only 13 percent of those in Mexico. And about 6 of every 1,000 infants in the United States die in the first year of life, compared to

about 21 per 1,000 in Mexico (Bureau of the Census 2005a:872, 2006a:837; Haub 2006).

Although Mexico is unquestionably a poor country, the gap between its richest and poorest citizens is one of the widest in the world (refer back to Figure 10-6, page 255). The World Bank reports that in 2006, 20 percent of Mexico's population survived on just $2 per day. At the same time, the wealthiest 10 percent of Mexico's people accounted for 43 percent of the entire nation's income. According to a *Forbes* magazine portrait of the world's wealthiest individuals, that year Mexico ranked 11th in terms of the number of the world's wealthiest who lived there (Kroll and Fass 2006; World Bank 2006b:291).

Political scientist Jorge Castañeda (1995:71) calls Mexico a "polarized society with enormous gaps between rich and poor, town and country, north and south, white and brown (or *criollos* and *mestizos*)." He adds that the country is also divided along lines of class, race, religion, gender, and age. We will examine stratification within Mexico by focusing on race relations and the plight of Mexican Indians, the status of Mexican women, and emigration to the United States and its impact on the U.S.–Mexican borderlands.

Race Relations in Mexico: The Color Hierarchy

Mexico's indigenous Indians account for an estimated 14 percent of the nation's population. More than 90 percent of them live in houses without sewers, compared with 21 percent of the population as a whole. And whereas just 10 percent of Mexican adults are illiterate, the proportion for Mexican Indians is 44 percent (Boudreaux 2002; *The Economist* 2004b; G. Thompson 2001b).

The subordinate status of Mexico's Indians is but one reflection of the nation's color hierarchy, which links social class to the appearance of racial purity. At the top of this hierarchy are the

A worker cleans the reflecting pool at the opulent Casa del Mar Hotel in San Jose del Cabo, Mexico. Though international tourism is a major industry in Mexico, most Mexicans have not benefited much from it. Mexican workers who are employed in the industry earn low wages, and their jobs are jeopardized by the travel industry's frequent boom and bust cycles.

criollos, the 10 percent of the population who are typically White, well-educated members of the business and intellectual elites, with familial roots in Spain. In the middle is the large, impoverished *mestizo* majority, most of whom have brown skin and a mixed racial lineage as a result of intermarriage. At the bottom of the color hierarchy are the destitute, full-blooded Mexican Indian minority and a small number of Blacks, some descended from 200,000 African slaves brought to Mexico. This color hierarchy is an important part of day-to-day life—enough so that some Mexicans in the cities use hair dyes, skin lighteners, and blue or green contact lenses to appear more White and European. Ironically, however, nearly all Mexicans are considered part Indian because of centuries of intermarriage (Castañeda 1995; DePalma 1995).

Many observers take note of widespread denial of prejudice and discrimination against people of color in Mexico. Schoolchildren are taught that the election of Benito Juárez, a Zapotec Indian, as president of Mexico in the 19th century proves that all Mexicans are equal. Yet there has been a marked growth in the last decade of formal organizations and voluntary associations representing indigenous Indians (DePalma 1995, 1996; Stavenhagen 1994; Utne 2003).

The Status of Women in Mexico

In 1975, Mexico City hosted the first international conference on the status of women, convened by the United Nations. Much of the discussion concerned the situation of women in developing countries; in that regard, the situation is mixed. Women now constitute 44 percent of the labor force—an increase from 31 percent in 1980, but still less than in industrial countries. Unfortunately, Mexican women are even more mired in the lowest-paying jobs than their counterparts in industrial nations. In the political

arena, though they rarely occupy top decision-making positions, women have significantly increased their representation in the national legislature, to 23 percent. Mexico now ranks 39th among 189 nations in this respect—well ahead of Great Britain, the United States, and France (Bureau of the Census 2006a:852; Inter-Parliamentary Union 2007).

Feminist sociologists emphasize that even when Mexican women work outside the home, they often are not recognized as active and productive household members, whereas men are typically viewed as heads of the household. As one consequence, women find it difficult to obtain credit and technical assistance in many parts of the country, and to inherit land in rural areas. Within manufacturing and service industries, women generally receive little training and tend to work in the least-automated and least-skilled jobs—in good part because there is little expectation that women will pursue career advancement, organize for better working conditions, or become active in labor unions (Kopinak 1995; Martelo 1996; see also G. Young 1993).

In recent decades, Mexican women have begun to organize to address an array of economic, political, and health issues. Since women continue to serve as the household managers for their families, even when they work outside the home, they are well aware of the consequences of the inadequate public services in lower-income urban neighborhoods. As far back as 1973, women in Monterrey—the nation's third-largest city—began protesting the continuing disruptions of the city's water supply. After individual complaints to city officials and the water authority proved fruitless, social networks of female activists began to emerge. These activists sent delegations to confront politicians, organized protest rallies, and blocked traffic as a means of getting media attention. Though their efforts brought improvements in Monterrey's water service, the issue of reliable and safe water remains a concern in Mexico and many developing countries (Bennett 1995).

The Borderlands

Growing recognition of the borderlands reflects the increasingly close and complex relationship between Mexico and the United States. The term **borderlands** refers to the area of common culture along the border between these two countries. Legal and illegal emigration from Mexico to the United States, day laborers crossing the border regularly to go to jobs in the United States, the implementation of the North American Free Trade Agreement, and the exchange of media across the border all make the notion of separate Mexican and U.S. cultures obsolete in the borderlands.

The economic position of the borderlands is rather complicated, as we can see in the emergence of *maquiladoras* on the Mexican side (see Figure 10-7, page 258). These are foreign-owned factories established just across the border in Mexico, where the companies that own them do not have to pay taxes or provide insurance and benefits to workers. The *maquiladoras* have attracted manufacturing jobs from other parts of North America to Mexico. As of the beginning of 2006, 1.1 million people were employed in the *maquiladoras,* where the daily

In 2000, a group of masked women demonstrated outside the Mexican Army's barracks in the state of Chiapas, demanding that the soldiers leave. The women were supporters of the Zapatista National Liberation Army, an insurgent group that protests economic injustices and discrimination against the Indian population in Chiapas.

take-home pay for entry-level workers was $4 to $5. Since many of these firms come from the United States and sell their products to Mexico's vast domestic market, their operations deepen the impact of U.S. consumer culture on Mexico's urban and rural areas (Federal Reserve Bank of Dallas 2006; *Migration News* 2005c).

The *maquiladoras* have contributed to Mexico's economic development, but not without some cost. Conflict theorists note that unregulated growth allows owners to exploit workers with jobs that lack security, possibilities for advancement, and decent wages. Moreover, many of the U.S.-owned factories require female job applicants to take a urine test to screen out those who are pregnant—a violation of Mexican law as well as of NAFTA, and the source of numerous cases of sex discrimination.

FIGURE 10–7
The Borderlands

MAPPING LIFE WORLDWIDE   www.mhhe.com/schaefer11

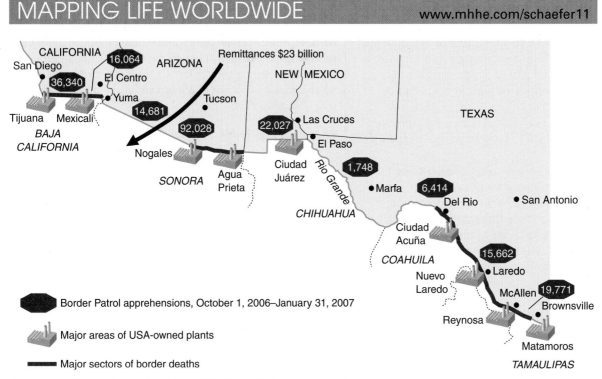

Source: Prepared by the author based on Dickerson 2007; Ellingwood 2001; G. Thompson 2001a.

Think About It
How do U.S. consumers benefit from the buildup of factories along the U.S.–Mexican border?

Social activists also complain that tens of thousands of Mexicans work on *maquiladora* assembly lines for very low wages, raising the issue of sweatshop labor noted earlier in this chapter (Dillon 1998; Dougherty and Holthouse 1999).

Ironically, the *maquiladoras* are now experiencing the same challenge from global trade as U.S. manufacturing plants did. Beginning in 2001, some companies began shifting their operations to China. While Mexican labor costs (wages plus benefits) are just $2 to $2.50 an hour, Chinese labor costs are even lower—50 cents to $1 an hour. Of the 700,000 new *maquiladora* jobs created in NAFTA's first seven years, 43 percent were eliminated between 2000 and 2003 (*Migration News* 2002, 2004).

When people in the United States think about the borderlands, they generally think about immigration, a controversial political issue in the United States—especially near the Mexican border. For its part, Mexico is concerned about the priorities and policies of its powerful northern neighbor. From the Mexican point of view, the United States too often regards Mexico simply as a reserve pool of cheap labor, encouraging Mexicans to cross the border when workers are needed but discouraging and cracking down on them when they are not. Some people, then, see immigration more as a labor market issue than a law enforcement issue. Viewed from the perspective of Immanuel Wallerstein's world systems analysis and dependency theory, it is yet another example of a core industrialized nation exploiting a developing country.

As we saw at the beginning of this case, the risks of immigration are considerable. Following September 11, 2001, when the U.S. government increased surveillance at common entry points along the border, migrants without proper documentation moved to more remote and dangerous locations. In all, about 500 illegal immigrants lose their lives every year while attempting to cross the long border, many of them from dehydration in the intense desert heat (LoMonaco 2006).

The social impact of emigration to the United States is felt throughout Mexico. According to sociological research, the earliest emigrants were typically married men of working age who came from the middle of the stratification system. They had enough financial resources to afford the costs and risks of emigration, yet were experiencing enough financial strain that entering the United States was attractive to them. Over time, kinship ties to migrants multiplied and emigration became less class-selective, with entire families making the trek to the United States. More recently, the occupational backgrounds of Mexican emigrants have widened further, reflecting not only changes in U.S. immigration policy but the continuing crisis in the Mexican economy (Massey 1998).

Many Mexicans who have come to the United States send some part of their earnings back across the border to family members still in Mexico. This substantial flow of money, sometimes referred to as **remittances** or *migradollars,* is estimated at a minimum of $23 billion a year and is surpassed only by oil as a source of income. If these funds went solely into the purchase of consumer goods, they would underscore the view of dependency theory, that Mexico's economy is little more than an extension of the economy of the United States. In fact, however, some of these migradollars are used by Mexicans to establish and maintain small business enterprises, such as handicraft workshops and farms. Consequently, the transfer of migradollars does stimulate the local and national economies of Mexico (Dickerson 2007).

We have seen that inequality is a problem not just in Mexico, but throughout the world. We turn now to an examination of an especially ugly form of social inequality, human rights abuse.

Use Your Sociological Imagination

Imagine a day when the border between the United States and Mexico is completely open. What would the two countries' economies be like? What would their societies be like?

social Policy
and Global Inequality

Universal Human Rights

The Issue

Poised on the third millennium, the world seemed capable of mighty feats, ranging from explorations of distant solar systems to the refinement of tiny genes within human cells. Yet at the same time came constant reminders of how quickly people and their fundamental human rights could be trampled.

Human rights refers to universal moral rights possessed by all people because they are human. The most important elaboration of human rights appears in the Universal Declaration of Human Rights, adopted by the United Nations in 1948. This declaration prohibits slavery, torture, and degrading punishment; grants everyone the right to a nationality and its culture;

affirms freedom of religion and the right to vote; proclaims the right to seek asylum in other countries to escape persecution; and prohibits arbitrary interference with one's privacy and the arbitrary taking of a person's property. It also emphasizes that mothers and children are entitled to special care and assistance.

What steps, if any, can the world community take to ensure the protection of these rights? Is it even possible to agree on what those rights are?

The Setting

At first, the United States opposed a binding obligation to the Universal Declaration of Human Rights. The government feared that the declaration would cause international scrutiny of the nation's civil rights controversies (at a time when racial segregation laws were still common). By the early 1960s, however, the United States had begun to use the declaration to promote democracy abroad (Forsythe 1990).

The 1990s brought the term *ethnic cleansing* into the world's vocabulary. In the former Yugoslavia, Serbs initiated a policy intended to "cleanse" Muslims from parts of Bosnia-Herzegovina, and ethnic Albanians from the province of Kosovo. Hundreds of thousands of people were killed in fighting there, while many others were uprooted from their homes. Moreover, reports surfaced of substantial numbers of rapes of Muslim, Croatian, and Kosovar women by Serbian soldiers. In 1996 a United Nations tribunal indicted eight Bosnian Serb military and police officers for rape, marking the first time that sexual assault was treated as a war crime under international law (Hagan et al. 2006; Power 2002).

Another human rights concern is the transnational crime of trafficking in humans. Each year an estimated 600,000 to 800,000 men, women, and children are transported across international borders for slavery or sexual exploitation. In 2000, Congress passed the Trafficking Victims Protection Act, which established minimum standards for the elimination of human trafficking. The act requires the State Department to monitor other countries' efforts to vigorously investigate, prosecute, and convict individuals who participate in trafficking—including government officials. Each year the department reports its findings, some of which are shown in Table 10-3. Tier 1 and tier 2 countries are thought to be largely in compliance with the act. Tier 2 watch nations are making efforts to comply, though trafficking remains a significant concern. Tier 3 countries are not compliant (Kapstein 2006; Kempadoo and Doezema 1998).

In the wake of the terrorist attacks of September 11, 2001, increased security and surveillance at U.S. airports and border crossings caused some observers to wonder whether human rights were not being jeopardized at home. At the same time,

Table 10-3

Human Trafficking Report

Tier 1 Full Compliance	Tier 2 Significant Effort	Tier 2 Watch Some Effort, but Trafficking Remains a Concern	Tier 3 Noncompliant, No Effort
Australia	Afghanistan	Armenia	Bolivia
Belgium	Algeria	Azerbaijan	Burma
Canada	Brazil	Bahrain	Cambodia
Colombia	Egypt	China	Cuba
Denmark	Iran	Dominican Republic	Ecuador
France	Israel	Greece	Jamaica
Germany	Japan	Haiti	Kuwait
Hong Kong	Libya	India	North Korea
Italy	Nigeria	Mexico	Qatar
Morocco	Oman	Nicaragua	Saudia Arabia
Norway	Romania	Philippines	Sudan
Poland	Turkey	Russia	Togo
South Korea	Vietnam	South Africa	United Arab Emirates
Spain	Yemen	Ukraine	Venezuela

Note: Tier 3 list is complete; others are incomplete.
Source: Department of State 2006b:Section IV.

thousands of noncitizens of Arab and south Asian descent were questioned for no other reason than their ethnic and religious backgrounds. A few were placed in custody, sometimes without access to legal assistance. As the war on terror moved overseas, human rights concerns escalated. In 2005, the United Nations' secretary-general Kofi Annan criticized the United States and Britain for equating people who were resisting the presence of foreign troops in Afghanistan and Iraq with terrorists. For the foreseeable future, it seems, the United States and other countries will walk a delicate tightrope between human rights and the need for security (Parker 2004; Steele 2005).

Sociological Insights

By its very title, the Universal Declaration of Human Rights emphasizes that such rights should be *universal*. Even so, cultural {p.76} relativism encourages understanding and respect for the distinctive norms, values, and customs of each culture. In some situations, conflicts arise between human rights standards and local social practices that rest on alternative views of human dignity. For example, is India's caste system an inherent violation of human rights? What about the many cultures of the world that view the subordinate status of women as an essential element in their traditions? Should human rights be interpreted differently in different parts of the world?

In 1993, the United States rejected such a view by insisting that the Universal Declaration of Human Rights set a single standard for acceptable behavior around the world. However, in the late 1990s, certain Asian and African nations were reviving arguments about cultural relativism in an attempt to block sanctions by the United Nations Human Rights Commission. For example, female genital mutilation, a practice that is common in more than 30 countries around the world, has been condemned in Western nations as a human rights abuse. This controversial practice often involves removal of the clitoris, in the belief that its excision will inhibit a young woman's sex drive, making her chaste and thus more desirable to her future husband. Though some countries have passed laws against the practice, they have gone largely unenforced. Immigrants from countries where genital mutilation is common often insist that their daughters undergo the procedure, to protect them from Western cultural norms that allow premarital sex. In this context, defining human rights becomes a challenge (Religious Tolerance 2005).

It is not often that a nation makes such a bold statement. Policymakers, including those in the United States, more frequently look at human rights issues from an economic perspective. Functionalists would point out how much more quickly we become embroiled in "human rights" concerns when oil is at stake, as in the Middle East, or when military alliances come into play, as in Europe. Governments ratify human rights but resist independent efforts to enforce them within their own borders (Hafner-Burton and Tsutsui 2005).

Because international human rights can be highly contextual, they may also be difficult to enforce within the formal requirements of a country's legal process. Despite the apparent torture exposed in digital camera shots from Iraq and Afghanistan, for example, numerous investigations by the British and U.S. military have been inconclusive. Either because of the tenets of military necessity in wartime or because of an inability to locate the victims, many apparent violations have gone unpunished (Klug 2005).

Policy Initiatives

Human rights issues come wrapped up in international diplomacy. For that reason, many national policymakers hesitate to interfere in human rights issues, especially if they conflict with what are regarded as more pressing national concerns. Stepping up to fill the gap are international organizations such as the United Nations and nongovernmental organizations (NGOs) like Médecins sans Frontières and Amnesty International. Most initiatives come from these international bodies.

Médecins sans Frontières (Doctors without Borders), the world's largest independent emergency medical aid organization, won the 1999 Nobel Peace Prize for its work in countries

A Chechen boy who witnessed his father's killing stands outside a refugee camp in Russia, where he and his brother are receiving mental health care from Doctors Without Borders. Civilian assassinations are one of the many violations of human rights that typically occur during wartime.

worldwide. Founded in 1971 and based in Paris, the organization has 5,000 doctors and nurses working in 80 countries. "Our intention is to highlight current upheavals, to bear witness to foreign tragedies and reflect on the principles of humanitarian aid," explains Dr. Rony Brauman, the organization's president (Spielmann 1992:12; also see Daley 1999).

In recent years, awareness has been growing of lesbian and gay rights as an aspect of universal human rights. In 1994, Amnesty International (1994:2) published a pioneering report in which it acknowledged that "homosexuals in many parts of the world live in constant fear of government persecution." The report examined abuses in Brazil, Greece, Mexico, Iran, the United States, and other countries, including cases of torture, imprisonment, and extrajudicial execution. Later in 1994, the United States issued an order that would allow lesbians and gay men to seek political asylum in the United States if they could prove they had suffered government persecution in their home countries solely because of their sexual orientation (Johnston 1994).

Ethnic cleansing in the former Yugoslavia, human rights violations in Iraq and Afghanistan, increased surveillance in the name of counterterrorism, violence against women inside and outside the family, government torture of lesbians and gay men—all these are vivid reminders that social inequality today can have life-and-death consequences. Universal human rights remain an ideal, not a reality.

Let's Discuss

1. Why do definitions of human rights vary?

2. Are violations of human rights excusable in time of war? In the aftermath of serious terrorist attacks such as those of September 11, 2001? Why or why not?

3. How well or poorly do you think the United States compares to other countries in terms of respect for human rights, both at home and abroad? Has the nation's record improved or declined in recent years?

GettingINVOLVED

To get involved in the debate over universal human rights, visit this text's Online Learning Center, which offers links to relevant Web sites. Check out the Social Policy section in the Online Learning Center as well; it provides survey data on U.S. public opinion regarding this issue.

www.mhhe.com/schaefer11

{ **MASTERING THIS CHAPTER** }

Summary

Worldwide, stratification can be seen both in the gap between rich and poor nations and in the inequality within countries. This chapter examined the global divide and stratification within the world economic system; the impact of *globalization, modernization,* and *multinational corporations* on developing countries; and the distribution of wealth and income in various nations.

1. Developing nations account for most of the world's population and most of its births, but they also bear the burden of most of its poverty, disease, and childhood deaths.

2. Former colonized nations are kept in a subservient position, subject to foreign domination, through the process of *neocolonialism.*

3. Drawing on the conflict perspective, sociologist Immanuel Wallerstein's *world systems analysis* views the global economic system as one divided between nations that control wealth (core nations) and those from which capital is taken (periphery nations).

4. According to *dependency theory,* even as developing countries make economic advances, they remain weak and subservient to core nations and corporations in an increasingly integrated global economy.

5. *Globalization,* or the worldwide integration of government policies, cultures, social movements, and financial markets through trade and the exchange of ideas, is a controversial trend that critics blame for contributing to the cultural domination of periphery nations by core nations.

6. *Multinational corporations* bring jobs and industry to developing nations, but they also tend to exploit workers in order to maximize profits.

7. Poverty is a worldwide problem that blights the lives of billions of people. In 2000 the United Nations launched the Millennium Project, whose goal is to eliminate extreme poverty worldwide by the year 2015.

8. Many sociologists are quick to note that terms such as *modernization* and even *development* contain an ethnocentric bias.

9. According to *modernization theory,* development in periphery countries will be assisted by innovations transferred from the industrialized world.

10. While Mexico is unquestionably a poor country, the gap between its richest and poorest citizens is one of the widest in the world.

11. The subordinate status of Mexico's Indians is but one reflection of the nation's color hierarchy, which links social class to the appearance of racial purity.

12. Growing recognition of the **borderlands** reflects the increasingly close and complex relationship between Mexico and the United States.

13. **Human rights** need to be identified and abuses of those rights corrected in countries throughout the world.

Critical Thinking Questions

1. How have multinational corporations and the trend toward globalization affected you, your family, and your community? List both the pros and the cons. Have the benefits outweighed the drawbacks?

2. Imagine that you have the opportunity to spend a year in Mexico studying inequality in that nation. How would you draw on specific research designs (surveys, observation, experiments, existing sources) to better understand and document stratification in Mexico?

3. How active should the U.S. government be in addressing violations of human rights in other countries? At what point, if any, does concern for human rights turn into ethnocentrism through failure to respect the distinctive norms, values, and customs of another culture?

Key Terms

Borderlands The area of common culture along the border between Mexico and the United States. (page 257)

Colonialism The maintenance of political, social, economic, and cultural dominance over a people by a foreign power for an extended period. (245)

Dependency theory An approach that contends that industrialized nations continue to exploit developing countries for their own gain. (246)

Globalization The worldwide integration of government policies, cultures, social movements, and financial markets through trade and the exchange of ideas. (246)

Gross national product (GNP) The value of a nation's goods and services. (248)

Human rights Universal moral rights possessed by all people because they are human. (259)

Modernization The far-reaching process by which periphery nations move from traditional or less developed institutions to those characteristic of more developed societies. (249)

Modernization theory A functionalist approach that proposes that modernization and development will gradually improve the lives of people in developing nations. (249)

Multinational corporation A commercial organization that is headquartered in one country but does business throughout the world. (246)

Neocolonialism Continuing dependence of former colonies on foreign countries. (245)

Remittances The monies that immigrants return to their families of origin. Also called *migradollars*. (259)

World systems analysis A view of the global economic system as one divided between certain industrialized nations that control wealth and developing countries that are controlled and exploited. (245)

Self-Quiz

Read each question carefully and then select the best answer.

1. The maintenance of political, social, economic, and cultural domination over a people by a foreign power for an extended period of time is referred to as

   a. neocolonialism.
   b. government-imposed stratification.
   c. colonialism.
   d. dependency.

2. In viewing the global economic system as divided between nations who control wealth and those from whom capital is taken, sociologist Immanuel Wallerstein draws on the

   a. functionalist perspective.
   b. conflict perspective.
   c. interactionist perspective.
   d. dramaturgical approach.

3. Which of the following nations would Immanuel Wallerstein classify as a *core* country within the world economic system?

   a. Germany
   b. South Korea
   c. Ireland
   d. Mexico

4. Which sociological perspective argues that multinational corporations can actually help the developing nations of the world?

   a. the interactionist perspective
   b. the feminist perspective
   c. the functionalist perspective
   d. the conflict perspective

5. Which of the following terms is used by contemporary social scientists to describe the far-reaching process by which peripheral nations move from traditional or less-developed institutions to those characteristic of more developed societies?

   a. dependency
   b. globalization
   c. industrialization
   d. modernization

6. In at least 22 nations around the world, the most affluent 10 percent receives at least what percentage of all income?

   a. 20 percent
   b. 30 percent
   c. 40 percent
   d. 50 percent

7. Karuna Chanana Ahmed, an anthropologist from India who has studied developing nations, calls which group the most exploited of oppressed people?

   a. children
   b. women
   c. the elderly
   d. the poor

8. Which of the following terms is used to refer to Mexico's large, impoverished majority, most of whom have brown skin and a mixed racial lineage due to intermarriage?

   a. criollo
   b. indio
   c. mestizo
   d. zapatista

9. In Mexico, women now constitute what percentage of the labor force?

   a. 15 percent
   b. 23 percent
   c. 35 percent
   d. 44 percent

10. Which of the following terms refers to the foreign-owned factories established just across the border in Mexico, where the companies that own them don't have to pay taxes or provide insurance or benefits for their workers?

    a. maquiladoras
    b. hombres
    c. mujeres
    d. toreadors

11. Colonial domination established patterns of economic exploitation leading to former colonies remaining dependent on more industrialized nations. Such continuing dependence and foreign domination are referred to as _____.

12. According to Immanuel Wallerstein's analysis, the United States is at the _____ while neighboring Mexico is on the _____ of the world economic system.

13. Wallerstein's world systems analysis is the most widely used version of _____ theory.

14. _____ factories are factories found throughout the developing world that are run by multinational corporations.

15. As _____ industries become a more important part of the international marketplace, many companies have concluded that the low costs of overseas operations more than offset the expense of transmitting information around the world.

16. Viewed from a(n) _____ perspective, the combination of skilled technology and management provided by multinationals and the relatively cheap labor available in developing nations is ideal for a global enterprise.

17. In 2000 the United Nations launched the _____ _____; its objective is to eliminate extreme poverty worldwide by the year 2015.

18. Modernization theory reflects the _____ perspective.

19. At the top of the color hierarchy in Mexico are the _____, the 10 percent of the population who are typically White, well-educated members of the business and intellectual elites, and who have familial roots in Spain.

20. The term _____ refers to the area of a common culture along the border between Mexico and the United States.

Online Learning Center

1. Test your knowledge of the information in this chapter by visiting the student center in the Online Learning Center at **www.mhhe.com/schaefer11** and taking the multiple-choice quiz. This quiz will not only test your knowledge; it will also give you immediate feedback on the questions that you answered incorrectly.

2. The governments of many industrialized countries—such as the United States—have had a history of subjecting native populations—such as Native Americans—to oppression and mistreatment. The Web site of the Museum Victoria allows you a glimpse into the historical oppression of Aboriginals in Australia. Explore the site at **www.museum.vic.gov.au/encounters.**

3. In this chapter you have begun to learn about the complex relationship between the United States and Mexico, including some information about the 1993 NAFTA agreement. The NAFTA page on the Public Citizen Web site (**www.citizen.org/trade/nafta**) provides a host of additional resources about this trade policy. Browse through the site in order to further your understanding of its wide-ranging financial and human impact.

*Note: Although all the URLs listed were current as of the printing of this book, these sites often change. Please check our Web site **(www.mhhe.com/schaefer11)** for updates, hyperlinks, and exercises related to these sites.*

HAVE YOU EVER SEEN A REAL INDIAN?

AMERICAN INDIAN
COLLEGE FUND
EDUCATION IS STRENGTH

This advertisement for the American Indian College Fund explodes common stereotypes about
Native Americans with its photograph of Blackfeet Indian Carly Kipp, a doctoral candidate in
veterinary medicine. Historically, prejudice and discrimination against members of minority
groups have prevented them from reaching their full potential.

11

Racial and Ethnic Inequality

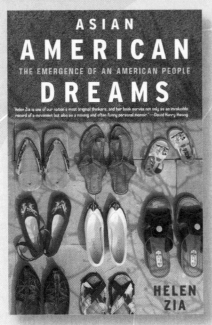

ASIAN
AMERICAN
THE EMERGENCE OF AN AMERICAN PEOPLE
DREAMS

"Helen Zia is one of our nation's most original thinkers, and her book serves not only as an invaluable record of a movement but also as a moving and often funny personal memoir." —David Henry Hwang

HELEN
ZIA

Ah so. No tickee, no washee. So sorry, so sollee.

Chinkee, Chink. Jap, Nip, zero, kamikaze. Dothead, flat face, flat nose, slant eye, slope. Slit, mamasan, dragon lady. Gook, VC, Flip, Hindoo.

By the time I was ten, I'd heard such words so many times I could feel them coming before they parted lips. I knew they were meant in the unkindest way. Still, we didn't talk about these incidents at home, we just accepted them as part of being in America, something to learn to rise above.

The most common taunting didn't even utilize words but a string of unintelligible gobbledygook that kids—and adults—would spew as they pretended to speak Chinese or some other Asian language. It was a mockery of how they imagined my parents talked to me.

Truth was that Mom and Dad rarely spoke to us in Chinese, except to scold or call us to dinner. Worried that we might develop an accent, my father insisted that we speak English at home. This, he explained, would lessen the hardships we might encounter and make us more acceptable as Americans.

I'll never know if my father's language decision was right. On the one hand, I, like most Asian Americans, have been complimented countless times on my spoken English by people who assumed I was a foreigner. "My, you speak such good English," they'd cluck. "No kidding, I ought to," I would think to myself, then wonder: should I thank them for assuming that English isn't my native language? Or should I correct them on the proper usage of "well" and "good"?

> Truth was that Mom and Dad rarely spoke to us in Chinese, except to scold or call us to dinner. Worried that we might develop an accent, my father insisted that we speak English at home.

More often than feeling grateful for my American accent, I've wished that I could jump into a heated exchange of rapid-fire Chinese, volume high and spit flying. But with a vocabulary limited to *"Ni hao?"* (How are you?) and *"Ting bu dong"* (I hear but don't understand), meaningful exchanges are woefully impossible. I find myself smiling and nodding like a dashboard ornament. I'm envious of the many people I know who grew up speaking an Asian language yet converse in English beautifully.

Armed with standard English and my flat New Jersey "a," I still couldn't escape the name-calling. I became all too familiar with other names and faces that supposedly matched mine—Fu Manchu, Suzie Wong, Hop Sing, Madame Butterfly, Charlie Chan, Ming the Merciless—the "Asians" produced for mass consumption. Their faces filled me with shame whenever I saw them on TV or in the movies. They defined my face to the rest of the world: a sinister Fu, Suzie the whore, subservient Hop Sing, pathetic Butterfly, cunning Chan, and warlike Ming. Inscrutable Orientals all, real Americans none.

(Zia 2000:109–110) Additional information about this excerpt can be found on the Online Learning Center at www.mhhe.com/schaefer11.

Helen Zia, the journalist and community activist who wrote this reminiscence from her childhood, is the successful daughter of Chinese immigrants to the United States. As her story shows, Zia experienced blatant prejudice against Chinese Americans, even though she spoke flawless English. In fact, all new immigrants and their families have faced stereotyping and hostility, whether they were White or non-White, Asian, African, or East European. In this multicultural society, those who are different from the dominant social group have never been welcome.

Today, millions of African Americans, Asian Americans, Hispanic Americans, and many other racial and ethnic minorities continue to experience the often bitter contrast between the "American dream" and the grim realities of poverty, prejudice, and discrimination. Like class, the social definitions of race and ethnicity still affect people's place and status in a stratification system, not only in this country but throughout the world. High incomes, a good command of English, and hard-earned professional credentials do not always override racial and ethnic stereotypes or protect those who fit them from the sting of racism.

What is prejudice, and how is it institutionalized in the form of discrimination? In what ways have race and ethnicity affected the experience of immigrants from other countries? What are the fastest-growing minority groups in the United States today? In this chapter we will focus on the meaning of race and ethnicity. We will begin by identifying the basic characteristics of a minority group and distinguishing between racial and ethnic groups. Then we will examine the dynamics of prejudice and discrimination. After considering four sociological perspectives on race and ethnicity, we'll take a look at common patterns of intergroup relations. The following section will describe the major racial and ethnic groups in the United States. Finally, in the Social Policy section we will explore the issue of global immigration.

Minority, Racial, and Ethnic Groups

Sociologists frequently distinguish between racial and ethnic groups. The term *racial group* describes a group that is set apart from others because of physical differences that have taken on social significance. Whites, African Americans, and Asian Americans are all considered racial groups in the United States. While race does turn on physical differences, it is the culture of a particular society that constructs and attaches social significance to those differences, as we will see later. Unlike racial groups, an *ethnic group* is set apart from others primarily because of its national origin or distinctive cultural patterns. In the United States, Puerto Ricans, Jews, and Polish Americans are all categorized as ethnic groups (see Table 11-1).

Minority Groups

A numerical minority is any group that makes up less than half of some larger population. The population of the United States includes thousands of numerical minorities, including television actors, green-eyed people, tax lawyers, and descendants of the Pilgrims who arrived on the *Mayflower*. However, these numerical minorities are not considered to be minorities in the sociological sense; in fact, the number of people in a group does not necessarily determine its status as a social minority (or a dominant group). When sociologists define a minority group, they are concerned primarily with the economic and political power, or powerlessness, of that group. A *minority group* is a subordinate group whose members have significantly less control or power over their own lives than the members of a dominant or majority group have over theirs.

Sociologists have identified five basic properties of a minority group: unequal treatment, physical or cultural traits, ascribed status, solidarity, and in-group marriage (Wagley and Harris 1958):

1. Members of a minority group experience unequal treatment compared to members of a dominant group. For example, the management of an apartment complex may refuse to rent to African Americans, Hispanics, or Jews. Social inequality may be created or maintained by prejudice, discrimination, segregation, or even extermination.

2. Members of a minority group share physical or cultural characteristics that distinguish them from the dominant group. Each society arbitrarily decides which characteristics are most important in defining groups.

3. Membership in a minority (or dominant) group is not voluntary; people are born into the group. Thus, race and ethnicity are considered *ascribed* statuses. {p.111

4. Minority group members have a strong sense of group solidarity. William Graham Sumner, writing in 1906, noted that people make distinctions between members of their own group (the *in-group*) and everyone else (the *out-group*). When a group is the object of long-term prejudice and discrimination, the feeling of "us versus them" can and often does become extremely intense. {p.137

5. Members of a minority group generally marry others from the same group. A member of a dominant group is often unwilling to marry into a supposedly inferior minority group. In addition, the minority group's sense of solidarity encourages marriage within the group and discourages marriage to outsiders.

Race

The term *racial group* refers to those minorities (and the corresponding dominant groups) set apart from others by obvious physical differences. But what is an "obvious" physical difference? Each society socially constructs which differences are important, while ignoring other characteristics that could serve as a basis for social differentiation. In the United States, we see differences in both skin color and hair color. Yet people learn informally that differences in skin color have a dramatic social and political meaning, while differences in hair color do not.

When observing skin color, many people in the United States tend to lump others rather casually into the traditional categories of "Black," "White," and "Asian." More subtle differences in skin color often go unnoticed. In many nations of Central America and South America, by contrast, people recognize color gradients on a continuum from light to dark skin color. Brazil has approximately 40 color groupings, while in other countries people may be described as "Mestizo Hondurans," "Mulatto Colombians," or "African Panamanians." What we see as "obvious" differences, then, are subject to each society's social definitions.

The largest racial minorities in the United States are African Americans (or Blacks), Native Americans (or American Indians), and Asian Americans (Japanese Americans, Chinese Americans, and other Asian peoples). Figure 11-1 (page 270) provides information about the population of racial and ethnic groups in the United States over the past five centuries.

Social Construction of Race In the United States, it was known as the "one-drop rule." If a person had even a single drop of "Black blood," that person was defined and viewed as Black, even if he or she *appeared* to be White. Clearly, race had social significance, enough so that White legislators established official standards about who was "Black" and who was "White."

The one-drop rule was a vivid example of the *social construction of race*—the process by which people come to define a group as a race based in part on physical characteristics, but also on historical, cultural, and economic factors. For example, in the 1800s, immigrant groups such as Italian and Irish Americans were not at first seen as being "White," but as foreigners who were not necessarily trustworthy. The social construction of race is an ongoing process that is subject to debate, especially in a diverse society such as the United States, where each year increasing numbers of children are born to parents of different racial backgrounds.

Recognition of Multiple Identities In the 2000 census, over 7 million people in the United States (or about 2.6 percent of the population) reported that they were of two or more races. Half the people classified as multiracial were under age 18, suggesting that this segment of the population will grow in the years to come. People who claimed both White and American Indian ancestry were the largest group of multiracial residents (N. Jones 2005).

This statistical finding of millions of multiracial people obscures how individuals are often asked to handle their identity. For example, the enrollment forms for government programs typically include only a few broad racial-ethnic categories. This approach to racial categorization is part of a long history that dictates single-race identities. Still, many individuals, especially young

Table 11-1

Racial and Ethnic Groups in the United States, 2004

Classification	Number in Thousands	Percentage of Total Population
Racial groups		
Whites (not Hispanic)	192,362	67.3%
Blacks/African Americans	37,772	12.2
Native Americans, Alaskan Native	2,151	0.8
Asian Americans	12,097	4.2
Chinese	2,830	1.0
Asian Indians	2,245	0.9
Filipinos	2,148	0.8
Vietnamese	1,268	0.4
Koreans	1,251	0.4
Japanese	832	0.3
Other	1,523	0.5
Ethnic groups		
White ancestry (single or mixed)		
Germans	42,842	15.2
Irish	30,525	10.8
English	24,509	8.7
Italians	15,638	5.6
Poles	8,977	3.2
French	8,310	3.0
Jews	5,200	1.8
Hispanics (or Latinos)	40,459	14.2
Mexican Americans	25,895	9.2
Central and South Americans	5,117	1.8
Puerto Ricans	3,874	1.4
Cubans	1,438	0.5
Other	4,136	1.4
Total Population	285,692	

Note: Percentages do not total 100 percent and figures under subheadings do not add up to figures under major headings because of overlap among groups (e.g., Polish American Jews or people of mixed ancestry, such as Irish and Italian). Hispanics may be of any race. White ancestry data and percentages are from the 2000 census.
Sources: Author based on American Community Survey 2005, 2007a, 2007b, 2007c; Brittingham and de la Cruz 2004; United Jewish Communities 2003.

Racial and Ethnic Groups in the United States, 1500–2100 (Projected)

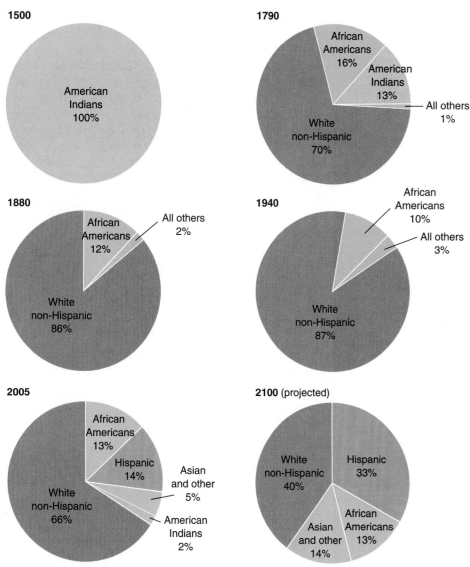

Sources: Author's estimate; American Community Survey 2006; Bureau of the Census 1975, 2004; Grieco and Cassidy 2001; Thornton 1987. Data for 2005 and 2100, African Americans and Asian and other are for non-Hispanics.

The racial and ethnic composition of what is today the United States has been undergoing change not just for the last 50 years, but for the last 500. Five centuries ago the land was populated only by indigenous Native Americans.

www.mhhe.com/schaefer11

Use Your Sociological Imagination

Using a TV remote control, how quickly do you think you could find a television show in which all the characters share your own racial or ethnic background? What about a show in which all the characters share a different background from your own—how quickly could you find one?

adults, struggle against social pressure to choose a single identity, and instead openly embrace multiple heritages. Tiger Woods, the world's best-known professional golfer, considers himself both Asian and African American.

As we saw in Chapter 5, a dominant or majority group has the power not only to define itself legally but to define a society's values. The interactionist William I. Thomas, observing how we assign social meanings, saw that the "definition of the situation" could mold the individual personality. To put it another way, people respond not only to the objective features of a situation or person but also to the *meaning* that situation or person has for them. Thus, we can create false images or stereotypes that become real in their consequences. **Stereotypes** are unreliable generalizations about all members of a group that do not recognize individual differences within the group.

In the last 30 years, critics have pointed out the power of the mass media to perpetuate false racial and ethnic stereotypes. Television is a prime example: Almost all the leading dramatic roles are cast as Whites, even in urban-based programs like *Friends* (see Chapter 7). Blacks tend to be featured mainly in crime-based dramas.

Ethnicity

An ethnic group, unlike a racial group, is set apart from others because of its national origin or distinctive cultural patterns. Among the ethnic groups in the United States are peoples with a Spanish-speaking background, referred to collectively as *Latinos* or *Hispanics*, such as Puerto Ricans, Mexican Americans, Cuban Americans, and other Latin Americans. Other ethnic groups in this country include Jewish, Irish, Italian, and Norwegian Americans. While these groupings are convenient, they serve to obscure differences *within* ethnic categories (as in the case of Hispanics), as well as to overlook the mixed ancestry of so many ethnic people in the United States.

The distinction between racial and ethnic minorities is not always clear-cut. Some members of racial minorities, such as Asian Americans, may have significant cultural differences from other racial groups. At the same time, certain ethnic minorities,

Today, some children of mixed-race families identify themselves as biracial or multiracial, rejecting efforts to place them in a single racial category.

such as Latinos, may have obvious physical differences that set them apart from other ethnic groups in the United States.

Despite categorization problems, sociologists continue to feel that the distinction between racial groups and ethnic groups is socially significant. In most societies, including the United States, socially constructed physical differences tend to be more visible than ethnic differences. Partly as a result of this fact, stratification along racial lines is more resistant to change than stratification along ethnic lines. Over time, members of an ethnic minority can sometimes become indistinguishable from the majority—although the process may take generations and may never include all members of the group. In contrast, members of a racial minority find it much more difficult to blend in with the larger society and gain acceptance from the majority.

Prejudice and Discrimination

In recent years, college campuses across the United States have been the scene of bias-related incidents. Student-run newspapers and radio stations have ridiculed racial and ethnic minorities; threatening literature has been stuffed under the doors of minority students; graffiti endorsing the views of White supremacist organizations such as the Ku Klux Klan have been scrawled on university walls. In some cases, there have even been violent clashes between groups of White and Black students (Bunzel 1992; Schaefer 2008). What causes such ugly incidents?

Prejudice

Prejudice is a negative attitude toward an entire category of people, often an ethnic or racial minority. If you resent your room-mate because he or she is sloppy, you are not necessarily guilty of prejudice. However, if you immediately stereotype your roommate on the basis of such characteristics as race, ethnicity, or religion, that is a form of prejudice. Prejudice tends to perpetuate false definitions of individuals and groups.

Sometimes prejudice results from *ethnocentrism*—the tendency to assume that one's own culture and way of life represent {p.75 the norm or are superior to all others. Ethnocentric people judge other cultures by the standards of their own group, which leads quite easily to prejudice against cultures they view as inferior.

FIGURE 11–2

Categorization of Reported Hate Crimes

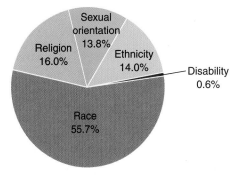

Source: Reported for 2005 in 2006. Department of Justice 2006b.

One important and widespread form of prejudice is *racism,* the belief that one race is supreme and all others are innately inferior. When racism prevails in a society, members of subordinate groups generally experience prejudice, discrimination, and exploitation. In 1990, as concern mounted about racist attacks in the United States, Congress passed the Hate Crimes Statistics Act. A *hate crime* is a criminal offense committed because of the offender's bias against a race, religion, ethnic group, national origin, or sexual orientation. In 2005 alone, more than 7,400 hate crimes were reported to authorities. As Figure 11-2 (page 271) shows, more than half those crimes against persons involved racial bias. Most were carried out by one or more individuals.

A particularly horrifying hate crime made the front pages in 1998: In Jasper, Texas, three White men with possible connections to race-hate groups tied up a Black man, beat him with chains, and then dragged him behind their truck until his body was dismembered. Numerous groups in the United States have been victims of hate crimes as well as generalized prejudice. In the wake of the terrorist attacks of September 11, 2001, hate crimes against Asian Americans and Muslim Americans escalated rapidly.

Discriminatory Behavior

Prejudice often leads to *discrimination,* the denial of opportunities and equal rights to individuals and groups because of prejudice or other arbitrary reasons. Say that a White corporate president with a prejudice against Asian Americans has to fill an executive position. The most qualified candidate for the job is a Vietnamese American. If the president refuses to hire this candidate and instead selects an inferior White candidate, he or she is engaging in an act of racial discrimination.

Prejudiced *attitudes* should not be equated with discriminatory *behavior.* Although the two are generally related, they are not identical; either condition can be present without the other. A prejudiced person does not always act on his or her biases. The White president, for example, might choose—despite his or her stereotypes—to hire the Vietnamese American. That would be prejudice without discrimination. On the other hand, a White corporate president with a completely respectful view of Vietnamese Americans might refuse to hire them for executive posts out of fear that biased clients would take their business elsewhere. In that case, the president's action would constitute discrimination without prejudice.

Sociologist Devah Pager's (2003) experiment, described in Chapter 2, documented racial discrimination in hiring.

Recall that a White job applicant with a prison record received slightly more callbacks than a Black applicant with no criminal record. Over time, the cumulative impact of such differential behavior contributes to significant differences in income. Figure 11-3 vividly illustrates the income inequality between White men and everyone else.

Sometimes racial and ethnic discrimination is overt. Internet forums like Craigslist.org or Roommate.com feature classified ads that state "African Americans and Arabians tend to clash with me" or "Clean, Godly Christian men only." While antidiscrimination laws prevent such notices from being published in the newspapers, existing law has not caught up with online bigotry in hiring and renting (Liptak 2006).

Discrimination persists even for the most educated and qualified minority group members from the best family backgrounds. Despite their talents and experiences, they sometimes encounter attitudinal or organizational bias that prevents them from reaching their full potential. The term *glass ceiling* refers to an invisible barrier that blocks the promotion of a qualified individual in a work environment because of the individual's gender, race, or ethnicity (Schaefer 2008; Yamagata et al. 1997).

In early 1995, the federal Glass Ceiling Commission issued the first comprehensive study of barriers to promotion in the United States. The commission found that glass ceilings continue to block women and minority group men from top management positions in the nation's industries. While White men constitute 47 percent of the paid labor force, they hold down a much higher proportion of top positions. Even in *Fortune* magazine's 2002 listing of the most diversified corporations, White men held more than 80 percent of both the board of directors seats and the top 50 paid positions in the firms. The existence of this glass ceiling results principally from the fears and prejudices

FIGURE 11–3

U.S. Median Income by Race, Ethnicity, and Gender

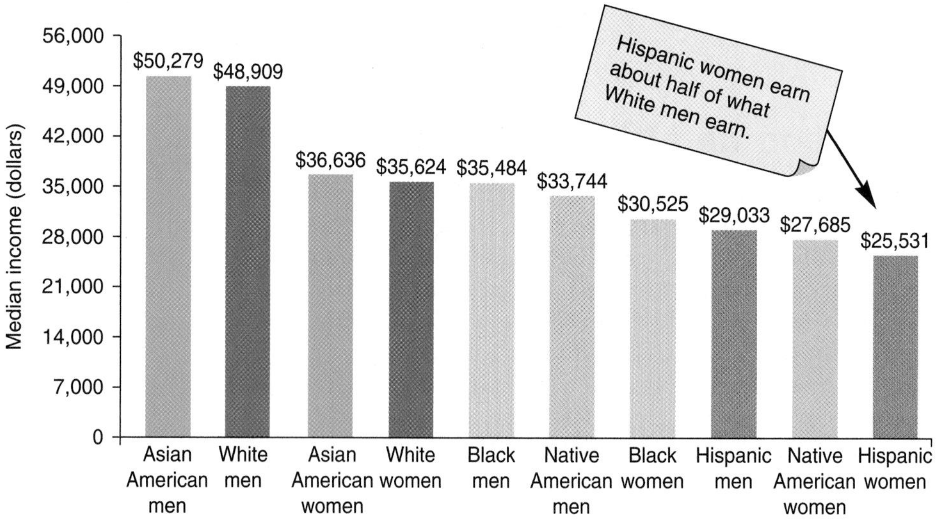

Note: Data released in 2006 for income earned in 2005. Includes only people working full-time, year-round, 25 years old and older. White refers to non-Hispanic Whites.

Sources: DeNavas-Walt et al. 2006; for Native Americans, author's estimate based on Bureau of the Census 2003b.

of many middle- and upper-level White male managers, who believe that the inclusion of women and minority group men in management circles will threaten their own prospects for advancement (Bureau of the Census 2005a:373; Department of Labor 1995a, 1995b; Hickman 2002).

The Privileges of the Dominant

One aspect of discrimination that is often overlooked is the privileges that dominant groups enjoy at the expense of others. For instance, we tend to focus more on the difficulty women have getting ahead at work and getting a hand at home than on the ease with which men avoid household chores and manage to make their way in the world. Similarly, we concentrate more on discrimination against racial and ethnic minorities than on the advantages members of the White majority enjoy. Indeed, most White people rarely think about their "Whiteness," taking their status for granted. But sociologists and other social scientists are becoming increasingly interested in what it means to be "White," for White privilege is the other side of the proverbial coin of racial discrimination.

The feminist scholar Peggy McIntosh (1988) became interested in White privilege after noticing that most men would not acknowledge that there were privileges attached to being male—even if they would agree that being female had its disadvantages. Did White people suffer from a similar blind spot regarding their own racial privilege? she wondered. Intrigued, McIntosh began to list all the ways in which she benefited from her Whiteness. She soon realized that the list of unspoken advantages was long and significant.

McIntosh found that as a White person, she rarely needed to step out of her comfort zone, no matter where she went. If she wished to, she could spend most of her time with people of her own race. She could find a good place to live in a pleasant neighborhood, buy the foods she liked to eat from almost any grocery store, and get her hair styled in almost any salon. She could attend a public meeting without feeling that she did not belong, that she was different from everyone else.

McIntosh discovered, too, that her skin color opened doors for her. She could cash checks and use credit cards without suspicion, browse through stores without being shadowed by security guards. She could be seated without difficulty in a restaurant. If she asked to see the manager, she could assume he or she would be of her own race. If she needed help from a doctor or a lawyer, she could get it.

McIntosh also realized that her Whiteness made the job of parenting easier. She did not need to worry about

protecting her children from people who didn't like them. She could be sure that their textbooks would show pictures of people who looked like them, and that their history texts would describe White people's achievements. She knew that the television programs they watched would include White characters.

Finally, McIntosh had to admit that others did not constantly evaluate her in racial terms. When she appeared in public, she didn't need to worry that her clothing or behavior might reflect poorly on White people. If she was recognized for an achievement, it was seen as her achievement, not that of an entire race. And no one ever assumed that the personal opinions she voiced should be those of all White people. Because McIntosh blended in with the people around her, she wasn't always onstage.

These are not all the privileges White people take for granted as a result of their membership in the dominant racial group in the United States. As Devah Pager's study (see page 41) showed, White job seekers enjoy a tremendous advantage over equally well-qualified—even better-qualified—Blacks. Whiteness *does* carry privileges—to a much greater extent than most White people realize.

Use Your Sociological Imagination

How often do you think people are privileged because of their race or ethnicity? How about yourself—how often are you privileged?

In U.S. retail stores, White customers have different experiences than Black customers. They are less likely than Blacks to have their checks or credit cards refused, and less likely to be viewed with suspicion by security personnel. Whiteness does confer privilege.

Prudence Hannis
Liaison Officer, National Institute of Science Research, University of Québec

Prudence Hannis is a First Nations (Native American) woman who serves as an official liaison between her people and Canadian researchers. In her position, she interacts with sociologists, anthropologists, political scientists, legal scholars, and researchers in health and medicine at several Canadian universities, all of whom wish to work with First Nations communities. Hannis is enthusiastic about her job, which gives her an opportunity to educate and sensitize would-be researchers who "never set foot in First Nations communities." In 10 years of work on behalf of the native peoples of Canada, Hannis has seen a dramatic change in their representation in Canadian research and policy. "We are everywhere in research efforts and policy consultation, but whether we are listened to is another matter," she notes.

Before taking her current position, Hannis served as a researcher and community activist with Québec Native Women. There she oversaw the women's health portfolio, organized seminars on sexual abuse for local communities, and produced a resource booklet on the subject. "The purpose of my job was to defend First Nations' women's concerns, to be their spokesperson when needed, to analyze critical situations for our sisters, and mostly, to determine ways in which women can empower themselves, their families, and their communities," she says.

Hannis has also worked for the Centre of Excellence on Women's Health, Consortium Université de Montréal, where she focused on First Nations women's health issues. A member of the Abenaki tribe, Hannis received her B.A. in sociology from the University of Québec at Montréal. She has found her background in the discipline to be invaluable. "Sociology is now, more than it has ever been, a part of my job," she says.

Let's Discuss

1. Explain the connection between Native Americans' ethnicity and their health.
2. In speaking of empowering First Nations women, what sociological perspective do you think Hannis is drawing on?

Institutional Discrimination

Discrimination is practiced not only by individuals in one-to-one encounters but also by institutions in their daily operations. Social scientists are particularly concerned with the ways in which structural factors such as employment, housing, health care, and government operations maintain the social significance of race and ethnicity. *Institutional discrimination* refers to the denial of opportunities and equal rights to individuals and groups that results from the normal operations of a society. This kind of discrimination consistently affects certain racial and ethnic groups more than others.

The Commission on Civil Rights (1981:9–10) has identified various forms of institutional discrimination:

- Rules requiring that only English be spoken at a place of work, even when it is not a business necessity to restrict the use of other languages.

- Preferences shown by law and medical schools in the admission of children of wealthy and influential alumni, nearly all of whom are White.

- Restrictive employment-leave policies, coupled with prohibitions on part-time work, that make it difficult for the heads of single-parent families (most of whom are women) to obtain and keep jobs.

A recent example of institutional discrimination occurred in the wake of the September 11, 2001, terrorist attacks on the United States. In the heat of demands to prevent terrorist takeovers of commercial airplanes, Congress passed the Aviation and Transportation Security Act, which was intended to strengthen airport screening procedures. The law stipulated that all airport screeners must be U.S. citizens. Nationally, 28 percent of all airport screeners were legal residents but not citizens of the United States; as a group, they were disproportionately Latino, Black, and Asian. Many observers noted that other airport and airline workers, including pilots, cabin attendants, and even armed National Guardsmen stationed at airports, need not be citizens. Efforts are now being made to test the constitutionality of the act. At the least, the debate over its fairness shows that even well-meant legal measures can have disastrous consequences for racial and ethnic minorities (H. Weinstein 2002).

In some cases, even ostensibly neutral institutional standards can have discriminatory effects. African American students at a midwestern state university protested a policy under which fraternities and sororities that wished to use campus facilities for a dance were required to post a $150 security deposit to cover possible damages. The Black students complained that the policy had a discriminatory impact on minority student organizations. Campus police countered that the university's policy applied to all student groups interested in using the facilities. However, since the overwhelmingly White fraternities and sororities at the school had their own houses, which they used for dances, the policy indeed affected only African American and other minority organizations.

Attempts have been made to eradicate or compensate for discrimination in the United States. The 1960s saw the passage of many pioneering civil rights laws, including the landmark 1964 Civil Rights Act (which prohibits discrimination in public accommodations and publicly owned facilities on the basis of race, color, creed, national origin, and gender). In two important rulings in 1987, the Supreme Court held that federal prohibitions against racial discrimination protect members of all ethnic minorities—including Hispanics, Jews, and Arab Americans—even though they may be considered White.

For more than 40 years, affirmative action programs have been instituted to overcome past discrimination. ***Affirmative action*** refers to positive efforts to recruit minority group members or women for jobs, promotions, and educational opportunities. Many people resent these programs, arguing that advancing one group's cause merely shifts the discrimination to another group. By giving priority to African Americans in admissions, for example, schools may overlook more qualified White candidates. In many parts of the country and many sectors of the economy, affirmative action is being rolled back, even though it was never fully implemented. We will discuss affirmative action in more detail in Chapter 18.

Discriminatory practices continue to pervade nearly all areas of life in the United States today. In part, that is because various individuals and groups actually *benefit* from racial and ethnic discrimination in terms of money, status, and influence. Discrimination permits members of the majority to enhance their wealth, power, and prestige at the expense of others. Less qualified people get jobs and promotions simply because they are members of the dominant group. Such individuals and groups will not surrender these advantages easily. We'll turn now

to a closer look at this functionalist analysis, as well as the conflict and interactionist perspectives on race and ethnicity.

Sociological Perspectives on Race and Ethnicity

Relations among racial and ethnic groups lend themselves to analysis from the three major sociological perspectives. Viewing race from the macro level, functionalists observe that racial prejudice and discrimination serve positive functions for dominant groups. Conflict theorists see the economic structure as a central factor in the exploitation of minorities. On the micro level, interactionist researchers stress the manner in which everyday contact between people from different racial and ethnic backgrounds contributes to tolerance or hostility.

Functionalist Perspective

What possible use could racial bigotry have? Functionalist theorists, while agreeing that racial hostility is hardly to be admired, point out that it serves positive functions for those who practice discrimination.

Anthropologist Manning Nash (1962) has identified three functions of racially prejudiced beliefs for the dominant group:

1. Racist views provide a moral justification for maintaining an unequal society that routinely deprives a minority group of its rights and privileges. Southern Whites justified slavery by believing that Africans were physically and spiritually subhuman and devoid of souls.

2. Racist beliefs discourage the subordinate minority from attempting to question its lowly status, which would be to question the very foundations of society.

3. Racial myths suggest that any major societal change (such as an end to discrimination) would only bring greater poverty to the minority and lower the majority's standard of living. As a result, racial prejudice grows when a society's value system (one underlying a colonial empire or slavery, for example) is threatened.

Although racial prejudice and discrimination may serve the powerful, such unequal treatment can also be dysfunctional for a society, and even for the dominant group. Sociologist Arnold Rose (1951) has outlined four dysfunctions associated with racism:

1. A society that practices discrimination fails to use the resources of all individuals. Discrimination limits the search for talent and leadership to the dominant group.

Before passage of the Civil Rights Act (1964), segregation of public accommodations was the norm throughout the South. Whites used the most up-to-date bathrooms, waiting rooms, and even drinking fountains, while Blacks ("Colored") were directed to older facilities in inferior condition. Such separate but unequal arrangements are a blatant example of institutional discrimination.

2. Discrimination aggravates social problems such as poverty, delinquency, and crime, and places the financial burden of alleviating those problems on the dominant group.

3. Society must invest a good deal of time and money to defend its barriers to the full participation of all members.

4. Racial prejudice and discrimination often undercut goodwill and friendly diplomatic relations between nations.

Conflict Perspective

Conflict theorists would certainly agree with Arnold Rose that racial prejudice and discrimination have many harmful consequences for society. Sociologists such as Oliver Cox (1948), Robert Blauner (1972), and Herbert M. Hunter (2000) have used the *exploitation theory* (or *Marxist class theory*) to explain the basis of racial subordination in the United States. As we saw in Chapter 9, Karl Marx viewed the exploitation of the lower class as a basic part of the capitalist economic system. From a Marxist point of view, racism keeps minorities in low-paying jobs, thereby supplying the capitalist ruling class with a pool of cheap labor. Moreover, by forcing racial minorities to accept low wages, capitalists can restrict the wages of *all* members of the proletariat. Workers from the dominant group who demand higher wages can always be replaced by minorities who have no choice but to accept low-paying jobs.

The conflict view of race relations seems persuasive in a number of instances. Japanese Americans were the object of little prejudice until they began to enter jobs that brought them into competition with Whites. The movement to keep Chinese immigrants out of the United States became most fervent during the latter half of the 19th century, when Chinese and Whites fought over dwindling work opportunities. Both the enslavement of Blacks and the extermination and removal westward of Native Americans were economically motivated.

However, the exploitation theory is too limited to explain prejudice in its many forms. Not all minority groups have been exploited to the same extent. In addition, many groups (such as the Quakers and the Mormons) have been victimized by prejudice for other than economic reasons. Still, as Gordon Allport (1979:210) concludes, the exploitation theory correctly "points a sure finger at one of the factors involved in prejudice, . . . rationalized self-interest of the upper classes."

One practice that fits both the conflict perspective and labeling theory is racial profiling. *Racial profiling* is any arbitrary action initiated by an authority based on race, ethnicity, or national origin rather than on a person's behavior. Generally, racial profiling occurs when law enforcement officers, including customs officials, airport security, and police, assume that people who fit a certain description are likely to be engaged in illegal activities. Beginning in the 1980s with the emergence of the crack cocaine market, skin color became a key characteristic in racial profiling. This practice is often based on very explicit stereotypes. For example, one federal antidrug initiative encouraged officers to look specifically for people with dreadlocks and for Latino men traveling together.

Today, authorities continue to rely on racial profiling despite overwhelming evidence that it is misleading. Though a federal study showed little difference nationwide in the likelihood of a person being stopped by officers, African Americans were twice as likely as Whites to have their vehicles searched, and Latinos five times more likely. A similar pattern emerged in the use of force against drivers: Police were three times more likely to use force against Latino and Black drivers than against White drivers. Yet in areas where minority group members were disproportionately targeted, Whites were more likely than Blacks to be found carrying drugs (Lichtblau 2003).

Research on the ineffectiveness of racial profiling, coupled with calls by minority communities to end the stigmatization, has led to growing demands to end the practice. But these efforts came to an abrupt halt after the September 11, 2001, terrorist attacks on the United States, when suspicions arose about Muslim and Arab immigrants. Foreign students from Arab countries were summoned for special questioning by authorities. Legal immigrants who were identified as Arab or Muslim were scrutinized for possible illegal activity and prosecuted for violations that authorities routinely ignored among immigrants of other

Too often, authorities treat individuals differently based solely on their race or ethnicity. This poster dramatizes the injustice of racial profiling, a practice in which a man who looks like the Reverend Martin Luther King Jr. (left) would be treated with more suspicion than the mass murderer Charles Manson (right).

ethnicities and faiths. In 2003, President George W. Bush barred federal agents from using race and ethnicity in their investigations, but cases involving terrorism and national security measures were specifically exempted (Withrow 2006).

Interactionist Perspective

A Hispanic woman is transferred from a job on an assembly line to a similar position working next to a White man. At first, the White man is patronizing, assuming that she must be incompetent. She is cold and resentful; even when she needs assistance, she refuses to admit it. After a week, the growing tension between the two leads to a bitter quarrel. Yet over time, each slowly comes to appreciate the other's strengths and talents. A year after they begin working together, these two workers become respectful friends. This story is an example of what interactionists call the *contact hypothesis* in action.

The **contact hypothesis** states that in cooperative circumstances, interracial contact between people of equal status will cause them to become less prejudiced and to abandon old stereotypes. People begin to see one another as individuals and discard the broad generalizations characteristic of stereotyping. Note the phrases *equal status* and *cooperative circumstances.* In the story just told, if the two workers had been competing for one vacancy as a supervisor, the racial hostility between them might have worsened (Allport 1979; Fine 2004).

As Latinos and other minorities slowly gain access to better-paying and more responsible jobs, the contact hypothesis may take on even greater significance. The trend in our society is toward increasing contact between individuals from dominant and subordinate groups. That may be one way of eliminating—or at least reducing—racial and ethnic stereotyping and prejudice. Another may be the establishment of interracial coalitions, an idea suggested by sociologist William Julius Wilson (1999b). To work, such coalitions would obviously need to be built on an equal role for all members.

Contact between individuals occurs on the micro level. Box 11-1 (page 278) examines the interactionist research on friendships that cross ethnic and racial lines.

Table 11-2 (page 278) summarizes the four major sociological perspectives on race. No matter what the explanation for racial and ethnic distinctions—functionalist, conflict, interactionist, or labeling theory—these socially constructed inequalities can have powerful consequences in the form of prejudice and discrimination. In the next section, we will see how inequality based on the ascribed characteristics of race and ethnicity can poison people's interpersonal relations, depriving whole groups of opportunities others take for granted.

Patterns of Intergroup Relations

Racial and ethnic groups can relate to one another in a wide variety of ways, ranging from friendships and intermarriages to hostility, from behaviors that require mutual approval to behaviors imposed by the dominant group.

One devastating pattern of intergroup relations is *genocide*—the deliberate, systematic killing of an entire people or nation. This term describes the killing of 1 million Armenians by Turkey beginning in 1915. It is most commonly applied to Nazi Germany's extermination of 6 million European Jews, as well as gays, lesbians, and the Romani people ("Gypsies"), during World War II. The term *genocide* is also appropriate in describing the United States' policies toward Native Americans in the 19th century. In 1800, the Native American (or American Indian) population of the United States was about 600,000; by 1850, it had been reduced to 250,000 through warfare with the U.S. cavalry, disease, and forced relocation to inhospitable environments.

The *expulsion* of a people is another extreme means of acting out racial or ethnic prejudice. In 1979, Vietnam expelled nearly 1 million ethnic Chinese, partly as a result of centuries of hostility between Vietnam and neighboring China. In a more recent example of expulsion (which had aspects of genocide), Serbian forces began a program of "ethnic cleansing" in 1991, in the newly independent states of Bosnia and Herzegovina. Throughout the former nation of Yugoslavia, the Serbs drove more than 1 million Croats and Muslims from their homes. Some they tortured and killed; others they abused and terrorized, in an attempt to "purify" the land (Cigar 1995; Petrovic 1994).

Genocide and expulsion are extreme behaviors. More typical intergroup relations follow four identifiable patterns: (1) amalgamation, (2) assimilation, (3) segregation, and (4) pluralism. Each pattern defines the dominant group's actions and the minority group's responses. Intergroup relations are rarely restricted to only one of the four patterns, although invariably one does tend to dominate. Think of these patterns primarily as ideal types.

Amalgamation

Amalgamation happens when a majority group and a minority group combine to form a new group. Through intermarriage over several generations, various groups in society combine to form a new group. This pattern can be expressed as A + B + C → D, where A, B, and C represent different groups in a society, and D signifies the end result, a unique cultural-racial group unlike any of the initial groups (Newman 1973).

The belief in the United States as a "melting pot" became compelling in the first part of the 20th century, particularly since that image suggested that the nation had an almost divine mission to amalgamate various groups into one people. However, in actuality, many residents were not willing to include Native Americans, Jews, African Americans, Asian Americans, and Irish Roman Catholics in the melting pot. Therefore, this pattern does not adequately describe dominant–subordinate relations in the United States.

Assimilation

In India, many Hindus complain about Indian citizens who copy the traditions and customs of the British. In France, people of Arab and African origin, many of them Muslim, complain they

11-1 Interracial and Interethnic Friendships

Do people really have close friends of different racial and ethnic backgrounds? Some sociologists have attempted to gauge the degree of White–Black interaction in the United States. But if these studies are not done carefully, they may overestimate the degree of "racial togetherness" in our society.

Sociologist Tom Smith, who directs the respected General Social Survey, has noticed that a high proportion of both White and African American respondents claim to have close friends of another race. But is that really true? When Smith and fellow researchers analyzed the survey data, they found that response rates varied with the way the question was phrased. When asked whether any of the friends they felt close to was Black, 42.1 percent of Whites said yes. Yet when asked to give the names of friends they felt close to, only 6 percent of Whites listed a close friend of a different race or ethnicity.

When asked the race of their best same-sex friend, most Americans choose someone of the same race as themselves. In a national study of adolescents, over 91 percent of non-Hispanic Whites claimed a non-Hispanic White as their best same-sex friend. (The General Social Survey yielded almost the same result for all adults.) Given the fact that over a third of the teens in the United States are either non-White or Hispanic, we might have expected to find more cross-race friendships. Members of mi-

> *A high proportion of both White and African American respondents claim to have close friends of another race.*

nority groups seem more willing than Whites to cross racial and ethnic boundaries, however. A slightly lower 85 percent of Black adolescents selected a Black for a best friend, and a markedly lower 62 percent of Mexican Americans named another Mexican American.

Interactionists have noted significant differences in interracial and interethnic friend-

ships. Regardless of one's racial or ethnic group, friendships that cross racial and ethnic boundaries are less likely than others to involve visits to each other's homes. They are also less likely than others to feature a sharing of personal problems.

In sum, careful research shows that to a great degree, our society's growing diversity is not reflected in our choice of friends.

Let's Discuss

1. How common are interracial and interethnic friendships where you live or go to school? Do the results of the two surveys described here strike you as familiar?
2. What might explain the gap between the percentage of Whites claiming to have a close friend who was Black and the percentage of Whites who listed a close friend of another race or ethnicity?

Sources: Hamm et al. 2005; Kao and Joyner 2004; T. Smith 1999.

---

are treated as second-class citizens—a charge that provoked riots in 2005. In Australia, Aborigines who have become part of the dominant society refuse to acknowledge their darker-skinned grandparents on the street. And in the United States, some Italian Americans, Polish Americans, Hispanics, and Jews have changed their ethnic-sounding family names to names that are typically found among White Protestant families.

Table 11-2

Sociological Perspectives on Race and Ethnicity

Perspective	Emphasis
Functionalist	The dominant majority benefits from the subordination of racial minorities.
Conflict	Vested interests perpetuate racial inequality through economic exploitation.
Interactionist	Cooperative interracial contacts can reduce hostility.
Labeling	People are profiled and stereotyped based on their racial and ethnic identity.

**Assimilation** is the process through which a person forsakes his or her own cultural tradition to become part of a different culture. Generally, it is practiced by a minority group member who wants to conform to the standards of the dominant group. Assimilation can be described as a pattern in which A + B + C → A. The majority, A, dominates in such a way that members of minorities B and C imitate it and attempt to become indistinguishable from it (Newman 1973).

Assimilation can strike at the very roots of a person's identity. Alphonso D'Abruzzo, for example, changed his name to Alan Alda. The British actress Joyce Frankenberg changed her name to Jane Seymour. Name changes, switches in religious affiliation, and dropping of native languages can obscure one's roots and heritage. However, assimilation does not necessarily bring acceptance to minority group individuals. A Chinese American such as Helen Zia (see the chapter-opening excerpt) may speak English fluently, achieve high educational standards, and become a well-respected professional or businessperson and _still_ be seen as different. Other Americans may reject her as a business associate, neighbor, or marriage partner.

Use Your Sociological Imagination

You have immigrated to another country with a very different culture. What steps might you take to assimilate?

Segregation

Separate schools, separate seating on buses and in restaurants, separate washrooms, even separate drinking fountains—these were all part of the lives of African Americans in the South when segregation ruled early in the 20th century. *Segregation* refers to the physical separation of two groups of people in terms of residence, workplace, and social events. Generally, a dominant group imposes this pattern on a minority group. Segregation is rarely complete, however. Intergroup contact inevitably occurs, even in the most segregated societies.

From 1948 (when it received its independence) to 1990, the Republic of South Africa severely restricted the movement of Blacks and other non-Whites by means of a wide-ranging system of segregation known as *apartheid.* Apartheid even included the creation of separate homelands where Blacks were expected to live. However, decades of local resistance to apartheid, combined with international pressure, led to marked political changes in the 1990s. In 1994, a prominent Black activist, Nelson Mandela, was elected South Africa's president in the first election in which Blacks (the majority of the nation's population) were allowed to vote. Mandela had spent almost 28 years in South African prisons for his anti-apartheid activities. His election was widely viewed as the final blow to South Africa's oppressive policy of segregation.

Long-entrenched social patterns are difficult to change, however. In the United States today, despite federal laws that forbid housing discrimination, residential segregation is still the norm, as a recent analysis of living patterns in metropolitan areas shows. Across the nation, neighborhoods remain divided along both racial and ethnic lines. The average White person lives in an area that is at least 83 percent White, while the average African American lives in a neighborhood that is mostly Black. The typical Latino lives in an area that is 42 percent Hispanic. Overall, segregation flourishes at the community and neighborhood level, despite the increasing diversity of the nation as a whole (Lewis Mumford Center 2001).

Whatever the country, residential segregation directly limits people's economic opportunity. Sociologists Douglas Massey and Nancy Denton (1993), in a book aptly titled *American Apartheid,* noted that segregation separates poor people of color from job opportunities and isolates them from successful role models. This pattern repeats itself the world over, from South Central Los Angeles to Oldham, England, and Soweto, South Africa.

This public housing development in suburban Paris is home to African and Asian immigrants, most of them Muslim. Such racial and ethnic enclaves are characterized by limited job opportunities and underfinanced schools. In many other parts of the world as well, the segregation of racial and ethnic minorities accentuates the gap between the haves and have-nots.

Pluralism

In a pluralistic society, a subordinate group does not have to forsake its lifestyle and traditions. *Pluralism* is based on mutual respect for one another's cultures among the various groups in a society. This pattern allows a minority group to express its own culture and still participate without prejudice in the larger society. Earlier, we described amalgamation as A + B + C → D, and assimilation as A + B + C → A. Using this same approach, we can conceive of pluralism as A + B + C → A + B + C. All the groups coexist in the same society (Newman 1973).

In the United States, pluralism is more of an ideal than a reality. There are distinct instances of pluralism—the ethnic neighborhoods in major cities, such as Koreatown, Little Tokyo, Andersonville (Swedish Americans), and Spanish Harlem—yet there are also limits to cultural freedom. To survive, a society must promote a certain consensus among its members regarding basic ideals, values, and beliefs. Thus, if a Romanian immigrant to the United States wants to move up the occupational ladder, he or she cannot avoid learning the English language.

Switzerland exemplifies the modern pluralistic state. There the absence of both a national language and a dominant religious faith leads to a tolerance for cultural diversity. In addition, various political devices safeguard the interests of ethnic groups in a way that has no parallel in the United States. By contrast, Great Britain has had difficulty achieving cultural pluralism in a multiracial society. East Indians, Pakistanis, and Blacks from the Caribbean and Africa experience prejudice and discrimination within the dominant White society there. Some British advocate cutting off all Asian and Black immigration, and a few even call for expulsion of those non-Whites currently living in Britain.

Race and Ethnicity in the United States

Few societies have a more diverse population than the United States; the nation is truly a multiracial, multiethnic society. Of course, that has not always been the case. The population of what is now the United States has changed dramatically since the arrival of European settlers in the 1600s, as Figure 11-1 (see page 270) showed. Immigration, colonialism, and in the case of Blacks, slavery determined the racial and ethnic makeup of our present-day society. Figure 11-4 shows where various racial and ethnic minorities are concentrated in the United States.

Racial Groups

The largest racial minorities in the United States are African Americans, Native Americans, and Asian Americans.

African Americans   "I am an invisible man," wrote Black author Ralph Ellison in his novel *Invisible Man* (1952:3). "I am a man of substance, of flesh and bone, fiber and liquids—and I might even be said to possess a mind. I am invisible, understand, simply because people refuse to see me."

Over five decades later, many African Americans still feel invisible. Despite their large numbers, they have long been treated as second-class citizens. Currently, by the standards of the fed-

FIGURE 11–4

Census 2000: The Image of Diversity

MAPPING LIFE NATIONWIDE   www.mhhe.com/schaefer11

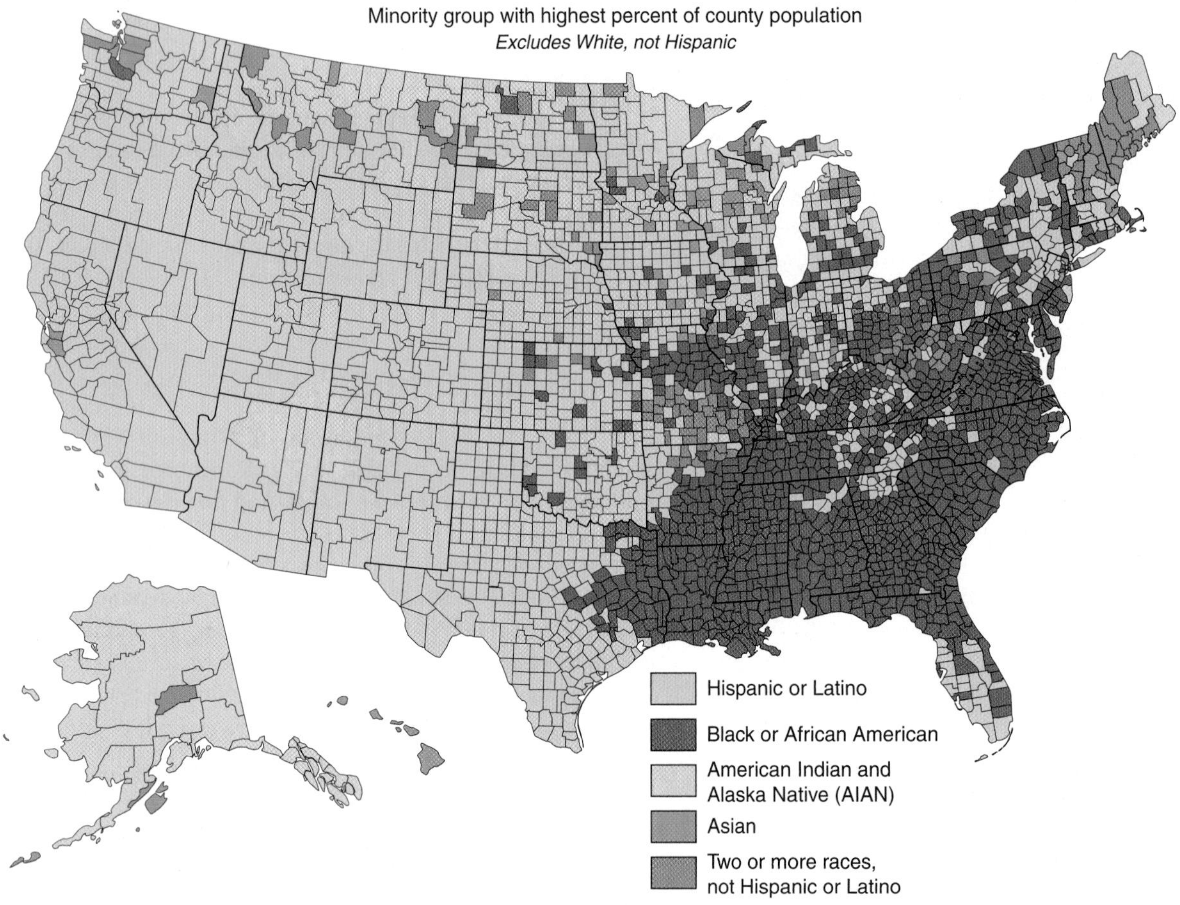

Minority group with highest percent of county population
Excludes White, not Hispanic

Hispanic or Latino
Black or African American
American Indian and Alaska Native (AIAN)
Asian
Two or more races, not Hispanic or Latino

Source: Brewer and Suchan 2001:20.

Think About It
The United States is a diverse nation. Why, in many parts of the country, can't people see that diversity in their own towns?

eral government, more than 1 out of every 4 Blacks—as opposed to 1 out of every 12 Whites—is poor.

Contemporary institutional discrimination and individual prejudice against African Americans are rooted in the history of slavery in the United States. Many other subordinate groups had little wealth and income, but as sociologist W. E. B. Du Bois (1909) and others have noted, enslaved Blacks were in an even more oppressive situation, because by law, they could not own property and could not pass on the benefits of their labor to their children. Today, increasing numbers of African Americans and sympathetic Whites are calling for *slave reparations* to compensate for the injustices of forced servitude. Reparations could include official expressions of apology from governments such as the United States, ambitious programs to improve African Americans' economic status, or even direct payments to descendants of slaves (D. Williams and Collins 2004).

The end of the Civil War did not bring genuine freedom and equality for Blacks. The Southern states passed "Jim Crow" laws to enforce official segregation, and the Supreme Court upheld them as constitutional in 1896. In addition, Blacks faced the danger of lynching campaigns, often led by the Ku Klux Klan, during the late 1800s and early 1900s. From a conflict perspective, Whites maintained their dominance formally through legalized segregation and informally by means of vigilante terror and violence (Franklin and Moss 2000).

A turning point in the struggle for Black equality came in 1954 with the unanimous Supreme Court decision in the case of *Brown v. Board of Education of Topeka, Kansas*. The Court outlawed segregation of public school students, ruling that "separate educational facilities are inherently unequal." In the wake of the *Brown* decision, there was a surge of activism on behalf of Black civil rights, including boycotts of segregated bus companies and sit-ins at restaurants and lunch counters that refused to serve Blacks.

During the 1960s, a vast civil rights movement emerged, with many competing factions and strategies for change. The Southern Christian Leadership Conference (SCLC), founded by Dr. Martin Luther King Jr., used nonviolent civil disobedience to oppose segregation. The National Association for the Advancement of Colored People (NAACP) favored use of the courts to press for equality for African Americans. But many younger Black leaders, most notably Malcolm X, turned toward an ideology of Black power. Proponents of **Black power** rejected the goal of assimilation into White middle-class society. They defended the beauty and dignity of Black and African cultures and supported the creation of Black-controlled political and economic institutions (Ture and Hamilton 1992).

Despite numerous courageous actions to achieve Black civil rights, Black and White citizens are still separate, still unequal. From birth to death, Blacks suffer in terms of their life chances. { p.230 Life remains difficult for millions of poor Blacks, who must attempt to survive in ghetto areas shattered by high unemployment and abandoned housing. Today the median household income of Blacks is still only 60 percent that of Whites, and the unemployment rate among Blacks is more than twice that of Whites.

Some African Americans—especially middle-class men and women—have made economic gains over the last 50 years. For example, data compiled by the Department of Labor show that the number of African Americans in management increased nationally from 2.4 percent of the total in 1958 to 6.0 percent in 2005. Yet Blacks still represent only 6 percent or less of all physicians, engineers, scientists, lawyers, judges, and marketing managers. In another occupation important to developing role models, African Americans and Hispanics together account for less than 11.7 percent of all editors and reporters in the United States (Bureau of the Census 2006a:388–389).

In many respects, the civil rights movement of the 1960s left institutionalized discrimination against African Americans untouched. Consequently, in the 1970s and 1980s, Black leaders worked to mobilize African American political power as a force for social change. Between 1970 and 2003, the number of African American elected officials increased sixfold. Even so, Blacks remain significantly *underrepresented*. That underrepresentation is especially distressing in view of the fact that sociologist W. E. B. Du Bois observed over 90 years ago that Blacks could not expect to achieve equal social and economic opportunities without first gaining political rights (Bureau of the Census 2006a:403; Green and Driver 1978).

Native Americans Today, about 2.2 million Native Americans represent a diverse array of cultures distinguishable by language, family organization, religion, and livelihood. The outsiders who came to the United States—European settlers and their descendants—came to know these native peoples' forefathers as "American Indians." By the time the Bureau of Indian Affairs (BIA) was organized as part of the War Department in

Whose history? Native Americans took to the streets in 2005 to protest Denver, Colorado's Columbus Day parade. The demonstrators, 200 strong, sought to remember those who lost their land and lives after White Europeans "discovered" the continent.

1824, Indian–White relations had already included three centuries of hostile actions that had led to the virtual elimination of native peoples (see Figure 11-1, page 270). During the 19th century, many bloody wars wiped out a significant part of the nation's Indian population. By the end of the century, schools for Indians—operated by the BIA or by church missions—prohibited the practice of Native American cultures. Yet at the same time, such schools did little to make the children effective competitors in White society.

Today, life remains difficult for members of the 554 tribal groups in the United States, whether they live in cities or on reservations. For example, one Native American teenager in six has attempted suicide—a rate four times higher than the rate for other teenagers. Traditionally, some Native Americans have chosen to assimilate and abandon all vestiges of their tribal cultures to escape certain forms of prejudice. However, by the 1990s, an increasing number of people in the United States were openly claiming a Native American identity. Since 1960, the federal government's count of Native Americans has tripled. According to the 2000 census, the Native American population increased 26 percent during the 1990s. Demographers believe that more and more Native Americans who previously concealed their identity are no longer pretending to be White (Grieco and Cassidy 2001).

The introduction of gambling on Indian reservations has transformed the lives of some Native Americans. Native Americans got into the gaming industry in 1988, when Congress passed the Indian Gambling Regulatory Act. The law stipulates that states must negotiate agreements with tribes interested in commercial gaming; they cannot prevent tribes from engaging in gambling operations, even if state law prohibits such ventures. The income from these lucrative operations is not evenly distributed, however. About two-thirds of recognized Indian tribes are not involved in gambling ventures. Those tribes that earn substantial revenues from gambling constitute only a small fraction of Native Americans (J. Taylor and Kalt 2005).

Use Your Sociological Imagination

www.mhhe.com/schaefer11

You are a Native American whose tribe is about to open a reservation-based casino. Will the casino further the assimilation of your people into mainstream society or encourage pluralism?

Asian Americans   Asian Americans are a diverse group, one of the fastest-growing segments of the U.S. population (up 69 percent between 1990 and 2000). Among the many groups of Americans of Asian descent are Vietnamese Americans, Chinese Americans, Japanese Americans, and Korean Americans (see Figure 11-5).

Asian Americans are held up as a *model* or *ideal minority* group, supposedly because despite past suffering from prejudice and discrimination, they have succeeded economically, socially,

and educationally without resorting to confrontations with Whites. The existence of a model minority seems to reaffirm the notion that anyone can get ahead in the United States with talent and hard work, and implies that those minorities that don't succeed are somehow responsible for their failure. Viewed from a conflict perspective, this attitude is yet another instance of "blaming the victims" (Hurh and Kim 1998).

The concept of a model minority ignores the diversity among Asian Americans: There are rich and poor Japanese Americans, rich and poor Filipino Americans, and so forth. In fact, Southeast Asians living in the United States have the highest rate of welfare dependency of any racial or ethnic group. Asian Americans have substantially more schooling than other ethnic groups, but their median income is only slightly higher than Whites' income, and their poverty rate is higher. In 2005, for every Asian American family with an annual income of $100,000 or more, there was another earning less than $25,000 a year. Moreover, even when Asian Americans are clustered at the higher-paying end of the stratification system, the glass ceiling may limit how far they can rise (DeNavas-Walt et al. 2006).

Vietnamese Americans   Each Asian American group has its own history and culture. Vietnamese Americans, for instance, came to the United States primarily during and after the Vietnam War—especially after the U.S. withdrawal from the conflict in 1975. Assisted by local agencies, refugees from the communist government in Vietnam settled throughout the United States, tens of thousands of them in small towns. But over time, Vietnamese Americans have gravitated toward the larger urban areas, establishing Vietnamese restaurants and grocery stores in their ethnic enclaves there.

FIGURE 11–5

Major Asian American Groups in the United States, 2005

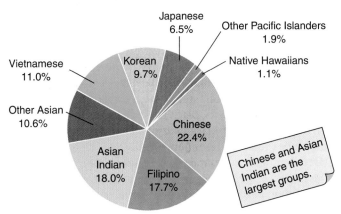

Source: Author's analysis of 2005 American Community Survey.

Think About It
Do Asian Americans really have a common identity?

In 1995, the United States resumed normal diplomatic relations with Vietnam. Gradually, the *Viet Kieu*, or Vietnamese living abroad, began to return to their old country to visit, but usually not to take up permanent residence. Today, more than 30 years after the end of the Vietnam War, sharp differences of opinion remain among Vietnamese Americans, especially the older ones, concerning the war and the present government of Vietnam (Lamb 1997).

Chinese Americans Unlike African slaves and Native Americans, the Chinese were initially encouraged to immigrate to the United States. From 1850 to 1880, thousands of Chinese immigrated to this country, lured by job opportunities created by the discovery of gold. However, as employment possibilities decreased and competition for mining jobs grew, the Chinese became the target of a bitter campaign to limit their numbers and restrict their rights. Chinese laborers were exploited, then discarded.

In 1882, Congress enacted the Chinese Exclusion Act, which prevented Chinese immigration and even forbade Chinese in the United States to send for their families. As a result, the Chinese population declined steadily until after World War II. More recently, the descendants of the 19th-century immigrants have been joined by a new influx from Hong Kong and Taiwan. These groups may contrast sharply in their degree of assimilation, desire to live in Chinatowns, and feelings about this country's relations with the People's Republic of China.

Currently, about 2.8 million Chinese Americans live in the United States. Some Chinese Americans have entered lucrative occupations, yet many immigrants struggle to survive under living and working conditions that belie the model-minority stereotype. New York City's Chinatown district is filled with illegal sweatshops in which recent immigrants—many of them Chinese women—work for minimal wages. Even in legal factories in the garment industry, hours are long and rewards are limited. A seamstress typically works 11 hours per day, 6 days a week, and earns about $10,000 a year. Other workers, such as hemmers and cutters, earn only $5,000 per year (Finder 1995; Lum and Kwong 1989).

Japanese Americans Approximately 1.3 million Japanese Americans live in the United States. As a people, they are relatively recent arrivals. In 1880, only 148 Japanese lived in the United States, but by 1920 there were more than 110,000. Japanese immigrants—called the *Issei*, or first generation—were usually males seeking employment opportunities. Many Whites saw them (along with Chinese immigrants) as a "yellow peril" and subjected them to prejudice and discrimination.

In 1941, the attack on Hawaii's Pearl Harbor by Japan had severe repercussions for Japanese Americans. The federal government decreed that all Japanese Americans on the West Coast must leave their homes and report to "evacuation camps." Japanese Americans became, in effect, scapegoats for the anger that other people in the United States felt concerning Japan's role in World War II. By August 1943, in an unprecedented application of guilt by virtue of ancestry, 113,000 Japanese Americans had been forced into hastily built camps. In striking contrast, only a few German Americans and Italian Americans were sent to evacuation camps (Hosokawa 1969).

This mass detention was costly for Japanese Americans. The Federal Reserve Board estimates their total income and property losses at nearly half a billion dollars. Moreover, the psychological effect on these citizens—including the humiliation of being labeled "disloyal"—was immeasurable. Eventually, children born in the United States to the *Issei*, called *Nisei*, were allowed to enlist in the Army and serve in Europe in a segregated combat unit. Others resettled in the East and Midwest to work in factories.

In 1983, a federal commission recommended government payments to all surviving Japanese Americans who had been held in detention camps. The commission reported that the detention was motivated by "race prejudice, war hysteria, and a failure of political leadership." It added that "no documented acts of espionage, sabotage, or fifth-column activity were shown

Despite their tourist appeal, Chinatowns offer their residents limited job opportunities in return for low wages and long hours.

to have been committed" by Japanese Americans. In 1988, President Ronald Reagan signed the Civil Liberties Act, which required the federal government to issue individual apologies for all violations of Japanese Americans' constitutional rights, and established a $1.25 billion trust fund to pay reparations to the approximately 77,500 surviving Japanese Americans who had been interned (Department of Justice 2000).

Korean Americans At nearly 1.3 million, the population of Korean Americans now exceeds that of Japanese Americans. Yet Korean Americans are often overshadowed by other groups from Asia.

Today's Korean American community is the result of three waves of immigration. The initial wave arrived between 1903 and 1910, when Korean laborers migrated to Hawaii. The second wave followed the end of the Korean War in 1953; most of these immigrants were wives of U.S. servicemen and war orphans. The third wave, continuing to the present, has reflected the admissions priorities set up in the 1965 Immigration Act. These well-educated immigrants arrive in the United States with professional skills. Yet because of language difficulties and discrimination, many must settle at least initially for positions of lower responsibility than those they held in Korea and must suffer through a period of disenchantment. Stress, loneliness, and family strife may accompany the pain of adjustment.

Like many other Asian American women, Korean American women commonly participate in the paid labor force, though in Korea women are expected to serve as mothers and homemakers only. While these roles carry over to the United States, Korean American women are also pressed to support their families while their husbands struggle to establish themselves financially. Many Korean American men begin small service and retail businesses and gradually involve their wives in the ventures. Making the situation even more difficult is the hostility Korean American–run businesses often encounter from their prospective customers (Hurh 1994, 1998; Kim 1999).

In the early 1990s, the apparent friction between Korean Americans and another subordinate racial group, African Americans, attracted nationwide attention. In New York City, Los Angeles, and Chicago, Korean American merchants confronted Blacks who were allegedly threatening them or robbing their stores. Black neighborhoods responded with hostility to what they perceived as the disrespect and arrogance of Korean American entrepreneurs. In South Central Los Angeles, the only shops in which to buy groceries, liquor, or gasoline were owned by Korean immigrants, who had largely replaced White businesspeople. African Americans were well aware of the dominant role that Korean Americans played in their local retail markets. During the 1992 riots in South Central Los Angeles, small businesses owned by Koreans were a particular target. More than 1,800 Korean businesses were looted or burned during the riots (Kim 1999).

Conflict between the two groups was dramatized in Spike Lee's 1989 movie *Do the Right Thing*. The situation stems from Korean Americans' position as the latest immigrant group to cater to the needs of inner-city populations abandoned by those who have moved up the economic ladder. This type of friction is not new; generations of Jewish, Italian, and Arab merchants have encountered similar hostility from what to outsiders seems an unlikely source—another oppressed minority.

Arab Americans Arab Americans are immigrants and their descendants who hail from the 22 nations of the Arab world. As defined by the League of Arab States, these are the nations of North Africa and what is popularly known as the Middle East, including Lebanon, Syria, Palestine, Morocco, Iraq, Saudi Arabia, and Somalia. Not all residents of those countries are Arab; for example, the Kurds, who live in northern Iraq, are not Arab. And some Arab Americans may have immigrated to the United States from non-Arab countries such as Great Britain or France, where their families have lived for generations.

The Arabic language is the single most unifying force among Arabs, although not all Arabs, and certainly not all Arab Americans, can read and speak Arabic. Moreover, the language has evolved over the centuries so that people in different parts of the Arab world speak different dialects. Still, the fact that the Qur'an (or Koran) was originally written in Arabic gives the language special importance to Muslims, just as the Torah's composition in Hebrew gives that language special significance to Jews.

Estimates of the size of the Arab American community differ widely. By some estimates, up to 3 million people of Arab ancestry reside in the United States. Among those who identify themselves as Arab Americans, the most common country of origin is Lebanon, followed by Syria, Egypt, and Palestine. In 2000, these four countries of origin accounted for two-thirds of all Arab Americans. As with other racial and ethnic groups, the Arab American population is concentrated in certain areas of the United States (see Figure 11-6). Their rising numbers have led to the development of Arab retail centers in several cities, including Dearborn and Detroit, Michigan; Los Angeles; Chicago; New York City; and Washington, D.C. (Wertsman 2001).

As a group, Arab Americans are extremely diverse. Many families have lived in the United States for several generations; others are foreign born. Their points of origin range from the metropolis of Cairo, Egypt, to the rural villages of Morocco. Despite the stereotype, most Arab Americans are *not* Muslim, and not all practice religion. Some Arab Americans are Christian. Nor can Arab Americans be characterized as having a specific family type, gender role, or occupational pattern (David 2004).

Despite this great diversity, profiling of potential terrorists at airports has put Arab and Muslim Americans under special surveillance. For years, a number of airlines and law enforcement authorities have used appearance and ethnic-sounding names to identify and take aside Arab Americans and search their belongings. After the terrorist attacks of September 2001, criticism of this practice declined as concern for the public's safety mounted.

Ethnic Groups

Unlike racial minorities, members of subordinate ethnic groups generally are not hindered by physical differences from assimilating into the dominant culture of the United States. However,

FIGURE 11–6

Distribution of the Arab American Population by State

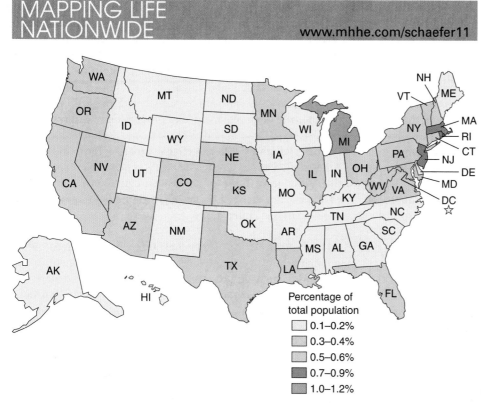

MAPPING LIFE NATIONWIDE

www.mhhe.com/schaefer11

Percentage of total population

- ☐ 0.1–0.2%
- ☐ 0.3–0.4%
- ☐ 0.5–0.6%
- ☐ 0.7–0.9%
- ☐ 1.0–1.2%

Source: Data for 2000 reported in Bureau of the Census 2003c.

high birthrates and levels of immigration—has intensified debates over public policy issues such as bilingualism and immigration.

The various Latino groups share a heritage of Spanish language and culture, which can cause serious problems in their assimilation. An intelligent student whose first language is Spanish may be presumed slow or even unruly by English-speaking schoolchildren, and frequently by English-speaking teachers as well. The labeling of Latino children as underachievers, as learn- {p.77} ing disabled, or as emotionally disturbed can act as a self-fulfilling prophecy for some children. Bilingual education aims at easing the educational difficulties experienced by Hispanic children and others whose first language is not English.

The educational difficulties of Latino students certainly contribute to the generally low economic status of Hispanics. In 2005 about 17 percent of all Hispanic households earned less than $15,000, compared to 12 percent of White non-Hispanic households. As of 2003, only 12 percent of Hispanic adults had completed college, compared to 28 percent of White non-Hispanics. In 2005 the poverty rate was 21.8 percent for Hispanics, compared to only 8.3 percent for White non-Hispanics. Overall, Latinos are not as affluent as White non-Hispanics, but a middle class is beginning to emerge (Bureau of the Census 2006a; DeNavas-Walt et al. 2006:33, 36, 48, 51; Tienda and Mitchell 2006).

members of ethnic minority groups still face many forms of prejudice and discrimination. Take, for instance, the country's largest ethnic groups—Latinos, Jews, and White ethnics.

Latinos   Together, the various groups included under the general category *Latinos* represent the largest minority in the United States. There are more than 40 million Hispanics in this country, including 26 million Mexican Americans, more than 3 million Puerto Ricans, and smaller numbers of Cuban Americans and people of Central and South American origin (see Figure 11-7). The latter group represents the fastest-growing and most diverse segment of the Hispanic community.

According to Census Bureau data, the Latino population now outnumbers the African American population in 6 of the 10 largest cities of the United States: Los Angeles, Houston, Phoenix, San Diego, Dallas, and San Antonio. Hispanics are now the majority of residents in cities such as Miami, Florida; El Paso, Texas; and Santa Ana, California. The rise in the Hispanic population of the United States—fueled by comparatively

Mexican Americans   The largest Latino population is Mexican Americans, who can be further subdivided into those

FIGURE 11–7

Major Hispanic Groups in the United States, 2005

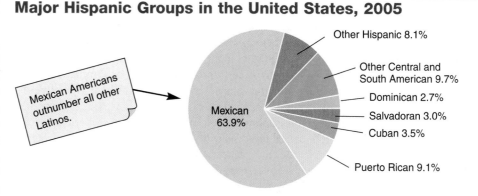

Mexican Americans outnumber all other Latinos.

- Mexican 63.9%
- Other Hispanic 8.1%
- Other Central and South American 9.7%
- Dominican 2.7%
- Salvadoran 3.0%
- Cuban 3.5%
- Puerto Rican 9.1%

Source: Author's analysis of 2005 American Community Survey.

descended from residents of the territories annexed after the Mexican American War of 1848 and those who have immigrated from Mexico to the United States. The opportunity for a Mexican to earn in one hour what it would take an entire day to earn in Mexico has pushed millions of legal and illegal immigrants north.

Aside from the family, the most important social organization in the Mexican American (or Chicano) community is the church, specifically the Roman Catholic church. This strong identification with the Catholic faith has reinforced the already formidable barriers between Mexican Americans and their predominantly White and Protestant neighbors in the Southwest. At the same time, the Catholic Church helps many immigrants to develop a sense of identity and assists their assimilation into the norms and values of the dominant culture of the United States. The complexity of the Mexican American community is underscored by the fact that Protestant churches—especially those that endorse expressive, open worship—have attracted increasing numbers of Mexican Americans.

Puerto Ricans The second-largest segment of Latinos in the United States is Puerto Ricans. Since 1917, residents of Puerto Rico have held the status of American citizens; many have migrated to New York and other eastern cities. Unfortunately, Puerto Ricans have experienced serious poverty both in the United States and on the island. Those who live in the continental United States earn barely half the family income of Whites. As a result, a reverse migration began in the 1970s, when more Puerto Ricans were leaving for the island than were coming to the mainland (Lemann 1991).

Politically, Puerto Ricans in the United States have not been as successful as Mexican Americans in organizing for their rights. For many mainland Puerto Ricans—as for many residents of the island—the paramount political issue is the destiny of Puerto Rico itself: Should it continue in its present commonwealth status, petition for admission to the United States as the 51st state, or attempt to become an independent nation? This question has divided Puerto Rico for decades and remains a central issue in Puerto Rican elections. In a 1998 referendum, voters supported a "none of the above" option, effectively favoring continuation of the commonwealth status over statehood or independence.

Cuban Americans Cuban immigration to the United States dates back as far as 1831, but it began in earnest following Fidel Castro's assumption of power in the Cuban revolution (1959). The first wave of 200,000 Cubans included many professionals with relatively high levels of schooling; these men and women were largely welcomed as refugees from communist tyranny. However, more recent waves of immigrants have aroused growing concern, partly because they were less likely to be skilled professionals. Throughout these waves of immigration, Cuban Americans have been encouraged to locate around the United States. Nevertheless, many continue to settle in (or return to) metropolitan Miami, Florida, with its warm climate and proximity to Cuba.

The Cuban experience in the United States has been mixed. Some detractors worry about the vehement anticommunism of Cuban Americans and the apparent growth of an organized crime syndicate that engages in the drug trade and ganglike violence. Recently, Cuban Americans in Miami have expressed concern over what they view as the indifference of the city's Roman Catholic hierarchy. Like other Hispanics, Cuban Americans are underrepresented in leadership positions within the church. Finally—despite many individual success stories—as a group, Cuban Americans in Miami remain behind "Anglos" (Whites) in income, rate of employment, and proportion of professionals.

Besides the ethnic differences that separate them from other Americans, Latinos must cope with gender role expectations that differ from those of mainstream American culture. Box 11-2 describes the special challenges young Latinas face as they grow up in the United States.

Jewish Americans Jews constitute almost 3 percent of the population of the United States. They play a prominent role in the worldwide Jewish community, because the United States has the world's largest concentration of Jews. Like the Japanese, many Jewish immigrants came to this country and became white-collar professionals in spite of prejudice and discrimination.

Anti-Semitism—that is, anti-Jewish prejudice—has often been vicious in the United States, although rarely so widespread and never so formalized as in Europe. In many cases, Jews have been used as scapegoats for other people's failures. Not surprisingly, Jews have not achieved equality in the United States. Despite high levels of education and professional training, they are still conspicuously absent from the top management of large corporations (except for the few firms founded by Jews). Until the late 1960s, many prestigious universities maintained restrictive quotas that limited Jewish enrollment. Private social clubs and fraternal groups frequently limit membership to gentiles (non-Jews), a practice upheld by the Supreme Court in the 1964 case *Bell v. Maryland.*

The Anti-Defamation League (ADL) of B'nai B'rith funds an annual tally of reported anti-Semitic incidents. Although the number has fluctuated, the 1994 tabulation reached the highest level in the 19 years the ADL has been recording them. In 2003 the total reported incidents of harassment, threats, vandalism, and assaults came to 1,557. Some incidents were inspired and carried out by neo-Nazi skinheads—groups of young people who champion racist and anti-Semitic ideologies. Such threatening behavior only intensifies the fears of many Jewish Americans, who find it difficult to forget the Holocaust—the extermination of 6 million Jews by the Nazi Third Reich during World War II (Anti-Defamation League 2004).

As is true for other minorities discussed in this chapter, Jewish Americans face the choice of maintaining ties to their long religious and cultural heritage or becoming as indistinguishable as possible from gentiles. Many Jews have tended to assimilate, as is evident from the rise in marriages between Jews and Christians. A study released in 2003 found that 47 percent of Jews who had married in the past five years chose to marry

research**IN***action*

11-2 Growing Up Latina

Being an adolescent in the United States is difficult—so many demands, so many perplexing changes. Add to this mix the challenges of being an immigrant and the demands escalate dramatically.

Adolescence is particularly challenging for Latinas, whose close-knit families tie them firmly to their cultural heritage at a time when other immigrant youths may be moving toward the mainstream. To get some perspective on what is happening in the lives of young Latinas, a group of researchers interviewed Spanish-speaking Latinas at an urban school in the Midwest. They found that Latinas are subject to harsher control than White non-Hispanics, both by their families and by their schoolmates, who consider them outsiders. Latinas are expected to help their families succeed by providing child care and doing household chores. The demands on them are much greater in the United States than they would be in their home countries, because in the United States virtually all adults in the family must work, often at odd hours.

The expectation that young Latinas will stay home when they are not at school effectively prevents them from working for wages, as so many other teenage girls do. Without money, they are hampered in their efforts to "look American," which makes them seem different to their peers at school. Latinas complain that they must wear inexpensive supermarket-brand tennis shoes, which separate them not only from other high school girls but from their brothers, who manage to acquire more expensive footwear through their jobs. Indeed, they lament, even Mexican Americans snub them. Added to these girls' household responsibilities is the close supervision they receive from their elders whenever they are not at home, especially at nonschool events.

The Latinas described by the researchers are typical teenage girls who are concerned with fitting in. They want to belong, but family expectations remove them from the very culture they want to assimilate with. Their plight reminds us of the special challenges many immigrant girls face, especially those who do not speak English. These girls struggle to overcome the stigma of being different. As one Latina put it, her classmates think Latinas "travel on burros" and are all called Maria.

At the same time these girls are trying to acquire an education, they are juggling two cultures, their families' and that of the larger society. One family event that Latinas look forward to is the **Quinceañera** (meaning "fifteen years"), or among Puerto Ricans, the **Quinceañero.** This very special birthday party is a celebration and formal acknowledgment of a young woman's passage to adulthood. The festive occasion may bring together the ex-

> *For those Latinas who go on to attend college, membership in a sorority can offer security on a campus where Hispanics are typically outnumbered.*

tended family, or it may be celebrated more formally as a debutante ball, with several families joining together to mark their daughters' fifteenth year. There is nothing quite like it in mainstream American culture.

For those Latinas who go on to attend college, membership in a sorority can offer security on a campus where Hispanics are typically outnumbered. Because many of the historically White sororities have been chilly at best toward Hispanics, Latinas have started their own social organizations. Today there are over 13 national Latina sororities on campuses throughout the nation, giving Latinas a much-needed sense of belonging as they develop their sense of identity as women, Hispanic Americans, and college-educated adults.

Members of the Latina sorority Sigma Pi Alpha pose for a group photo on the campus of their alma mater, California State University, Sacramento.

Let's Discuss

1. Did you attend a high school where Latinos or other immigrant students studied side by side with White non-Hispanics? If so, how wide was the cultural gap between mainstream and minority students? Did you notice any difference in the ability of different minority groups to fit in with the mainstream? What about the ability of girls versus boys to fit in?

2. Latina high school students clearly think they are handicapped in their efforts to fit in with mainstream adolescent culture. Might they feel the same way when they are 25 or 35 years old? What might be some strengths of the close family supervision they receive as adolescents?

Sources: Brodie et al. 2000; National Association of Latino Fraternal Organizations 2007; L. Williams et al. 2002.

a non-Jew. Many people in the Jewish community worry that intermarriage will lead to a rapid decline in those who identify themselves as "Jewish." Yet when asked which was the greater threat to Jewish life in the United States—intermarriage or anti-Semitism—only 41 percent of respondents replied that intermarriage was the greater threat; 50 percent selected anti-Semitism (American Jewish Committee 2001; United Jewish Communities 2003).

White Ethnics   A significant segment of the population of the United States is made up of White ethnics whose ancestors arrived from Europe within the last century. The nation's White ethnic population includes about 43 million people who claim at least partial German ancestry, 31 million Irish Americans, 16 million Italian Americans, and 9 million Polish Americans, as well as immigrants from other European nations. Some of these people continue to live in close-knit ethnic neighborhoods, while others have largely assimilated and left the "old ways" behind (Brittingham and de la Cruz 2004).

Many White ethnics today identify only sporadically with their heritage. *Symbolic ethnicity* refers to an emphasis on concerns such as ethnic food or political issues rather than on deeper ties to one's ethnic heritage. It is reflected in the occasional family trip to an ethnic bakery, the celebration of a ceremonial event such as St. Joseph's Day among Italian Americans, or concern about the future of Northern Ireland among Irish Americans. Except in cases in which new immigration reinforces old traditions, symbolic ethnicity tends to decline with each passing generation (Alba 1990; Gans 1979).

White ethnics and racial minorities have often been antagonistic to one another because of economic competition—an interpretation that agrees with the conflict approach to sociology. As Blacks, Latinos, and Native Americans emerge from the lower class, they must compete with working-class Whites for jobs, housing, and educational opportunities. In times of high unemployment or inflation, any such competition can easily generate intense intergroup conflict.

For practicing Jews, the Hebrew language is an important part of religious instruction. This teacher is showing flashcards of Hebrew alphabetic characters to deaf students.

In many respects, the plight of White ethnics raises the same basic issues as that of other subordinate people in the United States. How ethnic can people be—how much can they deviate from an essentially White, Anglo-Saxon, Protestant norm—before society punishes them for their willingness to be different? Our society does seem to reward people for assimilating, yet as we have seen, assimilation is no easy process. In the years to come, more and more people will face the challenge of fitting in, not only in the United States but around the world, as the flow of immigrants from one country to another continues to increase. In the Social Policy section that follows we will focus on global immigration and its implications for the future.

and Racial and Ethnic Inequality

Global Immigration

The Issue

Worldwide, immigration is at an all-time high. Each year, about 2.3 percent of the world's population, or 146 million people, move from one country to another (see Figure 11-8). A million of them enter the United States legally, to join the 12 percent of the population who are foreign born. Globally, these mass migrations have had a tremendous social impact. The constantly increasing numbers of immigrants and the pressure they put on job opportunities and welfare capabilities in the countries they enter raise troubling questions for many of the world's economic powers. Who should be allowed in? At what point should immigration be curtailed (Schmidley and Robinson 2003; Stalker 2000)?

The Setting

The migration of people is not uniform across time or space. At certain times, war or famine may precipitate large movements of people, either temporarily or permanently. Temporary disloca-

FIGURE 11–8

289

World Immigration Since 1500

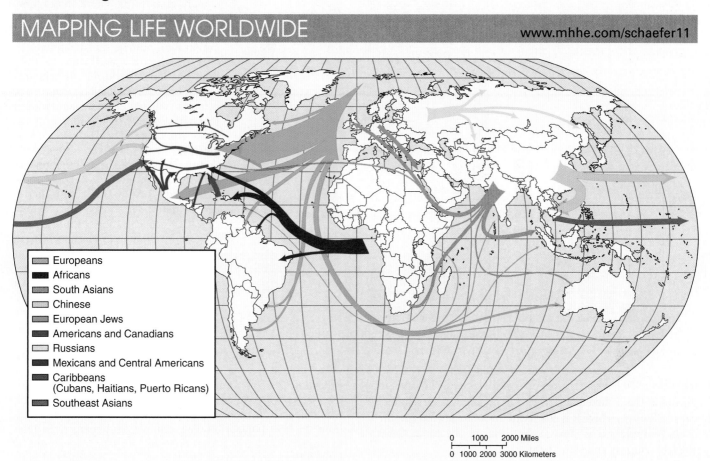

Legend:
- Europeans
- Africans
- South Asians
- Chinese
- European Jews
- Americans and Canadians
- Russians
- Mexicans and Central Americans
- Caribbeans (Cubans, Haitians, Puerto Ricans)
- Southeast Asians

0   1000   2000 Miles
0 1000 2000 3000 Kilometers

Source: Allen 2007:20.

Immigration has had a significant effect on virtually every country of the world because it has become either a source of migrants or an entry point of immigrants.

tions occur when people wait until it is safe to return to their home areas. However, more and more migrants who cannot make an adequate living in their home nations are making permanent moves to developed nations. The major migration streams flow into North America, the oil-rich areas of the Middle East, and the industrial economies of western Europe and Asia. Currently, seven of the world's wealthiest nations (including Germany, France, the United Kingdom, and the United States) shelter about one-third of the world's migrant population, but less than one-fifth of the world's total population. As long as disparities in job opportunities exist among countries, there is little reason to expect this international trend to reverse.

One consequence of global immigration is the emergence of *transnationals*—people or families who move across borders multiple times in search of better jobs and education. The industrial tycoons of the early 20th century, whose power outmatched that of many nation-states, were among the world's first transnationals. But today millions of people, many of very

modest means, move back and forth between countries much as commuters do between city and suburbs. More and more of these people have dual citizenship. Rather than being shaped by allegiance to one country, their identity is rooted in their struggle to survive—and in some instances prosper—by transcending international borders (Croucher 2004; Sassen 2005). We will take a closer look at these citizens of the world in the Social Policy section of Chapter 23.

Countries that have long been a destination for immigrants, such as the United States, usually have policies to determine who has preference to enter. Often, clear racial and ethnic biases are built into these policies. In the 1920s, U.S. policy gave preference to people from western Europe, while making it difficult for residents of southern and eastern Europe, Asia, and Africa to enter the country. During the late 1930s and early 1940s, the federal government refused to lift or loosen restrictive immigration quotas in order to allow Jewish refugees to escape the terror of the Nazi regime. In line with this policy, the SS *St. Louis,* with

Legal Migration to the United States, 1820–2010

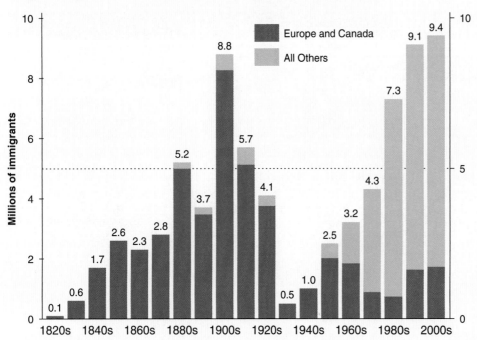

Sources: Author's estimates for the period 2000–2010; Bureau of the Census 2005a:11; Immigration and Naturalization Service 2002.

more than 900 Jewish refugees on board, was denied permission to land in the United States in 1939. The ship was forced to sail back to Europe, where it is estimated that at least a few hundred of its passengers later died at the hands of the Nazis (Morse 1967; G. Thomas and Witts 1974).

Since the 1960s, U.S. policy has encouraged the immigration of relatives of U.S. residents as well as of people who have desirable skills. This change has significantly altered the pattern of sending nations. Previously, Europeans dominated, but for the last 40 years, immigrants have come primarily from Latin America and Asia. Thus, an ever-growing proportion of the United States will be Asian or Hispanic (see Figure 11-9). To a large degrees, fear and resentment of growing racial and ethnic diversity is a key factor in opposition to immigration. In many nations, people are concerned that the new arrivals do not reflect their own cultural and racial heritage.

Sociological Insights

Research suggests that immigrants adapt well to life in the United States, becoming an asset to the nation's economy. In some areas, heavy immigration may drain a local community's resources, but in other areas it revitalizes the local economy. A national survey done in 2003 showed that 9 out of 10 immigrants believe that learning English is extremely important. Eighty-eight percent judge the United States to be better than their home country at offering "more opportunity to earn a good living" (DeParle 2007; Farkas et al. 2003; Fix et al. 2001; James P. Smith and Edmonston 1997).

Despite people's fears, immigration performs many valuable functions. For the receiving society, it alleviates labor shortages,

as it does in health care and technology in the United States. For the sending nation, migration can relieve an economy unable to support large numbers of people. Often overlooked is the large amount of money, called *remittances*, that immigrants send *back* to their home nations. Worldwide, immigrants send more than $300 billion a year back home to their relatives—an amount that represents a major source of income for developing nations (DeParle 2007b).

Immigration can be dysfunctional as well. Although studies generally show that it has a positive impact on the receiving nation's economy, areas that accept high concentrations of immigrants may find it difficult to meet short-term social service needs. And when migrants with skills or educational potential leave developing countries, their departure can be dysfunctional for those nations. No amount of payments sent back home can make up for the loss of valuable human resources from poor nations (P. Martin and Midgley 2003; Mosisa 2002).

Conflict theorists note how much of the debate over immigration is phrased in economic terms. But the debate intensifies when the arrivals are of a different racial and ethnic background from the host population. For example, Europeans often refer to "foreigners," but the term does not necessarily mean one of foreign birth. In Germany, "foreigners" refers to people of non-German ancestry, even if they were *born* in Germany; it does not refer to people of German ancestry born in another country, who may choose to return to their "mother country." Fear and dislike of "new" ethnic groups divides countries throughout the world.

The feminist perspective pays special attention to the role that women play in global immigration. Immigrant women face all the challenges that immigrant men do, plus some additional ones. Typically, they bear the responsibility for obtaining services for their families, particularly their children. Because the men are likely to be consumed with work, the women are left to navigate through the bureaucratic tangle of schools, city services, and medical facilities, as well as the unfamiliar stores and markets they must visit to feed their families. Women who need special medical services or are victims of domestic violence are often reluctant to seek outside help. Yet they are more likely than the men to serve as the liaison between their households and community and religious associations. Finally, because many new immigrants view the United States as a dangerous place to raise a family, women must be especially watchful over their children's lives (Hondagneu-Sotelo 2003).

Policy Initiatives

The long border with Mexico provides ample opportunity for illegal immigration into the United States. Throughout the 1980s, the public perception that the United States had lost control of its borders grew. Feeling pressure for immigration control, Congress ended a decade of debate by approving the Immigration Reform and Control Act of 1986. The act marked a historic change in the nation's immigration policy. For the first time, the hiring of illegal aliens was outlawed, and employers caught violating the law became subject to fines and even prison sentences. Just as significant a change was the extension of amnesty and legal status to many illegal immigrants already living in the United States. Almost 20 years later, however, the act appears to have had mixed results. Substantial numbers of illegal immigrants continue to enter the country each year, with an estimated 11 million present now at any given time—a marked increase since 2000 (Hoefer et al. 2006).

Recently, immigrants have staged massive marches to pressure Congress to speed the naturalization process and develop ways for illegal immigrants to gain legal residency. Counterdemonstrations by those who are opposed to illegal immigration have called for more resources with which to detect and deport illegal immigrants and strengthen the U.S.–Mexican border. Despite this widespread public dissatisfaction with the nation's immigration policy, however, little progress has been made. Congress has had difficulty reaching a bipartisan compromise that pleases both sides—both supporters of strict social control and those who would allow illegal immigrants to remain in the country legally, under some circumstances.

The entire world feels the overwhelming impact of globalization on immigration patterns. The European Union agreement of 1997 gave the governing commission authority to propose a Europewide policy on immigration. An EU policy that allows residents of one EU country to live and work in another EU country is expected to complicate efforts by sending nations, such as Turkey, to become members of the EU. Immigrants from Turkey's predominantly Muslim population are not welcome in many EU countries (Denny 2004).

In the wake of the attacks of September 11, 2001, on the World Trade Center and the Pentagon, immigration procedures were complicated by the need to detect potential terrorists. Illegal immigrants especially, but even legal immigrants, have felt increased scrutiny by government officials around the world. For would-be immigrants to many nations, the wait to receive the right to enter a country—even to join relatives—has increased substantially, as immigration officials scrutinize what were once routine applications more closely.

The intense debate over immigration reflects deep value conflicts in the cultures of many nations. One strand of our culture, for example, has traditionally emphasized egalitarian principles and a desire to help people in time of need. At the same time, hostility to potential immigrants and refugees—whether the Chinese in the 1880s, European Jews in the 1930s and 1940s, or Mexicans, Haitians, and Arabs today—reflects not only racial, ethnic, and religious prejudice, but a desire to maintain the dominant culture of the in-group by keeping out those viewed as outsiders.

Let's Discuss

1. Did you or your parents or grandparents immigrate to the United States from another nation? If so, when and where did your family come from, and why?

2. On balance, do the functions of immigration to the United States outweigh the dysfunctions?

3. Do you live, work, or study with recent immigrants to the United States? If so, are they well accepted in your community, or do they face prejudice and discrimination?

GettingINVOLVED

To get involved in the debate over global immigration, visit this text's Online Learning Center, which offers links to relevant Web sites. Check out the Social Policy section in the Online Learning Center as well; it provides survey data on U.S. public opinion regarding this issue.

www.mhhe.com/schaefer11

Summary

The social dimensions of race and ethnicity are important factors in shaping people's lives, both in the United States and in other countries. In this chapter, we examine the meaning of race and ethnicity and study the major *racial* and *ethnic groups* of the United States.

1. A *racial group* is set apart from others by physical differences; an *ethnic group* is set apart primarily by national origin or cultural patterns.

2. When sociologists define a *minority group,* they are concerned primarily with the economic and political power, or powerlessness, of the group.

3. The meaning people attach to the physical differences between races gives social significance to race, producing *stereotypes.*

4. *Prejudice* often leads to *discrimination,* but each can occur without the other.

5. *Institutional discrimination* results from the normal operations of a society.

6. Functionalists point out that discrimination is both functional and dysfunctional for a society. Conflict theorists explain racial subordination through *exploitation theory.* Interactionists pose the *contact hypothesis* as a means of reducing prejudice and discrimination.

7. *Racial profiling* is any arbitrary action initiated by an authority based on race, ethnicity, or national origin rather than on a person's behavior. Based on false stereotypes of certain racial and ethnic groups, the practice is not an effective way to fight crime.

8. Four patterns describe typical intergroup relations in North America and elsewhere: *amalgamation, assimilation, segregation,* and *pluralism.* Pluralism remains more of an ideal than a reality.

9. Contemporary prejudice and discrimination against African Americans are rooted in the history of slavery in the United States.

10. Asian Americans are commonly viewed as a *model* or *ideal minority,* a stereotype not necessarily beneficial to members of that group.

11. The various groups included under the general term *Latinos* represent the largest ethnic minority in the United States.

12. Worldwide, immigration is at an all-time high, fueling controversy not only in the United States but in the European Union. A new kind of immigrant, the *transnational,* moves back and forth across international borders in search of a better job or an education.

Critical Thinking Questions

1. Why is institutional discrimination even more powerful than individual discrimination? How would functionalists, conflict theorists, and interactionists study institutional discrimination?

2. Examine the relations between dominant and subordinate racial and ethnic groups in your hometown or your college. Can the community in which you grew up or the college you attend be viewed as a genuine example of pluralism?

3. What are some of the similarities and differences in the position of African Americans and Hispanics in the United States? What are some of the similarities and differences in the position of Asian Americans and Jewish Americans?

Affirmative action Positive efforts to recruit minority group members or women for jobs, promotions, and educational opportunities. (page 275)

Amalgamation The process through which a majority group and a minority group combine to form a new group. (277)

Anti-Semitism Anti-Jewish prejudice. (286)

Apartheid A former policy of the South African government, designed to maintain the separation of Blacks and other non-Whites from the dominant Whites. (279)

Assimilation The process through which a person forsakes his or her own cultural tradition to become part of a different culture. (278)

Black power A political philosophy, promoted by many younger Blacks in the 1960s, that supported the creation of Black-controlled political and economic institutions. (281)

Contact hypothesis An interactionist perspective which states that in cooperative circumstances, interracial contact between people of equal status will reduce prejudice. (277)

Discrimination The denial of opportunities and equal rights to individuals and groups because of prejudice or other arbitrary reasons. (272)

Ethnic group A group that is set apart from others primarily because of its national origin or distinctive cultural patterns. (268)

Ethnocentrism The tendency to assume that one's own culture and way of life represent the norm or are superior to all others. (271)

Exploitation theory A Marxist theory that views racial subordination in the United States as a manifestation of the class system inherent in capitalism. (276)

Genocide The deliberate, systematic killing of an entire people or nation. (277)

Glass ceiling An invisible barrier that blocks the promotion of a qualified individual in a work environment because of the individual's gender, race, or ethnicity. (272)

Hate crime A criminal offense committed because of the offender's bias against a race, religion, ethnic group, national origin, or sexual orientation. (272)

Institutional discrimination The denial of opportunities and equal rights to individuals and groups that results from the normal operations of a society. (274)

Minority group A subordinate group whose members have significantly less control or power over their own lives than the members of a dominant or majority group have over theirs. (268)

Model or **ideal minority** A minority group that despite past prejudice and discrimination, succeeds economically, socially, and educationally without resorting to confrontations with Whites. (282)

Pluralism Mutual respect for one another's cultures among the various groups in a society, which allows minorities to express their own cultures without experiencing prejudice. (279)

Prejudice A negative attitude toward an entire category of people, often an ethnic or racial minority. (271)

Quinceañera Among Latinos, a celebration of a young woman's fifteenth birthday. (287)

Racial group A group that is set apart from others because of physical differences that have taken on social significance. (268)

Racial profiling Any arbitrary action initiated by an authority based on race, ethnicity, or national origin rather than on a person's behavior. (276)

Racism The belief that one race is supreme and all others are innately inferior. (272)

Segregation The physical separation of two groups of people in terms of residence, workplace, and social events; often imposed on a minority group by a dominant group. (279)

Stereotype An unreliable generalization about all members of a group that does not recognize individual differences within the group. (270)

Symbolic ethnicity An ethnic identity that emphasizes concerns such as ethnic food or political issues rather than deeper ties to one's ethnic heritage. (288)

Read each question carefully and then select the best answer.

1. Sociologists have identified five basic properties of a minority group. Which of the following is *not* one of those properties?

    a. unequal treatment
    b. physical traits
    c. ascribed status
    d. cultural bias

2. The largest racial minority group in the United States is

    a. Asian Americans.
    b. African Americans.
    c. Native Americans.
    d. Jewish Americans.

3. Racism is a form of which of the following?

    a. ethnocentrism
    b. discrimination
    c. prejudice
    d. both b and c

4. Suppose that a White employer refuses to hire a Vietnamese American and selects an inferior White applicant. This illustrates an act of

    a. prejudice.
    b. ethnocentrism.
    c. discrimination.
    d. stigmatization.

5. Suppose that a workplace requires that only English be spoken, even when it is not a business necessity to restrict the use of other languages. This would be an example of

    a. prejudice.
    b. scapegoating.
    c. a self-fulfilling prophecy.
    d. institutional discrimination.

6. Working together as computer programmers for an electronics firm, a Hispanic woman and a Jewish man overcome their initial prejudices and come to appreciate each other's strengths and talents. This is an example of

    a. the contact hypothesis.
    b. a self-fulfilling prophecy.
    c. amalgamation.
    d. reverse discrimination.

7. Intermarriage over several generations, resulting in various groups combining to form a new group, would be an example of

    a. amalgamation.
    b. assimilation.
    c. segregation.
    d. pluralism.

8. Alphonso D'Abruzzo changed his name to Alan Alda. This is an example of

    a. amalgamation.
    b. assimilation.
    c. segregation.
    d. pluralism.

9. In which of the following racial or ethnic groups has one teenager in every six attempted suicide?

    a. African Americans
    b. Asian Americans
    c. Native Americans
    d. Latinos

10. Advocates of *Marxist class theory* argue that the basis for racial subordination in the United States lies within the capitalist economic system. Another representation of this point of view is reflected in which of the following theories?

    a. Exploitation
    b. Functionalist
    c. Interactionist
    d. Contact

11. Sociologists consider race and ethnicity to be _____ statuses, since people are born into racial and ethnic groups.

12. The one-drop rule was a vivid example of the social _____ of race—the process by which people come to define a group as a race based in part on physical characteristics, but also on historical, cultural, and economic factors.

13. _____ are unreliable generalizations about all members of a group that do not recognize individual differences within the group.

14. Sociologists use the term _____ to refer to a negative attitude toward an entire category of people, often an ethnic or racial minority.

15. When White Americans can use credit cards without suspicion, and browse through stores without being shadowed by security guards, they are enjoying _____ _____ .

16. _____ _____ refers to positive efforts to recruit minority group members or women for jobs, promotions, and educational opportunities.

17. After the Civil War, the Southern states passed "_____ _____" laws to enforce official segregation, and the Supreme Court upheld them as constitutional in 1896.

18. In the 1960s, proponents of _____ _____ rejected the goal of assimilation into White, middle-class society. They defended the beauty and dignity of Black and African cultures and supported the creation of Black-controlled political and economic institutions.

19. Asian Americans are held up as a(n) _____ or _____ minority group, supposedly because despite past suffering from prejudice and discrimination, they have succeeded economically, socially, and educationally without resorting to confrontations with Whites.

20. Together, the various groups included under the general category _____ represent the largest minority group in the United States.

{ TECHNOLOGY RESOURCES }

Online Learning Center

1. Be better prepared for your next quiz or exam by using the Flashcards at the student center in the Online Learning Center (**www.mhhe.com/schaefer11**). The Flashcards give you a fun and convenient way to brush up on the definitions of key terms and concepts from this chapter.

2. The Library of Congress maintains a Web site with information about African American History Month (**http://www.loc.gov/topics/africanamericans**). How familiar are you with this annual event, and with the African Americans who have helped to shape American society?

3. The Internet has quickly become an invaluable resource for Americans who wish to research their ethnic heritage. One useful site for Jewish Americans is JewishGen (**www.jewishgen.org**). Go to the site and link to one of the Special Interest Groups toward the bottom of the page. If you were a Jew descended from this region, how might you use these resources?

*Note: Although all the URLs listed were current as of the printing of this book, these sites often change. Please check our Web site (**www.mhhe.com/schaefer11**) for updates, hyperlinks, and exercises related to these sites.*

Reel Society Video Clips

Reel Society video clips, which appear on this book's Web site, can be used to spark discussion about the following topics from this chapter:

- Minority Groups
- Race
- Ethnicity
- Prejudice and Discrimination

This billboard in Hollywood, California, produced by the feminist advocacy group Guerrilla Girls, points out the gender inequities in the motion picture industry. In all categories, including makeup, the overwhelming majority of Oscars have been awarded to men.

12 Stratification by Gender

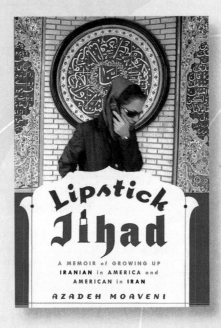

Lipstick Jihad

A MEMOIR of GROWING UP IRANIAN in AMERICA and AMERICAN in IRAN

AZADEH MOAVENI

" Young people sought Elvis's café [in Tehran, Iran] as refuge from the relentless ugliness that pervaded most public gathering places. Even in the rainy winter, people would crowd outside in the drizzle for an hour, smoking soggy cigarettes and waiting for a table. It was the only café in Tehran designed with innovative elegance and attracted young people starved for aesthetic beauty—the artists, writers, and musicians whose sensibilities suffered acutely in a city draped with grim billboards of war martyrs.

Elvis's coffeehouse inspired imitations all over the neighborhood and then the city. In early 2000, when Celine and I first began to haunt the tiny, modern nook, it was one of a kind. By the following summer of 2001, dozens of tastefully decorated cafés dotted the city, but Elvis's remained the original. In the Gandhi shopping complex, where it was located, at least six others sprang up, and the area became center stage in a café scene of shocking permissiveness. By that time, the dress code was so relaxed that everyone buzzed with tales of "You'll never believe what I saw this girl wearing!"; the fashion spring was likened to a silent coup.

Girls dressed in every color imaginable—veils of bright emerald, violet, buttercup—and in short, coat-like tunics called *manteaus* (also known by the Farsi word *roopoosh*) that hugged their curves, Capri pants that exposed long stretches of calf, pedicured toes in delicate sandals. They sat at the tables outside, in mixed groups, alone with boyfriends, laughing and talking into the late evening, past eleven. For a few weeks, Tehran actually had something like nightlife in public, not just sequestered parties inside people's houses. . . .

Often, once we finished discussing work, men, and the new styles of head scarf we coveted, Celine and I would sit and people-watch. The throng of students and young professionals flirted brazenly, and the coquettish slipping of veils produced nothing less than social theater. The Tehran of the revolution was one of the most sexualized milieus I had ever encountered. Even the chat rooms, Celine informed me, were rife with erotic discussion. People really, really wanted to talk about sex.

> *Often, once we finished discussing work, men, and the new styles of head scarf we coveted, Celine and I would sit and people-watch. The throng of students and young professionals flirted brazenly, and the coquettish slipping of veils produced nothing less than social theater.*

. . . Made neurotic by the innate oppressiveness of restriction, Iranians were preoccupied with sex in the manner of dieters constantly thinking about food. The subject meant to be *unmentionable*—to which end women were forced to wear veils, sit in the back of the bus, and order hamburgers from the special "women's line" at fast food joints—had somehow become the most mentioned of all. The constant exposure to covered flesh—whether it was covered hideously, artfully, or plainly—brought to mind, well, flesh.

The relaxing of the dress code encouraged this tendency, by breathing sexuality back into public space. Women walked down the street with their elbows, necks, and feet exposed, their figures outlined in form-fitting tunics. After two decades in exile, skin was finally back. And so imaginations flared, everyone eagerly thought about and talked about sex a lot, as though they were afraid if they didn't exploit the new permissiveness in dress and mood, they might wake up to find it had disappeared. "

(Moaveni 2005a:69–70, 71) Additional information about this excerpt can be found on the Online Learning Center at www.mhhe.com/schaefer11.

298 Azadeh Moaveni, the author of *Lipstick Jihad,* was born in California after her parents, both Iranian, fled the political turbulence of the Iranian revolution. In 1979, Islamic religious leaders overthrew the U.S.-backed monarchy that had ruled the country for decades. Almost overnight, the country was transformed from a relatively secular, Western-oriented society into a conservative Muslim state. Women who had been accustomed to dressing much as American women did were suddenly expected to cover themselves in dark robes. Young women, who had been required to attend school and serve in the armed forces under the old regime, were now forbidden even to appear in public without a male escort.

Though Moaveni grew up in the United States, she was conversant with her Persian cultural heritage, albeit from a distance. After graduating from college, she lived in Iran for two years, where she covered the country's affairs as a news correspondent. There she found a different society from the one her parents had fled a generation before. The lipstick jihad she refers to in the title of her book is an allusion to the recent relaxation of the strict standards for women's dress and behavior—a change that Iranian women effected by personally defying government sanctions. (*Jihad* is an Arabic term that stands for one's inner struggle against the forces of ungodliness.) Today, provocatively dressed Iranian women flirt with men in public cafés they would not have dared to visit—if the cafés had existed—25 years ago. But their place in society is still very much circumscribed by their gender (Moaveni 2005b).

How do gender roles differ from one culture to another? Are women in the United States still oppressed because of their gender? Have men's and women's positions in society changed? In this chapter we will study these and other questions by looking first at how various cultures, including our own, assign women and men to particular social roles. Then we will consider sociological explanations for gender stratification. We will

Azadeh Moaveni, author of *Lipstick Jihad,* was born in California to refugees from the Iranian revolution. In 1998 she moved to Iran and found a very different society from the one her parents had left in 1979.

see that around the world, women constitute an oppressed majority of the population. We'll learn that only recently have women begun to develop a collective consciousness of their oppression, and the way in which their gender combines with other factors to create social inequality. Finally, we will close the chapter with a Social Policy section on the controversy over a woman's right to abortion.

Social Construction of Gender

How many airline passengers do you think are startled on hearing a female captain's voice from the cockpit? What do we make of a father who announces that he will be late for work because his son has a routine medical checkup? Consciously or unconsciously, we are likely to assume that flying a commercial plane is a *man's* job and that most parental duties are, in fact, *maternal* duties. Gender is such a routine part of our everyday activities that we typically take notice only when someone deviates from conventional behavior and expectations.

Although a few people begin life with an unclear sexual identity, the overwhelming majority begin with a definite sex and

quickly receive societal messages about how to behave. In fact, virtually all societies have established social distinctions between females and males that do not inevitably result from biological differences between the sexes (such as women's reproductive capabilities).

In studying gender, sociologists are interested in the gender-role socialization that leads females and males to behave differently. In Chapter 4, *gender roles* were defined as expectations regarding the proper behavior, attitudes, and activities of males and females. The application of dominant gender roles leads to many forms of differentiation between women and men. Both sexes are physically capable of learning to cook and sew, yet most Western societies determine that women should perform those tasks. Both men and women are capable of learning to weld and to fly airplanes, but those functions are generally assigned to men.

Most people do not display strictly "masculine" or "feminine" qualities all the time. Indeed, such standards can be ambiguous. For instance, though men are supposed to be unemotional, they are allowed to become emotional when their favorite athletic team wins or loses a critical game. Yet our society still focuses on "masculine" and "feminine" qualities as if men and women must be evaluated in those terms. Despite recent inroads by women into male-dominated occupations, our construction of gender continues to define significantly different expectations for females and males (J. Howard and Hollander 1997; West and Zimmerman 1987).

Gender roles are evident not only in our work and behavior but also in how we react to others. We are constantly "doing gender" without realizing it. If the father mentioned earlier sits in the doctor's office with his son in the middle of a workday, he will probably receive approving glances from the receptionist and from other patients. "Isn't he a wonderful father?" runs through their minds. But if the boy's mother leaves *her* job and sits with the son in the doctor's office, she will not receive such silent applause.

We construct our behavior socially so as to create or exaggerate male–female differences. For example, men and women come in a variety of heights, sizes, and ages. Yet traditional norms regarding marriage and even casual dating tell us that in heterosexual couples, the man should be older, taller, and wiser than the woman. As we will see throughout this chapter, such social norms help to reinforce and legitimize patterns of male dominance.

Gender Roles in the United States

Gender-Role Socialization

Male babies get blue blankets; females get pink ones. Boys are expected to play with trucks, blocks, and toy soldiers; girls receive dolls and kitchen goods. Boys must be masculine—active, aggressive, tough, daring, and dominant—but girls must be feminine—soft, emotional, sweet, and submissive. These traditional gender-role patterns have been influential in the socialization of children in the United States.

An important element in traditional views of proper "masculine" and "feminine" behavior is **homophobia,** fear of and prejudice against homosexuality. Homophobia contributes significantly to rigid gender-role socialization, since many people stereotypically associate male homosexuality with femininity and lesbianism with masculinity. Consequently, men and women who deviate from traditional expectations about gender roles are often presumed to be gay. Despite the advances made by the gay liberation movement, the continuing stigma attached to homosexuality in our culture places pressure on all males (whether gay or not) to exhibit only narrow "masculine" behavior and on all females (whether lesbian or not) to exhibit only narrow "feminine" behavior (Seidman 1994; see also Lehne 1995).

It is *adults,* of course, who play a critical role in guiding children into those gender roles deemed appropriate in a society.

{ p.96 } Parents are normally the first and most crucial agents of socialization. But other adults, older siblings, the mass media, and religious and educational institutions also exert an important influence on gender-role socialization, in the United States and elsewhere.

It is not hard to test how rigid gender-role socialization can be. Just try transgressing some gender norm—say, by smoking a cigar in public if you are female, or by carrying a purse if you are male. That was exactly the assignment given to sociology students at the University of Colorado and Luther College in Iowa. Professors asked students to behave in ways that they thought violated the norms of how a man or woman should act. The students had no trouble coming up with gender-norm transgressions (see Table 12-1), and they kept careful notes on others' reactions to their behavior, ranging from amusement to disgust (Nielsen et al. 2000).

Women's Gender Roles How does a girl come to develop a feminine self-image, while a boy develops one that is masculine? In part, they do so by identifying with females and males in their families and neighborhoods and in the media. If a young girl regularly sees female television characters of all ages and body types, she is likely to grow up with a normal body image. And it will not hurt if the women she knows—her mother, sister, parents' friends, and neighbors—are comfortable with their body types, rather than constantly obsessed with their weight. In contrast, if this young girl sees only wafer-thin actresses and models on television, her self-image will be quite different. Even if she grows up to become a well-educated professional, she may

Table 12-1

An Experiment in Gender Norm Violation by College Students

Norm Violations by Women	Norm Violations by Men
Send men flowers	Wear fingernail polish
Spit in public	Needlepoint in public
Use men's bathroom	Throw Tupperware party
Buy jock strap	Cry in public
Buy/chew tobacco	Have pedicure
Talk knowledgeably about cars	Apply to baby-sit
Open doors for men	Shave body hair

Source: Nielsen et al. 2000:287.

In an experiment testing gender-role stereotypes, sociology students were asked to behave in ways that might be regarded as violations of gender norms, and to keep notes on how others reacted. This is a sample of their choices of behavior over a seven-year period. Do you agree that these actions test the boundaries of conventional gender behavior?

secretly regret falling short of the media stereotype—a shapely, sexy young woman in a bathing suit.

Television is far from alone in stereotyping women. Studies of children's books published in the United States in the 1940s, 1950s, and 1960s found that females were significantly underrepresented in central roles and illustrations. Virtually all female characters were portrayed as helpless, passive, incompetent, and in need of a strong male caretaker. Studies of picture books published from the 1970s through the 1990s found some improvement, but males still dominated the central roles. While males were portrayed as a variety of characters, females tended to be shown mostly in traditional roles, such as mother, grandmother, or volunteer, even if they also held nontraditional roles, such as working professional (Etaugh 2003).

Social research on gender roles reveals some persistent differences between men and women in North America and Europe. Women tend to feel pressure both to marry and to become a mother. Often, marriage is viewed as their true entry into adulthood. And women are expected not only to become mothers but to *want* to be mothers. Obviously, men play a role in marriage and parenthood, but these events do not appear to be as critical in the life course of a man. Society defines men's identities by their economic success. And even though many women today fully expect to have careers and achieve recognition in the labor force, success at work is not as important to their identity as it is for men (Doyle and Paludi 1998; Russo 1976).

Traditional gender roles have restricted females more severely than males. This chapter shows how women have been confined to subordinate roles in the political and economic institutions of the United States. Yet it is also true that gender roles have restricted males.

Men's Gender Roles Stay-at-home fathers? Until recent decades such an idea was unthinkable. Yet in a nationwide survey done in 2002, 69 percent of respondents said that if one parent stays home with the children, it makes no difference whether that parent is the mother or the father. Only 30 percent thought that the mother should be the one to stay home. But while people's conceptions of gender roles are obviously changing, the fact is that men who stay home to care for their children are still an unusual phenomenon. For every stay-at-home dad there are 38 stay-at-home moms (Jason Fields 2004:11–12; Robison 2002).

While attitudes toward parenting may be changing, studies show little change in the traditional male gender role. Men's roles are socially constructed in much the same way as women's are. Family, peers, and the media all influence how a boy or man comes to view his appropriate role in society. The male gender role, besides being antifeminine (show no "sissy stuff"), includes proving one's masculinity at work and sports—often by using force in dealing with others—as well as initiating and controlling all sexual relations.

What type of body image do the media promote to young women in the United States? Over the last 80 years, one-fourth of the winners of the Miss America pageant have been so thin, they would be considered undernourished by the World Health Organization (Byrd-Bredbenner and Murray 2003).

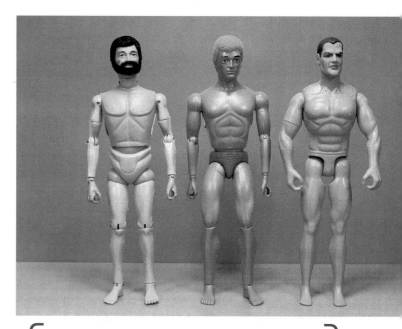

Society often exaggerates male–female differences in appearance and behavior. In 1964, the G.I. Joe doll (left) had a realistic appearance, but by 1992 (middle) it had begun to acquire the exaggerated muscularity characteristic of professional wrestlers (right). The change intensified the contrast with ultrathin female figures, like the Barbie doll (Angier 1998).

Gender roles serve to discourage men from entering certain low-paying female-dominated occupations, such as child care. Only 5 percent of day-care workers are male.

Males who do not conform to the socially constructed gender role face constant criticism and even humiliation, both from children when they are boys and from adults as men. It can be agonizing to be treated as a "chicken" or a "sissy" as a youth—particularly if such remarks come from one's father or brothers. And grown men who pursue nontraditional occupations, such as preschool teaching or nursing, must constantly deal with others' misgivings and strange looks. In one study, interviewers found that such men frequently had to alter their behavior in order to minimize others' negative reactions. One 35-year-old nurse reported that he had to claim he was "a carpenter or something like that" when he "went clubbing," because women weren't interested in getting to know a male nurse. The subjects made similar accommodations in casual exchanges with other men (Cross and Bagilhole 2002:215).

At the same time, boys who successfully adapt to cultural standards of masculinity may grow up to be inexpressive men who cannot share their feelings with others. They remain forceful and tough, but as a result they are also closed and isolated. In fact, a small but growing body of scholarship suggests that for men as well as women, traditional gender roles may be disadvantageous. In many communities across the nation, girls seem to outdo boys in high school, grabbing a disproportionate share of the leadership positions, from valedictorian to class president to yearbook editor—everything, in short, except captain of the boys' athletic teams. Their advantage continues after high school. In the 1980s, girls in the United States became more likely than boys to go to college. By 2004, women accounted for over 57 percent of college students nationwide. And in 2002, for the first time, more women than men in the United States earned doctoral degrees.

Some of this discrepancy in achievement can be explained by noting that men can earn good hourly wages with less formal schooling than women. Yet by a number of measures, girls appear to take schooling more seriously than boys. In 2003, for example, female students taking the Advanced Placement (AP) tests outnumbered male students in 19 out of 33 subjects. Overall, they accounted for 56 percent of students who took the AP tests. Educational professionals need to look more closely at men's underperformance in school, not to mention their overrepresentation in reported crime and illegal drug use (Bureau of the Census 2006a:171; Ripley 2005).

In the last 40 years, inspired in good part by the contemporary feminist movement (examined later in the chapter), increasing numbers of men in the United States have criticized the restrictive aspects of the traditional male gender role. Some men have taken strong public positions in support of women's struggle for full equality, and have even organized voluntary associations such as the National Organization for Men Against Sexism (NOMAS), founded in 1975 to support positive changes for men. Nevertheless, the traditional male gender role remains well entrenched as an influential element of our culture (Messner 1997; National Organization for Men Against Sexism 2007).

Use Your Sociological **Imagination**

You are living in a society in which there are no gender roles. What is your life like?

www.mhhe.com/schaefer11

Cross-Cultural Perspective

To what extent do actual biological differences between the sexes contribute to the cultural differences associated with gender? This question brings us back to the debate over "nature versus {pp.86–89 nurture." In assessing the alleged and real differences between men and women, it is useful to examine cross-cultural data.

The research of anthropologist Margaret Mead points to the importance of cultural conditioning—as opposed to biology—in defining the social roles of males and females. In *Sex and Temperament,* Mead ([1935] 2001; 1973) describes the typical behaviors of each sex in three different cultures in New Guinea.

Cultural conditioning is important in the development of gender-role differences. Among the Bororo, a semi-nomadic people of West Africa, the *male* gender role includes ceremonial dancing (shown here), body painting, and other forms of personal adornment.

In the first culture, both men and women play the role of nurturer. In the second, both sexes behave in a stereotypically male fashion. And in the third, the gender roles are reversed: women behave as we expect men to behave, and vice versa. If biology determined all differences between the sexes, then cross-cultural differences such as those described by Mead would not exist. Her findings confirm the influential role of culture and socialization in gender-role differentiation. There appears to be no innate or biological reason to designate completely different gender roles for men and women.

In any society, gender stratification requires not only individual socialization into traditional gender roles within the family, but the promotion and support of those traditional roles by other social institutions, such as religion and education. Moreover, even with all major institutions socializing the young into conventional gender roles, every society has women and men who resist and successfully oppose the stereotypes: strong women who become leaders or professionals, gentle men who care for children, and so forth. It seems clear that differences between the sexes are not dictated by biology. Indeed, the maintenance of traditional gender roles requires constant social controls—and those controls are not always effective.

We can see the social construction of gender roles in process in societies strained by war and social upheaval. By summer 2004, a year after the war in Iraq began, young girls in Baghdad seldom ventured out to the park or swimming pool. When they did, their parents made sure they were dressed conservatively, in loose clothing and perhaps a head scarf. The overthrow of Saddam Hussein's secular regime had emboldened Islamic fundamentalists, who had begun visiting schools, urging young

women to wear long sleeves and cover their heads. Though school officials resisted, many girls dropped out, some out of fear for their safety and others because of financial hardship. In the atmosphere of violence and lawlessness that followed the 2003 invasion, young women wondered what the future would hold for them, and whether they would ever have the opportunity to become educated professionals, as their mothers had (Sengupta 2004).

Sociological Perspectives on Gender

Cross-cultural studies indicate that societies dominated by men are much more common than those in which women play the decisive role. Sociologists have turned to all the major theoretical perspectives to understand how and why these social distinctions are established. Each approach focuses on culture rather than biology as the primary determinant of gender differences. Yet in other respects, advocates of these sociological perspectives disagree widely.

The Functionalist View

Functionalists maintain that gender differentiation has contributed to overall social stability. Sociologists Talcott Parsons and Robert Bales (1955) argued that to function most effectively, the family requires adults who specialize in particular roles. They viewed the traditional gender roles as arising out of the need to establish a division of labor between marital partners.

Parsons and Bales contended that women take the expressive, emotionally supportive role and men the instrumental, practical role, with the two complementing each other. *Instrumentality* refers to an emphasis on tasks, a focus on more distant goals, and a concern for the external relationship between one's family and other social institutions. *Expressiveness* denotes concern for the maintenance of harmony and the internal emotional affairs of the family. According to this theory, women's interest in expressive goals frees men for instrumental tasks, and vice versa. Women become anchored in the family as wives, mothers, and household managers; men become anchored in the occupational world outside the home. Of course, Parsons and Bales offered this framework in the 1950s, when many more women were full-time homemakers than is true today. These theorists did not explicitly endorse traditional gender roles, but they implied that dividing tasks between spouses was functional for the family as a unit.

Given the typical socialization of women and men in the United States, the functionalist view is initially persuasive. However, it would lead us to expect girls and women who have no interest in children to become baby-sitters and mothers. Similarly, males who love spending time with children might be programmed into careers in the business world. Such differentiation might harm the individual who does not fit into prescribed roles, as well as deprive society of the contributions of many talented people who feel confined by gender stereotyping. Moreover, the functionalist approach does not convincingly explain why men should be assigned categorically to the instrumental role, and women to the expressive role.

The Conflict Response

Viewed from a conflict perspective, the functionalist approach masks the underlying power relations between men and women. Parsons and Bales never explicitly presented the expressive and instrumental roles as being of unequal value to society, yet their inequality is quite evident. Although social institutions may pay lip service to women's expressive skills, men's instrumental skills are more highly rewarded, whether in terms of money or prestige. Consequently, according to feminists and conflict theorists, any division of labor by gender into instrumental and expressive tasks is far from neutral in its impact on women.

Conflict theorists contend that the relationship between females and males has traditionally been one of unequal power, with men in a dominant position over women. Men may originally have become powerful in preindustrial times because their size, physical strength, and freedom from childbearing duties allowed them to dominate women physically. In contemporary societies, such considerations are not so important, yet cultural beliefs about the sexes are long established, as anthropologist Margaret Mead and feminist sociologist Helen Mayer Hacker (1951, 1974) both stressed. Such beliefs support a social structure that places males in controlling positions.

Conflict theorists, then, see gender differences as a reflection of the subjugation of one group (women) by another group (men). If we use an analogy to Marx's analysis of class conflict, {pp.13–14, 222 we can say that males are like the bourgeoisie, or capitalists; they control most of the society's wealth, prestige, and power. Females are like the proletariat, or workers; they can acquire valuable resources only by following the dictates of their bosses. Men's work is uniformly valued; women's work (whether unpaid labor in the home or wage labor) is devalued.

The Feminist Perspective

A significant component of the conflict approach to gender {p.17 stratification draws on feminist theory. Although use of that term is comparatively recent, the critique of women's position in society and culture goes back to some of the earliest works that have influenced sociology. Among the most important are Mary Wollstonecraft's *A Vindication of the Rights of Women* (originally published in 1792), John Stuart Mill's *The Subjection of Women* (originally published in 1869), and

Conflict theorists emphasize that men's work is uniformly valued, while women's work (whether unpaid labor in the home or wage labor) is devalued. These women are making tents in a factory in Binghamton, New York.

Friedrich Engels's *The Origin of the Family, Private Property, and the State* (originally published in 1884).

Engels, a close associate of Karl Marx, argued that women's subjugation coincided with the rise of private property during industrialization. Only when people moved beyond an agrarian economy could males enjoy the luxury of leisure and withhold rewards and privileges from women. Drawing on the work of Marx and Engels, many contemporary feminist theorists view women's subordination as part of the overall exploitation and injustice that they see as inherent in capitalist societies. Some radical feminist theorists, however, view the oppression of women as inevitable in *all* male-dominated societies, whether they are labeled capitalist, socialist, or communist (L. Feuer 1989; Tuchman 1992).

Feminist sociologists would find little to disagree with in the conflict theorists' perspective, but are more likely to embrace a political agenda. Feminists would also argue that until recently, the very discussion of women and society, however well meant, was distorted by the exclusion of women from academic thought, including sociology. We have noted the many accom- {pp.14, 17 plishments of Jane Addams and Ida Wells-Barnett, but they generally worked outside the discipline, focusing on what we would now call applied sociology and social work. At the time, their efforts, while valued as humanitarian, were seen as unrelated to the research and conclusions being reached in academic circles, which of course were male academic circles (Andersen 2003; J. Howard 1999).

Feminist theorists today (including conflict theorists) emphasize that in the United States, male dominance goes far beyond the economic sphere. Throughout this textbook, we examine disturbing aspects of men's behavior toward women. The ugly realities of rape, wife battering, sexual harassment, and street harassment all illustrate and intensify women's subordinate position. Even if women reach economic parity with men, even if they win equal representation in government, genuine equality between the sexes cannot be achieved if these attacks remain as common as they are today.

Functionalist, conflict, and feminist theorists acknowledge that it is not possible to change gender roles drastically without making dramatic revisions in a culture's social structure. Functionalists perceive the potential for social disorder, or at least unknown social consequences, if all aspects of traditional gender stratification are disturbed. Yet for conflict and feminist theorists, no social structure is ultimately desirable if it is maintained by oppressing a majority of citizens. These theorists argue that gender stratification may be functional for men—who hold the power and privilege—but it is hardly in the interests of women.

The Interactionist Approach

While functionalists and conflict theorists who study gender stratification typically focus on macro-level social forces and institutions, interactionist researchers tend to examine gender stratification on the micro level of everyday behavior. As an example, studies show that men initiate up to 96 percent of all interruptions in cross-sex (male–female) conversations. Men are more likely than women to change the topic of conversation, to ignore topics chosen by members of the opposite sex, to minimize the contributions and ideas of members of the opposite sex, and to validate their own contributions. These patterns reflect the conversational (and in a sense, political) dominance of males. Moreover, even when women occupy a prestigious position, such as that of physician, they are more likely to be interrupted than their male counterparts (Ridgeway and Smith-Lovin 1999; Tannen 1990; West and Zimmerman 1983).

These findings regarding cross-sex conversations have been frequently replicated. They have striking implications when one considers the power dynamics underlying likely cross-sex interactions—employer and job seeker, college professor and student, husband and wife, to name just a few. From an interactionist perspective, these simple, day-to-day exchanges are one more battleground in the struggle for gender equality—as

women try to get a word in edgewise in the midst of men's interruptions and verbal dominance (Hollander 2002; Okamoto and Smith-Lovin 2001; Tannen 1994a, 1994b).

Table 12-2 summarizes the major sociological perspectives on gender.

Women: The Oppressed Majority

Many people, both male and female, find it difficult to conceive of women as a subordinate and oppressed group. Yet take a look at the political structure of the United States: Women remain noticeably underrepresented. As of mid-2006, for example, only 8 of the nation's 50 states had a female governor (Arizona, Connecticut, Delaware, Hawaii, Kansas, Louisiana, Michigan, and Washington).

Women have made slow but steady progress in certain political arenas. In 1981, out of 535 members of Congress, there were only 21 women: 19 in the House of Representatives and 2 in the Senate. In contrast, the Congress that held office in mid-2007 had 87 women: 71 in the House and 16 in the Senate. Yet the membership and leadership of Congress remain overwhelmingly male (Center for American Women and Politics 2007).

In October 1981, Sandra Day O'Connor was sworn in as the nation's first female Supreme Court justice. Still, no woman has ever served as president of the United States, vice president, or chief justice of the Supreme Court.

Sexism and Sex Discrimination

Just as African Americans are victimized by racism, women in our society suffer from sexism. **Sexism** is the ideology that one sex is superior to the other. The term is generally used to refer to male prejudice and discrimination against women. In Chapter 11, we noted that Blacks can suffer from both individual acts of racism and institutional discrimination. **Institutional discrimination** was defined as the denial of opportunities and equal rights to individuals and groups that results from the normal operations of a society. In the same sense, women suffer from both individual acts of sexism (such as sexist remarks and acts of violence) and institutional sexism.

It is not simply that particular men in the United States are biased in their treatment of women. All the major institutions of our society—including the government, armed forces, large corporations, the media, universities, and the medical establishment—are controlled by men. These institutions, in their normal, day-to-day operations, often discriminate against women and perpetuate sexism. For example, if the central office of a nationwide bank sets a policy that single women are a bad risk for loans—regardless of their incomes and investments—that bank will discriminate against women in state after state. It will do so even at branches where loan officers hold no personal biases toward women, but are merely "following orders." Box 12-1 dispels the sex-

Table 12-2

Sociological Perspectives on Gender

Theoretical Perspective	Emphasis
Functionalist	Gender differentiation contributes to social stability
Conflict	Gender inequality is rooted in the female–male power relationship
Feminist	Women's subjugation is integral to society and social structure
Interactionist	Gender distinctions are reflected in people's everyday behavior

12-1 Differences in Male and Female Physicians' Communication with Patients

When Perri Klass told her four-year-old son she would be taking him to the pediatrician, he replied, "Is she a nice doctor?" Klass, a professor of pediatrics, was struck by his innocent assumption that like his mother, all pediatricians were female. "Boys can be doctors too," she told him.

Not long ago, there would have been little potential for confusion on her son's part. Klass probably would not have been admitted to medical school, much less appointed a professor of medicine. But since the advent of the women's movement, the medical profession has been integrating women into its ranks. In the United States today, 42 percent of physicians under age 35 are female. Now, more than two dozen studies done over the past three and a half decades indicate that not only are women competent physicians; in some respects they are more effective than their male counterparts.

The female advantage is particularly noteworthy in physician–patient communication.

Female primary care physicians spend an extra two minutes talking with patients, or 10 percent more time than male primary care physicians. They also engage in more patient-centered communication, listening more, asking questions about patients' personal well-being, and counseling patients about the con-

> *Not only are women competent physicians; in some respects they are more effective than their male counterparts.*

cerns they bring to the doctor's office. Perhaps most important, female physicians tend to see their relationship with patients as an active partnership, one in which they discuss several treatment options with patients rather than recommending a single course of treatment. From a sociological point of view, these differ-

ences between female and male physicians correspond to the gender differences in communication style that interactionist researchers have noted.

In some respects, female and male physicians do not differ. Researchers noted no differences in the quality or amount of time the two groups spend on purely medical matters, or on the length of time they spend conversing socially with patients.

Let's Discuss

1. In your own experience, have you noted a gender difference in the way doctors communicate with their patients? Explain.
2. Why is the quality of a doctor's communication with patients important? What might be the benefit of female physicians' superior communication style?

Sources: John Carroll 2003; Klass 2003:319; Kotulak 2005; Roter et al. 2002.

---

ist myth that women cannot be good doctors, which medical schools used for years to justify their discriminatory admissions policies.

Our society is run by male-dominated institutions, yet with the power that flows to men come responsibility and stress. Men have higher reported rates of certain types of mental illness than women, and a greater likelihood of death due to heart attack or stroke. The pressure on men to succeed, and then to remain on top in the competitive world of work, can be especially intense. That is not to suggest that gender stratification is as damaging to men as it is to women. But it is clear that the power and privilege men enjoy are no guarantee of personal well-being.

Use Your Sociological **Imagination**

Think of organizations or institutions you belong to whose leadership positions are customarily held by men. What would those organizations be like if they were led by women?

Sexual Harassment

The courts recognize two kinds of sexual harassment. Formally defined, **sexual harassment** is behavior that occurs when work benefits are made contingent on sexual favors (as a quid pro quo), or when touching, lewd comments, or the exhibition of pornographic material creates a "hostile environment" in the workplace. In 1998, the Supreme Court ruled that harassment applies to people of the same sex as well as the opposite. The quid pro quo type of harassment is fairly easy to identify in a court of law. But the issue of hostile environment has become the subject of considerable debate both in courts and in the general public (Greenhouse 1998; Lewin 1998).

Sexual harassment must be understood in the context of continuing prejudice and discrimination against women. Whether it occurs in the federal bureaucracy, in the corporate world, or in universities, sexual harassment generally takes place in organizations in which White males are at the top of the hierarchy of authority, and women's work is valued less than men's. Studies have shown that African American women and Latinas are more likely than White women to experience sexual harassment. From a conflict perspective, it is not surprising that women—and especially women of color—are likely to become victims of sexual harassment. In terms of job security, these groups are typically an organization's most vulnerable employees (Shupe et al. 2002).

The Status of Women Worldwide

A detailed overview of the status of the world's women, issued by the United Nations in 2000, noted that women and men live in different worlds—worlds that differ in terms of access to education and work opportunities, as well as in health, personal security, and human rights. The Hindu culture of India, for example, makes life especially harsh for widows. When Hindu women marry, they join their husband's family. If the husband dies, the widow is the "property" of that family. In many cases, she ends up working as an unpaid servant; in others she is simply abandoned and left penniless. Ancient Hindu scriptures portray widows as "inauspicious" and advise that "a wise man should avoid her blessings like the poison of a snake" (Burns 1998:10).

Though Westerners tend to view Muslim societies as being similarly harsh toward women, that perception is actually an overgeneralization. Muslim countries are exceedingly varied and complex and do not often fit the stereotypes created by the Western media. For a detailed discussion of the status of Muslim women today, see Box 12-2.

Regardless of culture, however, women everywhere suffer from second-class status. It is estimated that women grow half the world's food, but they rarely own land. They constitute one-third of the world's paid labor force, but are generally found in the lowest-paying jobs. Single-parent households headed by women, which appear to be on the increase in many nations, are typically found in the poorest sections of the population. The feminization of poverty has become a global phenomenon. As in the United States, women around the world are underrepresented politically.

Despite these challenges, women are not responding passively. They are mobilizing, individually and collectively. Given the significant underrepresentation of women in government offices and national legislatures, however, the task is difficult, as we shall see in Chapter 17.

Not surprisingly, there is a link between the wealth of industrialized nations and the poverty of women in developing countries. Viewed from a conflict perspective or through the lens

{ pp.243–250 } of Immanuel Wallerstein's world systems analysis, the economies of developing nations are controlled and exploited by industrialized countries and multinational corporations based in those countries. Much of the exploited labor in developing nations, especially in the nonindustrial sector, is performed by women. Women workers typically toil long hours for low pay, but contribute significantly to their families' incomes (Jacobson 1993).

In industrial countries, women's unequal status can be seen in the division of housework, as well as the jobs they hold and the pay they earn. Sociologist Makiko Fuwa (2004) analyzed gender inequality in 22 industrial countries using data from the International Social Survey Programme. Fuwa looked first at how couples divided up their housework. Then she compared that data to societywide measures of women's presence in high-status occupations, as well as their wages relative to men's. Figure 12-1 shows that while gender differences in empowerment vary widely from one country to the next, equality between the sexes is rare.

Women in the Workforce of the United States

Almost 30 years ago, the U.S. Commission on Civil Rights (1976:1) concluded that the passage in the Declaration of

FIGURE 12–1

Gender Inequality in Industrial Nations

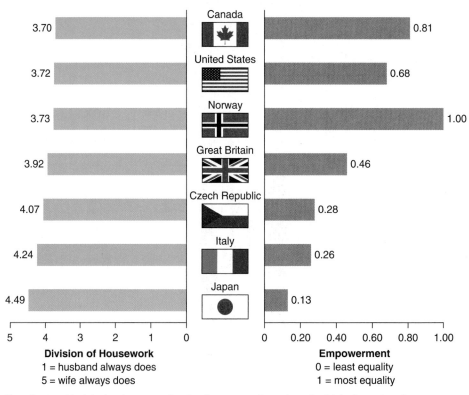

Notes: Housework includes laundry, grocery shopping, dinner preparation, and care for sick family members. Empowerment includes the proportions of women in parliament, in management, and in professional/technical positions, as well as gender inequality in income.
Source: Adapted from Fuwa 2004:757.

12-2 The Head Scarf and the Veil: Complex Symbols

The wearing of a veil or head scarf by women is common to many but not all Middle Eastern societies. However, Muslim women are not alone in their observance of certain standards for dress. All Muslims, men and women alike, are expected to cover themselves and avoid revealing clothes designed to accentuate the body's contours or emphasize its physical beauty. The Qur'an (or Koran) permits Muslims to wear revealing garments in private, with their families or with members of the same sex. In keeping with this religious prescription, some Muslim countries allow beaches and public pools to be set aside exclusively for use by men or women.

The Prophet Muhammad recommended that women cover all of their bodies except for the face, hands, and feet. The Koran adds that a woman's headcovering should fall over the upper chest and neck. A variety of women's outergarments comply with these guidelines for modest attire; collectively, they are referred to as the *hijab*. Accepted Muslim head coverings include both a simple head scarf and a face veil that actually covers the face. Face veils are dictated by cultural tradition, however—not by Islam.

In effect, the veil represents a rejection of the beauty myth (see Chapter 8), which is so prevalent in Western societies. While a Muslim woman's beauty is valued, it is not to be seen or exploited by the whole world. By covering themselves almost completely, Muslim women assure themselves and their families that their physical appearance will not play a role in their contacts outside the family. Rather, these women will be known only for their faith, their intellect, and their personalities.

In the 20th century, the veil was politicized by modernization movements that pitted Western cultural values against traditional Islamic values. In Turkey, for instance, the rise to power of President Kemal Atatürk in 1923 sparked a process of sweeping social change, in which government officials attempted to subordinate traditional ethnic and religious influences to their nationalistic goals. Though women weren't forbidden to wear the veil, they were not allowed to veil themselves in public places like schools. Not surprisingly, many Muslims resented these forced social changes. In recent decades, strict clergy in countries like Iran and Afghanistan have reinstituted the veil and other Islamic traditions.

In the United States today, Muslim women select from an array of traditional garments, including a long, loose tailored coat and a loose black overgarment that is worn with a scarf or perhaps a face veil. However, they are just as apt to wear an overblouse and a long skirt or loose pants, which they can buy at local clothing stores.

> *In effect, the veil represents a rejection of the beauty myth, which is so prevalent in Western societies.*

Researchers have identified three perspectives on the *hijab* among Muslim women in the United States and other non-Islamic countries. Younger, better-educated women who support wearing the *hijab* in public draw on Western ideas of individual rights, arguing in favor of veiling as a form of personal expression. In contrast, older, less well-educated women who support the *hijab* do so without referring to Western ideology; they cannot see why veiling should be an issue. A third group of women, of all ages and educational backgrounds, opposes the *hijab*.

In some non-Muslim countries, notably France, officials have come under fire for banning the *hijab* or the head scarf in public schools (see Chapter 4). The custom generally has not been an issue in the United States, though one 11-year-old had to go to federal

The head scarf—an expression of modesty, a woman's right as an individual, or a sign of oppression?

court to establish her right to wear a head scarf at school in Muskogee, Oklahoma. Interestingly, the U.S. Department of Justice supported her lawsuit.

Let's Discuss

1. Consider life in a society in which women wear veils. Can you see any advantages, from the woman's point of view? From the man's?
2. Do you find the Western emphasis on physical beauty oppressive? If so, in what ways?

Sources: al-Jadda 2006; Gole 1997; Haeri 2004; Killian 2003.

Independence proclaiming that "all men are created equal" has been taken too literally for too long—especially with respect to women's opportunities for employment. In this section we will see how gender bias has limited women's opportunities for employment outside the home, at the same time that it forces them to carry a disproportionate burden inside the home.

Labor Force Participation Women's participation in the paid labor force of the United States increased steadily throughout the 20th century (see Figure 12-2). No longer is the adult woman associated solely with the role of homemaker. Instead, millions of women—married and single, with and without children—are working in the paid labor force. In 2005, 59 percent of adult women in the United States held jobs outside the home, compared with 38 percent in 1960. A majority of women are now members of the paid labor force. Among new mothers, 56 percent return to the labor force within a year of giving birth. In 1975, only 31 percent went back to work (Bureau of the Census 2006a:377, 380).

Yet women entering the job market find their options restricted in important ways. Particularly damaging is occupational segregation, or confinement to sex-typed "women's jobs." For example, in 2005, women accounted for 97 percent of all dental hygienists and 85 percent of all librarians. Entering such sex-typed occupations places women in "service" roles that parallel the traditional gender-role standard under which housewives "serve" their husbands.

Women are *underrepresented* in occupations historically defined as "men's jobs," which often carry much greater financial rewards and prestige than women's jobs. For example, in 2005,

women accounted for approximately 45 percent of the paid labor force of the United States, yet they constituted only 13 percent of civil engineers, 23 percent of all dentists, and 30 percent of all computer systems analysts and physicians (see Table 12-3).

Such occupational segregation is not unique to the United States but typical of industrial countries. In Great Britain, for example, only 29 percent of computer analysts are women, while 81 percent of cashiers and 90 percent of nurses are women (Cross and Bagilhole 2002).

Women from all groups and men from minority groups sometimes encounter attitudinal or organizational bias that prevents them from reaching their full potential. As we saw in Chapter 11, the term ***glass ceiling*** refers to an invisible barrier that blocks the promotion of a qualified individual in a work environment because of the individual's gender, race, or ethnicity. A study of the Fortune 500 largest corporations in the United States showed that in 2006 less than 15 percent of the seats on their boards of directors were held by women. Furthermore, only 11 of the corporations had a female chief executive, while 489 had a male at the top (Catalyst 2007).

Table 12-3

U.S. Women in Selected Occupations, 2005: Women as a Percentage of All Workers in the Occupation

Underrepresented		Overrepresented	
Firefighters	3%	High school teachers	57%
Aircraft pilots	5	Cashiers	76
Civil engineers	13	Social workers	80
Police officers	14	File clerks	81
Clergy	16	Elementary teachers	82
Dentists	23	Librarians	85
Architects	24	Tellers	87
Computer systems analysts	30	Registered nurses	89
Lawyers	30	Receptionists	92
Physicians	32	Child care workers	95
Mail carriers	42	Secretaries	97
College teachers	44	Dental hygienists	97

Note: Women constitute 45 percent of the entire labor force.
Source: Data for 2005 reported in Bureau of the Census 2006a:388–391.

FIGURE 12–2

Trends in U.S. Women's Participation in the Paid Labor Force, 1890–2005

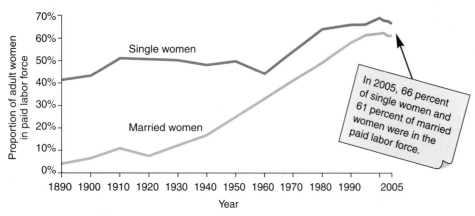

In 2005, 66 percent of single women and 61 percent of married women were in the paid labor force.

Sources: Bureau of the Census 1975; 2006a:379.

Compensation He works. She works. Both are physicians—a high-status occupation with considerable financial rewards. He makes $140,000. She makes $88,000.

These median earnings for physicians in the United States were released by the Census Bureau in 2004. They are typical of the results of the bureau's detailed study of occupations and income. Take air traffic controllers. He makes $67,000; she earns $56,000. Or housekeepers: he makes $19,000; she earns $15,000. What about teacher's assistants? He makes $20,000; she earns $15,000. Statisticians at the bureau looked at the median earnings for no fewer than 821 occupations ranging from dishwasher to chief executive. After adjusting for workers' age, education, and work experience, they came to an unmistakable conclusion: Across the board, there is a substantial gender gap in the median earnings of full-time workers.

Men do not always earn more than women for doing the same work. Researchers at the Census Bureau found 2 occupations out of 821 in which women typically earn about 1 percent more income than men: hazardous materials recovery and telecommunications line installation. These two occupations employed less than 1 out of every 1,000 workers the bureau studied. Forecasting analyses show no convincing evidence that the wage gap is narrowing (Lips 2003; Weinberg 2004).

While women may well be at a disadvantage in male-dominated occupations, the same is not true for men in female-dominated occupations. Sociologist Michelle Budig (2002) examined a national database containing career information on more than 12,000 men, collected over the course of 15 years. She found that men were uniformly advantaged in female occupations. Though male nurses, grade school teachers, and librarians may experience some scorn in the larger society, they are much more likely than women to be encouraged to become administrators. Observers of the labor force have termed this advantage for men in female-dominated occupations the *glass escalator*—quite a contrast to the glass ceiling (Jacobs 2003; C. L. Williams 1992, 1995).

Social Consequences of Women's Employment
Today, many women face the challenge of trying to juggle work and family. Their situation has many social consequences. For one thing, it puts pressure on child care facilities, public financing of day care, and even the fast-food industry, which provides many of the meals women used to prepare themselves. For another, it raises questions about what responsibility male wage earners have in the household.

Who does the housework when women become productive wage earners? Studies indicate that there is a clear gender gap in the performance of housework, although it has been narrowing. Women do more housework and spend more time on child care than men, whether on a workday or a nonworkday. Taken together, then, a woman's workday on and off the job is much longer than a man's (Sayer et al. 2004).

Sociologist Arlie Hochschild (1989, 1990, 2005) has used the phrase **second shift** to describe the double burden—work outside the home followed by child care and housework—that many women face and few men share equitably. On the basis of interviews with and observations of 52 couples over an eight-year period, Hochschild reports that the wives (and not their husbands) drive home from the office while planning domestic schedules and play dates for children—and then begin their second shift. Drawing on national studies, she concludes that women spend 15 fewer hours each week in leisure activities than their husbands. In a year, these women work an extra month of 24-hour days because of the second shift; over a dozen years, they work an extra year of 24-hour days. Hochschild found that the married couples she studied were fraying at the edges, and so were their careers and their marriages. With such reports in mind, many feminists have advocated greater governmental and { pp.102–103 } corporate support for child care, more flexible family leave policies, and other reforms designed to ease the burden on the nation's families (Moen and Roehling 2005).

The greater amounts of time women put into caring for their children, and to a lesser degree into housework, take a special toll on women who are pursuing careers. In a 2005 survey published in the *Harvard Business Review,* about 40 percent of women indicated that they had voluntarily left work for months or years, compared to only 24 percent of men. As Figure 12-3 (page 310) shows, women were much more likely than men to take time off for family reasons.

Though women in the United States have a long way to go toward equality in housework, they are doing as well as or better than women in most other countries, including industrial nations. By one measure, 30 percent of the couples in U.S. households share most of the housework, compared to 4 percent in Japan, 25 percent in Great Britain, 27 percent in Sweden, and 32 percent in Canada (C. Geist 2005).

Use Your Sociological Imagination

In your opinion, how important is it for a couple to share the housework?

www.mhhe.com/schaefer11

Emergence of a Collective Consciousness

Feminism is the belief in social, economic, and political equality for women. The feminist movement of the United States was born in upstate New York, in a town called Seneca Falls, in the summer of 1848. On July 19, the first women's rights convention began, attended by Elizabeth Cady Stanton, Lucretia Mott, and other pioneers in the struggle for women's rights. This first wave of *feminists,* as they are currently known, battled ridicule and scorn as they fought for legal and political equality for women. They were not afraid to risk controversy on behalf of their cause; in 1872, Susan B. Anthony was arrested for attempting to vote in that year's presidential election.

Why Leave Work?

| | Women | Five Top Reasons for Leaving | Men | |

Women — Percent
- Family time: 44%
- Change in career: 16%
- Earn a degree, other training: 23%
- Work not enjoyable, satisfying: 17%
- Not interested in field: *
- Moved away: 17%

Men — Percent
- Family time: 12%
- Change in career: 29%
- Earn a degree, other training: 25%
- Work not enjoyable, satisfying: 24%
- Not interested in field: 18%
- Moved away: *

* Not one of top 5 reasons

Note: Based on a representative Harris Interactive survey of "highly qualified" workers, defined as those with a graduate degree, a professional degree, or a high honors undergraduate degree.
Source: Figure adapted from Sylvia Ann Hewlett and Carolyn Burk Luce, 2005. "Off-Ramps and On-Ramps: Keeping Talented Women on the Road to Success," *Harvard Business Review,* March 2005. Copyright © 2005 by the Harvard Business School Publishing Corporation, all rights reserved. Reprinted by permission of Harvard Business Review.

Ultimately, the early feminists won many victories, among them the passage and ratification of the Nineteenth Amendment to the Constitution, which granted women the right to vote in national elections beginning in 1920. But suffrage did not lead to other reforms in women's social and economic position, and in the early and middle 20th century the women's movement became a much less powerful force for social change.

The second wave of feminism in the United States emerged in the 1960s and came into full force in the 1970s. In part, the movement was inspired by three pioneering books arguing for women's rights: Simone de Beauvoir's *The Second Sex,* Betty Friedan's *The Feminine Mystique,* and Kate Millett's *Sexual Politics.* In addition, the general political activism of the 1960s led women—many of whom were working for Black civil rights or against the war in Vietnam—to reexamine their own powerlessness. The sexism often found within allegedly progressive and radical political circles convinced many women that they needed to establish their own movement for women's liberation (Freeman 1973, 1975).

As more and more women became aware of sexist attitudes and practices, including attitudes they themselves had accepted through socialization into traditional gender roles, they began to challenge male dominance. A sense of sisterhood, much like the class consciousness that Marx hoped would emerge in the proletariat, became evident. Individual women identified their interests with those of the collectivity *women.* No longer were women happy in submissive, subordinate roles ("false consciousness" in Marxist terms).

One challenge this second wave of feminists faced was speaking to the needs of all women. At the time, many full-time homemakers feared that the movement was devaluing their traditional role in life. Moreover, the movement's most visible leaders were all White, and if they were not affluent, they generally were not poor. Consequently, many women "on the outside" of the core leadership group concluded that feminists were not speaking directly to the needs of poor African Americans, Latinos, and other minority groups (Breines 2007; P. Collins 2000).

National surveys done today, however, show that while women generally endorse feminist positions, they do not necessarily accept the label *feminist.* Fifty-seven percent of women considered themselves feminists in 1987; the proportion had dropped to about 25 percent in 2001. Feminism as a unified political cause, requiring one to accept a similar stance on everything from abortion to sexual harassment to pornography to welfare, has fallen out of favor. Both women and men prefer to express their views on these complex issues individually, rather than under a convenient umbrella like feminism. Still, feminism is very much alive in the growing acceptance of women in nontraditional roles, and even the basic acknowledgment that a married mother not only can work outside the home but perhaps *belongs* in the labor force. A majority of women say that given the choice, they would prefer to work outside the home rather than stay home and take care of a house and family, and about one-quarter of women prefer *Ms.* to *Miss* or *Mrs.* (Feminist Majority Foundation 2007; J. Robinson 2002).

The women's movement has undertaken public protests on a wide range of issues. Feminists have endorsed passage of the equal rights amendment, government subsidies for child care (see Chapter 4), affirmative action for women and minorities (see Chapter 18), federal legislation outlawing sex discrimination in education (see Chapter 16), greater representation of women in government (see Chapter 17), and the right to a legal abortion (discussed in the Social Policy section of this chapter).

Use Your Sociological Imagination

Do you know many people who refer to themselves explicitly as feminists? What about people who make it clear that they are not feminists—how many do you know?

Abigail E. Drevs
**Former Program and Volunteer
Coordinator, Y-ME Illinois**

For two and a half years Abigail Drevs served as the program and volunteer coordinator for the Illinois affiliate of Y-ME National Breast Cancer Organization. Y-ME's mission is to provide support and educational outreach through workshops and peer-led support groups, to ensure that no one faces breast cancer alone.

As the coordinator, Drevs was responsible for recruiting, training, and retaining the volunteers who staff the organization's support groups. She also presented workshops about breast cancer and how to detect it early. To make sure that services were available to all and that funding was being managed effectively, she met with community leaders and organizations, corporate partners, and medical institutions. "A typical work week, in one word, was juggling," she says. "In a small nonprofit, few people do the work of many."

Occasionally, Drevs traveled to conferences to network with other organizations dedicated to working with certain populations of breast cancer survivors, including young women. These organizations have banded together to develop a pilot program that will address young women's concerns with intimacy and infertility after breast cancer.

In Chicago, Drevs strove to raise the awareness of breast cancer among African American women from all walks of life. "As a middle-class white woman, the issue of race had been a very academic one in my experience," she says. "I read Studs Terkel and took racial disparities curricula, but never truly understood the issues until I became immersed in the community." Drevs's experience with Y-ME helped her to understand the position of thousands of underinsured African American women in that city—"limited access to health care, distrust of the system, and the importance of their community and social networks."

Asked what insights she has drawn from her training in sociology, Drevs replies, "It reaffirmed my belief that no one perspective is the only perspective. From fundamental social theory to social conflict to developing nations, there are many ways to explain something, and oftentimes, there is something that can be gained from each perspective."

Drevs is currently working for her alma mater, Dartmouth College, as the program manager for young alumni, students, and diversity at the Office of Alumni Relations. Her advice to current students of sociology: "Even if you don't major in this, make sure to take it with you wherever you go. Many of the world's problems can be traced to not communicating properly and not understanding another group's perspective. A good basis in sociology can serve you well, no matter what you do."

Let's Discuss

1. Do some research on breast cancer. Does the survival rate differ among different racial and ethnic groups? What about different social classes? Why are education and early detection important?
2. Relate what you have learned about breast cancer to what you have learned about gender. What social patterns does your research illustrate?

Intersection of Social Inequality

We have seen that, historically, women have been limited to specific roles and occupations by both tradition and law. Many women experience such differential treatment not only because of their gender, but because of their race and ethnicity. Moreover, a disproportionate share of this low-status group is also poor. The African American feminist Patricia Hill Collins (2000) has termed the convergence of social forces that contributes to their subordinate status the ***matrix of domination.*** Simply put, Whites dominate non-Whites; men dominate women; and the affluent dominate the poor (see Figure 12-4). Though gender, race, and social class are not the only sources of oppression, they do profoundly affect women and people of color in the United States. Other forms of categorization and stigmatization that can be included in the matrix include sexual orientation, religion, disability, and age.

Though feminists have addressed themselves to the needs of minority women, these women are oppressed much more by

FIGURE 12-4

Matrix of Domination

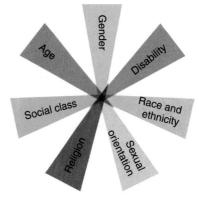

Source: Developed by author.

The matrix of domination illustrates how several social factors, including gender, social class, and race and ethnicity, can converge to create a cumulative impact on a person's social standing.

their race and ethnicity than by their gender. The question for Latinas (Hispanic women), African American women, Asian American women, and Native American women appears to be whether they should unite with their brothers against racism or challenge them for their sexism. The answer is that our society must eradicate both sexism and racism (Beisel and Kay 2004; C. Epstein 1999).

The discussion of gender roles among African Americans has always provoked controversy. Advocates of Black nationalism contend that feminism only distracts women from participating fully in the African American struggle. The existence of feminist groups among Blacks, in their view, simply divides the Black community, thereby serving the dominant White majority. In contrast, Black feminists such as bell hooks (1994) argue that little is to be gained by accepting the gender-role divisions of the dominant society, which place women in a separate, subservient position. Though the media commonly portray Black women in a negative light—as illiterates, welfare queens, or prostitutes—Black feminists emphasize that it is not solely Whites and the White-dominated media who focus on such negative images. Black men (most recently, Black male rap artists) have also portrayed African American women in a negative way (Raybon 1989; Threadcraft 2008).

Historically, Native Americans stand out as an exception to the patriarchal tradition in North America. At the time of the European settlers' arrival, Native American gender roles varied greatly from tribe to tribe. Southern tribes, for reasons unclear to today's scholars, were usually matriarchal and traced their descent through the mother. European missionaries, who sought to make the native peoples more like Europeans, set out to transform this arrangement, which was not entirely universal. Like members of other groups, some Native American women have resisted gender stereotypes (Marubbio 2006).

Latinas are usually considered as part of either the Hispanic or feminist movements, and their distinctive experience ignored. In the past, they have been excluded from decision making in the two social institutions that most affect their daily lives: the family and the church. Particularly in the lower class, the Hispanic family suffers from the pervasive tradition of male domination. And the Catholic Church relegates women to supportive roles, while reserving the leadership positions for men (Browne 2001; De Andra 2004). Box 11-2 (page 287) addresses the additional hardships that Latina immigrants to the United States experience.

To this point, much of our discussion has focused on the social effects of race and ethnicity, coupled with poverty, low incomes, and meager wealth. The matrix of domination highlights the confluence of these factors with gender discrimination, which we must include to fully understand the plight of women of color.

The Battle over Abortion from a Global Perspective

The Issue

Few issues seem to stir as much intense conflict as abortion. A critical victory in the struggle for legalized abortion in the United States came in 1973, when the Supreme Court granted women the right to terminate pregnancies. This ruling, known as *Roe v. Wade,* was based on a woman's right to privacy. The Court's decision was generally applauded by pro-choice groups, which believe women should have the right to make their own decisions about their bodies and should have access to safe and legal abortions. It was bitterly condemned by those opposed to abortion. For these pro-life groups, abortion is a moral and often a religious issue. In their view, human life begins at the moment of conception, so that its termination through abortion is essentially an act of murder.

The Setting

The debate that has followed *Roe v. Wade* revolves around prohibiting abortion altogether, or at the very least, limiting it. In 1979, for example, Missouri required parental consent for mi-

nors wishing to obtain an abortion, and the Supreme Court upheld the law. Parental notification and consent have become especially sensitive issues in the debate. Pro-life activists argue that the parents of teenagers should have the right to be notified about—and to permit or prohibit—abortions. In their view, parental authority deserves full support at a time when the traditional nuclear family is embattled. However, pro-choice activists counter that many pregnant teenagers come from troubled families where they have been abused. These young women may have good reason to avoid discussing such explosive issues with their parents.

Changing technology has had its impact on the debate. "Day-after" pills, which have been available in some nations since 1998, are now prescribed in the United States. These emergency contraception pills can prevent pregnancy after unprotected sex. In 2000, the U.S. government approved RU-486, an abortion-inducing pill that can be used in the first seven weeks of pregnancy. The regime requires doctor visits but no surgical procedures. In addition, doctors, guided by ultrasound, can now end a pregnancy as early as eight days after conception. Pro-life activists are concerned that the use of ultrasound technology will allow people to abort unwanted females in nations where a premium is placed on male offspring.

In the United States, people appear to support a woman's right to a legal abortion, but with reservations. According to a 2006 national survey, only 16 percent oppose a woman's right to a legal abortion under all circumstances. However, only 19 percent feel that abortion should be legal under *any* circumstances. These findings have held for the last 30 years (Benac 2006).

Sociological Insights

Sociologists see gender and social class as the defining issues surrounding abortion. The intense conflict over abortion reflects broader differences over women's position in society. Feminists involved in defending abortion rights typically believe that men and women are essentially similar; they support women's full participation in work outside the home and oppose all forms of sex discrimination. In contrast, most antiabortion activists believe that men and women are fundamentally different. In their view, men are best suited to the public world of work, while women are best suited to the demanding and crucial task of rearing children. These activists are troubled by women's growing participation in work outside the home, which they view as destructive to the family and ultimately to society.

In regard to social class, the first major restriction on the legal right to terminate a pregnancy affected poor people. In 1976, Congress passed the Hyde Amendment, which banned the use of Medicaid and other federal funds for abortions. The Supreme Court upheld this legislation in 1980. State laws also restrict the use of public funds for abortions (see Figure 12-5).

Another obstacle facing the poor is access to abortion providers. In the face of vocal pro-life sentiment, fewer and fewer hospitals throughout the world are allowing physicians to perform abortions, except in extreme cases. To avoid controversy, many medical schools have ceased to offer training in the procedure. Moreover, some doctors who work in clinics, intimidated by death threats and actual murders, have stopped performing abortions. For poor people in rural areas, this reduction in service makes it more difficult to locate and travel to a facility that will accommodate their wishes. Viewed from a conflict perspective, this is one more financial burden that falls especially heavily on low-income women.

FIGURE 12–5

313

Stratification by Gender

Restrictions on Public Funding for Abortion

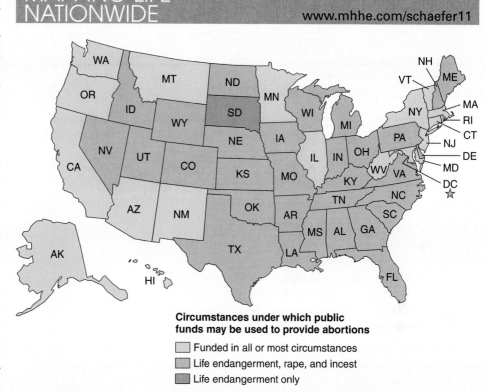

MAPPING LIFE NATIONWIDE

www.mhhe.com/schaefer11

Circumstances under which public funds may be used to provide abortions

☐ Funded in all or most circumstances
☐ Life endangerment, rape, and incest
☐ Life endangerment only

Note: As of January 17, 2007.
Source: NARAL Pro-Choice America 2007.

Policy Initiatives

In 1973 the Supreme Court supported the general right to terminate a pregnancy by a narrow 5–4 majority. Although pro-life activists continue to hope for an overruling of *Roe v. Wade*, they have focused in the interim on weakening the decision through tactics such as limiting the use of fetal tissue in medical experiments and prohibiting certain late-term abortions, which they term "partial-birth" abortions. The Supreme Court continues to hear cases involving such restrictions. In 2005, speculation arose over a potential narrowing of the applicability of *Roe v. Wade* following the appointment of new justices, who may hold more conservative positions than those they replaced.

What is the policy in other countries? As in the United States, many European nations responded to public opinion and liberalized abortion laws beginning in the 1970s. However, many of those nations limit the procedure to the first 12 weeks of a pregnancy. (The United States, by contrast, allows abortions up to about the 24th week and beyond.) Inspired by the strong antiabortion movement in the United States, antiabortion activists in Europe have become more outspoken, especially in Great Britain, France, Spain, Italy, and Germany (*The Economist* 2003c).

The policies of the United States and developing nations are intertwined. Throughout the 1980s and 1990s, antiabortion

The Global Divide on Abortion

☐ Nations where abortion is permitted in certain cases upon request

Note: Data current as of December 2004. Countries that prohibit abortion under any circumstances are Chile, El Salvador, Malta, and the Holy See (Vatican City).
Sources: Developed by the author based on Gonnut 2001; United Nations Population Division 1998, 2004, 2006.

members of Congress have often successfully blocked foreign aid to countries that might use the funds to encourage abortion. And yet those developing nations generally have the most restrictive abortion laws. As Figure 12-6 shows, it is primarily in Africa, Latin America, and parts of Asia that women are not allowed to terminate a pregnancy on request. As might be expected, illegal abortions are most common in those nations. An estimated quarter of the world's women live in countries where abortion is illegal or is permitted only if a woman's life is in jeopardy. Hence, 40 percent of abortions worldwide—about 20 million procedures each year—are performed illegally (Joynt and Ganeshananthan 2003).

Let's Discuss

1. Do you know anyone who has undergone an illegal abortion? If so, what were the circumstances? Was the woman's health endangered by the procedure?

2. Do you think teenage girls should have to get their parents' consent before having an abortion? Why or why not?

3. Under what circumstances should abortions be allowed? Explain your reasoning.

GettingINVOLVED

To get involved in the debate over abortion, visit this text's Online Learning Center, which offers links to relevant Web sites. Check out the Social Policy section in the Online Learning Center as well; it provides survey data on U.S. public opinion regarding this issue.

www.mhhe.com/schaefer11

Summary

Gender is an ascribed status that provides a basis for social differentiation. This chapter examines the social construction of gender, theories of stratification by gender, women as an oppressed majority group, and the intersection of social inequality.

1. In the United States, the social construction of gender continues to define significantly different expectations for females and males.

2. **Gender roles** show up in our work and behavior and in how we react to others.

3. Though females have been more severely restricted than men by traditional gender roles, those roles have also restricted males.

4. The research of anthropologist Margaret Mead points to the importance of cultural conditioning in defining the social roles of males and females.

5. Functionalists maintain that sex differentiation contributes to overall social stability, but conflict theorists charge that the relationship between females and males is one of unequal power, with men dominating women. This dominance shows up in people's everyday interactions.

6. As one example of their micro-level approach to the study of gender stratification, interactionists have analyzed men's verbal dominance over women through conversational interruptions.

7. Women around the world suffer from **sexism, institutional discrimination,** and **sexual harassment.**

8. As women have taken on more and more hours of paid employment outside the home, they have been only partially successful in getting their husbands to take on more homemaking duties, including child care.

9. Many women agree with the positions of the feminist movement but reject the label *feminist.*

10. Many women experience differential treatment not only because of their gender, but because of their race, ethnicity, and social class. Patricia Hill Collins has termed this convergence of social forces the **matrix of domination.**

11. The issue of abortion has bitterly divided the United States (as well as other nations), pitting pro-choice activists against pro-life activists.

Critical Thinking Questions

1. Imagine that you are assigned the opposite gender at birth, but that your race, ethnicity, religion, and social class remain the same. Drawing on the information contained in this chapter, describe how your life as a member of the opposite sex might differ from your life today.

2. In what ways is the social position of White women in the United States similar to that of African American women, Latinas (Hispanic women), and Asian American women? In what ways are women's social positions markedly different, given their racial and ethnic status?

3. Imagine that you have been asked to study political activism among women. How might you employ surveys, observations, experiments, and existing sources to better understand such activism?

Key Terms

Expressiveness Concern for the maintenance of harmony and the internal emotional affairs of the family. (page 302)

Feminism The belief in social, economic, and political equality for women. (309)

Gender role Expectations regarding the proper behavior, attitudes, and activities of males and females. (298)

Glass ceiling An invisible barrier that blocks the promotion of a qualified individual in a work environment because of the individual's gender, race, or ethnicity. (308)

Homophobia Fear of and prejudice against homosexuality. (299)

Institutional discrimination The denial of opportunities and equal rights to individuals and groups that results from the normal operations of a society. (304)

Instrumentality An emphasis on tasks, a focus on more distant goals, and a concern for the external relationship between one's family and other social institutions. (302)

Matrix of domination The cumulative impact of oppression because of race, gender, and class, as well as religion, sexual orientation, disability, and age. (311)

Second shift The double burden—work outside the home followed by child care and housework—that many women face and few men share equitably. (309)

Sexism The ideology that one sex is superior to the other. (304)

Sexual harassment Behavior that occurs when work benefits are made contingent on sexual favors (as a quid pro quo), or when touching, lewd comments, or the exhibition of pornographic material creates a "hostile environment" in the workplace. (305)

Read each question carefully and then select the best answer.

1. Both males and females are physically capable of learning to cook and sew, yet most Western societies determine that women should perform these tasks. This illustrates the operation of

   a. gender roles.
   b. sociobiology.
   c. homophobia.
   d. comparable worth.

2. An important element in traditional views of proper "masculine" and "feminine" behavior is fear of homosexuality. This fear, along with accompanying prejudice, is referred to as

   a. lesbianism.
   b. femme fatalism.
   c. homophobia.
   d. claustrophobia.

3. The most crucial agents of socialization in teaching gender roles in the United States are

   a. peers.
   b. teachers.
   c. media personalities.
   d. parents.

4. In examining cross-cultural data, anthropologist Margaret Mead found that

   a. biology is the most important factor in determining the social roles of males and females.
   b. cultural conditioning is the most important factor in defining the social roles of males and females.
   c. biology and cultural conditioning have an equal impact in determining the social roles of males and females.
   d. biology and cultural conditioning have a negligible impact in determining the social roles of males and females.

5. Which sociological perspective acknowledges that it is not possible to change gender roles drastically without dramatic revisions in a culture's social structure?

   a. the functionalist perspective
   b. the conflict perspective
   c. the interactionist perspective
   d. both a and b

6. The term *sexism* is generally used to refer to

   a. female prejudice and discrimination against men.
   b. male prejudice and discrimination against women.
   c. female discrimination against men and male discrimination against women equally.
   d. discrimination between members of the same sex.

7. Which of these statements is true?

   a. More boys than girls take AP exams.
   b. Women in the United States are more likely to attend college than men.
   c. Women in the United States are less likely to obtain doctoral degrees than men.
   d. all of the above

8. Which sociological perspective makes the distinction between instrumental and expressive roles?

   a. functionalist perspective
   b. conflict perspective
   c. interactionist perspective
   d. labeling theory

9. In what way do female physicians interact differently with patients than do male physicians?

   a. They take on an aggressive interactional style to compensate for their lack of authority.
   b. They have poor bedside manner.
   c. They spend 10 percent more time with patients.
   d. both a and c

10. The sense of sisterhood that became evident during the rise of the contemporary feminist movement resembled the Marxist concept of

    a. alienation.
    b. dialectics.
    c. class consciousness.
    d. false consciousness.

11. Talcott Parsons and Robert Bales contend that women take the _____, emotionally supportive role in the family and that men take the _____, practical role, with the two complementing each other.

12. A significant component of the _____ approach to gender stratification draws on feminist theory.

13. It is not simply that particular men in the United States are biased in their treatment of women. All the major institutions of our society—including the government, the armed forces, large corporations, the media, the universities, and the medical establishment—are controlled by men. This situation is symptomatic of institutional _____.

14. Women from all groups and men from minority groups sometimes encounter attitudinal or organizational bias that prevents them from reaching their full potential. This is known as the _____ _____.

15. Sociologist Arlie Hochschild has used the phrase _____ _____ to describe the double burden that many women face and few men share equitably: work outside the home followed by child care and housework.

16. Within the general framework of their theory, _____ sociologists maintain that gender differentiation has contributed to overall social stability.

17. Through the rise of contemporary _____, women are developing a greater sense of group solidarity.

18. _____ contributes significantly to rigid gender-role socialization, since many people stereotypically associate male homosexuality with femininity and lesbianism with masculinity.

19. In Margaret Mead's analysis of tribes in _____ _____, she indicates that gender roles vary from one culture to another.

20. The author of the pioneering argument for women's rights, *The Feminine Mystique*, is _____ _____.

Answers:
1 (a); 2 (c); 3 (d); 4 (b); 5 (d); 6 (b); 7 (b); 8 (a); 9 (c); 10 (c); 11 expressive; instrumental; 12 conflict; 13 discrimination; 14 glass ceiling; 15 second shift; 16 functionalist; 17 feminism; 18 Homophobia; 19 New Guinea; 20 Betty Friedan

---

{ TECHNOLOGY RESOURCES }

Online Learning Center

1. Few issues stir as much intense conflict as abortion. To find out how Americans feel about abortion, visit the student center of the Online Learning Center at **www.mhhe.com/schaefer11,** and click on the Social Policy link for this chapter. Read an overview of the abortion issue and then look at the colorful pie charts and graphs.

2. About Face (**www.about-face.org**) is an organization that brings public awareness to negative stereotypes of women in the media. Visit their site and explore the lists of "winners" and "offenders" in the media.

3. In this chapter you have learned about gender inequality based mainly on social statistics compiled in the United States. To access information on stratification by gender in hundreds of other countries, go to the GenderStats page at the World Bank's Web site (**devdata.worldbank.org/genderstats/home.asp**). How does the status of women in the United States compare to that of women in other developed countries? To that of women in developing countries?

*Note: Although all the URLs listed were current as of the printing of this book, these sites often change. Please check our Web site (**www.mhhe.com/schaefer11**) for updates, hyperlinks, and exercises related to these sites.*

Reel Society Video Clips

Reel Society video clips, which appear on this book's Web site, can be used to spark discussion about the following topics from this chapter:

- Gender Roles in the United States
- Cross-Cultural Perspective
- Sexism and Sex Discrimination
- The Status of Women Worldwide

This poster promoted 1999 as the United Nations' International Year of Older Persons. In April 2002, recognizing that soon every third person in the world would be over age 60, delegates to the Second World Assembly on Aging focused on ensuring that everyone, regardless of age, will have an active role to play in society.

13 Stratification by Age

tuesdays with **Morrie**

an old man, a young man,

and life's greatest lesson

Mitch Albom

"Later that day, we talked about aging. Or maybe I should say the fear of aging—another of the issues on my what's-bugging-my-generation list. On my ride from the Boston airport, I had counted the billboards that featured young and beautiful people. There was a handsome young man in a cowboy hat, smoking a cigarette, two beautiful young women smiling over a shampoo bottle, a sultry-looking teenager with her jeans unsnapped, and a sexy woman in a black velvet dress, next to a man in a tuxedo, the two of them snuggling a glass of scotch.

Not once did I see anyone who would pass for over thirty-five. I told Morrie I was already feeling over the hill, much as I tried desperately to stay on top of it. I worked out constantly. Watched what I ate. Checked my hairline in the mirror. I had gone from being proud to say my age—because of all I had done so young—to not bringing it up, for fear I was getting too close to forty and, therefore, professional oblivion.

Morrie had aging in better perspective.

"All this emphasis on youth—I don't buy it," he said. "Listen, I know what a misery being young can be, so don't tell me it's so great. All these kids who came to me with their struggles, their strife, their feelings of inadequacy, their sense that life was miserable, so bad they wanted to kill themselves . . .

"And, in addition to all the miseries, the young are not wise. They have very little understanding about life. Who wants to live every day when you don't know what's going on? When people are manipulating you, telling you to buy this perfume and you'll be beautiful, or this pair of jeans and you'll be sexy—and you believe them! It's such nonsense."

Weren't you *ever* afraid to grow old, I asked?

"Mitch, I *embrace* aging."

Embrace it?

"It's very simple. As you grow, you learn more. If you stayed at twenty-two, you'd always be as ignorant as you were at twenty-two. Aging is not just decay, you know. It's growth. It's more than the negative that you're going to die, it's also the positive that you understand you're going to die, and that you live a better life because of it."

Yes, I said, but if aging were so valuable, why do people always say, "Oh, if I were young again." You never hear people say, "I wish I were sixty-five."

He smiled. "You know what that reflects? Unsatisfied lives. Unfulfilled lives. Lives that haven't found meaning. Because if you've found meaning in your life, you don't want to go back. You want to go forward. You want to see more, do more. You can't wait until sixty-five. . . ."

All this emphasis on youth—I don't buy it," he said. "Listen, I know what a misery being young can be, so don't tell me it's so great. All these kids who came to me with their struggles, their strife, their feelings of inadequacy, their sense that life was miserable. . . .

(Albom 1997:117–118) Additional information about this excerpt can be found on the Online Learning Center at www.mhhe.com/schaefer11.

In *Tuesdays with Morrie,* journalist Mitch Albom (1997) recounted his final class with his favorite college professor, the respected Brandeis University sociologist Morrie Schwartz. Albom, who had graduated years before, contacted Schwartz when he learned the professor was dying of amyotrophic lateral sclerosis (ALS), also known as Lou Gehrig's disease. To his surprise, he found that his series of conversations with Morrie, held always on Tuesday, were more about life than death. From this sage man he learned that age has its benefits, and that growing old can also mean growing wise.

Age, like race or gender, is socially constructed. It is an ascribed status that dominates people's perceptions of others, obscuring individual differences. Rather than suggesting that a particular elderly person is no longer competent to drive, for instance, we may condemn the entire age group: "Those old codgers shouldn't be allowed on the road." Unless people can begin to look at the life course as a continuum, rather than as a series of finite stages with predictable consequences, such

stereotypical attitudes toward age and aging are not likely to change.

How do people's roles change as they age? What are the social implications of the growing number of elderly in the United States? How does ageism affect an older person's employment opportunities? In this chapter we will look at the process of aging throughout the life course. We will examine aging around the world, focusing primarily on the United States. After exploring various theories of the impact of aging, both on the individual and on society, we will discuss the role transitions typical of the major stages in the life course. In the process we will consider the challenges facing the "sandwich generation," middle-aged people who care for both their children and their aging parents. We will pay particular attention to the effects of prejudice and discrimination on older people, and to the rise of a political consciousness among the elderly. Finally, in the Social Policy section, we will discuss the controversial issue of the right to die.

Aging and Society

The Sherpas—a Tibetan-speaking Buddhist people in Nepal—live in a culture that idealizes old age. Almost all elderly members of the Sherpa culture own their homes, and most are in relatively good physical condition. Typically, older Sherpas value their independence and prefer not to live with their children. Among the Fulani of Africa, however, older men and women move to the edge of the family homestead. Since that is where people are buried, the elderly sleep over their own graves, for they are viewed socially as already dead. Like gender stratification, age stratification varies from culture to culture. One society may treat older people with great reverence, while another sees them as unproductive and "difficult" (M. Goldstein and Beall 1981; Stenning 1958; Tonkinson 1978).

It is understandable that all societies have some system of age stratification that associates certain social roles with distinct periods in life. Some of this age differentiation seems inevitable; it would make little sense to send young children off to war, or to expect most older citizens to handle physically demanding tasks, such as loading freight at shipyards. However, as is the case with stratification by gender, in the United States age stratification goes far beyond the physical constraints on human beings at different ages.

"Being old" is a master status that commonly overshadows all others in the United States. Thus, {p.197 the insights of labeling theory can help us

in analyzing the consequences of aging. Once people have been labeled "old," the designation has a major impact on how others perceive them, and even on how they view themselves. Negative stereotypes of the elderly contribute to their position as a mi-

In Korea, certain birthdays are celebrated as milestones, complete with a formal feast. At a 60th birthday celebration, for example, all the younger family members bow before the fortunate elder one by one, in order of their ages, and offer gifts. Later they compete with one another in composing poetry and singing songs to mark the occasion. Unfortunately, not all older people are so lucky; in many other cultures, being old is considered next to being dead.

nority group subject to discrimination, as we will see later in the chapter.

The model of five basic properties of a minority or subordi- {p.268 nate group (introduced in Chapter 11) can be applied to older people in the United States to clarify their subordinate status:

1. The elderly experience unequal treatment in employment, and may face prejudice and discrimination.

2. The elderly share physical characteristics that distinguish them from younger people. In addition, their cultural preferences and leisure-time activities often differ from those of the rest of society.

3. Membership in this disadvantaged group is involuntary.

4. Older people have a strong sense of group solidarity, as is reflected in the growth of senior citizens' centers, retirement communities, and advocacy organizations.

5. Older people generally are married to others of comparable age.

There is one crucial difference between older people and other subordinate groups, such as racial and ethnic minorities or women: *All* of us who live long enough will eventually assume the ascribed status of an older person (Barron 1953; Levin and Levin 1980; Wagley and Harris 1958).

Sociological Perspectives on Aging

Aging is one important aspect of socialization—the lifelong process through which an individual learns the cultural norms and values of a particular society. There are no clear-cut definitions for different periods of the aging cycle in the United States. *Old age* has typically been regarded as beginning at 65, which corresponds to the retirement age for many workers, but not everyone in the United States accepts that definition. With the increase in life expectancy, writers are beginning to refer to people in their 60s as the "young old," to distinguish them from those in their 80s and beyond (the "old old").

The particular problems of the elderly have become the focus of a specialized field of research and inquiry known as gerontology. *Gerontology* is the scientific study of the sociological and psychological aspects of aging and the problems of the aged. It originated in the 1930s, as an increasing number of social scientists became aware of the plight of the elderly.

Gerontologists rely heavily on sociological principles and theories to explain the impact of aging on the individual and society. They also draw on psychology, anthropology, physical education, counseling, and medicine in their study of the aging process. Two influential views of aging—disengagement theory and activity theory—can best be understood in terms of the sociological perspectives of functionalism and interactionism, respectively. The conflict perspective also contributes to our sociological understanding of aging.

Use Your Sociological Imagination

Time has passed, and you are now in your 70s or 80s. How does old age in your generation compare with your parents' or grandparents' experience of old age?

www.mhhe.com/schaefer11

Functionalist Approach: Disengagement Theory

After studying elderly people in good health and relatively comfortable economic circumstances, Elaine Cumming and William Henry (1961) introduced their *disengagement theory,* which implicitly suggests that society and the aging individual mutually sever many of their relationships. In keeping with the functionalist perspective, disengagement theory emphasizes that passing social roles on from one generation to another ensures social stability.

According to this theory, the approach of death forces people to drop most of their social roles—including those of worker, volunteer, spouse, hobby enthusiast, and even reader. Younger members of society then take on these functions. The aging person, it is held, withdraws into an increasing state of inactivity while preparing for death. At the same time, society withdraws from the elderly by segregating them residentially (in retirement homes and communities), educationally (in programs designed solely for senior citizens), and recreationally (in senior citizens' centers). Implicit in disengagement theory is the view that society should *help* older people to withdraw from their accustomed social roles.

Since it was first outlined more than four decades ago, disengagement theory has generated considerable controversy. Some gerontologists have objected to the implication that older people want to be ignored and put away—and even more to the idea that they should be encouraged to withdraw from meaningful social roles. Critics of disengagement theory insist that society *forces* the elderly into an involuntary and painful withdrawal from the paid labor force and from meaningful social relationships. Rather than voluntarily seeking to disengage, older employees find themselves pushed out of their jobs—in many instances, even before they are entitled to maximum retirement benefits (Dannefer 2004).

Although functionalist in its approach, disengagement theory ignores the fact that postretirement employment has been *increasing* in recent decades. In the United States, fewer than half of all employees actually retire from their career jobs. Instead, most move into a "bridge job"—employment that bridges the period between the end of a person's career and his or her retirement. Unfortunately, the elderly can easily be victimized in such "bridge jobs." Psychologist Kathleen Christensen (1990), warning of "bridges over troubled water," emphasizes that older employees do not want to end their working days as minimum-wage jobholders engaged in activities unrelated to their careers (Doeringer 1990; Hayward et al. 1987).

Dave Roberts admits to being a "people person," a trait that sociology courses fostered by showing how "everybody has differences; there are little bits of different cultures in all of us." He also had the benefit of "a lot of great teachers" at Florida State University, including Dr. Jill Quadagno in a course on aging. It was this class that sparked his interest in aging issues, which led to a certificate in gerontology in addition to a sociology degree in 1998. He realized that there was a good job market in working with the aging baby boom generation.

Volunteer work with the Meals on Wheels program steered him toward working with the elderly. Today Roberts is a social worker in a nursing home, where he is responsible for patients' care plans. In the course of his work, he meets regularly with patients, family members, and medical residents. Roberts finds that the concept of teamwork he learned in group projects in college has helped him in his job. Also, the projects he had to do in school taught him to work on a schedule. Perhaps most important, sociology has helped him "to grow as a person, to explore different angles, different theories. . . . I'm a better person."

His advice to sociology students: "Just give it a chance; they throw everything into an intro course. Don't get overwhelmed; take it as it comes."

Let's Discuss

1. What other types of employment might be open to a college graduate with a certificate in gerontology?
2. What might be the special rewards of working with the elderly?

Interactionist Approach: Activity Theory

Ask Ruth Vitow if she would like to trade her custom lampshade business in New York City for a condo in Florida, and you will get a quick response: "Deadly! I'd hate it." Vitow, in her 90s, vows to give up her business "when it gives me up." James Russell Wiggins has been working at a weekly newspaper in Maine since 1922. At age 95 he is now the editor. Vitow and Wiggins are among the 9 percent of the men and 3 percent of the women aged 75 years or older who are still participating in the nation's labor force (Himes 2001).

How important is it for older people to stay actively involved, whether at a job or in other pursuits? A tragic disaster in Chicago in 1995 showed that it can be a matter of life and death. An intense heat wave lasting more than a week—with a heat index exceeding 115 degrees on two consecutive days—resulted in 733 heat-related deaths. About three-fourths of the deceased were 65 and older. Subsequent analysis showed that older people who lived alone had the highest risk of dying, suggesting that support networks for the elderly literally help to save lives. Older Hispanics and Asian Americans had lower death rates from the heat wave than other racial and ethnic groups. Their stronger social networks probably resulted in more regular contact with family members and friends (Klinenberg 2002; Schaefer 1998a).

Often seen as an opposing approach to disengagement theory, *activity theory* suggests that those elderly people who remain active and socially involved will be best adjusted. Proponents of this perspective acknowledge that a 70-year-old person may not have the ability or desire to perform various social roles that he or she had at age 40. Yet they contend that old people have essentially the same need for social interaction as any other group.

The improved health of older people—sometimes overlooked by social scientists—has strengthened the arguments of activity theorists. Illness and chronic disease are no longer quite the scourge of the elderly that they once were. The recent emphasis on fitness, the availability of better medical care, greater control of infectious diseases, and the reduction of fatal strokes and heart attacks have combined to mitigate the traumas of growing old. Accumulating medical research also points to the importance of remaining socially involved. Among those who decline in their mental capacities later in life, deterioration is most rapid in those who withdraw from social relationships and activities. Fortunately, the aged are finding new ways to remain socially engaged, as evidenced by their increasing use of the Internet, especially to keep in touch with family and friends (Korczyk 2002).

Admittedly, many activities open to the elderly involve unpaid labor, for which younger adults may receive salaries. Unpaid elderly workers include hospital volunteers (versus aides and orderlies), drivers for charities such as the Red Cross (versus chauffeurs), tutors (as opposed to teachers), and craftspeople for charity bazaars (as opposed to carpenters and dressmakers). However, some companies have recently begun programs to hire retirees for full-time or part-time work.

Though disengagement theory suggests that older people find satisfaction in withdrawal from society, conveniently receding into the background and allowing the next generation to take over, proponents of activity theory view such withdrawal as harmful to both the elderly and society. Activity theorists focus on the potential contributions of older people to the maintenance of society. In their opinion, aging citizens will feel satisfied only when they can be useful and productive in society's

for those who suffer job-related injuries or illnesses. Working-class people also depend more heavily on Social Security benefits and private pension programs. During inflationary times, their relatively fixed incomes from these sources barely keep pace with the escalating costs of food, housing, utilities, and other necessities (Atchley and Barusch 2004).

According to the conflict approach, the treatment of older people in the United States reflects the many divisions in our society. The low status of older people is seen in prejudice and discrimination against them, in age segregation, and in unfair job practices—none of which are directly addressed by either disengagement or activity theory.

Conflict theorists have noted, too, that in the developing world, the transition from agricultural economies to industrialization and capitalism has not always been beneficial to the elderly. As a society's production methods change, the traditionally valued role of older people tends to erode. Their wisdom is no longer relevant in the new economy.

In sum, the three perspectives considered here take different views of the elderly. Functionalists portray older people as socially isolated, with reduced social roles; interactionists see them as involved in new networks and changing social roles; conflict theorists see them as victimized by social structure, with their social roles relatively unchanged but devalued. Table 13-1 (page 324) summarizes these perspectives.

Use Your Sociological Imagination

Have you noticed signs of second-class treatment of the elderly? If so, in what ways?

www.mhhe.com/schaefer11

These "silver surfers" still enjoy life to the fullest, just as they did when they were young. Staying active and involved has been shown to be healthy for the older population.

terms—primarily by working for wages (Civic Ventures 1999; Crosnoe and Elder Jr. 2002; Dowd 1980; Quadagno 2005).

The Conflict Approach

Conflict theorists have criticized both disengagement theorists and activity theorists for failing to consider the impact of social structure on aging patterns. Neither approach, they say, questions why social interaction must change or decrease in old age. In addition, they often ignore the impact of social class on the lives of the elderly.

The privileged upper class generally enjoys better health and vigor and less likelihood of dependency in old age. Affluence cannot forestall aging indefinitely, but it can soften the economic hardships people face in later years. Although pension plans, retirement packages, and insurance benefits may be developed to assist older people, those whose wealth allows them access to investment funds can generate the greatest income for their later years.

In contrast, the working class often faces greater health hazards and a greater risk of disability; aging is particularly difficult

Aging Worldwide

Around the world live more than 453 million people age 65 and over, who together constitute about 7 percent of the world's population. By 2050, one in every three of the world's people will be over 65. In an important sense, this trend toward the aging of the world's population represents a major success story, one that unfolded during the latter years of the 20th century. Through the efforts of national governments and international agencies, many societies have drastically reduced their incidence of disease, and with it their rate of death. As a result, these nations—particularly the industrialized countries of Europe and North America—have a high and steadily rising proportion of older members (see Figure 13-1, page 324).

Overall, Europe's population is older than that of any other continent. Though many European countries have long prided themselves on their generous pension programs, as the proportion of older people continues to rise, government officials have reluctantly begun to reduce pension benefits and raise the age at which

Table 13-1

Sociological Perspectives on Aging

Sociological Perspective	View of Aging	Social Roles	Portrayal of Elderly
Functionalist	Disengagement	Reduced	Socially isolated
Interactionist	Activity	Changed	Involved in new networks
Conflict	Competition	Relatively unchanged	Victimized, organized to confront their victimization

workers can receive them. Japan, too, has a relatively old population; the Japanese enjoy a life expectancy of 82 years, compared to 78 in the United States. But though four more years of life may sound like a bonus, it presents a real and growing challenge to Japanese society: see Box 13-1 (Vopel and Loichinger 2006).

In most developing countries, people over 60 are likely to be in poorer health than their counterparts in industrialized nations. Yet few of those countries are in a position to offer extensive financial support to the elderly. Ironically, though the modernization of the developing world has brought many social and economic advances, it has undercut the traditionally high status of the elderly. In many cultures, the earning power of younger adults now exceeds that of their older relatives (Haub 2006; He et al. 2005; Kinsella and Phillips 2005; Vidal 2004).

Role Transitions throughout the Life Course

As noted in Chapter 4 and throughout this textbook, socialization is a lifelong process. We simply do not experience {p.93 things the same way at different points in the life course. For example, one study found that even falling in love differs according to where we are in the life course. Young unmarried adults tend to treat love as a noncommittal game or an obsession characterized by possessiveness and dependency. People over the age of 50 are much more likely to see love as involving commitment, and they tend to take a practical approach to finding a partner who meets a set of rational criteria. The life course, then, affects the manner in which we relate to one another (Montgomery and Sorell 1997).

How we move through the life course varies dramatically, depending on our personal preferences and circumstances. Some of us marry early, others late; some have children and some don't. These individual patterns are influenced by social factors such as class, race, and gender. Only in the most general terms, then, can we speak of stages or periods in the life course (Shanahan 2000).

One transitional stage, identified by psychologist Daniel Levinson, begins at the time at which an individual gradually enters the adult world, perhaps by moving out of the parental home, beginning a career, or entering a marriage. The second transitional period, the midlife transition, typically begins at about age 40. Men and women often experience a stressful period of self-evaluation, commonly known as the *midlife crisis,* in which they realize that they have not achieved basic goals and ambitions and have little time left to do so. Thus, Levinson (1978, 1996) found that most adults surveyed experienced tumultuous midlife conflicts within the self and with the external world.

Not all the challenges at this time of life come from career or one's partner. In the next section we will examine a special challenge faced by a growing number of middle-aged adults: caring for two generations at once.

The Sandwich Generation

During the late 1990s social scientists focused on the *sandwich generation*—adults who simultaneously try to meet the com-

FIGURE 13–1

World's "Oldest" Countries versus the United States, 2006

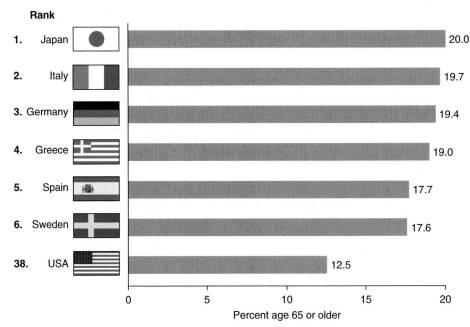

Rank		Percent age 65 or older
1.	Japan	20.0
2.	Italy	19.7
3.	Germany	19.4
4.	Greece	19.0
5.	Spain	17.7
6.	Sweden	17.6
38.	USA	12.5

Source: Bureau of the Census 2005d (projected).

13-1 Aging, Japanese Style

An electric water kettle is wired so that people in another location can determine whether it has been used in the previous 24 hours. This arrangement may seem a zany use of modern technology, but it symbolizes a change that is taking place around the globe: the growing needs of an aging population. The Japanese Welfare Network Ikebukuro Honcho installed these wired hotpots so that volunteers can monitor whether the elderly have prepared their morning tea. An unused pot initiates contacts to see whether the older person needs help. This technological monitoring system indicates not just the tremendous growth in Japan's elderly population, but the increasing numbers of elderly who live alone.

Indeed, Japan is struggling to confront the challenges posed by the world's most rapidly aging population. For generations, Japanese families have lived with and cared for their aging parents and grandparents. But this tradition of living under the same roof with one's elders is fading as more and more couples and even single adults strike out on their own. Hence the

need for the wired hotpots. Compared to the United States and Canada, Japan is less well equipped to deal with this social phenomenon. Assisted living, in-home services, and nursing homes are all much less common in Japan than they are in North America.

One challenge many aging couples face is the so-called "retired-husband syndrome." In their working days, most older Japanese

> An unused pot initiates contacts to see if the older person needs help.

men labored long hours in workplaces where women traditionally did not hold supervisory positions. When these men retire and begin to stay home full-time, some of them tend to treat their wives as subservient laborers. Moreover, many of them were so "married" to their jobs that they failed to develop hobbies or outside interests that might occupy them in retirement. Their wives, who have had free rein

around the house all their lives, often find sharing the home with their dictatorial husbands a real challenge. Though Japanese gender roles are changing as record numbers of women enter positions of real responsibility, the senior generation is still hampered by yesterday's stereotypes.

Let's Discuss

1. What do you think caused the change in housing patterns that has resulted in so many elderly Japanese living alone? Could the change in housing patterns be related to the change in life expectancy? How?
2. How might living alone contribute to the "retired-husband syndrome" noted among aging Japanese couples?

Sources: Crump 2006; Faiola 2005, 2006; Hani 1998; Haub 2006.

---

peting needs of their parents and their children. That is, caregiving goes in two directions: (1) to children, who even as young adults may still require significant direction, and (2) to aging parents, whose health and economic problems may demand intervention by their adult children.

Like the role of caring for children, the role of caring for aging parents falls disproportionately on women. Overall, women provide 60 percent of the care their parents receive, and even more as the demands of the role grow more intense and time consuming. Increasingly, middle-aged women and younger are finding themselves on the "daughter track," as their time and attention are diverted by the needs of their aging mothers and fathers (Gross 2005).

The last major transition identified by Levinson occurs after age 60—sometimes well after that age, given advances in health care, greater longevity, and gradual acceptance by society of older people. In fact, yesterday's 60 may be today's 70 or even 75. Nonetheless, there is a point at which people transition to a different lifestyle. As we will see, this is a time of dramatic changes in people's everyday lives.

Adjusting to Retirement

Retirement is a rite of passage that marks a critical transition from one phase of a person's life to another. Typically, symbolic

events are associated with this rite of passage, such as retirement gifts, a retirement party, and special moments on the last day on the job. The preretirement period itself can be emotionally charged, especially if the retiree is expected to train his or her successor (Atchley 1976).

From 1950 to the mid-1990s, the average age at retirement in the United States declined, but over the last few years it has reversed direction. In 2007, 8 percent of women and 14 percent of men over 70 were still working. A variety of factors explains this reversal: changes in Social Security benefits, an economic shift away from hard manual labor, and workers' concern with maintaining their health insurance and pension benefits. At the same time, longevity has increased, and the quality of people's health has improved (Bureau of Labor Statistics 2007).

Gerontologist Robert Atchley (1976) has identified several phases of the retirement experience:

- *Preretirement,* a period of anticipatory socialization as the person prepares for retirement
- *The near phase,* when the person establishes a specific departure date from his or her job
- *The honeymoon phase,* an often euphoric period in which the person pursues activities that he or she never had time for before

- *The disenchantment phase,* in which retirees feel a sense of let-down or even depression as they cope with their new lives, which may include illness or poverty
- *The reorientation phase,* which involves the development of a more realistic view of retirement alternatives
- *The stability phase,* a period in which the person has learned to deal with life after retirement in a reasonable and comfortable fashion
- *The termination phase,* which begins when the person can no longer engage in basic, day-to-day activities such as self-care and housework

Retirement is not a single transition, then, but rather a series of adjustments that varies from one person to another. The length and timing of each phase will differ for each individual, depending on such factors as financial status and health. A particular person will not necessarily go through all the phases identified by Atchley (Reitzes and Mutran 2006).

Some factors, such as being forced into retirement or being burdened with financial difficulties, can further complicate the retirement process. People who enter retirement involuntarily or without the necessary means may never experience the honey-moon phase. In the United States, many retirees continue in the paid labor force, often taking part-time jobs to supplement their

A sandwich-generation mom cares for her bedridden parent as her older child feeds the younger one. Increasingly, members of the baby boom generation find themselves caring for two generations at once.

pensions. Though most younger workers expect to retire before age 65, nearly three-fourths of older workers in the United States (those over the age of 50) anticipate that they will need to continue working after retirement (see Figure 13-2).

Like other aspects of life in the United States, the experience of retirement varies according to gender, race, and ethnicity. White males are most likely to benefit from retirement wages, as well as to have participated in a formal retirement preparation program. As a result, anticipatory socialization for retirement is most systematic for White men. In contrast, members of racial and ethnic minority groups—especially African Americans—are more likely to exit the paid labor force through disability than through retirement. Because of their comparatively lower incomes and smaller savings, men and women from racial and ethnic minority groups work intermittently after retirement more often than older Whites (National Institute on Aging 1999; Quadagno 2005).

During the reorientation and stability phases, an increasing number of elderly find they are living in neighborhoods where the majority of people are their own age. Box 13-2 (page 328) explores this social phenomenon, called naturally occurring retirement communities (NORCs).

Use Your Sociological Imagination

How have people close to you, such as relatives, personally handled their retirement from the labor force?

www.mhhe.com/schaefer11

Death and Dying

Among the role transitions that typically (but not always) come later in life is death. Until recently, death was viewed as a taboo topic in the United States. However, psychologist Elisabeth Kübler-Ross (1969), through her pioneering book *On Death and Dying,* greatly encouraged open discussion of the process of dying. Drawing on her work with 200 cancer patients, Kübler-Ross identified five stages of the experience: denial, anger, bargaining, depression, and finally acceptance.

Despite its popular appeal, the five-stage theory of dying has been challenged. Observers often cannot substantiate these stages. Moreover, research suggests that each person declines in his or her own way. Thus, one should not expect—much less counsel—a person to approach death in any particular way (R. Epstein 2005; Fitchett 1980).

Functionalists would see those who are dying as fulfilling distinct social functions. Gerontologist Richard Kalish (1985) lists

"Have you given much thought to what kind of job you want after you retire?"

on this concept. Hospice workers seek to improve the quality of a dying person's last days by offering comfort and by helping the person to remain at home, or in a homelike setting at a hospital or other special facility, until the end. Currently there are more than 2,800 hospice programs serving over 800,000 people a year through federal programs such as Medicare and Medicaid alone (Hospice Association of America 2006).

Although the Western ideal of the good death makes the experience of dying as positive as possible, some critics fear that acceptance of the concept of a good death may direct both individual efforts and social resources away from attempts to extend life. Still others argue that fatally ill older people should not just passively accept death, but should forgo further treatment in order to reduce public health care expenditures. Such issues are at the heart of current debates over the right to die and physician-assisted suicide (Counts 1977; Hospice Foundation of America 2005; Mahoney 1999).

among the tasks of the dying: completing unfinished business, such as settling insurance and legacy matters; restoring harmony to social relationships and saying farewell to friends and family; dealing with medical needs; and making funeral plans and other arrangements for survivors. In accomplishing these tasks, the dying person actively contributes to meeting society's need for smooth intergenerational transitions, role continuity, compliance with medical procedures, and minimal disruption of the social system, despite the loss of one of its members.

This functionalist analysis brings to mind the cherished yet controversial concept of a "good death." One researcher described a good death among the Kaliai, a people of the South Pacific. In that culture, the dying person calls together all his relatives, settles his debts, disposes of his possessions, and then announces that it is time for him to die (Counts 1977). The Kaliai concept of a good death has a parallel in Western societies, where people may speak of a "natural death," an "appropriate death," or "death with dignity." The practice of *hospice care,* introduced in London, England, in 1967, is founded

Recent studies in the United States suggest that in many varied ways, people have broken through the historic taboos about death and are attempting to arrange certain aspects of the idealized good death. For example, bereavement practices—once highly structured—are becoming increasingly varied and therapeutic. More and more people are actively addressing the

FIGURE 13–2

Expected Retirement Age

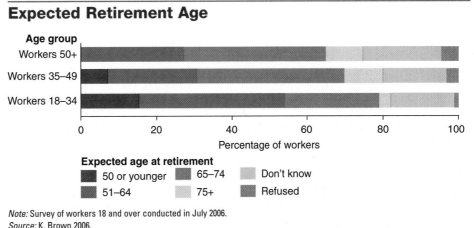

Note: Survey of workers 18 and over conducted in July 2006.
Source: K. Brown 2006.

Think About It
At what age do you expect to retire completely, without working for pay at all?

13-2 Naturally Occurring Retirement Communities (NORCs)

With recent improvements in health care, older Americans have gained new choices in where to live. Many do not reside in nursing homes or planned retirement communities. Instead, they congregate in areas that gradually become informal centers for senior citizens. Social scientists have dubbed such areas *naturally occurring retirement communities (NORCs)*. Using observation research, census data, and interviews, sociologists and urban planners have developed some interesting conclusions about NORCs.

NORCs can be as small as a single apartment building or as large as a neighborhood in a big city. Often, these settlements emerge as singles and young couples move out and older people move in. Sometimes couples simply remain where they are; as they grow older, the community becomes noticeably grayer. In time, business establishments that cater to the elderly, such as pharmacies, medical supply outlets, and small restaurants, relocate to the communities, making them even more attractive to older citizens.

The largest known NORC in the United States is Co-op City, a high-rise apartment complex in the Bronx, north of Manhattan. Built in the 1960s, the huge community was meant to house low-income workers and their families, in apartments that were relatively spacious by New York City's standards. More than three decades later, many of the buildings' first residents are still there, "aging in place," as the social workers say. Today, roughly 8,000 of Co-op City's 50,000 residents are age 65 or older.

Building managers readily admit that they could not cope with the needs of such a huge elderly population without the help they re-

> *NORCs can be as small as a single apartment building or as large as a neighborhood in a big city.*

ceive from the Senior Services Program. Begun by the United Hospital Fund and supported by the City Council and the New York State legislature, the program boasts a budget of $1.2 million and a staff of 40, including two nurses and four social workers. Through Senior Services, elderly residents can receive everything from Meals on Wheels and home health aides to field trips and exercise classes. With such comprehensive support, even many seriously ill seniors manage to stay out of nursing homes.

Unfortunately, residents of some high-rise communities are threatened by gentrification—the takeover of low-income neighborhoods by higher-income residents. In Chicago, a high-rise building known as Ontario Place is converting to a condominium, at prices that current residents cannot afford. About half the building's occupants are Russian immigrants; most of the others are elderly or disabled people living on fixed incomes. They are distressed not just because they will need to move, but because their community is being destroyed.

Let's Discuss

1. Can you think of a naturally occurring retirement community near your home or school? If so, describe the area. What kinds of services are available to elderly residents?
2. What can government or community activists do to help elderly people who are threatened by gentrification?

Sources: A. Feuer 2002; Lansprey 1995; Perry 2001; Sheehan 2005.

Coffins in Ghana sometimes reflect the way the dead lived their lives. This Methodist burial service honors a woman who died at age 85, leaving behind 11 children, 82 grandchildren, and 60 great-grandchildren. Her coffin, designed to resemble a mother hen, features 11 chicks nestling beneath the wings (Secretan 1995).

inevitability of death by making wills, leaving "living wills" (health care proxies that explain their feelings about the use of life-support equipment), donating organs, and providing instructions for family members about funerals, cremations, and burials. Given medical and technological advances and a breakthrough in open discussion and negotiation regarding death and dying, it is possible that good deaths may become a social norm in the United States (La Ganga 1999; J. Riley Jr. 1992).

Age Stratification in the United States

The "Graying of America"

When Lenore Schaefer, a ballroom dancer, tried to get on the *Tonight Show*, she was told she was "too young": she was in her early 90s. When she turned 101, she made it. But even at that age, Lenore is no longer unusual in our society. Today, people over 100 constitute, proportionately, the country's fastest-growing age group. They are part of the increasing proportion of the population of the United States that is composed of older people (Himes 2001; Rimer 1998).

As Figure 13-3 shows, in the year 1900, men and women age 65 and older constituted only 4.1 percent of the nation's population, but by 2010 that age group is expected to grow to 13.0 percent. According to current projections, the over-65 segment will continue to increase throughout this century. As the decades pass, the population of "old old" (people who are 85 and older) will increase at an ever-faster rate.

In 2010, 15.9 percent of non-Hispanic Whites are projected to be older than 65, compared to 8.7 percent of African Americans, 9.6 percent of Asian Americans, and 5.9 percent of Hispanics. In part, these differences reflect the shorter life spans of the latter groups. They also stem from immigration patterns among Asians and Hispanics, who tend to be young when they enter the country (Bureau of the Census 2006a:17).

The highest proportions of older people are found in Florida, Pennsylvania, Rhode Island, Iowa, West Virginia, and Arkansas. However, that will soon change. In 2000, Florida was the state most populated by the elderly, with 17.6 percent of the population over age 65. Yet as Figure 13-4 shows, in about another 25 years, more than half the states will have an even greater proportion of elderly than Florida does now.

The graying of the United States is a phenomenon that can no longer be ignored, either by social scientists or by government policymakers. Advocates

FIGURE 13–3

329

Stratification by Age

Actual and Projected Growth of the Elderly Population of the United States

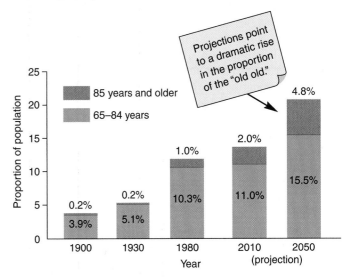

Sources: Hobbs and Damon 1996; He et al. 2005:9.

for the elderly have spoken out on a wide range of issues. Politicians court the votes of older people, since they are the age group most likely to register and vote. In fact, in the 2000 presidential race, people 55 or older made up 35 percent of the total vote (Holder 2006).

FIGURE 13–4

Twenty-Eight Floridas by 2030

MAPPING LIFE NATIONWIDE

www.mhhe.com/schaefer11

States where at least 20 percent of the population will be elderly

Source: Bureau of the Census 2005c.

There is significant variation in wealth and poverty among the nation's older people. Some individuals and couples find themselves poor in part because of fixed pensions and skyrocketing health care costs (see Chapter 19). Nevertheless, as a group, older people in the United States are neither homogeneous nor poor. The typical elderly person enjoys a standard of living that is much higher now than at any point in the nation's past. Class differences among the elderly remain evident, but tend to narrow somewhat: Those older people who enjoyed middle-class incomes while younger tend to remain better off after retirement, but less so than before (Denise Smith and Tillipman 2000).

To some extent, older people owe their overall improved standard of living to a greater accumulation of wealth—in the form of home ownership, private pensions, and other financial assets. But much of the improvement is due to more generous Social Security benefits. While modest when compared with other countries' pension programs, Social Security nevertheless provides 39 percent of all income received by older people in the United States. Still, about 10 percent of the nation's elderly population lives below the poverty line. At the extremes of poverty are those groups who were more likely to be poor at earlier points in the life cycle: female-headed households and racial and ethnic minorities (He et al. 2005).

Viewed from a conflict perspective, it is not surprising that older women experience a double burden; the same is true of elderly members of racial and ethnic minorities. For example, in 2005 the proportion of older Latinos with incomes below the poverty level (19.9 percent) was more than twice as large as the proportion of older non-Hispanic Whites (7.9 percent). Moreover, 23.3 percent of older African Americans fell below the federal government's poverty line (DeNavas-Walt et al. 2006:Table POV01).

Ageism

Physician Robert Butler (1990) became concerned 30 years ago when he learned that a housing development near his home in metropolitan Washington, D.C., barred the elderly. Butler coined the term *ageism* to refer to prejudice and discrimination based on a person's age. For example, we may choose to assume that someone cannot handle a rigorous job because he is "too old," or we may refuse to give someone a job with authority because she is "too young."

Ageism is especially difficult for the old, because at least youthful recipients of prejudice know that in time they will be "old enough." For many, old age symbolizes disease. With ageism all too common in the United States, it is hardly surprising that older people are barely visible on television. In 2002, the Senate Special Committee on Aging convened a panel on the media's portrayal of older people and sharply criticized media and marketing executives for bombarding audiences with negative images of the aged. The social consequences of such images are significant. Research shows that older people who have positive perceptions of aging live an average of 7.5 years longer than those who have negative perceptions (M. Gardner 2003; Levy et al. 2002; E. Ramirez 2002).

Use Your Sociological Imagination

It is September and you are channel-surfing through the new fall TV series. How likely are you to watch a television show that is based on older characters who spend a lot of time together?

Competition in the Labor Force

Participation in paid work is not typical after the age of 65. In 2007, 34 percent of men aged 65 to 69 and 25 percent of women participated in the paid labor force. While some people view these workers as experienced contributors to the labor force, others see them as "job stealers," a biased judgment similar to that directed against illegal immigrants. This mistaken belief not only intensifies age conflict but leads to age discrimination (Bureau of Labor Statistics 2007).

While firing people simply because they are old violates federal law, courts have upheld the right to lay off older workers for economic reasons. Critics contend that later, the same firms hire young, cheaper workers to replace experienced older workers. When economic growth began to slow in 2001 and companies cut back on their workforces, complaints of age bias grew sharply as older workers began to suspect they were bearing a disproportionate share of the layoffs. According to the Equal Employment Opportunity Commission, between 1999 and 2004, complaints of age discrimination rose more than 41 percent. However, evidence of a countertrend has emerged. Some firms have been giving larger raises to older workers, to encourage their retirement at the higher salary—a tactic that prompts younger workers to complain of age discrimination (Novelli 2004; Uchitelle 2003).

A controlled experiment conducted by the AARP confirmed that older people often face discrimination when applying for jobs. Comparable résumés for two applicants—one 57 years old and the other 32 years old—were sent to 775 large firms and employment agencies around the United States. In situations for which positions were actually available, the younger applicant received a favorable response 43 percent of the time. By contrast, the older applicant received favorable responses less than half as often (only 17 percent of the time). One Fortune 500 corporation asked the younger applicant for more information, while informing the older applicant that no appropriate positions were open (Bendick et al. 1993).

In contrast to the negative stereotypes, researchers have found that older workers can be an *asset* to employers. According to a study issued in 1991, older workers can be retrained in new technologies, have lower rates of absenteeism than younger employees, and are often more effective salespeople. The study focused on two corporations based in the United States (the

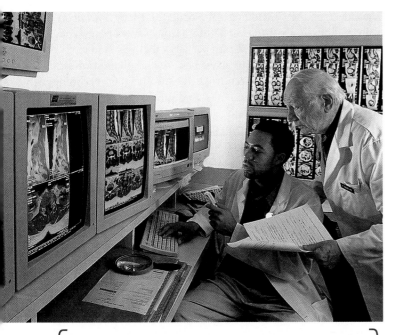

ers in the United States. The AARP has endorsed voter registration campaigns, nursing home reforms, and pension reforms. In acknowledgment of its difficulties recruiting members of racial and ethnic minority groups, the AARP recently began a Minority Affairs Initiative. The spokeswoman for the initiative, Margaret Dixon, became the AARP's first African American president in 1996 (Birnbaum 2005).

People grow old in many different ways. Not all the elderly face the same challenges or enjoy the same resources. While the AARP lobbies to protect the elderly in general, other groups work in more specific ways. For example, the National Committee to Preserve Social Security and Medicare, founded in 1982, successfully lobbied Congress to keep Medicare benefits for the ailing poor elderly. Other large special interest groups represent retired federal employees, retired teachers, and retired union workers (Quadagno 2005).

Still another manifestation of the new awareness of older people is the formation of organizations for elderly homosexuals. One

> About 30 percent of older workers choose to remain on the job past the usual retirement age. Research shows they can be retrained in new technologies and are more dependable than younger workers.

hotel chain Days Inns of America and the holding company Travelers Corporation of Hartford) and a British retail chain—all of which have long-term experience in hiring workers age 50 and over. Indeed, more and more U.S. corporations, from Borders to Home Depot, are actively trying to recruit retired people, recognizing their comparatively lower turnover rates and often superior work performance (Freudenheim 2005; Telsch 1991).

The Elderly: Emergence of a Collective Consciousness

During the 1960s, students at colleges and universities across the country, advocating "student power," collectively demanded a role in the governance of educational institutions. In the following decade, many older people became aware that *they* were being treated as second-class citizens and turned to collective action.

The largest organization representing the nation's elderly is the AARP, founded in 1958 by a retired school principal who was having difficulty getting insurance because of age prejudice. Many of the AARP's services involve discounts and insurance for its 37 million members (43 percent of Americans aged 50 or older), but the organization is also a powerful lobbying group. Recognizing that many elderly are still gainfully employed, it has dropped its full name, American Association of *Retired* Persons (Donnelly 2007).

The potential power of the AARP is enormous. It is the third-largest voluntary association in the United States (behind only the Roman Catholic church and the American Automobile Association), representing one out of every four registered vot-

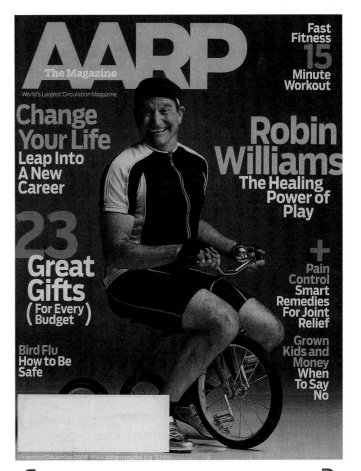

> The AARP is a major voice for the elderly. By featuring actor-comedian Robin Williams (born in 1953) on the cover of its widely distributed magazine, the organization is signaling a desire to represent the younger members of the older generation, as well as to portray the active lives many older people lead.

such group, Senior Action in a Gay Environment (SAGE), was established in New York City in 1977 and now oversees a nationwide network of community groups, as well as affiliates in Canada and Germany. Like more traditional senior citizens' groups, SAGE sponsors workshops, classes, dances, and food deliveries to the homebound. At the same time, the group must deal with special concerns, such as informing gay people of their rights, supporting gay people with Alzheimer's, and advocating for gays who face eviction (Senior Action in a Gay Environment 2007).

The elderly in the United States are better off today both financially and physically than ever before. Many of them have strong financial assets and medical care packages that will take care of almost any health need. But as we have seen, a significant segment is impoverished, faced with the prospect of declining health and mounting medical bills. And some older people must now add being aged to a lifetime of disadvantage. Like people in all other stages of the life course, the aged constitute a diverse group in the United States and around the world.

The Right to Die Worldwide

The Issue

On August 4, 1993, Dr. Jack Kevorkian, a retired pathologist, helped a 30-year-old Michigan man with Lou Gehrig's disease to commit suicide in a van. The patient died after inhaling carbon monoxide through a mask designed by Dr. Kevorkian; in doing so, he became the 17th person to commit suicide with Kevorkian's assistance. Kevorkian was openly challenging a Michigan law (aimed at him) that makes it a felony—punishable by up to four years in jail—to assist in a suicide. Since then Kevorkian has assisted in numerous other suicides, but not until he did it on television in 1998 did the charges brought against him result in his imprisonment for second-degree murder in 1999 until completing his sentence in 2007.

The issue of physician-assisted suicide is but one aspect of the larger debate in the United States and other countries over the ethics of suicide and euthanasia. The term *euthanasia* has been defined as the "act of bringing about the death of a hopelessly ill and suffering person in a relatively quick and painless way for reasons of mercy" (Council on Ethical and Judicial Affairs, American Medical Association 1992:2, 229). This type of mercy killing reminds us of the ideal of the "good death" discussed earlier in the chapter. The debate over euthanasia and assisted suicide often focuses on cases involving older people, though it can involve younger adults with terminal and degenerative diseases, or even children.

National surveys show that public opinion on this controversial practice is divided. In 2006, 69 percent of respondents said that a physician should be legally permitted to end a patient's life if both the patient and the patient's family make such a request. However, an earlier survey found that only half of respondents could even imagine a situation in which they themselves would request physician-assisted suicide (John Carroll 2003; Jost 2005).

The Setting

Many societies are known to have practiced *senilicide*—"killing of the aged"—because of extreme difficulties in providing basic

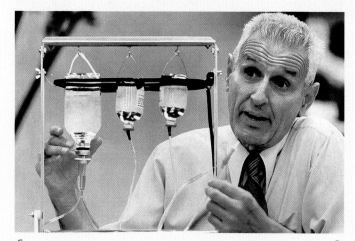

Dr. Jack Kevorkian with the apparatus that administers a lethal injection to those who want assistance in committing suicide.

necessities such as food and shelter. In a study of the treatment of the elderly in 41 nonindustrialized societies, Anthony Glascock (1990) found some form of "death-hastening" behavior in 21 of them. Killing of the elderly was evident in 14 of the societies, while abandoning of older people was evident in 8. Typically, death hastening occurs when older people become decrepit and are viewed as already dead. In these nonindustrialized cultures it is open and socially approved. Family members generally make decisions, often after open consultation with those who are about to die.

Currently, public policy in the United States does not permit *active euthanasia* (such as a deliberate injection of lethal drugs to a terminally ill patient) or physician-assisted suicide. Although suicide itself is no longer a crime, assisting suicide is illegal in at least 29 states. There is greater legal tolerance for *passive euthanasia* (such as disconnecting life-support equipment from a comatose patient).

Sociological Insights

Although formal norms concerning euthanasia may be in flux, informal norms seem to permit mercy killings. According to an estimate by the American Hospital Association, as many as 70 percent of all deaths in the United States are quietly negotiated, with patients, family members, and physicians agreeing not to use life-support technology. In an informal poll of internists, one in five reported that he or she had assisted or helped cause the death of a patient. In a period in which AIDS-related deaths are common, an AIDS underground is known to share information and assistance regarding suicide (Gibbs 1993; Martinez 1993).

Conflict theorists ask questions about the values raised by such decisions. By endorsing physician-assisted suicide, are we devaluing the disabled through an acceptance of their premature death? Critics note that we are all only temporarily able-bodied; disease or a speeding automobile can place any one of us among the disabled. By establishing a precedent for ending the lives of selected disabled people, we may unwittingly contribute to negative social views and labeling of all disabled people. Further reflecting the conflict perspective, gerontologist Elizabeth Markson (1992:6) argues that the "powerless, poor or undesirable are at special risk of being 'encouraged' to choose assisted death."

Critics of euthanasia charge that many of its supporters are guilty of ageism and other forms of bias. In a society that commonly discriminates against the elderly and people with disabilities, medical authorities and even family members may decide too quickly that such people should die "for their own good" or (in a view somewhat reminiscent of disengagement theory) "for the good of society." Some critics fear that society may use euthanasia to reduce health care costs, rather than striving to make life better for those near the end. Older people may even feel compelled to end their lives prematurely, to ease the emotional and financial burdens on family members and friends (Glascock 1990:45; *New York Times* 1993; Richman 1992).

Policy Initiatives

In the industrialized world, euthanasia is legal and widely accepted in only three countries: the Netherlands, where about 3,800 such procedures are carried out legally each year; Belgium,

which records about 350 procedures a year; and Switzerland, which records 200 a year. Unlike the Netherlands and Belgium, Switzerland allows foreigners to be euthanized; about 55 foreign nationals are euthanized there every year. While physician-assisted suicide is accepted by the public in all three countries, the so-called "suicide tourism" that occurs in Switzerland is controversial (*The Economist* 2005i).

In the United States, the only state to allow assisted suicide is Oregon, where the Death with Dignity Act became law in 1997. Since the law took effect, an average of about 40 terminally ill Oregonians have taken their lives each year; another 20 have obtained the necessary authorizations but chosen not to end their lives. Similar measures have failed to win support in at least 20 other states, where the issue has encountered sharp opposition. President George W. Bush's administration made an unsuccessful attempt to stop the prescription of lethal drugs to terminally ill patients in Oregon. In 2006 the Supreme Court ruled 6 to 3 that the federal government had overstepped its authority in punishing doctors in Oregon who had helped terminally ill patients to end their lives (Savage 2006).

Advances in technology now allow us to prolong life in ways that were unimaginable decades ago. But should people be forced or expected to prolong lives that are unbearably painful, or that are in effect "lifeless"? Unfortunately, medical and technological advances cannot provide answers to these complex ethical, legal, and political questions.

Let's Discuss

1. Why do you think "death-hastening" behavior is common in nonindustrialized countries?

2. In what ways are conflict theory and disengagement theory relevant to the debate over the "right to die"?

3. Do you think someone should be allowed to choose to die? Why or why not?

GettingINVOLVED

To get involved in the debate over the right to die, visit this text's Online Learning Center, which offers links to relevant Web sites. Check out the Social Policy section on the Online Learning Center as well; it provides survey data on U.S. public opinion regarding this issue.

www.mhhe.com/schaefer11

Summary

Age, like gender and race, is an ascribed status that forms the basis for social differentiation. This chapter examines sociological perspectives on aging, role transitions in the life course, age stratification in the United States, the growing political activism of the nation's elderly population, and the controversy surrounding the right to die.

1. Like other forms of stratification, age stratification varies from culture to culture.

2. In the United States, being old is a master status that seems to overshadow all others.

3. The particular problems of the aged have become the focus for a specialized area of research and inquiry known as *gerontology.*

4. *Disengagement theory* implicitly suggests that society should help older people to withdraw from their accustomed social roles. In contrast, *activity theory* suggests that the elderly person who remains active and socially involved will be better adjusted.

5. From a conflict perspective, the low status of older people is reflected in prejudice and discrimination against them and in unfair job practices.

6. About 40 percent of those who look after their elderly relatives still have children to care for; these people have been dubbed the *sandwich generation.*

7. As we age, we go through role transitions, including adjustment to retirement and preparation for death.

8. An increasing proportion of the population of the United States is composed of older people.

9. *Ageism* reflects a deep uneasiness about growing old on the part of younger people.

10. The AARP is a powerful lobbying group that backs legislation to benefit senior citizens.

11. The "right to die" often entails physician-assisted suicide, a controversial issue worldwide.

Critical Thinking Questions

1. Are there elderly students at your college or university? If so, how are they treated by younger students and by faculty members? Is there a subculture of older students? How do younger students view faculty members in their 50s and 60s?

2. Is age segregation functional or dysfunctional for older people in the United States? Is it functional or dysfunctional for society as a whole? What are the manifest functions, the latent functions, and the dysfunctions of age segregation?

3. If you were hired to run a senior center where you live, how would you use what you have learned in this chapter to better the lives of your community's seniors?

Activity theory An interactionist theory of aging that suggests that those elderly people who remain active and socially involved will be best adjusted. (page 322)

Ageism Prejudice and discrimination based on a person's age. (330)

Disengagement theory A functionalist theory of aging that suggests that society and the aging individual mutually sever many of their relationships. (321)

Euthanasia The act of bringing about the death of a hopelessly ill and suffering person in a relatively quick and painless way for reasons of mercy. (332)

Gerontology The scientific study of the sociological and psychological aspects of aging and the problems of the aged. (321)

Hospice care Treatment of the terminally ill in their own homes, or in special hospital units or other facilities, with the goal of helping them to die easily, without pain. (327)

Midlife crisis A stressful period of self-evaluation that begins at about age 40. (324)

Sandwich generation The generation of adults who simultaneously try to meet the competing needs of their parents and their children. (324)

Self-Quiz

Read each question carefully and then select the best answer.

1. Activity theory is associated with the
   a. functionalist perspective.
   b. conflict perspective.
   c. interactionist perspective.
   d. labeling perspective.

2. What is the one crucial difference between older people and other subordinate groups, such as racial and ethnic minorities or women?
   a. Older people do not experience unequal treatment in employment.
   b. Older people have a strong sense of group solidarity and other groups do not.
   c. All of us who live long enough will eventually assume the ascribed status of being an older person.
   d. Older people are generally married to others of comparable age and other minorities do not marry within their group.

3. Which field of study was originally developed in the 1930s as an increasing number of social scientists became aware of the plight of the elderly?
   a. sociology
   b. gerontology
   c. gerontocracy
   d. senilicide

4. Which sociological perspective is most likely to emphasize the important role of social networks in providing life satisfaction for the elderly?
   a. functionalist perspective
   b. conflict perspective
   c. interactionist perspective
   d. labeling theory

5. Elaine Cumming and William Henry introduced an explanation of the impact of aging known as
   a. disengagement theory.
   b. activity theory.
   c. labeling theory.
   d. the contact hypothesis.

6. According to psychologist Elisabeth Kübler-Ross, the first stage of the experience of dying that a person may undergo is
   a. denial.
   b. anger.
   c. depression.
   d. bargaining.

7. Which of the following statements about the elderly is correct?
   a. Being old is a master status.
   b. Once people are labeled as "old," the designation has a major impact on how others perceive them, and even on how they view themselves.
   c. Negative stereotypes of the elderly contribute to their position as a minority group subject to discrimination.
   d. all of the above

8. The text points out that the model of five basic properties of a minority or subordinate group can be applied to older people in the United States. Which of the following is *not* one of those basic properties?
   a. The elderly experience unequal treatment in employment and may face prejudice and discrimination.
   b. Statistically, the elderly represent a majority.
   c. Membership in this group is involuntary.
   d. Older people have a strong sense of group solidarity.

9. Which of the following theories argues that elderly people have essentially the same need for social interaction as any other group and that those who remain active and socially involved will be best adjusted?
   a. conflict theory
   b. functionalist theory
   c. activity theory
   d. disengagement theory

10. According to your text, which of the following statements is true?

    a. Functionalists portray the elderly as being socially isolated, with reduced social roles.

    b. Interactionists see older people as being involved in new networks of people and in changing social roles.

    c. Conflict theorists regard older people as being victimized by social structure, with their social roles relatively unchanged but devalued.

    d. all of the above

11. The elderly are _____ regarded in the traditional Sherpa (Tibet) culture.

12. In keeping with the _____ perspective of sociology, disengagement theory emphasizes that a society's stability is ensured when social roles are passed on from one generation to another.

13. The final phase of retirement, according to Robert Atchley, is the _____, which begins when the person can no longer engage in basic, day-to-day activities such as self-care and housework.

14. _____ theorists argue that both the disengagement and the activity perspectives often ignore the impact of social class in the lives of the elderly.

15. The fastest-growing age group in the United States is people over _____ years old.

16. _____ is the scientific study of the sociological and psychological aspects of aging and the problems of the aged. It originated in the 1930s as an increasing number of social scientists became aware of the plight of the elderly.

17. Based on a study of elderly people in good health and relatively comfortable economic circumstances, _____ theory suggests that society and the aging individual mutually sever many of their relationships.

18. During the late 1990s, social scientists focused on the _____ _____—adults who simultaneously try to meet the competing needs of their parents and their children.

19. In 2000, _____ was the state most populated by the elderly, with 17.6 percent of the population over age 65.

20. Physician Robert Butler coined the term _____ to refer to prejudice and discrimination based on a person's age.

Answers:
1 (c); 2 (b); 3 (b); 4 (c); 5 (a); 6 (a); 7 (d); 8 (b); 9 (c); 10 (d); 11 highly; 12 functionalist; 13 termination; 14 Conflict; 15 100; 16 Gerontology; 17 disengagement; 18 sandwich generation; 19 Florida; 20 ageism

Online Learning Center

1. Learn more about aging trends in your state by accessing the Interactive Map for this chapter in the student center of the Online Learning Center (**www.mhhe.com/schaefer11**). This map shows population projections for the elderly in 2030. Is your state one of those where at least 20 percent of the population will be age 65 or older?

2. Many social and political issues are coming to the forefront as the world's aged population increases. Global Action on Aging (**www .globalaging.org**) is an advocacy organization with numerous resources to help you understand the needs of aging people around the world.

3. How much do you know about the characteristics of older people in the United States? Familiarize yourself with the facts and trends by visiting the Web site of the Administration on Aging (**www.aoa .gov**). Start by clicking on "Statistics on the Aging Population" under the "Professionals" menu.

*Note: Although all the URLs listed were current as of the printing of this book, these sites often change. Please check our Web site (**www.mhhe.com/schaefer11**) for updates, hyperlinks, and exercises related to these sites.*

GO ON, TURN THE PAGE. HARRY'S USED TO BEING IGNORED.

Harry looked pretty sad when Barnardos first met him. His mum had overdosed and he'd been dumped on his dad. Then, when his father went missing for days on end, Harry would get shuffled from one abusive 'uncle' to another. And when no-one cared that he had stopped going to school, the only thing Harry learned was how to hate himself. But now, thanks to Barnardos, Harry's living with an experienced carer and is having intensive tutoring support. And he's feeling a whole lot happier.

You can help kids like Harry. This time, make a donation.

Barnardos
Caring for Australia's Children

Neglect hurts most when you ignore it.
Call 1800 061 000 or visit www.barnardos.org.au

BARFAD0505 Model used to protect privacy   A Company Ltd by Guarantee ABN 18 068 557 906. Registered Charity

---

KELLY WOULD LIKE TO FORGET HER PAST.

DON'T LET HER FORGET SHE HAS A FUTURE.

Sexually abused by her mother's many 'friends', living on the streets and stealing from shops. Exploited by prostitution, unable to read and embarrassed to confront people her own age. Kelly was just thirteen.

Now assisted by her Barnardos youth worker, Kelly has a safe place to live. As her literacy improves, her confidence grows. She is finally learning to live, feel and act like a normal teenager.

Like so many young people, Kelly has such potential. We just want to help her reach it.

Barnardos
Caring for Australia's Children

Help break the cycle of childhood neglect. Make a donation now.

Neglect hurts most when it's forgotten.
Call 1800 061 000 or visit www.barnardos.org.au

BARFAD0506B Model used to protect privacy   A Company Ltd by Guarantee ABN 18 068 557 906. Registered Charity

---

Not all children are lucky enough to grow up in a safe, loving family. These posters, sponsored by Barnardos, an Australian social service agency founded in 1921, call attention to the needs of abused and neglected children in Australia. But troubled families can be found everywhere in the world.

14 The Family and Intimate Relationships

annette lareau

unequal
childhoods

CLASS, RACE, AND FAMILY LIFE

"This provocative and often disturbing book will shape debates on the U.S. class system for decades to come."
SHARON HAYS, author of *Flat Broke with Children*

"A Black fourth-grader, Alexander Williams, is riding home from a school open house. His mother is driving their beige, leather-upholstered Lexus. It is 9:00 P.M. on a Wednesday evening. Ms. Williams is tired from work and has a long Thursday ahead of her. She will get up at 4:45 A.M. to go out of town on business and will not return before 9:00 P.M. On Saturday morning, she will chauffeur Alexander to a private piano lesson at 8:15 A.M., which will be followed by a choir rehearsal and then a soccer game. As they ride in the dark, Alexander's mother, in a quiet voice, talks with her son, asking him questions and eliciting his opinions.

Discussions between parents and children are a hallmark of middle-class child rearing. Like many middle-class parents, Ms. Williams and her husband see themselves as "developing" Alexander to cultivate his talents in a concerted fashion. Organized activities, established and controlled by mothers and fathers, dominate the lives of middle-class children. . . . By making certain their children have these and other experiences, middle-class parents engage in a process of *concerted cultivation*. From this, a robust sense of entitlement takes root in the children. . . .

Only twenty minutes away, in blue-collar neighborhoods, and slightly farther away, in public housing projects, childhood looks different. Mr.

> *Like many middle-class parents, Ms. Williams and her husband see themselves as "developing" Alexander to cultivate his talents in a concerted fashion. Organized activities, established and controlled by mothers and fathers, dominate the lives of middle-class children. . . .*

Yanelli, a white working-class father, picks up his son Little Billy, a fourth-grader, from an after-school program. They come home and Mr. Yanelli drinks a beer while Little Billy first watches television, then rides his bike and plays in the street. Other nights, he and his Dad sit on the sidewalk outside their house and play cards. . . . Many nights Little Billy's uncle stops by, sometimes bringing Little Billy's youngest cousin. In the spring, Little Billy plays baseball on a local team. For Little Billy, baseball is his only organized activity outside of school during the entire year. . . .

Farther away, a Black fourth-grade boy, Harold McAllister, plays outside on a summer evening in the public housing project in which he lives. His two male cousins are there that night, as they often are. After an afternoon spent unsuccessfully searching for a ball so they could play basketball, the boys had resorted to watching sports on television. Now they head outdoors for a twilight water balloon fight. Harold tries to get his neighbor, Miss Latifa, wet. People sit in white plastic lawn chairs outside the row of apartments. Music and television sounds waft through the open windows and doors.

The adults in the lives of Billy . . . and Harold want the best for them. Formidable economic constraints make it a major life task for these parents to put food on the table, arrange for housing, negotiate unsafe neighborhoods, take children to the doctor (often waiting for city buses that do not come), clean children's clothes, and get children to bed and have them ready for school the next morning. But unlike middle-class parents, these adults do not consider the concerted development of children, particularly through organized leisure activities, an essential aspect of good parenting. "

(Lareau 2003:1–3) Additional information about this excerpt can be found on the Online Learning Center at www.mhhe.com/schaefer11.

In this excerpt from *Unequal Childhoods: Class, Race, and Family Life,* Annette Lareau vividly illustrates how different types of stratification—class, race, gender, and age—define family life, molding the social relationships that develop among household members. Lareau, a sociologist who teaches at Temple University, based her book on the observation research she did in schools and homes. She also interviewed families from different social class backgrounds, both White and African American. Among these varied families, she found markedly different approaches to parenting—approaches, Lareau believes, that have much to do with their children's futures.

Just as stratification affects family life, so does the period in which a family lives. The family of today is not what it was a century ago, or even a generation ago. New roles, new gender distinctions, new child-rearing patterns have all combined to create new forms of family life. Today, for example, more and more women are taking the breadwinner's role, whether married or as a single parent. Blended families—the result of divorce and remarriage—are almost the norm. And many people are seeking intimate relationships outside marriage, whether it be in gay partnerships or in cohabiting arrangements.

This chapter addresses family and intimate relationships in the United States as well as other parts of the world. As we will see, family patterns differ from one culture to another, and even within the same culture. Despite the differences, however, the family is universal—found in every culture. A *family* can be defined as a set of people related by blood, marriage or some other agreed-upon relationship, or adoption, who share the primary responsibility for reproduction and caring for members of society.

What are families in different parts of the world like? How do people select their mates? When a marriage fails, how does the divorce affect the children? What are the alternatives to the nuclear family, and how prevalent are they? In this chapter we will look at the family and intimate relationships from the functionalist, conflict, and interactionist points of view. We'll examine variations in marital patterns and family life, including child rearing, paying particular attention to the increasing numbers of people in dual-income and single-parent families. We'll examine divorce in the United States, and consider diverse lifestyles such as cohabitation, lesbian and gay relationships, and marriage without children. In the Social Policy section we will confront the controversial issue of gay marriage.

Global View of the Family

Among Tibetans, a woman may be married simultaneously to more than one man, usually brothers. This system allows sons to share the limited amount of good land. Among the Betsileo of Madagascar, a man has multiple wives, each one living in a different village where he cultivates rice. Wherever he has the best rice field, that wife is considered his first or senior wife. Among the Yanomami of Brazil and Venezuela, it is considered proper to have sexual relations with your opposite-sex cousins if they are the children of your mother's brother or your father's sister. But if your opposite-sex cousins are the children of your mother's sister or your father's brother, the same practice is considered to be incest (Haviland et al. 2005; Kottak 2008).

As these examples illustrate, there are many variations in the family from culture to culture. Yet the family as a social institution exists in all cultures. Moreover, certain general principles concerning its composition, kinship patterns, and authority patterns are universal.

Composition: What Is the Family?

If we were to take our information on what a family is from what we see on television, we might come up with some very strange scenarios. The media don't always present a realistic view of the family. Moreover, many people still think of the family in very narrow terms—as a married couple and their unmarried children living together, like the family in the old *Cosby Show.* However, this is but one type of family, what sociologists refer to as a *nuclear family.* The term *nuclear family* is well chosen, since this type of family serves as the nucleus, or core, on which larger family groups are built.

Most people in the United States see the nuclear family as the preferred family arrangement. Yet by 2000, only about a third of the nation's family households fit this model. The proportion of households in the United States that is composed of married couples with children at home has decreased steadily over the last 40 years, and is expected to continue shrinking. At the same time, the number of single-parent households has increased (see Figure 14-1).

A family in which relatives—such as grandparents, aunts, or uncles—live in the same home as parents and their children is known as an *extended family.* Although not common, such living arrangements do exist in the United States. The structure of the extended family offers certain advantages over that of the nuclear family. Crises such as death, divorce, and illness put less strain on family members, since more people can provide assistance and emotional support. In addition, the extended family constitutes a larger economic unit than the nuclear family. If the

FIGURE 14–1

U.S. Households by Family Type, 1940–2010

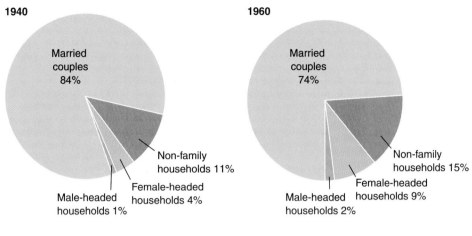

1940

Married couples 84%

Non-family households 11%

Male-headed households 1%

Female-headed households 4%

1960

Married couples 74%

Non-family households 15%

Male-headed households 2%

Female-headed households 9%

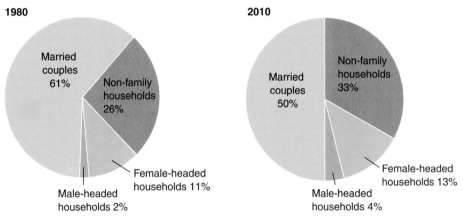

1980

Married couples 61%

Non-family households 26%

Male-headed households 2%

Female-headed households 11%

2010

Married couples 50%

Non-family households 33%

Male-headed households 4%

Female-headed households 13%

Note: Nonfamily households includes women and men living alone or exclusively with people to whom they are not related, as in a college dormitory, homeless shelter, or military base.

Source: Author's estimate based on Bureau of the Census 1996; Jason Fields 2004; see also McFalls 2003:23.

family is engaged in a common enterprise—a farm or a small business—the additional family members may represent the difference between prosperity and failure.

In considering these different family types, we have limited ourselves to the form of marriage that is characteristic of the United States—monogamy. The term ***monogamy*** describes a form of marriage in which one woman and one man are married only to each other. Some observers, noting the high rate of divorce in the United States, have suggested that "serial monogamy" is a more accurate description of the form that marriage takes in this country. In ***serial monogamy,*** a person may have several spouses in his or her lifetime, but only one spouse at a time.

Some cultures allow an individual to have several husbands or wives simultaneously. This form of marriage is known as ***polygamy.*** In fact, most societies throughout the world, past and present, have preferred polygamy to monogamy. Anthropologist George Murdock (1949, 1957) sampled 565 societies and found that in more than 80 percent, some type of polygamy was the

preferred form. While polygamy declined steadily through most of the 20th century, in at least five countries in Africa 20 percent of men still have polygamous marriages (Population Reference Bureau 1996).

There are two basic types of polygamy. According to Murdock, the most common—endorsed by the majority of cultures he sampled—is ***polygyny.*** Polygyny refers to the marriage of a man to more than one woman at the same time. The wives are often sisters, who are expected to hold similar values and have already had experience sharing a household. In polygynous societies, relatively few men actually have multiple spouses. Most individuals live in monogamous families; having multiple wives is viewed as a mark of status.

The other principal variation of polygamy is ***polyandry,*** in which a woman may have more than one husband at the same time. Such is the case in the culture of the Nyinba, described in Box 14-1 (page 344). Polyandry, however, is exceedingly rare today, though it is accepted in some extremely poor societies. Like many other societies, polyandrous cultures devalue the social worth of women.

Kinship Patterns: To Whom Are We Related?

Many of us can trace our roots by looking at a family tree or by listening to elderly family members talk about their lives—and about the lives of ancestors who died long before we were born. Yet a person's lineage is more than simply a personal history; it also reflects societal patterns that govern descent. In every culture, children encounter relatives to whom they are expected to show an emotional attachment. The state of being related to others is called ***kinship.*** Kinship is culturally learned, however, and is not totally determined by biological or marital ties. For example, adoption creates a kinship tie that is legally acknowledged and socially accepted.

The family and the kin group are not necessarily one and the same. Whereas the family is a household unit, kin do not always live together or function as a collective body on a daily basis. Kin groups include aunts, uncles, cousins, in-laws, and so forth. In a society such as the United States, the kinship group may come together only rarely, for a wedding or funeral. However, kinship ties frequently create obligations and responsibilities. We may feel compelled to assist our kin, and we feel free to call upon them for many types of aid, including loans and babysitting.

What Is a Family?

What makes a family? Not race, because families can be transracial. Not two generations, because families can be extended. Not the number or age of the members, because families can be big or small, young or old. Around the world, families may eat, dress, and worship differently, but all are united by a special intergenerational bond and an acknowledged responsibility to care for their kin.

German photographer Uwe Ommer (2000) took the photographs on this page and the next. For four years he traveled the world, visiting 130 countries on five continents in search of families who are typical of their societies. These three photographs, taken from Ommer's book *1000 Families,* only hint at the tremendous diversity of families around the world. The interracial family from Botswana (below) represents a departure from the norm in their society; in a country where politics is based on race, they feel they are outsiders. Still, their love for one another holds the family together. The thoroughly modern Syrian family (top right) has three children in college; of the three girls, one aspires to become a journalist, another an engineer, and the third a professional basketball player. The extended family from Armenia (bottom right) combines shoemaking, teaching, and farming to support three generations. Working with their hands and their heads, they are optimistic about the future and plan to have more children.

{Botswana}

342

{Syria}

{Armenia}

343

sociologyIN *the Global Community*

14-1 One Wife, Many Husbands: The Nyinba

The Nyinba culture of Nepal and Tibet is an agrarian society located in the remote valleys of the Himalaya Mountains, more than 9,000 feet above sea level. Despite the Nyinba's isolation, however, they have been closely studied. Scholars from around the world have traveled to the Himalayas to observe this people, one of the few remaining cultures on earth to practice polyandry.

In the physically challenging environment of the Himalayas, polyandry seems to work well. Because the land and climate make it difficult to sustain crops, farming is labor-intensive: many Nyinba laborers must work the fields to support a single family. Thus, a typical marriage involving three brothers and one wife provides the

> *Favoritism toward a particular husband is frowned on by the Nyinba. Thus, it is the wife's responsibility to see that each husband shares time with her in a rotational fashion.*

A Nyinba family threshing buckwheat in the field. At left is the wife; in the center, one of her five husbands (with raised mallet); at right, her mother-in-law.

necessary adult male laborers, yet minimizes the number of offspring—a necessity in a place where the food supply is limited.

While an outsider might suppose that Nyinba women dominate their families, in fact authority and inheritance rest on the husband or son. The birth of a son is celebrated, while the birth of a daughter, regardless of who might be the father, brings disappointment. Paternity appears to be a nonissue in this culture, since households are shared by brothers from the same family. The literal head of the household is the oldest brother, who typically chooses a wife from outside his extended family.

Favoritism toward a particular husband is frowned on by the Nyinba. Thus, it is the wife's responsibility to see that each husband shares time with her in a rotational fashion. Often, over the morning meal, she will indicate which husband will sleep with her that night. To avoid any confusion, the chosen husband will place his shoes outside her bedroom door.

As in any society (for example, the United States), not all Nyinba households conform to the social norm. If a family has only one son, he must of necessity marry monogamously—an unfortunate outcome in this society. If a wife is

unable to have children, a second wife, typically her sister or cousin, may be welcomed into the marriage.

Let's Discuss

1. Why would a monogamous marriage be considered an unfortunate one in the Nyinba culture?
2. What might be some other ways for a society to handle the physical constraints of life in a mountainous terrain?

Sources: Levine 1988; Stockard 2002.

How do we identify kinship groups? The principle of descent assigns people to kinship groups according to their relationship to a mother or father. There are three primary ways of determining descent. The United States follows the system of **bilateral descent,** which means that both sides of a person's family are regarded as equally important. For example, no higher value is given to the brothers of one's father than to the brothers of one's mother.

Most societies—according to George Murdock, 64 percent— give preference to one side of the family or the other in tracing descent. In **patrilineal** (from the Latin *pater,* "father") **descent,** only the father's relatives are significant in terms of property, inheritance, and emotional ties. Conversely, in societies that favor **matrilineal** (from the Latin *mater,* "mother") **descent,** only the mother's relatives are significant.

New forms of reproductive technology will necessitate a new way of looking at kinship. Today, a combination of biological and social processes can "create" a family member, requiring that more distinctions be made about who is related to whom.

Authority Patterns: Who Rules?

Imagine that you have recently married and must begin to make decisions about the future of your new family. You and your spouse face many questions. Where will you live? How will you furnish your home? Who will do the cooking, the shopping, the cleaning? Whose friends will be invited to dinner? Each time a decision must be made, an issue is raised: Who has the power to make the decision? In simple terms, who rules the family? Conflict theorists examine these questions in the context of tradi-{p.303} tional gender stratification, under which men have held a dominant position over women.

Societies vary in the way that power is distributed within the family. A society that expects males to dominate in all family decision making is termed a *patriarchy.* In patriarchal societies, such as Iran, the eldest male often wields the greatest power, although wives are expected to be treated with respect and kindness. A woman's status in Iran is typically defined by her relationship to a male relative, usually as a wife or daughter. In many patriarchal societies, women find it more difficult to obtain a divorce than a man does. In contrast, in a *matriarchy,* women have greater authority than men. Matriarchies, which are very uncommon, emerged among Native American tribal societies and in nations in which men were absent for long periods because of warfare or food-gathering expeditions (Farr 1999).

In a third type of authority pattern, the *egalitarian family,* spouses are regarded as equals. That does not mean, however, that all decisions are shared in such families. Wives may hold authority in some spheres, husbands in others. Many sociologists believe the egalitarian family has begun to replace the patriarchal family as the social norm in the United States.

Use Your Sociological Imagination

In your own family, which relatives do you have a significant relationship with? Which do you hardly ever see?

Though spouses in an egalitarian family may not share all their decisions, they regard themselves as equals. This pattern of authority is becoming more common in the United States.

Sociological Perspectives on the Family

Do we really need the family? A century ago, Friedrich Engels ([1884] 1959), a colleague of Karl Marx, described the family as the ultimate source of social inequality because of its role in the transfer of power, property, and privilege. More recently, conflict theorists have argued that the family contributes to societal injustice, denies women opportunities that are extended to men, and limits freedom in sexual expression and mate selection. In contrast, the functionalist perspective focuses on the ways in which the family gratifies the needs of its members and contributes to social stability. The interactionist view considers the intimate, face-to-face relationships that occur in the family.

Functionalist View

The family performs six paramount functions, first outlined more than 70 years ago by sociologist William F. Ogburn (Ogburn and Tibbits 1934):

1. **Reproduction.** For a society to maintain itself, it must replace dying members. In this sense, the family contributes to human survival through its function of reproduction.

2. **Protection.** Unlike the young of other animal species, human infants need constant care and economic security. In all cultures, the family assumes the ultimate responsibility for the protection and upbringing of children.

3. **Socialization.** Parents and other kin monitor a child's behavior and transmit the norms, values, and language of their culture to the child.

4. **Regulation of sexual behavior.** Sexual norms are subject to change both over time (for instance, in the customs for dating) and across cultures (compare strict Saudi Arabia to the more permissive Denmark). However, whatever the time period or cultural values of a society, standards of sexual behavior are most clearly defined within the family circle.

5. **Affection and companionship.** Ideally, the family provides members with warm and intimate relationships, helping them to feel satisfied and secure. Of course, a family member may find such rewards outside the family—from peers, in school, at work—and may even perceive the home as an unpleasant or abusive setting. Nevertheless, we expect our relatives to understand us, to care for us, and to be there for us when we need them.

6. **Provision of social status.** We inherit a social position because of the family background and reputation of our parents and siblings. The family presents the newborn child with an ascribed status based on race and ethnicity that helps to determine his or her place within society's stratification system. Moreover, family resources affect children's ability to pursue certain opportunities, such as higher education and special lessons.

Traditionally, the family has fulfilled a number of other functions, such as providing religious training, education, and recreational outlets. But Ogburn argued that other social institutions have gradually assumed many of those functions. Education once took place at the family fireside; now it is the responsibility of professionals working in schools and colleges. Even the family's traditional recreational function has been transferred to outside groups such as Little Leagues, athletic clubs, and Internet chat rooms.

Conflict View

Conflict theorists view the family not as a contributor to social stability, but as a reflection of the inequality in wealth and power that is found within the larger society. Feminist and conflict theorists note that the family has traditionally legitimized and perpetuated male dominance. Throughout most of human history—and in a wide range of societies—husbands have exercised overwhelming power and authority within the family. Not until the first wave of contemporary feminism in the United States, in the mid-1800s, was there a substantial challenge to the {p.17} historic status of wives and children as the legal property of husbands.

While the egalitarian family has become a more common pattern in the United States in recent decades—owing in good part to the activism of feminists beginning in the late 1960s and early 1970s—male dominance over the family has hardly disappeared. Sociologists have found that while married men are increasing their involvement in child care, their wives still perform a disproportionate amount of it. Furthermore, for every stay-at-home dad there are 38 stay-at-home moms (Fields 2004:11–12; Garcia-Moreno et al. 2005; Sayer et al. 2004). And unfortunately,

many husbands reinforce their power and control over wives and children through acts of domestic violence.

Conflict theorists also view the family as an economic unit that contributes to societal injustice. The family is the basis for transferring power, property, and privilege from one generation {pp.232–233} to the next. Although the United States is widely viewed as a land of opportunity, social mobility is restricted in important ways. Children inherit the privileged or less-than-privileged social and economic status of their parents (and in some cases, of earlier generations as well). As the chapter-opening excerpt showed, the social class of parents significantly influences children's socialization experiences and the degree of protection they receive. Thus, the socioeconomic status of a child's family will have a marked influence on his or her nutrition, health care, housing, educational opportunities, and in many respects, life chances as an adult. For this reason, conflict theorists argue that the family helps to maintain inequality.

Interactionist View

Interactionists focus on the micro level of family and other intimate relationships. They are interested in how individuals interact with one another, whether they are cohabiting partners or longtime married couples. For example, in a study of both Black and White two-parent households, researchers found that when fathers are more involved with their children (reading to them, helping them with homework, or restricting their television viewing), the children have fewer behavior problems, get along better with others, and are more responsible (Mosley and Thomson 1995).

Another interactionist study might examine the role of the stepparent. The increased number of single parents who remarry has sparked an interest in those who are helping to raise other people's children. Studies have found that stepmothers are more likely than stepfathers to accept the blame for bad relations with their stepchildren. Interactionists theorize that stepfathers (like most fathers) may simply be unaccustomed to interacting directly with children when the mother isn't there (Bray and Kelly 1999; Furstenberg and Cherlin 1991).

Feminist View

Because "women's work" has traditionally focused on family life, feminist sociologists have taken a strong interest in the family as a social institution. As we saw in Chapter 12, research on gender {p.309} roles in child care and household chores has been extensive. Sociologists have looked particularly closely at how women's work outside the home impacts their child care and housework—duties Arlie Hochschild (1989, 1990, 2005) has referred to as the "second shift." Today, researchers recognize that for many women, the second shift includes the care of aging parents as well.

Feminist theorists have urged social scientists and social agencies to rethink the notion that families in which no adult male is present are automatically a cause for concern, or even dysfunctional. They have also contributed to research on single

Interactionists are particularly interested in the ways in which mothers and fathers relate to each other and to their children. This mother and her two children are expressing a close and loving relationship, one of the foundations of a strong family.

women, single-parent households, and lesbian couples. In the case of single mothers, researchers have focused on the resiliency of many such households, despite economic stress. According to Velma McBride Murray and her colleagues (2001) at the University of Georgia, such studies show that among African Americans, single mothers draw heavily on kinfolk for material resources, parenting advice, and social support. Considering feminist research on the family as a whole, one researcher concluded that the family is the "source of women's strength" (L. Richardson et al. 2004).

Table 14-1

Sociological Perspectives on the Family

Theoretical Perspective	Emphasis
Functionalist	The family as a contributor to social stability Roles of family members
Conflict	The family as a perpetuator of inequality Transmission of poverty or wealth across generations
Interactionist	Relationships among family members
Feminist	The family as a perpetuator of gender roles Female-headed households

summingUP

Finally, feminists who take the interactionist perspective stress the need to investigate neglected topics in family studies. For instance, in a growing number of dual-income households, the wife earns a higher income than the husband. In 2005, a study of 58 married couples revealed that 26 percent of the wives earned more than their husbands. In 1981, the proportion was just 16 percent. Yet beyond individual case studies, little research has been done on how these families may differ from those in which the husband is the major breadwinner.

Table 14-1 summarizes the four major theoretical perspectives on the family.

Marriage and Family

Currently, over 95 percent of all men and women in the United States marry at least once during their lifetimes. Historically, the most consistent aspect of family life in this country has been the high rate of marriage. In fact, despite the high rate of divorce, there are some indications of a miniboom in marriages of late.

In this part of the chapter, we will examine various aspects of love, marriage, and parenthood in the United States and contrast them with cross-cultural examples. Though we're used to thinking of romance and mate selection as strictly a matter of individual preference, sociological analysis tells us that social institutions and distinctive cultural norms and values also play an important role.

Courtship and Mate Selection

"My rugby mates would roll over in their graves," says Tom Buckley of his online courtship and subsequent marriage to Terri Muir. But Tom and Terri are hardly alone these days in turning to the Internet for matchmaking services. A generation or two ago, most couples met in high school or college, but now that people are marrying later in life, the Internet has become the new meeting place for the romantically inclined. Today, thousands of Web sites offer to help people find mates. A 2005 survey found that 12 percent of couples who visited an online wedding site had met online. Success stories like these notwithstanding, online dating services are only as good as the people who use them. Subscribers' personal profiles—the basis for potential matches—often contain false or misleading information (Kapos 2005; B. Morris 1999:D1).

Internet romance is only the latest courtship practice. In the central Asian nation of Uzbekistan and many other traditional cultures, courtship is defined largely through the interaction of two sets of parents, who arrange marriages for their children. Typically, a young Uzbekistani woman will be socialized to eagerly anticipate her marriage to a man whom she has met only once, when he is presented to her family at the time of the final inspection of her dowry. In the United States, by contrast, courtship is conducted primarily by individuals who have a romantic interest in each other. In our culture, courtship often requires these individuals to rely heavily on intricate games, gestures, and signals. Despite such differences, courtship—whether in the United States, Uzbekistan, or elsewhere—is influenced by the norms and values of the larger society (C. J. Williams 1995).

One unmistakable trend in mate selection is that the process appears to be taking longer today than in the past. A variety of factors, including concerns about financial security and personal independence, has contributed to this delay in marriage. Most people are now well into their 20s before they marry, both in the United States and in other countries (see Figure 14-2).

Aspects of Mate Selection Many societies have explicit or unstated rules that define potential mates as acceptable or unacceptable. These norms can be distinguished in terms of endogamy and exogamy. ***Endogamy*** (from the Greek *endon*, "within") specifies the groups within which a spouse must be found and prohibits marriage with others. For example, in the United States, many people are expected to marry within their own racial, ethnic, or religious group, and are strongly discouraged or even prohibited from marrying outside the group. Endogamy is intended to reinforce the cohesiveness of the group by suggesting to the young that they should marry someone "of their own kind."

In contrast, ***exogamy*** (from the Greek *exo*, "outside") requires mate selection outside certain groups, usually one's own family or certain kinfolk. The ***incest taboo,*** a social norm common to virtually all societies, prohibits sexual relationships between certain culturally specified relatives. For those of us in the United States, this taboo means that we must marry outside the nuclear family. We cannot marry our siblings, and in most states we cannot marry our first cousins.

Endogamous restrictions may be seen as preferences for one group over another. In the United States, such preferences are most obvious in racial barriers. Until the 1960s, some states outlawed interracial marriage. Nevertheless, the number of marriages between African Americans and Whites in the United States has increased more than eight times in recent decades, jumping from 51,000 in 1960 to 422,000 in 2005. Moreover, 25 percent of married Asian American women and 12 percent of married Asian American men are married to a person who is not of Asian descent. Marriage across ethnic lines is even greater among Hispanics; 38 percent of all married Hispanics have a non-Hispanic spouse. But while all these examples of racial exogamy are noteworthy, endogamy is still the social norm in the United States (Bureau of the Census 1998, 2006a:52).

Another factor that influences the selection of a marriage partner is ***homogamy,*** the conscious or unconscious tendency to select a mate with personal characteristics similar to one's own. The "like marries like" rule can be seen in couples with similar personalities and cultural interests. However, mate selection is unpredictable. Though some people may follow the homogamous pattern, others observe the rule that opposites attract: One person is dependent and submissive—almost childishly so—while the other is dominant and controlling.

FIGURE 14–2

Percentage of People Ages 20 to 24 Ever Married, Selected Countries

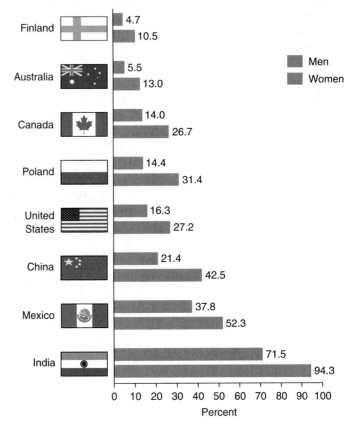

	Men	Women
Finland	4.7	10.5
Australia	5.5	13.0
Canada	14.0	26.7
Poland	14.4	31.4
United States	16.3	27.2
China	21.4	42.5
Mexico	37.8	52.3
India	71.5	94.3

Source: United Nations Population Division 2005.

Think About It

Why is the percentage of young women who are married particularly high in India, Mexico, and China? Particularly low in Finland and Australia?

Recently, the concept of homogamy has been incorporated into the process of seeking a date or marital partner online. The Internet dating site eHarmony, which claims to be the first to use a "scientific approach" to matching people based on a variety of abilities and interests, says that it "facilitates" 46 marriages a day. Sociologist Pepper Schwartz, who works as a consultant for the competing site PerfectMatch.com, has developed a 48-question survey that covers everything from prospective mates' decision-making style to their degree of impulsivity (Gottlieb 2006).

The Love Relationship Today's generation of college students seems more likely to "hook up" or cruise in large packs than to engage in the romantic dating relationships of their parents and grandparents. Still, at some point in their adult lives, the great majority of today's students will meet someone they love and enter into a long-term relationship that focuses on creating a family.

Interracial unions, which are becoming increasingly common and accepted, are blurring definitions of race. Would the children of this interracial couple be considered Black or White?

Parents in the United States tend to value love highly as a rationale for marriage, so they encourage their children to develop intimate relationships based on love and affection. Songs, films, books, magazines, television shows, and even cartoons and comic books reinforce the theme of love. At the same time, our society expects parents and peers to help a person confine his or her search for a mate to "socially acceptable" members of the opposite sex.

Though most people in the United States take the importance of falling in love for granted, the coupling of love and marriage is by no means a cultural universal. Many of the world's cultures give priority in mate selection to factors other than romantic feelings. In societies with *arranged marriages* engineered by parents or religious authorities, economic considerations play a significant role. The newly married couple is expected to develop a feeling of love *after* the legal union is formalized, if at all. Box 14-2 (page 350) describes the marriages that some immigrants to the United States arrange for their children.

In some societies, neither the parents nor the bride has a say in whom she marries. Since at least the 12th century, men in the central Asian nation of Kyrgyzstan have literally kidnapped their future wives from the street in a custom known as *ala kachuu*, which translates roughly as "grab and run." In its most benign form, this custom is a kind of elopement in which the man whisks off his girlfriend. Men do it to avoid the "bride price" that parents often demand in return for their consent. But as of 2005, one-third of the brides in Kyrgyzstan had been abducted against their will. Many of them—perhaps 80 percent—eventually assent to the kidnapping, often at their parents' urging. For these women, romantic love does not precede marriage, though love may well develop over time (Craig Smith 2005).

Use Your Sociological Imagination

Your parents and/or a matchmaker are going to arrange a marriage for you. What kind of mate will they select? Will your chances of having a successful marriage be better or worse than if you selected your own mate?

Variations in Family Life and Intimate Relationships

Within the United States, social class, race, and ethnicity create variations in family life. Studying these variations will give us a more sophisticated understanding of contemporary family styles in our country.

Social Class Differences Various studies have documented the differences in family organization among social classes in the United States. In the upper class, the emphasis is on lineage and maintenance of family position. If you are in the upper class, you are not simply a member of a nuclear family, but rather a member of a larger family tradition (think of the Rockefellers or the Kennedys). As a result, upper-class families are quite concerned about what they see as proper training for children.

Lower-class families do not often have the luxury of worrying about the "family name"; they must first struggle to pay their bills and survive the crises often associated with a life of poverty. Such families are more likely to have only one parent at home, which creates special challenges in child care and financial management. Children from lower-class families typically assume adult responsibilities—including marriage and parenthood—at an earlier age than children from affluent homes. In part, that is because they may lack the money needed to remain in school.

Social class differences in family life are less striking today than they once were. In the past, family specialists agreed that the contrasts in child-rearing practices were pronounced. Lower-class families were found to be more authoritarian in rearing children and more inclined to use physical punishment. Middle-class families were more permissive and more restrained in punishing their children. And compared to lower-class families, middle-class families tended to schedule more of their children's time, or even to overstructure it. However, these

research IN *action*

14-2 Arranged Marriage, American-Style

Leona Singh, a 25-year-old Californian, met her future mate, from Iowa, through her father. The two were introduced at a relative's home and later went out alone. Several months later, when they felt "90 percent certain" that their relationship would be a good one, the two Indian Americans married. Years later Leona looked back. "From the beginning, I felt there was a physical chemistry, but it took years to develop a mature bond, and I guess you could call that love" (Bellafante 2005:A15).

For many young people like Leona, the question is not "Does he or she love me?" but "Whom do my parents want me to marry?" In an *arranged marriage,* parents or matchmakers choose a marital partner for a young person based on considerations other than mutual attraction. Typically, couples whose marriages have been arranged don't even know each other. They are assumed to be compatible, however, since they have been carefully chosen to share the same social, economic, and cultural background.

> *In cultures in which arranged marriage is the norm, young people are socialized to expect and desire such unions.*

The idea of an arranged marriage seems strange to Western youths, who are brought up expecting to find Mr. or Ms. Right on their own—often through "love at first sight." But this romanticized approach to courtship has its drawbacks. In a romantic or sentimental marriage, a couple starts off on high ground, in love and dreaming about their hopes (or illusions) for the future. When some of their dreams fail to materialize after marriage, there is little likelihood that their relationship will improve, and a great danger of failure. In an arranged marriage, by contrast, a couple starts off on neutral ground, without unrealistic expectations. They then work to achieve the marital happiness they have been led to expect from their union. Mutual understanding develops as their relationship matures.

Historically, arranged marriages have not been unusual; even today they are common in many parts of Asia and Africa. In cultures in which arranged marriage is the norm, young people are socialized to expect and desire such unions. But what happens in cultures that

When the children of immigrants to the United States want a husband or wife, they often bow to their parents' wishes and select an arranged marriage.

send a very different message to youths? In the United States and Canada, for example, immigrants from countries such as India, Pakistan, and Bangladesh may want to arrange their children's marriages. Their sons and daughters, however, are growing up in a culture in which their schoolmates are obsessed with dating as a prelude to marriage. They listen as their friends engage in endless discussions of the latest episode of *Bachelor* or *Bachelorette.*

Studies of these young people, whose parents still cling to the tradition of arranging their children's marriages, document the challenges they face. Many of them do still embrace their parents' traditions. As one Princeton student of Indian ancestry put it, "In a lot of ways it's easier. I don't have pressure to look for a boyfriend" (Herschthal 2004). These youths will look to their parents and other relatives to find a mate, and may even accept a partner selected from their parents' country of origin. Nevertheless, though systematic, nationwide studies of this demographic group are lacking, the available research points to a trend away from arranged marriage, despite family objections.

In response to cultural pressure, some Indian immigrant families have replaced formally arranged marriage with *assisted marriage,* in

which the parents identify a limited number of potential mates for their children based on caste, family background, and geography. The children can then choose a mate from the candidates approved by their parents. Though these children may date on their own, when the time comes to marry they limit themselves to the very narrow field approved by their parents. Because of their continued reliance on arranged and now assisted marriage, Indian immigrants have the highest rate of ethnic endogamy of any major immigrant group in the United States: about 90 percent in 2003.

Let's Discuss

1. Can you, under any circumstances, imagine yourself accepting an arranged marriage? Take a poll of your classmates to see how many agree with you. Can you see an ethnic difference in the responses?

2. For Indian Americans as a group rather than as individuals, what might be some long-term benefits of arranged marriage? Might those benefits give them an advantage over other ethnic groups?

Sources: Bellafante 2005; Herschthal 2004; Talbani and Hasanali 2000; Zaidi and Shuraydi 2002.

FIGURE 14–3

Rise of Single-Parent Families in the United States, 1970–2001

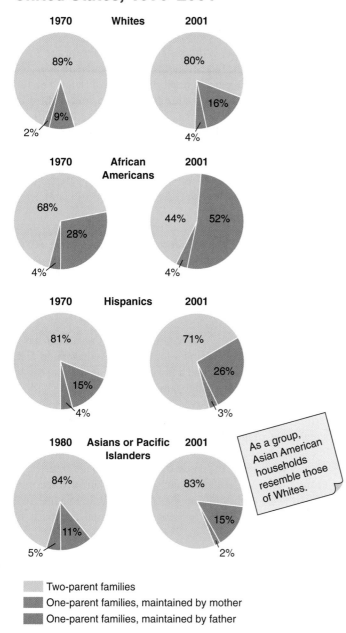

Whites

1970
89%
9%
2%

2001
80%
16%
4%

African Americans

1970
68%
28%
4%

2001
44%
52%
4%

Hispanics

1970
81%
15%
4%

2001
71%
26%
3%

Asians or Pacific Islanders

1980
84%
11%
5%

2001
83%
15%
2%

As a group, Asian American households resemble those of Whites.

■ Two-parent families
■ One-parent families, maintained by mother
■ One-parent families, maintained by father

Note: "Children" refers to children under 18. Early data for Asian Americans are for 1980. Hispanics can be of any race. Not included are unrelated people living together with no children present. All data exclude the 4 percent of children in nonparental households. *Source:* Bureau of the Census 1994:63; Kreider and Fields 2005:3.

differences may have narrowed as more and more families from all social classes turned to the same books, magazines, and even television talk shows for advice on rearing children (Luster et al. 1989; Tough 2006).

Among the poor, women often play a significant role in the economic support of the family. Men may earn low wages, may be unemployed, or may be entirely absent from the family. In

2005, 29 percent of all families headed by women with no husband present were below the government poverty line. The rate for married couples was only 5.1 percent (DeNavas-Walt et al. 2006:14).

Many racial and ethnic groups appear to have distinctive family characteristics. However, racial and class factors are often closely related. In examining family life among racial and ethnic minorities, keep in mind that certain patterns may result from class as well as cultural factors.

Racial and Ethnic Differences The subordinate status of racial and ethnic minorities in the United States profoundly affects their family lives. For example, the lower incomes of African Americans, Native Americans, most Hispanic groups, and selected Asian American groups make creating and maintaining successful marital unions a difficult task. The economic restructuring of the last 50 years, described by sociologist { p.229 } William Julius Wilson (1996) and others, has especially affected people living in inner cities and desolate rural areas, such as reservations. Furthermore, the immigration policy of the United States has complicated the successful relocation of intact families from Asia and Latin America.

The African American family suffers from many negative and inaccurate stereotypes. It is true that in a significantly higher proportion of Black than White families, no husband is present in the home (see Figure 14-3). Yet Black single mothers often belong to stable, functioning kin networks, which mitigate the pressures of sexism and racism. Members of these networks—predominantly female kin such as mothers, grandmothers, and aunts—ease financial strains by sharing goods and services. In addition to these strong kinship bonds, Black family life has emphasized deep religious commitment and high aspirations for achievement (Sarkisian and Gerstel 2004).

Like African Americans, Native Americans draw on family ties to cushion many of the hardships they face. On the Navajo reservation, for example, teenage parenthood is not regarded as the crisis that it is elsewhere in the United States. The Navajo trace their descent matrilineally. Traditionally, couples reside with the wife's family after marriage, allowing the grandparents to help with the child rearing. While the Navajo do not approve of teenage parenthood, the deep emotional commitment of their extended families provides a warm home environment for fatherless children (Dalla and Gamble 2001).

Sociologists also have taken note of differences in family patterns among other racial and ethnic groups. For example, Mexican American men have been described as exhibiting a sense of virility, personal worth, and pride in their maleness that is called ***machismo.*** Mexican Americans are also described as being more familistic than many other subcultures. ***Familism*** refers to pride in the extended family, expressed through the maintenance of close ties and strong obligations to kinfolk outside the immediate family. Traditionally, Mexican Americans have placed proximity to their extended families above other needs and desires.

These family patterns are changing, however, in response to changes in Latinos' social class standing, educational achievements, and occupations. Like other Americans, career-oriented Latinos in search of a mate but short on spare time are turning to Internet sites. As Latinos and other groups assimilate into the dominant culture of the United States, their family lives take on both the positive and negative characteristics associated with White households (Becerra 1999; Vega 1995).

Child-Rearing Patterns in Family Life

The Nayars of southern India acknowledge the biological role of fathers, but the mother's eldest brother is responsible for her children. In contrast, uncles play only a peripheral role in child care in the United States. Caring for children is a universal function of the family, yet the ways in which different societies assign this function to family members can vary significantly. Even within the United States, child-rearing patterns are varied. We'll take a look here at parenthood and grandparenthood, adoption, dual-income families, single-parent families, and stepfamilies.

Parenthood and Grandparenthood The socialization of children is essential to the maintenance of any culture. Consequently, parenthood is one of the most important (and most demanding) social roles in the United States. Sociologist Alice Rossi (1968, 1984) has identified four factors that complicate the { p.96 transition to parenthood and the role of socialization. First, there is little anticipatory socialization for the social role of caregiver. The normal school curriculum gives scant attention to the subjects most relevant to successful family life, such as child care and home maintenance. Second, only limited learning occurs during the period of pregnancy itself. Third, the transition to parenthood is quite abrupt. Unlike adolescence, it is not prolonged; unlike the transition to work, the duties of caregiving cannot be taken on gradually. Finally, in Rossi's view, our society lacks clear and helpful guidelines for successful parenthood. There is little consensus on how parents can produce happy and well-adjusted offspring—or even on what it means to be well-adjusted. For these reasons, socialization for parenthood involves difficult challenges for most men and women in the United States.

One recent development in family life in the United States has been the extension of parenthood, as adult children continue to live at home or return home after college. In 2003, 55 percent of men and 46 percent of women ages 18 to 24 lived with their parents. Some of these adult children were still pursuing an education, but in many instances, financial difficulties lay at the heart of these living arrangements. While rents and real estate prices have skyrocketed, salaries for younger workers have not kept pace, and many find themselves unable to afford their own homes. Moreover, with many marriages now ending in divorce—most commonly in the first seven years of marriage—divorced sons and daughters often return to live with their parents, sometimes with their own children (Jason Fields 2004:16).

Is this living arrangement a positive development for family members? Social scientists have just begun to examine the phenomenon, sometimes called the "boomerang generation" or the "full-nest syndrome" in the popular press. One survey in Virginia seemed to show that neither the parents nor their adult children were happy about continuing to live together. The children often felt resentful and isolated, but the parents suffered too: Learning to live without children in the home is an essential stage of adult life, and may even be a significant turning point for a marriage (*Berkeley Wellness Letter* 1990; Mogelonsky 1996).

In some homes, the full nest holds grandchildren. In 2002, 5.6 million children, or 8 percent of all children in the United States, lived in a household with a grandparent. In about a third of these homes, no parent was present to assume responsibility for the youngsters. Special difficulties are inherent in such relationships, including legal custodial concerns, financial issues, and emotional problems for adults and youths alike. Little surprise that support groups such as Grandparents as Parents have emerged to provide assistance (Cherlin 2006; Jason Fields 2003; H. Park 2005).

Adoption In a legal sense, ***adoption*** is a "process that allows for the transfer of the legal rights, responsibilities, and privileges of parenthood" to a new legal parent or parents (E. Cole 1985:638). In many cases, these rights are transferred from a biological parent or parents (often called birth parents) to an adoptive parent or parents.

Viewed from a functionalist perspective, government has a strong interest in encouraging adoption. Policymakers, in fact, have both a humanitarian and a financial stake in the process. In theory, adoption offers a stable family environment for children who otherwise might not receive satisfactory care. Moreover, government data show that unwed mothers who keep their babies tend to be of lower socioeconomic status, and often require public assistance to support their children. The government can lower its social welfare expenses, then, if children are transferred to economically self-sufficient families. From an interactionist perspective, however, adoption may require a child to adjust to a very different family environment and parental approach to child rearing.

About 4 percent of all people in the United States are adopted, about half of whom were adopted by persons not related to them at birth. There are two legal methods of adopting an unrelated person: the adoption may be arranged through a licensed agency, or in some states it may be arranged through a private agreement sanctioned by the courts. Adopted children may come from the United States or from abroad. In 2006 almost 21,000 children entered the United States as the adopted children of U.S. citizens. While the number of international adoptions remains substantial, it has declined in recent years. China, the source for about one-third of overseas adoptions, recently began to tighten the rules for foreigners. Applicants who are single, obese, or older than 50 may now be disqualified automatically (Belluck and Yardley 2006; Department of State 2007).

In some cases the adopters are not married. In 1995, an important court decision in New York held that a couple does not need to be married to adopt a child. Under this ruling, unmarried heterosexual couples, lesbian couples, and gay male couples

When nine-year-old Blake Brunson shows up for a basketball game, so do his *eight* grandparents—the result of his parents' remarriage. Blended families can be very supportive to children, but what message do they send to them on the permanency of marriage?

Idol winner Fantasia Barrino's song "Baby Mama" offers a tribute to young single mothers—a subject she knows about. Barrino was 17 when she became pregnant with her now three-year-old daughter. Though critics charged that the song sends the wrong message to teenage girls, Barrino says it is not about encouraging teens to have sex. Rather, she sees the song as an anthem for young mothers courageously trying to raise their children alone (Cherlin 2006).

In recent decades, the stigma attached to unwed mothers and other single parents has significantly diminished. ***Single-parent families,*** in which only one parent is present to care for the children, can hardly be viewed as a rarity in the United States. In 2001, a single parent headed about 20 percent of White families with children under 18, 29 percent of Hispanic families with children, and 56 percent of African American families with children (see Figure 14-3 on page 351).

The lives of single parents and their children are not inevitably more difficult than life in a traditional nuclear family. It is as inaccurate to assume that a single-parent family is necessarily

can all legally adopt children in New York. Writing for the majority, Chief Justice Judith Kaye argued that by expanding the boundaries of who can be legally recognized as parents, the state may be able to assist more children in securing "the best possible home." With this ruling, New York became the third state (after Vermont and Massachusetts) to recognize the right of unmarried couples to adopt children (Dao 1995).

For every child who is adopted, many more remain the wards of state-sponsored child protective services. At any given time, over half a million children in the United States are living in foster care. About 118,000 of these children are eligible for adoption (Koch 2006).

Dual-Income Families

The idea of a family consisting of a wage-earning husband and a wife who stays at home has largely given way to the dual-income household. Among married people between the ages of 25 and 34, 95 percent of the men and 68 percent of the women were in the labor force in 2005.

Why has there been such a rise in the number of dual-income couples? A major factor is economic need. In 2004 the median income for households with both partners employed was 91 percent more than in households in which only one person was working outside the home ($68,892 compared to $36,149). Of course, because of such work-related costs as child care, not all of a family's second wage is genuine additional income. Other factors that have contributed to the rise of the dual-income model include the nation's declining birthrate, the increase in the proportion of women with a college education, the shift in the economy of the United States from manufacturing to service industries, and the impact of the feminist movement in changing women's consciousness (Bureau of the Census 2006a:379; DeNavas-Walt et al. 2005:HINC-01 table).

Dad takes breakfast duty while Mom rushes off to work in this dual-income family. An increasing proportion of couples in the United States rejects the traditional nuclear family model of husband as breadwinner and wife as homemaker.

deprived as it is to assume that a two-parent family is always secure and happy. Nevertheless, life in a single-parent family can be extremely stressful, in both economic and emotional terms. A family headed by a single mother faces especially difficult problems when the mother is a teenager.

Why might low-income teenage women wish to have children and face the obvious financial difficulties of motherhood? Viewed from an interactionist perspective, these women tend to have low self-esteem and limited options; a child may provide a sense of motivation and purpose for a teenager whose economic worth in our society is limited at best. Given the barriers that many young women face because of their gender, race, ethnicity, and class, many teenagers may believe they have little to lose and much to gain by having a child.

According to a widely held stereotype, "unwed mothers" and "babies having babies" in the United States are predominantly African American. However, this view is not entirely accurate. African Americans account for a disproportionate share of births to unmarried women and teenagers, but the majority of all babies born to unmarried teenage mothers are born to White adolescents. Moreover, since 1980, birthrates among Black teenagers have declined steadily (J. Martin et al. 2005).

Although 82 percent of single parents in the United States are mothers, the number of households headed by single fathers more than quadrupled over the period 1980 to 2000. Though single mothers often develop social networks, single fathers are typically more isolated. In addition, they must deal with schools and social service agencies that are more accustomed to women as custodial parents (Jason Fields 2004).

Stepfamilies Approximately 45 percent of all people in the United States will marry, divorce, and then remarry. The rising rates of divorce and remarriage have led to a noticeable increase in stepfamily relationships.

The exact nature of blended families has social significance for adults and children alike. Certainly resocialization is required when an adult becomes a stepparent or a child becomes a stepchild and stepsibling. Moreover, an important distinction must be made between first-time stepfamilies and households where there have been repeated divorces, breakups, or changes in custodial arrangements.

In evaluating the rise of stepfamilies, some observers have assumed that children would benefit from remarriage because they would be gaining a second custodial parent, and would potentially enjoy greater economic security. However, after reviewing many studies of stepfamilies, sociologist Andrew J. Cherlin (2008:800) concluded that "the well-being of children in stepfamilies is no better, on average, than the well-being of children in divorced, single-parent households."

Stepparents can play valuable and unique roles in their stepchildren's lives, but their involvement does not guarantee an improvement in family life. In fact, standards may decline. Studies suggest that children raised in families with stepmothers are likely to have less health care, education, and money spent on their food than children raised by biological mothers. The measures are also negative for children raised by stepfathers, but only half as negative as in the case of stepmothers. These results don't mean that stepmothers are "evil"—it may be that the stepmother holds back out of concern for seeming too intrusive, or relies mistakenly on the biological father to carry out parental duties (Lewin 2000).

Divorce

"Do you promise to love, honor, and cherish . . . until death do you part?" Every year, people of all social classes and racial and ethnic groups make this legally binding agreement. Yet increasing numbers of these promises shatter in divorce.

Statistical Trends in Divorce

Just how common is divorce? Surprisingly, this is not a simple question; divorce statistics are difficult to interpret. The media frequently report that one out of every two marriages ends in divorce. But that figure is misleading, since many marriages last for decades. It is based on a comparison of all divorces that occur in a single year (regardless of when the couples were married) with the number of new marriages in the same year.

In the United States and many other countries, divorce began to increase in the late 1960s but then leveled off; since the late 1980s, it has declined by 30 percent (see Figure 14-4). This trend is due partly to the aging of the baby boomer population and the corresponding decline in the proportion of people of marriageable age. But it also indicates an increase in marital stability in recent years (Coontz 2006).

Getting divorced obviously does not sour people on marriage. About 63 percent of all divorcees in the United States have remarried. Women are less likely than men to remarry because many retain custody of their children after a divorce, which complicates a new adult relationship (Bianchi and Spain 1996; Saad 2004).

Some people regard the nation's high rate of remarriage as an endorsement of the institution of marriage, but it does lead to

Most households in the United States do not consist of two parents living with their unmarried children.

FIGURE 14–4

Trends in Marriage and Divorce in the United States, 1920–2006

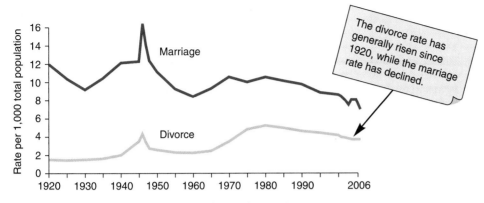

The divorce rate has generally risen since 1920, while the marriage rate has declined.

Sources: Bureau of the Census 1975:64; *National Vital Statistics Reports* 2007.

the new challenges of a kin network composed of both current and prior marital relationships. Such networks can be particularly complex if children are involved or if an ex-spouse remarries.

Factors Associated with Divorce

Perhaps the most important factor in the increase in divorce over the last hundred years has been the greater social *acceptance* of divorce. It's no longer considered necessary to endure an unhappy marriage. More important, various religious denominations have relaxed their negative attitudes toward divorce, so that most religious leaders no longer treat it as a sin.

The growing acceptance of divorce is a worldwide phenomenon. Only a decade ago, Sunoo, South Korea's foremost matchmaking service, had no divorced clients. Few Koreans divorced; those who did felt social pressure to resign themselves to the single life. But over the last seven years, South Korea's divorce rate has doubled. Today, 15 percent of Sunoo's membership is divorced (Onishi 2003).

In the United States, several factors have contributed to the growing social acceptance of divorce:

- Most states have adopted more liberal divorce laws in the last three decades. No-fault divorce laws, which allow a couple to end their marriage without fault on either side (by specifying adultery, for instance), accounted for an initial surge in the divorce rate after they were introduced in the 1970s, but appear to have had little effect beyond that.

- Divorce has become a more practical option in newly formed families, since families tend to have fewer children now than in the past.

- A general increase in family incomes, coupled with the availability of free legal aid to some poor people, has meant that more couples can afford costly divorce proceedings.

- As society provides greater opportunities for women, more and more wives are becoming less dependent on their husbands, both economically and emotionally. They may feel more able to leave a marriage if it seems hopeless.

Impact of Divorce on Children

Divorce is traumatic for all involved, but it has special meaning for the more than 1 million children whose parents divorce each year (see Box 14-3, page 356). Of course, for some of these children, divorce signals the welcome end to a very dysfunctional relationship. A national sample conducted by sociologists Paul R. Amato and Alan Booth (1997) showed that in about a third of divorces, the children benefit from parental separation because it lessens their exposure to conflict. But in about 70 percent of divorces, the parents engaged in a low level of conflict; in those cases, the realities of divorce appeared to be harder for the children to bear than living with the marital unhappiness.

Other researchers, using differing definitions of conflict, have found greater unhappiness for children living in homes with marital differences. Still, it would be simplistic to assume that children are automatically better off following the breakup of their parents' marriage. The interests of the parents do not necessarily serve children well.

Use Your Sociological Imagination

In a society that maximizes the welfare of all family members, how easy should it be for couples to divorce? How easy should it be to get married?

Diverse Lifestyles

Marriage is no longer the presumed route from adolescence to adulthood. In fact, it has lost much of its social significance as a rite of passage. The nation's marriage rate has declined since 1960 because people are postponing marriage until later in life, and because more couples, including same-sex couples, are deciding to form partnerships without marriage.

Cohabitation

In the United States, testing the marital waters by living together before making a commitment is a common practice among marriage-wary 20- and 30-somethings. The tremendous

researchINaction

14-3 The Lingering Impact of Divorce

What happens to the children of divorce? Early research suggested that the negative effects of divorce on children were confined to the first few years following a breakup. According to these studies, most children eventually adjusted to the change in family structure and went on to live normal lives. But recent studies suggest that the effects of divorce may linger much longer than scholars at first suspected, peaking in the adult years, when grown children are attempting to establish their own marriages and families.

A foremost proponent of this view is psychologist Judith A. Wallerstein, who has been conducting qualitative research on the effects of divorce on children since 1971. Wallerstein has been following the original 131 children in her study for 30 years; her subjects are now ages 28 to 43. She is convinced that these adult children of divorce have had greater difficulty than other adults in forming and maintaining intimate relationships because they have never witnessed the daily give-and-take of a successful marital partnership.

Another researcher, sociologist Paul R. Amato, agrees that divorce can affect children into adulthood, but for a different reason. Amato thinks that the parents' decision to end

their marriage lies at the root of the higher-than-normal divorce rate among their children. In this study, based on telephone interviews, children whose parents had divorced had a 30 percent divorce rate themselves, which is 12 to 13 percent higher than the divorce rate among children whose parents had *not* divorced. Significantly, children of parents who did not divorce had roughly the same divorce rate regardless of whether the level of conflict in

> *Recent studies suggest that the effects of divorce may linger much longer than scholars at first suspected.*

their parents' marriage was low or high. The parental example that a marriage contract can be broken—not the demonstration of poor relationship skills—is what makes an adult child more vulnerable than others to divorce, Amato thinks.

Sociologist Andrew J. Cherlin concedes that divorce can have lingering effects, but thinks the potential for harm has been exaggerated. Cherlin, who has conducted quantitative analyses of the effects of divorce on

thousands of children, finds that parental divorce does elevate children's risk of emotional problems, school withdrawal, and teen pregnancy. But most children, he emphasizes, do not develop those problems. Even Wallerstein admits that the ill effects of divorce do not apply across the board. Some children seem to be strengthened by the crisis, she observes, and go on to lead highly successful lives, both personally and professionally.

Let's Discuss

1. Do you know any adult children of divorce who have had difficulty establishing successful marriages? If so, what seems to be the problem, an inability to handle conflict or a lack of commitment to the marriage?

2. What practical conclusions should we draw from the research on children of divorce? Should couples stay together for the sake of their children?

Sources: Amato 2001; Amato and Sobolewski 2001; Bumiller 2000; Cherlin 2008; Marquardt 2005; J. Wallerstein et al. 2000. For a different view, see Hetherington and Kelly 2002.

---

increase in the number of male–female couples who choose to live together without marrying, a practice called **cohabitation,** is one of the most dramatic trends of recent years.

About half of all *currently* married couples in the United States say that they lived together before marriage. This percentage is likely to increase. The number of unmarried-couple households in the United States rose sixfold in the 1960s and increased another 72 percent between 1990 and 2000. Presently over 8 percent of opposite-sex couples are unmarried. Cohabitation is more common among African Americans and American Indians than among other racial and ethnic groups; it is least common among Asian Americans. Figure 14-5 (opposite) shows regional variations in cohabitation (Peterson 2003; T. Simmons and O'Connell 2003).

In much of Europe, cohabitation is so common that the general sentiment seems to be "Love, yes; marriage, maybe." In Iceland, 62 percent of all children are born to single mothers; in France, Great Britain, and Norway, the proportion is about 40 percent. Government policies in these countries make few legal

distinctions between married and unmarried couples or households (Lyall 2002; M. Moore 2006).

People commonly associate cohabitation only with college campuses or sexual experimentation. But according to a study done in Los Angeles, working couples are almost twice as likely to cohabit as college students. And census data show that in 2003, 45 percent of unmarried couples had one or more children present in the household. These cohabitants are more like spouses than dating partners. Moreover, in contrast to the common perception that people who cohabit have never been married, researchers report that about half of all people involved in cohabitation in the United States have been previously married. Cohabitation serves as a temporary or permanent alternative to matrimony for many men and women who have experienced their own or their parents' divorces (Jason Fields 2004; Popenoe and Whitehead 1999).

Periodically, legislators attempt to bolster the desirability of a lifelong commitment to marriage. In 2002, President George W. Bush backed funding for an initiative to promote marriage

FIGURE 14–5

357

The Family and Intimate Relationships

Unmarried-Couple Households by State

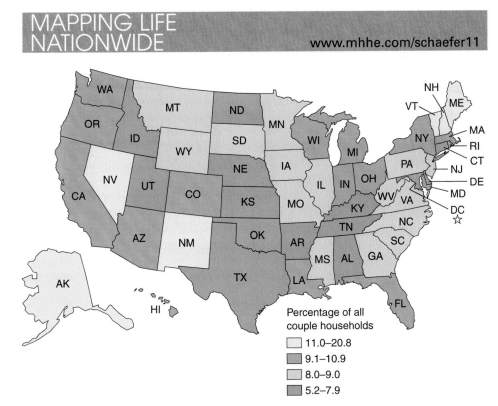

MAPPING LIFE NATIONWIDE

www.mhhe.com/schaefer11

Percentage of all couple households

- 11.0–20.8
- 9.1–10.9
- 8.0–9.0
- 5.2–7.9

Note: Data are for 2000 and include both opposite-sex and same-sex partners. U.S. average is 9.1 percent.
Source: T. Simmons and O'Connell 2003:4.

to marry to enjoy a satisfying life. Divorce, late marriage, and longevity also figure into this trend.

There are many reasons why a person may choose not to marry. Some singles do not want to limit their sexual intimacy to one lifetime partner. Some men and women do not want to become highly dependent on any one person —and do not want anyone depending heavily on them. In a society that values individuality and self-fulfillment, the single lifestyle can offer certain freedoms that married couples may not enjoy.

Remaining single represents a clear departure from societal expectations; indeed, it has been likened to "being single on Noah's Ark." A single adult must confront the inaccurate view that he or she is always lonely, is a workaholic, or is immature. These stereotypes help to support the traditional assumption in the United States and most other societies that to be truly happy and fulfilled, a person must get married and raise a family. To counter these societal expectations, singles have formed numerous support groups (Hertz 2006; Lundquist 2006).

among those who receive public assistance. Under the "Healthy Marriage Initiative," married couples would receive special monthly bonuses not available to others. The proposal garnered widespread support, though it drew some opposition from defenders of single-parent families. The debate became more heated when activists succeeded in legalizing gay marriage in Massachusetts: see the Social Policy section at the end of this chapter (S. Brown 2005; Cherlin 2003).

Remaining Single

Looking at TV programs today, you would be justified in thinking that most households are composed of singles. Although that is not the case, it is true that more and more people in the United States are *postponing* entry into a first marriage. Over one out of three households with children in the United States is a single-parent household. Even so, fewer than 4 percent of women and men in the United States are likely to remain single throughout their lives (Bureau of the Census 2006a:51).

The trend toward maintaining a single lifestyle for a longer period is related to the growing economic independence of young people. This trend is especially significant for women.
{ p.308 } Freed from financial needs, women don't necessarily need

Marriage without Children

There has been a modest increase in childlessness in the United States. According to census data, about 16 to 17 percent of women will now complete their childbearing years without having borne any children, compared to 10 percent in 1980. As many as 20 percent of women in their 30s expect to remain childless (Biddlecom and Martin 2006).

Childlessness within marriage has generally been viewed as a problem that can be solved through such means as adoption and artificial insemination. More and more couples today, however, choose not to have children and regard themselves as child-free rather than childless. They do not believe that having children automatically follows from marriage, nor do they feel that reproduction is the duty of all married couples. Childless couples have formed support groups (with names like No Kidding) and set up their own Web sites.

Economic considerations have contributed to this shift in attitudes; having children has become quite expensive. According to a government estimate made for 2004, the average middle-class family will spend $184,320 to feed, clothe, and shelter a child from birth to age 18. If the child attends college, that amount could double, depending on the college chosen. Aware of the financial pressures, some couples are having fewer children than they otherwise might, and others are weighing the advantages of a child-free marriage (Lino 2005).

Childless couples are beginning to question current practices in the workplace. While applauding employers' efforts to provide child care and flexible work schedules, some nevertheless express concern about tolerance of employees who leave early to take children to doctors, ballgames, or after-school classes. As more dual-career couples enter the paid labor force and struggle to balance career and familial responsibilities, conflicts with employees who have no children may increase (Biddlecom and Martin 2006).

Use Your Sociological Imagination

What would happen to our society if many more married couples suddenly decided not to have children? How would society change if cohabitation and/or singlehood became the norm?

Lesbian and Gay Relationships

Twenty-one-year-old Parke, a junior in college, grew up in a stable, loving family. A self-described fiscal conservative, he credits his parents with instilling in him a strong work ethic. Sound like an average child of an average family? The only break with tra-

ditional expectations in this case is that Parke is the son of a lesbian couple (P. L. Brown 2004).

The lifestyles of lesbians and gay men are varied. Some live in long-term, monogamous relationships; others live alone or with roommates. Some remain in "empty-shell" heterosexual marriages and do not publicly acknowledge their homosexuality. Others live with children from a former marriage or with adopted children. Based on election exit polls, researchers for the National Health and Social Life Survey and the Voter News Service estimate that 2 to 5 percent of the adult population identify themselves as either gay or lesbian. An analysis of the 2000 census shows a minimum of at least 600,000 gay households, and a gay and lesbian adult population approaching 10 million (Laumann et al. 1994b:293; David M. Smith and Gates 2001).

Gay and lesbian couples face discrimination on both a personal and a legal level. Their inability to marry denies them many rights that married couples take for granted, from the ability to make decisions for an incapacitated partner to the right to receive government benefits to dependents, such as Social Security payments. Though gay couples consider themselves families, just like the ones who live down the street, they are often treated as if they are not.

Precisely because of such inequities, many gay and lesbian couples are now demanding the right to marry. In the Social Policy section that follows, we will examine the highly controversial issue of gay marriage.

(social Policy)
and the Family

Gay Marriage

The Issue

In the United States, attitudes toward marriage are complex. As always, society and popular culture suggest that a young man or woman should find the perfect mate, settle down and marry, and live "happily ever after." But young people are also bombarded by messages implying the frequency of adultery and the acceptability of divorce. In this atmosphere, the idea of same-sex marriage strikes some people as only the latest of many attacks on traditional marriage. To others, it seems an overdue acknowledgment of the formal relationships that faithful, monogamous gay couples have long maintained.

The Setting

In 2004, in his State of the Union message, President George W. Bush warned "activist judges" against attempts to broaden the definition of marriage to include same-sex couples. The only re-

course to such measures, he said, would be a constitutional amendment banning same-sex unions.

What made gay marriage the focus of national attention? Events in two states brought the issue to the forefront. In 1999, Vermont gave gay couples the legal benefits of marriage through civil union, but stopped short of calling the arrangement a marriage. Then, in 2003, the Massachusetts Supreme Court ruled 4–3 that under the state's constitution, gay couples have the right to marry—a ruling the U.S. Supreme Court has refused to review.

Sociological Insights

Functionalists have traditionally seen marriage as a social institution that is closely tied to human reproduction. Same-sex marriage would at first appear not to fit that arrangement. But many same-sex couples are entrusted with the socialization of young children, whether or not their relationship is recognized by the state. Functionalists also wonder whether religious views toward marriage can be ignored. The courts have focused on civil marriage, but religious views are hardly irrelevant, even in a country like the United States, which observes a separation between religion and the state. Indeed, religious teachings have led even some staunch supporters of gay rights to oppose same-sex marriage on spiritual grounds.

Conflict theorists have charged that denial of the right to marry reinforces the second-class status of gays and lesbians. Some have compared the ban against gay marriage to past policies that until 1967 banned interracial marriage in 32 states (Liptak 2004a).

Interactionists generally avoid the policy question and focus instead on the nature of same-sex households. They ask many of the same questions about gay partner relations and child rearing that they raise about conventional couples. Of course, much less research has been done on same-sex households than on other families, but the studies published to date raise the same issues as those that apply to conventional married couples, plus a few more. For gay couples, the support or opposition of family, co-workers, and friends looms large (Dundas and Kaufman 2000; Dunne 2000).

Recently, national surveys of attitudes toward gay marriage have been showing volatile shifts in public opinion. Typically, people are more opposed to gay marriage than to civil union: about one-fifth of respondents favor legal recognition of gay marriage, while another fourth favor civil union. Still, as of 2006, a slight majority of the population endorsed a constitutional amendment to ban gay marriage (Gallup 2007a).

Policy Initiatives

The United States is not the first nation to consider this issue. Recognition of same-sex partnerships is not uncommon in Europe, including Belgium, Denmark, France, Germany, Great Britain, Italy, the Netherlands, Portugal, and Spain. Today, as many as 8 percent of all marriages in the Netherlands are same-sex. The trend is toward recognition in North America as well, since gay couples can marry legally in Canada.

Many nations strongly oppose such measures, however. For example, when Kofi Annan, then secretary general of the United Nations (UN), proposed extending the benefits that married UN employees receive to employees' same-sex partners in 2004, so many countries rose in protest that he reneged. Annan decided that such benefits would extend only to those UN employees whose member nations extend the same benefits to their citizens (Cowell 2005; Farley 2004; Wines 2005).

FIGURE 14–6

Discriminatory Marriage and Anti–Gay Discrimination Laws

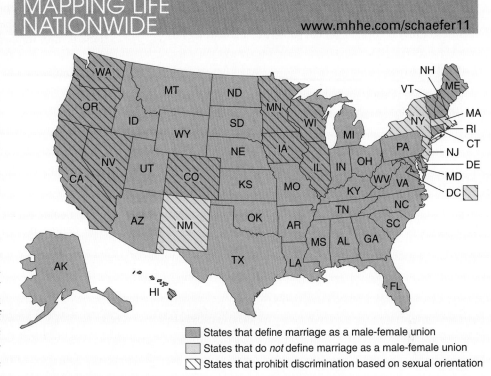

MAPPING LIFE NATIONWIDE

www.mhhe.com/schaefer11

■ States that define marriage as a male-female union
▫ States that do *not* define marriage as a male-female union
▨ States that prohibit discrimination based on sexual orientation

Note: Current as of June 2007. Vermont prohibits same-sex marriage but provides for same-sex civil union.
Source: Human Rights Campaign 2007.

In the United States, many local jurisdictions have passed legislation allowing for the registration of domestic partnerships, and have extended employee benefits to those relationships. Under such policies, a ***domestic partnership*** may be defined as two unrelated adults who share a mutually caring relationship, reside together, and agree to be jointly responsible for their dependents, basic living expenses, and other common necessities. Domestic partnership benefits can apply to couples' inheritance, parenting, pensions, taxation, housing, immigration, workplace fringe benefits, and health care. Even though the most passionate support for domestic partnership legislation has come from lesbian and gay male activists, the majority of those eligible for such benefits would be cohabiting heterosexual couples.

In the United States, marriage has traditionally been under the jurisdiction of state lawmakers. But recently, pressure has been mounting for national legislation. The Defense of Marriage Act, passed in 1996, provided that no state is obliged to recognize same-sex marriages performed in another state. However, some legal scholars doubt that the law could withstand a constitutional challenge, since it violates a provision in the Constitution that requires states to recognize one another's laws. In 2003, therefore, opponents of gay marriage proposed a constitutional amendment that would limit marriage to heterosexual couples. The measure was introduced in the Senate in 2006, but failed to receive sufficient support to come to a vote.

In the meantime, as Figure 14-6 shows (page 359), some states have moved to ban same-sex marriage, though they still prohibit discrimination against gays and lesbians. And though local jurisdictions such as the mayor's office in San Francisco may perform marriage ceremonies amid great publicity, the marriage certificates they confer on gay couples are of dubious legality.

Let's Discuss

1. If marriage is good for heterosexual couples and their families, why isn't it good for homosexual couples and their families?

2. How can interactionist studies of gay couples and their families inform policymakers who are dealing with the issue of gay marriage? Give a specific example.

3. Who are the stakeholders in the debate over gay marriage, and what do they stand to gain or lose? Whose interest do you think is most important?

GettingINVOLVED

To get involved in the debate over gay marriage, visit this text's Online Learning Center, which offers links to relevant Web sites. Check out the Social Policy section in the Online Learning Center as well; it provides survey data on U.S. public opinion regarding this issue.

www.mhhe.com/schaefer11

{ MASTERING THIS CHAPTER }

Summary

The *family,* in its many varying forms, is present in all human cultures. This chapter examines the state of marriage, the family, and other intimate relationships in the United States and considers alternatives to the traditional *nuclear family.*

1. *Families* vary from culture to culture and even within the same culture.

2. The structure of the *extended family* can offer certain advantages over that of the *nuclear family.*

3. Societies determine *kinship* by descent from both parents *(bilateral descent),* from the father only *(patrilineal descent),* or from the mother only *(matrilineal descent).*

4. Sociologists do not agree on whether the *egalitarian family* has replaced the patriarchal family as the social norm in the United States.

5. William F. Ogburn outlined six basic functions of the family: reproduction, protection, socialization, regulation of sexual behavior, companionship, and the provision of social status.

6. Conflict theorists argue that male dominance of the family contributes to societal injustice and denies women opportunities that are extended to men.

7. Interactionists focus on how individuals interact in the family and in other intimate relationships.

8. Feminists stress the need to broaden research on the family. Like conflict theorists, they see the family's role in socializing children as the primary source of sexism.

9. People select mates in a variety of ways. Some marriages are arranged; in other societies people choose their own mates. Some societies require mates to be chosen within a certain group *(endogamy)* or outside certain groups *(exogamy).* And consciously or unconsciously, many people look for a mate with similar personal characteristics *(homogamy).*

10. In the United States, family life varies with social class, race, and ethnicity.

11. Currently, in the majority of all married couples in the United States, both husband and wife work outside the home.

12. *Single-parent families* account for an increasing proportion of U.S. families.

13. Among the factors that contribute to the rising divorce rate in the United States are greater social acceptance of divorce and the liberalization of divorce laws in many states.

14. More and more people are living together without marrying, a practice known as *cohabitation.* People are also staying single longer, and some married couples are deciding not to have children.

15. The gay marriage movement, which would confer equal rights on gay and lesbian couples and their dependents, is strongly opposed by conservative religious and political groups.

Critical Thinking Questions

1. In an increasing proportion of couples in the United States, both partners work outside the home. What are the advantages and disadvantages of the dual-income model for women, for men, for children, and for society as a whole?

2. Take another look at the photo essay in Chapter 7, How Does Television Portray the Family? (see pages 160–161). Using your newly acquired understanding of the family in the United States, analyze the six programs illustrated in the essay.

3. Given the high rate of divorce in the United States, would it be more appropriate to view divorce as dysfunctional or as a normal part of our marriage system? What would be the implications of viewing divorce as normal rather than dysfunctional?

Key Terms

Adoption In a legal sense, a process that allows for the transfer of the legal rights, responsibilities, and privileges of parenthood to a new legal parent or parents. (page 352)

Bilateral descent A kinship system in which both sides of a person's family are regarded as equally important. (344)

Cohabitation The practice of living together as a male–female couple without marrying. (356)

Domestic partnership Two unrelated adults who share a mutually caring relationship, reside together, and agree to be jointly responsible for their dependents, basic living expenses, and other common necessities. (359)

Egalitarian family An authority pattern in which spouses are regarded as equals. (345)

Endogamy The restriction of mate selection to people within the same group. (348)

Exogamy The requirement that people select a mate outside certain groups. (348)

Extended family A family in which relatives—such as grandparents, aunts, or uncles—live in the same home as parents and their children. (340)

Familism Pride in the extended family, expressed through the maintenance of close ties and strong obligations to kinfolk outside the immediate family. (351)

Family A set of people related by blood, marriage or some other agreed-upon relationship, or adoption, who share the primary responsibility for reproduction and caring for members of society. (340)

Homogamy The conscious or unconscious tendency to select a mate with personal characteristics similar to one's own. (348)

Incest taboo The prohibition of sexual relationships between certain culturally specified relatives. (348)

Kinship The state of being related to others. (341)

Machismo A sense of virility, personal worth, and pride in one's maleness. (351)

Matriarchy A society in which women dominate in family decision making. (345)

Matrilineal descent A kinship system in which only the mother's relatives are significant. (344)

Monogamy A form of marriage in which one woman and one man are married only to each other. (341)

Nuclear family A married couple and their unmarried children living together. (340)

Patriarchy A society in which men dominate in family decision making. (345)

Patrilineal descent A kinship system in which only the father's relatives are significant. (344)

Polyandry A form of polygamy in which a woman may have more than one husband at the same time. (341)

Polygamy A form of marriage in which an individual may have several husbands or wives simultaneously. (341)

Polygyny A form of polygamy in which a man may have more than one wife at the same time. (341)

Serial monogamy A form of marriage in which a person may have several spouses in his or her lifetime, but only one spouse at a time. (341)

Single-parent family A family in which only one parent is present to care for the children. (353)

Read each question carefully and then select the best answer.

1. Alice, age seven, lives in a private home with her parents, her grand-mother, and her aunt. Alice's family is an example of a(n)

   a. nuclear family.
   b. dysfunctional family.
   c. extended family.
   d. polygynous family.

2. In which form of marriage may a person have several spouses in his or her lifetime, but only one spouse at a time?

   a. serial monogamy
   b. monogamy
   c. polygamy
   d. polyandry

3. The marriage of a woman to more than one man at the same time is referred to as

   a. polygyny.
   b. monogamy.
   c. serial monogamy.
   d. polyandry.

4. Which system of descent is followed in the United States?

   a. matrilineal
   b. patrilineal
   c. bilateral
   d. unilateral

5. According to the functionalist perspective, which of the following is *not* one of the paramount functions performed by the family?

   a. mediation
   b. reproduction
   c. regulation of sexual behavior
   d. affection and companionship

6. Which norm requires mate selection outside certain groups, usually one's own family or certain kinfolk?

   a. exogamy
   b. endogamy
   c. matriarchy
   d. patriarchy

7. According to the text's discussion of social class differences in family life and intimate relationships, which of the following statements is true?

   a. Social class differences in family life are more striking than they once were.
   b. The upper class emphasizes lineage and maintenance of family position.
   c. Among the poor, women usually play an insignificant role in the economic support of the family.
   d. In examining family life among racial and ethnic minorities, most patterns result from cultural, but *not* class, factors.

8. One recent development in family life in the United States has been the extension of parenthood as adult children continue to live at home or return home after college. The reason for this is

   a. the rising divorce rate.
   b. skyrocketing rent and real estate prices.
   c. financial difficulties.
   d. all of the above.

9. In the United States, the *majority* of all babies born to unmarried teenage mothers are born to whom?

   a. African American adolescents
   b. White adolescents
   c. Latina adolescents
   d. Asian American adolescents

10. Which of the following factors is associated with the high divorce rate in the United States?

    a. the liberalization of divorce laws
    b. the fact that contemporary families have fewer children than earlier families did
    c. the general increase in family incomes
    d. all of the above

11. The principle of _____ assigns people to kinship groups according to their relationship to an individual's mother or father.

12. _____ emerged among Native American tribal societies, and in nations in which men were absent for long periods because of warfare or food-gathering expeditions.

13. In the view of many sociologists, the _____ family has begun to replace the patriarchal family as the social norm in the United States.

14. As _____ theorists point out, the social class of couples and their children significantly influences the socialization experiences to which the children are exposed, and the protection they receive.

15. _____ focus on the micro level of family and other intimate relationships; for example, they are interested in whether people are cohabiting partners or are longtime married couples.

16. The rule of _____ specifies the groups within which a spouse must be found, and prohibits marriage with others.

17. Social class differences in family life are less striking today than they once were; however, in the past, _____-class families were found to be more authoritarian in rearing children and more inclined to use physical punishment.

18. Caring for children is a(n) _____ function of the family, yet the ways in which different societies assign this function to family members can vary significantly.

19. Viewed from the _____ perspective, the government has a strong interest in encouraging adoption.

20. The rising rates of divorce and remarriage have led to a noticeable increase in _____ relationships.

Online Learning Center

1. Visit the student center of the Online Learning Center at **www.mhhe.com/schaefer11** and link to "Audio Clips." Listen to Richard Schaefer, the author of this text, discuss how chat rooms are playing the role that singles' bars did in the 1980s. Professor Schaefer notes that sociologists are trying to determine whether the Internet is restructuring dating behavior or merely facilitating it.

2. More and more U.S. families include two income earners. In such households, spouses must find a way to balance their work and family obligations and accommodate each other's career needs. The Employment and Family Careers Institute at Cornell University has addressed the patterns and needs of dual-career families. Explore the institute's site (**www.human.cornell.edu/che/BLCC/index.cfm**) to learn more about this social trend.

3. U.S. families have undergone rapid change over the past few decades. To read about the latest trends, go to the Census Bureau's Web site (**www.census.gov**). Under Subjects A to Z, click on "Families/Households and Families Data."

*Note: Although all the URLs listed were current as of the printing of this book, these sites often change. Please check our Web site (**www.mhhe.com/schaefer11**) for updates, hyperlinks, and exercises related to these sites.*

Reel Society Video Clips

Reel Society video clips, which appear on this book's Web site, can be used to spark discussion about the following topics from this chapter:

- Authority Patterns: Who Rules?
- Sociological Perspectives on the Family
- Marriage and the Family
- Diverse Lifestyles

In this billboard, Volkswagen of France compares a secular event, the introduction of a new model ("Rejoice, my friends, for a new Golf is born"), to a sacred event. While such tongue-in-cheek references to religion may offend believers, they indicate the continuing relevance of religion, even in modern, industrialized societies.

15 Religion

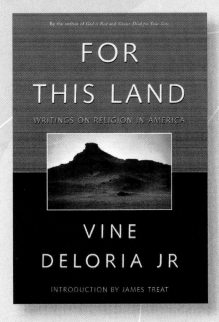

66 Growing up in a small mixed-blood community of seven hundred on the eastern edge of the Pine Ridge Reservation in South Dakota, I uncritically accepted the idea that the old Dakota religion and Christianity were both "true" and in some mysterious way compatible with each other. There were, to be sure, Christian fundamentalists with their intolerance and the old traditional Indians who kept their practices hidden, but the vast majority of the people in the vicinity more or less assumed that a satisfactory blend had been achieved that guaranteed our happiness.

Although my father was an Episcopal priest with a large number of chapels in a loosely organized Episcopal missionary district known (to Episcopalians) as "Corn Creek," he was far from an orthodox follower of the white man's religion. I always had the feeling that within the large context of "religion," which in a border town meant the Christian milieu, there was a special area in his spiritual life in which the old Dakota beliefs and practices reigned supreme. He knew thirty-three songs; some of them social, some ancient, and several spiritual songs used in a variety of ceremonial contexts. Driving to his chapels to hold Christian services he would open the window of the car and beat the side of the door with his hand for the drum beat and sing song after song. . . .

When I went to college I was exposed to a much larger canvas of human experience upon which various societies had left their religious mark. My first reaction was the belief that most of the religious traditions were simply wrong, that a few of them had come close to describing religious reality, but that it would take some intensive study to determine which religious traditions would best assist human beings in succeeding in the world. It was my good fortune to have as a religion and philosophy professor a Christian mystic who was trying to prove the deepest mysteries of the faith. He also had some intense personal problems which emerged again and again in his beliefs, indicating to me that religion and the specific individual path of life were always intertwined.

> *Although my father was an Episcopal priest with a large number of chapels in a loosely organized Episcopal missionary district known (to Episcopalians) as "Corn Creek," he was far from an orthodox follower of the white man's religion.*

Over several years and many profound conversations he was able to demonstrate to me that each religious tradition had developed a unique way to confront some problems and that they had something in common if only the search for truth and the elimination of many false paths. But his solution, after many years, became untenable for me. I saw instead religion simply as a means of organizing a society, articulating some reasonably apparent emotional truths, but ultimately becoming a staid part of social establishments that primarily sought to control human behavior and not fulfill human individual potential. It seemed as if those religions that placed strong emphasis on certain concepts failed precisely in the areas in which they claimed expertise. Thus religions of "love" could point to few examples of their efficacy; religions of "salvation" actually saved very few. The more I learned about world religions, the more respect I had for the old Dakota ways. 99

(Deloria 1999:273–275) Additional information about this excerpt can be found on the Online Learning Center at www.mhhe.com/schaefer11.

In this excerpt from *For This Land,* the late Vine Deloria—a Standing Rock Sioux—revealed his deep personal ties to the religion of his ancestors, undiluted by the overlays of missionary Christian theology. Even though his father was an Episcopal priest, Deloria was keenly aware of how tribal beliefs intruded to color his father's religious sensibility. He was also aware of the fact that Native American rites and customs had been appropriated by a generation of non-Indians seeking a kind of New Age "magic." For Deloria, Indian spiritual beliefs were an integral part of the Native American culture and helped to define that culture. Mixing those beliefs with the beliefs of other religions or systems of thought threatened to undermine the culture's strength.

Religion plays a major role in people's lives, and religious practices of some sort are evident in every society. That makes { p.59 religion a ***cultural universal,*** along with other common practices or beliefs found in every culture, such as dancing, food preparation, the family, and personal names. At present, an estimated 4 billion people belong to the world's many religious faiths (see Figure 15-1, opposite).

When religion's influence on other social institutions in a society diminishes, the process of ***secularization*** is said to be under way. During this process, religion will survive in the private sphere of individual and family life (as in the case of many Native American families); it may even thrive on a personal level. But at the same time, other social institutions—such as the economy, politics, and education—maintain their own sets of norms, independent of religious guidance (Stark and Iannaccone 1992).

What social purposes does religion serve? Does it help to hold society together or foster social change? What happens when religion mixes with politics? This chapter concentrates on the formal systems of religion that characterize modern industrial societies. We will begin with a brief description of the sociological perspectives on religion, followed by an overview of the world's major religions. Next, we will explore religion's role in societal integration, social support, social change, and social control. We'll examine three important components of religious behavior—belief, ritual, and experience—as well as the basic forms of religious organization, including new religious movements. In a special case study, we'll take a fascinating look at religion in India. The chapter will close with a Social Policy section on the controversy over religion in U.S. public schools.

Durkheim and the Sociological Approach to Religion

If a group believes that it is being directed by a "vision from God," sociologists do not attempt to prove or disprove the revelation. Instead, they assess the effects of the religious experience on the group. What sociologists are interested in is the social impact of religion on individuals and institutions.

Émile Durkheim was perhaps the first sociologist to recognize the critical importance of religion in human societies. He saw its appeal for the individual, but more important, he { p.12 stressed the *social* impact of religion. In Durkheim's view, religion is a collective act that includes many forms of behavior in which people interact with others. As in his work on suicide, Durkheim was not so interested in the personalities of religious believers as he was in understanding religious behavior within a social context.

Durkheim defined ***religion*** as a "unified system of beliefs and practices relative to sacred things." In his view, religion involves a set of beliefs and practices that are uniquely the property of religion, as opposed to other social institutions and ways of thinking. Durkheim ([1912] 2001) argued that religious faiths distinguish between certain transcending events and the everyday world. He referred to those realms as the *sacred* and the *profane.*

The *sacred* encompasses elements beyond everyday life that inspire awe, respect, and even fear. People become part of the sacred realm only by completing some ritual, such as prayer or sacrifice. Because believers have faith in the sacred, they accept what they cannot understand. In contrast, the *profane* includes the ordinary and commonplace. This concept can be confusing, however, because the same object can be either sacred or profane, depending on how it is viewed. A normal dining room table is profane, but becomes sacred to some Christians if it bears the elements of a communion. A candelabra becomes sacred to Jews if it is a menorah. For Confucians and Taoists, incense sticks are not mere decorative items, but highly valued offerings to the gods in religious ceremonies that mark the new and full moons.

Following the direction established by Durkheim almost a century ago, contemporary sociologists view religion in two different ways. They study the norms and values of religious faiths by examining their substantive beliefs. For example, it is possible to compare the degree to which Christian faiths interpret the Bible literally, or Muslim groups follow the Qur'an (or Koran), the sacred book of Islam. At the same time, sociologists examine religion in terms of the social functions it fulfills, such as providing social support or reinforcing social norms. By exploring both the beliefs and the functions of religion, we can better understand its impact on the individual, on groups, and on society as a whole.

FIGURE 15–1
Religions of the World

MAPPING LIFE WORLDWIDE

www.mhhe.com/schaefer11

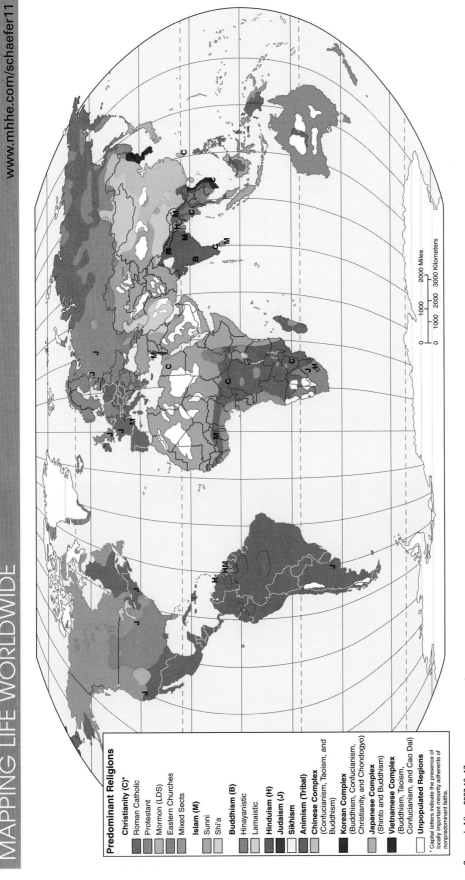

Predominant Religions

Christianity (C)*
- Roman Catholic
- Protestant
- Mormon (LDS)
- Eastern Churches
- Mixed Sects

Islam (M)
- Sunni
- Shi'a

Buddhism (B)
- Hinayanistic
- Lamaistic

Hinduism (H)
Judaism (J)
Sikhism
Animism (Tribal)
Chinese Complex
(Confucianism, Taoism, and Buddhism)
Korean Complex
(Buddhism, Confucianism, Christianity, and Chondogyo)
Japanese Complex
(Shinto and Buddhism)
Vietnamese Complex
(Buddhism, Taoism, Confucianism, and Cao Dai)
Unpopulated Regions

* Capital letters indicate the presence of locally important minority adherents of nonpredominant faiths.

Source: J. Allen 2007:16–17.

Religious adherence is one of the defining social characteristics of a culture.

Why Do Sociologists Study Religion?

Sociologists find religion a fascinating subject of study because it is a cultural universal whose collective expression can be manifested in so many different ways. For example, Christians worship one God and base their beliefs and values on the life and works of Jesus Christ. Within Christianity, Pentecostals (below) place special emphasis on their direct personal experience of God. Muslims (next page, top) are also monotheistic, but they base their beliefs on scriptural revelations about God in the Qur'an (Koran). Hindus (next page, bottom left) hold many aspects of life sacred, and emphasize the importance of being good in this life in order to advance in the next. Buddhists (next page, bottom right) strive to overcome worldly desires in order to reach a state of enlightenment.

Sociologists are interested in how widely and strongly such beliefs are held, and what influences individuals to adopt religious beliefs. They study the impact of the family, schools, the state, and the predominant culture, among other factors. Also of interest to sociologists are the ways in which people express their faith. Do they do so by attending services? By meditating privately? By performing rituals? At the societal level, sociologists consider what impact religious organizations have on society, and conversely, how a particular culture affects the practice of religion.

{Pentecostal Christians worshipping in Jacksonville, Illinois}

{Muslim men at prayer in Kurdistan, Iraq}

{Hindu holy man at the sacred Ganges River in India}

{Buddhist monks receiving food, Laos}

Worldwide, tremendous diversity exists in religious beliefs and practices. Overall, about 85 percent of the world's population adheres to some religion; only about 15 percent is nonreligious. This level of adherence changes over time, and also varies by country and age group. In the United States today, those who are nonreligious account for less than 10 to 14 percent of the population; in 1900, however, they constituted a mere 1.3 percent of all Americans. And in 2006, 19 percent of incoming U.S. college students had no religious preference, compared to only 10 percent of their mothers (Hout and Fischer 2002; Pryor et al. 2006; Winseman 2005).

Christianity is the largest single faith in the world; the second largest is Islam (see Table 15-1). Although global news events often suggest an inherent conflict between Christians and Muslims, the two faiths are similar in many ways. Both are monotheistic (that is, based on a single deity); both include a belief in prophets, an afterlife, and a judgment day. In fact, Islam recognizes Jesus as a prophet, though not the son of God. Both faiths impose a moral code on believers, which varies from fairly rigid proscriptions for fundamentalists to relatively relaxed guidelines for liberals.

The followers of Islam, called *Muslims,* believe that Islam's holy scriptures were received from Allah (God) by the prophet Mohammad nearly 1,400 years ago. They see Mohammad as the last in a long line of prophets, preceded by Adam, Abraham, Moses, and Jesus. Islam is more communal in its expression than

Christianity, particularly the more individualistic Protestant denominations. Consequently, in countries that are predominantly Muslim, the separation of religion and the state is not considered necessary or even desirable. In fact, Muslim governments often reinforce Islamic practices through their laws. Muslims do vary sharply in their interpretation of several traditions, some of which—such as the wearing of veils by women—are more cultural than religious in origin.

Like Christianity and Islam, Judaism is monotheistic. Jews believe that God's true nature is revealed in the Torah, which Christians know as the first five books of the Old Testament. According to these scriptures, God formed a covenant, or pact, with Abraham and Sarah, the ancestors of the tribes of Israel. Even today, Jews believe, this covenant holds them accountable to God's will. If they follow both the letter and spirit of the Torah, a long-awaited Messiah will one day bring paradise to earth. Although Judaism has a relatively small following compared to other major faiths, it forms the historical foundation for both Christianity and Islam. That is why Jews revere many of the same sacred Middle Eastern sites as Christians and Muslims.

Two other major faiths developed in a different part of the world, India. The earliest, Hinduism, originated around 1500 B.C. Hinduism differs from Judaism, Christianity, and Islam in that it embraces a number of gods and minor gods, although most worshippers are devoted primarily to a single deity, such as Shiva or Vishnu. Hinduism is also distinguished by a belief in reincarnation, or the perpetual rebirth of the soul after death. Unlike Judaism, Christianity, and Islam, which are based largely

Table 15-1

Major World Religions

summingUP

Faith	Current Following, in Millions (and Percent of World Population)	Primary Location of Followers Today	Founder (and Approximate Birth Date)	Important Texts (and Holy Sites)
Buddhism	379 (5.9%)	Southeast Asia, Mongolia, Tibet	Gautama Siddhartha (563 B.C.)	Triptaka (areas in Nepal)
Christianity	2,133 (33.1%)	Europe, North America, South America	Jesus (6 B.C.)	Bible (Jerusalem, Rome)
Hinduism	860 (13.3%)	India, Indian communities overseas	No specific founder (1500 B.C.)	Sruti and Smrti texts (seven sacred cities, including Vavansi)
Islam	1,309 (20.3%)	Middle East, Central Asia, North Africa, Indonesia	Mohammad (A.D. 570)	Qur'an, or Koran (Mecca, Medina, Jerusalem)
Judaism	15 (0.2%)	Israel, United States, France, Russia	Abraham (2000 B.C.)	Torah, Talmud (Jerusalem)

Sources: Author based on Barrett et al. 2006; Swatos 1998.

on sacred texts, Hindu beliefs have been preserved mostly through oral tradition.

A second religion, Buddhism, developed in the sixth century B.C. as a reaction against Hinduism. This faith is founded on the teachings of Siddhartha (later called Buddha, or "the enlightened one"). Through meditation, followers of Buddhism strive to overcome selfish cravings for physical or material pleasures, with the goal of reaching a state of enlightenment, or nirvana. Buddhists created the first monastic orders, which are thought to be the models for monastic orders in other religions, including Christianity. Though Buddhism emerged in India, its followers were eventually driven out of that country by the Hindus. It is now found primarily in other parts of Asia. (Contemporary adherents of Buddhism in India are relatively recent converts.)

Although the differences among religions are striking, they are exceeded by variations within faiths. Consider the differences within Christianity, from relatively liberal denominations such as Presbyterians or the United Church of Christ to the more conservative Mormons and Greek Orthodox Catholics. Similar divisions exist within Hinduism, Islam, and other world religions (Barrett et al. 2006; Swatos 1998).

Use Your Sociological Imagination

What evidence do you see of different religions in the area surrounding your college or university? What about on campus?

www.mhhe.com/schaefer11

Sociological Perspectives on Religion

Since religion is a cultural universal, it is not surprising that it plays a basic role in human societies. In sociological terms, it {p.16 performs both manifest and latent functions. Among its *manifest* (open and stated) functions, religion defines the spiritual world and gives meaning to the divine. It provides an explanation for events that seem difficult to understand, such as what lies beyond the grave. The *latent* functions of religion are unintended, covert, or hidden. Even though the manifest function of a church service is to offer a forum for religious worship, it might at the same time fulfill a latent social function as a meeting ground for unmarried members.

Functionalists and conflict theorists both evaluate religion's impact on human societies. We'll consider a functionalist view of religion's role in integrating society, providing social support, and promoting social change, and then look at religion from the conflict perspective, as a means of social control. Note that for the most part, religion's impact is best understood from a macro-level viewpoint that is oriented toward the larger society. Its social support function is an exception: it is best viewed on the micro, or individual, level.

Émile Durkheim viewed religion as an integrative force in human society—a perspective that is reflected in functionalist thought today. Durkheim sought to answer a perplexing question: "How can human societies be held together when they are generally composed of individuals and social groups with diverse interests and aspirations?" In his view, religious bonds often transcend these personal and divisive forces. Durkheim acknowledged that religion is not the only integrative force; nationalism or patriotism may serve the same end.

How does religion provide this "societal glue"? Religion, whether it be Buddhism, Islam, Christianity, or Judaism, gives meaning and purpose to people's lives. It offers certain ultimate values and ends to hold in common. Although they are subjective and not always fully accepted, these values and ends help society to function as an integrated social system. For example, funerals, weddings, bar and bat mitzvahs, and confirmations serve to integrate people into larger communities by providing shared beliefs and values about the ultimate questions of life.

Religion also serves to bind people together in times of crisis and confusion. Immediately after the terrorist attacks of September 11, 2001, on New York City and Washington, D.C., attendance at worship services in the United States increased dramatically. Muslim, Jewish, and Christian clerics made joint appearances to honor the dead and urge citizens not to retaliate against those who looked, dressed, or sounded different from others. A year later, however, attendance levels had returned to normal (D. Moore 2002).

The integrative power of religion can be seen, too, in the role that churches, synagogues, and mosques have traditionally played and continue to play for immigrant groups in the United States. For example, Roman Catholic immigrants may settle near a parish church that offers services in their native language, such as Polish or Spanish. Similarly, Korean immigrants may join a Presbyterian church that has many Korean American members and follows religious practices like those of churches in Korea. Like other religious organizations, these Roman Catholic and Presbyterian churches help to integrate immigrants into their new homeland.

Religion also strengthens social integration within specific faiths and denominations. In many faiths, members share certain characteristics that help to bind them together, including their race, ethnicity, and social class. Box 15-1 (page 372) examines the income and educational levels characteristic of specific denominations in the United States.

In some instances, religious loyalties are *dysfunctional;* that is, they contribute to tension and even conflict between groups or nations. During the Second World War, the German Nazis attempted to exterminate the Jewish people; approximately 6 million European Jews were killed. In modern times, nations such as Lebanon (Muslims versus Christians), Israel (Jews versus Muslims, as well as Orthodox versus secular Jews), Northern Ireland (Roman Catholics versus Protestants), and India (Hindus versus Muslims, and more recently, Sikhs) have been torn by clashes that are in large part based on religion. (See the case

researchIN*action*

15-1 Income and Education, Religiously Speaking

Sociologists have found that religions are distinguished not just by doctrinal issues, but by secular criteria as well. Research has consistently shown that denominations and faiths can be arranged in a hierarchy based on their members' social class. The associated differences in financial means have a noticeable impact on the religious bodies, affecting everything from the appearance of their houses of worship to their congregations' ability to undertake social outreach activities.

Analysis of the General Social Survey shows that Jews, Presbyterians, and Episcopalians claim a higher proportion of affluent members than other faiths and denominations (see the accompanying figure, top). Their relative affluence can often be seen in the architecture and furnishings of their houses of worship. Members of less affluent groups, such as Muslims and Baptists, may compensate for their lesser means by donating their

> *Research has consistently shown that denominations and faiths can be arranged in a hierarchy based on their members' social class.*

time and talent to outreach programs. Or they may pledge a higher proportion of their income to the church.

Of course, all religious groups draw some members from each social stratum. Group differences among the faiths reflect a variety of social factors. For example, some denominations have more followers in urban areas or in the Northeast, where salaries are generally higher. Nonetheless, the existence of these income differences means that religion can become a mechanism for signaling social mobility. A family that is moving up in wealth and power may seek out a faith that is associated with a higher social ranking, moving from, say, the Roman Catholic to the Episcopal church.

Educational differences among faiths and denominations are even more striking. In the United States, Jews are three times more likely than Baptists to have a college education (see the accompanying figure, bottom). But a closer

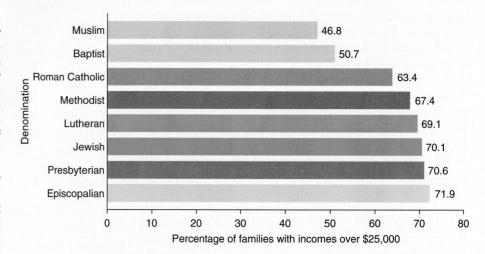

Percentage of families with incomes over $25,000

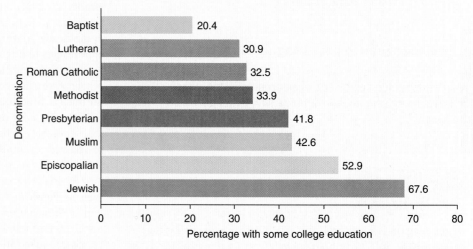

Percentage with some college education

look at the data reveals a more complex picture. Those whose faiths are associated with a lower level of formal schooling—Baptists, Lutherans, and Roman Catholics—also benefit from the strongest church-sponsored educational programs. So while members of these groups may have fewer years of schooling than others, they are much more likely to have been educated in an atmosphere that encourages allegiance to their faith.

Let's Discuss

1. Which faiths and denominations maintain houses of worship in your hometown? Do their facilities differ in terms of their size

and construction? If so, do the differences mirror the size of the congregations, or do they represent social class differences as well?

2. Beside religions, what other group affiliations might suggest a person's income or educational level?

Source: Based on author's analysis of the cumulative General Social Survey 1994–2004; see J. Davis et al. 2005.

study on page 382 for a more detailed discussion of religious conflict in India.)

Religious conflict (though on a less violent level) has been increasingly evident in the United States as well. Sociologist James Davison Hunter (1991) has referred to the "cultural war" taking place in the United States. In many communities, Christian fundamentalists, conservative Catholics, and Orthodox Jews have joined forces in a battle against liberal denominations for control of the secular culture. The battlefield is an array of familiar social issues, among them multiculturalism, child care (Chapter 4), abortion (Chapter 12), gay marriage (Chapter 14), school { pp.102, 312, 358 } prayer, media censorship, and government funding for the arts.

Religion and Social Support

Most of us find it difficult to accept the stressful events of life—the death of a loved one, serious injury, bankruptcy, divorce, and so forth—especially when something "senseless" happens. How can family and friends come to terms with the death of a talented college student, not even 20 years old?

Through its emphasis on the divine and the supernatural, religion allows us to "do something" about the calamities we face. In some faiths, adherents can offer sacrifices or pray to a deity in the belief that such acts will change their earthly condition. On a more basic level, religion encourages us to view our personal misfortunes as relatively unimportant in the broader perspective of human history—or even as part of an undisclosed divine purpose. Friends and relatives of the deceased college student may see his death as being "God's will," or as having some ultimate benefit that we cannot understand now. This perspective may be much more comforting than the terrifying feeling that any of us can die senselessly at any moment—and that there is no divine answer to why one person lives a long and full life, while another dies tragically at a relatively early age.

Faith-based community organizations have taken on more and more responsibilities in the area of social assistance. In fact, President George W. Bush created the Office of Faith-Based and Community Initiatives to give socially active religious groups access to government funding. From 2003 to 2005, the federal government's Compassion Capital Fund spent $100 million to support the community-oriented services of various religious groups. There is some evidence of such groups' effectiveness in helping others. Sociologist William Julius Wilson (1999b) has singled out faith-based organizations in 40 communities from California to Massachusetts as models of social reform. These organizations identify experienced leaders and assemble them into nonsectarian coalitions that are devoted to community development (DeParle 2005; Sager 2007).

Religion and Social Change

The Weberian Thesis

When someone seems driven to work and succeed, we often attribute the Protestant work ethic to that person. The term comes from the writings of Max Weber, who carefully examined the connection between religious allegiance

and capitalist development. Weber's findings appeared in his pioneering work *The Protestant Ethic and the Spirit of Capitalism* ([1904] 1958a).

Weber noted that in European nations with both Protestant and Catholic citizens, an overwhelming number of business leaders, owners of capital, and skilled workers were Protestant. In his view, this fact was no mere coincidence. Weber pointed out that the followers of John Calvin (1509–1564), a leader of the Protestant Reformation, emphasized a disciplined work ethic, this-worldly concerns, and a rational orientation to life that have become known as the **Protestant ethic.** One by-product of the Protestant ethic was a drive to accumulate savings that could be used for future investment. This "spirit of capitalism," to use Weber's phrase, contrasted with the moderate work hours, leisurely work habits, and lack of ambition that Weber saw as typical of the times.

Few books on the sociology of religion have aroused as much commentary and criticism as Weber's work. It has been hailed as one of the most important theoretical works in the field and an excellent example of macro-level analysis. Like Durkheim, Weber demonstrated that religion is not solely a matter of intimate personal beliefs. He stressed that the collective nature of religion has consequences for society as a whole.

Weber provided a convincing description of the origins of European capitalism. But this economic system has now been adopted by non-Calvinists in many parts of the world. Studies done in the United States today show little or no difference in achievement orientation between Roman Catholics and Protestants. Apparently, the "spirit of capitalism" has emerged as a generalized cultural trait rather than a specific religious tenet (Greeley 1989).

Conflict theorists caution that Weber's theory—even if it is accepted—should not be regarded as an analysis of mature capitalism, as reflected in the rise of multinational corporations. { p.247 } Marxists would disagree with Weber not on the origins of capitalism, but on its future. Unlike Marx, Weber believed that capitalism could endure indefinitely as an economic system. He added, however, that the decline of religion as an overriding force in society opened the way for workers to express their discontent more vocally (Collins 1980).

Liberation Theology

Sometimes the clergy can be found in the forefront of social change. Many religious activists, especially in the Roman Catholic Church in Latin America, support *liberation theology*—the use of a church in a political effort to eliminate poverty, discrimination, and other forms of injustice from a secular society. Advocates of this religious movement sometimes sympathize with Marxism. Many believe that radical change, rather than economic development in itself, is the only acceptable solution to the desperation of the masses in impoverished developing countries. Activists associated with liberation theology believe that organized religion has a moral responsibility to take a strong public stand against the oppression of the poor, racial and ethnic minorities, and women (C. Smith 1991).

The term *liberation theology* dates back to the publication in 1973 of the English translation of *A Theology of Liberation*. The book was written by a Peruvian priest, Gustavo Gutiérrez, who lived in a slum area of Lima during the early 1960s. After years of exposure to the vast poverty around him, Gutiérrez concluded that "in order to serve the poor, one had to move into political action" (R. M. Brown 1980:23; G. Gutiérrez 1990). Eventually, politically committed Latin American theologians came under the influence of social scientists who viewed the domination of capitalism and multinational corporations as central to the hemisphere's problems. One result was a new approach to theology that built on the cultural and religious traditions of Latin America rather than on models developed in Europe and the United States.

Liberation theology may be dysfunctional, however. Some Roman Catholic worshippers have come to believe that by focusing on political and governmental injustice, the clergy are no longer addressing their personal and spiritual needs. Partly as a result of such disenchantment, some Catholics in Latin America are converting to mainstream Protestant faiths or to Mormonism.

Use Your Sociological Imagination

The social support that religious groups provide is suddenly withdrawn from your community. How will your life or the lives of others change? What will happen if religious groups stop pushing for social change?

www.mhhe.com/schaefer11

Religion and Social Control: A Conflict View

Liberation theology is a relatively recent phenomenon that marks a break with the traditional role of churches. It was this traditional role that Karl Marx opposed. In his view, religion *impeded* social change by encouraging oppressed people to focus on otherworldly concerns rather than on their immediate poverty or exploitation. Marx described religion as an "opiate" that was particularly harmful to oppressed peoples. He felt that religion often drugged the masses into submission by offering a consolation for their harsh lives on earth: the hope of salvation in an ideal afterlife. For example, during the period of slavery in the United States, White masters forbade Blacks to practice native African religions, while encouraging them to adopt Christianity, which taught them that obedience would lead to salvation and eternal happiness in the hereafter. Viewed from a conflict perspective, Christianity may have pacified certain slaves and blunted the rage that often fuels rebellion.

Marx acknowledged that religion plays an important role in propping up the existing social structure. The values of religion, as already noted, tend to reinforce other social institutions and the social order as a whole. From Marx's perspective, however, religion's promotion of social stability only helps to perpetuate patterns of social inequality. According to Marx, the dominant religion reinforces the interests of those in power.

For example, contemporary Christianity reinforces traditional patterns of behavior that call for the subordination of the less powerful. The role of women in the church is an example of this uneven distribution of power. Assumptions about gender roles leave women in a subservient position both within Christian churches and at home. In fact, women find it as difficult to achieve leadership positions in many churches as they do in large corporations. A "stained glass ceiling" tends to stunt clergywomen's career development, even in the most liberal denominations.

Like Marx, conflict theorists argue that to whatever extent religion actually does influence social behavior, it reinforces existing patterns of dominance and inequality. From a Marxist perspective, religion keeps people from seeing their lives and societal conditions in political terms—for example, by obscuring the overriding significance of conflicting economic interests. {p.220} Marxists suggest that by inducing a "false consciousness" among the disadvantaged, religion lessens the possibility of collective political action that could end capitalist oppression and transform society.

Feminist Perspective

Drawing on the feminist approach, researchers and theorists have stressed the fundamental role women play in religious socialization. Most people develop their allegiance to a particular faith in their childhood, with their mothers playing a critical role in the process. Significantly, nonworshipping mothers tend to influence their children to be highly skeptical of organized religion.

On the other hand, women generally take a subordinate role in religious governance. Indeed, most faiths have a long tradition of exclusively male spiritual leadership. Furthermore, because most religions are patriarchal, they tend to reinforce men's dominance in secular as well as spiritual matters. Women do play a vital role as volunteers, staff, and religious educators, but even today, religious decision making and leadership typically fall to the men. Exceptions to this rule, such as the Shakers and Christian Scientists, as well as Hinduism with its long goddess heritage, are rare.

Nationally, women compose only 15.5 percent of U.S. clergy, though they account for 51 percent of students enrolled in theological institutions. Women clerics typically have shorter careers than men, often in related fields that do not involve congregational leadership, such as counseling. In faiths that restrict leadership positions to men, women still serve unofficially. For example, about 4 percent of Roman Catholic congregations are led by women who hold nonordained pastoral positions—a necessity in a church that faces a shortage of male priests (Adams 2007; Banerjee 2006; Bureau of the Census 2006a:388; Zelizer 2004).

Table 15-2 summarizes the four major sociological perspectives on religion.

Components of Religion

All religions have certain elements in common, yet those elements are expressed in the distinctive manner of each faith.

These patterns of religious behavior, like other patterns of social behavior, are of great interest to sociologists—especially interactionists—since they underscore the relationship between religion and society.

Religious beliefs, religious rituals, and religious experience all help to define what is sacred and to differentiate the sacred from the profane. Let's examine these three components of religion, as seen through the eyes of interactionists.

Belief

Some people believe in life after death, in supreme beings with unlimited powers, or in supernatural forces. *Religious beliefs* are statements to which members of a particular religion adhere. These views can vary dramatically from religion to religion.

In the late 1960s, something rather remarkable took place in the expression of religious beliefs in the United States. Denominations that held to relatively liberal interpretations of religious scripture (such as the Presbyterians, Methodists, and Lutherans) declined in membership, while those that held to more conservative interpretations grew in numbers. Furthermore, in most faiths, those members who held strict views of scripture became more outspoken, questioning those who remained open to a variety of newer interpretations. The term *fundamentalism* refers to a rigid adherence to fundamental religious doctrines. Often, fundamentalism is accompanied by a literal application of scripture or historical beliefs to today's world. The phrase "religious fundamentalism" was first applied to Protestant believers in the United States who took a literal interpretation of the Bible, but fundamentalism is found worldwide among most major religious groups, including Roman Catholicism, Islam, and Judaism. Fundamentalists vary immensely in their behavior. Some stress the need to be strict in their own personal faith but take little interest in broad social issues. Others are watchful of societal actions, such as government policies, that they see as conflicting with fundamentalist doctrine.

Most religions are patriarchal in both their ideology and their leadership. A significant exception to that pattern is the Christian Scientists, founded in the early twentieth century by Mary Baker Eddy.

The Adam and Eve account of creation found in Genesis, the first book of the Old Testament, is an example of a religious belief. Many people in the United States strongly adhere to this biblical explanation of creation, and even insist that it be taught in public schools. These people, known as *creationists,* are worried by the secularization of society, and oppose teaching that directly or indirectly questions biblical scripture. The Social Policy section at the end of this chapter examines the issue of religion in the schools in depth.

In general, spirituality is not as strong in industrialized nations as in developing nations. The United States is an exception to the trend toward secularization, in part because the government encourages religious expression (without explicitly supporting it) by allowing religious groups to claim charitable status, and even to receive federal aid for activities such as educational services. And although belief in God is relatively weak in formerly communist states such as Russia, surveys show a growth in spirituality in communist countries over the last 10 years (Norris and Inglehart 2004).

Table 15-2

Sociological Perspectives on Religion

summingUP

Theoretical Perspective	Emphasis
Functionalist	Religion as a source of social integration and unification
	Religion as a source of social support for individuals
Conflict	Religion as a potential obstacle to structural social change
	Religion as a potential source of structural social change (through liberation theology)
Interactionist	Individual religious expression through belief, ritual, and experience
Feminist	Religion as an instrument of women's subordination, except for their role in religious socialization

Religious rituals are practices required or expected of members of a faith. Rituals usually honor the divine power (or powers) worshipped by believers; they also remind adherents of their religious duties and responsibilities. Rituals and beliefs can be interdependent; rituals generally affirm beliefs, as in a public or private statement confessing a sin. Like any social institution, religion develops distinctive norms to structure people's behavior. Moreover, sanctions are attached to religious rituals, whether rewards (bar mitzvah gifts) or penalties (expulsion from a religious institution for violation of norms).

In the United States, rituals may be very simple, such as saying grace at a meal or observing a moment of silence to commemorate someone's death. Yet certain rituals, such as the process of canonizing a saint, are quite elaborate. Most religious rituals in our culture focus on services conducted at houses of worship. Attendance at a service, silent and spoken prayers, communion, and singing of spiritual hymns and chants are common forms of ritual behavior that generally take place in group settings. From an interactionist perspective, these rituals serve as important face-to-face encounters in which people reinforce their religious beliefs and their commitment to their faith.

For Muslims, a very important ritual is the *hajj*, a pilgrimage to the Grand Mosque in Mecca, Saudi Arabia. Every Muslim who is physically and financially able is expected to make this trip at least once. Each year 2 million pilgrims go to Mecca during the one-week period indicated by the Islamic lunar calendar. Muslims from all over the world make the *hajj*, including those in the United States, where many tours are arranged to facilitate the trip.

In recent decades, participation in religious rituals has tended to hold steady or decline in most countries. Figure 15-2 shows the change in religious participation in selected countries from 1981 to 2001.

Experience

In the sociological study of religion, the term ***religious experience*** refers to the feeling or perception of being in direct contact with the ultimate reality, such as a divine being, or of being over-

Pilgrims on *hajj* to the Grand Mosque in Mecca, Saudi Arabia. Islam requires all Muslims who are able to undertake a pilgrimage to the Holy Land.

come with religious emotion. A religious experience may be rather slight, such as the feeling of exaltation a person receives from hearing a choir sing Handel's "Hallelujah Chorus." But many religious experiences are more profound, such as a Muslim's experience on a *hajj*. In his autobiography, the late African American activist Malcolm X (1964:338) wrote of his *hajj* and how deeply moved he was by the way that Muslims in Mecca came together across race and color lines. For Malcolm X, the color blindness of the Muslim world "proved to me the power of the One God."

Another profound religious experience, for many Christians, is being "born again"—that is, at a turning point in one's life, making a personal commitment to Jesus. According to a 2005 national survey, 43 percent of people in the United States claim they have had a born-again Christian experience at some time in their lives. An earlier survey found that Southern Baptists (75 percent) were the most likely to report such experiences; in contrast, only 21 percent of Catholics and 24 percent of Episcopalians stated that they had been born again. The collective nature of religion, as emphasized by Durkheim, is evident in these statistics. The beliefs and rituals of a particular faith can create an atmosphere either friendly or indifferent to this type of religious experience. Thus, a Baptist would be encouraged to come forward and share such experiences with others, whereas an Episcopalian who claims to have been born again would receive much less interest (Newport 2004; Newport and Carroll 2005).

Use Your Sociological Imagination

Choose a religious tradition other than your own. How would your religious beliefs, rituals, and experience differ if you had been raised in that tradition?

Religious Organization

The collective nature of religion has led to many forms of religious association. In modern societies, religion has become increasingly formalized. Specific structures such as churches and synagogues have been constructed for religious worship; individuals have been trained for occupational roles within various fields. These developments make it possible to distinguish clearly between the sacred and secular parts of one's life—a distinction that could not be made easily in earlier times, when religion was largely a family activity carried out in the home.

Sociologists find it useful to distinguish between four basic forms of organization: the ecclesia, the denomination, the sect, and the new religious movement, or cult. We can see differences among these four forms of organization in their size, power, degree of commitment expected from members, and historical ties to other faiths.

Ecclesiae

An *ecclesia* (plural, *ecclesiae*) is a religious organization that claims to include most or all members of a society and is recognized as the national or official religion. Since virtually everyone belongs to the faith, membership is by birth rather than conscious decision. Examples of ecclesiae include Islam in Saudi Arabia and Buddhism in Thailand. However, significant differences exist within this category. In Saudi Arabia's Islamic regime, leaders of the ecclesia hold vast power over actions of the state. In contrast, the Lutheran church in contemporary Sweden holds no such power over the Riksdag (parliament) or the prime minister.

FIGURE 15-2

Religious Participation in Selected Countries, 1981 and 2001

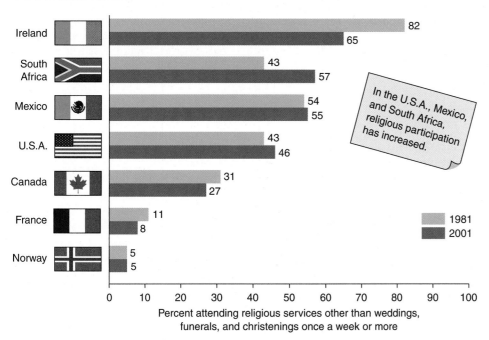

Note: World Values survey data for 2001.
Source: Norris and Inglehart 2004:74.

Think About It
Why did religious participation decrease in Ireland but increase in South Africa?

15-2 Islam in the United States

The growing presence of Islam in the United States is promoting better understanding of the significant diversity *within* Islam. Throughout the world, including the United States, Muslims are divided into a variety of sects, such as Sunni and Shia (or Shiite). These divisions sometimes result in antagonism, just as rivalries between Christian denominations can cause friction. Yet the Islamic faith is expressed in many different ways, even among Sunnis or Shia. To speak of Muslims as either Sunni or Shia would be like speaking of Christians as either Roman Catholic or Baptist.

The great majority of Muslims in the United States are Sunni Muslims—literally, those who follow the *Sunnah,* or way of the Prophet. Compared to other Muslims, Sunnis tend to be more moderate in their religious orthodoxy. The Shia, who come primarily from Iraq and Iran, are the second largest group. Shia Muslims are more attentive to guidance from accepted Islamic scholars than are Sunnis. In sufficient numbers, these two Muslim groups will choose to worship separately, even if they must cross ethnic or linguistic lines to do so. That certainly is the case in U.S. cities with large and varied Muslim communities.

Estimating the number of Muslim Americans in the United States is even more difficult than estimating the number of Arab Americans (see Chapter 11). There are no census data on Muslim Americans, and Islamic institutions such as mosques tend to operate autonomously. Even the most scientific analyses of the topic vary widely in their estimates. Based on the most recent studies, we can say that there are between 3 million and 5.7 million or more Muslims in the United States. About two-thirds of those residents are native-born citizens. In terms of ethnic and racial background, the estimated breakdown of Muslim Americans is as follows:

- 20–42 percent African American
- 24–33 percent South Asian (Afghan, Bangladeshi, Indian, and Pakistani)
- 12–32 percent Arab
- 10–22 percent "other" (Bosnian, Iranian, and Turk)

All scholars agree that the Muslim population in the United States is growing rapidly, through both immigration and religious conversion.

From these data, we can determine that African Americans who embrace Islam form a significant segment of the Muslim American community. The history of Black American Islam began in the 17th century, when members of some Muslim tribes were forcibly transported to the American colonies. An estimated 10 percent of African slaves were Muslim. Today's Black Islamic community emerged in the 20th century, however, based on the teachings of Elijah Muhammad. The Nation of Islam, a sect that focuses on the condition of Blacks in the United States as well as on the teachings of the Qur'an, was formed by Muhammad's fol-

> *To many Muslim Americans, the popular culture of the United States resembles a pagan cult that celebrates money and sex.*

lowers. Today, African American adherents of Islam reflect a variety of orientations, some unique to the United States and others tied to the larger Muslim community.

Though mosques are becoming more common in the United States, these houses of worship attract a different kind of attention than a traditional church with a steeple. To many people in the United States, the mosque repre-

Generally, ecclesiae are conservative, in that they do not challenge the leaders of a secular government. In a society with an ecclesia, the political and religious institutions often act in harmony and reinforce each other's power in their relative spheres of influence. In the modern world, ecclesiae are declining in power.

Denominations

A *denomination* is a large, organized religion that is not officially linked to the state or government. Like an ecclesia, it tends to have an explicit set of beliefs, a defined system of authority, and a generally respected position in society. Denominations claim as members large segments of a population. Generally, children accept the denomination of their parents and give little thought to membership in other faiths. Denominations also resemble ecclesiae in that they make few demands on members. However, there is a critical difference between these two forms of religious organization. Although the denomination is considered respectable and is not viewed as a challenge to the secular

government, it lacks the official recognition and power held by an ecclesia (Doress and Porter 1977).

The United States is home to a large number of denominations. In good measure, this diversity is a result of our nation's immigrant heritage. Many settlers brought with them the religious commitments native to their homelands. Some Christian denominations in the United States, such as the Roman Catholics, Episcopalians, and Lutherans, are the outgrowth of ecclesiae established in Europe. New Christian denominations also emerged, including the Mormons and Christian Scientists. Within the last generation, immigrants have increased the number of Muslims, Hindus, and Buddhists living in the United States.

Although by far the largest denomination in the United States is Roman Catholicism, at least 24 other Christian faiths have 1 million or more members. Protestants collectively accounted for about 49 percent of the nation's adult population in mid-2005, compared to 22 percent for Roman Catholics and 2 percent for Jews. There are also 5 million Muslims in the United States, and

sents not religious freedom and diversity, but a "foreign threat." Some communities have attempted to block the construction of Muslim religious centers. In return for a permit, local authorities may require that the buildings be stripped of the usual cultural symbols, perhaps even the traditional dome. On college campuses, administrators have responded more constructively to growing numbers of Muslim students, by hiring part-time imams (prayer leaders) to minister to their needs, dedicating space for daily prayer, and providing for Muslim dietary restrictions.

How does being Muslim in the United States differ from being Muslim in an Islamic country? In the United States, Muslim Americans reflect the diversity of the worldwide Islamic faith, but they practice their faith in a nation where Christianity is the dominant cultural influence. Some Islamic scholars argue that the democracy, religious diversity, and freedom of expression that Muslims experience in the United States have encouraged a stronger, more correct Islamic practice, uninhibited by the government interference that is characteristic of many Islamic states.

Other scholars contend that what makes the Muslim American experience unique is that followers must focus even more strongly on their religion in order to survive in a culture that is so permissive. Indeed, U.S. culture encourages many behaviors that are prohibited by Islamic law or cultural tradition. To many Muslim Americans, the popular culture of the United States resembles a pagan cult that celebrates money and sex. Muslim Americans,

In the United States, Muslim Americans must focus strongly on their faith to survive within the permissive mainstream culture. This Islamic school allows Muslim girls to play basketball without compromising their modesty.

then, feel both the freedom to practice their faith as they choose and the pressure to remain Muslim.

Let's Discuss

1. Is there a mosque in your community or a Muslim congregation on your campus? If so, are the members primarily Sunni or Shia? Immigrants or African Americans?

2. Should communities be allowed to block the construction of mosques or dictate their appearance? Would your answer be the same if your community tried to block the construction of a church or temple?

Sources: Ba-Yunus and Kone 2004; Belt 2002; Institute for Social Policy and Understanding 2004; P. King 2004; Leonard 2003; McCloud 1995; N. Paik 2001; T. Smith 2001.

large numbers of people adhere to Eastern faiths such as Buddhism (3 million) and Hinduism (1 million) (Barrett et al. 2006; Lindner 2006; T. Smith and Kim 2004). Box 15-2 takes a closer look at Islam in the United States.

Sects

A **sect** can be defined as a relatively small religious group that has broken away from some other religious organization to renew what it considers the original vision of the faith. Many sects, such as that led by Martin Luther during the Reformation, claim to be the "true church," because they seek to cleanse the established faith of what they regard as extraneous beliefs and rituals (Stark and Bainbridge 1985). Max Weber ([1916] 1958b:114) termed the sect a "believer's church," because affiliation is based on conscious acceptance of a specific religious dogma.

Sects are fundamentally at odds with society and do not seek to become established national religions. Unlike ecclesiae and denominations, they require intensive commitments and demonstrations of belief by members. Partly owing to their outsider status, sects frequently exhibit a higher degree of religious fervor and loyalty than more established religious groups. Recruitment focuses mainly on adults, and acceptance comes through conversion.

Sects are often short-lived. Those that are able to survive may become less antagonistic to society over time and begin to resemble denominations. In a few instances, sects have been able to endure over several generations while remaining fairly separate from society. Sociologist J. Milton Yinger (1970:226–273) uses the term **established sect** to describe a religious group that is the outgrowth of a sect, yet remains isolated from society. The Hutterites, Jehovah's Witnesses, Seventh-Day Adventists, and Amish are contemporary examples of established sects in the United States.

New Religious Movements or Cults

In 1997, 38 members of the Heaven's Gate cult were found dead in Southern California after a mass suicide timed to occur with the appearance of the Hale-Bopp comet. They believed the comet hid a spaceship on which they could catch a ride once they had broken free of their "bodily containers."

Partly as a result of the notoriety generated by such groups, the popular media have stigmatized the word *cult,* associating it with the occult and the use of intense and forceful conversion techniques. The stereotyping of cults as uniformly bizarre and unethical has led sociologists to abandon the term and refer instead to a *new religious movement (NRM).* While some NRMs exhibit strange behavior, many do not. They attract new members just like any other religion, and often follow teachings similar to those of established Christian denominations, though with less ritual.

Sects are difficult to distinguish from cults. A ***new religious movement (NRM)*** or ***cult*** is generally a small, secretive religious group that represents either a new religion or a major innovation of an existing faith. NRMs are similar to sects in that they tend to be small and are often viewed as less respectable than more established faiths. Unlike sects, however, NRMs normally do not result from schisms or breaks with established ecclesiae or denominations. Some cults, such as those focused on UFO sightings, may be totally unrelated to existing faiths. Even when a cult does accept certain fundamental tenets of a dominant faith—such as a belief in Jesus as divine or in Mohammad as a messenger of God—it will offer new revelations or insights to justify its claim to being a more advanced religion (Stark and Bainbridge 1979, 1985).

Like sects, NRMs may be transformed over time into other types of religious organizations. An example is the Christian Science Church, which began as a new religious movement under the leadership of Mary Baker Eddy. Today, this church exhibits the characteristics of a denomination. In fact, most major religions, including Christianity, began as cults. NRMs may be in the early stages of developing into a denomination or new religion, or they may just as easily fade away through the loss of members or weak leadership (J. Richardson and van Driel 1997).

Comparing Forms of Religious Organization

How can we determine whether a particular religious group falls into the sociological category of ecclesia, denomination, sect, or NRM? As we have seen, these types of religious organization have somewhat different relationships to society. Ecclesiae are recognized as national churches; denominations, although not officially approved by the state, are generally widely respected. In contrast, sects and NRMs are much more likely to be at odds with the larger culture.

Still, ecclesiae, denominations, and sects are best viewed as types along a continuum rather than as mutually exclusive categories. Table 15-3 summarizes some of the primary characteristics of these ideal types. Since the United States has no ecclesiae, sociologists studying this country's religions have focused on the denomination and the sect. These religious forms have been pictured on either end of a continuum, with denominations accommodating to the secular world and sects protesting against established religions. While NRMs are included in Table 15-3, they lie outside the continuum, because they generally define themselves in terms of a new view of life rather than in terms of existing religious faiths. In fact, one of the most controversial NRMs, the Church of Scientology, may not fully qualify as a religion (see Box 15-3).

Table 15-3

Characteristics of Ecclesiae, Denominations, Sects, and New Religious Movements

Characteristic	Ecclesia	Denomination	Sect	New Religious Movement (or Cult)
Size	Very large	Large	Small	Small
Wealth	Extensive	Extensive	Limited	Variable
Religious services	Formal, little participation	Formal, little participation	Informal, emotional	Variable
Doctrines	Specific, but interpretation may be tolerated	Specific, but interpretation may be tolerated	Specific, purity of doctrine emphasized	Innovative, pathbreaking
Clergy	Well-trained, full-time	Well-trained, full-time	Trained to some degree	Unspecialized
Membership	By virtue of being a member of society	By acceptance of doctrine	By acceptance of doctrine	By an emotional commitment
Relationship to the state	Recognized, closely aligned	Tolerated	Not encouraged	Ignored or challenged

Source: Adapted from Vernon 1962; see also Chalfant et al. 1994.

summing**UP**

15-3 The Church of Scientology: Religion or Quasi-Religion?

From the public statements of entertainers Tom Cruise, Kirstie Alley, and John Travolta to representations on *South Park*, probably no faith has come under as much scrutiny in the last 60 years, or been more misunderstood, than the Church of Scientology. Scientology bears little if any relationship to any other organized religious group, either historically or ideologically. Indeed, its detractors—and there are many, as we will see—question whether it should even be considered a religion.

The Church of Scientology was founded and continues to be based on the voluminous writings of L. Ron Hubbard (1911–1986). Hubbard described a spiritual system that he called Dianetics, in which the individual strives to achieve a heightened, positive state of mind. Essential to Dianetics is a process known as auditing, which is usually the first step in becoming a Scientologist. Auditing is a form of personal counseling in which the auditor, always a church member, measures a person's mental state using an Electropsychometer ("E-Meter"), a device developed by Hubbard.

Though Scientology affirms the existence of a Supreme Being, it does not describe the divine being or humans' relationship to that being. Hence, Scientology does not build on even the most basic elements of any other faith; it is truly a unique dogma. Though its concept of the *Thetan* is similar to the Judeo-Christian concept of the soul, unlike the soul, the Thetan is thought to live through many lifetimes in what is referred to as a "time track." Scientologists believe that with the passage of time, some of the Thetan's early experiences become increasingly obscured and must be identified through auditing.

Members of the Church of Scientology call it the only major new religion to have emerged in the twentieth century. They consider their faith to be similar to the Judeo-Christian and Eastern religions, particularly Buddhism. Skeptics find this claim to be far-fetched. The fact that an organization has declared its doctrine to be a religion does not make it so, they counter. Indeed, some scholars treat the Church of Scientology as a *quasi-religion*, a category that includes organizations that may see themselves as religious but are seen by

others as "sort of religious." Included in this category are Maharishi Mahesh Yogi's Transcendental Meditation (TM), introduced in 1958, and the New Age movements.

Though research on the Church of Scientology is admittedly limited, scholars are moving toward accepting it as a religion. As expressed in Dianetics, Scientology is a body of belief that offers an explanation for the world, a purpose for humankind, and answers to issues like salvation and the afterlife. Acknowledging this body of belief as a religion, however, would not mean that scholars regard it as an accurate worldview, any more than they might consider Episcopalian or Hindu doctrine to be accurate.

Organizationally, many scholars of religion find Scientology's method of financing its operations problematic. Most religious organizations seek voluntary contributions toward their operating expenses, along with payment for

> *Scientology bears little if any relationship to any other organized religious group, either historically or ideologically.*

specific services, such as child care programs and youth activities. They do not construe these monies as direct payments for instruction in their doctrine. In contrast, the Church of Scientology's doctrine includes the concept of "reciprocity," meaning that members are expected to pay for the spiritual benefits they receive through auditing and training.

Despite its apparent success and growing membership, Scientology is not a popular faith. In a 1995 national survey of born-again Christians, 81 percent of respondents said they thought Scientology had a negative impact on society. Ninety-two percent felt the same way about atheism.

Let's Discuss

1. What do you think of the practice of measuring a person's mental state with an Electropsychometer? If you were considering becoming a Scientologist, what

Religion or quasi-religion? Founded in the twentieth century, the Church of Scientology (shown here in Los Angeles, California) is a successful and growing religious organization.

questions would you ask your auditor about this device?
2. Do you agree that Scientology should be considered a religion? Why or why not?

Sources: Bromley and Bracey Jr. 1998; Hubbard 1950; Religious Tolerance 2007; Schaefer and Zellner 2007:280–306.

Advances in electronic communications have led to still another form of religious organization: the electronic church. Facilitated by cable television and satellite transmission, *televangelists* (as they are called) direct their messages to more people—especially in the United States—than are served by all but the largest denominations. While some televangelists are affiliated with religious denominations, most give viewers the impression that they are dissociated from established faiths.

At the close of the 1990s, the electronic church began to take on yet another dimension: the Internet. According to one 2005 survey, about 1 million weblogs, or blogs (that is, online opinion columns or diaries) have been established in the United States primarily to address people's views about religion or their personal spiritual experiences. People also use cyberspace to learn more about their faith, or even just to monitor the activities of their own places of worship (D. Cohen 2005).

Use Your Sociological Imagination

Suppose the political landscape in the United States has changed. The two mainstream parties, which once appealed to a broad cross-section of U.S. voters, have begun to champion specific religious beliefs. As you prepare to cast your vote, what are your concerns, both personal and societal? Assuming that one of the parties supports your religious views, would you vote for its candidates on that basis? What would you do if neither party was sympathetic to your beliefs?

CASE *study*

(RELIGION IN INDIA)

From a sociological point of view, the nation of India is large and complex enough that it might be considered a world of its own. Four hundred languages are spoken in India, 16 of which are officially recognized by the government. Besides the two major religions that originated there—Hinduism and Buddhism—several other faiths animate this society. Demographically the nation is huge, with over a billion residents. This teeming country is expected to overtake China as the most populous nation in the world in about three decades (Third World Institute 2005).

The Religious Tapestry in India

Hinduism and Islam, the two most important religions in India, were described on pages 370–371. Islam arrived in India in A.D. 1000, with the first of many Muslim invasions. It flowered there during the Mogul empire (1526–1857), the period when the Taj Mahal was built. Today, Muslims account for 13 percent of India's population; Hindus make up 83 percent.

The presence of one dominant faith influences how a society views a variety of issues, even secular ones. For example, India has emerged as a leader in biotechnology, due at least partly to the Hindu faith's tolerance of stem cell research and cloning—techniques that have been questioned in nations where Christianity dominates. Hinduism is open to the latest biomedical tech-

niques, as long as no evil is intended. The only legal prohibition is that fetuses cannot be terminated for the purpose of providing stem cells. Because of its respect for life in all its forms, Hinduism has no major conflict with engineered life forms of any kind, such as clones (Religion Watch 2006; Sengupta 2006).

Another religion, the Sikh faith, originated in the 15th century with a Hindu named Nanak, the first of a series of gurus (prophets). Sikhism shows the influence of Islam in India, in

Adherents of the Hindu religion participate in fire worship at the Ayyappa Pooja celebrations in Kerala, India. The Hindu faith is enormously influential in India, the country where most Hindus live.

that it is monotheistic (based on a belief in one god rather than many). It resembles Buddhism in its emphasis on meditation and spiritual transcendence of the everyday world. *Sikhs* (learners) pursue their goal of spiritual enlightenment through meditation with the help of a guru.

Sikh men have a characteristic mode of dress that makes them easy to identify. They do not cut their beards or hair, and they wrap their heads in turbans. (Because of their distinctive dress, the 400,000 Sikhs who live in the United States are often mistaken—and discriminated against—as Muslims.) Sikhs are highly patriotic. Though their 20 million members make up just 2 percent of India's population, they account for 25 percent of India's army. Their presence in the military gives them a much larger voice in the governance of the country than might be expected, given their numbers (Fausset 2003; Watson 2005).

Another faith that has been influential beyond its numbers in India is Jainism (pronounced *Jinism*). This religion was founded six centuries before the birth of Christ—about the same time as Buddhism—by a young Hindu named Mahavira. Offended by the Hindu caste system—the rigid social hierarchy that reduces some people to the status of outcastes based solely on their birth—and by the numerous Hindu deities, Mahavira left his family and his wealth behind to become a beggar monk. His teachings attracted many followers, and the faith grew and flourished until the Muslim invasions of the 12th century.

According to the Jain faith, there is no god; each person is responsible for his or her own spiritual well-being. By following a strict code of conduct, Jains believe they can ultimately free their souls from the endless cycle of death and rebirth and attain *nirvana* (spiritual enlightenment). Jains are required to meditate; forswear lying and stealing; limit their personal wealth; and practice self-denial, chastity, and nonviolence. Because they will not knowingly harm other living beings, including plants and animals, Jains shun meat, fish, or even vegetables whose harvest kills the entire plant, such as carrots and potatoes. They will not work in the military, in farming or fishing, or in the manufacture or sale of alcohol and drugs.

Though the Jains are a relatively small group (about 4 million), they exercise considerable influence in India through their business dealings and charitable contributions. Together with Christians and Buddhists, Jains make up 4 percent of India's population (Embree 2003).

Religion and the State in India

Religion was influential in India's drive to overturn British colonialism. The great Mohandas K. Gandhi (1869–1948) led the long struggle to regain India's sovereignty, which culminated in its independence in 1947. A proponent of nonviolent resistance, Gandhi persuaded Hindus and Muslims, ancient enemies, to join together in defying British domination. But his influence as a peacemaker could not override the Muslims' demand for a separate state of their own. Immediately after independence was granted, India was partitioned into two states, Pakistan for the Muslims and India for the Hindus. The new arrangement caused large-scale migrations of Indians, especially Muslims, from one nation to the other, and sparked boundary disputes that continue to this day. In many areas Muslims were forced to abandon places they considered sacred. In the chaotic months that followed, centuries of animosity between the two groups boiled over into riots, ending in Gandhi's assassination in January 1948.

Today, India is a secular state that is dominated by Hindus (see Figure 15-1 on page 367). Though the government is officially tolerant of the Muslim minority, tensions between Hindus and Muslims remain high in some states. Conflict also exists among various Hindu groups, from fundamentalists to more secular and ecumenical adherents (Embree 2003).

Many observers see religion as the moving force in Indian society. That certainly can be said of politics. When Indian political parties align themselves along religious lines, their actions polarize the nation's population. One party in particular, the Bharatiya Janata Party (BJP), is dominated by Hindu nationalists. The BJP, a major national party, led the coalition that controlled the Indian government from 1998 to 2004. Members of this party who manage to get elected to local office often tend to tolerate anti-Muslim violence. Today, however, India's prime minister is a Sikh, and its president is a Muslim woman—a combination that reflects the nation's political volatility. ●

socialPolicy
and Religion

Religion in the Schools

The Issue

Should public schools be allowed to sponsor organized prayer in the classroom? How about Bible reading, or just a collective moment of silence? Can athletes at public schools offer up a group prayer in a team huddle? Should students be able to initiate voluntary prayers at school events? Each of these situations has been an object of great dissension among those who see a role for prayer in the schools and those who want to maintain strict separation of church and state.

Another controversy concerns the teaching of theories about the origin of humans and the universe. Mainstream scientific thinking holds that humans evolved over billions of years from one-celled organisms, and that the universe came into being 15 billion years ago as a result of a "big bang." These theories are challenged by people who hold to the biblical account of the creation of humans and the universe some 10,000 years ago—a viewpoint known as *creationism.* Creationists, many of whom are Christian fundamentalists, want their belief taught in the schools as the only one—or at the very least, as an alternative to the theory of evolution.

Who has the right to decide these issues, and what is the "right" decision? Religion in the schools is one of the thorniest issues in U.S. public policy today.

The Setting

The issues just described go to the heart of the First Amendment's provisions regarding religious freedom. On the one hand, the government must protect the right to practice one's religion; on the other, it cannot take any measures that would seem to "establish" one religion over another (separation of church and state).

In the key case of *Engle v. Vitale,* the Supreme Court ruled in 1962 that the use of nondenominational prayer in New York schools was "wholly inconsistent" with the First Amendment's prohibition against government establishment of religion. In finding that organized school prayer violated the Constitution—even when no student was required to participate—the Court argued, in effect, that promoting religious observance was not a legitimate function of government or education. Subsequent Court decisions have allowed *voluntary* school prayer by students, but forbid school officials to *sponsor* any prayer or religious observance at school events. Despite these rulings, many public schools still regularly lead their students in prayer recitations or Bible reading (Firestone 1999).

The controversy over whether the biblical account of creation should be presented in school curricula recalls the famous "monkey trial" of 1925. In that trial, high school biology teacher John T. Scopes was convicted of violating a Tennessee law making it a crime to teach the scientific theory of evolution in public schools. Today, creationists have gone beyond espousing fundamentalist religious doctrine; they are attempting to reinforce their position regarding the origins of humanity and the universe with quasi-scientific data.

In 1987, the Supreme Court ruled that states could not compel the teaching of creationism in public schools if the primary purpose was to promote a religious viewpoint. In response, those who believe in the divine origin of life have recently advanced a concept called *intelligent design (ID),* the idea that life is so complex that it could only have been created by intelligent design. While this concept is not based explicitly on the biblical account of creation, fundamentalists feel comfortable with it. Supporters of intelligent design consider it a more accurate account of the origin of life than Darwinism, and hold that at the very least, ID should be taught as an alternative to the theory of evolution. But in 2005, in *Kitzmiller v. Dove Area School District,* a federal judge ended a Pennsylvania school district's plans to require teachers to present the concept in class. In essence, the judge found ID to be "a religious belief," a subtler but similar approach to creationism in that both find God's fingerprints in nature. The issue continues to be hotly debated and is expected to be the subject of future court cases (Clemmitt 2005; Goodstein 2005; Wallis 2005b).

Sociological Insights

Supporters of school prayer and of creationism feel that strict Court rulings have forced too great a separation between what Émile Durkheim called the *sacred* and the *profane.* They insist that the use of nondenominational prayer can in no way lead to the establishment of an ecclesia in the United States. Moreover, they believe that school prayer—and the teaching of creationism—can provide the spiritual guidance and socialization that many children today do not receive from parents or regular church attendance. Many communities also believe that schools should transmit the dominant culture of the United States by encouraging prayer.

Opponents of school prayer and creationism argue that a religious majority in a community might impose viewpoints specific to its faith at the expense of religious minorities. These critics question whether school prayer can remain truly voluntary. Drawing on the interactionist perspective and small-group research, they suggest that children will face enormous social pressure to conform to the beliefs and practices of the majority.

Policy Initiatives

School education is fundamentally a local issue, so most initiatives and lobbying have taken place at the local or state level. A significant departure from the local nature of this issue came in 2003, when President George W. Bush declared that schools whose policies prevent constitutionally protected school prayer risk losing their federal education funds. At the same time, federal courts were taking a hard line on religion in the schools. In a decision that the Supreme Court reversed in 2004, a federal appeals court ruled that reciting the phrase "under God" during the Pledge of Allegiance that opens each school day violates the U.S. Constitution (Religion News Service 2003).

Religion–school debates show no sign of ending. The activism of religious fundamentalists in the public school system raises the question: whose ideas and values deserve a hearing in classrooms? Critics see this campaign as one step toward sectarian religious control of public education. They worry that at some point in the future, teachers may not be able to use books or make statements that conflict with fundamentalist interpretations of the Bible. For advocates of a liberal education and of intellectual (and religious) diversity, this is a genuinely frightening prospect (Wilgoren 2005).

Let's Discuss

1. Was there organized prayer in any school you attended? Was creationism part of the curriculum?

Recently, advocates of the fundamentalist doctrine of creationism have clothed their argument in a concept called intelligent design.

2. Do you think that promoting religious observance is a legitimate function of education?

3. How might a conflict theorist view the issue of organized school prayer?

GettingINVOLVED

To get involved in the debate over religion in the schools, visit this text's Online Learning Center, which offers links to relevant Web sites. Check out the Social Policy section in the Online Learning Center as well; it provides survey data on U.S. public opinion regarding this issue.

www.mhhe.com/schaefer11

Summary

Religion is a *cultural universal* found throughout the world in various forms. This chapter examines the major world religions, the functions and dimensions of religion, and the four basic types of religious organization.

1. Émile Durkheim stressed the social impact of religion in attempting to understand individual religious behavior within the context of the larger society.

2. Eighty-five percent of the world's population adheres to some form of **religion.** Tremendous diversity exists in religious beliefs and practices, which may be heavily influenced by culture.

3. Religion helps to integrate a diverse society and provides social support in time of need.

4. Max Weber saw a connection between religious allegiance and capitalistic behavior in a religious orientation he termed the *Protestant ethic.*

5. In *liberation theology,* the teachings of Christianity become the basis for political efforts to alleviate poverty and social injustice.

6. From a Marxist point of view, religion serves to reinforce the social control of those in power. It discourages collective political action, which could end capitalist oppression and transform society.

7. Religious behavior is expressed through *religious beliefs, rituals,* and *experience.*

8. Sociologists have identified four basic types of religious organization: the *ecclesia,* the *denomination,* the *sect,* and the *new religious movement (NRM),* or *cult.*

9. Advances in communications have led to a new type of church organization, the electronic church. Televangelists now preach to more people than belong to many denominations, and roughly 2 million people a day use the Internet for religious purposes.

10. India is a secular state that is dominated by a religious majority, the Hindus. The creation of a separate nation, Pakistan, for the Muslim minority following India's independence in 1947 did not end the centuries-old strife between the two groups, which has worsened with their political polarization.

11. Today, the question of how much religion, if any, should be permitted in the U.S. public schools is a matter of intense debate.

Critical Thinking Questions

1. From a conflict point of view, explain how religion could be used to bring about social change. Can you think of an example?

2. What role do new religious movements (or cults) play in the organization of religion? Why are they so often controversial?

3. Do politics and religion mix? Explain your reasoning.

Creationism A literal interpretation of the Bible regarding the creation of humanity and the universe, used to argue that evolution should not be presented as established scientific fact. (page 384)

Cultural universal A common practice or belief found in every culture. (366)

Denomination A large, organized religion that is not officially linked to the state or government. (378)

Ecclesia A religious organization that claims to include most or all members of a society and is recognized as the national or official religion. (377)

Established sect A religious group that is the outgrowth of a sect, yet remains isolated from society. (379)

Fundamentalism Rigid adherence to fundamental religious doctrines, often accompanied by a literal application of scripture or historical beliefs to today's world. (375)

Intelligent design (ID) The idea that life is so complex, it could only have been created by intelligent design. (384)

Liberation theology Use of a church, primarily Roman Catholicism, in a political effort to eliminate poverty, discrimination, and other forms of injustice from a secular society. (373)

New religious movement (NRM) or cult A small, secretive religious group that represents either a new religion or a major innovation of an existing faith. (380)

Profane The ordinary and commonplace elements of life, as distinguished from the sacred. (366)

Protestant ethic Max Weber's term for the disciplined work ethic, this-worldly concerns, and rational orientation to life emphasized by John Calvin and his followers. (373)

Quasi-religion A scholarly category that includes organizations that may see themselves as religious but are seen by others as "sort of religious." (381)

Religion A unified system of beliefs and practices relative to sacred things. (366)

Religious belief A statement to which members of a particular religion adhere. (375)

Religious experience The feeling or perception of being in direct contact with the ultimate reality, such as a divine being, or of being overcome with religious emotion. (376)

Religious ritual A practice required or expected of members of a faith. (376)

Sacred Elements beyond everyday life that inspire awe, respect, and even fear. (366)

Sect A relatively small religious group that has broken away from some other religious organization to renew what it considers the original vision of the faith. (379)

Secularization The process through which religion's influence on other social institutions diminishes. (366)

Self-Quiz

Read each question carefully and then select the best answer.

1. Which of the following sociologists stressed the social impact of religion and was perhaps the first to recognize the critical importance of religion in human societies?

   a. Max Weber
   b. Karl Marx
   c. Émile Durkheim
   d. Talcott Parsons

2. A Roman Catholic parish church offers services in the native language of an immigrant community. This is an example of

   a. the integrative function of religion.
   b. the social support function of religion.
   c. the social control function of religion.
   d. none of the above.

3. Sociologist Max Weber pointed out that the followers of John Calvin emphasized a disciplined work ethic, this-worldly concerns, and a rational orientation to life. Collectively, this point of view has been referred to as

   a. capitalism.
   b. the Protestant ethic.
   c. the sacred.
   d. the profane.

4. The use of a church, primarily Roman Catholic, in a political effort to eliminate poverty, discrimination, and other forms of injustice evident in a secular society is referred to as

   a. creationism.
   b. ritualism.
   c. religious experience.
   d. liberation theology.

5. Many people in the United States strongly adhere to the biblical explanation of the beginning of the universe. Adherents of this point of view are known as

   a. liberationists.
   b. creationists.
   c. ritualists.
   d. experimentalists.

6. The Adam and Eve account of creation found in Genesis, the first book of the Old Testament, is an example of a religious

   a. ritual.
   b. experience.
   c. custom.
   d. belief.

7. Which of the following is not an example of an ecclesia?

    a. the Lutheran church in Sweden
    b. Islam in Saudi Arabia
    c. Buddhism in Thailand
    d. the Episcopal church in the United States

8. Religion defines the spiritual world and gives meaning to the divine. These are _____ functions of religion.

    a. manifest
    b. latent
    c. positive
    d. negative

9. Which sociological perspective emphasizes the integrative power of religion in human society?

    a. functionalist perspective
    b. conflict perspective
    c. interactionist perspective
    d. all of the above

10. John Calvin, a leader of the Protestant Reformation, emphasized

    a. disciplined work ethic.
    b. this-worldly concerns.
    c. a rational orientation to life.
    d. all of the above.

11. The _____ encompasses elements beyond everyday life that inspire awe, respect, and even fear, as compared to the _____, which includes the ordinary and the commonplace.

12. Religion defines the spiritual world and gives meaning to the divine. These are _____ functions of religion.

13. _____ is the largest single faith in the world; the second largest is _____.

14. _____ _____ are statements to which members of a particular religion adhere.

15. A(n) _____ is a religious organization that claims to include most or all members of a society and is recognized as the national or official religion.

16. Because they are _____, most religions tend to reinforce men's dominance in secular as well as spiritual matters.

17. The single largest denomination in the United States is _____ _____.

18. The "big bang" theory is challenged by _____, who hold to the biblical account of creation of humans and the universe.

19. Unlike ecclesiae and denominations, _____ require intensive commitments and demonstrations of belief by members.

20. A possible dysfunction of _____ _____ would be the belief that when Roman Catholics focus on political and governmental injustice, the clergy are no longer addressing their personal and spiritual needs.

Answers:
1 (c); 2(a); 3 (b); 4 (d); 5 (b); 6 (d); 7 (d); 8 (a); 9 (a); 10 (d); 11 sacred; profane; 12 manifest; 13 Christianity; Islam; 14 Religious beliefs; 15 ecclesia; 16 patriarchal; 17 Roman Catholicism; 18 creationists; 19 sects; 20 liberation theology

{ TECHNOLOGY RESOURCES }

Online Learning Center

1. How do you know what issues are most important as you prepare to read this chapter? The student center of the Online Learning Center at **www.mhhe.com/schaefer11** can help by providing a list of key learning objectives. Click on Learning Objectives as you get ready to read each chapter, and review the major ideas and concepts that you should absorb from your reading.

2. How much do you know about current government initiatives to provide social services through religious organizations? A page on the White House Web site provides more information, from the perspective of officials who favor these programs. Visit this site at **www.whitehouse.gov/government/fbci.**

3. An exhibit at the Web site of the Asia Society (**www.asiasociety .org/pressroom/rel-worldbuddhism.html**) allows you to learn more about a major world religion through art. Once you've entered the site, link to Buddhist art and the Trade Routes, at the top of the page, for numerous photographs and explanatory text.

*Note: Although all the URLs listed were current as of the printing of this book, these sites often change. Please check our Web site (**www.mhhe.com/schaefer11**) for updates, hyperlinks, and exercises related to these sites.*

Reel Society Video Clips

Reel Society video clips, which appear on this book's Web site, can be used to spark discussion about the following topics from this chapter:

- Durkheim and the Sociological Approach to Religion
- World Religions
- Sociological Explanations of Religion
- Components of Religion
- Research in Action: Islam in the United States

DURHAM COUNTY LITERACY COUNCIL

MY MOM IS A TERRIFIC STUDENT. SHE'S LEARNING TO READ.

The need for education isn't limited to school-age youths. This poster recognizes adults who strive to learn a skill most of us take for granted: reading. Nationwide, some 10 million adult Americans cannot read English. Some are immigrants from other countries; others suffer from learning disabilities or a disadvantaged upbringing.

16 Education

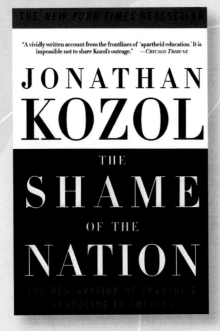

"Dear Mr. Kozol," said the eight-year-old, "we do not have the things you have. You have Clean things. We do not have. You have a clean bathroom. We do not have that. You have Parks and we do not have Parks. You have all the thing and we do not have all the thing. . . . Can you help us?"

The letter, from a child named Alliyah, came in a fat envelope of 27 letters from a class of third grade children in the Bronx.

. . . I had visited many elementary schools in the South Bronx and in one northern district of the Bronx as well. I had also made a number of visits to a high school where a stream of water flowed down one of the main stairwells on a rainy afternoon and where green fungus molds were growing in the office where the students went for counseling. . . .

In another elementary school, which had been built to hold 1,000 children but was packed to busting with some 1,500 boys and girls, the principal poured out his feelings to me in a room in which a plastic garbage bag had been attached somehow to cover part of the collapsing ceiling. "This," he told me, pointing to the garbage bag, then gesturing around him at the other indications of decay and disrepair one sees in ghetto schools much like it elsewhere, "would not happen to white children." . . .

In 1970, when substantial numbers of white children still attended New York City's schools, 400 doctors had been present to address the health needs of the children. By 1993, the number of doctors had been cut to 23, most of them part-time—a cutback that affected most acutely children in the city's poorest neighborhoods where medical provision was perennially substandard and health

> *I had also made a number of visits to a high school where a stream of water flowed down one of the main stairwells on a rainy afternoon and where green fungus molds were growing in the office where the students went for counseling.*

problems faced by children most extreme. During the 1990s, for example, the rate of pediatric asthma in the South Bronx, already one of the highest in the nation, was exacerbated when the city chose to build a medical waste incinerator in their neighborhood after a plan to build it on the East Side of Manhattan was abandoned in the face of protests from the parents of that area. Hospitalization rates for these asthmatic children in the Bronx were as much as 20 times more frequent than for children in the city's affluent communities. Teachers spoke of children who came into class with chronic wheezing and, at any moment of the day, might undergo more serious attacks, but in the schools I visited there were no doctors to attend to them. . . .

The disrepair and overcrowding of these schools in the South Bronx "wouldn't happen for a moment in a white suburban school district like Scarsdale," says former New York State Commissioner of Education Thomas Sobol, who was once the superintendent of the Scarsdale schools and is now a professor of education at Teachers College in New York. "I'm aware that I could never prove that race is at the heart of this if I were called to testify before a legislative hearing. But I've felt it for so long, and seen it operating for so long, I know it's true. . . ."

(Kozol 2005:39, 40–41, 42, 43) Additional information about this excerpt can be found on the Online Learning Center at www.mhhe.com/schaefer 11.

For several decades Jonathan Kozol, the author of this passage from *The Shame of the Nation,* toured public schools throughout the United States. He found that while White students in affluent suburban towns enjoyed state-of-the-art science labs, superb music and art programs, and elaborate athletic facilities, inner-city children were crowded into antiquated, decrepit buildings, deprived of even the most basic requirements—textbooks, classrooms, computers, counselors. An educator himself, Kozol challenged his readers to confront the social implications of this stark contrast in educational resources.

Education, like the family and religion, is a cultural universal. As such it is an important aspect of socialization—the lifelong process of learning the attitudes, values, and behavior considered appropriate to members of a particular culture. As we saw in Chapter 4, socialization can occur in the classroom or at home, through interactions with parents, teachers, friends, and even strangers. Exposure to books, films, television, and other forms of communication also promotes socialization. When learning is explicit and formalized—when some people consciously teach, while others adopt the role of learner—the process of socialization is called *education.* But students learn far more about their society at school than what is included in the curriculum.

This chapter focuses in particular on the formal systems of education that characterize modern industrial societies. Do public schools offer everyone a way up the socioeconomic ladder, or do they reinforce existing divisions among social classes? What is the "hidden curriculum" in U.S. schools? And what have sociologists learned about the latest trends in education, such as competency testing? We will begin with a discussion of four theoretical perspectives on education: functionalist, conflict, feminist, and interactionist. An examination of schools as formal organizations—as bureaucracies and subcultures of teachers and students—follows. One contemporary educational trend, homeschooling, merits special mention. The chapter closes with a Social Policy section on the controversial No Child Left Behind Act.

Sociological Perspectives on Education

Besides being a major industry in the United States, education is the social institution that formally socializes members of our society. In the last few decades, increasing proportions of people have obtained high school diplomas, college degrees, and advanced professional degrees. For example, the proportion of people age 25 or over with a high school diploma increased from 41 percent in 1960 to more than 85 percent in 2004. The proportion of those with a college degree rose from 8 percent in 1960 to about 29 percent in 2005. Figure 16-1 shows the proportion of the college-educated population in other countries (Bureau of the Census 2006a:144).

Throughout the world, education has become a vast and complex social institution that prepares citizens for the roles de-

FIGURE 16–1

Percentage of Adults Ages 25 to 64 Who Have Completed Higher Education (B.A./B.S.)

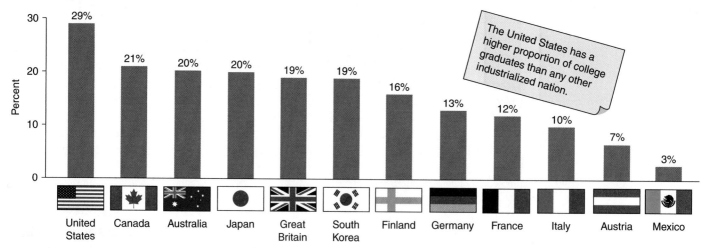

Source: Data for 2002 and 2003 released in Bureau of the Census 2006a:843.

manded by other social institutions, such as the family, government, and the economy. The functionalist, conflict, feminist, and interactionist perspectives offer distinctive views of education as a social institution.

Functionalist View

Like other social institutions, education has both manifest (open, stated) and latent (hidden) functions. The most basic *manifest* function of education is the transmission of knowledge. Schools teach students how to read, speak foreign languages, and repair automobiles. Another important manifest function is the bestowal of status. Because many believe this function is performed inequitably, we will consider it later, in the section on the conflict view of education.

In addition to these manifest functions, schools perform a number of *latent* functions: transmitting culture, promoting social and political integration, maintaining social control, and serving as an agent of change.

Transmitting Culture As a social institution, education performs a rather conservative function—transmitting the dominant culture. Schooling exposes each generation of young people to the existing beliefs, norms, and values of their culture. In our society, we learn respect for social control and reverence for established institutions, such as religion, the family, and the presidency. Of course, this statement is true of many other cultures as well. While schoolchildren in the United States are hearing about the accomplishments of George Washington and Abraham Lincoln, British children are hearing about the distinctive contributions of Queen Elizabeth I and Winston Churchill.

In Great Britain, the transmission of the dominant culture through schools goes far beyond learning about monarchs and prime ministers. In 1996, the government's chief curriculum adviser—noting the need to fill a void left by the diminishing authority of the Church of England—proposed that British schools should socialize students into a set of core values. The list included honesty, respect for others, politeness, a sense of fair play, forgiveness, punctuality, nonviolent behavior, patience, faithfulness, and self-discipline (Charter and Sherman 1996).

Sometimes nations reassess the ways in which they transmit culture to students. Recently the Chinese government revised the nation's history curriculum. Students are now taught that the Chinese Communist Party, not the United States, played a central role in defeating Japan in World War II. No mention is made of the estimated 30 million Chi-

nese who died from famine because of party founder Mao Zedong's disastrous Great Leap Forward (1958–1962), a failed effort to transform China's agrarian economy into an industrial powerhouse. In the urban, Western-oriented areas of Shanghai, textbooks acknowledge the technological advances made in Western industrial countries but avoid any criticism of past policies of the Chinese government (French 2004b; Kahn 2006b).

Use Your Sociological Imagination

In retrospect, what do you think of the version of U.S. history that you learned in high school?

Promoting Social and Political Integration Many institutions require students in their first year or two of college to live on campus to foster a sense of community among diverse groups. Education serves the latent function of promoting social and political integration by transforming a population composed of diverse racial, ethnic, and religious groups into a society whose members share—to some extent—a common identity. Historically, schools in the United States have played an important role in socializing the children of immigrants into the norms, values, and beliefs of the dominant culture. From a functionalist perspective, the common identity and social integration fostered by education contribute to societal stability and consensus (Touraine 1974).

Though the school that character Harry Potter attends in the film *Goblet of Fire* is fictitious, like real schools, it transmits a socially sanctioned culture to students.

In the past, the integrative function of education was most obvious in its emphasis on promoting a common language. Immigrant children were expected to learn English. In some instances, they were even forbidden to speak their native language {p.77 on school grounds. More recently, bilingualism has been defended both for its educational value and as a means of encouraging cultural diversity. However, critics argue that bilingualism undermines the social and political integration that education has traditionally promoted.

Maintaining Social Control

In performing the manifest function of transmitting knowledge, schools go far beyond teaching skills like reading, writing, and mathematics. Like other social institutions, such as the family and religion, education prepares young people to lead productive and orderly lives as adults by introducing them to the norms, values, and sanctions of the larger society.

Through the exercise of social control, schools teach students various skills and values essential to their future positions in the labor force. They learn punctuality, discipline, scheduling, and responsible work habits, as well as how to negotiate the complexities of a bureaucratic organization. As a social institution, education reflects the interests of both the family and another social institution, the economy. Students are trained for what is ahead, whether it be the assembly line or a physician's office. In effect, then, schools serve as a transitional agent of social control, bridging the gap between parents and employers in the life cycle of most individuals (Bowles and Gintis 1976; M. Cole 1988).

Schools direct and even restrict students' aspirations in a manner that reflects societal values and prejudices. School administrators may allocate ample funds for athletic programs but give much less support to music, art, and dance. Teachers and guidance counselors may encourage male students to pursue careers in the sciences but steer female students into careers as early childhood teachers. Such socialization into traditional gender roles can be viewed as a form of social control.

Serving as an Agent of Change

So far, we have focused on the conservative functions of education—on its role in transmitting the existing culture, promoting social and political integration, and maintaining social control. Yet education can also stimulate or bring about desired social change. Sex education classes were introduced to public {p.275 schools in response to the soaring pregnancy rate among teenagers. Affirmative action in admissions—giving

priority to females or minorities—has been endorsed as a means of countering racial and sexual discrimination. Project Head Start, an early childhood program that serves more than 907,000 children annually, has sought to compensate for the disadvantages in school readiness experienced by children from low-income families (Bureau of the Census 2006a:363).

Education also promotes social change by serving as a meeting ground where people can share distinctive beliefs and traditions. In 2006, U.S. campuses hosted just over 564,000 international students. While that is a large number, it represented the third successive decline over the preceding academic year. This reversal in the long-term trend may be temporary, but the tightening of visa requirements that followed the terrorist attacks of September 11, 2001, has made the United States appear to be less welcoming to foreign students than in the past. Educators worry that a sustained drop in the number of international students may adversely affect engineering and science programs, which find it difficult to attract qualified U.S. students. From a larger perspective, U.S. relations around the world are nurtured on our college campuses. Thus, a long-term decline in the number of international students could eventually weaken U.S. economic and diplomatic relationships (Arenson 2006).

Numerous sociological studies have revealed that additional years of formal schooling are associated with openness to new ideas and more liberal social and political viewpoints. Sociologist Robin Williams points out that better-educated people tend to have greater access to factual information, to hold more diverse opinions, and to possess the ability to make subtle distinc-

In response to a high pregnancy rate among adolescent girls, many schools now offer sex education courses that promote abstinence. When schools attempt to remedy negative social trends, they are serving as an agent of social change.

Ray Zapata
**Business Owner and Former Regent,
Texas State University**

Ray Zapata, investor, community activist, and restaurant owner, thinks his degree in sociology was the best preparation he could have received for a life spent in business and politics. A graduate of Angelo State University in Texas, Zapata finds that his understanding of society and social diversity has given him perspective on his community and helped him to cooperate with others from different backgrounds. "I think that I can pretty much fit anywhere, whether I'm in New York, London, or South Africa, and I think that's very, very important," he remarks.

Zapata was the second Hispanic to be appointed to the Board of Regents of the Texas State University system. As a regent, he was charged with overseeing both the financial and educational management of the system, which includes working with the state legislature to gain funding for new programs and facilities. During his term he presided over a half-billion-dollar construction program, including a major expansion at his alma mater, Angelo State.

More than the buildings that went up during his term, though, Zapata prides himself on the open admissions policy the Board instituted during his tenure. "If you put education out of reach of the working class or poor people in our society, then I think you lose an opportunity for great minds," he says. One of the most wonderful moments for this regent came when he watched a Hispanic woman who had worked as a janitor at Southwest State University graduate at the top of her class. Zapata wants to see more students like her, including senior citizens, on Texas State campuses. "Education will never hurt you at any age," he says.

Let's Discuss

1. How does an open admissions policy benefit society?
2. In what ways do the elderly benefit from education?

---

tions in analysis. Formal education stresses both the importance of qualifying statements (in place of broad generalizations) and {p.32} the need at least to question (rather than simply accept) established truths and practices. The scientific method, which relies on *testing* hypotheses, reflects the questioning spirit that characterizes modern education (R. Williams et al. 1964).

Conflict View

The functionalist perspective portrays contemporary education as a basically benign institution. For example, it argues that schools rationally sort and select students for future high-status positions, thereby meeting society's need for talented and expert personnel. In contrast, the conflict perspective views education as an instrument of elite domination. Conflict theorists point out the sharp inequalities that exist in the educational opportunities available to different racial and ethnic groups. In 2004, the nation marked the 50th anniversary of the Supreme Court's landmark decision *Brown v. Board of Education,* which declared unconstitutional the segregation of public schools. Yet today, African Americans are still 37 percent less likely than Whites, and Latinos 58 percent less likely than Whites, to have completed high school. Furthermore, Black and Latino schoolchildren continue to underperform White schoolchildren on nationally standardized tests (Bureau of the Census 2006a:143).

Conflict theorists also argue that the educational system socializes students into values dictated by the powerful, that schools stifle individualism and creativity in the name of maintaining order, and that the level of change they promote is relatively insignificant. From a conflict perspective, the inhibiting

effects of education are particularly apparent in the "hidden curriculum" and the differential way in which status is bestowed.

The Hidden Curriculum Schools are highly bureaucratic organizations, as we will see later. Many teachers rely on rules and regulations to maintain order. Unfortunately, the need for control and discipline can take precedence over the learning process. Teachers may focus on obedience to the rules as an end in itself, in which case students and teachers alike become victims of what Philip Jackson (1968) has called the *hidden curriculum.*

The term ***hidden curriculum*** refers to standards of behavior that are deemed proper by society and are taught subtly in schools. According to this curriculum, children must not speak until the teacher calls on them, and must regulate their activities according to the clock or bells. In addition, they are expected to concentrate on their own work rather than to assist other students who learn more slowly. A hidden curriculum is evident in schools around the world. For example, Japanese schools offer guidance sessions that seek to improve the classroom experience and develop healthy living skills. In effect, these sessions instill values and encourage behavior useful in the Japanese business world, such as self-discipline and openness to group problem solving and decision making (Okano and Tsuchiya 1999).

In a classroom that is overly focused on obedience, value is placed on pleasing the teacher and remaining quiet rather than on creative thought and academic learning. Habitual obedience to authority may result in the type of distressing behavior doc- {pp.185–186} umented by Stanley Milgram in his classic obedience studies.

Credentialism Fifty years ago, a high school diploma was the minimum requirement for entry into the paid labor force of the United States. Today, a college diploma is virtually the bare minimum. This change reflects the process of ***credentialism***—a term used to describe an increase in the lowest level of education needed to enter a field.

In recent decades, the number of occupations that are viewed as professions has risen. Credentialism is one symptom of this trend. Employers and occupational associations typically contend that such changes are a logical response to the increasing complexity of many jobs. However, in many cases, employers raise the degree requirements for a position simply because all applicants have achieved the existing minimum credential (D. Brown 2001; Hurn 1985).

Conflict theorists observe that credentialism may reinforce social inequality. Applicants from poor and minority backgrounds are especially likely to suffer from the escalation of qualifications, since they lack the financial resources needed to obtain degree after degree. In addition, upgrading of credentials serves the self-interest of the two groups most responsible for this trend. Educational institutions profit from prolonging the investment of time and money that people make by staying in school. Moreover, as C. J. Hurn (1985) has suggested, current jobholders have a stake in raising occupational requirements, since credentialism can increase the status of an occupation and lead to demands for higher pay. Max Weber anticipated this possibility as early as 1916, concluding that the "universal clamor for the creation of educational certificates in all fields makes for the formation of a privileged stratum in businesses and in offices" (Gerth and Mills 1958:240–241).

Use Your Sociological Imagination

How would you react if the job you have or plan to pursue suddenly required a higher-level degree? If suddenly the requirements were lowered?

www.mhhe.com/schaefer11

Bestowal of Status Both functionalist and conflict theorists agree that education performs the important function of bestowing status. As noted earlier, an increasing proportion of people in the United States are obtaining high school diplomas, college degrees, and advanced professional degrees. From a functionalist perspective, this widening bestowal of status is beneficial not only to particular recipients but to society as a {p.221 whole. According to Kingsley Davis and Wilbert E. Moore (1945), society must distribute its members among a variety of social positions. Education can contribute to this process by sorting people into appropriate levels and courses of study that will prepare them for positions in the labor force.

Conflict theorists are far more critical of the *differential* way in which education bestows status. They stress that schools sort pupils according to their social class backgrounds. Although the educational system helps certain poor children to move into middle-class professional positions, it denies most disadvantaged children the same educational opportunities afforded to children of the affluent. In this way, schools tend to preserve social class inequalities in each new generation (Giroux 1988; Pinkerton 2003).

Even a single school can reinforce class differences by putting students in tracks. The term ***tracking*** refers to the practice of placing students in specific curriculum groups on the basis of their test scores and other criteria. Tracking begins very early, often in reading groups during first grade. Most recent research on such ability groupings raises questions about its effectiveness, especially for low-ability students. Tracks can reinforce the disadvantages that children from less affluent families may face if they haven't been exposed to reading materials, computers, and other forms of educational stimulation during their early childhood years. To ignore the connection between tracking and students' race and social class is to fundamentally misunderstand how schools perpetuate the existing social structure (Lucas and Paret 2005; Sadker and Sadker 2003).

Tracking and differential access to higher education are evident in many nations around the world. Japan's educational system mandates equality in school funding and insists that all schools use the same textbooks. Nevertheless, only the more affluent Japanese families can afford to send their children to *juku,* or cram schools. These afternoon schools prepare high school students for examinations that determine admission into prestigious colleges (Efron 1997).

Conflict theorists hold that the educational inequalities produced by tracking are designed to meet the needs of modern capitalist societies. Samuel Bowles and Herbert Gintis (1976) have argued that capitalism requires a skilled, disciplined labor force, and that the educational system of the United States is structured

Studies conducted since 1987 suggest that the funding inequities between richer and poorer school districts have actually widened in recent years.

with that objective in mind. Citing numerous studies, they offer support for what they call the ***correspondence principle.*** According to this approach, schools promote the values expected of individuals in each social class and perpetuate social class divisions from one generation to the next. Thus, working-class children, assumed to be destined for subordinate positions, are likely to be placed in high school vocational and general tracks, which emphasize close supervision and compliance with authority. In contrast, young people from more affluent families are likely to be directed to college preparatory tracks, which stress leadership and decision making—the skills they are expected to need as adults.

Although the Chinese government is attempting to address educational inequalities, girls continue to receive less education than boys—especially in rural areas.

Feminist View

The educational system of the United States, like many other social institutions, has long been characterized by discriminatory treatment of women. In 1833, Oberlin College became the first institution of higher learning to admit female students—some 200 years after the first men's college was established. But Oberlin believed that women should aspire to become wives and mothers, not lawyers and intellectuals. In addition to attending classes, female students washed men's clothing, cared for their rooms, and served them at meals. In the 1840s, Lucy Stone, then an Oberlin undergraduate and later one of the nation's most outspoken feminist leaders, refused to write a commencement address because it would have been read to the audience by a male student.

In the 20th century, sexism in education showed up in many ways—in textbooks with negative stereotypes of women, counselors' pressure on female students to prepare for "women's work," and unequal funding for women's and men's athletic programs. But perhaps nowhere was educational discrimination more evident than in the employment of teachers. The positions of university professor and college administrator, which hold relatively high status in the United States, were generally filled by men. Public school teachers, who earn much lower salaries, were largely female.

Women have made great strides in one area: the proportion of women who continue their schooling. As recently as 1969, twice as many men as women received college degrees; today, women outnumber men at college commencements. Moreover, women's access to graduate education and to medical, dental, and law schools has increased dramatically in the last few decades as a result of the Education Act of 1972. Box 16-1 (page 398) examines the far-reaching effects of Title IX, the part of the act that concerns discrimination against women in education.

Much has been made of the superior academic achievement of girls and women. Today, researchers are beginning to examine the reasons for their comparatively strong performance in school—or to put it another way, for men's lackluster performance. Some studies suggest that men's aggressiveness, together with the fact that they do better in the workplace than women, even with less schooling, predisposes them to undervalue higher education. While the "absence of men" on many college campuses has captured headlines, it has also created a false crisis in public discourse. Few students realize their potential exclusively through formal education; other factors, such as ambition and personal talent, contribute to their success. And many students, including low-income and immigrant children, face much greater challenges than the so-called gender gap in education (Kimmel 2006; R. Wilson 2007).

In cultures in which traditional gender roles remain the social norm, women's education suffers appreciably. Since September 11, 2001, the growing awareness of the Taliban's repression of Afghan women has dramatized the gender disparities in education in developing nations. Research has demonstrated that women are critical to economic development and good governance, and that education is instrumental in preparing them for those roles. Educating women, especially young girls, yields high social returns by lowering birthrates and improving agricultural productivity through better management (I. Coleman 2004).

Interactionist View

In George Bernard Shaw's play *Pygmalion,* later adapted as the hit Broadway musical *My Fair Lady,* flower girl Eliza Doolittle is transformed into a "lady" by Professor Henry Higgins, who changes her manner of speech and teaches her the etiquette of "high society." When Eliza is introduced to society as an aristocrat, she is readily accepted. People treat her as a "lady" and she responds as one.

sociologyON*campus*

16-1 The Debate over Title IX

Few federal policies have had such a visible effect on education over the last 30 years as Title IX, which mandates gender equity in education in federally funded schools. Congressional amendments to the Education Act of 1972, together with guidelines for their implementation developed by the Department of Health, Education, and Welfare in 1974–1975, have brought significant changes for both men and women at all levels of schooling. Title IX eliminated sex-segregated classes, prohibited sex discrimination in admissions and financial aid, and mandated that girls receive more opportunities to play sports, in proportion to their enrollment and interest.

Today, Title IX is still one of the more controversial attempts ever made by the federal government to promote equality for all citizens. Its consequences for the funding of college athletics programs are hotly debated, while its real and lasting effects on college admissions and employment are often forgotten. Critics charge that men's teams have suffered from proportional funding of women's teams and athletic scholarships, since schools with tight athletic budgets can expand women's sports only at the expense of men's sports. To a certain extent, non-revenue-producing men's sports such as wrestling and golf do appear to have suffered as women's teams have been added. But the high expense of some men's sports, particularly football, would be beyond many schools' means even without Title IX expenditures. And the gains for women have

more than made up for the losses to men. In 1971, when there were few opportunities for women athletes on college campuses, only 300,000 girls participated in high school sports. In 2003, three decades after Title IX opened up college athletics to women, the figure was 2.7 million.

For minority women, however, the results have been less satisfactory. Most of the women's sports that have benefited from increases in scholarships over the last 20 years, like rowing and volleyball, traditionally have not been attractive to minority women. Twenty-

> *Critics charge that men's teams have suffered from proportional funding of women's teams and athletic scholarships.*

five years ago, just 2 percent of female college athletes were African American. Today, the percentage is a disappointing 2.7 percent.

Sociologists note, too, that the social effects of sports on college campuses are not all positive. Michael A. Messner, professor of sociology at the University of Southern California, points to some troubling results of a survey by the Women's Sports Foundation. The study shows that teenage girls who play sports simply for fun have more positive body images than girls who don't play sports. But those who are "highly involved" in sports are more likely

than other girls to take steroids and to become binge drinkers and risk takers. "Everyone has tacitly agreed, it seems, to view men's sports as the standard to which women should strive to have equal access," Messner writes. "Missing from the debate is any recognition that men's sports have become sources of major problems on campuses: academic cheating, sexual violence, alcohol abuse, steroid use, serious injuries and other health issues, to name just a few" (Messner 2002:B9). Messner is skeptical of a system that propels a lucky few college athletes to stardom each year while leaving the majority, many of them African American, without a career or an education. Certainly that was not the kind of equal opportunity legislators envisioned when they wrote Title IX.

Let's Discuss

1. Has Title IX had an effect on you personally? If so, explain. On balance, do you think the increase in women's participation in sports has been good for society as a whole?

2. Are the negative social effects of men's sports evident on your campus? If so, what changes would you recommend to address the problem?

Sources: Federal Register, June 4, 1975; V. Gutierrez 2002; H. Mason 2003; Messner 2002.

The labeling approach suggests that if we treat people in particular ways, they may fulfill our expectations. Children {p.197 who are labeled as "troublemakers" may come to view themselves as delinquents. Similarly, a dominant group's stereotyping of racial minorities may limit their opportunities to break away from expected roles.

Can the labeling process operate in the classroom? Because of their focus on micro-level classroom dynamics, interactionist researchers have been particularly interested in this question. Howard S. Becker (1952) studied public schools in low-income and more affluent areas of Chicago. He noticed that administrators expected less of students from poor neighborhoods, and wondered if teachers accepted their view. A decade later, in *Pyg-*

malion in the Classroom, psychologist Robert Rosenthal and school principal Lenore Jacobson (1968, 1992) documented what they referred to as a ***teacher-expectancy effect***—the impact that a teacher's expectations about a student's performance may have on the student's actual achievements. This effect is especially evident in the lower grades (through grade three).

In the first experiment, children in a San Francisco elementary school were administered a verbal and reasoning pretest. Rosenthal and Jacobson then *randomly* selected 20 percent of the sample and designated them as "spurters"—children of whom teachers could expect superior performance. On a later verbal and reasoning test, the spurters were found to score significantly higher than before. Moreover, teachers evaluated them as more interesting, more curious, and better-adjusted than their classmates. These results were striking. Apparently, teachers' perceptions that the students were exceptional led to noticeable improvements in their performance.

Studies in the United States have revealed that teachers wait longer for an answer from a student they believe to be a high achiever and are more likely to give such children a second chance. In one experiment, teachers' expectations were even shown to have an impact on students' athletic achievements. Teachers obtained better athletic performance—as measured in the number of sit-ups or push-ups performed—from those students of whom they *expected* higher numbers. Despite the controversial nature of these findings, researchers continue to document the existence of the teacher-expectancy effect. Interactionists emphasize that ability alone may be less predictive of academic success than one might think (Babad and Taylor 1992; Brint 1998; R. Rosenthal and Jacobsen 1992:247–262).

Table 16-1 summarizes the four major theoretical perspectives on education.

Use Your Sociological Imagination

What kinds of labels do school authorities apply to students? What is the outcome of those labels?

www.mhhe.com/schaefer11

Schools as Formal Organizations

Nineteenth-century educators would be amazed at the scale of schools in the United States in the 21st century. For example, California's public school system, the largest in the nation, currently enrolls as many children as there were in secondary schools in the entire country in 1950 (Bureau of the Census 1975:368; 2006a).

In many respects, today's schools, when viewed as an example of a formal organization, are similar to factories, hospitals, and business firms. Like those organizations, schools do not operate autonomously; they are influenced by the market of potential students. This statement is especially true of private schools, but could have broader impact if acceptance of voucher plans and other school choice programs increases. The parallels between schools and other types of formal organizations will become more apparent as we examine the bureaucratic nature of schools, teaching as an occupation, and the student subculture (K. Dougherty and Hammack 1992).

Bureaucratization of Schools

It simply is not possible for a single teacher to transmit culture and skills to children of varying ages who will enter many diverse occupations. The growing number of students being served by school systems and the greater degree of specialization required within a technologically complex society have combined to bureaucratize schools.

Max Weber noted five basic characteristics of bureaucracy, all { pp.141–143 of which are evident in the vast majority of schools, whether at the elementary, secondary, or even college level:

1. **Division of labor.** Specialized experts teach particular age levels and specific subjects. Public elementary and secondary schools now employ instructors whose sole responsibility is to work with children with learning disabilities or physical impairments.

2. **Hierarchy of authority.** Each employee of a school system is responsible to a higher authority. Teachers must report to principals and assistant principals, and may also be supervised by department heads. Principals are answerable to a superintendent of schools, and the superintendent is hired and fired by a board of education.

3. **Written rules and regulations.** Teachers and administrators must conform to numerous rules and regulations in the performance of their duties. This bureaucratic trait can become dysfunctional; the time invested in completing required forms could instead be spent in preparing lessons or conferring with students.

4. **Impersonality.** As class sizes have swelled at schools and universities, it has become more difficult for teachers to give personal attention to each student. In fact, bureaucratic norms may actually encourage teachers to treat all students in the same way, despite the fact that students have distinctive personalities and learning needs.

Table 16-1

Sociological Perspectives on Education

summingUP

Theoretical Perspective	Emphasis
Functionalist	Transmission of the dominant culture
	Integration of society
	Promotion of social norms, values, and sanctions
	Promotion of desirable social change
Conflict	Domination by the elite through unequal access to schooling
	Hidden curriculum
	Credentialism
	Bestowal of status
Interactionist	Teacher-expectancy effect
Feminist	Treatment of female students
	Role of women's education in economic development

5. **Employment based on technical qualifications.** At least in theory, the hiring of instructors is based on professional competence and expertise. Promotions are normally dictated by written personnel policies; people who excel may be granted lifelong job security through tenure.

Functionalists take a generally positive view of the bureaucratization of education. Teachers can master the skills needed to work with a specialized clientele, since they no longer are expected to cover a broad range of instruction. The chain of command within schools is clear. Students are presumably treated in an unbiased fashion because of uniformly applied rules. Finally, security of position protects teachers from unjustified dismissal. In general, then, functionalists stress that the bureaucratization of education increases the likelihood that students, teachers, and administrators will be dealt with fairly —that is, on the basis of rational and equitable criteria.

Despite efforts to establish positive relationships among students and between teachers and students, many young people view their schools as impersonal institutions.

In contrast, conflict theorists argue that the trend toward more centralized education has harmful consequences for disadvantaged people. The standardization of educational curricula, including textbooks, will generally reflect the values, interests, and lifestyles of the most powerful groups in our society, and may ignore those of racial and ethnic minorities. In addition, the disadvantaged, more so than the affluent, will find it difficult to sort through complex educational bureaucracies and to organize effective lobbying groups. Therefore, in the view of conflict theorists, low-income and minority parents will have even less influence over citywide and statewide educational administrators than they have over local school officials (Bowles and Gintis 1976; Katz 1971).

Sometimes schools can seem overwhelmingly bureaucratic, with the effect of stifling rather than nourishing intellectual curiosity in students. This concern has led many parents and policymakers to push for school choice programs—allowing parents to choose the school that suits their children's needs, and forcing schools to compete for their "customers."

In the United States, another significant countertrend to the bureaucratization of schools is the availability of education over the Internet. Increasingly, colleges and universities are reaching out via the Web, offering entire courses and even majors to students in the comfort of their homes. Online curricula provide flexibility for working students and others who may have difficulty attending conventional classes because of distance or disability. Research on this type of learning is just beginning, so the question of whether teacher–student contact can thrive online remains to be settled. Computer-mediated instruction may also

have an impact on instructors' status as employees, which we will discuss next, as well as on alternative forms of education like adult education and homeschooling.

Use Your Sociological Imagination

How would you make your school less bureaucratic? What would it be like?

Teachers: Employees and Instructors

Whether they serve as instructors of preschoolers or graduate students, teachers are employees of formal organizations with bureaucratic structures. There is an inherent conflict in serving as a professional in a bureaucracy. The organization follows the principles of hierarchy and expects adherence to its rules, but professionalism demands the individual responsibility of the practitioner. This conflict is very real for teachers, who experience all the positive and negative consequences of working in bureaucracies (see Table 6-2, page 143).

A teacher undergoes many perplexing stresses every day. While teachers' academic assignments have become more specialized, the demands on their time remain diverse and contradictory. Conflicts arise from serving as an instructor, a disciplinarian, and an employee of a school district at the same time. In too many schoools, discipline means dealing with violence (see Box 16-2). Burnout is one result of these stresses: 40 to

research**IN**action

16-2 Violence in the Schools

Littleton, Colorado; Red Lake, Minnesota; Jonesboro, Arkansas; West Paducah, Kentucky; Pearl, Mississippi; Edinboro, Pennsylvania; Springfield, Oregon—these are now more than just the names of small towns and medium-size cities. They resonate with the sound of gunshots, of kids killing kids on school grounds. As a result, people no longer perceive schools as safe havens. But how accurate is that impression?

Studies of school violence put the recent spate of school killings in perspective:

- A child has less than a one in a million chance of being killed at school.
- Ninety-nine percent of violent deaths of school-aged children in 1992–1999 occurred *outside* school grounds.
- Fewer students are now being found with guns in school.
- With the exception of 1999, school-associated violent deaths declined every year from 1992 through 2000.
- Twenty-three times more children are killed in gun *accidents* than in school killings.

Schools, then, are safer than neighborhoods, but people are still unnerved by the perception of an alarming rise in schoolyard violence generated by heavy media coverage of recent incidents. Some conflict theorists object to the huge outcry about recent violence in schools. After all, they note, violence in and around inner-city schools has a long history. It seems that only when middle-class White children are the victims does school violence become a plank on the national policy agenda. When violence hits the middle class, the problem is viewed not as an extension of delinquency, but as a structural issue in need of legislative remedies, such as gun control.

The issues of gun control and school safety received renewed attention in 2007 when a lone gunman killed 32 people in a dormitory and a classroom building at Virginia Tech in Blacksburg, Virginia. His rampage was the worst incident of violence on a college campus since 1966, when a student at the University of Texas at Austin carried a rifle to the observation deck of the school's clock tower and shot dozens of people in the quad below, leaving a death toll of 16.

> *A child has less than a one in a million chance of being killed at school.*

Feminists observe that virtually all the offenders in these incidents are male, and in some instances, such as the case in Jonesboro, the victims are disproportionately female. The precipitating factor in the violence is often a broken-off dating relationship—yet another example of the violence of men against women (or in this case, boys against girls).

Increasingly, efforts to prevent school violence are focusing on the ways in which the socialization of young people contributes to violence. For example, the *Journal of the American Medical Association* published a study of Second Step, a violence prevention curriculum for elementary school students that teaches social skills related to anger management, impulse control, and empathy. The study evaluated the impact of the program on urban and suburban elementary school students and found that it appeared to lead to a moderate decrease in physically aggressive behavior and an increase in neutral and prosocial behavior at school.

Some people believe that a key ingredient in the prevention of violence, in or out of school, is greater parental supervision of and responsibility for their children. In her book *A Tribe Apart,* Patricia Hersch documents the lives of eight teens growing up in a Virginia suburb over a three-year period. Her conclusion: Children need meaningful adult relationships in their lives. And former Secretary of Education Richard Riley cites studies showing that youths who feel connected to their parents and schools are less likely to engage in high-risk behaviors.

Let's Discuss

1. Has a shooting or other violent episode ever occurred at your school? If so, how did students react? Do you feel safer at school than at home, as experts say you are?
2. What steps have administrators at your school taken to prevent violence? Have they been effective, or should other steps be taken?

Sources: Department of Education 1999, 2004; Donohue et al. 1998; Hersch 1998; National Center for Education Statistics 2002.

---

50 percent of new teachers quit the profession within five years (G. Gordon 2004).

Given these difficulties, does teaching remain an attractive profession in the United States? In 2006, 4.8 percent of first-year college students indicated that they were interested in becoming elementary school teachers, and 4.8 percent, high school teachers. These figures are dramatically lower than the 13 percent of first-year male students and 38 percent of first-year female students who held those occupational aspirations in 1968 (Astin et al. 1994; Pryor et al. 2006:32).

Undoubtedly, economic considerations enter into students' feelings about the attractiveness of teaching. In 2007 the average salary for all public elementary and secondary school teachers in the United States was reported at $46,600, placing teachers somewhere near the average of all the nation's wage earners. In most other industrial countries, teachers' salaries are higher in relation to the general standard of living. Of course, teachers' salaries vary considerably from state to state (see Figure 16-2, page 402), and even more from one school district to another. Nevertheless, the economic reward for teaching is miniscule

Average Salary for Teachers

MAPPING LIFE NATIONWIDE

www.mhhe.com/schaefer11

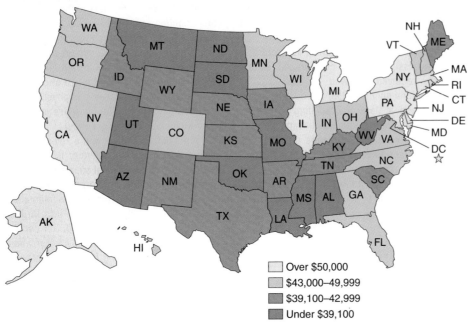

Over $50,000

$43,000–49,999

$39,100–42,999

Under $39,100

Source: American Federation of Teachers 2007.

State averages for teacher salaries range from a low of $34,039 in South Dakota to a high of $57,760 in Massachusetts.

compared to some career options: The CEO of a major corporation makes more money in a day than the average teacher makes in a year (American Federation of Teachers 2007; Herring 2006).

The status of any job reflects several factors, including the level of education required, financial compensation, and the respect given the occupation by society. The teaching profession (see Table 9-2, page 224) is feeling pressure in all three of these areas. First, the level of formal schooling required for teaching remains high, and the public has begun to call for new competency examinations. Second, the statistics just cited demonstrate that teachers' salaries are significantly lower than those of many professionals and skilled workers. Finally, the overall prestige of the teaching profession has declined in the last decade. Many teachers have become disappointed and frustrated and have left the educational world for careers in other professions.

Student Subcultures

An important latent function of education relates directly to student life: Schools provide for students' social and recreational needs. Education helps toddlers and young children develop interpersonal skills that are essential during adolescence and adulthood. In their high school and college years, students may meet future husbands and wives and establish lifelong friendships.

When people observe high schools, community colleges, or universities from the outside, students appear to constitute a cohesive, uniform group. However, the student subculture is actually complex and diverse. High school cliques and social groups may crop up according to race, social class, physical attractiveness, placement in courses, athletic ability, and leadership roles in the school and community. In his classic community study of "Elmtown," August B. Hollingshead (1975) found some 259 distinct cliques in a single high school. The cliques, whose average size was five, were centered on the school itself, on recreational activities, and on religious and community groups.

Amid these close-knit and often rigidly segregated cliques, gay and lesbian students are particularly vulnerable. Peer group pressure to conform is intense at this age. Although coming to terms with one's sexuality is difficult for all adolescents, it can be downright dangerous for those whose sexual orientation does not conform to societal expectations.

Teachers and administrators are becoming more sensitized to these issues. Perhaps more important, some schools are creating gay–straight alliances (GSAs), school-sponsored support groups that bring gay teens together with sympathetic straight peers. Begun in Los Angeles in 1984, these programs numbered nearly 3,000 nationwide in 2005; most were founded after the murder of Matthew Shepard, a gay college student, in 1998. In some districts parents have objected to these organizations, but the same court rulings that protect the right of conservative Bible groups to meet on school grounds also protect GSAs. In 2003, the gay–straight movement reached a milestone when the New York City public schools moved an in-school program for gays, bisexuals, and transgender students to a separate school of their own. The Harvey Milk High School was named in memory of San Francisco's first openly gay city supervisor, who was assassinated in 1978 (Gay, Lesbian and Straight Education Network 2007).

We can find a similar diversity of student groups at the college level. Burton Clark and Martin Trow (1966) and more recently, Helen Lefkowitz Horowitz (1987) have identified four distinctive subcultures among college students:

1. The *collegiate* subculture focuses on having fun and socializing. These students define what constitutes a "reasonable" amount of academic work (and what amount of work is "ex-

cessive" and leads to being labeled as a "grind"). Members of the collegiate subculture have little commitment to academic pursuits. Athletes often fit into this subculture.

2. The *academic* subculture identifies with the intellectual concerns of the faculty and values knowledge for its own sake.

3. The *vocational* subculture is interested primarily in career prospects, and views college as a means of obtaining degrees that are essential for advancement.

4. Finally, the *nonconformist* subculture is hostile to the college environment, and seeks out ideas that may or may not relate to academic studies. This group may find outlets through campus publications or issue-oriented groups.

Each college student is eventually exposed to these competing subcultures and must determine which (if any) seems most in line with his or her feelings and interests.

The typology used by the researchers reminds us that school is a complex social organization—almost like a community with different neighborhoods. Of course, these four subcultures are not the only ones evident on college campuses in the United States. For example, one might find subcultures of Vietnam veterans or former full-time homemakers at community colleges and four-year commuter institutions. And as more and more students from minority groups decide to continue their formal education beyond high school, subcultures based on race and ethnicity will become more evident. As Figure 16-3 shows, tomorrow's high school graduates will be a diverse group.

Sociologist Joe R. Feagin has studied a distinctive collegiate subculture: Black students at predominantly White universities. These students must function academically and socially within universities where there are few Black faculty members or Black administrators, where harassment of Blacks by campus police is common, and where the curricula place little emphasis on Black contributions. Feagin (1989:11) suggests that "for minority students life at a predominantly White college or university means long-term encounters with pervasive whiteness." In Feagin's view, African American students at such institutions experience both blatant and subtle racial discrimination, which has a cumulative impact that can seriously damage the students' confidence (see also Feagin et al. 1996).

Use Your Sociological Imagination

What distinctive subcultures can you identify at your college?

Homeschooling

When most people think of school, they think of bricks and mortar and the teachers, administrators, and other employees

Student subcultures are more diverse today than they were in the past. Many adults are returning to college to obtain further education, advance their careers, or change their line of work.

who staff school buildings. But for an increasing number of students in the United States, home is the classroom and the teacher is a parent. More than 2 million students are now being educated at home. That is about 4 percent of the K–12 school population. For these students, the issues of bureaucratization and social structure are less significant than they are for public school students (Ray 2006).

In the 1800s, after the establishment of public schools, families that taught their children at home lived in isolated environments or held strict religious views that were at odds with the secular environment of public schools. But today, homeschooling is attracting a broader range of families not necessarily tied to organized religion. Poor academic quality, peer

FIGURE 16–3

Public High School Graduates by Race and Ethnicity, 2014 (projected)

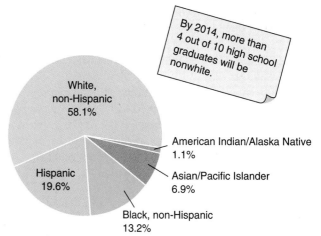

By 2014, more than 4 out of 10 high school graduates will be nonwhite.

White, non-Hispanic 58.1%

American Indian/Alaska Native 1.1%

Asian/Pacific Islander 6.9%

Black, non-Hispanic 13.2%

Hispanic 19.6%

Note: Percentages do not add to 100 due to rounding error.
Source: Western Interstate Commission for Higher Education 2003.

pressure, and school violence are motivating many parents to teach their children at home. The recent publicity given to school shooting sprees seems to have accelerated the move toward homeschooling.

While supporters of homeschooling believe children can do just as well or better in homeschools as in public schools, critics counter that because homeschooled children are isolated from the larger community, they lose an important chance to improve their socialization skills. But proponents of homeschooling claim their children benefit from contact with others besides their own age group. They also see homeschools as a good alternative for children who suffer from attention-deficit/hyperactivity disorder (ADHD) and learning disorders (LDs). Such children often do better in smaller classes, which present fewer distractions to disturb their concentration.

Quality control is an issue in homeschooling. While homeschooling is legal in all 50 states, 10 states require no notification that a child will be homeschooled, and another 14 require notification only. Other states may require parents to submit their children's curricula or test scores for professional evaluation. Despite the lack of uniform standards, a research review by the Home School Legal Defense Association (2005) reports that homeschooled students score higher than others on standardized tests, in every subject and every grade.

Who are the people who are running homeschools? In general, they tend to have higher-than-average incomes and educational levels. Most are two-parent families, and their children watch less television than average—both factors that are likely to support superior educational performance. The same students, with the same support from their parents, would probably do just as well in the public schools. As research has repeatedly shown, small classes are better than big classes, and strong parental and community involvement is key (R. Cox 2003:28).

social Policy and Education

No Child Left Behind Act

The Issue

The consensus was clear: Too many public schools in the United States were failing to educate their students—failing to meet even minimum performance standards. In the 2000 presidential election campaign, President George W. Bush had promised to "leave no child behind" if he were elected. The president had advocated an educational reform plan that he had instituted in the Texas public schools while he was governor of that state. In 2001, the U.S. House of Representatives voted 381–41, and the Senate 87–10, to approve the president's No Child Left Behind (NCLB) Act, an initiative designed to improve the performance of public schools in the United States. The NCLB increased federal standards of accountability for states, school districts, and schools, and gave parents more flexibility in choosing which schools their children would attend.

The apparent consensus for educational reform soon disappeared, however. Supporters charged that the act was not being enforced stringently enough; others felt the legislation went too far. What does this state of affairs say about the NCLB in particular, and about the school reform movement in general?

The Setting

The NCLB must be viewed in the context of the United States' unusual educational system. In this country, unlike most others, public schools are locally run and financed, albeit with some federal and state aid. The United States does not have a national education program that follows a common curriculum. Until the 1940s, in fact, the federal government had very little involvement with public education. But in the 1990s, public concern over poor student performance in the United States, compared to that of other countries, led to the establishment of national educational standards.

The NCLB built on those national standards, and for the first time set penalties for failure to meet them. States are now required to conduct annual assessments of all public school students, grades K–12. The resulting performance data must be cross-tabulated by students' race, ethnicity, gender, social class, and disability. Schools whose students do not perform well on the required tests are subject to restructuring, and their students are eligible to transfer to different schools. Theoretically, the testing requirements and the penalties associated with substandard performance should reduce the achievement gap between advantaged and disadvantaged students, allowing the nation to "leave no child behind." The program's ambitious goal is for every student in the nation to be proficient in reading and mathematics by the year 2014.

The NCLB has created a national debate about how best to offer high-quality schooling to all children. Some critics have charged that the program has no substance—that the required testing is just an academic exercise. Others charge that it overemphasizes reading and math at the expense of other subjects, such as art, music, and social studies. Indeed, many principals have reworked their curricula and staff to emphasize the subjects that are tested under the NCLB. Finally, state and local educators have complained bitterly about federal intrusion into local schools. They insist that they need more federal funding if they are to have any hope of complying with the act (Wallis and Steptoe 2007).

Sociological Insights

From a functionalist point of view, the development of common curricular objectives promotes social integration. Because the NCLB requires scores to be broken out by gender, race, income, ethnicity, and disability, it prevents schools from disguising low achievement by disadvantaged students. The result should be better educational achievement across the board. Conflict theorists support the need to educate all students, regardless of their socioeconomic status, but they question the wisdom of pursuing that goal through testing programs.

Even before the NCLB, educational testing was a hot issue. From preschool screening through entry-level professional examinations, the practice has always been controversial. Critics have raised serious questions about the reliability and validity of such tests. Recall from Chapter 2 that *validity* refers to the degree to which a scale or measure truly reflects the phenomenon under study. Does an aptitude test really measure the likelihood of future academic success, for instance? *Reliability* refers to the extent to which a measure provides consistent results. If an exam supposedly measures a student's readiness to study high school algebra, it should yield the same result, no matter who administers and scores it.

Reliability and validity are major issues in constructing any test; rarely are these concerns totally resolved. Scholars who design standardized tests are constantly tweaking the questions to improve the tests' reliability and validity. From preschool to graduate and professional programs, the reliability and validity of tests affect everything from the allocation of funds to admissions decisions in highly competitive programs. With high-stakes testing—testing that determines whether a public school closes or remains open, for instance—these issues become even more important.

Policy Initiatives

National policy efforts like the NCLB overlay a patchwork of state and local programs. Educational reformers have yet to come up with a solution that fits all schools in all states. Former Representative Dick Gephardt, a Democrat who voted for the act, has complained that the program does not do what it claimed it would: "We were all fooled into it. It is a fraud." Still, many educators see the NCLB as their best hope so far for improving the nation's schools. According to Peggy Hinckley, an Indiana School superintendent, "We are living in a results-

A statue of President George W. Bush stands outside Hamilton High School in Ohio, where the president signed the No Child Left Behind Act in 2002. Two years later, Hamilton High was labeled a failing school under the act's tough standards.

oriented society. Everybody is looking for results and we will do whatever we can to achieve them" (Dobbs 2004:29; Schrag 2004:40).

In 2007, an independent commission advocated maintaining the 2014 goals, even though by its own estimate, only a small portion of the nation's schools would reach the objectives. By that time, only 13 percent of the nation's eighth graders are expected to reach the mathematics objectives. A maximum of 33 percent of all third graders are expected to meet the reading objectives (Tommy G. Thompson and Barnes 2007:69).

Let's Discuss

1. What are the public schools like in the community where you live? Are some schools in trouble because of high-stakes testing? Does the school system have adequate funding, or are administrators forced to cut corners to stay within budget?

2. What do you think of the practice of restructuring or closing schools whose students do not perform well on national tests? What will be the short-term effect on individual students? The long-term effect on students and schools?

3. Can you think of a better way to improve the nation's public schools?

To get involved in the debate over the No Child Left Behind program, visit this text's Online Learning Center, which offers links to relevant Web sites. Check out the Social Policy section of the Online Learning Center as well; it provides survey data on U.S. public opinion regarding this issue.

www.mhhe.com/schaefer11

{ MASTERING THIS CHAPTER }

Summary

Education is a cultural universal found throughout the world, although in varied forms. This chapter examines sociological views of education and analyzes schools as an example of formal organizations.

1. The transmission of knowledge and bestowal of status are manifest functions of education. Among the latent functions are transmitting culture, promoting social and political integration, maintaining social control, and serving as an agent of social change.

2. In the view of conflict theorists, education serves as an instrument of elite domination by creating standards for entry into occupations, bestowing status unequally, and subordinating the role of women.

3. Teacher expectations about a student's performance can sometimes have an impact on the student's actual achievements.

4. Today, most schools in the United States are organized in a bureaucratic fashion. Weber's five basic characteristics of bureaucracy are all evident in schools.

5. Homeschooling has become a viable alternative to traditional public and private schools. An estimated 1.6 million or more American children are now educated at home.

6. The No Child Left Behind Act is a controversial initiative designed to improve the performance of public schools in the United States by increasing federal standards of accountability. Critics charge that the program is underfunded, that it overemphasizes reading and math, and that the tests used to determine whether a school is meeting federal standards are flawed.

Critical Thinking Questions

1. What are the functions and dysfunctions of tracking in schools? Viewed from an interactionist perspective, how would tracking of high school students influence the interactions between students and teachers? In what ways might tracking have positive and negative impacts on the self-concepts of various students?

2. Are the student subcultures identified in this text evident on your campus? What other student subcultures are present? Which subcultures have the highest (and the lowest) social status? How might functionalists, conflict theorists, and interactionists view the existence of student subcultures on a college campus?

Key Terms

Correspondence principle The tendency of schools to promote the values expected of individuals in each social class and to prepare students for the types of jobs typically held by members of their class. (page 397)

Credentialism An increase in the lowest level of education required to enter a field. (396)

Education A formal process of learning in which some people consciously teach while others adopt the social role of learner. (392)

Hidden curriculum Standards of behavior that are deemed proper by society and are taught subtly in schools. (395)

Reliability The extent to which a measure produces consistent results. (405)

Teacher-expectancy effect The impact that a teacher's expectations about a student's performance may have on the student's actual achievements. (398)

Tracking The practice of placing students in specific curriculum groups on the basis of their test scores and other criteria. (396)

Validity The degree to which a measure or scale truly reflects the phenomenon under study. (405)

Self-Quiz

Read each question carefully and then select the best answer.

1. Which sociological perspective emphasizes that the common identity and social integration fostered by education contribute to overall societal stability and consensus?

   a. the functionalist perspective
   b. the conflict perspective
   c. the interactionist perspective
   d. labeling theory

2. Which one of the following was introduced into school systems to promote social change?

   a. sex education classes
   b. affirmative action programs
   c. Project Head Start
   d. all of the above

3. The correspondence principle was developed by

   a. Max Weber.
   b. Karl Marx and Friedrich Engels.
   c. Samuel Bowles and Herbert Gintis.
   d. James Thurber.

4. The student subculture that is hostile to the college environment and seeks out ideas that may or may not relate to studies is called the

   a. collegiate subculture.
   b. academic subculture.
   c. vocational subculture.
   d. nonconformist subculture.

5. Most recent research on ability grouping raises questions about its

   a. effectiveness, especially for lower-achieving students.
   b. failure to improve the prospects of higher-achieving students.
   c. ability to improve the prospects of lower- and higher-achieving students.
   d. both a and b

6. The most basic *manifest* function of education is

   a. transmitting knowledge.
   b. transmitting culture.
   c. maintaining social control.
   d. serving as an agent of change.

7. Fifty years ago, a high school diploma was the minimum requirement for entry into the paid labor force of the United States. Today, a college diploma is virtually the bare minimum. This change reflects the process of

   a. tracking.
   b. credentialism.
   c. the hidden curriculum.
   d. the correspondence principle.

8. Samuel Bowles and Herbert Gintis have argued that capitalism requires a skilled, disciplined labor force and that the educational system of the United States is structured with that objective in mind. Citing numerous studies, they offer support for what they call

   a. tracking.
   b. credentialism.
   c. the correspondence principle.
   d. the teacher-expectancy effect.

9. The teacher-expectancy effect is most closely associated with

   a. the functionalist perspective.
   b. the conflict perspective.
   c. the interactionist perspective.
   d. anomie theory.

10. Sociologist Max Weber noted five basic characteristics of bureaucracy, all of which are evident in the vast majority of schools, whether at the elementary, secondary, or even college level. Which of the following is *not* one of them?

    a. division of labor
    b. written rules and regulations
    c. impersonality
    d. shared decision making

408 11. The _____ perspective stresses the importance of education in transmitting culture, maintaining social control, and promoting social change.

12. In the past, the integrative function of education was most obvious through its emphasis on promoting a common _____.

13. The _____ subculture identifies with the intellectual concerns of the faculty and values knowledge for its own sake.

14. _____ and _____ are major issues in constructing any test, but rarely are they totally resolved.

15. Women's education tends to suffer in those cultures with traditional _____ _____.

16. Schools provide a variety of _____ functions, such as transmitting culture, promoting social and political integration, and maintaining social control.

17. Sociologist _____ _____ points out that better-educated people tend to have greater access to information, to hold more diverse opinions, and to possess the ability to make subtle distinctions in analysis.

18. The term _____ _____ refers to standards of behavior that are deemed proper by society and are taught subtly in schools. According to this curriculum, children must not speak until the teacher calls on them and must regulate their activities according to the clock or the bell.

19. _____ is the practice of placing students in specific curriculum groups on the basis of their test scores and other criteria.

20. Of the four distinctive subcultures among college students discussed in the text, the _____ subculture is interested primarily in career prospects, and views college as a means of obtaining degrees that are essential for advancement.

Online Learning Center

1. An effective and visually interesting way to reinforce your understanding of the key points from this chapter is to view the PowerPoint slides for this chapter in the student center of the Online Learning Center (**www.mhhe.com/schaefer11**). The slides include tables and figures from the chapter, as well as links that allow you to navigate to particular topics.

2. Humanitarian organizations are concerned about access to education in developing countries. To find out about charitable efforts to improve basic education in the world's poorest countries, go to the Oxfam Web site (**www.oxfam.org.uk**) and explore the section on education.

3. You can find out how teachers themselves view major issues in U.S. education by visiting the Web site of the American Federation of Teachers (**www.aft.org**). Information on teacher salaries, which you can access by linking to Salary Surveys on the left-hand side of the page, may be especially interesting.

*Note: Although all the URLs listed were current as of the printing of this book, these sites often change. Please check our Web site (**www.mhhe.com/schaefer11**) for updates, hyperlinks, and exercises related to these sites.*

Reel Society Video Clips

Reel Society video clips, which appear on this book's Web site, can be used to spark discussion about the following topics from this chapter:

- Sociological Perspectives on Education
- Schools as Formal Organizations

Politically oriented messages are often meant for international as well as local consumption. In 2005 the Saudi Arabian government launched a public relations campaign featuring slogans like "Islam Is Moderation" and "Say No to Terrorism." On this poster, the English translation appears in much larger type than the Arabic message.

17 Government and Politics

inside

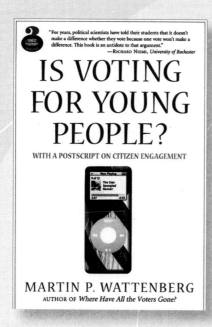

"For years, political scientists have told their students that it doesn't make a difference whether they vote because one vote won't make a difference. This book is an antidote to that argument."
—RICHARD NIEMI, *University of Rochester*

IS VOTING FOR YOUNG PEOPLE?

WITH A POSTSCRIPT ON CITIZEN ENGAGEMENT

MARTIN P. WATTENBERG
AUTHOR OF *Where Have All the Voters Gone?*

"Voting is for Old People," proclaimed a T-shirt printed and distributed in 2004 by Urban Outfitters, a popular American clothing company. At Harvard's Kennedy School of Government, the perceived message of the shirt hit a raw nerve. Its director issued a public statement criticizing the slogan, saying that it could not be further from the truth—that voting is for everyone. In response, Urban Outfitters said they never intended to discourage anyone from voting. Rather, they asserted that their goal was to draw attention to the relative lack of participation of young adults in politics, a problem that many analysts and politicians acknowledge but few seem to be genuinely concerned about. . . .

Over the last three decades, politics and voting have indeed become more and more the province of the elderly, which will be shown to be the case not only in the United States but also *throughout the world's advanced industrialized democracies.* There is in fact a rift between politicians and young adults, although not one of mutual contempt but rather of mutual neglect. Many young people don't vote simply because they don't follow politics. Moreover, because so many young people don't follow politics and don't vote, parties and politicians frequently don't bother with young people, thereby further widening the age bias in electoral participation.

All too often, low turnout rates among the young are considered to be a natural part of political life, and hence not worth fretting about. Scholars often write of a life cycle pattern in which people become more aware of the political world as they age, and hence are more likely to vote. As such, it is often thought that today's young nonvoters will eventually show up at the polls and have their voices heard.

> *All too often, low turnout rates among the young are considered to be a natural part of political life, and hence not worth fretting about.*

If such a life cycle truly exists, it ought to be consistently found in: (1) different eras; and (2) across a wide range of democracies. The data . . . from a number of countries in the 1970s contradict the life cycle hypothesis. . . .

Communications technology is one . . . aspect of political life that has undergone transformation throughout the world's advanced industrialized societies . . . in recent years. . . . Changes in media habits from generation to generation have led to a new situation in which young people are far less likely to be exposed to news about public affairs than their elders. Young adults have not consciously decided to avoid political news in recent years; rather, having been socialized in a markedly different communications environment, they just have not picked up the same media habits that their parents and grandparents did. These media habits, which older people developed long ago in a different world, continue to serve them well in today's political environment—making them substantially more likely to follow politics and become familiar with the issues of the day. And the more one learns about public affairs and follows current events, the more one is likely to realize the stakes involved at the polls.

(Wattenberg 2008:1–2, 3) Additional information about this excerpt can be found on the Online Learning Center at www.mhhe.com/schaefer11.

412 In this excerpt from *Is Voting for Young People?* Martin P. Wattenberg, a professor of political science at the University of California at Irvine, confronts the generation gap in politics, not only in the United States but in industrialized countries around the world. Wattenberg thinks that the absence of young people from the voting booth reflects a generational difference in the way that citizens use the mass media. Few young people nowadays read the newspapers, so few know much about politics or think that it has any relevance for them. Most spend their time surfing the Internet, downloading music to their iPods and MP3s, text-messaging and snapping photos using their cell phones. Only in countries where these technological marvels are not available to the average youth is apathy among young people not a noteworthy phenomenon.

Those who vote (or who choose not to) operate within the framework of the existing political system, be it local, state, national, or international. By *political system,* sociologists mean the social institution that is founded on a recognized set of procedures for implementing and achieving society's goals, such as the allocation of valued resources. Like religion and the family, the political system is a cultural universal: It is found in every society. In the United States, the political system holds the ultimate responsibility for addressing the social policy is-

sues examined in this textbook: child care, the AIDS crisis, welfare reform, and so forth.

Are young people more interested in what's playing on their portable media players than in the political issues contronting their nation? How does government maintain its power, and how do political parties and public interest groups attempt to exert theirs? Does our campaign finance system put some groups at a disadvantage? In this chapter we will analyze the impact of government on people's lives from a sociological point of view. We will begin with a macro-level analysis of the sources of political power and authority, and the four major types of government in which that power and authority is exerted. We will see how politics works, with particular attention to citizens' participation and the changing role of women and minority groups. We'll look at two models of power in the United States, the elite and the pluralist models. Then we'll touch briefly on war, peace, and terrorism, and see how political activists have begun using the Internet to promote their causes. Finally, the Social Policy section will explore the controversy over campaign financing, an issue that vividly illustrates the close relationship between government and the moneyed elite who seek to influence the political process.

Power and Authority

In any society, someone or some group—whether it be a tribal chief, a dictator, or a parliament—makes important decisions about how to use resources and how to allocate goods. One cultural universal, then, is the exercise of power and authority. Inevitably, the struggle for power and authority involves *politics,* which political scientist Harold Lasswell (1936) tersely defined as "who gets what, when, and how." In their study of politics and government, sociologists are concerned with social interactions among individuals and groups and their impact on the larger political and economic order.

Power

{ p.220 Power lies at the heart of a political system. According to Max Weber, *power* is the ability to exercise one's will over others. To put it another way, whoever can overcome the resistance of others and control their behavior is exercising power. Power relations can involve large organizations, small groups, or even people in an intimate association.

Because Weber developed his conceptualization of power in the early 1900s, he focused primarily on the nation-state and its sphere of influence. Today scholars recognize that the trend toward globalization has brought new opportunities, and with

them new concentrations of power. Power is now exercised on a global as well as a national stage, as countries and multinational corporations vie to control access to resources and manage the distribution of capital (Sernau 2001; Schaefer 2008b).

There are three basic sources of power within any political system: force, influence, and authority. *Force* is the actual or threatened use of coercion to impose one's will on others. When leaders imprison or even execute political dissidents, they are applying force; so, too, are terrorists when they seize or bomb an embassy or assassinate a political leader. *Influence,* on the other hand, refers to the exercise of power through a process of persuasion. A citizen may change his or her view of a Supreme Court nominee because of a newspaper editorial, the expert testimony of a law school dean before the Senate Judiciary Committee, or a stirring speech by a political activist at a rally. In each case, sociologists would view such efforts to persuade people as examples of influence. Now let's take a look at the third source of power, *authority.*

Types of Authority

The term *authority* refers to institutionalized power that is recognized by the people over whom it is exercised. Sociologists commonly use the term in connection with those who hold legitimate power through elected or publicly acknowledged positions.

"Which country is the least mad at us?"

This cartoon, published in 1957, is still relevant today. The extent of the tension between the United States and foreign countries should not be exaggerated, however. Though other countries may resent the United States' preeminent power and influence, they do not necessarily dislike the people of the United States.

A person's authority is often limited. Thus, a referee has the authority to decide whether a penalty should be called during a football game, but has no authority over the price of tickets to the game.

Max Weber ([1913] 1947) developed a classification system for authority that has become one of the most useful and frequently cited contributions of early sociology. He identified three ideal types of authority: traditional, rational-legal, and charismatic. Weber did not insist that only one type applies to a given society or organization. All can be present, but their relative importance will vary. Sociologists have found Weber's typology valuable in understanding different manifestations of legitimate power within a society.

Traditional Authority

Until the middle of the last century, Japan was ruled by a revered emperor whose absolute power was passed down from generation to generation. In a political system based on *traditional authority,* legitimate power is conferred by custom and accepted practice. A king or queen is accepted as ruler of a nation simply by virtue of inheriting the crown; a tribal chief rules because that is the accepted practice. The ruler may be loved or hated, competent or destructive; in terms of legitimacy, that does not matter. For the traditional leader, authority rests in custom, not in personal characteristics, technical competence, or even written law. People accept the ruler's au-

thority because that is how things have always been done. Traditional authority is absolute when the ruler has the ability to determine laws and policies.

Rational-Legal Authority

The U.S. Constitution gives Congress and our president the authority to make and enforce laws and policies. Power made legitimate by law is known as *rational-legal authority.* Leaders derive their rational-legal authority from the written rules and regulations of political systems, such as a constitution. Generally, in societies based on rational-legal authority, leaders are thought to have specific areas of competence and authority but are not thought to be endowed with divine inspiration, as in certain societies with traditional forms of authority.

Charismatic Authority

Joan of Arc was a simple peasant girl in medieval France, yet she was able to rally the French people and lead them into major battles against English invaders. How was this possible? As Weber observed, power can be legitimized by the *charisma* of an individual. The term *charismatic authority* refers to power made legitimate by a leader's exceptional personal or emotional appeal to his or her followers.

Charisma lets a person lead or inspire without relying on set rules or traditions. In fact, charismatic authority is derived more from the beliefs of followers than from the actual qualities of leaders. So long as people *perceive* a leader as having qualities that set him or her apart from ordinary citizens, that leader's authority will remain secure and often unquestioned.

Unlike traditional rulers, charismatic leaders often become well known by breaking with established institutions and advocating dramatic changes in the social structure and the economic system. Their strong hold over their followers makes it easier to build protest movements that challenge the dominant norms and values of a society. Thus, charismatic leaders such as Jesus, Joan of Arc, Gandhi, Malcolm X, and Martin Luther King, Jr., all used their power to press for changes in accepted social behavior. But so did Adolf Hitler, whose charismatic appeal turned people toward violent and destructive ends in Nazi Germany.

Observing from an interactionist perspective, sociologist Carl Couch (1996) points out that the growth of the electronic media has facilitated the development of charismatic authority. During the 1930s and 1940s, the heads of state of the United States, Great Britain, and Germany all used radio to issue direct appeals to citizens. Now, television and the Internet allow leaders to "visit" people's homes and communicate with them. In both Taiwan and South Korea in 1996, troubled political leaders facing reelection campaigns spoke frequently to national audiences and exaggerated military threats from neighboring China and North Korea, respectively. Later in this chapter we will discuss the impact that the Internet may be having on political campaigns.

As we noted earlier, Weber used traditional, rational-legal, and charismatic authority as ideal types. In reality, particular leaders

For Joshua Johnston, deciding on a major was easy: Everything he was interested in fell into the area of sociology. Johnston, an avid people watcher, appreciates the discipline's focus on everyday social life. "Whether the subject is conspicuous consumption or people standing against the walls in elevators, you can see it all around you," he says.

A graduate of the University of Washington (2003), Johnston is now an aide to a congressional representative from the Seattle area. "I am the person that people work with when they want a meeting with the congressman or they would like him to attend an event," he explains. "A lot of my job is event coordinating and planning." Johnston's week begins with a Monday morning conference at which he schedules upcoming meetings and events. Working with labor unions is another of his responsibilities, one he particularly enjoys: "They are hard-working men and women who are trying to support their families and make an honest living." Once or twice a week, Johnston spends the evening at a community event.

Johnston appreciates the opportunity to work on issues that are important to people in the Pacific Northwest, such as salmon recovery. One of his first assignments as a congressional aide was to organize a hearing on the issue, so that congressional representatives from the area could hear expert opinions on the topic. He also relishes the chance to meet well-known politicians. When Al Gore visited Seattle to talk about climate change, Johnston worked with Gore's staff to set up the event. He has also met John Edwards and Barack Obama.

Of all the topics Johnston studied in his sociology courses, he finds his knowledge of social networks to be most helpful on the job. "We all have to work with social networks, and we need the tools to be able to work effectively within them," he notes. But he also sees a broader benefit to majoring in sociology: "Sociology has given me the tools that I need to be able to think critically about a subject," he explains. "Above all else, I think this is the one tool that has been the most important to me in my life. Being able to think critically about a subject has given me the chance to analyze why I believe a certain thing, and then have true conviction when people ask me a question about my beliefs."

Let's Discuss

1. How has your study of sociology helped to clarify your thinking on issues that are important to you?
2. Relate what you have learned about networking to the field of politics. In what kind of politics is networking especially useful? How have new technologies that support networking changed politics?

and political systems combine elements of two or more of these forms. Presidents Franklin D. Roosevelt, John F. Kennedy, and Ronald Reagan wielded power largely through the rational-legal basis of their authority. At the same time, they were unusually charismatic leaders who commanded the personal loyalty of large numbers of citizens.

Use Your Sociological Imagination

What would our government be like if it were founded on traditional rather than rational-legal authority? What difference would it make to the average citizen?

www.mhhe.com/schaefer11

Types of Government

Each society establishes a political system through which it is governed. In modern industrial nations, these formal systems of government make a significant number of critical political decisions. We will survey five basic types of government here: monarchy, oligarchy, dictatorship, totalitarianism, and democracy.

Monarchy

A **monarchy** is a form of government headed by a single member of a royal family, usually a king, queen, or some other hereditary ruler. In earlier times, many monarchs claimed that God had granted them a divine right to rule. Typically, they governed on the basis of traditional forms of authority, sometimes accompanied by the use of force. By the beginning of the 21st century, however, monarchs held genuine governmental power in only a few nations, such as Monaco. Most monarchs now have little practical power; they serve primarily ceremonial purposes.

Oligarchy

An **oligarchy** is a form of government in which a few individuals rule. A rather old method of governing that flourished in ancient Greece and Egypt, oligarchy now often takes the form of military rule. In developing nations in Africa, Asia, and Latin America, small factions of military officers will forcibly seize power, either from legally elected regimes or from other military cliques.

Strictly speaking, the term *oligarchy* is reserved for governments that are run by a few selected individuals. However, the People's Republic of China can be classified as an oligarchy if we stretch the meaning of the term. In China, power rests in the

North Korea has a totalitarian government whose leadership attempts to control all aspects of people's lives. This billboard, a blatant example of government propaganda, portrays the country's ruthless leader as a benevolent father figure.

(Monarchies and oligarchies may also achieve this type of dominance.) *Totalitarianism* involves virtually complete government control and surveillance over all aspects of a society's social and political life. Germany during Hitler's reign, the Soviet Union in the 1930s, and North Korea today are classified as totalitarian states.

Political scientists Carl Friedrich and Zbigniew Brzezinski (1965:22) have identified the traits that are typical of totalitarian states. They include the widespread use of ideological propaganda and state control of the media and the economy.

Democracy

In a literal sense, *democracy* means government by the people. The word *democracy* originated in two Greek roots—*demos*, meaning "the populace" or "the common people," and *kratia*, meaning "rule." Of course, in large, populous nations such as the United States, government by the people is impractical at the national level. Americans cannot vote on every important issue that comes before Congress. Consequently, popular rule is generally maintained through *representative democracy*, a form of government in which certain individuals are selected to speak for the people.

The United States is commonly classified as a **representative democracy**, since the elected members of Congress and state legislatures make our laws. However, critics have questioned how *representative* our democracy really is. Do Congress and the state legislatures genuinely represent the masses? Are the people of the United States legitimately self-governing, or has our government become a forum for powerful elites? We will explore these issues in the remainder of the chapter.

Political Behavior in the United States

Citizens of the United States take for granted many aspects of their political system. They are accustomed to living in a nation with a Bill of Rights, two major political parties, voting by secret ballot, an elected president, state and local governments distinct from the national government, and so forth. Yet each society has its own ways of governing itself and making decisions. Just as U.S. residents expect Democratic and Republican candidates to compete for public office, residents of Cuba and the People's Republic of China are accustomed to one-party rule by the Communist Party. In this section, we will examine several aspects of political behavior within the United States.

Participation and Apathy

In theory, a representative democracy will function most effectively and fairly if an informed and active electorate communicates its views to government leaders. Unfortunately, that is hardly the case in the United States. Virtually all citizens are familiar with the basics of the political process, and most tend to identify to some extent with a political party. (In 2007, about 34 percent of registered voters in the United States saw themselves

hands of a large but exclusive ruling *group*, the Communist Party. In a similar vein, drawing on conflict theory, one might argue that many industrialized nations of the West should be considered oligarchies (rather than democracies), since only a powerful few—leaders of big business, government, and the military—actually rule. Later in this chapter, we will examine the "elite model" of the U.S. political system in greater detail.

Dictatorship and Totalitarianism

A *dictatorship* is a government in which one person has nearly total power to make and enforce laws. Dictators rule primarily through the use of coercion, which often includes torture and executions. Typically, they *seize* power rather than being freely elected (as in a democracy) or inheriting power (as in a monarchy). Some dictators are quite charismatic and manage to achieve a certain popularity, though their supporters' enthusiasm is almost certainly tinged with fear. Other dictators are bitterly hated by the people over whom they rule.

Frequently, dictators develop such overwhelming control over people's lives that their governments are called *totalitarian*.

as Democrats, 36 percent as independents, and 29 percent as Republicans.) However, only a small minority of citizens, often members of the higher social classes, actually participate in political organizations on a local or national level. Studies reveal that only 8 percent of Americans belong to a political club or organization. Not more than one in five has ever contacted an official of national, state, or local government about a political issue or problem (Gallup 2007a; Orum 2001).

By the 1980s, it had become clear that many people in the United States were beginning to be turned off by political parties, politicians, and big government. The most dramatic indication of this growing alienation came from voting statistics. Today, voters of all ages and races appear to be less enthusiastic than ever about elections, even presidential contests. For example, in the presidential election of 1896, almost 80 percent of eligible voters in the United States went to the polls. Yet by the 2000 election, turnout had fallen to less than 60 percent of all eligible voters. Obviously, even modestly higher voter turnout could dramatically change election outcomes, as we saw in the razor-thin margin in the 2000 presidential election (Holder 2006).

While a few nations still command high voter turnout, it is increasingly common to hear national leaders of other countries complain of voter apathy. Still, among the 140 countries that have held parliamentary elections since 1945, the United States ranks only 114th in voter turnout. No other industrial nation has recorded a lower average turnout (see Figure 17-1).

In the end, political participation makes government accountable to the voters. If participation declines, government operates with less of a sense of accountability to society. This issue is most serious for the least powerful individuals and groups in the United States. Voter turnout has been particularly low among members of racial and ethnic minorities. In post-election surveys, fewer African Americans and Hispanics than Whites report that they actually voted. Many more potential voters fail to register to vote. The poor—whose focus understandably is on survival—are traditionally underrepresented among voters as well. The low turnout found among these groups is explained at least in part by their common feeling of powerlessness. Yet these low statistics encourage political power brokers to continue to ignore the interests of the less affluent and the nation's minorities. The segment of the voting population that has shown the most voter apathy is the young: see Box 17-1 (Holder 2006).

Use Your Sociological Imagination

Were you brought up to consider political involvement an important civic duty? If so, do you take that duty seriously by informing yourself about the issues and voting?

www.mhhe.com/schaefer11

Race and Gender in Politics

Because politics is synonymous with power and authority, we should not be surprised that political strength is lacking in marginalized groups, such as women and racial and ethnic minori-

FIGURE 17-1

Voter Turnout Worldwide

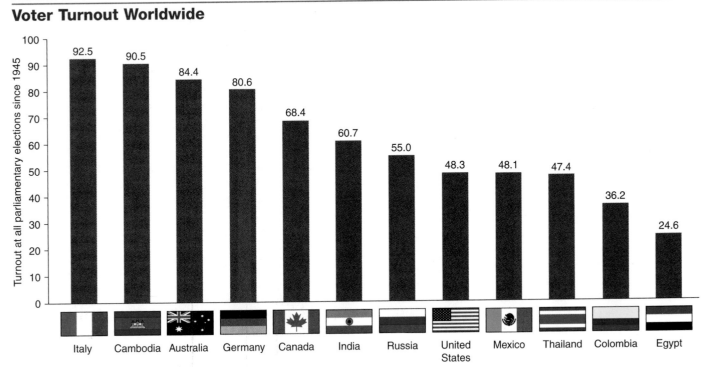

Source: International Institute for Democracy and Electoral Assistance 2005.

17-1 Why Don't More Young People Vote?

All through the 1960s, young people in the United States participated actively in a range of political issues, from pushing civil rights to protesting the Vietnam War. They were especially disturbed by the fact that young men were barred from voting but were being drafted to serve in the military and were dying for their country. In response to these concerns, the 26th Amendment to the Constitution was ratified in 1971, lowering the voting age from 21 to 18.

Now, more than 30 years later, we can consider the available research and see what happened. Frankly, what is remarkable is what did *not* happen. First, young voters (those between ages 18 and 21) have not united in any particular political sentiment. We can see in the way the young vote the same divisions of race, ethnicity, and gender that are apparent among older age groups.

Second, while the momentum for lowering the voting age came from college campuses, the majority of young voters are not students at all. Many are already part of the workforce and either live with their parents or have established their own households.

Third, and particularly troubling, is their relatively low turnout. The 2004 presidential election, held against a background of war in Iraq and an economic slump at home, did pique the interest of young voters. In that election, 51 percent of voters under age 30 turned out, compared to 42 percent in 2000. But turnout among that group was 55 percent in 1972.

What lies behind this voter apathy among the young? The popular explanation is that people—especially young people—are alienated from the political system, turned off by the shallowness and negativity of candidates and campaigns. True, studies have documented

> *While the momentum for lowering the voting age came from college campuses, the majority of young voters are not students at all.*

that young voters are susceptible to cynicism and distrust, but those qualities are not necessarily associated with voter apathy. Numerous studies show that the relationship between how people perceive the candidates and issues and their likelihood of voting is a very complex one. Young people do vote as they age. Any disaffection with the voting booth certainly is not permanent, as political scientist Martin Wattenberg, author of *Is Voting for Young People?* would agree.

Other explanations for the lower turnout among the young seem more plausible. First, the United States is virtually alone in requiring citizens to vote twice, in effect. They must first *register* to vote, often at a time when issues are not on the front burner and candidates haven't even declared. Second, while citizens in the United States tend to be more active than those in other countries in politics at the community level, young people often feel unmoved by local issues such as public school financing.

Let's Discuss

1. How often do you vote? If you do not vote, what accounts for your apathy? Are you too busy to register? Are community issues uninteresting to you?

2. Do you think voter apathy is a serious social problem? What might be done to increase voter participation in your age group and community?

Sources: Alwin 2002; Clymer 2000; A. Goldstein and Morin 2002; Higher Education Research Institute 2004; Jamieson et al. 2002; Patterson 2005; Y. Rosenberg 2004; Wattenberg 2008.

ties. Nationally, women did not get the vote until 1920. Most Chinese Americans were turned away from the polls until 1926. And African Americans were disenfranchised until 1965, when national voting rights legislation was passed. Predictably, it has taken these groups some time to develop their political power and begin to exercise it effectively.

While the rising tide of African American and Latino voters has been well publicized, less attention has been paid to Native

> Minnesota Democrat Keith Ellison created quite a stir in 2007 when he became the first person to take the Congressional oath of office on a Qur'an instead of a Bible. The newly elected member of the House of Representatives, who is Muslim, thought the Qur'an would make his oath more meaningful than a Bible. Speaker of the House Nancy Pelosi (left) responded by borrowing Thomas Jefferson's two-volume Qur'an for the occasion— a reminder that diversity is nothing new in U.S. politics.

social INEQUALITY ● ● ●

17-2 American Indians: First Here, Among the Last to Vote

The native peoples of the United States have had a long struggle to gain the right to vote. Beginning with the Constitution, they have held an ambiguous status: American Indians clearly were not citizens, but neither were they regarded as sovereign nations. After the end of the Indian–Cavalry wars in the 19th century, the federal government made an effort to assimilate surviving Native Americans. In 1887, the United States extended citizenship to those Indians who had "adopted the habits of civilized life." Though perhaps a quarter of tribal peoples qualified for citizenship in this way, very few voted. Later the government took other actions to extend citizenship to Native Americans, including those who had served in World War I, but with little success.

In 1924 Congress passed the Indian Citizenship Act, which provided for the enfranchisement of all Native Americans. However, most states with large tribal populations managed to prevent Indians from voting, either by physically barring them from the polls or by instituting literacy tests. Another means of blocking their vote was based on the legal concept of "guardianship." Most states have laws that bar people who are under court-appointed guardianship from voting. For decades, several states argued successfully that American Indians were still under legal guardianship.

> *Ironically, Native Americans are often criticized for having too much influence on politics—not through the voting booth, but through their lobbying efforts.*

Most of these overt forms of voting discrimination faded away in the 1960s. Yet today, civil rights groups are still fighting political attempts to draw the boundaries of voting districts in such a way as to minimize the impact of Indian voters. Little wonder that American Indians who have been elected to public office are the exception rather than the rule. In the entire history of the nation, only 11 Native Americans have ever been elected to Congress; one of them, from Oklahoma, is serving now. Ironically, Native Americans are often criticized for having *too much* influence on politics—not through the voting booth, but through their lobbying efforts, which are funded by casino gambling profits.

Let's Discuss

1. Why would politicians want to minimize the impact of Native American voters?
2. Are voting rights more important to groups of people, such as minority groups, than they are to individuals? Why or why not?

Sources: McCool et al. 2007; M. Nelson 2007; Wilkins 2007.

American voters. Box 17-2 considers their struggle to exercise their right to vote, and to elect members of their own ethnicity to public office.

Progress toward the inclusion of minority groups in government has been slow. As of mid-2007, only 16 out of 100 U.S. senators were women. One senator was an African American, 3 were Latinos, and 2 were Asian Americans, leaving 78 White non-Hispanic men. Among the 435 members of the U.S. House of Representatives, 314 were White non-Hispanic men. Seventy were women, 40 were African Americans (including 10 women), 23 were Latinos (including 7 Latinas), 4 were Asian Americans (including 1 woman), 1 was an Asian Indian, and 1 was an American Indian. These numbers, though low, represent a high-water mark for most of these groups.

Today, with record-high numbers of Blacks and Latinos holding elective office, many critics still decry what has been termed "fiesta politics." White power brokers tend to visit racial and ethnic minority communities only when they need electoral support, making a quick appearance on a national or ethnic holiday to get their pictures taken and then vanishing. When the election is over, they too often forget to consult the residents who supported them about community needs and concerns.

Female politicians may be enjoying more electoral success now than in the past, but there is evidence that the media cover them differently from male politicians. A content analysis of newspaper coverage of recent gubernatorial races showed that reporters wrote more often about a female candidate's personal life, appearance, or personality than a male candidate's, and less often about her political positions and voting record. Furthermore, when political issues were raised in newspaper articles, reporters were more likely to illustrate them with statements made by male candidates than by female candidates (Devitt 1999).

Figure 17-2 (opposite) shows the representation of women in selected national legislatures. While the proportion of women in national legislatures has increased in the United States and many other nations, women still do not account for half the members of the national legislature in any country. The African Republic of Rwanda ranks the highest, with 48.8 percent of its legislative seats held by women. Overall, the United States ranked 84th among 189 nations in the proportion of women serving as national legislators in 2007 (Paxton et al. 2006).

To remedy this situation, many countries have adopted quotas for female representatives. In some, the government sets aside a certain percentage of seats for women, usually from 10 to 30 percent. In others, political parties have decided that 20 to 40 percent of their candidates should be women. Thirty-two countries now have some kind of female quota system (Vasagar 2005).

{ p.304

Models of Power Structure in the United States

Who really holds power in the United States? Do "we the people" genuinely run the country through our elected representatives? Or is it true that behind the scenes, a small elite controls both the government and the economic system? It is difficult to determine the location of power in a society as complex as the United States. In exploring this critical question, social scientists have developed two basic views of our nation's power structure: the power elite and the pluralist models.

Power Elite Models

Karl Marx believed that 19th-century representative democracy was essentially a sham. He argued that industrial societies were dominated by relatively small numbers of people who owned factories and controlled natural resources. In Marx's view, government officials and military leaders were essentially servants of this capitalist class and followed their wishes. Therefore, any key decisions made by politicians inevitably reflected the interests of the dominant bourgeoisie. Like others who hold an *elite model* of power relations, Marx believed that society is ruled by a small group of individuals who share a common set of political and economic interests.

Mills's Model Sociologist C. Wright Mills, referred to earlier in this chapter, took this model a step further in his pioneering work *The Power Elite* ([1956] 2000b). Mills described a small group of military, industrial, and government leaders who controlled the fate of the United States—the *power elite.* Power rested in the hands of a few, both inside and outside government.

A pyramid illustrates the power structure of the United States in Mills's model (see Figure 17-3a, page 420). At the top are the corporate rich, leaders of the executive branch of government, and heads of the military (whom Mills called the "warlords"). Directly below are local opinion leaders, members of the legislative branch of government, and leaders of special-interest groups. Mills contended that these individuals and groups would basically follow the wishes of the dominant power elite. At the bottom of the pyramid are the unorganized, exploited masses.

The power elite model is, in many respects, similar to the work of Karl Marx. The most striking difference is that Mills believed that the economically powerful coordinate their maneuvers with the military and political establishments to serve their common interests. Yet, reminiscent of Marx, Mills argued that the corporate rich were perhaps the most powerful element of the power elite (first among "equals"). And the powerless masses at the bottom of Mills's power elite model certainly bring to mind Marx's portrait of the oppressed workers of the world, who have "nothing to lose but their chains."

A fundamental element in Mills's thesis is that the power elite not only includes relatively few members but also operates as a self-conscious, cohesive unit. Although not necessarily diabolical

FIGURE 17–2

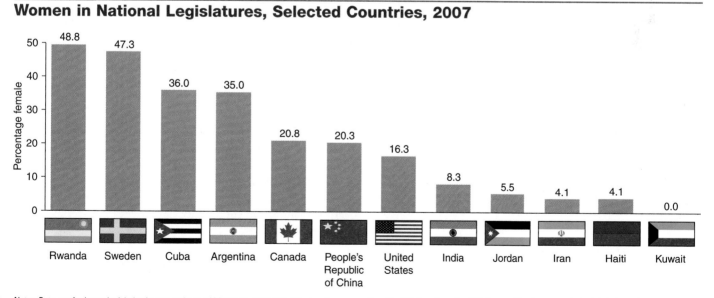

Women in National Legislatures, Selected Countries, 2007

Notes: Data are for lower legislative houses only, as of March 31, 2007; data on upper houses, such as the U.S. Senate or the U.K. House of Lords, are not included. In 2005, the all-male Kuwaiti Parliament granted women the right to vote and serve in elected offices, which could allow women to run for office as soon as 2007.
Source: Inter-Parliamentary Union 2007.

Power Elite Models

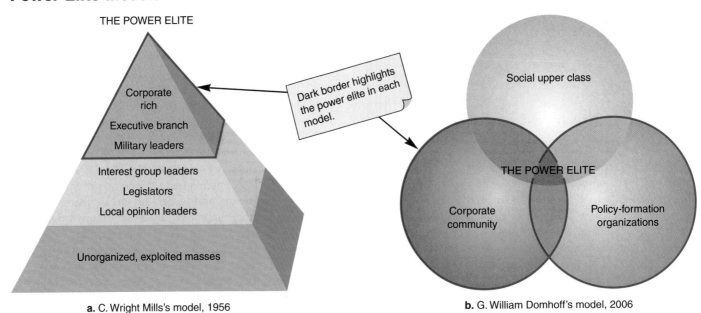

THE POWER ELITE

Corporate rich

Executive branch

Military leaders

Interest group leaders

Legislators

Local opinion leaders

Unorganized, exploited masses

Dark border highlights the power elite in each model.

Social upper class

THE POWER ELITE

Corporate community

Policy-formation organizations

a. C. Wright Mills's model, 1956

b. G. William Domhoff's model, 2006

Source: Left, author based on C. W. Mills [1956] 2000b; right, Domhoff 2006:105.

or ruthless, the elite comprises similar types of people who interact regularly with one another and have essentially the same political and economic interests. Mills's power elite is not a conspiracy, but rather a community of interest and sentiment among a small number of influential people (A. Hacker 1964).

Admittedly, Mills failed to clarify when the elite opposes protests and when it tolerates them; he also failed to provide detailed case studies that would substantiate the interrelationships among members of the power elite. Nevertheless, his challenging theories forced scholars to look more critically at the democratic political system of the United States.

In commenting on the scandals that have rocked major corporations such as Enron and Arthur Andersen over the last decade, observers have noted that members of the business elite *are* closely interrelated. In a study of the members of the boards of directors of Fortune 1,000 corporations, researchers found that each director can reach *every* other board of directors in just 3.7 steps. That is, by consulting acquaintances of acquaintances, each director can quickly reach someone who sits on each of the other 999 boards. Furthermore, the face-to-face contact directors regularly have in their board meetings makes them a highly cohesive elite. Finally, the corporate elite is not only wealthy, powerful, and cohesive; it is also overwhelmingly White and male (G. Davis 2003, 2004; Kentor and Jang 2004; Mizruchi 1996; Schaefer 2008b; Strauss 2002).

Domhoff's Model Over the last three decades, sociologist G. William Domhoff (2006) has agreed with Mills that a powerful elite runs the United States. He finds that it is still largely White,

male, and upper class, as he wrote in his book with Richard L. Zweigenhaft (2006). But Domhoff stresses the role played both by elites of the corporate community and by the leaders of policy-formation organizations, such as chambers of commerce and labor unions. Many of the people in both groups are also members of the social upper class.

While these groups overlap, as Figure 17-3b shows, they do not necessarily agree on specific policies. Domhoff notes that in the electoral arena, two different coalitions have exercised influence. A *corporate-conservative coalition* has played a large role in both political parties, generating support for particular candidates through direct-mail appeals. A *liberal-labor coalition* is based in unions, local environmental organizations, a segment of the minority group community, liberal churches, and the university and arts communities (Zweigenhaft and Domhoff 2006).

Pluralist Model

Several social scientists insist that power in the United States is shared more widely than the elite models indicate. In their view, a pluralist model more accurately describes the nation's political system. According to the ***pluralist model,*** many competing groups within the community have access to government, so that no single group is dominant.

The pluralist model suggests that a variety of groups play a significant role in decision making. Typically, pluralists make use of intensive case studies or community studies based on observation research. One of the most famous—an investigation of decision making in New Haven, Connecticut—was reported by Robert Dahl (1961). Dahl found that although the number of people involved in any important decision was rather small, community power was nonetheless diffuse. Few political actors exercised decision-making power on all issues. One individual or group might be influential in a battle over urban renewal, but have little impact on educational policy.

The pluralist model, however, has not escaped serious questioning. Domhoff (1978, 2006) reexamined Dahl's study of decision making in New Haven and argued that Dahl and other pluralists had failed to trace how local elites who were prominent in decision making belonged to a larger national ruling class. In addition, studies of community power, such as Dahl's work in New Haven, can examine decision making only on issues that become part of the political agenda. They fail to address the potential power of elites to keep certain matters entirely out of the realm of government debate.

Dianne Pinderhughes (1987) has criticized the pluralist model for failing to account for the exclusion of African Americans from the political process. Drawing on her studies of Chicago politics, Pinderhughes points out that the residential and occupational segregation of Blacks and their long political disenfranchisement violates the logic of pluralism—which would hold that such a substantial minority should always have been influential in community decision making. This critique applies to many cities across the United States, where other large racial and ethnic minorities, among them Asian Americans, Puerto Ricans, and Mexican Americans, are relatively powerless.

Historically, pluralists have stressed ways in which large numbers of people can participate in or influence governmental decision making. New communications technologies like the Internet are increasing the opportunity to be heard, not just in countries such as the United States but in developing countries the world over. One common point of the elite and pluralist perspectives stands out, however: in the political system of the United States, power is unequally distributed. All citizens may be equal in theory, yet those who are high in the nation's power structure are "more equal." New communications technology may or may not change that distribution of power.

Perhaps the ultimate test of power, no matter what a nation's power structure, is the decision to go to war. Because the rank and file of any army is generally drawn from the lower classes—the least powerful groups in society—such a decision has life-and-death consequences for people far removed from the center of power. In the long run, if the general population is not convinced that war is necessary, military action is unlikely to succeed. Thus, war is a risky way in which to address conflict between nations. In the following section we will contrast war and peace as ways of addressing societal conflict, and more recently, the threat of terrorism.

War and Peace

Conflict is a central aspect of social relations. Too often it becomes ongoing and violent, engulfing innocent bystanders as well as intentional participants. Sociologists Theodore Caplow and Louis Hicks (2002:3) have defined **war** as conflict between organizations that possess trained combat forces equipped with

Pluralism can be seen in action in the activity of lobbying groups attempting to influence public policy. The highly publicized battle over stem-cell research is one example; it has pitted conservative religious groups against health advocacy groups, dividing political leaders in the process. Though legislation to support the controversial research technique had the backing of several prominent Republican lawmakers, including Senator Orrin Hatch (R-Utah), shown here with actor and activist Michael J. Fox, it fell victim to a presidential veto in 2006.

On Earth Day 2004, ecologically aware students at the University of Wisconsin, Madison, hopped on their bicycles and joined local residents at the Hummer dealership. Protesters were hoping to disrupt sales of the huge gas-guzzling vehicles by blocking traffic. When public interest groups seek to exert their power through such mass protests, they are demonstrating a belief in the pluralist model of the United States' power structure.

deadly weapons. This meaning is broader than the legal definition, which typically requires a formal declaration of hostilities.

War

Sociologists approach war in three different ways. Those who take a global view study how and why two or more nations become engaged in military conflict. Those who take a nation-state view stress the interaction of internal political, socioeconomic, and cultural forces. And those who take a micro view focus on the social impact of war on individuals and the groups they belong to (Kiser 1992).

The internal decision-making process that leads to war has been much studied. During the Vietnam War, Presidents Johnson and Nixon both misled Congress, painting a falsely optimistic picture of the likely outcome. Based on their intentional distortions, Congress appropriated the military funds the two administrations requested. But in 1971 the *New York Times* published a set of classified documents now known as "The Pentagon Papers," which revealed the real prospects for the war. Two years later—over Nixon's veto—Congress passed the War Powers Act, which requires the president to notify Congress of the reasons for committing combat troops to a hostile situation (Patterson 2003).

Though the decision to go to war is made by government leaders, public opinion plays a significant role in its execution. By 1971, the number of U.S. soldiers killed in Vietnam had surpassed 50,000, and antiwar sentiment was strong. Surveys done at that time showed the public was split roughly equally on the question of whether war was an appropriate way to settle differences between nations (see Figure 17-4). This division in public opinion continued until the United States became involved in the Gulf War following Iraq's invasion of Kuwait in 1990. Since then, U.S. sentiment has been more supportive of war as a means of resolving disputes.

A major change in the composition of the U.S. military is the growing presence of women. Over 202,000 women, or about 15 percent of U.S. military forces, are now in uniform, serving not just as support personnel but as an integral part of combat units. The first casualty of the war in Iraq, in fact, was Private First Class Lori Piestewa, a member of the Hopi tribe and a descendant of Mexican settlers in the Southwest (Department of Defense 2006).

From a micro point of view, war can bring out the worst as well as the best in people. In 2004, graphic images of the abuse of Iraqi prisoners by U.S. soldiers at Iraq's Abu Ghraib prison shocked the world. For social scientists, the deterioration of the guards' behavior brought to mind Philip Zimbardo's mock prison experiment, done in 1971. Though the results of the experiment, highlighted in Chapter 5, have been applied primarily to civilian correctional facilities, Zimbardo's study was actually funded by the Office of Naval Research. In July 2004, the U.S. military began using a documentary film about the experiment to train military interrogators to avoid mistreatment of prisoners (Zarembo 2004; Zimbardo 2004).

Peace

Sociologists have considered *peace* both as the absence of war and as a proactive effort to develop cooperative relations among nations. While we will focus here on international relations, we should note that in the 1990s, 90 percent of the world's armed conflicts occurred *within* rather than between states. Often, outside powers became involved in these internal conflicts, either as supporters of particular factions or in an attempt to broker a peace accord. In at least 28 countries where such conflicts occurred—none of which would be considered core nations in world systems analysis—at least 10,000 people died (Kriesberg 1992; Dan Smith 1999).

Sociologists and other social scientists who draw on sociological theory and research have tried to identify conditions that deter war. One of their findings is that international trade may act as a deterrent to armed conflict. As countries exchange goods, people, and then cultures, they become more integrated and less likely to threaten each other's security. Viewed from this perspective, not just trade but immigration and foreign exchange programs have a beneficial effect on international relations.

FIGURE 17–4

U.S. Public Opinion on the Necessity of War, 1971–2004

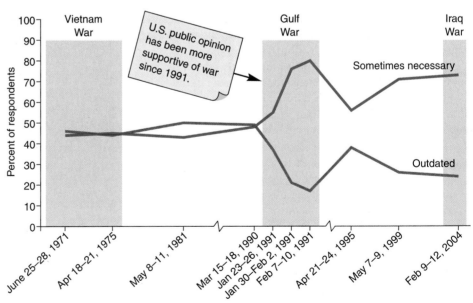

Note: Respondents replied to the following question: "Some people feel that war is an outmoded way of settling differences between nations. Others feel that wars are sometimes necessary to settle differences. With which point of view do you agree?"
Source: Arora 2004.

Another means of fostering peace is the activity of international charities and activist groups called nongovernmental organizations (NGOs). The Red Cross and Red Crescent, Doctors Without Borders, and Amnesty International donate their services wherever they are needed, without regard to nationality. In the last decade or more, these global organizations have been expanding in number, size, and scope. By sharing news of local conditions and clarifying local issues, they often prevent conflicts from escalating into violence and war. Some NGOs have initiated cease-fires, reached settlements, and even ended warfare between former adversaries.

Finally, many analysts stress that nations cannot maintain their security by threatening violence. Peace, they contend, can best be maintained by developing strong mutual security agreements between potential adversaries (Etzioni 1965; Shostak 2002).

In recent years, the United States has begun to recognize that its security can be threatened not just by nation-states, but by political groups that operate outside the bounds of legitimate authority. Indeed, terrorism is now considered the foremost threat to U.S. security—one the U.S. military is unaccustomed to fighting.

A representative of the International Red Crescent Society delivers an aid parcel in the southern Iraqi town of Safwan. The Red Crescent provides emergency aid to victims of war and disaster in Muslim communities. Such nongovernmental organizations (NGOs) help to bind countries together, promoting peaceful relations.

Use Your Sociological Imagination

Do you hear much discussion of how to promote worldwide peace, or do the conversations you hear focus more on ending a particular conflict?

www.mhhe.com/schaefer11

Terrorism

Acts of terror, whether perpetrated by a few or by many people, can be a powerful political force. Formally defined, *terrorism* is the use or threat of violence against random or symbolic targets in pursuit of political aims. For terrorists, the end justifies the means. They believe the status quo is oppressive, and desperate measures are essential to end the suffering of the deprived. Convinced that working through the formal political process will not effect the desired political change, terrorists insist that illegal actions—often directed against innocent people—are needed. Ultimately, they hope to intimidate society and thereby bring about a new political order.

An essential aspect of contemporary terrorism involves use of the media. Terrorists may wish to keep secret their individual identities, but they want their political messages and goals to receive as much publicity as possible. Drawing on Erving Goffman's dramaturgical approach, sociologist Alfred McClung Lee has likened terrorism to the theater, where certain scenes are played out in predictable fashion. Whether through calls to the media, anonymous manifestos, or other means, terrorists typically admit responsibility for and defend their violent acts.

Figure 17-5 (page 424) shows the global reach of terrorism. Since September 11, 2001, governments worldwide have renewed their efforts to fight terrorism. Though the public generally regards increased surveillance and social control as a necessary evil, these measures have nonetheless raised governance issues. For example, some citizens in the United States and elsewhere have questioned whether measures such as the USA Patriot Act of 2001 threaten civil liberties. Citizens also complain about the heightened anxiety created by the vague alerts issued by the federal government from time to time. Worldwide, immigration and the processing of refugees have slowed to a crawl, separating families and preventing employers from filling job openings. As these efforts to combat political violence illustrate, the term *terrorism* is an apt one (R. Howard and Sawyer 2003; Lee 1983; R. Miller 1988).

Political Activism on the Internet

By any measure, the Internet has emerged as a force to be reckoned with in politics. While television and newspapers remain the primary sources of political news, use of the Internet for news gathering more than doubled between the 2002 and 2006

The Global Reach of Terrorism

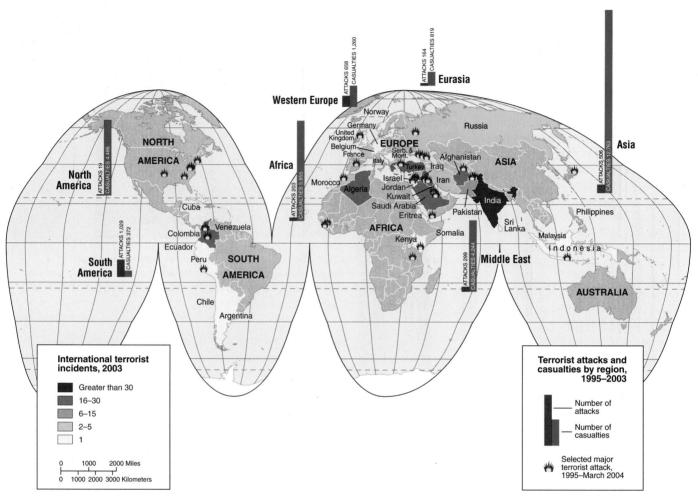

International terrorist incidents, 2003

- Greater than 30
- 16–30
- 6–15
- 2–5
- 1

0   1000   2000 Miles

0 1000 2000 3000 Kilometers

Terrorist attacks and casualties by region, 1995–2003

- Number of attacks
- Number of casualties
- Selected major terrorist attack, 1995–March 2004

Source: National Geographic 2005:17.

elections. Increasingly, surfing the net is the way people "watch" television news shows and "read" the daily paper. The majority of Internet users now look for information about candidates' positions online. During the 2006 election, 41 percent of them went online to check the accuracy of candidates' claims. Many people also visit video-sharing sites like YouTube, which provide up-to-the-minute clips of candidates' appearances that may or may not be flattering.

Not only is the Internet affecting the way people get their news; it is changing the way they think about politics. In one survey, 43 percent of Internet users said the information they received online affected their vote. Modern technology may not eliminate voter apathy, but it is one more way to motivate people to get involved in politics (Rainie and Horrigan 2007).

Is reliance on the Internet a healthy development? A national survey taken in 2007 shows that the general public is divided on this issue. Forty-five percent of respondents said that the "citizen journalism" acquired through Internet Web sites and cell phone cameras is more reliable than traditional journalism. Only 48 percent saw those outlets as less reliable than traditional news organizations (Gallup 2007c).

On the Internet, political activity is not limited to traditional party politics, and certainly not to domestic politics. In far-flung places including China, Mexico, Indonesia, Kosovo, and Malaysia, citizens are making themselves heard through *cyberactivism* or Net Activism—the use of the Internet for political purposes. In China, 10,000 members of the fast-growing Falun Gong religious sect surprised government officials with a mass rally or-

{ The Web site for Greenpeace, an international organization of environmental activists, encourages interested citizens to get involved in public affairs. }

ganized on the web. In Kosovo, the staff of *Koha Ditore*, a dissident newspaper, took to the Web after Serbian soldiers closed their office. And in Mexico, the revolutionary Zapatista movement gained support from an online campaign for self-rule in the state of Chiapas.

As these incidents illustrate, organizers find the Web especially useful in circumventing the restrictive controls of authoritarian regimes. In fact, groups branded as terrorists in a variety of states have used the Web to their advantage. Web sites can be established outside a country's borders, beyond the control of government officials yet still accessible to the country's citizens. What is more, government officials who would like to clamp down on such activities are constrained by their desire to reap the commercial benefits of the Web. For example, Chinese offi-

cials have decided to advance information technology despite the challenges it poses to government control. The technology is simply too important to China's economic modernization for the government to suppress it. From a conflict perspective, then, the Internet seems to have the potential to level the playing field for opposition groups—or at least to minimize the ruling party's clout (Crossette 1999; Hick and McNutt 2002; Piller 2001).

Also growing in importance are borderless organizations that unite people of like mind—from peace activists to terrorists—around the world. These are very tightly knit communities, notes Professor Juan Enriquez of Harvard University. Labor groups and environmental organizations such as Greenpeace have become particularly adept at using e-mail to mobilize activists quickly, wherever they are needed. The result: a completely new kind of power structure, compared to the more familiar face-to-face approach of Washington lobbyists. "The new people with power are those with credibility and an e-mail list," says political consultant Jennifer Laszlo. "You have no idea who they are, where they are, what color they are" (Engardio 1999:145).

Use Your Sociological Imagination

Imagine a future in which everyone in the United States has access to the Internet, and the Internet is the foremost political medium. How would government in that society differ from government today?

social Policy
and Politics

Campaign Financing

The Issue

November 23, 1999
Question: How do you reconcile your position on campaign finance reform with all the money you are spending on television
advertisements?
Hillary Rodham Clinton: I believe we ought to have, you know,
more public financing of campaigns. We don't have it yet, does
that mean I shouldn't raise money?
(Washington Transcript Service 1999:17).

In her successful bid for election to the U.S. Senate, Hillary Rodham Clinton was not the first politician to criticize campaign financing methods while at the same time raising millions of
dollars to pay her expenses. Over the last few decades, many seasoned representatives have left office bemoaning the amount of
time they had to spend raising money. Nor, as we shall see, are
attempts to regulate campaign financing new.

The Setting

Regulation of campaign contributions has a long history, beginning with efforts to bar the requirement that government employees contribute to their bosses' campaign funds. More
recently, the focus on both the state and national levels has been
on remedying the shortcomings of the Federal Campaign Act of
1974, which placed restrictions on so-called *hard money,* or donations made to specific candidates for national office. Hard
money is now limited to $10,000 per organization or $2,000 per
individual donor per election cycle (the primary and election
being separate cycles). These limits were intended to keep national candidates or elected officials from being "bought" by the
wealthy or by powerful special-interest groups.

But soon after passage of the act, contributors and potential
recipients—that is, politicians—found loopholes in the new law.
In 2002, Congress passed the Bipartisan Campaign Reform Act
(BCRA) to address some of those shortcomings. For the first
time, limitations were placed on contributions of *soft money*—
donations to the major political parties, leadership committees,
and political action committees by corporations and special-
interest groups. Now, no soft money is permitted in federal elections, and its use in state and local elections is limited.

Under the BCRA, major political parties are still allowed to
spend soft money freely on *independent expenditures,* or purchases made on behalf of a political position rather than an individual candidate. This *issue advocacy money,* as it has been
called, has become an important way of supporting a particular
candidate while escaping contribution limits. To support a pro-
environment, or "green," candidate, for example, donors would

purchase television ads expressing concern about the environment and pollution.

Soon after the BCRA was passed, political pundits began to
speculate on how politicians might still amass huge campaign
war chests, regardless of the new restrictions. Some speculated
that the law would encourage political parties and political interest groups to rely more on direct mail, phone banks, voter
mobilization drives, and other unregulated activities. Few
thought that the massive amounts that had once been raised as
soft money would disappear from politics. Indeed, in 2004, the
Democratic and Republican parties each raised 10 times what
they did in 1992. Undoubtedly, new ways will be found to channel such huge amounts of money in a way that conforms to the
BCRA. And predictably, these new innovations in spending will
be followed by fresh cries for reform (Campaign Legal Center
2004).

Sociological Insights

Functionalists would say that political contributions keep the
public involved in the democratic process and connected to the
candidates. Issue advocacy money also offers voters a way to
express their views on issues directly, rather than through the
candidates. But conflict theorists would counter that since
money brings influence, this use of material wealth allows
donors to influence government policymakers in ways that tend
to preserve their own wealth. In increasing numbers of cases,
candidates like the multimillionaires Ross Perot and Steve
Forbes have used their own private fortunes to finance their
campaigns—an approach that allows them to sidestep public
disclosure requirements.

Interactionists would point out the symbolic significance
of the public perception that big money drives elections in
the United States. Accurate or not, this impression encourages voter apathy, which is reflected in low turnout at the polls.
What good does participating in politics do, voters may wonder,
when special interests can spend millions to counteract their
efforts?

Policy Initiatives

Surveys have regularly shown that the majority of U.S. voters
want campaign finance reform, but are unsure how to achieve it.
One proposal that has been advanced at the state level is to require that the names of donors be made public through posting
on the Internet. Another is to place restrictions on how much
money anyone can give to any organization for political purposes. While these reform proposals have gained much public
sympathy, however, the courts have generally ruled that Internet

posting may invade donors' privacy, discouraging them from making campaign contributions. Financial limits may also restrict people's freedom to participate in the political process (McDermott 1999; Simon 1999).

On the national level, traditional reform groups—Common Cause, the League of Women Voters, and Ralph Nader's organization Public Citizen—continue to call for tighter limits on contributions by both individuals and organizations. But other interest groups, including the American Civil Liberties Union and the Cato Institute, claim that limiting anyone's involvement in the political process is unfair. The BCRA addresses citizens' complaints that politicians are routinely "bought" by wealthy special interests. Yet it also raises the specter of limits on citizens' freedom to support the candidates of their choice. With voter apathy on the rise, such limits may be too high a price to pay for campaign finance reform.

"I PREFER NOT TO THINK OF MYSELF AS A FORMER CONGRESSMAN, BUT RATHER AS A FUTURE LOBBYIST."

The high cost of financing political campaigns tends to create a too-cozy relationship between elected officials and lobbyists for special-interest groups.

Let's Discuss

1. Did you vote in the most recent election? Does your vote count, or do special-interest groups wield more power than voters like you?

2. Do you work for or contribute to political candidates? What about groups that promote special issues, like school prayer, gun control, and free trade? Which is more important to you, the candidate or the issue?

3. Would strict across-the-board spending limits on all candidates for public office help to make the political process more democratic? What about limits on political contributions of all kinds?

GettingINVOLVED

To get involved in the debate over campaign financing, visit this text's Online Learning Center, which offers links to relevant Web sites. Check out the Social Policy section of the Online Learning Center as well; it provides survey data on U.S. public opinion regarding this issue.

www.mhhe.com/schaefer11

Summary

Every society must have a *political system* in order to allocate valued resources. This chapter examined the sources of *power* and *authority* in such systems; the four major types of government; political behavior, including voter apathy and women's representation in government; two basic models of power structure in the United States; *war* and *peace*; political activism on the Internet; and campaign finance reform.

1. There are three basic sources of *power* within any political system: *force, influence,* and *authority.*

2. Max Weber identified three ideal types of authority: *traditional, rational-legal,* and *charismatic.*

3. There are four basic types of government: *monarchy, oligarchy, dictatorship,* and *democracy.*

4. Political participation makes government accountable to its citizens, but voters display a great deal of apathy both in the United States and in other countries.

5. Women are still underrepresented in politics, but are becoming more successful at winning election to public office.

6. Advocates of the *elite model* of the U.S. power structure see the nation as being ruled by a small group of individuals who share common political and economic interests (a *power elite*), whereas advocates of a *pluralist model* believe that power is shared more widely among conflicting groups.

7. *War* may be defined as conflict between organizations that possess trained combat forces equipped with deadly weapons—a definition that includes conflict with terrorist organizations.

8. Around the world, the Internet has become a potent political arena, one that dissident groups can use to oppose the power of authoritarian regimes.

9. Despite legislative efforts to reform campaign financing methods, wealthy donors and special-interest groups still wield enormous power in U.S. government through their contributions to candidates, political parties, and issue advocacy.

Critical Thinking Questions

1. In many places in the world, the United States is considered a model political system. Drawing on material presented in earlier chapters of this textbook, discuss the values and beliefs on which this political system is founded. Have those values and beliefs changed over time? Has the system itself changed?

2. Who really holds power in the college or university you attend? Describe the distribution of power at your school, drawing on the elite and pluralist models where relevant.

3. Imagine that you have joined your state representative's legislative staff as a summer intern. She has assigned you to a committee that is working on solutions to the problem of school violence. How could you use what you have learned about sociology to conceptualize the problem? What type of research would you suggest the committee undertake? What legislative solutions might you recommend?

Key Terms

Authority Institutionalized power that is recognized by the people over whom it is exercised. (page 412)

Charismatic authority Power made legitimate by a leader's exceptional personal or emotional appeal to his or her followers. (413)

Democracy In a literal sense, government by the people. (415)

Dictatorship A government in which one person has nearly total power to make and enforce laws. (415)

Elite model A view of society as being ruled by a small group of individuals who share a common set of political and economic interests. (419)

Force The actual or threatened use of coercion to impose one's will on others. (412)

Influence The exercise of power through a process of persuasion. (412)

Monarchy A form of government headed by a single member of a royal family, usually a king, queen, or some other hereditary ruler. (414)

Oligarchy A form of government in which a few individuals rule. (414)

Peace The absence of war, or more broadly, a proactive effort to develop cooperative relations among nations. (422)

Pluralist model A view of society in which many competing groups within the community have access to government, so that no single group is dominant. (420)

Political system The social institution that is founded on a recognized set of procedures for implementing and achieving society's goals. (412)

Politics In Harold Lasswell's words, "who gets what, when, and how." (412)

Power The ability to exercise one's will over others. (412)

Power elite A small group of military, industrial, and government leaders who control the fate of the United States. (419)

Rational-legal authority Power made legitimate by law. (413)

Representative democracy A form of government in which certain individuals are selected to speak for the people. (415)

Terrorism The use or threat of violence against random or symbolic targets in pursuit of political aims. (423)

Totalitarianism Virtually complete government control and surveillance over all aspects of a society's social and political life. (415)

Traditional authority Legitimate power conferred by custom and accepted practice. (413)

War Conflict between organizations that possess trained combat forces equipped with deadly weapons. (421)

Self-Quiz

Read each question carefully and then select the best answer.

1. Which one of the following is a cultural universal?

    a. religion
    b. the political system
    c. family
    d. all of the above

2. A king or queen is accepted as ruler of a nation simply by virtue of inheriting the crown. This is an example of

    a. totalitarianism.
    b. charismatic authority.
    c. traditional authority.
    d. rational-legal authority.

3. Totalitarian states typically control which of the following institutions?

    a. family
    b. economy
    c. politics
    d. all of the above

4. G. William Domhoff's model is an example of

    a. an elite theory of power.
    b. a pluralist theory of power.
    c. a functionalist theory of power.
    d. an interactionist theory of power.

5. Almost _____ percent of eligible voters in the United States went to the polls in the presidential election of 1896, as compared to less than _____ percent in the 2000 election.

    a. 75; 25
    b. 80; 60
    c. 15; 10
    d. 73; 70

6. Political scientist Harold Lasswell defined *politics* as

    a. the struggle for power and authority.
    b. the allocation of valued resources.
    c. who gets what, when, and how.
    d. a cultural universal.

7. What are the three basic sources of power within any political system?

    a. force, influence, and authority
    b. force, influence, and democracy
    c. force, legitimacy, and charisma
    d. influence, charisma, and bureaucracy

8. Which of the following is *not* part of the classification system of authority developed by Max Weber?

    a. traditional authority
    b. pluralist authority
    c. legal-rational authority
    d. charismatic authority

9. According to C. Wright Mills, power rests in the hands of the

    a. people.
    b. representative democracy.
    c. aristocracy.
    d. power elite.

10. The use or threat of violence against random or symbolic targets in pursuit of political aims is referred to as

    a. politics.
    b. power.
    c. authority.
    d. terrorism.

430

11. _____ is the actual or threatened use of coercion to impose one's will on others.

12. In most of today's _____, kings and queens have little practical power.

13. The elite model of political power implies that the U.S. has a(n) _____ as its form of government.

14. As of mid-2007, only _____ out of 100 United States senators were women.

15. Sexism has been the most serious barrier to women interested in holding public office. To remedy this situation, many countries have adopted _____ for female representatives.

16. _____ is the exercise of power through a process of persuasion.

17. Joan of Arc, Gandhi, Malcolm X, Adolf Hitler, and Martin Luther King, Jr., all possessed _____ authority.

18. _____ involves virtually complete government control and surveillance over all aspects of a society's social and political life.

19. The United States is commonly classified as a(n) _____ _____, because the elected members of Congress and state legislatures make our laws.

20. Advocates of the _____ model suggest that competing groups within the community have access to government, so that no single group is dominant.

Answers:
1 (d); 2 (c); 3 (d); 4 (a); 5 (b); 6 (c); 7 (a); 8 (b); 9 (d); 10 (d); 11 Force; 12 monarchies; 13 oligarchy; 14 16; 15 quotas; 16 Influence; 17 charismatic; 18 Totalitarianism; 19 representative democracy; 20 pluralist

Online Learning Center

1. Visit the student center in the Online Learning Center at **www.mhhe.com/schaefer11** and link to Use Your Sociological Imagination. You will be asked to consider some of the personal implications of this chapter's material by discussing your attitudes toward political involvement as a civic duty.

2. Monarchy is a form of government that has changed a great deal over the past few centuries. Visit the Web site of the British Monarchy (**www.royal.gov.uk**) to see how one famous monarchy has changed over time.

3. Exploring the government's regulations and recommendations for travel to different countries can tell you a lot about the political relationship between the United States and other nations. To take a look at travel guidelines issued by the United States government, visit the U.S. Department of State Web site at **travel.state.gov /travel/travel_1744.html.** Click on Tips for Traveling Abroad for links to country-specific information.

*Note: Although all the URLs listed were current as of the printing of this book, these sites often change. Please check our Web site **(www.mhhe.com/schaefer11)** for updates, hyperlinks, and exercises related to these sites.*

Reel Society Video Clips

Reel Society video clips, which appear on this book's Web site, can be used to spark discussion about the following topic from this chapter:

• Power and Authority

EXCLUSIVE BOOK EXCERPT
AL-QAEDA'S PLOT TO ATTACK THE NYC SUBWAY
By Ron Suskind

Why the world's biggest democracy is the next great economic superpower—and what it means for America

INDIA INC.

www.time.com AOL Keyword: TIME

This 2006 cover from *Time* magazine salutes the rapid growth of information technology in India. More than ever before, the world marketplace is in flux, and the repercussions of economic change are being felt around the globe.

18 The Economy and Work

Technology, Jobs and Your Future

THE END OF WORK

The Decline of the Global Labor Force and the Dawn of the Post-Market Era

JEREMY RIFKIN

FOREWORD BY ROBERT L. HEILBRONER

"Thorough, thought-provoking and as radical as reality itself." *Newsday*

"Percy Barnevik is the chief executive officer of Asea Brown Boveri, a 29-billion-dollar-a-year Swiss-Swedish builder of electric generators and transportation systems, and one of the largest engineering firms in the world. Like other global companies, ABB has recently re-engineered its operations, cutting nearly 50,000 workers from the payroll, while increasing turnover 60 percent in the same time period. Barnevik asks, "Where will all these [unemployed] people go?" He predicts that the proportion of Europe's labor force employed in manufacturing and business services will decline from 35 percent today to 25 percent in ten years from now, with a further decline to 15 percent twenty years down the road. Barnevik is deeply pessimistic about Europe's future: "If anybody tells me, wait two or three years and there will be a hell of a demand for labor, I say, tell me where? What jobs? In what cities? Which companies? When I add it all together, I find a clear risk that the 10% unemployed or underemployed today could easily become 20 to 25%." . . .

For some, particularly the scientists, engineers, and employers, a world without work will signal the beginning of a new era in history in which human beings are liberated, at long last, from a life of back-breaking toil and mindless repetitive tasks. For others, the workerless society conjures up the notion of a grim future of mass unemployment and global destitution, punctuated by increasing social unrest and upheaval. On one point virtually all of the contending parties agree. We are, indeed, entering into a new period in history—one in which machines increasingly replace human beings in the process of making and moving goods and providing services. . . .

> *For some, particularly the scientists, engineers, and employers, a world without work will signal the beginning of a new era in history in which human beings are liberated, at long last, from a life of back-breaking toil and mindless repetitive tasks.*

Most workers feel completely unprepared to cope with the enormity of the transition taking place. The rash of current technological breakthroughs and economic restructuring initiatives seem to have descended on us with little warning. Suddenly, all over the world, men and women are asking if there is a role for them in the new future unfolding across the global economy. Workers with years of education, skills, and experience face the very real prospect of being made redundant by the new forces of automation and information. What just a few short years ago was a rather esoteric debate among intellectuals and a small number of social writers around the role of technology in society is now the topic of heated conversation among millions of working people. They wonder if they will be the next to be replaced by the new thinking machines. . . .

The new high-technology revolution could mean fewer hours of work and greater benefits for millions. For the first time in modern history, large numbers of human beings could be liberated from long hours of labor in the formal marketplace, to be free to pursue leisure-time activities. The same technological forces could, however, as easily lead to growing unemployment and a global depression."

(Rifkin 1995a:11–13) Additional information about this excerpt can be found on the Online Learning Center at www.mhhe.com/schaefer11.

In his book *The End of Work,* social activist Jeremy Rifkin imagines what the economy will look like after automation and high technology have rendered human labor more and more obsolete. Economic forces have a huge impact on our lives—from questions as basic as whether we can put food on the table to more soul-searching concerns, such as "How can I be more productive?" Rifkin's view is that we must be prepared to deal with the inevitable dysfunctions and dislocations that accompany a major transformation of the global economic system.

The term *economic system* refers to the social institution through which goods and services are produced, distributed, and consumed. As with social institutions such as the family, religion, and government, the economic system shapes other aspects of the social order and is in turn influenced by them. Throughout this textbook, you have been reminded of the economy's impact on social behavior—for example, on individual and group behavior in factories and offices. You have {p.13 studied the work of Karl Marx and Friedrich Engels,

who emphasized that a society's economic system can promote social inequality. And you have learned that foreign investment {p.252 in developing countries can intensify inequality among residents.

This chapter will present a sociological analysis of the impact of the economy on people's lives. What makes work satisfying? How has the trend toward deindustrialization changed the work people do? What will the workforce of the 21st century look like? We will begin to answer these questions with a macro-level analysis of two ideal types of economic system—capitalism and socialism—and the real-world institution known as the informal economy. A case study on China, a socialist society that has been moving toward capitalism, follows. Next, we will examine various aspects of work, including worker alienation and worker satisfaction. We will also look at the ways in which the world's economies are changing. Finally, in the Social Policy section we will explore the new trend toward global offshoring, an important issue in today's workplace.

Economic Systems

The sociocultural evolution approach developed by Gerhard {p.123 Lenski categorizes preindustrial society according to the way in which the economy is organized. The principal types of preindustrial society, as you recall, are hunting-and-gathering societies, horticultural societies, and agrarian societies.

As we noted in Chapter 5, the *industrial revolution*—which {p.124 took place largely in England during the period 1760 to 1830—brought about changes in the social organization of the workplace. People left their homesteads and began working in central locations such as factories. As the industrial revolution proceeded, a new form of social structure emerged: the *industrial society,* a society that depends on mechanization to produce its goods and services.

Two basic types of economic system distinguish contemporary industrial societies: capitalism and socialism. As described in the following sections, capitalism and socialism serve as ideal types of economic system. No nation precisely fits either model. Instead, the economy of each individual state represents a mixture of capitalism and socialism, although one type or the other is generally more useful in describing a society's economic structure.

Capitalism

In preindustrial societies, land functioned as the source of virtually all wealth. The industrial revolution changed all that. It required that certain individuals and institutions be willing to take substantial risks in order to finance new inventions, machinery, and business enterprises. Eventually, bankers, industrialists, and other holders of large sums of money replaced landowners as

the most powerful economic force. These people invested their funds in the hope of realizing even greater profits, and thereby became owners of property and business firms.

The transition to private ownership of business was accompanied by the emergence of the capitalist economic system. *Capitalism* is an economic system in which the means of production are held largely in private hands and the main incentive for economic activity is the accumulation of profits. In practice, capitalist systems vary in the degree to which the government regulates private ownership and economic activity (D. Rosenberg 1991).

Immediately following the industrial revolution, the prevailing form of capitalism was what is termed *laissez-faire* ("let them do"). Under the principle of laissez-faire, as expounded and endorsed by British economist Adam Smith (1723–1790), people could compete freely, with minimal government intervention in the economy. Business retained the right to regulate itself and operated essentially without fear of government interference (Smelser 1963).

Two centuries later, capitalism has taken on a somewhat different form. Private ownership and maximization of profits still remain the most significant characteristics of capitalist economic systems. However, in contrast to the era of laissez-faire, capitalism today features government regulation of economic relations. Without restrictions, business firms can mislead consumers, endanger workers' safety, and even defraud the companies' investors—all in the pursuit of greater profits. That is why the government of a capitalist nation often monitors prices, sets safety and environmental standards for industries, protects the rights of consumers, and regulates collective bargaining between labor unions and management. Yet under capitalism as an ideal type, government rarely takes over ownership of an entire industry.

Contemporary capitalism also differs from laissez-faire in another important respect: Capitalism tolerates monopolistic practices. A **monopoly** exists when a single business firm controls the market. Domination of an industry allows the firm to effectively control a commodity by dictating pricing, quality standards, and availability. Buyers have little choice but to yield to the firm's decisions; there is no other place to purchase the product or service. Monopolistic practices violate the ideal of free competition cherished by Adam Smith and other supporters of laissez-faire capitalism.

Some capitalistic nations, such as the United States, outlaw monopolies through antitrust legislation. Such laws prevent any business from taking over so much of the competition in an industry that it controls the market. The U.S. federal government allows monopolies to exist only in certain exceptional cases, such as the utility and transportation industries. Even then, regulatory agencies scrutinize these officially approved monopolies to protect the public. The protracted legal battle between the Justice Department and Microsoft, owner of the dominant operating system for personal computers, illustrates the uneasy relationship between government and private monopolies in capitalistic countries.

Conflict theorists point out that although *pure* monopolies are not a basic element of the economy of the United States, competition is much more restricted than one might expect in what is called a *free enterprise system*. In numerous industries, a few companies largely dominate the field and keep new enterprises from entering the marketplace.

A worker mines for coltan with sweat and a stick. The sudden increase in demand for the metal by U.S. computer manufacturers caused incursions into the Congo by neighboring countries hungry for capital to finance a war. Too often, globalization can have unintended consequences for a nation's economy and social welfare.

As we have seen in earlier chapters, globalization and the rise of multinational corporations have spread the capitalistic pursuit of profits around the world. Especially in developing countries, governments are not always prepared to deal with the sudden influx of foreign capital and its effects on their economies. One particularly striking example of how unfettered capitalism can harm developing nations is found in the Democratic Republic of Congo (formerly Zaire). The Congo has significant deposits of the metal columbite-tantalite—coltan, for short—which is used in the production of electronic circuit boards. Until the market for cell phones, pagers, and laptop computers heated up recently, U.S. manufacturers got most of their coltan from Australia. But at the height of consumer demand, they turned to miners in the Congo to increase their supply.

Predictably, the escalating price of the metal—as much as $400 a kilogram at one point, or more than three times the average Congolese worker's yearly wages—attracted undesirable attention. Soon the neighboring countries of Rwanda, Uganda, and Burundi, at war with one another and desperate for resources to finance the conflict, were raiding the Congo's national parks, slashing and burning to expose the coltan underneath the forest floor. Indirectly, the sudden increase in the demand for coltan was financing war and the rape of the environment. U.S. manufacturers have

In the movie *Jerry Maguire,* Tom Cruise plays a successful sports agent who is fired for placing the well-being of the athletes he represents ahead of his agency's bottom line. Filmmakers often portray capitalists as selfish people who profit unfairly from the labor of others—an image that corporate scandals continue to reinforce.

Amy Wang
Product Manager, Norman International Company

When Amy Wang entered the University of Texas at Austin in 1999, she didn't know what subject she wanted to major in, but she soon became fascinated by sociology. "Sociology was intriguing in the sense that it combined everything in life," she explains. "I am a people person and I enjoy knowing and learning about all aspects of how people live and interact in society." Wang particularly enjoyed the criminology course she took, as well as another on the sociology of gender, which she found to be eye-opening.

Wang's employer, Norman International Company, is a manufacturer of fine, hand-crafted interior window furnishings. In launching a new product, Wang works closely with a research and development team based in China. Part of her job is to research the domestic market and suggest which options are likely to be popular with U.S. consumers—a task in which she puts her training in doing sociological research to good use. After the R&D team has finalized a new product's specifications, Wang outsources the production of samples to vendors in China. When the product is finally ready for sale, she coordinates the company's U.S.-based operations, including information systems, advertising, and shipping, to ensure a smooth introduction.

Wang, who was born in Taiwan, grew up in a suburb of Dallas, where she became assimilated to mainstream U.S. culture. When she began work with Norman International, the company sent her to southern China for a month and a half to meet the R&D team and work with them closely on a new product. "It was an exciting experience, because it was the first time I had been to China," she remembers. "I was absorbing all of the cultural differences and their way of life. It is very different than the U.S. and I really appreciated my life in the States afterwards."

Wang believes that her background in sociology helps her to adjust to different cultures when she travels on the job. She also thinks that a familiarity with the interactionist perspective fosters teamwork, which is essential to success in business. "Not only do you have to do your job well, but you have to get along with your co-workers so that projects can be finished efficiently," she emphasizes. In a global marketplace, that insight is especially important.

Let's Discuss

1. Given what you have learned about globalization, how likely do you think it is that you will someday be working abroad, on either a temporary or a permanent basis? Do you feel ready for that challenge?
2. What kind of cultural differences might complicate business relations between employees in two different countries—for example, the United States and China?

---

since cut off their sources in the Congo in an effort to avoid abetting the destruction. But their action has only penalized legitimate miners in the impoverished country (Austin 2002; Delawala 2002).

Socialism

{p.13} Socialist theory was refined in the writings of Karl Marx and Friedrich Engels. These European radicals were disturbed by the exploitation of the working class that emerged during the industrial revolution. In their view, capitalism forced large numbers of people to exchange their labor for low wages. The owners of an industry profit from the labor of workers primarily because they pay workers less than the value of the {p.219} goods produced.

As an ideal type, a socialist economic system attempts to eliminate such economic exploitation. Under *socialism,* the means of production and distribution in a society are collectively rather than privately owned. The basic objective of the economic system is to meet people's needs rather than to maximize profits. Socialists reject the laissez-faire philosophy that free competition benefits the general public. Instead, they believe that the central government, acting as the representative of the people, should make basic economic decisions. Therefore, government ownership of all major industries—including steel production, automobile manufacturing, and agriculture—is a primary feature of socialism as an ideal type.

In practice, socialist economic systems vary in the extent to which they tolerate private ownership. For example, in Great Britain, a nation with some aspects of both a socialist and a capitalist economy, passenger airline service is concentrated in the government-owned corporation British Airways. Yet private airlines are allowed to compete with it.

Socialist societies differ from capitalist nations in their commitment to social service programs. For example, the U.S. government provides health care and health insurance to the elderly and poor through the Medicare and Medicaid programs. But socialist countries typically offer government-financed medical care to *all* citizens. In theory, the wealth of the people as a collectivity is used to provide health care, housing, education, and other key services to each individual and family.

Marx believed that socialist states would eventually "wither away" and evolve into *communist* societies. As an ideal type, *communism* refers to an economic system under which all property is communally owned and no social distinctions are made on the basis of people's ability to produce. In recent decades, the Soviet Union, the People's Republic of China, Vietnam, Cuba,

Table 18-1

Characteristics of the Three Major Economic Systems

Economic System	Characteristics	Contemporary Examples
Capitalism	Private ownership of the means of production Accumulation of profits the main incentive	Canada Mexico United States
Socialism	Collective ownership of the means of production Meeting people's needs the basic objective	Germany Russia Sweden
Communism	Communal ownership of all property No social distinctions made on basis of people's ability to produce	Cuba North Korea Vietnam

Note: Countries listed in column 3 are typical of one of the three economic systems, but not perfectly so. In practice, the economies of most countries include a mix of elements from the three major systems.

and nations in Eastern Europe were popularly thought of as examples of communist economic systems. However, this usage represents an incorrect application of a term with sensitive political connotations. All nations known as communist in the 20th century actually fell far short of the ideal type.

By the early 1990s, Communist parties were no longer ruling the nations of Eastern Europe. The first major challenge to Communist rule came in 1980, when Poland's Solidarity movement—led by Lech Walesa and backed by many workers—questioned the injustices of that society. Though martial law forced Solidarity underground, the movement eventually negotiated the end of Communist Party rule, in 1989. Over the next two years, Communist parties were overthrown by popular uprisings in the Soviet Union and throughout Eastern Europe. The former Soviet Union, Czechoslovakia, and Yugoslavia were then subdivided to accommodate ethnic, linguistic, and religious differences.

As of 2007, China, Cuba, and Vietnam remained socialist societies ruled by Communist parties. Even in those countries, however, capitalism had begun to make inroads. In China, fully 25 percent of the country's production originated in the private business sector. (See the case study Capitalism in China, pages 439–441, for a fuller discussion.)

As we have seen, capitalism and socialism serve as ideal types of economic system. In reality, the economy of each industrial society—including the United States, the European Union, and Japan—includes certain elements of both capitalism and socialism (see Table 18-1). Whatever the differences—whether a society more closely fits the ideal type of capitalism or socialism—all industrial societies rely chiefly on mechanization in the production of goods and services.

The Informal Economy

In many countries, one aspect of the economy defies description as either capitalist or socialist. In the *informal economy,* trans-

fers of money, goods, or services take place but are not reported to the government. Examples of the informal economy include trading services with someone—say, a haircut for a computer lesson; selling goods on the street; and engaging in illegal transactions, such as gambling or drug deals. Participants in this type of economy avoid taxes and government regulations.

In developing nations, the informal economy represents a significant and often unmeasured part of total economic activity. Yet because this sector of the economy depends to a large extent on the labor of women, work in the informal economy is undervalued or even unrecognized the world over. Box 18-1 (page 438) explains how the informal economy operates in Nepal.

Functionalists contend that bureaucratic regulations sometimes contribute to the rise of an informal economy. In the developing world, governments often set up burdensome business regulations that overworked bureaucrats must administer. When requests for licenses and permits pile up, delaying business projects, legitimate entrepreneurs find they need to "go underground" to get anything done. Despite its apparent efficiency, this type of informal economy is dysfunctional for a country's overall political and economic well-being. Since informal firms typically operate in remote locations to avoid detection, they cannot easily expand when they become profitable. And given the limited protection for their property and contractual rights, participants in the informal economy are less likely than others to save and invest their income.

Whatever functions an informal economy may serve, it is in some respects dysfunctional for workers. Working conditions in these illegal businesses are often unsafe or dangerous, and the jobs rarely provide any benefits to those who become ill or cannot continue to work. Perhaps more significant, the longer a worker remains in the informal economy, the less likely that person is to make the transition to the regular economy. No matter how efficient or productive a worker, employers expect to see experience in the formal economy on a job application. Experience as a successful street vendor or self-employed cleaning person does not carry much weight with interviewers (Venkatesh 2006).

Use Your Sociological Imagination

Some of your relatives are working full-time in the informal economy—for example, babysitting, lawn cutting, house cleaning—and are earning all their income that way. What will be the consequences for them in terms of job security and health care? Will you try to persuade them to seek formal employment, regardless of how much money they are making?

sociologyIN *the Global Community*

18-1 Working Women in Nepal

Nepal, a small and mountainous Asian country of about 25 million people, has a per capita gross domestic product (GDP) of just $1,530 per year. (The comparable figure in the United States is $41,950.) But gross domestic product seriously understates the true production level in Nepal, for several reasons. Among the most important is that many Nepalese women work in the informal economy, whose activities are not included in the GDP.

Because women's work is undervalued in this traditional society, it is also underreported and underestimated. Official figures state that women account for 27 percent of GDP and form 40 percent of the labor force. But Nepalese women are responsible for 60 percent of additional nonmarket production—

> *Because women's work is undervalued in this traditional society, it is also underreported and underestimated.*

that is, work done in the informal economy—and 93 percent of the housework (see figure).

Most female workers cultivate corn, rice, and wheat on the family farm, where they spend hours on labor-intensive tasks such as fetching water and feeding livestock. Because much of the food they raise is consumed at home, however, it is considered to be nonmarket production. At home, women concentrate on food processing and preparation, caregiving, and other household tasks, such as clothes making. Childbearing and rearing and elder care are particularly crucial activities. Yet none of these chores are considered part of GDP; instead, they are dismissed as "women's work," both by economists and by the women themselves.

Gender Contributions to GDP and Household Maintenance in Nepal

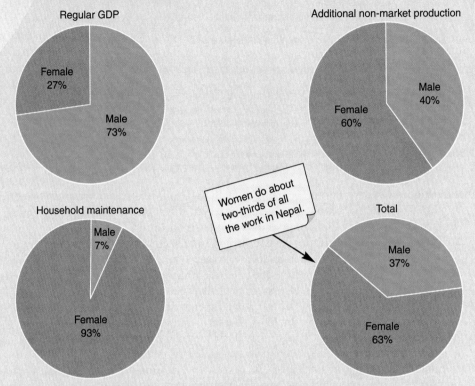

Source: Survey by S. Acharya as cited in Mahbub ul Haq Human Development Centre 2000:54.

The figures on housework and nonmarket production in Nepal come from an independent economic study. To compile them, researchers had to adapt the conventional accounting system by adding a special account dedicated to household maintenance activities. When they did so, women's "invisible work" suddenly became visible and valuable. Not just in Nepal but in every country, economists need to expand their definitions of work and the labor force to account for the tremendous contributions women make to the world economy.

Let's Discuss

1. In your own family, is "women's work" taken for granted? Have you ever tried to figure out what it would cost your family to pay for all the unpaid work women do?

2. Why is recognizing women's work important? How might life for both men and women change if the true economic value of women's work were recognized?

Sources: Acharya 2000; Haub 2006; Mahbub ul Haq Human Development Centre 2000:54–57.

CASE*study* (CAPITALISM IN CHINA)

Today's China is not the China of past generations; it stands on the brink of becoming the world's largest economy (see Figure 18-1). In this country where the Communist Party once dominated people's lives, few now bother to follow party proceedings. Instead, after a decade of rapid economic growth, most Chinese are more interested in acquiring the latest consumer goods. Ironically, it was party officials' decision to transform China's economy by opening it up to capitalism that reduced the once omnipotent institution's influence.

The Road to Capitalism

When the communists assumed leadership of China in 1949, they cast themselves as the champions of workers and peasants and the enemies of those who exploited workers, namely landlords and capitalists. Profit making was outlawed, and those who engaged in it were arrested. By the 1960s, China's economy was dominated by huge state-controlled enterprises, such as factories. Even private farms were transformed into community-owned organizations. Peasants essentially worked for the government, receiving payment in goods based on their contribution to the collective good. In addition, they could receive a small plot of land on which to produce food for their families or for exchange with others. But while the centralization of production for the benefit of all seemed to make sense ideologically, it did not work well economically.

In the 1980s, the government eased restrictions on private enterprise somewhat, permitting small businesses with no more than seven employees. But business owners could not hold policymaking positions in the party, at any level. Late in the decade, party leaders began to make market-oriented reforms, revising the nation's legal structure to promote private business. For the first time, private entrepreneurs were allowed to compete with some state-controlled businesses. By the mid-1990s, impressed with the results of the experiment, party officials had begun to hand some ailing state-controlled businesses over to private entrepreneurs, in hopes they could be turned around.

The Chinese Economy Today

Today, the entrepreneurs who weathered government harassment during the Communist Party's early years are among the nation's wealthiest capitalists. Some even hold positions on government advisory boards. The growing free-market economy they spawned has brought significant inequality to Chinese workers, however, especially between urban and rural workers. Though the move toward market-driven development has been slowing, questions are still being raised about the accumulation of wealth by a few (Sicular et al. 2006).

Chinese capitalists have had to compete with multinational corporations, which can operate more easily in China now, thanks to government economic reforms. General Motors (GM) first became interested in China in 1992, hoping to use the nation's low-cost labor to manufacture cars for overseas markets. But more and more, foreign-owned enterprises like GM are selling to the Chinese market. By 2006, GM's Chinese operation was

FIGURE 18–1

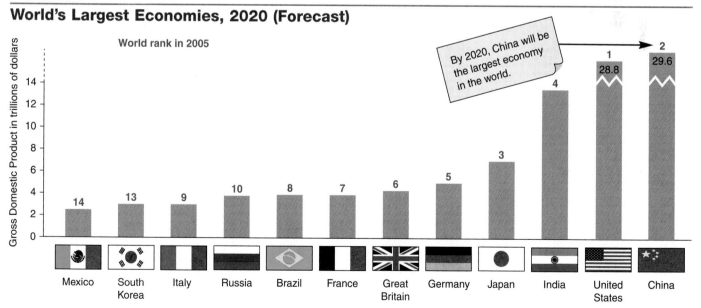

Source: *The Economist* 2006a.
Note: Data standardized in terms of estimated purchasing power parity to eliminate differences in buying power. Countries ranked in 2005, when Spain was ranked 11, Canada 12.

This burgeoning metropolis isn't located in the United States or Europe, but in China. Shanghai has experienced rapid economic growth over the last decade, spurred by an influx of investment by multinational corporations.

Pollution is common in urban areas, and environmental problems are extraordinary (M. Elliott 2006; French 2006, 2007).

For the average worker, party membership is less important now than in the past. Instead, managerial skill and experience are much in demand. Hong Kong sociologist Xiaowei Zang (2002) surveyed 900 workers in a key industrial city and found that party members still had an advantage in government and state-owned companies, where they earned higher salaries than other workers. But in private businesses, seniority and either managerial or entrepreneurial experience were what counted. As might be expected, being male and well educated also helped.

Women have been slower to advance in the workplace than men. Traditionally, Chinese women have been relegated to subservient roles in the patriarchal family structure. Commu-

producing 6 million automobiles a year, at a profit much higher than in the United States (Kahn 2003; Krebs 2006).

nist Party rule has allowed them to make significant gains in employment, income, and education, although not as quickly as promised. For rural women in China, the growth of a market economy has meant a choice between working in a factory or on a farm. Still, despite recent economic changes, emerging research

Chinese Workers in the New Economy

For Chinese workers, the loosening of state control over the economy has meant a rise in occupational mobility, which was severely limited in the early days of Communist Party rule. The new markets created by private entrepreneurs are allowing ambitious workers to advance their careers by changing jobs or even cities. On the other hand, many middle-aged urban workers have lost their jobs to rural migrants seeking higher wages. Moreover, the privately owned factories that churn out lawn chairs and power tools for multinational corporations offer limited opportunities and very long hours. Wages average only $75 a month—⅙ what factory workers earn in Mexico, and ¹⁄₄₀ of U.S. workers' wages.

Serious social problems have accompanied China's massive economic growth. Because safety is not a priority in many businesses, workers suffer from high injury rates. Harsh working conditions contribute to rapid turnover in the labor force. There is no pension system in China, so retirees must struggle to find other ways to support themselves.

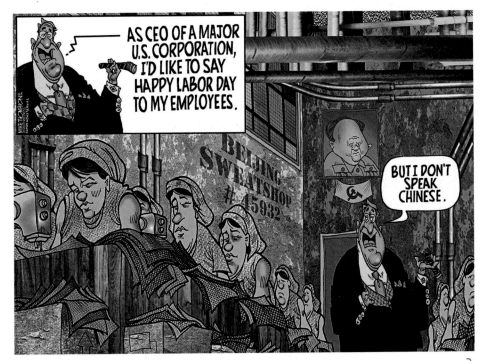

For better or worse, the expansion of capitalism in China has linked U.S. businesses to that expanding economy.

shows that Chinese women receive lower wages than men who work in the same job sectors (Wang and Cai 2006).

With the growth of a middle class and increased education, many Chinese are seeking the same opportunities as their Western counterparts. The struggle has been particularly visible in the Chinese people's desire for open, unrestricted access to the World Wide Web. China requires even U.S.-based companies like Google, Yahoo, Microsoft, and Cisco Systems to alter their search engines and blogging tools so as to block access to unapproved Web sites. In most countries of the world, a Web search for images of Tiananmen Square will call up photos of the 1989 crackdown on student protesters, in which soldiers in tanks attacked unarmed students. But on the other side of what has been dubbed the Great Firewall of China, the same search yields only photos of visiting diplomats—including those from the United States—posing in the square (Grossman and Beech 2006). ●

Use Your Sociological Imagination

How have you been touched personally by the growth of capitalism in China?

Work and Alienation

"A moron could learn this job, it's so easy," says one Burger King worker in George Ritzer's study of the fast-food industry (2000:137). Doing repetitive tasks that take minimal skills can be demoralizing, leading to a sense of alienation and isolation in the workplace. Jeremy Rifkin, as we saw in the chapter-opening excerpt, took this concern a step further: As work becomes more and more automated, human skills become obsolete and workers lose their jobs altogether, or are forced into low-skills service jobs (Rifkin 1996).

All the pioneers of sociological thought were concerned about the negative impact on workers of the changes brought about by the industrial revolution. Émile Durkheim ([1893] 1933) argued that as labor becomes more and more differentiated, individuals experience *anomie,* or loss of direction. Workers can't feel as much fulfillment from performing one specialized task in a factory as they did when they were totally responsible for creating a product. Clearly, the impersonality of bureaucratic organizations can produce a cold and uncaring workplace. But the most penetrating analysis of the dehumanizing aspects of industrialization was offered by Karl Marx.

Marx's View

Marx believed that as the process of industrialization advanced, workers were robbed of any meaningful relationship to their work. The emphasis on the specialization of tasks, he believed, contributed to a growing sense of alienation among industrial workers. The term ***alienation*** refers to a condition of estrange-

ment or dissociation from the surrounding society. Consider today's telemarketers, who make "cold calls" to sell people products and services. Do they feel a part of the financial institution that employs them? But it wasn't just the monotonous repetition of the same tasks that concerned Marx. In his view, an even deeper cause of alienation was the *powerlessness* of workers in a capitalist economic system. Workers had no control over their occupational tasks, the products of their labor, or the distribution of profits. Moreover, they were constantly producing property that was owned by others (the members of the capitalist class) (Erikson 1986).

The solution to the problem of workers' alienation, according to Marx, was to give workers greater control over the workplace and the products of their labor. Marx didn't focus on the limited reform of factory life; rather, he envisioned a revolutionary overthrow of capitalist oppression. After a transition to collective ownership of the means of production (socialism), the ideal of communism would eventually be achieved. Yet the trend in capitalist societies has been toward concentration of ownership by giant corporations. Currently, about 49 percent of the paid U.S. labor force is employed by business firms with more than 500 workers. Through mergers and acquisitions, such corporations become even larger, and individual workers find themselves dwarfed by firms of overwhelming size and power (Bureau of the Census 2002:482).

When Marx wrote about work and alienation in 1844, the physical conditions of labor were much harsher than they are today. Yet his writings inspired research that persists today, even though the majority of workers now enjoy safer, more comfortable surroundings. Most studies of alienation have focused on how structural changes in the economy serve to increase or decrease worker satisfaction. In fact, the growth of the size of businesses, the emergence of huge franchise chains, and the dominance of multinational corporations have only increased the isolation of laborers. Large business organizations report an escalation in episodes of "desk rage," in which employees or angry ex-employees act out their frustrations, disrupting the workplace and often raising other workers' alienation in the process (Hodson and Sullivan 1995; Hymowitz and Silverman 2001).

Marx focused on alienation among the proletariat, whom he viewed as powerless to effect change in capitalist institutions. But by the 1980s, the term *burnout* was increasingly being used to describe the stress experienced by a wide range of workers, including professionals, self-employed persons, and even unpaid volunteers. The concept of work-related anxiety now covers alienation even among more affluent workers, who have a greater degree of control over their working conditions. From a conflict perspective, we have masked the fact that alienation falls most heavily on the lower and working classes by making it appear to be endemic, from the boardroom to the shop floor.

Worker Satisfaction

In general, people with greater responsibility for a finished product (such as white-collar professionals and managers) experience

What Is Our Work?

Sociologists are interested not only in how economies are organized, but in the many different ways workers earn their daily keep. Author Ferdinand Protzman (2006) traveled the world for *National Geographic* to study people at work. The photographs in his book capture variations in the way people work, from hunting and gathering in the field or on the seashore to running the vast machinery of industry. On a seemingly endless assembly line in Dehui City, China (below), factory workers process chicken parts. In Yemen (opposite page, top), women collect clover for cattle feed. In Salt Lake City, Utah (opposite, bottom left), miners at the Bingham Canyon copper mine pose in front of a giant shovel. And in Costa Rica (opposite, bottom right), men collect turtle eggs.

{China}

{Yemen}

{United States}

{Costa Rica}

more satisfaction than those with less responsibility. For women and men working in blue-collar jobs, the repetitive nature of work can be particularly unsatisfying. The automobile assembly line is commonly cited as an extreme example of monotonous work. Studs Terkel (1974:159), in his book *Working*, gives a first-person account of a spot welder's labor:

> I stand in one spot, about a two- or three-feet area, all night. The only time a person stops is when the line stops. We do about thirty-two jobs per car, per unit, forty-eight units per hour, eight hours a day. Thirty-two times forty-eight times eight. Figure it out, that's how many times I push that button.

Robert Blauner's (1964) classic research study revealed that printers—who often work in small shops and supervise apprentices—were more satisfied with their work than laborers who performed repetitive tasks on automobile assembly lines.

Working at the checkout counter may help to pay the bills, but it isn't likely to provide much job satisfaction—especially in a large supermarket where workers enjoy little responsibility or personal recognition.

Factors in Job Satisfaction

A number of general factors can reduce the level of dissatisfaction of contemporary industrial workers. Higher wages give workers a sense of accomplishment apart from the task before them. A shorter workweek is supposed to increase the amount of time people can devote to recreation and leisure, reducing some of the discontent of the workplace. But the number of hours Americans work actually *increased* in the 1990s, by the equivalent of about one workweek. Short staffing because of low unemployment rates may have accounted for part of the increase in hours worked; however, many Americans took a second job during this period, just to make ends meet (Gerson and Jacobs 2004).

Numerous studies have shown that positive relationships with co-workers can make a boring job tolerable or even enjoyable. In his often cited "banana time" study, sociologist Donald Roy (1959) examined worker satisfaction in a two-month participant observation of a small group of machine operators. Drawing on the interactionist perspective, Roy carefully recorded the social interactions among members of his work group, including many structured "times" and "themes" designed to break up long days of simple, repetitive work. For example, the workers divided their food breaks into coffee time, peach time, banana time, fish time, Coke time, and lunch time—each of which occurred daily and involved distinctive responsibilities, jokes, and insults. Roy (1959:166) concluded that his observations "seem to support the generally accepted notion that one key source of job satisfaction lies in the informal interaction shared by members of a work

group." The patterned conversation and horseplay of these workers reduced the monotony of their workdays.

Sociologist George Ritzer (1977, 2000) has suggested that the relatively positive impression many workers present is misleading. In his view, manual workers are so deeply alienated that they come to expect little from their jobs. Their satisfaction comes from nonwork tasks, and any job-related gratification results from receiving wages. Ritzer's interpretation explains why manual workers—although they say they are satisfied with their occupations—would not choose the same line of work if they could begin their lives over.

Job Satisfaction in Japan

One of the major economic developments of the 1980s was the emergence of Japan as an industrial giant. In earlier decades, many people had attributed Japan's economic accomplishments to low wages combined with the production of inexpensive goods. However, in the 1980s Japanese salaries were comparable to those of other industrial nations. A more likely explanation of Japan's remarkable success at that time focused instead on the unusual pride Japanese workers took in their products. In Japanese plants and factories, workers are expected to assume the role of quality-control inspector. Although employees perform specialized production tasks, they can still identify with the finished product.

For a long time, the collectivist orientation of Japanese culture heavily influenced its economic system. An individual was perceived as an extension of his or her family, business, or community, and as bound together with others in a common purpose. In contrast to U.S. firms, most Japanese companies maintained an ideal of "lifetime employment" for some of their employees. Because they made substantial investments in training, they were reluctant to lay off employees during a business slump. The employer–employee relationship was paramount. Companies even operated reception halls, gymnasiums and swimming pools, mortgage-lending institutions, and cultural programs for the benefit of their workers.

By the close of the 1990s this situation had changed. A severe economic recession had hit Japan, resulting in record unemployment. While joblessness was still low compared to European countries, almost twice as many people were looking for jobs as there were job openings. Companies facing the impact of a lingering recession and increased competition from abroad set aside the notion of lifetime employment. Interactionists observed that Japanese men—accustomed to job security—were so embarrassed over losing a job that they would keep it secret from their families for days, if not weeks (see Chapter 4). Men in their 50s were looking for work along with recent college graduates. As a result of the restructuring, the bonds between workers and employers are currently weakening. The feelings of worker isolation that Marx and Ritzer wrote about in Europe and North America are becoming increasingly evident in Japan (French 2002).

Use Your Sociological Imagination

In thinking about the work you will seek after graduation, which is more important to you, job satisfaction or salary?

Changing Economies

As advocates of the power elite model point out, the trend in capitalist societies has been toward concentration of ownership by giant corporations, especially multinational ones. In the following sections, we will examine two outgrowths of this trend in the United States, deindustrialization and the changing face of the workforce, as well as a countertrend: the rise of microfinancing in developing countries. As these trends show, any change in the economy has social and political implications.

Microfinancing

In some respects it offers a small solution to a big problem. *Microfinancing* is lending small sums of money to the poor so they can work their way out of poverty. Borrowers use the money to get small businesses off the ground—to buy the tools, equipment, and bamboo to make stools, yarn to weave into

cloth, or cows to produce milk. The products they produce are then sold in the local shops. Typically, microloans are made for less than $100, often for as little as $12. The recipients are people who ordinarily would not be able to qualify for banking services.

Sometimes referred to as "banking the unbanked," microfinancing was the brainchild of Bangladeshi economist Muhammad Yunus. In 1976, in the midst of a devastating famine in Bangladesh, Yunus founded the Grameen (meaning "Village") Bank. The idea came to him when he reached into his pocket to lend $27 to a group of villagers who had asked him for help. Working through local halls or meeting places, the Grameen Bank has now extended credit to nearly 7 million people. The idea has spread, and has even been underwritten by multinational organizations such as the International Monetary Fund and for-profit banks like Citigroup. Estimates are that microfinancing will have reached 60 million people by 2007.

Microfinancing works well in countries that have experienced severe economic devastation. At the start of 2002, after decades of conflict and military occupation, Afghanistan did not have a single functioning bank. Five years later, with the help of the World Bank and other donors, Afghans could get microloans and other financial services in 22 of the country's 34 provinces. The new microlenders are the first evidence of a formal financial sector that Afghanistan has seen in years. Their funds have helped to start businesses and allowed farmers to convert from opium growing to other crops.

Because an estimated 90 percent of the recipients of microcredit are women, feminist theorists are especially interested in the growth of microfinancing. Women's economic status has been found to be critical to the well-being of their children, and

In 2006 Muhammad Yunus, founder of the Grameen Bank, was awarded the Nobel Peace Prize for his work in championing the concept of microfinancing. The small loans his bank makes to the poor, many of them women, have improved the quality of life of countless families.

18-2 Affirmative Action

Jessie Sherrod began picking cotton in the fields of Mississippi when she was eight years old, earning $1.67 for a 12-hour day. Today she is a Harvard-educated pediatrician who specializes in infectious diseases. But the road from the cotton fields to the medical profession was hardly an easy one. "You can't make up for 400 years of slavery and mistreatment and unequal opportunity in 20 years," she says angrily. "We had to ride the school bus for five miles . . . and pass by a white school to get to our black elementary school. Our books were used books. Our instructors were not as good. We didn't have the proper equipment. How do you make up for that?" (Stolberg 1995:A14). Some people think it should be done through affirmative action programs.

The term *affirmative action* first appeared in an executive order issued by President John

> *Critics warn against hiring and admissions quotas, complaining that they constitute a kind of "reverse discrimination" against White males.*

F. Kennedy in 1961. That order called for contractors to "take affirmative action to ensure that applicants are employed, and that employees are treated during employment, without regard to their race, creed, color, or national origin." In 1967, the order was amended by President Lyndon Johnson to prohibit discrimination on the basis of sex as well, but affirmative action remained a vague concept. Currently, **affirmative action** refers to positive efforts to recruit minority group members or women for jobs, promotions, and educational opportunities.

Sociologists—especially conflict theorists—view affirmative action as a legislative attempt to reduce the inequality embedded in the social structure by increasing opportunities for groups who were deprived in the past,

such as women and African Americans. Despite the clear disparity in earnings between White males and other groups, however, many people doubt that everything done in the name of affirmative action is desirable. Critics warn against hiring and admissions quotas, complaining that they constitute a kind of "reverse discrimination" against White males. Thus, though a majority of 60 percent of respondents to a 2004 national survey favored affirmative action in college admissions, an analysis of the responses revealed clear racial and gender differences. Among Blacks, 87 percent favored affirmative action; among Hispanics, the rate was 77 percent. But fewer White women—60 percent—approved of the programs, and only 49 percent of White men did.

Affirmative action became a prominent issue in state and national political campaigns in 1996, when California's voters approved by a 54 to 46 percent margin the California Civil Rights Initiative. Better known as Proposition 209, this measure amends the state constitution to *prohibit* any program that gives preference to women and minorities in college admissions, hiring, promotion, or government contracts. In other words, it aims to abolish affirmative action programs. The courts have since upheld the measure. In 1998, voters in Washington state passed a similar anti–affirmative action measure.

In 2003, focusing specifically on college admissions in a pair of decisions involving policies at the University of Michigan, the Supreme Court ruled that colleges may consider race and ethnicity as one factor in their admissions decisions. However, they cannot

assign a specific value to being a minority candidate in such a way that race becomes the overriding factor in a decision. The ruling allowed many colleges and universities to continue their existing affirmative action policies. But critics complained that it permits blatant favoritism toward the children of alumni, who are more likely than others to be White, while subjecting programs that favor disadvantaged minority candidates to much greater scrutiny.

Let's Discuss

1. Is affirmative action part of the admissions policy at the college or university you attend? If so, do you think the policy has helped to level the playing field? Might it have excluded some qualified White applicants?

2. Take a poll of your classmates. What percentage of the class supports affirmative action in hiring and college admissions? How does that group break down in terms of gender, race, and ethnicity?

Sources: Pew Research Center 2004; Stolberg 1995; University of Michigan 2003.

the key to a healthy household environment. In developing countries, where women often are not treated as well as men, being entrusted with credit is particularly empowering to them. In recognition of these social and economic contributions of microfinancing, the United Nations proclaimed 2005 the International Year of Microcredit (Dugger 2006; Flynn 2007; World Bank 2006c).

The Changing Face of the Workforce

The workforce in the United States is constantly changing. During World War II, when men were mobilized to fight abroad, women entered the workforce in large numbers. And with the rise of the civil rights movement in the 1960s, minorities found numerous job opportunities opening to them. Box 18-2 (opposite) takes a closer look at the active recruitment of women and minorities into the workplace, known as *affirmative action*.

While predictions are not always reliable, sociologists and labor specialists foresee a workforce increasingly composed of women and racial and ethnic minorities. In 1960 there were twice as many men in the labor force as women. From 1984 to 2014, however, 54 percent of new workers are expected to be women. The dynamics for minority-group workers are even more dramatic, as the number of Black, Latino, and Asian American workers continues to increase at a faster rate than the number of White workers (Toossi 2005:26).

More and more, then, the workforce reflects the diversity of the population, as ethnic minorities enter the labor force and immigrants and their children move from marginal jobs or employment in the informal economy to positions of greater visi- { pp.233–234 } bility and responsibility. The impact of this changing labor force is not merely statistical. A more diverse workforce means that relationships between workers are more likely to cross gender, racial, and ethnic lines. Interactionists note that

people will soon find themselves supervising and being supervised by people very different from themselves. In response to these changes, 75 percent of businesses had instituted some type of cultural diversity training program as of 2000 (Melia 2000).

Deindustrialization

What happens when a company decides it is more profitable to move its operations out of a long-established community to another part of the country, or out of the country altogether? People lose jobs; stores lose customers; the local government's tax base declines and it cuts services. This devastating process has occurred again and again in the last decade or so.

The term *deindustrialization* refers to the systematic, widespread withdrawal of investment in basic aspects of productivity, such as factories and plants. Giant corporations that deindustrialize are not necessarily refusing to invest in new economic opportunities. Rather, the targets and locations of investment change, and the need for labor decreases as advances in technology continue to automate production. First, companies may move their plants from the nation's central cities to the suburbs. The next step may be relocation from suburban areas of the Northeast and Midwest to the South, where labor laws place more restrictions on unions. Finally, a corporation may simply relocate *outside* the United States to a country with a lower rate of prevailing wages. General Motors, for example, decided to build a multibillion-dollar plant in China rather than in Kansas City or even in Mexico (Lynn 2003).

Although deindustrialization often involves relocation, in some instances it takes the form of corporate restructuring, as companies seek to reduce costs in the face of growing worldwide competition. When such restructuring occurs, the impact on the bureaucratic hierarchy of formal organizations can be significant. A large corporation may choose to sell off or entirely abandon less

Gutted factories like this one in Boston, Massachusetts (left) contrast with the glamorous corporate campus of Google Corporation (right) in Mountain View, California. Deindustrialization and the rise of high technology have shifted the U.S. labor market, displacing many workers in the process.

productive divisions and to eliminate layers of management viewed as unnecessary. Wages and salaries may be frozen and fringe benefits cut—all in the name of restructuring. Increasing reliance on automation also spells the end of work as we have known it.

The term *downsizing* was introduced in 1987 to refer to reductions taken in a company's workforce as part of deindustrialization. Viewed from a conflict perspective, the unprecedented attention given to downsizing in the mid-1990s reflected the continuing importance of social class in the United States. Conflict theorists note that job loss has long been a feature of deindustrialization among blue-collar workers. But when large numbers of middle-class managers and other white-collar employees with substantial incomes began to be laid off, suddenly the media began expressing great concern over downsizing. The Social Policy section that follows highlights the latest version of this issue, the outsourcing of service jobs at U.S. companies to workers in foreign countries (Meyerson 2006).

The social costs of deindustrialization and downsizing cannot be overemphasized. Plant closings lead to substantial unemployment in a community, which can have a devastating impact on both the micro and macro levels. On the micro level, the unemployed person and his or her family must adjust to a loss of spending power. Painting or re-siding the house, buying health insurance or saving for retirement, even thinking about having another child must be put aside. Both marital happiness and family cohesion may suffer as a result. Although many dismissed workers eventually reenter the paid labor force, they must often accept less desirable positions with lower salaries and fewer benefits (DePalma 2002). Unemployment and underemployment are tied to many of the social problems discussed throughout this textbook, among them the need for child care and the controversy over welfare. In the minds of many displaced workers in the United States, the source of all these ills is the offshoring of U.S. jobs to overseas workers—the subject of the following Social Policy section. {pp. 102, 234

Use Your Sociological Imagination

Do you see any evidence of deindustrialization or downsizing in your hometown?

(social Policy)
and the Economy

Global Offshoring

The Issue

Anney Unnikrishnan's situation is not unusual. In fact, she is one of thousands of Indians who work in global call centers, answering phone calls from all over the world or dialing out to solicit business. Anney received her MBA in India before taking the entrance exams to Purdue University. But after concluding that she couldn't afford Purdue, she realized that because U.S. corporations were setting up shop in India, she didn't need to emigrate to the United States. Anney sums up what she considers her enviable position in this way: "So I still get my rice and sambar (a traditional Indian dish). . . . I don't need to . . . learn to eat coleslaw and cold beef . . . and I still work for a multinational. Why should I go to America?" (Friedman 2005:28).

Offshoring is global: it occurs not just between North America and India, but between North America and Europe (see Box 10-2 on page 253) and between other industrial and developing countries. Online services in the United States enlist Romanians to represent well-to-do video game players. Japan enlists Chinese speakers of Japanese—a legacy of Japan's bitter occupation of China—to create databases or develop floor plans for Japanese construction firms. In Africa, over 54,000 people work in call centers, some specializing in French and others serving the English-speaking market. People all over the world are affected by this issue (Friedman 2005; Lacey 2005).

The Setting

U.S. firms have been *outsourcing* certain types of work for generations. For example, moderate-sized businesses such as furniture stores and commercial laundries have long relied on outside trucking firms to make deliveries to their customers. The new trend toward *offshoring* carries this practice one step further, by transferring other types of work to foreign contractors. Now, even large companies are turning to overseas firms, many of them located in developing countries. Offshoring has become the latest tactic in the time-worn business strategy of raising profits by reducing costs.

Offshoring began when U.S. companies started transferring manufacturing jobs to foreign factories, where wage rates were much lower. But the transfer of work from one country to another is no longer limited to manufacturing. Office and professional jobs are being exported, too, thanks to advanced telecommunications and the growth of skilled, English-speaking labor forces in developing nations with relatively low wage scales. The trend includes even those jobs that require considerable training, such as accounting and financial analysis, computer programming, claims adjustment, telemarketing, and hotel and airline reservations. Today, when you call a toll-free number to reach a customer service representative, chances are that the person who answers the phone will not be speaking from the United States.

In 2003, an estimated 1.5 million service jobs were done in lower-wage countries for customers in higher-wage economies. By 2008, that number is expected to reach 4.1 million. Even without further technological breakthroughs, the total could eventually climb to over 160 million jobs worldwide. These substantial increases in overseas outsourcing would be accompanied, of course, by further job reductions in the industrialized countries (McKinsey Global Institute 2005).

Sociological Insights

Because offshoring, like outsourcing in general, tends to improve the efficiency of business operations, it can be viewed as functional to society. Offshoring also increases economic interdependence in the production of goods and services, both among enterprises located just across town from one another and among those across the globe.

Conflict theorists question whether this aspect of globalization furthers social inequality. While moving high-tech work to India does help to lower a company's costs, the impact on those technical and service workers who are displaced is clearly devastating. Certainly middle-class workers in industrial countries are alarmed by the trend. Though economists favor some assistance for workers who have been displaced by offshoring, they oppose broad-based efforts to block the practice.

There is a downside to offshoring for foreigners, as well. Although outsourcing is a significant source of employment for India's upper middle class, hundreds of millions of other Indians have seen little to no positive impact from the trend. Most households in India do not possess any form of high technology: only about 1 out of 10 have a telephone, and just 3 out of 1,000 a computer. Instead of improving these people's lives, the new business centers have siphoned water and electricity away from those who are most in need. Even the high-tech workers are experiencing negative consequences. Many suffer from stress disorders such as stomach problems and difficulty sleeping; more than half quit their jobs before the end of a year. On the other hand, the new call centers have brought significant improvements in India's infrastructure, particularly in telecommunications and power generation. The long-term impact of offshoring on India and other developing nations is difficult to predict (Waldman 2004a, 2004b, 2004c).

Policy Initiatives

Alan S. Blinder (2006), former vice chairman of the Federal Reserve, predicts that offshoring will become the "third Industrial Revolution"—a life-altering shift in the way goods and services are produced and consumed. Blinder says we have barely seen

the "tip of the offshoring iceberg." While offshoring may not lead to large-scale unemployment, it will likely produce a shift in Western labor markets. Jobs that are easily outsourced, like accounting and computer programming, will migrate to developing countries, leaving those that must be done on site, like nursing and construction, at home.

Despite concerns over the impact of offshoring on the labor force, little legislative action has been taken. Most policymakers, while they bemoan the loss of jobs, see offshoring as part of the "natural" process of globalization, one more manifestation of the gains that come from international trade. In their view, the resulting dislocation of workers at home is just another job

The number of jobs that can be offshored is growing. Some U.S.-based online tutoring services have begun to employ foreigners such as Somit Basak. Based in New Delhi, India, Basak earns about $200 a month, or $1.40 an hour—very little compared to the $20 or $30 an hour that online tutors in the United States earn.

change—one that more and more workers will have to adjust to at some point during their lifetimes.

Let's Discuss

1. Do you know anyone whose job has been transferred to a foreign country? If so, was the person able to find a comparable job in the same town, or did he or she have to relocate? How long was the person unemployed?

2. What do you think should be done, if anything, about the growing trend toward offshoring? Do you see it as a serious political issue?

3. How might the number of foreign students who are educated in the United States contribute to the trend toward offshoring? On balance, do you think the gain from training foreign students outweighs the loss from exported jobs?

GettingINVOLVED

To get involved in the debate over global offshoring, visit this text's Online Learning Center, which offers links to relevant Web sites. Check out the Social Policy section on the Online Learning Center as well; it provides survey data on U.S. public opinion regarding this issue.

www.mhhe.com/schaefer11

{ **MASTERING THIS CHAPTER** }

Summary

The *economic system* of a society has an important influence on social behavior and on other social institutions. This chapter examines the major economic systems, the rise of *capitalism* in China, work and *alienation* from work, the changing economy, and the trend toward global *offshoring*.

1. With the industrial revolution, a new form of social structure emerged: the *industrial society.*

2. Systems of *capitalism* vary in the degree to which the government regulates private ownership and economic activity, but all emphasize the profit motive.

3. The basic objective of *socialism* is to eliminate economic exploitation and meet people's needs.

4. Marx believed that *communism* would evolve naturally out of socialism.

5. In developing nations, the *informal economy* represents a significant part of total economic activity. Yet because this sector depends largely on women's work, it is undervalued.

6. In the 1980s, the Chinese Communist Party began allowing Chinese entrepreneurs to experiment with capitalist ventures. Today, multinational corporations are capitalizing on China's huge workforce to produce goods and services for sale not just to those in industrial nations, but to the people of China.

7. Industrial jobs can lead to a sense of *alienation* in the workplace. Karl Marx expected that powerless workers would eventually overthrow the capitalist system.

8. *Affirmative action* is intended to remedy the effects of discrimination against minority groups and women in education and the workplace. The concept is controversial, however, because some people see it as reverse discrimination against majority groups.

9. The world's economies are changing, both in the United States and abroad. In developing countries, *microfinancing* is improving the lives of millions of poor people. In the United States, workers are coping with *deindustrialization* and employers are training an increasingly diverse workforce.

10. *Offshoring,* or the transfer of work to foreign contractors, has become a global phenomenon involving both developed and developing nations. Today, even professional services can be outsourced to nations like India, which possess a large, well-educated English-speaking population that will work for comparatively low wages.

Critical Thinking Questions

1. The United States has long been put forward as the model of a capitalist society. Drawing on material in earlier chapters of this textbook, discuss the values and beliefs that have led people in the United States to cherish a laissez-faire, capitalist economy. To what degree have those values and beliefs changed over the past hundred years? What aspects of socialism are now evident in the nation's economy? Have our values and beliefs changed to support certain principles traditionally associated with socialist societies?

2. Describe some of the service workers in the college or university you attend. Do you see any sign of alienation in the workplace?

3. Imagine that you have been assigned to study possible changes in the economy of the city nearest you. How could you use surveys, observation research, experiments, and existing sources to complete the task?

Key Terms

Affirmative action Positive efforts to recruit minority group members or women for jobs, promotions, and educational opportunities. (page 446)

Alienation A condition of estrangement or dissociation from the surrounding society. (441)

Capitalism An economic system in which the means of production are held largely in private hands, and the main incentive for economic activity is the accumulation of profits. (434)

Communism As an ideal type, an economic system under which all property is communally owned and no social distinctions are made on the basis of people's ability to produce. (436)

Deindustrialization The systematic, widespread withdrawal of investment in basic aspects of productivity, such as factories and plants. (447)

Downsizing Reductions taken in a company's workforce as part of deindustrialization. (448)

Economic system The social institution through which goods and services are produced, distributed, and consumed. (434)

Industrial society A society that depends on mechanization to produce its goods and services. (434)

Informal economy Transfers of money, goods, or services that are not reported to the government. (437)

Laissez-faire A form of capitalism under which people compete freely, with minimal government intervention in the economy. (434)

Microfinancing Lending small sums of money to the poor so they can work their way out of poverty. (445)

Monopoly Control of a market by a single business firm. (435)

Offshoring The transfer of work to foreign contractors. (448)

Socialism An economic system under which the means of production and distribution are collectively owned. (436)

Self-Quiz

Read each question carefully and then select the best answer.

1. Which two basic types of economic system distinguish contemporary industrial societies?
   a. capitalism and communism
   b. capitalism and socialism
   c. socialism and communism
   d. capitalism and dictatorship

2. According to the discussion of capitalism in the text, which of the following statements is true?
   a. The means of production are held largely in private hands.
   b. The main incentive for economic activity is the accumulation of profits.
   c. The degree to which the government regulates private ownership and economic activity will vary.
   d. all of the above

3. Which sociological perspective points out that while *pure* monopolies are not a basic element of the economy of the United States, competition is much more restricted than one might expect in what is called a *free enterprise system*?
   a. the functionalist perspective
   b. the conflict perspective
   c. the interactionist perspective
   d. labeling theory

4. Which of the following is *not* an example of the informal economy?
   a. trading a haircut for a computer lesson
   b. selling illegal drugs on the street
   c. working as a computer programmer for a major corporation
   d. providing child care out of a private home, without reporting the income to the IRS

5. The systematic, widespread withdrawal of investment in basic aspects of productivity such as factories and plants is called
   a. deindustrialization.
   b. downsizing.
   c. postindustrialization.
   d. gentrification.

6. Karl Marx is associated with which of the following concepts?
   a. anomie
   b. assimilation
   c. apartheid
   d. alienation

7. Sociologists and labor specialists foresee a workforce increasingly composed of
   a. women.
   b. racial minorities.
   c. ethnic minorities.
   d. all of the above.

8. Currently, _____ _____ refers to positive efforts to recruit minority group members or women for jobs, promotions, and educational opportunities.

   a. equal rights
   b. affirmative action
   c. work programs
   d. equal action

9. The principle of laissez-faire was expounded and endorsed by the British economist

   a. John Maynard Keynes.
   b. Adam Smith.
   c. Paul Samuelson.
   d. Arthur Scargill.

10. Which sociologist, using the interactionist perspective, noted that "one key source of job satisfaction lies in the informal interaction shared by members of a work group"?

   a. Robert Blauner
   b. Donald Roy
   c. George Ritzer
   d. Karl Marx

11. The term _____ _____ refers to the social institution through which goods and services are produced, distributed, and consumed.

12. The principle of_____-_____, as expounded and endorsed by the British economist Adam Smith, was the prevailing form of capitalism immediately following the industrial revolution.

13. Under _____, the means of production and distribution in a society are collectively rather than privately owned, and the basic objective of the economic system is to meet people's needs rather than to maximize profits.

14. _____ is an economic system under which all property is communally owned and no social distinctions are made based on people's ability to produce.

15. The term _____ was introduced in 1987 to refer to reductions taken in a company's workforce as part of deindustrialization.

16. A(n) _____ society depends on mechanization to produce its goods and services.

17. _____ theorists point out that while pure monopolies are not a basic element of the economy of the United States, competition is much more restricted than one might expect in what is called a free enterprise system.

18. Émile Durkheim argued that as labor becomes more and more differentiated, individuals experience _____, or loss of direction.

19. Most studies of _____ have focused on factors that serve to increase or decrease worker satisfaction.

20. Some capitalist nations, such as the United States, outlaw _____ through antitrust legislation.

Answers:
1 (b); 2 (d); 3 (b); 4 (c); 5 (a); 6 (d); 7 (d); 8 (b); 9 (b); 10 (b); 11 economic system; 12 laissez-faire; 13 socialism; 14 Communism; 15 downsizing; 16 industrial; 17 Conflict; 18 anomie; 19 alienation; 20 monopolies

Online Learning Center

1. Now that you've studied topics related to the economy and work, this may be a good time to do some thinking about your future career possibilities. Materials in the student center of the Online Learning Center at **www.mhhe.com/schaefer11** can help. Link to Career Opportunities under Course-Wide Content for information on career possibilities for social science majors.

2. The Bureau of Labor Statistics (**www.bls.gov**) compiles many informative statistics on the U.S. labor force. Explore the site to learn about the current unemployment rate, both in the United States and in your home state.

3. Have you now or in the past been one of the many Americans who must balance work and family responsibilities? If so, information from a PBS special on juggling work and family (**hedricksmith .com/site_workfamily/index.html**) may be helpful. Or, visit the site simply to gain insights on the challenges these working Americans face.

*Note: Although all the URLs listed were current as of the printing of this book, these sites often change. Please check our Web site (**www.mhhe.com/schaefer11**) for updates, hyperlinks, and exercises related to these sites.*

Reel Society Video Clips

Reel Society video clips, which appear on this book's Web site, can be used to spark discussion about the following topics from this chapter:

- Economic Systems
- Changing Economies

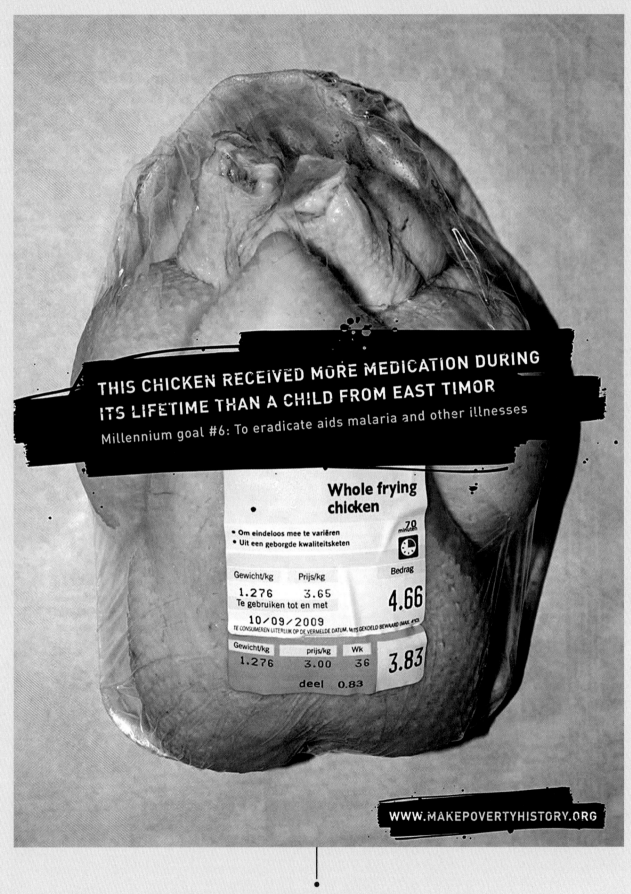

This advertisement for the One Campaign points out that in the United States, chickens receive more antibiotics than the children of many developing countries. For too many people, social inequality can have life-threatening consequences.

19 Health and Medicine

THE SCALPEL
AND THE
SILVER BEAR

The First Navajo
Woman Surgeon
Combines
Western Medicine
and
Traditional Healing

LORI ARVISO ALVORD, M.D.
AND
ELIZABETH COHEN VAN PELT

“ I knew that Navajo people mistrusted Western medicine, and that Navajo customs and beliefs, even Navajo ways of interacting with others, often stood in direct opposition to the way I was trained at Stanford to deliver medical care. I wanted to make a difference in the lives of my people, not only by providing surgery to heal them but also by making it easier for them to understand, relate to, and accept Western medicine. By speaking some Navajo with them, by showing respect for their ways, and by being one of them, I could help them. I watched my patients. I listened to them. Slowly I began to develop better ways to heal them, ways that respected their culture and beliefs. I desired to incorporate these traditional beliefs and customs into my practice. . . .

Navajo patients simply didn't respond well to the brusque and distanced style of Western doctors. To them it is not acceptable to walk into a room, quickly open someone's shirt and listen to their heart with a stethoscope, or stick something in their mouth or ear. Nor is it acceptable to ask probing and personal questions. As I adapted my practice to my culture, my patients relaxed in situations that could otherwise have been highly stressful to them. As they became more comfortable and at ease, something even more remarkable—astonishing, even—happened. When patients were trusting and accepting before surgery, their operations seemed to be more successful. If they were anxious, distrustful, and did not understand, or had resisted treatment, they seemed to have more operative or postoperative complications. Could this be happening? The more I watched, the more I saw it was indeed true. Incorporating Navajo philosophies of balance and symmetry, respect and connectedness into my practice, benefited my patients and allowed everything in my two worlds to make sense.

Navajos believe in *hózhǫ́* or *hózhǫ́ni*—"Walking in Beauty"—a worldview in which everything in life is connected and influences everything else. A stone thrown into a pond can influence the life of a deer in the forest, a human voice and a spoken word can influence events around the world, and all things possess spirit and power. So Navajos make every effort to live in harmony and balance with everyone and everything else. Their belief system sees sickness as a result of things falling out of balance, of losing one's way on the path of beauty. In this belief system, religion and medicine are one and the same. . . .

As I have modified my Western techniques with elements of Navajo culture and philosophy, I have seen the wisdom and truth of Navajo medicine too, and how Navajo patients can benefit from it. In this way I am pulling the strands of my life even closer together. The results have been dazzling—*hózhǫ́ni*. It has been beautiful. ”

> *Navajos believe in hózhǫ́ or hózhǫ́ni—"Walking in Beauty"—a worldview in which everything in life is connected and influences everything else.*

(Alvord and Van Pelt 1999:13–15) Additional information about this excerpt can be found on the Online Learning Center at www.mhhe.com/schaefer11.

455

In this excerpt from *The Scalpel and the Silver Bear,* Dr. Lori Arviso Alvord, the first Navajo woman to become a surgeon, describes her effort to bridge the cultural gap between Western medicine and traditional Native American healing. Dropping the impersonal clinical manner she had learned in medical school, Alvord reached out to her Navajo patients, acknowledging their faith in holistic healing practices. Her account communicates the wonder she felt as she watched their health improve. By walking in beauty, Dr. Alvord had become a healer as well as a surgeon.

Dr. Alvord's account illustrates the powerful effect of culture on both health and medicine. Culture affects the way people interact with doctors and healers, the way they relate to their families when they are sick, and even the way they think about health. Are some health problems peculiar to certain cultures? Who defines what illness is? How does health care vary from one social class to another and from one nation to another? In this chapter, we will consider first the relationship between culture and health. Then we will present a sociological overview of health, illness, health care, and medicine as a social institution. We will begin by examining how functionalists, conflict theorists, interactionists, and labeling theorists look at health-related issues. Then we will study the distribution of diseases in a society by social class, race and ethnicity, gender, and age.

We'll look too at the evolution of the U.S. health care system. Sociologists are interested in the roles people play in the health care system and the organizations that deal with issues of health and sickness. Therefore, we will analyze the interactions among physicians, nurses, and patients; alternatives to traditional health care; and the role of government in providing health services to the needy. The chapter continues with an examination of mental illness that contrasts the medical and labeling approaches to mental disorders. Finally, the Social Policy section explores the AIDS crisis, both at home and abroad.

Culture and Health

The communities people live in have an impact on their health. In rural areas, for example, residents must travel many miles to see a doctor. The nearest hospital may be hundreds of miles away. On the other hand, people who live in the country escape many of the stresses and strains that plague people who live in cities.

Culture, too, contributes to differences in medical care and even how health is defined. In Japan, for instance, organ transplants are rare. The Japanese do not generally favor harvesting organs from brain-dead donors. Researchers have shown that diseases, too, are rooted in the shared meanings of particular cultures. The term **culture-bound syndrome** refers to a disease or illness that cannot be understood apart from its specific social context (Shepherd 2003; U.S. Surgeon General 1999b).

In the United States, a culture-bound syndrome known as anorexia nervosa has received increasing attention over the last few decades. First described in England in the 1860s, this condition is characterized by an intense fear of becoming obese and a distorted image of one's body. Those who suffer from anorexia nervosa (primarily young women in their teenage years or 20s) lose weight drastically through self-induced semistarvation. Anorexia nervosa is best understood in the context of Western culture, which typically views the slim, youthful body as healthy and beautiful, and the fat person as ugly and lacking in self-discipline.

Until recently, U.S. researchers dealt with the concept of culture-bound syndromes only in cross-cultural studies. However, recent increases in immigration, along with efforts by the medical establishment to reach out to immigrant communities, have led to a belated recognition that not everyone views medicine in the same way. Medical practitioners are now being trained to recognize cultural beliefs that are related to medicine. Table 19-1 gives some examples.

Culture can also influence the relative incidence of a disease or disorder. In *The Scalpel and the Silver Bear,* Dr. Lori Arviso Alvord writes of the depression and alcoholism that attend life on the reservation. These diseases, she says, are born from "historical grief": "Navajo children are told of the capture and murder of their forefathers and mothers, and then they too must share in the legacy. . . ." Not just for the Navajo, Alvord writes, but for Black Americans as well, the weight of centuries of suffering, injustice, and loss too often manifests itself in despair and addiction. The rate of alcoholism mortality among Native Americans served by the Indian Health Service is five times that of the general population of the United States (Alvord and Van Pelt 1999:12).

Sociological Perspectives on Health and Illness

How can we define health? Imagine a continuum with health on one end and death on the other. In the preamble to its 1946 constitution, the World Health Organization defined **health** as a "state of complete physical, mental, and social well-being, and not merely the absence of disease and infirmity" (Leavell and Clark 1965:14).

In this definition, the "healthy" end of the continuum represents an ideal rather than a precise condition. Along the continuum, people define themselves as healthy or sick on the basis of criteria established by themselves and relatives, friends, co-workers, and medical practitioners. Because health is relative,

Table 19-1   **457**

Cultural Challenges to Medicine

Culture	Cultural Challenge	Implications for Medical Decision Making and Treatment
Central Americans	May consider pain a consequence of "earthly misconduct" or imbalance of nature.	May give the impression of acquiescing to a doctor's suggestion (through silence or nodding) because of reluctance to disagree with a person of such authority.
Ethiopians, Eritreans	Traditionally have viewed pregnancy as a dangerous state, blaming sorcery for miscarriages and other bad outcomes.	May have little knowledge or understanding of treatment procedures. A patient who is asked to sign consent forms may become very anxious.
Koreans	May seek care from a *hanui,* a traditional herbal medicine doctor.	Often keep bad medical news from a family member who is ill, believing that such information would wipe out hope.

Source: Adapted from Levine 2006:31.

then, we can view it in a social context and consider how it varies in different situations or cultures.

Why is it that you may consider yourself sick or well when others do not agree? Who controls definitions of health and illness in our society, and for what ends? What are the consequences of viewing yourself (or of being viewed) as ill or disabled? By drawing on four sociological perspectives—functionalism, conflict theory, interactionism, and labeling theory—we can gain greater insight into the social context that shapes definitions of health and the treatment of illness.

Functionalist Approach

Illness entails breaks in our social interactions, both at work and at home. From a functionalist perspective, being sick must therefore be controlled, so that not too many people are released from their societal responsibilities at any one time. Functionalists contend that an overly broad definition of illness would disrupt the workings of a society.

Sickness requires that one take on a social role, if only temporarily. The *sick role* refers to societal expectations about the attitudes and behavior of a person viewed as being ill. Sociolo- {p.15 gist Talcott Parsons (1951, 1975), well known for his contributions to functionalist theory, outlined the behavior required of people who are considered sick. They are exempted from their normal, day-to-day responsibilities and generally do not suffer blame for their condition. Yet they are obligated to try to get well, which includes seeking competent professional care. Attempting to get well is particularly important in the world's developing countries. Modern automated industrial societies can absorb a greater degree of illness or disability than horticultural or agrarian societies, in which the availability of workers is far more critical (Conrad 2005).

According to Parsons's theory, physicians function as "gatekeepers" for the sick role. They either verify a patient's condition as "illness" or designate the patient as "recovered." The ill person

becomes dependent on the physician, because the latter can control valued rewards (not only treatment of illness, but also excused absences from work and school). Parsons suggests that the physician–patient relationship is somewhat like that between parent and child. Like a parent, the physician helps the patient to enter society as a full and functioning adult (Segall 1976).

The concept of the sick role is not without criticism. First, patients' judgments regarding their own state of health may be related to their gender, age, social class, and ethnic group. For example, younger people may fail to detect warning signs of a dangerous illness, while the elderly may focus too much on the

In U.S. society, people who are sick are supposed to stay home and rest until they feel better. Though different societies have different expectations of a person who is seen as being ill, all recognize the significance of the *sick role.*

What Is Medical Care?

Sociologists are interested in how people decide they need medical attention, what kind of care they expect to get, and whom they trust to deliver it. The answers to these questions vary dramatically from one culture to another. In the United States, for example, people typically do not seek dental care from a sidewalk practitioner. Yet for many residents of India, street dentists (below) are an affordable alternative to Western-style dentistry. People from different cultures also seek different remedies for their illnesses, from Western pharmaceuticals to the herbal treatments and folk remedies common in Asia (opposite, top left and right). Likewise, the type of medical practitioner people visit varies from culture to culture. In the United States, robotic machines can now diagnose illness (opposite, bottom left); in Mexico, people continue to visit the *curandero,* or folk healer, (opposite, bottom right).

{India}

{Asia}

{Indonesia}

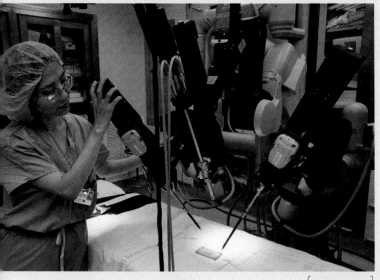

{United States}

{Mexico}

459

slightest physical malady. Second, the sick role may be more applicable to people who are experiencing short-term illnesses than to those with recurring, long-term illnesses. Finally, even simple factors, such as whether a person is employed, seem to affect one's willingness to assume the sick role—as does the impact of socialization into a particular occupation or activity. For example, beginning in childhood, athletes learn to define certain ailments as "sports injuries" and therefore do not regard themselves as "sick." Nonetheless, sociologists continue to rely on Parsons's model for functionalist analysis of the relationship between illness and societal expectations of the sick (Curry 1993).

www.mhhe.com/schaefer11

Use Your Sociological **Imagination**

Describe some situations you have witnessed that illustrate different definitions of the "sick role."

Conflict Approach

Conflict theorists observe that the medical profession has assumed a preeminence that extends well beyond whether to excuse a student from school or an employee from work. Sociologist Eliot Freidson (1970:5) has likened the position of medicine today to that of state religions yesterday—it has an officially approved monopoly of the right to define health and illness and to treat illness. Conflict theorists use the term *medicalization of society* to refer to the growing role of medicine as a major institution of social control (Conrad and Schneider 1992; McKinlay and McKinlay 1977; Zola 1972, 1983).

The Medicalization of Society Social control involves techniques and strategies for regulating behavior in order to enforce the distinctive norms and values of a culture. Typically, we {p.184 think of informal social control as occurring within families and peer groups, and formal social control as being carried out by authorized agents such as police officers, judges, school administrators, and employers. Viewed from a conflict perspective, however, medicine is not simply a "healing profession"; it is a regulating mechanism.

How does medicine manifest its social control? First, medicine has greatly expanded its domain of expertise in recent decades. Physicians now examine a wide range of issues, among them sexuality, old age, anxiety, obesity, child development, alcoholism, and drug addiction. We tolerate this expansion of the boundaries of medicine because we hope that these experts can bring new "miracle cures" to complex human problems, as they have to the control of certain infectious diseases.

The social significance of this expanding medicalization is that once a problem is viewed using a *medical model*—once medical experts become influential in proposing and assessing

relevant public policies—it becomes more difficult for common people to join the discussion and exert influence on decision making. It also becomes more difficult to view these issues as being shaped by social, cultural, or psychological factors, rather than simply by physical or medical factors (Caplan 1989; Conrad and Schneider 1992; Starr 1982).

Second, medicine serves as an agent of social control by retaining absolute jurisdiction over many health care procedures. It has even attempted to guard its jurisdiction by placing health care professionals such as chiropractors and nurse-midwives outside the realm of acceptable medicine. Despite the fact that midwives first brought professionalism to child delivery, they have been portrayed as having invaded the "legitimate" field of obstetrics, both in the United States and Mexico. Nurse-midwives have sought licensing as a way to achieve professional respectability, but physicians continue to exert power to ensure that midwifery remains a subordinate occupation (Friedland 2000).

The growing concern about obesity among the young has focused attention on their eating habits and their need for exercise.

Inequities in Health Care The medicalization of society is but one concern of conflict theorists as they assess the workings of health care institutions. As we have seen throughout this textbook, in analyzing any issue, conflict theorists seek to determine who benefits, who suffers, and who dominates at the expense of others. Viewed from a conflict perspective, glaring inequities exist in health care delivery in the United States. For example, poor areas tend to be underserved because medical services concentrate where people are wealthy.

Similarly, from a global perspective, obvious inequities exist in health care delivery. Today, the United States has about 266 physicians per 10,000 people, while African nations have fewer than 1 per 10,000. This situation is only worsened by the ***brain drain***—the immigration to the United States and other industrialized nations of skilled workers, professionals, and technicians who are desperately needed in their home countries. As part of this brain drain, physicians, nurses, and other health care professionals have come to the United States from developing countries such as India, Pakistan, and various African states. Conflict theorists view their emigration out of the Third World as yet another way in which the world's core industrialized nations enhance their quality of life at the expense of developing countries. One way the developing countries suffer is in lower life expectancy. In Africa and much of Latin America and Asia, life expectancy is far lower than in industrialized nations (Bureau of the Census 2006a:110; World Bank 2006a).

Conflict theorists emphasize that inequities in health care have clear life-and-death consequences. From a conflict perspective, the dramatic differences in infant mortality rates around the world (see Figure 19-1) reflect, at least in part, unequal distribution of health care resources based on the wealth or poverty of various communities and nations. Still, despite the wealth of the United States, at least 39 nations have *lower* infant mortality rates, among them Canada, Sweden, and Japan. Conflict theorists point out that unlike the United States, these countries offer some form of government-supported health care for all citizens, which typically leads to greater availability and use of prenatal care.

Interactionist Approach

From an interactionist point of view, patients are not passive; often, they actively seek the services of a health care practitioner. In examining health, illness, and medicine as a social institution, then, interactionists engage in micro-level study of the roles played by health care professionals and patients. Interactionists are particularly interested in how physicians learn to play their occupational role. According to Brenda L. Beagan (2001), the technical language students learn in medical school becomes the basis for the script they follow as novice physicians. The familiar white coat is their costume—one that helps them to appear confident and professional at the same time that it identifies them as doctors to patients and other staff members. Beagan found that many medical students struggle to project the appearance of competence they think their role demands.

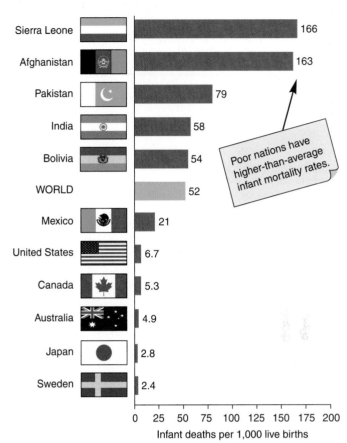

Infant Mortality Rates in Selected Countries

	Infant deaths per 1,000 live births
Sierra Leone	166
Afghanistan	163
Pakistan	79
India	58
Bolivia	54
WORLD	52
Mexico	21
United States	6.7
Canada	5.3
Australia	4.9
Japan	2.8
Sweden	2.4

Poor nations have higher-than-average infant mortality rates.

Source: Haub 2006.

Sometimes patients play an active role in health care by *failing* to follow a physician's advice. For example, some patients stop taking medications long before they should. Some take an incorrect dosage on purpose, and others never even fill their prescriptions. Such noncompliance results in part from the prevalence of self-medication in our society; many people are accustomed to self-diagnosis and self-treatment. On the other hand, patients' active involvement in their health care can sometimes have very *positive* consequences. Some patients read books about preventive health care techniques, attempt to maintain a healthful and nutritious diet, carefully monitor any side effects of medication, and adjust the dosage based on perceived side effects. Finally, as Box 19-1 (page 462) shows, physicians may *change* their approach to a patient based on the patient's wishes.

Labeling Approach

Labeling theory helps us to understand why certain people are { p.197 *viewed* as deviants, "bad kids," or criminals, whereas others whose behavior is similar are not. Labeling theorists also suggest that the designation "healthy" or "ill" generally involves social definition by others. Just as police officers, judges, and

19-1 To Inform or Not to Inform? How Race and Ethnicity Affect Views of Patient Autonomy

Should patients be told the seriousness of their illness? Should they be included in the decisions about what medical care they receive? In the last 25 years, the principle of patient autonomy has become a fundamental ideal of medical care in the United States. According to this principle, "people have the right to make informed decisions about their medical care; consequently, they need the truth about their diagnosis, their prognosis, and the risks and benefits of possible treatments." While the ideal of patient autonomy has won wide acceptance from physicians, policymakers, and the general public, some critics argue that the current focus on patient autonomy reflects an ethnocentric cultural bias that ignores other values, such as family integrity and physician responsibility.

The question of how race and ethnicity influence attitudes toward patient autonomy was studied by a team of researchers, including an internal medicine specialist and ethicist, anthropologists, translators, a statistician, and a law professor. At 31 senior centers in Los Angeles County, the researchers administered questionnaires to 800 people of diverse ethnic backgrounds, all of them age 65 or over. The major finding of the study was that there are marked differences by race and ethnicity in attitudes toward patient autonomy. While 88 percent of African Americans and 87 percent of White Americans believe that a patient should be informed of a diagnosis of cancer, the same is true of only 65 percent of Mexican Americans and 47 percent of Korean Americans. Moreover, 69 percent of Whites and 63 percent of African Americans believe that a patient should be informed of a terminal prognosis, compared with 48 percent of Mexican Americans and 35 percent of Korean Americans.

> *Navajos believe that physicians and other healers should never offer a terminal diagnosis or use any negative language that could trouble or hurt a patient.*

One reason why Korean Americans are especially opposed to hearing a terminal prognosis is their belief in the unity of mind and body. Truth-telling is like a death sentence to traditional Koreans, because of their view that the body will react to ominous news received by the mind. Many Korean Americans believe that physicians should always be optimistic and positive in their communications with patients.

Similarly, a separate study of residents of a Navajo Indian reservation in Arizona revealed that Navajo culture places a high value on thinking and speaking in a positive way. For Navajos, language can shape reality. Consequently, Navajos believe that physicians and other healers should never offer a terminal diagnosis or use any negative language that could trouble or hurt a patient. One highly regarded medicine man notes that the mention of death to a patient "is sharper than any needle" (Carrese and Rhodes 1995:828).

Let's Discuss

1. How has terminal illness been handled in your family? Have relatives who were dying been told the truth about their condition, or has it been withheld from them? Do you think your family's cultural background influenced the decision?
2. Which is more important, the patient's right to know or the patient's faith in the chance of recovery?

Sources: Blackhall et al. 1995; Carrese and Rhodes 1995; Commonwealth Fund 2002; Monmaney 1995.

---

other regulators of social control have the power to define certain people as criminals, health care professionals (especially physicians) have the power to define certain people as sick. Moreover, like labels that suggest nonconformity or criminality, labels that are associated with illness commonly reshape how others treat us and how we see ourselves. Our society attaches serious consequences to labels that suggest less-than-perfect physical or mental health (Becker 1963; C. Clark 1983; H. Schwartz 1987).

A historical example illustrates perhaps the ultimate extreme in labeling social behavior as a sickness. As enslavement of Africans in the United States came under increasing attack in the 19th century, medical authorities provided new rationalizations for the oppressive practice. Noted physicians published articles stating that the skin color of Africans deviated from "healthy" white skin coloring because Africans suffered from congenital leprosy. Moreover, the continuing efforts of enslaved Africans to escape from their White masters were classified as an example of the "disease" of drapetomania (or "crazy runaways"). The prestigious *New Orleans Medical and Surgical Journal* suggested that the remedy for this "disease" was to treat slaves kindly, as one might treat children. Apparently, these medical authorities would not entertain the view that it was healthy and sane to flee slavery or join in a slave revolt (Szasz 1971).

By the late 1980s, the power of one particular label—"person {p.112 with AIDS"—had become quite evident. As we saw in our discussion of the late Arthur Ashe, this label often functions as a master status that overshadows all other aspects of a person's life. Once someone is told that he or she has tested positive for HIV, the virus associated with AIDS, that person is forced to confront immediate and difficult questions: Should I tell my family members, my sexual partner(s), my friends, my co-workers, my employer? How will these people respond? People's intense fear of the disease has led to prejudice and discrimination—even social ostracism—against those who have (or are suspected of having) AIDS. A person who has AIDS must deal not only with the serious medical consequences of the disease, but with the distressing social consequences associated with the label.

According to labeling theorists, we can view a variety of life experiences as illnesses or not. Recently, premenstrual syndrome, posttraumatic disorders, and hyperactivity have been labeled medically recognized disorders. In addition, the medical community continues to disagree over whether chronic fatigue syndrome constitutes a medical illness.

Probably the most noteworthy medical example of labeling is the case of homosexuality. For years, psychiatrists classified being gay or lesbian not as a lifestyle but as a mental disorder subject to treatment. This official sanction by the psychiatry profession became an early target of the growing gay and lesbian rights movement in the United States. In 1974, members of the American Psychiatric Association voted to drop homosexuality from the standard manual on mental disorders (Adam 1995; Monteiro 1998).

Table 19-2 summarizes four major sociological perspectives on health and illness. Though they may seem quite different, two common themes unite them. First, any person's health or illness is more than an organic condition, since it is subject to the interpretation of others. The impact of culture, family and friends, and the medical profession means that health and illness are not purely biological occurrences, but sociological occurrences as well. Second, since members of a society (especially industrial societies) share the same health care delivery system, health is a group and societal concern. Although health may be defined as the complete well-being of an individual, it is also the result of his or her social environment, as the next section will show (Cockerham 2007).

Social Epidemiology and Health

Social epidemiology is the study of the distribution of disease, impairment, and general health status across a population. Initially, epidemiology concentrated on the scientific study of epidemics, focusing on how they started and spread. Contemporary social epidemiology is much broader in scope, concerned not only with epidemics but also with nonepidemic diseases, injuries, drug addiction and alcoholism, suicide, and mental illness. Recently, epidemiologists took on the new role of tracking bioterrorism. In 2001 they mobilized to trace the anthrax outbreak and prepare for any terrorist use of smallpox or other lethal microbes. Epidemiologists draw on the work of a wide variety of scientists and researchers, among them physicians, sociologists, public health officials, biologists, veterinarians, demographers, anthropologists, psychologists, and meteorologists.

Researchers in social epidemiology commonly use two concepts: *incidence* and *prevalence*. **Incidence** refers to the number of new cases of a specific disorder that occur within a given population during a stated period, usually a year. For example, the incidence of AIDS in the United States in 2004 was 44,108 cases. In contrast, **prevalence** refers to the total number of cases of a specific disorder that exist at a given time. The prevalence of HIV/AIDS in the United States through 2006 was about one million cases (Bureau of the Census 2006a:120; Centers for Disease Control and Prevention 2006).

When disease incidence figures are presented as rates, or as the number of reports per 100,000 people, they are called **morbidity rates.** (The term **mortality rate** refers to the incidence of *death* in a given population.) Sociologists find morbidity rates useful because they reveal that a specific disease occurs more frequently among one segment of a population than another. As we shall see, social class, race, ethnicity, gender, and age can all affect a population's morbidity rates.

Social Class

Social class is clearly associated with differences in morbidity and mortality rates. Studies in the United States and other countries have consistently shown that people in the lower classes have higher rates of mortality and disability than others. One study concluded that Americans whose family incomes were less than $10,000 could expect to die seven years sooner than those with incomes of at least $25,000 (Pamuk et al. 1998).

Why is class linked to health? Crowded living conditions, substandard housing, poor diet, and stress all contribute to the

Table 19-2

Sociological Perspectives on Health and Illness

	Functionalist	Conflict	Interactionist	Labeling
Major emphasis	Control of the number of people who are considered sick	Overmedicalization Gross inequities in health care	Doctor–patient relationship Interaction of medical staff	Definition of illness and health
Controlling factors	Physician as gatekeeper	Medical profession Social inequities	Medical profession	Medical profession
Proponents	Talcott Parsons	Paul Starr Thomas Szasz Irving Zola	Doug Maynard	Thomas Szasz

summingUP

{ When people who do not have health insurance seek medical care, their condition is often more critical than it would be if they had been receiving regular preventive care from a primary care provider. And the care they receive, especially if it is delivered in an emergency room, is much more expensive than the care delivered in a doctor's office. }

In the view of Karl Marx and contemporary conflict theorists, capitalist societies such as the United States care more about maximizing profits than they do about the health and safety of industrial workers. As a result, government agencies do not take forceful action to regulate conditions in the workplace, and workers suffer many preventable job-related injuries and illnesses. Research also shows that the lower classes are more vulnerable to environmental pollution than the affluent, not only where they work but where they live (see Chapter 21).

Use Your Sociological Imagination
Does the cost of health care affect the way you receive medical services?

www.mhhe.com/schaefer11

ill health of many low-income people in the United States. In certain instances, poor education may lead to a lack of awareness of measures necessary to maintain good health. Financial strains are certainly a major factor in the health problems of less affluent people.

What is particularly troubling about social class differences is that they appear to be cumulative. Little or no health care in childhood or young adulthood is likely to mean more illness later in life. The longer that low income presents a barrier to adequate health care, the more chronic and difficult to treat illness becomes (Prus 2007).

Another reason for the link between social class and health is that the poor—many of whom belong to racial and ethnic minorities—are less able than others to afford quality medical care. As Figure 19-2 shows, the affluent are more likely than others to have health insurance, either because they can afford it or because they have jobs that provide it. This situation has been deteriorating over time, as employer-provided coverage (the most common form of health insurance) declined steadily from 2000 to 2005 (E. Gould 2006).

Another factor in the link between class and health is evident at the workplace: The occupations of people in the working and lower classes of the United States tend to be more dangerous than those of more affluent citizens. Miners, for example, risk injury or death from explosions and cave-ins; they are also vulnerable to respiratory diseases such as black lung. Workers in textile mills who are exposed to toxic substances may contract a variety of illnesses, including one commonly known as *brown lung disease*. In recent years, the nation has learned of the perils of asbestos poisoning, a particular worry for construction workers (Berkman 2004; R. Hall 1982; J. Scott 2005).

Race and Ethnicity

The health profiles of many racial and ethnic minorities reflect the social inequality evident in the United States. The poor economic and environmental conditions of groups such as African Americans, Hispanics, and Native Americans are manifested in high morbidity and mortality rates for these groups. It is true that some afflictions, such as sickle-cell anemia among Blacks,

FIGURE 19–2

Percentage of People without Health Insurance

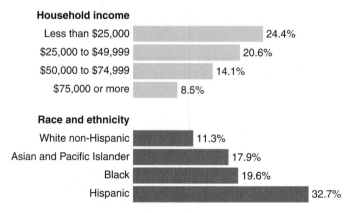

Household income

Less than $25,000	24.4%
$25,000 to $49,999	20.6%
$50,000 to $74,999	14.1%
$75,000 or more	8.5%

Race and ethnicity

White non-Hispanic	11.3%
Asian and Pacific Islander	17.9%
Black	19.6%
Hispanic	32.7%

Note: Based on 2-year average 2003–2004.
Source: DeNavas-Walt et al. 2006:22.

have a clear genetic basis. But in most instances, environmental factors contribute to the differential rates of disease and death.

In many respects, the mortality rates for African Americans are distressing. Compared with Whites, Blacks have higher death rates from heart disease, pneumonia, diabetes, and cancer. The death rate from stroke is twice as high among African Americans. Such epidemiological findings reflect in part the fact that a high proportion of Blacks are found among the nation's lower classes. According to the National Center for Health Statistics (2007), Whites can expect to live 78.3 years. In contrast, life expectancy for Blacks is 73.1 years.

As noted earlier, infant mortality is regarded as a primary indicator of health care. There is a significant gap in the United States between the infant mortality rates of African Americans and Whites. Generally, the rate of infant death is more than twice as high among Blacks. African Americans account for 15 percent of all live births in the nation but 29 percent of infant deaths. Puerto Ricans and Native Americans have infant mortality rates that are lower than African Americans' but higher than Whites' (MacDorman et al. 2005).

The medical establishment is not exempt from racism. Unfortunately, the media often focus on obvious forms of racism, such as hate crimes, while overlooking more insidious forms in social institutions like the medical establishment. One review of more than 100 studies conducted over the last decade concluded that minorities receive inferior care even when they are insured. Despite having access to care, Blacks, Latinos, and American Indians are treated unequally as a result of racial prejudice and differences in the quality of various health care plans. Furthermore, national clinical studies have shown that even allowing for differences in income and insurance coverage, racial and ethnic minorities are less likely than other groups to receive both standard health care and life-saving treatment for conditions such as HIV infection (Caesar and Williams 2002; Smedley et al. 2002; Steyerberg et al. 2005).

The roots of this unequal treatment extend back to slavery. Scholars from a variety of disciplines have investigated the history of African American health care and found some shocking abuses of the Hippocratic oath. Box 19-2 (page 466) details the deliberate misuse of medicine that lies at the foundation of what some have called *medical apartheid*.

Drawing on the conflict perspective, sociologist Howard Waitzkin (1986) suggests that racial tensions also contribute to the medical problems of Blacks. In his view, the stress that results from racial prejudice and discrimination helps to explain the higher rates of hypertension found among African Americans (and Hispanics) compared to Whites. Hypertension—twice as common in Blacks as in Whites—is believed to be a critical factor in Blacks' high mortality rates from heart disease, kidney disease, and stroke (Morehouse Medical Treatment and Effectiveness Center 1999).

Some Mexican Americans and many other Latinos adhere to cultural beliefs that make them less likely to use the established medical system. They may interpret their illnesses according to traditional Latino folk medicine, or **curanderismo**—a form of holistic health care and healing. *Curanderismo* influences how one approaches health care and even how one defines illness. Most Hispanics probably use folk healers, or *curanderos,* infrequently, but perhaps 20 percent rely on home remedies. Some define such illnesses as *susto* (fright sickness) and *atague* (or fighting attack) according to folk beliefs. Because these complaints often have biological bases, sensitive medical practitioners need to deal with them carefully in order to diagnose and treat illnesses accurately. Moreover, it would be a mistake to blame the poor health care that Latinos receive on cultural differences. Latinos are much more likely to seek treatment for pressing medical problems at clinics and emergency rooms than they are to receive regular preventive care through a family physician (Council on Scientific Affairs 1999; Durden and Hummer 2006; Trotter and Chavira 1997).

Gender

A large body of research indicates that compared with men, women experience a higher prevalence of many illnesses, although they tend to live longer. There are some variations—for example, men are more likely to have parasitic diseases, whereas women are more likely to become diabetic—but as a group, women appear to be in poorer health than men.

The apparent inconsistency between the ill health of women and their greater longevity deserves an explanation, and researchers have advanced a theory. Women's lower rate of cigarette smoking (reducing their risk of heart disease, lung cancer, and emphysema), lower consumption of alcohol (reducing the risk of auto accidents and cirrhosis of the liver), and lower rate of employment in dangerous occupations explain about one-third of their greater longevity than men. Moreover, some clinical studies suggest that the differences in morbidity may actually be less pronounced than the data show. Researchers argue that women are much more likely than men to seek treatment, to be diagnosed as having a disease, and thus to have their illnesses reflected in the data examined by epidemiologists.

From a conflict perspective, women have been particularly vulnerable to the medicalization of society, with everything from birth to beauty being treated in an increasingly medical context. Such medicalization may contribute to women's higher morbidity rates compared to those of men. Ironically, even though women have been especially affected by medicalization, medical researchers have often excluded them from clinical studies. Female physicians and researchers charge that sexism lies at the heart of such research practices, and insist there is a desperate need for studies of female subjects (Bates 1999; McDonald 1999; Vidaver et al. 2000).

Age

Health is the overriding concern of the elderly. Most older people in the United States report having at least one chronic illness, but only some of those conditions are potentially life threatening or require medical care. At the same time, health problems can affect the quality of life of older people in important ways.

social**INEQUALITY**

19-2 Medical Apartheid

Numerous studies have shown that even when medical care is accessible to African Americans, many are reluctant to trust the U.S. medical establishment. From seeking medical care to giving blood or signing an organ donation card, Black Americans are less likely than others to participate in life-saving medical programs. Unfortunately, there appears to be good reason for their reluctance to take advantage of a world-class medical system: a long and continuing history of mistreatment. Banned from medical schools, denied access to "White blood" as soldiers until after World War II, and prohibited from joining the American Medical Association until the 1960s, Blacks have long suffered from explicit discrimination at the hands of the medical establishment.

Even so, their wary attitude toward medicine has more to do with the way African Americans have been treated as patients. In the notorious Tuskegee syphilis study, begun by the federal government in 1932, doctors knowingly infected Black men from Alabama with syphilis in order to observe the disease's progression. Despite the discovery of antibiotic treatments for the disease in 1945, the men did not receive medical treatment until the press exposed the unethical program in 1972. This deliberate abuse of African Americans' human rights has made contemporary Blacks particularly leery of the medical establishment.

Regrettably, Tuskegee was not an isolated case, nor was it the first or the last. For generations before Tuskegee, medical practitioners' role with respect to people of color was either to verify their worth as slaves, by certifying them as healthy, or to determine whether they were truly sick or feigning illness to avoid slave labor. Even after Tuskegee was exposed, the abuse continued. In Baltimore in 1991, in a program that was applauded by some observers as a way to "reduce the underclass," researchers implanted the now-defunct birth control device Norplant in African American teenagers. And from 1992 to 1997, in a study meant to determine whether there is a biological or genetic basis for violent behavior, researchers at Columbia University misled the parents of their young subjects, all of whom were Black males, by telling them that the children would undergo no more than a series of

> *In the notorious Tuskegee syphilis study, begun by the federal government in 1932, doctors knowingly infected Black men from Alabama with syphilis in order to observe the disease's progression.*

tests and questions. In fact, the boys were given potentially risky doses of the same drug found in the now-banned Fen-phen weight-loss pill, which causes heart irregularities.

Given these ethical violations, the Black community's suspicious attitude toward the medical community is understandable. Unfortunately, their absence from research trials has also hurt them. Only 1 percent of the nearly 20 million Americans currently enrolled in biomedical studies and clinical trials is Black. Yet research shows that in well-managed clinical trials, African Americans' participation is no different from that of Whites; they are simply less likely than other groups to be included. Thus, Blacks often miss out on the latest medical breakthroughs. Virtually no Blacks were included in the original studies of the HIV inhibitor AZT, for example. Because the Food and Drug Administration had little evidence of its impact on Black patients when the drug came into widespread use in 1991, the agency erroneously reported that it was ineffective in the treatment of African Americans.

In sum, medical abuse of the African American community is not some distant historical fact. Observers maintain that rather than leaving the issue to journalists and historians, the medical profession should acknowledge the flagrant mistakes of the past, along with the more subtle ones of today. For this community to be healed, the focus must shift from Black Americans' well-publicized concerns about medicine to the demonstrated untrustworthiness of U.S. medical research.

Let's Discuss

1. Do you know anyone who has experienced deliberately inferior or unethical medical treatment? If so, do you think that racism was the reason for the mistreatment? Were any other factors involved?
2. Drawing on what you have learned in this course, what, other than racism, do you think might explain the behavior of the doctors who agreed to participate in experiments that clearly violated their professional oaths?

Sources: Centers for Disease Control and Prevention 2007; Goodwin 2006; Head 2007; Jecker 2000; Reverby 2000; Washington 2007.

Almost half of older people in the United States are troubled by arthritis, and many have visual or hearing impairments that can interfere with the performance of everyday tasks.

Older people are also especially vulnerable to certain mental health problems. Alzheimer's disease, the leading cause of dementia in the United States, afflicts an estimated 5.9 million people age 65 or over—that is, 13 percent of that segment of the population. While some individuals with Alzheimer's exhibit only mild symptoms, the risk of severe problems resulting from the disease rises substantially with age (Alzheimer's Association 2007:5).

Not surprisingly, older people in the United States (ages 75 and older) are five times more likely to use health services and to be hospitalized than younger people (ages 15–24). The disproportionate use of the U.S. health care system by older people is a critical factor in all discussions about the cost of health care and possible reforms of the health care system (Bureau of the Census 2006a:112).

In sum, to achieve greater access and reduce health disparities, federal health officials must overcome inequities that are rooted not just in age, but in social class, race and ethnicity, and gender.

FIGURE 19–3

Availability of Physicians by State

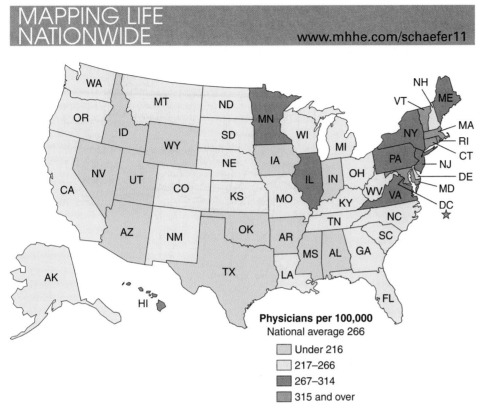

MAPPING LIFE
NATIONWIDE

www.mhhe.com/schaefer11

Physicians per 100,000
National average 266

Under 216
217–266
267–314
315 and over

Source: Data for 2004 in Bureau of the Census 2006a:110.

If that were not enough, they must also deal with a geographical disparity in health care resources. Figure 19-3 shows the differences in the presence of physicians from one state to another. Dramatic differences in the availability of physicians, hospitals, and nursing homes also exist between urban and rural areas in the same state.

Health Care in the United States

As the entire nation is well aware, the costs of health care have skyrocketed in the last 35 years. In 1997, total expenditures for health care in the United States crossed the trillion-dollar threshold—more than four times the 1980 figure (see Figure 19-4, page 468). In 2000, the amount spent on health care equaled that spent on education, defense, prisons, farm subsidies, food stamps, and foreign aid combined. By the year 2015, total expenditures for health care in the United States are expected to exceed $3.8 trillion. The rising costs of medical care are especially burdensome in the event of catastrophic illnesses or confinement to a nursing home. Bills of tens of thousands of dollars are not unusual in the treatment of cancer, Alzheimer's disease, and other chronic illnesses requiring custodial care.

The health care system of the United States has moved far beyond the days when general practitioners living in a neighbor-hood or community typically made house calls and charged modest fees for their services. How did health care become a big business involving nation-wide hospital chains and marketing campaigns? How have these changes reshaped the interactions between doctors, nurses, and patients? We will address these questions in the next section of the chapter.

A Historical View

Today, state licensing and medical degrees confer an authority on medical professionals that is maintained from one generation to the next. However, health care in the United States has not always followed this model. The "popular health movement" of the 1830s and 1840s emphasized preventive care and what is termed "self-help." Strong criticism was voiced of "doctoring" as a paid occupation. New medical philosophies or sects established their own medical schools and challenged the authority and methods of more traditional doctors. By the 1840s, most states had repealed medical licensing laws.

In response, through the leadership of the American Medical Association (AMA), founded in 1848, "regular" doctors attacked lay practitioners, sectarian doctors, and female physicians in general. (For a different view, see Navarro 1984.) Once they had institutionalized their authority through standardized programs of education and licensing, they conferred it on all who successfully completed their programs. The authority of the physician no longer depended on lay attitudes or on the person occupying the sick role; increasingly, it was built into the structure of the medical profession and the health care system. As the institutionalization of health care proceeded, the medical profession gained control over both the market for its services and the various organizational hierarchies that govern medical practice, financing, and policymaking. By the 1920s, physicians controlled hospital technology, the division of labor of health personnel, and indirectly, other professional practices such as nursing and pharmacy (R. Coser 1984).

Physicians, Nurses, and Patients

Traditionally, physicians have held a position of dominance in their dealings with both patients and nurses. The functionalist and interactionist perspectives offer a framework for understanding the professional socialization of physicians as it relates to patient care. Functionalists suggest that established physicians and medical school professors serve as mentors or role models

Total Health Care Expenditures in the United States, 1970–2015 (projected)

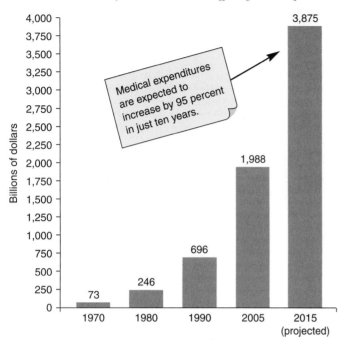

Medical expenditures are expected to increase by 95 percent in just ten years.

Billions of dollars

1970	1980	1990	2005	2015 (projected)
73	246	696	1,988	3,875

Sources: Centers for Medicare and Medicaid Services 2007 (2005–2015 data); Health Care Financing Administration 2001 (1970–1990 data).

Think About It

What social changes in the United States might account for the rise in health care costs from $73 billion in 1970 to $1.9 trillion in 2005?

who transmit knowledge, skills, and values to the passive learner—the medical student. Interactionists emphasize that students are molded by the medical school environment as they interact with their classmates.

Both approaches argue that the typical training of physicians in the United States leads to rather dehumanizing physician–patient encounters. As Dr. Lori Arviso Alvord writes in *The Scalpel and the Silver Bear,* "I had been trained by a group of physicians who placed much more emphasis on their technical abilities and clinical skills than on their abilities to be caring and sensitive" (Alvord and Van Pelt 1999:13). Despite many efforts to formally introduce a humanistic approach to patient care into the medical school curriculum, patient overload and cost-cutting by hospitals have tended to undercut positive relations. Moreover, widespread publicity about malpractice suits and high medical costs has further strained the physician–patient relationship.

Interactionists have closely examined compliance and negotiation between physician and patient. They concur with Talcott Parsons's view that the relationship is generally asymmetrical, with doctors holding a position of dominance and controlling rewards.

Just as physicians have maintained dominance in their interactions with patients, they have controlled interactions with nurses. Despite their training and professional status, nurses commonly take orders from physicians. Traditionally, the relationship between doctors and nurses has paralleled the male dominance of the United States: Most physicians have been male, while virtually all nurses have been female.

Like other women in subordinate roles, nurses have been expected to perform their duties without challenging the authority of men. Psychiatrist Leonard Stein (1967) refers to this process as the *doctor–nurse game.* According to the rules of this "game," the nurse must never openly disagree with the physician. When she has recommendations concerning a patient's care, she must communicate them indirectly, in a deferential tone. For example, if asked by a hospital's medical resident, "What sleeping medication has been helpful to Mrs. Brown in the past?" (an indirect request for a recommendation), the nurse will respond with a disguised recommendation, such as "Pentobarbital mg 100 was quite effective night before last." Her careful response allows the physician to authoritatively restate the same prescription as if it were *his* idea.

Like nurses, female physicians have traditionally found themselves in a subordinate position because of gender. In fall 2004, while 49 percent of all new medical school students in the United States were female, only 31 percent of all faculty members at medical schools were female (Association of American Medical Colleges 2005a, 2005b).

A study of male and female medical residents suggests that the increasing number of women physicians may alter the traditional doctor–patient relationship. Male residents were found to be more focused on the intellectual challenges of medicine and the prestige associated with certain medical specialties. In contrast, female residents were more likely to express a commitment to caring for patients and devoting time to them. In terms of the functionalist analysis of gender stratification offered by sociolo-{p.15} gists Talcott Parsons and Robert Bales, male residents took the *instrumental,* achievement-oriented role, while female residents took the *expressive,* interpersonal-oriented role. As women continue to enter and move higher in the hierarchies of the medical profession, sociological studies will surely be done to see if these apparent gender differences persist. Box 12-1 on page 305 discusses one such difference, the gender difference in doctor–patient communication style.

Patients have traditionally relied on medical personnel to inform them of health care issues, but increasingly they are turning to the media for health care information. Recognizing this change, pharmaceutical firms are advertising their prescription drugs directly to potential customers through television and magazines. The Internet is another growing source for patient information.

Medical professionals are understandably suspicious of these new sources of information. A study published in the *Journal of the American Medical Association* in 2001 found that health information on the Internet is often incomplete and inaccurate, even on the best sites. Nevertheless, there is little doubt that Web research is transforming an increasing proportion of patient–physician encounters, as patients arrive for their doctor's appointments armed with the latest printout from the Internet (Berland 2001).

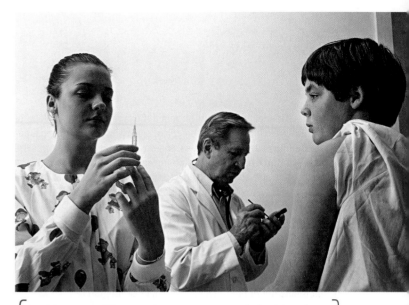

As if the status differences between nurses and physicians were not clear to all, the cheery uniform of nurses and the formal white doctor's coat reinforce the distinction.

www.mhhe.com/schaefer11

Use Your Sociological Imagination

If you were a patient, would you put yourself entirely in the physician's hands? Or would you do some research about your illness on your own? If you were a doctor, would you want your patient checking medical information on the Internet? Explain your positions.

Alternatives to Traditional Health Care

In traditional forms of health care, people rely on physicians and hospitals for the treatment of illness. Yet at least one out of every three adults in the United States attempts to maintain good health or respond to illness through the use of alternative health care techniques. For example, in recent decades interest has been growing in *holistic* (also spelled *wholistic*) medical principles, first developed in China. **Holistic medicine** refers to therapies in which the health care practitioner considers the person's physical, mental, emotional, and spiritual characteristics. The

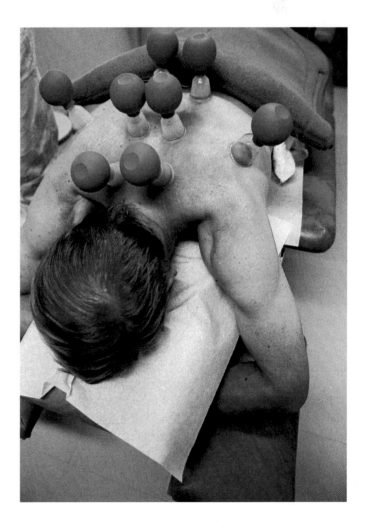

Health care takes many forms around the world. Cupping—a traditional practice used in ancient China, India, Egypt, and Greece—survives in modern Finland. Physiotherapists there use suction cups to draw out blood in order to lower patients' blood pressure, improve their circulation, and relieve muscular pain.

When Lola Adedokun entered Dartmouth College, she was thinking of concentrating in biology and premedical studies. But after taking a sociology course on racial disparities, she realized that sociology was the only subject that offered courses on topics she was passionate about. Eventually, she settled on sociology, along with a special social science major in health policy that she created herself.

Today, Adedokun is a consultant on a number of health-related research projects. One, funded by the National Institutes of Health (NIH), is a follow-up study of an international training program for researchers and clinicians working on HIV/AIDS. Another, funded by the Centers for Disease Control and Prevention (CDC), focuses on the sexual behaviors of heterosexuals at high risk of contracting HIV. "Understanding human behavior and human sexual behavior as well as the cultural and social issues that drive this behavior is essential," she explains. Adedokun is also a graduate research assistant at the National Center for Children in Poverty, where she conducts and analyzes interviews with families, children, and mental health professionals.

Each week is different for this self-employed researcher. Often she works from home, conducting interviews over the phone and analyzing data on her own computer. At other times she works at her clients' offices, using their proprietary software. Adedokun also trains teams of interviewers and serves as a liaison between agencies. "I have a lot of face-to-face contact interviewing clients and researching people from high-risk communities," she says. "The nature of the work is much like

the field of sociology—it is vast and broad, and I'm thinking about it all the time. In that way, my work does not feel like work."

Travel has been one of the high points in Adedokun's career. "The most amazing opportunity I have had in the last few years was traveling to Asia, Africa, and Latin America to conduct interviews with some of the world's leading HIV/AIDS researchers," she says. "I was able to truly get a sense of the challenges and the achievements that these researchers have encountered."

Asked what advice she would give to current students of sociology, Adedokun replies, "One piece of advice is that you would be doing yourself a disservice to distance yourself from this important material. It is the fundamentals of sociology that will be most relevant to any area that you choose to pursue in your future," she continues, "so ask questions, debate, discuss, and argue, as the knowledge that you will pull from that will prove to be the greatest academic lessons you may ever learn."

Let's Discuss

1. What social issue or problem do you feel passionate about, and how can sociology help to address it?
2. Adedokun is a self-starter who created her own major and is now pursuing a career on her own. Have you ever considered creating your own career path, rather than relying on large institutions to map your future? What might be the benefits of such an approach? The drawbacks?

---

individual is regarded as a totality rather than a collection of interrelated organ systems. Treatment methods include massage, chiropractic medicine, acupuncture (which involves the insertion of fine needles into surface points), respiratory exercises, and the use of herbs as remedies. Nutrition, exercise, and visualization may also be used to treat ailments that are generally treated through medication or hospitalization (Sharma and Bodeker 1998).

The Navajo concept of *hózhǫ́* (walking in beauty) is another example of a holistic approach to health (see the chapter introduction). Practitioners of holistic medicine do not necessarily function totally outside the traditional health care system. Some, like Dr. Lori Arviso Alvord, have medical degrees and rely on X-rays and EKG machines for diagnostic assistance. Others who staff holistic clinics, often referred to as *wellness clinics,* reject the use of medical technology. The recent resurgence of holistic medicine comes amid widespread recognition of the value of nutrition and the dangers of overreliance on prescription drugs (especially those used to reduce stress, such as Valium).

The medical establishment—professional organizations, research hospitals, and medical schools—has generally served as

a stern protector of traditionally accepted health care techniques. However, a major breakthrough occurred in 1992 when the federal government's National Institutes of Health—the nation's major funding source for biomedical research—opened an Office of Alternative Medicine, empowered to accept grant requests. Possible areas of study include herbal medicine, mind–body control techniques, and the use of electromagnetism to heal bones. A national study published in *The Journal of the American Medical Association* indicates that 46 percent of the general public uses alternative medicine. Most of it is not covered by insurance. In fact, out-of-pocket expenses for alternative medicine match all out-of-pocket expenses for traditional physicians' services (Eisenberg et al. 1998; Winnick 2005).

On the international level, the World Health Organization (WHO) has begun to monitor the use of alternative medicine around the world. According to WHO, 80 percent of people who live in the poorest countries in the world use some form of alternative medicine, from herbal treatments to the services of a faith healer. In most countries, these treatments are largely unregulated, even though some of them can be fatal. For example,

Kavakava, an herbal tea used to relieve anxiety in the Pacific Islands, can be toxic to the liver in concentrated form. Yet other alternative treatments have been found to be effective in the treatment of serious diseases, such as malaria and sickle-cell anemia. WHO's goal is to compile a list of such practices, as well as to encourage the development of universal training programs and ethical standards for practitioners of alternative medicine. To date, the organization has published findings on about 100 of the 5,000 plants believed to be used as herbal remedies (McNeil 2002).

The Role of Government

Not until the 20th century did health care receive federal aid. The first significant involvement was the 1946 Hill-Burton Act, which provided subsidies for building and improving hospitals, especially in rural areas. A far more important change came with the enactment in 1965 of two wide-ranging government assistance programs: Medicare, which is essentially a compulsory health insurance plan for the elderly, and Medicaid, which is a noncontributory federal and state insurance plan for the poor. These programs greatly expanded federal involvement in health care financing for needy men, women, and children.

Given the high rates of illness and disability among elderly people, Medicare has had a huge impact on the health care system. Initially, Medicare simply reimbursed health care providers such as physicians and hospitals for the billed costs of their services. However, in 1983, as the overall costs of Medicare increased dramatically, the federal government introduced a price-control system. Under this system, private hospitals often transfer patients whose treatment may be unprofitable to public facilities. In fact, many private hospitals have begun to conduct "wallet biopsies"—that is, to investigate the financial status of potential patients. Those judged undesirable are then refused admission or dumped. Though a federal law passed in 1987 made it illegal for any hospital receiving Medicare funds to dump patients, the practice continues (E. Gould 2007; D. Light 2004b).

Mental Illness in the United States

The words *mental illness* and *insanity* evoke dramatic and often inaccurate images of emotional problems. Though the media routinely emphasize the most violent behavior of those with disturbances, mental health and mental illness can more appropriately be viewed as a continuum of behavior that we ourselves move along. Using a less sensational definition, we can consider a person to have a mental disorder "if he or she is so disturbed that coping with routine, everyday life is difficult or impossible." The term **mental illness** should be reserved for a disorder of the brain that disrupts a person's thinking, feeling, and ability to interact with others (Coleman and Cressey 1980:315; National Alliance for the Mentally Ill 2000).

How prevalent is mental illness? According to the World Bank, mental disorders are a significant cause of disability in industrial economies. In the United States, about one out of every four Americans suffers from some form of mental illness. Yet in industrial countries, less than half of all serious cases receive any kind of treatment. In developing nations, the percentage is only one-fifth (World Health Organization 2004).

People in the United States have traditionally maintained a negative and suspicious view of those with mental disorders. Holding the status of "mental patient" or even "former mental patient" can have unfortunate and undeserved consequences. Voting rights are denied in some instances, acceptance for jury duty is problematic, and past emotional problems are an issue in divorce and custody cases. Moreover, content analysis of network television programs and films shows that mentally ill characters are uniformly portrayed in a demeaning and derogatory fashion; many are labeled as "criminally insane," "wackos," or "psychos." From an interactionist perspective, a key social institution is shaping social behavior by manipulating symbols and intensifying people's fears about the mentally ill (J. Klein 2003).

In April 2007, in the aftermath of a deadly shooting rampage at Virginia Tech, reporters raised questions about potential warning signs of mental illness in the shooter's behavior. Apparently the Virginia Tech senior had made some disturbing statements to classmates and professors, and had even been ordered to receive psychiatric counseling two years earlier. This troubling episode highlights many shortcomings of the U.S. mental health system. First, officials are poorly prepared to detect any type of mental health issue, much less the more dramatic ones. Second, mental health services and adequate follow-up care are even more limited in availability than treatments for diagnosed physical illnesses. And third, the stigmatization of mental illness and mental health services discourages many people from seeking help.

Theoretical Models of Mental Disorders

In studying mental illness, we can draw on both a medical model and a more sociological approach derived from labeling theory. Each model rests on distinctive assumptions regarding treatment of people with mental disorders.

According to the *medical model,* mental illness is rooted in biological causes that can be treated through medical intervention. Problems in brain structure or in the biochemical balance in the brain, sometimes due to injury and sometimes due to genetic inheritance, are thought to be at the bottom of these disorders. The U.S. Surgeon General (1999a) released an exhaustive report on mental health in which he declared that the accumulated weight of scientific evidence leaves no doubt about the physical origins of mental illness.

That is not to say that social factors do not contribute to mental illness. Just as culture affects the incidence and prevalence of illness in general, its treatment, and the expression of certain culture-bound syndromes, so too it can affect mental illness. In fact, the very definition of mental illness differs from one culture to the next. Mainstream U.S. culture, for instance,

Social factors such as war can jeopardize a person's mental health. Many people who once lived in war zones, like these Sundanese fleeing the horrors of genocide in Darfur, later suffer from symptoms of severe mental trauma, including depression, nightmares, and flashbacks to violent events.

considers hallucinations highly abnormal. But many traditional cultures view them as evidence of divine favor, and confer a special status on those who experience them. As we have noted throughout this textbook, a given behavior may be viewed as normal in one society, disapproved of but tolerated in a second, and labeled as sick and heavily sanctioned in a third.

In contrast to the medical model, *labeling theory* suggests that some behaviors that are viewed as mental illnesses may not really be illnesses, since the individual's problems arise from living in society and not from physical maladies. For example, the U.S. Surgeon General's report (1999a:5) notes that "bereavement symptoms" of less than two months' duration do not qualify as a mental disorder, but beyond that they may be redefined. Sociologists would see this approach to bereavement as labeling by those with the power to affix labels rather than as an acknowledgment of a biological condition.

Psychiatrist Thomas Szasz (1974), in his book *The Myth of Mental Illness,* which first appeared in 1961, advanced the view that numerous personality disorders are not diseases, but simply patterns of conduct labeled as disorders by significant others. The response to Szasz's challenging thesis was sharp: The commissioner of the New York State Department of Hygiene demanded his dismissal from his university position because Szasz did not "believe" in mental illness. But many sociologists embraced his model as a logical extension of examining individual behavior in a social context.

In sum, the medical model is persuasive because it pinpoints the causes of mental illness and offers treatment for disorders.

Yet proponents of the labeling perspective maintain that mental illness is a distinctively social process, whatever other processes are involved. From a sociological perspective, the ideal approach to mental illness integrates the insights of labeling theory with those of the medical approach (Horwitz 2002).

Patterns of Care

For most of human history, those who suffered from mental disorders were deemed the responsibility of their families. Yet mental illness has been a matter of governmental concern much longer than physical illness has. That is because severe emotional disorders threaten stable social relationships and entail prolonged incapacitation. As early as the 1600s, European cities began to confine the insane in public facilities along with the poor and criminals. Prisoners, indignant at being forced to live with "lunatics," resisted this approach. The isolation of the mentally ill from others in the same facility and from the larger society soon made physicians the central and ultimate authority over their welfare.

A major policy development in caring for those with mental disorders came with the passage of the Community Mental Health Centers Act (1963). The CMHC program, as it is known, not only increased federal government involvement in the treatment of the mentally ill. It also established community-based mental health centers to treat clients on an *outpatient* basis, thereby allowing them to continue working and living at home. The program showed that outpatient treatment could be more effective than the institutionalized programs of state and county mental hospitals.

Expansion of the federally funded CMHC program decreased inpatient care. By the 1980s, community-based mental health care had replaced hospitalization as the typical form of treatment. Across the United States, deinstitutionalization of the mentally ill reached dramatic proportions. State mental hospitals had held almost 560,000 long-term patients in 1955; by 1998 they had fewer than 63,000. Deinstitutionalization was conceived as a social reform that would effectively reintegrate the mentally ill into the outside world. But the authentic humanitarian concern behind deinstitutionalization proved to be a convenient front for politicians whose goal was simply cost cutting (Bureau of the Census 2002:117; Grob 1995).

In a marked shift from public policy over the last three decades, several states have recently made it easier to commit mental patients to hospitals involuntarily. These changes have come in part because community groups and individual residents have voiced increasing fear and anger about the growing number of mentally ill homeless people living in their midst, many of them on the streets. All too often, the severely mentally ill end up in jail or prison after committing crimes that lead to their prosecution. Ironically, family members of these mentally ill men and women complain that they cannot get adequate treatment for their loved ones *until* they have committed violent acts. Nevertheless, civil liberties advocates and voluntary associations of mentally ill people worry about the risks of denying people their constitutional rights, and cite horror stories about the abuses people have experienced during institutionalization (Marquis and Morain 1999; Shogren 1994).

At a community mental health center, outpatients create a newsletter for their day program. In the 1980s, community-based mental health care replaced hospitalization as the typical form of treatment for people with serious mental illnesses.

www.mhhe.com/schaefer11

Use Your Sociological Imagination

How are your views of mental illness different from or similar to your views of physical illness?

(social|Policy)
and Health

The AIDS Crisis

The Issue

In his novel *The Plague*, Albert Camus (1948:34) wrote, "There have been as many plagues as wars in history, yet always plagues and wars take people equally by surprise." Regarded by many as the distinctive plague of the modern era, AIDS certainly caught major social institutions—particularly the government, the health care system, and the economy—by surprise when it was first noticed by medical practitioners in the 1970s. It has since spread around the world. While encouraging new therapies have been developed to treat AIDS, there is currently no way to eradicate the disease by medical means. Therefore, it is essential to protect people by reducing the transmission of the fatal virus. But how is that to be done, and whose responsibility is it? What is the role of social institutions in preventing the spread of AIDS?

The Setting

AIDS is the acronym for *acquired immune deficiency syndrome*. Rather than being a distinct disease, AIDS is actually a predisposition to disease that is caused by a virus, the human immunodeficiency virus (HIV). The virus gradually destroys the body's immune system, leaving the carrier vulnerable to infections such as pneumonia that those with healthy immune systems can generally resist. Transmission of the virus from one person to another appears to require either intimate sexual contact or exchange of blood or bodily fluids (whether from contaminated hypodermic needles or syringes, transfusions of infected blood, or transmission from an infected mother to her child before or during birth).

The first cases of AIDS in the United States were reported in 1981. While the numbers of new cases and deaths have recently

474 shown some evidence of decline, an estimated 1.4 million people were living with AIDS or HIV by December 2006. Women account for a growing proportion of new cases; racial and ethnic minorities, for 70 percent. Worldwide, AIDS is stabilizing, with only gradual increases in reported cases; an estimated 39.5 million people are now infected (see Figure 19-5). The disease is not evenly distributed; those areas least equipped to deal with it—the developing nations of sub-Saharan Africa—face the greatest challenge (Centers for Disease Control and Prevention 2006; Glanton 2007).

Sociological Insights

Dramatic crises like the AIDS epidemic are likely to bring about certain transformations in a society's social structure. From a functionalist perspective, if established social institutions cannot meet a crucial need, new social networks are likely to emerge to perform that function. In the case of AIDS, self-help groups—especially in the gay communities of major cities—have organized to care for the sick, educate the healthy, and lobby for more responsive public policies.

The label "person with AIDS" or "HIV-positive" often functions as a master status. People who have AIDS or are infected with the virus face a powerful dual stigma. Not only are they associated with a lethal and contagious disease, but they have a disease that disproportionately afflicts already stigmatized groups, such as gay males and intravenous drug users. This link to stigmatized groups delayed recognition of the severity of the AIDS epidemic. The media took little interest in the disease until it seemed to be spreading beyond the gay community.

Viewed from a conflict perspective, policymakers were slow to respond to the AIDS crisis because those in high-risk groups—gay men and IV drug users—were comparatively powerless. Furthermore, studies show that African Americans and Latinos are diagnosed later and are slower to get treatment than other racial and ethnic groups. New programs have been launched to address this disparity in treatment (Glanton 2007).

On the micro level of social interaction, observers once forecasted that AIDS would lead to a more conservative sexual climate—among both homosexuals and heterosexuals—in which people would be much more cautious about becoming

FIGURE 19–5

Adults and Children Living with HIV/AIDS

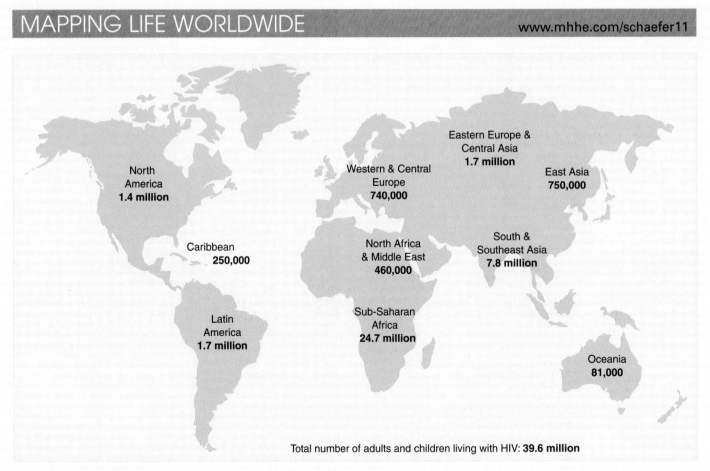

MAPPING LIFE WORLDWIDE   www.mhhe.com/schaefer11

North America
1.4 million

Caribbean
250,000

Latin America
1.7 million

Western & Central Europe
740,000

Eastern Europe & Central Asia
1.7 million

East Asia
750,000

North Africa & Middle East
460,000

South & Southeast Asia
7.8 million

Sub-Saharan Africa
24.7 million

Oceania
81,000

Total number of adults and children living with HIV: **39.6 million**

Note: Midpoint estimates for December 2006.
Source: UNAIDS 2007a.

involved with new partners. Yet it appears that many sexually active people in the United States have not heeded precautions about "safe sex." Data from studies conducted in the early 1990s indicated a growing complacency about AIDS, even among those who were most vulnerable (Bernstein 2004).

Policy Initiatives

AIDS has struck all societies, but not all nations can respond in the same manner. Studies done in the United States show that today, people with HIV or AIDS who receive appropriate medical treatment are living longer than they did in the past. This advance may put additional pressure on policymakers to address the issues raised by the spread of AIDS.

In some nations, cultural practices may prevent people from dealing realistically with the AIDS epidemic. They may not be likely to take the necessary preventive measures, including open discussion of sexuality, homosexuality, and drug use. Prevention has shown signs of working among target groups, such as drug users, pregnant women, and gay men and lesbians, but preventive initiatives are few and far between in developing nations.

Despite an increase in the availability of AIDS drugs in nonindustrial countries, concern remains about equity in the global fight against HIV/AIDS. In 2007, activists criticized pharmaceutical companies for delaying the delivery of new AIDS medicines to countries like Thailand, because of suspicion that those nations planned to produce their own generic versions. Officials in the affected countries responded that the corporations' efforts to lower drug prices in their countries were insufficient (Japsen 2007).

The high cost of drug treatment programs has generated intensive worldwide pressure on the major pharmaceutical companies to lower the prices to patients in developing nations, especially in sub-Saharan Africa. Bowing to this pressure, several of the companies have now agreed to make the combination therapies available at cost. As a result, the accessibility of HIV treatment has increased steadily, though it has hardly become universal. By the beginning of 2007, only 28 percent of those in need in sub-Saharan Africa had gained access to the drugs—still, a significant increase from 2 percent in 2003. Clearly, the prevention and diagnosis of HIV/AIDS must be accelerated, but we must also improve access to treatment for the tens of millions of people already living with the disease (UNAIDS 2007b).

Finally, while the increase in AIDS victims is leveling off, and strides have been made in treating survivors, one sobering fact still looms large. Within a few years, the global death toll from AIDs will exceed that of the dreaded Black Death in the 14th century (Kristof 2006).

Let's Discuss

1. Do the people you know take few risks sexually because of the danger of becoming infected with the AIDS virus? If not, why not?

2. Look at the map in Figure 19-5. Why do you think North Africa and the Middle East had only 460,000 people living with AIDS in 2006, while sub-Saharan Africa had 24.7 million? List as many factors as you can that might account for the disparity.

3. Aside from the obvious humanitarian reasons, why should the United States help developing countries in the fight against AIDS?

GettingINVOLVED

To get involved in the debate over the AIDS crisis, visit this text's Online Learning Center, which offers links to relevant Web sites. Check out the Social Policy section on the Online Learning Center as well; it provides survey data on U.S. public opinion regarding this issue.

www.mhhe.com/schaefer11

Summary

The meanings of **health,** sickness, and disease are shaped by social definitions of behavior. This chapter considers the relationship between culture and health, several sociological perspectives on health and illness, the distribution of diseases in a society, the evolution of the U.S. health care system, and the sociological dimension of mental health and **mental illness.** It closes with a discussion of the AIDS crisis.

1. The effect of culture on health can be seen in the existence of **culture-bound syndromes,** as well as in cultural differences in medical care and the **incidence** and **prevalence** of certain diseases.

2. According to Talcott Parsons's functionalist perspective, physicians function as "gatekeepers" for the **sick role,** either verifying a person's condition as "ill" or designating the person as "recovered."

3. Conflict theorists use the term *medicalization of society* to refer to medicine's growing role as a major institution of social control.

4. Labeling theorists suggest that the designation of a person as "healthy" or "ill" generally involves social definition by others. These definitions affect how others see us and how we view ourselves.

5. Contemporary **social epidemiology** is concerned not only with epidemics but with nonepidemic diseases, injuries, drug addiction and alcoholism, suicide, and mental illness.

6. Studies have consistently shown that people in the lower classes have higher rates of mortality and disability than others.

7. Racial and ethnic minorities have higher rates of morbidity and mortality than Whites. Women tend to be in poorer health than men but live longer. Older people are especially vulnerable to mental health problems, such as Alzheimer's disease.

8. The preeminent role of physicians in the U.S. health care system has given them a position of dominance in their dealings with nurses and patients.

9. Many people use alternative health care techniques, such as **holistic medicine** and self-help groups.

10. Mental disorders may be viewed from two different perspectives, the medical model and the sociological model, which is based on labeling theory. In the United States, society has traditionally taken a negative, suspicious attitude toward people with mental disorders.

11. Around the world, the AIDS epidemic has increased mortality rates, strained health care systems, and devastated those communities hardest hit by the disease.

Critical Thinking Questions

1. Sociologist Talcott Parsons has argued that the doctor–patient relationship is similar to that between parent and child. Does this view seem accurate? Should the doctor–patient relationship be more egalitarian? How might functionalist and conflict theorists differ in their views of the power of physicians in the U.S. health care system?

2. How would the process of classifying a person as mentally ill differ under the medical model and the sociological model? Draw on Erving Goffman's concept of stigmatization (see Chapter 8).

3. Relate what you have learned about social epidemiology to the question of universal health care coverage. If the United States were to adopt a system of universal coverage, what might be the effect on the incidence and prevalence of disease among Americans of all classes, races and ethnicities, genders, and ages? What might be the ultimate effect of such changes on health care costs?

Brain drain The immigration to the United States and other industrialized nations of skilled workers, professionals, and technicians who are desperately needed in their home countries. (page 461)

Culture-bound syndrome A disease or illness that cannot be understood apart from its specific social context. (456)

Curanderismo Latino folk medicine, a form of holistic health care and healing. (465)

Health As defined by the World Health Organization, a state of complete physical, mental, and social well-being, and not merely the absence of disease and infirmity. (456)

Holistic medicine Therapies in which the health care practitioner considers the person's physical, mental, emotional, and spiritual characteristics. (469)

Incidence The number of new cases of a specific disorder that occur within a given population during a stated period. (463)

Mental illness A disorder of the brain that disrupts a person's thinking, feeling, and ability to interact with others. (471)

Morbidity rate The incidence of disease in a given population. (463)

Mortality rate The incidence of death in a given population. (463)

Prevalence The total number of cases of a specific disorder that exist at a given time. (463)

Sick role Societal expectations about the attitudes and behavior of a person viewed as being ill. (457)

Social epidemiology The study of the distribution of disease, impairment, and general health status across a population. (463)

Self-Quiz

Read each question carefully and then select the best answer.

1. Which sociologist developed the concept of the sick role?

   a. Émile Durkheim
   b. Talcott Parsons
   c. C. Wright Mills
   d. Erving Goffman

2. Regarding health care inequities, the conflict perspective would note that

   a. physicians serve as "gatekeepers" for the sick role, either verifying a patient's condition as "illness" or designating the patient as "recovered."
   b. patients play an active role in health care by failing to follow a physician's advice.
   c. emigration out of the Third World by physicians is yet another way that the world's core industrialized nations enhance their quality of life at the expense of developing countries.
   d. the designation "healthy" or "ill" generally involves social definition by others.

3. Which one of the following nations has the lowest infant mortality rate?

   a. the United States
   b. Mozambique
   c. Canada
   d. Sweden

4. Compared with Whites, Blacks have higher death rates from

   a. heart disease.
   b. diabetes.
   c. cancer.
   d. all of the above

5. Which theorist notes that capitalist societies, such as the United States, care more about maximizing profits than they do about the health and safety of industrial workers?

   a. Thomas Szasz
   b. Talcott Parsons
   c. Erving Goffman
   d. Karl Marx

6. Which program is essentially a compulsory health insurance plan for the elderly?

   a. Medicare
   b. Medicaid
   c. Blue Cross
   d. Healthpac

7. Which of the following is a criticism of the sick role?

   a. Patients' judgments regarding their own state of health may be related to their gender, age, social class, and ethnic group.
   b. The sick role may be more applicable to people experiencing short-term illnesses than to those with recurring long-term illnesses.
   c. Even such simple factors as whether a person is employed or not seem to affect the person's willingness to assume the sick role.
   d. all of the above

8. Which of the following terms do conflict theorists use in referring to the growing role of medicine as a major institution of social control?

   a. the sick role
   b. the medicalization of society
   c. medical labeling
   d. epidemiology

9. Which sociological perspective emphasizes that a patient should not always be viewed as passive, but instead as someone who often plays an active role in his or her health care?

   a. the functionalist perspective
   b. the conflict perspective
   c. the interactionist perspective
   d. the labeling approach

10. Which of the following statements is *not* true?

   a. Compared with men, women experience a higher prevalence of many illnesses.
   b. Men are more likely than women to have parasitic diseases.
   c. As a group, women appear to be in better health than men.
   d. Women are more likely than men to become diabetic.

11. _____ affects the way people interact with doctors and healers, the way they relate to their families when they are sick, and even the way they think about health.

12. From a(n) _____ perspective, "being sick" must be controlled so as to ensure that not too many people are released from their societal responsibilities at any one time.

13. The immigration to the United States and other industrialized nations of skilled workers, professionals, and technicians who are desperately needed by their home countries is known as the _____ _____.

14. Traditionally, the relationship between doctors and nurses has paralleled _____ dominance of the larger society.

15. According to the _____ model, mental illness is rooted in biological causes that can be treated through medical intervention.

16. Sociologists find it useful to consider _____ rates because they reveal that a specific disease occurs more frequently among one segment of a population compared with another.

17. The system of reimbursement used by Medicare has contributed to the controversial practice of "_____," under which patients whose treatment may be unprofitable are transferred by private hospitals to public facilities.

18. As defined by the World Health Organization, _____ is a "state of complete physical, mental, and social well-being, and not merely the absence of disease and infirmity."

19. Social _____ is the study of the distribution of disease, impairment, and general health status across a population.

20. _____ refers to the number of new cases of a specific disorder occurring within a given population during a stated period, usually a year.

Answers:

1 (b); 2 (c); 3 (d); 4 (d); 5 (d); 6 (a); 7 (d); 8 (d); 9 (b); 10 (c); 11 Culture; 12 functionalist; 13 brain drain; 14 male; 15 medical; 16 morbidity; 17 dumping; 18 health; 19 epidemiology; 20 Incidence

Online Learning Center

1. A good way to help prepare for an exam or review for a class discussion is to study the outline and summary for this chapter. Outlines and summaries for all chapters in this book are available in the student center at the Online Learning Center. Go to **www.mhhe.com/schaefer11** and link to Chapter Outline or Chapter Summary.

2. The University of Michigan is the home of a research institute whose focus is on health inequalities. To view some enlightening figures that illustrate the connections among race, class, and health, visit the Michigan Center for the Study of Health Inequalities (**www.sph.umich.edu/miih/index2.html**).

3. Attention-deficit/hyperactivity disorder (ADHD) has been a prominent news item in recent years. Visit the Web site of the National Resource Center on ADHD (**www.help4adhd.org**) to learn more about this health disorder, and use your sociological imagination to view it from a sociological perspective.

*Note: Although all the URLs listed were current as of the printing of this book, these sites often change. Please check our Web site (**www.mhhe.com/schaefer11**) for updates, hyperlinks, and exercises related to these sites.*

Reel Society Video Clips

Reel Society video clips, which appear on this book's Web site, can be used to spark discussion about the following topic from this chapter:

• Social Epidemiology and Health

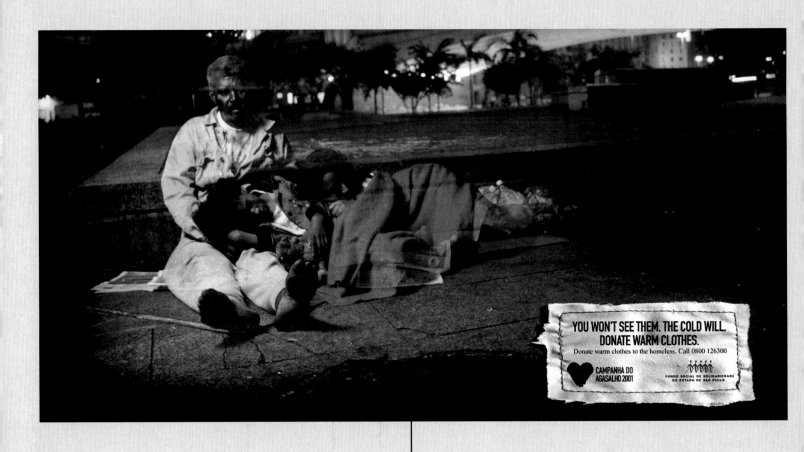

Homelessness is a major social problem not just in the United States, but in cities around the world. This poster, published in the city of São Paulo, Brazil, appeals for clothing donations to keep those who sleep on the street warm. As the photograph suggests, whole families, including children, may become homeless.

20 Communities and Urbanization

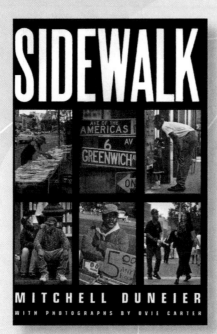

SIDEWALK

AVE OF THE AMERICAS
6 AV
GREENWICH
ON
5.00

MITCHELL DUNEIER

WITH PHOTOGRAPHS BY OVIE CARTER

" It is not hard to understand why Hakim Hasan came to see himself as a public character. Early one July morning, a deliveryman pulled his truck up to the curb behind Hakim's vending table on Greenwich Avenue off the corner of Sixth Avenue [in lower Manhattan] and carried a large box of flowers over to him.

"Can you hold these until the flower shop opens up?" the deliveryman asked.

"No problem," responded Hakim as he continued to set up the books on his table. "Put them right under there."

When the store opened for business, he brought them inside and gave them to the owner.

"Why did that man trust you with the flowers?" I later asked.

"People like me are the eyes and ears of this street," he explained, echoing [sociologist] Jane Jacobs again. "Yes, I could take those flowers and sell them for a few hundred dollars. But that deliveryman sees me here every day. I'm as dependable as any store-owner." . . .

Another day, I was present at the table when a traffic officer walked by to give out parking tickets.

"Are any of these your cars?" she asked Hakim.

"Yes, that one, and that one," said Hakim, pointing.

"What is that all about?" I asked.

"The day I met her, we got into an argument," he explained. "She was getting ready to give the guy across the street a ticket. I say, 'You can't do this!' She said, 'Why not?' I say, ''Cause I'm getting ready to put a quarter in.' She said, 'You can't do that.' I guess that, because of the way I

> *Early one July morning, a deliveryman pulled his truck up to the curb behind Hakim's vending table on Greenwich Avenue off the corner of Sixth Avenue [in lower Manhattan] and carried a large box of flowers over to him.*

made my argument, she didn't give out the ticket, and from that point onward we became friends. And when she comes on the block, she asks me, for every car on the block that has a violation sign, 'Is that your car?' Meaning, 'Is it someone you know?' And depending on whether I say yes or no, that's it—they get a ticket." . . .

"Are these things part of your job description as a vendor?" I asked him once.

"Let me put it to you this way, Mitch," he replied. "I kind of see what I loosely call my work on the sidewalk as going far, far beyond just trying to make a living selling books. That sometimes even seems secondary. Over time, when people see you on the sidewalk, there is a kind of trust that starts. They've seen you so long that they walk up to you. There have been occasions when I've had to have directions translated out of Spanish into French to get somebody to go someplace!"

It is not only directions and assistance that I have seen Hakim give out. He also tells people a great deal about books—so much so that he once told me he was thinking of charging tuition to the people who stand in his space on the sidewalk. "

(Duneier 1999:17–18) Additional information about this excerpt can be found on the Online Learning Center at www.mhhe.com/schaefer11.

This excerpt from *Sidewalk,* by the sociologist Mitchell Duneier, describes the social position of Hakim Hasan, a sidewalk book vendor in New York City's Greenwich Village. The author, who for two years lived just around the corner from Hasan's table, was so fascinated by street life in the Village that he decided to do observation research on it. As Duneier explains in his book, street vendors like Hasan are just as much a part of the neighborhood as the shopkeepers who occupy the storefronts behind them—even if they don't have a mailing address. In fact, their presence on the street, day in and day out, contributes to the neighborhood's safety and stability (Duneier 1999).

This chapter explores communities of all sorts, from rural towns to inner-city neighborhoods and the suburbs that surround them. In sociological terms, a **community** may be defined as a spatial or political unit of social organization that gives people a sense of belonging. That sense of belonging can be based either on shared residence in a particular city or neighborhood, such as Greenwich Village, or on a common identity, such as that of street vendors, homeless people, or gays and lesbians. Whatever the members have in common, communities give people the feeling that they are part of something larger than themselves (Dotson 1991; see also Hillery 1955).

The anthropologist George Murdock (1949) has observed that the community is one of only two truly universal units of social organization (the other being the family). How did communities originate? Why have large cities grown at the expense of small villages in many areas of the world today? And why, even in nations like the United States, are many residents of large and prosperous communities homeless? In this chapter

Sociologist Mitchell Duneier *(right)* did participant observation as he worked the tables of sidewalk vendors in Greenwich Village.

we will begin to answer these questions by tracing the development of communities from their ancient origins to the birth of the modern city and its growth through technological change. In particular, we will examine the rapid and dramatic urbanization that occurred around the world during the 20th century. Then we will study two different sociological views of urbanization, one stressing its functions and the other its dysfunctions. We'll compare rural, suburban, and urban communities in the United States today. Finally, in the Social Policy section, we'll analyze the disturbing phenomenon of homelessness, an all-too-familiar feature of community life.

How Have Communities Changed?

The nature of community has changed greatly over the course of history—from early hunting-and-gathering societies to highly modernized postindustrial cities. For most of human history, people used basic tools and knowledge to survive. They satisfied their need for an adequate food supply through hunting, foraging for fruits or vegetables, fishing, and herding. In comparison with later industrial societies, then, early civilizations were much { p.123 more dependent on the physical environment and much less able to alter that environment to their advantage. Even when they discovered how to cultivate food rather than forage for it, their use of tools and thus the amount of food they could produce were limited. Gradually, however, farming communities began to accumulate a surplus of food, which allowed some people to turn to the production of other goods and services. This

economic breakthrough laid the foundation for social stratification and the eventual rise of preindustrial cities.

Preindustrial Cities

It is estimated that beginning about 10,000 B.C., permanent settlements free from dependence on crop cultivation emerged. By today's standards, these early communities would barely qualify as cities. The **preindustrial city,** as it is termed, generally had only a few thousand people living within its borders, and was characterized by a relatively closed class system and limited mobility. In these early cities, status was usually based on ascribed characteristics such as family background, and education was limited to members of the elite. All the residents relied on perhaps 100,000 farmers and their own part-time farming to provide the needed agricultural surplus. The Mesopotamian city of

Ur had a population of about 10,000 and was limited to roughly 220 acres of land, including the canals, the temple, and the harbor.

Why were these early cities so small and relatively few in number? Several key factors restricted urbanization:

- **Reliance on animal power (both humans and beasts of burden) as a source of energy for economic production.** This factor limited the ability of humans to make use of and alter the physical environment.

- **Modest levels of surplus produced by the agricultural sector.** Between 50 and 90 farmers may have been required to support one city resident (K. Davis [1949] 1995).

- **Problems in transportation and the storage of food and other goods.** Even an excellent crop could easily be lost as a result of such difficulties.

- **Hardships of migration to the city.** For many peasants, migration was both physically and economically impossible. A few weeks of travel was out of the question without more sophisticated food storage techniques.

- **Dangers of city life.** Concentrating a society's population in a small area left it open to attack from outsiders, as well as more susceptible to extreme damage from plagues and fires.

A sophisticated social organization was also an essential precondition for urban existence. Specialized social roles brought people together in new ways through the exchange of goods and services. A well-developed social organization ensured that those relationships were clearly defined and generally acceptable to all parties.

Industrial and Postindustrial Cities

Imagine how harnessing the energy of air, water, and other natural resources could change a society. Advances in agricultural technology led to dramatic changes in community life, but so did {p.124 the process of industrialization. The *industrial revolution,* which began in the middle of the 18th century, focused on the application of nonanimal sources of power to labor tasks. Industrialization had a wide range of effects on people's lifestyles, as well as on the structure of communities. Emerging urban settlements became centers not only of industry but of banking, finance, and industrial management.

The factory system that developed during the industrial revolution led to a much more refined division of labor than was evident in preindustrial cities. The many new occupations that were

created produced a complex set of relationships among workers. Thus, the *industrial city* was not merely more populous than its predecessors; it was based on very different principles of social organization (see Table 20-1, page 484).

In comparison with preindustrial cities, industrial cities had a more open class system and more social mobility. After initiatives in industrial cities by women's rights groups, labor unions, and other political activists, formal education gradually became available to many children from poor and working-class families. While ascribed characteristics such as gender, race, and ethnicity remained important, a talented or skilled individual had greater opportunity to better his or her social position. In these and other respects, the industrial city was genuinely a different world from the preindustrial urban community.

In the latter part of the 20th century, a new type of urban community emerged. The *postindustrial city* is a city in which {p.124 global finance and the electronic flow of information dominate the economy. Production is decentralized and often takes place outside urban centers, but control is centralized in multinational corporations whose influence transcends urban and even national boundaries. Social change is a constant feature of the postindustrial city. Economic restructuring and spatial change seem to occur each decade, if not more frequently. In the postindustrial world, cities are forced into increasing competition for economic opportunities, which deepens the plight of the urban poor (E. Phillips 1996; D. A. Smith and Timberlake 1993).

Sociologist Louis Wirth (1928, 1938) argued that a relatively large and permanent settlement leads to distinctive patterns of

Over the centuries, communities of all sizes have undergone significant social change. Like the Canadian city of Toronto, many have become increasingly diverse in race and ethnicity.

behavior, which he called **urbanism.** He identified three critical factors that contribute to urbanism: the size of the population, population density, and the heterogeneity (variety) of the population. A frequent result of urbanism, according to Wirth, is that we become insensitive to events around us and restrict our attention to the primary groups to which we are emotionally attached.

Table 20-1 summarizes the differences among preindustrial, industrial, and postindustrial cities.

www.mhhe.com/schaefer11

Use Your Sociological Imagination

What would the ideal city of the future look like? Describe its architecture, public transportation, neighborhoods, schools, and workplaces. What kinds of people would live and work there?

Urbanization

Urbanization has become a central aspect of life in the United States, north, south, east, and west. Only four states (Maine, Mississippi, Vermont, and West Virginia) are truly rural—that is, more than half their population lives in towns of fewer than 2,500 residents (Bureau of the Census 2004:3–4, 28).

Urbanization can be seen throughout the rest of the world, too. In 1900, only 10 percent of the world's people lived in urban areas, but by 2000, around 50 percent of them did. By the year 2025, the number of city dwellers could reach 5 billion. During the 19th and early 20th centuries, rapid urbanization occurred primarily in Europe and North America. But since World War II, the population of cities in developing countries has exploded: see Figure 20-1 (Koolhaas et al. 2001:3).

Some metropolitan areas have spread so far that they have connected with other urban centers. Such a densely populated area, containing two or more cities and their suburbs, has become known as a **megalopolis.** An example is the 500-mile corridor stretching from Boston south to Washington, D.C., which includes New York City, Philadelphia, and Baltimore and accounts for one-sixth of the total population of the United States. Even when the megalopolis is divided into autonomous political jurisdictions, it can be viewed as a single economic entity. The megalopolis is also evident in Great Britain, Germany, Italy, Egypt, India, Japan, and China.

Functionalist View: Urban Ecology

Human ecology is an area of study that is concerned with the interrelationships between people and their environment. Human ecologists have long been interested in how the physical environment shapes people's lives (for example, how rivers can serve as a barrier to residential expansion) and in how people influence the surrounding environment (for example, how air-conditioning has accelerated the growth of major metropolitan areas in the Southwest). **Urban ecology** focuses on such relationships as they emerge in urban areas. Although the urban ecological approach focuses on social change in cities, it is nev-

Table 20-1

Comparing Types of Cities

summingUP

Preindustrial Cities (through 18th century)	Industrial Cities (18th through mid-20th century)	Postindustrial Cities (beginning late 20th century)
Closed class system—pervasive influence of social class at birth	Open class system—mobility based on achieved characteristics	Wealth based on ability to obtain and use information
Economic realm controlled by guilds and a few families	Relatively open competition	Corporate power dominates
Beginnings of division of labor in the creation of goods	Elaborate specialization in manufacturing of goods	Sense of place fades, transnational networks emerge
Pervasive influence of religion on social norms	Influence of religion limited as society becomes more secularized	Religion becomes more fragmented; greater openness to new religious faiths
Little standardization of prices, weights, and measures	Standardization enforced by custom and law	Conflicting views of prevailing standards
Population largely illiterate, communication by word of mouth	Emergence of communication through posters, bulletins, and newspapers	Emergence of extended electronic networks
Schools limited to elites and designed to perpetuate their privileged status	Formal schooling open to the masses and viewed as a means of advancing the social order	Professional, scientific, and technical personnel become increasingly important

Sources: Based on E. Phillips 1996:132–135; Sjoberg 1960:323–328.

FIGURE 20–1

485

Communities and Urbanization

Global Urbanization 2015 (projected)

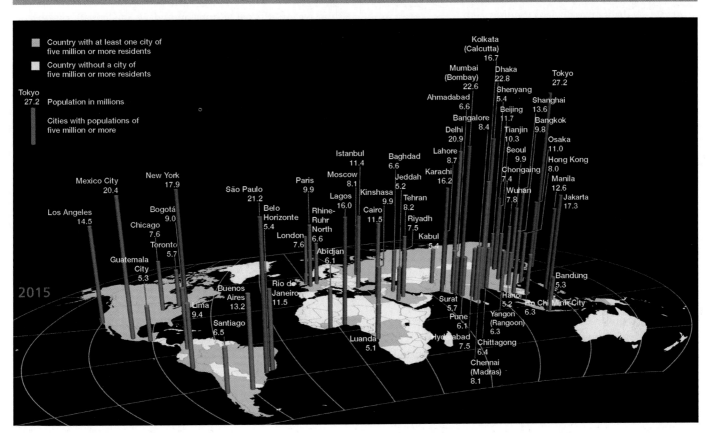

■ Country with at least one city of five million or more residents

□ Country without a city of five million or more residents

Tokyo 27.2 Population in millions

Cities with populations of five million or more

2015

Mexico City 20.4
New York 17.9
Los Angeles 14.5
Bogotá 9.0
Chicago 7.6
Toronto 5.7
Guatemala City 5.3
Buenos Aires 13.2
Lima 9.4
Santiago 6.5
São Paulo 21.2
Belo Horizonte 5.4
Rio de Janeiro 11.5
London 7.6
Paris 9.9
Rhine-Ruhr North 6.6
Abidjan 6.1
Istanbul 11.4
Moscow 8.1
Lagos 16.0
Kinshasa 9.9
Cairo 11.5
Luanda 5.1
Baghdad 6.6
Jeddah 5.2
Tehran 8.2
Riyadh 7.5
Kabul 5.4
Lahore 8.7
Karachi 16.2
Surat 5.7
Pune 6.1
Hyderabad 7.5
Chennai (Madras) 8.1
Chittagong 6.4
Kolkata (Calcutta) 16.7
Mumbai (Bombay) 22.6
Ahmadabad 6.6
Bangalore 8.4
Delhi 20.9
Dhaka 22.8
Shenyang 5.4
Beijing 11.7
Tianjin 10.3
Chongqing 7.4
Wuhan 7.8
Yangon (Rangoon) 6.3
Hanoi 5.2
Ho Chi Minh City 6.3
Tokyo 27.2
Shanghai 13.6
Bangkok 9.8
Osaka 11.0
Seoul 9.9
Hong Kong 8.0
Manila 12.6
Jakarta 17.3
Bandung 5.3

Source: National Geographic 2005:104–105.

ertheless functionalist in orientation because it emphasizes how different elements in urban areas contribute to social stability.

Early urban ecologists such as Robert Park (1916, 1936) and Ernest Burgess (1925) concentrated on city life but drew on the approaches used by ecologists who study plant and animal communities. With few exceptions, urban ecologists trace their work back to the **concentric-zone theory** devised in the 1920s by Burgess (see Figure 20-2a, page 486). Using Chicago as an example, Burgess proposed a theory for describing land use in industrial cities. At the center, or nucleus, of such a city is the central business district. Large department stores, hotels, theaters, and financial institutions occupy this highly valued land. Surrounding this urban center are zones devoted to other types of land use, which illustrate the growth of the urban area over time.

Note that the creation of zones is a *social* process, not the result of nature alone. Families and business firms compete for the most valuable land; those who possess the most wealth and power are generally the winners. The concentric-zone theory proposed by Burgess represented a dynamic model of urban growth. As urban growth proceeded, each zone would move even farther from the central business district.

Because of its functionalist orientation and its emphasis on stability, the concentric-zone theory tended to understate or ignore certain tensions that were apparent in metropolitan areas. For example, the growing use by the affluent of land in a city's peripheral areas was uncritically approved, while the arrival of African Americans in White neighborhoods in the 1930s was described by some sociologists in terms such as *invasion* and *succession.* Moreover, the urban ecological perspective gave little thought to gender inequities, such as the establishment of men's softball and golf leagues in city parks, without any programs for women's sports. Consequently, the urban ecological approach has been criticized for its failure to address issues of gender, race, and class.

By the middle of the 20th century, urban populations had spilled beyond traditional city limits. No longer could urban ecologists focus exclusively on *growth* in the central city, for large numbers of urban residents were abandoning the cities to live in suburban areas. As a response to the emergence of more than one focal point in some metropolitan areas, Chauncy D. Harris and Edward Ullman (1945) presented the **multiple-nuclei theory** (see Figure 20-2b). In their view, all urban growth does not radiate outward from a central business district. Instead, a metropolitan area may have many centers of development, each of which reflects a particular urban need or activity. Thus, a city may have a financial district, a manufacturing zone, a waterfront area, an entertainment center, and so forth. Certain types of business firms and certain types of housing will naturally cluster around each distinctive nucleus (Squires 2002).

The rise of suburban shopping malls is a vivid example of the phenomenon of multiple nuclei within metropolitan areas. Initially, all major retailing in urban areas was located in the central business district. Each residential neighborhood had its own grocers, bakers, and butchers, but people traveled to the center of the city to make major purchases at department stores. However, as metropolitan areas expanded and the suburbs became more populous, increasing numbers of people began to shop nearer their homes. Today, the suburban mall is a significant retailing and social center in communities across the United States.

In a refinement of the multiple-nuclei theory, contemporary urban ecologists have begun to study what journalist Joel Garreau (1991) has called "edge cities." These communities, which have grown up on the outskirts of major metropolitan areas, are economic and social centers with identities of their own. By any standard of measurement—height of buildings, amount of office space, presence of medical facilities, presence of leisure-time facilities, or of course, population—edge cities qualify as independent cities rather than large suburbs (R. Lang and LeFurgy 2007).

Whether metropolitan areas include edge cities or multiple nuclei, more and more of them are characterized by spread-out development and unchecked growth. In recent years, Las Vegas has been the most dramatic example. By 2007 the city had grown to nine times its size in 1950, and its population had exploded from less than 25,000 to about 600,000. The social consequences of such rapid growth are equally dramatic, from a shortage of affordable housing and an inadequate number of food pantries to an overstretched water supply, poor health care delivery, and impossible traffic. Today's cities are very different from the preindustrial cities of a thousand years ago (Las Vegas 2006).

Use Your Sociological Imagination

Consider the spatial arrangements in your everyday life from the point of view of urban ecology. How do man-made constructions and barriers affect your travel patterns?

Conflict View: New Urban Sociology

Contemporary sociologists point out that metropolitan growth is not governed by waterways and rail lines, as a purely ecological interpretation might suggest. From a conflict perspective, communities are human creations that reflect people's needs, choices, and decisions—though some people have more influ-

FIGURE 20–2

Comparison of Ecological Theories of Urban Growth

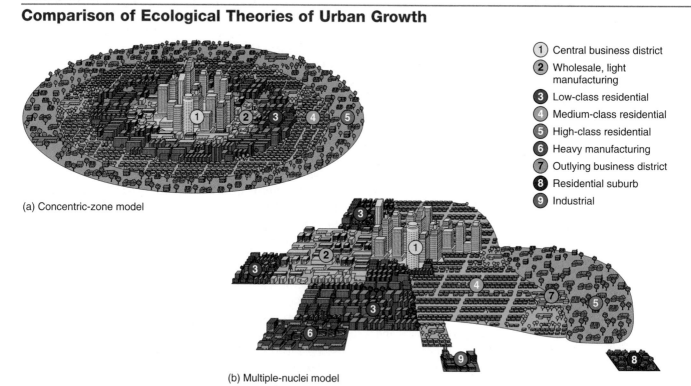

(a) Concentric-zone model

(b) Multiple-nuclei model

1. Central business district
2. Wholesale, light manufacturing
3. Low-class residential
4. Medium-class residential
5. High-class residential
6. Heavy manufacturing
7. Outlying business district
8. Residential suburb
9. Industrial

Source: Adapted from C. Harris and Ullmann 1945:13.

Between 2000 and 2006, metropolitan Las Vegas grew by more than 400,000 people, to a total population of over 1.7 million. Cities that are undergoing such rapid growth give rise to both multiple-nuclei and edge cities.

ence over those decisions than others. Drawing on conflict theory, an approach called the **new urban sociology** considers the interplay of local, national, and worldwide forces and their effect on local space, with special emphasis on the impact of global economic activity (Gottdiener and Hutchison 2006).

New urban sociologists note that proponents of the ecological approaches have typically avoided examining the social forces, largely economic in nature, that have guided urban growth. For example, central business districts may be upgraded or abandoned, depending on whether urban policymakers grant substantial tax exemptions to developers. The suburban boom in the post–World War II era was fueled by highway construction and federal housing policies that channeled investment capital into the construction of single-family homes rather than affordable rental housing in the cities. Similarly, while some observers suggest that the growth of sun-belt cities is due to a "good business climate," new urban sociologists counter that the term is actually a euphemism for hefty state and local government subsidies and antilabor policies intended to draw manufacturers (Gottdiener and Feagin 1988; M. Smith 1988).

The new urban sociology draws on the conflict perspective and, more specifically, on sociologist Immanuel Wallerstein's { pp.245–246 *world systems analysis.* Wallerstein argues that certain industrialized nations (among them the United States, Japan, and Germany) hold a dominant position at the *core* of the global economic system. At the same time, the poor developing countries of Asia, Africa, and Latin America lie on the *periphery*

of the global economy, controlled and exploited by core industrialized nations.

Using world systems analysis, new urban sociologists consider urbanization from a global perspective. They view cities not as independent and autonomous entities, but as the outcome of decision-making processes directed or influenced by a society's dominant classes and by core industrialized nations. New urban sociologists note that the rapidly growing cities of the world's developing countries were shaped first by colonialism and then by a global economy controlled by core nations and multinational corporations. The outcome has not been beneficial to the poorest citizens, as Box 20-1 (page 488) shows. An unmistakable feature of many cities in developing countries is the existence of large squatter settlements just outside city limits (Gottdiener and Feagin 1988; D. A. Smith 1995).

The urban ecologists of the 1920s and 1930s were aware of the role that the larger economy played in urbanization, but their theories emphasized the impact of local rather than national or global forces. In contrast, through their broad, global emphasis on social inequality and { pp.229, 246, 447 conflict, new urban sociologists concentrate on such topics as the existence of an underclass, the power of multinational corporations, deindustrialization, homelessness, and residential segregation.

For example, developers, builders, and investment bankers are not especially interested in urban growth when it means providing housing for middle- or low-income people. Their lack of interest contributes to the problem of homelessness. These urban elites counter that the nation's housing shortage and the plight of the homeless are not their fault, and insist that they do not have the capital needed to construct and support such housing. But affluent people *are* interested in growth, and they *can* somehow find capital to build new shopping centers, office towers, and ballparks. Why, then, can't they provide the capital for affordable housing, ask new urban sociologists?

Part of the answer is that developers, bankers, and other powerful real estate interests view housing in quite a different manner from tenants and most homeowners. For a tenant, an apartment is shelter, housing, a home. But for developers and investors—many of them large (and sometimes multinational) corporations—an apartment is simply a housing investment. These financiers and owners are concerned primarily with maximizing profit, not with solving social problems (Feagin 1983; Gottdiener and Hutchison 2006).

As we have seen throughout this textbook in studying such varied issues as deviance, race and ethnicity, and aging, no single

20-1 Squatter Settlements

Bariadas, favelas, bustees, kampungs, and *bidonvilles:* The terms vary depending on the nation and language, but the meaning is the same—"squatter settlements." In **squatter settlements,** areas occupied by the very poor on the fringe of cities, housing is constructed by the settlers themselves from discarded material, including crates from loading docks and loose lumber from building projects. While the term *squatter settlement* has wide use, many observers prefer to use a less pejorative term, such as *autonomous settlements.*

This type of settlement is typical of cities in the world's developing nations. In such countries, new housing has not kept pace with the combined urban population growth resulting from births and migration from rural areas. Squatter settlements also swell when city dwellers are forced out of housing by astronomical jumps in rent. By definition, squatters living on vacant land are trespassers and can be legally evicted. However, given the large number of poor people who live in such settlements (by UN estimates, 40 or 50 percent of inhabitants of cities in many developing nations), governments generally look the other way.

Obviously squatters live in substandard housing, yet that is only one of the many problems they face. Residents do not receive most public services, since their presence cannot be legally recognized. Police and fire protection, paved streets, and sanitary sewers are virtually nonexistent. In some countries, squatters may have trouble voting or enrolling their children in public schools.

Despite such conditions, squatter settlements are not always as bleak as they may appear from the outside. You can often find a

> *Squatter settlements are not always as bleak as they may appear from the outside.*

well-developed social organization there, rather than a disorganized collection of people. Typically, a thriving "informal economy" develops: residents establish small, home-based businesses such as grocery stores, jewelry shops, and the like. Local churches, men's clubs, and women's clubs are often established in specific neighborhoods within settlements. In addition, certain areas may form governing councils or membership associations. These governing bodies may face the usual problems of municipal governments, including charges of corruption and factional splits.

Squatter settlements remind us that respected theoretical models of social science in the United States may not directly apply to other cultures. The various ecological models of urban growth, for example, would not explain a metropolitan expansion that locates the poorest people on the urban fringes. Furthermore, solutions that are logical in a highly industrialized nation may not be relevant in developing nations. Planners in developing nations, rather than focusing on large-scale solutions to urban problems, must think in terms of providing basic amenities, such as water or electrical power for the ever-expanding squatter settlements.

Let's Discuss

1. Do you know of any "squatters" in your own community? If so, describe them and the place where they live.
2. Given the number of homeless people in the United States, why aren't there more squatters?

Sources: Castells 1983; Neuwirth 2004; Patton 1988; T. Phillips 2005; Yap 1998.

---

theoretical approach necessarily offers the only valuable perspective. As Table 20-2 shows, urban ecology and the new urban sociology offer significantly different ways of viewing urbanization, both of which enrich our understanding of this complex phenomenon.

Types of Communities

Communities vary substantially in the degree to which their members feel connected and share a common identity. Ferdinand Tönnies ([1887]1988) used the term *Gemeinschaft* to de-
{ p.121 scribe a close-knit community where social interaction among people is intimate and familiar. This is the kind of place where people in a coffee shop will stop talking whenever anyone enters, because they are sure to know whoever walks through the door. A shopper at the small grocery store in this town would expect to know every employee, and probably every other customer as well. In contrast, the ideal type of the *Gesellschaft* describes modern urban life, in which people have little in common with others. Social relationships often result from interactions focused on immediate tasks, such as purchasing a product. In the United States, contemporary city life generally resembles a *Gesellschaft.*

The following sections will examine different types of communities found in the United States, focusing on the distinctive characteristics and problems of central cities, suburbs, and rural areas.

Central Cities

In terms of both land and population, the United States is the fourth-largest nation in the world. Yet three-quarters of the population is concentrated in a mere 1.5 percent of the nation's land area. In 2000 some 226 million people—or 79 percent of the nation's population—lived in metropolitan areas. Even those who live outside central cities, such as residents of suburban and rural communities, find that urban centers heavily influence their lifestyles (Bureau of the Census 2003a:34).

Urban Dwellers Many urban residents are the descendants of European immigrants—Irish, Italians, Jews, Poles, and others—who came to the United States in the 19th and early 20th centuries. The cities socialized these newcomers to the norms, values, and language of their new homeland and gave them an opportunity to work their way up the economic ladder. In addition, a substantial number of low-income African Americans and Whites came to the cities from rural areas in the period following World War II.

Even today, cities in the United States are the destinations of immigrants from around the world—including Mexico, Ireland, Cuba, Vietnam, and Haiti—as well as of migrants from the U.S. commonwealth of Puerto Rico. Yet unlike those who came to this country 100 years ago, current immigrants are arriving at a time of growing urban decay. Thus they have more difficulty finding employment and decent housing.

Urban life is noteworthy for its diversity, so it would be a serious mistake to see all city residents as being alike. Sociologist Herbert J. Gans (1991) has distinguished five types of people found in cities:

1. **Cosmopolites.** These residents remain in cities to take advantage of unique cultural and intellectual benefits. Writers, artists, and scholars fall into this category.

2. **Unmarried and childless people.** Such people choose to live in cities because of the active nightlife and varied recreational opportunities.

3. **Ethnic villagers.** These urban residents prefer to live in their own tight-knit communities. Typically, immigrant groups

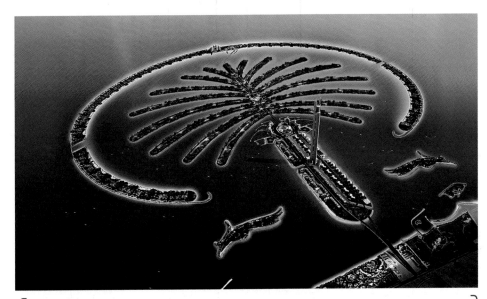

The only limit to urban expansion is the imagination. This proposed development for the city of Dubai in the United Arab Emirates, called Palm Island, would be situated on an entirely man-made landform in the Arabian Gulf.

isolate themselves in such neighborhoods to avoid resentment from well-established urban dwellers.

4. **The deprived.** Very poor people and families have little choice but to live in low-rent, often run-down urban neighborhoods.

5. **The trapped.** Some city residents wish to leave urban centers but cannot because of their limited economic resources and prospects. Gans includes the "downward mobiles" in this category—people who once held higher social positions, but who are forced to live in less prestigious neighborhoods owing to loss of a job, death of a wage earner, or old age.

To this list we can add a sixth type, people who live in naturally occurring retirement communities (see Box 13-2, page 328). These varied categories remind us that the city represents a

Table 20-2

Sociological Perspectives on Urbanization

summingUP

	Urban Ecology	New Urban Sociology
Theoretical perspective	Functionalist	Conflict
Primary focus	Relationship of urban areas to their spatial setting and physical environment	Relationship of urban areas to global, national, and local forces
Key source of change	Technological innovations such as new methods of transportation	Economic competition and monopolization of power
Initiator of actions	Individuals, neighborhoods, communities	Real estate developers, banks and other financial institutions, multinational corporations
Allied disciplines	Geography, architecture	Political science, economics

choice (even a dream) for certain people and a nightmare for others.

Issues Facing Cities Within any city in the United States, people and neighborhoods vary greatly. Yet all residents of a central city—regardless of social class, racial, and ethnic differences—face certain common problems. Crime, air pollution, noise, unemployment, overcrowded schools, inadequate public transportation—these unpleasant realities and many more are an increasingly common feature of contemporary urban life.

Perhaps the single most dramatic reflection of the nation's urban ills has been the apparent death of entire neighborhoods. In some urban districts, business activity seems virtually nonexistent. Visitors can walk for blocks and find little more than deteriorated, boarded-up, abandoned, and burned-out buildings. Vacant factories mark the sites of businesses that relocated a generation ago. Such urban devastation has contributed greatly to the growing problem of homelessness.

Residential segregation has also been a persistent problem in cities across the United States. Segregation has resulted from the policies of financial institutions, the business practices of real estate agents, the actions of home sellers, and even urban planning initiatives (for example, decisions about where to locate public housing). Sociologists Douglas Massey and Nancy Denton (1993) have used the term *American apartheid* to refer to such residential patterns. In their view, we no longer perceive segregation as a problem, but rather accept it as a feature of the urban landscape. For subordinate minority groups, segregation means not only limited housing opportunities but reduced access to employment, retail outlets, and medical services.

Another critical problem for the cities has been mass transportation. Since 1950, the number of cars in the United States has multiplied twice as fast as the number of people. Growing traffic congestion in metropolitan areas has led many cities to recognize the need for safe, efficient, and inexpensive mass transit systems. However, the federal government has traditionally given much more assistance to highway programs than to public transportation. Conflict theorists note that such a bias favors the relatively affluent (automobile owners) as well as corporations such as auto manufacturers, tire makers, and oil companies. Meanwhile, low-income residents of metropolitan areas, who are much less likely to own cars than members of the middle and upper classes, face higher fares on public transit along with deteriorating service (J. W. Mason 1998; Reschovsky 2004).

Use Your Sociological Imagination

You have fast-forwarded to a future in which there are no central cities—just sprawling suburbs and isolated rural communities. What are the economic and social effects of the disappearance of the downtown area?

www.mhhe.com/schaefer11

C stands for "congestion." In 2003, to alleviate gridlock, officials of the city of London began to charge vehicles about $16 a day to enter designated congestion zones. At least initially, significant traffic reductions resulted, leading cities such as Singapore, Stockholm, Oslo, and Rome to copy the idea. The revenue from the fees is used to pay for more buses, road improvements, and upgraded bicycle paths.

Suburbs

The term *suburb* derives from the Latin *sub urbe*, meaning "under the city." Until recent times, most suburbs were just that—tiny communities totally dependent on urban centers for jobs, recreation, and even water.

Today, the term **suburb** defies simple definition. The term generally refers to any community near a large city—or as the Census Bureau would say, any territory within a metropolitan area that is not included in the central city. By that definition, more than 138 million people, or about 51 percent of the population of the United States, live in the suburbs (Kleniewski 2002).

Three social factors differentiate suburbs from cities. First, suburbs are generally less dense than cities; in some suburbs, no more than two dwellings may occupy an acre of land. Second, the suburbs consist almost exclusively of private space. For the most part, private ornamental lawns replace common park

Christie Taylor works at the African American Health Coalition, a community-based organization in Portland, Oregon. As program coordinator there, she runs a support group, develops educational programs on nutrition and community-specific health problems, engages guest speakers, and works within the community to promote awareness of the coalition's work. Taylor also manages several annual events, including a Health Disparities Conference that brings members of the community together with government representatives, policymakers, and health care providers.

For Taylor, a typical week is spent working with community members and collaborating with local organizations. She creates newsletters and flyers to attract new clients and keep regular clients up to date on the coalition's programs. She meets with community leaders to track the programs' progress and look for development opportunities. And she works with local organizations that support the coalition by sponsoring its programs and providing venues for special events.

A graduate of the University of Wisconsin at La Crosse, Taylor decided to major in sociology because "it opened my eyes to look at what was going on around me in a whole new way." She began to understand how people's experiences affect them, and how over time those experiences can affect whole groups of people. Taylor says the discipline gave her "the ability to take in new information that may seem foreign, or not be congruent with what I had always understood." As an

example, she describes an internship she did at the Drug Court in La Crosse, which exposed her to "an entirely different and very effective way of treating drug addiction and the crime it causes. It was refreshing," she says, "and opened my eyes to look for innovative solutions to established problems."

This openness to new experiences has served her well in her work outside the academic walls. "Being from Wisconsin and accustomed to more traditional Midwestern cuisine, I was unsure of my ability to coordinate nutrition programs that would be cultural specific to African Americans," she admits. Nevertheless, she took the challenge and found that she was equal to it: "My training in sociology taught me cultural competence and the skill set to understand and work well with all kinds of people."

Let's Discuss

1. Have you ever worked in a community of people whose cultural background was different from your own? If so, what were the challenges and the rewards? Were you prepared for them?
2. Communities may have problems, but they are also a source of great strength to their members. What aspects of the African American community are especially supportive to those who belong to it?

---

areas. Third, suburbs have more exacting building design codes than cities, and those codes have become increasingly precise in the last decade. While the suburbs may be diverse in population, their design standards give the impression of uniformity.

Distinguishing between suburbs and rural areas can also be difficult. Certain criteria generally define suburbs: Most people work at urban (as opposed to rural) jobs, and local governments provide services such as water supply, sewage disposal, and fire protection. In rural areas, those services are less common, and a greater proportion of residents is employed in farming and related activities.

Suburban Expansion   Whatever the precise definition of a suburb, it is clear that suburbs have expanded. In fact, suburbanization was the most dramatic population trend in the United States throughout the 20th century. Suburban areas grew at first along railroad lines, then at the termini of streetcar tracks, and by the 1950s along the nation's growing system of freeways and expressways. The suburban boom has been especially evident since World War II.

Proponents of the new urban sociology contend that initially, industries moved their factories from central cities to suburbs to

reduce the power of labor unions. Subsequently, many suburban communities induced businesses to relocate there by offering them subsidies and tax incentives. As sociologist William Julius Wilson (1996) has observed, federal housing policies contributed to the suburban boom by withholding mortgage capital from inner-city neighborhoods, by offering favorable mortgages to military veterans, and by assisting the rapid development of massive amounts of affordable tract housing in the suburbs. Moreover, federal highway and transportation policies provided substantial funding for expressway systems (which made commuting to the cities much easier), while undermining urban communities by building freeway networks through their heart.

All these factors contributed to the movement of the (predominantly White) middle class out of the central cities, and as we shall see, out of the suburbs as well. From the perspective of new urban sociology, suburban expansion is far from a natural ecological process; rather, it reflects the distinct priorities of powerful economic and political interests.

Suburban Diversity   In the United States, race and ethnicity remain the most important factors that distinguish cities from

The growth of the Hispanic population in small towns and agricultural areas has been a welcome countertrend to the stagnation of most rural areas in the United States. This community in Beardstown, Illinois, is thriving.

suburbs. Nevertheless, the common assumption that suburbia includes only prosperous Whites is far from correct. The last 20 years have witnessed the diversification of suburbs in terms of race and ethnicity. For example, by 2000, 34 percent of Blacks in the United States, 46 percent of Latinos, and 53 percent of Asians lived in the suburbs. Like the rest of the nation, members of racial and ethnic minorities are becoming suburban dwellers (El Nasser 2001; Frey 2001).

But are the suburban areas re-creating the racial segregation of the central cities? A definite pattern of clustering, if not outright segregation, is emerging. A study of suburban residential patterns in 11 metropolitan areas found that Asian Americans and Hispanics tend to reside in the same socioeconomic areas as Whites—that is, affluent Hispanics live alongside affluent Whites, poor Asians near poor Whites, and so on. However, the case for African Americans is quite distinct. Suburban Blacks live in poorer suburbs than Whites, even after taking into account differences in their income, education, and homeownership.

Again, in contrast to prevailing stereotypes, the suburbs include a significant number of low-income people from all backgrounds—White, Black, and Hispanic. Poverty is not conventionally associated with the suburbs, partly because the suburban poor tend to be scattered among more affluent people. In some instances, suburban communities intentionally hide social problems such as homelessness so they can maintain a "respectable image." Soaring housing costs have contributed to suburban poverty, which is rising at a faster rate than urban poverty (Puentes and Warren 2006).

Rural Areas

As we have seen, the people of the United States live mainly in urban areas. Yet according to the 2000 census, 59 million Americans, or 21 percent of the population, live in rural areas. There

is quite a range in the number of rural residents from state to state: In California, less than 6 percent of residents live in rural areas; in Vermont, more than 60 percent (Bureau of the Census 2006a).

Rural Diversity

As with the suburbs, it would be a mistake to view these rural communities as fitting one set image. Turkey farms, coal-mining towns, cattle ranches, and gas stations along interstate highways are all part of the rural landscape in the United States. And though globalization usually brings to mind the world's financial capitals, rural areas, including those in the United States, also play a fundamental role in the global economy. Like their urban counterparts, rural communities have adjusted to world competition. U.S. farmers now produce 40 percent of the world's supply of soybeans. In response to global concerns over oil shortages, they developed ethanol, a gasoline substitute produced from agricultural feed or grains like corn and wheat (Flora and Flora with Fey 2004).

Historically, rural areas have also been ethnically and racially diverse. In the 19th century, several immigrant groups, such as the Scandinavians, were attracted to rural areas and the opportunities they offered for farming. In the 20th century, South Asian immigrants, particularly Vietnamese Americans, migrated to sparsely settled coastal areas to take jobs in the fishing industry. And well into the 1920s, the Black population of the United States was concentrated largely in the rural South.

Recently, the catastrophic Hurricane Katrina, which devastated Gulf Coast cities and towns in 2005, has contributed to a rural resurgence in the deep South. Faced with the slow reconstruction of New Orleans and other hard-hit cities, many displaced residents have relocated from the coast to rural areas further inland. African Americans in particular have begun to gravitate toward communities that offer jobs in the fish farming industry. These small rural communities have become an economic and social magnet for displaced Gulf residents (Eaton 2007; Kandell 2005).

Rural Challenges

Today, many rural areas are facing problems that were first associated with the central cities, and are now evident in the suburbs. Overdevelopment, gang warfare, and drug trafficking can be found on the policymaking agenda far outside major metropolitan areas. While the magnitude of the problems may not be as great as in the central cities, rural resources cannot begin to match those that city mayors can marshall in an attempt to address social ills (Graham 2004; Osgood and Chambers 2003).

The postindustrial revolution has been far from kind to the rural communities of the United States. Of the fewer than 3 mil-

research IN *action*

20-2 Wal-Mart: The Store Wars

No organization exists in a vacuum, especially not a corporate giant. Executives of Wal-Mart know that. The epitome of the superstore, Wal-Mart has become the center of controversy in towns and cities across the United States, despite the familiar smiley-face logo and its red, white, and blue corporate image. The reason: A new Wal-Mart can have powerfully negative effects on the surrounding community.

Wal-Mart was founded in 1962 by Sam Walton, whose strategy was to locate new stores in rural communities, where competition from other retailers was weak and unions were not organized. Over the years, as the enormously successful discount chain expanded to become the world's largest corporation, Wal-Mart began to move into the fringes of metropolitan areas as well. But the residents of the communities Wal-Mart moved into did not always welcome their new neighbor.

In Ashland, Virginia, a community of 7,200 people, residents worried that Wal-Mart would destroy the small-town atmosphere they treasured. Would their cozy grocery store, known for its personal service, survive the discount giant's competition? Would their quaint and charming Main Street fall into decline? Would full-time jobs with full benefits give way to part-time employment? (Studies have shown that superstores ultimately *reduce* employment.) Ashland's grassroots opposition to Wal-Mart, chronicled in the PBS documentary *Store Wars,* ultimately lost its battle because of Wal-Mart's promised low prices and increased tax revenues. But citizens in many other communities have won, at least temporarily.

On the urban fringes, too, residents have mobilized to stop new superstores. In Bangor, Maine, environmentalists raised an alarm over a proposed Wal-Mart superstore, to be located next to a marsh that sheltered endangered wildlife. Activists in Riverside, California, also challenged Wal-Mart, again on environmental grounds.

But the issue is more complicated in these areas, because communities on the urban fringe are hardly untouched by economic development. Wal-Mart's proposed site in Bangor, for instance, is not far from the Bangor Mall. And the huge new houses that dot the suburbs surrounding new stores, built on lots carved out of farmland or forest, have had an environmental impact themselves. In fact, the trend toward the superstore seems to parallel the emergence of the megalopolis, whose boundaries push farther and farther outward, eating up open space in the process. Recognizing the drawbacks of urban sprawl, some

> *In Ashland, Virginia, residents worried that Wal-Mart would destroy the small-town atmosphere they treasured.*

planners are beginning to advocate "smart growth"—restoring the central city and its older suburbs rather than abandoning them for the outer rings.

Recently, the debate over Wal-Mart's economic impact has expanded to include health care. Given their wage level, a large proportion of Wal-Mart's employees cannot afford health insurance. In the state of Maryland, frustrated legislators passed a law requiring the state's largest private employers to spend a minimum of 8 percent of their payroll on employee health care. The law, which was later overturned in court, was aimed squarely at Wal-Mart, the only large employer in the state that was not spending the required amount on health insurance. Whatever the outcome of this contro-

versy, there is no denying the social impact of the nation's largest employer.

Not all communities reject superstores. In countries like Mexico, where the economic outlook has been poor recently, people have welcomed Wal-Mart. From Tijuana to Cancún, in fact, public reaction to the U.S. chain's arrival has been almost universally positive. Mexican shoppers appreciate Wal-Mart's wide selection and low prices.

Wal-Mart executives are unapologetic about the chain's rapid expansion. They argue that their aggressive competition has lowered prices and raised working people's standard of living. And they say they have given back to the communities where their stores are located by donating money to educational institutions and local agencies. To counter criticism, executives have launched an advertising campaign that promotes Wal-Mart's community-oriented image. Even though public opinion of the corporation continues to be negative, around the world the huge chain still draws ever increasing crowds of loyal customers.

Let's Discuss

1. Is there a Wal-Mart, Home Depot, or some other superstore near you? If so, was its opening a matter of controversy in your community?

2. What do you think of the "smart growth" movement? Should communities attempt to redirect business and residential development, or should developers be free to build wherever and whatever they choose?

Sources: Halebsky 2004; Hansen 2004; *Maine Times* 2001; PBS 2005; Pantesco 2006; Saporito 2003; Smart Growth 2005; Wal-Mart 2007; Wal-Mart Watch 2007.

lion farm and ranch operators nationwide, little more than a third consider agriculture their principal occupation. Farm residents now represent less than 1 percent of the nation's population, compared to 95 percent in 1790. The depopulation of farming areas has been especially hard on the youngest residents. It is not uncommon for rural children to travel 90 minutes each way to school, compared to a nationwide one-way commute of less than 26 minutes for urban workers (Department of Agriculture 2004; Dillon 2004).

While the press often notes the consolidation of rural school districts, rural educational problems are not limited to the elementary schools. From Washington state to rural West Virginia, college-age youths often have only limited access to two-year colleges. Although long-distance learning opportunities have expanded to meet their needs, college-bound residents of rural areas are more likely than their urban counterparts to face a patchwork of programs (Hebel 2006).

Economic stagnation and resulting depopulation have been particularly stark in the northern Rockies and western Great Plains. These areas do not benefit much from tourism, and though agriculture thrives there, the income from farming flows disproportionately to large agribusinesses. Even food processing, an obvious potential source of employment, is lacking; area produce is shipped elsewhere to be processed (Florio 2006).

In desperation, residents of depressed rural areas have begun to encourage prison construction, which they once discouraged, to bring in badly needed economic development. Ironically, in regions where the prison population has declined, communities have been hurt yet again by their dependence on a single industry (Kilborn 2001).

The construction of large businesses can create its own problems, as small communities that have experienced the arrival of large discount stores, such as Wal-Mart, Target, Home Depot, or Costco, have discovered. Although many residents welcome the new employment opportunities and the convenience of one-stop shopping, local merchants see their longtime family businesses endangered by formidable 200,000-square-foot competitors with a national reputation. Even when such discount stores provide a boost to a town's economy (and they do not always do so), they can undermine the town's sense of community and identity. Box 20-2 (page 493) chronicles the "store wars" that often ensue.

On a more positive note, advances in electronic communications have allowed some people in the United States to work wherever they wish. For those who are concerned about quality-of-life issues, working at home in a rural area that has access to the latest high-tech services is the perfect arrangement. No matter where people make their homes—whether in the city, the suburbs, or a country village—economic and technological change will have an impact on their quality of life.

Use Your Sociological Imagination

Have you seen rural areas change? If so, in what ways? In your opinion, are the changes you have seen for the better or worse?

www.mhhe.com/schaefer11

Seeking Shelter Worldwide

The Issue

A chance meeting brought two old classmates together. In late 1997, Prince Charles encountered Clive Harold during a tour of the offices of a magazine sold by the homeless in London. But while Prince Charles can call several palaces home, Harold is homeless. This modern-day version of *The Prince and the Pauper* intrigued many people with its message that "it can happen to anyone." Harold had been a successful author and journalist until his marriage fell apart and alcohol turned his life inside out (*Chicago Tribune* 1997).

The issue of inadequate shelter manifests itself in many ways, for all housing problems can be considered relative. To a middle-class family in the United States, it may mean a somewhat smaller house than they need, because that is all they can afford. For a single working adult in Tokyo, it may mean having to commute two hours to a full-time job. For many people worldwide, however, the housing problem means finding shelter of any kind that they can afford, in a place where anyone would reasonably wish to live. Prince Charles of Buckingham Palace and Clive Harold, homeless person, are extreme examples of a continuum that is present in all communities and all societies. What can be done to ensure adequate shelter for those who can't afford it?

The Setting

Homelessness is evident in both industrialized and developing countries. According to estimates, on any given night, the number of homeless persons in the United States is at least 750,000 (see Figure 20-3), only about half of whom are sheltered. As many as 3.5 million Americans may experience homelessness at some time each year (Housing and Urban Development 2007; National Alliance to End Homelessness 2007).

In Third World countries, rapid population growth has outpaced the expansion of housing by a wide margin, leading to a rise in homelessness. For example, estimates of homelessness in Mexico City range from 10,000 to 100,000, and do not include the many people living in caves or squatter settlements (see Box

FIGURE 20–3

Homeless Estimates by State

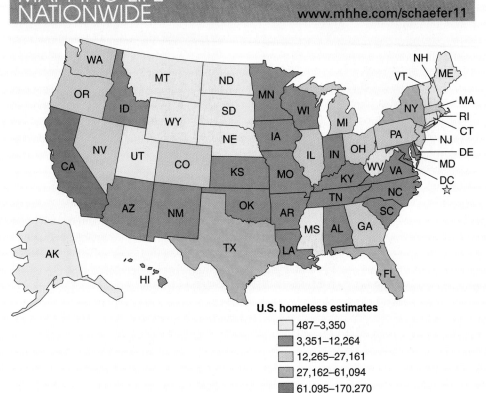

MAPPING LIFE
NATIONWIDE

www.mhhe.com/schaefer11

U.S. homeless estimates

- ☐ 487–3,350
- ☐ 3,351–12,264
- ☐ 12,265–27,161
- ☐ 27,162–61,094
- ☐ 61,095–170,270

Source: Based on 2005 data reported by National Alliance to End Homelessness 2007:3.

Though homelessness tends to be concentrated in the more populous states, such as California, hundreds of homeless people can be found in every state.

20-1, page 488). By 1998, in urban areas alone, 600 million people around the world were either homeless or inadequately housed (M. Davis 2005; G. Goldstein 1998; Ross 1996).

Sociological Insights

Both in the United States and around the world, homelessness {pp.112, 191 functions as a master status that largely defines a person's position in society. In this case, homelessness means that in many important respects, the individual is *outside* society. Without a home address and telephone, it is difficult to look for work or even apply for public assistance. Moreover, the master status of being homeless carries a serious stigma that can lead to prejudice and discrimination. Poor treatment of people suspected of being homeless is common in stores and restaurants, and many communities have reported acts of random violence against homeless people.

The profile of homelessness has changed significantly over the last 40 years. In the past, most homeless people were older White males living as alcoholics in skid-row areas. However, today's homeless are comparatively younger, with an average age in the low 30s. Overall, an estimated 59 percent of homeless peo-

ple in the United States are from racial and ethnic minority groups. Moreover, a 25-city survey done in 2004 found that the homeless population is growing faster than the increase in emergency food and shelter space (Housing and Urban Development 2007; U.S. Conference of Mayors 2004).

Changing economic and residential patterns account for much of this increase in homelessness. In recent decades, the process of urban renewal has included a noticeable boom in **gentrification.** This term refers to the resettlement of low-income city neighborhoods by prosperous families and business firms. In some instances, city governments have promoted gentrification by granting lucrative tax breaks to developers who convert low-cost rental units into luxury apartments and condominiums. Conflict theorists note that although the affluent may derive both financial and emotional benefits from gentrification and redevelopment, the poor often end up being thrown out on the street.

Policy Initiatives

The major federal program intended to assist the homeless is the McKinney Homeless Assistance Act, passed in 1987. This act authorizes federal aid for emergency food, shelter, physical and mental health care, job training, and education for homeless children and adults. Thus far, most policymakers have been content to steer the homeless toward large, overcrowded, unhealthy shelters. Yet many neighborhoods and communities have resisted plans to open large shelters or even smaller residences for the homeless, often raising the familiar cry of "Not in my backyard!"

According to an analysis by the National Law Center on Homelessness and Poverty (2006), the 1990s saw a growing trend toward the adoption of anti-homeless public policies and the "criminalization" of homeless people. Many cities have enacted curbs on panhandling, sitting on sidewalks, standing near automated teller machines, and other behavior sometimes evident among the homeless. At the same time, more and more policymakers—especially conservative officials—have advocated cutbacks in government funding for the homeless and argued that voluntary associations and religious organizations should assume a more important role in addressing the problem (Archibold 2006a, 2006b).

Though new policy proposals have not received much attention, opinion polls show that homelessness is part of the national consciousness. In a 2005 national survey, 53 percent of respondents said they thought that the problem of homelessness was very serious; 36 percent, somewhat serious; and only 11 percent, not serious. People typically did not blame the victims; 56 percent of respondents said they thought the homeless were the victims of circumstances beyond their control, while only 38 percent saw them as responsible for their situation (Roper Center 2005; Ryan 1976).

Innovative programs to address homelessness have encountered some skepticism. The city of Portland, Oregon, has begun an ambitious program to house the homeless without stipulating that they be alcohol- and drug-free. Preliminary results suggest that recovery rates go up and unemployment drops in such housing programs, and that they are more cost effective than crime and drug intervention programs (Citizens Commission on Homelessness 2004; NewsHour 2007).

Developing nations have special problems. They have understandably given highest priority to economic productivity, as measured by jobs with living wages. Unfortunately, even the most ambitious economic and social programs may be overwhelmed by minor currency fluctuations, a drop in the value of a nation's major export, or an influx of refugees from a neighboring country. Some of the reforms implemented have included promoting private (as opposed to government-controlled) housing markets, allowing dwellings to be places of business as well, and loosening restrictions on building materials.

All three of those short-term solutions have shortcomings, however. Private housing markets invite exploitation; mixed residential/commercial use may only cause good housing to deteriorate faster; and the use of marginal building materials leaves low-income residential areas more vulnerable to calamities such as floods, fires, and earthquakes. Large-scale rental housing under government supervision, the typical solution in North America and Europe, has been successful only in economically advanced city-states such as Hong Kong and Singapore (Speak and Tipple 2006; Strassman 1998).

This modest house, made of concrete blocks, was designed for use in Haiti by Habitat for Humanity. Since its founding in 1976, Habitat for Humanity International has built over 200,000 houses for a million people in a hundred countries, including the United States.

In sum, though homeless people in the United States and abroad are not getting the shelter they need, they lack the political clout to gain policymakers' attention.

Let's Discuss

1. Have you ever worked as a volunteer in a shelter or soup kitchen? If so, were you surprised by the type of people who lived or ate there? Has anyone you know ever had to move into a shelter?

2. Is gentrification of low-income housing a problem where you live? Have you ever had difficulty finding an affordable place to live?

3. What kind of assistance is available to homeless people in the community where you live? Does the help come from the government, from private charities, or both? What about housing assistance for people with low incomes, such as rent subsidies—is it available?

GettingINVOLVED

To get involved in the debate over homelessness, visit this text's Online Learning Center, which offers links to relevant Web sites. Check out the Social Policy section on the Online Learning Center as well; it provides survey data on U.S. public opinion regarding this issue.

{ MASTERING THIS CHAPTER }

Summary

A *community* is a spatial or political unit of social organization that gives people a sense of belonging. This chapter explains how communities have changed and analyzes the process of urbanization from both the functionalist and conflict perspectives. It describes various types of communities, including the central cities, the *suburbs,* and rural areas.

1. Stable communities began to develop when people stayed in one place to cultivate crops; eventually, surplus production enabled cities to emerge.

2. Over time, cities changed and developed with their economies. In the industrial revolution, the *preindustrial city* of agricultural societies gave way to the *industrial city;* the advent of the Information Age brought with it the *postindustrial city.*

3. Urbanization is evident not only in the United States but throughout the world; by 2000, 50 percent of the world's population lived in urban areas.

4. The *urban ecological* approach is functionalist because it emphasizes how different elements in urban areas contribute to social stability.

5. Drawing on conflict theory, *new urban sociology* emphasizes the interplay of a community's political and economic interests, as well as the impact of the global economy on communities in the United States and other countries.

6. Many urban residents are immigrants from other nations who tend to live together in ethnic neighborhoods.

7. In the last three decades, cities have confronted an overwhelming array of economic and social problems, including crime, unemployment, and the deterioration of schools and public transit systems.

8. Suburbanization was the most dramatic population trend in the United States throughout the 20th century. In recent decades, *suburbs* have become more racially and ethnically diverse.

9. Rural communities are economically, ethnically, and racially diverse. Though farming—once the mainstay of rural areas—has declined, new groups are moving in to take advantage of the opportunities rural areas offer.

10. Soaring housing costs, unemployment, cutbacks in public assistance, and rapid population growth have contributed to rising homelessness around the world. Most social policy is directed toward sending the homeless to large shelters.

Critical Thinking Questions

1. How can the functionalist and conflict perspectives be used to examine solutions to the issues faced by cities and other communities?

2. How has your home community (your city, town, or neighborhood) changed over the years you have lived there? Have there been significant changes in the community's economic base or its racial and ethnic profile? Have the community's social problems intensified or lessened? Is unemployment currently a major problem? What are the community's future prospects?

3. Imagine that you have been asked to study the issue of homelessness in the largest city in your state. How might you draw on surveys, observation research, experiments, and existing sources to study this issue?

Key Terms

Community A spatial or political unit of social organization that gives people a sense of belonging, based either on shared residence in a particular place or on a common identity. (page 482)

Concentric-zone theory A theory of urban growth devised by Ernest Burgess that sees growth in terms of a series of rings radiating from the central business district. (485)

Gentrification The resettlement of low-income city neighborhoods by prosperous families and business firms. (495)

Human ecology An area of study that is concerned with the interrelationships between people and their environment. (484)

Industrial city A relatively large city characterized by open competition, an open class system, and elaborate specialization in the manufacturing of goods. (483)

Megalopolis A densely populated area containing two or more cities and their suburbs. (484)

Multiple-nuclei theory A theory of urban growth developed by Harris and Ullman that views growth as emerging from many centers of development, each of which reflects a particular urban need or activity. (485)

New urban sociology An approach to urbanization that considers the interplay of local, national, and worldwide forces and their effect on local space, with special emphasis on the impact of global economic activity. (487)

Postindustrial city A city in which global finance and the electronic flow of information dominate the economy. (483)

Preindustrial city A city of only a few thousand people that is characterized by a relatively closed class system and limited mobility. (482)

Squatter settlement An area occupied by the very poor on the fringe of a city, in which housing is constructed by the settlers themselves from discarded material. (488)

Suburb According to the Census Bureau, any territory within a metropolitan area that is not included in the central city. (490)

Urban ecology An area of study that focuses on the interrelationships between people and their environment in urban areas. (484)

Urbanism A term used by Louis Wirth to describe distinctive patterns of social behavior evident among city residents. (484)

World systems analysis Immanuel Wallerstein's view of the global economic system as one divided between certain industrialized nations that control wealth and developing countries that are controlled and exploited. (487)

Read each question carefully and then select the best answer.

1. Louis Wirth argued that a relatively large and permanent settlement leads to distinctive patterns of behavior, which he called

   a. squatting.
   b. linear development.
   c. urbanism.
   d. gentrification.

2. In comparison with industrial cities, preindustrial cities had

   a. relatively open class systems.
   b. extensive social mobility.
   c. a largely illiterate population.
   d. all of the above

3. Robert Park and Ernest Burgess are associated with

   a. the functionalist perspective.
   b. the conflict perspective.
   c. the linear-development model.
   d. multiple-nuclei theory.

4. Urbanization in preindustrial cities was restricted by

   a. the ease of migration to the city.
   b. high levels of surplus produced by the agricultural sector.
   c. reliance on animal power as a source of energy for economic production.
   d. all of the above

5. The new urban sociology draws generally on the conflict perspective and more specifically on sociologist Immanuel Wallerstein's

   a. concentric-zone theory.
   b. multiple-nuclei theory.
   c. concept of edge cities.
   d. world systems analysis.

6. According to Herbert Gans, residents who remain in the city to take advantage of unique cultural and intellectual benefits of the city are called

   a. cosmopolites.
   b. ethnic villagers.
   c. urban villagers.
   d. the trapped.

7. World systems analysis is closely aligned with

   a. the concentric-zone theory.
   b. the multiple-nuclei theory.
   c. new urban sociology.
   d. zone sector theory.

8. The most dramatic population trend in the United States throughout the 20th century was

   a. urbanization.
   b. suburbanization.
   c. the move to the sun belt.
   d. the move to the "old homestead" in rural areas.

9. In which type of city is there a greater openness to new religious faiths?

   a. preindustrial city
   b. industrial city
   c. postindustrial city
   d. edge city

10. Which of these results from gentrification, according to conflict theorists?

    a. low-income families receive tax breaks
    b. locally owned businesses suffer
    c. poor people are displaced
    d. pollution increases

11. The 500-mile corridor stretching from Boston south to Washington, D.C., which accounts for one-sixth of the total population of the United States, is an example of a(n) _____.

12. A less pejorative term for squatter settlements is _____ _____.

13. The urban ecological model is criticized by some for referring to the arrival of African Americans in white neighborhoods in the 1930s as an example of _____ and _____.

14. The emergence of squatter settlements is often accompanied by a thriving "_____ economy."

15. _____ _____ is concerned with the interrelationships between people and their environment.

16. According to the concentric-zone theory, at the core of the city is the _____ business district.

17. Ferdinand Tönnies used the term _____ to describe a close-knit community where social interaction among people is intimate and familiar.

18. Studies have shown that superstores, such as Wal-Mart, ultimately _____ employment.

19. A study of suburban residential patterns found that _____ Americans and _____ tend to reside in equivalent socioeconomic areas with Whites; however, _____ Americans are found in poorer suburbs than Whites.

20. While some observers suggest that the growth of sun-belt cities is due to a "good business climate," _____ theorists counter that this term is actually a euphemism for hefty government subsidies and antilabor policies.

Answers:
1 (c); 2 (c); 3 (a); 4 (c); 5 (d); 6 (a); 7 (c); 8 (b); 9 (c); 10 (c); 11 megalopolis; 12 autonomous settlements; 13 invasion; succession; 14 informal; 15 Human ecology; 16 central; 17 *Gemeinschaft*; 18 reduce; 19 Asian; Hispanics; African; 20 conflict

TECHNOLOGY RESOURCES

Online Learning Center

1. You can assess your knowledge of the material in this chapter at any point by completing the true–false quiz at the student center in the Online Learning center. It will give you immediate feedback on incorrect answers. You can even take the quiz before reading the chapter, as a way of familiarizing yourself with some of the key topics.

2. Although you have probably heard of Habitat for Humanity—the organization that builds homes for poor families—you may not be aware of the breadth of their activities. Find out more at their Web site **www.habitat.org.**

3. Learn more about patterns of urbanization throughout the world from data at NationMaster.com (**www.nationmaster.com**). Start by clicking on "Statistics" at the top of the page, and then "Geography." Link to "Largest City Population" and examine the graph.

*Note: Although all the URLs listed were current as of the printing of this book, these sites often change. Please check our Web site (**www.mhhe.com/schaefer11**) for updates, hyperlinks, and exercises related to these sites.*

STOP ST. LAWRENCE CEMENT. SUPPORT HVPC.

Industrial production can cause serious environmental damage to our air, land, and water. This poster, sponsored by the Hudson Valley Preservation Committee, urges the citizens of New York to oppose the construction of a new coal-powered cement plant on the banks of the Hudson River.

21

Population and the Environment

inside

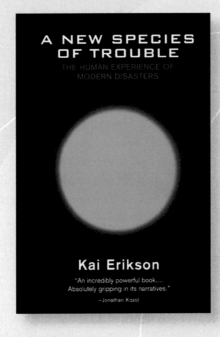

A NEW SPECIES OF TROUBLE

THE HUMAN EXPERIENCE OF MODERN DISASTERS

Kai Erikson

"An incredibly powerful book.... Absolutely gripping in its narratives." – Jonathan Kozol

" Over the past twenty years, research errands of one kind or another have taken me to a number of communities still stunned by the effects of a recent disaster. These include a valley in West Virginia known as Buffalo Creek, devastated by a fearsome flood; an Ojibwa Indian reserve in Canada called Grassy Narrows, plagued by contamination of the waterways along which members of the band had lived for centuries; a town in South Florida named Immokalee, where three hundred migrant farm workers were robbed of the only money most of them had ever saved; a group of houses in Colorado known as East Swallow, threatened by vapors from silent pools of gasoline that had gathered in the ground below; and the neighborhoods surrounding Three Mile Island.

In one respect, at least, these events were altogether different. A flood. An act of larceny. A toxic poisoning. A gasoline spill. A nuclear accident. My assignment in each of those cases was to learn enough about the people who thought they had been damaged by the blow to appear on their behalf in a court of law, so each was a separate research effort, and each resulted in a separate research report.

In another respect, though, it was clear from the beginning that those scenes of trouble had much in common. I was asked to visit them in the first place, obviously, because the persons who issued the invitations thought they could see resemblances there. And just as obviously, I was drawn to them because they touched a corresponding set of curiosities and preoccupations in me. Moreover, common themes seemed to come into focus as I moved from one place to another, so that those separate happen-

> *Soon after the black wall of water and debris ground its way down Buffalo Creek, attorneys for the coal company involved called the disaster "an act of God."*

ings (and the separate stories told of them) began to fuse into a more inclusive whole. One of the excitements of sociological work in general is to watch general patterns—dim and shapeless at first—emerge from a wash of seemingly unconnected details. . . .

In particular: Soon after the black wall of water and debris ground its way down Buffalo Creek, attorneys for the coal company involved called the disaster "an act of God." . . . However people elsewhere may look upon that . . . reasoning, the residents of Buffalo Creek understood it to be blasphemy. They knew that one does not blame God lightly for the wrongdoings of humankind, . . . and they knew, too, that the phrase itself reflected a degree of indifference bordering on contempt. On both of those counts they reacted with fury.

I thought then that the sharpness of the reaction had a lot to do with cultural particulars: the immediacy of Appalachian spirituality, the paternalism of Appalachian coal camps, the communality of Appalachian society. I would suggest now, though, that the people of the valley were drawing on local languages and sensibilities to express feelings that are far more general, for people elsewhere seem to respect a profound difference between those disasters that can be understood as the work of nature and those that need to be understood as the work of humankind. "

(Erikson 1994:11–12, 19) Additional information about this excerpt can be found on the Online Learning Center at www.mhhe.com/schaefer11.

In this passage from *A New Species of Trouble,* Kai Erikson explains how he brought his sociological imagination to bear on five seemingly unrelated disasters. Each, he realized, had been caused not by natural forces, but by human disregard for the natural world or for other human beings. But while ignorance or negligence is often thought to be at the bottom of such catastrophes, Erikson saw a larger, more sweeping process at work. Consumerism and rapid increases in population, he thought, lay at the bottom of these calamities. Economically, people and their ever-increasing wants and needs had begun to outstrip the capacity of the environment to tolerate their encroachments. Through overpopulation, overconsumption, overbuilding, and overgrazing, people were beginning to overwhelm their physical environment.

What is the relationship between population and the environment? Are humans in danger of overpopulating the world, causing an environmental catastrophe in the process? How does rapid population growth contribute to the movement of large groups of people from one part of the world to another? What do sociologists have to say about population policy and environmental issues? In this chapter, because we cannot begin to understand the deterioration of our physical environment without grasping the effects of human behavior, we will take a sociological overview of world population and some related environmental issues. We will begin with Thomas Robert Malthus's controversial analysis of population trends and Karl Marx's critical response to it. A brief overview of world population history follows. We'll pay particular attention to the current problem of overpopulation, and the prospects for and potential consequences of stable population growth in the United States. We'll see, too, how population growth fuels the migration of large numbers of people from one area of the world to another.

Later in the chapter, we will examine the environmental problems facing the world in the 21st century, and will draw on the functionalist and conflict perspectives to better understand environmental issues. It is important not to oversimplify the relationship between population and the environment. Rising population, in itself, does not necessarily destroy the environment, while stable population growth alone is no guarantee of healthful air or water. Nevertheless, as will be evident in the second half of the chapter and in the Social Policy section on world population policy, increases in population can strain our environmental resources and present difficult choices for policymakers.

Demography: The Study of Population

The study of population issues engages the attention of both natural and social scientists. The biologist explores the nature of reproduction and casts light on factors that affect *fertility,* the level of reproduction in a society. The medical pathologist examines and analyzes trends in the causes of death. Geographers, historians, and psychologists also have distinctive contributions to make to our understanding of population. Sociologists, more than these other researchers, focus on the *social* factors that influence population rates and trends.

In their study of population issues, sociologists are aware that the norms, values, and social patterns of a society profoundly affect various elements of population, such as fertility, *mortality* (the death rate), and migration. Fertility is influenced by people's age of entry into sexual unions and by their use of contraception—both of which, in turn, reflect the social and religious values that guide a particular culture. Mortality is shaped by a nation's level of nutrition, acceptance of immunization, and provisions for sanitation, as well as its general commitment to health care and health education. Migration from one country to another can depend on marital and kinship ties, the relative degree of racial and religious tolerance in various societies, and people's evaluation of their employment opportunities.

Demography is the scientific study of population. It draws on several components of population, including size, composition, and territorial distribution, to understand the social consequences of population change. Demographers study geographical variations and historical trends in their effort to develop population forecasts. They also analyze the structure of a population—the age, gender, race, and ethnicity of its members. A key figure in this analysis was Thomas Malthus.

Malthus's Thesis and Marx's Response

The Reverend Thomas Robert Malthus (1766–1834), who was educated at Cambridge University, spent his life teaching history and political economy. He strongly criticized two major institutions of his time—the church and slavery—yet his most significant legacy to contemporary scholars is his still-controversial *Essays on the Principle of Population,* published in 1798.

Essentially, Malthus held that the world's population was growing more rapidly than the available food supply. He argued that food supply increases in arithmetic progression (1, 2, 3, 4, and so on), whereas population expands by geometric progression (1, 2, 4, 8, and so on). According to his analysis, the gap between food supply and population will continue to grow over time. Even though the food supply will increase, it will not increase nearly enough to meet the needs of an expanding world population.

Malthus advocated population control to close the gap between rising population and the food supply, yet he explicitly denounced artificial means of birth control because they were not sanctioned by religion. For Malthus, one appropriate way to control population was to postpone marriage. He argued that couples must take responsibility for the number of children they choose to bear; without such restraint, the world would face widespread hunger, poverty, and misery (Malthus et al. [1824] 1960; Petersen 1979).

Karl Marx strongly criticized Malthus's views on population. Marx pointed to the nature of economic relations in Europe's industrial societies as the central problem. He could not accept the Malthusian notion that rising world population, rather than capitalism, was the cause of social ills. In Marx's opinion, there was no special relationship between world population and the supply of resources (including food). If society were well ordered, increases in population would lead to greater wealth, not to hunger and misery.

Of course, Marx did not believe that capitalism operated under these ideal conditions. He maintained that capitalism devoted resources to the financing of buildings and tools rather than to the equitable distribution of food, housing, and other necessities of life. Marx's work is important to the study of population because he linked overpopulation to the unequal distribution of resources—a topic that will be taken up later in this chapter. His concern with the writings of Malthus also testifies to the importance of population in political and economic affairs.

The insights of Malthus and Marx regarding population issues have come together in what is termed the *neo-Malthusian view,* best exemplified by the work of Paul Ehrlich (1968; Ehrlich and Ehrlich 1990), author of *The Population Bomb.* Neo-Malthusians agree with Malthus that population growth is outstretching the world's natural resources. However, in contrast to the British theorist, they insist that birth control measures are needed to regulate population increases. Showing a Marxist bent, neo-Malthusians condemn the developed nations, which despite their low birthrates consume a disproportionately large share of world resources. While rather pessimistic about the future, these theorists stress that birth control and sensible use of resources are essential responses to rising world population (J. Tierney 1990; Weeks 2008).

Studying Population Today

The relative balance of births and deaths is no less important today than it was during the lifetime of Malthus and Marx. The suffering that Malthus spoke of is certainly a reality for many people of the world. Malnutrition remains the largest contributing factor to illness and death among children in developing countries. Almost 18 percent of these children will die before age five—a rate over 11 times higher than in developed nations. Warfare and large-scale migration intensify problems of population and food supply. For example, recent strife in Afghanistan, the Congo, and Iraq has caused maldistribution of food supplies, leading to regional health concerns. Combating world hunger may require reducing human births, dramatically in-

As this crowded street in Delhi, India, suggests, India will soon become the most populous country in the world. Not all developing countries are choked by their populations, however; population patterns can vary dramatically from country to country.

creasing the world's food supply, or perhaps both. The study of population-related issues, then, seems to be essential.

In the United States and most other countries, the census is the primary mechanism for collecting population information. A *census* is an enumeration, or counting, of a population. The Constitution of the United States requires that a census be held every 10 years to determine congressional representation. This periodic investigation is supplemented by *vital statistics,* or records of births, deaths, marriages, and divorces that are gathered through a registration system maintained by governmental units. In addition, other government surveys provide up-to-date information on commercial developments, educational trends, industrial expansion, agricultural practices, and the status of groups such as children, the elderly, racial minorities, and single parents.

In administering a nationwide census and conducting other types of research, demographers employ many of the skills and techniques described in Chapter 2, including questionnaires,

Kelsie Wilson-Dorsett was born in the Bahamas, where she received her primary and secondary education. She graduated from McMaster University in Hamilton, Ontario, with a combined honors degree in sociology and political science. In studying for her master's degree in sociology at the University of Western Ontario in London, she specialized in demography.

Currently, Wilson-Dorsett holds the positions of Deputy Director, Department of Statistics and Head of the Social Statistics Division, Government of Bahamas, where she oversees the country's census, vital statistics, and other surveys. In this position, she is responsible for the execution of the Bahamas' first Living Conditions Survey (BLCS), which when completed will enable the government to establish a poverty line and to measure the incidence and extent of poverty in that country.

Wilson-Dorsett's study of sociology is directly related to her current job. She states, "The study of sociology has enabled me to put meaning to the figures which come into my office and has provided me with avenues to interpret these figures and determine the direction of future data collection. The analysis of census data, for instance, allows me to see where my country was several years ago, where it is now, and where it is likely to be in the years ahead."

Let's Discuss

1. What challenges do you think Wilson-Dorsett might encounter as she oversees a national census in a country like the Bahamas?
2. What other areas of specialization in sociology would be helpful to someone interpreting the results of a project such as the Living Conditions Survey (BLCS)?

interviews, and sampling. The precision of population projections depends on the accuracy of a series of estimates demographers must make. First, they must determine past population trends and establish a current base population. Next, birthrates and death rates must be determined, along with estimates of future fluctuations. In projecting a nation's population trends for the future, demographers must consider migration as well, since a significant number of individuals may enter and leave a country.

Elements of Demography

Demographers communicate population facts with a language derived from the basic elements of human life—birth and death. The **birthrate** (or more specifically, the *crude birthrate*) is the number of live births per 1,000 population in a given year. In 2006, for example, there were 14 live births per 1,000 people in the United States. The birthrate provides information on the reproductive patterns of a society.

One way demographers can project future growth in a society is to make use of the **total fertility rate (TFR).** The TFR is the average number of children born alive to any woman, assuming that she conforms to current fertility rates. The TFR reported for the United States in 2006 was 2.0 live births per woman, compared to nearly 8 births per woman in a developing country such as Niger.

Mortality, like fertility, is measured in several different ways. The **death rate** (also known as the *crude death rate*) is the number of deaths per 1,000 population in a given year. In 2006, the United States had a death rate of 8.0 per 1,000 population. The **infant mortality rate** is the number of deaths of infants under one year old per 1,000 live births in a given year. This particular measure serves as an important indicator of a society's level of health care (see Figure 19-1, page 461); it reflects prenatal nutrition, delivery procedures, and infant screening measures. The infant mortality rate also functions as a useful indicator of future population growth, since those infants who survive to adulthood will contribute to further population increases.

A general measure of health used by demographers is **life expectancy,** the median number of years a person can be expected to live under current mortality conditions. Usually the figure is reported as life expectancy *at birth.* At present, Japan reports a life expectancy at birth of 82 years—slightly higher than the United States' figure of 78 years. In contrast, life expectancy at birth is less than 40 in several developing nations, including Botswana (see Figure 21-1).

The **growth rate** of a society is the difference between births and deaths, plus the difference between *immigrants* (those who enter a country to establish permanent residence) and *emigrants* (those who leave a country permanently) per 1,000 population. For the world as a whole, the growth rate is simply the difference between births and deaths per 1,000 population, since worldwide immigration and emigration must of necessity be equal. In 2006, the United States had a growth rate of 0.6 percent, compared to an estimated 1.2 percent for the entire world (Haub 2006).

World Population Patterns

One important aspect of demographic work involves a study of the history of population. But how is that possible? After all, official national censuses were relatively rare before 1850. Re-

FIGURE 21-1

505

Population and the Environment

Life Expectancy in Selected Countries

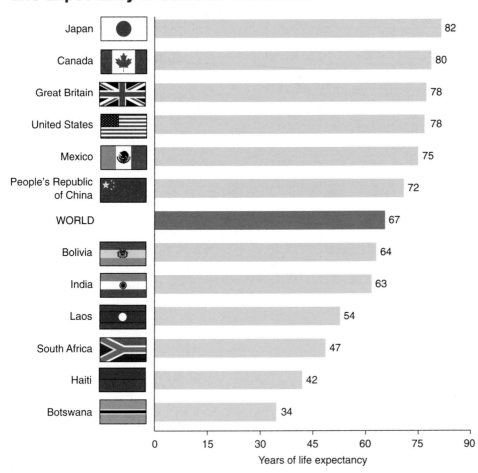

Japan 82
Canada 80
Great Britain 78
United States 78
Mexico 75
People's Republic of China 72
WORLD 67
Bolivia 64
India 63
Laos 54
South Africa 47
Haiti 42
Botswana 34

Years of life expectancy

Source: Estimates for 2006 by Population Reference Bureau; Haub 2006.

while death rates fell, birthrates remained high; as a result, this period of European history brought unprecedented population growth. By the late 1800s, however, the birthrates of many European countries had begun to decline, and the rate of population growth had also decreased.

The changes in birthrates and death rates that occurred in 19th-century Europe serve as an example of *demographic transition.* Demographers use the term **demographic transition** to describe changes in birthrates and death rates that occur during a nation's development, resulting in new patterns of vital statistics. In many nations today, we are seeing a demographic transition from high birthrates and death rates to low birthrates and death rates. As Figure 21-2 (page 506) shows, this process typically takes place in three stages:

1. Pretransition stage: high birthrates and death rates with little population growth.

2. Transition stage: declining death rates—primarily the result of reductions in infant deaths—along with high to medium fertility, resulting in significant population growth.

3. Posttransition stage: low birthrates and death rates with little population growth.

searchers interested in early population must turn to archeological remains, burial sites, baptismal and tax records, and oral history sources. In the next section we will see what such detective work has told us about changes in population over time.

Demographic Transition

On October 13, 1999, in a maternity clinic in Sarajevo, Bosnia-Herzegovina, Helac Fatina gave birth to a son who has been designated the 6 billionth person on this planet. Until modern times, relatively few humans lived in the world. One estimate places the global population of a million years ago at only 125,000 people. As Table 21-1 (page 506) indicates, in the last 200 years the world's population has exploded (World Health Organization 2000:3).

The phenomenal growth of population in recent times can be accounted for by changing patterns in births and deaths. Beginning in the late 1700s—and continuing until the mid-1900s—death rates in northern and western Europe gradually decreased. People were beginning to live longer because of advances in food production, sanitation, nutrition, and public health care. But

The demographic transition should be regarded not as a "law of population growth," but rather as a generalization of the population history of industrial nations. This concept helps us to understand world population problems better. About two-thirds of the world's nations have yet to pass fully through the second stage of the demographic transition. Even if such nations make dramatic advances in fertility control, their populations will nevertheless increase greatly because of the large base of people already at prime childbearing age.

The pattern of demographic transition varies from nation to nation. One particularly useful distinction is the contrast between the rapid transition now occurring in developing nations—which include about two-thirds of the world's population—and that which occurred over the course of almost a century in more industrialized countries. In developing nations, the demographic transition has involved a rapid decline in death rates without adjustments in birthrates.

Specifically, in the post–World War II period, the death rates of developing nations began a sharp decline. This revolution in "death control" was triggered by antibiotics, immunization,

Throughout the world, population patterns vary widely. As this scene in Warsaw, the capital of Poland, suggests, Eastern Europe has been losing population as the birthrate falls and young people emigrate to other countries. In Africa, by contrast, the population is growing. Over the next four decades, the country of Somalia is expected to double in population.

FIGURE 21–2

Demographic Transition

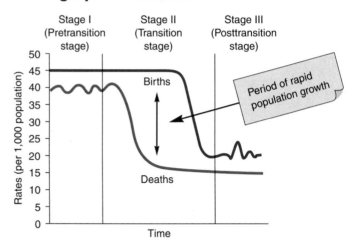

Demographers use the concept of *demographic transition* to describe changes in birthrates and death rates that occur during a nation's development. This graph shows the pattern that took place in presently developed nations. In the first stage, both birthrates and death rates were high, so that there was little population growth. In the second stage, the birthrate remained high while the death rate declined sharply, which led to rapid population growth. By the last stage, which many developing countries have yet to enter, the birthrate had declined as well, reducing population growth.

insecticides (such as DDT, used to strike at malaria-bearing mosquitoes), and largely successful campaigns against such fatal diseases as smallpox. Substantial medical and public health technology was imported almost overnight from more developed nations. As a result, the drop in death rates that had taken a century in Europe was telescoped into two decades in many developing countries.

Birthrates had little time to adjust. Cultural beliefs about the proper size of families could not possibly change as quickly as the falling death rates. For centuries, couples had given birth to as many as eight or more children, knowing that perhaps only two or three would survive to adulthood. Families were more willing to accept technological advances that prolonged life than to abandon fertility patterns that reflected time-honored tradition and religious training. The result was an astronomical "population explosion" that was well under way by the middle 1900s. By the middle 1970s, however, demographers had

Table 21-1

Estimated Time for Each Successive Increase of 1 Billion People in World Population

Population Level	Time Taken to Reach New Population Level	Year of Attainment
First billion	Human history before 1800	1804
Second billion	123 years	1927
Third billion	32 years	1959
Fourth billion	15 years	1974
Fifth billion	13 years	1987
Sixth billion	12 years	1999
Seventh billion	13 years	2012
Eighth billion	14 years	2026
Ninth billion	16 years	2042

Source: Bureau of the Census 2007d.

observed a slight decline in the growth rate of many developing nations, as family planning efforts began to take hold (Kent and Haub 2005).

The Population Explosion

Apart from war, rapid population growth has been perhaps the dominant international social problem of the past 40 years. Often this issue is referred to in emotional terms as the "population bomb" or the "population explosion." Such striking language is not surprising, given the staggering increases in world population recorded during the 20th century (refer to Table 21-1). The population of our planet rose from 1 billion around the year 1800 to 6.7 billion by 2008.

Beginning in the 1960s, governments in certain developing nations sponsored or supported campaigns to encourage family planning. In good part as the result of government-sponsored birth control campaigns, Thailand's total fertility rate fell from 6.1 births per woman in 1970 to only 1.7 in 2006. In China, the government's strict one-child policy actually produced a negative growth rate in some urban areas (see Box 21-1, page 508). Yet even if family planning efforts are successful in reducing fertility rates, the momentum toward growing world population is well established. Developing nations face the prospect of continued population growth, since a substantial proportion of their population is approaching the childbearing years (see the top half of Figure 21-3).

A **population pyramid** is a special type of bar chart that shows the distribution of a population by gender and age; it is generally used to illustrate the population structure of a society. As Figure 21-3 shows, a substantial portion of the population of Afghanistan consists of children under age 15, whose childbearing years are still to come. Thus, the built-in momentum for population growth is much greater in Afghanistan (and in many other developing countries in other parts of the world) than in Western Europe or the United States.

Consider the population data for India, which in 2000 surpassed 1 billion residents. Sometime around 2026, India's population will exceed China's. The substantial momentum for growth that is built into India's age structure means that the nation will face a staggering increase in population in the coming decades, even if its birthrate declines sharply (Bureau of the Census 2007c).

Population growth is not a problem in all nations. Today, a handful of countries are even adopting policies that encourage growth. One such country is Japan, where the total fertility rate has fallen sharply. Nevertheless, a global perspective underscores the serious consequences that could result from continued population growth overall.

Sadly, in the last 25 years, the spread of the once unknown disease of AIDS has begun to restrict population growth. The Social Policy section at the end of Chapter 19 considers the AIDS health crisis and its devastating effects on African communities.

FIGURE 21–3

Population Structure of Afghanistan and the United States, 2010

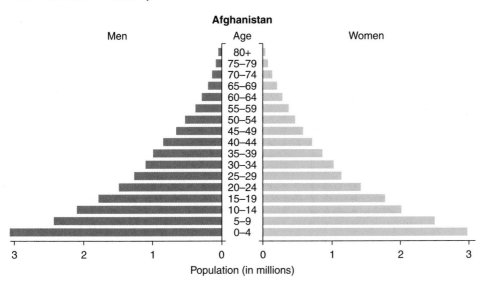

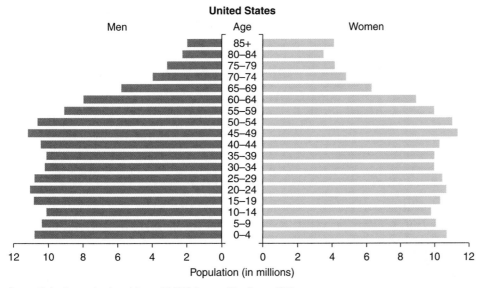

Source: Projections updated as of August 24, 2006. Bureau of the Census 2007c.

21-1 Population Policy in China

In a residential district in Shanghai, a member of the local family planning committee knocks on the door of a childless couple. Why, she inquires, have they not started a family?

Such a question would have been unthinkable in 1979, when family planning officials, in an attempt to avoid a looming population explosion, began resorting to sterilization to enforce the government rule of one child per family. Since then, the government has quietly begun to grant exceptions to the one-child policy to adults who are only children themselves. In 2002 it extended the privilege to all families, but at a price. A new family planning law imposes "social compensation fees" to cover the cost to society of an additional child. The fee, which is substantial, is equivalent to 20 years' worth of a rural farm family's income.

Chinese families are beset, too, by the unforeseen results of their attempts to circumvent the one-child policy. In the past, in an effort to ensure that their one child would be a male capable of perpetuating the family line, many couples chose to abort female fetuses, or quietly allowed female infants to die of neglect. As a result, among children one to four years old, China's sex ratio (the ratio of males to females) is now about 119 to 100—well above the normal rate at birth of 105 to 100. This difference in birthrates translates into 1.7 million fewer female births per year than normal—and down the line, to many fewer childbearers than normal.

As a result of the rising sex ratio, Chinese officials have begun to worry about a future with too few women. The government now pays the parents of daughters to speak with other parents in an attempt to persuade them to raise girls. Officials have also increased the criminal penalties doctors face for performing

This billboard, photographed in China, promotes the government's policy of allowing only one child per family. For several decades, the People's Republic of China has been struggling with a population explosion that threatens to outstrip the nation's ability to provide for all its citizens.

prenatal scans and aborting pregnancies for purposes of sex selection.

Another legacy of the one-child policy is a shortage of caretakers for the elderly. Coupled with improvements in longevity, the generation-long decline in births has greatly increased the

> _A new family planning law imposes "social compensation fees" equivalent to 20 years' income._

ratio of dependent elders to able-bodied children. The migration of young adults to other parts of China has further compromised the care of the elderly. To compound the crisis, barely one in four of China's elders receives

any pension at all. No other country in the world faces the prospect of caring for such a large population of seniors with so little social support.

Let's Discuss

1. Does any government, no matter how overpopulated a country is, have a right to sterilize people who do not voluntarily limit the size of their families? Why or why not?

2. What do you think has been the most dramatic consequence of the one-child policy?

Sources: Glenn 2004; N. Riley 2004; Yardley 2005.

Use Your Sociological **Imagination**

You are living in a country that is so heavily populated, basic resources such as food, water, and living space are running short. What will you do? How will you respond to the crisis if you are a government social planner? A politician?

Fertility Patterns in the United States

Over the last four decades, the United States and other industrial nations have passed through two different patterns of population growth—the first marked by high fertility and rapid growth (stage II in the theory of demographic transition), the second marked by declining fertility and little growth (stage III). Sociol-

IT'S THE POPULATION CONTROL WORKER AGAIN, MOM.

AIDS

AIDS has had a dramatic impact on the death rates in many developing countries, particularly in Africa.

ogists are keenly aware of the social impact of these fertility patterns.

The Baby Boom

The most recent period of high fertility in the United States has often been referred to as the *baby boom*. During World War II, large numbers of military personnel were separated from their spouses. When they returned, the annual number of births began to rise dramatically. Still, the baby boom was not a return to the large families common in the 1800s. In fact, there was only a slight increase in the proportion of couples having three or more children. Instead, the boom resulted from a striking decrease in the number of childless marriages and one-child families. Although a peak was reached in 1957, the nation maintained a relatively high birthrate of over 20 live births per 1,000 population until 1964. By 2006 the birthrate had fallen to 14 live births per 1,000 population (Bureau of the Census 1975; Haub 2006).

It would be a mistake to attribute the baby boom solely to the return home of large numbers of soldiers. High wages and general prosperity during the postwar period encouraged many married couples to have children and purchase homes. In addition, several sociologists—as well as feminist author Betty Friedan (1963)—have noted the strong societal pressure on women during the 1950s to marry and become mothers and homemakers (Bouvier 1980).

Stable Population Growth

Although the total fertility rate of the United States has remained low over the last two decades, the nation continues to grow in size because of two factors: the momentum built into our age structure by the postwar population boom and continued high rates of immigration. Because of the upsurge of births

beginning in the 1950s, there are now many more people in their childbearing years than in older age groups (in which most deaths occur). This growth of the childbearing population represents a "demographic echo" of the baby boom generation. Consequently, the number of people born each year in the United States continues to exceed the number who die. In addition, the nation allows a large number of immigrants to enter each year; immigrants currently account for between one-fourth and one-third of annual growth.

Despite these trends, some analysts in the 1980s and early 1990s projected relatively low fertility levels and moderate net migration over the coming decades. As a result, it seemed possible that the United States might reach *zero population growth (ZPG).* ZPG is the state of a population in which the number of births plus immigrants equals the number of deaths plus emigrants. In the recent past, although some nations have achieved ZPG, it has been relatively short-lived. Yet today, projections of population change between 2006 and 2050 indicate that 46 countries, including 19 in Europe, are showing a *decline* in population (Balter 2006; Haub 2006).

What would a society with stable population growth be like? In demographic terms, it would be quite different from the United States of the 1990s. There would be relatively equal numbers of people in each age group, and the median age of the population might perhaps be as high as 38 (compared to 35 in 2000). As a result, the population pyramid of the United States (as shown in Figure 21-3) would look more like a rectangle.

There would also be a much larger proportion of older people, especially age 75 and over. These citizens would place a greater demand on the nation's social service programs and health care institutions. On a more positive note, the economy would be less volatile under ZPG, since the number of entrants into the paid labor force would remain stable. ZPG would also lead to changes in family life. With fertility rates declining, women would devote fewer years to child rearing and to the social roles of motherhood; the proportion of married women entering the labor force would continue to rise (McFalls 2007; Weeks 2008).

Population and Migration

Along with births and deaths, migration is one of the three factors that affect population growth or decline. The term *migration* refers to the relatively permanent movement of people, with the purpose of changing their place of residence (Prehn 1991). Migration usually describes movement over a sizable distance, rather than from one side of a city to another.

As a social phenomenon, migration is fairly complex; it results from a variety of factors. The most important tend to be economic—financial failure in the "old country" and a perception of greater economic opportunity and prosperity in the new homeland. Other factors that contribute to migration include racial and religious bigotry, dislike for prevailing political regimes, and desire to reunite one's family. All these forces combine to *push* some individuals out of their homelands and *pull* them to areas they believe to be more attractive.

International Migration

International migration—changes of residence across national boundaries—has been a significant force in redistributing the world's population during certain periods of history. For example, the composition of the United States has been significantly {pp.289–290} altered by immigrants who came here beginning in the 19th century and continuing through the present. Their entry was encouraged or restricted by various immigration policies.

Today, at the beginning of the twenty-first century, legal immigrants to the United States account for about 45 to 60 percent of the nation's growth. To some observers, this nation is already overpopulated. Recognizing that additional people place greater strain on our natural resources, members of one respected environmental organization, the Sierra Club, have debated taking an official position against the present immigration rate. Thus far, rather than enter the politically charged debate over immigration, the majority of the club's members have preferred to remain neutral (Schaefer 2008).

In the last decade, immigration has become a controversial issue throughout much of Europe. Western Europe in particular has become a desirable destination for individuals and families from former colonies or former communist-bloc countries who are fleeing the poverty, persecution, and warfare of their native lands. Currently, there are 20 million legal immigrants in western Europe, along with an estimated 2 million illegal immigrants. The number of immigrants and refugees has been increasing at a time of widespread unemployment and housing shortages, provoking a striking rise in antiforeign (and often openly racist) sentiment in Germany, France, and other countries. Right-wing forces in Germany (including members of the skinhead counterculture) have mounted more than 3,500 attacks on foreigners in recent years. Immigrants from eastern Europe and Asia are often the targets, and attacks have been made as well on Germany's small Jewish community.

Developing countries in Asia and Africa are also encountering difficulties as thousands of displaced people seek assistance and asylum. At the end of 2006, an estimated 12 million people worldwide were refugees or asylum seekers—a number equivalent to the population of Michigan or the Netherlands. Half these people came from two areas, Palestine and Afghanistan. Needless to say, the political and economic problems of developing nations (see Chapter 10) are only intensified by such massive migration, begun under desperate conditions (U.S. Committee for Refugees and Immigrants 2006).

Internal Migration

Migratory movements within societies can vary in important ways. In traditional societies, migration often represents a way of life, as people move to accommodate the changing availability of fertile soil and wild game. In industrial societies, people may relocate because of job transfers or because they believe that a particular region offers better employment opportunities or a more desirable climate.

Although nations typically have laws and policies governing movement across their borders, the same is not true of internal movement. Generally, the residents of a country are legally free to move from one locality to another. Of course, that is not the case in all nations; historically, the Republic of South Africa restricted the movement of Blacks and other non-Whites through the system of segregation known as *apartheid* (refer back to Chapter 11).

We can identify three distinctive trends in recent internal migrations within the United States:

1. *Suburbanization.* During the period 1980–1990, the suburban population grew 14 percent while the total population of the United States rose only 10 percent. The urban population had remained constant at about one-third since 1950, but the share of the population living in rural areas declined from 44 percent in 1950 to 20 percent in 1994 (Bureau of the Census 1996:38).

Within days of the terrorist attack on the World Trade Center in New York, thousands of Afghan refugees had fled to Pakistan in anticipation of U.S. retaliation. Catastrophic conflicts such as war and terrorist attacks often trigger massive international migrations.

2. *"Sunning of America."* Significant numbers of people have moved from the "snow belt" of the north central and northeastern states to the "sun belt" in the South and West. Since 1970, the sun belt has absorbed almost two-thirds of the population growth of the United States. Individuals and families move to the sun belt because of its expanding economy and desirable climate. Businesses are attracted by the comparatively inexpensive energy supplies, increased availability of labor, and relative weakness of labor unions there. Since 2000, internal immigration to some areas of the South and Arizona and Nevada has remained high (see Figure 21-4).

3. *Rural life rebound.* In the early 1990s, nonmetropolitan counties gained in population, though the trend began to level off in 1998. This migration to rural areas, which reversed a longstanding trend toward urbanization, reflected concern about the quality of life in the cities and suburbs. It has dropped off as the outskirts of metropolitan areas spread out and many downtown areas experienced a rebirth (K. Johnson 1999; Schachter 2001).

Use Your Sociological Imagination

What would happen if present patterns of migration, both internal and international, reversed themselves? How would your hometown change? What would be the effect on the nation's economy? Would your own life change?

Sociological Perspectives on the Environment

Sociologists and others may debate the potential impact of population growth, but increases in population, together with the

FIGURE 21–4

Where Americans Have Moved Since 2000

MAPPING LIFE NATIONWIDE
www.mhhe.com/schaefer11

Percent change in population from 2000 to 2006 by county

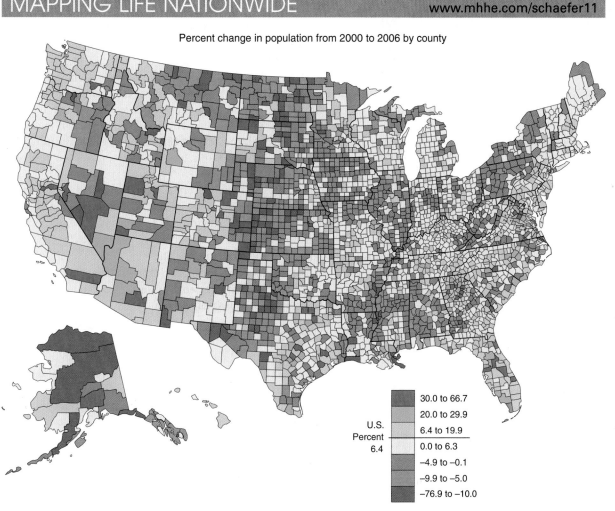

U.S. Percent 6.4

| 30.0 to 66.7 |
| 20.0 to 29.9 |
| 6.4 to 19.9 |
| 0.0 to 6.3 |
| −4.9 to −0.1 |
| −9.9 to −5.0 |
| −76.9 to −10.0 |

Source: Bureau of the Census 2007e.

In a makeshift recycling center, a Chinese woman uses a hammer to open an old cathode ray tube. She wants the copper that is inside, but in the process she will release several pounds of lead into the soil and groundwater. Scientists have found alarmingly high levels of toxic heavy metals in the rivers that flow by such rural recycling operations.

economic development that accompanies them, have already had serious environmental consequences. We can see signs of despoliation almost everywhere: Our air, our water, and our land are being polluted, whether we live in St. Louis, Mexico City, or Lagos, Nigeria. But though environmental problems may be easy to identify, devising socially and politically acceptable solutions to them is much more difficult. In this section we will see what sociologists have to say about the trade-off between economic growth and development and its effects on the environment. In the section that follows we will look more closely at specific environmental problems.

Human Ecology

Human ecology is an area of study that is concerned with interrelationships between people and their environment. As the environmentalist Barry Commoner (1971:39) put it, "Everything is connected to everything else." Human ecologists focus on how the physical environment shapes people's lives and on how people influence the surrounding environment.

In an application of the human ecological perspective, sociologists and environmentalists have identified several relationships between the environment and people. Among them are the following:

1. **The environment provides the resources essential for life.** These include air, water, and materials used to create shelter, transportation, and needed products. If human societies exhaust these resources—for example, by polluting the water supply or cutting down rain forests—the consequences could be dire.

2. **The environment serves as a waste repository.** More so than other living species, humans produce a huge quantity and variety of waste products—bottles, boxes, papers, sewage, garbage, and so on. Various types of pollution have become more common because human societies are generating more wastes than the environment can safely absorb.

3. **The environment "houses" our species.** It is our home, our living space, the place where we reside, work, and play. At times we take this truism for granted, but not when day-to-day living conditions become unpleasant and difficult. If our air is "heavy," if our tap water turns brown, if toxic chemicals seep into our neighborhood, we remember why it is vital to live in a healthful environment.

There is no shortage of illustrations of the interconnectedness of people and their environment. For example, scientific research has linked pollutants in the physical environment to people's health and behavior. The increasing prevalence of asthma, lead poisoning, and cancer have all been tied to human alterations to the environment. Similarly, the rise in melanoma (skin cancer) diagnoses has been linked to global warming. And ecological changes in our food and diet have been related to early obesity and diabetes.

With its view that "everything is connected to everything else," human ecology stresses the trade-offs inherent in every decision that alters the environment. In facing the environmental challenges of the twenty-first century, government policymakers and environmentalists must determine how they can fulfill humans' pressing needs for food, clothing, and shelter while at the same time preserving the environment as a source of resources, a waste repository, and our home.

Conflict View of the Environment

In Chapter 10 we drew on world systems analysis to show how a growing share of the human and natural resources of developing countries is being redistributed to the core industrialized nations. This process only intensifies the destruction of natural resources in poorer regions of the world. From a conflict perspective, less affluent nations are being forced to exploit their mineral deposits, forests, and fisheries in order to meet their debt obligations. The poor turn to the only means of survival available to them: They plow mountain slopes, burn plots in tropical forests, and overgraze grasslands (Livernash and Rodenburg 1998).

Brazil exemplifies this interplay between economic troubles and environmental destruction. Each year more than 5.7 million acres of forest are cleared for crops and livestock. The elimination of the rain forest affects worldwide weather patterns, heightening the gradual warming of the earth. These socioeconomic patterns, with their harmful environmental consequences, are evident not only in Latin America but in many regions of Africa and Asia (*National Geographic* 2002).

Conflict theorists are well aware of the environmental implications of land use policies in the Third World, but they contend that focusing on the developing countries is ethnocentric. Who, they ask, is more to blame for environmental deterioration: the poverty-stricken and "food-hungry" populations of the world or the "energy-hungry" industrialized nations? These theorists point out that the industrialized nations of North America and Europe account for only 12 percent of the world's population but are responsible for 60 percent of worldwide consumption. The money their residents spend on ocean cruises each year could provide clean drinking water for everyone on the planet. Ice cream expenditures in Europe alone could be used to immunize every child in the world. Thus, conflict theorists charge, the most serious threat to the environment comes from the global consumer class (G. Gardner et al. 2004).

Allan Schnaiberg (1994) further refines this analysis by criticizing the focus on affluent consumers as the cause of environmental troubles. In his view, a capitalist system creates a "treadmill of production" because of its inherent need to build ever-expanding profits. This treadmill necessitates creating an increasing demand for products, obtaining natural resources at minimal cost, and manufacturing products as quickly and cheaply as possible—no matter what the long-term environmental consequences.

Environmental Justice

In a stretch of land along the lower Mississippi River in Louisiana, one factory after another pours its industrial waste into the water, raising pollution counts to dangerous levels. It is no accident that the people who live nearby are African American. Poor and lacking in political clout, the communities that border these industrial sites are no match for the powerful business interests that built them (Bullard 1993).

Observations like this one have given rise to *environmental justice,* a legal strategy based on claims that racial minorities are subjected disproportionately to environmental hazards. The approach has had some success. In 1998 a chemical company called Shintech dropped plans to build a plastics plant in a poor black community in Mississippi after opponents filed a civil rights complaint with the Environmental Protection Agency (EPA). EPA administrator Carol Browner praised the company's decision: "The principles applied to achieve this solution should be incorporated into any blueprint for dealing with environmental justice issues in communities across the nation" (Associated Press 1998:18; Pellow and Brulle 2007).

Following reports from the EPA and other organizations documenting the discriminatory location of hazardous waste sites,

President Bill Clinton issued an executive order in 1994 that requires all federal agencies to ensure that low-income and minority communities have access to better information about their environment, and an opportunity to participate in shaping government policies that affect their health. Initial efforts to implement the policy have aroused widespread opposition because of the delays it imposes in establishing new industrial sites. Some observers question the wisdom of an order that slows economic development in areas that are in dire need of employment opportunities. Others point out that such businesses employ few unskilled or less skilled workers, and only make the environment less livable (Pellow 2002).

Meanwhile, the poor and oppressed continue to bear the brunt of environmental pollution. In the 1990s, the federal government, unable to find a disposal site for spent nuclear fuel, turned to tribal reservations. Agents eventually persuaded a tiny band of Goshute Indians in Skull Valley, Utah, to accept more than 44,000 barrels of the hot, highly radioactive substance, which will remain dangerous for an estimated 10,000 years. The government dropped the plan only after opposition from surrounding towns and cities, whose residents objected to the movement of the material through their communities. This was not the first time the nation attempted to persuade the impoverished tribe to accept environmentally objectionable installations. The military's nerve gas storage facility resides on or near the reservation, along with the Intermountain Power Project, which generates coal-fired electrical power for consumers in California (Eureka County 2006; Foy 2006).

Sociologists, then, have emphasized both the interconnectedness of humans and the environment and the divisiveness of race and

From her apartment in Harlem, New York, environmental activist Millicent Redick looks out over a hazy skyline. Redick's home is located near a bus depot, whose fumes have been linked to her children's asthma.

21-2 The Mysterious Fall of the Nacirema

Chapter 3 opened with anthropologist Horace Miner's description of the strange rituals practiced by the Nacirema (*American* spelled backward). Sixteen years after Miner first described the culture, American Studies scholar Neil B. Thompson wrote a follow-up article, "The Mysterious Fall of the Nacirema," that was in effect the culture's epitaph.

The Nacirema, Thompson wrote, were master engineers who had created extensive networks of "narrow ribbons, called streets," which covered the landscape. From the air, the ribbons around major population centers could be seen to be very elaborate. The purpose of these networks, Thompson speculated, might have been to promote the centralization of government or to separate "persons of lower caste" from others, in neighborhoods referred to as "ottehgs."

A special group of highly privileged priests, called the "ssenisub community," directed such massive projects. The priests lived in gated areas secured by electronic alarm systems. The ssenisub enjoyed complete freedom in creating their vast engineering marvels. "There is no evidence," Thompson wrote, "to suggest that any restraints—moral, sociological, or engineering—were placed on their self-determined enterprises."

Looking back over the last 300 "solar cycles" of the culture, Thompson noted that the Nacirema had devoted a great deal of time and attention to changing the color of the air and water. For the first 250 cycles they had little

> *Looking back over the last 300 "solar cycles" of the culture, Thompson noted that the Nacirema had devoted a great deal of time and attention to changing the color of the air and water.*

success, "but during the short period before the fall of the culture, they mastered their art magnificently," changing the water from bluish-green to reddish-brown and the air from blue to grayish-yellow.

To accomplish this great engineering feat, the Nacirema built huge plants near large cities. "These plants constantly produced a variety of reagents . . . which were then pumped into the rivers and lakes or released into the atmosphere in the form of hot gases." To solve the problem of what to do with the by-products of these processes, the Nacirema distributed them to people's homes, where they were kept for a short time before being sent to a landfill.

Thompson wrote his article in 1972. To date, archeologists have not been able to explain the demise of this fascinating culture.

Let's Discuss

1. Have you ever visited a foreign culture and been struck by something that seemed odd to you, but perfectly normal to everyone else? If so, did you discuss your reaction with others? Could they see your point of view?

2. If all of us could step back and take an objective look at what we are doing to the environment, would our society change for the better? Why or why not?

Sources: Miner 1956; N. Thompson 1972.

---

social class in their work on humans and their alteration of the environment. Scientists, too, have taken different approaches, disagreeing sharply on the likely outcomes of environmental change. Of course, when their disagreements threaten to affect government policy and economic regulations, they become highly politicized. For some perspective on this struggle between environmental preservation and economic self-interest, let's revisit the Nacirema, introduced in the opening excerpt for Chapter 3. Box 21-2 presents this unusual culture through the eyes of environmentalists.

Use Your Sociological Imagination

Your community has been designated as a site for burial of toxic waste. How will you react? Will you organize a protest? Or will you make sure the authorities carry out the project safely? How can such sites be chosen fairly?

Environmental Problems

Unfortunately, the environmental problems caused by unbridled development have effects far beyond the places where they are created. Witness Muhammad Ali, a Bangladeshi man who has had to flee flood waters five times in the last decade. Scientists believe that global warming is to blame, both for worsening monsoons and for the raging waters of the Jamuna River, swollen by abnormally high glacier melt from the Himalayas. Every time the river floods, Ali tears down his house, made of tin and bamboo, and moves to higher ground. But he is running out of land to move to. "Where we are standing, in five days it will be gone," he says. "Our future thinking is that if this problem is not taken care of, we will be swept away" (Goering 2007).

We will discuss the enormous challenge of global warming later in this section. First, we will discuss three broad areas of environmental concern—two of which, air and water pollution, are thought to be contributors to global warming.

Air Pollution

Worldwide, more than 1 billion people are exposed to potentially health-damaging levels of air pollution. Unfortunately, in cities around the world, residents have come to accept smog and polluted air as normal. Urban air pollution is caused primarily by emissions from automobiles and secondarily by emissions from electric power plants and heavy industries. Smog not only limits visibility; it can lead to health problems as uncomfortable as eye irritation and as deadly as lung cancer. Such problems are especially severe in developing countries. The World Health Organization estimates that up to 700,000 premature deaths *per year* could be prevented if pollutants were brought down to safer levels (Carty 1999; World Resources Institute 1998).

People are capable of changing their behavior, but they are also unwilling to make such changes permanent. During the 1984 Olympics in Los Angeles, residents were asked to carpool and stagger their work hours to relieve traffic congestion and improve the quality of the air athletes would breathe. These changes resulted in a remarkable 12 percent drop in ozone levels. But when the Olympians left, people reverted to their normal behavior and the ozone levels climbed back up. Similarly, in the 2008 Olympics, China is prepared to take drastic action to ensure that Beijing's high levels of air pollution do not mar the games. For a two-month period, all construction work in the city will cease, polluting factories and power plants will close down, and roads will be swept and sprayed with water several times a day. But this temporary solution will hardly solve China's ongoing problem (Ni 2006).

Water Pollution

Throughout the United States, dumping of waste materials by industries and local governments has polluted streams, rivers, and lakes. Consequently, many bodies of water have become unsafe for drinking, fishing, and swimming. Around the world, pollution of the oceans is an issue of growing concern. Such pollution results regularly from waste dumping, and is made worse by fuel leaks from shipping and occasional oil spills. When the oil tanker *Exxon Valdez* ran aground in Prince William Sound, Alaska, in 1989, its cargo of 11 million gallons of crude oil spilled into the sound and washed onto the shore, contaminating 1,285 miles of shoreline. All together, about 11,000 people {p.45 joined in a massive cleanup effort that cost over $2 billion. Globally, oil spills occur regularly. In 2002 the oil tanker *Prestige* spilled twice as much fuel as the *Valdez,* greatly damaging coastal areas in Spain and France (ITOPF 2006).

Less dramatic than large-scale accidents or disasters, but more common in many parts of the world, are problems with the basic water supply. Worldwide, over 1.1 billion people lack safe and adequate drinking water, and 2.6 billion have no acceptable means of sanitation—a problem that further threatens the quality of water supplies. The health costs of unsafe water are enormous (United Nations Development Programme 2006).

Global Warming

In 1896, the Swedish scientist Svante Arrhemius was the first to speculate that the earth's surface temperatures could warm significantly as industrial gases (that is, carbon dioxide) turned the planet's atmosphere into a virtual greenhouse. Arrhemius anticipated by a century present-day observations that global warming of the air and oceans is under way. At the time, his idea received little attention, and being from Scandinavia, he was not overly concerned about rising temperatures.

A century later, with water levels rising from melting polar icepacks, deserts expanding, tropical storms becoming more fierce, and the frequency and intensity of deadly droughts increasing, concern over global warming has heated up. According to a 2007 national survey, 60 percent of the American public believes that global warming has already begun, while only 26 percent think it will not happen in their lifetime, if ever. Though most people agree that they should make their homes more energy efficient, switch to mass transit, or drive a hybrid car, 58 percent do not think the government should impose tough new energy restrictions on industries and utilities (J. Carroll 2007; Duncan 2006; Intergovernmental Panel on Climate Change 2007).

In truth, climate change remains low on policymakers' list of concerns. The problem seems abstract, and in many countries, officials think that the real impact of any action they may take depends on decisive action by other nations. The Kyoto Protocol was intended to reduce global emissions of heat-trapped gases, which can contribute to global warming and climate change. To date, 169 countries have signed the accord, but the United States, which produces 24 percent of the world's carbon dioxide, is not one of them. Opponents of the protocol argue that doing so would place the nation at a disadvantage in the global marketplace. Thirty-five other developed nations have agreed to a 5 percent reduction in the greenhouse gases they produce—a goal they must reach by 2012 (Landler 2005).

In writing about the global environment, activists often assert, "We're all in this together." Though we are all in this together, the reality is that globally, the most vulnerable countries tend to be the poorest. Developing nations are more likely than others to have economies that are built on limited resources or a small number of crops vulnerable to drought, flood, and fluctuations in worldwide demand (Revkin 2007).

What are the causes of this global environmental crisis? Some observers, such as Paul Ehrlich and Anne Ehrlich, see the pressure of world population growth as the central factor in environmental deterioration. They argue that population control is essential in preventing widespread starvation and environmental decay. Barry Commoner, a biologist, counters that the primary cause of environmental ills is the increasing use of technological innovations that are destructive to the environment—among them plastics, detergents, synthetic fibers, pesticides, herbicides, and chemical fertilizers. Conflict theorists see the despoliation of the environment through the lens of world systems analysis (Commoner 1971, 1990; Ehrlich 1968; Ehrlich and Ehrlich 1990; Ehrlich and Ellison 2002).

Vacation in an unspoiled paradise! Increasingly, people from developed countries are turning to ecotourism as an environmentally friendly way to see the world. The new trend bridges the interests of environmentalists and businesspeople, especially in developing countries. These birdwatchers are vacationing in Belize.

Use Your Sociological Imagination

As you think about all the problems facing our society, how often do you consider global warming? How often do your friends give it much thought?

www.mhhe.com/schaefer11

The Impact of Globalization

Globalization can be both good and bad for the environment. On the negative side, it can create a race to the bottom, as polluting companies relocate to countries with less stringent environmental standards. Similarly, globalization allows multinationals to reap the resources of developing countries for short-term profit. From Mexico to China, the industrialization that often accompanies globalization has increased pollution of all types.

Yet globalization can have a positive impact, as well. As barriers to the international movement of goods, services, and people fall, multinational corporations have an incentive to carefully consider the cost of natural resources. Overusing or wasting resources makes little sense, especially when they are in danger of depletion (Kwong 2005).

and Population

World Population Policy

The Issue

Six billion and counting: The world's population is growing as you read, threatening the earth's ability to sustain it. Social planners who have grappled with this problem have suggested a policy that provides for a reasonable amount of population growth. But just what is reasonable growth, and how can it be implemented? Social policies that address population growth touch on the most sensitive aspects of people's lives: sexuality, childbearing, and family relationships. For this reason, reaching a global consensus on population issues has been difficult.

The Setting

Beginning in the 1950s, delegates to international conferences sponsored by the United Nations became concerned about the negative consequences of rapid population growth. As we saw earlier, the introduction of modern medicine to developing countries had caused a rapid fall in death rates, but birthrates remained high. To reduce the birthrates, planners devised programs aimed at encouraging family planning and limiting the number of children couples had through contraception.

But such programs were controversial. In many developing countries, the traditional culture placed great value on large families. Children were seen as a source of support for their aging parents. To compensate for high infant mortality rates, couples generally had more children than they expected to survive to adulthood. Some government officials, reluctant to deny poor people their means of support in old age, hoped instead that rising living standards would eventually allow people to limit the size of their families.

Population planning programs came under fire in the United States as well, from antiabortion activists in particular. Public financial aid, they charged, should not be used to support family planning clinics that provided abortion counseling or services. In 1984, under President Ronald Reagan, U.S. delegates to the World Population Conference in Mexico City announced that the United States would no longer support international population planning programs that provided abortion services (Ashford 2001:8; Rayman-Read 2001).

Sociological Insights

Functionalists would note that the best course of action for a community might differ from the best course of action for a society. In developing nations, parents see children as potential laborers, and ultimately as a means of broadening the family's economic base through their marriage. Under such conditions, having fewer children may not appear to be a rational choice. Yet for a country that is struggling to provide clean water, food, and

A nurse in Zambia, Africa, instructs a client in how to use birth control pills. Family planning clinics have helped to slow the population growth rate in developing nations.

shelter to its people, high population growth is dysfunctional. Even so, officials of a developing nation may resent powerful industrial nations that attempt to influence (and may appear to dictate) their population policy.

Because the burden of implementing population policy falls particularly on women, sociologists who take the feminist perspective have focused considerable attention on population policy. Early on, feminists charged that workers in government-funded population control programs were distributing contraceptives without sufficient concern for their health risks. In such programs, they added, women were often pressured to adopt certain contraceptive methods not for their own needs, but so the clinics could meet government quotas. Too often, feminist critics complained, population control workers ignored sociocultural influences on sexuality and childbearing—influences that often ran counter to the contraceptives they were distributing (Ashford 2001).

Critics who take the conflict perspective have questioned why the United States and other industrialized nations are so enthusiastic about controlling the population of developing countries. In line with Marx's response to Malthus, they argue that neither large families nor population growth is the cause of hunger and misery. Rather, the unjust economic domination of the world by developed states results in an unequal distribution of the world's resources and in widespread poverty in developing nations (Fornos 1997).

Policy Initiatives

The Mexico City policy established during Ronald Reagan's presidency was overturned during President Bill Clinton's administration. However, in 2001, President George W. Bush reinstated it. Today, the Bush administration requires health workers who receive U.S. government funding to refrain from discussing abortion, either publicly or with their patients. To the extent that international family planning services depend on U.S. government funding, they are clearly hampered by this gag rule, which has politicized otherwise nonpartisan public health programs (Geyer 2004; Purdum 2002).

Setting aside restrictions such as the Mexico City policy, more funding is needed in those countries where government re-

sources are overtaxed. In sub-Saharan Africa, less than 10 percent of women of childbearing age use contraceptives, compared to 83 percent in China. Family planning is still sparse in poverty-stricken rural areas the world over (Haub and Herstad 2002).

Let's Discuss

1. What are the social and cultural attitudes toward family planning in your community? Do people tend to have large families or small ones? What are the reasons they give for their choices?

2. Which perspective on population policy—functionalist, feminist, or conflict—makes the most sense to you? Why?

3. Do you think the U.S. government has a right to dictate abortion policy to other countries? Explain.

GettingINVOLVED

To get involved in the debate over population policy, visit this text's Online Learning Center, which offers links to relevant Web sites. Check out the Social Policy section of the Online Learning Center as well; it provides survey data on U.S. public opinion regarding this issue.

www.mhhe.com/schaefer11

MASTERING THIS CHAPTER

Summary

The size, composition, and distribution of the population have an important influence on many of the policy issues presented in this book. This chapter examines various elements of population, the current problem of overpopulation, the possibility of *zero population growth,* and the environmental problems facing our planet.

1. Thomas Robert Malthus suggested that the world's population was growing more rapidly than the available food supply, and that the gap would increase over time. However, Karl Marx saw capitalism, rather than rising world population, as the real cause of social ills.

2. The primary mechanism for obtaining population information in the United States and most other countries is the *census.*

3. Roughly two-thirds of the world's nations have yet to pass fully through the second stage of *demographic transition.* Thus they continue to experience significant population growth.

4. Developing nations face the prospect of continued population growth because a substantial portion of their population is approaching childbearing age. Some developed nations have begun to stabilize their population growth, however.

5. The most important factors in *migration* tend to be economic—financial failure in the "old country" and a perception of greater economic opportunity elsewhere.

6. The human ecological perspective suggests that the natural environment serves three basic functions: It provides essential resources, serves as a waste repository, and houses our species.

7. Conflict theorists charge that the most serious threat to the environment comes from Western industrialized nations.

8. *Environmental justice* addresses the disproportionate subjection of minorities to environmental hazards.

9. Four broad areas of environmental concern include air and water pollution, global warming, and globalization. Though globalization can contribute to environmental woes, it can also have beneficial effects.

10. World population policy is controversial both in developing countries, where planners' attempts to limit population growth may run counter to traditional cultural values, and in developed countries such as the United States, where funding of international population programs has been politicized.

Critical Thinking Questions

1. Select one of the social policy issues examined in this textbook and analyze in detail how the size, composition, and distribution of the population of the United States influence that issue.

2. Some European nations are experiencing population declines: Their death rates are low and their birthrates are even lower than in stage III of the demographic transition model. Does this pattern suggest that there is a fourth stage in the demographic transition? What are the implications of negative population growth for an industrialized nation in the 21st century?

3. Imagine that you have been asked to study the issue of air pollution in the largest city in your state. How might you draw on surveys, observation research, experiments, and existing sources to study the issue?

Key Terms

Birthrate The number of live births per 1,000 population in a given year. Also known as the *crude birthrate.* (page 504)

Census An enumeration, or counting, of a population. (503)

Death rate The number of deaths per 1,000 population in a given year. Also known as the *crude death rate.* (504)

Demographic transition A term used to describe the change from high birthrates and death rates to low birthrates and death rates. (505)

Demography The scientific study of population. (502)

Environmental justice A legal strategy based on claims that racial minorities are subjected disproportionately to environmental hazards. (513)

Fertility The level of reproduction in a society. (502)

Growth rate The difference between births and deaths, plus the difference between immigrants and emigrants, per 1,000 population. (504)

Human ecology An area of study that is concerned with the interrelationships between people and their environment. (512)

Infant mortality rate The number of deaths of infants under one year old per 1,000 live births in a given year. (504)

Life expectancy The median number of years a person can be expected to live under current mortality conditions. (504)

Migration The relatively permanent movement of people, with the purpose of changing their place of residence. (509)

Population pyramid A special type of bar chart that shows the distribution of a population by gender and age. (507)

Total fertility rate (TFR) The average number of children born alive to any woman, assuming that she conforms to current fertility rates. (504)

Vital statistics Records of births, deaths, marriages, and divorces gathered through a registration system maintained by governmental units. (503)

Zero population growth (ZPG) The state of a population in which the number of births plus immigrants equals the number of deaths plus emigrants. (509)

Read each question carefully and then select the best answer.

1. Which of the following argued that food supply increases in an arithmetic progression, whereas population expands by a geometric progression?
   a. Thomas Robert Malthus
   b. Karl Marx
   c. Émile Durkheim
   d. Max Weber

2. The final stage in demographic transition is marked by
   a. high birthrates and high death rates.
   b. high birthrates and low death rates.
   c. low birthrates and high death rates.
   d. low birthrates and low death rates.

3. The most recent period of high fertility in the United States, which began after the end of World War II, has often been referred to as the
   a. baby bust.
   b. baby boom.
   c. population bomb.
   d. age of Aquarius.

4. In studying population, which of the following would most interest a sociologist?
   a. the impact of natural disasters on population trends
   b. the relationship between climate and fertility
   c. availability of natural resources, such as oil and arable land, and how it influences mortality rates
   d. social factors that influence population rates and trends

5. For Thomas Robert Malthus, the appropriate way to control population was to
   a. use artificial means of birth control.
   b. postpone marriage.
   c. pass legislation prohibiting families from having more than one child.
   d. all of the above

6. Paul Ehrlich's work would be an example of the
   a. functionalist perspective.
   b. conflict perspective.
   c. interactionist perspective.
   d. neo-Malthusian view.

7. Karl Marx's work is important to the study of population because he linked overpopulation to
   a. migration.
   b. demographic transition.
   c. the sick role.
   d. the distribution of resources.

8. The first stage of the demographic transition is called the
   a. pretransition stage.
   b. transition stage.
   c. posttransition stage.
   d. initiation stage.

9. According to sociologists and environmentalists, which one of the following is not a basic function that the natural environment serves for humans?
   a. It provides the resources essential for life.
   b. It serves as a waste depository.
   c. It provides a natural setting for social inequalities.
   d. It "houses" our species.

10. Conflict theorists would contend that blaming developing countries for the world's environmental deterioration contains an element of
    a. ethnocentrism.
    b. xenocentrism.
    c. separatism.
    d. goal displacement.

11. Drawing on several components, including size, composition, and territorial distribution, _____ is the scientific study of population.

12. _____ _____ are records of births, deaths, marriages, and divorces that are gathered through a registration system maintained by governmental units.

13. The _____ _____ is the number of live births per 1,000 population in a given year.

14. A general measure of health used by demographers is _____ _____.

15. In demography the letters TFR stand for _____ _____ _____.

16. The growth rate of a society is the difference between births and deaths, plus the difference between _____ and _____.

17. In an application of the _____ _____ perspective, sociologists suggest that the natural environment serves three basic functions for humans and for many animal species.

18. In the United States and most other countries, the _____ is the primary mechanism for collecting population information.

19. Regarding environmental problems, four broad areas of concern stand out: _____ pollution, _____ pollution, _____ _____, and _____.

20. Neo-Malthusians are _____ in their condemnation of developed nations, which, despite their low birthrates, consume a disproportionately large share of world resources.

{ TECHNOLOGY RESOURCES }

Online Learning Center

1. Try the crossword puzzle in the student center of the Online Learning Center (**www.mhhe.com/schaefer11**). Working the puzzle is a great way to test your familiarity with the terms and concepts related to population and the environment. It's also an enjoyable way to review for exams.

2. The Earthwatch Institute strives to protect the environment by organizing volunteers to participate in environmental research. To learn about the issues that concern this group, go to its Web site (**www.earthwatch.org**).

3. The Population Reference Bureau offers a wealth of information for anyone curious abut demographic patterns around the world. Explore these resources at **www.prb.org.**

*Note: Although all the URLs listed were current as of the printing of this book, these sites often change. Please check our Web site (**www.mhhe.com/schaefer11**) for updates, hyperlinks, and exercises related to these sites.*

Reel Society Video Clips

Reel Society video clips, which appear on this book's Web site, can be used to spark discussion about the following topics from this chapter:

- Demography: The Study of Population
- Environmental Problems

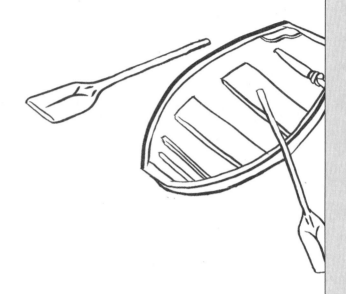

HELP

NEED FOOD, WATER, ELECTRICITY,

$80 BILLION IN FEDERAL AID (MINIMUM), 4 MILLION CUBIC FT. OF CONCRETE FILL FOR DAMAGED LEVEES, ARCHITECTS, LANDSCAPE CONSULTANTS, URBAN PLANNERS ~~YOGA~~ DONATED SHOES + CLOTHES DONATED BLANKETS

1 CITY,
1.2 MILLION POP.
(+10,031 PETS (APPROX.))
217,000 HOMES (APPROX.)

BULLDOZERS, CRANES, DUMP TRUCKS, GARBAGE TRUCKS, EXCAVATION CREWS, CONSTRUCTION CREWS, WATER VACUUMS (BIG ONES PREFERRED)

PLUMBING SPECIALISTS, ALUMINUM SIDING, FIBERGLASS INSULATION, CEDAR 2×4s, SEALANTS, HOUSE PAINT

POWER SAWS, HAMMERS, NAILS, BROOMS, MOPS, SCREWDRIVERS, LIGHT BULBS, FARMING SOIL, SOIL VITAMINS, MIRACLE-GROW + DUCT TAPE

This poster was created for The Hurricane Poster Project. All profits from the sale of this poster have been donated directly to The Red Cross to assist New Orleans in its recovery from Hurricane Katrina.

www.thehurricaneposterproject.com   www.redcross.org

This moving appeal on behalf of the city of New Orleans was conceived for the Hurricane Poster Project, a collective effort by the art and graphic design industry. Proceeds from the online sale of the limited-edition posters were donated to the Red Cross.

22

Collective Behavior and Social Movements

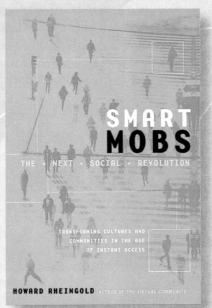

SMART MOBS

THE · NEXT · SOCIAL · REVOLUTION

TRANSFORMING CULTURES AND
COMMUNITIES IN THE AGE
OF INSTANT ACCESS

HOWARD RHEINGOLD AUTHOR OF *THE VIRTUAL COMMUNITY*

“ On January 20, 2001, President Joseph Estrada of the Philippines became the first head of state in history to lose power to a smart mob. More than 1 million Manila residents, mobilized and coordinated by waves of text messages, assembled at the site of the 1986 "People Power" peaceful demonstrations that had toppled the Marcos regime. Tens of thousands of Filipinos converged on Epifanio de los Santas Avenue, known as "Edsa," within an hour of the first text message volleys: "Go 2EDSA, Wear blck." Over four days, more than a million citizens showed up, mostly dressed in black. Estrada fell. The legend of "Generation Txt" was born.

Bringing down a government without firing a shot was a momentous early eruption of smart mob behavior. It wasn't, however, the only one.

• On November 30, 1999, autonomous but internetworked squads of demonstrators protesting the meeting of the World Trade Organization used "swarming" tactics, mobile phones, Web sites, laptops, and handheld computers to win the "Battle of Seattle."

• In September 2000, thousands of citizens in Britain, outraged by a sudden rise in gasoline prices, used mobile phones, SMS, email from laptop PCs, and CB radios in taxicabs to coordinate dispersed groups that blocked fuel delivery at selected service stations in a wildcat political protest. . . .

• Since 1992, thousands of bicycle activists have assembled monthly for "Critical Mass" moving demonstrations, weaving through San Francisco streets en masse. Critical Mass operates through loosely linked networks, alerted by mobile phone and email trees, and breaks up into smaller, tele-coordinated groups when appropriate. . . .

Location-sensing wireless organizers, wireless networks, and community supercomputing collectives all have one thing in common: *They enable people to act together in new ways and in situations where collective action was not possible before.* . . .

> *Bringing down a government without firing a shot was a momentous early eruption of smart mob behavior. It wasn't, however, the only one.*

As indicated by their name, smart mobs are not always beneficial. Lynch mobs and mobocracies continue to engender atrocities. The same convergence of technologies that opens new vistas of cooperation also makes possible a universal surveillance economy and empowers the bloodthirsty as well as the altruistic. Like every previous leap in technological power, the new convergence of wireless computation and social communication will enable people to improve life and liberty in some ways and to degrade it in others. The same technology has the potential to be used as both a weapon of social control and a means of resistance. Even the beneficial effects will have side effects. ”

(Rheingold 2003:157–158, viii) Additional information about this excerpt can be found on the Online Learning Center at www.mhhe.com/schaefer11.

In this excerpt from *Smart Mobs,* Howard Rheingold (2003) describes a new phenomenon in which strangers linked by mobile communications devices converge spontaneously to achieve some common goal. Rheingold, an acknowledged authority on the social implications of new technologies, has identified an emergent social behavior, one sociologists would recognize as a form of *collective behavior.* Practically all behavior can be thought of as collective behavior, but sociologists have given distinct meaning to the term. Neil Smelser (1981:431), a sociologist who specializes in this field of study, has defined **collective behavior** as the "relatively spontaneous and unstructured behavior of a group of people who are reacting to a common influence in an ambiguous situation." Rumors are a form of collective behavior; so is public opinion—people's reactions to shared events such as wars and elections.

What guides and governs collective behavior? Why do people participate in fads, and what causes mass panics? How do new social movements spread their message to others? In this chapter we will examine a number of sociological theories of collective behavior, including the emergent-norm, value-added, and assembling perspectives. We will give particular attention to certain types of collective behavior, among them crowd behavior, disaster behavior, fads and fashions, panics and crazes, rumors, public opinion, and social movements. We will also look at the role communications technology plays in globalizing collective behavior. Sociologists study collective behavior because it incorporates activities that we all engage in on a regular basis. Moreover, they acknowledge the crucial role that social movements can play in mobilizing discontented members of a society and initiating social change. In the Social Policy section, we will focus on the role that the social movement for disability rights plays in promoting change.

Theories of Collective Behavior

In 1979, 11 rock fans died of suffocation after a crowd outside Cincinnati's Riverfront Stadium pushed to gain entrance to a concert by The Who. In 1989, when thousands of soccer fans forced their way into a stadium to see the English Cup semifinals, more than 90 people were trampled to death or smothered. In 2000, fans surged forward at a Pearl Jam concert in Denmark, killing eight men. And in 2003, 100 people died after a pyrotechnics display by Great White ignited a fire at a nightclub in West Warwick, Rhode Island. Many had watched excitedly as flames engulfed the bandstand, thinking they were part of the act.

Collective behavior is usually unstructured and spontaneous. This fluidity makes it more difficult for sociologists to generalize about people's behavior in such situations. Nevertheless, sociologists have developed various theoretical perspectives that can help us to study—and deal with in a constructive manner—crowds, riots, fads, and other types of collective behavior.

Police arrive at a 2000 Pearl Jam concert in Roskilde, Denmark, where eight people died when the crowd surged suddenly toward the outdoor stage.

Emergent-Norm Perspective

Early writings on collective behavior implied that crowds are basically ungovernable. However, that is not always the case. In many situations, crowds are effectively governed by norms and procedures, including queuing, or waiting in line. We routinely encounter queues when we await service in a fast-food restaurant or bank, or when we enter or exit a movie theater or football stadium. Normally, physical barriers, such as guardrails and checkout counters, help to regulate queuing. When massive crowds are involved, ushers or security personnel may be present to assist in the orderly movement of the crowd. Nevertheless, there are times when such measures prove inadequate, as the examples just given and the one that follows demonstrate.

On December 28, 1991, people began gathering outside the City College gymnasium in New York City to see a heavily promoted charity basketball game featuring rap stars and other celebrities. By late afternoon, more than 5,000 people had arrived for the 6:00 P.M. game, even though the gym could accommodate only 2,730 spectators. Although the crowd was divided into separate lines for ticket holders and those wishing to buy tickets at the door, restlessness and discontent swept through both lines and sporadic fights broke out. The arrival of celebrities only added to the commotion and tension.

Doors to the gymnasium were finally opened one hour before game time, but only 50 people were admitted to the lobby at one time. Once their tickets had been taken, spectators proceeded down two flights of stairs, through a single unlocked entrance and into the gym. Those farther back in the crowd experienced the disconcerting feeling of moving forward, then stopping for a period, then repeating the process again and again. Well past the publicized starting time, huge crowds still stood outside, pressing to gain entrance to the building.

Finally, with the arena more than full, the doors to the gym were closed. As rumors spread outside the building that the game was beginning, more than 1,000 frustrated fans, many with valid tickets, poured through the glass doors into the building and headed for the stairs. Soon the stairwell became a horrifying mass of people surging against locked metal doors to the gym and crushed against concrete walls. The result was a tragedy: 9 young men and women eventually died, and 29 were injured through the sheer pressure of bodies pressing against one another and against walls and doors (Mollen 1992).

Sociologists Ralph Turner and Lewis Killian (1987) have offered a view of collective behavior that is helpful in assessing a tragic event like this one. It begins with the assumption that a large crowd, such as a group of rock or soccer fans, is governed by expectations of proper behavior just as much as four people playing doubles tennis. But during an episode of collective behavior, a definition of what behavior is appropriate or not emerges from the crowd. Turner and Killian call this view the **emergent-norm perspective.** Like other social norms, the emer-
{ p.69 gent norm reflects shared convictions held by members of the group and is enforced through sanctions. The new norm of proper behavior may arise in what seems at first to be an ambiguous situation. There is latitude for a wide range of acts within a general framework established by the emergent norm (for a critique of this perspective, see McPhail 1991).

Using the emergent-norm perspective, we can see that fans outside the charity basketball game at City College found themselves in an ambiguous situation. Normal procedures of crowd control, such as orderly queues, were rapidly dissolving. Simultaneously, a new norm was emerging: It is acceptable to push forward, even if the people in front protest. Some members of the crowd—especially those with valid tickets—may have felt that their push forward was justified as a way of ensuring that they would get to see the game. Others pushed forward simply to relieve the physical pressure of those pushing behind them. Even individuals who rejected the emergent norm may have felt afraid to oppose it, fearing ridicule or injury. Thus, conforming
{ p.185 behavior, which we usually associate with highly structured situations, was evident in this rather chaotic crowd, as it had been at the concerts by The Who, Pearl Jam, and Great White and at the soccer game in England. But it would be misleading to assume that these fans acted simply as a united, collective unit in creating a dangerous situation.

Value-Added Perspective

Neil Smelser (1962) proposed a different sociological explanation for collective behavior. He used the **value-added model** to explain how broad social conditions are transformed in a definite pattern into some form of collective behavior. This model outlines six important determinants of collective behavior: structural conduciveness, structural strain, a generalized belief, a precipitating factor, mobilization for action, and the exercise of social control.

In Smelser's view, certain elements must be present for an incident of collective behavior to take place. He used the term *structural conduciveness* to indicate that the organization of society can facilitate the emergence of conflicting interests. Structural conduciveness was evident in the former East Germany in 1989, just a year before the collapse of the ruling Communist Party and the reunification of Germany. The government of East Germany was extremely unpopular, and there was growing freedom to publicly express and be exposed to new and challenging viewpoints. Such structural conduciveness makes collective behavior possible, though not inevitable.

The second determinant of collective behavior, *structural strain,* occurs when the conduciveness of the social structure to potential conflict gives way to a perception that conflicting interests do, in fact, exist. The intense desire of many East Germans to travel to or emigrate to western European countries placed great strain on the social control exercised by the Communist Party. Such structural strain contributes to what Smelser calls a *generalized belief*—a shared view of reality that redefines social action and serves to guide behavior. The overthrow of Communist rule in East Germany and other Soviet-bloc nations occurred in part as a result of a generalized belief that the Communist regimes were oppressive and that popular resistance *could* lead to social change.

Smelser suggests that a specific event or incident, known as a *precipitating factor,* triggers collective behavior. The event may grow out of the social structure, but whatever its origins, it contributes to the strains and beliefs shared by a group or community. For example, studies of race riots have found that interracial fights or arrests and searches of minority individuals by police officers often precede disturbances. The 1992 riots in South Central Los Angeles, which claimed 58 lives, were sparked by the acquittal of four White police officers charged after the videotaped beating of Rodney King, a Black construction worker.

According to Smelser, the four determinants just identified are necessary for collective behavior to occur. In addition to these factors, the group must be *mobilized for action.* An extended thundershower or severe snowstorm may preclude such mobilization. People are more likely to come together on weekends than on weekdays, and in the evening rather than during the day.

The *manner in which social control is exercised*—both formally and informally—can be significant in determining whether the preceding factors will end in collective behavior. Stated simply, social control may prevent, delay, or interrupt a collective outburst. In some instances, those using social control may be guilty of misjudgments that intensify the severity of an outbreak. Many observers believe that the Los Angeles police did not respond fast enough when the rioting began in 1992, which allowed the level of violence to escalate.

Sociologists have questioned the validity of both the emergent-norm and value-added perspectives because of their imprecise definitions and the difficulty of testing them empirically. For example, some have criticized the emergent-norm perspective for being too vague in defining what constitutes a norm; others have challenged the value-added model for its lack of specificity in defining generalized belief and structural strain. Of these two theories, the emergent-norm perspective appears to offer a more useful explanation of societywide episodes of collective behavior, such as crazes and fashions, than the value-added approach (M. Brown and Goldin 1973; Quarantelli and Hundley 1975; K. Tierney 1980).

Smelser's value-added model, however, represents an advance over earlier theories that treated crowd behavior as being dominated by irrational, extreme impulses. The value-added approach firmly relates episodes of collective behavior to the overall social structure of a society (for a critique, see McPhail 1994).

Antiwar protesters in Seoul, South Korea, rally against the war in Iraq. According to the assembling perspective, nonperiodic assemblies like this one are relatively spontaneous, loosely organized reactions to galvanizing events.

Assembling Perspective

A series of football victory celebrations at the University of Texas that had spilled over into the main streets of Austin came under the scrutiny of sociologists (Snow et al. 1981). Some participants had actively tried to recruit passersby for the celebrations by thrusting out open palms "to get five," or by yelling at drivers to honk their horns. In fact, encouraging further assembling became a preoccupation of the celebrators. Whenever spectators were absent, participants were relatively quiet. As we have seen, a key determinant of collective behavior is mobilization for action. How do people come together to undertake collective action?

Clark McPhail, perhaps the most prolific researcher of collective behavior in the last three decades, sees people and organizations consciously responding to one another's actions. Building on the interactionist approach, McPhail and Miller (1973) introduced the concept of the assembling process. In their *assembling perspective* they sought to examine how and why people move from different points in space to a common location. Before the advent of new technologies, the process of assembling for collective action was slower and more deliberate than it is today, but McPhail's approach still applies.

A basic distinction has been made between two types of assemblies. *Periodic assemblies* include recurring, relatively routine gatherings of people such as work groups, college classes, and season ticket holders in an athletic series. These assemblies are characterized by advance scheduling and recurring attendance of the majority of participants. For example, members of an introductory sociology class may gather for lectures every Monday, Wednesday, and Friday morning at 10 A.M. In contrast, *nonperiodic assemblies* include demonstrations, parades, and gatherings at the scene of fires, accidents, and arrests. Such assemblies, which result from casually transmitted information, are generally less formal than periodic assemblies. One example would be an organized rally held at Gallaudet University in 1988 to back a deaf person for president of the school for deaf students—see the photo of the campaign leaflet on the opposite page (McPhail 2006; D. L. Miller 2000).

These three approaches to collective behavior give us deeper insight into relatively spontaneous and unstructured situations. Although episodes of collective behavior may seem irrational to outsiders, norms emerge among the participants, and organized efforts are made to assemble at a certain time and place.

Use Your Sociological Imagination

Think about the practice of assembling to attend class or to study in the library. On a daily basis, how is this practice affected by the direct or indirect actions of your fellow students, co-workers, relatives, or teammates?

www.mhhe.com/schaefer11

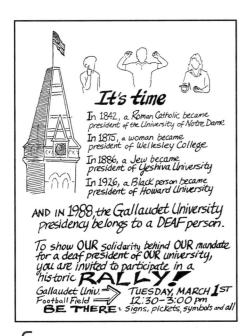

Gallaudet University in Washington, D.C., is the only four-year liberal arts college for deaf students in the United States. The leaflet shown on the left was distributed in 1988 as part of a successful effort by students, faculty, and alumni to force the appointment of the university's first deaf president. In 2007, after that president's retirement, students protested once again over the election process (right).

Forms of Collective Behavior

Do you remember the Ninja Turtles? Did you collect Beanie Babies when you were young? Any grunge clothes or tube tops lurking in your closet? These are all fads and fashions that depend on collective behavior. Using the emergent-norm, value-added, and assembling perspectives along with other aspects of sociological study, sociologists have investigated many forms of collective behavior—not only fads and fashions but also crowds, disaster behavior, panics and crazes, rumors, and public opinion. In this section we will study all these forms of collective behavior. The section that follows will be devoted to the most significant form of collective behavior, social movments.

Crowds

A *crowd* is a temporary gathering of people in close proximity who share a common focus or interest. Spectators at a baseball game, participants at a pep rally, and rioters are all examples of a crowd. Sociologists have been interested in what characteristics are common to crowds. Of course, it can be difficult to generalize, since the nature of crowds varies dramatically. Think about how hostages on a hijacked airplane might feel, as opposed to participants in a religious revival.

Like other forms of collective behavior, crowds are not totally lacking in structure. Even during riots, participants are governed by identifiable social norms and exhibit definite patterns of behavior. In fact, crowds are no more emotional, suggestible, or destructive than any other social gathering. Sociologists Richard

Berk and Howard Aldrich (1972) analyzed patterns of vandalism in 15 cities in the United States during the riots of the 1960s. They found that the stores of merchants who were perceived as exploitative were likely to be attacked, while private homes and public agencies with positive reputations were more likely to be spared. Apparently, looters had reached a collective agreement as to what constituted a "proper" or "improper" target for destruction. Today, this type of information can be shared instantly via text messaging.

The emergent-norm perspective suggests that during urban rioting, a new social norm that basically condones looting is accepted, at least temporarily. The norms of respect for private property—as well as norms involving obedience to the law—are replaced by a concept of all goods being community property. All desirable items, including those behind locked doors, can be used for the "general welfare." In effect, the emergent norm allows looters to take what they regard as properly theirs—a scenario that was played out in Baghdad after the collapse of Saddam Hussein's regime in 2003. Yet not everyone participates in the free-for-all. Typically, most community residents reject the new norm, and either stand by passively or attempt to stop the wholesale theft (Couch 1968; Quarantelli and Dynes 1970; see also McPhail 1991, 2006).

Disaster Behavior

Newspapers, television reports, and even rumors bring word of many disasters around the world. The term *disaster* refers to a sudden or disruptive event or set of events that overtaxes a community's resources, so that outside aid is necessary. Traditionally, disasters have been catastrophes related to nature, such as earthquakes, floods, and fires. Yet in an industrial age, natural disasters have been joined by such "technological disasters" as airplane crashes, industrial explosions, nuclear meltdowns, and massive chemical poisonings. The distinction between the two types of disaster is not clear-cut, however. As environmentalists have observed, many human practices either contribute to or trigger natural disasters. Building in flood plains, clear-cutting forests, and erecting rigid structures in earthquake zones all create the potential for disaster (Abramovitz 2001a, 2001b).

Disaster Research Sociologists have made enormous strides in disaster research, despite the problems inherent in this type of investigation. The work of the Disaster Research Center at the University of Delaware has been especially important. The center has teams of trained researchers prepared to leave for the site of any disaster on four hours' notice. Their field kits include identification material, recording equipment, and interview guidelines for use in various types of disasters. En route to the scene, these researchers try to become informed about the conditions they may encounter. Upon arrival, they establish a communication post to coordinate fieldwork and maintain contact with the center's headquarters.

Since its founding in 1963, the Disaster Research Center has conducted about 600 field studies of natural and technological disasters in the United States and other nations. Its research has been used to develop effective planning in the delivery of emergency health care, the establishment and operation of rumor-control centers, the coordination of mental health services after disasters, and the implementation of disaster-preparedness and emergency-response programs. The center has also provided training and field research for graduate students, who maintain a professional commitment to disaster research and often go on to work for disaster service organizations such as the Red Cross and civil defense agencies (Disaster Research Center 2005).

Case Studies: Collapse of the World Trade Center and Hurricane Katrina Two devastating but very different disasters have provided fascinating case studies for researchers to examine. One was the collapse of the World Trade Center following the terrorist attack of September 11, 2001, which caused nearly three thousand deaths and billions of dollars worth of property damage. The other was the unprecedented destruction caused by Hurricane Katrina in August 2005, which left hundreds of thousands of people homeless.

Sociologists who have studied such disasters have found some common patterns in people's response. Disasters are often followed by the creation of an emergency operations group, which coordinates both public services and some private-sector services, such as food distribution. Decision making becomes more centralized during these periods than it is in normal times. Such was the case on September 11, 2001. New York City's well-designed Emergency Management Center, located in the World

Trade Center, was destroyed when the building collapsed and all power at nearby City Hall was cut off. Yet within hours, both an incident command post and a new emergency operations center had been established to direct the search and recovery effort at the 16-acre site. Shortly thereafter came a victims' center, information kiosks, and an office for issuing death certificates, staffed around the clock by counselors, as well as facilities for serving meals to rescue workers. To identify potential hazards to rescuers and survey what had become a gigantic crime scene, police and public safety officials turned to computer maps and aerial photographs. They also designated places where victims could be identified, human resource functions relocated, and charitable contributions collected (Wachtendorf 2002).

Hurricane Katrina was an entirely different kind of disaster. Though unlike 9/11, the storm's arrival was expected, its path of destruction was much greater, covering 90,000 square miles—an enormous area compared to the World Trade Center. In the four

A helicopter hovers over a flooded New Orleans neighborhood, searching for survivors on the rooftops. In the days that followed the storm, federal, state, and local authorities struggled to coordinate their rescue efforts, as thousands of stranded residents went without food or water.

When a terrorist attack destroyed New York City's emergency command center, officials quickly set up a new one to direct the search and recovery effort. Even in times of unimaginable disaster, people respond in predictable ways.

years since 9/11, all levels of government in the United States had worked to improve their response to disasters, whatever the origin. Because of well-publicized government responses to other disasters, both at home and overseas, the public had come to expect virtually instant rescues. But while the destruction of low-lying coastal areas in the Southeast by a catastrophic hurricane could have been anticipated, days passed before authorities managed to mount a full-scale rescue effort in response to Katrina. With streets flooded and communications knocked out, stranded residents waited on their rooftops for food, water, or a helicopter lift, wondering where the rescue teams were.

What went wrong? A monumental lack of coordination stymied government authorities. Confusion reigned among the numerous agencies involved in the effort, including the Federal Emergency Management Agency (FEMA), which had been reorganized under the authority of the Department of Homeland Security less than two years earlier; the National Guard, with a different command structure in each state; the active-duty military; and literally thousands of city, county, and state governments, each with its own sphere of authority. Part of the problem was that when federal officials revised the nation's emergency response plan following 9/11, they relied on local government to manage in the first few days after a disaster. But

Katrina overwhelmed both local police and National Guard units stationed near the Gulf. In this case, the centralization of decision making that typically follows a disaster occurred over a period of days, not hours. In reviewing what happened, federal officials may decide to revise their emergency response plan and re-examine laws governing change-of-command authority, to expedite federal and military aid when necessary.

The long-term recovery from Katrina was even more complicated than the rescue operation. In contrast to the World Trade Center's collapse, Hurricane Katrina had a disproportionately large effect on the poor, who possessed few if any resources to draw on in the emergency. Lacking a nest egg, these families had little choice in where to relocate, and they faced much more difficulty than others in finding permanent shelter and employment.

Disaster research has shown that in the wake of calamity, maintaining and restoring communications is vital not just to directing relief efforts, but to reducing survivors' anxiety. On September 11, most cell phones in Manhattan were rendered useless by the destruction of communications towers and relay stations. To contact loved ones or to plan their escape from a city clogged with emergency vehicles, people stood in line at pay phones. In the days to follow, families seeking information about their loved ones posted fliers at makeshift information centers. Following Hurricane Katrina, survivors who had been dispersed to shelters across the nation—often without knowing whether family members were alive or dead—turned to special Web sites to find their kin, business associates, teachers, and even pets. In the aftermath of unimaginable disaster, people and organizations responded in predictable ways (Dreifus 2003, 2004; M. Hall 2005; P. Light 2005).

Fads and Fashions

An almost endless list of objects and behavior patterns seems temporarily to catch the fancy of adults and children. Think about Silly Putty, Hula Hoops, the Rubik's Cube, break dancing, Sudoku puzzles, Nintendo video, and mosh pits. Fads and fashions are sudden movements toward the acceptance of some lifestyle or particular taste in clothing, music, or recreation (Aguirre et al. 1988; R. Johnson 1985).

Fads are temporary patterns of behavior involving large numbers of people; they spring up independently of preceding trends and do not give rise to successors. In contrast, *fashions* are pleasurable mass involvements that feature a certain amount of acceptance by society and have a line of historical continuity (J. Lofland 1981, 1985). Thus, punk haircuts would be considered a fashion, part of the constantly changing standards of hair length and style, whereas dancing the Macarena would be considered a fad of the mid-1990s.

Typically, when people think of *fashions,* they think of clothing, particularly women's clothing. In reality, fads and fashions enter every aspect of life in which choices are not dictated by sheer necessity—vehicles, sports, music, drama, beverages, art, and even the selection of pets. Any area of our lives that is subject to continuing change is open to fads and fashions. There is

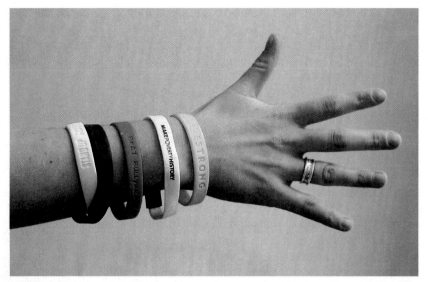

Plastic bracelets are the latest fad in charity fund-raising. In return for a modest contribution, those who support a particular charity receive an elastic armband bearing an inspirational motto or slogan. People collect the bracelets and wear several at once.

a clear commercial motive behind these norms of collective behavior. For example, in about seven months of 1955, retailers sold over $100 million of Davy Crockett items (worth over $700 million in 2002 dollars), including coonskin caps, toy rifles, knives, camping gear, cameras, and jigsaw puzzles. In 1999 Nintendo took in $5 billion from sales of Pokémon paraphernalia, ranging from virtual pets to compact discs (S. King 1999).

Fads and fashions allow people to identify with something different from the dominant institutions and symbols of a culture. Members of a subculture can break with tradition while remaining "in" with a significant reference group of peers. Fads are generally short-lived and tend to be viewed with amusement or lack of interest by most nonparticipants. Fashions, in contrast, often have wider implications, because they can reflect (or give the impression of) wealth and status.

Use Your Sociological Imagination

List some current fads and fashions. Now think back to when you were in elementary school. Can you name at least two fads from that time that seem to have faded away?

Panics and Crazes

Panics and crazes both represent responses to some generalized belief. A **craze** is an exciting mass involvement that lasts for a relatively long period (J. Lofland 1981, 1985). For example, in late 1973, a press release from a Wisconsin congressman described how the federal bureaucracy had failed to contract for enough toilet paper for government buildings. Then, on December 19, as part of his nightly monologue, *Tonight Show* host Johnny Carson suggested that it would not be strange if the entire nation experienced a shortage of toilet paper. Millions of people took his humorous comment seriously and immediately began stockpiling the item out of fear that it would soon be unavailable. Shortly thereafter, as a consequence of this craze, a shortage of toilet paper actually did occur. Its effects were felt into 1974 (Malcolm 1974; *Money* 1987).

In contrast, a **panic** is a fearful arousal or collective flight based on a generalized belief that may or may not be accurate. In a panic, people commonly think there is insufficient time or inadequate means to avoid injury. Panics often occur on battlefields, in overcrowded burning buildings, or during stock market crashes. The key distinction between panics and crazes is that panics are flights *from* something, whereas crazes are movements *to* something.

One of the most famous cases of panic in the United States was touched off by a media event: the 1938 Halloween eve radio dramatization of H. G. Wells's science fiction novel *The War of the Worlds.* This broadcast told realistically of an invasion from Mars, with interplanetary visitors landing in northern New Jersey and taking over New York City 15 minutes later. The announcer indicated at the beginning of the broadcast that the account was fictional, but about 80 percent of the listeners tuned in late. Many became frightened by what they assumed to be a news report.

Some accounts have exaggerated the extent of people's reactions to *The War of the Worlds.* One report concluded that "people all over the United States were praying, crying, fleeing frantically to escape death from the Martians." In contrast, a CBS national survey of listeners found that only 20 percent were genuinely scared by the broadcast. Although perhaps a million people *reacted* to the program, many reacted by switching to other stations to see if the "news" was being carried elsewhere. This "invasion from outer space" set off a limited panic rather than mass hysteria (Roger Brown 1954; Cantril 1940; Houseman 1972).

It is often believed that people who are engaged in panics or crazes are unaware of their actions, but that is certainly not the case. As the emergent-norm perspective suggests, people take cues from one another as to how to act during such forms of collective behavior. Even in the midst of an escape from a life-threatening situation, such as a fire in a crowded theater, people do not tend to run in a headlong stampede. Rather, they adjust their behavior on the basis of the perceived circumstances and the conduct of others who are assembling in a given location. To outside observers studying the events, people's decisions may seem foolish (pushing against a locked door) or suicidal (jumping from a balcony). Yet for that individual at that moment, the action may genuinely seem appropriate—or the only desperate choice available (L. Clarke 2002; Quarantelli 1957).

Rumors

The e-mail carried the subject line "Travelers Beware!" Its message was to warn those planning to go to Mardi Gras in New Orleans in 1997 that a highly organized crime ring there was drugging tourists, removing organs from their bodies, and selling them on the black market. The rumor circulated the country via e-mail and fax, causing an avalanche of calls to the New Orleans Police Department. Of course, an investigation turned up absolutely no evidence of an organ-snatching ring. The department finally set up a Web site to squash the rumors.

New Orleans wasn't the first city to be struck with this rumor. Similar stories targeted visitors to Houston and Las Vegas. It was said that a visitor to Las Vegas woke up one morning in a bathtub full of ice minus one kidney. Some version of the organ-snatching tale has swept through numerous countries, repeated by thousands of people. No one has ever been able to verify the story or to offer proof of its truth (Emery 1997).

Not all rumors we hear are as astonishing as the one about kidney snatchers. But none of us is immune to hearing or starting rumors. A **rumor** is a piece of information gathered informally that is used to interpret an ambiguous situation. Rumors serve a function by providing a group with a shared belief. As a group strives for consensus, members eliminate those rumors that are least useful or credible. Sociologist Tamotsu Shibutani (1966) sees this process as being akin to the survival of the fittest or strongest rumor. Rumors are also a means of adapting to change. If a business is about to be taken over by another firm, rumors will usually abound as to the significance the move will have for personnel. Gradually, such rumors are either verified or discarded, but the very exchange of rumors allows people to cope with changes over which they have little control. Scary rumors probably spread the fastest, because fear induces stress and stress is reduced by sharing the fear with others. Moreover, some people enjoy provoking fear in others (D. E. Miller 2006; Renard 2003; Rosnow and Fine 1976).

The attack on the Pentagon and the World Trade Center produced a flurry of rumors. According to one false account, a police officer "surfed" a steel beam down 86 floors as one of the towers collapsed. Given the role of the media in covering the event, many rumors centered on them. For example, one rumor suggested that a CNN film of Palestinians dancing in the streets after the attack was actually file footage photographed during the Gulf War. In Pakistan, rumors spread that the vivid photos of the hijacked planes crashing into the World Trade Center had actually been staged. Like these examples, rumors often reinforce people's ideologies and their suspicion of the mass media.

Publics and Public Opinion

The least organized and most individualized form of collective behavior is the public. The term **public** refers to a dispersed group of people, not necessarily in contact with one another, who share an interest in an issue. As the term is used in the study of collec-

"Did you hear that?" Rumors are a common type of social interaction that underscores shared understandings—even if the information they convey is incorrect.

tive behavior, the public does not include everyone. Rather, it is a collective of people who focus on some issue, engage in discussion, agree or disagree, and sometimes dissolve when the issue has been decided (Blumer 1955, 1969; R. Turner and Killian 1987).

The term **public opinion** refers to expressions of attitudes on matters of public policy that are communicated to decision makers. The last part of this definition is particularly important. Theorists of collective behavior see no public opinion without both a public and a decision maker. In studying public opinion, we are not concerned with the formation of an *individual's* attitudes on social and political issues. Instead, we focus on the ways in which a public's attitudes are communicated to decision makers, and on the ultimate outcome of the public's attempts to influence policymaking (R. Turner and Killian 1987).

Polls and surveys play a major role in assessing public opinion. Using the techniques for developing reliable questionnaire and { p.37 interview schedules, survey specialists conduct studies of public opinion for business firms (market analyses), the government, the mass media (program ratings), and of course, politicians. Survey data have become extremely influential not only in preselecting the products we buy but in determining which political candidates are likely to win an election and even which potential Supreme Court nominees should be selected (Brower 1988).

Today's political polls are well-constructed surveys based on representative sampling techniques. As a result, their projections of presidential elections often fall within a few percentage points of the actual vote. In marked contrast to these polls, some surveys are downright misleading. Telephone companies have marketed call-in "polls" using 1-900 numbers. Television viewers or newspaper readers are asked to call one number to register an opinion on an issue, or a second number to register an alternative opinion. Many problems are inherent in this type of "polling." The { p.35 sample that emerges is hardly representative, since it includes only those people who happened to see the commercial or advertisement for the poll and who felt strongly enough about the issue to spend the typical charge of $1 for a 1-900 call.

Although such factors as the physical environment, population, technology, and social inequality serve as sources of change, it is the *collective* effort of individuals organized in social movements that ultimately leads to change. Sociologists use the term ***social movements*** to refer to organized collective activities to bring about or resist fundamental change in an existing group or society (Benford 1992). Herbert Blumer (1955:19) recognized the special importance of social movements when he defined them as "collective enterprises to establish a new order of life."

In many nations, including the United States, social movements have had a dramatic impact on the course of history and the evolution of the social structure. Consider the actions of abolitionists, suffragists, civil rights workers, and activists opposed to the war in Vietnam. Members of each social movement stepped outside traditional channels for bringing about social change, yet had a noticeable influence on public policy. In Eastern Europe, equally dramatic collective efforts helped to topple Communist regimes in a largely peaceful manner, in nations that many observers had thought were "immune" to such social change (Ramet 1991).

Though social movements imply the existence of conflict, we can also analyze their activities from a functionalist perspective. Even when they are unsuccessful, social movements contribute to the formation of public opinion. Initially, people thought the ideas of Margaret Sanger and other early advocates of birth control were radical, yet contraceptives are now widely available in the United States. Moreover, functionalists view social movements as training grounds for leaders of the political establishment. Such heads of state as Cuba's Fidel Castro and South Africa's Nelson Mandela came to power after serving as leaders of revolutionary movements. Poland's Lech Walesa, Russia's Boris Yeltsin, and the Czech playwright Vaclav Havel all led protest movements against Communist rule and later became leaders of their countries' governments.

Because social movements know no borders, even nationalistic movements like those led by Castro and Walesa are deeply influenced by global events. Increasingly, social movements are taking on an international dimension from the start. Global enterprises, in particular, lend themselves to targeting through international mobilization, whether they are corporations like McDonald's or governmental bodies like the World Trade Organization. Global activism is not new, however; it began with the writing of Karl Marx, who sought to mobilize oppressed peoples in other industrialized countries. Today, activist networking

Social movements are not limited to local issues; globalization and the rise of the Internet have facilitated international protests. In December 2005, these South Koreans traveled to Hong Kong to protest against free trade at a meeting of the World Trade Organization.

is facilitated by the Internet and by relatively cheap travel costs. Participation in transnational activism is much wider now than in the past, and passions are quicker to ignite (Della Porta and Tarrow 2005; Tarrow 2005).

How and why do social movements emerge? Obviously, people are often discontented with the way things are. But what causes them to organize at a particular moment in a collective effort to effect change? Sociologists rely on two explanations for why people mobilize: the relative deprivation and resource mobilization approaches.

Use Your Sociological Imagination

What social moments are most visible on your campus? In the community where you live?

www.mhhe.com/schaefer11

Relative Deprivation Approach

Those members of a society who feel most frustrated and disgruntled by social and economic conditions are not necessarily the worst off in an objective sense. Social scientists have long recognized that what is most significant is the way in which people *perceive* their situation. As Karl Marx pointed out, although the misery of the workers was important to their perception of their oppressed state, so was their position *in relation to* the capitalist ruling class (Marx and Engels [1847] 1955).

The term *relative deprivation* is defined as the conscious feeling of a negative discrepancy between legitimate expectations and present actualities (J. Wilson 1973). In other words, things aren't as good as you hoped they would be. Such a state may be characterized by scarcity rather than a complete lack of necessities (as we saw in the distinction between absolute and relative poverty in Chapter 9). A relatively deprived person is dissatisfied because he or she feels downtrodden relative to some appropriate reference group. Thus, blue-collar workers who live in two-family houses on small plots of land—though hardly at the bottom of the economic ladder—may nevertheless feel deprived in comparison to corporate managers and professionals who live in lavish homes in exclusive suburbs.

In addition to the feeling of relative deprivation, two other elements must be present before discontent will be channeled into a social movement. People must feel that they have a *right* to {p.245 their goals, that they deserve better than what they have. For example, the struggle against European colonialism in Africa intensified when growing numbers of Africans decided that it was legitimate for them to have political and economic independence. At the same time, the disadvantaged group must perceive that its goals cannot be attained through conventional means. This belief may or may not be correct. Whichever is the case, the group will not mobilize into a social movement unless there is a shared perception that members can end their relative deprivation only through collective action (Morrison 1971).

Critics of this approach have noted that people don't need to feel deprived to be moved to act. In addition, this approach fails to explain why certain feelings of deprivation are transformed into social movements, whereas in other similar situations, no collective effort is made to reshape society. Consequently, in recent years, sociologists have paid increasing attention to the forces needed to bring about the emergence of social movements (Alain 1985; Finkel and Rule 1987; Orum 1989).

Resource Mobilization Approach

It takes more than desire to start a social movement. It helps to have money, political influence, access to the media, and personnel. The term *resource mobilization* refers to the ways in which a social movement utilizes such resources. The success of a movement for change will depend in good part on what resources it has and how effectively it mobilizes them (see also Gamson 1989; Staggenborg 1989a, 1989b).

Sociologist Anthony Oberschall (1973:199) has argued that to sustain social protest or resistance, there must be an "organizational base and continuity of leadership." As people become part of a social movement, norms develop to guide their behavior. Members of the movement may be expected to attend regular meetings of organizations, pay dues, recruit new adherents, and boycott "enemy" products or speakers. An emerging social movement may give rise to special language or new words for familiar terms. In recent years, social movements have been responsible for such new terms of self-reference as *Blacks* and *African Americans* (used to replace *Negroes*), *senior citizens* (used to replace *old folks*), *gays* (used to replace *homosexuals*), and *people with disabilities* (used to replace *the handicapped*).

Activists march in Washington, D.C., to protest the Supreme Court's historic *Roe v. Wade* ruling. Like most of the demonstrations held in the nation's capital, the annual pro-life event is the culmination of year-round planning and preparation. Social movements don't just happen; they require careful mobilization of resources.

Leadership is a central factor in the mobilization of the discontented into social movements. Often, a movement will be led by a charismatic figure, such as Dr. Martin Luther King Jr. As {p.413} Max Weber described it in 1904, *charisma* is that quality of an individual that sets him or her apart from ordinary people. Of course, charisma can fade abruptly, which helps to account for the fragility of certain social movements (A. Morris 2000).

Yet many social movements do persist over long periods because their leadership is well organized and ongoing. Ironically, as Robert Michels (1915) noted, political movements that are fighting for social change eventually take on some of the aspects of bureaucracy that they were organized to protest. Leaders tend to dominate the decision-making process without directly consulting followers. The bureaucratization of social movements is not inevitable, however. More radical movements that advocate major structural change in society and embrace mass actions tend not to be hierarchical or bureaucratic (Fitzgerald and Rodgers 2000).

Why do certain individuals join a social movement while others who are in similar situations do not? Some of them are recruited to join. Karl Marx recognized the importance of {p.219} recruitment when he called on workers to become *aware* of their oppressed status and to develop a class consciousness. Like theorists of the resource-mobilization approach, Marx held that a social movement (specifically, the revolt of the proletariat) would require leaders to sharpen the awareness of the oppressed. They would need to help workers to overcome feelings of *false consciousness,* or attitudes that do not reflect workers' objective position, in order to organize a revolutionary movement. Similarly, one of the challenges faced by women's liberation activists of the late 1960s and early 1970s was to convince women that they were being deprived of their rights and of socially valued resources.

Gender and Social Movements

Sociologists point out that gender is an important element in understanding social movements. In our male-dominated society, women find it more difficult than men to assume leadership positions in social movement organizations. Though women often serve disproportionately as volunteers in these movements, their work is not always recognized, nor are their voices as easily heard as men's. Moreover, gender bias causes the real extent of women's influence to be overlooked. Traditional examination of the sociopolitical system tends to focus on such male-dominated corridors of power as legislatures and corporate boardrooms, to the neglect of more female-dominated domains such as households, community-based groups, and faith-based networks. But efforts to influence family values, child rearing, relationships between parents and schools, and spiritual values are clearly significant to a culture and society (Ferree and Merrill 2000; Noonan 1995).

Scholars of social movements now realize that gender can affect even the way we view organized efforts to bring about or resist change. For example, an emphasis on using rationality and cold logic to achieve goals helps to obscure the importance of passion and emotion in successful social movements. It would be difficult to find any movement—from labor battles to voting rights to animal rights—in which passion was not part of the consensus-building force. Yet calls for a more serious study of the role of emotion are frequently seen as applying only to the women's movement, because emotion is traditionally thought of as being feminine (Ferree and Merrill 2000; V. Taylor 1995).

New Social Movements

Beginning in the late 1960s, European social scientists observed a change in both the composition and the targets of emerging social movements. Previously, traditional social movements had focused on economic issues, often led by labor unions or by people who shared the same occupation. However, many social movements that have become active in recent decades—including the contemporary women's movement, the peace movement, and the environmental movement—do not have the social class roots typical of the labor protests in the United States and Europe over the past century (Tilly 1993, 2004).

The term *new social movements* refers to organized collective activities that address values and social identities, as well as improvements in the quality of life. These movements may be involved in developing collective identities. Many have complex agendas that go beyond a single issue, and even cross national boundaries. Educated, middle-class people are significantly represented in some of these new social movements, such as the women's movement and the movement for lesbian and gay rights. Box 22-1 describes some new social movements in India.

New social movements generally do not view government as their ally in the struggle for a better society. While they typically do not seek to overthrow the government, they may criticize, protest, or harass public officials. Researchers have found that members of new social movements show little inclination to accept established authority, even scientific or technical authority. This characteristic is especially evident in the environmental and anti–nuclear power movements, whose activists present their own experts to counter those of government or big business (Garner 1996; Polletta and Jasper 2001; A. Scott 1990).

The environmental movement is one of many new movements with a worldwide focus. In their efforts to reduce air and water pollution, curtail global warming, and protect endangered animal species, environmental activists have realized that strong regulatory measures within a single country are not sufficient. Similarly, labor union leaders and human rights advocates cannot adequately address exploitative sweatshop conditions in a developing country if a multinational corporation can simply move the factory to another country, where workers earn even less. Whereas traditional views of social movements tended to emphasize resource mobilization on a local level, new social movement theory offers a broader, global perspective on social and political activism. Table 22-1 (page 536) summarizes the sociological approaches that have contributed to social movement theory. Each has added to our understanding of the development of social movements.

22-1 Women and New Social Movements in India

In the sixty years since India gained its independence from Great Britain in 1947, a variety of new social movements has emerged. These grassroots efforts deal primarily with women's rights, discrimination against the untouchables *(dalits)*, environmental issues, and farming problems. Though they tend to be most visible in the media when their demonstrations occur in cities, most of these movements are based in India's vast rural areas, where about three quarters of the nation's 1.1 billion people live.

Sociologists and other scholars have emphasized the central role that women play in starting these movements and creating social networks with activists in neighboring villages and adjacent states. Sometimes these movements connect to form nationwide networks through the assistance of the Women's Development Program (WDP). Founded by UNICEF in 1984, the WDP helps women to improve their quality of life, freeing them from dependence on slow and cumbersome government bureaucracies.

One notable social movement occurred in the Indian textile industry. In the mid-1980s, 5,000 striking textile workers came home from Bombay to mobilize support in their rural villages and gather food for strikers in the city. As the strike wore on, some remained in their villages and sought employment on government drought-relief projects. However, there weren't enough jobs for rural residents, much less for these new migrants from Bombay.

This experience was the origin of a new social movement in rural India. With unemployment threatening an expanded population in rural areas, activists formed what came to be called the *Shoshit, Shetkari, Kashtakari, Kamgar, Mukti Sangharsh (SSKKMS)*, which means "exploited peasants, toilers, workers liberation struggle." The initial goal of the movement was to provide drought relief for villagers, but the deeper goal was to bring more power to rural areas.

The SSKKMS was unusual compared to other social movements in India: about half its participants and many of its leaders were women. This was no accident, for the movement also sought to address gender inequities. At a

> *The initial goal of the movement was to provide drought relief for villagers, but the deeper goal was to bring more power to rural areas.*

meeting in 1986, Indutai Patankar—a pioneer in the rural women's movement—declared:

> We have gathered here to discuss our problems as women and a rural poor. . . . Not only do we work twice as hard as men but we also do not get equal wages, no child care. . . . We have to organize as women with the other oppressed toilers in urban and rural areas (Desai 1996:214).

Some men have joined the women of the SSKKMS in their political activism, using direct-action tactics such as roadblocks.

The Working Women's Forum is another example of Indian women's efforts to mobilize themselves and their resources for better wages and working conditions. Women have also marched on government offices to demand that at least a third of the seats in Parliament and the state assemblies be reserved for them. And they have begun to improve their families' lot through microfinance programs (see Chapter 18). Clearly, Indian women's traditional role of maintaining their households' health and nutrition is critical to their families' survival. Thus, their leadership in seeking improved living conditions is winning them new respect in India's patriarchal society. From the environment to the voting booth, from untouchables' rights to workers' rights, women's social movements are an increasingly common feature of Indian politics.

Let's Discuss

1. Why do you think so many of India's women participate in new social movements? Describe their goals.
2. What would happen if "powerless" people in the United States formed a similar social movement? Would it succeed? Why or why not?

Sources: Bystydzienski and Sekhon 1999; Daley-Harris 2002; Desai 1996; Ray 1999; Subramaniam 2006; Working Women's Forum 2007.

Use Your Sociological Imagination

Try to imagine a society without any social movements. Under what conditions could such a society exist? Would you want to live in it?

Communications and the Globalization of Collective Behavior

Many of the examples that we have used to illustrate collective behavior reflect the impact of communications technology—from radio broadcasts proclaiming that Martians have landed to the use of text messaging to organize impromptu political protests. Mobile communications devices are only the latest innovation in a wave of new communications technology that has transformed collective behavior.

How might some of the theoretical perspectives we examined earlier in this chapter apply to technology's role in collective behavior? Although Neil Smelser's value-added perspective did not explicitly refer to communications technology, its emphasis on people needing to be mobilized for action takes on new meaning today, with global text messaging and the Internet. With relatively little effort and expense, we can now reach a large number of people around the world in a short period. Looking at this new technology from the assembling perspective, we could

research**IN***action*

22-2 Organizing for Controversy on the Web

Concern about the spread of terrorism is not limited to border checks. Worldwide, government leaders are concerned about people using the Internet to incite terrorist acts. But where do you draw the line between legitimate political activity on behalf of respectable causes and criminal activity that seeks to create havoc among innocent civilians?

Thirty-one-year-old Babar Ahmad is a case in point. The British-born mechanical engineer was arrested in London in 2004 on the charge that his Web sites were a fundraising front for Islamic extremists, including Chechen rebels, the Taliban militia, and al Qaeda affiliates. Still in prison in 2007, Ahmad was relying on supporters to publicize his struggle to be released from custody. He maintains that he is being persecuted not for promoting terrorism, but for speaking his mind. As one supporter declared,

> *Where do you draw the line between legitimate political activity on behalf of respectable causes and criminal activity that seeks to create havoc among innocent civilians?*

Supporters of Babar Ahmad, a British citizen imprisoned for using the Internet to promote Islamic causes, pray together near a London court.

the war in Iraq is not an information war being fought on the Internet.

In truth, the Internet has become host to more and more Islamic extremist Web sites, many of which are technologically advanced, and even more important, written in English. These Web sites have been garnering support for Islamic causes outside the Middle East. Such sites are not the only ones in cyberspace that tie extremist beliefs to religion. Ku Klux Klan Web sites have also been growing in number, complete with online "news shows" and streaming video.

Equally disturbing are sites that promote what many see as self-destructive behavior. The Internet allows people who are engaged in unusual activities, such as collecting parking meters, to network and become a virtual group. More troubling still for many doctors and par-

ents are the slick Web sites that encourage anorexia and bulimia (disorders characterized by little or no eating or by overeating and purging) and self-mutilation. Internet chatrooms that support those engaged in these life-threatening behaviors are flourishing. Participants are urged to "go public" and send in for a beaded bracelet that shows support for their behavior, like the charity bracelets shown on page 530.

To counteract these sites, members of the medical community have established Web sites to promote recovery and safe behavior. Their actions illustrate the double-edged nature of free expression. On the street or on the Internet, social movements may be seen either as promoting desirable social change or as

supporting negative behaviors that many people find objectionable.

Let's Discuss

1. Have you ever been involved in a social or political movement whose legitimacy some people considered questionable? If so, what was the movement, and what were the objections to it? Did you consider the objections to be legitimate?

2. Can any social movement ever be totally free from controversy? Would you want to live in a society in which controversy is not tolerated?

Sources: FreeBaborAhmad 2007; Thomasrobb.com 2007; Tibbles 2007; Whitlock 2005.

536

consider the Internet's listservs and chatrooms as examples of nonperiodic assemblies. Without face-to-face contact or even simultaneous interaction, people can develop an identity with a large collective of like-minded people via the Internet (Calhoun 1998).

We have seen that rumors fly on the Internet. One click of the Send button can forward a message to every person in an address book. Multiply this potential by the millions of e-mail account holders to get an idea of the reach of the Internet in distributing rumors. We have seen, too, how Internet rumors can stir panics. In the same way, people can be exposed almost instantly to the latest crazes, fads, and fashions. And people are constantly being encouraged to call a telephone number or log on to a Web site to register their public opinion on some policy issue.

summingUP

Table 22-1

Contributions to Social Movement Theory

Approach	Emphasis
Relative deprivation approach	Social movements are especially likely to arise when rising expectations are frustrated.
Resource mobilization approach	The success of social movements depends on which resources are available and how effectively they are used.
New social movement theory	Social movements arise when people are motivated by value issues and social identity questions.

Can one be part of a "crowd" via the new communications technology? Television and the Internet, as contrasted with books and newspapers, often convey a false sense of intimacy reinforced by immediacy. We seem to be personally hurt by the death of Princess Diana or moved by the troubles of the Kennedy family. Therefore, the latest technology brings us together to act and react in an electronic global village (Della Porta and Tarrow 2005; Garner 1999).

This sense of online togetherness extends to social movements, which more and more are being mounted on the Web. Through the instantaneous communication that is possible over the Internet, Mexican Zapatistas and other groups of Indigenous Peoples can transform their cause into an international lobbying effort, and Greenpeace organizers can link environmental activists throughout the world. Sociologists have begun to call such electronic enhancement of established social movements *computer-mediated communication (CMC)*. Electronic communication strengthens a group's solidarity, allowing fledgling social movements to grow and develop faster than they might otherwise. Thus the face-to-face contact that once was critical to a social movement is no longer necessary (Castells 1997; Niezen 2005). As Box 22-2 suggests, however, the legitimacy of such online movements is a matter of opinion.

The new global communications technology also helps to create enclaves of similarly minded people. Web sites are not autonomous and independent; they are connected by a global electronic network. One Web site generally lists a variety of other sites that serve as links. For example, seeking out information on domestic partnerships may lead you to an electronic enclave that is supportive of cohabitation between men and women or, alternatively, to an enclave that is supportive of gay and lesbian couples. New developments in communications technology have clearly broadened the way we interact with one another (Calhoun 1998).

social Policy

and Social Movements

Disability Rights

The Issue

In the early 1960s, Ed Roberts joined forces with some other young adults who wanted to attend the University of California at Berkeley. Members of the group had more than their educational aspirations in common: all had disabilities. The university, reluctant to admit them at first, finally agreed, and found living quarters for them in the infirmary. Dubbed the Rolling Quads, these students proved they could succeed in college despite the extraordinary challenges they faced. Berkeley's administrators, convinced they were there to stay, awarded them their own student center. Eventually, the group turned their attention to the surrounding community, establishing the Berkeley Center for Independent Living, which became a model for hundreds of other independent living centers. Their activism marked the beginning of advocacy for people with disabilities (Brannon 1995).

Since then, the effort to ensure not only the health but also the rights of people with disabilities has been growing steadily. Like members of other advocacy organizations, the women and men of the disability rights movement are working to challenge negative stereotypes of disabled people; to gain a greater voice in the agency and public policy decisions that affect them; and to reshape laws, institutions, and environments so that people with disabilities can be fully integrated into mainstream society. According to disability rights activists, there is an important distinction between organizations *for* disabled people and organizations *of* disabled people. Because people with disabilities do not control the service providers, charitable associations, and parents' groups that work for their welfare, those organizations do not stress the goals of independence and self-help that are important to people with disabilities (Scotch 1989, 2001).

One of the obstacles the disability rights movement faces is the invisibility of many disabilities. Most of us are unaware of how many people struggle, some silently, with unseen disabilities. Table 22-2 challenges you to match some famous people with their disabilities.

The Setting

In 1990, working with a presidentially appointed council, organizations representing people with disabilities achieved passage of the Americans with Disabilities Act (ADA). In many respects the most sweeping antidiscrimination legislation since the Civil Rights Act (1964), the ADA took effect in 1992. The act defines a disability as a condition that substantially limits a major life activity, such as walking or seeing. It prohibits bias against people with disabilities in employment, transportation, public accommodations, and telecommunications. Businesses with more than 25 employees

In 2004, in *Tennessee v. Lane and Jones,* the Supreme Court upheld George Lane's rights as a person with a disability. Lane, who had to crawl up two flights of stairs at the Folk County Courthouse, sued to eliminate the architectural barriers in his state's court system. He won despite the fact that the federal and state governments have historically been deemed immune to lawsuits.

cannot refuse to hire a qualified applicant with a disability. Instead, they must make reasonable accommodations that will allow workers with disabilities to do their jobs. Nor can commercial establishments such as offices, buildings, hotels, theaters, supermarkets, and dry cleaners deny service to people with disabilities.

The responsibility for enforcing the ADA has been given to several federal agencies. For example, the Equal Employment Opportunity Commission oversees employment of people with disabilities; the Department of Transportation is responsible for enforcing transportation requirements (Burgdorf Jr. 2005).

Table 22-2

Can You Match the Person with the Disability?

All the famous people listed in this table have at least one disability. Match each person with one or more disabilities; then check your answers below.

Match the people in Column A with the disabilities in Column B

Column A	Column B
1._____ Lance Armstrong	A. Attention Deficit Disorder
2._____ Beethoven	B. Bipolar Disorder
3._____ Ray Charles	C. Blind
4._____ Tom Cruise	D. Cancer
5._____ Patrick Dempsey	E. Deaf
6._____ Michael J. Fox	F. Dwarfism
7._____ Magic Johnson	G. Epilepsy
8._____ Frida Kahlo	H. HIV/AIDS
9._____ Jay Leno	I. Learning Disability
10._____ John Lennon	J. Multiple Sclerosis
11._____ John Mellencamp	K. Quadriplegic
12._____ "Mini-me"	L. Parkinson's Disease
13._____ Napoleon	M. Polio
14._____ Christopher Reeve	N. Spina Bifida
15._____ Franklin Delano Roosevelt	O. Stuttering
16._____ Axl Rose	
17._____ Charles Schwab	
18._____ Steven Spielberg	
19._____ Sting	
20._____ Montel Williams	
21._____ Robin Williams	
22._____ Bruce Willis	
23._____ Stevie Wonder	

Source: Meyer 2007.

Answers: 1. D, 2. E, 3. C, 4. I, 5. G, 6. L, 7. H, 8. M, 9. I, 10. A, 11. N, 12. F, 13. G, 14. K, 15. M, 16. B, 17. I, 18. I, 19. B, 20. J, 21. A, 22. O, 23. C.

Sociological Insights

From a labeling perspective, the ADA represents a significant framing of the issue of disability rights. Through its civil rights approach to disabilities, it seeks to humanize the way society sees and treats people with disabilities. In other nations, such as Great Britain, disability is seen as an entitlement issue: that is, people with disabilities can expect to receive certain benefits from the government. That is quite different from the perspective that the disabled must not be denied certain rights—rights that everyone should possess, whether disabled or not. As activist Mark Johnson has put it, "Black people fought for the right to ride in the front of the bus. We're fighting for the right to get on the bus" (Shapiro 1993:128; see also Albrecht 1995, 1997; Gooding 1994).

Conflict theorists see the mobilization of resources on behalf of people with disabilities as part of a 40-year-long civil rights movement, one that has also benefited racial and ethnic minorities, women, and gays and lesbians. Interactionists focus on the everyday relationships between people with and without disabilities. More and more, they point out, people with disabilities are being seen as *people* rather than as wheelchair occupants or guide-dog owners.

Policy Perspectives

Today, policymakers and the courts are confronting issues that weren't even considered 20 years ago, when disability activists mobilized to pass the ADA. In the past, the courts have often ruled that citizens cannot sue the federal or state governments. Yet in 2004, in *Tennessee v. Lane and Jones,* the Supreme Court upheld the right of individuals with disabilities to gain physical access to the courts. Despite such victories, however, the groups who worked for the ADA's passage feel that federal agencies are still too cautious in enforcing the law (Burgdorf Jr. 2005; National Council on Disability 2004).

New on the agenda of disability rights activists is the concept of **visitability,** or the accessibility of private homes to visitors with disabilities. In the mid-1990s, cities such as Atlanta, Georgia, and Austin, Texas, as well as some cities in Great Britain, passed construction ordinances that encouraged the installation of accommodations such as no-step entrances, wide doorways, and grab bars in the bathroom. The idea is that all environments should be accessible to those with disabilities, not just public places such as classrooms and courtrooms. Many people consider such ordinances to be unnecessary interference from the government, but others see them as a long-overdue recognition that people with disabilities should be able to move freely throughout the country (Buchholz 2003; *Ragged Edge* 1998).

The passage of the ADA in the United States sparked similar actions in several other countries, including Great Britain. The European Union has mandated that by the end of 2006, all EU member countries must put in place laws that protect people with disabilities against discrimination in employment and training. As in the United States, disability rights activists in Europe have raised concerns about the interpretation and lax enforcement of the law (Ruebain 2005; Cooper 2005).

Disability rights activists are encouraged by the progress they have made since the ADA's passage. Studies show that a little more than 15 years later, people with disabilities feel empowered and enjoy access to better employment opportunities. However, we must remember that civil rights activists felt a measure of optimism after passage of the Civil Rights Act more than 40 years ago—and the nation still has a long way to go in enforcing that legislation (Albrecht 2005; Meyer 2008).

Let's Discuss

1. Think of someone you know who has a disability. Could that person easily visit your home? If not, what are the barriers that would make a visit difficult?

2. Why do you think the Supreme Court ruled as it did in *Tennessee v. Lane and Jones*? Do some research: What legal principle or precedent did the Supreme Court consider more important than the immunity of government from citizens' lawsuits?

3. Contrast the British approach to disabilities as entitlements with the U.S. emphasis on disability rights. What might be the benefits and the drawbacks of each approach?

GettingINVOLVED

To get involved in the debate over disability rights, visit this text's Online Learning Center, which offers links to relevant Web sites. Check out the Social Policy section in the Online Learning Center as well; it provides survey data on U.S. public opinion regarding this issue.

www.mhhe.com/schaefer11

{ MASTERING THIS CHAPTER }

Summary

Collective behavior is the relatively spontaneous and unstructured behavior of a group that is reacting to a common influence in an ambiguous situation. This chapter examines sociological theories used to understand collective behavior and forms of collective behavior, with particular attention to *social movements* and their important role in promoting social change.

1. Turner and Killian's *emergent-norm perspective* suggests that new forms of proper behavior may emerge from a crowd during an episode of collective behavior.

2. Smelser's *value-added model* of collective behavior outlines six important determinants of such behavior: structural conduciveness, structural strain, generalized belief, precipitating factor, mobilization of participants for action, and operation of social control.

3. The *assembling perspective* introduced by McPhail and Miller sought to examine how and why people move from different points in space to a common location.

4. In *crowds* people are in relatively close contact and interaction for a period and are focused on something of common interest.

5. Researchers are interested in how groups interact in times of *disaster.*

6. *Fads* are temporary patterns of behavior involving large numbers of people; *fashions* have more historical continuity.

7. The key distinction between a *panic* and a *craze* is that a panic is a flight *from* something, whereas a craze is a mass movement *toward* something.

8. A *rumor* is a piece of information used to interpret an ambiguous situation. It serves a social function by providing a group with a shared belief.

9. *Publics* represent the most individualized and least organized form of collective behavior. *Public opinion* is the expression of attitudes on public policy to decision makers.

10. *Social movements* are more structured than other forms of collective behavior and persist over longer periods.

11. A group will not mobilize into a social movement without a shared perception that its *relative deprivation* can be ended only through collective action.

12. The success of a social movement depends in good part on effective *resource mobilization.*

13. *New social movements* tend to focus on more than just economic issues, and often cross national boundaries.

14. Advances in communications technology—especially the Internet—have had a major impact on various forms of collective behavior.

15. The disability rights movement, which began at the University of California in Berkeley in the 1960s, achieved a major victory with passage of the Americans with Disabilities Act in 1990. The act, which prohibits discrimination against people with disabilities in employment, transportation, public accommodations, and telecommunications, has prompted significant changes in employment and public accommodations.

Critical Thinking Questions

1. Are the emergent-norm, value-added, and assembling perspectives aligned with or reminiscent of functionalism, conflict theory, or interactionism? What aspects of each of these theories of collective behavior (if any) seem linked to the broader theoretical perspectives?

2. Without using any of the examples given in this textbook, list at least two examples of each of the following types of collective behavior: crowds, disasters, fads, fashions, panics, crazes, rumors, publics, and social movements. Explain why each example belongs in its assigned category. Distinguish among these types of collective behavior based on the types and degrees of social structure and interaction connected with them.

3. Select one social movement that is currently working for change in the United States. Analyze that movement, drawing on the concepts of relative deprivation, resource mobilization, and false consciousness.

Key Terms

Assembling perspective A theory of collective behavior introduced by McPhail and Miller that seeks to examine how and why people move from different points in space to a common location. (page 526)

Collective behavior In the view of sociologist Neil Smelser, the relatively spontaneous and unstructured behavior of a group of people who are reacting to a common influence in an ambiguous situation. (524)

Craze An exciting mass involvement that lasts for a relatively long period. (530)

Crowd A temporary gathering of people in close proximity who share a common focus or interest. (527)

Disaster A sudden or disruptive event or set of events that overtaxes a community's resources, so that outside aid is necessary. (527)

Emergent-norm perspective A theory of collective behavior proposed by Turner and Killian that holds that a collective definition of appropriate and inappropriate behavior emerges during episodes of collective behavior. (525)

Fad A temporary pattern of behavior that involves large numbers of people and is independent of preceding trends. (529)

False consciousness A term used by Karl Marx to describe an attitude held by members of a class that does not accurately reflect their objective position. (534)

Fashion A pleasurable mass involvement that has a line of historical continuity. (529)

New social movement An organized collective activity that addresses values and social identities, as well as improvements in the quality of life. (534)

Nonperiodic assembly A nonrecurring gathering of people that often results from word-of-mouth information. (526)

Panic A fearful arousal or collective flight based on a generalized belief that may or may not be accurate. (530)

Periodic assembly A recurring, relatively routine gathering of people, such as a college class. (526)

Public A dispersed group of people, not necessarily in contact with one another, who share an interest in an issue. (531)

Public opinion Expressions of attitudes on matters of public policy that are communicated to decision makers. (531)

Relative deprivation The conscious feeling of a negative discrepancy between legitimate expectations and present actualities. (533)

Resource mobilization The ways in which a social movement utilizes such resources as money, political influence, access to the media, and personnel. (533)

Rumor A piece of information gathered informally that is used to interpret an ambiguous situation. (531)

Social movement An organized collective activity to bring about or resist fundamental change in an existing group or society. (532)

Value-added model A theory of collective behavior proposed by Neil Smelser to explain how broad social conditions are transformed in a definite pattern into some form of collective behavior. (525)

Visitability The accessibility of private homes to visitors with disabilities. (539)

Self-Quiz

Read each question carefully and then select the best answer.

1. The early writings on collective behavior imply that crowds are basically
   a. functional.
   b. value-added.
   c. structured.
   d. ungovernable.

2. The emergent-norm perspective has been criticized for being too vague in defining what constitutes a
   a. riot.
   b. crowd.
   c. belief.
   d. norm.

3. In sociological terms, which of the following constitute a crowd?
   a. spectators at a baseball game
   b. participants at a college pep rally
   c. urban rioters
   d. all of the above

4. The least organized and most individualized form of collective behavior is represented by
   a. rumors.
   b. publics.
   c. fashions.
   d. panics.

5. Which sociological perspective would be most likely to emphasize that rumors serve a function by providing a group with a shared belief?

- **a.** the functionalist perspective
- **b.** the conflict perspective
- **c.** the interactionist perspective
- **d.** labeling theory

6. From the point of view of theorists of collective behavior, there can be no public opinion unless there is both

- **a.** a public and mass media.
- **b.** a decision maker and mass media.
- **c.** a public and a decision maker.
- **d.** relative deprivation and resource mobilization.

7. The most all-encompassing type of collective behavior is

- **a.** public opinion.
- **b.** social movements.
- **c.** rumors.
- **d.** crowds.

8. From the point of view of social scientists, call-in telephone "polls" using 1-900 numbers are misleading because

- **a.** of the Hawthorne effect.
- **b.** the sample that emerges is hardly representative.
- **c.** they rely on improper resource mobilization.
- **d.** all of the above

9. "Collective enterprises to establish a new order of life" refers to

- **a.** public opinion.
- **b.** social movements.
- **c.** rumors.
- **d.** crowds.

10. The resource mobilization perspective would be most interested in looking at the influence of _____ on social movements.

- **a.** tenacity
- **b.** desire
- **c.** emotion
- **d.** money

11. Like other social norms, the emergent norm reflects shared convictions held by members of a group, and is enforced through _____.

12. Building on the _____ perspective, Clark McPhail and David Miller introduced the concept of the assembling process.

13. The term _____ refers to a sudden or disruptive event or set of events that overtaxes a community's resources, so that outside aid is necessary.

14. Members of a(n) _____ may adopt a fad or fashion in order to break with tradition while remaining "in" with (accepted by) a significant reference group of peers.

15. In the wake of many natural and technological disasters, decision making becomes more _____ than in normal times.

16. The _____ perspective emphasizes that even when unsuccessful, social movements contribute to the formation of public opinion.

17. A relatively deprived person is dissatisfied because he or she feels deprived relative to some appropriate _____ group.

18. As Max Weber described it in 1904, _____ is the quality of an individual that sets him or her apart from ordinary people.

19. As Robert Michels pointed out, social movements often become more _____ over time.

20. The SSKKMS movement was unusual when compared to other social movements in India in that about one-half of its participants, and many of its leaders, were _____.

Answers:
1 (d); 2 (d); 3 (d); 4 (b); 5 (a); 6 (c); 7 (b); 8 (b); 9 (b); 10 (d); 11 sanctions; 12 interactionist; 13 disaster; 14 subculture; 15 centralized; 16 functionalist; 17 reference; 18 charisma; 19 bureaucratic; 20 women

Online Learning Center

1. Your introductory sociology course may be drawing to a close, which means that it's a good time to start reviewing materials from earlier in the text. Two resources in the student center at the Online Learning Center—Name that Sociologist and What Perspective Am I—can be a big help. Try out these activities at **www.mhhe.com /schaefer11.**

2. Some people feel overwhelmed by our culture's emphasis on consumerism. The Center for a New American Dream is a social movement whose goal—among others—is to help Americans reduce the role of consumerism in their lives. To see how members of this movement aim to change society, visit the center's Web site (**www .newdream.org).**

3. What are some of the urban legends that you've heard recently? Can you discern an untrue urban legend from a true story? The Urban Legends Reference Pages at snopes.com (**www.snopes.com**) maintains a large index of urban legends, along with codes indicating whether or not they are true.

Note: Although all the URLs listed were current as of the printing of this book, these sites often change. Please check our Web site **(www.mhhe.com/schaefer11)** *for updates, hyperlinks, and exercises related to these sites.*

Reel Society Video Clips

Reel Society video clips, which appear on this book's Web site, can be used to spark discussion about the following topic from this chapter:

• Social Movements

In 2002, amid charges that wealthy nations were dumping cheap milk and other commodities on poor countries, the global charity Oxfam launched a campaign to ensure fair trade with nations that depend on a single crop, such as wheat, coffee, or rice. These photos of well-known personalities were taken to advertise the effort beginning in 2005. From left to right: singer/actress Alanis Morissette, actor Colin Firth, and Chris Martin (Coldplay).

23 Globalization, Technology, and Social Change

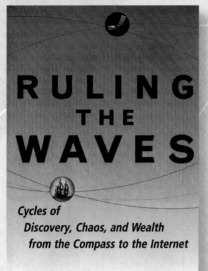

RULING THE WAVES

*Cycles of
Discovery, Chaos, and Wealth
from the Compass to the Internet*

DEBORA L. SPAR

"Chuck D is an unlikely hero of the digital age. With hit albums such as *Yo! Bum Rush the Show* and *Fear of a Black Planet,* the founder of the rap group Public Enemy would seem to inhabit a world far removed from the more conspicuous pioneers of cyberspace, from the Netscapes and Yahoos! and AOLs. In 1998, however, Chuck D stormed into cyberspace. Rather than giving his latest songs to Def Jam, the label that had produced his music for over a decade, the rap artist instead released his music directly onto the Internet, at www.public-enemy.com. It shouldn't have been such a big deal, really: one artist, a handful of songs, and a funky distribution method that probably reached several thousand fans. But in the music business this was very big news. For Chuck D had taken one of the industry's most sacred practices and thrown it, quite literally, into space. With just a couple of songs, he challenged how music was sold and, even more fundamentally, how it was owned. "This is the beginning," proclaimed the rapper, "of the end of domination."

As far as Chuck D was concerned, putting music online was a matter of power, of using new technologies to right old wrongs and give recording artists the influence and money that was rightfully theirs. To the recording industry, however, it was heresy. . . .

Had Chuck D been an isolated case, the studios most likely could have looked the other way. They could have dismissed Chuck D as a simple renegade, a rapper gone bad, and forgotten him and his web site. But the problem was that Chuck D, potentially, was everywhere. In cyberspace, any recording artist could distribute his or her music online; any musician could become a mini-studio, circumventing the record labels and their complex, clunky rules. . . .

> *It shouldn't have been such a big deal, really: one artist, a handful of songs, and a funky distribution method that probably reached several thousand fans. But in the music business this was very big news.*

Matters reached a head in 1999, when a nineteen-year-old college dropout named Shawn Fanning joined Chuck D in storming the frontier. Backed by his uncle in Boston, Fanning created Napster, a revolutionary system that allowed thousands—even millions—of users to trade their music online. Within months of its release, Napster had become a social phenomenon and a massive commercial threat. Universities complained that Napster was suddenly consuming huge chunks of their Internet bandwidth, and the music industry condemned it as piracy of the most blatant sort: "STEALING," as one music lawyer described it, "in big letters." Ironic foes such as Prince and the rock band Metallica joined the labels in pursuit of these new pirates, while prophets predicted the death of the recorded music industry. "A revolution has occurred in the way music is distributed," wrote one observer, "and the big record companies are in a state of panic."

(Spar 2001:327–329) Additional information about this excerpt can be found on the Online Learning Center at www.mhhe.com/schaefer11.

In this selection from *Ruling the Waves: Cycles of Discovery, Chaos, and Wealth from the Compass to the Internet,* political scientist Debora L. Spar (2001) describes the economic repercussions of a recent change in the way popular music is distributed. To students, the advent of Napster meant that suddenly, free music was available to them over the Internet. But to recording artists and record companies, Napster was a revolutionary new technology with the potential to shift the balance of power from the corporate giants that produced popular music to the artists who created and performed it. The global distribution of digitized music via the Internet, then, changed both the way people behaved—how they selected, obtained, and listened to music—and the cultural institution that is the music business.

The invention of the personal computer and its worldwide integration into people's day-to-day lives is another example of the social change that often follows the introduction of a new technology. *Social change* has been defined as significant alteration over time in behavior patterns and culture (W. Moore 1967). But what constitutes a "significant" alteration? Certainly the dramatic rise in formal education documented in Chapter 16 represents a change that has had profound social consequences. Other social changes that have had long-term and important consequences include the emergence of slavery as a system of stratification (see Chapter 9), the industrial revolution (Chapters 5 and 20), the increased participation of women in the paid labor forces of the United States and Europe (Chapter 12), and the worldwide population explosion (Chapter 21). In many instances, the social movements covered in Chapter 22 have played an important role in promoting social change.

How does social change happen? Is the process unpredictable, or can we make certain generalizations about it? Why do some people resist social change? What changes are likely to follow the technologies of the future? And what have been the negative effects of the sweeping technological changes of the last century? In this chapter we will examine the process of social change, with special emphasis on the impact of technological advances. Efforts to explain long-term social changes have led to the development of theories of change; we will consider the evolutionary, functionalist, and conflict approaches to change. We will see how vested interests attempt to block changes that they see as threatening. We'll see, too, that the process of globalization means that these social changes often happen on a global scale. We'll look at various aspects of our technological future, such as the Internet, computerized surveillance, and biotechnology. Taken together, the impact of these technological changes may be approaching a level of magnitude comparable to that of the industrial revolution. Finally, in the Social Policy section we'll discuss a controversial effect of global social change, the creation of *transnationals*—immigrants with an allegiance to more than one nation.

Theories of Social Change

A new millennium provides the occasion to offer explanations of *social change,* which we have defined as significant alteration over time in behavior patterns and culture. Social change can occur so slowly as to be almost undetectable to those it affects, but it can also happen with breathtaking rapidity. As Table 23-1 shows, some changes that have occurred in U.S. society over the past century and a half have been relatively slow or slight; others have been rapid or striking in magnitude.

Explanations of social change are clearly a challenge in the diverse and complex world we inhabit today. Nevertheless, theorists from several disciplines have sought to analyze social change. In some instances, they have examined historical events to arrive at a better understanding of contemporary changes. We will review three theoretical approaches to change—evolutionary, functionalist, and conflict theory—and then take a look at resistance to social change.

Evolutionary Theory

The pioneering work of Charles Darwin (1809–1882) in biological evolution contributed to 19th-century theories of social change. Darwin's approach stresses a continuing progression of successive life forms. For example, human beings came at a later stage of evolution than reptiles and represent a more complex form of life. Social theorists seeking an analogy to this biological model originated *evolutionary theory,* in which society is viewed as moving in a definite direction. Early evolutionary theorists generally agreed that society was progressing inevitably toward a higher state. As might be expected, they concluded in ethnocentric fashion that their own behavior and culture were more advanced than those of earlier civilizations.

{ p.11 Auguste Comte (1798–1857), a founder of sociology, was an evolutionary theorist of change. He saw human societies as moving forward in their thinking, from mythology to the scientific method. Similarly, Émile Durkheim ([1893]1933) maintained that society progressed from simple to more complex forms of social organization.

Today, evolutionary theory influences sociologists in a variety of ways. For example, it has encouraged sociobiologists to investigate the behavioral links between humans and other animals. It has also influenced human ecology, the study of the interaction between communities and their environment (Maryanski 2004).

Functionalist Theory

Because functionalist sociologists focus on what *maintains* a system, not on what changes it, they might seem to offer little to the study of social change. Yet as the work of sociologist Talcott Par-

Table 23-1

The United States: A Changing Nation

Population	1850	1940	1960	2010
Total in millions	23.2	132.1	180.7	308.9
Percentage under age 15	41%	25%	31%	20%

Education	1850	1940	1960	2005
Percentage not completing high school	88%	18%	13%	15%
Percentage ages 19–24 enrolled in higher education	Under 1%	8%	40%	46%

Labor Force Participation	1850	1940	1960	2005
Men working in their 20s	94%	88%	86%	86%
Women working in their 20s	22%	39%	74%	72%

Health	1850	1940	1960	2010
Physicians per 100,000 population	176	133	150	265
Life expectancy at birth, in years	38	63	70	78.5

Technology	1870	1940	1960	2005
Copyrights issued	5,600	176,997	243,926	157,700
Patents issued	12,127	42,238	47,170	121,600

Family	1890	1940	1960	2004
Median age at first marriage				
Men	26	24	23	24
Women	22	22	20	22
Number of children born per family	3.25	2.7	3.65	2.04

Note: Data are comparable, although definitions vary. Definition of the United States changes between 1850 and 1940 and between 1940 and 1960. Earliest date for children born per family is 1905.
Source: Author, based on federal data collected in Bureau of the Census 2006a:8, 13, 66, 75, 110, 140, 143, 376, 507; Kreider 2005:8; Sutch and Carter 2006:1–28/29, 391, 401–402, 440, 541, 685, 697, 709, 2–441/442, and 3–424/425, 427/428.

Think About It
Which of the social changes shown in this table surprises you the most? Which category do you think will change the most in the next 20 years?

sons demonstrates, functionalists have made a distinctive contribution to this area of sociological investigation.

Parsons (1902–1979), a leading proponent of functionalist theory, viewed society as being in a natural state of equilibrium. {p.15 By "equilibrium," he meant that society tends toward a state of stability or balance. Parsons would view even prolonged labor strikes or civilian riots as temporary disruptions in the status quo rather than as significant alterations in social structure. Therefore, according to his **equilibrium model,** as changes occur in one part of society, adjustments must be made in other parts. If not, society's equilibrium will be threatened and strains will occur.

Reflecting the evolutionary approach, Parsons (1966) maintained that four processes of social change are inevitable. The first, *differentiation,* refers to the increasing complexity of social organization. The transition from "medicine man" to physician, nurse, and pharmacist is an illustration of differentiation in the field of health. This process is accompanied by *adaptive upgrading,* in which social institutions become more specialized in their purposes. The division of physicians into obstetricians, internists, surgeons, and so forth is an example of adaptive upgrading.

The third process Parsons identified is the *inclusion* of groups that were previously excluded because of their gender, race, ethnicity, and social class. Medical schools have practiced inclusion by admitting increasing numbers of women and African Americans. Finally, Parsons contends that societies experience *value generalization,* the development of new values that tolerate and legitimate a greater range of activities. The acceptance of preventive and alternative medicine is an example of value generalization: Society has broadened its view of health care. All four processes identified by Parsons stress consensus—societal agreement on the nature of social organization and values (B. Johnson 1975; Wallace and Wolf 1980).

Though Parsons's approach explicitly incorporates the evolutionary notion of continuing progress, the dominant theme in his model is stability. Society may change, but it remains stable through new forms of integration. For example, in place of the kinship ties that provided social cohesion in the past, people develop laws, judicial processes, and new values and belief systems.

Functionalists assume that social institutions would not persist unless they continued to contribute to society. This assumption leads them to conclude that drastically altering institutions will threaten societal equilibrium. Critics note that the functionalist approach virtually disregards the use of coercion by the powerful to maintain the illusion of a stable, well-integrated society (Gouldner 1960).

Conflict Theory

The functionalist perspective minimizes the importance of change. It emphasizes the persistence of social life, and sees change as a means of maintaining society's equilibrium (or balance). In contrast, conflict theorists contend that social institutions and practices persist because powerful groups have the ability to maintain the status quo. Change has crucial significance, since it is needed to correct social injustices and inequalities.

Karl Marx accepted the evolutionary argument that societies develop along a particular path. However, unlike Comte and Spencer, he did not view each successive stage as an inevitable improvement over the previous one. History, according to Marx, proceeds through a series of stages, each of which exploits a class of people. Ancient society exploited slaves; the estate system of feudalism exploited serfs; modern capitalist society exploits the working class. Ultimately, through a socialist revolution led by the proletariat, human society will move toward the final stage of development: a classless communist society, or "community of free individuals," as Marx described it in 1867 in *Das Kapital* (see Bottomore and Rubel 1956:250).

On the outskirts of Buenos Aires, Argentina, a shantytown forms a stark contrast to the gleaming skyscrapers in the wealthy downtown area. Marxists and conflict theorists see social change as a way of overcoming the kind of social inequality evident in this photograph.

As we have seen, Marx had an important influence on the development {p.13 of sociology. His thinking offered insights into such institutions as the economy, the family, religion, and government. The Marxist view of social change is appealing because it does not restrict people to a passive role in responding to inevitable cycles or changes in material culture. Rather, Marxist theory offers a tool for those who wish to seize control of the historical process and gain their freedom from injustice. In contrast to functionalists' emphasis on stability, Marx argues that conflict is a normal and desirable aspect of social change. In fact, change must be encouraged as a means of eliminating social inequality (Lauer 1982).

One conflict theorist, Ralf Dahrendorf (1958), has noted that the contrast between the functionalist perspective's emphasis on stability and the conflict perspective's focus on change reflects the contradictory nature of society. Human societies are stable and long-lasting, yet they also experience serious conflict. Dahrendorf found that the functionalist approach and the conflict approach were ultimately compatible, despite their many points of disagreement. Indeed, Parsons spoke of new functions that result from social change, and Marx recognized the need for change so that societies could function more equitably.

Table 23-2 summarizes the differences between the three major theories of social change.

Use Your Sociological Imagination

Which theory of social change most concerns you? Why?

Resistance to Social Change

Efforts to promote social change are likely to meet with resistance. In the midst of rapid scientific and technological innovations, many people are frightened by the demands of an ever-changing society. Moreover, certain individuals and groups have a stake in maintaining the existing state of affairs.

Social economist Thorstein Veblen (1857–1929) coined the term **vested interests** to refer to those people or groups who will suffer in the event of social change. For example, the American Medical Association (AMA) has taken strong stands against na-{p.460 tional health insurance and the professionalization of midwifery. National health insurance could lead to limits on physicians' income, and a rise in the status of midwives could threaten the preeminent position of doctors as deliverers of babies. In general, those with a disproportionate share of society's wealth, status, and power, such as members of the American Medical Association, have a vested interest in preserving the status quo (Starr 1982; Veblen 1919).

Economic and Cultural Factors

Economic factors play an important role in resistance to social change. For example, it can be expensive for manufacturers to meet high standards for the safety of products and workers, and for the protection of the environment. Conflict theorists argue that in a capitalist economic system, many firms are not willing to pay the price of meeting strict safety and environmental standards. They may resist social change by cutting corners or by pressuring the government to ease regulations.

Communities, too, protect their vested interests, often in the name of "protecting property values." The abbreviation *NIMBY* stands for "not in my backyard," a cry often heard when people protest landfills, prisons, nuclear power facilities, and even bike trails and group homes for people with developmental disabilities. The targeted community may not challenge the need for the facility, but may simply insist that it be located elsewhere. The "not in my backyard" attitude has become so common that it is almost impossible for policymakers to find acceptable locations for facilities such as hazardous waste dumps (Jasper 1997).

Like economic factors, cultural factors frequently shape resistance to change. William F. Ogburn (1922) distinguished between material and nonmaterial aspects of culture. *Material culture* includes inventions, artifacts, and technology; *nonmaterial culture* encompasses ideas, norms, communications, and so-{p.63 cial organization. Ogburn pointed out that one cannot devise methods for controlling and using new technology before the introduction of a technique. Thus, nonmaterial culture typically must respond to changes in material culture. Ogburn introduced the term **culture lag** to refer to the period of maladjustment when the nonmaterial culture is still struggling to adapt to new material conditions. One example is the Internet. Its rapid uncontrolled growth raises questions about whether to regulate it, and if so, how much.

In certain cases, changes in material culture can strain the relationships between social institutions. For example, new means of birth control have been developed in recent decades. Large families are no longer economically necessary, nor are they commonly endorsed by social norms. But certain religious faiths, among them Roman Catholicism, continue to extol large families and to disapprove of methods of limiting family size, such as contraception and abortion. This issue represents a lag between aspects of material culture (technology) and nonmaterial culture (religious beliefs). Conflicts may also emerge between religion and other social institutions, such as government and the educational system, over the dissemination of birth control and family-planning information (M. Riley et al. 1994a, 1994b).

"Not in my backyard!" say these demonstrators, objecting to the placement of a new incinerator in a Hartford, Connecticut, neighborhood. The NIMBY phenomenon has become so common that it is almost impossible for policymakers to find acceptable locations for incinerators, landfills, and hazardous waste dumps.

Resistance to Technology

Technological innovations are examples of changes in material {p.124 culture that often provoke resistance. The *industrial revolution,* which took place largely in England during the period 1760 to 1830, was a scientific revolution focused on the application of nonanimal sources of power to labor tasks. As this revolution proceeded, societies came to rely on new inventions that facilitated agricultural and industrial production, and on new sources of energy such as steam. In some industries, the introduction of power-driven machinery reduced the need for factory workers and made it easier for factory owners to cut wages.

Strong resistance to the industrial revolution emerged in some countries. In England, beginning in 1811, masked craft workers took extreme measures: They mounted nighttime raids on factories and destroyed some of the new machinery. The government hunted these rebels, known as **Luddites,** and ultimately banished or hung them. In a similar effort in France, angry workers threw their wooden shoes *(sabots)* into factory machinery to destroy it, giving rise to the term *sabotage.* While the resistance of the Luddites and the French workers was short-lived and unsuccessful, they have come to symbolize resistance to technology.

Are we now in the midst of a second industrial revolution, with a contemporary group of Luddites engaged in resisting? Many sociologists believe that we are living in a *postindustrial so-*{p.124 *ciety.* It is difficult to pinpoint exactly when this era began. Generally, it is viewed as having begun in the 1950s, when for the first time the majority of workers in industrial societies

Table 23-2

Sociological Perspectives on Social Change

summingUP

Evolutionary	Social change moves society in a definite direction, frequently from simple to more complex.
Functionalist	Social change must contribute to society's stability. Modest adjustments must be made to accommodate social change.
Conflict	Social change can correct social injustices and inequalities.

became involved in services rather than in the actual manufacture of goods (D. Bell 1999; Fiala 1992).

Just as the Luddites resisted the industrial revolution, people in many countries have resisted postindustrial technological changes. The term *neo-Luddites* refers to those who are wary of technological innovations, and who question the incessant expansion of industrialization, the increasing destruction of the natural and agrarian world, and the "throw-it-away" mentality of contemporary capitalism, with its resulting pollution of the environment. Neo-Luddites insist that whatever the presumed benefits of industrial and postindustrial technology, such technology has distinctive social costs, and may represent a danger to both the future of the human species and our planet (Bauerlein 1996; Rifkin 1995; Sale 1996; Snyder 1996).

Even today, many people will resist a new technology, either because they find it difficult to use or because they suspect that it will complicate their lives. Both these objections are especially true of new information and media technologies. Whether it is TiVo, the iPhone, or even the latest microwave oven or digital camera, many consumers are leery of these so-called "must-have" items.

In 2007 the Pew Research Center released a report that sorted U.S. residents into 10 categories based on their use of information and communications technologies (ICTs) (see Table 23-3). According to the report, about 31 percent of the adult population falls into the top 4 categories, from the "Omnivores," who use these devices as a means of self-expression, to the "Productivity Enhancers," who use them to get the job done. Middle-of-the-road users, who represent about 20 percent of the population, take advantage of new technologies but aren't as excited about them. They range from the "Mobile Centrics," who are strongly attached to their cell phones, to the "Connected but Hassled." Close to half the people in the nation have few if any technology devices, or if they do, they are not wedded to them. Typically, younger people embrace technological change more than older people, who tend either to be indifferent toward new technologies or to find them annoying.

Use Your Sociological Imagination

What kind of change do you find the hardest to accept? The easiest?

Global Social Change

We are at a truly dramatic time in history to consider global social change. Maureen Hallinan (1997), in her presidential address to the American Sociological Association, asked those present to consider just a few of the recent political events: the collapse of communism; terrorism in various parts of the world, including the United States; major regime changes and severe

Table 23-3

Contours of Communication

Omnivores: 8% of American adults constitute the most active participants in the information society, consuming information goods and services at a high rate and using them as a platform for participation and self-expression.

The Connectors: 7% of the adult population surround themselves with technology and use it to connect with people and digital content. They get a lot out of their mobile devices and participate actively in online life.

Lackluster Veterans: 8% of American adults make up a group who are not at all passionate about their abundance of modern ICTs. Few like the intrusiveness their gadgets add to their lives and not many see ICTs adding to their personal productivity.

Productivity Enhancers: 9% of American adults happily get a lot of things done with information technology, both at home and at work.

Mobile Centrics: 10% of the general population are strongly attached to their cell phones and take advantage of a range of mobile applications.

Connected but Hassled: 9% of American adults fit into this group. They have invested in a lot of technology, but the connectivity is a hassle for them.

Inexperienced Experimenters: 8% of adults have less ICT on hand than others. They feel competent in dealing with technology, and might do more with it if they had more.

Light but Satisfied: 15% of adults have the basics of information technology, use it infrequently, and it does not register as an important part of their lives.

Indifferents: 11% of adults have a fair amount of technology on hand, but it does not play a central role in their daily lives.

Off the Net: 15% of the population, mainly older Americans, is off the modern information network.

Note: From a Pew Internet and American Life Project survey conducted in April 2006.
Source: Horrigan 2007:vii.

Think About It
What category would you place yourself in?

economic disruptions in Africa, the Middle East, and Eastern Europe; the spread of AIDS; and the computer revolution. Just a few months after her remarks came the first verification of the cloning of a complex animal, Dolly the sheep.

In this era of massive social, political, and economic change on a global scale, is it possible to predict change? Some technological changes seem obvious, but the collapse of communist governments in the former Soviet Union and Eastern Europe in the early 1990s took people by surprise. Yet prior to the Soviet collapse, sociologist Randall Collins (1986, 1995), a conflict theorist, had observed a crucial sequence of events that most observers had missed.

In seminars as far back as 1980, and in a book published in 1986, Collins had argued that Soviet expansionism had resulted in an overextension of resources, including disproportionate spending on military forces. Such an overextension will strain a regime's stability. Moreover, geopolitical theory suggests that nations in the middle of a geographic region, such as the Soviet Union, tend to fragment into smaller units over time. Collins predicted that the coincidence of social crises on several frontiers would precipitate the collapse of the Soviet Union.

And that is just what happened. In 1979, the success of the Iranian revolution had led to an upsurge of Islamic fundamentalism in nearby Afghanistan, as well as in Soviet republics with substantial Muslim populations. At the same time, resistance to Communist rule was growing both throughout Eastern Europe and within the Soviet Union itself. Collins had predicted that the rise of a dissident form of communism within the Soviet Union might facilitate the breakdown of the regime. Beginning in the late 1980s, Soviet leader Mikhail Gorbachev chose not to use military power and other types of repression to crush dissidents in Eastern Europe. Instead, he offered plans for democratization and social reform of Soviet society, and seemed willing to reshape the Soviet Union into a loose federation of somewhat autonomous states. But in 1991, six republics on the western periphery declared their independence, and within months the entire Soviet Union had formally disintegrated into Russia and a number of other independent nations.

In her address, Hallinan (1997) cautioned that we need to move beyond the restrictive models of social change—the linear view of evolutionary theory and the assumptions about equilibrium in functionalist theory. She and other sociologists have looked to the "chaos theory" advanced by mathematicians to understand erratic events as a part of change. Hallinan noted that upheavals and major chaotic shifts do occur, and that sociologists must learn to predict their occurrence, as Collins did with the Soviet Union. For example, imagine the dramatic nonlinear social change that will result from major innovations in communications and biotechnology—topics we will discuss next.

Technology and the Future

Technology is cultural information about how to use the material resources of the environment to satisfy human needs and desires. Technological advances—the airplane, the automobile, the television, the atomic bomb, and more recently, the computer, digital media, and the cellular phone—have brought striking changes to our cultures, our patterns of socialization, our social institutions, and our day-to-day social interactions. Technological innovations are, in fact, emerging and being accepted with remarkable speed.

In the last generation alone, industrial countries have seen a major shift in consumer technologies. No longer do we buy electronic devices to last for even ten years. Increasingly, we buy them with the expectation that within as little as three years, we will need to upgrade to an entirely new technology, whether it be a hand-held device or a home computer. Of course, there are those people who either reject the latest gadgets or become frustrated trying to adapt to them. And then there are the "tech-no's"—people who resist the worldwide movement toward electronic networking. Those who become tech-no's are finding that it is a life choice that sets them apart from their peers, much like deciding to be "child free" (Darlin 2006; Kornblum 2007).

In the following sections, we will examine various aspects of our technological future and consider their impact on social change, including the social strain they will cause. We will focus in particular on recent developments in computer technology, electronic censorship, and biotechnology.

Computer Technology

The last decade witnessed an explosion of computer technology in the United States and around the world. Its effects were particularly noteworthy with regard to the Internet, the world's largest computer network. In 2007 the Internet reached 1.1 billion users, compared to just 50 million in 1996. Box 23-1 (page 552) sketches the worldwide access to and use of the Internet (Internet World Stats 2007).

The Internet evolved from a computer system built in 1962 by the U.S. Defense Department to enable scholars and military researchers to continue their government work even if part of the nation's communications system were destroyed by a nuclear attack. Until recently, it was difficult to gain access to the Internet without holding a position at a university or a government research laboratory. Today, however, virtually anyone can reach the Internet with a phone line, a computer, and a modem. People buy and sell cars, trade stocks, auction off items, research new medical remedies, vote, and track down long-lost friends online—to mention just a few of the thousands of possibilities (Reddick and King 2000).

Unfortunately, not everyone can get onto the information highway, especially not the less affluent. Moreover, this pattern of inequality is global. The core nations that Immanuel Wallerstein described in his world systems analysis have a virtual monopoly on information technology; the peripheral nations of Asia, Africa, and Latin America depend on the core nations both for technology and for the information it provides. For example, North America, Europe, and a few industrialized nations in other regions possess almost all the world's *Internet hosts*—computers that are connected directly to the worldwide network.

What is the solution to this global disconnect between the haves and the have-nots? Some people have suggested giving everyone a computer—or at least, everyone who can't afford one. Box 23-2 (page 553) takes a look at this interesting proposal.

Privacy and Censorship in a Global Village

As we saw in the chapter-opening excerpt, new technologies like the personal computer and the Internet have brought about

research IN action

23-1 The Internet's Global Profile

The old notion of an Internet accessed primarily in the United States and dominated by English-only content is passé. In fact, usage patterns are changing so fast, generalizing about global use of the Internet requires careful research and phrasing.

For example, Figure A, Internet Users by World Region, shows an Internet that is dominated by users in Asia and Europe, two relatively populous continents. However, Figure B, Internet Penetration by World Region, shows a dramatically different picture, one in which the proportion of people in each region who access the Internet is highest in North America and Australia. That is, numerically, most Internet users live in Asia and Europe, but the likelihood of a person being an Internet user is greatest in North America and Australia. Figure B shows dramatically low Internet use in Africa, where less than 4 percent of residents can access the global network.

Though English is still the primary language of Internet users, as Figure C shows, use of the Chinese language has become much more

> *The old notion of an Internet accessed primarily in the United States and dominated by English-only content is passé.*

common. Chinese usage on the Internet increased nearly 400 percent between 2000 and 2007, compared to only 140 percent for English. Interestingly, 67 percent of all Japanese speakers use the Internet, compared to only 29 percent of all English speakers, though in absolute terms speakers of Japanese are a significantly smaller group.

Let's Discuss

1. In surfing the Web, how often do you encounter a Web site that is written in a language you do not read or speak? Do you think that experience will become increasingly common in the future?
2. Why do you think the use of Chinese on the Internet has increased so dramatically in less than a decade? What kind of information would you expect to find in Chinese? Who would use it?

Source: All data taken from Internet World Stats 2007 as of March 19, 2007.

FIGURE A
Internet Users by World Region

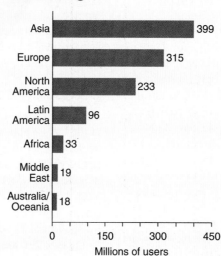

Region	Millions of users
Asia	399
Europe	315
North America	233
Latin America	96
Africa	33
Middle East	19
Australia/Oceania	18

FIGURE B
Internet Penetration by World Region

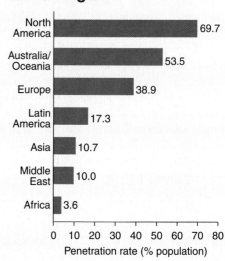

Region	Penetration rate (% population)
North America	69.7
Australia/Oceania	53.5
Europe	38.9
Latin America	17.3
Asia	10.7
Middle East	10.0
Africa	3.6

FIGURE C
Internet Top 10 Languages

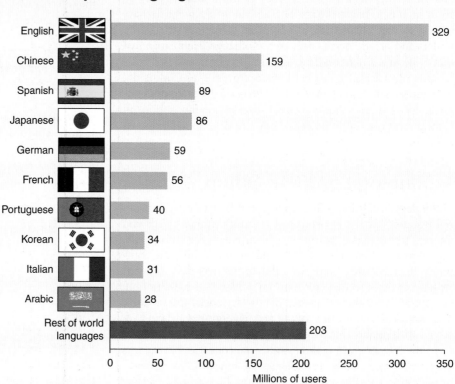

Language	Millions of users
English	329
Chinese	159
Spanish	89
Japanese	86
German	59
French	56
Portuguese	40
Korean	34
Italian	31
Arabic	28
Rest of world languages	203

23-2 One Laptop per Child

A decade ago, some colleges debated requiring entering freshmen to arrive on campus with a laptop. Others experimented with giving a laptop or iPod to every student. Such efforts were aimed at the privileged few—a fraction of the college students in the United States, and a minuscule percentage of young adults worldwide. But what if we were to give a free laptop to every child in the world?

In January 2005, Nicholas Negroponte of the Massachusetts Institute of Technology announced his revolutionary idea for just such a giveaway. For several years he had been trying to develop a low-cost computer, called the XO, for the 1.2 billion children of the developing world. Negroponte claims his prototype could sell for $100, complete with wireless hook-up and a battery with a five-year lifespan. His intention is to persuade foundations and the governments of industrial countries to fund the distribution, so that the laptop would be available for free.

Critics in the computer business have called the idea "wacky," referring to Negroponte as a "cyberevangelist." They question the plausibility of offering a laptop with wi-fi networking capability at such a low price. Others have argued that people in the developing world won't be able to handle the sophisticated technology. Supporters of expanding the availability of computers around the globe see such concerns as elitist, if not racist.

Whether the XO ever emerges from the laboratory to be distributed globally remains to be seen. Nonetheless, Negroponte's idea has launched some remarkable discussions and has led to serious soul-searching among executives of the established corporate giants. Feeling the heat, computer manufacturers, software developers, and telecommunications giants are discussing the possibility of truly open-source (that is, free) operating systems, or of allowing a single computer to be accessed by many people at once. Some corporations have discussed making expensive computer-based archives available free of access charges. In short, Negroponte's concept has challenged industry leaders to think of new, innovative ways of bringing information technology to those who need it most—young people with few, if any, material resources.

What if we were to give a free laptop to every child in the world?

The XO computer

Let's Discuss

1. Do you know any students who can't afford to buy a computer or upgrade to a new model? What would an XO computer mean to them?

2. From a purely business point of view, what would be the pros and cons of giving a free XO to every needy child in the developing world? Would the social benefits of such an action outweigh the business costs and benefits?

Sources: The Economist 2006c; J. Markoff 2006, 2007; Nocera 2006; One Laptop Per Child 2007; Read 2006.

---

sweeping social change. While much of that change has been beneficial, there have been some negative effects. Recent advances in computer technology have made it increasingly easy for business firms, government agencies, and even criminals to retrieve and store information about everything from our buying habits to our Web-surfing patterns. In public places, at work, and on the Internet, surveillance devices now track our every move, be it a keystroke or an ATM withdrawal. At the same time that these innovations have increased others' power to monitor our behavior, they have raised fears that they might be misused for criminal or undemocratic purposes. In short, new technologies threaten not just our privacy, but our freedom from crime and censorship (O'Harrow Jr. 2005).

In recent years, concern about the criminal misuse of personal information has been underscored by the accidental loss of some huge databases. In 2006, for example, the theft of a laptop computer from the home of an employee of the Veterans' Administration compromised the names, Social Security numbers, and dates of birth of up to 26.5 million veterans. Unfortunately, technologies that facilitate the sharing of information have also created new types of crime.

From a sociological point of view, the complex issues of privacy and censorship can be considered illustrations of culture lag. As usual, the material culture (technology) is changing faster than the nonmaterial culture (norms for controlling the use of technology). Too often, the result is an anything-goes approach to the use of new technologies.

Legislation regarding the surveillance of electronic communications has not always upheld citizens' right to privacy. In 1986, the federal government passed the Electronic Communications Privacy Act, which outlawed the surveillance of telephone calls except with the permission of both the U.S.

554 attorney general and a federal judge. Telegrams, faxes, and e-mail did not receive the same degree of protection, however. In 2001, one month after the terrorist attacks of September 11, Congress passed the USA PATRIOT Act, which relaxed existing legal checks on surveillance by law enforcement officers. Federal agencies are now freer to gather data electronically, including credit card receipts and banking records (Eckenwiler 1995).

Sociologists' views on the use and abuse of new technologies differ depending on their theoretical perspective. Functionalists take a generally positive view of the Internet, pointing to its manifest function of facilitating communication. From their perspective, the Internet performs the latent function of empowering those with few resources—from hate groups to special interest organizations—to communicate with the masses. Conflict theorists, in contrast, stress the danger that the most powerful groups in a society will use technology to violate the privacy of the less powerful. Indeed, officials in the People's Republic of China have attempted to censor online discussion groups and Web postings that are critical of the government (see Chapter 18). The same abuses can occur in the United States, civil liberties advocates remind us, if citizens are not vigilant in protecting their right to privacy (Magnier 2004).

If anything, however, people seem to be less vigilant today about maintaining their privacy than they were before the information age. Young people who have grown up browsing the Internet seem to accept the existence of the "cookies" and "spyware" they may pick up while surfing. They have become accustomed to adult surveillance of their conversation in electronic chat rooms. Many see no risk in providing personal information about themselves to the strangers they meet online. Little wonder that college professors find their students do not appreciate the political significance of their right to privacy (Turkle 2004).

www.mhhe.com/schaefer11

Use Your Sociological Imagination

Do you hold strong views regarding the privacy of your electronic communications? If your safety were in jeopardy, would you be willing to sacrifice your privacy?

Biotechnology and the Gene Pool

Another field in which technological advances have spurred global social change is biotechnology. Sex selection of fetuses, genetically engineered organisms, cloning of sheep and cows—these have been among the significant yet controversial scientific advances in the field of biotechnology in recent years. George {p.136 Ritzer's concept of McDonaldization applies to the entire area of biotechnology. Just as the fast-food concept has permeated society, no phase of life now seems exempt from therapeutic or medical intervention. In fact, sociologists view many aspects of biotechnology as an extension of the recent trend toward the medicalization of society, discussed in Chapter 19. Through genetic manipulation, the medical profession is expanding its turf still further (Clarke et al. 2003).

Today's biotechnology holds itself out as totally beneficial to human beings, but it is in constant need of monitoring. As we will see, biotechnological advances have raised many difficult ethical and political questions, among them the desirability of tinkering with the gene pool, which could alter our environment in unexpected and unwanted ways (D. Weinstein and Weinstein 1999).

One startling biotechnological advance is the possibility of altering human behavior through genetic engineering. Fish and plant genes have already been mixed to create frost-resistant potato and tomato crops. More recently, human genes have been implanted in pigs to provide humanlike kidneys for organ transplants.

One of the latest developments in genetic engineering is gene therapy. Geneticists working with mouse fetuses have managed to disable genes that carry an undesirable trait and replace them with genes carrying a desirable trait. Such advances raise staggering possibilities for altering animal and human life forms. Still, gene therapy remains highly experimental, and must be considered a long, long shot (Kolata 1999).

The debate on genetic engineering escalated in 1997 when scientists in Scotland announced that they had cloned a sheep. After many unsuccessful attempts, they had finally been able to

Though the USA PATRIOT Act was intended to protect citizens from terrorism, in practice it has raised concerns about the potential violation of their privacy.

23-3 The Human Genome Project

Together with geneticists, pathologists, and microbiologists, sociologist Troy Duster of New York University has been grappling with the ethical, legal, and social issues raised by the Human Genome Project since 1989. An original member of the oversight committee appointed to deal with such matters, he does not expect that his work will be done anytime in the near future.

Duster, who is also past president of the American Sociological Association, has been asked to explain why his committee is taking so long to conclude its work. In reply, he lists the many issues raised by the massive project. First, he is concerned that the medical breakthroughs made possible by the project will not benefit all people equally. He notes that biotechnology firms have used the project's data to develop a test for cystic fibrosis in White Americans, but not for the same syndrome in Zuni Indians. Biotechnology companies are profit-making ventures, not humanitarian organizations. So while the scientists involved in the Human Genome Project hope to map the genes of all the world's peoples, not everyone may benefit from the project in practical ways.

Duster's committee has also struggled with the question of informed consent—making sure that everyone who donates genes to the project will do so voluntarily, after being informed of the risks and benefits. In Western societies, scientists commonly obtain such consent from the individuals who participate in their research. But according to Duster, many non-Western societies do not acknowledge the individual's right to make such decisions. Instead, a leader makes the decision for the group as a whole. "When Western-trained researchers descend upon a village," Duster asks, "who should they turn to for consent?" (Duster 2002:69). And what if the answer is no?

Race, too, is a knotty problem for Duster's committee. DNA analysis shows conclusively that there is no genetic difference between the races. Given that analysis, many geneticists do not want to invest more time and effort in research on racial differences. As a sociologist, Duster knows that race is socially constructed. Yet he also knows that for millions of people around the world, race has a significant effect on their health and well-being. More to the point, he knows that a group's economic and political power helps to determine which diseases scientists study.

On the other hand, Duster worries that some researchers may be putting too much emphasis on biological differences between the races. He notes that those racial groups who are socially disadvantaged suffer much higher

> *A group's economic and political power helps to determine which diseases scientists study.*

rates of disease than advantaged groups. In the United States, for example, African American men suffer from prostate cancer at twice the rate of White men. Yet in the Caribbean and sub-Saharan Africa, Black men have a much lower rate of prostate cancer than American men, White or Black. How can genes explain this disparity? Duster suspects that the explanation for African Americans' higher disease rates lies not in their genes, but in their stressful environment, where they are routinely subjected to racial profiling and other forms of institutional discrimination. "We may be 99.9 percent alike at the level of DNA," Duster writes, "but if that were the end of the story,

Troy Duster, a sociologist at NYU, also teaches and directs the American Cultures Center at the University of California, Berkeley.

we could all pack up and go home" (Duster 2002:70).

Let's Discuss

1. What other criteria besides the power of a racial or ethnic group could be used to determine how much research is done on diseases that affect the group?
2. What should a researcher do if a tribal leader refuses to allow members of the tribe to participate in a research project?

Sources: Dreifus 2005; Duster 2002; Human Genome Project 2006.

replace the genetic material of a sheep's egg with DNA from an adult sheep, creating a lamb that was a clone of the adult. The very next year, Japanese researchers successfully cloned cows. These developments raised the possibility that in the near future, scientists may be able to clone human beings.

William F. Ogburn probably could not have anticipated such scientific developments when he wrote of culture lag 70 years earlier. However, the successful cloning of sheep illustrates again how quickly material culture can change, and how nonmaterial culture moves more slowly in absorbing such changes.

While cloning grabs the headlines, controversy has been growing concerning genetically modified (GM) food. This issue arose in Europe but has since spread to other parts of the world, including the United States. The idea behind the technology is to increase food production and make agriculture more economical. But critics use the term *Frankenfood* (as in "Frankenstein") to refer to everything from breakfast cereals made from genetically engineered grains to "fresh" GM tomatoes. Members of the anti-biotech movement object to tampering with nature, and are concerned about the possible health effects of GM food. Supporters of genetically modified food include not just biotech companies, but those who see the technology as a way to help feed the burgeoning populations of Africa and Asia (Golden 1999; Schurman 2004).

Another form of biotechnology with a potentially wide-ranging impact is the Human Genome Project. This effort involves teams of scientists around the world in sequencing and mapping all 30,000 to 40,000 human genes in existence, collectively known as the *human genome.* Supporters say that the re-

In Spain, Greenpeace members protest the European Union's proposed approval of a strain of genetically modified corn. The insect-resistant sweet corn produces a substance that is toxic to corn borers and earworms but not to humans. Nevertheless, transnational activists have raised questions about its potential health effects. Their vocal opposition has disrupted international trade and caused friction between the United States and Europe.

sulting knowledge could revolutionize doctors' ability to treat and even prevent disease. But sociologists worry about the ethical implications of such research. Box 23-3 (page 556) provides an overview of the many issues the project has raised.

Use Your Sociological Imagination

Are you concerned about the safety of your food or water? Have any of your friends ever expressed an opinion on this matter?

www.mhhe.com/schaefer11

Transnationals

The Issue

Imagine that as you leave your college commencement ceremony, diploma in hand, a stranger approaches and offers you a job. If you are willing to relocate to a foreign, non-English-speaking country, he says, you can earn $300,000 a year for the kind of work you have always thought of as menial labor. You can do the job for one year or several years. The only catch is that you must enter the country illegally, and remain there until you are ready to give up your job. The opportunity he is describing isn't new to you. In fact, you have many friends and relatives who have done exactly that.

The lure of fast, easy money that is described in this story may seem incredible to you, but it is real for many people in developing nations. Incomes in developing nations are so low that the wages an immigrant can earn in the United States, even at the most menial job, seem like a fortune. Back in the home country, their purchasing power is the equivalent of a $300,000 income in the United States—a huge economic incentive to immigrate. But while the opportunity to become rich may encourage even highly skilled foreigners to immigrate, these migrant workers—even those with legal status—enjoy far fewer rights than native-born workers.

The Setting

Figure 23-1 (page 558) shows the worldwide movement of workers with and without the legal right to immigrate. Several areas, such as the European Union, have instituted international agreements that provide for the free movement of laborers. But in most other parts of the world, immigration restrictions give foreign workers only temporary status. Despite such legal restrictions, the labor market has become an increasingly global one. Just as globalization has integrated government policies, cultures, social movements, and financial markets, it has unified what once were discrete national labor markets.

Globalization has changed the immigrant experience as well as the labor market. In generations past, immigrants read foreign-language newspapers to keep in touch with events in their home countries. Today, the Internet gives them immediate access to their countries and kinfolk. In this global framework, immigrants are less likely than they were in the past to think of themselves as residents of just one country. *Transnationals* are immigrants who sustain multiple social relationships that link their societies of origin with their societies of settlement.

Immigrants from the Dominican Republic, for example, identify with the United States, but at the same time they maintain close ties to their Caribbean homeland, returning periodically for extended stays with relatives and friends. While there,

they deliver *remittances (migradollars)* to needy family members. Dominican villages reflect these close ties, both in billboards that promote special long-distance service to the United States and in the presence of expensive household appliances bought with migradollars. In poor countries, transnational remittances —worth more than $300 billion a year worldwide—are easily the most reliable source of foreign income, worth nearly three times the combined value of all foreign aid budgets (DeParle 2007b; Tilly 2007; World Bank 2006b).

Sociological Insights

Sociologists did not begin to investigate transnationalism until the early 1990s. They are finding that new technologies which facilitate international travel and communications are accelerating the transnational movement of workers. Two other forces tend to promote transnationalism: Nationalism encourages émigrés to express continued allegiance to their homelands, and multiculturalism has legitimized the expression of those loyalties in receiving nations. Finally, international human rights organizations have joined faith-based groups in stressing universal human rights, regardless of a person's citizenship status. Whether these diverse influences will further the emergence of a global workforce composed of global citizens or simply fuel nationalistic fervor remains to be seen (Waldinger and Fitzgerald 2004).

As with other issues, sociologists differ in their opinion of transnationals, depending on their theoretical perspective. Functionalists see the free flow of immigrants, even when it is legally restricted, as one way for economies to maximize their use of human labor. Given the law of supply and demand, they note, countries with too few workers will inevitably attract laborers, while those with too many will become unattractive to residents.

Conflict theorists charge that globalization and international migration have increased the economic gulf between developed and developing nations. Today, residents of North America, Europe, and Japan consume 32 times more resources than the billions of people who live in developing countries. Through tourism and the global reach of the mass media, people in the poorer countries have become aware of the affluent lifestyle common in developed nations—and of course, many of them now aspire to it (Diamond 2003).

Sociologists who follow world systems analysis (see Chapter 10) suggest that the global flow of people, not just goods and resources, should be factored into the relationship between core and periphery societies. The global economic system, with its sharp contrast between have and have-not nations, is responsible for the creation of the informal social networks that link

Labor Migration

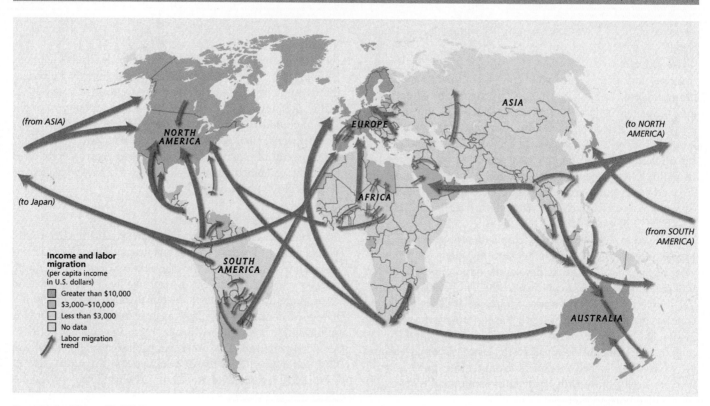

MAPPING LIFE WORLDWIDE   www.mhhe.com/schaefer11

Income and labor migration
(per capita income in U.S. dollars)
- Greater than $10,000
- $3,000–$10,000
- Less than $3,000
- No data
- Labor migration trend

Source: National Geographic 2005:16.

those seeking a better life with those who already enjoy prosperity.

Interactionists are interested in the day-to-day relationships transnationals have with the people around them, from those of their country of origin to those of the host country and fellow workers from other countries. The members of these global networks provide one another with mutual support and trust. Just as interesting is the question of how migrants see themselves—how they see their own identities as well as those of their children. In effect, transnationals negotiate their identities, depending on which social network they belong to at the moment. Some sociologists note that while being a transnational can be exhilarating, it can also isolate a person, even in a city of millions. Others worry that transnationals may become so cosmopolitan that they will lose touch with their national identities (Calhoun 2003; Plüss 2005; Rajan and Sharma 2006; Tilly 2007).

Policy Initiatives

The International Labor Organization has complained that the intense economic competition created by globalization is unraveling the social welfare systems of many countries. The United

States is now only 25th on the Economic Security Index (Sweden is the most secure country). In general, Western European nations are among the most secure; Eastern European countries that once belonged to the Soviet Union are among the least secure. To alleviate the pressure created by a failing social service system, workers will often move to countries that offer both good jobs and good social services—a trend that strains receiving nations' safety nets. In 2005, voters in both France and the Netherlands rejected the proposed European Union constitution, in part because of concerns about a potential influx of workers from developing countries like Turkey (Standing 2004).

Another unresolved transnational issue is voter eligibility. Not all nations allow dual citizenship; even those countries that do may not allow absent nationals to vote. The United States and Great Britain are rather liberal in this regard, permitting dual citizenship and allowing émigrés to continue to vote. Mexico, in contrast, has been reluctant to allow citizens who have emigrated to vote. Mexican politicians worry that the large number of Mexicans who live abroad (especially those in the United States) might vote differently from local voters, causing different outcomes (Sellers 2004).

Finally, the controversial issue of illegal immigration has yet to be settled, perhaps because of culture lag. That is, both public attitudes and government policies (nonmaterial culture) have not kept pace, much less adjusted to, the increasing ease of migration around the globe (material culture). Though globalization has created a global labor market—one that many countries depend on, legal or illegal—the general public's attitude toward illegal immigrants remains hostile, especially in the United States.

Let's Discuss

1. Suppose you live in an impoverished developing country and have the opportunity to earn a much higher income by immigrating to the United States. Will you do it, even if it means entering the country illegally and working long hours doing menial labor? If so, how will you justify your decision to those who condemn illegal immigration?

2. The U.S. economy depends on the cheap labor immigrants provide. Should immigrants receive the same social services that U.S. citizens receive? What about their children who are born in the United States (and therefore are U.S. citizens)? Explain your reasoning.

3. Globalization has increased international trade and development at the same time that it has strained nations' social service systems, as migrant workers flow toward countries offering the most extensive social protection. On balance, do you think its overall effect has been beneficial or harmful? What might be done to alleviate the harmful effects of globalization?

GettingINVOLVED

To get involved in the debate over transnationals, visit this text's Online Learning Center, which offers links to relevant Web sites. Check out the Social Policy section in the Online Learning Center as well; it provides survey data on U.S. public opinion regarding this issue.

www.mhhe.com/schaefer11

{ MASTERING THIS CHAPTER }

Summary

Social change is significant alteration over time in behavior patterns and culture, including norms and values. *Technology* is information about how to use the material resources of the environment to satisfy human needs and desires. This chapter examines sociological theories of social change, resistance to change, global social change, and the impact of technology on society's future.

1. Early advocates of the *evolutionary theory* of social change believed that society was progressing inevitably toward a higher state.

2. Talcott Parsons, a leading advocate of functionalist theory, viewed society as being in a natural state of equilibrium or balance.

3. Conflict theorists see change as having crucial significance, since it is needed to correct social injustices and inequalities.

4. In general, those with a disproportionate share of society's wealth, status, and power, called *vested interests,* have a stake in preserving the status quo and will resist change.

5. The period of maladjustment when a nonmaterial culture is still struggling to adapt to new material conditions is known as *culture lag.*

6. We are living in a time of sweeping social, political, and economic change—change that occurs not just on a local or national basis, but on a global scale.

7. The core industrialized nations have a virtual monopoly on information technology, making the peripheral nations dependent on them both for technology and for the information it provides.

8. Computer technology has made it increasingly easy for any individual, business firm, or government agency to retrieve more and more information about any of us, thereby infringing on our privacy.

9. Advances in biotechnology have raised difficult ethical questions about genetic engineering and the sex selection of fetuses.

10. Globalization has increased the international migration of laborers, producing a new kind of immigrant. *Transnationals* are immigrants who sustain multiple social relationships that link their societies of origin with their societies of settlement.

1. In the last few years we have witnessed phenomenal growth in the use of cellular phones around the world. Analyze this form of material culture in terms of culture lag. Consider usage, government regulation, and privacy issues.

2. Consider one of the technological advances discussed in the section on technology and the future. Analyze this new technology, focusing on whether it is likely to increase or reduce inequality in the coming decades. Whenever possible, address issues of gender, race, ethnicity, and class, as well as inequality between nations.

3. In what ways has social interaction in your college community been affected by the technological advances examined in this chapter? Are particular subcultures more or less likely to employ new forms of electronic communication?

Key Terms

Culture lag A period of maladjustment when the nonmaterial culture is still struggling to adapt to new material conditions. (page 549)

Equilibrium model The functionalist view that society tends toward a state of stability or balance. (547)

Evolutionary theory A theory of social change that holds that society is moving in a definite direction. (546)

Luddites Rebellious craft workers in 19th-century England who destroyed new factory machinery as part of their resistance to the industrial revolution. (549)

Social change Significant alteration over time in behavior patterns and culture, including norms and values. (546)

Technology Cultural information about how to use the material resources of the environment to satisfy human needs and desires. (551)

Transnational An immigrant who sustains multiple social relationships that link his or her society of origin with the society of settlement. (557)

Vested interests Those people or groups who will suffer in the event of social change, and who have a stake in maintaining the status quo. (548)

Self-Quiz

Read each question carefully and then select the best answer.

1. Nineteenth-century theories of social change reflect the pioneering work in biological evolution done by
   a. Albert Einstein.
   b. Charles Darwin.
   c. Harriet Martineau.
   d. Benjamin Franklin.

2. The writings of Auguste Comte and Émile Durkheim are examples of
   a. cyclical theory.
   b. evolutionary theory.
   c. interactionist theory.
   d. conflict theory.

3. The acceptance of preventive medicine is an example of the process that Parsons called
   a. differentiation.
   b. value generalization.
   c. inclusion.
   d. adaptive upgrading.

4. The term *vested interests* was coined by social economist
   a. William F. Ogburn.
   b. Talcott Parsons.
   c. Auguste Comte.
   d. Thorstein Veblen.

5. Which of the following theorists argued that conflict is a normal and desirable aspect of social change?
   a. Karl Marx
   b. Talcott Parsons
   c. Émile Durkheim
   d. all of the above

6. The abbreviation "NIMBY" stands for "not in my backyard," a cry often heard when people protest
   a. landfills.
   b. prisons.
   c. nuclear power facilities.
   d. all of the above

7. Which sociologist introduced the concept of culture lag?
   a. William F. Ogburn
   b. Talcott Parsons
   c. Auguste Comte
   d. Thorstein Veblen

8. Which term refers to an immigrant who sustains multiple social relationships that link his or her society of origin with the society of settlement?
   a. transnational
   b. transglobal
   c. global citizen
   d. none of the above

9. Internationally, which langu
   a. English
   b. Russian
   c. German
   d. Japanes

10. Which sociological pers
    economies to maximize their
    a. functionalist
    b. conflict
    c. interactionist
    d. feminist

11. Early evolutionary theorists concluded in a(n) _____ fashion that their own behavior and culture were more advanced than those of earlier civilizations.

12. Talcott Parsons used the term _____ to refer to the increasing complexity of social organization.

13. _____ argued that conflict is a normal and desirable aspect of social change.

14. _____ is information about how to use the material resources of the environment to satisfy human needs and desires.

15. The _____ is the world's largest computer network.

16. The term _____ refers to those who are wary of technological innovations, and who question the incessant expansion of industrialization, the increasing destruction of the natural and agrarian world, and the "throw-it-away" mentality of contemporary capitalism..

17. The nation of _____ saw its Internet usage increase by nearly 400 percent between the years 2000 and 2007.

18. In January 2005 _____ _____ of the Massachusetts Institute of Technology announced his revolutionary idea for a low-cost laptop for the 1.2 billion children of the developing world.

19. The _____ perspective would stress the danger that the most powerful groups in a society will use technology to violate the privacy of the less powerful.

20. Regarding privacy on the Internet, young people who have grown up browsing the Internet seem to accept the existence of _____ and _____ that they may pick up while surfing.

Answers:
1 (b); 2 (b); 3 (b); 4 (d); 5 (a); 6 (d); 7 (a); 8 (b); 9 (a); 10 (a); 11 ethnocentric; 12 differentiation; 13 Marx; 14 Technology; 15 Internet; 16 neo-Luddites; 17 China; 18 Nicholas Negroponte; 19 conflict; 20 cookies; spyware

{ TECHNOLOGY RESOURCES }

Online Learning Center

1. Test your preparation for a final exam with resources in the student center of the Online Learning Center at **www.mhhe.com/schaefer11.** Click on the Final Exam link under Course-Wide Content and answer 75 multiple-choice and true-false questions from throughout the course.

2. One way that the Internet has helped to bring about enormous social changes is through Web sites like Changemakers.net (**www.changemakers.net**), an organization that seeks to promote positive social change, using the Internet as a communication tool.

3. Are you fully aware of the extent to which technology has changed during the past hundred years? The Smithsonian exhibition "America on the Move" (**americanhistory.si.edu/onthemove/exhibition**), which tracks changes in transportation technology since 1876, may hold some surprises for you.

*Note: Although all the URLs listed were current as of the printing of this book, these sites often change. Please check our Web site **(www.mhhe.com/schaefer11)** for updates, hyperlinks, and exercises related to these sites.*

Reel Society Video Clips

Reel Society video clips, which appear on this book's Web site, can be used to spark discussion about the following topic from this chapter:

• Theories of Social Change

glossary

Numbers following the definitions indicate pages where the terms were identified. Consult the index for further page references.

A

Absolute poverty   A minimum level of subsistence that no family should be expected to live below. (226)

Achieved status   A social position that a person attains largely through his or her own efforts. (112, 215)

Activity theory   An interactionist theory of aging that suggests that those elderly people who remain active and socially involved will be best adjusted. (322)

Adoption   In a legal sense, a process that allows for the transfer of the legal rights, responsibilities, and privileges of parenthood to a new legal parent or parents. (352)

Affirmative action   Positive efforts to recruit minority group members or women for jobs, promotions, and educational opportunities. (275, 446)

Ageism   A term coined by Robert N. Butler to refer to prejudice and discrimination based on a person's age. (330)

Agrarian society   The most technologically advanced form of preindustrial society. Members are engaged primarily in the production of food, but increase their crop yields through technological innovations such as the plow. (123)

Alienation   A condition of estrangement or dissociation from the surrounding society. (142, 441)

Amalgamation   The process through which a majority group and a minority group combine to form a new group. (277)

Anomie   Durkheim's term for the loss of direction felt in a society when social control of individual behavior has become ineffective. (12, 194)

Anomie theory of deviance   Robert Merton's theory of deviance as an adaptation of socially prescribed goals or of the means governing their attainment, or both. (195)

Anticipatory socialization   Processes of socialization in which a person "rehearses" for future positions, occupations, and social relationships. (95)

Anti-Semitism   Anti-Jewish prejudice. (286)

Apartheid   A former policy of the South African government, designed to maintain the separation of Blacks and other non-Whites from the dominant Whites. (279)

Applied sociology   The use of the discipline of sociology with the specific intent of yielding practical applications for human behavior and organizations. (21)

Argot   Specialized language used by members of a group or subculture. (73)

Ascribed status   A social position assigned to a person by society without regard for the person's unique talents or characteristics. (111, 215)

Assembling perspective   A theory of collective behavior introduced by McPhail and Miller that seeks to examine how and why people move from different places to a common location. (526)

Assimilation   The process through which a person forsakes his or her own cultural tradition to become part of a different culture. (278)

Authority   Institutionalized power that is recognized by the people over whom it is exercised. (412)

B

Basic sociology   Sociological inquiry conducted with the objective of gaining a more profound knowledge of the fundamental aspects of social phenomena. Also known as *pure sociology.* (22)

Bilateral descent   A kinship system in which both sides of a person's family are regarded as equally important. (344)

Bilingualism   The use of two or more languages in a particular setting, such as the workplace or schoolroom, treating each language as equally legitimate. (77)

Birthrate   The number of live births per 1,000 population in a given year. Also known as the *crude birthrate.* (504)

Black power   A political philosophy, promoted by many younger Blacks in the 1960s, that supported the creation of Black-controlled political and economic institutions. (281)

Borderlands   The area of common culture along the border between Mexico and the United States. (257)

Bourgeoisie   Karl Marx's term for the capitalist class, comprising the owners of the means of production. (219)

Brain drain   The immigration to the United States and other industrialized nations of skilled workers, professionals, and technicians who are desperately needed in their home countries. (461)

Bureaucracy   A component of formal organization that uses rules and hierarchical ranking to achieve efficiency. (141)

Bureaucratization   The process by which a group, organization, or social movement becomes increasingly bureaucratic. (145)

C

Capitalism   An economic system in which the means of production are held largely in private hands and the main incentive for economic activity is the accumulation of profits. (219, 434)

Caste   A hereditary rank, usually religiously dictated, that tends to be fixed and immobile. (216)

Causal logic   The relationship between a condition or variable and a particular consequence, with one event leading to the other. (34)

Census   An enumeration, or counting, of a population. (503)

Charismatic authority   Max Weber's term for power made legitimate by a leader's exceptional personal or emotional appeal to his or her followers. (413)

Class   A group of people who have a similar level of wealth and income. (220)

Class consciousness   In Karl Marx's view, a subjective awareness held by members of a class regarding their common vested interests and need for collective political action to bring about social change. (220)

Classical theory   An approach to the study of formal organizations that views workers as being motivated almost entirely by economic rewards. (145)

Class system   A social ranking based primarily on economic position in which achieved characteristics can influence social mobility. (216)

Clinical sociology   The use of the discipline of sociology with the specific intent of altering social relationships or restructuring social institutions. (21)

Closed system   A social system in which there is little or no possibility of individual social mobility. (232)

Coalition   A temporary or permanent alliance geared toward a common goal. (138)

Code of ethics   The standards of acceptable behavior developed by and for members of a profession. (43)

Cognitive theory of development   Jean Piaget's theory that children's thought progresses through four stages of development. (93)

Cohabitation   The practice of living together as a male–female couple without marrying. (356)

Collective behavior   In the view of sociologist Neil Smelser, the relatively spontaneous and unstructured behavior of a group of people who are reacting to a common influence in an ambiguous situation. (524)

Colonialism   The maintenance of political, social, economic, and cultural dominance over a people by a foreign power for an extended period. (245)

Communism   As an ideal type, an economic system under which all property is communally owned and no social distinctions are made on the basis of people's ability to produce. (436)

Community   A spatial or political unit of social organization that gives people a sense of belonging, based either on shared residence in a particular place or on a common identity. (482)

Concentric-zone theory   A theory of urban growth devised by Ernest Burgess that sees growth in terms of a series of rings radiating from the central business district. (485)

Conflict perspective   A sociological approach that assumes that social behavior is best understood in terms of tension between groups over power or the allocation of resources, including housing, money, access to services, and political representation. (16)

Conformity   Going along with peers—individuals of our own status who have no special right to direct our behavior. (185)

Contact hypothesis   An interactionist perspective which states that in cooperative circumstances, interracial contact between people of equal status will reduce prejudice. (277)

Content analysis   The systematic coding and objective recording of data, guided by some rationale. (43)

Control group   The subjects in an experiment who are not introduced to the independent variable by the researcher. (40)

Control theory   A view of conformity and deviance that suggests that our connection to members of society leads us to systematically conform to society's norms. (189)

Control variable   A factor that is held constant to test the relative impact of an independent variable. (36)

Corporate welfare   Tax breaks, direct payments, and grants that the government makes to corporations. (234)

Correlation   A relationship between two variables in which a change in one coincides with a change in the other. (34)

Correspondence principle   A term used by Bowles and Gintis to refer to the tendency of schools to promote the values expected of individuals in each social class and to prepare students for the types of jobs typically held by members of their class. (397)

Counterculture   A subculture that deliberately opposes certain aspects of the larger culture. (74)

Craze   An exciting mass involvement that lasts for a relatively long period. (530)

Creationism   A literal interpretation of the Bible regarding the creation of humanity and the universe, used to argue that evolution should not be presented as established scientific fact. (384)

Credentialism   An increase in the lowest level of education required to enter a field. (396)

Crime   A violation of criminal law for which some governmental authority applies formal penalties. (200)

Cross-tabulation   A table that shows the relationship between two or more variables. (51)

Crowd   A temporary gathering of people in close proximity who share a common focus or interest. (527)

Cultural relativism   The viewing of people's behavior from the perspective of their own culture. (76)

Cultural transmission   A school of criminology that argues that criminal behavior is learned through social interactions. (196)

Cultural universal   A common practice or belief found in every culture. (59, 366)

Culture   The totality of learned, socially transmitted customs, knowledge, material objects, and behavior. (58)

Culture-bound syndrome   A disease or illness that cannot be understood apart from its specific social context. (456)

Culture lag   A period of maladjustment when the nonmaterial culture is still struggling to adapt to new material conditions. (63, 549)

Culture shock   The feeling of surprise and disorientation that people experience when they encounter cultural practices that are different from their own. (74)

Curanderismo   Latino folk medicine, a form of holistic health care and healing. (465)

Death rate   The number of deaths per 1,000 population in a given year. Also known as the *crude death rate.* (504)

Degradation ceremony   An aspect of the socialization process within some total institutions, in which people are subjected to humiliating rituals. (96)

Deindustrialization   The systematic, widespread withdrawal of investment in basic aspects of productivity, such as factories and plants. (447)

Democracy   In a literal sense, government by the people. (415)

Demographic transition   A term used to describe the change from high birthrates and death rates to low birthrates and death rates. (505)

Demography   The scientific study of population. (502)

Denomination   A large, organized religion that is not officially linked to the state or government. (378)

Dependency theory   An approach that contends that industrialized nations continue to exploit developing countries for their own gain. (246)

Dependent variable   The variable in a causal relationship that is subject to the influence of another variable. (33)

Deviance   Behavior that violates the standards of conduct or expectations of a group or society. (190)

Dictatorship   A government in which one person has nearly total power to make and enforce laws. (415)

Differential association   A theory of deviance proposed by Edwin Sutherland that holds that violation of rules results from exposure to attitudes favorable to criminal acts. (196)

Differential justice   Differences in the way social control is exercised over different groups. (199)

Diffusion   The process by which a cultural item spreads from group to group or society to society. (63)

Disaster   A sudden or disruptive event or set of events that overtaxes a community's resources, so that outside aid is necessary. (527)

Discovery   The process of making known or sharing the existence of an aspect of reality. (59)

Discrimination   The denial of opportunities and equal rights to individuals and groups because of prejudice or other arbitrary reasons. (272)

Disengagement theory   A functionalist theory of aging introduced by Cumming and Henry that suggests that society and the aging individual mutually sever many of their relationships. (321)

Domestic partnership   Two unrelated adults who share a mutually caring relationship, reside together, and agree to be jointly responsible for their dependents, basic living expenses, and other common necessities. (359)

Dominant ideology   A set of cultural beliefs and practices that helps to maintain powerful social, economic, and political interests. (71, 166, 222)

Downsizing   Reductions taken in a company's workforce as part of deindustrialization. (448)

Dramaturgical approach   A view of social interaction, popularized by Erving Goffman, in which people are seen as theatrical performers. (19, 91)

Dyad   A two-member group. (140)

Dysfunction   An element or process of a society that may disrupt the social system or reduce its stability. (16)

Ecclesia   A religious organization that claims to include most or all members of a society and is recognized as the national or official religion. (377)

Economic system   The social institution through which goods and services are produced, distributed, and consumed. (434)

Education   A formal process of learning in which some people consciously teach while others adopt the social role of learner. (392)

Egalitarian family   An authority pattern in which spouses are regarded as equals. (345)

Elite model   A view of society as being ruled by a small group of individuals who share a common set of political and economic interests. (419)

Emergent-norm perspective   A theory of collective behavior proposed by Turner and Killian that holds that a collective definition of appropriate and inappropriate behavior emerges during episodes of collective behavior. (525)

Endogamy   The restriction of mate selection to people within the same group. (348)

Environmental justice   A legal strategy based on claims that racial minorities are subjected disproportionately to environmental hazards. (513)

Equilibrium model   Talcott Parsons's functionalist view that society tends toward a state of stability or balance. (547)

Established sect   J. Milton Yinger's term for a religious group that is the outgrowth of a sect, yet remains isolated from society. (379)

Estate system   A system of stratification under which peasants were required to work land leased to them by nobles in exchange for military protection and other services. Also known as *feudalism.* (216)

Esteem   The reputation that a specific person has earned within an occupation. (223)

Ethnic group   A group that is set apart from others primarily because of its national origin or distinctive cultural patterns. (268)

Ethnocentrism   The tendency to assume that one's own culture and way of life represent the norm or are superior to all others. (75, 271)

Ethnography   The study of an entire social setting through extended systematic observation. (39)

Euthanasia   The act of bringing about the death of a hopelessly ill and suffering person in a relatively quick and painless way for reasons of mercy. (332)

Evolutionary theory   A theory of social change that holds that society is moving in a definite direction. (546)

Exogamy   The requirement that people select a mate outside certain groups. (348)

Experiment   An artificially created situation that allows a researcher to manipulate variables. (40)

Experimental group   The subjects in an experiment who are exposed to an independent variable introduced by a researcher. (40)

Exploitation theory   A Marxist theory that views racial subordination in the United States as a manifestation of the class system inherent in capitalism. (276)

Expressiveness   Concern for the maintenance of harmony and the internal emotional affairs of the family. (302)

Extended family   A family in which relatives—such as grandparents, aunts, or uncles—live in the same home as parents and their children. (340)

Face-work   A term used by Erving Goffman to refer to the efforts people make to maintain the proper image and avoid public embarrassment. (91)

Fad   A temporary pattern of behavior that involves large numbers of people and is independent of preceding trends. (529)

False consciousness   A term used by Karl Marx to describe an attitude held by members of a class that does not accurately reflect their objective position. (220, 534)

Familism   Pride in the extended family, expressed through the maintenance of close ties and strong obligations to kinfolk outside the immediate family. (351)

Family   A set of people related by blood, marriage or some other agreed-upon relationship, or adoption, who share the primary responsibility for reproduction and caring for members of society. (340)

Fashion   A pleasurable mass involvement that has a line of historical continuity. (529)

Feminism   The belief in social, economic, and political equality for women. (309)

Feminist view   A sociological approach that views inequity in gender as central to all behavior and organization. (17)

Fertility   The level of reproduction in a society. (502)

Folkway   A norm governing everyday behavior whose violation raises comparatively little concern. (68)

Force   The actual or threatened use of coercion to impose one's will on others. (412)

Formal norm   A norm that has been written down and that specifies strict punishments for violators. (68)

Formal organization   A group designed for a special purpose and structured for maximum efficiency. (141)

Formal social control   Social control that is carried out by authorized agents, such as police officers, judges, school administrators, and employers. (187)

Functionalist perspective   A sociological approach that emphasizes the way in which the parts of a society are structured to maintain its stability. (15)

Fundamentalism   Rigid adherence to fundamental religious doctrines, often accompanied by a literal application of scripture or historical beliefs to today's world. (375)

Gatekeeping   The process by which a relatively small number of people in the media industry control what material eventually reaches the audience. (165)

Gemeinschaft   A term used by Ferdinand Tönnies to describe a close-knit community, often found in rural areas, in which strong personal bonds unite members. (121)

Gender role   Expectations regarding the proper behavior, attitudes, and activities of males or females. (97, 298)

Generalized other   A term used by George Herbert Mead to refer to the attitudes, viewpoints, and expectations of society as a whole that a child takes into account in his or her behavior. (90)

Genocide   The deliberate, systematic killing of an entire people or nation. (277)

Gentrification   The resettlement of low-income city neighborhoods by prosperous families and business firms. (495)

Gerontology   The scientific study of the sociological and psychological aspects of aging and the problems of the aged. (321)

Gesellschaft   A term used by Ferdinand Tönnies to describe a community, often urban, that is large and impersonal, with little commitment to the group or consensus on values. (122)

Glass ceiling   An invisible barrier that blocks the promotion of a qualified individual in a work environment because of the individual's gender, race, or ethnicity. (272, 308)

Globalization   The worldwide integration of government policies, cultures, social movements, and financial markets through trade and the exchange of ideas. (22, 246)

Goal displacement   Overzealous conformity to official regulations of a bureaucracy. (142)

Gross national product (GNP)   The value of a nation's goods and services. (248)

Group   Any number of people with similar norms, values, and expectations who interact with one another on a regular basis. (117, 136)

Groupthink   Uncritical acceptance of or conformity to the prevailing viewpoint. (141)

Growth rate   The difference between births and deaths, plus the difference between immigrants and emigrants, per 1,000 population. (504)

Hate crime   A criminal offense committed because of the offender's bias against a race, religion, ethnic group, national origin, or sexual orientation. (272)

Hawthorne effect   The unintended influence that observers of experiments can have on their subjects. (40)

Health   As defined by the World Health Organization, a state of complete physical, mental, and social well-being, and not merely the absence of disease and infirmity. (456)

Hidden curriculum   Standards of behavior that are deemed proper by society and are taught subtly in schools. (395)

Holistic medicine   Therapies in which the health care practitioner considers the person's physical, mental, emotional, and spiritual characteristics. (469)

Homogamy   The conscious or unconscious tendency to select a mate with personal characteristics similar to one's own. (348)

Homophobia   Fear of and prejudice against homosexuality. (299)

Horizontal mobility   The movement of an individual from one social position to another of the same rank. (232)

Horticultural society   A preindustrial society in which people plant seeds and crops rather than merely subsist on available foods. (123)

Hospice care   Treatment of the terminally ill in their own homes, or in special hospital units or other facilities, with the goal of helping them to die easily, without pain. (327)

Human ecology   An area of study that is concerned with the interrelationships between people and their environment. (484, 512)

Human relations approach   An approach to the study of formal organizations that emphasizes the role of people, communication, and participation in a bureaucracy and tends to focus on the informal structure of the organization. (145)

Human rights   Universal moral rights possessed by all people because they are human. (259)

Hunting-and-gathering society   A preindustrial society in which people rely on whatever foods and fibers are readily available in order to survive. (123)

Hypothesis   A speculative statement about the relationship between two or more variables. (33)

Ideal type   A construct or model for evaluating specific cases. (13, 141)

Impression management   A term used by Erving Goffman to refer to the altering of the presentation of the self in order to create distinctive appearances and satisfy particular audiences. (91)

Incest taboo   The prohibition of sexual relationships between certain culturally specified relatives. (348)

Incidence   The number of new cases of a specific disorder that occur within a given population during a stated period. (463)

Income   Salaries and wages. (214)

Independent variable   The variable in a causal relationship that causes or influences a change in a second variable. (33)

Index crimes   The eight types of crime reported annually by the FBI in the *Uniform Crime Reports:* murder, rape, robbery, assault, burglary, theft, motor vehicle theft, and arson. (200)

Industrial city   A relatively large city characterized by open competition, an open class system, and elaborate specialization in the manufacturing of goods. (483)

Industrial society   A society that depends on mechanization to produce its goods and services. (124, 434)

Infant mortality rate   The number of deaths of infants under one year old per 1,000 live births in a given year. (504)

Influence   The exercise of power through a process of persuasion. (412)

Informal economy   Transfers of money, goods, or services that are not reported to the government. (437)

Informal norm   A norm that is generally understood but not precisely recorded. (68)

Informal social control   Social control that is carried out casually by ordinary people through such means as laughter, smiles, and ridicule. (187)

In-group   Any group or category to which people feel they belong. (137)

Innovation   The process of introducing a new idea or object to a culture through discovery or invention. (59)

Institutional discrimination   The denial of opportunities and equal rights to individuals and groups that results from the normal operations of a society. (274, 304)

Instrumentality   An emphasis on tasks, a focus on more distant goals, and a concern for the external relationship between one's family and other social institutions. (302)

Intelligent design (ID)   The idea that life is so complex, it could only have been created only by intelligent design. (384)

Interactionist perspective   A sociological approach that generalizes about everyday forms of social interaction in order to explain society as a whole. (18)

Intergenerational mobility   Changes in the social position of children relative to their parents. (232)

Interview   A face-to-face or telephone questioning of a respondent to obtain desired information. (37)

Intragenerational mobility   Changes in social position within a person's adult life. (232)

Invention   The combination of existing cultural items into a form that did not exist before. (59)

Iron law of oligarchy   A principle of organizational life developed by Robert Michels, under which even a democratic organization will eventually develop into a bureaucracy ruled by a few individuals. (145)

Kinship   The state of being related to others. (341)

Labeling theory   An approach to deviance that attempts to explain why certain people are viewed as deviants while others engaged in the same behavior are not. (197)

Labor union   Organized workers who share either the same skill or the same employer. (150)

Laissez-faire   A form of capitalism under which people compete freely, with minimal government intervention in the economy. (434)

Language   An abstract system of word meanings and symbols for all aspects of culture; includes gestures and other nonverbal communication. (65)

Latent function   An unconscious or unintended function that may reflect hidden purposes. (16)

Law   Governmental social control. (68, 189)

Liberation theology   Use of a church, primarily Roman Catholicism, in a political effort to eliminate poverty, discrimination, and other forms of injustice from a secular society. (373)

Life chances   Max Weber's term for the opportunities people have to provide themselves with material goods, positive living conditions, and favorable life experiences. (230)

Life course approach   A research orientation in which sociologists and other social scientists look closely at the social factors that influence people throughout their lives, from birth to death. (94)

Life expectancy   The median number of years a person can be expected to live under current mortality conditions. (504)

Looking-glass self   A concept used by Charles Horton Cooley that emphasizes the self as the product of our social interactions. (89)

Luddites   Rebellious craft workers in nineteenth-century England who destroyed new factory machinery as part of their resistance to the industrial revolution. (549)

Machismo   A sense of virility, personal worth, and pride in one's maleness. (351)

Macrosociology   Sociological investigation that concentrates on large-scale phenomena or entire civilizations. (15)

Manifest function   An open, stated, and conscious function. (16)

Mass media   Print and electronic means of communication that carry messages to widespread audiences. (158)

Master status   A status that dominates others and thereby determines a person's general position in society. (112)

Material culture   The physical or technological aspects of our daily lives. (63)

Matriarchy   A society in which women dominate in family decision making. (345)

Matrilineal descent   A kinship system in which only the mother's relatives are significant. (344)

Matrix of domination   The cumulative impact of oppression because of race, gender, and class, as well as religion, sexual orientation, disability, and age. (311)

McDonaldization   The process by which the principles of the fast-food restaurant are coming to dominate more and more sectors of American society as well as of the rest of the world. (136)

Mean   A number calculated by adding a series of values and then dividing by the number of values. (50)

Mechanical solidarity   A collective consciousness that emphasizes group solidarity, characteristic of societies with minimal division of labor. (121)

Median   The midpoint or number that divides a series of values into two groups of equal numbers of values. (50)

Megalopolis   A densely populated area containing two or more cities and their suburbs. (484)

Mental illness   A disorder of the brain that disrupts a person's thinking, feeling, and ability to interact with others. (471)

Microfinancing   Lending small sums of money to the poor so they can work their way out of poverty. (445)

Microsociology   Sociological investigation that stresses the study of small groups, often through experimental means. (15)

Midlife crisis   A stressful period of self-evaluation that begins at about age 40. (324)

Migration   The relatively permanent movement of people, with the purpose of changing their place of residence. (509)

Minority group   A subordinate group whose members have significantly less control or power over their own lives than the members of a dominant or majority group have over theirs. (268)

Mode   The single most common value in a series of scores. (50)

Model or **ideal minority**   A minority group that despite past prejudice and discrimination, succeeds economically, socially, and educationally without resorting to confrontations with Whites. (282)

Modernization   The far-reaching process by which periphery nations move from traditional or less developed institutions to those characteristic of more developed societies. (249)

Modernization theory   A functionalist approach that proposes that modernization and development will gradually improve the lives of people in developing nations. (249)

Monarchy   A form of government headed by a single member of a royal family, usually a king, queen, or some other hereditary ruler. (414)

Monogamy   A form of marriage in which one woman and one man are married only to each other. (341)

Monopoly   Control of a market by a single business firm. (435)

Morbidity rate   The incidence of disease in a given population. (463)

Mores   Norms deemed highly necessary to the welfare of a society. (68)

Mortality rate   The incidence of death in a given population. (463)

Multinational corporation   A commercial organization that is headquartered in one country but does business throughout the world. (246)

Multiple-nuclei theory   A theory of urban growth developed by Harris and Ullman that views growth as emerging from many centers of development, each of which reflects a particular urban need or activity. (485)

Narcotizing dysfunction   The phenomenon in which the media provide such massive amounts of coverage that the audience becomes numb and fails to act on the information, regardless of how compelling the issue. (164)

Natural science   The study of the physical features of nature and the ways in which they interact and change. (5)

Neocolonialism   Continuing dependence of former colonies on foreign countries. (245)

Net neutrality   The principle that the government should remain nonselective or neutral toward online content. (128)

New religious movement (NRM) or **cult**   A small, secretive religious group that represents either a new religion or a major innovation of an existing faith. (380)

New social movement   An organized collective activity that addresses values and social identities, as well as improvements in the quality of life. (534)

New urban sociology   An approach to urbanization that considers the interplay of local, national, and worldwide forces and their effect on local space, with special emphasis on the impact of global economic activity. (487)

Nonmaterial culture   Ways of using material objects, as well as customs, beliefs, philosophies, governments, and patterns of communication. (63)

Nonperiodic assembly   A nonrecurring gathering of people that often results from word-of-mouth information. (526)

Nonverbal communication   The sending of messages through the use of gestures, facial expressions, and postures. (18)

Norm   An established standard of behavior maintained by a society. (67)

Nuclear family   A married couple and their unmarried children living together. (340)

Obedience   Compliance with higher authorities in a hierarchical structure. (185)

Objective method   A technique for measuring social class that assigns individuals to classes on the basis of criteria such as occupation, education, income, and place of residence. (223)

Observation   A research technique in which an investigator collects information through direct participation and/or by closely watching a group or community. (39)

Offshoring   The transfer of work to foreign contractors. (448)

Oligarchy   A form of government in which a few individuals rule. (414)

Open system   A social system in which the position of each individual is influenced by his or her achieved status. (232)

Operational definition   An explanation of an abstract concept that is specific enough to allow a researcher to assess the concept. (33)

Opinion leader   Someone who influences the opinions and decisions of others through day-to-day personal contact and communication. (173)

Organic solidarity A collective consciousness that rests on mutual interdependence, characteristic of societies with a complex division of labor. (121)

Organized crime The work of a group that regulates relations between criminal enterprises involved in illegal activities, including prostitution, gambling, and the smuggling and sale of illegal drugs. (201)

Out-group A group or category to which people feel they do not belong. (137)

Panic A fearful arousal or collective flight based on a generalized belief that may or may not be accurate. (530)

Patriarchy A society in which men dominate in family decision making. (345)

Patrilineal descent A kinship system in which only the father's relatives are significant. (344)

Peace The absence of war or, more broadly, a proactive effort to develop cooperative relations among nations. (422)

Percentage A portion of 100. (50)

Periodic assembly A recurring, relatively routine gathering of people, such as a college class. (526)

Personality A person's typical patterns of attitudes, needs, characteristics, and behavior. (86)

Peter principle A principle of organizational life, originated by Laurence J. Peter, according to which every employee within a hierarchy tends to rise to his or her level of incompetence. (143)

Pluralism Mutual respect for one another's cultures among the various groups in a society, which allows minorities to express their own cultures without experiencing prejudice. (279)

Pluralist model A view of society in which many competing groups within the community have access to government, so that no single group is dominant. (420)

Political system The social institution that is founded on a recognized set of procedures for implementing and achieving society's goals. (412)

Politics In Harold Lasswell's words, "who gets what, when, and how." (412)

Polyandry A form of polygamy in which a woman may have more than one husband at the same time. (341)

Polygamy A form of marriage in which an individual may have several husbands or wives simultaneously. (341)

Polygyny A form of polygamy in which a man may have more than one wife at the same time. (341)

Population pyramid A special type of bar chart that shows the distribution of a population by gender and age. (507)

Postindustrial city A city in which global finance and the electronic flow of information dominate the economy. (483)

Postindustrial society A society whose economic system is engaged primarily in the processing and control of information. (124)

Postmodern society A technologically sophisticated society that is preoccupied with consumer goods and media images. (125)

Power The ability to exercise one's will over others. (220, 412)

Power elite A term used by C. Wright Mills to refer to a small group of military, industrial, and government leaders who control the fate of the United States. (419)

Preindustrial city A city of only a few thousand people that is characterized by a relatively closed class system and limited mobility. (482)

Prejudice A negative attitude toward an entire category of people, often an ethnic or racial minority. (271)

Prestige The respect and admiration that an occupation holds in a society. (223)

Prevalence The total number of cases of a specific disorder that exist at a given time. (463)

Primary group A small group characterized by intimate, face-to-face association and cooperation. (136)

Profane The ordinary and commonplace elements of life, as distinguished from the sacred. (366)

Professional criminal A person who pursues crime as a day-to-day occupation, developing skilled techniques and enjoying a certain degree of status among other criminals. (201)

Proletariat Karl Marx's term for the working class in a capitalist society. (219)

Protestant ethic Max Weber's term for the disciplined work ethic, this-worldly concerns, and rational orientation to life emphasized by John Calvin and his followers. (373)

Public A dispersed group of people, not necessarily in contact with one another, who share an interest in an issue. (531)

Public opinion Expressions of attitudes on matters of public policy that are communicated to decision makers. (531)

Qualitative research Research that relies on what is seen in field or naturalistic settings more than on statistical data. (39)

Quantitative research Research that collects and reports data primarily in numerical form. (39)

Quasi-religion A scholarly category that includes organizations that may see themselves as religious but are seen by others as "sort of religious." (381)

Questionnaire A printed or written form used to obtain information from a respondent. (37)

Quinceañera Among Latinos, a celebration of a young woman's fifteenth birthday. (287)

Racial group A group that is set apart from others because of physical differences that have taken on social significance. (268)

Racial profiling Any arbitrary action initiated by an authority based on race, ethnicity, or national origin rather than on a person's behavior. (276)

Racism The belief that one race is supreme and all others are innately inferior. (272)

Random sample A sample for which every member of an entire population has the same chance of being selected. (35)

Rational-legal authority Power made legitimate by law. (413)

Reference group Any group that individuals use as a standard for evaluating themselves and their own behavior. (138)

Relative deprivation The conscious feeling of a negative discrepancy between legitimate expectations and present actualities. (533)

Relative poverty A floating standard of deprivation by which people at the bottom of a society, whatever their lifestyles, are judged to be disadvantaged *in comparison with the nation as a whole*. (226)

Reliability The extent to which a measure produces consistent results. (35, 405)

Religion According to Émile Durkheim, a unified system of beliefs and practices relative to sacred things. (366)

Religious belief A statement to which members of a particular religion adhere. (375)

Religious experience The feeling or perception of being in direct contact with the ultimate reality, such as a divine being, or of being overcome with religious emotion. (376)

Religious ritual A practice required or expected of members of a faith. (376)

Remittances The monies that immigrants return to their families of origin. Also called *migradollars*. (259)

Representative democracy A form of government in which certain individuals are selected to speak for the people. (415)

Research design A detailed plan or method for obtaining data scientifically. (37)

Resocialization The process of discarding former behavior patterns and accepting new ones as part of a transition in one's life. (95)

Resource mobilization The ways in which a social movement utilizes such resources as money, political influence, access to the media, and personnel. (533)

Rite of passage A ritual marking the symbolic transition from one social position to another. (93)

Role conflict The situation that occurs when incompatible expectations arise from two or more social positions held by the same person. (116)

Role exit The process of disengagement from a role that is central to one's self-identity in order to establish a new role and identity. (116)

Role strain The difficulty that arises when the same social position imposes conflicting demands and expectations. (116)

Role taking The process of mentally assuming the perspective of another and responding from that imagined viewpoint. (90)

Routine activities theory The notion that criminal victimization increases when motivated offenders and suitable targets converge. (196)

Rumor A piece of information gathered informally that is used to interpret an ambiguous situation. (531)

Sacred Elements beyond everyday life that inspire awe, respect, and even fear. (366)

Sample A selection from a larger population that is statistically representative of that population. (35)

Sanction A penalty or reward for conduct concerning a social norm. (69, 185)

Sandwich generation The generation of adults who simultaneously try to meet the competing needs of their parents and their children. (324)

Sapir-Whorf hypothesis A hypothesis concerning the role of language in shaping our interpretation of reality. It holds that language is culturally determined. (65)

Science The body of knowledge obtained by methods based on systematic observation. (5)

Scientific management approach Another name for the classical theory of formal organizations. (145)

Scientific method A systematic, organized series of steps that ensures maximum objectivity and consistency in researching a problem. (32)

Secondary analysis A variety of research techniques that make use of previously collected and publicly accessible information and data. (41)

Secondary group A formal, impersonal group in which there is little social intimacy or mutual understanding. (136)

Second shift The double burden—work outside the home followed by child care and housework—that many women face and few men share equitably. (309)

Sect A relatively small religious group that has broken away from some other religious organization to renew what it considers the original vision of the faith. (379)

Secularization The process through which religion's influence on other social institutions diminishes. (366)

Segregation The physical separation of two groups of people in terms of residence, workplace, and social events; often imposed on a minority group by a dominant group. (279)

Self According to George Herbert Mead, a distinct identity that sets us apart from others. (89)

Serial monogamy A form of marriage in which a person may have several spouses in his or her lifetime, but only one spouse at a time. (341)

Sexism The ideology that one sex is superior to the other. (304)

Sexual harassment Behavior that occurs when work benefits are made contingent on sexual favors (as a quid pro quo), or when touching, lewd comments, or the exhibition of pornographic material creates a "hostile environment" in the workplace. (305)

Sick role Societal expectations about the attitudes and behavior of a person viewed as being ill. (457)

Significant other A term used by George Herbert Mead to refer to an individual who is most important in the development of the self, such as a parent, friend, or teacher. (91)

Single-parent family A family in which only one parent is present to care for the children. (353)

Slavery A system of enforced servitude in which some people are owned by other people. (215)

Small group A group small enough for all members to interact simultaneously—that is, to talk with one another or at least be well acquainted. (138)

Social change Significant alteration over time in behavior patterns and culture, including norms and values. (546)

Social constructionist perspective An approach to deviance that emphasizes the role of culture in the creation of the deviant identity. (197)

Social control The techniques and strategies for preventing deviant human behavior in any society. (184)

Social epidemiology The study of the distribution of disease, impairment, and general health status across a population. (463)

Social inequality A condition in which members of society have different amounts of wealth, prestige, or power. (22, 214)

Social institution An organized pattern of beliefs and behavior centered on basic social needs. (119)

Social interaction The ways in which people respond to one another. (110)

Socialism An economic system under which the means of production and distribution are collectively owned. (436)

Socialization The lifelong process in which people learn the attitudes, values, and behaviors appropriate for members of a particular culture. (86)

Social mobility Movement of individuals or groups from one position in a society's stratification system to another. (232)

Social movement An organized collective activity to bring about or resist fundamental change in an existing group or society. (532)

Social network A series of social relationships that links a person directly to others, and through them indirectly to still more people. (117)

Social role A set of expectations for people who occupy a given social position or status. (113)

Social science The study of the social features of humans and the ways in which they interact and change. (5)

Social structure The way in which a society is organized into predictable relationships. (110)

Societal-reaction approach Another name for *labeling theory*. (197)

Society A fairly large number of people who live in the same territory, are relatively independent of people outside it, and participate in a common culture. (58)

Sociobiology The systematic study of how biology affects human social behavior. (63)

Sociocultural evolution Long-term trends in societies resulting from the interplay of continuity, innovation, and selection. (123)

Sociological imagination An awareness of the relationship between an individual and the wider society, both today and in the past. (4)

Sociology The scientific study of social behavior and human groups. (4)

Squatter settlement An area occupied by the very poor on the fringe of a city, in which housing is constructed by the settlers themselves from discarded material. (488)

Status A term used by sociologists to refer to any of the full range of socially defined positions within a large group or society. (111)

Status group A term used by Max Weber to refer to people who have the same prestige or lifestyle, independent of their class positions. (220)

Stereotype An unreliable generalization about all members of a group that does not recognize individual differences within the group. (167, 270)

Stigma   A label used to devalue members of certain social groups. (191)

Stratification   A structured ranking of entire groups of people that perpetuates unequal economic rewards and power in a society. (214)

Subculture   A segment of society that shares a distinctive pattern of mores, folkways, and values that differs from the pattern of the larger society. (73)

Suburb   According to the Census Bureau, any territory within a metropolitan area that is not included in the central city. (490)

Survey   A study, generally in the form of an interview or questionnaire, that provides researchers with information about how people think and act. (37)

Symbol   A gesture, object, or word that forms the basis of human communication. (89)

Symbolic ethnicity   An ethnic identity that emphasizes concerns such as ethnic food or political issues rather than deeper ties to one's ethnic heritage. (288)

Teacher-expectancy effect   The impact that a teacher's expectations about a student's performance may have on the student's actual achievements. (398)

Technology   Cultural information about the ways in which the material resources of the environment may be used to satisfy human needs and desires. (63, 123, 551)

Telecommuter   An employee who works full-time or part-time at home rather than in an outside office, and who is linked to supervisor and colleagues through computer terminals, phone lines, and fax machines. (148)

Terrorism   The use or threat of violence against random or symbolic targets in pursuit of political aims. (423)

Theory   In sociology, a set of statements that seeks to explain problems, actions, or behavior. (10)

Total fertility rate (TFR)   The average number of children born alive to any woman, assuming that she conforms to current fertility rates. (504)

Total institution   A term coined by Erving Goffman to refer to an institution that regulates all aspects of a person's life under a single authority, such as a prison, the military, a mental hospital, or a convent. (95)

Totalitarianism   Virtually complete government control and surveillance over all aspects of a society's social and political life. (415)

Tracking   The practice of placing students in specific curriculum groups on the basis of their test scores and other criteria. (396)

Traditional authority   Legitimate power conferred by custom and accepted practice. (413)

Trained incapacity   The tendency of workers in a bureaucracy to become so specialized that they develop blind spots and fail to notice obvious problems. (142)

Transnational   An immigrant who sustains multiple social relationships that link his or her society of origin with the society of settlement. (557)

Transnational crime   Crime that occurs across multiple national borders. (202)

Triad   A three-member group. (140)

Underclass   The long-term poor who lack training and skills. (229)

Urban ecology   An area of study that focuses on the interrelationships between people and their environment in urban areas. (484)

Urbanism   A term used by Louis Wirth to describe distinctive patterns of social behavior evident among city residents. (484)

Validity   The degree to which a measure or scale truly reflects the phenomenon under study. (35, 405)

Value   A collective conception of what is considered good, desirable, and proper—or bad, undesirable, and improper—in a culture. (70)

Value-added model   A theory of collective behavior proposed by Neil Smelser to explain how broad social conditions are transformed in a definite pattern into some form of collective behavior. (525)

Value neutrality   Max Weber's term for objectivity of sociologists in the interpretation of data. (45)

Variable   A measurable trait or characteristic that is subject to change under different conditions. (33)

Verstehen   The German word for "understanding" or "insight"; used by Max Weber to stress the need for sociologists to take into account the subjective meanings people attach to their actions. (12)

Vertical mobility   The movement of an individual from one social position to another of a different rank. (232)

Vested interests   Veblen's term for those people or groups who will suffer in the event of social change, and who have a stake in maintaining the status quo. (548)

Victimization survey   A questionnaire or interview given to a sample of the population to determine whether people have been victims of crime. (204)

Victimless crime   A term used by sociologists to describe the willing exchange among adults of widely desired, but illegal, goods and services. (200)

Visitability   The accessibility of private homes to visitors with disabilities. (539)

Vital statistics   Records of births, deaths, marriages, and divorces gathered through a registration system maintained by governmental units. (503)

Voluntary association   An organization established on the basis of common interest, whose members volunteer or even pay to participate. (146)

War   Conflict between organizations that possess trained combat forces equipped with deadly weapons. (421)

Wealth   An inclusive term encompassing all a person's material assets, including land, stocks, and other types of property. (214)

White-collar crime   Illegal acts committed by affluent, "respectable" individuals in the course of business activities. (201)

World systems analysis   Immanuel Wallerstein's view of the global economic system as one divided between certain industrialized nations that control wealth and developing countries that are controlled and exploited. (245, 487)

Zero population growth (ZPG)   The state of a population in which the number of births plus immigrants equals the number of deaths plus emigrants. (509)

references

ABC News. 2007. "Iraq: Where Things Stand: March 19, 2007." Accessed March 30 (http://abc.go.com/).

Abercrombie, Nicholas, Bryan S. Turner, and Stephen Hill, eds. 1990. *Dominant Ideologies.* Cambridge, MA: Unwin Hyman.

———, Stephen Hill, and Bryan S. Turner. 1980. *The Dominant Ideology Thesis.* London: George Allen and Unwin.

Aberle, David E., A. K. Cohen, A. K. Davis, M. J. Leng, Jr., and F. N. Sutton. 1950. "The Functional Prerequisites of a Society." *Ethics* 60 (January): 100–111.

Abrahamson, Mark. 1978. *Functionalism.* Englewood Cliffs, NJ: Prentice Hall.

Abramovitz, Janet N. 2001a. "Averting Unnatural Disasters." Pp. 123–142 in *State of the World 2001,* edited by Lester R. Brown, Christopher Flavin, and Hilary French. New York: Norton.

———. 2001b. *Unnatural Disasters.* Washington DC: Worldwatch Institute.

Abramson, Jeffrey. 1994. *We, the Jury. The Jury System and the Ideal of Democracy.* New York: Basic Books.

Acharya, Menna. 2000. *Labor Market Developments and Poverty: With Focus on Economic Opportunities for Women.* Kathmandu, Nepal: Tanka Prasad Acharya Foundation/FES.

Acosta, R. Vivian, and Linda Jean Carpenter. 2001. "Women in Intercollegiate Sport: A Longitudinal Study: 1977–1998." Pp. 302–308 in *Sport in Contemporary Society: An Anthology,* 6th ed., edited by D. Stanley Eitzen. New York: Worth.

Adam, Barry D. 1995. *The Rise of a Gay and Lesbian Movement.* Rev. ed. New York: Twayne.

Adams, Jimi. 2007. "Stained Glass Makes the Ceiling Visible: Organizational Opposition to Women in Congregational Leadership." *Gender and Society* 21 (February):80–115.

Addams, Jane. 1910. *Twenty Years at Hull-House.* New York: Macmillan.

———. 1930. *The Second Twenty Years at Hull-House.* New York: Macmillan.

Adler, Freda. 1975. *Sisters in Crime: The Rise of the New Female Criminal.* New York: McGraw-Hill.

———, Gerhard O. W. Mueller, and William S. Laufer. 2004. *Criminology and the Criminal Justice System.* 5th ed. New York: McGraw-Hill.

Adler, Patricia A. 1993. *Wheeling and Dealing: An Ethnography of an Upper-Level Drug Dealing and Smuggling Community.* 2d ed. New York: Columbia University Press.

———, and Peter Adler. 1991. *Backboards and Blackboards.* New York: Columbia University Press.

———, and ———. 1998. *Peer Power: Preadolescent Culture and Identity.* New Brunswick, NJ: Rutgers University Press.

———, and ———. 2003. "The Promise and Pitfalls of Going into the Field." *Contexts* (Spring):41–47.

———, and ———. 2004. *Paradise Laborers: Hotel Work in the Global Economy.* Ithaca, NY: Cornell University Press.

———, and ———. 2005. "Self-Injurers as Loners: The Social Organization of Solitary Deviance." *Deviant Behavior.*

———, ———, and John M. Johnson. 1992. "Street Corner Society Revisited." *Journal of Contemporary Ethnography* 21 (April):3–10.

Adler, Patti, and Peter Adler. 2008. "Of Rhetoric and Representation: The Four Faces of Ethnography." *Sociological Quarterly* (No. 1).

AFL-CIO. 2001. *More Workers Are Choosing a Voice at Work.* Accessed April 18 (www.aflcio.org/ voiceatwork/morejoin/htm).

Aguirre, Benigno E., E. L. Quarantelli, and Jorge L. Mendoza. 1988. "The Collective Behavior of Fads: The Characteristics, Effects, and Career of Streaking." *American Sociological Review* 53 (August):569–584.

Alain, Michel. 1985. "An Empirical Validation of Relative Deprivation." *Human Relations* 38 (8):739–749.

Alba, Richard D. 1990. *Ethnic Identity: The Transformation of White America.* New Haven, CT: Yale University Press.

Albas, Daniel, and Cheryl Albas. 1988. "Aces and Bombers: The Post-Exam Impression Management Strategies of Students." *Symbolic Interaction* 11 (Fall):289–302.

Albiniak, P. 2000. "TV's Drug Deal." *Broadcasting and Cable,* January 17, pp. 3, 148.

Albom, Mitch. 1997. *Tuesdays with Morrie.* New York: Doubleday.

Albrecht, Gary L. 1995. "Review of Disability Laws, Enabling Acts: Disability Rights in Britain and America." *Contemporary Sociology* 24 (5):627–629.

———. 1997. "Disability Is Area Rich with Sociological Opportunity." *Footnotes* 25 (December): 6.

———. 2004. "Disability: Sociological Perspectives." Pp. 3710–3713 in *International Encyclopedia of the Social and Behavioral Sciences,* edited by Neil J. Smelser and Paul B. Baltes. New York: Elsevier.

———, ed. 2005. *Encyclopedia of Disability.* Thousand Oaks, CA: Sage.

Alfino, Mark, John S. Caputo, and Robin Wynyard. 1998. *McDonaldization Revisited: Critical Essays on Consumer Culture.* Westport, CT: Praeger.

al-Jadda, Souheila. 2006. "A Veil Doesn't Mean 'Oppressed.'" *USA Today,* June 22, p. 13A.

Al Jazeera. 2006. Home page. Accessed January 30 (http://english.alijeera.net/HomePage).

Allen, Bem P. 1978. *Social Behavior: Fact and Falsehood.* Chicago: Nelson-Hall.

Allen, John L. 2007. *Student Atlas of World Politics.* 7th ed. New York: McGraw-Hill.

Allport, Gordon W. 1979. *The Nature of Prejudice.* 25th anniversary ed. Reading, MA: Addison-Wesley.

Alvord, Lori Arviso, and Elizabeth Cohen Van Pelt. 1999. *The Scalpel and the Silver Bear.* New York: Bantam.

Alwin, Duane F. 2002. "Generations X, Y, and Z: Are They Changing America?" *Contexts* (Fall/ Winter):42–51.

Alzheimer's Association. 2007. *Alzheimer's Disease Facts and Figures.* Chicago: Alzheimer's Association.

Amato, Paul R. 2001. "What Children Learn from Divorce." *Population Today,* January, pp. 1, 4.

———, and Alan Booth. 1997. *A Generation at Risk.* Cambridge, MA: Harvard University Press.

———, and Juliana M. Sobolewski. 2001. "The Effects of Divorce and Marital Discord on Adult Children's Psychological Well-Being." *American Sociological Review* 66 (December):900–921.

American Academy of Cosmetic Surgery. 2007. "2006 Procedural Survey Shows 3% Increases in Men Seeking Cosmetic Surgery." Accessed February 17 (www.medicalnewstoday.com).

American Bar Association. 1997. *Section of the Individual Rights and Responsibilities: Section of Litigation (Capital Punishment).* Chicago: Division for Policy Administration, ABA.

American Community Survey. 2005. *American Community Survey 2004.*

———. 2006. *American Community Survey 2005.* Accessed at www.census.gov.

———. 2007a. *The American Community—Asians: 2004.* Issued February 2004. Washington, DC: U.S. Government Printing Office.

———. 2007b. *The American Community—Blacks: 2004.* Issued February 2004. Washington, DC: U.S. Government Printing Office.

———. 2007c. *The American Community—Hispanics: 2004.* Issued February 2004. Washington, DC: U.S. Government Printing Office.

American Federation of Teachers. 2007. *Survey and Analysis of Teacher Salary Trends 2005.* Washington, DC: AFT.

American Jewish Committee. 2001. "2000 Annual Survey of American Jewish Opinion." Accessed October 25 (www.ajc.org/pre/survey2000.htm).

American Lung Association. 2003. "Scenesmoking." Accessed December 19 (www.scenesmoking.org).

American Sociological Association. 1997. *Code of Ethics.* Washington, DC: American Sociological Association. Available at www.asanet. org/ members/ecoderev.html.

———. 2001. *Data Brief: Profile of ASA Membership.* Washington, DC: American Sociological Association.

———. 2005. "Need Today's Data Yesterday." Accessed December 17 (www.asanet.org).

———. 2006a. *Careers in Sociology with an Undergraduate Degree in Sociology.* 7th ed. Washington, DC: ASA.

———. 2006b. *A National Survey of Seniors Majoring in Sociology.* Washington, DC: ASA.

———. 2008. *2007 Guide to Graduate Departments of Sociology.* Washington, DC: ASA.

Amnesty International. 1994. *Breaking the Silence: Human Rights Violations Based on Sexual Orientation.* New York: Amnesty International.

———. 2007. "Amnesty International: Facts and Figures on the Death Penalty." Accessed February 17 (www.amnesty.org).

Andersen, Margaret. 1997. *Thinking about Women: Sociological Perspectives on Sex and Gender.* 4th ed. Boston: Allyn and Bacon.

Anderson, Elijah. 1990. *Streetwise: Race, Class, and Change in an Urban Community.* Chicago: University of Chicago Press.

Anderson, John Ward, and Molly Moore. 1993. "The Burden of Womanhood." *Washington Post National Weekly Edition* 10 (March 22–28):6–7.

Angier, Natalie. 1998. "Drugs, Sports, Body Image and G.I. Joe." *New York Times,* December 22, sec. D, pp. 1, 3.

Anti-Defamation League. 2004. "ADL Audit, Anti-Semitic Incidents 2003." Press release, March 24. Accessed February 24, 2007 (www.adl.org).

Appelbaum, Richard, and Peter Dreier. 1999. "The Campus Anti-Sweatshops Movement." *The American Prospect* (September/October):71–78.

Archibold, Randal C. 2006a. "Appeals Court Bars Arrests of Homeless in Los Angeles." *New York Times,* April 15, p. A9.

———. 2006b. "Las Vegas Rule Makes Feeding Homeless Illegal." *New York Times,* July 28, pp. A1, A23.

Arenson, Karen W. 2006. "A Decline in Foreign Students Is Revised." *New York Times,* November 13, p. A19.

Argetsinger, Amy, and Jonathan Krim. 2002. "Stopping the Music." *Washington Post National Weekly Edition* 20 (December 2), p. 20.

Armer, J. Michael, and John Katsillis. 1992. "Modernization Theory." Pp. 1299–1304 in *Encyclopedia of Sociology,* Vol. 4, edited by Edgar F. Borgatta and Marie L. Borgatta. New York: Macmillan.

Arora, Raksha. 2004. "Is War Still Necessary in the 21st Century?" Gallup Poll Tuesday Briefing May 11 (www.gallup.com).

Ashford, Lori S. 2001. "New Population Policies: Advancing Women's Health and Rights." *Population Bulletin* 56 (March).

Asian American Journalists Association. 2007. "Media Advisory: Coverage on Virginia Tech Shooting Incident." Accessed May 16 (www.aaja.org).

Associated Press. 1998. "Environmental Test Case Averted." *Christian Science Monitor,* September 21, p. 18.

———. 2007. "Exxon Mobil Appealing $2.5 Billion Compensation for *Valdez* Spill." *Anchorage Daily News* (January 17, 2007).

Association of American Medical Colleges. 2005a. *Facts Applicants, Matriculates and Graduates.* Accessed May 26 (www.aamc.org/data/facts/start.htm).

———. 2005b. *U.S. Medical School Faculty, 2003.* Accessed May 26 (www.aamc.org/data/faculty roster/reports.htm).

Astin, Alexander, Sarah A. Parrott, William S. Korn, and Linda J. Sax. 1994. *The American Freshman: Thirty Year Trends.* Los Angeles: Higher Education Research Institute.

Atchley, Robert C. 1976. *The Sociology of Retirement.* New York: Wiley.

———, and Amanda S. Barusch. 2004. *Social Forces and Agency: An Introduction to Social Gerontology.* 10th ed. Belmont, CA: Thomson.

Austin, April. 2002. "Cellphones and Strife in Congo." *Christian Science Monitor,* December 5, p. 11.

Axtell, Roger E. 1990. *Do's and Taboos around the World.* 2d ed. New York: John Wiley and Sons.

Azumi, Koya, and Jerald Hage. 1972. *Organizational Systems.* Lexington, MA: Heath.

Babad, Elisha Y., and P. J. Taylor. 1992. "Transparency of Teacher Expectancies Across Language, Cultural Boundaries." *Journal of Educational Research* 86:120–125.

Baby Name Wizard. 2007. "Name Voyager." Accessed January 19 (www.babynamewizard.com).

Baer, Douglas, James Curtis, and Edward Grabb. 2000. *Has Voluntary Association Activity Declined? A Cross-National Perspective.* Paper presented at the annual meeting of the American Sociological Association, Washington, DC.

Baggett, Connie. 2007. "Report: Alcohol Caused College Student's Death." *Press-Register* (Malside) February 23.

Bainbridge, William Sims. 1999. "Cyberspace: Sociology's Natural Domain." *Contemporary Sociology* 28 (November):664–667.

Baker, Therese L. 1999. *Doing Social Research.* 3d ed. New York: McGraw-Hill.

Baldauf, Scott. 2006. "India's Superman Saves the Universe and Aces an IQ Test." *Christian Science Monitor* (July 10).

Balter, Michael. 2006. "The Baby Deficit." *Science* 312 (June 30), pp. 1894–1897.

Banerjee, Neela. 2006. "Clergywomen Find Hard Path to Bigger Pulpit." *New York Times,* August 26, pp. A1, A11.

Barboza, David. 2006. "Citing Public Sentiment, China Cancels Release of 'Geisha.'" *New York Times,* February 1, p. B6.

Barley, Stephen R., and Gideon Kunda. 2004. *Gurus, Hired Guns, and Warm Bodies: Itinerant Experts in a Knowledge Economy.* Princeton: Princeton University Press.

Barnes, Ken. 2007. "The Good, the Bad and the Digital." *USA Today* (January 5), p. 3D.

Barr, Cameron W. 2002. "Top Arab TV Network to Hit US Market." *Christian Science Monitor,* December 26, pp. 1, 7.

Barrett, David B., Todd M. Johnson, and Peter F. Crossing. 2006. "The 2005 Annual Megacensus of Religions." Pp. 282–283 in 2006 *Book of the Year.* Chicago: Encyclopedia Britannica.

Barron, Milton L. 1953. "Minority Group Characteristics of the Aged in American Society." *Journal of Gerontology* 8:477–482.

Barton, Bernadette. 2006. *Stripped: Inside the Lives of Exotic Dancers.* New York: New York University Press.

Basso, Keith H. 1972. "Ice and Travel among the Fort Norman Slave: Folk Taxonomies and Cultural Rules." *Language in Society* 1 (March): 31–49.

Bates, Colleen Dunn. 1999. "Medicine's Gender Gap." *Shape,* October.

Bauerlein, Monika. 1996. "The Luddites Are Back." *Utne Reader* (March/April):24, 26.

Baum, Katrina. 2006. "Identity Theft, 2004." *Bureau of Justice Statistics Bulletin* (April).

Bauman, Kurt J. 1999. "Extended Measures of Well-Being: Meeting Basic Needs." *Current Population Reports,* ser. P-70, no. 67. Washington, DC: U.S. Government Printing Office.

Ba-Yunus, Ilyas, and Kassim Kone. 2004. "Muslim Americans: A Demographic Report." Pp. 299–322 in *Muslims in the American Public Square,* edited by Zahid H. Bukhari et al. Walnut Creek, CA: Alta Mira Press.

Bazar, Emily. 2007. "Wider Death Penalty Sought." *USA Today* (February 7), p. A1.

BBC News. 2005a. "Indonesian Village Report: January 12, 2005." Accessed January 19 (www.theworld.org).

Beagan, Brenda L. 2001. " 'Even If I Don't Know What I'm Doing I Can Make It Look Like I Know What I'm Doing': Becoming a Doctor in the 1990s." *Canadian Review of Sociology and Anthropology* 38:275–292.

Bearman, Peter S., James Moody, and Katherine Stovel. 2004. "Chains of Affection: The Structure of Adolescent Romantic and Sexual Networks." *American Journal of Sociology* 110 (July):44–91.

Becerra, Rosina M. 1999. "The Mexican-American Family." Pp. 153–171 in *Ethnic Families in America: Patterns and Variations,* 4th ed., edited by Charles H. Mindel, Robert W. Habenstein, and Roosevelt Wright, Jr. Upper Saddle River, NJ: Prentice Hall.

Becker, Anne E. 2007. "Facets of Acculturation and Their Diverse Relations to Body Shape Concerns in Fiji" *International Journal of Eating Disorders* 40 (No. 1).

Becker, Howard S. 1952. "Social Class Variations in the Teacher-Pupil Relationship." *Journal of Educational Sociology* 25 (April):451–465.

———. 1963. *The Outsiders: Studies in the Sociology of Deviance.* New York: Free Press.

———, ed. 1964. *The Other Side: Perspectives on Deviance.* New York: Free Press.

———. 1973. *The Outsiders: Studies in the Sociology of Deviance.* Rev. ed. New York: Free Press.

Beech, Hannah. 2005. "Sex, Please—We're Young and Chinese." *Time,* December 11, p. 61.

Beeghley, Leonard. 1978. *Social Stratification in America: A Critical Analysis of Theory and Research.* Santa Monica, CA: Goodyear Publishing.

Beisel, Nicola and Tamara Kay. 2004. "Abortion, Race, and Gender in Nineteenth-Century America." *American Sociological Review* 69(4): 498–518.

Bell, Daniel. 1953. "Crime as an American Way of Life." *Antioch Review* 13 (Summer):131–154.

———. 1999. *The Coming of Post-Industrial Society: A Venture in Social Forecasting.* With new foreword. New York: Basic Books.

Bell, Wendell. 1981. "Modernization." Pp. 186–187 in *Encyclopedia of Sociology.* Guilford, CT: DPG Publishing.

Bellafante, Ginia. 2005. "Young South Asians in America Embrace 'Assisted' Marriages." *New York Times,* August 23, pp. A1, A15.

Belluck, Pam, and Jim Yardley. 2006. "China Tightens Adoption Rules for Foreigners." *New York Times,* September 20, p. A1.

Belt, Don. 2002. "The World of Islam." *National Geographic* (January):26–85.

Benac, Nancy. 2006. "Abortion Opinions Stay the Same as Laws Change." *Chicago Sun-Times,* March 13, p. 42.

Bendick, Marc, Jr., Charles W. Jackson, and J. Horacio Romero. 1993. *Employment Discrimination against Older Workers: An Experimental Study of Hiring Practices.* Washington, DC: Fair Employment Council of Greater Washington.

Bendix, B. Reinhard. 1968. "Max Weber." Pp. 493–502 in *International Encyclopedia of the Social Sciences,* edited by David L. Sills. New York: Macmillan.

Benford, Robert D. 1992. "Social Movements." Pp. 1880–1887 in *Encyclopedia of Sociology,* vol. 4, edited by Edgar F. Borgatta and Marie Borgatta. New York: Macmillan.

Bennett, Vivienne. 1995. "Gender, Class, and Water: Women and the Politics of Water Service in Monterrey, Mexico." *Latin American Perspectives* 22 (September), pp. 76–99.

Bergen, Raquel Kennedy. 2006. *Marital Rape: New Research and Directions.* Harrisburg, PA: VAW Net.

Berger, Peter, and Thomas Luckmann. 1966. *The Social Construction of Reality.* New York: Doubleday.

Berk, Richard A., and Howard E. Aldrich. 1972. "Patterns of Vandalism during Civil Disorders as an Indicator of Selection of Targets." *American Sociological Review* 37 (October):533–547.

Berkeley Wellness Letter. 1990. "The Nest Refilled." 6 (February):1–2.

Berkman, Lisa F. 2004. "The Health Divide." *Contexts* (Fall):38–43.

Berland, Gretchen K. 2001. "Health Information on the Internet: Accessibility, Quality, and Readability in English and Spanish." *Journal of the American Medical Association* 285 (March 23):2612–2621.

Berlin, Brent, and Paul Kay. 1991. *Basic Color Terms: Their Universality and Evolution.* Berkeley, CA: University of California Press.

Berman, Paul. 2003. *Terror and Liberalism.* New York: W.W. Norton.

Bernasek, Anna. 2006. "A Poverty Line That's Out of Date and Out of Favor." *New York Times,* August 14, p. 8.

Bernstein, Sharon. 2004. "Under the Radar, HIV Worsens." *Los Angeles Times,* October 16, pp. A1, A12.

Bhagat, Chetan. 2007. *One Night at the Call Centre.* London: Black Swan.

Bianchi, Suzanne M., and Daphne Spain. 1996. "Women, Work, and Family in America." *Population Bulletin* 51 (December).

Biddlecom, Ann, and Steven Martin. 2006. "Childless in America." *Contexts* 5 (Fall): 54.

Bielby, Denise D., and William T. Bielby. 2002. "Hollywood Dreams, Harsh Realities: Writing for Film and Television." *Contexts* 1 (Fall/Winter): 21–25.

Birnbaum, Jeffrey H. 2005. "Listen to the Wallet." *Washington Post National Weekly Edition,* April 4, p. 11.

Black, Donald. 1995. "The Epistemology of Pure Sociology." *Law and Social Inquiry* 20 (Summer): 829–870.

Blackhall, Leslie J., et al. 1995. "Ethnicity and Attitudes toward Patient Autonomy." *Journal of the American Medical Association* 274 (September 13): 820–825.

Blau, Peter M., and Otis Dudley Duncan. 1967. *The American Occupational Structure.* New York: Wiley.

———, and Marshall W. Meyer. 1987. *Bureaucracy in Modern Society.* 3d ed. New York: Random House.

Blauner, Robert. 1964. *Alienation and Freedom.* Chicago: University of Chicago Press.

———. 1972. *Racial Oppression in America.* New York: Harper and Row.

Blinder, Alan S. 2006. "Offshoring: The Next Industrial Revolution." *Foreign Affairs* (March/April).

Blumer, Herbert. 1955. "Collective Behavior." Pp. 165–198 in *Principles of Sociology,* 2d ed., edited by Alfred McClung Lee. New York: Barnes and Noble.

———. 1969. *Symbolic Interactionism: Perspective and Method.* Englewood Cliffs, NJ: Prentice Hall.

Boase, Jeffery, John B. Horrigan, Barry Wellman, and Lee Rainie. 2006. *The Strength of Internet Ties.* Washington, DC: Pew Internet and American Life Project.

Bonczar, Thomas P., and Tracy L. Snell. 2005. "Capital Punishment, 2004." *Bureau of Justice Statistics Bulletin* (November).

Bordt, Rebecca. 2005. "Using a Research Article to Facilitate a Deep Structure Understanding or Discrimination." *Teaching Sociology* 33 (October):403–410.

Bornschier, Volker, Christopher Chase-Dunn, and Richard Rubinson. 1978. "Cross-National Evidence of the Effects of Foreign Investment and Aid on Economic Growth and Inequality: A Survey of Findings and a Reanalysis." *American Journal of Sociology* 84 (November):651–683.

Borosage, Robert L. 2003. "Class Welfare: Bush Style." *American Prospect* 14 (March):15–18.

Bottomore, Tom, and Maximilien Rubel, eds. 1956. *Karl Marx: Selected Writings in Sociology and Social Philosophy.* New York: McGraw-Hill.

Boudreaux, Richard. 2002. "Indian Rights Law Is Upheld in Mexico." *Los Angeles Times,* September 7, p. A3.

Boushey, Heather. 2005. *Student Debt: Bigger and Bigger.* Washington, DC: Center for Economic and Policy Research.

Bouvier, Leon F. 1980. "America's Baby Boom Generation: The Fateful Bulge." *Population Bulletin* 35 (April).

Bowles, Samuel, and Herbert Gintis. 1976. *Schooling in Capitalistic America: Educational Reforms and the Contradictions of Economic Life.* New York: Basic Books.

Brannigan, Augustine. 1992. "Postmodernism." Pp. 1522–1525 in *Encyclopedia of Sociology,* vol. 3, edited by Edgar F. Borgatta and Marie L. Borgatta. New York: Macmillan.

Brannon, Rush. 1995. "The Use of the Concept of Disability Culture: A Historian's View." *Disability Studies* 15 (Fall):3–15.

Braverman, Amy. 2002. "Open Door Sexuality." *University of Chicago Magazine* 95 (October): 20–21.

Braxton, Greg. 2007. "Is Prime Time Quietly Becoming Colorblind?" *Chicago Tribune,* March 20, sec. 5, p. 3.

Bray, James H., and John Kelly. 1999. *Stepfamilies: Love, Marriage, and Parenting in the First Decade.* New York: Broadway Books.

Breines, Winifred. 2007. "Struggling to Connect: White and Black Feminism in the Movement Years." *Contexts* 6 (Winter): 18–24.

Brewer, Cynthia A., and Trudy A. Suchan. 2001. *Mapping Census 2000: The Geography of U.S. Diversity.* Washington, DC: U.S. Government Printing Office.

Brint, Steven. 1998. *Schools and Societies.* Thousand Oaks, CA: Pine Forge Press.

Brittingham, Angela, and G. Patricia de la Cruz. 2004. *Ancestry: 2000. Census Brief* C2KBR-35. Washington, DC: U.S. Government Printing Office.

Brodie, Mollyann, Annie Steffenson, Jamie Valdez, Rebecca Levin, and Roberto Suro. 2000. *2002 National Survey of Latinos.* Menlo Park, CA: Henry J. Kaiser Foundation and Pew Hispanic Center.

Bromley, David G., and Mitchell L. Bracey, Jr. 1998. "The Church of Scientology: A Quasi-Religion." Pp. 141–156 in *Sects, Cults, and Spiritual Communities: A Sociological Analysis,* edited by William W. Zellner and Marc Petrowsky. Westport, CT: Praeger.

Brower, Brock. 1988. "The Pernicious Power of the Polls." *Money,* March 17, pp. 144–163.

Brown, David K. 2001. "The Social Sources of Educational Credentialism: Status Cultures, Labor Markets, and Organizations." *Sociology of Education* 74 (Extra Issue):19–34.

Brown, Michael, and Amy Goldin. 1973. *Collective Behavior: A Review and Reinterpretation of the Literature.* Pacific Palisades, CA: Goodyear.

Brown, Patricia Leigh. 2004. "For Children of Gays, Marriage Brings Joy." *New York Times,* March 19, p. A13.

Brown, Robert McAfee. 1980. *Gustavo Gutierrez.* Atlanta: John Knox.

Brown, Roger W. 1954. "Mass Phenomena." Pp. 833–873 in *Handbook of Social Psychology,* vol. 2, edited by Gardner Lindzey. Reading, MA: Addison-Wesley.

Brown, S. Kathi. 2006. *Attitudes Toward Work and Job Security.* Washington, DC: AARP.

Brown, Susan I. 2005. "How Cohabitation Is Reshaping American Families." *Contexts* (Summer):33–37.

Browne, Irene, ed. 2001. *Latinas and African American Women at Work: Race, Gender, and Economic Inequlity.* New York: Russell Sage Foundation.

Buchholz, Barbara Ballinger. 2003. "Expanded Access." *Chicago Tribune,* January 26, sec. 16, pp. 1R, 5R.

Budig, Michelle J. 2002. "Male Advantage and the Gender Composition of Jobs: Who Rides the Glass Escalator?" *Social Problems* 49 (2):258–277.

Bullard, Robert, D. 1993. *Dumping in Dixie: Race, Class, and Environmentalist Quality.* 2d ed. Boulder, CO: Westin Press.

Bulle, Wolfgang F. 1987. *Crossing Cultures? Southeast Asian Mainland.* Atlanta: Centers for Disease Control.

Bumiller, Elisabeth. 2000. "Resolute Adversary of Divorce." *New York Times,* December 16, pp. A17, A19.

Bunzel, John H. 1992. *Race Relations on Campus: Stanford Students Speak.* Stanford, CA: Portable Stanford.

Bureau of Justice Statistics. 2004. *First Release from State Prisons 2001.* Washington, DC: Bureau of Justice Statistics.

Bureau of Labor Statistics. 2005. *Union Members in 2004.* Accessed February 28 (www.bls.gov).

———. 2006a. "Characteristics of Minimum Wage Workers: 2005." Accessed February 10, 2007 (www.bls.gov).

———. 2006b. "Number of Jobs Held, Labor Market Activity, and Earnings Growth Among the Youngest Baby Boomers: Results from a Longitudinal Survey." *News.* August 25, 2006. Washington, DC: BLS.

———. 2007. "Labor Force (Demographic) Data." February 13. Accessed February 28 (www.bls.gov).

Bureau of the Census. 1975. *Historical Statistics of the United States, Colonial Times to 1970.* Washington, DC: U.S. Government Printing Office.

———. 1994. *Statistical Abstract of the United States, 1994.* Washington, DC: U.S. Government Printing Office.

———. 1996. "Percent Distribution of Projected Households by Type: 1995 to 2010." Released May 1996. Accessed March 1, 2006 (www.census.gov).

———. 1998. "Race of Wife by Race of Husband." Internet release of June 10.

———. 2002. *Statistical Abstract of the United States, 2002.* Washington, DC: U.S. Government Printing Office.

———. 2003a. *Statistical Abstract of the United States, 2003.* Washington, DC: U.S. Government Printing Office.

———. 2003b. *Characteristics of American Indians and Alaska Natives. By Tribe and Language: 2000.* Washington, DC: U.S. Government Printing Office.

———. 2003c. TM-PCT023 *Percent of Persons of Arab Ancestry 2000.* Accessed March 4, 2004 (http://factfinder.census.gov).

———. 2003d. *Summary Tables on Language Use and English Ability, 2000* (PHC-T-20). Accessed January 14, 2004 (www.census.gov/population/www/cen2000/phc-t20.html).

———. 2004a. *Statistical Abstract of the United States, 2004–2005.* Washington, DC: U.S. Government Printing Office.

———. 2004b. *U.S. Interim Projections by Age, Sex, Race, and Hispanic Origin.* Released March 18, 2004 (www.census.gov/ipc/www/usinterimproj).

———. 2005a. *Statistical Abstract of the United States 2006.* Washington, DC: U.S. Government Printing Office.

———. 2005c. *Florida, California and Texas Future Population Growth,* Census Bureau Reports, CB05-52. Washington, DC: U.S. Government Printing Office.

———. 2005d. "International Data Base." Accessed April 26 (www.census.gov/ipc/www/idbnew.html).

———. 2005f. "American Fact Finder: Places with United States." Accessed December 12 (http://factfinder.census.gov).

———. 2005g. "Hurricane Katrina Disaster Area." Accessed December 15 (www.census.gov).

———. 2006a. *Statistical Abstract of the United States 2007.* Washington, DC: U.S. Government Printing Office.

———. 2007b. "Income Historical Tables—Families." Accessed March 1 (www.census.gov).

———. 2007c. "International Data Base." Accessed May 1 (www.census.gov/ipc/www/idbnew.html).

———. 2007d. "World Population Information." Accessed May 1 (www.census.gov/ipc/www/world.html).

———. 2007e. "Percentage Change in Population for Countries and Puerto Rico Municipios: April 1, 2000 to July 1, 2006." Accessed May 1 (www.census.gov/popest/gallery/maps/chg 0006.html).

Burgdorf, Robert L., Jr. 2005. "Americans with Disabilities Act of 1990 (United States)." Pp. 93–101 in *Encyclopedia of Disability,* edited by Gary Albrecht. Thousand Oaks, CA: Sage.

Burgess, Ernest W. 1925. "The Growth of the City." Pp. 47–62 in *The City,* edited by Robert E. Park, Ernest W. Burgess, and Roderick D. McKenzie. Chicago: University of Chicago Press.

Burns, John R. 1998. "Once Widowed in India, Twice Scorned." *New York Times,* March 29, p. A1.

Butler, Daniel Allen. 1998. *"Unsinkable": The Full Story.* Mechanicsburg, PA: Stackpole Books.

Butler, Robert N. 1990. "A Disease Called Ageism." *Journal of American Geriatrics Society* 38 (February):178–180.

Byrd-Bredbenner, Carol, and Jessica Murray. 2003. "Comparison of the Anthropometric Measurements of Idealized Female Body Images in Media Directed to Men, Women, and Mixed Gender Audiences." *Topics in Clinical Nutrition* 18 (2):117–129.

Bystydzienski, Jill M., and Joti Sekhon. 1999. *Democratization and Women's Grassroots Movements.* Bloomington: Indiana University Press.

Caesar, Lena G., and David R. Williams. 2002. *The ASHA Leader Online: Socioculture and the Delivery of Health Care: Who Gets What and Why.* Accessed December 1 (www.asha.org).

Calhoun, Craig. 1998. "Community without Propinquity Revisited." *Sociological Inquiry* 68 (Summer):373–397.

———. 2003. "Belonging in the Cosmopolitan Imaginary." *Ethnicities* 3 (December):531–553.

Campaign Legal Center. 2004. "National Party Finances." *Weekly Reports* (November 19).

Campbell, Mary, Robert Haveman, Gary Sandefur, and Barbara Wolte. 2005. "Economic Inequality and Educational Attainment Across a Generation." *Focus* 23 (Spring):11–15.

Camus, Albert. 1948. *The Plague.* New York: Random House.

Cantril, Hadley. 1940. *The Invasion from Mars: A Study in the Psychology of Panic.* Princeton, NJ: Princeton University Press.

Caplan, Ronald L. 1989. "The Commodification of American Health Care." *Social Science and Medicine* 28 (11):1139–1148.

Caplow, Theodore, and Louis Hicks. 2002. *Systems of War and Peace.* 2d ed. Lanham, MD: University Press of America.

Carey, Anne R., and Elys A. McLean. 1997. "Heard It Through the Grapevine?" *USA Today,* September 15, p. B1.

Carrese, Joseph A., and Lorna A. Rhodes. 1995. "Western Bioethics on the Navaho Reservation: Benefit or Harm?" *Journal of the American Medical Association* 274 (September 13):826–829.

Carroll, John. 2003. "The Good Doctor." *American Way* (July 15):26–31.

Carroll, Joseph. 2005. "Who Supports Marijuana Legalization?" November 1. Accessed January 19, 2007 (www.galluppoll.com).

———. 2006. "Public Continues to Support Right-to-Die for Terminally Ill Patients." Accessed June 26, 2007 (www.gallup.com).

———. 2006. "Public: National Anthem Should Be Sung in English." Gallup Poll, May 3, 2006.

———. 2007. "Americans Assess What They Can Do to Reduce Global Warming." April 24. Accessed May 2 (www.galluppoll.com).

Carty, Win. 1999. "Greater Dependence on Cars Leads to More Pollution in World's Cities." *Population Today* 27 (December):1–2.

Castañeda, Jorge G. 1995. "Ferocious Differences." *Atlantic Monthly* 276 (July):68–69, 71–76.

Castells, Manuel. 1983. *The City and the Grass Roots.* Berkeley: University of California Press.

———. 1997. *The Power of Identity.* Vol. 1 of *The Information Age: Economy, Society and Culture.* London: Blackwell.

———. 1998. *End of Millennium.* Vol. 3 of *The Information Age: Economy, Society and Culture.* London: Blackwell.

———. 2000. *The Information Age: Economy, Society and Culture* (3 vols.). 2d ed. Oxford and Malden, MA: Blackwell.

———. 2001. *The Internet Galaxy: Reflections on the Internet, Business, and Society.* New York: Oxford University Press.

Catalano, Shannon M. 2006. *Criminal Victimization, 2005.* Washington, DC: U.S. Government Printing Office.

Catalyst. 2007. *2006 Census of Women Corporate Officers, Top Earners, and Directors of the Fortune 500.* New York: Catalyst.

574

CBS News. 1979. Transcript of *Sixty Minutes* segment, "I Was Only Following Orders." March 31, pp. 2–8.

Center for Academic Integrity. 2006. *CAI Research.* Accessed January 10 (www.academicintegrity.org).

Center for American Women and Politics. 2007. *Fact Sheet: Women in the U.S. Congress 2007 and Statewide Elective Women 2007.* Rutgers, NJ: CAWP.

Centers for Disease Control and Prevention. 2006. "Twenty-Five Years of HIV/AIDS—United States, 1981–2006." *MMWR Weekly* 55 (June 2): 585–589.

———. 2007. "U.S. Public Health Service Syphilis Study at Tuskegee." Accessed April 25 (www.cdc.gov).

Centers for Medicare and Medicaid Services. 2007. "NHE Projections 2006–2016." Accessed April 25 (www.cms.hhs.gov).

Cerulo, Karen A., Janet M. Ruane, and Mary Chagko. 1992. "Technological Ties that Bind: Media Generated Primary Groups." *Communication Research* 19:109–129.

Chalfant, H. Paul, Robert E. Beckley, and C. Eddie Palmer. 1994. *Religion in Contemporary Society.* 3d ed. Itasca, IL: F. E. Peacock.

Chambliss, William. 1973. "The Saints and the Roughnecks." *Society* 11 (November/December): 24–31.

Charter, David, and Jill Sherman. 1996. "Schools Must Teach New Code of Values." *London Times,* January 15, p. 1.

Chase-Dunn, Christopher, and Peter Grimes. 1995. "World-Systems Analysis." Pp. 387–417 in *Annual Review of Sociology, 1995,* edited by John Hagan. Palo Alto, CA: Annual Reviews.

———, Yukio Kawano, and Benjamin D. Brewer. 2000. "Trade Globalization Since 1795: Waves of Integration in the World System." *American Sociological Review* 65 (February):77–95.

Cherlin, Andrew J. 2003. "Should the Government Promote Marriage?" *Contexts* 2 (Fall): 22–29.

———. 2006. On Single Mothers "Doing" Family. *Journal of Marriage and Family* 68 (November): 800–803.

———. 2008. *Public and Private Families: An Introduction.* 5th ed. New York: McGraw-Hill.

Chesney-Lind, Meda. 1989. "Girls' Crime and Woman's Place: Toward a Feminist Model of Female Delinquency." *Crime and Delinquency* 35:5–29.

Chicago Tribune. 1997. "In London, Prince Meets a Pauper, an Ex-Classmate." December 5, p. 19.

Children Now. 2004. *Fall Colors: 2003–04 Prime Time Diversity Report.* Oakland, CA: Children Now.

Chin, Ko-lin. 1996. *Chinatown Gangs: Extortion, Enterprise, and Ethnicity.* New York: Oxford University Press.

China Daily. 2004. "Starbucks Takes Aim at China Chain." Accessed July 21 (www2.chinadaily.com.cn).

Christensen, Kathleen. 1990. "Bridges over Troubled Water: How Older Workers View the Labor Market." Pp. 175–207 in *Bridges to Retirement,* edited by Peter B. Doeringer. Ithaca, NY: IRL Press.

Chronic Poverty Research Center. 2005. "Chronic Poverty." Accessed March 3, 2006 (www.chronicpoverty.org).

Chu, Henry. 2005. "Tractors Crush Heart of a Nation." *Los Angeles Times,* July 10, p. A9.

Cigar, Norman. 1995. *Genocide in Bosnia: The Policy of "Ethnic Cleansing."* College Station, TX: Texas A & M University Press.

Citizens Commission on Homelessness. 2004. *Home Again.* Portland, OR: Bureau of Housing and Community Development.

Civic Ventures. 1999. *The New Face of Retirement: Older Americans, Civic Engagement, and the Longevity Revolution.* Washington, DC: Peter D. Hart Research Associates.

Clark, Burton, and Martin Trow. 1966. "The Organizational Context." Pp. 17–70 in *The Study of College Peer Groups,* edited by Theodore M. Newcomb and Everett K. Wilson. Chicago: Aldine.

Clark, Candace. 1983. "Sickness and Social Control." Pp. 346–365 in *Social Interaction: Readings in Sociology,* 2d ed., edited by Howard Robboy and Candace Clark. New York: St. Martin's.

Clarke, Adele E., Janet K. Shim, Laura Maro, Jennifer Ruth Fusket, and Jennifer R. Fishman. 2003. "Bio Medicalization: Technoscientific Transformations of Health, Illness, and U.S. Biomedicine." *American Sociological Review* 68 (April):161–194.

Clarke, Lee. 2002. "Panic: Myth or Reality?" *Contexts* 1 (Fall):21–26.

Clawson, Dan, and Naomi Gerstel. 2002. "Caring for Our Young: Child Care in Europe and the United States." *Contexts* 1 (Fall/Winter):23–35.

Clemmitt, Marcia. 2005. "Intelligent Design." *CQ Researcher* 15 (July 29):637–660.

———. 2006. "Cyber Sociology." *CQ Researcher* 16 (July 28), pp. 625–648.

Clinard, Marshall B., and Robert F. Miller. 1998. *Sociology of Deviant Behavior.* 10th ed. Fort Worth: Harcourt Brace.

Clymer, Adam. 2000. "College Students Not Drawn to Voting or Politics, Poll Shows." *New York Times,* January 2, p. A14.

Cockerham, William C. 2007. *Medical Sociology.* 10th ed. Upper Saddle River, NJ: Prentice Hall.

Cohen, Debra Nussbaum. 2005. "Questions, Answers and Minutiae of the Faithful Can Be Found in the Blogosphere." *New York Times,* March 5, p. A13.

Cohen, Lawrence E., and Marcus Felson. 1979. "Social Change and Crime Rate Trends: A Routine Activities Approach." *American Sociological Review* 44:588–608.

Cole, Elizabeth S. 1985. "Adoption, History, Policy, and Program." Pp. 638–666 in *A Handbook of Child Welfare,* edited by John Laird and Ann Hartman. New York: Free Press.

Cole, Mike. 1988. *Bowles and Gintis Revisited: Correspondence and Contradiction in Educational Theory.* Philadelphia: Falmer.

Coleman, Isobel. 2004. "The Payoff from Women's Rights." *Foreign Affairs* 83 (May/June):80–95.

Coleman, James William. 2006. *The Criminal Elite: Understanding White-Collar Crime.* 6th ed. New York: Worth.

———, and Donald R. Cressey. 1980. *Social Problems.* New York: Harper and Row.

Collins, Patricia Hill. 2000. *Black Feminist Thought: Knowledge, Consciousness, and the Politics of Empowerment.* Revised 10th Anniv. 2nd ed. New York: Routledge.

Collins, Randall. 1975. *Conflict Sociology: Toward an Explanatory Sociology.* New York: Academic.

———. 1980. "Weber's Last Theory of Capitalism: A Systematization." *American Sociological Review* 45 (December):925–942.

———. 1986. *Weberian Sociological Theory.* New York: Cambridge University Press.

———. 1995. "Prediction in Macrosociology: The Case of the Soviet Collapse." *American Journal of Sociology* 100 (May):1552–1593.

Columbia Accident Investigation Board. 2003. "*Columbia* Accident Investigation Report Board Report: Volume I." Washington, DC: CAIB, NASA.

Commission on Civil Rights. 1976. *A Guide to Federal Laws and Regulations Prohibiting Sex Discrimination.* Washington, DC: U.S. Government Printing Office.

———. 1981. *Affirmative Action in the 1980s: Dismantling the Process of Discrimination.* Washington, DC: U.S. Government Printing Office.

Commoner, Barry. 1971. *The Closing Circle.* New York: Knopf.

———. 1990. *Making Peace with the Planet.* New York: Pantheon.

Commonwealth Fund. 2002. *Unequal Treatment: Confronting Racial and Ethnic Disparities in Health Care.* Washington, DC: National Academy of Sciences.

Comstock, P., and M. B. Fox. 1994. "Employer Tactics and Labor Law Reform." Pp. 90–109 in *Restoring the Promise of American Labor Law,* edited by S. Friedman, R. W. Hurd, R. A. Oswald, and R. L. Seeber. Ithaca, NY: ILR Press.

Conrad, Peter, ed. 2005. *The Sociology of Health and Illness: Cultural Perspectives.* 7th ed. New York: Worth.

———, and Joseph W. Schneider. 1992. *Deviance and Medicalization: From Badness to Sickness.* Expanded ed. Philadelphia: Temple University Press.

Cooley, Charles. H. 1902. *Human Nature and the Social Order.* New York: Scribner.

Coontz, Stephanie. 2006. "A Pop Quiz on Marriage." *New York Times,* February 19, p. 12.

Cooper, Jeremy. 2005. "Disability Law: Europe." Pp. 444–449 in *Encyclopedia of Disability,* edited by Gary Albrecht. Thousand Oaks, CA: Sage.

Cornell, S. E., and D. Hartmann. 2001. "Pluralism, Race and Ethnicity in Selected African Countries." In *Race and Ethnicity: Critical Concepts in Sociology,* vol. 1, edited by H. Goulbourne. London & New York: Routledge.

Coser, Lewis A. 1977. *Masters of Sociological Thought: Ideas in Historical and Social Context.* 2d ed. New York: Harcourt, Brace and Jovanovich.

Coser, Rose Laub. 1984. "American Medicine's Ambiguous Progress." *Contemporary Sociology* 13 (January):9–13.

Côté, James E. 2000. *Arrested Adulthood: The Changing Nature of Identity and Maturity in the Late World.* New York: New York University.

Couch, Carl J. 1968. "Collective Behavior: An Examination of Some Stereotypes." *Social Problems* 15:310–322.

———. 1996. *Information Technologies and Social Orders.* Edited with an introduction by David R. Maines and Shing-Ling Chien. New York: Aldine de Gruyter.

Council on Ethical and Judicial Affairs, American Medical Association. 1992. "Decisions Near the End of Life." *Journal of the American Medical Association* 267 (April 22–29): 2229–2333.

Council on Scientific Affairs. 1999. "Hispanic Health in the United States." *Journal of the American Medical Association* 265 (January 9): 248–252.

Counts, D. A. 1977. "The Good Death in Kaliai: Preparation for Death in Western New Britain." *Omega* 7:367–372.

Cowell, Alan. 2005. "Gay Britons Signing Up as Unions Become Legal." *New York Times,* December 5.

Cox, Oliver C. 1948. *Caste, Class, and Race: A Study in Social Dynamics.* Detroit: Wayne State University Press.

Cromwell, Paul F., James N. Olson, and D'Aunn Wester Avarey. 1995. *Breaking and Entering: An Ethnographic Analysis of Burglary.* Newbury Park, CA: Sage.

Crosnoe, Robert, and Glen H. Elder Jr. 2002. "Successful Adaptation in the Later Years: A Life Course Approach to Aging." *Social Psychology Quarterly* (No. 4), pp. 309–328.

Cross, Simon, and Barbara Bagilhole. 2002. "Girls' Jobs for the Boys? Men, Masculinity and Non-Traditional Occupations." *Gender, Work, and Organization* 9 (April):204–226.

Crossette, Barbara. 1999. "The Internet Changes Dictatorship's Rules." *New York Times,* August 1, sec. 4, p. l.

Croteau, David, and William Hoynes. 2003. *Media/Society: Industries, Images, and Audiences.* 3d ed. Thousand Oaks, CA: Pine Forge.

———. 2006. *The Business of the Media: Corporate Media and the Public Interest.* 2d ed. Thousand Oaks, CA: Pine Forge.

Croucher, Sheila L. 2004. *Globalization and Belonging: The Politics of Identity in a Changing World.* Lanham, MD: Rowman and Littlefield.

Crouse, Kelly. 1999. "Sociology of the *Titanic.*" *Teaching Sociology Listserv.* May 24.

Crowe, Jerry, and Valli Herman. 2005. "NBA Lists Fashion Do's and Don'ts." *Los Angeles Times,* October 19, pp. A1, A23.

Crump, Andy. 2006. "Suicide in Japan." *Lancet* 367 (April 8): 1143.

Cuff, E. C., W. W. Sharrock, and D. W. Francis, eds. 1990. *Perspectives in Sociology.* 3d ed. Boston: Unwin Hyman.

Cullen, Francis T., Jr., and John B. Cullen. 1978. *Toward a Paradigm of Labeling Theory,* ser. 58. Lincoln: University of Nebraska Studies.

Cumming, Elaine, and William E. Henry. 1961. *Growing Old: The Process of Disengagement.* New York: Basic Books.

Currie, Elliot. 1985. *Confronting Crime: An American Challenge.* New York: Pantheon.

———. 1998. *Crime and Punishment in America.* New York: Metropolitan Books.

Curry, Timothy Jon. 1993. "A Little Pain Never Hurt Anyone: Athletic Career Socialization and the Normalization of Sports Injury." *Symbolic Interaction* 26 (Fall):273–290.

Curtiss, Susan. 1977. *Genie: A Psycholinguistic Study of a Modern Day "Wild Child."* New York: Academic Press.

———. 1985. "The Development of Human Cerebral Lateralization." Pp. 97–116 in *The Dual Brain,* edited by D. Frank Benson and Eran Zaidel. New York: Guilford.

Dahl, Robert A. 1961. *Who Governs?* New Haven, CT: Yale University Press.

Dahrendorf, Ralf. 1958. "Toward a Theory of Social Conflict." *Journal of Conflict Resolution* 2 (June):170–183.

———. 1959. *Class and Class Conflict in Industrial Sociology.* Stanford, CA: Stanford University Press.

Daley, Suzanne. 1999. "Doctors' Group of Volunteers Awarded Nobel." *New York Times,* October 16, pp. A1, A6.

Daley-Harris, Sam, ed. 2002. *Pathways out of Poverty: Innovations in Microfinance for the Poorest Families.* Bloomfield, CT: Komarian Press.

Dalla, Rochelle L., and Wendy C. Gamble. 2001. "Teenage Mothering and the Navajo Reservation: An Examination of Intergovernmental Perceptions and Beliefs." *American Indian Culture and Research Journal* 25 (1):1–19.

Dallas Federal Reserve Bank. 2006. "Maquiladora Industry Update." Accessed February 19, 2007 (http://www.dallasfed.org/data/data/mag_charts.pdf).

Daniels, Arlene Kaplan. 1987. "Invisible Work." *Social Problems* 34 (December):403–415.

———. 1988. *Invisible Careers.* Chicago: University of Chicago Press.

Daniszewski, John. 2003. "Al-Jazeera TV Draws Flak Outside—and Inside—the Arab World." *Los Angeles Times,* January 5, pp. A1, A5.

Dannefer, Dale. 2004. "Age Stratification." Pp. 278–283 in *International Encyclopedia of the Social and Behavioral Sciences,* edited by Neil J. Smelser and Paul B. Baltes. New York: Elsevier.

Dao, James. 1995. "New York's Highest Court Rules Unmarried Couples Can Adopt." *New York Times,* November 3, pp. A1, B2.

Darlin, Damon. 2006. "It's O.K to Fall Behind the Technology Curve." *New York Times,* December 30, p. B6.

Darwin, Charles. 1859. *On the Origin of Species.* London: John Murray.

Dash, Erich. 2006. "Executive Pay: A Special Project." *New York Times,* April 9, sec. 3, pp. 1, 5.

David, Gary. 2004. "Scholarship on Arab Americans Distorted Past 9/11." *Al Jadid* (Winter/Spring): 26–27.

Davies, Christie. 1989. "Goffman's Concept of the Total Institution: Criticisms and Revisions." *Human Studies* 12 (June):77–95.

Davis, Darren W. 1997. "The Direction of Race of Interviewer Effects Among African-Americans: Donning the Black Mask." *American Journal of Political Science* 41 (January):309–322.

———, and Brian D. Silver. 2003. "Stereotype Threat and Race of Interviewer Knowledge." *American Journal of Political Science* 47 (January): 33–45.

Davis, Donald B., and Karen A. Polonko. 2001. *Telework America 2001 Summary.* Accessed March 3, 2003 (www.workingfromanywhere.org/telework/twa2001.htm).

Davis, Gerald. 2003. *America's Corporate Banks Are Separated by Just Four Handshakes.* Accessed March 7 (www.bus.umich.edu/research/davis.html).

———. 2004. "American Cronyism: How Executive Networks Inflated the Corporate Bubble." *Contexts* (Summer):34–40.

Davis, James A. 1982. "Up and Down Opportunity's Ladder." *Public Opinion* 5 (June/July):11–15, 48–51.

———, and Tom W. Smith. 2001. *General Social Surveys, 1972–2000.* Storrs, CT: The Roper Center.

———, Tom W. Smith, and Peter V. Marsden. 2005. *General Social Surveys, 1972–2004: Cumulative Codebook.* Chicago: National Opinion Research Center.

Davis, Kingsley. 1940. "Extreme Social Isolation of a Child." *American Journal of Sociology* 45 (January):554–565.

———. 1947. "A Final Note on a Case of Extreme Isolation." *American Journal of Sociology* 52 (March):432–437.

———. [1949] 1995. *Human Society.* Reprint, New York: Macmillan.

———, and Wilbert E. Moore. 1945. "Some Principles of Stratification." *American Sociological Review* 10 (April):242–249.

Davis, Mike. 2005. *Planet of Slums.* London: Verso.

Davis, Nanette J. 1975. *Sociological Constructions of Deviance: Perspectives and Issues in the Field.* Dubuque, IA: Wm. C. Brown.

De Anda, Roberto M. 2004. *Chicanas and Chicanos in Contemporary Society.* 2nd ed. Lanham, MD: Rowman and Littlefield.

Death Penalty Information Center. 2007a. "Number of Executions by State and Region Since 1976." Accessed February 16 (www.deathpenaltyinfo.org).

———. 2007b. "Descriptions of Execution Methods." Accessed February 18 (www.deathpenaltyinfo.org).

Deegan, Mary Jo, ed. 1991. *Women in Sociology: A Bio-Biographical Sourcebook.* Westport, CT: Greenwood.

———. 2003. "Textbooks, the History of Sociology, and the Sociological Stock of Knowledge." *Sociological Theory* 21 (November):298–305.

Deflem, Mathieu. 2005. "'Wild Beasts Without Nationality': The Uncertain Origins of Interpol, 1898–1910." Pp. 275–285 in *Handbook of Transnational Crime and Justice,* edited by Philip Rerchel. Thousand Oaks, CA: Sage.

Delaney, Kevin J. 2005. "Big Mother Is Watching." *Wall Street Journal,* November 26, pp. A1, A6.

576

Delawala, Imtyaz. 2002. "What Is Coltran?" January 21, 2002 (www.abcnews.com).

Della Porta, Donatella, and Sidney Tarrow, eds. 2005. *Transnational Protest and Global Activism.* Lanham, MD: Rowman and Littlefield.

Deloria, Vine, Jr. 1999. *For This Land: Writings on Religion in America.* New York: Routledge.

DeNavas-Walt, Carmen, Bernadette D. Proctor, and Cheryl Miller. 2005. "Income, Poverty and Health Insurance Coverage in the United States: 2004." *Current Population Reports,* ser. P-60, no. 229. Washington, DC: U.S. Government Printing Office.

———. 2006. "Income, Poverty, and Health Insurance Coverage in the United States 2005." *Current Population Reports,* ser. P-60, no. 231. Washington, DC: U.S. Government Printing Office.

Denny, Charlotte. 2004. "Migration Myths Hold No Fears." *Guardian Weekly* (February 26):12.

Denzin, Norman K. 2004. "Postmodernism." Pp. 581–583 in *Encyclopedia of Social Theory,* edited by George Ritzer. Thousand Oaks, CA: Sage.

DePalma, Anthony. 1995. "Racism? Mexico's in Denial." *New York Times,* June 11, p. E4.

———. 1996. "For Mexico Indians, New Voice but Few Gains." *New York Times,* January 13, pp. B1, B2.

———. 2002. "White-Collar Layoffs, Downsized Dreams." *New York Times,* December 5, pp. A1, A38.

DeParle, Jason. 2005. "Hispanic Group Thrives on Federal Aid." *New York Times,* May 3, pp. A1, A16.

———. 2007a. "A Good Provider Is One Who Leaves." *New York Times Magazine* (April 22), pp. 50–57, 72, 122–123.

———. 2007b. "In a World on the Move, a Tiny Land Strains to Cope." *New York Times* (June), p. A1.

Department of Agriculture. 2004. *2002 Census of Agriculture: Preliminary Report AC-02-A-PR.* Washington, DC: U.S. Government Printing Office.

Department of Defense. 2006. "Selected Manpower Statistics Fiscal Year 2005." Washington, DC: Department of Defense.

Department of Education. 1999. *Report on State Implementation of the Gun-Free Schools Act. School Year 1997–98.* Rockville, MD: Westat.

———. 2004. *Crime and Safety in America's Public Schools.* Washington, DC: U.S. Government Printing Office.

———. 2006. *Integrated Postsecondary Education Data Systems, Completions, 1995–2004.* Washington, DC: NCES.

Department of Energy. 2004. *Permanent Markers Implementation Plan.* Carlsbad, NM: Carlsbad Field Office, Department of Energy.

Department of Homeland Security. 2006. *The Federal Response to Hurricane Katrina: Lessons Learned.* Washington, DC: U.S. Government Printing Office.

Department of Justice. 2000. *The Civil Liberties Act of 1988: Redress for Japanese Americans.* Accessed June 29 (http://www.usdoj.gov/crt/ora/main.html).

———. 2006a. *Crime in the United States, 2005.* Washington, DC: U.S. Government Printing Office.

———. 2006b. *Hate Crime Statistics, 2006.* Washington, DC: U.S. Government Printing Office.

Department of Labor. 1995a. *Good for Business: Making Full Use of the Nation's Capital.* Washington, DC: U.S. Government Printing Office.

———. 1995b. *A Solid Investment: Making Full Use of the Nation's Human Capital.* Washington, DC: U.S. Government Printing Office.

Department of State. 2006a. *Trafficking in Persons Report 2006.* Washington, DC: U.S. Department of State.

———. 2007. "Immigrant Visas Issued to Orphans Coming to the US." Accessed May 15 (http://travel.state.gov/family/adoption/stats/stats_451.html).

Derné, Steve. 2003. "Arnold Schwarzenegger, Ally McBeal, and Arranged Marriages: Globalization on the Ground Media." *Contexts* 2 (Summer): 12–18.

Desai, Manisha. 1996. "If Peasants Build Their Own Dams, What Would the State Have Left to Do?" Pp. 209–224 in *Research in Social Movements, Conflicts and Change,* vol. 19, edited by Michael Dobkowski and Isidor Wallimann. Greenwich, CT: JAI Press.

Devitt, James. 1999. *Framing Gender on the Campaign Trail: Women's Executive Leadership and the Press.* New York: Women's Leadership Conference.

Diamond, Jared. 2003. "Globalization, Then." *Los Angeles Times,* September 14, pp. M1, M3.

Diamond, Shari Seidman, and Mary R. Rose. 2005. "Real Juries." Pp. 255–284 in *Annual Review of Law and Social Science 2005.* Palo Alto, CA: Annual Reviews.

Dickerson, Marla. 2007. "Mexico's Economy Loses Steam." *Los Angeles Times,* February 17.

Dillon, Sam. 1998. "Sex Bias at Border Plants in Mexico Reported by U.S." *New York Times,* January 13, p. A6.

———. 2004. "Education Can Be Long, Hard Haul for Nation's Rural Kids." *Chicago Tribune,* May 28, p. 13.

DiMaggio, Paul, Eszter Hargittai, W. Russell Neuman, and John P. Robinson. 2001. "Social Implications of the Internet." Pp. 307–336 in *Annual Review of Sociology, 2001,* edited by Karen S. Cook and John Hogan. Palo Alto, CA: Annual Reviews.

Directors Guild of America. 2002. *Diversity Hiring Special Report.* Los Angeles: DGA.

Disaster Research Center. 2005. *Who Are We? DRC.* Accessed June 10 (www.udel.edu/DRC/about.html).

Dobbs, Michael. 2004. "'No Child' Law Leaves a Good Deal Behind." *Washington Post National Weekly Edition,* May 9, p. 29.

Dodds, Klaus. 2000. *Geopolitics in a Changing World.* Harlow, England: Pearson Education.

Doeringer, Peter B., ed. 1990. *Bridges to Retirement: Older Workers in a Changing Labor Market.* Ithaca, NY: ILR Press.

Domhoff, G. William. 1978. *Who Really Rules? New Haven and Community Power Reexamined.* New Brunswick, NJ: Transaction.

———. 2006. *Who Rules America?* 5th ed. New York: McGraw-Hill.

Dominick, Joseph R. 2005. *The Dynamics of Mass Communication: Media in the Digital Age.* 8th ed. New York: McGraw-Hill.

Donnelly, Sally B. 2007. "Growing Younger." *Time* (January bonus section): A13–A14.

Donohue, Elizabeth, Vincent Schiraldi, and Jason Ziedenberg. 1998. *School House Hype: School Shootings and Real Risks Kids Face in America.* New York: Justice Policy Institute.

Doress, Irwin, and Jack Nusan Porter. 1977. *Kids in Cults: Why They Join. Why They Stay, Why They Leave.* Brookline, MA: Reconciliation Associates.

Dotson, Floyd. 1991. "Community." P. 55 in *Encyclopedic Dictionary of Sociology.* 4th ed. Guilford, CT: Dushkin.

Dougherty, John, and David Holthouse. 1999. "Bordering on Exploitation." Accessed March 5 (www.phoenixnewtime.com/issies/1998-07-09/feature.html).

Dougherty, Kevin, and Floyd M. Hammack. 1992. "Education Organization." Pp. 535–541 in *Encyclopedia of Sociology,* vol. 2, edited by Edgar F. Borgatta and Marie L. Borgatta. New York: Macmillan.

Dowd, James J. 1980. *Stratification among the Aged.* Monterey, CA: Brooks/Cole.

Doyle, James A., and Michele A. Paludi. 1998. *Sex and Gender: The Human Experience.* 4th ed. New York: McGraw-Hill.

Dreifus, Claudia. 2003. "A Conversation with Lee Clarke." *New York Times,* May 20, Science Times Section, p. 2.

———. 2004. "A Sociologist with an Advanced Degree in Calamity." *New York Times,* September 7, p. D2.

———. 2005. "A Sociologist Confronts 'the Messy Stuff' of Race, Genes and Disease." *New York Times,* October 18.

Du Bois, W. E. B. 1909. *The Negro American Family.* Atlanta University. Reprinted 1970. Cambridge, MA: M.I.T. Press.

———. [1940] 1968. *Dusk of Dawn.* New York: Harcourt, Brace. Reprint, New York: Schocken Books.

Dugger, Celia. 2006. "Peace Prize to Pioneer of Loans for Those Too Poor to Borrow." *New York Times* (October 14), pp. A1, A6.

Dukes, Richard L., Tara M. Bisel, Karoline N. Burega, Eligio A. Lobato, and Matthew D. Owens. 2003. "Expression of Love, Sex, and Hurt in Popular Songs: A Content Analysis of All-Time Greatest Hits." *Social Science Journal:*643–650.

Duncan, Emma. 2006. "The Heat Is On: A Survey of Climate Change." *The Economist* (September 9), special section.

Dundas, Susan, and Miriam Kaufman. 2000. "The Toronto Lesbian Family Study." *Journal of Homosexuality* 40 (20):65–79.

Duneier, Mitchell. 1994a. "On the Job, but Behind the Scenes." *Chicago Tribune,* December 26, pp. 1, 24.

———. 1994b. "Battling for Control." *Chicago Tribune,* December 28, pp. 1, 8.

———. 1999. *Sidewalk.* New York: Farrar, Straus and Giroux.

Dunne, Gillian A. 2000. "Opting into Motherhood: Lesbians Blurring the Boundaries and Transforming the Meaning of Parenthood and Kinship." *Gender and Society* 14 (February):11–35.

Durden, T. Elizabeth, and Robert A. Hummer. 2006. "Access to Healthcare Among Working-Aged Hispanic Adults in the United States." *Social Science Quarterly* 87 (December): 1319–1343.

Durkheim, Émile. [1893] 1933. *Division of Labor in Society.* Translated by George Simpson. Reprint, New York: Free Press.

———. [1895] 1964. *The Rules of Sociological Method.* Translated by Sarah A. Solovay and John H. Mueller. Reprint, New York: Free Press.

———. [1897] 1951. *Suicide.* Translated by John A. Spaulding and George Simpson. Reprint, New York: Free Press.

———. [1912] 2001. *The Elementary Forms of Religious Life.* A new translation by Carol Cosman. New York: Oxford University Press.

Duster, Troy. 2002. "Sociological Stranger in the Land of the Human Genome Project." *Contexts* 1 (Fall):69–70.

Dykman, Jason. 2006. "America by the Numbers." *Time* 168 (October): 41–54.

Eaton, Leslie. 2007. "Urban to Care, Storm Evacuees Give Farm a Try." *New York Times* (April 28): A1, A9.

Ebaugh, Helen Rose Fuchs. 1988. *Becoming an Ex: The Process of Role Exit.* Chicago: University of Chicago Press.

Eckenwiler, Mark. 1995. "In the Eyes of the Law." *Internet World* (August):74, 76–77.

The Economist. 2003a. "Race in Brazil: Out of Eden." (July 5):31–32.

———. 2003b. "The One Where Pooh Goes to Sweden." (April 5):59.

———. 2003c. "The War That Never Ends." 360 (January 18):24–26.

———. 2004b. "Battle on the Home Front." (February 21):8–10.

———. 2005a. "Back to the Beach?" (January 8):54–55.

———. 2005b. "We Are Tous Québécois." (January 8):39.

———. 2005c. "Behind the Digital Divide." (March 2):22–25.

———. 2005f. "The Hidden Wealth of the Poor." (November 5):1–14.

———. 2005g. "Not Here, Surely?" 377 (December 10):31–32.

———. 2005h. "The Conundrum of the Glass Ceiling." 376 (July 23): 63–65.

———. 2005i. "The Policeman's Dilemma." 377 (October 15): 58–59.

———. 2006a. "The World's Largest Economies." (April 1):84.

———. 2006b. "Freelancers of the World, Unite!" 381 (November 11): 76.

———. 2006c. "Splitting the Digital Difference." (September 23), 3–4

———. 2007a. "Giving to Charity: Bring Back the Victorians." 382 (February 17): 56–57.

Edwards, Harry. 1973. *Sociology of Sport.* Homewood, IL: Dorsey Press.

Efron, Sonni. 1997. "In Japan, Even Tots Must Make the Grade." *Los Angeles Times,* February 16, pp. A1, A17.

Ehrenreich, Barbara. 2001. *Nickel and Dimed: On (Not) Getting By in America.* New York: Metropolitan.

Ehrlich, Paul R. 1968. *The Population Bomb.* New York: Ballantine.

———, and Anne H. Ehrlich. 1990. *The Population Explosion.* New York: Simon and Schuster.

———, and Katherine Ellison. 2002. "A Looming Threat We Won't Face." *Los Angeles Times,* January 20, p. M6.

Eisenberg, David M., et al. 1998. "Trends in Alternative Medicine Use in the United States, 1990–1997." *Journal of the American Medical Association* 280 (November 11): 1569–1636.

Eitzen, D. Stanley. 2006. *Fair and Foul: Beyond the Myths and Paradoxes of Sport.* 3d ed. Lanham, MD: Rowman and Littlefield.

Ellingwood, Ken. 2001. "Results of Crackdown and Border Called Mixed." *Los Angeles Times,* August 4, p. B9.

Elliot, Michael. 2007. "The Chinese Century." *Time* 169 (January 22): 22–32.

Elliott, Barry J. 1999. "Road Rage: Media Hype or Serious Road Safety Issue?" Accessed December 14, 2005 (www.drivers.com).

Ellison, Ralph. 1952. *Invisible Man.* New York: Random House.

El Nasser, Haya. 2001. "Minorities Reshape Suburbs." *USA Today,* July 9, p. 1A.

Ely, Robin J. 1995. "The Power of Demography: Women's Social Construction of Gender Identity at Work." *Academy of Management Journal* 38 (3):589–634.

Embree, Ainslie. 2003. "Religion." Pp. 101–220 in *Understanding Contemporary India,* edited by Sumit Ganguly and Neil DeVotta. Boulder, CO: Lynne Rienner.

Emery, David. 1997. "The Kidney Snatchers." Accessed December 21, 1999 (http://urbanlegends.about.com/culture/urbanlegends/library/blkid.htm).

Engardio, Pete. 1999. "Activists Without Borders." *BusinessWeek,* October 4, pp. 144–145, 148, 150.

Engels, Friedrich [1884] 1959. "The Origin of the Family, Private Property, and the State." Pp. 392–394, excerpted in *Marx and Engels: Basic Writings on Politics and Philosophy,* edited by Lewis Feuer. Garden City, NY: Anchor.

Entine, Jon, and Martha Nichols. 1996. "Blowing the Whistle on Meaningless 'Good Intentions.' " *Chicago Tribune,* June 20, sec. 1, p. 21.

Epstein, Cynthia Fuchs. 1999. "The Major Myth of the Women's Movement." *Dissent* (Fall):83–111.

Epstein, Robert. 2005. "Psychology's Top 10 Misguided Ideas." *Psychology Today* 38 (January/February):55–58, 60.

Erard, Michael. 2005. "How Linguistics and Missionaries Share a Bible of 6,912 Languages." *New York Times,* July 10, p. D3.

Ericson, Nels. 2001. "Substance Abuse: The Nation's Number One Health Problem." *OJJDP Fact Sheet* 17 (May):1–2.

Erikson, Kai. 1966. *Wayward Puritans: A Study in the Sociology of Deviance.* New York: Wiley.

———. 1986. "On Work and Alienation." *American Sociological Review* 51 (February):1–8.

———. 1994. *A New Species of Trouble: The Human Experience of Modern Disasters.* New York: Norton.

Etaugh, Claire. 2003. "Witches, Mothers and Others: Females in Children's Books." *Hilltopics* (Winter): 10–13.

Etzioni, Amitai. 1964. *Modern Organization.* Englewood Cliffs, NJ: Prentice Hall.

———. 1965. *Political Unification.* New York: Holt, Rinehart, and Winston.

Eureka County. 2006. "EPA Hears Testimony on Proposed Radiation Rule." *Nuclear Waste Office Newsletter* (Eureka County Yucca Mountain Information Office) 11 (Winter).

Faiola, Anthony. 2005. "Their Husbands Made Them Sick." *Washington Post National Weekly Edition* 23 (October 24): 18.

———. 2006. "Japan's Vulnerable Elderly." *Washington Post National Weekly Edition* 23 (February 27): 18.

FAIR. 2001. "Fear and Favor 2000." Accessed December 29, 2001 (www.FAIR.org).

Faith, Nazila. 2005. "Iranian Cleric Turns Blogger in Campaign for Reform." *New York Times,* January 16, p. 4.

Fallows, Deborah. 2006. *Pew Internet Project Data.* Washington, DC: Pew Internet and American Life Project.

Farkas, Steve, Ann Duffett, and Jean Johnson, with Leslie Moyer and Jackie Vine. 2003. *Now That I'm Here: What America's Immigrants Have to Say About Life in the U.S. Today.* New York: Public Agenda.

Farley, Maggie. 2004. "U.N. Gay Policy Is Assailed." *Los Angeles Times,* April 9, p. A3.

Farr, Grant M. 1999. *Modern Iran.* New York: McGraw-Hill.

Farrar, Melissa. 2005. "Road Rage and Aggressive Driving." Unpublished paper, DePaul University, Chicago.

Fausset, Richard. 2003. "Sikhs Mark New Year, Fight Post-September 11 Bias." *Los Angeles Times,* April 14, pp. B1, B7.

Feagin, Joe R. 1983. *The Urban Real Estate Game: Playing Monopoly with Real Money.* Englewood Cliffs, NJ: Prentice Hall.

———. 1989. *Minority Group Issues in Higher Education: Learning from Qualitative Research.* Norman, OK: Center for Research on Minority Education, University of Oklahoma.

———. 2001. "Social Justice and Sociology: Agenda for the Twenty-First Century." *American Sociological Review* 66 (February):1–20.

———, Harnán Vera, and Nikitah Imani. 1996. *The Agony of Education: Black Students at White Colleges and Universities.* New York: Routledge.

Featherman, David L., and Robert M. Hauser. 1978. *Opportunity and Change.* New York: Aeodus.

578 *Federal Register,* June 4, 1975.

Feinglass, Joe. 1987. "Next, the McDRG." *The Progressive* 51 (January):28.

Feketekuty, Geza. 2001. "Globalization—Why All the Fuss?" P. 191 in *2001 Britannica Book of the Year.* Chicago: Encyclopedia Britannica.

Fellmann, Jerome D., Arthur Getis, and Judith Getis. 2007. *Human Geography.* 9th ed. New York: McGraw-Hill.

Felson, David, and Akis Kalaitzidis. 2005. "A Historical Overview of Transnational Crime." Pp. 3–19 in *Handbook of Transnational Crime and Justice,* edited by Philip Reichel. Thousand Oaks, CA: Sage.

Felson, Marcus. 2002. *Crime and Everyday Life.* 3d ed. Thousand Oaks, CA: Pine Forge Press.

Feminist Majority Foundation. 2007. "Feminists Are the Majority." Accessed February 25 (www.feminist.org).

Ferree, Myra Marx. 2005. "It's Time to Mainstream Research on Gender." *Chronicle of Higher Education* 51 (August 21):B10.

———, and David A. Merrill. 2000. "Hot Movements, Cold Cognition: Thinking about Social Movements in Gendered Frames." *Contemporary Society* 29 (May):454–462.

Feuer, Alan. 2002. "High-Rise Colony of Workers Evolves for Their Retirement." *New York Times,* August 5, pp. A1, A15.

Feuer, Lewis S. 1989. *Marx and Engels: Basic Writings on Politics and Philosophy.* New York: Anchor Books.

Fiala, Robert. 1992. "Postindustrial Society." Pp. 1512–1522 in *Encyclopedia of Sociology,* vol. 3, edited by Edgar F. Borgatta and Marie L. Borgatta. New York: Macmillan.

Fields, Jason. 2003. "Children's Living Arrangements and Characteristics: March 2002." *Current Population Reports,* ser. P-20, no. 547. Washington, DC: U.S. Government Printing Office.

———. 2004. "America's Families and Living Arrangements: 2003." *Current Population Reports,* ser. P-20, no. 553. Washington, DC: U.S. Government Printing Office.

Fields, Jessica. 2005. "'Children Having Children': Race, Innocence, and Sexuality Education." *Social Problems* 52 (4):549–571.

Finder, Alan. 1995. "Despite Tough Laws, Sweatshops Flourish." *New York Times,* January 6, pp. A1, B4.

Fine, Gary Alan. 1987. *With the Boys: Little League Baseball and Preadolescent Culture.* Chicago: University of Chicago Press.

———. 2004. "Forgotten Classic: The Robbers Cave Experiment." *Sociological Forum* 19 (December): 663–666.

Finkel, Steven E., and James B. Rule. 1987. "Relative Deprivation and Related Psychological Theories of Civil Violence: A Critical Review." *Research in Social Movements* 9:47–69.

Firestone, David. 1999. "School Prayer Is Revived as an Issue in Alabama." *New York Times,* July 15, p. A14.

Fiss, Peer C., and Paul M. Hirsch. 2005. "The Discourse of Globalization: Framing of an Emerging Concept." *American Sociological Review* (February):29–52.

Fitchett, George. 1980. "It's Time to Bury the Stage Theory of Death and Dying." *Oncology Nurse Exchange II* (Fall).

Fitzgerald, Kathleen J., and Diane M. Rodgers. 2000. "Radical Social Movement Organization: A Theoretical Model." *The Sociological Quarterly* 41 (4):573–592.

Fix, Michael, Wendy Zimmerman, and Jeffry S. Passel. 2001. *The Integration of Immigrant Families in the United States.* Washington, DC: The Urban Institute.

Flacks, Richard. 1971. *Youth and Social Change.* Chicago: Markham.

Fletcher, Connie. 1995. "On the Line: Women Cops Speak Out." *Chicago Tribune Magazine,* February 19, pp. 14–19.

Flora, Cornelia Butter, and Jan L. Flora, with Susan Fey. 2004. *Rural Communities: Legacy and Change.* 2d ed. Boulder, CO: Westview.

Florio, Gwen. 2006. "Vacant Seat Tough to Fill If 'Districts' Empty, Too." *USA Today,* January 24, p. 3A.

Flynn, Patrice. 2007. "Microfinance: The Newest Finance Technology of the Washington Consensus." *Challenge* 50 (March/April): 110–121.

Fornos, Werner. 1997. *1997 World Population Overview.* Washington, DC: The Population Institute.

Förster, Michael, and Marco Mira d'Ercole. 2005. *Income Distribution and Poverty in OECD Countries in the Second Half of the 1990s.* Paris: OECD.

Forsythe, David P. 1990. "Human Rights in U.S. Foreign Policy: Retrospect and Prospect." *Political Science Quarterly* 105(3):435–454.

Fortune. 2005. "Fortune Global 500." 152 (July 25), 97–142.

———. 2007. "Global 500." (July 14).

Foy, Paul. 2006. "Interior Rejects Goshute Nuclear Waste Stockpile." *Indian Country Today* (September 18), 20:1.

Frank, Thomas. 2007. "TSA Union Fight Threatens Anti-Terror Bill." *USA Today* (March 1), p. 4a.

Franklin, John Hope, and Alfred A. Moss. 2000. *From Slavery to Freedom: A History of African Americans.* 8th ed. Upper Saddle River, NJ: Prentice Hall.

FreeBabarAhmad. 2007. "Home Page." Accessed May 7 (www.freebabarahmad.com).

Free Lancers Union. 2007. "About Us." Accessed February 10 (www.freelancersunion.org).

Freeman, Jo. 1973. "The Origins of the Women's Liberation Movement." *American Journal of Sociology* 78 (January):792–811.

———. 1975. *The Politics of Women's Liberation.* New York: McKay.

Freidson, Eliot. 1970. *Profession of Medicine.* New York: Dodd, Mead.

French, Howard W. 2000. "The Pretenders." *New York Times Magazine,* December 3, pp. 86–88.

———. 2002. "Teaching Japan's Salarymen to Be Their Own Men." *New York Times,* November 27, p. A4.

———. 2003a. "Insular Japan Needs, but Resists, Immigration." *New York Times,* July 24, pp. A1, A3.

———. 2003b. "Japan's Neglected Resource: Female Workers." *New York Times,* July 25.

———. 2004a. "Despite an Act of Clemency, China Has Its Eye on the Web." *New York Times,* June 27, p. 6.

———. 2004b. "China's Textbooks Twist and Omit History." *New York Times* (December 6), p. A10.

———. 2006. "Chinese Success Story Chokes on It's own Growth." *New York Times,* December 19, pp. A1, A10.

———. 2007. "China Scrambles for Stability as It's Works Age." *New York Times,* March 22, pp. A1, A8.

Freudenburg, William R. 2005. "Seeing Science, Courting Conclusions: Reexamining the Intersection of Science, Corporate Cash, and the Law." *Sociological Forum* 20 (March):3–33.

Freudenheim, Milt. 2005. "Help Wanted: Oldest Workers Please Apply." *New York Times,* March 23, pp. A1, C3.

Frey, William H. 2001. *Melting Pot Suburbs: A Census 2000 Study of Suburban Diversity.* Washington, DC: The Brookings Institution.

Fridlund, Alan. J., Paul Erkman, and Harriet Oster. 1987. "Facial Expressions of Emotion; Review of Literature 1970–1983." Pp. 143–224 in *Nonverbal Behavior and Communication,* 2d ed., edited by Aron W. Seigman and Stanley Feldstein. Hillsdale, NJ: Lawrence Erlbaum Associates.

Friedan, Betty. 1963. *The Feminine Mystique.* New York: Dell.

Friedland, Jonathon. 2000. "An American in Mexico Champions Midwifery as a Worthy Profession." *Wall Street Monitor,* February 15, pp. A1, A12.

Friedman, Thomas L. 2005. *The World Is Flat: A Brief History of the Twenty-first Century.* New York: Farrar, Straus and Giroux.

Friedrich, Carl J., and Zbigniew Brzezinski. 1965. *Totalitarian Dictatorship and Autocracy.* 2d ed. Cambridge, MA: Harvard University Press.

Fujimoto, Kayo. 2004. "Feminine Capital: The Forms of Capital in the Female Labor Market in Japan." *Sociological Quarterly* 45 (1):91–111.

Furstenberg, Frank, and Andrew Cherlin. 1991. *Divided Families: What Happens to Children When Parents Part.* Cambridge, MA: Harvard University Press.

Furstenberg, Sheela Kennedy, Jr., Vonnie C. McCloyd, Rubén G. Rumbaut, and Richard A. Setterstein, Jr. 2004. "Growing Up Is Harder to Do." *Contexts* 3:33–41.

Fuwa, Makiko. 2004. "Macro-Level Gender Inequality and the Division of Household Labor in 22 Countries." *American Sociological Review* 69 (December):751–767.

Gallup. 2004. *The Gallup Poll of Baghdad.* Omaha, NE: Gallup.

———. 2006. "Party Affiliation May 12–13, 2006." Accessed June 2 (www.gallup.com).

———. 2006a. "Can You Hear Me? An Overview of The Gallup Organization's Poll of the Muslim World." Omaha, NE: Gallup World Poll.

———. 2007a. "Death Penalty." Accessed February 17, 2007 (www.gallup.com).

———. 2007b. "Homosexual Relations." January 23, 2007. Accessed March 2 (www.gallup.com).

———. 2007c. "Media Use and Evaluation." Accessed April 19 (www.gallup.com).

Gamson, Joshua. 1989. "Silence, Death, and the Invisible Enemy: AIDS Activism and Social Movement 'Newness.'" *Social Problems* 36 (October):351–367.

———, and Pearl Latteier. 2004. "Do Media Monsters Devour Diversity?" *Contexts* (Summer): 26–32.

Gans, Herbert J. 1979. "Symbolic Ethnicity: The Future of Ethnic Groups and Cultures in America." *Ethnic and Racial Studies* 2 (January): 1–20.

———. 1991. *People, Plans, and Policies: Essays on Poverty, Racism, and Other National Urban Problems.* New York: Columbia University Press and Russell Sage Foundation.

———. 1995. *The War against the Poor: The Underclass and Antipoverty Policy.* New York: Basic Books.

Ganzeboom, Harry B. G., Ruud Luijkx, Donald J. Treiman. 1989. "Inter-genera-tional Class Mobility in Comparative Perspective." *Research in Social Stratification and Mobility* (8), pp. 3–79.

Ganzeboom, Harry B. G., Donald J. Treiman, and Woult C. Ultee. 1991. "Comparative Intergenerational Stratification Research." Pp. 277–302 in *Annual Review of Sociology, 1991*, edited by W. Richard Scott. Palo Alto, CA: Annual Reviews.

Garcia-Moreno, Claudia, Henrica A. F. M. Jansen, Mary Ellsberg, Lori Heise, and Charlotte Watts. 2005. *WHO Multi-country Study on Women's Health and Domestic Violence Against Women.* Geneva, Switzerland: WHO.

Gardner, Gary, Erik Assadourian, and Radhika Sarin. 2004. "The State of Consumption Today." Pp. 3–21 in *State of the World 2004,* edited by Brian Halweil and Lisa Mastny. New York: W. W. Norton.

Gardner, Marilyn. 2003. "This View of Seniors Just Doesn't 'Ad' Up." *Christian Science Monitor,* January 15, p. 15.

Garfinkel, Harold. 1956. "Conditions of Successful Degradation Ceremonies." *American Journal of Sociology* 61 (March):420–424.

Garner, Roberta. 1996. *Contemporary Movements and Ideologies.* New York: McGraw-Hill.

———. 1999. "Virtual Social Movements." Presented at Zaldfest: A conference in honor of Mayer Zald. September 17, Ann Arbor, MI.

Garreau, Joel. 1991. *Edge City: Life on the New Frontier.* New York: Doubleday.

Gay, Lesbian and Straight Education Network. 2007. "About GLSEN." Accessed April 11 (www.glsen.org).

Gecas, Viktor. 2004. "Socialization, Sociology of." Pp. 14525–14530 in *International Encyclopedia of the Social and Behavioral Sciences,* edited by Neil J. Smelser and Paul B. Baltes. Cambridge, MA: Elsevier.

Geist, Claudia. 2005. "The Welfare State and the Home: Regime Differences in the Domestic Division of Labour." *European Sociological Review 2005* 21(1):23–4.

Geist, Eric L., Vasily V. Titov, and Costas E. Synolakis. 2006. "Tsunami: Wave of Change." *Scientific American* 294 (January):56–63.

Gentleman, Amelia. 2006. "Bollywood Captivated by the Call Centre Culture." *Guardian Weekly* (June 2): 17.

———. 2007. "Police Ignore Serial Killings in Delhi Slum, Exposing Unequal Justice for India's Poor." *New York Times,* January 7, p. 8.

Gerson, Kathleen, and Jerry A. Jacobs. 2004. "The Work-Home Crunch." *Contexts* 3 (Fall):29–37.

Gerth, H. H., and C. Wright Mills. 1958. *From Max Weber: Essays in Sociology.* New York: Galaxy.

Gertner, Jon. 2005. "Our Ratings, Ourselves." *New York Times Magazine,* April 10, pp. 34–41, 56, 58, 64–65.

Geyer, Georgie Anne. 2004. "U.S. Refusal to Supply Population Funds Based on Misinformation." *Chicago Tribune,* July 23, p. 25.

Gibbs, Nancy. 1993. "Rx for Death." *Time,* May 31, pp. 34–39.

Giddens, Anthony. 1991. *Modernity and Self-Identity: Self and Society in the Late Modern Age.* Cambridge, UK: Polity.

Giordano, Peggy C. 2003. "Relationships in Adolescence." Pp. 257–281 in *Annual Review of Sociology, 2003,* edited by Karen S. Cook and John Hagan. Palo Alto, CA: Annual Reviews.

———, Stephen A. Cernkovich, and Alfred DeMaris. 1993. "The Family and Peer Relations of Black Adolescents." *Journal of Marriage and Family* 55 (May): 277–287.

Giroux, Henry A. 1988. *Schooling and the Struggle for Public Life: Critical Pedagogy in the Modern Age.* Minneapolis: University of Minnesota Press.

Gitlin, Todd. 2002. *Media Unlimited: How the Torrent of Images and Sounds Overwhelms Our Lives.* New York: Henry Holt and Company.

Glanton, Dahleen. 2007. "Law AIDS Awareness adds to crisis." *Chicago Tribune,* February 7, p. 3.

Glascock, Anthony P. 1990. "By Any Other Name, It Is Still Killing: A Comparison of the Treatment of the Elderly in American and Other Societies." Pp. 44–56 in *The Cultural Context of Aging: Worldwide Perspective,* edited by Jay Sokolovsky. New York: Bergen and Garvey.

Glaze, Lauren E, and Seri Palla. 2005. "Probation and Parole in the United States, 2004." *Bureau of Justice Statistics Bulletin* (November).

Glenn, David. 2004. "A Dangerous Surplus of Sons?" *Chronicle of Higher Education* 50 (April 30):A14–A16, A18.

Global Alliance for Workers and Communities. 2003. *About Us.* Accessed April 28 (www.theglobalalliance.org).

Goering, Laurie. 2007. "The First Refugees of Global Warming." *Chicago Tribune,* May 2, pp. 1, 25.

Goffman, Erving. 1959. *The Presentation of Self in Everyday Life.* New York: Doubleday.

———. 1961. *Asylums: Essays on the Social Situation of Mental Patients and Other Inmates.* Garden City, NY: Doubleday.

———. 1963. *Stigma: Notes on Management of Spoiled Identity.* Englewood Cliffs, NJ: Prentice Hall.

———. 1979. *Gender Advertisements.* Cambridge, MA: Harvard University Press.

Golden, Daniel. 2006. *The Price of Admission: How America's Ruling Class Buys Its Way into Elite Colleges—and Who Gets Left Outside the Gates.* New York: Crown.

Golden, Frederic. 1999. "Who's Afraid of Frankenfood?" *Time,* November 29, pp. 49–50.

Goldstein, Amy, and Richard Morin. 2002. "The Squeaky Wheel Gets the Grease." *Washington Post National Weekly Edition 20,* October 28, p. 34.

Goldstein, Greg. 1998. "World Health Organization and Housing." Pp. 636–637 in *The Encyclopedia of Housing,* edited by Willem van Vliet. Thousand Oaks, CA: Sage.

Goldstein, Melvyn C., and Cynthia M. Beall. 1981. "Modernization and Aging in the Third and Fourth World: Views from the Rural Hinterland in Nepal." *Human Organization* 40 (Spring): 48–55.

Gole, Nilofer. 1997. "Lifting the Veil—Reform vs. Tradition in Turkey—An Interview." *Manushi,* May 1.

Gonnut, Jean Pierre. 2001. Interview. June 18, 2001.

Gonzalez, David. 2003. "Latin Sweatshops Pressed by U.S. Campus Power." *New York Times,* April 4, p. A3.

Gooding, Caroline. 1994. *Disability Laws, Enabling Acts: Disability Rights in Britain and America.* Boulder, CO: Westview.

Goodman, Peter S., and Akiko Kashiwagi. 2002. "In Japan, Housewives No More." *Washington Post National Weekly Edition,* November 4, pp. 18–19.

Goodstein, Laurie. 2005. "Issuing Rebuke, Judge Rejects Teaching of Intelligent Design." *New York Times,* December 21, pp. A1, A21.

Goodwin, Michele. 2006. *Black Markets: The Supply and Demand of Body Parts.* New York: Cambridge University Press.

Gordon, Gary. 2004. "Teacher Retention Statistics with Great Principals." *Gallup Poll Tuesday Briefing,* February 17. Accessed March 18 (www.gallup.com).

Gordon, Raymond G., Jr., ed. 2005. *Ethnologue: Languages of the World.* 15th ed. Dallas, TX: SIL International.

Gottdiener, Mark, and Joe R. Feagin. 1988. "The Paradigm Shift in Urban Sociology." *Urban Affairs Quarterly* 24 (December):163–187.

———, and Ray Hutchison. 2006. *The New Urban Sociology.* 3d ed. Boulder, CO: Westview.

Gottfredson, Michael, and Travis Hirschi. 1990. *A General Theory of Crime.* Palo Alto, CA: Stanford University Press.

Gottlieb, Lori. 2006. "How Do I Love Thee?" *Atlantic Monthly* (March): 58, 60, 62–68, 70.

Gould, Elise. 2006. *Health Insurance Erodes for Working Families: Employer-Presided Coverage Declines for Fifth Consecutive Year.* Washington, DC: Economic Policy Institute.

———. 2007. "The Health-Finance Debate Reaches a Fever Pitch." *Chronicle of Higher Education* (April 13): B14, B15.

Gould, Larry A. 2002. "Indigenous People Policing Indigenous People: The Potential Psychological and Cultural Costs." *Social Science Journal* 39:171–188.

Gouldner, Alvin. 1960. "The Norm of Reciprocity." *American Sociological Review* 25 (April):161–177.

580

———. 1970. *The Coming Crisis of Western Sociology.* New York: Basic Books.

Graham, Judith. 2004. "Kids of Addicts Bear Scars as Meth Sweeps Rural Areas." *Chicago Tribune,* March 7, pp. 1, 14.

Gramsci, Antonio. 1929. *Selections from the Prison Notebooks.* Antonio Gramsci. Edited and translated by Quintin Hoare and Geoffrey Nowell Smith. London: Lawrence and Wishort.

Greeley, Andrew M. 1989. "Protestant and Catholic: Is the Analogical Imagination Extinct?" *American Sociological Review* 54 (August):485–502.

Green, Dan S., and Edwin D. Driver. 1978. "Introduction." Pp. 1–60 in *W. E. B. DuBois on Sociology and the Black Community,* edited by Dan S. Green and Edwin D. Driver. Chicago: University of Chicago Press.

Greenblatt, Alan. 2005. "Upward Mobility." *CQ Researcher* 15 (April 29).

Greenhouse, Linda. 1998. "High Court Ruling Says Harassment Includes Same Sex." *New York Times,* March 5, pp. A1, A17.

———. 2005. "Justices Say U.S. May Prohibit the Use of Medical Marijuana." *New York Times,* June 7, pp. A1, A15.

Grieco, Elizabeth M., and Rachel C. Cassidy. 2001. "Overview of Race and Hispanic Origin." *Current Population Reports Series* CENBR/01–1. Washington, DC: U.S. Government Printing Office.

Grier, Peter. 2005. "Rich-Poor Gap Gaining Attention." *Christian Science Monitor,* June 14.

Griswold, Wendy. 2004. *Cultures and Societies in a Changing World.* 2d ed. Thousand Oaks, CA: Pine Forge Press.

Grob, Gerald N. 1995. "The Paradox of Deinstitutionalization." *Society* 32 (July/August): 51–59.

Groening, Chad. 2007. "Media Coverage of Virginia Tech Massacre Shows Anti-Gun Bias, Says Watchdog." Accessed May 16 (www.onenewsnow.com).

Gross, Jane. 2005. "Forget the Career. My Parents Need Me at Home." *New York Times,* November 24: A1, A20.

Grossman, Ler, and Hannah Beech. 2006. "Google Under the Gun." *Time,* February 13, p. 53.

Groza, Victor, Daniela F. Ileana, and Ivor Irwin. 1999. *A Peacock or a Crow: Stories, Interviews, and Commentaries on Romanian Adoptions.* Euclid, OH: Williams Custom Publishing.

Guterman, Lila. 2000. "Why the 25-Year-Old Battle over Sociology Is More than Just 'An Academic Sideshow.'" *Chronicle of Higher Education,* July 7, pp. A17–A18.

Gutiérrez, Gustavo. 1990. "Theology and the Social Sciences." Pp. 214–225 in *Liberation Theology at the Crossroads: Democracy or Revolution?,* edited by Paul E. Sigmund. New York: Oxford University Press.

Gutierrez, Valerie. 2002. "Minority Women Get Left Behind by Title IX." *Los Angeles Times,* June 23, pp. D1, D12.

Hacker, Andrew. 1964. "Power to Do What?" Pp. 134–146 in *The New Sociology,* edited by Irving Louis Horowitz. New York: Oxford University Press.

Hacker, Helen Mayer. 1951. "Women as a Minority Group." *Social Forces* 30 (October):60–69.

———. 1974. "Women as a Minority Group, Twenty Years Later." Pp. 124–134 in *Who Discriminates against Women?* edited by Florence Denmark. Beverly Hills, CA: Sage.

Haeri, Shaykh Fadhilalla. 2004. *The Thoughtful Guide to Islam.* Alresford, UK: O Books.

Hafner-Burton, Emilie M., and Kiyoteru Tsutsui. 2005. "Human Rights in a Globalizing World: The Paradox of Empty Promises." *American Journal of Sociology* 110 (March):1373–1411.

Hagan, John, Heather Schoenfeld, and Alberto Palloni. 2006. "The Science of Human Rights, War Crimes, and Humanitarian Emergencies." Pp. 329–349 in *Annual Review of Sociology 2006,* edited by Karen S. Cook and Douglas S. Massey. Palo Alto, CA: Annual Reviews.

Halebsky, Stephen. 2004. "Superstores and the Politics of Retail Development." *City and Community* 5 (June):115–134.

Hall, Mimi. 2005. "Senators 'to Demand Answers' on Slow Action." *USA Today,* September 6, p. 4A.

Hall, Robert H. 1982. "The Truth about Brown Lung." *Business and Society Review* 40 (Winter 1981–82):15–20.

Haller, Max, Wolfgang Konig, Peter Krause, and Karin Kurz. 1990. "Patterns of Career Mobility and Structural Positions in Advanced Capitalist Societies: A Comparison of Men in Austria, France, and the United States." *American Sociological Review* 50 (October): 579–603.

Hallinan, Maureen T. 1997. "The Sociological Study of Social Change." *American Sociological Review* 62 (February):1–11.

Hamilton, Brady E., Joyce A. Martin, and Stephanie J. Ventura. 2006. "Births: Preliminary Data for 2005." *National Vital Statistics Reports* 55 (December 28): 1–20.

Hamilton, Brady E., Joyce A. Martin, Stephanie J. Ventura, Paul D. Sutton, and Fay Menacker. 2005. "Births: Preliminary Data for 2004." *National Vital Statistics Reports* 54 (December 29).

Hamm, Jill V., B. Bradford Brown, and Daniel J. Heck. 2005. "Bridging the Ethnic Divide: Students and School Characteristics in African American, Asian-Descent, Latino, and White Adolescents' Cross-Ethnic Friend Nominations." *Journal of Research on Adolescence* 15 (1):21–46.

Hani, Yoko. 1998. "Hot Pots Wired to Help the Elderly." *Japan Times Weekly International Edition,* April 13, p. 16.

Hank, Karsten. 2001. "Changes in Child Care Could Reduce Job Options for Eastern German Mothers." *Population Today* 29 (April):3, 6.

Hansen, Brian. 2004. "Big-Box Stores." *CQ Researcher* 14 (September 10).

Hanson, Ralph E. 2005. *Mass Communication: Living in a Media World.* New York: McGraw-Hill.

Hare, A. Paul. 1992. "Group Size." Pp. 788–791 in *Encyclopedia of Sociology,* vol 2, edited by Edgar F. Borgatta and Marie L. Borgatta. New York: Macmillan.

Harlow, Harry F. 1971. *Learning to Love.* New York: Ballantine.

Harrington, Michael. 1962. *The Other America: Poverty in the United States.* Baltimore: Penguin.

———. 1980. "The New Class and the Left." Pp. 123–138 in *The New Class,* edited by B. Bruce Briggs. Brunswick, NJ: Transaction.

Harris, Chauncy D., and Edward Ullman. 1945. "The Nature of Cities." *Annals of the American Academy of Political and Social Science* 242 (November):7–17.

Harris, Judith Rich. 1998. *The Nurture Assumption: Why Children Turn Out the Way They Do.* New York: Free Press.

Hartman, Chris, and Jake Miller. 2001. *Bail Outs That Work for Everyone.* Boston: United for a Fair Economy.

Haskins, Ron. 2006. "Welfare Reform, 10 Years Later." *Poverty Research Insights* (Fall).

Haub, Carl. 2004. *World Population Data Sheet, 2004.* Washington, DC: Population Reference Bureau.

———. 2006. *2006 World Population Data Sheet.* Washington, DC: Population Reference Bureau.

———, and Britt Herstad. 2002. *Family Planning Worldwide: 2002 Data Sheet.* Washington, DC: Population Reference Bureau.

Hauser, Robert M., and David B. Grusky. 1988. "Cross-National Variation in Occupational Distributions, Relative Mobility Chances, and Intergenerational Shifts in Occupational Distributions." *American Sociological Review* 53 (October):723–741.

Haviland, William A. 2002. *Cultural Anthropology.* 10th ed. Belmont, CA: Wadsworth.

———, Harald E. L. Prins, Dana Walrath, and Bunny McBride. 2005. *Cultural Anthropology— The Human Challenge.* New York: McGraw-Hill.

Hayden, H. Thomas. 2004. "What Happened at Abu Ghraib." Accessed August 7 (www.military.com).

Hayward, Mark D., William R. Grady, and Steven D. McLaughlin. 1987. "Changes in the Retirement Process." *Demography* 25 (August):371–386.

He, Wan, Manisha Sengupta, Victoria A. Velkoff, and Kimberly A. DeBarros. 2005. "65+ in the United States: 2005." *Current Population Reports,* ser. P-23, no. 209. Washington, DC: U.S. Government Printing Office.

Head, John F. 2007. "Why, Even Today, Many Banks Are Wary about American Medicine." *Crisis* (January), pp. 48–49.

Health Care Financing Administration. 2001. *National Health Care Expenditures Projections.* Accessed August 10 (www.hcfa.gov/stats/NHE-proj/).

Hebel, Sara. 2006. "In Rural America, Few People Harvest 4-Year Degrees." *Chronicle of Higher Education* 53 (November 3), pp. A21–A24.

Heckert, Druann, and Amy Best. 1997. "Ugly Duckling to Swan: Labeling Theory and the Stigmatization of Red Hair." *Symbolic Interaction* 20 (4):365–384.

Hedley, R. Alan. 1992. "Industrialization in Less Developed Countries." Pp. 914–920 in *Encyclopedia of Sociology,* vol. 2, edited by Edgar F. Borgatta and Marie L. Borgatta. New York: Macmillan.

Heilman, Madeline E. 2001. "Description and Prescription: How Gender Stereotypes Prevent Women's Ascent up the Organizational Ladder." *Journal of Social Issues* 57 (4):657–674.

Hellmich, Nanci. 2001. "TV's Reality: No Vast American Waistlines." *USA Today,* October 8, p. 7D.

Henly, Julia R. 1999. "Challenges to Finding and Keeping Jobs in the Low-Skilled Labor Market." *Poverty Research News* 3 (1):3–5.

Herring, Hubert B. 2006. "A Teacher's Year, A C.E.O.'s Day: The Pay's Similar." *New York Times,* September 5, p. 2.

Hersch, Patricia. 1998. *A Tribe Apart: A Journey into the Heart of the American Adolescence.* New York: Fawcett Books.

Herschthal, Eric. 2004. "Indian Students Discuss Pros, Cons of Arranged Marriages." *Daily Princetonian* (October 20).

Hertz, Rosanna. 2006. *Single by Chance. Mothers by Choice.* New York: Oxford University Press.

Hetherington, E. Mavis, and John Kelly. 2002. *For Better or For Worse.* New York: Norton.

Hewlett, Sylvia Ann, and Carolyn Buck Luce. 2005. "Off-Ramps and On-Ramps: Keeping Talented Women on the Road to Success." *Harvard Business Review* (March):43–53.

Hick, Steven F., and John G. McNutt. 2002. *Advocacy, Activism, and the Internet.* Chicago: Lyceum.

Hickman, Jonathan. 2002. "America's 50 Best Corporations for Minorities." *Fortune* 146 (July 8):110–120.

Higher Education Research Institute. 2004. *Trends in Political Attitudes and Voting Behavior Among College Freshmen and Early Career College Graduates: What Issues Could Drive This Election?* Los Angeles: HERI, University of California, Los Angeles.

Hill, Michael R., and Susan Hoecker-Drysdale, eds. 2001. *Harriet Martineau: Theoretical and Methodological Perspectives.* New York: Routledge.

Hillery, George A. 1955. "Definitions of Community: Areas of Agreement." *Rural Sociology* (2):111–123.

Himes, Vristine L. 2001. "Elderly Americans." *Population Bulletin* 56 (December).

Hipp, John R., Daniel J. Bauer, Patrick J. Curran, and Kenneth A. Bollen. 2004. "Crimes of Opportunity or Crimes of Emotion? Testing Two Explanations of Seasoned Change in Crime." *Social Forces* 82 (4):1333–1372.

Hirsch, Barry, and David Macpherson. 2006. "Union Membership and Coverage Database." Accessed April 12 (www.unionstats.com).

Hirsch, Paul M., and Michaela De Soucey. 2006. "Organizational Restructuring and Its Consequences: Rhetorical and Structural." Pp. 171–189 in *Annual Review of Sociology 2006,* edited by Karen S. Cook and Douglas S. Massey. Palo Alto, CA: Annual Reviews.

Hirschi, Travis. 1969. *Causes of Delinquency.* Berkeley: University of California Press.

Hirst, Paul, and Grahame Thompson. 1996. *Globalization in Question: The International Economy and the Possibilities of Governance.* Cambridge, UK: Polity Press.

Hitlin, Steven, and Jane Allyn Piliavin. 2004. "Values: Reviving a Dormant Concept." Pp. 359–393 in *Annual Review of Sociology, 2004,* edited by Karen S. Cook and John Hagan. Palo Alto, CA: Annual Reviews.

Hobbs, Frank B., and Bonnie L. Damon. 1996. *65+ in the United States.* Washington, DC: U.S. Government Printing Office.

Hochschild, Arlie Russell. 1990. "The Second Shift: Employed Women Are Putting in Another Day of Work at Home." *Utne Reader* 38 (March/April): 66–73.

———. 2005. *The Commercialization of Intimate Life: Notes from Home and Work.* Berkeley: University of California Press.

———, with Anne Machung. 1989. *The Second Shift: Working Parents and the Revolution at Home.* New York: Viking Penguin.

Hodge, Robert W., and Peter H. Rossi. 1964. "Occupational Prestige in the United States, 1925–1963." *American Journal of Sociology* 70 (November):286–302.

Hodson, Randy, and Teresa A. Sullivan. 1995. *The Social Organization of Work.* 2d ed. Belmont, CA: Wadsworth.

Hoefer, Michael, Nancy Rytina, and Christopher Campbell. 2006. Estimates of the Unauthorized Immigrant Population Residing in the United States: January 2005. Rev. Number 2006. Washington, DC: Policy Directorate Office of Immigration Statistics.

Hoffman, Adonis. 1997. "Through an Accurate Prism." *Los Angeles Times,* August 8, p. M1.

Hoffman, Lois Wladis. 1985. "The Changing Genetics/Socialization Balance." *Journal of Social Issues* 41 (Spring):127–148.

Holden, Constance. 1980. "Identical Twins Reared Apart." *Science* 207 (March 21):1323–1328.

———. 1987. "The Genetics of Personality." *Science* 257 (August 7):598–601.

Holder, Kelly. 2006. "Voting and Registration in the Election of November 2004." *Current Population Reports,* ser. P-20, no. 556. Washington, DC: U.S. Government Printing Office.

Hollander, Jocelyn A. 2002. "Resisting Vulnerability: The Social Reconstruction of Gender in Interaction." *Social Problems* 49 (4):474–496.

Hollingshead, August B. 1975. *Elmtown's Youth and Elmtown Revisited.* New York: Wiley.

Homans, George C. 1979. "Nature versus Nurture: A False Dichotomy." *Contemporary Sociology* 8 (May):345–348.

Home School Legal Defense Association. 2005. "State Laws" and "Academic Statistics on Homeschooling." Accessed May 12 (www.hslda.org).

Hondagneu-Sotelo, Pierrette, ed. 2003. *Gender and U.S. Immigration: Contemporary Trends.* Berkeley: University of California Press.

hooks, bell. 1994. "Black Students Who Reject Feminism." *The Chronicle of Higher Education,* July 13, 60:A44.

Horgan, John. 1993. "Eugenics Revisited." *Scientific American* 268 (June):122–128, 130–133.

Horovitz, Bruce. 2003. "Smile! You're the Stars of the Super Ad Bowl." *USA Today,* January 24, pp. B1, B2.

Horowitz, Helen Lefkowitz. 1987. *Campus Life.* Chicago: University of Chicago Press.

Horrigan, John B. 2007. *A Typology of Information and Communication Technology Users.* Washington, DC: Pew Internet and American Life Project.

Horwitz, Allan V. 2002. *Creating Mental Illness.* Chicago: University of Chicago Press.

Hosokawa, William K. 1969. *Nisei: The Quiet Americans.* New York: Morrow.

Hospice Association of America. 2006. *Hospice Facts and Statistics.* March. Washington, DC: Hospice Association of America.

Hospice Foundation of America. 2005. *What Is Hospice?* Accessed April 28 (www.hospicefoundation.org/what_is).

Houseman, John. 1972. *Run Through.* New York: Simon and Schuster.

Housing and Urban Development. 2007. *The Annual Homeless Assessment Report to Congress.* Washington, DC: U.S. Government Printing Office.

Hout, Michael. 1988. "More Universalism, Less Structural Mobility: The American Occupational Structure in the 1980s." *American Journal of Sociology* 91 (May):1358–1400.

———, and Claude S. Fischer. 2002. "Why More Americans Have No Religious Preference: Politics and Generations." *American Sociological Review* 67 (April):165–190.

Howard, Judith A. 1999. "Border Crossings between Women's Studies and Sociology." *Contemporary Sociology* 28 (September):525–528.

———, and Jocelyn Hollander. 1997. *Gendered Situations, Gendered Selves.* Thousand Oaks, CA: Sage.

Howard, Michael C. 1989. *Contemporary Cultural Anthropology.* 3d ed. Glenview, IL: Scott, Foresman.

Howard, Russell D., and Reid L. Sawyer. 2003. *Terrorism and Counterterrorism: Understanding the New Security Environment.* Guilford, CT: McGraw-Hill/Dushkin.

Huang, Gary. 1988. "Daily Addressing Ritual: A Cross-Cultural Study." Presented at the annual meeting of the American Sociological Association, Atlanta.

Hubbard, L. Ron. 1950. *Dianetics.* Hollywood, CA: Bridge.

Huber, Bettina J. 1985. *Employment Patterns in Sociology: Recent Trends and Future Prospects.* Washington, DC: American Sociological Association.

Huddy, Leonie, Joshua Billig, John Bracciodieta, Lois Hoeffler, Patrick J. Moynihan, and Patricia Pugliani. 1997. "The Effect of Interviewer Gender on the Survey Response." *Political Behavior* 19 (September):197–220.

Huff, Charlotte. 2007. "Survival of the Fittest." *American Way* (May 1), pp. 30, 32, 34.

Huffstutter, P. J. 2003. "See No Evil." *Los Angeles Times,* January 12, pp. 12–15, 43–45.

Hughes, Everett. 1945. "Dilemmas and Contradictions of Status." *American Journal of Sociology* 50 (March):353–359.

Human Genome Project. 2006. "Human Genome Project Information." Accessed May 15, 2007 (www.ornl.gov).

582

Human Rights Campaign. 2007. "State Prohibitions on Marriage for Same-Sex Couples and Statewide Anti-Discrimination Laws and Policies." Accessed March 1 (www.hrc.org).

Hunt, Darnell. 1997. *Screening the Los Angeles "Riots": Race, Seeing, and Resistance.* New York: Cambridge University Press.

Hunter, Herbert M., ed. 2000. *The Sociology of Oliver C. Cox: New Perspectives: Research in Race and Ethnic Relations,* vol. 2. Stamford, CT: JAI Press.

Hunter, James Davison. 1991. *Culture Wars: The Struggle to Define America.* New York: Basic Books.

Huntington, Samuel P. 1993. "The Clash of Civilizations?" *Foreign Affairs* 72 (Summer): 22–49.

Hurh, Won Moo. 1994. *Korean Immigrants in America: A Structural Analysis of Ethnic Confinement and Adhesive Adaptation.* Rutherford, NJ: Fairleigh Dickinson University Press.

———. 1998. *The Korean Americans.* Westport, CT: Greenwood Press.

———, and Kwang Chung Kim. 1998. "The 'Success' Image of Asian Americans: Its Validity, and Its Practical and Theoretical Implications." *Ethnic and Racial Studies* 12 (October):512–538.

Hurn, Christopher J. 1985. *The Limits and Possibilities of Schooling,* 2d ed. Boston: Allyn and Bacon.

Hymowitz, Carol, and Rachel Emma Silverman. 2001. "Can Work Place Stress Get Worse?" *Wall Street Monitor,* January 16, pp. B1, B4.

Igo, Sarah E. 2007. *The Average American: Surveys, Citizens, and the Making of a Mass Public.* Cambridge, MA: Harvard University Press.

Immervoll, Herwig. 2006. "Can Parents Afford to Work?" Presentation at University of Antwerp for OECD, January 16.

Immigration and Naturalization Service. 2002. *1999 Statistical Yearbook of the Immigration and Naturalization Service.* Washington, DC: U.S. Government Printing Office.

Inglehart, Ronald, and Wayne E. Baker. 2000. "Modernization, Cultural Change, and the Persistence of Traditional Values." *American Sociological Review* 65 (February):19–51.

Innocence Project. 2007. "Facts on Post-Conviction DNA Exonerations." Accessed February 17 (www.innocenceproject.org).

Institute for Social Policy and Understanding. 2004. *The USA PATRIOT Act: Impact on the Arabs and Muslim American Community.* Clinton Township, MI: ISPU.

Instituto del Tercer Mundo. 2005. *The World Guide 2005/2006.* Oxford: New Internationalist Publications.

Intergovernmental Panel on Climate Change. 2007. *Working Group I Report: The Physical Science Basis.* Paris: World Meteorological Organization and United Nations Environment Programme.

International Crime Victim Survey. 2004. *Nationwide Surveys in the Industrialized Countries.* Accessed February 20 (www.ruljis.leidenuniv.nl/group/jfcr/www/icvs).

International Institute for Democracy and Electoral Assistance. 2005. "Turnout in the World—Country by Country Performance." Modified March 7, 2005. Accessed April 19, 2007 (www.idea.int).

International Monetary Fund. 2000. *World Economic Outlook: Asset Prices and the Business Cycle.* Washington, DC: International Monetary Fund.

Internet Crime Complaint Center. 2006. "IC3 Internet Crime Report." Accessed February 18, 2007 (www.IC3.gov).

Internet World Stats. 2007. "Usage and Population Statistics." Accessed May 8 (www.internetworldstats.com).

Inter-Parliamentary Union. 2007. *Women in National Parliaments.* January 31. Accessed February 9 (www.ipu.org).

Iraq Analysis Group. 2007. "About Iraq Analysis Group." Accessed January 19, 2007 (Iraqanalysis.org).

ITOPF. 2006. "Statistics: International Tanker Owners Pollution Federation Limited." Accessed May 2 (www.itopf.com/stats.html).

Jackson, Elton F., Charles R. Tittle, and Mary Jean Burke. 1986. "Offense-Specific Models of the Differential Association Process." *Social Problems* 33 (April):335–356.

Jackson, Matthew O., and Brian W. Rogers. 2007. "Relating Network Structure to Diffusion Properties through Stochastic Dominance." *The B.E. (Berkeley Electronic Press) Journal of Theoretical Economics,* Vol. 7 (No. 1). Available at http://www.bepress.com/bejte/vol7/iss1/art6.

Jackson, Philip W. 1968. *Life in Classrooms.* New York: Holt.

Jacobs, Jerry. 2003. "Detours on the Road to Equality: Women, Work and Higher Education." *Contexts* (Winter):32-41.

Jacobson, Jodi. 1993. "Closing the Gender Gap in Development." Pp. 61–79 in *State of the World,* edited by Lester R. Brown. New York: Norton.

Jamieson, Arnie, Hyon B. Shin, and Jennifer Day. 2002. "Voting and Registration in the Election of November 2000." *Current Population Reports,* ser. P-20, no. 542. Washington, DC: U.S. Government Printing Office.

Janis, Irving. 1967. *Victims of Groupthink.* Boston: Houghton Mifflin.

Japsen, Bruce. 2007. "Abbott, Activists Tangle." *Chicago Tribune* (April 28), sec. 3, pp. 1, 2.

Jargowsky, Paul A. 2003. *Stunning Progress, Hidden Problems: The Dramatic Decline of Concentrated Poverty in the 1990s.* Washington, DC: Brookings Institution.

———, and Rebecca Yang. 2006. "The 'Underclass' Revisited: A Social Problem in Decline." *Journal of Urban Affairs* 28 (No. 1), pp. 55–70.

Jasper, James M. 1997. *The Art of Moral Protest: Culture, Biography, and Creativity in Social Movements.* Chicago: University of Chicago Press.

Jecker, Nancy. 2000. "Review of Medical Apartheid." *New England Journal of Medicine* (November 23).

Jencks, Christopher, Joe Swingle, and Scott Winship. 2006. "Welfare Redux." *American Prospect* (March):36–40.

Jenkins, Richard. 1991. "Disability and Social Stratification." *British Journal of Sociology* 42 (December):557–580.

Joffe, Josef. 2006. "The Perils of Soft Power." *New York Times,* May 14, pp. 15–16, 18.

Johnson, Anne M., Jane Wadsworth, Kaye Wellings, and Julie Field. 1994. *Sexual Attitudes and Lifestyles.* Oxford: Blackwell Scientific.

Johnson, Benton. 1975. *Functionalism in Modern Sociology: Understanding Talcott Parsons.* Morristown, NJ: General Learning.

Johnson, Julia Overturf. 2005. "Who's Minding the Kids? Child Care Arrangements: Winter 2002." *Current Population Reports,* ser. P-70, no. 101. Washington, DC: U.S. Government Printing Office.

Johnson, Kenneth M. 1999. "The Rural Rebound." *Reports on America* 1 (September).

Johnson, Richard A. 1985. *American Fads.* New York: Beech Tree.

Johnston, David Cay. 1994. "Ruling Backs Homosexuals on Asylum." *New York Times,* June 12, pp. D1, D6.

Jones, Nicholas A. 2005. *We the People of More Than One Race in the United States.* Census 2000 Special Reports, CENSR-22. Washington, DC: U.S. Government Printing Office.

Jones, Stephen R. G. 1992. "Was There a Hawthorne Effect?" *American Journal of Sociology* 98 (November):451–568.

Joseph, Jay. 2004. *The Gene Illusion: Genetic Research in Psychiatry and Psychology under the Microscope.* New York: Algora Books.

Jost, Kenneth. 2005. "Right to Die." *CQ Researcher* (May 13).

Joynt, Jen, and Vasugi Ganeshananthan. 2003. "Abortion Decisions." *Atlantic Monthly* 291 (April):38–39.

Juhasz, Anne McCreary. 1989. "Black Adolescents' Significant Others." *Social Behavior and Personality* 17 (2):211–214.

Kahn, Joseph. 2003. "Made in China, Bought in China." *New York Times,* January 5, sec. 3, pp. 1, 10.

———. 2006a. "A Sharp Debate Erupts in China over Ideologies." *New York Times,* March 12, pp. 1, 8.

———. 2006b. "Where's Mao? Chinese Revise History Books." *New York Times,* September 1, pp. A1, A6.

Kaiser Family Foundation. 2005. *Sex on TV4.* Santa Barbara, CA: Kaiser Family Foundation.

Kalish, Richard A. 1985. *Death, Grief, and Caring Relationships.* 2d ed. Monterey, CA: Brooks/Cole.

Kalita, S. Mitra. 2006. "On the Other End of the Line." *Washington Post National Week Edition,* January 9, pp. 20–21.

Kamenetz, Anya. 2006. *Generation Debt.* New York: Riverhead.

Kandel, William. 2005. "Rural Hispanics at a Glance." *Economic Information Bulletin* (December).

Kao, Grace, and Kara Joyner. 2004. "Do Race and Ethnicity Matter among Friends? Activities among Interracial, Interethnic, and Interethnic Adolescent Friends." *Sociology Quarterly* 45 (3):557–573.

Kapos, Shia. 2005. "Bloom Falls Off the Rose for Internet Matchups." *Chicago Tribune,* February 14, sec. 4, pp. 1, 7.

Kapstein, Ethan B. 2006. "The New Global Slave Trade." *Foreign Affairs* 85 (November/December): 103–115.

Katel, Peter. 2005. "Ending Poverty." *CQ Researcher* 15 (September 9):733–760.

Katovich, Michael A. 1987. Correspondence. June 1.

Katz, Michael. 1971. *Class, Bureaucracy, and the Schools: The Illusion of Educational Change in America.* New York: Praeger.

Kaufman, Sarah. 2006. "The Criminalization of New Orleanians in Katrina's Wake." Accessed April 4 (www.ssrc.org).

Kempadoo, Kamala, and Jo Doezema, eds. 1998. *Global Sex Workers: Rights, Resistance, and Redefinition.* New York: Routledge.

Kent, Mary M., and Carl Haub. 2005. "Global Demographic Divide." *Population Bulletin* 60 (December).

Kentor, Jeffrey, and Yong Suk Jang. 2004. "Yes, There Is a (Growing) Transnational Business Community." *International Sociology* 19 (September), 355–368.

Kerbo, Harold R. 2003. *Social Stratification and Inequality: Class Conflict in Historical, Comparative, and Global Perspective.* 5th ed. New York: McGraw-Hill.

———. 2006. *World Poverty: The Roots of Global Inequality and the Modern World System.* New York: McGraw-Hill.

Kilborn, Peter T. 2001. "Rural Towns Turn to Prisons to Reignite Their Economies." *New York Times,* August 1, pp. A1, A11.

Kiley, David. 2006. "Best Global Brands." *Business Week* (August 7), pp. 54–56, 60, 62, 64, 66.

Killian, Caitlin. 2003. "The Other Side of the Veil: North Africa Women in France Respond to the Headscarf Affair." *Gender and Society* (August 17):576–590.

Kim, Kwang Chung. 1999. *Koreans in the Hood: Conflict with African Americans.* Baltimore: Johns Hopkins University Press.

Kimmel, Michael. 2006. "A War Against Boys?" *Dissent* (Fall):65–70.

King, Leslie. 1998. "France Needs Children: Pronatalism, Nationalism, and Women's Equity." *Sociological Quarterly* 39 (Winter):33–52.

King, Peter H. 2004. "Their Spiritual Thirst Found a Desert Spring." *Los Angeles Times,* August 4, pp. A1, A10, A11.

King, Sharon A. 1999. "Mania for 'Pocket Monsters' Yields Billions for Nintendo." *New York Times,* April 26, pp. A1, A18.

Kinsella, Kevin, and David R. Phillips. 2005. "Global Aging: The Challenge of Success." *Population Bulletin* 60 (March).

Kinsey, Alfred C., Wardell B. Pomeroy, and Paul H. Gebhard. 1953. *Sexual Behavior in the Human Female.* Philadelphia: Saunders.

———, Wardell B. Pomeroy, and Clyde E. Martin. 1948. *Sexual Behavior in the Human Male.* Philadelphia: Saunders.

Kirp, David L. 2004. "Life Way After Head Start." *New York Times,* November 21, pp. 31–33, 38.

Kiser, Edgar. 1992. "War." Pp. 2243–2247 in *Encyclopedia of Sociology,* edited by Edgar F. Borgatta and Marie L. Borgatta. New York: Macmillan.

Kitchener, Richard F. 1991. "Jean Piaget: The Unknown Sociologist." *British Journal of Sociology* 42 (September):421–442.

Klass, Perri. 2003. "This Side of Medicine." P. 319 in *This Side of Doctoring: Reflection for Women in Medicine,* edited by Eliza Lo Chin. New York: Oxford University Press.

Klein, Julia M. 2003. "Film: Depicting Mental Illness." *Chronicle of Higher Education* 49 (June 27):B15–B16.

Klein, Naomi. 1999. *No Logo: Money, Marketing, and the Growing Anti-Corporate Movement.* New York: Picador (St. Martin's Press).

Kleiner, Art. 2003. "Are You In with the In Crowd?" *Harvard Business Review* 81 (July):86–92.

Kleinknecht, William. 1996. *The New Ethnic Mobs: The Changing Face of Organized Crime in America.* New York: Free Press.

Kleniewski, Nancy. 2002. *Cities, Change, and Conflict: A Political Economy of Urban Life.* 2d ed. Belmont, CA: Wadsworth.

Klinenberg, Eric. 2002. *Heat Wave: A Social Autopsy of Disaster in Chicago.* Chicago: University of Chicago Press.

Klug, Heinz. 2005. "Transnational Human Rights: Exploring the Persistence and Globalization of Human Rights." Pp. 85–103 in *Annual Review of Law and Social Sciences.* Palo Alto, CA: Annual Reviews.

Koch, Wendy. 2006. "Relatives Open Hearts and Homes." *USA Today,* March 20, p. 3A.

Kochhar, Rakesh. 2004. *The Wealth of Hispanic Households: 1996 to 2002.* Washington, DC: Pew Hispanic Center.

Kolata, Gina. 1999. *Clone: The Road to Dolly and the Path Beyond.* New York: William Morrow.

Koolhaas, Rem, et al. 2001. *Mutations.* Barcelona, Spain: Actar.

Kopinak, Kathryn. 1995. "Gender as a Vehicle for the Subordination of Women Maquiladora Workers in Mexico." *Latin American Perspectives* 22 (Winter):30–48.

Korczyk, Sophie M. 2002. *Back to Which Future: The U.S. Aging Crisis Revisited.* Washington, DC: AARP.

Kornblum, Janet. 2007. "Meet the 'Tech-No's': People Who Reject Plugging into the Highly Wired World." *USA Today* (January 11), pp. A1, A2.

Kottak, Conrad. 2008. *Anthropology: The Explanation of Human Diversity.* 12th ed. New York: McGraw-Hill.

Kotulak, Ronald. 2005. "Increase in Women Doctors Changing the Face of Medicine" *Chicago Tribune,* January 12, pp. 1, 4.

Kozol, Jonathan. 2005. *The Shame of the Nation: The Restoration of Apartheid Schooling.* New York: Crown.

Kraybill, Donald B. 2008. "Amish." In *Encyclopedia of Race, Ethnicity, and Society,* edited by Richard T. Schaefer. Thousand Oaks, CA: Sage.

Krebs, Michelle. 2006. "Chinese Lessons: What GM Has Learned in China." Inside Line.

Kreider, Rose M. 2005. "Number, Timing, and Duration of Marriages and Divorces: 2001." *Current Population Reports,* pp. 70–97. Washington, DC: U.S. Government Printing Office.

———, and Jason Fields. 2005. "Living Arrangements of Children: 2001." *Current Population Reports,* ser. P-70, no. 104. Washington, DC: U.S. Government Printing Office.

Kriesberg, Louis. 1992. "Peace." Pp. 1432–1436 in *Encyclopedia of Sociology,* edited by Edgar F. Borgatta and Marie L. Borgatta. New York: Macmillan.

Kristof, Nicholas D. 1998. "As Asian Economies Shrink, Women Are Squeezed Out." *New York Times,* June 11, pp. A1, A12.

———. 2006. "Race Against Death." *New York Times,* June 4, sect. wk, p. 15.

Kroeger, Brooke. 2004. "When a Dissertation Makes a Difference." Accessed January 15, 2005 (www.racematters.org/devahpager.htm).

Kroll, Luisa, and Allison Fass. 2006. "The World's Billionaires." *Forbes* (March 9).

Kübler-Ross, Elisabeth. 1969. *On Death and Dying.* New York: Macmillan.

Kwong, Jo. 2005. "Globalization's Effects on the Environment." *Society* 42 (January/February): 21–28.

Labaton, Stephan. 2003. "10 Wall St. Firms Settle with U.S. in Analyst Inquiry." *New York Times,* April 29, pp. A1, C4.

Lacey, Marc. 2005. "Accents of Africa: A New Outsoaring Frontier." *New York Times,* February 2, pp. C1, C6.

Ladner, Joyce. 1973. *The Death of White Sociology.* New York: Random Books.

La Ganga, Maria L. 1999. "Trying to Figure the Beginning of the End." *Los Angeles Times,* October 15, pp. A1, A28, A29.

Lague, David. 2006. "Official Union Set Up in China at Wal-Mart." *New York Times,* July 31, pp. C1, C8.

Lamb, David. 1997. "Viet Kieu: A Bridge Between Two Worlds." *Los Angeles Times,* November 4, pp. A1, A8.

Landler, Mark. 2005. "Mixed Feelings as Kyoto Pact Takes Effect." *New York Times,* February 16, pp. C1, C3.

———, and Michael Barbaro. 2006. "No, Not Always." *New York Times,* August 2, pp. C1, C4.

Landtman, Gunnar. [1938] 1968. *The Origin of Inequality of the Social Class.* New York: Greenwood (original edition 1938, Chicago: University of Chicago Press).

Lang, Eric. 1992. "Hawthorne Effect." Pp. 793–794 in *Encyclopedia of Sociology,* vol. 2, edited by Edgar F. Borgatta and Marie L. Borgatta. New York: Macmillan.

Lang, Robert E., and Jennifer B. LeFurgy. 2007. *Boomburbs: The Rise of America's Accidental Crisis.* Washington, DC: Brookings Institution.

584

Lansprey, Susan. 1995. "AAAs and 'Naturally Occurring Retirement Communities' (NORCs)." Accessed August 4, 2003 (www.aoa.gov/housing/norcs.html).

Lareau, Annette. 2003. *Unequal Childhoods: Class, Race, and Family Life.* Berkeley: University of California Press.

Laska, Shirley. 2005. "The Role of Social Science Research in Disaster Preparedness and Response." Testimony before U.S. House of Representatives, Science Committee, Subcommittee on Research.

Lasn, Kalle. 2003. "Ad Spending Predicted for Steady Decline." *Adbusters* (January/February).

Lasswell, Harold D. 1936. *Politics: Who Gets What, When, How.* New York: McGraw-Hill.

Las Vegas. 2006. "Statistics" and "History." Accessed April 27, 2007 (www.lasvegasnevada.gov).

Lauer, Robert H. 1982. *Perspectives on Social Change.* 3d ed. Boston: Allyn and Bacon.

Laumann, Edward O., John H. Gagnon, and Robert T. Michael. 1994a. "A Political History of the National Sex Survey of Adults." *Family Planning Perspectives* 26 (February):34–38.

———, John H. Gagnon, Robert T. Michael, and Stuart Michaels. 1994b. *The Social Organization of Sexuality: Sexual Practices in the United States.* Chicago: University of Chicago Press.

Lazarsfeld, Paul, Bernard Beretson, and H. Gaudet. 1948. *The People's Choice.* New York: Columbia University Press.

———, and Robert K. Merton. 1948. "Mass Communication, Popular Taste, and Organized Social Action." Pp. 95–118 in *The Communication of Ideas,* edited by Lymon Bryson. New York: Harper and Brothers.

Lear, Norman, and Robert W. McChesney. 2006. "Does Big Media Need to Get Bigger?" *Los Angeles Times,* August 5, p. B17.

Leavell, Hugh R., and E. Gurney Clark. 1965. *Preventive Medicine for the Doctor in His Community: An Epidemiologic Approach.* 3d ed. New York: McGraw-Hill.

Lee, Alfred McClung. 1983. *Terrorism in Northern Ireland.* Bayside, NY: General Hall.

Lehne, Gregory K. 1995. "Homophobia among Men: Supporting and Defining the Male Role." Pp. 325–336 in *Men's Lives,* edited by Michael S. Kimmel and Michael S. Messner. Boston: Allyn and Bacon.

Lemann, Nicholas. 1991. "The Other Underclass." *Atlantic Monthly* 268 (December):96–102, 104, 107–108, 110.

Lengermann, Patricia Madoo, and Jill Niebrugge-Brantley. 1998. *The Women Founders: Sociology and Social Theory, 1830–1930.* Boston: McGraw-Hill.

Lenhart, Amanda, Mary Madden, and Paul Hitlin. 2005. *Teens and Technology.* Washington, DC: Pew Internet and American Life Project.

———. 2007. *Social Networking Websites and Teens: An Overview.* Washington, DC: Pew Internet and American Life Project.

Lenski, Gerhard. 1966. *Power and Privilege: A Theory of Social Stratification.* New York: McGraw-Hill.

Leonard, Koren Isakser. 2003. *Muslims in the United States: The State of Research.* New York: Russell Sage Foundation.

Leonhardt, David. 2004. "As Wealthy Fill Top Colleges Concerns Grow Over Fairness." *New York Times,* April 22, pp. A1, A12.

———. 2007. "Middle-Class Squeeze Comes with Nuances." *New York Times,* April 25, pp. C1, C12.

Levin, Jack, and William C. Levin. 1980. *Ageism.* Belmont, CA: Wadsworth.

Levine, Nancy. 1988. *The Dynamics of Polyandry: Kinship, Domesticity, and Population on the Tibetan Border.* Chicago: University of Chicago Press.

Levine, Susa. 2006. "Culturally Sensitive Medicine." *Washington Post National Weekly Edition* 23 (March 26), p. 31.

Levinson, Daniel J. 1978. *The Seasons of a Man's Life.* With Charlotte N. Darrow et al. New York: Knopf.

———. 1996. *The Season of a Woman's Life.* With Judy D. Levinson. New York: Knopf.

Levitt, Steven D., and Stephen J. Dubner. 2005. *Freakonomics: A Rogue Economist Explores the Hidden Side of Everything.* New York: William Morrow.

Levy, Becca R., Martin D. Slade, Suzanne R. Kunkel, and Stanislav V. Kasl. 2002. "Longevity Increased by Positive Self-Perceptions of Aging." *Journal of Personality and Social Psychology* 83 (2):261–270.

Lewin, Tamar. 1998. "Debate Centers on Definition of Harassment." *New York Times,* March 22, pp. A1, A20.

———. 2000. "Differences Found in Care with Stepmothers." *New York Times,* August 17, p. A16.

Lewis Mumford Center. 2001. *Ethnic Diversity Grows, Neighborhood Integration Is at a Standstill.* Albany, NY: Lewis Mumford Center.

Lictblau, Eric. 2003. "Bush Issues Racial Profiling Ban but Exempts Security Inquiries." *New York Times,* June 18, pp. A1, A14.

Lieberman, David. 2007. "View of Media Ownership Limits Changes." *USA Today,* January 29, pp. B1–B2.

Lieberson, Stanley. 2000. *A Matter of Taste: How Names, Fashions, and Culture Change.* New Haven, CT: Yale University Press.

Light, Donald W. 2004. "Dreams of Success: A New History of the American Health Care System." *Journal of Health and Social Behavior* 45 (Extra Issue):1–24.

Light, Paul C. 2005. "Katrina's Lesson in Readiness." *Washington Post,* September 1.

Lim, Louisa. 2007. "Digital Culture: China's 'Gold Farmers' Play a Grim Game." May 14, 2007 broadcast on NPR. Accessed at www.npr.org.

Lin, Nan, and Wen Xie. 1988. "Occupational Prestige in Urban China." *American Journal of Sociology* 93 (January):793–832.

Lindner, Eileen, ed. 2006. *Yearbook of American and Canadian Churches, 2006.* Nashville: Abingdon Press.

Linn, Susan, and Alvin F. Poussaint. 1999. "Watching Television: What Are Children Learning About Race and Ethnicity?" *Child Care Information Exchange* 128 (July):50–52.

Lino, Mark. 2005. *Expenditures on Children by Families, 2004.* Washington, DC: U.S. Department of Agriculture, Center for Nutrition Policy and Promotion.

Lips, Hilary M. 2003. "The Gender Pay Gap: Concrete Indicator of Woman's Progress Toward Equality." *Analysis of Social Issues and Public Policy* 3 (1):87–109.

Lipson, Karen. 1994. "'Nell' Not Alone in the Wilds." *Los Angeles Times,* December 19, pp. F1, F6.

Liptak, Adam. 2004a. "Bans on Interracial Unions Offer Perspective on Gay Ones." *New York Times,* March 17, p. A16.

———. 2006. "The Ads Discriminate, but Does the Web?" *New York Times,* March 5, p. 16.

Liska, Allen E., and Steven F. Messner. 1999. *Perspectives on Crime and Deviance.* 3d ed. Upper Saddle River, NJ: Prentice Hall.

Little, Kenneth. 1988. "The Role of Voluntary Associations in West African Urbanization." Pp. 211–230 in *Anthropology for the Nineties: Introductory Readings,* edited by Johnnetta B. Cole. New York: Free Press.

Liveplasma.com. 2006. "Music Maps." Accessed January 30 (www.liveplasma.com).

Livernash, Robert, and Eric Rodenburg. 1998. "Population Change, Resources, and the Environment." *Population Bulletin* 53 (March).

Livingstone, Sonia. 2004. "The Challenge of Changing Audiences." *European Journal of Communication* 19 (March):75–86.

Loeb, Susanna, Bruce Fuller, Sharon Lynn Kagan, and Bidemi Carrol. 2004. "Child Care in Poor Communities: Early Learning Effects of Type, Quality, and Stability." *Child Development* 75 (January/February):47–65.

Lofland, John. 1981. "Collective Behavior: The Elementary Forms." Pp. 441–446 in *Social Psychology: Sociological Perspectives,* edited by Morris Rosenberg and Ralph Turner. New York: Basic Books.

———. 1985. *Protests: Studies of Collective Behavior and Social Movements.* Rutgers, NJ: Transaction.

Lofland, Lyn H. 1975. "The 'Thereness' of Women: A Selective Review of Urban Sociology." Pp. 144–170 in *Another Voice,* edited by M. Millman and R. M. Kanter. New York: Anchor/Doubleday.

LoMonaco, Claudine. 2006. "U.S.-Mexico Border: The Season of Death Dispatches June 27, 2006." Accessed February 19, 2007 (www.pbs.org).

Lucas, Samuel R., and Morcel Paret. 2005. "Law, Race, and Education in the United States." Pp. 203–231 in *Annual Review of Law and Society.* Palo Alto, CA: Annual Reviews.

Lukacs, Georg. 1923. *History and Class Consciousness.* London: Merlin.

Lum, Joann, and Peter Kwong. 1989. "Surviving in America: The Trials of a Chinese Immigrant Woman." *Village Voice* 34 (October 31):39–41.

Lumpe, Lora. 2003. "Taking Aim at the Global Gun Trade." *Amnesty Now* (Winter):10–13.

Lundquist, Jennifer Hickes. 2006. "Choosing Single Motherhood." *Contexts* 5 (Fall): 64–67.

Lupton, Deborah. 1999. "Monster in Metal Cocoons: 'Road Rage' and Cyborg Bodies." *Body and Soul* 3 (N.1):57–92.

———. 2001. "Constructing 'Road Rage' as News: An Analysis of Two Australian Newspapers." *Australian Journal of Communication* 28 (N.3):25–36.

Luster, Tom, Kelly Rhoades, and Bruce Haas. 1989. "The Relation between Parental Values and Parenting Behavior: A Test of the Kohn Hypothesis." *Journal of Marriage and the Family* 51 (February):139–147.

Lyall, Sarah. 2002. "For Europeans, Love, Yes; Marriage, Maybe." *New York Times,* March 24, pp. 1–8.

Lynn, Barry C. 2003. "Trading with a Low-Wage Tiger." *The American Prospect* 14 (February): 10–12.

M

MacCoun, Robert J. 1989. "Experimental Research on Jury Decision-Making." *Science* 244 (June 2), pp. 1046–1050.

MacDorman, Marian, et al. 2005. "Explaining the 2001–2002 Infant Mortality Increase: Data from the Linked Death/Infant Death Data Set." *National Vital Statistics Reports* 53 (January 24).

Mack, Raymond W., and Calvin P. Bradford. 1979. *Transforming America: Patterns of Social Change.* 2d ed. New York: Random House.

MacLeod, Scott, and Vivienne Walt. 2005. "Live from Qatar." *Time,* Bonus Section, June, pp. A6–A8.

Maggi, Laura. 2007. "Enough Thousands March to Protest City's Alarming Murder Rate." *The Times-Picayune,* January 12, 2007.

Magnier, Mark. 2004. "China Clamps Down on Web News Discussion." *Los Angeles Times,* February 26, p. A4.

Mahbub ul Haq Human Development Centre. 2000. *Human Development in South Asia 2000.* Oxford, England: Oxford University Press for Mahbub ul Haq Human Development Centre.

Mahoney, Robert J. 1999. "Lessens from a Rose: Sociological Reflections on Eight Years of Long Term Care." *Illness, Crisis and Loss* 7 (1):77–90.

Maine Times. 2001. Article on Wal-Mart's Plan to Build Near the Penja. January 4.

Malcolm, Andrew H. 1974. "The 'Shortage' of Bathroom Tissue: A Classic Study in Rumor." *New York Times,* February 3, p. 29.

Malcolm X, with Alex Haley. 1964. *The Autobiography of Malcolm X.* New York: Grove.

Malthus, Thomas Robert, Julian Huxley, and Frederick Osborn. [1824] 1960. *Three Essays on Population.* Reprint. New York: New American Library.

Mangum, Garth L., Stephen L. Magnum, and Andrew M. Sum. 2003. *The Persistence of Poverty in the United States.* Baltimore: Johns Hopkins University Press.

Mantel, Barbara. 2005. "No Child Left Behind." *CQ Researcher* 15 (May 27).

Marcus, Itamar, and Barbara Crook. 2007. "Hamas Mickey Mouse Creator: Islamic Rule Will Benefit Christians and Jews." Accessed May 16 (www.pmw.org.il).

Marijuana Policy Project. 2004. *State-by-State Medical Marijuana Laws: How to Remove the Threat of Arrest.* Washington, DC: MPP.

———. 2007. *Marijuana Policy Project.* Accessed February 17 (www.mpp.org).

Mark, Gloria, Victor M. Gonzalez, and Justin Harris. 2005. "No Task Left Behind? Examining the Nature of Fragmented Work." Paper presented at CHI 2005, Portland, Oregon.

Markoff, John. 2006. "For $150, Third-World Laptop Stirs a Big Debate." *New York Times,* November 30, pp. A1, C6.

———. 2007. "At Davos, the Squabble Resumes on How to Wire the Third World." *New York Times,* January 29, pp. C1, C2.

Markson, Elizabeth W. 1992. "Moral Dilemmas." *Society* 29 (July/August):4–6.

Marquardt, Elizabeth. 2005. *Between Two Worlds: The Inner Lives of Children of Divorce.* New York: Institute for American Values.

Marquis, Julie, and Dan Morain. 1999. "A Tortuous Path for the Mentally Ill." *Los Angeles Times,* November 21, pp. A1, A22, A23.

Marr, Phebe. 2003. "Civics 101, Taught by Saddam Hussein: First, Join the Paramilitary." *New York Times,* April 20.

Marshall, Tyler. 2003. "Kuwait's Klatch of the Titans." *Los Angeles Times,* February 12, pp. A1, A5.

Martelo, Emma Zapata. 1996. "Modernization, Adjustment, and Peasant Production." *Latin American Perspectives* 23 (Winter):118–130.

Martin, Dominique, Jean-Luc Metzger, and Philippe Pierre. 2006. "The Sociology of Globalization: Theoretical and Methodological Reflections." *International Sociology* 21 (July): 499–521.

Martin, Joyce A., Brady E. Hamilton, Paul D. Sutton, Stephanie J. Ventura, Fay Menacker, and Martha L. Munson. 2005. "Births: Final Data for 2003." *National Vital Statistics Reports* 54 (September 8).

Martin, Marvin. 1996. "Sociology Adapting to Changes." *Chicago Tribune,* July 21, sec. 18, p. 20.

Martin, Philip, and Elizabeth Midgley. 2003. "Immigration: Shaping and Reshaping America." *Population Bulletin* 58 (June).

Martin, Susan E. 1994. "Outsider Within the Station House: The Impact of Race and Gender on Black Women Politics." *Social Problems* 41 (August): 383–400.

Martineau, Harriet. [1837] 1962. *Society in America.* Edited, abridged, with an introductory essay by Seymour Martin Lipset. Reprint. Garden City, NY: Doubleday.

———. [1838] 1989. *How to Observe Morals and Manners.* Philadelphia: Leal and Blanchard. Sesquentennial edition, edited by M. R. Hill, Transaction Books.

Martinez, Elizabeth. 1993. "Going Gentle into That Good Night: Is a Rightful Death a Feminist Issue?" *Ms.* 4 (July/August):65–69.

Marubbio, M. Elise. 2006. *Killing the Indian Maiden: Images of Native American Women in Film.* Lexington, KY: University Press of Kentucky.

Marx, Karl, and Friedrich Engels. [1847] 1955. *Selected Work in Two Volumes.* Reprint, Moscow: Foreign Languages Publishing House.

Maryanski, Alexandra R. 2004. "Evaluation Theory." Pp. 257–263 in *Encyclopedia of Social Theory,* edited by George Ritzer. Thousand Oaks, CA: Sage.

Mason, Heather. 2003. "What Do Americans See in Title IX's Future?" *Gallup Poll Tuesday Briefing.* Accessed January 28, 2003 (www.gallup.com).

Mason, J. W. 1998. "The Buses Don't Stop Here Anymore." *American Prospect* 37 (March):56–62.

Massey, Douglas S. 1998. "March of Folly: U.S. Immigration Policy After NAFTA." *The American Prospect* (March/April):22–23.

———, and Nancy A. Denton. 1993. *American Apartheid: Segregation and the Making of the Underclass.* Cambridge, MA: Harvard University Press.

McCall, Tommy. 2006. "Pay for Performance? Sometimes, but Not Always." *New York Times,* April 9, sec. 3, p. 6.

McCarthy, Ellen. 2004. "A Voice for the Mideast." *Washington Post National Weekly Edition* 22 (October 25):30–31.

McChesney, Robert W. 2004. *The Problem of the Media: U.S. Communication Politics in the 21st Century.* New York: Monthly Review Press.

McCloud, Aminah Beverly. 1995. *African American Islam.* New York: Routledge.

McCool, Daniel, Susan M. Olsen, and Jennifer L. Robinson. 2007. *Native Vote: American Indians, the Voting Rights Act, and the Rights Vote.* New York: Cambridge University Press.

McDermott, Kevin. 1999. "Illinois Bill Would Repeal Law Requiring Listing of Campaign Donors on Internet." *St. Louis Post-Dispatch,* November 25, p. A1.

McDonald, Kim A. 1999. "Studies of Women's Health Produce a Wealth of Knowledge on the Biology of Gender Differences." *Chronicle of Higher Education* 45 (June 25):A19, A22.

McFalls, Joseph A., Jr. 2003. "Population: A Lively Introduction." *Population Bulletin* 58 (December).

———. 2007. *Population: A Lively Introduction.* 5th ed. Washington, DC: Population Reference Bureau.

McFarland, Daniel A., and Reuben J. Thomas. 2006. "Bowling Young: How Youth Voluntary Associations Influence Adult Political Participation." *American Sociological Review* 71 (June): 401–425.

McGue, Matt, and Thomas J. Bouchard, Jr. 1998. "Genetic and Environmental Influence on Human Behavioral Differences." Pp. 1–24 in *Annual Review of Neurosciences.* Palo Alto, CA: Annual Reviews.

McIntosh, Peggy. 1988. "White Privilege and Male Privilege: A Personal Account of Coming to See Correspondence Through Work and Women's Studies." Working Paper No. 189, Wellesley College Center for Research on Women, Wellesley, MA.

McKinlay, John B., and Sonja M. McKinlay. 1977. "The Questionable Contribution of Medical Measures to the Decline of Mortality in the United States in the Twentieth Century." *Milbank Memorial Fund Quarterly* 55 (Summer): 405–428.

McKinsey Global Institute. 2005. "The Emerging Global Labor Market." Accessed April 24 (www.mckinsey.com).

McLuhan, Marshall. 1964. *Understanding Media: The Extensions of Man.* New York: New American Library.

———, and Quentin Fiore. 1967. *The Medium Is the Message: An Inventory of Effects.* New York: Bantam Books.

586

McNeil, Donald G., Jr. 2002. "W.H.O. Moves to Make AIDS Drugs More Accessible to Poor Worldwide." *New York Times,* August 23, p. D7.

———. 2004. "Plan to Battle AIDS Worldwide Is Falling Short." *New York Times,* March 28, pp. 1, 14.

McPhail, Clark. 1991. *The Myth of the Madding Crowd.* New York: De Gruyter.

———. 1994. "The Dark Side of Purpose in Riots: Individual and Collective Violence." *Sociological Quarterly* 35 (January):i–xx.

———. 2006. "The Crowd and Collective Behavior: Bringing Symbolic Interaction Back In." *Symbolic Interaction* 29 (Issue 4): 433–464.

———, and David Miller. 1973. "The Assembling Process: A Theoretical Empirical Examination." *American Sociological Review* 38 (December): 721–735.

Mead, George H. 1934. In *Mind, Self and Society,* edited by Charles W. Morris. Chicago: University of Chicago Press.

———. 1964a. In *On Social Psychology,* edited by Anselm Strauss. Chicago: University of Chicago Press.

———. 1964b. "The Genesis of the Self and Social Control." Pp. 267–293 in *Selected Writings: George Herbert Mead,* edited by Andrew J. Reck. Indianapolis: Bobbs-Merrill.

Mead, Margaret. 1973. "Does the World Belong to Men—Or to Women?" *Redbook* 141(October): 46–52.

———. [1935] 2001. *Sex and Temperament in Three Primitive Societies.* New York: Perennial, Harper-Collins.

MediaGuardian. 2001. "Censorship of News in Wartime Is Still Censorship." October 15. Accessed January 25, 2003 (http://media.guardian.co.uk/attack/story/0,1301,57445,00.html).

Meier, Robert F., and Gilbert Geis. 1997. *Victimless Crime? Prostitution, Drugs, Homosexuality, Abortion.* Los Angeles: Roxbury Books.

Melia, Marilyn Kennedy. 2000. "Changing Times." *Chicago Tribune,* January 2, sec. 17, pp. 12–15.

Mendez, Jennifer Bickman. 1998. "Of Mops and Maids: Contradictions and Continuities in Bureaucratized Domestic Work." *Social Problems* 45 (February):114–135.

Menzel, Peter. 1994. *Material World.* Berkeley: University of California Press.

Merton, Robert. 1948. "The Bearing of Empirical Research upon the Development of Social Theory." *American Sociological Review* 13 (October): 505–515.

———. 1968. *Social Theory and Social Structure.* New York Free Press.

———, and Alice S. Kitt. 1950. "Contributions to the Theory of Reference Group Behavior." Pp. 40–105 in *Continuities in Social Research: Studies in the Scope and Methods of the American Soldier,* edited by Robert K. Merton and Paul L. Lazarsfeld. New York: Free Press.

Messner, Michael A. 1997. *Politics of Masculinities: Men in Movements.* Thousand Oaks, CA: Sage.

———. 2002. "Gender Equity in College Sports: 6 Views." *Chronicle of Higher Education.* 49 (December 6):B9–B10.

———, Margaret Carlisle Duncan, and Nicole Williams. 2006. "This Revolution Is Not Being Televised." *Contexts* 5 (Summer): 34–38.

Meyer, Karen. 2007. "Match the Disability." April 31. Unpublished paper. Chicago: DePaul University.

———. 2008. "Americans with Disabilities Act." In *Encyclopedia of Race, Ethnicity, and Society,* edited by Richard T. Schaefer. Thousand Oaks, CA: Sage.

Meyers, Thomas J. 1992. "Factors Affecting the Decision to Leave the Old Order Amish." Presented at the annual meeting of the American Sociological Association, Pittsburgh.

Meyerson, Harold. 2006. "How Capitalism Works Now." *Prospect Magazine* 17 (November): 54–55.

Michals, Jennifer M. 2003. "The Price We Pay to Get Richer: A Look at Student Indebtedness." Unpublished M.A. paper, DePaul University, Chicago, IL.

Michels, Robert. 1915. *Political Parties.* Glencoe, IL: Free Press (reprinted 1949).

Migration News. 2002c. "Mexico: Bush, IDs, Remittances" (December). Accessible online at http://migration.ucdavis.edu.

———. 2004. "NAFTA at 10." *Migration News* 11 (January). Accessible online at http://migration.ucdavis.edu.

———. 2005. "Maquiladoras" (July). Accessible online at http://migration.ucdavis.edu.

Milgram, Stanley. 1963. "Behavioral Study of Obedience." *Journal of Abnormal and Social Psychology* 67 (October):371–378.

———. 1975. *Obedience to Authority: An Experimental View.* New York: Harper and Row.

Miller, Dan E. 2006. "Rumor: An Examination of Some Stereotypes." *Symbolic Interaction* 28 (Issue 4): 505–519.

Miller, David L. 2000. *Introduction to Collective Behavior and Collective Action.* 2d ed. Prospect Heights, IL: Waveland Press.

———, and JoAnne DeRoven Darlington. 2002. *Fearing for the Safety of Others: Disasters and the Small World Problem.* Paper presented at Midwest Sociological Society, Milwaukee, WI.

Miller, Jacqueline W., Timothy S. Naimi, Robert D. Brewer, and Sherry Everett Jones. 2007. "Binge Drinking and Associated Health Risk Behaviors Among High School Students." *Pediatrics* 119 (January): 76–85.

Miller, Reuben. 1988. "The Literature of Terrorism." *Terrorism* 11 (1):63–87.

Mills, C. Wright. [1959] 2000a. *The Sociological Imagination. 40th Anniversary Edition: New Afterword by Todd Gitlin.* New York: Oxford University Press.

———. [1956] 2000b. *The Power Elite.* A New Edition. Afterword by Alan Wolfe. New York: Oxford University Press.

Miner, Horace. 1956. "Body Ritual among the Nacirema." *American Anthropologist* 58 (June): 503–507.

Minnesota Center for Twin and Family Research. 2007. "Minnesota Center for Twins and Family Research." Accessed January 29 (www.psych.umn.edu).

Mirapaul, Matthew. 2001. "How the Net Is Documenting a Watershed Moment." *New York Times,* October 15, p. E2.

Mizruchi, Mark S. 1996. "What Do Interlocks Do? An Analysis, Critique, and Assessment of Research on Interlocking Directorates." Pp. 271–298 in *Annual Review of Sociology,* 1996, edited by John Hagan and Karen Cook. Palo Alto, CA: Annual Reviews.

Moaddel, Mansoor. 2007. "What the Iraqi Study Group Missed: The Iraqi People." *Footnotes* 35 (January): 1, 4.

Moaveni, Azadeh. 2005a. *Lipstick Jihad. A Memoir of Growing Up Iranian in America and American in Iran.* New York: Public Affairs.

———. 2005b. "Fast Times in Tehran." *Time* (June 12): 38–42.

Moeller, Susan D. 1999. *Compassion Fatigue.* London: Routledge.

Moen, Phyllis, and Patricia Roehling. 2005. *The Career Mystique: Cracks in the American Dream.* Lanham, MD: Rowman and Littlefield.

Mogelonsky, Marcia. 1996. "The Rocky Road to Adulthood." *American Demographics* 18 (May): 26–29, 32–35, 56.

Mokhtarian, Patricia L., Ilan Salomon, and Sangho Choo. 2005. "Measuring the Measurable: Why Can't We Agree on the Number of Telecommuters in the U.S." *Quality and Quantity* 35: 423–452.

Mollen, Milton. 1992. *"A Failure of Responsibility": Report to Mayor David N. Dinkins on the December 28, 1991, Tragedy at City College of New York.* New York: Office of the Deputy Mayor for Public Safety.

Monaghan, Peter. 1993. "Sociologist Jailed Because He 'Wouldn't Snitch' Ponders the Way Research Ought to Be Done." *Chronicle of Higher Education* 40 (September 1):A8, A9.

Monahan, Mary T. 2007. *2007 Identity Fraud Survey Report: Identity Fraud Is Dropping, Continued Vigilance Necessary.* Pleasanton, CA: Javelin Strategy and Research.

Money. 1987. "A Short History of Shortages." 16 (Fall, special issue):42.

Monmaney, Terence. 1995. "Ethnicities' Medical Views Vary, Study Says." *Los Angeles Times,* September 13, pp. B1, B3.

Monteiro, Lois A. 1998. "Ill-Defined Illnesses and Medically Unexplained Symptoms Syndrome." *Footnotes* 26 (February):3, 6.

Montgomery, Marilyn J., and Gwendolyn T. Sorrell. 1997. "Differences in Love Attitudes Across Family Life Stages." *Family Relations* 46:55–61.

Montopoli, Brian. 2006. "Wal-Mart's German Flop." August 2. Accessed January 23, 2007 (www.cbsnews.com).

Moore, David W. 2002. "Americans' View of Influence of Religion Settling Back to Pre-September 11 Levels." *Gallup Poll Tuesday Briefing.* December 31.

Moore, Molly. 2006. "Romance, but not Marriage." *Washington Post National Weekly Edition* (November 27): 18.

Moore, Wilbert E. 1967. *Order and Change: Essays in Comparative Sociology.* New York: Wiley.

———. 1968. "Occupational Socialization." Pp. 861–883 in *Handbook of Socialization Theory and Research,* edited by David A. Goslin. Chicago: Rand McNally.

Morehouse Medical Treatment and Effectiveness Center. 1999. *A Synthesis of the Literature: Racial and Ethnic Differences in Acccess to Medical Care.* Menlo Park, CA: Henry J. Kaiser Family Foundation.

Morin, Richard. 2000. "Will Traditional Polls Go the Way of the Dinosaur?" *Washington Post National Weekly Edition* 17 (May 15):34.

Morris, Aldon. 2000. "Reflections on Social Movement Theory: Criticisms and Proposals." *Contemporary Sociology* 29 (May):445–454.

Morris, Bonnie Rothman. 1999. "You've Got Romance! Seeking Love on Line." *New York Times,* August 26, p. D1.

Morrison, Denton E. 1971. "Some Notes toward Theory on Relative Deprivation, Social Movements, and Social Change." *American Behavioral Scientist* 14 (May/June):675–690.

Morse, Arthur D. 1967. *While Six Million Died: A Chronicle of American Apathy.* New York: Ace.

Morselli, Carlo, Pierre Tremblay, and Bill McCarthy. 2006. "Mentors and Criminal Achievement." *Criminology* 44 (No. 1): 17–43.

Mosisa, Abraham T. 2002. "The Role of Foreign-Born Workers in the U.S. Economy." *Monthly Labor Review* (May), pp. 3–14.

Mosley, J., and E. Thomson. 1995. Pp. 148–165 in *Fatherhood: Contemporary Theory, Research and Social Policy,* edited by W. Marsiglo. Thousand Oaks, CA: Sage.

Moss, Michael, and Ford Fessenden. 2002. "New Tools for Domestic Spying, and Qualms." *New York Times,* December 10, pp. A1, A18.

Mueller, G. O. 2001. "Transnational Crime: Definitions and Concepts." Pp. 13–21 in *Combating Transnational Crime: Concepts, Activities, and Responses,* edited by P. Williams and D. Vlassis. London: Franklin Cass.

Murdock, George P. 1945. "The Common Denominator of Cultures." Pp. 123–142 in *The Science of Man in the World Crisis,* edited by Ralph Linton. New York: Columbia University Press.

———. 1949. *Social Structure.* New York: Macmillan.

———. 1957. "World Ethnographic Sample." *American Anthropologist* 59 (August): 664–687.

Murphy, Caryle. 1993. "Putting Aside the Veil." *Washington Post National Weekly Edition* 10 (April 12–18):10–11.

Murphy, Dean E. 1997. "A Victim of Sweden's Pursuit of Perfection." *Los Angeles Times,* September 2, pp. A1, A8.

Murray, Velma McBride, Amanda Willert, and Diane P. Stephens. 2001. "The Half-Full Glass: Resilient African American Single Mothers and Their Children." *Family Focus,* June, pp. F4–F5.

NAACP Legal Defense and Educational Fund. 2006. *Death Row U.S.A. Fall 2006.* Washington, DC: NAACP Legal Defense and Educational Fund.

NACCRRA (National Association of Child Care Resource and Referral Agencies). 2006. *Breaking the Piggy Bank: Parents and the High Price of Child Care.* Arlington, VA: NACCRRA.

———. 2007. "Child Care in America." Accessed January 31 (www.naccrra.org).

NARAL Pro-Choice America. 2007. *Who Decided? A State-by-State Report on the Status of Women's Reproductive Rights.* Accessed February 25 (www.naral.org).

Nash, Manning. 1962. "Race and the Ideology of Race." *Current Anthropology* 3 (June):285–288.

National Advisory Commission on Criminal Justice. 1976. *Organized Crime.* Washington, DC: U.S. Government Printing Office.

National Alliance for the Mentally Ill. 2000. "What Is Mental Illness?" Accessed January 18 (www.nami.org/disorder/whatis. html).

National Alliance to End Homelessness. 2007. *Homeless Counts.* Washington, DC: National Alliance to End Homelessness.

National Association of Latino Fraternal Organizations. 2007. "Member Organizations." Accessed February 21 (www.nalfo.org).

National Center for Education Statistics. 2002. *Indicators of School Crime and Safety.* Washington, DC: U.S. Government Printing Office.

National Center for Health Statistics. 2007. *Health, United States 2006.* Washington, DC: U.S. Government Printing Office.

National Council on Disability. 2004. *Righting the ADA.* Washington, DC: NCD.

National Geographic. 2002. "A World Transformed." *National Geographic* (September): map.

———. 2005. *Atlas of the World.* 8th ed. Washington, DC: *National Geographic.*

National Institute on Aging. 1999. *Early Retirement in the United States.* Washington, DC: U.S. Government Printing Office.

National Law Center on Homelessness and Poverty. 1996. *Mean Sweeps: A Report on Anti-Homeless Laws, Litigation, and Alternatives in 50 United States Cities.* Washington, DC: National Law Center on Homelessness and Poverty.

———. 2006. *A Dream Denied: The Criminalization Of Homelessness in U.S. Cities.* Washington, DC: National Law Center on Homelessness and Poverty.

National Organization for Men Against Sexism. 2007. Home page. Accessed February 25 (www.nomas.org).

National Right to Work Legal Defense Foundation. 2007. *Right to Work States.* Accessed February 10 (www.nrtw.org/rtws.htm).

National Vital Statistics Reports. 2007. "Births, Marriages, Divorces, and Deaths: Provisional Data for July 2006." *National Vital Statistics Reports* 55 (February 28).

Navarro, Mireya. 2002. "Trying to Get Beyond the Role of the Maid." *New York Times,* May 16, pp. E1, E4.

Navarro, Vicente. 1984. "Medical History as Justification Rather Than Explanation: A Critique of Starr's *The Social Transformation of American Medicine.*" *International Journal of Health Services* 14 (4):511–528.

Neary, Ian. 2003. "Burakumin at the End of History." *Social Research* 70 (Spring):269–294.

Nelson, Emily. 2004. "Goodbye, 'Friends'; Hello, New Reality." *Wall Street Journal,* February 9, pp. B6, B10.

Nelson, Michael. 2007. "Politics of Tribal Recognition: Casinos, Culture, and Controversy." Pp. 65–85 in *Interest Group Politics,* 7th ed., edited by Allan J. Cigler and Burdett A. Loomis. Washington, DC: CQ Press.

Neuman, W. Lawrence. 2000. *Social Research Methods: Qualitative and Quantitative Approaches.* Boston: Allyn and Bacon.

Neuwirth, Robert. 2004. *Shadow Cities: A Billion Squatters, a New Urban World.* New York: Routledge.

Newman, William M. 1973. *American Pluralism: A Study of Minority Groups and Social Theory.* New York: Harper and Row.

Newport, Frank. 2004. "A Look at Americans and Religion." Accessed April 14 (www.gallup.com).

———, and Joseph Carroll. 2005. "Another Look at Evangelicals in America Today." December 2. Accessed March 4, 2007 (www.gallup.com).

Newsday. 1997. "Japan Sterilized 16,000 Women." September 18, p. A19.

NewsHour. 2007. "New National Approach Focuses on Chronically Homeless." Accessed April 28 (www.pbs.org).

New York Times. 1993. "Dutch May Broaden Euthanasia Guidelines." February 17, p. A3.

Ni, Ching-Ching. 2006. "Beijing Focuses on Cleaning Up the Air for Its Olympic Moment." *Los Angeles Times,* August 9, p. A8.

NICHD. 1998. *Early Childhood Care.* Accessed October 19, 2000 (www.nichd.nih.gov/publications/pubs/early_child_care.htm).

Nielsen, Joyce McCarl, Glenda Walden, and Charlotte A. Kunkel. 2000. "Gendered Heteronormativity: Empirical Illustrations in Everyday Life." *Sociological Quarterly* 41(2): 283–296.

Niezen, Ronald. 2005. "Digital Identity: The Construction of Virtual Selfhood in the Indigenous Peoples' Movement." *Comparative Studies in Society and History,* 47 (No. 3): 532–551.

Nixon, Howard L., II. 1979. *The Small Group.* Englewood Cliffs, NJ: Prentice Hall.

Nocera, Joe. 2006. "Computer CARE Packages." *New York Times,* April 29, pp. B1, B8.

Nolan, Patrick, and Gerhard Lenski. 2006. *Human Societies: An Introduction to Macrosociology.* 10th ed. Boulder, CO: Paradigm.

Noonan, Rita K. 1995. "Women Against the State: Political Opportunities and Collective Action Frames in Chile's Transition to Democracy." *Sociological Forum* 10:81–111.

Norris, Poppa, and Ronald Inglehart. 2004. *Sacred and Secular: Religion and Politics Worldwide.* Cambridge: Cambridge University Press.

Nossiter, Adam. 2007. "Storm Left New Orleans Ripe for Violence." *New York Times,* January 11.

Novelli, William D. 2004. "Common Sense: The Case for Age Discrimination Law." *Global Report on Aging,* pp. 4, 7. Washington, DC: AARP.

Nussbaum, Bruce. 2006. "Can Wal-Mart Make It in India?" November 28. Accessed January 23, 2007 (www.businessweek.com).

Oberschall, Anthony. 1973. *Social Conflict and Social Movements.* Englewood Cliffs, NJ: Prentice Hall.

O'Connor, Anne-Marie. 2004. "Time of Blogs and Bombs." *Los Angeles Times,* December 27, pp. E1, E14–E15.

O'Donnell, Jayne, and Richard Willing. 2003. "Prison Time Gets Harder for White-Collar Crooks." *USA Today,* May 12, pp. A1, A2.

O'Donnell, Mike. 1992. *A New Introduction to Sociology.* Walton-on-Thames, United Kingdom: Thomas Nelson and Sons.

Office of Justice Programs. 1999. "Transnational Organized Crime." *NCJRS Catalog* 49 (November/December):21.

Ogburn, William F. 1922. *Social Change with Respect to Culture and Original Nature.* New York: Huebsch (reprinted 1966, New York: Dell).

———, and Clark Tibbits. 1934. "The Family and Its Functions." Pp. 661–708 in *Recent Social Trends in the United States,* edited by Research Committee on Social Trends. New York: McGraw-Hill.

O'Hare, William P., and Brenda Curry White. 1992. "Is There a Rural Underclass?" *Population Today* 20 (March):6–8.

O'Harrow, Jr., Robert. 2005. "Mining Personal Data." *Washington Post National Weekly Edition* (February 6), pp. 8–10.

Okamoto, Dina G., and Lynn Smith-Lovin. 2001. "Changing the Subject: Gender, Status, and the Dynamics of Topic Change." *American Sociological Review* 66 (December):852–873.

Okano, Kaori, and Motonori Tsuchiya. 1999. *Education in Contemporary Japan: Inequality and Diversity.* Cambridge: Cambridge University Press.

Oliver, Melvin L., and Thomas M. Shapiro. 1995. *Black Wealth/White Wealth: New Perspectives on Racial Inequality.* New York: Routledge.

Ommer, Uwe. 2000. *1000 Families: The Family Album of Planet Earth.* Cologne, Germany: Taschen for Unicef.

One Laptop per Child. 2007. "One Laptop per Child" and "Internet World Users by Language." Accessed May 8 (www.laptop.org).

Onishi, Norimitso. 2003. "Divorce in South Korea: Striking a New Attitude." *New York Times,* September 21, p. 19.

Ormond, James. 2005. "The McDonaldization of Football." Accessed January 23, 2006 (http://courses.essex.ac.uk/sc/sc111).

Orum, Anthony M. 1989. *Introduction to Political Sociology: The Social Anatomy of the Body Politic.* 3d ed. Englewood Cliffs, NJ: Prentice Hall.

———. 2001. *Introduction to Political Sociology.* 4th ed. Upper Saddle River, NJ: Prentice Hall.

Osberg, Lars, and Timothy Smeeding. 2006. "'Fair' Inequality? Attitudes Toward Pay Differentials: The United States in Comparative Perspective." *American Sociological Review* 71 (June): 450–473.

Osgood, D. Wayne, and Jeff M. Chambers. 2003. "Community Correlates of Rural Youth Violence." *Juvenile Justice Bulletin* (May):1–9.

Osnos, Evan. 2007. "Chinese Blogger's Crusade Has Starbucks Feeling Heat." *Chicago Tribune,* January 28, pp. 1, 10.

Ouchi, William. 1981. *Theory Z: How American Businesses Can Meet the Japanese Challenge.* Reading, MA: Addison-Wesley.

Pace, David. 2006. "FEC Won't Regulate Internet Politics." May 27. Associated Press.

Page, Charles H. 1946. "Bureaucracy's Other Face." *Social Forces* 25 (October):89–94.

Pager, Devah. 2003. "The Mark of a Criminal Record." *American Journal of Sociology* 108 (March):937–975.

———, and Lincoln Quillian. 2005. "Walking the Talk? What Employers Say Versus What They Do." *American Sociological Review* 70 (June): 355–380.

Paik, Nancy. 2001. *One Nation: Islam in America.* Accessed March 15 (www.channelonenews.com/special/islam/media.html).

Pamuk, E., D. Makui, K. Heck, C. Reuban, and K. Lochren. 1998. *Health, United States 1998 with Socioeconomic Status and Health Chartbook.* Hyattsville, MD: National Center for Health Statistics.

Pantesco, Joshua. 2006. "Federal Judge Strikes Down Maryland Wal-Mart Health Care Law." *Jurist Legal News and Research* (University of Pittsburgh School of Law) (July 19).

Park, Hwa-Ok. 2005. "Grandmothers Raising Grandchildren: Family Well-Being and Economic Assistance." *Focus* 24 (Fall):19–27.

Park, Robert E. 1916. "The City: Suggestions for the Investigation of Human Behavior in the Urban Environment." *American Journal of Sociology* 20 (March):577–612.

———. 1922. *The Immigrant Press and Its Control.* New York: Harper.

———. 1936. "Succession, an Ecological Concept." *American Sociological Review* 1 (April):171–179.

Parker, Alison. 2004. "Inalienable Rights: Can Human-Rights Law Help to End U.S. Mistreatment of Noncitizens?" *American Prospect* (October):A11–A13.

Parsons, Talcott. 1951. *The Social System.* New York: Free Press.

———. 1966. *Societies: Evolutionary and Comparative Perspectives.* Englewood Cliffs, NJ: Prentice Hall.

———. 1975. "The Sick Role and the Role of the Physician Reconsidered." *Milbank Medical Fund Quarterly Health and Society* 53 (Summer): 257–278.

———, and Robert Bales. 1955. *Family: Socialization and Interaction Process.* Glencoe, IL: Free Press.

Passero, Kathy. 2002. "Global Travel Expert Roger Axtell Explains Why." *Biography,* July, pp. 70–73, 97–98.

Patterson, Thomas E. 2003. *We the People.* 5th ed. New York: McGraw-Hill.

———. 2005. "Young Voters and the 2004 Election." Cambridge, MA: Vanishing Voter Project, Harvard University.

Pattillo-McCoy, Mary. 1999. *Black Picket Fences: Privilege and Peril among the Black Middle Class.* Chicago: University of Chicago Press.

Patton, Carl V., ed. 1988. *Spontaneous Shelter: International Perspectives and Prospects.* Philadelphia: Temple University Press.

Paxton, Pamela, Melanie M. Hughes, and Jennifer L. Green. 2006. "The International Women's Movement and Women's Political Representation, 1893–2003." *American Sociological Review* 71 (December): 898–920.

PBS. 2005. "Store Wars: When Wal-Mart Comes to Town." Accessed August 31 (www.pbs.org).

Pear, Robert. 1997. "Now, the Archenemies Need Each Other." *New York Times,* June 22, sec. 4, pp. 1, 4.

Pearlstein, Steven. 2001. "Coming Soon (Maybe): Worldwide Recession." *Washington Post National Weekly Edition* 19 (November 12):18.

Pellow, David Naguib. 2002. *Garbage Wars: The Struggle for Environmental Justice in Chicago.* Cambridge, MA: MIT Press.

———, and Robert J. Brulle. 2007. "Poisoning the Planet. The Struggle for Environmental Justice." *Contexts* 6 (No. 1), pp. 37–41.

Pelton, Tom. 1994. "Hawthorne Works' Glory Now Just So Much Rubble." *Chicago Tribune,* April 18, pp. 1, 6.

Perrow, Charles. 1986. *Complex Organizations.* 3d ed. New York: Random House.

Perry, Joellen. 2001. "For Most, There's No Place Like Home." *U.S. News and World Report* 130 (June 4):66.

Peter, Laurence J., and Raymond Hull. 1969. *The Peter Principle.* New York: Morrow.

Petersen, William. 1979. *Malthus.* Cambridge, MA: Harvard University Press.

Peterson, Karen S. 2003. "Unmarried with Children: For Better or Worse." *USA Today,* August 18, pp. 1A, 8A.

Petrášová, Alexandra. 2006. *Social Protection in the European Union.* Brussels: European Union.

Petrovic, Drazen. 1994. "Ethnic Cleansing—An Attempt at Methodology." *EJIL* 5: 1–19.

Pew Internet Project. 2007. "Demographics of Internet Users." Accessed February 13 (http://www.pewinternet.org/trends/User_Demo_1.11.07.htm).

Pew Research Center. 2004. "Conflicted Views of Affirmative Action." News release, May 14, 2004. Washington, DC: Pew Research Center.

Phillips, E. Barbara. 1996. *City Lights: Urban–Suburban Life in the Global Society.* New York: Oxford University Press.

Phillips, Susan A. 1999. *Wallbangin': Graffiti and Gangs in L.A.* Chicago: University of Chicago Press.

Phillips, Tom. 2005. "Farewell to the Favelas?" *Guardian Weekly* 173 (November 17), p. 29.

Piaget, Jean. 1954. *The Construction of Reality in the Child.* Translated by Margaret Cook. New York: Basic Books.

Pierre, Robert E. 2002. "When Welfare Reform Stops Working." *Washington Post National Weekly Edition,* January 13, pp. 29–30.

Piller, Charles. 2001. "Terrorists Taking Up Cyberspace." *Los Angeles Times,* February 8, pp. A1, A14, A15.

———. 2006. "An Alert Unlike Any Other." *Los Angeles Times,* May 3, pp. A1, A8.

Pinderhughes, Dianne. 1987. *Race and Ethnicity in Chicago Politics: A Reexamination of Pluralist Theory.* Urbana: University of Illinois Press.

Pinkerton, James P. 2003. "Education: A Grand Compromise." *Atlantic Monthly* 291 (January/February):115–116.

Plomin, Robert. 1989. "Determinants of Behavior." *American Psychologist* 44 (February):105–111.

Plüss, Caroline. 2005. "Constructing Globalized Ethnicity." *International Sociology* 20 (June):201–224.

Polletta, Francesca, and James M. Jasper. 2001. "Collective Identity and Social Movements." Pp. 283–305 in *Annual Review of Sociology, 2001,* edited by Karen S. Cook and Leslie Hogan. Palo Alto, CA: Annual Reviews.

Poniewozik, James. 2001. "What's Wrong with This Picture?" *Time* 157 (May 28):80–81.

Popenoe, David, and Barbara Dafoe Whitehead. 1999. *Should We Live Together? What Young Adults Need to Know About Cohabitation Before Marriage.* Rutgers, NJ: The National Marriage Project.

Population Reference Bureau. 1996. "Speaking Graphically." *Population Today* 24 (June/July):b.

Power, Samantha. 2002. *A Problem from Hell: America and the Age of Genocide.* New York: Perennial.

Prah, Pamela M. 2005. "Labor Unions' Future." *CQ Researcher* 15 (September 2):709–731.

Prehn, John W. 1991. "Migration." Pp. 190–191 in *Encyclopedia of Sociology,* 4th ed. Guilford, CT: Dushkin.

Price, Jay. 2006. "Hired Guns Unaccountable." *News and Observer* (Raleigh, NC), March 23.

Prus, Steven G. 2007. "Age, SES, and Health: A Population Level Analysis of Health Irregularities over the Lifecourse." *Sociology of Health and Illness* 29 (March):275–296.

Pryor, John H., Sylvia Hurtado, Victor B. Saenz, Jessica S. Korn, José Luis Santos, and William Korn. 2006. *The American Freshman: National Norms for Fall 2006.* Los Angeles: Higher Education Research Institute, UCLA.

Puentes, Robert, and David Warrenn. 2006. *One-Fifth of America: A Comprehensive Guide to American's First Suburbs.* Washington, DC: Brookings Institution.

Purdum, Todd S. 2002. "U.S. Blocks Money for Family Clinics Promoted by U.N." *New York Times,* July 23, pp. A1, A6.

Quadagno, Jill. 2005. *Aging and the Life Course: An Introduction to Social Gerontology.* 3d ed. New York: McGraw-Hill.

Quarantelli, Enrico L. 1957. "The Behavior of Panic Participants." *Sociology and Social Research* 41 (January):187–194.

———, and Russell R. Dynes. 1970. "Property Norms and Looting: Their Patterns in Continuity Crises." *Phylon* (Summer):168–182.

———, and James R. Hundley, Jr. 1975. "A Test of Some Propositions about Crowd Formation and Behavior." Pp. 538–554 in *Readings in Collective Behavior,* edited by Robert R. Evans. Chicago: Rand McNally.

Quart, Alissa. 2003. *Branded: The Buying and Selling of Teenagers.* New York: Perseus.

Quinney, Richard. 1970. *The Social Reality of Crime.* Boston: Little, Brown.

———. 1974. *Criminal Justice in America.* Boston: Little, Brown.

———. 1979. *Criminology.* 2d ed. Boston: Little, Brown.

———. 1980. *Class, State and Crime.* 2d ed. New York: Longman.

Ragged Edge. 1998. "Austin, Texas Becomes Second City in the Nation to Require Basic Access in Single Family Homes." *Ragged Edge* (November/December):5.

Rainie, Lee. 2001. *The Commons of the Tragedy.* Washington, DC: Pew Internet and American Life Project.

———. 2005. *Sports Fantasy Leagues Online.* Washington, DC: Pew Internet and American Life Project.

———, and John Horrigan. 2007. *Election 2006 Online.* Washington, DC: Pew Research Center.

Rajan, Gita, and Shailja Sharma. 2006. *New Cosmopolitanisms: South Asians in the US.* Stanford, CA: Stanford University Press.

Rakowitz, Susan, and J. Sabini. 1995. *Social Psychology.* 2d rev. ed. New York: W.W. Norton.

Ramet, Sabrina. 1991. *Social Currents in Eastern Europe: The Source and Meaning of the Great Transformation.* Durham, NC: Duke University Press.

Ramirez, Eddy. 2002. "Ageism in the Media Is Seen as Harmful to Health of the Elderly." *Los Angeles Times,* September 5, p. A20.

Ray, Brian D. 2006. "Research Facts on Homeschooling." Accessed April 11, 2007 (www.Nheri.org).

Ray, Raka. 1999. *Fields of Protest: Women's Movement in India.* Minneapolis: University of Minnesota Press.

Raybon, Patricia. 1989. "A Case for 'Severe Bias.'" *Newsweek* 114 (October 2):11.

Rayman-Read, Alyssa. 2001. "The Sound of Silence." *The American Prospect* (Fall Special Supplement):A20–A24.

Read, Brock. 2006. "Can Technology Save the Developing World?" *Chronicle of Higher Education* 52 (July 21), pp. A27–A29.

Reddick, Randy, and Elliot King. 2000. *The Online Student: Making the Grade on the Internet.* Fort Worth: Harcourt Brace.

Reinharz, Shulamit. 1992. *Feminist Methods in Social Research.* New York: Oxford University Press.

Reitzes, Donald C., and Elizabeth J. Mutran. 2006. "Lingering Identities in Retirement." *Sociological Quarterly* 47: 333–359.

Religion News Service. 2003. "New U.S. Guidelines on Prayer in Schools Get Mixed Reaction." *Los Angeles Times,* February 15, p. B24.

Religion Watch. 2006. "Hinduism Shaping India's Pragmatic Use of Biotechnology." April.

Religious Tolerance. 2005. "Female Genital Mutilation (FGM): Informational Materials." Accessed March 15 (www.religioustolerance.org).

———. 2007. "Prejudice of Americans towards Various Religions." Accessed January 7, 2007 (www.religioustolerance.org/amer_intol.htm).

Remnick, David. 1998. "Bad Seeds." *New Yorker* 74 (July 20):28–33.

Renard, J. B. 2003. "Rumors and Urban Legends." *International Encyclopedia of the Social and Behavioral Sciences.* Amsterdam: Elsevier.

Reschovsky, Clara. 2004. *Journey to Work: 2000.* Census 2000 Brief C2KBR-23. Washington, DC: U.S. Government Printing Office.

Reverby, Susan M., ed. 2000. *Tuskegee's Truths: Rethinking the Tuskegee Syphilis Study.* Chapel Hill, NC: University of North Carolina Press.

Revkin, Andrew C. 2007. "Wealth and Poverty, Drought and Flood: Report from Four Fronts in the War on Warming." *New York Times,* April 3, pp. D4–D5.

Rheingold, Howard. 2003. *Smart Mobs: The Next Social Revolution.* Cambridge, MA: Perseus.

Richardson, James T., and Barend van Driel. 1997. "Journalists' Attitudes toward New Religious Movements." *Review of Religious Research* 39 (December):116–136.

Richardson, Laurel, Verta Taylor, and Nancy Whittier, eds. 2004. *Feminist Frontiers.* 6th ed. New York: McGraw-Hill.

Richman, Joseph. 1992. "A Rational Approach to Rational Suicide." *Suicide and Life-Threatening Behavior* 22 (Spring):130–141.

Rideout, Victoria, Donald F. Roberts, and Ulla G. Foehr. 2005. *Executive Summary: Generation M: Media in the Lives of 8–18-Year-Olds.* Menlo Park, CA: Kaiser Family Foundation.

Ridgeway, Cecilia L., and Lynn Smith-Lovin. 1999. "The Gender System and Interaction." Pp. 191–216 in *The Annual Review of Sociology 1999,* edited by Karen Cook and John Hagan. Palo Alto, CA: Annual Reviews.

Riding, Alan. 1998. "Why 'Titanic' Conquered the World." *New York Times,* April 26, sec. 2, pp. 1, 28, 29.

———. 2005. "Unesco Adopts New Plan Against Cultural Invasion." *New York Times,* October 21, p. B3.

Rifkin, Jeremy. 1995a. "Afterwork." *Utne Reader* (May/June):52–62.

———. 1995b. *The End of Work; The Decline of the Global Labor Force and the Dawn of the Post-Market Era.* New York: Tarcher/ Putnam.

———. 1996. "Civil Society in the Information Age." *The Nation* 262 (February 26):11–12, 14–16.

Riley, John W., Jr. 1992. "Death and Dying." Pp. 413–418 in *Encyclopedia of Sociology,* vol. 1, edited by Edgar F. Borgatta and Marie L. Borgatta. New York: Macmillan.

Riley, Matilda White, Robert L. Kahn, and Anne Foner. 1994a. *Age and Structural Lag.* New York: Wiley InterScience.

———, Robert L. Kahn, and Anne Foner, in association with Karin A. Mock. 1994b. "Introduction: The Mismatch between People and Structures." Pp. 1–36 in *Age and Structural Lag,* edited by Matilda White Riley, Robert L. Kahn, and Anne Foner. New York: Wiley InterScience.

Riley, Nancy E. 2004. "China's Population: New Trends and Challenges." *Population Bulletin* 59 (June).

590

Rimer, Sara. 1998. "As Centenarians Thrive, 'Old' Is Redefined." *New York Times,* June 22, pp. A1, A14.

Ripley, Amanda. 2005. "Who Says a Woman Can't Be Einstein?" *Time* (March 7):51–60.

Ritzer, George. 1977. *Working: Conflict and Change.* 2d ed. Englewood Cliffs, NJ: Prentice Hall.

———. 2000. *The McDonaldization of Society.* New Century Edition. Thousand Oaks, CA: Pine Forge Press.

———. 2002. *McDonaldization: The Reader.* Thousand Oaks, CA: Pine Forge Press.

———. 2004a. *The McDonaldization of Society.* Revised New Century Edition. Thousand Oaks, CA: Pine Forge Press.

———. 2004b.*The Globalization of Nothing.* Thousand Oaks, CA: Pine Forge Press.

Rivoli, Pietra. 2005. *The Travels of a T-Shirt in the Global Economy: An Economist Examines the Markets, Power, and Politics of World Trade.* Hoboken, NJ: John Wiley.

Roan, Shari. 1995. "Under Pressure, Isolation: Jury Stress Sparks Concerns." *Los Angeles Times,* August 22, pp. A1, A28.

Roberson, Debi, Ian Davies, and Jules Davidoff. 2000. "Color Categories Are Not Universal: Replications and New Evidence From Stone Age Culture." *Journal of Experimental Psychology* 129 (3):369–398.

Roberts, D. F., Lisa Henriksen, Peter G. Christiansson, and Marcy Kelly. 1999. "Substance Abuse in Popular Movies and Music." Accessible online (www.whitehousedrugpolicy.gov/news/press/042899.html). Washington, DC: Office of Juvenile Justice.

Robertson, Roland. 1988. "The Sociological Significance of Culture: Some General Considerations." *Theory, Culture, and Society* 5 (February):3–23.

Robison, Jennifer. 2002. "Feminism—What's in a Name?" Accessed February 25, 2007 (www.galluppoll.com).

———. 2002. "Should Mothers Work?" *Gallup Poll Tuesday Briefing.* Accessed August 17 (www.gallup.com).

Roethlisberger, Fritz J., and W. J. Dickson. 1939. *Management and the Worker.* Cambridge, MA: Harvard University Press.

Roper Center. 2005. "Associated Press/Ipsos-Public Affairs Poll." February 2005. Accessed at www.ropercenter.uconn.edu

Rose, Arnold. 1951. *The Roots of Prejudice.* Paris: UNESCO.

Rose, Peter I., Myron Glazer, and Penina Migdal Glazer. 1979. "In Controlled Environments: Four Cases of Intense Resocialization." Pp. 320–338 in *Socialization and the Life Cycle,* edited by Peter I. Rose. New York: St. Martin's.

Rosenberg, Douglas H. 1991. "Capitalism." Pp. 33–34 in *Encyclopedic Dictionary of Sociology,* 4th ed., edited by Dushkin Publishing Group. Guilford, CT: Dushkin.

Rosenberg, Howard. 2003. "Snippets of the 'Unique' Al Jazeera." *Los Angeles Times,* April 4, pp. E1, E37.

Rosenberg, Yuval. 2004. "Lost Youth." *American Demographics* (March):18–19.

Rosenthal, Elizabeth. 2001. "College Entrance in China: 'No' to the Handicapped." *New York Times,* May 23, p. A3.

Rosenthal, Robert, and Lenore Jacobson. 1968. *Pygmalion in the Classroom.* New York: Holt.

———. 1992. *Pygmalion in the Classroom: Teacher Expectations and Pupils' Intellectual Development.* Newly expanded edition. Bancy Felin, UK: Crown House.

Rosnow, Ralph L., and Gary L. Fine. 1976. *Rumor and Gossip: The Social Psychology of Hearsay.* New York: Elsevier.

Ross, John. 1996. "To Die in the Street: Mexico City's Homeless Population Booms as Economic Crisis Shakes Social Protections." *SSSP Newsletter* 27 (Summer):14–15.

Rossi, Alice S. 1968. "Transition to Parenthood." *Journal of Marriage and the Family* 30(February): 26–39.

———. 1984. "Gender and Parenthood." *American Sociological Review* 49 (February):1–19.

Rossi, Peter H. 1987. "No Good Applied Social Research Goes Unpunished." *Society* 25 (November/December):73–79.

Rossides, Daniel W. 1997. *Social Stratification: The Interplay of Class, Race, and Gender.* 2d ed. Upper Saddle River, NJ: Prentice Hall.

Roszak, Theodore. 1969. *The Making of a Counterculture.* Garden City, NY: Doubleday.

Roter, Debra L., Judith A. Hall, and Yutaka Aoki. 2002. "Physician Gender Effects in Medical Communication: A Meta-analytic Review." *Journal of the American Medical Association* 288 (August 14):756–764.

Roy, Donald F. 1959. "'Banana Time': Job Satisfaction and Informal Interaction." *Human Organization* 18 (Winter):158–168.

Ruane, Janet M., and Karen A. Cerulo. 2004. *Second Thoughts: Seeing Conventional Wisdom Through the Sociological Eye.* Thousand Oaks, CA: Pine Forge.

Rubin, Alissa J. 2003. "Pat-Down on the Way to Prayer." *Los Angeles Times,* November 25, pp. A1, A5.

Ruebain, David. 2005. "Disability Discrimination Act of 1995 (United Kingdom)." Pp. 420–422 in *Encyclopedia of Disability,* edited by Gary Albrecht. Thousand Oaks, CA: Sage.

Russo, Nancy Felipe. 1976. "The Motherhood Mandate." *Journal of Social Issues* 32:143–153.

Ryan, William. 1976. *Blaming the Victim.* Rev. ed. New York: Random House.

Rymer, Russ. 1993. *Genie: An Abused Child's Flight from Science.* New York: HarperCollins.

Saad, Lydia. 2004. "Divorce Doesn't Last." *Gallup Poll Tuesday Briefing,* March 30 (www.gallup.com).

Sabbathday Lake. 2004. Interview by author with Sabbathday Lake Shaker Village. July 28.

Sachs, Jeffrey D. 2005a. *The End of Poverty: Economic Possibilities for Our Time.* New York: Penguin.

———. 2005b. "Can Extreme Poverty Be Eliminated?" *Scientific American* 293 (September): 56–65.

Sadker, Myra Pollack, and David Miller Sadker. 2003. *Teachers, Schools and Society,* 6th ed. New York: McGraw-Hill.

Sagarin, Edward, and Jose Sanchez. 1988. "Ideology and Deviance: The Case of the Debate over the Biological Factor." *Deviant Behavior* 9 (1):87–99.

Sager, Rebecca. 2007. "The Faith-Based Initiative." *Footnotes* (April), p. 3.

Said, Edward W. 2001. "The Clash of Ignorance." *The Nation* (October 22).

Sale, Kirkpatrick. 1996. *Rebels against the Future: The Luddites and Their War on the Industrial Revolution* (with a new preface by the author). Reading, MA: Addison-Wesley.

Salem, Richard, and Stanislaus Grabarek. 1986. "Sociology B.A.s in a Corporate Setting: How Can They Get There and of What Value Are They?" *Teaching Sociology* 14 (October):273–275.

Samuelson, Paul A., and William D. Nordhaus. 2005. *Economics.* 18th ed. New York: McGraw-Hill.

Sanders, Edmund. 2004. "Coming of Age in Iraq." *Los Angeles Times,* August 14, pp. A1, A5.

Saporito, Bill. 2003. "Can Wal-Mart Get Any Bigger?" *Time,* January 13, pp. 38–43.

Sarkisian, Natalia, and Naomi Gerstel. 2004. "Kin Support among Blacks and Whites: Race and Family Organizations." *American Sociological Review* 69 (December):812–837.

Sassen, Saskia. 2005. "New Global Classes: Implications for Politics." Pp. 143–170 in *The New Egalitarianism,* edited by Anthony Giddens and Patrick Diamond. Cambridge: Polity.

Savage, David G. 2006. "Supreme Court Upholds Oregon Right-to-Die Law." *Los Angeles Times,* January 18, pp. A1, A14.

Sayer, Liana C., Suzanne M. Bianchi, and John P. Robinson. 2004. "Are Parents Investing Less in Children? Trends in Mothers' and Fathers' Time with Children." *American Journal of Sociology* 110 (July):1–43.

Scarce, Rik. 1994. "(No) Trial (But) Tribulations: When Courts and Ethnography Conflict." *Journal of Contemporary Ethnography* 23 (July):123–149.

———. 1995. "Scholarly Ethics and Courtroom Antics: Where Researchers Stand in the Eyes of the Law." *American Sociologist* 26 (Spring):87–112.

———. 2005. "A Law to Protect Scholars." *Chronicle of Higher Education* (August 12):324.

Schachter, Jason. 2001. "Geographical Mobility: Population Characteristics." *Current Population Reports,* ser. P-20, no. 538. Washington, DC: U.S. Government Printing Office.

Schaefer, Richard T. 1998a. "Differential Racial Mortality and the 1995 Chicago Heat Wave." Presentation at the annual meeting of the American Sociological Association, August, San Francisco.

———. 1998b. *Alumni Survey.* Chicago: Department of Sociology, DePaul University.

———. 2006. *Racial and Ethnic Relations.* 10th ed. Upper Saddle River, NJ: Prentice Hall.

————. 2008a. *Race and Ethnicity in the United States.* 11th ed. Upper Saddle River, NJ: Prentice Hall.

————. 2008b. "'Power' and 'Power Elite.'" In *Encyclopedia of Social Problems,* edited by Vincent Parrillo. Thousand Oaks, CA: Sage.

————, and William W. Zellner. 2007. *Extraordinary Groups.* 8th ed. New York: Worth.

Scharnberg, Kirsten. 2002. "Tattoo Unites WTC's Laborers." *Chicago Tribune,* July 22, pp. 1, 18.

Schmidley, A. Dianne, and J. Gregory Robinson. 2003. *Measuring the Foreign-Born Population in the United States with the Current Population Survey: 1994–2002.* Washington, DC: Population Division, Bureau of the Census.

Schnaiberg, Allan. 1994. *Environment and Society: The Enduring Conflict.* New York: St. Martin's.

Schrag, Peter. 2004. "Bush's Education Fraud." *American Prospect* 15 (February):38–41.

Schulman, Gary I. 1974. "Race, Sex, and Violence: A Laboratory Test of the Sexual Threat of the Black Male Hypothesis." *American Journal of Sociology* 79 (March): 1260–1272.

Schur, Edwin M. 1965. *Crimes without Victims: Deviant Behavior and Public Policy.* Englewood Cliffs, NJ: Prentice Hall.

————. 1968. *Law and Society: A Sociological View.* New York: Random House.

————. 1985. "'Crimes without Victims': A 20 Year Reassessment." Paper presented at the annual meeting of the Society for the Study of Social Problems.

Schurman, Rachel. 2004. "Fighting 'Frankenfoods': Industry Opportunity Structures and the Efficacy of the Anti-Biotech Movement in Western Europe." *Social Problems* 51 (2):243–268.

Schwartz, Howard D., ed. 1987. *Dominant Issues in Medical Sociology.* 2d ed. New York: Random House.

Schwartz, John. 2004. "Leisure Pursuits of Today's Young Man." *New York Times,* March 29.

————. 2005. "NASA Shuts Down Shuttle Program, over Foam Debris." *New York Times,* July 28, pp. A1, A19.

Schwartz, Shalom H., and Anat Bardi. 2001. "Value Hierarchies Across Cultures: Taking a Similarities Perspective." *Journal of Cross-Cultural Perspective* 32 (May):268–290.

Scotch, Richard. 1989. "Politics and Policy in the History of the Disability Rights Movement." *The Milbank Quarterly* 67 (Supplement 2):380–400.

————. 2001. *From Good Will to Civil Rights: Transforming Federal Disability Policy.* 2d ed. Philadelphia: Temple University Press.

Scott, Alan. 1990. *Ideology and the New Social Movements.* London: Unwin Hyman.

Scott, Gregory. 2001. "Broken Windows behind Bars: Eradicating Prison Gangs through Ecological Hardening and Symbolic Cleansing." *Corrections Management Quarterly* 5 (Winter):23–36.

————. 2005. "Public Symposium: HIV/AIDS, Injection Drug Use and Men Who Have Sex with Men." Pp. 38–39 in *Scholarship with a Mission,* edited by Susanna Pagliaro. Chicago: DePaul University.

Scott, Jenny. 2005. "Life at the Top in America Isn't Better, It's Longer." *New York Times,* May 16, pp. A1, A19–A20.

Scott, W. Richard. 2003. *Organizations: Rational, Natural, and Open Systems.* 5th ed. Upper Saddle River, NJ: Prentice Hall.

————. 2004. "Reflections on a Half-Century of Organizational Sociology." Pp. 1–21 in *Annual Review of Sociology 2004,* edited by Karen S. Cook and John Hagan. Palo Alto, CA: Annual Reviews.

Seabrook, Jeremy. 2005. "In Death, Imperialism Lives On." *Guardian Weekly Edition,* July 7, p. 5.

Secretan, Thierry. 1995. *Going into Darkness: Fantastic Coffins from Africa.* London: Thames and Hudson.

Segall, Alexander. 1976. "The Sick Role Concept: Understanding Illness Behavior." *Journal of Health and Social Behavior* 17 (June): 163–170.

Segerstråle, Ullica. 2000. *Defense of the Truth: The Battle for Science in the Sociobiology Debate and Beyond.* New York: Oxford University Press.

Seidman, Steven. 1994. "Heterosexism in America: Prejudice against Gay Men and Lesbians." Pp. 578–593 in *Introduction to Social Problems,* edited by Craig Calhoun and George Ritzer. New York: McGraw-Hill.

Sellers, Frances Stead. 2004. "Voter Globalization." *Washington Post National Weekly Edition,* November 29, p. 22.

Sengupta, Somini. 2004. "For Iraqi Girls, Changing Land Narrows Lines." *New York Times,* June 27, pp. A1, A11.

————. 2006. "Report Shows Muslims Near Bottom of Social Ladder." *New York Times,* November 29, p. A4.

Senior Action in a Gay Environment (SAGE). 2007. Home page. Accessed February 28 (www.sageusa.org).

Sernau, Scott. 2001. *Worlds Apart: Social Inequalities in a New Century.* Thousand Oaks, CA: Pine Forge Press.

Shanahan, Michael J. 2000. "Pathways to Adulthood in Changing Socities: Variability and Mechanisms in Life Cause Perspective." Pp. 667–692 in *Annual Review of Sociology 2000,* edited by Karen S. Cook. Palo Alto, CA: Annual Reviews.

Shapiro, Joseph P. 1993. *No Pity: People with Disabilities Forging a New Civil Rights Movement.* New York: Times Books.

Sharma, Hari M., and Gerard C. Bodeker. 1998. "Alternative Medicine." Pp. 228–229 in *Britannica Book of the Year 1998.* Chicago: Encyclopaedia Britannica.

Sheehan, Charles. 2005. "Poor Seniors Take On Plans of Condo Giant." *Chicago Tribune,* March 22, pp. 1, 9.

Shenon, Philip. 1995. "New Zealand Seeks Causes of Suicides by Young." *New York Times,* July 15, p. 3.

Shepherd, Jean. 2003. *Japan Performs First Transplants from Brain-Dead Donor.* Accessed June 14 (www.pntb.org/ff-rndwrld.html).

Shibutani, Tamotshu. 1966. *Improvised News: A Sociological Study of Rumor.* Indianapolis: Bobbs-Merrill.

Shin, Hyon B., and Rosalind Bruno. 2003. "Language Use and English-Speaking Ability: 2000." *Census 2000 Brief,* C2KBR-29. Washington, DC: U.S. Government Printing Office.

Shinkai, Hiroguki, and Ugljea Zvekic. 1999. "Punishment." Pp. 89–120 in *Global Report on Crime and Justice,* edited by Graeme Newman. New York: Oxford University Press.

Shipler, David K. 2005. *The Working Poor: Invisible in America.* New York: Alfred A. Knopf.

Shogren, Elizabeth. 1994. "Treatment against Their Will." *Los Angeles Times,* August 18, pp. A1, A14–A15.

Shorrucks, Anthony, James Davies, Susanna Sandström, and Edward Wolff. 2006. *The World Distribution of Household Wealth.* Helsinki, Finland: United Nations University and World Institute for Development Economics Research.

Shortliffe, E. H., and V. L. Patel. 2004. "Internet: Psychological Perspectives." Pp. 7852–7855 in *International Encyclopedia of the Social and Behavioral Sciences,* edited by Neil J. Smelser and Paul B. Baltes. New York: Elsevier.

Shostak, Arthur B. 2002. "Clinical Sociology and the Art of Peace Promotion: Earning a World Without War." Pp. 325–345 in *Using Sociology: An Introduction from the Applied and Clinical Perspectives,* edited by Roger A. Straus. Lanham, MD: Rowman and Littlefield.

Shupe, Anson D., and David G. Bromley. 1980. "Walking a Tightrope." *Qualitative Sociology* 2:8–21.

Shupe, Ellen I., Lilia M. Cortina, Alexandra Ramos, Louisa F. Fitzgerald, and Jan Salisbury. 2002. "The Incidence and Outcomes of Sexual Harassment Among Hispanic and Non-Hispanic White Women: Comparison Across Levels of Cultural Affiliation." *Psychology of Women Quarterly* 26 (No. 4): 298–308.

Shuraydi, Muhammad, and Arshia U. Zaidi. 2002. "Perceptions of Arranged Marriages by Young Pakistani Muslim Women Living in a Western Society." *Journal of Comparative Family Studies* 33 (Autumn): 37–57.

Sicular, Terry, Ximing Yue, Bjorn Gustafsson, and Shi Li. 2006. *The Urban-Rural Income Gap and Inequality in China.* Research Paper No. 2006/135, United Nations University—World Institute for Development Economic Research.

Silicon Valley Cultures Project. 2004. The Silicon Valley Cultures Project Web site. Accessed February 3, 2005 (www2.sjsu.edu/depts/anthropology/svcp).

Silver, Ira. 1996. "Role Transitions, Objects, and Identity." *Symbolic Interaction* 10 (1):1–20.

Simmel, Georg. [1917] 1950. *Sociology of Georg Simmel.* Translated by K. Wolff. Glencoe, IL: Free Press (originally written in 1902–1917).

Simmons, Ann M. 1998. "Where Fat Is a Mark of Beauty." *Los Angeles Times,* September 30, pp. A1, A12.

Simmons, Tavia, and Martin O'Connell. 2003. "Married-Couple and Unmarried-Partner Households: 2000." *Census 2000 Special Reports* CENBR-5. Washington, DC: U.S. Government Printing Office.

Simon, Joshua M. 1999. "Presidential Candidates Face Campaign Finance Issue." *Harvard Crimson,* July 2.

Simons, Marlise. 1997. "Child Care Sacred as France Cuts Back the Welfare State." *New York Times,* December 31, pp. A1, A6.

Sjoberg, Gideon. 1960. *The Preindustrial City: Past and Present.* Glencoe, IL: Free Press.

Slavin, Robert E., and A. Cheung. 2003. *Effective Reading Programs for English Language Learners: A Best-Evidence Synthesis.* Baltimore, MD: Johns Hopkins University, Center for Research on the Education of Students Placed at Risk.

Smart, Barry. 1990. "Modernity, Postmodernity, and the Present." Pp. 14–30 in *Theories of Modernity and Postmodernity,* edited by Bryan S. Turner. Newbury Park, CA: Sage.

Smart Growth. 2005. "About Smart Growth." Accessed May 31 (www.smartgrowth.org.).

Smedley, Brian D., Adrienne Y. Stith, and Alan R. Nelson, eds. 2002. *Unequal Treatment: Confronting Racial and Ethnic Disparities in Health Care.* Washington, DC: Institutional Medicine.

Smelser, Neil. 1962. *Theory of Collective Behavior.* New York: Free Press.

———. 1963. *The Sociology of Economic Life.* Englewood Cliffs, NJ: Prentice Hall.

———. 1981. *Sociology.* Englewood Cliffs, NJ: Prentice Hall.

Smith, Christian. 1991. *The Emergence of Liberation Theology: Radical Religion and Social Movement Theory.* Chicago: University of Chicago Press.

Smith, Craig S. 2005. "Abduction, Often Violent, a Kyrgyz Wedding Rite." *New York Times,* April 30, pp. A1, A7.

———. 2006a. "Romania's Orphans Face Widespread Abuse, Group Says." *New York Times,* May 10, p. A3.

———. 2006b. "Warm and Fuzzy TV, Brought to You by Hamas." *New York Times,* January 13, pp. A1, A4.

Smith, Dan. 1999. *The State of the World Atlas.* 6th ed. London: Penguin.

Smith, David A. 1995. "The New Urban Sociology Meets the Old: Rereading Some Classical Human Ecology." *Urban Affairs Review* 20 (January): 432–457.

———, and Michael Timberlake. 1993. "World Cities: A Political Economy/Global Network Approach." Pp. 181–207 in *Urban Sociology in Transition,* edited by Ray Hutchison. Greenwich, CT: JAI Press.

Smith, David M., and Gary J. Gates. 2001. *Gay and Lesbian Families in the United States: Same-Sex Unmarried Partner Households.* Washington, DC: Human Rights Campaign.

Smith, Denise, and Hava Tillipman. 2000. "The Older Population in the United States." *Current Population Reports,* ser. P-20, no. 532. Washington, DC: U.S. Government Printing Office.

Smith, James P., and Barry Edmonston, eds. 1997. *The New America: Economic, Demographic, and Fiscal Effects of Immigration.* Washington, DC: National Academy Press.

Smith, Michael Peter. 1988. *City, State, and Market.* New York: Basil Blackwell.

Smith, Tom. 1999. *GSS News: Trendlets: An Inter-Racial Friendship.* Accessed December 17, 2001 (www.icpsr.uonich.edu/GSS/about/news/trends.htm).

———. 2001. *Estimating the Muslim Population in the United States.* New York: American Jewish Committee.

———. 2003. *Coming of Age in 21st Century America: Public Attitudes Toward the Importance and Timing of Transition to Adulthood.* Chicago: National Opinion Research Center.

———, and Seokho Kim. 2004. "The Vanishing Protestant Majority." *GSS Social Change Report No. 49.* Chicago: NORC.

Smith, Vicki. 2004. "Review of Gurus, Hired Guns, and Warm Bodies." *Administrative Science Quarterly* 49 (December): 651–654.

Snell, Tracy L. 2006. "Capital Punishment, 2005." *Bureau of Justice Statistics Bulletin* (December), p. 31.

Snow, David A., Louis A. Zurcher, Jr., and Robert Peters. 1981. "Victory Celebrations as Theater: A Dramaturgical Approach to Crowd Behavior." *Symbolic Interaction* 4:21–42.

Snyder, Thomas D. 1996. *Digest of Education Statistics 1996.* Washington, DC: U.S. Government Printing Office.

Sorokin, Pitirim A. [1927] 1959. *Social and Cultural Mobility.* New York: Free Press.

Spar, Debora. 2001. *Ruling the Waves: Cycles of Discovery, Chaos, and Wealth from the Compass to the Internet.* Harcourt.

Speak, Suzanne, and Graham Tipple. 2006. "Perceptions, Persecution and Pity: The Limitations of Interventions for Homelessness in Developing Countries." *International Journal of Urban and Regional Research* 30 (March): 172–188.

Spielmann, Peter James. 1992. "11 Population Groups on 'Endangered' List." *Chicago Sun-Times,* November 23, p. 12.

Spitzer, Steven. 1975. "Toward a Marxian Theory of Deviance." *Social Problems* 22 (June):641–651.

Squires, Gregory D., ed. 2002. *Urban Sprawl: Causes, Consequences and Policy Responses.* Washington, DC: Urban Institute.

Staggenborg, Suzanne. 1989a. "Stability and Innovation in the Women's Movement: A Comparison of Two Movement Organizations." *Social Problems* 36 (February):75–92.

———. 1989b. "Organizational and Environmental Influences on the Development of the Pro-Choice Movement." *Social Forces* 36 (September): 204–240.

Stalker, Peter. 2000. *Workers Without Frontiers.* Boulder, CO: Lynne Rienner.

Standing, Guy. 2004. *Economic Security for a Better World.* Geneva: International Labour Organization.

Stanley, Alessandra. 2007. "Deadly Rampage and No Loss for Words." *New York Times,* April 17.

Stark, Rodney, and William Sims Bainbridge. 1979. "Of Churches, Sects, and Cults: Preliminary Concepts for a Theory of Religious Movements." *Journal for the Scientific Study of Religion* 18 (June):117–131.

———, and William Sims Bainbridge. 1985. *The Future of Religion.* Berkeley: University of California Press.

———, and Laurence R. Iannaccone. 1992. "Sociology of Religion." Pp. 2029–2037 in *Encyclopedia of Sociology,* vol. 4, edited by Edgar F. Borgatta and Marie L. Borgatta. New York: Macmillan.

Starr, Paul. 1982. *The Social Transformation of American Medicine.* New York: Basic Books.

Stavenhagen, Rodolfo. 1994. "The Indian Resurgence in Mexico." *Cultural Survival Quarterly,* Summer/Fall, pp. 77–80.

Steele, Jonathan. 2005. "Annan Attacks Britain and U.S. over Erosion of Human Rights." *Guardian Weekly,* March 16, p. 1.

Stein, Leonard I. 1967. "The Doctor-Nurse Game." *Archives of General Psychology* (Volume 16): 699–703.

Stenning, Derrick J. 1958. "Household Viability among the Pastoral Fulani." Pp. 92–119 in *The Developmental Cycle in Domestic Groups,* edited by John R. Goody. Cambridge, England: Cambridge University Press.

Stevenson, David, and Barbara L. Schneider. 1999. *The Ambitious Generation: America's Teenagers, Motivated but Directionless.* New Haven, CT: Yale University Press.

Steyerberg, Ewout, Craig Earle, Bridget Neville, and Jane Weeks. 2005. "Racial Differences in Surgical Evaluation, Treatment, and Outcome of Loco-regional Esophageal Cancer: A Population-Based Analysis of Elderly Patients." *Journal of Clinical Oncology* 23:510–517.

Stockard, Janice E. 2002. *Marriage in Culture.* Belmont, CA: Thomson Wadsworth.

Stolberg, Sheryl. 1995. "Affirmative Action Gains Often Come at a High Cost." *Los Angeles Times,* March 29, pp. A1, A13–A16.

Stone, Brad. 2007. "Using Web Cams but Few Inhibitions, the Young Turn to Risky Social Sites." *New York Times,* January 2, pp. C1, C2.

Strassman, W. Paul. 1998. "Third World Housing." Pp. 589–592 in *The Encyclopedia of Housing,* edited by Willem van Vliet. Thousand Oaks, CA: Sage.

Strauss, Gary. 2002. "'Good Old Boys' Network Still Rules Corporate Boards." *USA Today,* November 1, pp. B1, B2.

Street, Marc D. 1997. "Groupthink: An Examination of Theoretical Issues, Implications, and Future Research Systems." *Small Group Research* 28 (February):72–93.

Stutzman, Frederic. 2007. "An Evaluation of Identity-Sharing Behavior in Social Network Communities." *IMba* 3.

Subramaniam, Mangala. 2006. *The Power of Women's Organization: Gender, Caste, and Class in India.* Lanham, MD: Lexington Books.

Suitor, J. Jill, Staci A. Minyard, and Rebecca S. Carter. 2001. "'Did You See What I Saw?' Gender Differences in Perceptions of Avenues to Prestige Among Adolescents." *Sociological Inquiry* 71 (Fall):437–454.

Sullivan, Harry Stack. [1953] 1968. *The Interpersonal Theory of Psychiatry.* Edited by Helen Swick Perry and Mary Ladd Gawel. New York: W.W. Norton.

Sullivan, Kevin. 2006. "Bridging the Digital Divide." *Washington Post National Weekly Edition* 25 (July 17), pp. 11–12.

Sumner, William G. 1906. *Folkways*. New York: Ginn.

Sunstein, Cass. 2002. *Republic.com*. Rutgers, NJ: Princeton University Press.

Sunwolf, and David R. Seibold. 1998. "Jurors' Intuitive Rules for Deliberation: A Structurational Approach to Communication in Jury Decision Making." *Communication Monographs* 65 (December): 282–307.

Sutch, Richard, and Susan B. Carter. 2006. *Historical Statutes of US: Earliest Time to the Present*. Cambridge University Press.

Sutcliffe, Bob. 2002. *100 Ways of Seeing an Unequal World*. London: Zed Books.

Sutherland, Edwin H. 1937. *The Professional Thief*. Chicago: University of Chicago Press.

———. 1940. "White-Collar Criminality." *American Sociological Review* 5 (February):1–11.

———. 1949. *White Collar Crime*. New York: Dryden.

———. 1983. *White Collar Crime: The Uncut Version*. New Haven, CT: Yale University Press.

———, Donald R. Cressey, and David F. Luckenbill. 1992. *Principles of Criminology*. 11th ed. New York: Rowman and Littlefield.

Swatos, William H., Jr., ed. 1998. *Encyclopedia of Religion and Society*. Lanham, MD: Alta Mira.

Sweet, Kimberly. 2001. "Sex Sells a Second Time." *Chicago Journal* 93 (April):12–13.

Swiss Re. 2005. "Catastrophes." *The Economist* (March 26):98.

Szasz, Thomas S. 1971. "The Same Slave: An Historical Note on the Use of Medical Diagnosis as Justificatory Rhetoric." *American Journal of Psychotherapy* 25 (April):228–239.

———. 1974. *The Myth of Mental Illness*. Rev. ed. New York: Harper and Row.

Talbani, Aziz, and Parveen Hasanali. 2000. "Adolescent Females between Tradition and Modernity: Gender Role Socialization in South Asian Immigrant Culture." *Journal of Adolescence* 23:615–627.

Tannen, Deborah. 1990. *You Just Don't Understand: Women and Men in Conversation*. New York: Ballantine.

———. 1994a. *Talking from 9 to 5*. New York: William Morris.

———. 1994b. *Gender and Discourse*. New York: Oxford University Press.

Tapscott, Don. 1998. *Growing Up Digital: The Rise of the Net Generation*. New York: McGraw-Hill.

Tarrow, Sidney. 2005. *The New Transnational Activism*. Boulder, CO: Rowman and Littlefield.

Taylor, Jonathan B., and Joseph P. Kalt. 2005. *American Indians on Reservations: A Data Book of Socioeconomic Change between the 1990 and 2000 Censuses*. Cambridge, MA: The Harvard Project on American Indian Development.

Taylor, Verta. 1995. "Watching for Vibes: Bringing Emotions into the Study of Feminist Organizations." Pp. 223–233 in *Feminist Organizations:*

Harvest of the New Women's Movement, edited by Myra Marx Ferree and Patricia Yancy Martin. Philadelphia: Temple University Press.

Tedeschi, Bob. 2004. "Social Networks: Will Users Pay to Get Friends?" *New York Times*, February 9, pp. C1, C3.

———. 2006. "Those Born to Shop Can Now Use Cellphones." *New York Times,* January 2.

Telsch, Kathleen. 1991. "New Study of Older Workers Finds They Can Become Good Investments." *New York Times,* May 21, p. A16.

Terkel, Studs. 1974. *Working*. New York: Pantheon.

Tessler, Joelie. 2006. "Privacy Erosion: A 'Net' Loss." *CQ Weekly* (February 20), p. 480.

Third World Institute. 2005. *The World Guide 2005–2006*. Oxford, England. New Internationalist Publishers.

Thomas, Gordon, and Max Morgan Witts. 1974. *Voyage of the Damned*. Greenwich, CT: Fawcett Crest.

Thomas, Pradip N., and Zaharom Nain. 2004. *Who Owns the Media: Global Trends and Local Resistance*. London: WACC/Zed Books.

Thomas, R. Murray. 2003. "New Frontiers in Cheating." In *Encyclopedia Britannica 2003 Book of the Year*. Chicago: Encyclopedia Britannica.

Thomas, William I. 1923. *The Unadjusted Girl*. Boston: Little, Brown.

Thomasrobb.com. 2007. "WhitePride Tv." Accessed May 7 (http://thomasrobb.com).

Thompson, Clive. 2005. "Meet the Life Hackers." *New York Times Magazine*, October 16, pp. 40–45.

Thompson, Ginger. 2001a. "Chasing Mexico's Dream into Squalor." *New York Times*, February 11, pp. 1, 6.

———. 2001b. "Why Peace Eludes Mexico's Indians." *New York Times,* March 11, sec. WK, p. 16.

Thompson, Neil B. 1972. "The Mysterious Fall of the Nacirema." *Natural History* (December).

Thompson, Tommy G., and Roy E. Barnes. 2007. *Beyond NCLB: Fulfilling the Promise to Our Nation's Children*. Washington, DC: Aspen Institute.

Thompson, Tony. 2005. "Romanians Are Being Paid to Play Computer Games for Westerners." *Guardian Weekly*, March 25, p. 17.

Thomson Gale. 2007. "Association Unlimited." Accessed February 10 (www.gale.com).

Thornton, Russell. 1987. *American Indians Holocaust and Survival: A Population History Since 1492*. Norman: University of Oklahoma Press.

Threadcraft, Shatema. 2008. "Welfare Queen." In *Encyclopedia of Race, Ethnicity and Society,* edited by Richard T. Schaefer. Thousand Oak, CA: Sage.

Tibbles, Kevin. 2007. "Web Sites Encourage Eating Disorders." *Today,* February 18. Accessed May 7 (www.msabc.msn.com).

Tienda, Marta, and Faith Mitchell, eds. 2006. *Hispanics and the Future of America*. Washington, DC: National Academics Press.

Tierney, John. 1990. "Betting the Planet." *New York Times Magazine,* December 2, pp. 52–53, 71, 74, 76, 78, 80–81.

———. 2003. "Iraqi Family Ties Complicate American Efforts for Change." *New York Times,* September 28, pp. A1, A22.

Tierney, Kathleen. 1980. "Emergent Norm Theory as 'Theory': An Analysis and Critique of Turner's Formulation." Pp. 42–53 in *Collective Behavior: A Source Book,* edited by Meredith David Pugh. St. Paul, MN: West.

Tilly, Charles. 1993. *Popular Contention in Great Britain 1758–1834*. Cambridge, MA: Harvard University Press.

———. 2004. *Social Movements, 1768–2004*. Boulder, CO: Paradigm.

———. 2007. "Trust Networks in Transnational Migration." *Sociological Forum* 22 (March): 3–24.

Tolbert, Kathryn. 2000. "In Japan, Traveling Alone Begins at Age 6." *Washington Post National Weekly Edition* 17 (May 15):17.

Tonkinson, Robert. 1978. *The Mardudjara Aborigines*. New York: Holt.

Tönnies, Ferdinand. [1887] 1988. *Community and Society*. Rutgers, NJ: Transaction.

Toossi, Mitra. 2005. "Labor Force Projections to 2014: Returning Boomers." *Monthly Labor Review* (November):25–44.

Tough, Paul. 2006. "What It Takes to Make a Student." *New York Times Magazine* (November 26).

Touraine, Alain. 1974. *The Academic System in American Society*. New York: McGraw-Hill.

Treiman, Donald J. 1977. *Occupational Prestige in Comparative Perspective*. New York: Academic Press.

Trotter III, Robert T., and Juan Antonio Chavira. 1997. *Curanderismo: Mexican American Folk Healing*. Athens, GA: University of Georgia Press.

Trumbull, Mark. 2006. "America's Younger Workers Losing Ground on Income." *Christian Science Monitor,* February 27.

Tuchman, Gaye. 1992. "Feminist Theory." Pp. 695–704 in *Encyclopedia of Sociology,* vol. 2, edited by Edgar F. Borgatta and Marie L. Borgatta. New York: Macmillan.

Tumin, Melvin M. 1953. "Some Principles of Stratification: A Critical Analysis." *American Sociological Review* 18 (August):387–394.

———. 1985. *Social Stratification*. 2d ed. Englewood Cliffs, NJ: Prentice Hall.

Ture, Kwame, and Charles Hamilton. 1992. *Black Power: The Politics of Liberation*. Rev. ed. New York: Vintage Books.

Turek, Melanie. 2006. "The Number of Telecommuters Is on the Rise." November 27. Accessed February 10, 2007 (www.collaborationloop.com).

Turkle, Sherry. 2004. "How Computers Change the Way We Think." *Chronicle of Higher Education* 50 (January 30):B26–B28.

Turner, Bryan S., ed. 1990. *Theories of Modernity and Postmodernity*. Newbury Park, CA: Sage.

Turner, C. F., et al. 1998. "Adolescent Sexual Behavior, Drug Use, and Violence Increased Reporting with Computer Survey Technology." *Science* 280:867–873.

Turner, Ralph, and Lewis M. Killian. 1987. *Collective Behavior*. 3d ed. Englewood Cliffs, NJ: Prentice Hall.

Turner, S. Derek, and Mark Cooper. 2006. *Out of the Picture: Minority and Female TV Station Ownership in the United States*. Washington, DC: Free Press.

Uchitelle, Louis. 2003. "Older Workers Are Thriving Despite Recent Hard Times." *New York Times,* September 8, pp. A1, A13.

UNAIDS. 2007a. "Global Facts and Figures." Accessed April 23 (www.unaids.org).

———. 2007b. "Access to HIV Therapy Grew Significantly." April 17. Accessed April 23 (www.unaids.org).

United Jewish Communities. 2003. *The National Jewish Population Survey 2000–2001.* New York: UJC.

United Nations. 2005a. *The Millennium Development Goals Report.* Washington, DC: United Nations.

———. 2005b. *In Larger Freedom: Towards Development, Security and Human Rights for All.* New York: United Nations.

United Nations Development Programme. 1995. *Human Development Report 1995.* New York: Oxford University Press.

———. 2000. *Poverty Report 2000: Overcoming Human Poverty.* Washington, DC: UNDP.

———. 2006. *Human Development Report 2006. Beyond Scarcity: Power, Poverty and the Global Water Crisis.* New York: UNDP.

United Nations Office on Drugs and Crime. 2005. "The United Nations Convention Against Transnational Organized Crime and Its Protocols." Accessed March 18, 2005 (www.unodc.org).

United Nations Population Division. 1998. *World Abortion Policies.* New York: Department of Economic and Social Affairs, UNPD.

———. 2004. *World Population Monitoring 2002: Reproductive Rights and Reproductive Health.* New York: United Nations.

———. 2005. *World Fertility Report 2003.* New York: UNPD.

———. 2006. *World Population Policies 2005.* New York: United Nations.

University of Michigan. 2003. *Information on Admissions Lawsuits.* Accessed August 8 (www.umich.edu/~urel/admissions).

Urbina, Ian. 2002. "Al Jazeera: Hits, Misses and Ricochets." *Asia Times,* December 25.

U.S. Committee for Refugees and Immigrants. 2006. *World Refugee Swing 2006.* Washington, DC: US Committee for Refugees and Immigrants.

U.S. Conference of Mayors. 2004. *Hunger and Homeless Survey.* Washington, DC: United States Conference of Mayors and SODEXHO USA.

U.S. English. 2007. "Making English the Official Language." Accessed January 23 (www.us-english.org/inc/).

U.S. Surgeon General. 1999a. *Surgeon General's Report on Mental Health.* Washington, DC: U.S. Government Printing Office.

———. 1999b. "Overview of Cultural Diversity and Mental Health Services." In Chapter 2 of *Surgeon General's Report on Mental Health.* Washington, DC: U.S. Government Printing Office.

U.S. Trade Representative. 2007. "Trade Promotion Authority Delivers Jobs, Growth, Prosperity, and Security at Home." January 31 Fact Sheet. Accessed February 19 (www.ustr.gov).

Utne, Leif. 2003. "We Are All Zapatistas." *Utne Reader* (November–December):36–37.

Vaisse, Justin. 2004. *U.S.-France Analysis Series.* Washington, DC: Brookings Institution.

van den Berghe, Pierre. 1978. *Race and Racism: A Comparative Perspective.* 2d ed. New York: Wiley.

van Vucht Tijssen, Lieteke. 1990. "Women between Modernity and Postmodernity." Pp. 147–163 in *Theories of Modernity and Postmodernity,* edited by Bryan S. Turner. London: Sage.

Vasagar, Jeeran. 2005. "'At Last Rwanda Is Known for Something Positive.'" *Guardian Weekly,* July 22, p. 18.

Vaughan, Diane. 1996. *The Challenger Launch Decision: Risky Technology, Culture, and Deviance at NASA.* Chicago: University of Chicago Press.

———. 1999. "The Dark Side of Organizations: Mistake, Misconduct, and Disaster." Pp. 271–305 in *Annual Review of Sociology,* edited by Karen J. Cook and John Hagan. Palo Alto, CA: Annual Reviews.

Vaupel, James W., and Elke Loichinger. 2006. "Redistributing Work in Aging Europe." *Science* 312 (June 30): 1911–1913.

Veblen, Thorstein. [1899] 1964. *Theory of the Leisure Class.* New York: Macmillan. New York: Penguin.

———. 1919. *The Vested Interests and the State of the Industrial Arts.* New York: Huebsch.

Vega, William A. 1995. "The Study of Latino Families: A Point of Departure." Pp. 3–17 in *Understanding Latino Families: Scholarship, Policy, and Practice,* edited by Ruth E. Zambrana. Thousand Oaks, CA: Sage.

Venkatesh, Sudhir Alladi. 2000. *American Project: The Rise and Fall of a Modern Ghetto.* Cambridge, MA: Harvard University Press.

———. 2006. *Off the Books: The Underground Economy of Urban Poor.* Cambridge, MA: Harvard University Press.

Vernon, Glenn. 1962. *Sociology and Religion.* New York: McGraw-Hill.

Vidal, John. 2004. "One in Three People Will Be Elderly by 2050." *Guardian Weekly,* April 1, p. 5.

Vidaver, R. M., et al. 2000. "Women Subjects in NIH-Funded Clinical Research Literature: Lack of Progress in Both Representation and Analysis by Sex." *Journal of Women's Health Gender-Based Medicine* 9 (June):495–504.

Villarreal, Andrés. 2004. "The Social Ecology of Rural Violence: Land Scarcity, the Organization of Agricultural Production, and the Presence of the State." *American Journal of Sociology* 110 (September):313–348.

Wachtendorf, Tricia. 2002. "A Changing Risk Environment: Lessons Learned from the 9/11 World Trade Center Disaster." Presentation at the Sociological Perspectives on Disasters, Mt. Macedon, Australia, July.

Wages for Housework Campaign. 1999. *Wages for Housework Campaign.* Circular. Los Angeles.

Wagley, Charles, and Marvin Harris. 1958. *Minorities in the New World: Six Case Studies.* New York: Columbia University Press.

Waite, Linda. 2000. "The Family as a Social Organization: Key Ideas for the Twentieth Century." *Contemporary Sociology* 29 (May):463–469.

Waitzkin, Howard. 1986. *The Second Sickness: Contradictions of Capitalist Health Care.* Chicago: University of Chicago Press.

Waldinger, Roger, and David Fitzgerald. 2004. "Transnationalism in Question." *American Journal of Sociology* 109 (March):1177–1195.

Waldman, Amy. 2004a. "India Takes Economic Spotlight, and Critics Are Unkind." *New York Times,* March 7, p. 3.

———. 2004b. "Low-Tech or High, Jobs Are Scarce in India's Boon." *New York Times,* May 6, p. A3.

———. 2004c. "What India's Upset Vote Reveals: The High Tech Is Skin Deep." *New York Times,* May 15, p. A5.

Waldrop, Judith, and Sharon M. Stern. 2003. *Disability Status: 2000.* Census 2000 Brief C2KBR-17. Washington, DC: U.S. Government Printing Office.

Wallace, Ruth A., and Alison Wolf. 1980. *Contemporary Sociological Theory.* Englewood Cliffs, NJ: Prentice Hall.

Wallerstein, Immanuel. 1974. *The Modern World System.* New York: Academic Press.

———. 1979a. *Capitalist World Economy.* Cambridge, England: Cambridge University Press.

———. 1979b. *The End of the World as We Know It: Social Science for the Twenty-First Century.* Minneapolis: University of Minnesota Press.

———. 2000. *The Essential Wallerstein.* New York: The New Press.

Wallerstein, Judith S., Judith M. Lewis, and Sandra Blakeslee. 2000. *The Unexpected Legacy of Deviance.* New York: Hyperion.

Wallerstein, Michael, and Bruce Western. 2000. "Unions in Decline? What Has Changed and Why." Pp. 355–377 in *Annual Review of Political Science,* edited by Nelson Polsby. Palo Alto, CA: Annual Reviews.

Wallis, Claudia. 2005a. "A Snapshot of Teen Sex." *Time,* February 7, p. 58.

———. 2005b. "The Evolution Wars." *Time,* August 15, pp. 26–35.

Wallis, Claudia and Sonia Steptoe. 2007. "How to Fix No Child Left Behind." *Time* 169 (June 4): 34–41.

Wall Street Journal. 2006. "The Web's Worst New Idea." *Wall Street Journal* (May 18).

Wal-Mart. 2007. "Wal-Mart News: Our Commitment to Communities." Accessed April 27 (www.walmartstores.com).

———. 2007a. "The 'Ten-Foot Attitude.'" Accessed January 23 (www.wal-martchina.com).

Wal-Mart Watch. 2007. *Wal-Mart Watch: Breaking News.* Accessed April 27 (www.walmartwatch.com).

———. 2007. "Results of Wal-Mart Watch/Westhill 2007 Public Opinion Survey." Accessed March 29 (www.walmartwatch.com).

Wang, Meiyan, and Fand Cai. 2006. *Gender Wage Differentials in China's Urban Labor Market.* Research Paper No. 2006/141. United Nations University World Institute for Development Economics Research.

Washington, Harriet. 2007. *Medical Apartheid: The Dark History of Medical Experimentation on Black Americans from Colonial Times to Present.* New York: Doubleday.

Washington Transcript Service. 1999. "Hillary Rodham Clinton Holds News Conference on Her New York Senatorial Bid." November 23.

Watson, Paul. 2005. "Defying Tradition." *Los Angeles Times,* April 24, p. 56.

Wattenberg, Martin P. 2008. *Is Voting for Young People?* New York: Pearson Longman.

Watts, Duncan J. 2004. "The 'New' Science of Networks." Pp. 243–270 in *Annual Review of Sociology 2004,* edited by Karen S. Cook and John Hagan. Palo Alto, CA: Annual Reviews.

Weber, Max. [1913–1922] 1947. *The Theory of Social and Economic Organization.* Translated by A. Henderson and T. Parsons. New York: Free Press.

———. [1904] 1949. *Methodology of the Social Sciences.* Translated by Edward A. Shils and Henry A. Finch. Glencoe, IL: Free Press.

———. [1904] 1958a. *The Protestant Ethic and the Spirit of Capitalism.* Translated by Talcott Parsons. New York: Scribner.

———. [1916] 1958b. *The Religion of India: The Sociology of Hinduism and Buddhism.* New York: Free Press.

Wechsler, Henry, J. E. Lee, M. Kuo, M. Seibring, T. F. Nelson, and H. Lee. 2002. "Trends in College Binge Drinking During a Period of Increased Prevention Efforts: Findings from Four Harvard School of Public Health College Alcohol Surveys: 1993–2001." *Journal of American College Health* 50 (5):203–217.

———, Mark Seibring, I-Chao Liu, and Marilyn Ahl. 2004. "Colleges Respond to Student Binge Drinking: Reducing Student Demand or Limiting Access." *Journal of American College Health* 52 (4):159–168.

Weeks, John R. 2002. *Population: An Introduction to Concepts and Issues.* 8th ed. Belmont, CA: Wadsworth.

———. 2005. *Population: An Introduction to Concepts and Issues.* 9th ed. Belmont, CA: Wadsworth.

Weil, Nancy. 1998. "Internet Tax Freedom Act Heads to Full House." June 19. Accessed January 30, 2007 (www.cnn.com).

Weinberg, Daniel H. 2004. *Evidence from Census 2000 About Earnings by Detailed Occupation for Men and Women.* CENSR-15. Washington, DC: U.S. Government Printing Office.

Weinstein, Deena, and Michael A. Weinstein. 1999. "McDonaldization Enframed." Pp. 57–69 in *Resisting McDonaldization,* edited by Barry Smart. London: Sage.

Weinstein, Henry. 2002. "Airport Screener Curb Is Regretful." *Los Angeles Times,* November 16, pp. B1, B14.

Weinstein, Michael A., and Deena Weinstein. 2002. "Hail to the Shrub." *American Behavioral Scientist* 46 (December):566–580.

Weisbrot, Mark, Dean Baker, and David Rusnick. 2005. *The Scorecard on Development: 25 Years of Diminished Progress.* Washington, DC: Center for Economic and Policy Research.

Wells-Barnett, Ida B. 1970. *Crusade for Justice: The Autobiography of Ida B. Wells.* Edited by Alfreda M. Duster. Chicago: University of Chicago Press.

Wentz, Laurel, and Claire Atkinson. 2005. "'Apprentice' Translators Hope for Hits All Over Globe." *Advertising Age,* February 14, pp. 3, 73.

Wertsman, Vladimir. 2001. "Arab Americans: A Comparative and Critical Analysis of Leading Reference Sources." *Multicultural Review* (June):42–57.

West, Candace, and Don H. Zimmerman. 1983. "Small Insults: A Study of Interruptions in Cross Sex Conversations between Unacquainted Persons." Pp. 86–111 in *Language, Gender, and Society,* edited by Barrie Thorne, Cheris Kramarae, and Nancy Henley. Rowley, MA: Newbury House.

———. 1987. "Doing Gender." *Gender and Society* 1 (June):125–151.

Western Interstate Commission for Higher Education. 2003. *Knocking at the College Door—2003.* Boulder, CO: WICHE.

Whitlock, Craig. 2005. "The Internet as Bully Pulpit." *Washington Post National Weekly Edition* 22 (August 22):9.

Whyte, William Foote. 1981. *Street Corner Society: Social Structure of an Italian Slum.* 3d ed. Chicago: University of Chicago Press.

Whyte, William H., Jr. 1952. "Groupthink." *Fortune,* March, pp. 114–117, 142, 146.

Wickman, Peter M. 1991. "Deviance." Pp. 85–87 in *Encyclopedic Dictionary of Sociology,* 4th ed., edited by Dushkin Publishing Group. Guilford, CT: Dushkin.

Wilford, John Noble. 1997. "New Clues Show Where People Made the Great Leap to Agriculture." *New York Times,* November 18, pp. B9, B12.

Wilgoren, Jodi. 2005. "In Kansas, Darwinism Goes on Trial Once More." *New York Times,* May 6, p. A14.

Wilkins, David E. 2007. *American Indian Politics and the American Political System.* 2d ed. Lanham, MD: Rowman and Littlefield.

Wilkinson, Alec. 2007. "No Obstacles." *New Yorker* (April 16): 106–108, 110, 112–114, 116.

Williams, Carol J. 1995. "Taking an Eager Step Back." *Los Angeles Times,* June 3, pp. A1, A14.

Williams, Christine L. 1992. "The Glass Escalator: Hidden Advantages for Men in the 'Female' Professions." *Social Problems* 39 (3):253–267.

———. 1995. *Still a Man's World: Men Who Do Women's Work.* Berkeley: University of California Press.

Williams, David R., and Chiquita Collins. 2004. "Reparations." *American Behavioral Scientist* 47 (March):977–1000.

Williams, Robin M., Jr. 1970. *American Society.* 3d ed. New York: Knopf.

———, with John P. Dean and Edward A. Suchman. 1964. *Strangers Next Door: Ethnic Relations in American Communities.* Englewood Cliffs, NJ: Prentice Hall.

Williams, L. Susan, Sandra D. Alvarez, and Kevin S. Andrado Hauck. 2002. "My Name is Not Maria: Young Latinas Seeking Home in the Heartland." *Social Problems* 49(4):563–584.

Williams, Wendy M. 1998. "Do Parents Matter? Scholars Need to Explain What Research Really Shows." *Chronicle of Higher Education* 45 (December 11):B6–B7.

Wilson, Edward O. 1975. *Sociobiology: The New Synthesis.* Cambridge, MA: Harvard University Press.

———. 1978. *On Human Nature.* Cambridge, MA: Harvard University Press.

———. 2000. *Sociobiology: The New Synthesis.* Cambridge, MA: Belknap Press, Harvard University Press.

Wilson, John. 1973. *Introduction to Social Movements.* New York: Basic Books.

Wilson, Robin. 2007. "The New Gender Divide." *Chronicle of Higher Education* 53 (January 26): A36–A39.

Wilson, William Julius. 1980. *The Declining Significance of Race: Blacks and Changing American Institutions.* 2d ed. Chicago: University of Chicago Press.

———. 1987. *The Truly Disadvantaged: The Inner City, the Underclass and Public Policy.* Chicago: University of Chicago Press.

———. 1996. *When Work Disappears: The World of the New Urban Poor.* New York: Knopf.

———. 1999. *The Bridge over the Racial Divide: Rising Inequality and Coalition Politics.* Berkeley: University of California Press.

———, J. M. Quane, and B. H. Rankin. 2004. "Underclass." In *International Encyclopedia of Social and Behavioral Sciences.* New York: Elsevier.

———, and Richard P. Taub in collaboration with Reuben A. Buford May and Mary Pattillo. 2006. "Groveland: A Stable African American Community." Pp. 128–160 in *There Goes the Neighborhood* by William Julius Wilson and Richard P. Taub. New York: Alfred A. Knopf.

Wines, Michael. 2005. "Same-Sex Unions to Become Legal in South Africa." *USA Today,* December 2, p. A6.

Winnick, Terri A. 2005. "From Quackery to 'Complementary' Medicine: The American Medical Profession Confects Alternative Therapies." *Social Problems* 52 (1):38–61.

Winseman, Albert L. 2005. "Religion in America: Who Has None?" December 6, 2005. Accessed March 4, 2007 (www.gallup.com).

Wirth, Louis. 1928. *The Ghetto.* Chicago: University of Chicago Press.

———. 1931. "Clinical Sociology." *American Journal of Sociology* 37 (July):49–60.

———. 1938. "Urbanism as a Way of Life." *American Journal of Sociology* 44 (July):1–24.

Withrow, Brian L. 2006. *Racial Profiling: From Rhetoric to Reason.* Upper Saddle River, NJ: Prentice Hall.

Witte, Griff. 2005. "The Vanishing Middle Class." *Washington Post National Weekly Edition,* September 27:6–9.

596 Wolf, Naomi. 1992. *The Beauty Myth: How Images of Beauty Are Used Against Women.* New York: Anchor.

Wolf, Richard. 2006. "How Welfare Reform Changed America." *USA Today,* July 18, pp. 1A, 6A.

Wolff, Edward N. 2002. *Top Heavy.* Updated ed. New York: New Press.

Wolraich, M., et al. 1998. "Guidance for Effective Discipline." *Pediatrics* 101 (April):723–728.

Wood, Julia T. 1994. *Gendered Lives: Communication, Gender and Culture.* Belmont, CA: Wadsworth.

Working Women's Forum. 2007. Home page. Accessed May 7 (www.workingwomensforum.org).

World Bank. 2000. *World Development Report 2000/2001.* Washington, DC: World Bank.

———. 2001. *World Development Report 2002. Building Instructions for Markets.* New York: Oxford University Press.

———. 2003a. *World Development Report 2003: Sustainable Development in a Dynamic World.* Washington, DC: World Bank.

———. 2006a. *World Development Indicators 2006.* New York: World Bank.

———. 2006b. *Global Economic Prospects 2006.* Washington, DC: World Bank.

———. 2006c. "Microfinance Comes of Age." December 7. Accessed April 24, 2007 (www.Worldbank.org).

———. 2007a. *World Development Indicators 2007.* New York: World Bank.

———. 2007b. *Repositioning Nutrition as Central to Development: A Strategy for Large-Scale Action.* Washington, DC: World Bank.

World Development Forum. 1990. "The Danger of Television." 8 (July 15):4.

World Economic Forum. 2007. *The Global Information Technology Report 2006–2007.* Davos, Switzerland: World Economic Forum.

World Health Organization. 2000. *The World Health Report 2000. Health Systems: Improving Performance.* Geneva, Switzerland: WHO.

———. 2004. "Prevalence, Severity, and Unmet Need for Treatment of Mental Disorders in the World Health Organization World Mental Health Surveys." *Journal of the American Medical Association* (June 2):2581–2590.

———. 2006. "Pesticides Are a Leading Suicide Method." Accessed December 4 (www.who.org).

World Resources Institute. 1998. *1998–1999 World Resources: A Guide to the Global Environment.* New York: Oxford University Press.

Wortham, Robert A. 2005. "The Early Sociological Legacy of W. E. B. DuBois." Pp. 74–95 in *Diverse Histories of American Sociology,* edited by Anthony J. Blasi. Boston: Brill.

Wright, Charles R. 1986. *Mass Communication: A Sociological Perspective.* 3d ed. New York: Random House.

Wright, Eric R., William P. Gronfein, and Timothy J. Owens. 2000. "Deinstitutionalization, Social Rejection, and the Self-Esteem of Former Mental Patients." *Journal of Health and Social Behavior* (March).

Wright, Erik Olin, David Hachen, Cynthia Costello, and Joy Sprague. 1982. "The American Class Structure." *American Sociological Review* 47 (December):709–726.

Yamagata, Hisashi, Kuang S. Yeh, Shelby Stewman, and Hiroko Dodge. 1997. "Sex Segregation and Glass Ceilings: A Comparative Statistics Model of Women's Career Opportunities in the Federal Government over a Quarter Century." *American Journal of Sociology* 103 (November):566–632.

Yap, Kioe Sheng. 1998. "Squatter Settlements." Pp. 554–556 in *The Encyclopedia of Housing,* edited by Willem van Vliet. Thousand Oaks, CA: Sage.

Yardley, Jim. 2005. "Fearing Future, China Starts to Give Girls Their Due." *New York Times,* January 31, p. A3.

Yinger, J. Milton. 1970. *The Scientific Study of Religion.* New York: Macmillan.

Young, Alfred A., Jr., 2007. "Herbert Gans and the Politics of Urban Ethnography in the (Continued) Age of the Underclass." *City and Community* 6 (March): 7–20.

Young, Alford A., Jr., and Donald R. Deskins, Jr. 2001. "Early Traditions of African-American Sociological Thought." Pp. 445–477 in *Annual Review of Sociology, 2001,* edited by Karen S. Cook and John Hagan. Palo Alto, CA: Annual Reviews.

Young, Gay. 1993. "Gender Inequality and Industrial Development: The Household Connection." *Journal of Comparative Family Studies* 124 (Spring):3–20.

Young, Kevin, ed. 2004. *Sporting Bodies, Damaged Selves.* New York: Elsevier.

Zarembo, Alan. 2004. "A Theater of Inquiry and Evil." *Los Angeles Times,* July 15, pp. A1, A24, A25.

Zellner, William M. 1995. *Counter Cultures: A Sociological Analysis.* New York: St. Martin's Press.

Zernike, Kate. 2002. "With Student Cheating on the Rise, More Colleges Are Turning to Honor Codes." *New York Times,* November 2, p. A10.

Zia, Helen. 2000. *Asian American Dreams: The Emergence of an American People.* New York: Farrar, Straus, and Giroux.

Zimbardo, Philip G. 1972. "Pathology of Imprisonment." *Society* 9 (April):4, 6, 8.

———. 2004. "Power Turns Good Soldiers into 'Bad Apples.'" *Boston Globe,* May 9. Also available at www.prisonexp.org.

———. 2005. "What Do You Believe Is True Even Though You Cannot Prove It?" *New York Times,* January 4, p. D3.

———. 2007. "Revisiting the Stanford Prison Experiment: A Lesson in the Power of the Situation." *Chronicle of Higher Education* 53 (March 20):B6, B7.

———, Craig Haney, W. Curtis Banks, and David Jaffe. 1974. "The Psychology of Imprisonments: Privation, Power, and Pathology." In *Doing Unto Others: Joining, Molding, Conforming, Helping, and Loving,* edited by Zick Rubin. Englewood Cliffs, NJ: Prentice Hall.

———, Ann L. Weber, and Robert Johnson. 2003. *Psychology: Core Concepts.* 4th ed. Boston: Allyn and Bacon.

Zimmerman, Ann, and Emily Nelson. 2006. "With Profits Elusive, Wal-Mart to Exit Germany." *Wall Street Journal* (July 29): A1, A6.

Zola, Irving K. 1972. "Medicine as an Institution of Social Control." *Sociological Review* 20 (November):487–504.

———. 1983. *Socio-Medical Inquiries.* Philadelphia: Temple University Press.

Zweigenhaft, Richard L., and G. William Domhoff. 2006. *Diversity in the Power Elite: How It Happened, Why It Matters.* 2d ed. New York: Rowman and Littlefield

acknowledgments

Chapter 1

P. 3: Quotation from Barbara Ehrenreich. 2001. "Evaluation" pp. 6, 197–198 from *Nickel and Dimed: On (Not) Getting By in America.* Copyright 2001 by Barbara Ehrenreich. Reprinted by permission of Henry Holt and Company, LLC, and by permission of International Creative Management, Inc.

P. 18: Figure 1-3 From Out of Code by Perry Perez in Jerry Crowe and Valli Herman. 2005. "NBA Lists Fashion Do's & Don't's," *Los Angeles Times* (October 19):A23. Copyright 2005 Los Angeles Times. Reprinted by permission.

Chapter 2

P. 31: Quotation from Patricia A. Adler and Peter Adler. 2004. *Paradise Laborers: Hotel Work in the Global Economy.* © 2004 by Cornell University. Used by permission of the publisher, Cornell University Press.

P. 36: Figure 2-4, Author's analysis of General Social Survey 2004 in J. A. Davis et al. 2005. Used by permission of National Opinion Research Center.

P. 37: Cartoon, DOONESBURY " 1989 G. B. Trudeau. Reprinted with permission of UNIVERSAL PRESS SYNDICATE. All rights reserved.

P. 41: Figure from Devah Pager, "The Mark of a Criminal Record," *American Journal of Sociology.* Copyright © 2003 by the University of Chicago Press via the Copyright Clearance Center.

P. 42: Figure from Laura Wattenberg. 2006. *The Baby Name Wizard.* Used by permission.

P. 48: Figure 2-5 From Henry J. Kaiser Family Foundation. February 2005. Executive Summary of Sex on TV 4:4; a Biennial Report of the Kaiser Family Foundation (#7399). This information was reprinted with permission from the Henry J. Kaiser Family Foundation. The Kaiser Family Foundation, based in Menlo Park, CA, is a nonprofit, private operating foundation focusing on the major health care issues facing the nation and is not associated with Kaiser Permanente or Kaiser Industries.

P. 50, 51: Figures 2-6, 2-7 From The Gallup Poll, "Who Supports Marijuana Legalization," by Joseph Carroll. Copyright © 2005 The Gallup Organization, Princeton, NJ. All rights reserved. Reprinted with permission.

Chapter 3

P. 57: Quotation from Horace Miner. 1956. "Body Ritual among the Nacirema." *American Anthropologist,* vol. 58 (1956), pp. 503–504. © 1956 American Anthropological Association. Used with permission.

P. 66: Figure 3-1 From Michael Erard. 2005. "How Linguists and Missionaries Share a Bible of 6,912 Languages," *New York Times* (July 19): D4. New York Times Copyright © 2005 by The New York Times Co. Reprinted with permission.

P. 71: Figure 3-3 As reported in Astin et al. 1994; Pryor et al. 2006. From UCLA Higher Education Research Institute. 2006. The American Freshman: National Norms for Fall '06. Reprinted by permission of UCLA.

P. 75: Cartoon by Sidney Harris. © ScienceCartoonsPlus.com.

P. 75: Figure 3-4 From Jerome Fellmann et al. 2007. *Human Geography* 9e, © 2007. Reprinted by permission of the McGraw-Hill Companies.

Chapter 4

P. 85: Quotation from Mary Pattillo-McCoy. 1999. *Black Picket Fences: Privilege and Peril among the Black Middle Class.* Copyright 1999. Reprinted by permission of University of Chicago Press.

P. 87: Figure 4-1 From Susan Curtiss. 1977. *Genie: a Psycholinguistic Study of a Modern-Day "Wild Child,"* p. 275. Copyright Academic Press. Reprinted with permission of Elsevier.

P. 92: Quotation from Daniel Albas and Cheryl Albas. 1988. "Aces and Bombers: The Post-Exam Impression Management Strategies of Students." *Symbolic Interaction* Copyright 1988 by University of California Press—Journals. Reproduced by permission of University of California Press—Journals via Copyright Clearance Center.

P. 95: Table 4-2 From Tom Smith. 2003. "Coming of Age in 21st Century America: Public Attitudes Toward the Importance and Timing of Transition to Adulthood." Based on the 2002 General Social Survey of 1,398 people. Used by permission of National Opinion Research Center.

P. 100: Table 4-3 Adapted from Jill Suitor, Staci A. Minyard, and Rebecca S. Carter, "Did You See What I Saw? Gender Difference in Perceptions of Avenues to Prestige Among Adolescents," *Sociological Inquiry* 71 (Fall 2001):445, Table 2. University of Texas Press. Reprinted by permission of Blackwell Publishing Ltd.

P. 103: Figure 4-4 From Herwig Immervoll. 206. "Can Parents Afford to Work?" January 16, 2006. © OECD 2006 (Organisation for Economic Co-operation and Development).

Chapter 5

P. 109: Quotation from Philip G. Zimbardo. 1972. "Pathology of Imprisonment," *Society,* 9 (April):4. Copyright © 1972 by Transaction Publishers. Reprinted by permission of the publisher. And quotation from P. G. Zimbardo, C. Haney, W. C. Banks, & D. Jaffe. 1974. "The Psychology of Imprisonment: Privation, Power, and Pathology." In Z. Rubin (Ed.), *Doing Unto Others: Explorations in Social Behavior,* 1974:61–63. Used by permission of Philip G. Zimbardo, Inc.

P. 118: Figure adapted from Peter S. Bearman, James Moody, and Katherine Stovel. 2004. "Chains of Affection: The Structure of Adolescent Romantic and Sexual Networks," Figure 2, p. 58. *American Journal of Sociology* Copyright 2004. Used by permission of University of Chicago Press via the Copyright Clearance Center.

P. 122: Cartoon © The New Yorker Collection 1986 Dean Vietor from cartoonbank.com. All rights reserved.

P. 127: Cartoon by TOLES © 2000 The Washington Post. Reprinted with permission of UNIVERSAL PRESS SYNDICATE. All rights reserved.

P. 128: Figure 5-2 Adapted from Frederic Stutzman, "An Evaluation of Identity-sharing Behavior in Social Network Communities," *International Digital Media and Art Journal* 3 (No. 1), 2007. Used with permission of IDMAA/Frederic Stutzman.

Chapter 6

P. 135: Quotations from George Ritzer. 2004. *The McDonaldization of Society,* Revised New Century Edition. 2004a: 1-4, 10–11. Copyright © 2004 by Sage Publications. Reproduced with permission of Pine Forge Press, a Division of Sage Publications, Inc. via Copyright Clearance Center.

P. 138: Cartoon © The New Yorker Collection 1979 Robert Weber from cartoonbank.com. All rights reserved.

P. 143: Cartoon by Chris Wildt. www.CartoonStock.com.

P. 147: Figure 6-1 From James Allan Davis and Tom W. Smith. 2001. *General Social Surveys 2001:* 347. Published by the Roper Center, Storrs, CT. Reprinted by permission of National Opinion Research Center.

P. 150: Figure 6-2 From Barry T. Hirsch and David A. MacPherson, "Union Membership and Coverage Database from the Current Population Survey: Note," *Industrial and Labor Relations Review* 56 (2), Jan. 2003, pp. 349–354, and accompanying database at www.unionstats.com. Used by permission.

Chapter 7

P. 157: Quotation from Don Tapscott. 1999. *Growing Up Digital: The Rise of the Net Generation.* © 1999. Reprinted by permission of the McGraw-Hill Companies.

P. 169: Figure 7-2 Adapted from Michael A. Messner, Margaret Carlisle Duncan and Nicole William. 2006. "The Revolution Is Not Being Televised," *Contexts,* (Summer 2006), p. 35. American Sociological Association. Copyright 2006 by University of California Press—Journals. Used by permission of University of California Press—Journals via the Copyright Clearance Center.

P. 170: Figure 7-3 Adapted from *National Geographic Atlas of the World* 8e. National Geographic Society, 2005. The Fuller Projection Map design is a trademark of the Buckminster Fuller Institute™ © 1938, 1967 & 1992. All rights reserved. www.bfi.org. NG Maps/National Geographic Image Collection. Used by permission of National Geographic Image Sales and the Buckminster Fuller Institute.

P. 171: Figure 7-4 From the Pew Internet & American Life Project. Reprinted with permission.

P. 173: Figure 7-5 From liveplasma.com. Used by permission.

P. 177: Cartoon by Daryl Cagle 2004. © Daryl Cagle and Politicalcartoons.com All rights reserved.

Chapter 8

P. 183: Quotation from Bernadette Barton. 2006. *Stripped: Inside the Lives of Exotic Dancers,* p. 1, 2. Used with permission of New York University Press.

P. 188: Figure from Henry Wechsler et al. 2002. "Trends in College Binge Drinking During a Period of Increased Prevention Efforts," *Journal of American College Health,* 2002:208. Copyright © 2002 Heldref Publications. Reprinted with permission of the Helen Dwight Reid Educational Foundation. Published by Heldref Publications, 1319 18th St. NW, Washington, DC 20036-1802.

P. 191: Cartoon © The New Yorker Collection 2002 Alex Gregory from cartoonbank.com. All rights reserved.

P. 195: Table 8-1 From Robert K. Merton. 1968. *Social Theory and Social Structure.* Adapted by permission of The Free Press, a Division of Simon & Schuster Adult Publishing Group. Copyright © 1967, 1968 by Robert K. Merton. All rights reserved.

P. 202: Cartoon by Sidney Harris. © ScienceCartoonsPlus.com.

P. 206: Figure 8-3 From Death Penalty Information Center 2006. Used with permission.

Chapter 9

P. 213: Quotation from David K. Shipler. 2005. *The Working Poor: Invisible in America.* Copyright © 2004, 2005 by David K. Shipler. Used by permission of Alfred A. Knopf, a division of Random House, Inc.

P. 224: Table 9-2 From James. A. Davis and Peter B. Marsden. 2005. *General Social Surveys, 1972–2004: Cumulative Codebook.* Chicago: National Opinion Research Center. Used by permission.

P. 225: Figure 9-3 From "America by the Numbers," Project directed by Jackson Dykman, *TIME,* 10/30/06, p. 48–49. © 2006 Time Inc. Reprinted by permission.

P. 226: Figure 9-4, Data on wealth from Edward N. Wolff. 2002. "Recent Trends in the Distribution of Household Wealth Ownership." In *Back to Shared Prosperity: The Growing Inequality of Wealth and Income in America,* ed. Ray Marshall. New York: M.E. Sharpe. Reprinted by permission of the author.

P. 227: Figure 9-6 From Michael Förster and Marco Mira d'Ercole. 2005. *Income Distribution and Poverty in OECD Countries in the Second Half of the 1990s* (2005), Table 8. © OECD 2005 (Organisation for Economic Cooperation and Development).

P. 231: Cartoon by Harley Schwadron. Reprinted with permission.

P. 235: Cartoon by Mike Konopacki. Used with permission, Mike Konopacki, Huck/Konopacki Labor Cartoons.

Chapter 10

P. 241: Quotation from Steve Derné. 2003. "Schwarzenegger, McBeal and Arranged Marriages: Globalization on the Ground in India" in *Contexts,* a publication of the American Sociological Association. Copyright 2003 of University of California Press—Journals. Used by permission of University of California Press—Journals via the Copyright Clearance Center.

P. 243: Figure 10-1 Adapted from Bob Sutcliffe. 2002. *100 Ways of Seeing an Unequal World,* Fig 1, p. 18. London: Zed Books. Reprinted by permission.

P. 244: Figure 10-2 Adapted in part from John R. Weeks. 2002, 2005. *Population: An Introduction to Concepts and Issues,* with InfoTrac 8th ed. and 9th ed. Belmont, CA: Wadsworth. © 2002 and © 2005. Reprinted with permission of Wadsworth, a division of Thomson Learning, www.thomsonrights.com. Fax (800) 730-2215. And adapted in part from Carl Haub. 2006. *World Population Data Sheet 2006.* Used by permission of Population Reference Bureau.

P. 248: Table 10-1 Adapted in part from *Fortune.* 2007. FORTUNE Global 500, http://money.cnn.com/magazines/fortune/global500/2007/full_list/index.html. © 2007 Time Inc. All rights reserved. And adapted in part from World Bank. 2007. *World Development Indicators 2007.* Copyright 2007 by World Bank. Used by permission of the World Bank via the Copyright Clearance Center.

P. 250: Figure 10-4 From Chronic Poverty Research Center. 2005. Administered by Institute for Development Policy and Management, School of Environment and Development, University of Manchester, UK. Used by permission.

P. 253: Table from *The Global Information Technology Report* 2006-2007. Reproduced with permission of Palgrave Macmillan.

P. 255: Figure 10-6, Data from World Bank. 2005. *World Development Indicators 2005.* Copyright 2005 by World Bank. Used by permission of the World Bank via Copyright Clearance Center.

Chapter 11

P. 267: Quotation from Helen Zia. 2000. *Asian American Dreams: The Emergence of an American People.* Copyright © 2000 by Helen Zia. Reprinted by permission of Farrar, Straus & Giroux, LLC.

P. 289: Figure 11-8 From John L. Allen. 2007. *Student Atlas of World Geography* 7e. Copyright © 2007 by The McGraw-Hill Companies, Inc. All rights reserved. Reprinted by permission of McGraw-Hill/Contemporary Learning Series.

Chapter 12

P. 297: Quotation from Azadeh Moaveni. 2005. *Lipstick Jihad: A Memoir of Growing up Iranian in America and American in Iran.* Copyright © 2005 by Azadeh Moaveni. Reprinted by permission of PublicAffairs, a member of the Perseus Books Group LLC.

P. 299: Table 12-1 From Joyce McCarl Nielsen, et al. 2000. "Gendered Heteronormativity: Empirical Illustrations in Everyday Life," *Sociological Quarterly* 41 (No. 2):287. © 2000 by Blackwell Publishing, reprinted by permission.

P. 306: Figure 12-1 From Makiko Fuwa. 2004. "Macro-level Gender Inequality and the Division of Household Labor in 22 Countries." *American Sociological Review* 69: December 2004, Table 2, page 757. Used by permission of the American Sociological Association and the author.

P. 313: Figure 12-5 From NARAL Pro-Choice America Foundation 2007. Used by permission of NARAL, Washington, DC.

Chapter 13

P. 319: Quotation from *Tuesdays with Morrie* by Mitch Albom, copyright © 1997 by Mitch Albom. Used by permission of Doubleday, a division of Random House, Inc. and the David Black Agency.

P. 327: Figure 13-2 © AARP. Reprinted by permission of the American Association of Retired Persons.

P. 327: Cartoon © The New Yorker Collection 2006 Barbara Smaller from cartoonbank.com. All rights reserved.

Chapter 14

P. 339: Quotation from Annette Lareau. 2003. *Unequal Childhoods: Class, Race, and Family Life.* Copyright 2003 The Regents of the University of California. Used by permission of the University of California Press via Copyright Clearance Center.

P. 341: Figure 14-1 In part from Joseph A. McFalls, Jr. 2003. "Population: A Lively Introduction." 4e, *Population Bulletin* 58 (December):23. Used by permission of the Population Reference Bureau.

P. 348: Figure 14-2 From *World Fertility Report 2003.* © 2004 United Nations Population Division. Used by permission.

P. 354: Cartoon by Signe Wilkinson, Cartoon Arts International. Used by permission of Signe Wilkinson, Cartoonists & Writers Syndicate/cartoonweb.com.

P. 359: Figure 14-6 From Human Rights Campaign accessed at www.hrc.org, "Statewide Anti-Discrimination Laws and Policies" and "Statewide Discriminatory Marriage Laws". Used with permission.

Chapter 15

P. 365: Quotation from Vine Deloria, Jr. 1999. *For This Land: Writings on Religion in America:*273–275. Copyright © 1999 by Vine Deloria. Reproduced by permission of Routledge Publishing Inc. a division of Taylor & Francis Group.

P. 367: Figure 15-1 from John L. Allen. 2007. *Student Atlas of World Geography* 7e. Copyright © 2007 by The McGraw-Hill Companies, Inc. All rights reserved. Reprinted by permission of McGraw-Hill/Contemporary Learning Series.

P. 377: Figure 15-2 Adapted from Pippa Norris and Ronald Inglehart. 2004. *Sacred and Secular: Religion and Politics Worldwide*: Table 3.6, p.74. Cambridge University Press © 2004. Reprinted with permission of Cambridge University Press.

P. 385: Cartoon by Mike Keefe, The Denver Post.

Chapter 16

P. 391: Quotation from Jonathan Kozol. 2005. *The Shame of the Nation*. © Jonathan Kozol 2005. Reprinted by permission of Crown/Three Rivers Press, a division of Random House, Inc. and the author.

P. 396: Cartoon by Kirk Anderson. Used by permission of Kirk Anderson, www.kirktoons.com.

P. 403: Figure 16-3 Western Interstate Commission for Higher Education, 2003. Used by permission of WICHE.

Chapter 17

P. 411: Quotation from Martin P. Wattenberg. 2008. *Is Voting for Young People?* pp. 1–2, 3. Copyright © 2008 by Pearson Education, Inc. Reprinted by permission.

P. 413: Cartoon © The New Yorker Collection 1957 Chon Day from cartoonbank.com. All rights reserved.

P. 416: Figure 17-1 © International Institute for Democracy and Electoral Assistance, www.idea.int. Used by permission.

P. 419: Figure 17-2 From Inter-Parliamentary Union (IPU), 2007, Women in National Parliaments, www.ipu.org/wmn-e/classif.htm. Used by permission.

P. 420: Figure 17-3 (right) From G. William Domhoff. 2006. *Who Rules America*, 5th ed. © 2006 by The McGraw-Hill Companies, Inc. Reproduced by permission of the publisher.

P. 422: Figure 17-4 From 1971–2004 The Gallup Poll. All rights reserved. Reprinted with permission from The Gallup Organization.

P. 424: Figure 17-5 Adapted from *National Geographic Atlas of the World* 8e. National Geographic Society, 2005. NG Maps/National Geographic Image Collection. Used by permission.

P. 425: Screenshot from www.greenpeace.org. Used by permission.

P. 427: Cartoon by Drew Sheneman. © Tribune Media Services, Inc. All rights reserved. Reprinted with permission.

Chapter 18

P. 433: Quotation from Jeremy Rifkin. 1995. *The End of Work*. Copyright © 1995 by Jeremy Rifkin. Used by permission of Jeremy P. Tarcher, an imprint of Penguin Group USA Inc.

P. 438: Figure From S. Acharya. 2000. In Mahbub ul Haq Human Development Centre, *Human Development in South Asia 2000: The Gender Question*:54. Oxford University Press, Karachi. Reprinted by permission.

P. 439: Figure 18-1 Copyright 2006 by The Economist Newspaper Group. Reproduced with permission of The Economist via Copyright Clearance Center.

P. 440: Cartoon by Mike Thompson, Copley News Service. Reprinted with permission.

P. 446: Cartoon by MIKE PETERS EDTCTN (NEW) © KING FEATURES SYNDICATE.

P. 446: Quotation from Sheryl Stolberg. 1995. "Affirmative Action Gains Often Come at a High Cost," *Los Angeles Times*, March 29, 1995:A14. Copyright 1995 Los Angeles Times. Reprinted by permission.

Chapter 19

P. 455: Quotation from *The Scalpel and the Silver Bear*, by Lori Arviso Alvord & Elizabeth Cohen Van Pelt, copyright © 1999 by Lori Arviso Alvord & Elizabeth Cohen Van Pelt. Used by permission of Bantam Books, a division of Random House, Inc. and the author.

P. 457: Table 19-1 From Susan Levine, "Reshaping Bedside Manner in a Diverse World" by Susan Levine, *The Washington Post*, February 26, 2006. In "Culturally Sensitive Medicine," *Washington Post* National Weekly Edition, 23, March 26, 2006, p. 31. © 2006 The Washington Post, reprinted with permission.

P. 461: Figure 19-1 From Carl Haub. 2006. *World Population Data Sheet 2006*. Used by permission of Population Reference Bureau.

P. 468: Cartoon by Sidney Harris. © ScienceCartoonsPlus.com.

Chapter 20

P. 481: Quotation from Mitchell Duneier. 1999. *Sidewalk*. Copyright © 1999 by Mitchell Duneier. Reprinted by permission of Farrar, Straus & Giroux, LLC and the author.

P. 484: Table 20-1 Based on Gideon Sjoberg. 1960. *The Preindustrial City: Past and Present*, 1960: 323-328. Adapted with permission of The Free Press, a Division of Simon & Schuster Adult Publishing Group. Copyright © 1960 by The Free Press. Copyright © renewed 1968 by Gideon Sjoberg. All rights reserved. And based on E. Barbara Phillips. 1996. *City Lights: Urban-Suburban Life in the Global Society*, 2/e. Copyright © 1981 by E. Barbara Phillips and Richard T. LeGates, 1996 by E. Barbara Phillips. Oxford University Press. Used by permission.

P. 485: Figure 20-1 Adapted from *National Geographic Atlas of the World* 8e. National Geographic Society, 2005. NG Maps/National Geographic Image Collection. Used by permission.

P. 486: Figure 20-2 Adapted from Chauncy Harris and Edward Ullmann. 1945. "The Nature of Cities," *Annals of the American Academy of Political and Social Science*, 242 (November):13. Reprinted by permission of American Academy of Political and Social Science, Philadelphia.

P. 495: Figure 20-3 2007 Homelessness Research Institute at the National Alliance to End Homelessness. Used with permission.

Chapter 21

P. 501: Quotation from Kai Erikson. 1994. *A New Species of Trouble: The Human Experience of Modern Disasters*. Copyright © 1994 by Kai Erikson. Used by permission of W. W. Norton Company, Inc.

P. 505: Figure 21-1 From Carl Haub. 2005. *World Population Data Sheet 2005*. Used by permission of Population Reference Bureau.

P. 509: Cartoon by Signe Wilkinson/Philadelphia Daily News. Used by permission of Cartoonists & Writers Syndicate.

P. 514: Quotation from Neil B. Thompson. 1972. Reprinted from *Natural History*, December 1972; copyright © Natural History Magazine, Inc. 1972. Used with permission.

P. 515: Cartoon by Mike Luckovich. Reprinted by permission of Mike Luckovich and Creators Syndicate, Inc.

Chapter 22

P. 523: Quotation from Howard Rheingold. 2003. *Smart Mobs, The Next Social Revolution: Transforming Cultures and Communities in the Age of Instant Access*. Copyright © 2003 Howard Rheingold. Reprinted by permission of Basic Books, a member of Perseus Books LLC.

P. 527: Figure reprinted by permission of the publisher from John B. Christiansen and Sharon N. Barnartt, *Deaf President Now! The 1988 Revolution at Gallaudet University* (Washington D.C.: Gallaudet University Press, 1995) p. 22. Copyright 1995 by Gallaudet University.

P. 535: Quotation from Manisha Desai. 1996. "If Peasants Build Their Own Dams, What Would the State Have Left to Do?" *Research in Social Movements, Conflicts and Change*, 19:214, ed. Michael Dobkowski and Isidor Wallimann. Greenwich, CT: JAI Press. Used with permission from Elsevier.

P. 539: Table 22-2 From Karen Meyer, "Match the Disability." April 30, 2007. Chicago: DePaul University.

Chapter 23

P. 545: Quotation from Debora L. Spar. 2001. *Ruling the Waves: Cycles of Discovery, Chaos and Wealth from the Compass to the Internet*. Copyright © 2001 by Debora L. Spar. Reprinted by permission of Harcourt, Inc.

P. 550: Table 23-3 From the Pew Internet & American Life Project. Reprinted with permission.

P. 554: Cartoon © Matt Wuerker. Reprinted by permission.

P. 558: Figure 23-1 Adapted from *National Geographic Atlas of the World* 8e. National Geographic Society, 2005. NG Maps/National Geographic Image Collection. Used by permission.

photo credits

Chapter 1: CO1, © United Air Lines, Inc. All rights Reserved. By permission of Fallon Minneapolis. Photography: © 2005 Kevin Peterson (left) and Matthew Phillips/Jupiter (right); pp. 6 and 7, © 1994 Peter Menzel www.menzelphoto.com. From the book Material World, Sierra Club Books; p. 9, © Win McNamee/Getty Images; p. 10, © Kyle Niemi/U.S. Coast Guard via Getty Images; p. 11, © AJ Mast/AP Images; p. 12, © Spencer Arnold/Getty Images; p. 13 (left), Bibliothèque Nationale de France; p. 13 (middle), The Granger Collection, New York; p. 13 (right), © Imagno/Getty Images; p. 14, Jane Addams Memorial Collection (JAMC neg. 613), Special Collections, The University Library, The University of Illinois at Chicago; p. 16, © Earl & Nazima Kowall/Corbis; p. 17 (bottom), Department of Special Collections, The University of Chicago Library; p. 20, © Gavin Lawrence/Getty Images; p. 21, © Topham/The Image Works. **Chapter 2:** CO2, © 1990 Erika Rothenberg; p. 35, © Van Bucher/Photo Researchers, Inc.; p. 38, © 2003 The Gallup Poll; p. 39, © Robert Fried/Alamy; p. 40, Courtesy of AT&T Archives and History Center; p. 44, © Stephen Shugerman/Getty Images; p. 45, © John Gaps III/AP Images; p. 47, © Bob Daemmrich/The Image Works; p. 49, © Peter Parks/AFP/Getty Images. **Chapter 3:** CO3, © Mike Clark /AFP/Getty Images; p. 57, © Don Farrall/Getty Images; p. 59, © UPPA/Zuma Press; p. 60, © Eddie Gerald/Lonely Planet Images; p. 61 (top), AP Images; p. 61 (bottom), © Patrick Zachmann/Magnum Photos, Inc.; p. 63, © José Fuste Raga/AGE Fotostock; p. 67, Courtesy of the Oneida Nation; p. 68, AP I mages; p. 69, © Topham/The Image Works; p. 71, © Sebastian D'Souza/AFP/Getty Images; p. 74, © Mark Henley/Panos Pictures; p. 78, © Andre Jenny/Alamy. **Chapter 4:** CO4, © David H. Wells/The Image Works; p. 88, © Bob DeBris/Corbis; p. 89, © Margot Granitsas/The Image Works; p. 90, © AP Images; p. 91, © Ryan McVay/Getty Images; p. 94 (top), © Thomas S. England/Photo Researchers, Inc.; p. 94 (bottom), © AP Images; p. 96, © A. Ramey/PhotoEdit; p. 97, © Dennis Macdonald/Index Stock; p. 98, © Carlos Osorio/AP Images; p. 99, Collection of Richard Schaefer; p. 101, © Jim West/The Image Works; p. 103, Courtesy of Communicare, Perth, Australia. **Chapter 5:** CO5, Courtesy of America's Promise; p. 109, Courtesy of Phil Zimbardo, Stanford University; p. 111, © Don Murray-Pool/Getty Images; p. 112, © Vincent DeWitt/Stock Boston, LLC; p. 114, © Scott Fisher/Woodfin Camp & Associates; p. 115 (top), © Chung Sung-Jun/Getty Images; p. 115 (bottom), © Stan Honda/AFP/Getty Images; p. 116, © Anna Clopet/Corbis; p. 119, © AP Images; p. 121, © Charles & Josette Lenars/Corbis; p. 122, © Pablo Corral V/Corbis; p. 125 (top), © David Frazier/Photo Edit; p. 125 (bottom), © Vladimir Sichov/SIPA Press. **Chapter 6:** CO6, Photofest; p. 137, © Viviane Moos/Corbis; p. 139 (top), Courtesy of the New York Unicycle Club; p. 139 (bottom), Photofest; p. 142, © AP Images; p. 144, © Koichi Kamoshida/Getty Images; p. 147, © Kenneth Jarecke/Woodfin Camp & Associates; p. 148, © Reter R. Hvizdak/The Image Works. **Chapter 7:** CO7, Courtesy of Michael Horse; p. 159, © Khalil Hamra; p. 160 (left), © CBS/Photofest; p. 160 (right), © ABC/Photofest; p. 161 (top left), © NBC/Photofest; p. 161 (top right), © Fox Broadcasting/Photofest; p. 161(bottom left), © HBO/Photofest; p. 161 (bottom right), © CBS/Warner Bros./Photofest; p. 162 (left), Photo by Stan Wayman/Time Magazine, Copyright Time Inc./Time Life Pictures/Getty Images; p. 162 (middle left), PEOPLE Weekly © Time Inc. All Rights Reserved; p. 162 (middle right), © Vince Bucci/Getty Images; p. 162 (right), By Peter Travers from Rolling Stone, June 15, 1989 © Rolling Stone, LLC 1989. All Rights Reserved. Reprinted by Permission; p. 163 (top), Courtesy Nicole Martorano Van Cleve; p. 163 (bottom), © Columbia Pictures/Topham/The Image Works; p. 166 (top), © SPPS/Atlaspress; p. 166 (bottom), © Ellen Emendorp/The New York Times; p. 167, Photofest; p. 168, Ron Tom/© UPN/Everett Collection; p. 175, © Frederic Stevens/SIPA Press; p. 176 (left), © Editorial Image, LLC; p. 176 (right), © Royalty Free/Corbis; p. 176 (bottom), © Jeffery Aaronson/Still Media. **Chapter 8:** CO8, Finish Government; p. 183, Photo by Editorial Image, LLC; p. 185, © Lehtikuva/Jussi Nukari; p. 186, From the film OBEDIENCE © 1968 by Stanley Milgram; © renewed 1991 by Alexandra Milgram and distributed by Penn State Media Sales.; p. 187, © George Steinmetz; p. 190 (top), © Duane Burleson/AP Images; p. 190 (bottom), The Herald Bulletin, John P. Cleary/AP Images; p. 192, © Jerry Alexander/Getty Images; p. 193 (top), © Mohsen Shandiz/Corbis; p. 193 (bottom), Kevin Moloney for The New York Times; p. 196, © AP Images; p. 197, © Jeff Spielman/Photographer's Choice/Getty Images; p. 198, © Michael Newman/PhotoEdit; p. 199, © David Pollack/Corbis; p. 203, Courtesy Tiffany Zapata-Mancilla. **Chapter 9:** CO9, ConAgra Foods Feeding Children Better Foundation. Courtesy of The Ad Council; p. 217, Courtesy Jessica Houston Su; p. 219 (top), © Roger Ball/Corbis; p. 219 (bottom), © Bettmann/Corbis; p. 221, © Steven S. Miric/Super-Stock; p. 222, © Paul A. Souders/Corbis; p. 229, © Rubber Ball Productions/Index Stock; p. 230, © AP Images; p. 233 (top), © Stockbyte/Getty Images; p. 233 (bottom), © Suzanne Opton. **Chapter 10:** CO10, Courtesy of Pieni-m Oy; p. 241, © Margo Silver/Stone/Getty; p. 242, © Alan Dejecacion/Getty; p. 243 (left), Nati Harnik/AP Images; p. 243 (right), © Photofusion Picture Library/Alamy; p. 247, © K. Hamilton/Corbis; p. 249, © Catherine Karnow/Woodfin Camp & Associates; p. 252, Agency: Springer & Jacoby Werbung GmbH, Hamburg; creative directors: Betina Olf, Timm Weber; copywriter: Sven Keitel; art director: Claudia Todt; photographer: Jan Burwick; p. 255, © Stuart Franklin/Magnum Photos, p. 257, © Gregory Bull/AP Images; p. 258, © Eduardo Verdugo/

AP Images; p. 261, © Simon C. Roberts/NB Pictures/Contact Press Images. **Chapter 11:** CO11, © Courtesy of the American Indian College Fund; p. 271 (left), © John Lund/Sam Diephuis/Blend Image/Getty Images; p. 271 (right), © Motofish Images/Corbis; p. 273, © Tom McCarthy/PhotoEdit; p. 275, © Elliot Erwitt/Magnum Photos; p. 276, Courtesy of Devito/Verdi, New York, NY; p. 279, © Alexandra Boulat/VII/AP Images; p. 281, David Zalubowski/AP Images; p. 283, © Roy Ooms/Masterfile; p. 287, Courtesy of Sigma Pi Alpha Sorority, Inc.; p. 288, © Photo by David Bohrer. Copyright 2002, Los Angeles Times. Reprinted with permission. **Chapter 12:** CO12, Courtesy www.guerillagirls.com; p. 298, Courtesy of Azadeh Moaveni; p. 300 (left), © Laura Farr/Zuma Press; p. 300 (right), Picture provided by Harrison G. Pope, Jr. adapted from THE ADONIS COMPLEX by Harrison G. Pope, Jr., Katherine Phillips, Roberto Olivardia. The Free Press, © 2000; p. 301, © Gideon Mendel/Corbis; p. 302, © Steve McCurry/Magnum; p. 303, © Bob Mahoney/The Image Works; p. 307, John Birdsall/The Image Works; p. 311, Courtesy Abigail E. Drevs. **Chapter 13:** CO13, United Nation; p. 320, © Robert Brenner/PhotoEdit; p. 323, © Catherine Karnow/Woodfin Camp & Associates; p. 326, © Spencer Grant/PhotoEdit; p. 328, © Thierry Secretan/Woodfin Camp & Associates; p. 331 (top), © Gabe Palmer/Corbis; p. 331 (bottom), Photo by Editorial Image, LLC; p. 332, Detroit News. **Chapter 14:** CO14, Courtesy of Barnardos; pp. 342 and 343, Uwe Ommer from 1000 families; p. 344, © Thomas L. Kelly; p. 345, © Ariel Skelley/Corbis; p. 347, © Richard Hutchings; p. 349, © Colin Young-Wolff/PhotoEdit; p. 350, © Arif Ali/AFP/Getty Images; p. 353 (top), © Lori Waselchuck/New York Times Pictures/Redux; p. 353 (bottom), © Blair Seitz/Photo Researchers, Inc. **Chapter 15:** CO15, © Thomas Coex/AFP/Getty Images; p. 368, © Journal-Courier/Steve Warmouski/The Image Works; p. 369 (top), © Sebastian Bolesch/Peter Arnold, Inc.; p. 369 (bottom left), © Lindsay Hebberd/Corbis; p. 369 (bottom right), © Jorgen Schytte/Peter Arnold, Inc.; p. 375, © Corbis; p. 376, AP Images; p. 379, © Robert Davis; p. 381, © Max Jourdan/AA World Travel/Tophoto/The Image Works; p. 382, © Dinodia/The Image Works. **Chapter 16:** CO16, Courtesy of Durham Literacy Center; p. 391, Photo by Editorial Image, LLC; p. 393, © Warner Bros./courtesy Everett Collection; p. 394, © Mary Kate Denny/PhotoEdit, Inc.; p. 397, © Marc Ribound/Magnum Photos; p. 400, © Dennis MacDonald/Alamy; p. 403, © Chuck Savage/Corbis; p. 405, Chicago Tribune photo by Candice C. Cruisic. All rights reserved. Used with permission. **Chapter 17:** CO17, © Mike Nelson/epa/Corbis; p. 411, Photo by Editorial Image, LLC; p. 414, Courtesy Joshua Johnston; p. 415, © Joren Gerhard/Corbis Sygma; p. 417, © Win McNamee/Getty Images; p. 421 (top), Haraz Ghanbari/AP Images; p. 421 (bottom), © Jaron Berman Photography; p. 423, © Yannis Behrakis/Reuters/Landov. **Chapter 18:** CO18, © Photomontage by Arthur Hochstein/Time & Life Pictures/Getty Images; p. 435 (top), © Ramadhan Khamis/Panapress; p. 435 (bottom), © Andrew Cooper/Columbia Tri Star/The Kobal Collection; p. 437, Courtesy Amy Wang; p. 440, © Jose Fuste Raga/Corbis; p. 442, © Edward Burtynsky; p. 443 (top), © Steve McCurry/Magnum; p. 443 (bottom left), © Joel Sartore/National Geographic Image Collection; p. 443 (bottom right), © Steve Winter/National Geographic Image Collection; p. 444, © Chuck Keeler/Stone/Getty Images; p. 445, © Jesus Castillo/ITSPress/Atlas Press #1LDN; p. 447 (left), © Age Fotostock/SuperStock; p. 447 (right), © Erin Lubin/Bloomberg News/Landov; p. 449, © Manan Vatsyayana/AFP/Getty Images. **Chapter 19:** CO19, Courtesy of Marsel van Oosten. Agency: Cygnus X-3; Art Director: Marsel van Oosten, Mathieu Winkel; Copywriter: Arjen de Jong, Reny Panoet; Photographer: Mathieu Winkel; Client: NCDO; p. 457, © Stephen Derr/The Image Bank/Getty Images; p. 458, © Stacey Stowe/Redux; p. 459 (top left), © Robert Harding Picture Library Ltd/Alamy; p. 459 (top right), © Richard C. Paddock; p. 459 (bottom left), © Chris Hondros/Newsmakers/Getty Images; p. 459 (bottom right), © Reuters/Corbis; p. 460, © Bob Daemmrich/The Image Works; p. 464, © Ryan McVay/Photodisc Green/Getty; p. 469 (top), © Creatas/SuperStock; p. 469 (bottom), © Stephanie Maze/Woodfin Camp & Associates; p. 470, Courtesy Lola Adedokun; p. 472: © Mustafa Ozer/AFP/Getty Images; p. 473, © Rhonda Sidney/Stock Boston. **Chapter 20:** CO20, Courtesy of Newcomm Bates, Brazil; p. 482, © Ovie Carter; p. 483, © Mark Henley/Panos Pictures; p. 487, © Sarah Leen/National Geographic/Getty Images; p. 489, © dpa/Landov; p. 490, Max Nash/AP Images; p. 491, Courtesy Christie Taylor; p. 492, © Steve Warmowski/The Image Works; p. 496, © Steffan Hacker/Habitat for Humanity. **Chapter 21:** CO21, Courtesy of Pirtle Design; p. 503, © Jon Arnold Images/SuperStock; p. 506, © Josef Polleross/The Image Works; p. 508, © Goh Chai Hin/AFP/Getty Images; p. 510, AP Images; p. 512, Basel Action Network; p. 513, © Jennifer S. Altman; p. 516, © Macduff Everton/Corbis; p. 517, © A. Ramey/Woodfin Camp & Associates. **Chapter 22:** CO22, © Matt Dorfman; p. 524, AP Images; p. 526, © Chung Sung-Jun/Getty Images; p. 527, © Joshua Roberts/Getty Images; p. 528, AP Images; p. 529, AP Images; p. 530, © Scott Barbour/Reportage/Getty Images; p. 531, © Raoul Minsart/Super Stock; p. 532, © Ryan Pyle/Corbis; p. 533, AP Images; p. 536, © Peter Macdiarmid/Getty Images; p. 538, AP Images. **Chapter 23:** CO23, Courtesy of the Make Trade Fair Campaign, Oxfam and Greg Williams, Photographer; p. 548, © 2002 Joseph Rodriguez/Stockphoto.com; p. 549, © Jim West/jimwestphoto.com; p. 553, Courtesy of One Laptop per Child; p. 555, Courtesy of Troy Duster; p. 556, © Pedro Armestre/Reuters.

name index

subject index

Applications of Sociology's Major Theoretical Approaches

Sociology provides comprehensive coverage of the major sociological perspectives. This summary table includes a sample of the topics in the text that have been explored using the major approaches. The numbers in parentheses indicate the pertinent chapters.

FUNCTIONALIST PERSPECTIVE

Defined and explained (1)
Adoption (14)
AIDS and social networks (5)
AIDS crisis (19)
Anomie theory of deviance (8)
Bilingualism (3)
Bureaucratization of
   schools (16)
Campaign financing (17)
Cow worship in India (1)
Culture (3, 16)
Davis and Moore's view of
   stratification (9)
Death penalty (8)
Disengagement theory of
   aging (13)
Dominant ideology (3)
Durkheim's view of deviance (8)
Dysfunctions of racism (11)
Ethnocentrism (3)
Family (14)
Formal organizations (6)
Functions of dying (13)
Functions of racism (11)
Gans's functions of poverty (9)
Gay marriage (14)
Gender stratification (12)
Global immigration (11)
Health and illness (19)
Human ecology (21)
Human rights (10)
In-groups and out-groups (6)
Integrative function of
   religion (15)
Internet (23)
Media and social norms (7)
Media and socialization (7)
Media and status conferral (7)
Media concentration (7)
Media promotion of
   consumption (7)
Modernization theory (10)
Multinational corporations (10)
Narcotizing effect of the
   media (7)
No Child Left Behind Act (16)
Offshoring (18)
Population policy (21)
Racial prejudice and
   discrimination (11)
Regulating the Internet (5)
Rumors (22)
Social change (16, 23)
Social control (8, 16)
Social institutions (5)
Socialization in schools (4, 16)
Sports (1)
Subcultures (3)
Transnationals (23)
Urban ecology (20)

CONFLICT PERSPECTIVE

Defined and explained (1)
Abortion (12)
Access to health care (19)
Access to technology (23)
Affirmative action (18)
Age stratification (13)
AIDS crisis (5, 19)
Bilingualism (3)
Bureaucratization of
   schools (16)
Campaign financing (17)
Capitalism (15, 18)
Corporate welfare (9)
Correspondence principle (16)
Credentialism (16)
Culture (3)
Day care funding (4)
Death penalty (8)
Deviance (8)
Disability as a master status (5)
Disability rights (22)
Dominant ideology (3, 7, 9)
Downsizing (18)
Elite model of the U.S. power
   structure (17)
Environmental issues (21)
Exploitation theory of
   discrimination (11)
Family (14)
Gay marriage (12)
Gender equity in education (16)
Gender stratification (12)
Global immigration (11)

Hidden curriculum (16)
Iron Law of Oligarchy (6)
Labor unions (6)
Marx's view of stratification (9)
Matrix of domination (12)
Media concentration (7)
Media gatekeeping (7)
Media stereotypes (7)
Medicalization of society (19)
Model minority (11)
Multinational corporations (10)
New urban sociology (20)
No Child Left Behind Act (16)
Offshoring (18)
Population policy (21)
Poverty (9)
Privacy and technology (23)
Racism and health (19)
Regulating the Internet (5)
Religion and social control (15)
Right to die (13)
School violence (16)
Social change (23)
Social control (8)
Social institutions (5)
Socialization in schools (4)
Sports (1)
Subcultures (3)
Tracking (16)
Transnationals (23)
Victimless crimes (8)
White-collar crime (8)
World systems
   analysis (10, 20, 23)

INTERACTIONIST PERSPECTIVE

Defined and explained (1)
Activity theory of aging (13)
Adolescent sexual networks (5)
Adoption (14)
Affirmative action (18)
AIDS and its impact (5)
AIDS crisis (19)
Campaign financing (17)
Charismatic authority (17)
Conspicuous consumption (9)
Contact hypothesis (11)
Culture (3)
Differential association (8)
Disability rights (22)
Dramaturgical approach (4, 17)
Electronic communication (7)
Family (14)

Gay marriage (12)
Gender stratification (12)
Health and illness (19)
Human relations approach (6)
Interracial and interethnic
   friendships (11)
Media concentration (7)
NBA dress code (1)
Obedience (8)
Presentation of the self (4)
Regulating the Internet (5)
Routine activities theory (8)
Small groups (6)
Social institutions (5)
Sports (1)
Tattoo symbols of 9/11 (1)
Teacher-expectancy effect (16)
Teenage pregnancy (14)
Transnationals (23)
Unions (6)

FEMINIST PERSPECTIVE

Defined and explained (1)
Day care funding (4)
Deviance (8)
Dominant ideology (3)
Ethnographic research (2)
Family (14)
Gender gap in education (16)
Gender stratification (12)
Language (3)
Media stereotypes (7)
Population policy (21)
Pornography (7)
Rape (8)
Religion and social control (15)
School violence (16)
Sports (1)
Victimless crimes (8)

LABELING THEORY

Defined and explained (8)
AIDS and labeling (5, 19)
AIDS crisis (19)
Disabilities and labeling (5)
Disability rights (22)
Health and illness (19)
Mental illness (19)
Road rage (8)
Societal reaction approach (8)
Teacher-expectancy effect (16)
Victimless crimes (8)